1987 Annual Edition
West's Federal Taxation:

# Corporations, Partnerships, Estates, and Trusts.

# 1987 Annual Edition
# West's Federal Taxation:
# Corporations, Partnerships, Estates, and Trusts.

*General Editor*

WILLIAM H. HOFFMAN, JR., J.D., Ph.D., C.P.A.

*Contributing Authors*

D. LARRY CRUMBLEY, Ph.D., C.P.A.
Texas A & M University

STEVEN C. DILLEY, J.D., Ph.D., C.P.A.
Michigan State University

PATRICA C. ELLIOTT, D.B.A., C.P.A.
University of New Mexico

WILLIAM H. HOFFMAN, JR., J.D., Ph.D., C.P.A.
University of Houston

JEROME S. HORVITZ, J.D., LL.M. in Taxation
University of Houston

MARILYN PHELAN, J.D., D.B.A., C.P.A.
Texas Tech University

WILLIAM A. RAABE, Ph.D., C.P.A.
University of Wisconsin-Milwaukee

BOYD C. RANDALL, J.D., Ph.D.
Brigham Young University

W. EUGENE SEAGO, J.D., Ph.D., C.P.A.
Virginia Polytechnic Institute and State University

JAMES E. SMITH, Ph.D., C.P.A.
College of William and Mary

WILLIS C. STEVENSON, Ph.D., C.P.A.
University of Wisconsin-Madison

EUGENE WILLIS, Ph.D., C.P.A.
University of Illinois at Urbana

**WEST PUBLISHING CO.**
ST. PAUL • NEW YORK • LOS ANGELES • SAN FRANCISCO

Copy editor: Deborah Smith
Text composition: York Graphic Services

*Library of Congress Cataloging in Publication Data*

Hoffman, William H
    West's Federal taxation.
    Includes index.
    1.  Taxation—United States—Law.  I.  Title.
KF6335.H63      343'.73'04      76-54355
**ISBN** 0-314-99653-2
**ISSN** 0272-0329
**1987 ANNUAL EDITION**

# PREFACE

This work was inspired by and designed to relieve the absence, perceived by the authors, of suitable textual material for a second course in Federal taxation—the follow-up to a course outlining the Federal income taxation of individuals. This text, as the basis for a second course offered at either the undergraduate or graduate level or as a tool for self-study, contains an introduction to tax research and discussions of the Federal income tax treatment of taxpayers other than individuals and the treatment of those property transfers subject to Federal and state gift and death taxes.

Throughout the text the authors stress the practical application of the materials through a liberal use of examples, most of which have been classroom tested and found to be effective learning devices. At the same time, the evolution of specific statutory provisions through the interaction of case law, political compromise, and economic considerations is discussed to offer the student a broad base for understanding and applying the tax law. Our text does not purport to be a treatise on historical and fiscal policy considerations; its primary concern is tax practice. For this reason, such discussions of the law's development were minimized. Of course, this minimization does not compromise the subject matter's presentation.

At the center of the practical application of tax law is tax planning—the legal minimization of the tax burden. The authors are sensitive to this facet of tax law education; therefore, all chapters conclude with a special section—"Tax Planning Considerations."

The authors are of the opinion that any advanced Federal tax course should offer the student the opportunity to learn and utilize the methodology of tax research; therefore, Chapter 1 is devoted in part to this topic, and each Chapter contains several research projects. The effectiveness of the text does not, however, depend upon the use of these research materials. They may be omitted without diminishing the presentation of all other topics.

Many of our users are not aware of the useful material contained in the appendixes to the text. In addition to the usual Subject Index, the following items are included: Tax Rates and Tables (Appendix A); Tax Forms (Appendix B); Glossary of Tax Terms (Appendix C); Table of Code Sections Cited (Appendix D-1); Table of Regulations Cited (Appendix D-2); Table of Revenue Procedures and Revenue Rulings Cited (Appendix D-3); and, Table of Cases Cited (Appendix E).

I am delighted to have the opportunity, as editor, to coordinate the efforts of our authors in this, the 1987 Annual Edition of *West's Federal Taxation: Corporations, Partnerships, Estates and Trusts*. The nine years that have elapsed since our text first was made available to the academic and professional communities has more than justified the hope that it would fulfill a real need.

In addition to the usual updating to reflect the changes in the tax law, the 1987 Annual Edition incorporates an *Instructor's Guide*. The so-called

"IG" contains the following materials:

- —Instructor's Summaries that can be used as lecture outlines and provide the instructor with teaching aids and information not contained in the text.

- —Incorporated as part of the Instructor's Summaries are selected queries that facilitate the use of WESTLAW, a computerized compilation of legal sources (judicial, legislative, and administrative) pertinent to the area of taxation. WESTLAW, a service available from West Publishing Co., provides a sophisticated short cut for carrying out in-depth analysis of various tax issues.

- —Improved and additional Examination Questions with solutions thereto.

- —The solutions to the Research Problems contained in the text.

- —The solutions to the Comprehensive Tax Return Problems contained in the text.

The *Solutions Manual* continues to contain the answers to the Discussion Questions and Problems.

I am extremely grateful to the users of our text who were kind enough to provide me with constructive comments concerning its effectiveness both as a teaching and as a learning device.

In particular, I would like to thank the following professors for the reviews and comments they made regarding the 1986 Annual Edition:

Philip R. Fink, The University of Toledo
C. Douglass Izard, University of Tennessee
Raymond J. Levesque, Bentley College
David M. Maloney, University of Virginia
Kent W. Meyer, The California State University
William Resler, University of Washington
Herbert C. Sieg, Illinois State University
Roy Soll, Florida Atlantic University
Tom White, College of Charleston

Needless to say, such input eased my editorial task considerably.

Lastly, I appreciate the invaluable assistance rendered by my wife, Bonnie S. Hoffman, M.S.Accounting, C.P.A.

WILLIAM H. HOFFMAN, JR.

Houston, Texas
March, 1986

# CONTENTS IN BRIEF

# TABLE OF CONTENTS

## CHAPTER 1. UNDERSTANDING AND WORKING WITH THE FEDERAL TAX LAW

## CHAPTER 2. CORPORATIONS: INTRODUCTION AND OPERATING RULES

### CHAPTER 3. CORPORATIONS: ORGANIZATION AND CAPITAL STRUCTURE

## CHAPTER 7. CORPORATE ACCUMULATIONS

## CHAPTER 8. S CORPORATIONS

### CHAPTER 9.   PARTNERSHIPS:
### FORMATION AND OPERATION

### CHAPTER 10.   PARTNERSHIPS:
### TRANSFER OF PARTNERSHIP INTERESTS;
### FAMILY AND LIMITED PARTNERSHIPS

## CHAPTER 11. THE FEDERAL GIFT AND ESTATE TAXES

THE FEDERAL GIFT TAX—Continued

### CHAPTER 12.  VALUATION AND LIQUIDITY PROBLEMS

# CHAPTER 13. INCOME TAXATION OF TRUSTS AND ESTATES

# CHAPTER 14. TAX ADMINISTRATION AND PRACTICE

TAX ADMINISTRATION—Continued

## APPENDIXES

# 1987 Annual Edition
## West's Federal Taxation:
# Corporations, Partnerships, Estates, and Trusts.

# Understanding and Working with the Federal Tax Law

1

## CHAPTER OBJECTIVES

—Describe the influence of economic, social, equity, and political considerations on the evolution of the Federal tax law.
—Describe how the IRS (as the protector of the revenue) and the courts (as the interpreter of Congressional intent) have influenced the Federal tax law.
—Aid the reader in dealing with the complexity of the Federal income tax as it currently exists.
—Familiarize the reader with tax law sources (i.e., statutory, administrative, and judicial).
—Explain how to locate and cite appropriate tax law sources.
—Assess the weight of tax law sources.
—Identify and resolve tax problems.
—Explain the importance of particular tax planning measures.
—Learn about computer-assisted tax research.

# THE WHYS OF THE TAX LAW

The Federal tax law is a mixture of statutory provisions, administrative pronouncements, and court decisions. Anyone who has attempted to work with this body of knowledge would have to admit to the law's disturbing complexity. For the person who has to wade through rule upon rule to find the solution to a tax problem, it may be of some consolation to know that the law's complexity can be explained. There is a reason for the formulation of every rule. Knowing these reasons, therefore, is a considerable step toward understanding the Federal tax law.

At the outset one should stress that the Federal tax law does not have as its sole objective the raising of revenue. Although the fiscal needs of the government are important, other considerations exist that explain certain portions of the law. Economic, social, equity, and political factors also play a significant role. Added to these factors is the marked impact the Internal Revenue Service and the courts have had and will continue to have on the evolution of Federal tax law. These matters are treated in the first part of this chapter, and wherever appropriate, the discussion is related to subjects covered later in the text.

## ECONOMIC CONSIDERATIONS

The use of the tax system in an effort to accomplish economic objectives appears to have become increasingly popular in recent years. Generally, this involves utilization of tax legislation to amend the Internal Revenue Code[1] and looks toward measures designed to help control the economy or to encourage certain activities and businesses.

*Control of the Economy.* One of the better known provisions of the tax law that purports to aid in controlling the economy is the investment tax credit. By providing a tax credit for investment in qualified property, so the logic goes, businesses will be encouraged to expand. The resulting expansion stimulates the economy and generates additional employment. As a safety valve against overexpansion, the investment credit can be suspended for a period of time or completely terminated.[2] Because the amount

---

1. The Internal Revenue Code is a compilation of Federal tax legislation.
2. Since the investment tax credit first was enacted in 1962, it has been suspended once and repealed once. The credit was reinstated in 1971, and its benefits were expanded under the Tax Reduction Act of 1975, the Revenue Act of 1978, and the Economic Recovery Tax Act of 1981. Some restriction of the credit, however, did occur as the result of the Tax Equity and Fiscal Responsibility Act of 1982 (TEFRA). Except for the TEFRA retrenchment, which was more motivated by budgetary constraints, all of these changes were justified in terms of the effect they would have on the nation's economy.

of the credit allowed varies with the recovery period of the property, provision is made for recapture of some or all of the credit in the event the property is disposed of prematurely.[3]

A further incentive towards capital formation is the degree to which a capital investment can be recovered with a tax benefit. For many years the tax law had recognized this consideration with provisions allowing accelerated methods of depreciation when writing off the cost of most tangible personalty (e. g., machinery, equipment) acquired for use in a trade or business.[4] The Economic Recovery Tax Act of 1981 goes much further by generally allowing shorter recovery periods and more generous recovery amounts under a newly established accelerated cost recovery system (ACRS). Additionally, beginning in 1982, taxpayers are allowed to expense certain capital asset acquisitions. In other words, limited amounts may be deducted in the year the asset(s) is purchased and placed in service. Thus, the taxpayer derives an immediate tax benefit from the property acquisition and does not have to await (under ACRS) recoupment of cost over a prescribed period of time.

> **Example 1.** In 1985, T purchases a machine for $5,000 for use in his trade or business. The machine is classified as five-year property under ACRS. At T's election, he may expense the $5,000 in 1985 rather than capitalize the amount and deduct its cost over a five-year period.

Of more immediate impact on the economy is a change in the tax rate structure. By lowering tax rates, taxpayers are able to obtain additional spendable funds. An increase in tax rates creates the opposite effect. An illustration of this approach was the passage of the Revenue Act of 1978. Among the many changes provided by this legislation was a decrease (from 48 percent to 46 percent) in the maximum rate of tax applicable to corporations. Also modified was the amount of taxable income (from the excess of $50,000 to the excess of $100,000) to which the maximum rate applies. The Economic Recovery Tax Act of 1981 further pursued this policy by significantly reducing the tax rates applicable to individuals over a three-year period and providing modest reductions of corporate rates for 1982 and 1983. Also, the penalty tax on personal holding companies was lowered from 70 percent to 50 percent.[5]

*Encouragement of Certain Activities.* Without passing judgment on the wisdom of any such choices, it is quite clear that the tax law does encourage certain types of economic activity or segments of the economy. If, for example, one assumes that technological progress is fostered, the favorable treatment allowed research and development expenditures can be explained. Under the tax law such expenditures can be deducted in the year incurred or, as an alternative, capitalized and amortized over a period of 60 months or more. In terms of timing the tax saving, such options usually are

---

3. The maximum credit is allowed for investments in qualifying property having a recovery period of five or more years.
4. The Tax Reform Act of 1969 severely restricted the use of accelerated depreciation methods with most depreciable real estate.
5. See Chapters 2 and 7.

preferable to a capitalization of the cost with a write-off over the estimated useful life of the asset created.[6]

The Economic Recovery Tax Act of 1981 further recognized the need to stimulate, through the use of the tax laws, technological progress. In addition to the favorable write-off treatment noted above, certain incremental research and development costs now qualify for a 25 percent tax credit.

> **Example 2.** In 1985, T Corporation (a 46 percent bracket taxpayer) incurs incremental research and development expenditures of $100,000. If the proper election is made, these expenses can be written off in 1985 with a tax saving of $46,000 [$100,000 (expenses incurred) × 46% (applicable tax bracket)]. To this can be added the tax credit of $25,000 [$100,000 (qualifying incremental expenses) × 25%] for an overall tax benefit of $71,000 ($46,000 + $25,000).

The encouragement of technological progress also can explain why the tax law places the inventor in an advantageous position. Not only can patents qualify as capital assets, but under certain conditions their disposition automatically carries favorable long-term capital gain treatment.

Is it desirable to encourage the conservation of energy resources? Considering the world energy situation and our own reliance on the consumption of foreign oil production, the answer to this question has to be obvious. The concern over energy usage was a prime consideration that led to the enactment in 1978 of the Energy Tax Act. The result of this legislation was to make available to taxpayers various tax savings (in the form of tax credits) for energy conservation expenditures made to personal residence and business property.

Are ecological considerations a desirable objective? If they are, this explains why the tax law permits a 60-month amortization period for costs incurred in the installation of pollution control facilities.

Would it be advantageous to the economy to stimulate the development of residential rental property and the rehabilitation of low-income rental housing? The tax law definitely favors these activities, since taxpayers incurring such costs are allowed to use rapid depreciation methods.

Is saving desirable for the economy? Saving leads to capital formation and thus makes funds available to finance home construction and industrial expansion. The tax law provides incentives to encourage savings through preferential treatment accorded to private retirement plans. Not only are contributions to Keogh (H.R. 10) plans and Individual Retirement Accounts (IRAs) deductible, but income from such contributions accumulates on a tax-free basis. As noted in a following section, the encouragement of private-sector pension plans can be justified under social considerations as well.

Is it wise to stimulate U. S. exports of goods and services abroad? Considering the pressing and continuing problem of a deficit in the U. S. balance of payments, the answer should be clear. Along this line, Congress has created a unique type of organization designed to encourage domestic exports of goods, called Foreign Sales Corporations (FSCs). A portion of the

---

**6.** If the asset developed has no estimated useful life, no write-off would be available without the two options allowed by the tax law.

export income from such eligible FSCs is exempt from Federal income taxes. Further, a domestic corporation is allowed a 100 percent dividends received deduction for distributions from an FSC out of earnings attributable to certain foreign trade income. Also in an international setting, Congress has deemed it advisable to establish incentives for those U. S. citizens who accept employment in overseas locations. Under the Economic Recovery Tax Act of 1981, such persons receive generous tax breaks through special treatment of their foreign-source income and certain housing costs.

An item previously mentioned can be connected to the encouragement of U. S. foreign trade. Because one of this country's major exportable products is its technology, can it not be said that the favoritism accorded to research and development expenditures (see above) also serves to foster international trade?

*Encouragement of Certain Industries.* No one can question the proposition that a sound agricultural base is necessary for a well-balanced national economy. Undoubtedly this can explain why farmers are accorded special treatment under the Federal tax system. Among these benefits are the following: the election to expense rather than capitalize soil and water conservation expenditures, fertilizers, and land clearing costs; the possibility of obtaining long-term capital gain treatment on the disposition of livestock held for draft, breeding, or dairy purposes; the availability of the investment tax credit on certain farm structures; and the election to defer the recognition of gain on the receipt of crop-insurance proceeds.

The tax law also operates to favor the development of natural resources by permitting the use of percentage depletion on the extraction and sale of oil and gas and specified mineral deposits[7], a write-off (rather than a capitalization) of certain exploration costs, and the possibility of long-term capital gain treatment on the sale of timber, coal, or domestic iron ore. The railroad and bank industries also are singled out for special tax treatment. All of these provisions can be explained, in whole or in part, by economic considerations.

*Encouragement of Small Business.* At least in the U. S., a consensus exists that what is good for small business is good for the economy as a whole. This assumption has led to a definite bias in the tax law favoring small business. How else can one explain why the owner of a family business can elect to write off a capital expenditure for 1985 of up to $5,000 while Exxon is limited to the same amount?[8]

In the corporate tax area, several provisions can be explained by their motivation to benefit small business. One provision, for example, enables a shareholder in a small business corporation to obtain an ordinary deduction for any loss recognized on a stock investment. Normally, such a loss would receive the less attractive capital loss treatment. This apparent favoritism is to encourage additional equity investments in small business

---

7. The tax advantages of percentage depletion were severely curtailed by legislation passed in 1975.

8. Previously, an individual filing a joint return could claim bonus depreciation of 20% on a qualifying investment of up to $20,000. Other taxpayers (including corporations) were allowed 20% of up to $10,000 of investment.

corporations.[9] Another provision permits the shareholders of a small business corporation to make a special election that generally will avoid the imposition of the corporate income tax.[10] Furthermore, such an election enables the corporation to pass through to its shareholders any of its operating losses and investment tax credits.[11]

The tax rates applicable to corporations tend to favor small business insofar as size is relative to the amount of taxable income generated in any one year. Since the full corporate tax rate of 46 percent applies only to taxable income in excess of $100,000, corporations that stay within these limits are subject to lower average tax rates.

> **Example 3.** For calendar year 1986, X Corporation has taxable income of $100,000 and Y Corporation has taxable income of $200,000. Based on this information, the corporate income tax is $25,750 for X Corporation and $71,750 for Y Corporation (see Example 25 in Chapter 2). By comparison, then, X Corporation is subject to an average tax rate of 25.75% (i. e., $25,750 ÷ $100,000) while Y Corporation is subject to a rate of 35.875% (i. e., $71,750 ÷ $200,000).

Furthermore, for taxable years beginning after 1984, the $20,250 savings that results from the graduated rate structure is phased out for large corporations with taxable income in excess of one million dollars. This is accomplished by imposing an additional five percent tax on taxable income in excess of one million dollars. This extra tax continues until the full $20,250 savings is recovered.

Another provision specifically designed to aid small business involves the LIFO inventory procedures. Enacted by the Economic Recovery Tax Act of 1981, such procedures are available only to those businesses with average gross receipts of less than two million dollars.

One of the justifications given for the enactment of the tax law governing corporate reorganizations (see Chapter 6) was the economic benefit it would provide for small businesses. By allowing corporations to combine without adverse tax consequences, small corporations would be in a position to compete more effectively with larger concerns.

*Budget Deficit Considerations.* Many people have become increasingly concerned over mounting budget deficits. In 1984 Congress modestly reacted to this concern by enacting the Deficit Reduction Act. Designed to raise additional revenue, some of the major changes made by this legislation are summarized as follows:

—Increase the write-off period for certain real property from 15 to 18 years.

—Freeze the amount of business asset acquisitions that can be expensed (rather than capitalized and depreciated) at $5,000 per year (refer to page 1-2 in this chapter). Such amount was scheduled to increase to $7,500 in 1984.

---

9. Known as Section 1244 stock, this subject is covered in Chapter 3.
10. Known as the S corporation election, the subject is discussed extensively in Chapter 8.
11. In general, an operating loss can benefit only the corporation incurring the loss through a carryback or carryforward to profitable years. Consequently, the shareholders of the corporation usually cannot take advantage of any such loss.

—Curtail the benefits to be derived from income averaging (see page 1-11 in this chapter).

—Postpone scheduled increases in the amount of income that can be excluded from the income tax by U. S. residents working overseas (refer to page 1-4 in this chapter).

Although a provision in the tax law can be justified on nonrevenue grounds, budget deficit considerations can dictate a contrary treatment.

**Example 4.** In the Economic Recovery Tax Act of 1981, Congress included in the tax law a provision that would have allowed taxpayers to exclude from taxation up to 15% of certain interest income. This provision, to have become effective for tax years beginning after 1984, was justified on the economic grounds that it would encourage savings and would aid financial institutions in acquiring capital resources. Apparently Congress had second thoughts about an interest exclusion when it took into consideration the potential revenue loss. The Deficit Reduction Act of 1984 rescinded the exclusion before it ever took effect.

Budget deficit considerations undoubtedly will play an ever-increasing role in shaping future tax policy. The Deficit Reduction Act of 1984 may be just the tip of the iceberg.

## SOCIAL CONSIDERATIONS

Some of the tax laws can be explained by looking to social considerations. This is particularly the case when dealing with the Federal income tax of individuals. Notable examples and the rationale behind each are summarized as follows:

—The nontaxability of certain benefits provided to employees through accident and health plans financed by employers. It would appear socially desirable to encourage such plans, since they provide medical benefits in the event of an employee's illness or injury.

—The nontaxability to the employee of some of the premiums paid by an employer for group term insurance covering the life of the employee. These arrangements can be justified in that they provide funds for the family unit to help it readjust following the loss of wages caused by the employee's death.

—The tax treatment to the employee of contributions made by an employer to qualified pension or profit-sharing plans.[12] The contribution and any income it generates will not be taxed to the employee until the funds are distributed. Private retirement plans should be encouraged, since they supplement the subsistence income level the employee otherwise would have under the Social Security system.[13]

---

12. These arrangements also benefit the employer by allowing it a tax deduction when the contribution is made to the qualified plan.
13. The same rationale explains the availability of similar arrangements for self-employed persons (the H.R. 10 or Keogh type of plan).

—The deduction allowed for contributions to qualified charitable organizations.[14] The deduction attempts to shift some of the financial and administrative burden of socially desirable programs from the public (the government) to the private (the citizens) sector.

—The credit allowed for amounts spent to furnish care for certain minor or disabled dependents to enable the taxpayer to seek or maintain gainful employment. Who could deny the social desirability of encouraging taxpayers to provide care for their children while they work?

—The disallowance of a tax deduction for certain expenditures that are deemed to be contrary to public policy. This disallowance extends to such items as fines, penalties, illegal kickbacks, and bribes to government officials.[15] Social considerations dictate that these activities should not be encouraged by the tax law. Permitting the deduction would supposedly encourage these activities.

—The imposition of the Federal estate tax on large estates.[16] From one viewpoint, it would be socially undesirable to permit large accumulations of wealth to pass by death from generation to generation without being subject to some type of transfer tax.[17]

Many other examples could be included but the conclusion would be unchanged: Social considerations do explain a significant part of the Federal tax law.


## EQUITY CONSIDERATIONS

The concept of equity is, of course, relative. Reasonable persons can, and often do, disagree about what is fair or unfair. In the tax area, moreover, equity is most often tied to a particular taxpayer's personal situation. To illustrate, it may be difficult for Ms. Jones to understand why none of the rent she pays on her apartment is deductible when her brother, Mr. Jones, is able to deduct a large portion of the monthly payments he makes on his personal residence in the form of interest and taxes.[18]

In the same vein, compare the tax treatment of a corporation with that of a partnership. Although the two businesses may be of equal size, similarly situated, and competitors in the production of goods or services, they are not comparably treated under the tax law. The corporation is subject to a separate Federal income tax; the partnership is not. Whether the differences in tax treatment logically can be justified in terms of equity is beside

---

**14.** The charitable contribution deduction available to corporations is discussed in Chapter 2.

**15.** Recent disclosures involving large corporations with international operations have highlighted this policy.

**16.** As noted in Chapter 11, the statutory definition of "large," under prior law, was any amount in excess of the $60,000 exemption allowed each decedent.

**17.** Portions of Chapter 11 are devoted to procedures that formerly permitted taxpayers to pass wealth from one generation to another with minimal tax consequences.

**18.** The encouragement of home ownership can be justified both on economic and social grounds. In this regard, it is interesting to note that some state income tax laws allow a form of relief (e. g., tax credit) to the taxpayer who rents his or her personal residence.

the point. The point is that the tax law can and does make a distinction between these business forms.

Equity, then, is not what appears fair or unfair to any one taxpayer or group of taxpayers. It is, instead, what the tax law recognizes. Some recognition of equity does exist, however, and offers an explanation of part of the law. The concept of equity appears in tax provisions that alleviate the effect of multiple taxation, postpone the recognition of gain when the taxpayer lacks the ability or wherewithal to pay the tax, mitigate the effect of the application of the annual accounting period concept, and help taxpayers to cope with the eroding result of inflation.

*Alleviating the Effect of Multiple Taxation.* The same income earned by a taxpayer may be subject to taxes imposed by different taxing authorities. If, for example, the taxpayer is a resident of New York City, income might generate Federal, State of New York, and City of New York income taxes. To compensate for this apparent inequity, the Federal tax law allows a taxpayer to claim a deduction for state and local income taxes. The deduction, however, does not neutralize the effect of multiple taxation, since the benefit derived depends on the taxpayer's Federal income tax bracket.[19]

Equity considerations can explain the Federal tax treatment of certain income from foreign sources. Since double taxation results when the same income is subject to both foreign and U. S. income taxes, the tax law permits the taxpayer to choose either a credit or a deduction for the foreign taxes paid.

The imposition of a separate income tax on corporations also leads to multiple taxation of the same income.

> **Example 5.** During the current year M Corporation has net income of $100,000, of which $5,000 was received as dividends from stock it owns in the Xerox Corporation. Assume M Corporation distributes the after-tax income to its shareholders (all individuals). At a minimum, the distribution received by the shareholders will be subject to two income taxes: the corporate income tax when the income is earned by M Corporation and the individual income tax when the balance is distributed to the shareholders as a dividend. The $5,000 M Corporation receives from the Xerox Corporation fares even worse. Because it is paid from income earned by the Xerox Corporation, it has been subjected to a third income tax (i. e., the corporate income tax imposed on the Xerox Corporation).[20]

The tax law attempts to alleviate the effect of double taxation by granting noncorporate shareholders a $100 ($200 on a joint return) exclusion for dividends received from certain domestic corporations. This exclusion would be available for each of the individual shareholders of M Corporation.[21] In the case of corporate shareholders, for whom triple taxa-

---

**19.** A tax credit, rather than a deduction, would eliminate the effects of multiple taxation on the same income.

**20.** The result materializes because the tax law permits no deduction to a corporation for the dividend distributions it makes. See Chapter 2.

**21.** Dividends in excess of $100 ($200 on a joint return) will still be subject to the double tax. The exclusion, therefore, provides only a limited degree of equity.

tion is possible, the law provides a deduction for dividends received from certain domestic corporations. The deduction, usually 85 percent of the dividends, would be allowed to M Corporation for the $5,000 it received from the Xerox Corporation. (See the discussion in Chapter 2.)

In the area of the Federal estate tax, several provisions reflect attempts through the law to compensate for the effect of multiple taxation. Some degree of equity is achieved, for example, by allowing a limited credit against the estate tax for state and foreign death taxes imposed on the same transfer. Other estate tax credits are available and can be explained on the same grounds.[22]

*The Wherewithal to Pay Concept.* Quite simply, the wherewithal to pay concept recognizes the inequity of taxing a transaction when the taxpayer lacks the means with which to pay the tax. It is particularly suited to situations when the taxpayer's economic position has not changed significantly as a result of a transaction.

> **Example 6.** T Corporation holds unimproved land held as an investment. The land has a basis to T Corporation of $60,000 and a fair market value of $100,000. The land is exchanged for a building (worth $100,000) that the corporation will use in its business.[23]

> **Example 7.** T Corporation owns a warehouse that it uses in its business. At a time when the warehouse has an adjusted basis of $60,000, it is destroyed by fire. T Corporation collects the insurance proceeds of $100,000 and, within two years of the end of the year in which the fire occurred, uses all of the proceeds to purchase a new warehouse.[24]

> **Example 8.** T, a sole proprietor, decides to incorporate his business. In exchange for the business's assets (adjusted basis of $60,000 and a fair market value of $100,000), T receives all of the stock of X Corporation, a newly created corporation.[25] The X Corporation stock is worth $100,000.

> **Example 9.** R, S, and T want to develop unimproved land owned by T. The land has a basis to T of $60,000 and a fair market value of $100,000. The RST Partnership is formed with the following investment: land worth $100,000 transferred by T, $100,000 in cash by R, and $100,000 cash by S. Each party receives a one-third interest in the RST Partnership.[26]

> **Example 10.** A Corporation and B Corporation decide to consolidate to form C Corporation.[27] Pursuant to the plan of reorganization, T

---

22. See Chapter 11.
23. The nontaxability of like-kind exchanges applies to the exchange of property held for investment or used in a trade or business for property to be similarly held or used.
24. The nontaxability of gains realized from involuntary conversions applies when the proceeds received by the taxpayer are reinvested within a prescribed period of time in property similar or related in service or use to that converted. Involuntary conversions take place as a result of casualty losses, theft losses, and condemnations by a public authority.
25. Transfers of property to controlled corporations are discussed in Chapter 3.
26. The formation of a partnership is discussed in Chapter 9.
27. Corporate reorganizations are discussed in Chapter 6.

exchanges her stock in A Corporation (basis of $60,000 and fair market value of $100,000) for stock in C Corporation worth $100,000.

In all of the above examples, either T Corporation or T had a realized gain of $40,000 [i. e., $100,000 (fair market value of the property received) − $60,000 (basis of the property given up)].[28] It would seem inequitable to force the taxpayer to recognize any of this gain for two reasons. First, without disposing of the property or interest acquired, the taxpayer would be hard-pressed to pay the tax.[29] Second, the taxpayer's economic situation has not changed significantly. To illustrate by referring to Example 8, can it be said that T's position as sole shareholder of X Corporation is much different from his prior status as owner of a sole proprietorship?[30]

Several warnings are in order concerning the application of the wherewithal to pay concept. Recognized gain is merely postponed and not necessarily avoided. Because of the basis carryover to the new property or interest acquired in these nontaxable transactions, the gain element is still present and might be recognized upon a subsequent taxable disposition of the property.[31] Referring to Example 8, suppose T later sold the stock in X Corporation for $100,000. Because T's basis in the stock is $60,000 (the same basis as in the assets transferred), the sale results in a recognized gain of $40,000. Also, many of the provisions previously illustrated prevent the recognition of realized losses. Since such provisions are automatic in application (i. e., not elective with the taxpayer), they could operate to the detriment of a taxpayer who wishes to obtain a deduction for a loss. The notable exception deals with involuntary conversions (Example 7). Here, nonrecognition treatment is elective with the taxpayer and will not apply to a realized loss if it is otherwise deductible.

One last comment about the wherewithal to pay concept is in order. Although it has definitely served as a guideline in shaping part of the tax law, it is not a hard-and-fast principle that is followed in every case. Only when the tax law specifically provides for no tax consequences will this result materialize.

**Example 11.** T exchanges stock in A Corporation (basis of $60,000 and fair market value of $100,000) for stock in B Corporation (fair

---

**28.** Realized gain can be likened to economic gain. However, the Federal income tax is imposed only on that portion of realized gain considered to be recognized under the law. Generally, recognized (or taxable) gain can never exceed realized gain.

**29.** If the taxpayer ends up with other property (boot) as part of the transfer, gain may be recognized to this extent. The presence of boot, however, helps solve the wherewithal to pay problem; it provides property, other than the property or interest central to the transaction, with which to pay the tax.

**30.** The results reached in Examples 8 and 9 also can be justified on economic grounds. To the extent possible, the tax laws should not interfere with the exercise of taxpayer judgment as to the form in which a business is to be conducted. Taxpayers, for example, might be deterred from incorporating a business or forming a partnership if these events were treated as taxable exchanges.

**31.** The recognition of gain might be completely or partially avoided if the property interest is passed by death. The heir or estate assumes an income tax basis in the property equal to the fair market value on date of death (or alternate valuation date when elected). In essence, any appreciation escapes the income tax. For a further discussion of the planning potential of this approach, see Chapter 12.

market value of $100,000). The exchange is not pursuant to a reorganization. Under these circumstances, T's realized gain of $40,000 is recognized for Federal income tax purposes.[32]

The result reached in Example 11 seems harsh in that the exchange does not place T in a position to pay the tax on the $40,000 gain. How can this result be reconciled with that reached in Example 10 when the exchange was nontaxable? In other words, why does the tax law apply the wherewithal to pay concept to the exchange of stock pursuant to a corporate reorganization (Example 10) but not to certain other stock exchanges (Example 11)?

Recall that the wherewithal to pay concept is particularly suited to situations in which the taxpayer's economic position has not changed significantly as a result of a transaction. In Example 10, T's stock investment in A Corporation really continues in the form of the C Corporation stock, since C was formed through a consolidation of A and B Corporations.[33] However, continuation of investment is not the case in Example 11. Here T's ownership in A Corporation has ceased, and an investment in an entirely different corporation has been substituted.

*Mitigating the Effect of the Annual Accounting Period Concept.* For purposes of effective administration of the tax law it is necessary for all taxpayers to report to and settle with the Federal government at periodic intervals. Otherwise, taxpayers would remain uncertain as to their tax liabilities, and the government would have difficulty judging revenues and budgeting expenditures. The period selected for final settlement of most tax liabilities, in any event an arbitrary determination, is one year. At the close of each year, therefore, a taxpayer's position becomes complete for that particular year. Referred to as the annual accounting period concept, its effect is to divide, for tax purposes, each taxpayer's life into equal annual intervals.

The finality of the annual accounting period concept could lead to dissimilarity in tax treatment for taxpayers who are, from a long-range standpoint, in the same economic position. Compare, for example, two individual taxpayers, C and D. Over a four-year period, C has annual income of $10,000 for the first three years and $100,000 in the fourth year. During the same period, D has income of $32,500 per year. Which taxpayer is better off? Considering the progressive nature of the Federal income tax, D's overall tax liability will be much less than that incurred by C. Is this a fair result in view of the fact that each taxpayer earned the same total income (i. e., $130,000) over the four-year period? It is easy to see, therefore, why the income averaging provision of the tax law can be explained on the basis of equitable considerations. Keep in mind, however, that the income averaging provision does not violate the annual accounting period concept but merely operates to mitigate its effect. By income averaging, C

---

**32.** The exchange of stock does not qualify for nontaxable treatment as a like-kind exchange (refer to Example 6).

**33.** This continuation is known as the "continuity of interest" concept. It forms the foundation for all nontaxable corporate reorganizations. This concept is discussed at length in Chapter 6.

would compute the tax on the $100,000 received in the fourth year by a special and favorable procedure without disturbing the finality of any of the returns filed or the taxes paid for the preceding three years.

The same reasoning used to support income averaging can be applied to explain the special treatment accorded by the tax law to net operating losses, excess capital losses, and excess charitable contributions.[34] Carry-back and carryover procedures help mitigate the effect of limiting a loss or a deduction to the accounting period in which it is realized. With such procedures, a taxpayer may be able to salvage a loss or a deduction that might otherwise be wasted.

**Example 12.** R and S are two sole proprietors and have experienced the following results during the past four years:

|  | Profit (or Loss) | |
| --- | --- | --- |
| Year | R | S |
| 1982 | $ 50,000 | $ 150,000 |
| 1983 | 60,000 | 60,000 |
| 1984 | 70,000 | 70,000 |
| 1985 | 50,000 | (50,000) |

Although R and S have the same profit of $230,000 over the period from 1982–1985, the finality of the annual accounting period concept places S at a definite disadvantage for tax purposes. The net operating loss procedure, therefore, offers S some relief by allowing him to apply some or all of his 1985 loss to the earlier profitable years (in this case 1982). Thus, he would be in a position with a net operating loss carry-back to obtain a refund for some of the taxes he paid on the $150,000 profit reported for 1982.

Mitigation of the annual accounting period concept also explains in part the preferential treatment the tax law accords to long-term capital gains. Often the gain from the disposition of an asset is attributable to appreciation that has developed over a long period of time. In view of the impracticality of taxing such appreciation as it occurs, the law looks to the year of realization as the taxable event.[35] Long-term capital gain treatment, therefore, represents a method of achieving relief from the bunching effect of forcing a gain to be recognized in the tax year of realization.[36]

The installment method of recognizing gain on the sale of property allows a taxpayer to spread tax consequences over the payout period.[37] The

---

**34.** The tax treatment of these items, as they relate to corporations, is discussed in Chapter 2.

**35.** Postponing the recognition of gain until the year it is realized is consistent with the wherewithal to pay concept. It would be difficult, for example, to pay a tax on the appreciation of an asset before its sale or other disposition has provided the necessary funds.

**36.** The law arbitrarily sets "more than six months" as the holding period necessary for long-term capital gain treatment. In this sense, it does seem unusual to tax appreciation which, for example, has materialized over a period of ten years in the same manner as that occurring during six months and one day.

**37.** Under the installment method, each payment received by the seller represents a return of basis (the nontaxable portion) and profit from the sale (the taxable portion).

harsh effect of taxing all the gain in the year of sale is thereby avoided. The installment method can also be explained by the wherewithal to pay concept, since recognition of gain is tied to the collection of the installment notes received from the sale of the property. Tax consequences, then, tend to correspond to the seller's ability to pay the tax.[38]

**Example 13.** In 1985, T sold unimproved real estate (cost of $40,000) for $100,000. Under the terms of the sale, T receives two notes from the purchaser, each for $50,000 (plus interest). One note is payable in 1986 and the other note in 1987. Without the installment method, T would have to recognize and pay a tax on the gain of $60,000 for the year of the sale (i. e., 1985). This is a rather harsh result, since none of the sale proceeds will be received until 1986 and 1987. With the installment method and presuming the notes are paid when each comes due, T recognizes half of the gain (i. e., $30,000) in 1986 and the remaining half in 1987.

The annual accounting period concept also has been modified to apply to situations in which taxpayers may have difficulty in accurately assessing their tax positions by year-end. In many such cases, the law permits taxpayers to treat transactions taking place in the next year as having occurred in the prior year.

**Example 14.** T, a calendar year individual taxpayer, is a participant in an H.R. 10 (Keogh) retirement plan. (See Appendix C for a definition of a Keogh plan.) Under the plan, T contributes 20% of her net self-employment income, such amount being deductible for Federal income tax purposes. On April 10, 19X5, T determines that her net self-employment income for calendar year 19X4 was $80,000, and consequently, she contributes $16,000 (20% × $80,000) to the plan. Even though the $16,000 contribution was made in 19X5, the law permits T to claim it as a deduction for tax year 19X4. Requiring T to make the contribution by December 31, 19X4, in order to obtain the deduction for that year would place the burden on her of arriving at an accurate determination of net self-employment income long before her income tax return needs to be prepared and filed.

Similar exceptions to the annual accounting period concept cover certain charitable contributions by accrual basis corporations (Chapter 2), dividend distributions by S corporations (Chapter 8), and the dividend deduction allowed in applying the tax on unreasonable accumulation of corporate earnings and the tax on personal holding companies (Chapter 7).

*Coping With Inflation.* During periods of inflation, bracket creep has plagued the working person. Because of the progressive nature of the income tax, any wage adjustment to compensate for inflation can increase the income tax bracket of the recipient. The overall impact is an erosion of purchasing power. The Reagan Administration recognized this problem in

---

**38.** Undoubtedly, this explains why, until recently, the installment method was not available on the sales of realty and the casual sales of personalty when the payments in the year of the sale exceeded 30% of the selling price.

1981 and provided for the solution (the indexation procedure) through the Economic Recovery Tax Act. However, indexation was not made effective until 1985.

For 1985, the tax brackets, personal and dependency exemptions, and the zero bracket amounts were adjusted upward by 4.1 percent. The 4.1 percent adjustment was derived from the increase in the average consumer price index over previous years. Any increase that is not a multiple of $10 shall be rounded to the nearest multiple of $10. If such increase is a multiple of $5, it shall be increased to the next multiple of $10. In 1986, the inflation indexing is 3.7 percent higher than the rate for 1985.

> **Example 15.** For 1985, the personal and dependency exemption amounts were increased from $1,000 to $1,040 [$1,000 + (.041 × $1,000) rounded to the nearest multiple of $10]. For 1986, the exemption amount is $1,080 ($1,040 × 1.037 rounded to the nearest multiple of $10). Single taxpayers enjoyed a zero bracket amount (ZBA) increase in 1985 from $2,300 to $2,390 [$2,300 + (.041 × $2,300) rounded to the nearest multiple of $10]. The ZBA for a single taxpayer in 1986 is $2,480 ($2,390 × 1.037 rounded to the nearest multiple of $10). For married persons filing joint returns in 1985, the ZBA moved from $3,400 to $3,540 [$3,400 + (.041 × $3,400) rounded to the nearest multiple of $10]. In 1986, the ZBA for married persons filing jointly is $3,670 ($3,540 × 1.037).

A similar expansion of the tax brackets will help, somewhat but not entirely, taxpayers whose incomes have been raised to offset inflation from being pushed into a higher tax bracket.

> **Example 16.** A married couple with two children and an adjusted gross income of $30,000 in 1985 would have their taxes drop by $115 in 1986 if their income does not change. A four-person family earning $40,000 in 1986 will get a $180 tax reduction as a result of indexing.

The Consumer Price Index is to be based on an average as of the close of the 12-month period ending on September 30 of each calendar year. Since this text was printed before this cutoff date, the indexation adjustment for 1987 was not available.

## POLITICAL CONSIDERATIONS

A large segment of the Federal tax law is made up of statutory provisions. Since these statutes are enacted by Congress, is it any surprise that political considerations do influence tax law? For purposes of discussion, the effect of political considerations on the tax law is divided into the following topics: special interest legislation, political expediency, the flat tax proposal, and state and local government influences.

*Special Interest Legislation.* There is no doubt that certain provisions of the tax law largely can be explained by looking to the political influence some pressure groups have exerted on Congress. Is there any other reason why, for example, prepaid subscription and dues income are not taxed until earned while prepaid rents are taxed to the landlord in the year received?

Along the same line are those tax provisions sponsored by individual members of Congress at the obvious instigation of a particularly influential constituent. In one case, for example, the effective date in proposed legislation that would reinstate the investment tax credit was moved back several months. It was well-known by all that the member of Congress initiating the change had a constituent with substantial capital expenditures that otherwise would not have qualified for the credit.

Special interest legislation is not necessarily to be condemned if it can be justified on economic or social grounds. At any rate, it is an inevitable product of our political system.

*Political Expediency.* Various tax reform proposals rise and fall in favor depending upon the shifting moods of the American public. That Congress is sensitive to popular feeling is an accepted fact. There are, therefore, certain provisions of the tax law that can be explained on the basis of political necessity existing at the time of enactment. With the public paying higher prices for gasoline and the major oil companies reporting larger profits, is it any wonder why, in 1980, Congress chose to impose a special excise tax on producers and royalty owners (i. e., the Crude Oil Windfall Profit Tax Act)?

Measures that deter more affluent taxpayers from obtaining so-called preferential tax treatment have always had popular appeal and, consequently, the support of Congress. Provisions such as the minimum tax, the imputed interest rules, and the limitation on the deductibility of interest on investment indebtedness can be explained on this basis. In the same vein are the provisions imposing penalty taxes on corporations that unreasonably accumulate earnings or that are classified as personal holding companies (see Chapter 7).

Other changes partially founded on the basis of political expediency include lowering individual income tax rates, increasing the amount of the dependency exemption, and instituting an earned income credit.

*The Flat Tax.* Political pressure that would call for a drastic revision of our current tax system is mounting. Any such modification would be founded upon the following assumptions:

—The income tax provisions in the tax law have become extremely complex.

—Such complexity has a negative effect on taxpayer morale and encourages taxpayer noncompliance.

Called the "flat tax," the new approach would eliminate many exclusions, deductions, and credits with a corresponding reduction in the tax rates. Ideally, the flat tax would be revenue-neutral, and its impact on any one taxpayer would depend upon the circumstances involved. It is likely that the tax liability of some would increase while the liability for others would diminish or disappear. One such proposal (designated FAST, for Fair And Simple Tax) has been introduced in Congress by Representative Jack Kemp (R–N.Y.) and Senator Robert Kasten (R–Wis.). Some of the FAST provisions are as follows:

—A higher level of income is exempted from any tax at all (e. g., $5,875 for single taxpayers, $14,375 for a family of four).

—Personal and dependency exemptions would be increased from $1,000 to $2,000 each.

—Twenty percent of wages up to $40,000 would be exempt. As wages approach $100,000, the exemptions would be phased out.

—Taxpayers at all levels would pay the same effective tax rate (approximately 25 percent).

—The only deductions retained would be for interest payments, medical expenses, real property taxes, and charitable contributions.

—The distinction between capital gains and ordinary income would be retained.

—The tax benefits for pension plans would be continued.

Because the Kemp–Kasten Bill retains certain deductions and favors some types of income, it does not meet the definition of a *pure* flat tax. But if certain exceptions are in order, where is the line to be drawn? One would not expect, for example, the home building industry to accept the nondeductibility of interest on mortgages and real property taxes. Besides, is not the encouragement of home ownership part of the American dream? Herein lies the flaw of the flat tax approach. In the political atmosphere in which Congress functions, the replacement of our current income tax system with a pure flat tax appears to be neither feasible nor likely.

*State and Local Influences.* Political considerations have played a major role in the exclusion from gross income of interest received on state and local obligations. In view of the furor that has been raised by state and local political figures every time any kind of modification of this tax provision has been proposed, one might well regard it as sacred.

Somewhat less apparent has been the influence state law has had in shaping our present Federal tax law. Of prime import in this regard has been the effect of the community property system employed in eight states.[39] At one time the tax position of the residents of these states was so advantageous that many common law states actually adopted community property systems.[40] Needless to say, the political pressure placed on Congress to correct the disparity in tax treatment was considerable. To a large extent this was accomplished in the Revenue Act of 1948 which extended many of the community property tax advantages to residents of common law jurisdictions.[41] Thus, common law states avoided the trauma of dis-

---

**39.** The states with community property systems are Louisiana, Texas, New Mexico, Arizona, California, Washington, Idaho, Nevada and Wisconsin (effective January 1, 1986). The rest of the states are classified as common law jurisdictions. The difference between common law and community property systems centers around the property rights possessed by married persons. In a common law system, each spouse owns whatever he or she earns. Under a community property system, one-half of the earnings of each spouse is considered owned by the other spouse. Assume, for example, H and W are husband and wife and their only income is the $40,000 annual salary H receives. If they live in New York (a common law state), the $40,000 salary belongs to H. If, however, they live in Texas (a community property state), the $40,000 salary is divided equally, in terms of ownership, between H and W.

**40.** Such states included Michigan, Oklahoma, and Pennsylvania.

**41.** The major advantage extended was the provision allowing married taxpayers to file joint returns and compute the tax liability as if the income had been earned one-half by each spouse. This result is automatic in a community property state, since half of the income earned by one spouse belongs to the other spouse. The income-splitting benefits of a joint return are incorporated as part of the tax rates applicable to married taxpayers.

carding the time-honored legal system familiar to everyone. The impact of community property law on the Federal estate and gift taxes is further explored in Chapters 11 and 12.

## INFLUENCE OF THE INTERNAL REVENUE SERVICE

The influence of the IRS is recognized in many areas beyond its obvious role in the issuance of the administrative pronouncements that make up a considerable portion of our tax law. In its capacity as the protector of the national revenue, the IRS has been instrumental in securing the passage of much legislation designed to curtail the most flagrant tax avoidance practices (to close tax loopholes). In its capacity as the administrator of the tax laws, the IRS has sought and obtained legislation to make its job easier (to attain administrative feasibility).

*The IRS as Protector of the Revenue.* Innumerable examples can be given of provisions in the tax law that stemmed from the direct influence of the IRS applied to preclude the use of a loophole as a means of avoiding the tax consequences intended by Congress. Working within the letter of existing law, ingenious taxpayers and their advisers devise techniques that accomplish indirectly what cannot be accomplished directly. As a consequence, legislation is enacted to close the loophole that taxpayers have located and exploited. The following summarizes some tax law that can be explained in this fashion and is discussed in the chapters to follow:

—The use of a related corporation to carry out a stock redemption and, in this manner, convert dividend income into long-term capital gain. This led to the enactment of Section 304 (discussed in Chapter 4).

—The use of preferred stock to bail out corporate profits as long-term capital gains rather than as dividend income. This led to the enactment of Section 306 (discussed in Chapter 4).

—The liquidation of a corporation before it has realized much, if any, income from the property it has developed. The procedure avoided ordinary income at the corporate level, while the distributions in liquidation gave the shareholders preferentially treated capital gains. This led to the collapsible corporation rules of Section 341 (discussed in Chapter 5).

In addition, the IRS has secured from Congress legislation of a more general nature that enables it to make adjustments based upon the substance, rather than the formal construction, of what a taxpayer has done. One provision, for example, authorizes the IRS to establish guidelines on the thin capitalization issue—when will corporate debt be recognized as debt for tax purposes and when will it be reclassified as equity or stock (see the discussion of thin capitalization in Chapter 3).[42] Another provision permits the IRS to make adjustments to a taxpayer's method of accounting when the method used by the taxpayer does not clearly reflect income (briefly discussed in Chapter 3 in connection with transfers to controlled

---

**42.** Section 385.

corporations and in Chapter 5 with reference to corporate liquidations).[43] The IRS also has been granted the authority to allocate income and deductions among businesses owned or controlled by the same interests when the allocation is necessary to prevent the evasion of taxes or to clearly reflect the income of each business.[44]

> **Example 17.** X Corporation and Y Corporation are brother-sister corporations (i. e., the stock of each is owned by the same shareholders), and both use the calendar year for tax purposes. For tax year 19X1, $10,000 of the income earned by X Corporation is claimed by Y Corporation. As a result, each corporation reports taxable income of $100,000 for the year.[45] Since the parties have not clearly reflected the taxable income of each business, the IRS can reallocate the $10,000 of income to X Corporation. After the reallocation, X Corporation has taxable income of $110,000 and Y Corporation has taxable income of $90,000.

Also of a general nature is the authority Congress has given the IRS to prevent taxpayers from acquiring corporations to obtain a tax advantage when the principal purpose of such acquisition was the evasion or avoidance of the Federal income tax.[46] The provision of the tax law that provides this authority is discussed briefly in Chapter 6.

*Administrative Feasibility.* Some of the tax law is justified on the grounds that it simplifies the task of the IRS in collecting the revenue and administering the law. With regard to collecting the revenue, the IRS long ago realized the importance of placing taxpayers on a pay-as-you-go basis. Elaborate withholding procedures apply to wages, while the tax on other types of income may have to be paid at periodic intervals throughout the year. The IRS has been instrumental in convincing the courts that accrual basis taxpayers should pay taxes on prepaid income in the year received and not when earned. The approach may be contrary to generally accepted accounting principles, but it is consistent with the wherewithal to pay concept.

Of considerable aid to the IRS in collecting revenue are the numerous provisions that impose interest and penalties on taxpayers for noncompliance with the tax law. Provisions such as the penalties for failure to pay a tax or to file a return that is due, the negligence penalty for intentional disregard of rules and regulations, and various penalties for civil and criminal fraud serve as deterrents to taxpayer noncompliance. This aspect of the tax law is discussed in Chapter 14.

One of the keys to an effective administration of our tax system is the audit process conducted by the IRS. To carry out this function, the IRS is aided by provisions that reduce the chance of taxpayer error or manipula-

---

**43.** Section 446(b).
**44.** Section 482.
**45.** By shifting $10,000 of income to Y Corporation, the taxpayers hoped to have the income taxed in the 40% bracket (the rate applicable to taxable income between $75,000–$100,000) rather than in the 46% bracket (the rate applicable to taxable income in excess of $100,000). See Chapter 2 for a further discussion of the income tax rates applicable to corporations.
**46.** Section 269.

tion and therefore simplify the audit effort that is necessary. An increase in the amount of the zero bracket amount, for example, reduces the number of individual taxpayers who will be in a position of claiming excess itemized deductions. With fewer deductions to check, therefore, the audit function is simplified.[47] The same objective can be used to explain the $155,800 unified estate and gift tax credit in 1986 and the $10,000 annual gift tax exclusion (see Chapter 11). These provisions decrease the number of tax returns that must be filed (as well as reduce the taxes paid) and thereby save audit effort.[48]

The audit function of the IRS has been simplified by provisions of the tax law dealing with the burden of proof. Suppose, for example, the IRS audits a taxpayer and questions a particular deduction. Who has the burden of proving the propriety of the deduction? Except in the case of fraud (see Chapter 14), the burden is always on the taxpayer.

## INFLUENCE OF THE COURTS

In addition to interpreting statutory provisions and the administrative pronouncements issued by the IRS, the Federal courts have influenced tax law in two other respects.[49] First, the courts have formulated certain judicial concepts that serve as guides in the application of various tax provisions. Second, certain key decisions have led to changes in the Internal Revenue Code. Understanding this influence helps to explain some of our tax law.

*Judicial Concepts Relating to Tax Law.* It is difficult to rank the tax concepts developed by the courts in order of importance. If this were done, however, one must place near the top of the list the concept of substance over form. Variously described as the "telescoping" or "collapsing" process or the "step transaction approach," it involves determining the true substance of what occurred. In a transaction involving many steps, any one step may be collapsed (or disregarded) to arrive directly at the result reached.

> **Example 18.** In 19X1, Mrs. G, a widow, wants to give $20,000 to S without incurring any gift tax liability.[50] She knows that the law permits her to give up to $10,000 each year per person without any tax consequences (the annual exclusion). With this in mind, the following steps are taken: a gift by Mrs. G to S of $10,000 (nontaxable because of

---

**47.** The same justification was given by the IRS when it proposed to Congress the $100-per-event limitation on personal casualty and theft losses. Imposition of the limitation eliminated many casualty and theft loss deductions and, as a consequence, saved the IRS considerable audit time. After 1982, an additional limitation equal to 10% of adjusted gross income applies to the total of nonbusiness losses after reduction by the floor of $100 for each loss.
**48.** Particularly in the case of nominal gifts among family members, taxpayer compliance in reporting and paying a tax on such transfers would be questionable. The absence of the $10,000 gift tax exclusion would, therefore, create a serious enforcement problem for the IRS.
**49.** A great deal of case law is devoted to ascertaining Congressional intent. The courts, in effect, ask: What did Congress have in mind when it enacted a particular tax provision?
**50.** The example assumes that Mrs. G has exhausted her unified transfer tax credit. See Chapter 11.

the $10,000 annual exclusion), a gift by Mrs. G to B of $10,000 (also nontaxable), and a gift by B to S of $10,000 (nontaxable because of B's annual exclusion). Regarding only the form of what Mrs. G and B have done, all appears well taxwise. In substance, however, what has happened? By collapsing the steps involving B, it is apparent that Mrs. G has made a gift of $20,000 to S and, therefore, has not avoided the Federal gift tax.

The substance over form concept plays an important role in transactions involving corporations. The liquidation-reincorporation problem, discussed in Chapter 6, is an ideal example of its possible application.

Another leading tax concept developed by the courts deals with the interpretation of statutory tax provisions that operate to benefit taxpayers. The courts have established the rule that these relief provisions are to be narrowly construed against taxpayers if there is any doubt about their application. Suppose, for example, X Corporation wants to be treated as an S corporation (see Chapter 8) but has not literally satisfied the statutory requirements for making the required election. Because S corporation status is a relief provision favoring taxpayers, chances are the courts will deny X Corporation this treatment. Other examples of the narrow construction of relief provisions that are covered in subsequent chapters are ordinary loss treatment on the stock of a small business corporation (Section 1244 in Chapter 3) and the definition of property for purposes of the 12-month liquidation (Section 337 in Chapter 5).

Important in the area of corporate-shareholder dealings (see the discussion of constructive dividends in Chapter 4) and in the resolution of valuation problems for estate and gift tax purposes (see Chapter 12) is the arm's length concept. Particularly in dealings between related parties, transactions can be tested by questioning whether the taxpayers acted in an "arm's length" manner. The question to be asked is: Would unrelated parties have handled the transaction in the same way?

> **Example 19.** The sole shareholder of a corporation leases property to it for a monthly rental of $500. To test whether the corporation should be allowed a rent deduction for this amount, the IRS and the courts will apply the arm's length concept. Would the corporation have paid $500 a month in rent if the same property had been leased from an unrelated party (rather than from the sole shareholder)?

The continuity of interest concept originated with the courts but has, in many situations, been incorporated into statutory provisions of the tax law. Primarily concerned with business readjustments, the concept permits tax-free treatment only if the taxpayer retains a substantial continuing interest in the property transferred to the new business. Due to the continuing interest retained, tax consequences should not result from the transfer because the position of the taxpayer has not changed. This concept applies to transfers to controlled corporations (Section 351 in Chapter 3), corporate reorganizations (Section 368 in Chapter 6), and transfers to partnerships (Section 721 in Chapter 9). Further, this approach may enable a taxpayer to avoid recapture of the investment tax credit when property is transferred to a partnership or a corporation [Section 47(b) in Chapters 3 and 9]. The continuity of interest concept helps explain the results reached in Examples 8 through 10 of this chapter. This concept is further discussed in Chapter 6.

Also developed by the courts, the business purpose concept has principal application to transactions involving corporations. Under this concept, some sound business reason must be present that motivates the transaction in order for the prescribed tax treatment to ensue. The avoidance of taxation is not considered to be a sound business purpose.

> **Example 20.** B and C are equal shareholders in X Corporation. They have recently had a disagreement and have, therefore, reached an impasse on how the future operations of X Corporation are to be conducted. This shareholder disagreement on corporate policy constitutes a sound business purpose and would justify a division of X Corporation in a way that will permit B and C to go their separate ways. Whether the division of X Corporation would be nontaxable to the parties involved would depend on compliance with the applicable statutory provisions dealing with corporate reorganizations. The point is, however, that compliance with statutory provisions would not be enough to insure nontaxability without a business purpose for the transaction.

The business purpose concept is discussed further in Chapter 6.

*Judicial Influence on Statutory Provisions.* Some court decisions have been of such consequence that Congress has incorporated them into statutory tax law. One illustration of this influence appears in Example 21.

> **Example 21.** In 19X0, T claimed a capital loss of $100,000 for Z Corporation stock that had become worthless during the year. Because of the absence of any offsetting gains, the capital loss deduction produced no income tax saving for T either in 19X0 or in future years. In 19X5, T institutes a lawsuit against the former officers of Z Corporation for their misconduct that resulted in the corporation's failure and thereby led to T's $100,000 loss. In settlement of the suit, the officers pay $50,000 to T. The IRS argued that the full $50,000 should be taxed as gain to T. Because the stock in Z Corporation was written off in 19X0, it had a zero basis for tax purposes. The $50,000 recovery received by T on the stock was, therefore, all gain. Although the position of the IRS was logical and conformed to the tax statutes as they then existed, it was not equitable. The court stated that T should not be taxed on the recovery of an amount previously deducted unless the deduction produced a tax saving. Since the $100,000 capital loss deduction in 19X0 produced no tax benefit, none of the $50,000 received in 19X5 results in gain.

The decision reached by the courts in Example 21, known as the tax benefit rule, has since become part of the statutory tax law.[51] The tax benefit rule is discussed later in connection with transfers to controlled corporations (Chapter 3) and corporate liquidations (Chapter 5).

Court decisions sometimes produce uncertainty in the tax law. Although such decisions may reach the right result, they do not produce the guidelines necessary to enable taxpayers to comply. In many situations, then, Congress may be compelled to add certainty to the law by enacting

---

51. Section 111.

statutory provisions specifying when a particular tax consequence will or will not materialize. Illustrations of this type of judicial "cause" and the statutory "effect" are as follows:

—When a stock redemption will be treated as an exchange or as a dividend (see Chapter 4).[52]

—Whether the liquidating corporation, in substance, made the sale of property distributed to its shareholders or whether the shareholders, in fact, made the sale (see Chapter 5).[53]

—What basis a parent corporation will have in the assets received from a subsidiary that is liquidated shortly after its acquisition (see Chapter 5).[54]

—When the income earned by a short-term trust will be shifted from the person creating the trust (i. e., the grantor) to the beneficiary of the trust (see Chapter 13).[55]

Some of the statutory provisions can be explained by the negative effect a particular court decision has had on Congress. In one decision, for example, it was held that the transfer of a liability to a controlled corporation should be treated as "boot" received by the transferor (see Chapter 3). Congress apparently disagreed with this treatment and promptly enacted legislation to change the result.[56]

## SUMMARY

In addition to its obvious revenue-raising objective, the Federal tax law has developed in response to several other factors:

—*Economic considerations.* Here, the emphasis is on tax provisions that help regulate the economy and encourage certain activities and types of businesses.

—*Social considerations.* Some tax provisions are designed to encourage or discourage certain socially desirable or undesirable practices.

—*Equity considerations.* Of principal concern in this area are tax provisions that alleviate the effect of multiple taxation, recognize the wherewithal to pay concept, mitigate the effect of the annual accounting period concept, and recognize the eroding effect of inflation.

—*Political considerations.* Of significance in this regard are tax provisions that represent special interest legislation, reflect political expediency, and illustrate the effect of state law.

—*Influence of the IRS.* Many tax provisions are intended to aid the IRS in the collection of the revenue and in the administration of the tax law.

---

**52.** Section 302(b)(2) and (3) (the "substantially disproportionate" and "complete termination of an interest" types of stock redemptions).
**53.** Section 337 (the 12-month liquidation).
**54.** Section 338 (the single-transaction approach).
**55.** Sections 671 through 678 (the grantor trust problem).
**56.** Section 357(a).

*—Influence of the Courts.* Court decisions have established a body of judicial concepts relating to tax law and have, on occasion, led Congress to enact statutory provisions to either clarify or negate their effect.

These factors explain various tax provisions and thereby help in understanding why the tax law developed to its present state. The next step involves learning to work with the tax law.

# WORKING WITH THE TAX LAW— TAX SOURCES

Learning to work with the tax law involves the following three basic steps:

—Familiarity with the sources of the law.

—Application of research techniques.

—Effective use of planning procedures.

Statutory, administrative, and judicial sources of the tax law are considered first.

## STATUTORY SOURCES OF THE TAX LAW

*Origin of the Internal Revenue Code.* Prior to 1939, the statutory provisions relating to tax were contained in the individual revenue acts enacted by Congress. Because of the inconvenience and confusion that resulted from dealing with many separate acts, in 1939 Congress codified all of the Federal tax laws. Known as the Internal Revenue Code of 1939, the codification arranged all Federal tax provisions in a logical sequence and placed them in a separate part of the Federal statutes. A further rearrangement took place in 1954 and resulted in the Internal Revenue Code of 1954 which continues in effect to the present day.

The following observations will help to clarify the significance of the codification procedure:

—With some exceptions, neither the 1939 nor the 1954 Code substantially changed the tax law existing on the date of enactment. Much of the 1939 Code, for example, was incorporated into the 1954 Code; the major change was the reorganization and renumbering of the tax provisions.[57]

—Statutory amendments to the tax law are integrated into the Code. The Deficit Reduction Act of 1984, for example, became part of the Internal Revenue Code of 1954.

*The Legislative Process.* Federal tax legislation generally originates in the House of Representatives where it is first considered by the House Ways and Means Committee. Tax bills originate in the Senate when they

---

57. This point is important in assessing judicial decisions interpreting provisions of the Internal Revenue Code of 1939. If the same provision was included in the Internal Revenue Code of 1954 and has not been subsequently amended, the decision has continuing validity.

are attached as riders to other legislative proposals.[58] If acceptable to the Committee, the proposed bill is referred to the whole House of Representatives for approval or disapproval. Approved bills are sent to the Senate where they are referred to the Senate Finance Committee for further consideration.[59] The next step involves referral from the Senate Finance Committee to the whole Senate. Assuming no disagreement between the House and Senate, passage by the Senate means referral to the President for approval or veto. If the bill is approved or if the President's veto is overridden, the bill becomes law and part of the Internal Revenue Code.

When the Senate version of the bill differs from that passed by the House,[60] the Joint Conference Committee, including members of both the House Ways and Means Committee and the Senate Finance Committee, is called upon to resolve these differences. The result, usually a compromise of the two versions, is then voted on by both the House and Senate. Acceptance by both bodies precedes referral to the President for approval or veto.

The typical legislative process dealing with tax bills is summarized below:

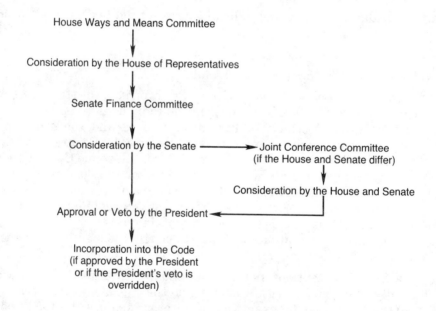

House Ways and Means Committee

↓

Consideration by the House of Representatives

↓

Senate Finance Committee

↓

Consideration by the Senate ———→ Joint Conference Committee
(if the House and Senate differ)

↓

Consideration by the House and Senate

↓

Approval or Veto by the President ←———

↓

Incorporation into the Code
(if approved by the President
or if the President's veto is
overridden)

---

**58.** The Tax Equity and Fiscal Responsibility Act of 1982 (TEFRA) originated in the Senate; its constitutionality was unsuccessfully challenged in the courts (one case was pursued by former Houston Congressman Ron Paul). The Senate version of the Deficit Reduction Act of 1984 was attached as an amendment to the Federal Boat Safety Act.

**59.** Some tax provisions are commonly referred to by the number of the bill designated in the House when first proposed or by the name of the member of Congress sponsoring the legislation. For example, the Self-Employed Individuals Tax Retirement Act of 1962 (refer to Example 14 in this chapter) is popularly known as H.R. 10 (i. e., House of Representatives Bill No. 10) or as the Keogh Act (i. e., Keogh being one of the members of Congress sponsoring the bill).

**60.** This is frequently the case with major tax bills. One factor contributing to a different Senate version is the latitude each individual senator has to make amendments to a bill when the Senate as a whole is voting on a bill referred to it by the Senate Finance Committee. Less latitude is allowed in the House of Representatives. Thus, the whole House either accepts or rejects what is proposed by the House Ways and Means Committee, and changes from the floor are not commonplace.

Referrals from the House Ways and Means Committee, the Senate Finance Committee, and the Joint Conference Committee are usually accompanied by Committee Reports. Because these Committee Reports often explain the provisions of the proposed legislation, they are a valuable source in ascertaining the intent of Congress. What Congress has in mind when it considers and enacts tax legislation is, of course, the key to interpreting such legislation. Since Regulations normally are not issued immediately after a statute is enacted, taxpayers and the courts look to legislative history materials to ascertain Congressional intent.

The role of the Joint Conference Committee indicates the importance of compromise to the legislative process. The practical effect of the compromise process is illustrated by reviewing what happened in the Economic Recovery Tax Act of 1981 concerning the change in the carryover period of unused investment tax credits.

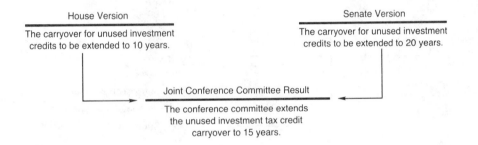

*Arrangement of the Code.* In working with the Code it helps to understand the format followed. Note, for example, the following partial table of contents:

Subtitle A.　Income Taxes

　　Chapter 1.　Normal Taxes and Surtaxes

　　　　Subchapter A.　Determination of Tax Liability

　　　　　　Part I.　Tax on Individuals

　　　　　　　　Sections 1–5

　　　　　　Part II.　Tax on Corporations

　　　　　　　　Sections 11–12

* * *

In referring to a provision of the Code, the key is usually the section number involved. In designating Section 2(a) (dealing with the status of a surviving spouse), for example, it would be unnecessary to include Subtitle A, Chapter 1, Subchapter A, Part I. Merely mentioning Section 2(a) will suffice, since the section numbers run consecutively and do not begin again with each new Subtitle, Chapter, Subchapter, or Part. However, not all Code section numbers are used. Notice that Part I ends with Section 5 and

Part II starts with Section 11 (i. e., at present there are no Sections 6, 7, 8, 9, and 10).[61]

Among tax practitioners, a common way of referring to some specific area of income taxation is by Subchapter designation. More common Subchapter designations include Subchapter C ("Corporate Distributions and Adjustments"), Subchapter K ("Partners and Partnerships"), and Subchapter S ("Tax Treatment of S Corporations and Their Shareholders"). Particularly in the last situation, it is much more convenient to describe the effect of the applicable Code provisions involved (Sections 1361 through 1379) as S corporation status rather than as the "Tax Treatment of S Corporations and Their Shareholders."

*Citing the Code.* Code sections often are broken down into subparts.[62] Section 2(a)(1)(A) serves as an example.

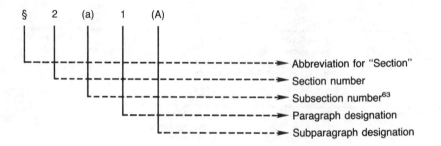

Broken down as to content, § 2(a)(1)(A) becomes:

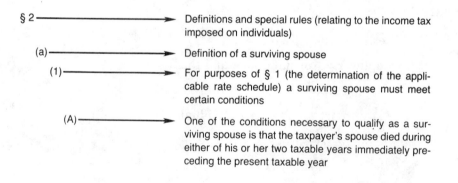

§ 2 ⟶ Definitions and special rules (relating to the income tax imposed on individuals)

(a) ⟶ Definition of a surviving spouse

(1) ⟶ For purposes of § 1 (the determination of the applicable rate schedule) a surviving spouse must meet certain conditions

(A) ⟶ One of the conditions necessary to qualify as a surviving spouse is that the taxpayer's spouse died during either of his or her two taxable years immediately preceding the present taxable year

Throughout the remainder of the text, references to Code sections are in the form just given. The symbols "§" and "§ §" are used in place of "Section" and "Sections." Unless otherwise stated, all Code references are to

---

**61.** When the 1954 Code was drafted, the omission of section numbers was intentional. This provided flexibility to incorporate later changes into the Code without disrupting its organization. When Congress does not leave enough space, subsequent Code Sections are given A, B, C, etc., designations. A good example is the treatment of § § 280A through 280G.
**62.** Some Code Sections do not necessitate subparts. See, for example, § 482.
**63.** Some Code Sections omit the subsection designation and use, instead, the paragraph designation as the first subpart. See, for example, § 212(1) and § 1221(1).

the Internal Revenue Code of 1954. The format followed in the remainder of text is summarized as follows:

| *Complete Reference* | *Text Reference* |
|---|---|
| Section 2(a)(1)(A) of the Internal Revenue Code of 1954 | § 2(a)(1)(A) |
| Sections 1 and 2 of the Internal Revenue Code of 1954 | §§ 1 and 2 |
| Section 12(d) of the Internal Revenue Code of 1939[64] | § 12(d) of the Internal Revenue Code of 1939 |

## ADMINISTRATIVE SOURCES OF THE TAX LAW

The administrative sources of the Federal tax law can be grouped as follows: Treasury Department Regulations, Revenue Rulings and Procedures, and other administrative pronouncements. All are issued either by the U. S. Treasury Department or by one of its instrumentalities [e. g., the Internal Revenue Service (IRS) or a District Director]. The role played by the IRS in this process is considered in greater depth in Chapter 14.

*Treasury Department Regulations.* Regulations are issued by the U. S. Treasury Department under authority granted by Congress.[65] Interpretative by nature, they provide taxpayers with considerable guidance on the meaning and application of the Code. Although not issued by Congress, Regulations do carry considerable weight and are an important factor to consider in complying with the tax law.

Since Regulations interpret the Code, they are arranged in the same sequence. Regulations are, however, prefixed by a number that designates the type of tax or administrative, procedural, or definitional matter to which they relate. For example, the prefix 1 designates the Regulations under the income tax law. Thus, the Regulations under Code § 2 would be cited as Reg. § 1.2 with subparts added for further identification. However, these subparts often have no correlation in their numbering with the Code subsections. The prefix 20 designates estate tax Regulations; 25 covers gift tax Regulations; 31 relates to employment taxes; and 301 refers to Regulations dealing with procedure and administration. This listing is not all-inclusive.

New Regulations and changes to existing Regulations usually are issued in proposed form before they are finalized. The time interval between the proposal of a Regulation and its finalization permits taxpayers and other interested parties to comment on the propriety of the proposal. Proposed Regulations under Code § 2, for example, would be cited as Prop.Reg. § 1.2.

Sometimes temporary Regulations are issued by the Treasury Department relating to elections and other matters where speed is critical. Tem-

---

**64.** Section 12(d) of the Internal Revenue Code of 1939 is the predecessor to § 2 of the Internal Revenue Code of 1954. Keep in mind that the 1954 Code has superseded the 1939 Code. The reason for referring to a provision of the 1939 Code is set forth in Footnote 57 of this chapter.

**65.** § 7805.

porary Regulations usually are necessitated due to legislation recently enacted by Congress that takes effect immediately.

Proposed and final Regulations are published in the *Federal Register* and are reproduced in major tax services. Final Regulations are issued as Treasury Decisions (T.D.).

*Revenue Rulings and Revenue Procedures.* Revenue Rulings are official pronouncements of the National Office of the IRS and, like Regulations, are designed to provide interpretation of the tax law. However, they do not carry the same legal force and effect of Regulations and usually deal with more restricted problems. Both Revenue Rulings and Revenue Procedures serve an important function in that they afford guidance to both IRS personnel and taxpayers in handling routine tax matters.

Although letter rulings (discussed below) are not the same as Revenue Rulings, a Revenue Ruling often results from a specific taxpayer's request for a letter ruling. If the IRS believes that a taxpayer's request for a letter ruling deserves official publication because of its widespread impact, the holding will be converted into a Revenue Ruling. In making this conversion, names, identifying facts, and money amounts will be changed to disguise the identity of the requesting taxpayer. The IRS then will issue what would have been a letter ruling as a Revenue Ruling.

Revenue Procedures are issued in the same manner as are Revenue Rulings, but they deal with the internal management practices and procedures of the IRS. Familiarity with these procedures can increase taxpayer compliance and assist the efficient administration of the tax laws by the IRS.

Both Revenue Rulings and Revenue Procedures are published weekly by the U. S. Government in the *Internal Revenue Bulletin* (I.R.B.). Semiannually, the Bulletins for a six-month period are gathered together, reorganized by Code Section classification, and published in a bound volume designated *Cumulative Bulletin* (C.B.).[66] The proper form for citing Rulings and Procedures depends on whether the item has been published in the *Cumulative Bulletin* or is available in I.R.B. form. Consider, for example, the following transition:

| | |
|---|---|
| Temporary Citation | Rev.Rul. 85–63, I.R.B. No. 21, 10. *Explanation:* Revenue Ruling Number 63, appearing on page 10 of the 21st weekly issue of the *Internal Revenue Bulletin* for 1985. |
| Permanent Citation | Rev.Rul. 85–63, 1985–1 C.B. 292 *Explanation:* Revenue Ruling Number 63, appearing on page 292 of volume 1 of the *Cumulative Bulletin* for 1985. |

---

**66.** Usually only two volumes of the *Cumulative Bulletin* are published each year. However, when major tax legislation has been enacted by Congress, other volumes might be published containing the Congressional Committee Reports supporting the Revenue Act. See, for example, the two extra volumes for 1984 dealing with the Deficit Reduction Act of 1984. The 1984–3 *Cumulative Bulletin,* Volume 1, contains the text of the law itself; 1984–3, Volume 2, contains the Committee Reports. This makes a total of four volumes of the *Cumulative Bulletin* for 1984: 1984–1; 1984–2; 1984–3, Volume 1; and 1984–3, Volume 2.

Since the first volume of the 1985 *Cumulative Bulletin* was not published until the end of 1985, the I.R.B. citation must be used until that time. After the publication of the *Cumulative Bulletin,* the C.B. citation is proper. The basic portion of both citations (i. e., Rev.Rul. 85–63) indicates that this was the 63rd Revenue Ruling issued by the IRS during 1985.

Revenue Procedures are cited in the same manner, except that "Rev.Proc." is substituted for "Rev.Rul." Procedures, like Rulings, are published in the *Internal Revenue Bulletin* (the temporary source) and later transferred to the *Cumulative Bulletin* (the permanent source).

*Other Administrative Pronouncements.* Treasury Decisions (T.D.s) are issued by the Treasury Department to promulgate new Regulations, to amend or otherwise change existing Regulations, or to announce the position of the Government on selected court decisions. Like Revenue Rulings and Revenue Procedures, T.D.s are published in the *Internal Revenue Bulletin* and subsequently transferred to the *Cumulative Bulletin.*

Technical Information Releases (T.I.R.) are usually issued to announce the publication of various IRS pronouncements (e. g., Revenue Rulings, Revenue Procedures).

Individual rulings are issued upon a taxpayer's request and describe how the IRS will treat a proposed transaction for tax purposes. They apply only to the taxpayer who asks for and obtains the ruling.[67] Though this procedure may sound like the only real way to carry out effective tax planning, the IRS limits the issuance of individual rulings to restricted, preannounced areas of taxation. Thus, it is not possible to obtain a ruling on many of the problems that are particularly troublesome for taxpayers.[68] For example, the IRS will not issue a ruling as to whether compensation paid to shareholder-employees is reasonable (see Chapter 4) or whether § 269 applies [i. e., the acquisition of a corporation to evade or avoid income tax (see Chapter 5)]. The main reason the IRS will not rule in certain areas is that such areas involve fact-oriented situations.

Individual rulings are not published by the government and, at one time, were "private" (i. e., the content of the ruling was made available only to the taxpayer requesting the ruling). However, Federal legislation and the courts have forced the IRS to modify its position on the confidentiality of individual rulings.[69]

The Tax Reform Act of 1976 now requires the IRS to make individual rulings available for public inspection after identifying details are deleted.[70] Published digests of private letter rulings can be found in *Private Letter Rulings* (published by Prentice-Hall), *BNA Daily Tax Reports,* and Tax Analysts & Advocates *TAX NOTES. IRS Letter Rulings Reports* (pub-

---

**67.** In this regard, individual rulings differ from Revenue Rulings, which are applicable to *all* taxpayers.

**68.** Rev.Proc. 86–3, I.R.B. No. 1, 26, contains a listing of areas in which the IRS will not issue advance rulings. From time to time, subsequent Revenue Procedures are issued that modify or amplify Rev.Proc. 86–3.

**69.** The Freedom of Information Act as interpreted by *Tax Analysts and Advocates v. U. S.,* 74–2 USTC ¶ 9635, 34 AFTR2d 74–5731, 505 F.2d 350 (CA–DC, 1974), and *Tax Analysts and Advocates v. U. S.,* 75–2 USTC ¶ 9869, 37 AFTR2d 76–352, 405 F.Supp. 1065 (D.Ct.D.C., 1975).

**70.** § 6110.

lished by Commerce Clearing House) contains both digests and full texts of all letter rulings.

The National Office of the IRS releases Technical Advice Memoranda (TAMs) weekly. Although letter rulings are responses to requests by taxpayers, Technical Advice Memoranda are initiated by IRS personnel during audits. Technical Advice Memoranda give the IRS's determination of an issue somewhat like letter rulings. They deal with completed rather than proposed transactions and are often requested in relation to exempt organizations and employee plans. However, TAMs are issued by the National Office of the IRS to field personnel, whereas letter rulings are issued to taxpayers at their request. TAMs are not officially published and may not be cited or used as precedent according to § 6110(j)(3).

Both letter rulings and Technical Advice Memoranda are issued with multi-digit file numbers. Consider, for example, the following Technical Advice Memorandum dealing with the alternative minimum tax: DOC 8423006. The first two digits refer to the year (84 = 1984), the next two digits indicate the week of issuance (23 = the twenty-third week), and the last three digits represent the number of ruling issued during such week (sixth ruling during the twenty-third week).

Like individual rulings, determination letters are issued at the request of taxpayers and provide guidance concerning the application of the tax law. They differ from individual rulings in that the issuing source is the District Director rather than the National Office of the IRS. Also, determination letters usually involve completed (as opposed to proposed) transactions. Determination letters are not published but are made known only to the party making the request.

The following examples illustrate the distinction between individual rulings and determination letters:

> **Example 22.** The shareholders of X Corporation and Y Corporation want assurance that the consolidation of the corporations into Z Corporation will be a nontaxable reorganization (see Chapter 6). The proper approach would be to request from the National Office of the IRS an individual ruling concerning the income tax effect of the proposed transaction.

> **Example 23.** T operates a barber shop in which he employs eight barbers. To properly comply with the rules governing income tax and payroll tax withholdings, T wants to know whether the barbers working for him are employees or independent contractors. The proper procedure would be to request from the appropriate District Director a determination letter on the status of such persons.

## JUDICIAL SOURCES OF THE TAX LAW

*The Judicial Process in General.* After a taxpayer has exhausted some or all of the remedies available within the IRS (i. e., no satisfactory settlement has been reached at the agent or at the conference level discussed in Chapter 14), the dispute can be taken to the Federal courts. The dispute is first considered by a court of original jurisdiction (known as a trial court) with any appeal (either by the taxpayer or the IRS) taken to the

**Figure I**

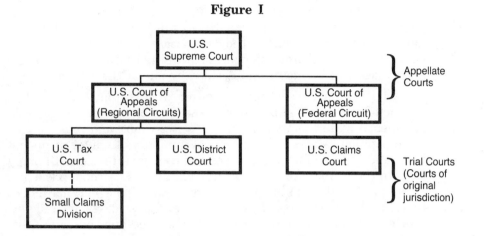

appropriate appellate court. In most situations the taxpayer has a choice of any of four trial courts: a Federal District Court, the U. S. Claims Court, the U. S. Tax Court, or the Small Claims Division of the U. S. Tax Court. The trial and appellate court scheme for Federal tax litigation is illustrated in Figure I.

The broken line between the U. S. Tax Court and the Small Claims Division indicates that there is no appeal from the Small Claims Division. Currently, the jurisdiction of the Small Claims Division of the U. S. Tax Court is limited to $10,000 or less. The proceedings of the Small Claims Division are informal, and its decisions are not precedents for any other court decision and are not reviewable by any higher court. Proceedings can be more timely and less expensive in the Small Claims Division.

American law, following English law, is frequently "made" by judicial decisions. Under the doctrine of *stare decisis,* each case (except in the Small Claims Division) has precedential value for future cases with the same controlling set of facts. Most Federal and state appellate court decisions and some decisions of trial courts are published. More than 3,000,000 judicial opinions have been published in the United States; over 30,000 cases are published each year.[71] Published court reports are organized by jurisdiction (Federal or state) and level of court (appellate or trial).

*Trial Courts.* Differences between the various trial courts (courts of original jurisdiction) are summarized as follows:

—There is only one Claims Court and only one Tax Court, but there are many Federal District Courts. The taxpayer does not select the District Court that will hear the dispute but must sue in the one that has jurisdiction.

—The U. S. Claims Court has jurisdiction in judgment upon any claim against the United States that is based on the Constitution, any Act of Congress, or any regulation of an executive department.

---

71. Jacobstein and Mersky, *Fundamentals of Legal Research,* 3rd Edition (Mineola, N.Y.: The Foundation Press, Inc. 1985).

—Each District Court has only one judge, the Claims Court has 16 judges, and the Tax Court has 19. In the case of the Tax Court, however, the whole court will decide a case (i. e., the court sits *en banc*) only when more important or novel tax issues are involved. Most cases will be heard and decided by one of the 19 judges.

—The Claims Court meets most often in Washington, D.C., while a District Court meets at a prescribed seat for the particular district. Since each state has at least one District Court and many of the more populous states have more, the problem of travel inconvenience and expense for the taxpayer and counsel (present with many suits in the Claims Court) is largely eliminated. Although the Tax Court is officially based in Washington, D.C., the various judges travel to different parts of the country and hear cases at predetermined locations and dates. Although this procedure eases the distance problem for the taxpayer, it could mean a delay before the case comes to trial and is decided.

—The Tax Court hears only tax cases; the Claims Court and District Courts hear nontax litigation as well. This difference, plus the fact that many Tax Court justices have been appointed from IRS or Treasury Department positions, has led some to conclude that the Tax Court has more expertise in tax matters.

—The only court in which a taxpayer can obtain a jury trial is in a District Court. But since juries can decide only questions of fact and not questions of law, even those taxpayers who choose the District Court route often do not request a jury trial. In such event, the judge will decide all issues. Note that a District Court decision is controlling only in the district in which the court has jurisdiction.

—In order for the Claims Court or a District Court to have jurisdiction, the taxpayer must pay the tax deficiency assessed by the IRS and sue for a refund. If the taxpayer wins (assuming no successful appeal by the Government), the tax paid plus appropriate interest thereon will be recovered. In the case of the Tax Court, however, jurisdiction is usually obtained without first paying the assessed tax deficiency. In the event the taxpayer loses in the Tax Court (and no appeal is taken or any appeal is unsuccessful), the deficiency must be paid with appropriate interest.

—Appeals from a District Court or a Tax Court decision are to the appropriate U. S. Court of Appeals. Appeals from the Claims Court go to the Court of Appeals for the Federal Circuit.

*Appellate Courts.* Regarding appeals from a trial court, the listing on the next page indicates the Court of Appeals of appropriate jurisdiction.

Two of these Courts of Appeals are of recent vintage and may cause some confusion for one who conducts tax research. The Eleventh Court of Appeals came into being in late 1981 and comprises states (i. e., Alabama, Florida, and Georgia) that formerly were within the jurisdiction of the Fifth Court of Appeals. The reason for the division was the increase in population in some of the Sun Belt states and the enormity of the geographical area previously covered by the Fifth Court of Appeals. The Court

| First | Seventh |
|---|---|
| Maine | Illinois |
| Massachusetts | Indiana |
| New Hampshire | Wisconsin |
| Rhode Island | |
| Puerto Rico | Eighth |
| | Arkansas |
| Second | Iowa |
| Connecticut | Minnesota |
| New York | Missouri |
| Vermont | Nebraska |
| | North Dakota |
| Third | South Dakota |
| Delaware | |
| New Jersey | Ninth |
| Pennsylvania | Alaska |
| Virgin Islands | Arizona |
| | California |
| District of Columbia | Hawaii |
| Washington, D.C. | Idaho |
| | Montana |
| Fourth | Nevada |
| Maryland | Oregon |
| North Carolina | Washington |
| South Carolina | Guam |
| Virginia | |
| West Virginia | Tenth |
| | Colorado |
| Fifth | Kansas |
| Canal Zone | New Mexico |
| Louisiana | Oklahoma |
| Mississippi | Utah |
| Texas | Wyoming |
| | |
| Sixth | Eleventh |
| Kentucky | Alabama |
| Michigan | Florida |
| Ohio | Georgia |
| Tennessee | |

Federal Circuit

All of the jurisdictions (where the case originates in the Claims Court)

of Appeals for the Federal Circuit was created in late 1982 and was given jurisdiction over all appeals from the U. S. Claims Court. Previously, such appeals went directly to the U. S. Supreme Court, thus bypassing the Court of Appeals level. As a matter of identification, the same legislation that established the Court of Appeals for the Federal Circuit changed the name of what used to be the U. S. Court of Claims to the U. S. Claims Court.

If the Government loses at the trial court level (i. e., District Court, Tax Court, or Claims Court), it need not (and frequently does not) appeal. The fact that an appeal is not made, however, does not indicate that the IRS agrees with the result and will not litigate similar issues in the future. There could be a number of reasons for the Service's failure to appeal. First, the current litigation load may be heavy, and as a consequence, the

IRS may decide that available personnel should be assigned to other, more important, cases. Second, the IRS may determine that this is not a good case to appeal. Such might be true if the taxpayer is in a sympathetic position or the facts are particularly strong in his or her favor. In such event, the IRS may wait to test the legal issues involved with a taxpayer who has a much weaker case. Third, if the appeal is from a District Court or the Tax Court, the Court of Appeals of jurisdiction could have some bearing on whether or not the decision is made to go forward with an appeal. Based on past experience and precedent, the IRS may conclude that the chance for success on a particular issue might be more promising in another Court of Appeals. The IRS will wait for a similar case to arise in a different appellate court.

District Courts, the Tax Court, and the Claims Court must abide by the precedents set by the Court of Appeals of jurisdiction. A particular Court of Appeals need not follow the decisions of another Court of Appeals. All courts, however, must follow the decisions of the U. S. Supreme Court.

Because the Tax Court is a national court (i. e., it hears and decides cases from all parts of the country), the observation made in the previous paragraph has caused problems. For many years the Tax Court followed a policy of deciding cases based on what it thought the result should be, even though the appeal of its decision might have been to a Court of Appeals that had previously decided a similar case differently. A few years ago this policy was changed. Now the Tax Court will still decide a case as it feels the law should be applied *only* if the Court of Appeals of appropriate jurisdiction has not yet passed on the issue or has previously decided a similar case in accordance with the Tax Court's decision.[72] If the Court of Appeals of appropriate jurisdiction has previously held otherwise, the Tax Court will conform under the *Golsen* rule even though it disagrees with the holding.

> **Example 24.** Taxpayer T lives in Texas and sues in the Tax Court on Issue A. The Fifth Court of Appeals, the appellate court of appropriate jurisdiction, has already decided that, based on similar facts and involving a different taxpayer, Issue A should be resolved against the Government. Although the Tax Court feels that the Fifth Court of Appeals is wrong, under the *Golsen* rule it will render judgment for T. Shortly thereafter, Taxpayer U, a resident of New York, in a comparable case, sues in the Tax Court on Issue A. Assume further that the Second Court of Appeals, the appellate court of appropriate jurisdiction, has never expressed itself on Issue A. Presuming the Tax Court has not reconsidered its position on Issue A, it will decide against Taxpayer U. Thus, it is entirely possible for two taxpayers suing in the same court to end up with opposite results merely because they live in different parts of the country.

Appeal to the U. S. Supreme Court is by Writ of Certiorari. If the Court accepts jurisdiction, it will grant the Writ (i. e., *Cert. Granted*). Most often, it will deny jurisdiction (i. e., *Cert. Denied*). For whatever reason or rea-

---

72. *Jack E. Golsen*, 54 T.C. 742 (1970).

sons, the Supreme Court rarely hears tax cases. The Court usually grants certiorari to resolve a conflict among the Courts of Appeals (e. g., two or more appellate courts have assumed opposing positions on a particular issue). The granting of a Writ of Certiorari indicates that at least four members of the Supreme Court believe that the issue is of sufficient importance to be heard by the full court.

The role of appellate courts is limited to a review of the record of trial compiled by the trial courts. Thus, the appellate process usually involves a determination of whether or not the trial court applied the proper law in arriving at its decision. Rarely will an appellate court disturb a lower court's fact-finding determination.

The result of an appeal could be any of a number of possibilities. The appellate court could approve (affirm) or disapprove (reverse) the lower court's finding, and it could also send the case back for further consideration (remand). When many issues are involved, it is not unusual to encounter a mixed result. Thus, the lower court could be affirmed (i. e., *aff'd.*) on Issue A and reversed (i. e., *rev'd.*) on Issue B, and Issue C could be remanded (i. e., *rem'd.*) for additional fact finding.

When more than one judge is involved in the decision-making process, disagreement is not uncommon. In addition to the majority view, there could be one or more judges who concur (i. e., agree with the result reached but not with some or all of the reasoning) or dissent (i. e., disagree with the result). In any one case it is, of course, the majority view that controls. But concurring and dissenting views can have influence on other courts or, at some subsequent date when the composition of the court has changed, even on the same court.

Having concluded a brief description of the judicial process, it is appropriate to consider the more practical problem of the relationship of case law to tax research. As previously noted, court decisions are an important source of tax law. The ability to cite a case and to locate it is, therefore, a must in working with the tax law.

*Judicial Citations—The U. S. Tax Court.*  A good starting point is with the U. S. Tax Court (formerly the Board of Tax Appeals). The Court issues two types of decisions: Regular and Memorandum. The distinction between the two involves both substance and form. In terms of substance, Memorandum decisions deal with situations necessitating only the application of already established principles of law; however, Regular decisions involve novel issues not previously resolved by the Court. In actual practice, however, this distinction is not always preserved. Not infrequently, Memorandum decisions will be encountered that appear to warrant Regular status and vice versa. At any rate, do not conclude that Memorandum decisions possess no value as precedents. Both represent the position of the Tax Court and, as such, can be relied upon.

Another important distinction between the Regular and Memorandum decisions issued by the Tax Court arises in connection with form. The Memorandum decisions officially are published in mimeograph form only, but Regular decisions are published by the U. S. Government in a series designated *Tax Court of the United States Reports*. Each volume of these reports covers a six-month period (April 1 through September 30 and October 1 through March 31) and is given a succeeding volume number. But, as was true of the *Cumulative Bulletin,* there is usually a time lag between the date a decision is rendered and the date it appears in bound form. A temporary citation might be necessary to aid the researcher in locating a recent Regular decision. Consider, for example, the temporary and permanent citations for *John F. Knowlton,* a decision filed on February 6, 1985:

| | |
|---|---|
| Temporary Citation | *John F. Knowlton,* 84 T.C. __, No. 11 (1985). |
| | *Explanation:* Page number left blank because not yet known |
| Permanent Citation | *John F. Knowlton,* 84 T.C. 160 (1985). |
| | *Explanation:* Page number now available |

Both citations tell us that the case ultimately will appear in Volume 84 of the *Tax Court of the United States Reports.* But until this volume is bound and made available to the general public, the page number must be left blank. Instead, the temporary citation identifies the case as being the 11th Regular decision issued by the Tax Court since Volume 83 ended. With this information, the decision can be easily located in either of the special Tax Court services published by Commerce Clearing House or Prentice-Hall. Once Volume 84 is released, the permanent citation can be substituted and the number of the case dropped.

Before 1943, the Tax Court was called the Board of Tax Appeals, and its decisions were published as the *United States Board of Tax Appeals Reports* (B.T.A.). These forty-seven volumes cover the period from 1924 to 1942. For example, the citation *Karl Pauli,* 11 B.T.A. 784 (1928) refers to the eleventh volume of the *Board of Tax Appeals Reports,* page 784, issued in 1928.

One further distinction between Regular and Memorandum decisions of the Tax Court involves the IRS procedure of acquiescence (i. e., "A" or "Acq.") or nonacquiescence (i. e., "NA" or "Nonacq."). If the IRS loses in a Regular decision, it will usually indicate whether it agrees or disagrees with the result reached by the Court. The acquiescence or nonacquiescence will be published in the *Internal Revenue Bulletin* and the *Cumulative Bulletin.* The procedure is not followed for Memorandum decisions or for the decisions of other courts. The IRS can retroactively revoke an acquiescence. The IRS sometimes issues an announcement that it will *or* will not follow a decision of another Federal court on similar facts.

Although Memorandum decisions are not published by the U. S. Government, they are published by Commerce Clearing House (CCH) and Prentice-Hall (P–H). Consider, for example, the three different ways that *Walter H. Johnson* can be cited:

> *Walter H. Johnson,* T.C.Memo. 1975–245
> > The 245th Memo. Decision issued by the Tax Court in 1975
>
> *Walter H. Johnson,* 34 TCM 1056
> > Page 1056 of Vol. 34 of the *CCH Tax Court Memorandum Decisions*
>
> *Walter H. Johnson,* P–H T.C.Mem.Dec. ¶ 75,245
> > Paragraph 75,245 of the *P–H T.C. Memorandum Decisions*

Note that the third citation contains the same information as the first. Thus, ¶ 75,245 indicates the following information about the case: year 1975, 245th T.C. Memo. Decision.[73]

*Judicial Citations—The U. S. District Court, Claims Court, and Court of Appeals.*  District Court, Claims Court, Court of Appeals, and Supreme Court decisions dealing with Federal tax matters are reported in both the CCH *U. S. Tax Cases* (USTC) and the P–H *American Federal Tax Reports* (AFTR) series.

Federal District Court decisions, dealing with *both* tax and nontax issues, also are published by West Publishing Company in its Federal Supplement Series. Examples of how a District Court case can be cited in three different forms appear as follows:

*Simons-Eastern Co. v. U. S.,* 73–1 USTC ¶ 9279 (D.Ct.Ga., 1972).

> *Explanation:* Reported in the first volume of the *U. S. Tax Cases* (i. e., USTC) published by Commerce Clearing House for calendar year 1973 (i. e., 73–1) and located at paragraph 9279 (i. e., ¶ 9279).

*Simons-Eastern Co. v. U. S.,* 31 AFTR2d 73–640 (D.Ct.Ga., 1972).

> *Explanation:* Reported in the 31st volume of the second series of the *American Federal Tax Reports* (i. e., AFTR2d) published by Prentice-Hall and commencing on page 640. The "73" preceding the page number indicates the year the case was published but is a designation used only in recent decisions.

*Simons-Eastern Co. v. U. S.,* 354 F.Supp. 1003 (D.Ct.Ga., 1972).

> *Explanation:* Reported in the 354th volume of the *Federal Supplement Series* (i. e., F.Supp.) published by West Publishing Company and commencing on page 1003.

In all of the above citations note that the name of the case is the same (Simons-Eastern Co. being the taxpayer) as is the reference to the Federal District Court of Georgia (i. e., D.Ct.Ga.,) and the year the decision was rendered (i. e., 1972).[74]

Decisions of the Claims Court (previously called the Court of Claims) and the Courts of Appeals are published in the USTCs, AFTRs, and a West Publishing Company reporter designated as the Federal Second Series (F.2d). Illustrations of the different forms follow:

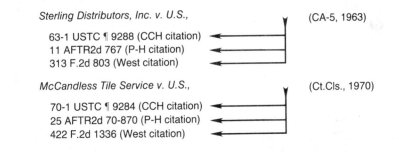

*Sterling Distributors, Inc. v. U.S.,*   (CA-5, 1963)

63-1 USTC ¶ 9288 (CCH citation)
11 AFTR2d 767 (P-H citation)
313 F.2d 803 (West citation)

*McCandless Tile Service v. U.S.,*   (Ct.Cls., 1970)

70-1 USTC ¶ 9284 (CCH citation)
25 AFTR2d 70-870 (P-H citation)
422 F.2d 1336 (West citation)

---

**73.**  In this text the Prentice-Hall citation for Memorandum decisions of the U. S. Tax Court is omitted. Thus, *Walter H. Johnson* would be cited as: 34 TCM 1056, T.C.Memo. 1975–245.
**74.**  In the text the case will be cited in the following form: *Simons-Eastern Co. v. U. S.,* 73–1 USTC ¶ 9279, 31 AFTR2d 73–640, 354 F.Supp. 1003 (D.Ct.Ga., 1972).

Note that *Sterling Distributors, Inc.* is a decision rendered by the Fifth Court of Appeals in 1963 (i. e., CA–5, 1963) while *McCandless Tile Service* is one rendered in 1970 by the Court of Claims (i. e., Ct. Cls., 1970), the predecessor of the Claims Court.

Beginning in October of 1982, decisions of the new Claims Court are reported by West Publishing Company in a series designated *Claims Court Reporter.* Thus, the Claims Court decision in *Recchie v. U. S.* appears as follows:

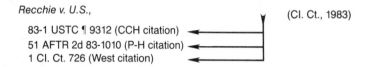

*Recchie v. U.S.,*                                                      (Cl. Ct., 1983)

83-1 USTC ¶ 9312 (CCH citation)
51 AFTR 2d 83-1010 (P-H citation)
1 Cl. Ct. 726 (West citation)

*Judicial Citations—The U. S. Supreme Court.* Like all other Federal tax cases (except those rendered by the U. S. Tax Court), Supreme Court decisions are published by Commerce Clearing House in the USTCs and by Prentice-Hall in the AFTRs. The U. S. Government Printing Office also publishes these decisions in the *United States Supreme Court Reports* (i. e., U. S.) as does West Publishing Company in its *Supreme Court Reporter* (i. e., S.Ct.) and the Lawyer's Co-Operative Publishing Company in its *United States Reports, Lawyer's Edition* (i. e., L.Ed.). The following is an illustration of the different ways the same decision can be cited:

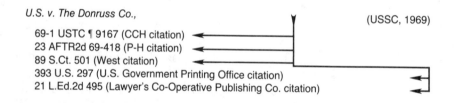

*U.S. v. The Donruss Co.,*                                              (USSC, 1969)

69-1 USTC ¶ 9167 (CCH citation)
23 AFTR2d 69-418 (P-H citation)
89 S.Ct. 501 (West citation)
393 U.S. 297 (U.S. Government Printing Office citation)
21 L.Ed.2d 495 (Lawyer's Co-Operative Publishing Co. citation)

The parenthetical reference (USSC, 1969) identifies the decision as having been rendered by the U. S. Supreme Court in 1969. The citations given in this text for Supreme Court decisions will be limited to the CCH (i. e., USTC), P–H (i. e., AFTR), and the West (i. e., S.Ct.) versions.

# WORKING WITH THE TAX LAW— TAX RESEARCH

Tax research is the method whereby one determines the best available solution to a situation that possesses tax consequences. In other words, it is the process of finding a competent and professional conclusion to a tax problem. The problem might originate either from completed or proposed transactions. In the case of a completed transaction, the objective of the research would be to determine the tax result of what has already taken place. For example, was the expenditure incurred by the taxpayer deductible or not deductible for tax purposes? When dealing with proposed transactions, however, the tax research process is directed toward the determination of possible tax consequences. To the extent that tax research leads to a choice of alternatives or otherwise influences the future actions of the taxpayer, it becomes the key to effective tax planning.

Tax research involves the following procedures:

—Identifying and refining the problem.

—Locating the appropriate tax law sources.

—Assessing the validity of the tax law sources.

—Arriving at the solution or at alternative solutions with due consideration given to nontax factors.

—Effectively communicating the solution to the taxpayer or the taxpayer's representative.

—Following up on the solution (where appropriate) in the light of new developments.

These procedures are diagrammed in Figure II. The broken lines reflect those steps of particular interest when tax research is directed toward proposed, rather than completed, transactions.

**Figure II**

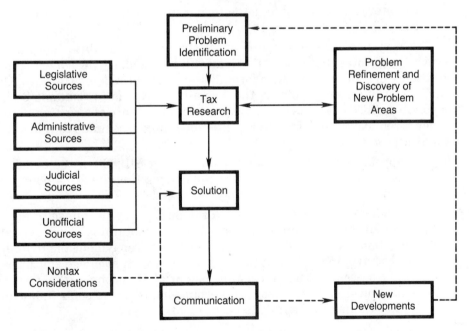

## IDENTIFYING THE PROBLEM

Problem identification must start with a compilation of the relevant facts involved.[75] In this regard, *all* of the facts that might have a bearing on the

---

**75.** For an excellent discussion of the critical role of facts in carrying out tax research, see Ray M. Sommerfeld and G. Fred Streuling, *Tax Research Techniques,* Tax Study No. 5 (New York, N.Y.: The American Institute of Certified Public Accountants, 1981), Chapter 2.

problem must be gathered, because any omission could modify the solution to be reached. To illustrate, consider what appears to be a very simple problem.

> **Example 25.**  A widowed mother advances $52,000 to her son in 19X0 to enable him to attend a private college. Seven years later, the mother claims a bad debt deduction for the $42,000 the son has not repaid. The problem: Is the mother entitled to a bad debt deduction?

*Refining the Problem.*  Before a bad debt deduction can arise, it must be established that a debt really existed. In a related-party setting (e. g., mother and son), the IRS may contend that the original advance was not a loan but, in reality, a gift. Of key significance in this regard would be whether or not the lender (i. e., the mother) had an honest and real expectation of payment by the borrower (i. e., the son).[76] Indicative of this repayment expectation is whether the parties preserved the formalities of a loan, including the following:

—The borrower issued a written instrument evidencing the obligation.

—Interest was provided for as part of the loan arrangement.

—The note specified a set due date.

—Collateral was available to the lender in the event of default by the borrower.[77]

The very presence of some or all of the above formalities does not, however, guarantee that a bona fide loan will be found. By the same token, the absence of some or all of such formalities does not condemn the advance to a gift classification. Applying the formalities criteria to Example 25 is not possible, since key facts (e. g., the presence or absence of a written note) are not given. Nevertheless, several inferences might be made that lead to a loan interpretation:

—It appears that the son has repaid at least $10,000 of the $52,000 that he borrowed. If the parties intended a gift of the full amount of the loan, why was partial repayment made?

—Although one would not expect a son on his way to college to have assets to serve as collateral for a loan, the obtaining of additional education could reinforce any expectation of repayment the mother might have. In most situations, the person with a college education would possess a higher earning potential than one without such education. Needless to say, this would improve the son's financial ability to make repayments on the loan.

*Further Refinement of the Problem.*  Whether the advance constitutes a loan or a gift may be a result that cannot be reached with any degree of certainty. In either event, however, the researcher must ascertain the tax consequences of each possibility.

If the advance ultimately is determined to be a gift, it will be subject to

---

**76.** *William F. Mercil,* 24 T.C. 1150 (1955), and *Evans Clark,* 18 T.C. 780 (1952), *aff'd.* 53–2 USTC ¶ 9452, 44 AFTR 70, 205 F.2d 353 (CA–2, 1953).

**77.** *Arthur T. Davidson,* 37 TCM 725, T.C.Memo. 1978–167.

the Federal gift tax.[78] Whether or not a gift tax would be generated because of the transfer would depend upon how much of the unified transfer tax credit the mother has available to absorb the gift tax on $42,000 [$52,000 (total gift)—$10,000 (annual exclusion)].[79] But whether the transfer results in a gift tax or not, it would have to be reported on Form 709 (United States Gift Tax Return), since the amount of the gift exceeds the annual exclusion.

Even if it is assumed that the mother made a gift to the son in 19X0, does not the intervention of seven years preclude the IRS from assessing any gift tax that might be due as a result of such transfer?[80] Further research would indicate that the statute of limitations on assessments does not begin to run when a tax return was due but not filed.[81]

To complete the picture, what are the tax consequences if the advance is treated as a bona fide loan? Aside from the bad debt deduction aspects (covered later in this chapter), the Deficit Reduction Act of 1984 provides more immediate tax ramifications that are summarized as follows:[82]

—If interest is not provided for, interest will be imputed with the following effect:

    (a) The lender (i. e., the mother) must recognize interest income as to the imputed value.

    (b) Since the lender has not received the interest, a gift of such interest is deemed to have taken place from the lender to the borrower.

    (c) The borrower (i. e., son) is entitled to deduct (as an itemized expense) the amount of interest deemed paid to the lender (i. e., mother).

—If interest is provided for but the rate is lower than market (as determined by the yield on certain U. S. government securities), the differential will be treated as noted above.

—For gift loans of $100,000 or less, the imputed element cannot exceed the net investment income of the borrower.

## LOCATING THE APPROPRIATE TAX LAW SOURCES

Once the problem is clearly defined, what is the next step? Although this is a matter of individual judgment, most involved tax research begins with the index volume of the tax service. If the problem is not complex, the

---

**78.** The transfer does not fall within the unlimited gift tax exclusion of § 2503(e)(1)(2)(A), since the mother did not pay the amount directly to an educational institution. Besides, the exclusion covers only tuition payments and not other costs attendant to going to college (e. g., room and board).

**79.** This, in turn, depends upon the amount of taxable gifts the mother has made in the past. For a discussion of the mechanics of the Federal gift tax, see Chapter 11.

**80.** Throughout the discussion of Example 25, the assumption has been made that if a gift occurred, it took place in 19X0. Such need not be the case. Depending upon the mother's intent, she could have decided to make a gift of the unpaid balance anytime after the loan was made (e. g., 19X1, 19X2, etc.)

**81.** See § 6501(c)(3) and the discussion of the statute of limitations in Chapter 14.

**82.** § 7872.

researcher may bypass the tax service and turn directly to the Internal Revenue Code and the Treasury Regulations. For the beginner, this procedure saves time and will solve many of the more basic problems. If the researcher does not have a personal copy of the Code or Regulations, resorting to the appropriate volume(s) of a tax service will be necessary.[83]

The major tax services available are as follows:

*Standard Federal Tax Reporter,* Commerce Clearing House.

*Federal Taxes,* Prentice-Hall.

Mertens, *Law of Federal Income Taxation,* Callaghan and Co.

*Tax Coordinator,* Research Institute of America.

*Tax Management Portfolios,* Bureau of National Affairs.

Rabkin and Johnson, *Federal Income, Gift and Estate Taxation,* Matthew Bender, Inc.

*Working With the Tax Services.* In this text it is not feasible to teach the use of any particular tax service; this can be learned only by practice.[84] However, several important observations can be made about the use of tax services that cannot be overemphasized. First, never forget to check for current developments. The main text of any service is not revised frequently enough to permit reliance on that portion as the *latest* word on any subject. Where such current developments can be found depends, of course, on which service is being used. Both the Commerce Clearing House and Prentice-Hall services contain a special volume devoted to current matters. Second, when dealing with a tax service synopsis of a Treasury Department pronouncement or a judicial decision, remember there is no substitute for the original source.

To illustrate, do not base a conclusion solely on a tax service's commentary on *Simons-Eastern Co. v. U. S.*[85] If the case is vital to the research, look it up. It is possible that the facts of the case are distinguishable from those involved in the problem being researched. This is not to say that the case synopsis contained in the tax service is wrong; it might just be misleading or incomplete.

*Tax Periodicals.* Additional sources of tax information are the various tax periodicals. The best means of locating a journal article pertinent to a tax problem is through Commerce Clearing House's *Federal Tax Articles.* This three-volume service includes a subject index, a Code Section number index, and an author's index. Also, the P–H tax service has a topical "Index to Tax Articles" section that is organized using the P–H paragraph index system.

---

**83.** Several of the major tax services publish paperback editions of the Code and Treasury Regulations which can be purchased at modest prices. These editions are usually revised twice each year.

**84.** The representatives of the various tax services are prepared to provide the users of their services with printed booklets and individual instruction on the utilization of such materials.

**85.** Cited in Footnote 74.

The following are some of the more useful tax periodicals:

The Journal of Taxation
Warren, Gorham and Lamont
210 South Street
Boston, MA 02111

Tax Law Review
Warren, Gorham and Lamont
210 South Street
Boston, MA 02111

Taxation for Accountants
Warren, Gorham and Lamont
210 South Street
Boston, MA 02111

TAXES—The Tax Magazine
Commerce Clearing House, Inc.
4025 West Peterson Avenue
Chicago, IL 60646

National Tax Journal
21 East State Street
Columbus, OH 43215

The Tax Adviser
1211 Avenue of the Americas
New York, NY 10036

The Practical Accountant
Institute of Continuing Professional
   Development
964 - 3rd Avenue
New York, NY 10155

Journal of Corporate Taxation
Warren, Gorham and Lamont
210 South Street
Boston, MA 02111

Trusts and Estates
Communication Channels Inc.
6255 Barfield Road
Atlanta, GA 30328

Estate Planning
Warren, Gorham and Lamont
210 South Street
Boston, MA 02111

Journal of Partnership Taxation
Warren, Gorham and Lamont
210 South Street
Boston, MA 02111

The Tax Executive
1300 North 17th Street
Arlington, VA 22209

Oil and Gas Tax Quarterly
Matthew Bender & Co.
235 East 45th Street
New York, NY 10017

The International Tax Journal
Panel Publishers
14 Plaza Road
Greenvale, NY 11548

The Tax Lawyer
American Bar Association
1800 M Street, N. W.
Washington, DC 20036

Journal of the American Taxation Association
American Accounting Association
5717 Bessie Drive
Sarasota, FL 33583

## ASSESSING THE VALIDITY OF TAX LAW SOURCES

After a source has been located, the next procedure is to assess such source in light of the problem at hand. Proper assessment involves careful interpretation of the tax law with consideration as to the law's relevance and validity. In connection with validity, an important step is to check for recent changes in the tax law.

*Interpreting the Internal Revenue Code.* The language of the Code can be extremely difficult to comprehend fully. For example, a subsection [§ 341(e)] relating to collapsible corporations contains *one* sentence of more than 450 words (twice as many as in the Gettysburg Address). Within this same subsection are two other sentences of 300 and 340 words. One author has noted ten common pitfalls in interpreting the Code:[86]

---

86. H. G. Wong, "Ten Common Pitfalls in Reading the Internal Revenue Code," *The Practical Accountant* (July–August 1972), pp. 30–33.

1. Determine the limitations and exceptions to a provision. Do not permit the language of the Code section to carry greater or lesser weight than was intended. See Example 26.

2. Just because a section fails to mention an item does not necessarily mean that the item is excluded. See Example 26.

3. Read definitional clauses carefully. Note, for example, that § 7701(a)(3) defines a corporation as including "associations." This inclusion, further developed in Chapter 2, becomes essential in determining how professional associations are to be treated for Federal income tax purposes.

4. Do not overlook small words such as "and" and "or." There is a world of difference between these two words.[87]

5. Read the Code section completely; do not jump to conclusions.

6. Watch out for cross-referenced and related provisions, since many sections of the Code are interrelated.[88]

7. Congress is at times not careful when reconciling new Code provisions with existing sections. Conflicts among sections, therefore, do arise. See Example 26.

8. Be alert for hidden definitions; terms in a particular Code section may be defined in the same section *or in a separate section.*[89]

9. Some answers might not be found in the Code; therefore, a researcher may have to consult the Regulations and/or judicial decisions.[90]

10. Take careful note of measuring words such as "less than 50 percent;" "exceeds 35 percent;" "at least 80 percent;" and "more than 80 percent."[91]

---

**87.** Sections 357(b)(1)(A) and (B) are connected by "or" which means, as noted in Chapter 3, a liability transferred to a controlled corporation can be treated as boot to the transferor even though there was no tax avoidance purpose [§ 357(b)(1)(A)] as long as the transfer lacked a bona fide business purpose [§ 357(b)(1)(B)]. In contrast, § § 542(a)(1) and (2) are joined by "and" which means, as noted in Chapter 7, that a corporation cannot be classified as a personal holding company unless it satisfies both the adjusted ordinary gross income requirement [§ 542(a)(1)] *and* the stock ownership requirement [§ 542(a)(2)].

**88.** For example, consider § 331(a)(1), which sets forth the general rule on the effect to a shareholder of a complete liquidation of the corporation (see Chapter 5). Such a liquidation shall be treated "as in full payment in exchange for the stock." Section 331(c) cross references this rule with §§ 1001 and 1002. Considered as a whole, therefore, the shareholder's gain or loss is the difference between the fair market value of the liquidating distribution and his or her adjusted basis in the stock.

**89.** For example, § 337(f) mentions special treatment for LIFO inventories sold during the 12-month liquidation of a corporation (see Chapter 5). To determine what this special treatment will be, however, one must refer to § 336(b).

**90.** The Code is silent concerning the deductibility of education expenses. Such deductibility, however, falls under the general provision of § 162(a) (the allowance for "all the ordinary and necessary expenses paid or incurred during the taxable year in carrying on any trade or business . . ."). Guidelines for their deductibility can be found in Reg. § 1.162–5. As another example, the Code says nothing concerning the application of the tax benefit rule to corporate liquidations. Here, reference to judicial decisions would be necessary (see Chapter 5).

**91.** Compare § 302(b)(2)(B) with § 303(b)(2)(A), both discussed in Chapter 4. Also, compare § 332(b)(1) (see Chapter 5) with § 1239(b)(2) (see Chapter 3).

The following example illustrates some of the problems a researcher could encounter in interpreting the Code:

**Example 26.** In 1985, X Corporation liquidates and distributes its only asset, depreciable real estate that has appreciated in value, to its sole shareholder (an individual). Does X Corporation have any gain to recognize because of the liquidating distribution? The applicable § 336 states: "Except as provided in subsection (b) of this section (dealing with LIFO inventory) and § 453B (relating to disposition of installment obligations), no gain or loss shall be recognized to a corporation on the distribution of property in complete liquidation." Since depreciable real estate is not an installment obligation, it would appear that no gain will be recognized to X Corporation. Further research, however, leads to § 1250, dealing with the recapture as ordinary income of certain depreciation claimed on real estate upon its disposition. The exceptions to the application of § 1250, contained in subsection (d), do not include the type of liquidating distribution described above. Furthermore, subsection (i) of § 1250 provides: "This section shall apply notwithstanding any other provision of this subtitle." Thus, § 1250 controls, and X Corporation will be subject to its recapture rules. In spite of the fact that § 336 specifically provides for nonrecognition of gain or loss for all liquidating distributions of property other than installment obligations and LIFO inventory, § 1250 will prevail.

Example 26 illustrates many of the pitfalls noted. One in particular, number 7, really explains why the apparent inconsistencies in these Code Sections developed. Quite simply, § 1250 was enacted after § 336. Rather than amend § 336 and other Code Sections similarly affected by the new provision, Congress included § 1250(i) as a means of accomplishing the same objective. The result is, of course, a lack of cross-referencing and possible confusion on the part of a reader of the Code.

*Assessing the Validity of a Treasury Regulation.* It is often stated that Treasury Regulations have the force and effect of law. This statement is certainly true for most Regulations, but there have been judicial decisions that have held a Regulation or a portion thereof invalid, usually on the grounds that the Regulation is contrary to the intent of Congress upon the enactment of a particular Code Section.

Keep in mind the following observations when assessing the validity of a Regulation:

—In a challenge, the burden of proof is on the taxpayer to show that the Regulation is wrong. However, a court may invalidate a Regulation that varies from the language of the statute and has no support in the Committee Reports.

—If the taxpayer loses the challenge, the imposition of a penalty under § 6653(a) can result. This provision deals with the "intentional disregard of rules and regulations" on the part of the taxpayer and is further explained in Chapter 14.

—Some Regulations merely reprint or rephrase what Congress has stated in its Committee Reports issued in connection with the enactment of tax legislation. Such Regulations are "hard and solid" and almost impossible to overturn, because they clearly reflect the intent of Congress.

—In some Code Sections, Congress has given to the "Secretary or his delegate" the authority to prescribe Regulations to carry out the details of administration or to otherwise complete the operating rules. Under such circumstances, it could almost be said that Congress is delegating its legislative powers to the Treasury Department. Regulations issued pursuant to this type of authority truly possess the force and effect of law and are often called "legislative Regulations."[92]

*Assessing the Validity of Other Administrative Sources of the Tax Law.* Revenue Rulings issued by the IRS carry less weight than Treasury Department Regulations. Rulings are important, however, in that they reflect the position of the IRS on tax matters. In any dispute with the IRS on the interpretation of tax law, therefore, taxpayers should expect agents to follow the results reached in any applicable Rulings.

Revenue Rulings further tell the taxpayer the IRS's reaction to certain court decisions. Recall that the IRS follows a practice of either acquiescing (i. e., agreeing) or nonacquiescing (i. e., not agreeing) with the *Regular* decisions of the U. S. Tax Court. This practice does not mean that a particular decision of the Tax Court is of no value if, for example, the IRS has nonacquiesced in the result. It does, however, indicate that the IRS will continue to litigate the issue involved.

The validity of individual (formerly private) rulings issued by the IRS is discussed in Chapter 14.

*Assessing the Validity of Judicial Sources of the Tax Law.* The judicial process as it relates to the formulation of tax law has already been described. How much reliance can be placed on a particular decision depends upon the following variables:

—The level of the court. A decision rendered by a trial court (e. g., a Federal District Court) carries less weight than one issued by an appellate court (e. g., the Fifth Court of Appeals). Unless Congress changes the Code, decisions by the U. S. Supreme Court represent the last word on any tax issue.

—The legal residence of the taxpayer. If, for example, a taxpayer lives in Texas, a decision of the Fifth Court of Appeals means more than one rendered by the Second Court of Appeals. This is the case, since any appeal from a U. S. District Court or the U. S. Tax Court would be to the Fifth Court of Appeals and not to the Second Court of Appeals.[93]

---

**92.** These are to be distinguished from "interpretative" Regulations, which purport to reflect the meaning of a particular Code Section. Examples of "legislative" Regulations would be those dealing with consolidated returns issued under §§ 1501 through 1505. As a further example, note the authority granted to the Treasury Department by § 385 to issue Regulations setting forth guidelines on when corporate debt can be reclassified as equity (see Chapter 3).

**93.** Before October 1, 1982, an appeal from the then designated U. S. Court of Claims (i. e., the other trial court) was made directly to the U. S. Supreme Court.

—Whether the decision represents the weight of authority on the issue. In other words, is it supported by the results reached by other courts?

—The outcome or status of the decision on appeal. For example, was the decision appealed and, if so, with what result?

In connection with the last two variables, the use of a manual citator or a computer search is invaluable to tax research.[94] Such use of a manual citator is illustrated in the appendix to this chapter.

*Assessing the Validity of other Sources.* Primary sources of tax law include the Constitution, legislative history materials, statutes, treaties, Treasury Regulations, IRS pronouncements, and judicial decisions. The IRS considers only primary sources to constitute substantial authority. However, a researcher might wish to refer to secondary materials such as legal periodicals, treatises, legal opinions, general counsel memoranda, technical memoranda, and written determinations. In general, secondary sources are not authority. Reg. § 1.6661–3(b)(2) summarizes the opinion of the IRS as follows:

> In determining whether there is substantial authority (other than in cases described in paragraph (b)(4)(i) of this section), only the following will be considered authority: Applicable provisions of the Internal Revenue Code and other statutory provisions; temporary and final regulations construing such statutes; court cases; administrative pronouncements (including revenue rulings and revenue procedures); tax treaties and regulations thereunder, and Treasury Department and other official explanations of such treaties; and Congressional intent as reflected in committee reports, joint explanatory statements of managers included in conference committee reports, and floor statements made prior to enactment by one of a bill's managers. Conclusions reached in treatises, legal periodicals, legal opinions or opinions rendered by other tax professionals, descriptions of statutes prepared after enactment (such as "General Explanations" prepared by the Staff of the Joint Committee on Taxation), general counsel memoranda, (other than those published in pre-1955 volumes of the Cumulative Bulletin), actions on decisions, technical memoranda, written determinations (except as provided in paragraph (b)(4)(i) of this section), and proposed regulations are not authority. The authorities underlying such expressions of opinion where applicable to the facts of a particular case, however, may give rise to substantial authority for the tax treatment of an item.

An individual ruling or determination letter is substantial authority only to the taxpayer to whom it is issued.

---

**94.** The major manual citators are published by Commerce Clearing House, Prentice-Hall, and Shepard's Citations, Inc.

## ARRIVING AT THE SOLUTION OR AT ALTERNATIVE SOLUTIONS

Returning to Example 25, assume the researcher decides that the loan approach can be justified from the factual situation involved. Does this lead to a bad debt deduction for the mother? Before this question can be resolved, the loan needs to be classified as either a business or a nonbusiness debt. One of the reasons why this classification is important is that a nonbusiness bad debt cannot be deducted until it becomes entirely worthless. Unlike a business debt, no deduction for partial worthlessness is allowed.[95]

It is very likely that the loan the mother made in 19X0 falls into the nonbusiness category. Unless exceptional circumstances exist (e. g., the lender was in the trade or business of lending money), loans in a related-party setting invariably are treated as nonbusiness. The probability is therefore high that the mother would be relegated to nonbusiness bad debt status.

The mother has the burden of proving that the remaining unpaid balance of $42,000 is *entirely* worthless.[96] In this connection, what collection effort, if any, has the mother made? But would any such collection effort be fruitless? Perhaps the son is insolvent, ill, unemployed, or has disappeared for parts unknown.

Even if the debt is entirely worthless, one further issue remains to be resolved. In what year did the worthlessness occur? It could be, for example, that worthlessness took place in a year before it was claimed.[97]

A clear-cut answer may not be possible as to a bad debt deduction for the mother as to year 19X7 (seven years after the advance was made). This does not, however, detract from the value of the research. Often a guarded judgment is the best possible solution to a tax problem.

## COMMUNICATING TAX RESEARCH

Once satisfied that the problem has been researched adequately, the researcher may need to prepare a memo setting forth the result. The form such a memo takes could depend on a number of considerations. For example, is any particular procedure or format recommended for tax research memos by either an employer or an instructor? Is the memo to be given directly to the client or will it first pass to the researcher's employer? Whatever form it takes, a good research memo should contain the following elements:

—A clear statement of the issue.

—In more complex situations, a short review of the factual pattern that raises the issue.

—A review of the tax law sources (e. g., Code, Regulations, Rulings, judicial authority).

—Any assumptions made in arriving at the solution.

---

**95.** See § 166 and the discussion on "Investor Losses" in Chapter 3.
**96.** Compare *John K. Sexton,* 48 TCM 512, T.C.Memo. 1984–360 with *Stewart T. Oatman,* 45 TCM 214, T.C.Memo. 1982–684.
**97.** *Ruth Wertheim Smith,* 34 TCM 1474, T.C.Memo. 1975–339.

—The solution recommended and the logic or reasoning in its support.

—The references consulted in the research process.

In short, a good tax memo should tell the reader what was researched, the results of that research, and the justification for the recommendation made.[98]

# WORKING WITH THE TAX LAW— TAX PLANNING

Tax research and tax planning are inseparable. The primary purpose of effective tax planning is to reduce the taxpayer's total tax bill. This does not mean that the course of action selected must produce the lowest possible tax under the circumstances; the minimization of tax payments must be considered in context with the legitimate business goals of the taxpayer.

A secondary objective of effective tax planning works toward a deferment or postponement of the tax. Specifically, this objective aims to accomplish any one or more of the following: eradicating the tax entirely; eliminating the tax in the current year; deferring the receipt of income; converting ordinary income into capital gains; proliferating taxpayers (i. e., forming partnerships and corporations or making lifetime gifts to family members); eluding double taxation; avoiding ordinary income; or creating, increasing, or accelerating deductions. However, this second objective should be pursued with considerable reservation. Although the maxim "A bird in the hand is worth two in the bush" has general validity, there are frequent cases in which the rule breaks down. For example, a tax election in one year, although it accomplishes a current reduction in taxes, could saddle future years with a disadvantageous tax position.

## NONTAX CONSIDERATIONS

There is an honest danger that tax motivations can take on a significance that is not in conformity with the true values involved. In other words, tax considerations can operate to impair the exercise of sound business judgment by the taxpayer. Thus, the tax planning process can become a medium through which to accomplish ends that are socially and economically objectionable. Ostensibly, a pronounced tendency exists for planning to move toward the opposing extremes of either not enough or too much emphasis on tax considerations. The happy medium—a balance that recognizes the significance of taxes, but not beyond the point at which planning serves to detract from the exercise of good business judgment—turns out to be the promised land that is seldom reached.

The remark is often made that a good rule to follow is to refrain from pursuing any course of action that would not be followed were it not for certain tax considerations. This statement is not entirely correct, but it does illustrate the desirability of preventing business logic from being

---

**98.** See Chapter 6 of Sommerfeld and Streuling, *Tax Research Techniques,* cited in Footnote 75.

"sacrificed at the altar of tax planning." In this connection, the following comment is significant:

> The lure of a quick tax dollar is often the only justification for a transaction that might have been accomplished with much sounder economic results and equivalent tax savings if more careful and deliberate consideration had been given to the problem. Certainly in this atmosphere of the tax-controlled economy a very heavy obligation is cast upon the tax adviser to give serious consideration as to whether a proposed action achieves a desirable economic result apart from tax savings or whether the immediate tax advantages may be more than offset by later economic or personal disadvantage. We cannot afford to develop successful cures that are killing our patients.[99]

## TAX EVASION AND TAX AVOIDANCE

A fine line exists between legal tax planning and illegal tax planning—tax avoidance versus tax evasion. Tax avoidance is merely tax minimization through legal techniques. In this sense, tax avoidance becomes the proper objective of all tax planning. Evasion, while also aimed at the elimination or reduction of taxes, connotes the use of subterfuge and fraud as a means to an end. Popular usage, probably because of the common goals that are involved, has linked these two concepts to the extent that any true distinctions have been obliterated in the minds of many. Consequently, the taint created by the association of tax avoidance and tax evasion has deterred some taxpayers from properly taking advantage of the planning possibilities. The now-classic verbiage of Judge Learned Hand in *Commissioner v. Newman* reflects the true values the individual should have:

> Over and over again courts have said that there is nothing sinister in so arranging one's affairs as to keep taxes as low as possible. Everybody does so, rich or poor; and all do right, for nobody owes any public duty to pay more than the law demands: taxes are enforced extractions, not voluntary contributions. To demand more in the name of morals is mere cant.[100]

## FOLLOW-UP PROCEDURES

Because tax planning usually involves a proposed (as opposed to a completed) transaction, it is predicated upon the continuing validity of the advice based upon the tax research. A change in the tax law (either legislative, administrative, or judicial) could alter the original conclusion. Addi-

---

**99.**  Norris Darrell, "Some Responsibilities of the Tax Adviser in Regard to Tax Minimization Devices," *Proceedings of the New York University Eighth Annual Institute on Federal Taxation* (Albany, N.Y.: Matthew Bender & Co., 1950), pp. 988–989. For a more detailed discussion of tax planning, see F. W. Norwood, S. W. Chisholm, F. Burke, and D. M. Vaughan, *Federal Taxation: Research, Planning, and Procedure* (Englewood Cliffs, N.J.: Prentice-Hall, Inc., 1979), Chapter 6.

**100.**  *Comm. v. Newman,* 47–1 USTC ¶ 9175, 35 AFTR 857, 159 F.2d 848 (CA–2, 1947).

tional research may be necessary to test the solution in light of current developments.

Under what circumstances does a tax practitioner have an obligation to inform a client as to changes in the tax law? The legal and ethical aspects of this question are discussed in Chapter 14.

## TAX PLANNING—A PRACTICAL APPLICATION

Returning to the facts in Example 25, what should be done to help protect the mother's bad debt deduction?

—All formalities should be present as to the loan (e. g., written instrument, definite and realistic due date).

—Upon default, the lender (mother) should make a reasonable effort to collect from the borrower (son). If not, the mother should be in a position to explain why any such effort would be to no avail.

—If interest is provided for, it should be paid.

—Any interest paid (or imputed under § 7872) should be recognized as income by the mother.

—Because of the annual exclusion of $10,000, it appears doubtful that actual (or imputed) interest would necessitate the filing by the mother of a Federal gift tax return. But should one be due, it should be filed.

—If § 7872 applies (not enough or no interest is provided for), the son should keep track of his net investment income. This is advisable, since the income the mother must recognize might be limited by such amount.

Throughout the text, each chapter concludes with observations on TAX PLANNING CONSIDERATIONS. Such observations are not all-inclusive but are intended to illustrate some of the ways in which the material covered can be effectively utilized to minimize taxes.

## COMPUTER-ASSISTED TAX RESEARCH

The computer is being used more and more frequently in the day-to-day practice of tax professionals, students, and educators. Many software vendors offer tax return software programs for individual, corporate, partnership, and fiduciary returns. The use of computers, however, is not limited to the role of batch-processed tax returns and computer timesharing for quantitative tax and problem-solving planning and calculations.

Predictions are that the microcomputer will become the revolutionary tool of the future—much like the electronic calculator did in the seventies. Electronic spreadsheets are being used to replace the fourteen-column worksheet. The electronic spreadsheet approach can be used for retirement planning, 1040 projections, real estate projections, partnership allocations, consolidated tax return problems, compensation planning—anytime projections and calculations are needed. Internally prepared tax-related programs are used by many public accounting firms. Software is available for the microcomputer for estate planning calculations.

LEXIS, a computerized legal data bank, has been available since 1973 as a complement to the conventional manual research approach (available in at least one-half of the more than seventy graduate tax programs). WESTLAW, a competitive system from West Publishing Company, has been operational since 1975. Prentice-Hall has a national computer network, called PHINET, which makes its looseleaf service accessible by computer. WESTLAW, LEXIS, and PHINET are in actuality document retrieval systems that cannot interpret the law.

Users have access to these computerized data banks through special terminals and long-distance telephone lines. A user selects key words, phrases, or numbers and types the search request on the keyboard on the terminal. A display screen then shows the full text or portions of the various documents containing the words, phrases, or numbers in the search request. A printer can be used to obtain hard copy of any documents or portions of a document. For example, a researcher can obtain the decisions of a particular judge or court over a specified time period. It is also possible to access judicial opinions containing specific words or phrases of statutory language. These computer-assisted tax systems can be used as a citator by collecting all judicial decisions that have cited a particular decision or statute as well as all decisions that have a specific combination of two or more earlier decisions or statutes.

Computer-assisted tax research is useful in searching for facts because human indexing evolves around legal theories rather than fact patterns. Computer searching also is useful in finding new court decisions not yet in the printed indexes. Because computer searching probably does not find as many relevant cases as does manual searching, a combination of manual and computer searching can be quite effective.

# APPENDIX—USE OF CITATOR

## ILLUSTRATION OF THE USE OF THE P–H CITATOR

### Background

The Prentice-Hall *Federal Tax Citator* is a separate multi-volume service with two loose-leaf current matters sections. Cases that are reported by the *Citator* are divided into the various issues involved. Since the researcher may be interested in only one or two issues, only those cases involving the particular issue need to be checked.

The volumes of the P–H *Federal Tax Citator* and the period of time covered by each are:

Volume 1 (1863–1941)
Volume 2 (1942–1948)
Volume 3 (1948–1954)
Volume 1, Second Series (1954–1977)
Loose-leaf, two volumes (1977 to present)

## Figure III

Prentice-Hall Citator Symbols*

COURT DECISIONS

Judicial History of the Case

a    affirmed (by decision of a higher court)

d    dismissed (appeal to a higher court dismissed)

m    modified (decision modified by a higher court, or on rehearing)

r    reversed (by a decision of a higher court)

s    same case (e. g., on rehearing)

rc    related case (companion cases and other cases arising out of the same subject matter are so designated)

x    certiorari denied (by the Supreme Court of the United States)

(C or G)    The Commissioner or Solicitor General has made the appeal

(T)    Taxpayer has made the appeal

(A)    Tax Court's decision acquiesced in by Commissioner

(NA)    Tax Court's decision nonacquiesced in by Commissioner

sa    same case affirmed (by the cited case)

sd    same case dismissed (by the cited case)

sm    same case modified (by the cited case)

sr    same case reversed (by the cited case)

sx    same case-certiorari denied

Syllabus of the Cited Case

iv    four (on all fours with the cited case)

f    followed (the cited case followed)

e    explained (comment generally favorable, but not to a degree that indicates the cited case is followed)

k    reconciled (the cited case reconciled)

n    dissenting opinion (cited in a dissenting opinion)

g    distinguished (the cited case distinguished either in law or on the facts)

l    limited (the cited case limited to its facts. Used when an appellate court so limits a prior decision, or a lower court states that in its opinion the cited case should be so limited)

c    criticized (adverse comment on the cited case)

q    questioned (the cited case not only criticized, but its correctness questioned)

o    overruled

* Reproduced from the Federal Taxes Citator with the permission of the publisher, Prentice-Hall, Inc., Englewood Cliffs, N. J. 07632

Through the use of symbols, the *Citator* indicates whether a decision is followed, explained, criticized, questioned, or overruled by a later court decision. These symbols are reproduced in Figure III.

## Example

Determine the background and validity of *Adda v. Comm.*, 37 AFTR 654, 171 F.2d 457 (CA–4, 1948).

## Solution

Turning directly to the case itself (reproduced as Figure IV), note the two issues involved (i. e., "1." and "2."). For purposes of emphasis, these issues have been bracketed and identified as such by a marginal notation added to Figure IV. The reason for the division of the issues becomes apparent when the case is traced through the *Citator*.

Refer to Volume 3 for the AFTR Series (covering the period from October 7, 1948, through July 29, 1954) of the P–H *Federal Tax Citator*. Reference to the case is located on page 5505. This page is reproduced in Figure V.

Correlating the symbols reproduced in Figure III with the shaded portion of Figure V reveals the following information about *Adda v. Comm.*:

Application for certiorari (i. e., appeal to the U. S. Supreme Court) filed by the taxpayer (T) on March 1, 1949.

Certiorari was denied (x) by the U. S. Supreme Court on April 18, 1949.

The trial court decision is reported in 10 T.C. 273 and was affirmed on appeal (sa) to the Fourth Court of Appeals.

During the time frame of Volume 3 of the *Citator* (October 7, 1948, through July 29, 1954), one decision (*Milner Hotels, Inc.*) has agreed "on all fours with the cited case" (iv). One decision (*Comm. v. Nubar*) has limited the cited case to its facts (1), and two decisions (*The Scottish American Investment Co., Ltd.* and *Zareh Nubar*) have distinguished the cited case on issue number one (g–1).

Reference to Volume 1 of the *Citator* Second Series (covering the period from 1954 through 1977) shows the *Adda v. Comm.* case on page 25. This page is reproduced in Figure VI.

Correlating the symbols reproduced in Figure III with the shaded portion of Figure VI reveals the following additional information about *Adda v. Comm.*

The case was cited without comment in two rulings and two cases: *Rev.Rul. 56–145, Rev.Rul. 56–392, Balanovski,* and *Liang.*

It was followed in *Asthmanefrin Co.* (f–1).

It was distinguished in *deVegvar* and *Purvis* (g–1).

It was reconciled in *deKrause* (k–1).

Reference to the "Court Decisions" section of the loose-leaf Volume 1 for the *Citator* covering the period from 1977 to the present shows that *Adda v. Comm.* was cited in *Robert E. Cleveland* and *Judith C. Connelly,* each case limited to its facts (1). The loose-leaf Volume 2 contains a "Supplementary Compilation" section and a "Current Monthly Supplement"

## Figure IV

### ADDA v. COMMISSIONER OF INTERNAL REVENUE    457

Cite as 171 F.2d 457

### ADDA v. COMMISSIONER OF INTERNAL REVENUE

No. 5796.

United States Court of Appeals
Fourth Circuit.

Dec. 3, 1948.

**1. Internal revenue ⟐792**

ISSUE 1. Where nonresident alien's brother residing in United States traded for alien's benefit on commodity exchanges in United States at authorization of alien, who vested full discretion in brother with regard thereto, and many transactions were effected through different brokers, several accounts were maintained, and substantial gains and losses realized, transactions constituted a "trade or business," profits of which were "capital gains" taxable as income to the alien. 26 U.S.C.A. § 211(b).

See Words and Phrases, Permanent Edition, for other judicial constructions and definitions of "Capital Gains" and "Trade or Business".

**2. Internal revenue ⟐792**

ISSUE 2. The exemption of a nonresident alien's commodity transactions in the United States provided for by the Internal Revenue Code does not apply where alien has agent in United States using his own discretion in effecting transactions for alien's account. 26 U.S.C.A. § 211(b).

On Petition to Review the Decision of The Tax Court of the United States.

Petition by Fernand C. A. Adda to review a decision of the Tax Court redetermining a deficiency in income tax imposed by the Commissioner of Internal Revenue.

Decision affirmed.

Rollin Browne and Mitchell B. Carroll, both of New York City, for petitioner.

Irving I. Axelrad, Sp. Asst. to Atty. Gen. (Theron Lamar Caudle, Asst. Atty. Gen., and Ellis N. Slack and A. F. Prescott, Sp. Assts. to Atty. Gen., on the brief), for respondent.

Before PARKER, Chief Judge, and SOPER and DOBIE, Circuit Judges.

PER CURIAM.

[1, 2] This is a petition by a non-resident alien to review a decision of the Tax Court. Petitioner is a national of Egypt, who in the year 1941 was residing in France. He had a brother who at that time was residing in the United States and who traded for petitioner's benefit on commodity exchanges in the United States in cotton, wool, grains, silk, hides and copper. This trading was authorized by petitioner who vested full discretion in his brother with regard thereto, and it resulted in profits in the sum of $193,857.14. The Tax Court said: "While the number of transactions or the total amount of money involved in them has not been stated, it is apparent that many transactions were effected through different brokers, several accounts were maintained, and gains and losses in substantial amounts were realized. This evidence shows that the trading was extensive enough to amount to a trade or business, and the petitioner does not contend, nor has he shown, that the transactions were so infrequent or inconsequential as not to amount to a trade or business." We agree with the Tax Court that, for reasons adequately set forth in its opinion, this income was subject to taxation, and that the exemption of a non-resident alien's commodity transactions in the United States, provided by section 211(b) of the Internal Revenue Code, 26 U.S.C.A. § 211 (b), does not apply to a case where the alien has an agent in the United States using his own discretion in effecting the transactions for the alien's account. As said by the Tax Court, "Through such transactions the alien is engaging in trade or business within the United States, and the profits on these transactions are capital gains taxable to him." Nothing need be added to the reasoning of the Tax Court in this connection, and the decision will be affirmed on its opinion.

Affirmed.

## Figure V

**ADAMSON, JAMES H. & MARION C. v U. S., — F Supp —, 36 AFTR 1529, 1946 P.-H. ¶ 72,418 (DC Calif) (See Adamson v U. S.)**

**ADAMSON, R. R., MRS., — BTA —, 1934 (P.-H.) BTA Memo. Dec. ¶ 34,370**

**ADAMSON v U. S., 26 AFTR 1188 (DC Calif, Sept 8, 1939)**
iv—Coggan, Linus C., 1939 (P.-H.) BTA Memo. Dec. page 39—806

**ADAMSON; U. S. v, 161 F(2d) 942, 35 AFTR 1404 (CCA 9)**
1—Lazier v U. S., 170 F(2d) 524, 37 AFTR 545, 1948 P.-H. page 73,174 (CCA 8)
1—Grace Bros., Inc. v Comm., 173 F(2d) 178, 37 AFTR 1014, 1949 P.-H. page 72,433 (CCA 9)
1—Briggs; Hofferbert v, 178 F(2d) 744, 38 AFTR 1219, 1950 P.-H. page 72,267 (CCA 4)
1—Rogers v Comm., 180 F(2d) 722, 39 AFTR 115, 1950 P.-H. page 72,531 (CCA 3)
1—Lamar v Granger, 99 F Supp 41, 40 AFTR 270, 1951 P.-H. page 72,945 (DC Pa)
1—Herbert v Riddell, 103 F Supp 383, 41 AFTR 975, 1952 P.-H. page 72,383 (DC Calif)
1—Hudson, Galvin, 20 TC 737, 20-1953 P.-H. TC 418

**ADAMSON v U. S., — F Supp —, 36 AFTR 1529, 1946 P.-H. ¶ 72,418 (DC Calif, Jan 28, 1946)**

**ADAMS-ROTH BAKING CO., 8 BTA 458**
1—Gunderson Bros. Engineering Corp., 16 TC 129, 16-1951 P.-H. TC 72

**ADAMSTON FLAT GLASS CO. v COMM., 162 F(2d) 875, 35 AFTR 1579 (CCA 6)**
4—Forrest Hotel Corp. v. Fly, 112 F Supp 789, 43 AFTR 1080, 1953 P.-H. page 72,856 (DC Miss)

**ADDA v COMM., 171 F(2d) 457, 37 AFTR 654, 1948 P.-H. ¶ 72,655 (CCA 4, Dec 3, 1948)**
Cert. filed, March 1, 1949 (T)
No cert. (G) 1949 P-H ¶ 71,050
x—Adda v Comm., 336 US 952, 69 S Ct 883, 93 L Ed 1107, April 18, 1949 (T)
sa—Adda, Fernand C. A., 10 TC 273 (No. 33), ¶ 10.33 P.-H. TC 1948
iv—Milner Hotels, Inc., N. Y., 173 F(2d) 567, 37 AFTR 1170, 1949 P.-H. page 72,528 (CCA 6)
1—Nubar; Comm. v, 185 F(2d) 588, 39 AFTR 1315, 1950 P.-H. page 73,423 (CCA 4)
g-1—Scottish Amer. Invest. Co., Ltd., The, 12 TC 59, 12-1949 P.-H. TC 32
g-1—Nubar, Zareh, 13 TC 579, 13-1949 P.-H. TC 318

**ADDA, FERNAND C. A., 10 TC 273 (No. 33), ¶ 10.33 P.-H. TC 1948 (A) 1918-2 CB 1**
a—Adda v Comm., 171 F(2d) 457, 37 AFTR 654, 1948 P.-H. ¶ 72,655 (CCA 4)
1—Nubar; Comm. v, 185 F(2d) 588, 39 AFTR 1315, 1950 P.-H. page 73,423 (CCA 4)
g-1—Scottish Amer. Invest. Co., Ltd., The, 12 TC 59, 12-1949 P.-H. TC 32
g-1—Nubar, Zareh, 13 TC 579, 13-1949 P.-H. TC 318

**ADDA, FERNAND C. A., 10 TC 1291 (No. 168), ¶ 10.168 P.-H. TC 1948 (A) 1953-1 CB 3, 1953 P.-H. ¶ 76,453 (NA) 1948-2 CB 5, 1948 P.-H. ¶ 76,434 withdrawn**
1—Scottish Amer. Invest. Co., Ltd., The, 12 TC 59, 12-1949 P.-H. TC 32

**ADDA INC., 9 TC 199 (A) 1949-1 CB 1, 1949 P.-H. ¶ 76,260 (NA) 1947-2 CB 6 withdrawn**
a—Adda, Inc.; Comm. v, 171 F(2d) 367, 37 AFTR 641, 1948 P.-H. ¶ 72,654 (CCA 2)
a—Adda, Inc.; Comm. v, 171 F(2d) 367, 37 AFTR 641, 1949 P.-H. ¶ 72,303 (CCA 2)
e-1—G.C.M. 26069, 1949-2 CB 38, 1949 P.-H. page 76,226
3—Koshland, Execx.; U.S. v, 208 F(2d) 640, — AFTR —, 1953 P.-H. page 73,597 (CCA 9)
4—Kent, Otis Beall, 1954 (P. H.) TC Memo. Dec. page 54—47

**ADDA, INC.; COMM. v, 171 F(2d) 367, 37 AFTR 641, 1948 P.-H. ¶ 72,654 (CCA 2, Dec 6, 1948)**
sa—Adda, Inc., 9 TC 199
s—Adda, Inc.; Comm. v, 171 F(2d) 367, 37 AFTR 641, 1949 P.-H. ¶ 72,303 (CCA 2) reh. den.
e-1—G.C.M. 26069, 1949-2 CB 39, 1949 P.-H. page 76,227
e-2—G.C.M. 26069, 1949-2 CB 39, 1949 P.-H. page 76,227

**ADDA, INC.; COMM. v, 171 F(2d) 367, 37 AFTR 641, 1949 P.-H. ¶ 72,303 (CCA 2, Dec 6, 1948) reh. den.**
sa—Adda, Inc., 9 TC 199
s—Adda, Inc.; Comm. v, 171 F(2d) 367, 37 AFTR 641, 1948 P.-H. ¶ 72,654 (CCA 2)

**ADDISON-CHEVROLET SALES, INC. v CHAMBERLAIN, L. A. & NAT. BANK OF WASH., THE, — F Supp —, — AFTR —, 1954 P.-H. ¶ 72,550 (DC DC) (See Campbell v Chamberlain)**

**ADDISON v COMM., 177 F(2d) 521, 38 AFTR 821, 1949 P.-H. ¶ 72,637 (CCA 8, Nov 3, 1949)**
sa—Addison, Irene D., — TC —, 1948 (P.-H.) TC Memo. Dec. ¶ 48,177
1—Roberts, Supt. v U. S., 115 Ct Cl 439, 87 F Supp 937, 38 AFTR 1314, 1950 P.-H. page 72,292
1—Cold Metal Process Co., The, 17 TC 934, 17-1951 P.-H. TC 512
1—Berger, Samuel & Lillian, 1954 (P.-H.) TC Memo. Dec. page 54—232
2—Urquhart, George Gordon & Mary F., 20 TC 948, 20-1953 P.-H. TC 536

**ADDISON, IRENE D., — TC —, 1948 (P.-H.) TC Memo. Dec. ¶ 48,177**
App (T) Jan 14. 1949 (CCA 8)
a—Addison v Comm., 177 F(2d) 521, 38 AFTR 821, 1949 P.-H. ¶ 72,637 (CCA 8)
1—Urquhart, George Gordon & Mary F., 20 TC 948, 20-1953 P.-H. TC 536

**ADDITON, HARRY L. & ANNIE S., 3 TC 427**
1—Lum, Ralph E., 12 TC 379, 12-1949 P.-H. TC 204
1—Christie, John A. & Elizabeth H., — TC —, 1949 (P.-H.) TC Memo. Dec. page 49—795

**ADDRESSOGRAPH - MULTIGRAPH CORP., 1945 (P.-H.) TC Memo. Dec. ¶ 45,058**
f-10—Rev. Rul. 54-71, 1954 P.-H. page 76.453

**ADDRESSOGRAPH-MULTIGRAPH CORP. v U. S., 112 Ct Cl 201, 78 F Supp 111, 37 AFTR 53, 1948 P.-H. ¶ 72,504 (June 1, 1948)**
No cert (G) 1949 P-H ¶ 71,041
1—New Oakmont Corp., The v U. S., 114 Ct Cl 686, 86 F Supp 901, 38 AFTR 924, 1949 P.-H. page 73,181

**ADELAIDE PARK LAND, 25 BTA 211**
g—Amer. Security & Fidelity Corp., — BTA —, 1940 (P.-H.) BTA Memo. Dec. page 40—571

**ADELPHI PAINT & COLOR WORKS, INC., 18 BTA 436**
1—Neracher, William A., — BTA —, 1939 (P.-H.) BTA Memo. Dec. page 39—350
1—Lyman-Hawkins Lumber Co., — BTA —, 1939 (P.-H.) BTA Memo. Dec. page 39—350

**ADEMAN v U. S., 174 F(2d) 283, 37 AFTR 1406 (CCA 9, April 25, 1949)**

**ADICONIS, NOELLA L. (PATNAUDE), 1953 (P.-H.) TC Memo. Dec. ¶ 53,305**

**ADJUSTMENT BUREAU OF ST. LOUIS ASSN., OF CREDIT MEN, 21 BTA 232**
1—Cook County Loss Adjustment Bureau, — BTA —, 1940 (P.-H.) BTA Memo. Dec. page 40—331

**ADKINS, CHARLES I., — BTA —, 1933 (P.-H.) BTA Memo. Dec. ¶ 33,457**

**ADLER v COMM., 77 F(2d) 733, 16 AFTR 162 (CCA 5)**
g-2—McEuen v Comm., 196 F(2d) 130, 41 AFTR 1172, 1952 P.-H. page 72,604 (CCA 5)

## Figure VI

### ADASKAVICH—ADELSON      25

ADASKAVICH, STEPHEN A. v U.S., 39 AFTR2d
77-517, 422 F Supp 276 (DC Mont) (See Wiegand,
Charles J., Jr. v U.S.)

AD. AURIEMA, INC., 1943 P-H TC Memo ¶ 43,422
   e-1—Miller v U.S., 13 AFTR2d 1515, 166 Ct Cl 257, 331
     F2d 859

ADAY v SUPERIOR CT. OF ALAMEDA COUNTY, 8
AFTR2d 5367, 13 Cal Reptr 415, 362 P2d 47 (Calif,
5-11-61)

ADCO SERVICE, INC., ASSIGNEE v CYBERMATICS,
INC., 36 AFTR2d 75-6342 (NJ) (See Adco Service,
Inc., Assignee v Graphic Color Plate)

ADCO SERVICE, INC., ASSIGNEE v GRAPHIC
COLOR PLATE, 36 AFTR2d 75-6342 (NJ, Supr Ct,
11-10-75)

ADCO SERVICE, INC., ASSIGNEE v GRAPHIC
COLOR PLATE, INC., 36 AFTR2d 75-6342 (NJ) (See
Adco Service, Inc., Assignee v Graphic Color Plate)

ADDA v COMM., 171 F2d 457, 37 AFTR 654 (USCA 4)
   Rev. Rul. 56-145, 1956-1 CB 613
   1—Balanovski, U.S. v., 236 F2d 304, 49 AFTR 2013
     (USCA 2)
   1—Liang, Chang Hsiao, 23 TC 1045, 23-1955 P-H TC
     624
   f-1—Asthmanefrin Co., Inc., 25 TC 1141, 25-1956 P-H
     TC 639
   g-1—de Vegvar, Edward A. Neuman. 28 TC 1061,
     28-1957 P-H TC 599
   g-1—Purvis, Ralph E. & Patricia Lee, 1974 P-H TC
     Memo 74-669
   k-1—deKrause, Piedad Alvarado, 1974 P-H TC Memo
     74-1291
   1—Rev. Rul. 56-392, 1956-2 CB 971

ADDA, FERNAND C.A., 10 TC 273, ¶ 10,133 P-H TC
1948
   1—Balanovski; U.S. v., 236 F2d 303, 49 AFTR 2012
     (USCA 2)
   1—Liang, Chang Hsiao, 23 TC 1045, 23-1955 P-H TC
     624
   g-1—de Vegvar, Edward A. Neuman, 28 TC 1061,
     28-1957 P-H TC 599
   g-1—Purvis, Ralph E. & Patricia Lee, 1974 P-H TC
     Memo 74-669
   k-1—deKrause, Piedad Alvarado, 1974 P-H TC Memo
     74-1291

ADDA, INC., 9 TC 199
   Pardee, Marvin L., Est. of, 49 TC 152, 49 P-H TC 107
     [See 9 TC 206-208]
   f-1—Asthmanefrin Co., Inc., 25 TC 1141, 25-1956 P-H
     TC 639
   1—Keil Properties, Inc. (Dela), 24 TC 1117, 24-1955 P-H
     TC 615
   1—Saffan, Samuel, 1957 P-H TC Memo 57—701
   1—Rev. Rul. 56-145, 1956-1 CB 613
   1—Rev. Rul. 56-392, 1956-2 CB 971
   4—Midler Court Realty, Inc., 61 TC 597, 61 P-H TC
     368

ADDA, INC.; COMM. v, 171 F2d 367, 37 AFTR 641
(USCA 2)
   1—Pardee, Marvin L., Est. of, 49 TC 152, 49 P-H TC
     107
   1—Saffan, Samuel, 1957 P-H TC Memo 57-701
   2—Midler Court Realty, Inc., 61 TC 597, 61 P-H TC
     368

ADDELSTON, ALBERT A. & SARAH M., 1965 P-H TC
Memo ¶ 65,215

ADDISON v COMM., 177 F2d 521, 38 AFTR 821 (USCA
8)
   g-1—Industrial Aggregate Co. v U.S., 6 AFTR2d 5963,
     284 F2d 645 (USCA 8)
   1—Sturgeon v McMahon, 155 F Supp 630, 52 AFTR
     789 (DC NY)
   1—Gilmore v U.S., 16 AFTR2d 5211, 5213, 245 F Supp
     384, 386 (DC Calif)
   1—Waldheim & Co., Inc., 25 TC 599, 25-1955 P-H TC
     332
   g-1—Galewitz, Samuel & Marian, 50 TC 113, 50 P-H TC
     79
   1—Buder, G. A., Est. of, 1963 P-H TC Memo 63-345
   e-1—Rhodes, Lynn E. & Martha E., 1963 P-H TC
     Memo 63-1374
   2—Shipp v Comm., 217 F2d 402, 46 AFTR 1170 (USCA
     9)

ADDISON—Contd.
   g-2—Industrial Aggregate Co. v U.S., 6 AFTR2d 5964,
     284 F2d 645 (USCA 8)
   e-2—Buder, Est. of v Comm., 13 AFTR2d 1238, 330
     F2d 443 (USCA 8)
   2—Iowa Southern Utilities Co. v Comm., 14 AFTR2d
     5063, 333 F2d 385 (USCA 8)
   2—Kelly, Daniel, S.W., 23 TC 687, 23-1955 P-H TC 422
   f-2—Morgan, Joseph P., Est. of, 37 TC 36, 37, 37-1961
     P-H TC 26, 27
   n-2—Woodward, Fred W. & Elsie M., 49 TC 385, 49
     P-H TC 270

ADDISON, IRENE D., 1948 P-H TC Memo ¶ 48,177
   1—Waldheim & Co., Inc., 25 TC 599, 25-1955 P-H TC
     332
   f-1—Morgan, Joseph P., Est. of, 37 TC 36, 37, 37-1961
     P-H TC 26, 27
   1—Buder, G. A., Est. of, 1963 P-H TC Memo 63-345
   e-1—Rhodes, Lynn E. & Martha E., 1963 P-H TC
     Memo 63-1374

ADDISON, JOHN MILTON, BKPT; U.S. v, 20 AFTR2d
5630, 384 F2d 748 (USCA 5) (See Rochelle Jr., Trtee;
U.S. v)

ADDRESSOGRAPH - MULTIGRAPH CORP., 1945
P-H TC Memo ¶ 45,058
   Conn. L. & P. Co., The v U.S., 9 AFTR2d 679, 156 Ct
     Cl 312, 314, 299 F2d 264
   Copperhead Coal Co., Inc., 1958 P-H TC Memo 58-33
   1—Seas Shipping Co., Inc. v Comm., 19 AFTR2d 596,
     371 F2d 529 (USCA 2)
   e-1—Hitchcock, E. R., Co., The v U.S., 35 AFTR2d
     75-1207, 514 F2d 487 (USCA 2)
   f-2—Vulcan Materials Co. v U.S., 25 AFTR2d 70-446,
     308 F Supp 57 (DC Ala)
   f-3—Marlo Coil Co. v U.S., 1969 P-H 58,133 (Ct Cl
     Comr Rep)
   4—United Gas Improvement Co. v Comm., 240 F2d 318,
     50 AFTR 1354 (USCA 3)
   10—St. Louis Co. (Del) (in Dissolution) v U.S., 237 F2d
     156, 50 AFTR 257 (USCA 3)

ADDRESSOGRAPH - MULTIGRAPH CORP. v U.S.,
112 Ct Cl 201, 78 F Supp 111, 37 AFTR 53
   f-1—St. Joseph Lead Co. v U.S., 9 AFTR2d 712, 299
     F2d 350 (USCA 2)
   e-1—Central & South West Corp. v U.S., 1968 P-H
     58,175 (Ct Cl Comr Rep)
   1—Smale & Robinson, Inc. v U.S., 123 F Supp 469, 46
     AFTR 375 (DC Calif)
   1—St. Joseph Lead Co. v U.S., 7 AFTR2d 401, 190 F
     Supp 640 (DC NY)
   1—Eisenstadt Mfg. Co., 28 TC 230, 28-1957 P-H TC 132
   f-2—St. Joseph Lead Co. v U.S., 9 AFTR2d 712, 299
     F2d 350 (USCA 2)
   f-3—Consol, Coppermines Corp. v U.S., 8 AFTR2d
     5873, 155 Ct Cl 736, 296 F2d 745

ADELAIDE PARK LAND, 25 BTA 211
   g—Custom Component Switches, Inc. v U.S., 19
     AFTR2d 560 (DC Calif) [See 25 BTA 215]
   O'Connor, John C., 1957 P-H TC Memo 57-190

ADELBERG, MARVIN & HELEN, 1971 P-H TC Memo
¶ 71,015

ADELMAN v U.S., 27 AFTR2d 71-1464, 440 F2d 991
(USCA 9, 5-3-71)
   sa—Adelman v U.S., 24 AFTR2d 69-5769, 304 F Supp
     599 (DC Calif)

ADELMAN v U.S., 24 AFTR2d 69-5769, 304 F Supp 599
(DC Calif, 9-30-69)
   a—Adelman v U.S., 27 AFTR2d 71-1464, 440 F2d 991
     (USCA 9)

ADELSON, SAMUEL; U.S. v, 52 AFTR 1798 (DC RI)
   (See Sullivan Co., Inc.; U.S. v)

ADELSON v U.S., 15 AFTR2d 246, 342 F2d 332 (USCA
9, 1-13-65)
   sa—Adelson v U.S., 12 AFTR2d 5010, 221 F Supp 31
     (DC Calif)
   g-1—Greenlee, L. C. & Gladys M., 1966 P-H TC Memo
     66-985
   f-1—Cochran, Carol J., 1973 P-H TC Memo 73-459
   f-1—Marchionni, Siro L., 1976 P-H TC Memo 76-1321
   f-2—Krist, Edwin F. v Comm., 32 AFTR2d 73-5663, 483
     F2d 1351 (USCA 2)
   f-2—Fugate v U.S., 18 AFTR2d 5607, 259 F Supp 401
     (DC Tex) [See 15 AFTR2d 249, 342 F2d 335]

section. When using the loose-leaf volumes for the *Citator,* be sure to refer to the "Current Monthly Supplement" in Volume 2. Otherwise, very recent citations might be overlooked.

Except as otherwise noted, it would appear that *Adda v. Comm.* has withstood the test of time.

## PROBLEM MATERIALS

### Discussion Questions

1. As a general rule, the investment tax credit is not allowed for property purchased for use outside the U. S. Explain why this restriction exists.

2. For many years, a proposal has been before Congress that would allow a taxpayer to claim a tax credit for tuition paid to send a dependent to a private school. Is there any justification (e. g., social, economic, equity) for such a proposal?

3. State the manner in which the following tax provisions encourage small business:

    (a) Expensing capital acquisitions.

    (b) The nature of a shareholder's loss on a stock investment.

    (c) The tax rates applicable to corporations.

    (d) Nontaxable corporate reorganizations.

4. Although death taxes imposed on large estates can be justified on the grounds of social desirability, can such taxes carry economic implications? Explain.

5. Some states that impose a state income tax allow the taxpayer a deduction for any Federal income taxes paid. What is the justification for such an approach?

6. A provision of the Code allows a taxpayer a deduction for Federal income tax purposes for state and local income taxes paid. Does this provision eliminate the effect of multiple taxation of the same income? Why or why not? In this connection, consider the following:

    (a) Taxpayer, an individual, has itemized deductions less than the zero bracket amount.

    (b) Taxpayer is in the 30% tax bracket for Federal income tax purposes. The 50% tax bracket.

    (c) The state imposing the income tax allows a deduction for Federal income taxes paid.

7. During the current year X Corporation distributes $10,000 as dividends to its shareholder(s). In terms of alleviating the effect of multiple taxation, discuss the following suppositions:

    (a) X Corporation has 50 equal shareholders, all individuals.

    (b) X Corporation has one shareholder, an individual.

    (c) X Corporation has two shareholders, an individual and another corporation.

8. T operates a profitable sole proprietorship, and because the business is expanding, she would like to transfer it to a newly created corporation. T is concerned, however, over the possible tax consequences that would result from incorporating. Please comment.

9. Assume the same facts as in Question 8. T is also worried that once she incorporates, the business will be subject to the Federal corporate income tax. Any suggestions? *Yes it will. what about subchapter S ?*

10. There is a measure of support for what has been designated a "flat tax." Under this approach, most deductions would be disallowed and the income tax would be imposed upon gross income (i. e., gross receipts less cost of goods sold). As a part of the change, the income tax rates would be significantly reduced.

    (a) What are the positive aspects of such a tax? *Simple, easily collected, & determined*

    (b) What are the negative implications? *Regressive, ignores political reality, ignores social consequences.*

11. In situations in which the tax law recognizes the wherewithal to pay concept, discuss the effect of the following:

    (a) The basis to the transferor of property received in an exchange.

    (b) The recognition by the transferor of any realized loss on the transfer.

    (c) The receipt of "boot" or other property by the transferor.

12. Can it be said that the application of the wherewithal to pay concept permanently avoids the recognition of any gain or loss by a transferor? Explain. *no Only postponed*

13. T, an individual, exchanges 100 shares of X Corporation stock for 100 shares of Y Corporation stock. Such exchange is not pursuant to a nontaxable reorganization. Does the wherewithal to pay concept shield T from the recognition of gain or loss? Why?

14. W operates a service business as a sole proprietor. For tax purposes, she recognizes income using the cash method but deducts expenses as they accrue.

    (a) What is W trying to accomplish?

    (b) Is this proper procedure?

    (c) Does the IRS have any recourse?

15. The tax law provides relief for taxpayers who, over a period of years, go from rags to riches. Does it do anything for the reverse situation (i. e., riches to rags)? Why is this a problem in the first place?

16. Prior tax law made the installment sales provision unavailable if the seller received more than 30% of the sales price as a down payment in the year of the sale. Can such a rule be justified? Why or why not?

17. State the manner in which the annual accounting period concept is mitigated by the tax provisions relating to:

    (a) Income averaging.

    (b) Net operating loss carrybacks and carryovers.

    (c) Excess charitable contribution carryovers.

    (d) Long-term capital gains.

18. U, a calendar year cash basis taxpayer, is a participant in an H.R.10 (Keogh) retirement plan for self-employed persons. To get the deduction for 19X5, U makes his contribution on December 30, 19X5.

    (a) Why was there an element of urgency in U's action?

    (b) Was U misinformed about the tax law? Explain.

19. Give an example of how the community property system has affected the Federal tax law.

20. In what way does the wherewithal to pay concept aid the IRS in the collection of tax revenue?

21. Describe how administrative feasibility is achieved for the IRS by each of the following tax provisions:

    (a) The zero bracket amount allowed to individual taxpayers.

    (b) The $155,800 unified transfer tax credit allowed for estate tax purposes in 1986.

    (c) The $10,000 annual exclusion allowed for gift tax purposes.

    (d) The burden of proof in the audit of a taxpayer.

22. What is meant by the concept of substance over form? Why is it variously described as the "telescoping," "collapsing," or "step transaction" approach?

23. What is meant by the concept that statutory relief provisions of the tax law are to be narrowly construed? Where did the concept originate?

24. When does the tax benefit rule apply? With what effect?

25. W Corporation loans $10,000 to Z Corporation with no provision for interest. W Corporation and Z Corporation are owned by the same shareholders. In what manner might the IRS restructure this transaction with adverse tax consequences to W Corporation?

26. Under what circumstances can court decisions lead to changes in the Code?

27. The Deficit Reduction Act of 1984 became part of the Internal Revenue Code of 1954. Explain the meaning of this statement.

28. Judicial decisions interpreting a provision of the Internal Revenue Code of 1939 are no longer of any value in view of the enactment of the Internal Revenue Code of 1954. Assess the validity of this statement.

29. Trace through Congress the path usually followed by a tax bill.

30. What is the function of the Joint Conference Committee of the House Ways and Means Committee and the Senate Finance Committee?

31. Why are Committee Reports of Congress important as a source of tax law?

32. What is a Proposed Regulation? How would a Proposed Regulation under § 541 be cited?

33. Distinguish between Treasury Regulations and Revenue Rulings, between Revenue Rulings and Revenue Procedures, and between Revenue Rulings and individual (i. e., "private") rulings.

34. What is the difference, if any, between the *Internal Revenue Bulletin* (I.R.B.) and the *Cumulative Bulletin* (C.B.)

35. Explain the fact-finding determination of a Federal Court of Appeals.

36. Taxpayer lives in Michigan. In a controversy with the IRS, taxpayer loses at the trial court level. Describe the appeal procedure under the following different assumptions:

    (a) The trial court was the Small Claims Division of the U. S. Tax Court.

    (b) The trial court was the U. S. Tax Court.

    (c) The trial court was a U. S. District Court.

    (d) The trial court was the U. S. Claims Court.

37. Suppose the U. S. Government loses a tax case in the U. S. District Court of Idaho but does not appeal the result. What does the failure to appeal signify?

38. Because the U. S. Tax Court is a national court, it always decides the same issue in a consistent manner. Assess the validity of this statement.

39. Explain the following abbreviations:

(a) CA–2          (d) *rev'd.*          (g) *acq.*          (j) AFTR          (m) USSC

(b) Cls.Ct.       (e) *rem'd.*         (h) B.T.A.          (k) F.2d          (n) S.Ct.

(c) *aff'd.*       (f) *Cert. denied*    (i) USTC           (l) F.Supp.       (o) D.Ct.

40. What is the difference between a Regular and a Memorandum decision of the U. S. Tax Court?

41. What is a "legislative Regulation"?

42. In assessing the validity of a court decision, discuss the significance of the following:

(a) The decision was rendered by the U. S. District Court of Wyoming. Taxpayer lives in Wyoming.

(b) The decision was rendered by the U. S. Claims Court. Taxpayer lives in Wyoming.

(c) The decision was rendered by the Second Court of Appeals. Taxpayer lives in California.

(d) The decision was rendered by the U. S. Supreme Court.

(e) The decision was rendered by the U. S. Tax Court. The IRS has acquiesced in the result.

(f) Same as (e) except that the IRS has issued a nonacquiescence as to the result.

43. Is tax avoidance illegal? Explain.

44. Where can a researcher locate tax articles discussing a particular Code Section?

## Problems

1. T owns some real estate (basis of $100,000 and fair market value of $60,000) that she would like to sell to her son, S, for $60,000. T is aware, however, that losses on sales between certain related parties are disallowed for Federal income tax purposes [§ 267(a)(1)]. T therefore sells the property to P (an unrelated party) for $60,000. On the same day, P sells the same property to S for the same amount. Is T's realized loss of $40,000 deductible? Explain.

2. X and Y, individual taxpayers, are neighbors and good friends who own homes in a recently constructed residential subdivision in Chicago, Illinois. Each paid $80,000 for the residence, and the property is worth approximately this amount. X sells his residence to Y for $80,000 and immediately leases the property back for a fair rental value. Y follows the same procedure. After the transfers are completed, each is the other person's landlord but both continue to occupy the same premises.

(a) Through the sale and leaseback procedure, what were X and Y trying to accomplish?

(b) On what basis, if any, could the IRS challenge this procedure?

3. T, a cash basis and calendar year individual taxpayer, has enjoyed modest success as a trial attorney in handling damage claims on a contingent fee basis. At a point when T has several lawsuits pending, she incorporates her practice. T transfers all of her business assets (including the contingent fee claims from the pending lawsuits) to T Corporation, a newly formed professional association, in return for all of its stock. Subsequent to the incorporation, the lawsuits are resolved in favor of T's clients and $300,000 is paid to T Corporation in settlement of her contingent fee claims.

(a) What was T trying to accomplish by incorporating her professional practice?

(b) Does the IRS have any defense(s)?

4.  T Corporation is in the construction business and uses the completed contract method (see the *Glossary of Tax Terms* in Appendix C) for reporting gain from the projects it completes. Prior to the completion of a number of particularly lucrative contracts, T Corporation is liquidated and all of its assets (including the contracts) are distributed to the shareholders. Subsequently, the gain from these contracts is reported by T Corporation's shareholders.

(a) What were the parties trying to accomplish by liquidating T Corporation?

(b) Does the IRS have any defense?

5.  P exchanges some real estate (basis of $80,000 and fair market value of $100,000) for other real estate owned by R (basis of $120,000 and fair market value of $90,000) and $10,000 in cash. The real estate involved is unimproved and is held by P and R, before and after the exchange, as investment property.

(a) What is P's realized gain on the exchange? Recognized gain?

(b) What is R's realized loss? Recognized loss?

(c) Support your results to (a) and (b) under the wherewithal to pay concept as applied to like-kind exchanges (§ 1031).

6.  In 19X5, T (an individual) incurred and paid personal medical expenses of $2,400 and reported adjusted gross income of $36,000. Because of the 5% limitation of § 213, T deducted only $600 of these medical expenses [$2,400 − (5% × $36,000) = $600] on her 19X5 tax return. In 19X6, T is reimbursed by her insurance company for $1,000 of the $2,400 medical expenses paid in 19X5.

(a) How much, if any of the reimbursement is income to T in 19X6?

(b) What concept, if any, would preclude T from filing an amended return for 19X5 and eliminating the medical expense deduction because of the later reimbursement?

7.  In late 19X2, T, a cash basis and calendar year unmarried individual, received a state income tax refund of $800 for tax year 19X1. On her Federal income tax return for 19X1, T had itemized deductions in excess of the zero bracket amount of $600. Comment on the treatment of the $800 income tax refund in connection with the following alternatives:

(a) T should file an amended Federal income tax return for 19X1 claiming only the zero bracket amount (i. e., not itemize her excess deductions from adjusted gross income).

(b) T should offset her income tax refund against any state income taxes she pays in 19X2.

(c) T should include some or all of the refund in her gross income for 19X2.

(d) T should disregard the refund for income tax purposes.

8.  T sells property (basis of $20,000) to V Corporation for $30,000. Based on the following conditions, how could the IRS challenge this transaction?

(a) T is the sole shareholder of V Corporation.

(b) T is the son of the sole shareholder of V Corporation.

(c) T is neither a shareholder in V Corporation nor related to any of its shareholders.

9. Using the legend provided, classify each of the following statements (*Note:* more than one answer per statement may be appropriate):

**Legend**

D = Applies to the U. S. District Court
T = Applies to the U. S. Tax Court
C = Applies to the U. S. Claims Court
A = Applies to the U. S. Court of Appeals
U = Applies to the U. S. Supreme Court
N = Applies to none of the above

     (a) Decides only Federal tax matters.
*T* (b) Decisions are reported in the F.2d Series.
*U A C D* (c) Decisions are reported in the USTCs.
*U A C D* (d) Decisions are reported in the AFTRs.
*U* (e) Appeal is by Writ of Certiorari.
*C* (f) Court meets generally in Washington, D.C.
*D* (g) A jury trial is available.
*D C T* (h) Trial courts.
*A* (i) Appellate courts.
*C* (j) Appeal is to the U. S. Court of Appeals for the Federal Circuit.
*T* (k) Has a Small Claims Division.
*T* (l) The only trial court where the taxpayer does not have to first pay the tax assessed by the IRS.

10. Identify the governmental unit that produces the following tax sources:
*Treasury* (a) Proposed Regulations.
*IRS* (b) Revenue Procedures.
*IRS* (c) Letter rulings. *(National Ofa )*
*IRS* (d) Determination letters. - *(District Directors )*
*IRS* (e) Technical Advice Memoranda.

11. Locate the following Internal Revenue Code citations and give a brief description of each:

     (a) § 104(a)(1).
     (b) § 195(b).
     (c) § 1371(b)(1).

12. Locate the following Regulation citations and give a brief description of each:

     (a) Reg. § 1.48–9(f)(6).
     (b) Reg. § 1.191–1(d).
     (c) Reg. § 1.535–2(d).

13. Locate the following Proposed Regulation citations and give a brief description of each:

     (a) Prop.Reg. § 1.44F–2(a)(1).
     (b) Prop.Reg. § 1.83–6(e).
     (c) Prop.Reg. § 1.174–2(a)(1).

14. Determine the acquiescence/nonacquiescence position of the IRS with respect to *Leland Adkins*, 51 T.C. 957 (1969).

15. Locate the following tax services in your library and indicate the name of the publisher and whether the service is organized by topic or Code Section:

    (a) *Federal Taxes.*

    (b) *Standard Federal Tax Reporter.*

    (c) *Tax Coordinator 2d.*

    (d) *Mertens Law of Federal Income Taxation.*

    (e) *Tax Management Portfolios.*

    (f) Rabkin & Johnson, *Federal Income, Gift & Estate Taxation.*

## Research Problems

*Research Problem 1.* Are the following Regulations valid:

(a) Reg. § 20.2056(b)–5(c).

(b) Reg. § 1.562–1(a).

*Research Problem 2.* Must the Internal Revenue Service treat similarly situated taxpayers consistently?

*Research Problem 3.* Determine the disposition of the following decisions at the Supreme Court level:

(a) *International Business Machines Corp. v. U. S.*, 343 F.2d 914 (Ct.Cl., 1965).

(b) *Knetsch v. U. S.*, 348 F.2d 932 (Ct.Cl., 1965).

(c) *American Society of Travel Agents, Inc. v. Blumenthal*, 566 F.2d 145 (CA–D.C., 1977).

(d) *Litchfield Securities v. U. S.*, 324 F.2d 667 (CA–2, 1963).

(e) *Wilson Bros. & Co. v. Comr.*, 170 F.2d 423 (CA–9, 1948).

*Research Problem 4.* Did the IRS agree or disagree with the following court decisions:

(a) *C. Blake McDowell, Inc.*, 67 T.C. 1043 (1977).

(b) *West Coast Ice Co.*, 49 T.C. 345 (1968).

(c) *Dwinwell & Co.*, 33 T.C. 827 (1960).

(d) *Henry Schwartz Corp.*, 60 T.C. 728 (1973).

*Research Problem 5.* T is a participating physician in a medical plan offered by the SC Corporation. Under a deferred compensation plan, T enters into a supplemental agreement designating 30% of his scheduled fees to be paid to him and the remainder to go into the deferred compensation plan. SC has established a trust with itself as the settlor (i.e., grantor) and beneficiary, and three physicians (including T) as trustees. The trustees purchased retirement annuity policies to provide for the payment of benefits under the plan. These benefits become payable to T (or his beneficiaries) when he retires, dies, becomes disabled, or leaves SC. Are the 70% amounts placed into the trust taxable to T under the constructive receipt doctrine or the economic benefit doctrine?

*Research Problem 6.* In December of 19X3, T, a cash basis and calendar year taxpayer, embezzles $200,000 from a bank where he is employed as an assistant cashier. T disappears for parts unknown and goes on a three-month spending spree. In 19X4, T is apprehended by law enforcement authorities and forced to make restitution of the $150,000 still not spent. Comment on T's income tax position, with special reference to the mitigation of the annual accounting period concept.

*Partial list of research aids:*

Code § § 61, 172, 1301–1305, and 1341.

*Bernard A. Yerkie,* 67 T.C. 388 (1976).

*Research Problem 7.* Complete the following citations to the extent the research materials are available to you:

(a) *Eisner v. Macomber,* —— S.Ct. 189 (——, 1920).

(b) *Cowden v. Comm.,* —— AFTR2d —— (CA–5, 1961).

(c) *Tougher v. Comm.,* —— USTC —— (CA–9, 1971).

(d) *York v. Comm.,* 261 F.2d —— (——, 1958).

(e) —— *v.* ——, 66–2 USTC ¶ 9537 (CA–4, 1966).

(f) *C. F. Kahler,* 18 T.C. —— (1952).

(g) *Pir M. Toor,* 36 TCM 1616, T.C.Memo. ——-——.

(h) ——, 47 B.T.A. 886 (1942).

(i) Rev.Rul. 72–312, —— C.B. 22.

(j) Rev.Rul. 86– ——, I.R.B. No. 9, 4.

(k) Rev.Rul. ——, 1969–2 C.B. 29.

*Research Problem 8.* By using the research materials available to you, answer the following questions:

(a) Has Prop.Reg. § 1.79–1(d)(7) been finalized?

(b) What happened to *Barry D. Pevsner,* P–H T.C.Mem.Dec. ¶ 79, 311, on appeal?

(c) Does Rev.Rul. 60–97 still represent the position of the IRS on the issue involved?

(d) What is the underlying Code Section for Reg. § 1.9101–1? Summarize this Regulation.

# Corporations: Introduction and Operating Rules 2

## CHAPTER OBJECTIVES

—Summarize the income tax treatment of various forms of conducting a business.

—Determine when an entity will be treated as a corporation for Federal income tax purposes.

—Review the general income tax provisions applicable to individuals.

—Establish the tax rules peculiar to corporations.

—Describe the procedural aspects of filing and reporting for corporate taxpayers.

—Evaluate the corporate form as a means of conducting a trade or business.

# THE TAX TREATMENT OF
# VARIOUS BUSINESS FORMS

Business operations can be conducted in a number of different forms. Among the various possibilities are the following:

—Sole proprietorships.

—Partnerships.

—Trusts and estates.

—Subchapter S corporations (also known as S corporations).

—Regular corporations (also called Subchapter C or C corporations).

For Federal income tax purposes the distinction between these forms of business organizations becomes very important. A brief summary of the tax treatment of each form will highlight these distinctions.

1. Sole proprietorships are not separate taxable entities from the individual who owns the proprietorship. The owner of the business will, therefore, report all business transactions on his or her individual income tax return.

2. Partnerships are not subject to the income tax. Under the conduit concept, the various tax attributes of the partnership's operations flow through to the individual partners to be reported on their personal income tax returns (see Example 1). Although a partnership is not a tax-paying entity, it is a reporting entity. Form 1065 is used to aggregate partnership transactions for the tax year and to allocate their pass-through to the individual partners. The tax consequences of the partnership form of business organization are outlined in Subchapter K of the Internal Revenue Code and are the subject of Chapters 9 and 10.

3. The income tax treatment of trusts and estates is in some respects similar and in others dissimilar to the partnership approach. In terms of similarity, income is taxed only once. However, tax may be imposed on the entity. Unlike a partnership, therefore, a trust or an estate may be subject to the Federal income tax. Whether the income will be taxed to a trust or an estate or to its beneficiaries generally depends on whether the income is retained by the entity or distributed to the beneficiaries. In the event of distribution, a modified form of the conduit principle is followed to preserve for the beneficiary the character of certain income (e. g., nontaxable

interest on municipal bonds). The income taxation of trusts and estates is treated in Chapter 13.[1]

4. Subchapter S of the Code permits certain corporations to elect special tax treatment. Such special treatment generally means avoidance of any income tax at the corporate level. Subchapter S corporations, called S corporations, are treated like partnerships in that the owners of the entity report most of the corporate tax attributes (e.g., income, losses, capital gains and losses, § 1231 gains and losses, charitable contributions, tax-exempt interest) on their individual returns. S corporations and their shareholders are the subject of Chapter 8.

5. The regular corporate form of doing business carries with it the imposition of the corporate income tax. For Federal income tax purposes, therefore, the corporation is recognized as a separate tax-paying entity. This produces what is known as a double tax effect: Income is taxed to the corporation as earned and taxed again to the shareholders as dividends when distributed. Also, the tax attributes of various types of income lose their identity as they pass through the corporate entity. In other words, the corporation does not act as a conduit when making distributions to its shareholders.

**Example 1.** During the current year X Company recognizes a long-term capital gain and receives tax-exempt interest, both of which are distributed to its owners. If X Company is a regular corporation, the distribution to the shareholders constitutes a dividend. The fact that it originated from long-term capital gain and tax-exempt interest is of no consequence.[2] On the other hand, if X Company is a partnership or an S corporation, the long-term capital gain and tax-exempt interest retain their identity as they pass through to the individual partners.

The tax consequences of operating a business in the regular corporate form fall within Subchapter C of the Code and are the subject of this chapter and Chapters 3 through 6.[3] Corporations that either unreasonably accumulate earnings or meet the definition of a personal holding company may be subject to further taxation. These so-called penalty taxes are im-

---

1. The tax treatment of Real Estate Investment Trusts (i. e., REIT's) presents peculiar problems and is not covered in this text. See § § 856–858. For further reading on this subject see: Kelley, "Real Estate Investment Trusts", *32nd N.Y.U. Tax Institute*, Vol. II (1974), p. 1637, and Allen, "REIT Provisions Substantially Changed by TRA," 46 *Journal of Taxation* (February 1977), p. 114.

2. As noted in Chapter 4, such items will, however, affect the distributing corporation's earnings and profits.

3. Special rules apply to cooperative organizations (§ § 521–522), banking institutions (Subchapter H), insurance companies (Subchapter L), and regulated investment companies (Subchapter M). In the interest of space and because of limited applicability, these rules are not discussed in this text. For further reading on the subjects, see Clark, "The Federal Income Taxation of Financial Intermediaries," 84 *Yale Law Journal* (July 1975), p. 1603; Ian and Pusey, "Selected Tax Planning Ideas for Savings and Loan Associations," 10 *Tax Adviser* (May 1979), p. 260; and Pehrson, Chiechi, and Adney, "Insurance Companies and the Income Tax," 10 *Tax Adviser* (July 1979), p. 414.

posed in addition to the corporate income tax and are discussed in Chapter 7.

Clearly, then, the form of organization chosen to carry on a trade or business has a significant effect on Federal income tax consequences. Though tax considerations may not control the choice, it could be unfortunate if they are not taken into account.

# WHAT IS A CORPORATION?

The first step in any discussion of the Federal income tax treatment of corporations must be definitional. More specifically, what is a corporation? At first glance the answer to this question would appear to be quite simple. Merely look to the appropriate state law to determine whether the entity has satisfied the specified requirements for corporate status. Have articles of incorporation been drawn up and filed with the state regulatory agency? Has a charter been granted? Has stock been issued to shareholders? These are all points to consider.

Compliance with state law, although important, may not tell the full story as to whether or not an entity is to be recognized as a corporation for tax purposes. On the one hand, a corporation qualifying under state law may be disregarded as a taxable entity if it is a mere "sham." On the other hand, an organization not qualifying as a regular corporation under state law may be taxed as a corporation under the association approach. These two possibilities are discussed in the following sections.

*Disregard of Corporate Entity.* In most cases, the IRS and the courts will recognize a corporation legally constituted under state law. In exceptional situations, however, the corporate entity may be disregarded because it lacks substance.[4] The key to such treatment rests with the degree of business activity conducted at the corporate level. Thus, the more the corporation does in connection with its trade or business, the less likely it will be treated as a sham and disregarded as a separate entity.

> **Example 2.** C and D are joint owners of a tract of unimproved real estate that they wish to protect from future creditors. Consequently, C and D form R Corporation, to which they transfer the land in return for all of the latter's stock. The corporation merely holds title to the land and conducts no other activities. In all respects, R Corporation meets the requirements of a corporation under applicable state law.

> **Example 3.** Assume the same facts as in Example 2. In addition to holding title to the land, R Corporation leases the property, collects rents, and pays the property taxes thereon.

---

**4.** The reader should bear in mind that the textual discussion relates to the classification of an entity for *Federal* income tax purposes. State corporate income taxes or other corporate taxes (e. g., franchise taxes) may still be imposed. An entity may quite possibly be treated as a corporation for state tax purposes and not for Federal or vice versa. This will become even more apparent when dealing with S corporations (Chapter 8), such status not being recognized by some states.

R Corporation probably would not be recognized as a separate entity under the facts set forth in Example 2. In Example 3, however, the opposite should prove true. It appears that enough activity has taken place at the corporate level to warrant the conclusion that R Corporation should be treated as a real corporation for Federal income tax purposes.[5]

Whether the IRS or the taxpayers will attempt to disregard the corporate entity must, of course, depend on the circumstances of each particular situation. More often than not, the IRS may be trying to disregard (or "collapse") a corporation to make the corporation's income taxable directly to the shareholders.[6] In other situations, a corporation might be trying to avoid the corporate income tax or to permit its shareholders to take advantage of excess corporate deductions and losses.[7]

Theoretically speaking, the disregard-of-corporate-entity approach should be equally available to both the IRS and the taxpayers. From a practical standpoint, however, taxpayers have enjoyed considerably less success than has the IRS.[8] Courts generally conclude that since the taxpayers created the corporation in the first place, they later should not be permitted to disregard it in order to avoid taxes.

*Associations Taxed as Corporations.* Section 7701(a)(3) defines a corporation to include "associations, joint stock companies, and insurance companies." What Congress intended by the inclusion of "associations" in the definitions has never been entirely clear. Judicial decisions have clarified the status of associations and the relationship between associations and corporations.

The designation given to the entity under state law is not controlling. In one case, what was a business trust under state law was deemed to be an association (and therefore taxable as a corporation) for Federal income tax purposes.[9] In another case, a partnership of physicians was held to be an association even though state law prohibited the practice of medicine in the corporate form.[10]

Whether or not an entity will be considered an association for Federal income tax purposes depends upon the number of corporate characteristics it possesses. According to court decisions and Regulation § 301.7701–2(a), corporate characteristics include the following:

1. Associates.

2. An objective to carry on a business and divide the gains therefrom.

3. Continuity of life.

---

5. A classic case in this area is *Paymer v. Comm.*, 45–2 USTC ¶ 9353, 33 AFTR 1536, 150 F.2d 334 (CA–2, 1945). Here, two corporations were involved. The Court chose to disregard one corporate entity but to recognize the other.

6. See, for example, *Floyd Patterson*, 25 TCM 1230, T.C.Memo. 1966–239, *aff'd.* in 68–2 USTC ¶ 9471, 22 AFTR2d 5810 (CA–2, 1968).

7. An election under Subchapter S would accomplish this if it were timely made and the parties qualified. See Chapter 8.

8. See, for example, *Rafferty Farms, Inc. v. U. S.*, 75–1 USTC ¶ 9271, 35 AFTR2d 75–811, 511 F.2d 1234 (CA–8, 1975), and *Collins v. U. S.*, 75–2 USTC ¶ 9553, 36 AFTR2d 75–5175, 514 F.2d 1282 (CA–5, 1975).

9. *Morrissey v. Comm.*, 36–1 USTC ¶ 9020, 16 AFTR 1274, 56 S.Ct. 289 (USSC, 1936).

10. *U. S. v. Kintner*, 54–2 USTC ¶ 9626, 47 AFTR 995, 216 F.2d 418 (CA–9, 1954).

4. Centralized management.

5. Limited liability.

6. Free transferability of interests.

The Regulations state that an unincorporated organization shall not be classified as an association unless it possesses more corporate than non-corporate characteristics. In making the determination, the characteristics common to both corporate and noncorporate business organizations shall be disregarded.[11]

Both corporations and partnerships generally have associates (i. e., shareholders and partners) and an objective to carry on a business and divide the gains. In testing whether a particular partnership is an association, these criteria would be disregarded. It then becomes a matter of determining whether the partnership possesses a majority of the remaining corporate characteristics (see items 3 through 6). Does the partnership terminate upon the withdrawal or death of a partner (i. e., no continuity of life)? Is the management of the partnership centralized or do all partners participate therein? Are all partners individually liable for the debts of the partnership or is the liability of some limited to their actual investment in the partnership (i. e., limited partnership)? May a partner freely transfer his or her interest without the consent of the other partners? Courts have ruled that any partnership lacking two or more of these characteristics will not be classified as an association. Conversely, any partnership having three or more of these characteristics will be classified as an association.[12]

In the case of trusts, the first two characteristics listed above would have to be considered in testing for association status. The conventional type of trust often does not have associates and usually restricts its activities to investments as opposed to carrying on a trade or business. These characteristics, however, are common to corporations. Consequently, whether a trust qualifies as an association depends upon the satisfaction of the first two corporate characteristics.

From a taxpayer's standpoint, the desirability of association status turns on the tax implications involved. In some cases, the parties may find it advantageous to have the entity taxed as a corporation while in others they may not. These possibilities are explored at length in the TAX PLANNING CONSIDERATIONS portion of this chapter.

# AN INTRODUCTION TO THE INCOME TAXATION OF CORPORATIONS

## AN OVERVIEW OF CORPORATE VERSUS INDIVIDUAL INCOME TAX TREATMENT

In any discussion of how corporations are treated under the Federal income tax, the best approach is to compare such treatment with that applicable to individual taxpayers.

---

11. Reg. § 301.7701–2(a)(3).
12. See *Zuckman v. U. S.*, 75–2 USTC ¶ 9778, 36 AFTR2d 6193, 524 F.2d 729 (Ct.Cls., 1975), and *P. G. Larson*, 66 T.C. 159 (1976).

*Similarities.* The gross income of a corporation is determined in much the same manner as it is determined for individuals. Thus, gross income includes compensation for services rendered, income derived from a business, gains from dealings in property, interest, rents, royalties, dividends— to name only a few such items [§ 61(a)]. Both individuals and corporations are entitled to exclusions from gross income; however, fewer exclusions are allowed in the case of corporate taxpayers. Interest on municipal bonds would be excluded from gross income whether the bondholder is an individual or a corporate taxpayer (§ 103).

Gains and losses from property transactions are handled similarly. For example, whether a gain or loss is capital or ordinary depends upon the nature of the asset in the hands of the taxpayer making the taxable disposition. Code § 1221, in defining what is not a capital asset, makes no distinction between corporate and noncorporate taxpayers. In the area of nontaxable exchanges, corporations are like individuals in that no gain or loss is recognized by them on a like-kind exchange (§ 1031) and recognized gain may be deferred on an involuntary conversion of property (§ 1033).[13] For obvious reasons, the nonrecognition of gain provisions dealing with the sale of a personal residence (§ § 121 and 1034) do not apply to corporations. But both corporations and individuals are vulnerable to the disallowance of losses on sales of property to related parties [§ 267(a)(1)] or on the wash sales of securities (§ 1091). However, the wash sales rules do not apply to individuals who are traders or dealers in securities or to corporations that are dealers, if the sales of the securities are in the ordinary course of the corporation's business. Upon the sale or other taxable disposition of depreciable property, the recapture rules (e. g., § § 1245 and 1250) generally make no distinctions between corporate and noncorporate taxpayers. [However, § 291(a) does cause a corporation to have more recapture on § 1250 property. Under § 291(a), 20 percent of the excess of the amount that would be recaptured under § 1245 over the amount recaptured under § 1250 is ordinary income to a corporation on the disposition of § 1250 property.]

The business deductions of corporations also parallel those available to individuals. Therefore, deductions will be allowed for all ordinary and necessary expenses paid or incurred in carrying on a trade or business under the general rule of § 162(a). Specific provision is made for the deductibility of interest (§ 163), certain taxes (§ 164), losses (§ 165), bad debts (§ 166), accelerated cost recovery (§ 168), charitable contributions (§ 170), net operating losses (§ 172), research and experimental expenditures (§ 174), and other less common deductions. No deduction will be permitted for interest paid or incurred on amounts borrowed to purchase or carry tax-exempt securities [§ 265(2)]. The same holds true for expenses contrary to public policy [e. g., § § 162(c) and (f)] and certain unpaid expenses and interest between related parties [§ 267(a)(2)].

Many of the tax credits available to individuals also can be claimed by corporations. This is certainly the case with two of the most important— the investment tax credit (§ 38) and the foreign tax credit (§ 33). Not avail-

---

**13.** For definitions of terms such as "like-kind exchange" and "involuntary conversion," see the Glossary of Tax Terms in Appendix C.

able to corporations are certain credits that are personal in nature, such as the child care credit (§ 21), the credit for the elderly (§ 22), the political contributions credit (§ 24), and the earned income credit (§ 32).

Corporations generally have the same choices of accounting periods and methods as do individual taxpayers. Like an individual, a corporation may choose a calendar year or a fiscal year for reporting purposes (§ 441). Corporations, however, do enjoy greater flexibility in the selection of a tax year. For example, corporations usually can have different tax years from those of their shareholders. Also, newly formed corporations (as new taxpayers) generally have a choice of any approved accounting period without having to obtain the consent of the IRS. Permissible accounting methods include the cash or accrual method [§ 446(c)], the installment method (§ 453), or, for use in conjunction with long-term contracts, the percentage of completion or the completed contract method (Reg. § 1.451–3).

*Dissimilarities.* Significant variations exist, however, in the income taxation of corporations and individuals. A major variation is that different tax rates apply to corporations (§ 11) and to individuals (§ 1). Corporate tax rates are discussed in a later section of this chapter.

All allowable corporate deductions are treated as business deductions. Thus, the determination of adjusted gross income (§ 62), so essential in the case of individual taxpayers, has no relevance to corporations. Taxable income simply is computed by subtracting from gross income all allowable deductions and losses. As such, corporations need not be concerned with itemized deductions (e. g., §§ 211–220) or the zero bracket amount [§ 63(d)]. Likewise, the deduction for personal and dependency exemptions (§§ 151 through 154) is not available.

Because corporations can have only business deductions and losses, the $100 floor on the deductible portion of personal casualty and theft losses and the limitation that nonbusiness casualty losses will be deductible only to the extent such losses exceed 10 percent of AGI do not apply [§ 165(c)]. Also, expenses paid or incurred on property held for the production of income or in connection with the determination, collection, or refund of any tax would be deductible as a business expense [i. e., § 162(a) applies rather than § 212].

> **Example 4.** During 19X6, X, a calendar year taxpayer with AGI of $10,000, suffers a casualty loss of $4,000 and pays $300 to a CPA for the preparation of a 19X5 Federal income tax return. If X is an individual, only $2,900 ($4,000 − $100 − $1,000) of the casualty loss can be deducted (assuming the loss is personal and there has been no actual insurance recovery and none is reasonably anticipated). Chances are the casualty loss and the $300 tax return preparation fee can only be claimed as an itemized deduction and would not be available if X chose not to itemize. On the other hand, if X is a corporation, both items would be deductible in full as business expenses under § 162.

## SPECIFIC PROVISIONS COMPARED

—Although the capital gains and losses of individuals and corporations are computed in the same manner, their tax treatment is substantially different [e. g., §§ 1201(a), 1211(a), and 1212(a)].

—Recapture of depreciation rules differ somewhat for corporations and individuals. Although depreciation recapture for § 1245 assets is computed in the same manner for individuals as it is for corporations, corporations are subject to additional recapture on § 1250 assets [§ 291(a)(1)].

—The percentages used to determine the maximum charitable contribution allowance are not the same for corporate and noncorporate taxpayers [§ 170(b)(2)].

—Net operating losses of individuals and corporations require different adjustments for carryback and carryover purposes [§ 172(d)(4), (5), and (6)].

—Corporations are entitled to certain special deductions. The most important of these are the deduction for dividends received from other domestic corporations (§ 243) and the write-off of organizational expenditures (§ 248). Corporations are not allowed the $100 dividend exclusion available to individuals (§ 116).

These differences in the income tax treatment of corporate and individual taxpayers are discussed in depth in the sections to follow.

## CAPITAL GAINS AND LOSSES

Capital gains and losses result from the taxable sales or exchanges of capital assets. Whether such gains and losses would be long-term or short-term depends upon the holding period of the assets sold or exchanged. Each year a taxpayer's long-term capital gains and losses are combined and the result is either a *net* long-term capital gain or a *net* long-term capital loss. A similar aggregation is made with short-term capital gains and losses, the result being a *net* short-term capital gain or a *net* short-term capital loss (§ 1222). The following combinations and results are possible:

1.  A net long-term capital gain and a net short-term capital loss. These are combined and the result is either a net capital gain or a net capital loss. Net capital gains receive preferential tax treatment. Net capital losses of corporate and noncorporate taxpayers are treated differently (see below).

2.  A net long-term capital gain and a net short-term capital gain. No further combination is made. Net long-term capital gains receive preferential tax treatment, and net short-term capital gains are taxed as ordinary income.

3.  A net long-term capital loss and a net short-term capital gain. These are combined and the result is either capital gain net income or a net capital loss. Net short-term capital gains in excess of the net long-term capital loss are taxed as ordinary income.

4.  A net long-term capital loss and a net short-term capital loss. No further combination is made.

*Capital Gains.* In the case of an individual taxpayer, long-term capital gains are included in gross income with an offsetting 60 percent net capital gain deduction (§ 1202).

**Example 5.** T, an individual, has the following capital transactions during 19X3: a long-term capital gain of $10,000 and a short-term capital gain of $4,000. T includes the $10,000 long-term capital gain in gross income and claims a $6,000 capital gain deduction. The short-term capital gain of $4,000 also must be included in gross income (see combination 2).

The treatment of long-term capital gains in the hands of corporate taxpayers differs from the above example in two respects. First, the 60 percent net capital gain deduction is not available. Second, net capital gains for corporations may be taxed at an alternative tax rate of 28 percent [§ 1201(a)]. Consequently, a corporation for computation purposes can either include the full net capital gain in the regular tax computation or exclude it and compute the tax on the net capital gain at the alternative 28 percent rate and add the result to the regular tax liability.

**Example 6.** Assume the same facts as in Example 5, except that T is a corporate taxpayer. T Corporation includes the $10,000 of long-term capital gain in gross income, but with no offsetting net capital gain deduction. Using the alternative tax computation, T adds $2,800 (i. e., 28% × $10,000) to its regular tax liability, which is computed without the net capital gain in the tax base. In either case, the short-term capital gain of $4,000 also must be included in gross income.

Whether corporate taxpayers should use the alternative tax computation depends, of course, on the tax savings generated.

**Example 7.** During 19X4, T Corporation has taxable income of $100,000 without the inclusion of a net capital gain of $1,000. Since T Corporation has reached the 46% income tax bracket (see the discussion later in the chapter on the corporate income tax rates), it should use the alternative tax. Consequently, $280 (28% of $1,000) should be added to T Corporation's regular income tax liability on $100,000.

**Example 8.** Assume the same facts as in Example 7, except that T Corporation has taxable income of only $24,000. Because it is only in the 15% tax bracket level, the $1,000 net capital gain should be included in T Corporation's gross income and the alternative tax method not used.

*Capital Losses.* Differences also exist between corporate and noncorporate taxpayers in the income tax treatment of net capital losses (see combinations 1, 3, and 4 described previously). Generally, noncorporate taxpayers can deduct up to $3,000 of such net losses against other income [§ 1211(b)]. However, if the net loss is a long-term capital loss, it will require $2 of loss to generate $1 of deduction. Any remaining capital losses can be carried forward to future years until absorbed by capital gains or by the $3,000 (with exceptions noted above) deduction [§ 1212(b)]. Carryovers do not lose their identity but remain either long-term or short-term.

**Example 9.** T, an individual, incurs a net long-term capital loss of $7,500 for calendar year 19X8. Assuming adequate taxable income, T may deduct $3,000 of this loss on his 19X8 return. The remaining $1,500 (i. e., $7,500 − $6,000) of the loss is carried to 19X9 and years thereafter until completely deducted. The $1,500 will be carried forward as a long-term capital loss.

Unlike individuals, corporate taxpayers are not permitted to claim any net capital losses as a deduction against ordinary income [§ 1211(a)]. Capital losses, therefore, can be used only as an offset against capital gains. Corporations may, however, carry back net capital losses to three preceding years, applying them first to the earliest year in point of time. Carryforwards are allowed for a period of five years from the year of the loss [§ 1212(a)]. When carried back or forward, a long-term capital loss becomes a short-term capital loss.

> **Example 10.**  Assume the same facts as in Example 9, except that T is a corporation. None of the $7,500 long-term capital loss incurred in 19X8 can be deducted in that year. T Corporation may, however, carry the loss back to years 19X5, 19X6, and 19X7 (in this order) and apply it to any capital gains recognized in these years. If the carryback does not exhaust the loss, it may be carried forward to calendar years 19X9, 19X0, 19X1, 19X2, and 19X3 (in this order). Either a carryback or a carryforward of the long-term capital loss converts it to a short-term capital loss.

## RECAPTURE OF DEPRECIATION

Corporations have more recapture of depreciation under § 1250 than do individuals. Depreciation recapture for § 1245 property is computed in the same manner for individuals and for corporations; however, under § 291(a)(1) for sales of depreciable real estate that is § 1250 property, 20 percent of the excess of any amount that would be treated as ordinary income under § 1245 over the amount treated as ordinary income under § 1250 is additional ordinary income.

> **Example 11.**  A corporation purchased an office building on January 3, 1982, for $300,000. Accelerated depreciation was taken in the amount of $117,000 before the building was sold on January 5, 1986, for $250,000. Straight-line depreciation would have been $80,000 (using a 15-year recovery period under ACRS). Because the building is § 1245 recovery property, the gain of $67,000 [$250,000 − ($300,000 − $117,000)] is recaptured to the extent of all depreciation taken. Thus, all gain is ordinary income under § 1245.

> **Example 12.**  Assume the building is residential rental property. It is now § 1250 property; thus, gain recaptured under § 1250 is $37,000 ($117,000 − $80,000). For an individual taxpayer, the remaining gain of $30,000 would be § 1231 gain. However, for a corporate taxpayer,

§ 291(a)(1) causes additional § 1250 ordinary income of $6,000, computed as follows:

| | |
|---|---:|
| Section 1245 recapture | $ 67,000 |
| Less gain recaptured under § 1250 | 37,000 |
| Excess § 1245 gain | $ 30,000 |
| Percentage that is ordinary gain | 20% |
| Additional § 1250 gain | $ 6,000 |
| Ordinary income ($37,000 + $6,000) | $ 43,000 |
| Section 1231 gain ($67,000 − $37,000 − $6,000) | 24,000 |
| Total gain | $ 67,000 |

**Example 13.** Assume the building is commercial property and straight-line depreciation was used. An individual would report all gain of $30,000 [$250,000 − ($300,000 − $80,000 depreciation)] as § 1231 gain. However, a corporate taxpayer would recapture as ordinary income, under § 291, 20% of the depreciation recapture under § 1245 (20% of $30,000). Thus, $6,000 would be ordinary income and $24,000 would be § 1231 gain.

## CHARITABLE CONTRIBUTIONS

No deduction will be allowed to either corporate or noncorporate taxpayers for a charitable contribution unless the recipient is a qualified charitable organization within the meaning of § 170(c). Generally, a deduction will be allowed only for the year in which the payment is made. However, an important exception is made in the case of *accrual basis corporations*. Here the deduction may be claimed in the year preceding payment if the contribution has been authorized by the board of directors by the end of that year and is, in fact, paid on or before the 15th day of the third month of the next year [§ 170(a)(2)].

**Example 14.** On December 28, 19X5, XYZ Company, a calendar year accrual basis taxpayer, authorizes a $5,000 donation to the Atlanta Symphony Association (a qualified charitable organization). The donation is made on March 14, 19X6. If XYZ Company is a partnership, the contribution can be deducted only in 19X6.[14]

**Example 15.** Assume the same facts as in Example 14, except that the XYZ Company is a corporation. Presuming the December 28, 19X5, authorization was made by its board of directors, XYZ Company may claim the $5,000 donation as a deduction for calendar year 19X5. If it was not, the deduction may still be claimed for calendar year 19X6.

---

14. Each partner will pick up his or her allocable portion of the charitable contribution deduction as of December 31, 19X6 (the end of the partnership's tax year). See Chapter 9.

*Property Contributions.*  Property contributions are governed by the following rules:

1.  Generally, the measure of the deduction is the fair market value of the property on the date of its donation.

2.  The deduction for "ordinary income property" that has appreciated in value is generally limited to the adjusted basis of the property. A corporate taxpayer may deduct the property's basis plus one-half of the appreciated value of ordinary income property (not to exceed twice the basis of the property) if the property is used in a manner related to the exempt purpose of the donee and the donee uses the property solely for the care of the ill, needy, or infants. In addition, a corporation may deduct the property's basis plus one-half of the appreciated value of ordinary income property for gifts of scientific property to colleges and universities for use in research, provided the following conditions are met: (a) the property was constructed by the taxpayer; (b) the gift was made within two years of the substantial completion of construction; (c) the donee is the original user of the property; (d) at least 80 percent of the property's use by the charitable organization will be for research or experimentation; and (e) the property was not transferred in exchange for money, other property, or services. The donor corporation must secure a written statement that requirements for the use of property for the ill, needy, or infants or for research purposes have been met. "Ordinary income property" is defined as property that would not have yielded long-term capital gain if sold or otherwise disposed of in a taxable exchange [§ 170(e)(1)(A)].[15]

3.  Normally, appreciated property, which if sold would have resulted in a long-term capital gain to the donor, can be claimed at its fair market value on the date of contribution. This rule is, however, subject to two exceptions. The first exception involves the charitable contribution of tangible personal property, the use of which by the donee is unrelated to the purpose or function constituting the basis for its tax-exempt status.[16] The second exception relates to the donation of long-term capital gain property (except certain "qualified" stock) to certain private foundations.[17] In either of these situations, the deduction is limited to the fair market value of the property less 40 percent ($^{28}/_{46}$, or 60.87 percent, in the case of a corporation) of the long-term gain that would have been recognized had such property been sold [§ 170(e)(1)(B)].

**Example 16.**  X donates an art collection (basis of $40,000 and fair market value of $100,000) to the Atlanta Symphony Associa-

---

15.  Section 1231 property (i. e., depreciable property and real estate used in a trade or business and held over six months) would not be ordinary income property except to the extent of its recapture potential under §§ 1245 and 1250. See "recapture of depreciation" in the Glossary of Tax Terms in Appendix C.

16.  Tangible personalty excludes real estate and intangible property (e. g., stocks and bonds).

17.  As defined in § 509(a).

tion (a qualified charitable organization) to help raise funds for a special summer concert program. The art collection is tangible personal property, and its use is not related to the purpose or function constituting the basis for the Atlanta Symphony Association's exempt status. If X is an individual, the measure of the charitable contribution is $76,000 [$100,000 (fair market value of the collection) − $24,000 (40% × $60,000 capital gain potential)]. If X is a corporation, the deduction is $63,478 [$100,000 − $36,522 ($28/_{46}$ × $60,000)]. Both results are predicated on the assumption that the art collection is a capital asset held for more than six months. If not, the deduction for corporate and noncorporate taxpayers would be limited to $40,000 (i. e., the lower of the fair market value of the property or the property's adjusted basis on the date of its donation).

*Limitations Imposed on Charitable Contribution Deductions.* Like individuals, corporations are not permitted an unlimited charitable contribution deduction.[18] For any one year a corporate taxpayer is limited to 10 percent of taxable income, computed without regard to the charitable contribution deduction, any net operating loss carryback or capital loss carryback, and the dividends received deduction [§ 170(b)(2)]. Any contributions in excess of the 10 percent limitation may be carried forward to the five succeeding tax years. Any carryforward must be added to subsequent contributions and will be subject to the 10 percent limitation. In applying this limitation, the current year's contributions must be deducted first, with excess deductions from previous years deducted in order of time [§ 170(d)(2) and Reg. § 1.170–2(g)].

**Example 17.** During 19X4, T Corporation (a calendar year taxpayer) had the following income and expenses:

| | |
|---|---:|
| Income from operations | $ 140,000 |
| Expenses from operations | 110,000 |
| Dividends received | 10,000 |
| Charitable contributions made in May 19X4 | 5,000 |

For purposes of the 10% limitation *only,* T Corporation's taxable income is $40,000 [$140,000 − $110,000 + $10,000]. Consequently, the allowable charitable deduction for 19X4 is $4,000 (10% × $40,000). The $1,000 unused portion of the contribution can be carried forward to 19X5, 19X6, 19X7, 19X8, and 19X9 (in that order) until exhausted.

**Example 18.** Assume the same facts as in Example 17. In 19X5, T Corporation has taxable income (for purposes of the 10% limitation) of $50,000 and makes a charitable contribution of $4,500. The maximum deduction allowed for 19X5 would be $5,000 (10% × $50,000). The first $4,500 of the allowed deduction must be allocated to the contribution made in 19X5, and $500 of the balance is carried over from 19X4. The remaining $500 of the 19X4 contribution may be carried over to 19X6, etc.

---

18. The percentage limitations applicable to individuals are set forth in § 170(b)(1).

## NET OPERATING LOSSES

The net operating loss of a corporation, which may be carried back three years and forward 15 to offset taxable income for those years, is not subject to the adjustments required for individual taxpayers. A corporation does not adjust its tax loss for the year for capital gains and losses as do individual taxpayers. This is true because a corporation is not permitted a deduction for net capital losses, and the capital gain is not subject to a capital gain deduction. A corporation does not make adjustments for nonbusiness deductions as do individual taxpayers. Further, a corporation is allowed to include the dividends received deduction (see below) in computing its net operating loss [§ 172(d)].

**Example 19.** In 19X5, X Corporation has gross income (including dividends) of $200,000 and deductions of $300,000 excluding the dividends received deduction. X Corporation had received taxable dividends of $100,000 from Y Corporation, a domestic corporation that is not a member of a controlled group with X Corporation. X Corporation has a net operating loss of $185,000, computed as follows:

| | | |
|---|---|---|
| Gross income (including dividends) | | $ 200,000 |
| Less: | | |
| Business deductions | $ 300,000 | |
| Dividends received deduction | | |
| (85% of $100,000) | 85,000 | 385,000 |
| Taxable income (or loss) | | $ (185,000) |

The net operating loss is carried back three years to 19X2. (X Corporation may forgo the carryback option and elect instead to carry forward the loss.) Assume X Corporation had taxable income of $40,000 in 19X2. The carryover to 19X3 is $145,000, computed as follows:

| | |
|---|---|
| Taxable income for 19X2 | $ 40,000 |
| Less net operating loss carryback | 185,000 |
| Taxable income for 19X2 after net operating loss carryback (carryover to 19X3) | $ (145,000) |

It is advisable to forgo the carryback option and elect instead to carry forward the loss if taxable income in future years is anticipated to be in substantially higher brackets than in the carryback years.

**Example 20.** Assume X Corporation in Example 19 had taxable income of $20,000, $25,000, and $25,000, respectively, for 19X2, 19X3, and 19X4. X Corporation anticipates taxable income in 19X6 of $215,000 because of the development of a new product. If it carries back its $185,000 loss, $70,000 of the loss will be used to save $10,500 in taxes (all income in the carryback years was taxed at 15%, assuming these years were after 1982). After deducting the remaining loss of $115,000 to offset taxable income in 19X6, X Corporation's income for

19X6 would be $100,000. Tax for 19X6 would be $25,750 (see Example 25 for computation). However, if X Corporation had carried forward the entire loss of $185,000, its taxable income for 19X6 would be only $30,000 ($215,000 − $185,000). Tax on $30,000 is $4,650 (15% of $25,000 plus 18% of $5,000). By forgoing the tax saving of $10,500 for the previous three tax years, X Corporation will save an additional $21,100 ($25,750 − $4,650) in 19X6.

## DEDUCTIONS AVAILABLE ONLY TO CORPORATIONS

*Dividends Received Deduction.* A corporation is allowed a deduction equal to (a) 85 percent of the amount of dividends received from domestic corporations or (b) 100 percent of the amount of dividends received from corporations that are members of an affiliated group with the recipient corporation.[19]

The purpose of the 85 percent dividends received deduction is to prevent triple taxation. Absent the deduction, income paid to a corporation in the form of a dividend would be subject to taxation for a second time (once to the distributing corporation) with no corresponding deduction to the distributing corporation. Later, when the recipient corporation paid the income to its individual shareholders, such income would again be subject to taxation with no corresponding deduction to the corporation. The dividends received deduction alleviates some of this inequity by causing only a small amount of dividend income to be subject to taxation at the corporate level.

The dividends received deduction is limited to 85 percent of the taxable income of a corporation computed without regard to the net operating loss, the dividends received deduction, and any capital loss carryback to the current tax year. However, the taxable income limitation does not apply if the corporation has a net operating loss for the current taxable year [§ § 246(b)(1) and (2)].

**Example 21.** In the current year, T Corporation has the following income and expenses:

| | |
|---|---|
| Gross income from operations | $ 400,000 |
| Expenses from operations | 340,000 |
| Dividends received from domestic corporations | 200,000 |

The dividends received deduction is $170,000 (85% × $200,000) unless 85% of taxable income is less. Because taxable income (for this purpose) is $260,000 ($400,000 − $340,000 + $200,000), and 85% of $260,000 is $221,000, the full $170,000 will be allowed.

**Example 22.** Assume the same facts as in Example 21, except that T Corporation's gross income from operations is $320,000 (instead of $400,000). The usual dividends received deduction of $170,000

---

19. § 243(a).

(85% × $200,000) is now limited to 85% of the taxable income. Since 85% of $180,000 ($320,000 − $340,000 + $200,000) is $153,000, this amount is the dividends received deduction (i. e., $153,000 is less than $170,000). The full $170,000 cannot be claimed, because it does not generate or add to a net operating loss. (Taxable income of $180,000 less $170,000 does not result in a net operating loss.)

**Example 23.**  Assume the same facts as in Example 21, except that T Corporation's gross income from operations is $300,000 (instead of $400,000). The usual dividends received deduction of $170,000 can now be claimed under the net operating loss exception. Taxable income of $160,000 ($300,000 − $340,000 + $200,000) less $170,000 generates a net operating loss of $10,000.

In summary, Example 21 reflects the general rule that the dividends received deduction is 85 percent of the qualifying dividends. Example 22 presents the exception whereby the deduction may be limited to 85 percent of taxable income. Example 23 presents the situation in which the taxable income exception will not apply, because allowance of the full deduction generates or adds to a net operating loss.

*Deduction of Organizational Expenditures.*  Expenses incurred in connection with the organization of a corporation normally are chargeable to a capital account. That they benefit the corporation during its existence seems clear. But how can they be amortized when most corporations possess unlimited life? The lack of a determinable and limited estimated useful life would, therefore, preclude any tax write-off. Code § 248 was enacted to solve this problem.

Under § 248, a corporation may elect to amortize organizational expenditures over a period of 60 months or more. The period begins with the month in which the corporation begins business.[20] Organizational expenditures subject to the election include legal services incident to organization (e. g., drafting the corporate charter, bylaws, minutes or organizational meetings, terms of original stock certificates), necessary accounting services, expenses of temporary directors and of organizational meetings of directors or shareholders, and fees paid to the state of incorporation.[21] Expenditures that do not qualify include those connected with issuing or selling shares of stock or other securities (e. g., commissions, professional fees, and printing costs) or with the transfer of assets to a corporation. Such expenditures reduce the amount of capital raised and are not deductible at all.

To qualify for the election, the expenditure must be *incurred* before the end of the taxable year in which the corporation begins business. In this regard, the corporation's method of accounting is of no consequence. Thus,

---

**20.**  The month in which a corporation begins business may not be immediately apparent. See Reg. § 1.248–1(a)(3). For a similar problem in the Subchapter S area see Reg. § 1.1372–2(b)(1) and Chapter 8.

**21.**  Reg. § 1.248–1(b).

an expense incurred by a cash basis corporation in its first tax year would qualify even though not paid until a subsequent year.[22]

The election is made in a statement attached to the corporation's return for its first taxable year. The return and statement must be filed no later than the due date of the return (including any extensions). The statement must set forth the description and amount of the expenditure involved, the date such expenditures were incurred, the month in which the corporation began business, and the number of months (not less than 60) over which such expenditures are to be deducted ratably.[23]

If the election is not made on a timely basis, organizational expenditures cannot be deducted until the corporation ceases to do business and liquidates. These expenditures will be deductible if the corporate charter limits the life of the corporation.

**Example 24.** T Corporation, an accrual basis taxpayer, was formed and began operations on May 1, 19X5. The following expenses were incurred during its first year of operations (May 1–December 31, 19X5):

| | |
|---|---|
| Expenses of temporary directors and of organizational meetings | $ 500 |
| Fee paid to the state of incorporation | 100 |
| Accounting services incident to organization | 200 |
| Legal services for drafting the corporate charter and bylaws | 400 |
| Expenses incident to the printing and sale of stock certificates | 300 |

Assume T Corporation makes a timely election under § 248 to amortize qualifying organizational expenses over a period of 60 months. The monthly amortization would be $20 [($500 + $100 + $200 + $400) ÷ 60 months], and $160 ($20 × 8 months) would be deductible for tax year 19X5. Note that the $300 of expenses incident to the printing and sale of stock certificates does not qualify for the election. These expenses cannot be deducted at all but reduce the amount of the capital realized from the sale of stock.

Organizational expenditures are to be distinguished from "start-up" expenditures covered by § 195. Start-up expenditures refer to various investigation expenses involved in entering a new business, whether they be incurred by a corporate or a noncorporate taxpayer. Such expenditures (e. g., travel, market surveys, financial audits, legal fees), at the election of the taxpayer, can be amortized over a period of 60 months or longer rather than capitalized as part of the cost of the business acquired.

---

**22.** Reg. § 1.248–1(a)(2).
**23.** Reg. § 1.248–1(c).

# DETERMINING THE
# CORPORATE INCOME TAX LIABILITY

## CORPORATE INCOME TAX RATES

Unlike the income tax rates applicable to noncorporate taxpayers, the corporate rates are only mildly progressive. The rates are as follows:

| Taxable Income | Rates |
|---|---|
| $     1–$   25,000 | 15% |
| 25,001–    50,000 | 18 |
| 50,001–    75,000 | 30 |
| 75,001–  100,000 | 40 |
| Over $100,000 | 46 |
| Excess over $1,000,000 | For tax years beginning after 1983, an additional tax of 5% of the excess (but not to exceed $20,250)[24] |

**Example 25.** T Corporation, a calendar year taxpayer has taxable income of $150,000 in 1986. Its income tax liability would be computed as follows:

| | |
|---|---|
| 15% of $25,000 | $  3,750 |
| 18% of $25,000 | 4,500 |
| 30% of $25,000 | 7,500 |
| 40% of $25,000 | 10,000 |
| 46% of $50,000 | 23,000 |
| Total tax | $ 48,750 |

**Example 26.** Z Corporation, a calendar year taxpayer, has taxable income of $1,200,000 for 1986. Under § 11 (as amended by the Deficit Reduction Act of 1984), it would compute its corporate income tax as follows:

| | |
|---|---|
| Tax on first $100,000 | $  25,750 |
| Tax on next $1,100,000 at 46% | 506,000 |
| Additional tax on amount in excess of $1,000,000 (5% × $200,000) | 10,000 |
| Total tax | $ 541,750 |

A short-cut approach for determining the income tax liability of a corporation with taxable income *in excess of $100,000* (but less than $1,000,000) would be to start with $25,750 and add 46 percent of the amount beyond $100,000. Thus, in Example 25 the tax would be $25,750 plus $23,000 (i. e., 46 percent of $50,000) or $48,750. Taxable income will have to be prorated

---

**24.** § 11(b). The additional tax does not apply after the taxable income of a corporation reaches $1,405,000. At this level, therefore, a corporation will be subject to the 46% rate on all of its taxable income.

for fiscal year corporations whenever there is a change in tax rates from one calendar year to another.[25]

## MINIMUM TAX    *see handout*

A corporation is subject to the minimum tax on certain tax preferences as are individuals; however, the tax is computed differently for corporations and is added to a corporation's regular tax liability rather than being an alternative tax as in the case of individuals.

The minimum tax for individuals, an alternative tax that applies only if it exceeds the regular tax, is imposed at a flat rate of 20 percent on the amount of alternative minimum taxable income in excess of $30,000 ($40,000 for a joint return). Alternative minimum taxable income is adjusted gross income plus tax preferences reduced by certain deductions, such as medical expenses in excess of 10 percent of AGI, casualty losses, wagering losses, charitable contributions, interest on a principal residence, and certain other investment interest. Tax preferences for individuals are essentially the same as for corporations; however, there are additional preferences for individuals, such as dividends excluded under the dividend exclusion provision (§ 116).

A corporation is liable for a 15 percent minimum tax on tax preferences in excess of the greater of $10,000 or its regular tax liability.[26] The following are included as items of tax preferences for corporations:[27]

—Accelerated depreciation on real property and on leased personal property in excess of what would have been allowed under the straight-line method. For leased personal property, ACRS recovery must use a period in computing straight-line depreciation of 5 years for 3-year property, 8 years for 5-year property, 15 years for 10-year property, and 22 years for 15-year public utility property.[28]

—Deductions for certified pollution control facilities in excess of normal depreciation.

—The excess of the deduction allowed financial institutions for a reasonable addition to a bad debt reserve over the deduction based on actual experience.

—The excess of depletion allowable over the adjusted basis of the property at year-end (figured before deducting depletion for the year).

—Excess of net long-term capital gain over net short-term capital loss multiplied by a fraction, the numerator of which is the highest tax rate of the corporation for the taxable year minus the alternative tax rate of 28 percent, and the denominator of which is 46 percent (i.e., $^{(46-28)}/_{46} = {}^{18}/_{46}$, or 39.13 percent).

**Example 27.** T Corporation has taxable income of $105,000 plus a net long-term capital gain of $100,000. Its regular tax liability is $56,050 [$28,050 + $28,000 (28% × $100,000)]. T Corporation had

---

25.  § 15.
26.  § 56(a).
27.  See § 57(a).
28.  § 57(a)(12)(A).

accelerated depreciation on real property of $21,750 in excess of what would have been permitted under the straight-line method. Tax preferences total $60,880 [$21,750 (excess accelerated depreciation) + $39,130 ($100,000 net long-term capital gains $\times$ $^{18}/_{46}$)]. Tax preferences exceed regular tax liability by $4,830 ($60,880 − $56,050). This excess of $4,830 multiplied by 15% produces a minimum tax of $724.50. This is added to T Corporation's regular tax liability of $56,050 for a total tax liability of $56,774.50.

For tax years beginning after 1984, only 59⅚ percent of the following tax preferences are included in the minimum tax base:

—Accelerated depreciation on real property where there has been a 20 percent increase in depreciation recapture on dispositions after 1984.

—Rapid amortization of certified pollution control facilities placed in service after 1984 where there has been a 20 percent reduction in the rapid amortization.

—A financial institution's excess bad debt deduction where it has been reduced 20 percent after 1984.

—For coal and iron ore, where the depletion deduction has been reduced 15 percent, 71.6 percent of the percentage depletion deduction.

For controlled groups, discussed in Chapter 3, the $10,000 reduction on the amount of the tax preferences subject to the minimum tax must be divided among the component members of the group in proportion to their respective regular tax liability for the taxable year.

A corporation must file Form 4626 if it has tax preferences in excess of $10,000.

## PROCEDURAL MATTERS

### FILING REQUIREMENTS FOR CORPORATIONS

A corporation must file a return regardless of whether or not it has taxable income [§ 6012(a)(2)]. If a corporation was not in existence throughout an entire annual accounting period, it is required to file a return for that fraction of a year during which it was in existence. In addition, the corporation must file a return even though it has ceased to do business if it has valuable claims for which it will bring suit. It is relieved of filing returns once it ceases business and dissolves, retaining no assets, whether or not under state law it is treated as a corporation for certain limited purposes connected with the winding up of its affairs, such as for the purpose of suing and being sued.[29]

The corporate return is filed on Form 1120 unless the corporation is a small corporation entitled to file the shorter Form 1120–A. Form 1120–A may be filed by corporations having gross receipts or sales, total income (gross profit plus other income including gains on sales of property), or

---

29.  Reg. § 1.6012–2(a)(2).

total assets not exceeding $250,000 each, if the following additional requirements are met: The corporation may not be involved in a dissolution or liquidation, may not be a member of a controlled group under § § 1561 and 1563, may not file a consolidated return, may not have ownership in a foreign corporation, and may not have foreign shareholders who directly or indirectly own 50 percent or more of its stock.

Corporations electing under Subchapter S (see Chapter 8) file on Form 1120S. Forms 1120, 1120–A, and 1120S are reproduced in Appendix B.

The return must be filed on or before the fifteenth day of the third month following the close of a corporation's accounting year. Corporations can receive an automatic extension of six months for filing the corporate return by filing Form 7004 by the due date for the return.[30] However, the IRS may terminate the extension by mailing a 10-day notice to the taxpayer corporation.

A corporation must make payments of estimated tax if its tax liability can reasonably be expected to exceed $40; the payments must be at least 90 percent of the corporation's final tax.[31] These payments can be made in four installments due on or before the fifteenth day of the fourth month, the sixth month, the ninth month, and the twelfth month of the corporate taxable year.[32] The full amount of the unpaid tax is due on the due date of the return.

A corporation failing to pay 90 percent of its final tax liability as estimated tax payments will be subjected to a nondeductible penalty on the amount by which the installments are less than 90 percent of the tax due unless the installments are based on (1) tax liability for the prior year, (2) tax liability on the prior year's income computed using tax rates for the current year, or (3) 90 percent of the tax that would be due on its income computed on an annualized basis.

A *large* corporation (defined as one with taxable income in excess of one million dollars in any of three preceding taxable years) cannot rely on exceptions (1) and (2).

## RECONCILIATION OF TAXABLE INCOME AND FINANCIAL NET INCOME

Taxable income and financial net income for a corporation are seldom the same amount. For example, a difference may arise if the corporation uses accelerated cost recovery system (ACRS) for tax purposes and straight-line depreciation for financial purposes. Consequently, cost recovery allowable for tax purposes may differ from book depreciation.

Many items of income for accounting purposes, such as proceeds from a life insurance policy on the death of a corporate officer and interest on municipal bonds, may not be taxable income. Some expense items for financial purposes, such as expenses to produce tax-exempt income, estimated warranty reserves, a net capital loss, and Federal income taxes, may not be deductible for tax purposes.

---

30. § 6081.
31. § 6655(b).
32. Reg. § 1.6154.

Schedule M–1 on the last page of Form 1120 is used to reconcile financial net income (net income after Federal income taxes) with taxable income (as computed on the corporate tax return before the deduction for a net operating loss and for the dividends received deduction). In the left-hand column of Schedule M–1, net income per books is added to the Federal income tax liability for the year, the excess of capital losses over capital gains (which cannot be deducted in the current year), taxable income that is not income in the current year for financial purposes, and expenses recorded on the books that are not deductible on the tax return. In the right-hand column, income recorded on the books that is not currently taxable or is tax-exempt and deductions for tax purposes that are not expenses for financial purposes are deducted from the left-hand column total to arrive at taxable income (before the net operating loss deduction and the dividends received deduction).

**Example 28.** During 1985, T Corporation had the following transactions:

| | |
|---|---:|
| Net income per books (after tax) | $ 91,650 |
| Taxable income | 50,000 |
| Federal income tax liability [(15% × $25,000) + (18% × $25,000)] | 8,250 |
| Interest income from tax-exempt bonds | 5,000 |
| Interest paid on loan, the proceeds of which were used to purchase the tax-exempt bonds | 500 |
| Life insurance proceeds received through the death of a key employee | 50,000 |
| Premiums paid on the keyman life insurance policy | 2,600 |
| Excess of capital losses over capital gains | 2,000 |

For book and tax purposes, T Corporation determines depreciation under the straight-line method. T Corporation's Schedule M–1 for the current year is as follows:

| **Schedule M–1** Reconciliation of Income Per Books With Income Per Return | | | | |
|---|---:|---|---|---:|
| Do not complete this schedule if the total assets on line 14, column (d), of Schedule L are less than $25,000. | | | | |
| 1 Net income per books | 91,650 | 7 Income recorded on books this year not included in this return (itemize) | | |
| 2 Federal income tax | 8,250 | | | |
| 3 Excess of capital losses over capital gains | 2,000 | a Tax-exempt interest $ 5,000 | | |
| 4 Income subject to tax not recorded on books this year (itemize) | | Life insurance proceeds on keyman 50,000 | | 55,000 |
| | | 8 Deductions in this tax return not charged against book income this year (itemize) | | |
| 5 Expenses recorded on books this year not deducted in this return (itemize) | | a Depreciation . . $ | | |
| a Depreciation . . $ | | b Contributions carryover $ | | |
| b Contributions carryover $ | | | | |
| Interest on tax-exempt bonds | 500 | | | |
| Premiums on life insurance | 2,600 | 9 Total of lines 7 and 8 | | 55,000 |
| 6 Total of lines 1 through 5 | 105,000 | 10 Income (line 28, page 1)—line 6 less line 9 | | 50,000 |

Schedule M–2 reconciles unappropriated retained earnings at the beginning of the year with unappropriated retained earnings at year-end. Beginning balance plus net income per books, as entered on line 1 of Sched-

ule M–1, less dividend distributions during the year equals ending retained earnings. Other sources of increases or decreases in retained
earnings are also listed on Schedule M–2.

> **Example 29.** Assume the same facts as in Example 28. T Corpora-
> tion's beginning balance in unappropriated retained earnings is
> $125,000, and during the year T Corporation distributed a cash divi-
> dend of $30,000 to its shareholders. Based on these further assump-
> tions, T Corporation's Schedule M–2 for the current year follows:

| Schedule M–2 | Analysis of Unappropriated Retained Earnings Per Books (line 24, Schedule L) | | | |
|---|---|---|---|---|
| | Do not complete this schedule if the total assets on line 14, column (d), of Schedule L are less than $25,000. | | | |
| 1 Balance at beginning of year | 125,000 | 5 Distributions: **a** Cash | | 30,000 |
| 2 Net income per books | 91,650 | **b** Stock | | |
| 3 Other increases (itemize) _____ | | **c** Property | | |
| _____ | | 6 Other decreases (itemize)_____ | | |
| _____ | | _____ | | |
| _____ | | _____ | | |
| _____ | | 7 Total of lines 5 and 6 | | 30,000 |
| 4 Total of lines 1, 2, and 3 | 216,650 | 8 Balance at end of year (line 4 less line 7) | | 186,650 |

## FORM 1120–A ILLUSTRATED

The Cash-Carry Flower Shop, Inc., was incorporated on July 1, 1982. All of
its stock is owned by various unrelated parties. The corporation is engaged
in the business of selling fresh cut flowers and plants. Its employer identification number is 89-2134657, and its business address is 1349 Brentwood
Lane, Fairfield, MD 20715. The corporation uses the accrual method of
accounting and reports on a calendar year basis for tax purposes. For 1985,
the corporation made estimated tax payments of $6,000, and there were no
1984 overpayments that could be allowed as a credit.

The corporate books and records reflect the following profit and loss
items for 1985:

| Account | Debit | Credit |
|---|---|---|
| Gross sales | | $ 248,000 |
| Sales returns and allowances | $    7,500 | |
| Cost of goods sold | 144,000 | |
| Interest income (taxable) | | 942 |
| Compensation of officers | 23,000 | |
| Salaries and wages | 24,320 | |
| Rents | 6,000 | |
| Taxes | 3,320 | |
| Interest expense | 1,340 | |
| Contributions | 1,820 | |
| Advertising | 3,000 | |
| Federal income tax accrued | 5,486 | |
| Net income per books after tax | 29,156 | |
| Total | $ 248,942 | $ 248,942 |

In arriving at cost of goods sold, the purchases amount was $134,014. Also
considered were other costs of $9,466 for items relating to the sale of flow-
ers and plants, such as flower pots, vases, stands, boxes, wire strands, and
tissue paper.

| Form **1120-A** | **U.S. Short-Form Corporation Income Tax Return** To see if you qualify to file Form 1120-A, see Instructions. | | | | | OMB No. 1545-0890 | |
|---|---|---|---|---|---|---|---|
| Department of the Treasury Internal Revenue Service | For calendar 1985 or tax year beginning \_\_\_\_\_, 1985, ending \_\_\_\_\_, 19\_\_\_ ▶ For Paperwork Reduction Act Notice, see page 1 of the instructions. | | | | | 19**85** | |

| See Instructions for list of principal business: | **A** Activity Flower Sh **B** Product or service Flowers **C** Code 5995 | Use IRS label. Otherwise please type or machine print | Name Cash-Carry Flower Shop, Inc. Number and street 1349 Brentwood Lane City or town, state, and ZIP code Fairfield, MD 20715 | | **D** Employer identification number (EIN) 89-2134657 **E** Date incorporated 7-1-82 **F** Total assets (see Specific Instructions) |
|---|---|---|---|---|---|

| | | Dollars | Cents |
|---|---|---|---|
| | | $ 65,841 | |

**G** Check method of accounting: (1) ☐ Cash (2) ☒ Accrual (3) ☐ Other (specify) ▶ \_\_\_\_\_

**H** Check box if there has been a change in address from the previous year . . . . . . . . . . . . . ▶ ☐

| | | | | | |
|---|---|---|---|---|---|
| **Income** | **1 a** Gross receipts or sales 248,000 | **b** Less returns and allowances 7,500 | Balance ▶ | **1c** | 240,500 |
| | **2** Cost of goods sold and/or operations (see instructions) . . . . . . . . . . | | | **2** | 144,000 |
| | **3** Gross profit (line 1c less line 2) . . . . . . . . . . . . . . . . . | | | **3** | 96,500 |
| | **4** Domestic corporation dividends subject to the 85% deduction . . . . . . . | | | **4** | |
| | **5** Interest . . . . . . . . . . . . . . . . . . . . . . . . . . | | | **5** | 942 |
| | **6** Gross rents . . . . . . . . . . . . . . . . . . . . . . . . . | | | **6** | |
| | **7** Gross royalties . . . . . . . . . . . . . . . . . . . . . . . . | | | **7** | |
| | **8** Capital gain net income (attach separate Schedule D (Form 1120)) . . . . . | | | **8** | |
| | **9** Net gain or (loss) from Form 4797, line 17, Part II (attach Form 4797) . . . . | | | **9** | |
| | **10** Other income (see instructions) . . . . . . . . . . . . . . . . . | | | **10** | |
| | **11**      TOTAL income—Add lines 3 through 10 . . . . . . . . . . . . ▶ | | | **11** | 97,442 |

| | | | | | |
|---|---|---|---|---|---|
| **Deductions** | **12** Compensation of officers (see instructions) . . . . . . . . . . . . . . | | | **12** | 23,000 |
| | **13 a** Salaries and wages 24,320 | **b** Less jobs credit \_\_\_\_\_ | Balance ▶ | **13c** | 24,320 |
| | **14** Repairs . . . . . . . . . . . . . . . . . . . . . . . . . . | | | **14** | |
| | **15** Bad debts (If reserve method is used, answer Question K on page 2) . . . . . | | | **15** | |
| | **16** Rents . . . . . . . . . . . . . . . . . . . . . . . . . . . | | | **16** | 6,000 |
| | **17** Taxes . . . . . . . . . . . . . . . . . . . . . . . . . . . | | | **17** | 3,320 |
| | **18** Interest . . . . . . . . . . . . . . . . . . . . . . . . . . | | | **18** | 1,340 |
| | **19** Contributions (see instructions for 10% limitation) . . . . . . . . . . . | | | **19** | 1,820 |
| | **20** Depreciation (attach Form 4562) . . . . . . . . | **20** | | | |
| | **21** Less depreciation claimed elsewhere on return . . . . | **21a** | **21b** | | |
| | **22** Other deductions (attach schedule) . . . . . . . . . . . . . . . . | | | **22** | 3,000 |
| | **23**      TOTAL deductions—Add lines 12 through 22 . . . . . . . . . . . ▶ | | | **23** | 62,800 |
| | **24** Taxable income before net operating loss deduction and special deductions (line 11 less line 23) . . . . | | | **24** | 34,642 |
| | **25** Less: **a** Net operating loss deduction (see instructions) . . . | **25a** | | | |
| |          **b** Special deductions (see instructions) . . . . . | **25b** | **25c** | | |

| | | | | | |
|---|---|---|---|---|---|
| | **26** Taxable income (line 24 less line 25c) . . . . . . . . . . . . . . . | | | **26** | 34,642 |
| | **27**      TOTAL TAX (from Part I, line 6 on page 2) . . . . . . . . . . . . | | | **27** | 5,486 |

| | | | | | |
|---|---|---|---|---|---|
| **Tax and Payments** | **28** Payments: | | | | |
| |    **a** 1984 overpayment allowed as a credit . . . . . | | | | |
| |    **b** 1985 estimated tax payments . . . . . | 6,000 | | | |
| |    **c** Less 1985 refund applied for on Form 4466 . . (      ) | 6,000 | | | |
| |    **d** Tax deposited with Form 7004 . . . . . . . . | | | | |
| |    **e** Credit from regulated investment companies (attach Form 2439) . . . | | | | |
| |    **f** Credit for Federal tax on gasoline and special fuels (attach Form 4136) . . . | | | **28** | 6,000 |
| | **29** Enter any **PENALTY** for underpayment of estimated tax—Check ▶ ☐ if Form 2220 is attached . . . | | | **29** | |
| | **30** TAX DUE—If the total of lines 27 and 29 is larger than line 28, enter AMOUNT OWED . . . . . . . | | | **30** | |
| | **31** OVERPAYMENT—If line 28 is larger than the total of lines 27 and 29, enter AMOUNT OVERPAID . . ▶ | | | **31** | 514 |
| | **32** Enter amount of line 31 you want: **Credited to 1986 estimated tax** ▶ 514     Refunded ▶ | | | **32** | |

| Please Sign Here | Under penalties of perjury, I declare that I have examined this return, including accompanying schedules and statements, and to the best of my knowledge and belief, it is true, correct, and complete. Declaration of preparer (other than taxpayer) is based on all information of which preparer has any knowledge. | | |
|---|---|---|---|
| | ▶ Signature of officer | Date | ▶ Title |

| Paid Preparer's Use Only | Preparer's signature ▶ | Date | Check if self-employed ☐ | Preparer's social security number |
|---|---|---|---|---|
| | Firm's name (or yours, if self-employed) and address ▶ | | E.I. No. ▶ ZIP code ▶ | |

Form **1120-A** (1985)

Comparative balance sheets for the Cash-Carry Flower Shop, Inc., appear as follows:

| Assets | January 1, 1985 | December 31, 1985 |
|---|---|---|
| Cash | $ 20,540 | $ 18,352 |
| Inventories | 2,530 | 2,010 |
| Federal bonds | 13,807 | 45,479 |
| Total assets | $ 36,877 | $ 65,841 |

Form 1120-A (1985)    **Part I**   **Tax Computation (See Instructions)** Page 2     Enter EIN ▶    89-2134657

| | | |
|---|---|---|
| 1 Income tax (see instructions to figure the tax, enter lesser of this tax or alternative tax from Schedule D). Check if from Schedule D ▶ ☐ . | 1 | 5,486 |
| 2 General business credit. Check if from ☐ Form 3800 ☐ Form 3468 ☐ Form 5884 ☐ Form 6478 ☐ Form 8007. | 2 | |
| 3 Line 1 less line 2 . . . . . . . . . . . . . . | 3 | 5,486 |
| 4 Tax from recomputing prior-year investment credit (attach Form 4255) . . . . . . . . . | 4 | |
| 5 Minimum tax on tax preference items (see instructions—attach Form 4626) . . . . . . . . | 5 | |
| 6 Total tax—Add lines 3 through 5. Enter here and on line 27, page 1 . . . . . . . . . . | 6 | 5,486 |

**Additional Information** (See instruction F)

I Was a deduction taken for expenses connected with:

  (1) An entertainment facility (boat, resort, ranch, etc.)? Yes ☐ No ☒

  (2) Employees' families at conventions or meetings? Yes ☐ No ☒

J Did any individual, partnership, estate or trust at the end of the tax year own, directly or indirectly, 50% or more of the corporation's voting stock? (For rules of attribution, see section 267(c).) If "Yes," complete (1) and (2) . . . . . . . . Yes ☐ No ☒

  (1) Attach a schedule showing name, address, and identifying number.

  (2) Enter "highest amount owed;" include loans and accounts receivable/payable:

    (a) Enter highest amount owed by the corporation to such owner during the year ▶ . . . .

    (b) Enter highest amount owed to the corporation by such owner during the year ▶ . . . .

K If the reserve method is used for bad debts, complete (1) and (2) for the current year:

  (1) Amount added to the reserve account:

    (a) Current year's provision ▶

  (b) Recoveries ▶ . . . . . . .

  (2) Amount charged against the reserve account ▶

L If an amount for cost of goods sold and/or operations is entered on line 2, page 1, complete (1) and (2):

  (1) Purchases ▶ . . . . . . . .    134,014

  (2) Other costs (attach schedule) ▶ . .    9,466

M At any time during the tax year, did you have an interest in or a signature or other authority over a financial account in a foreign country (such as a bank account, securities account, or other financial account)? (See instruction F for filing requirements for Form TD F 90-22.1.) . . . . Yes ☐ No ☒

If "Yes," write in the name of the foreign country

▶

N During this tax year was any part of your accounting/tax records maintained on a computerized system? . . . . . . . . . . Yes ☐ No ☒

O Enter amount of cash distributions and the book value of property (other than cash) distributions made in this tax year ▶

**Part II**   **Balance Sheets**

| | (a) Beginning of tax year | (b) End of tax year |
|---|---|---|
| **Assets** | | |
| 1 Cash . . . . . . . . . . | 20,540 | 18,352 |
| 2 Trade notes and accounts receivable . . . . . . | | |
|   a Less allowance for bad debts . . . . . . . | ( ) | ( ) |
| 3 Inventories . . . . . . . . . . | 2,530 | 2,010 |
| 4 Federal and State government obligations . . . . . . | 13,807 | 45,479 |
| 5 Other current assets (attach schedule) . . . . . | | |
| 6 Loans to stockholders . . . . . . . . | | |
| 7 Mortgage and real estate loans . . . . . . | | |
| 8 Depreciable, depletable, and intangible assets . . . . | | |
|   a Less accumulated depreciation, depletion, and amortization . | ( ) | ( ) |
| 9 Land (net of any amortization) . . . . . . | | |
| 10 Other assets (attach schedule) . . . . . . | | |
| 11 Total assets . . . . . . . . . | 36,877 | 65,841 |
| **Liabilities and Stockholders' Equity** | | |
| 12 Accounts payable . . . . . . . . . | 6,415 | 6,223 |
| 13 Other current liabilities (attach schedule) . . . . | | |
| 14 Loans from stockholders . . . . . . . . | | |
| 15 Mortgages, notes, bonds payable . . . . . . | | |
| 16 Other liabilities (attach schedule). . . . . . | | |
| 17 Capital stock (Preferred and Common stock) . . . . | 20,000 | 20,000 |
| 18 Paid-in or capital surplus . . . . . . | | |
| 19 Retained earnings . . . . . . . . | 10,462 | 39,618 |
| 20 Less cost of treasury stock . . . . . . . | ( ) | ( ) |
| 21 Total liabilities and stockholders' equity. . . . . . . | 36,877 | 65,841 |

**Part III**   **Reconciliation of Income Per Books With Income Per Return (See Instructions)**

| | | |
|---|---|---|
| 1 Enter net income per books . . . . . . . | 29,156 | |
| 2 Federal income tax . . . . . . . . | 5,486 | |
| 3 Income subject to tax not recorded on books this year (itemize) | | |
| 4 Expenses recorded on books this year not deducted in this return (itemize) . . . . . . . . | | |

| | |
|---|---|
| 5 Income recorded on books this year not included in this return (itemize) | |
| 6 Deductions in this tax return not charged against book income this year (itemize) | |
| 7 Income (line 24, page 1). Enter the sum of lines 1, 2, 3, and 4 less the sum of lines 5 and 6 . . . . | 34,642 |

| Liabilities and Equity | January 1, 1985 | December 31, 1985 |
|---|---|---|
| Accounts payable | $ 6,415 | $ 6,223 |
| Capital stock | 20,000 | 20,000 |
| Retained earnings | 10,462 | 39,618 |
| Total Liabilities and Equity | $ 36,877 | $ 65,841 |

The completed Form 1120–A for the Cash-Carry Flower Shop, Inc., is reproduced above.

Although most of the entries of Form 1120–A for Cash-Carry Flower Shop, Inc., are self-explanatory, the following additional comments should be helpful:

—To arrive at the cost of goods sold figure appearing on line 2 (page 1), the instructions require that the preparer answer question L in Part I (page 2). Other costs (e. g., flower pots, vases, stands) relating to cost of goods sold should be added to purchases and supported by a schedule. Thus, $2,530 (beginning inventory) + $134,014 (purchases) + $9,466 (other costs) − $2,010 (ending inventory) = $144,000 (cost of goods sold).

—The charitable contributions listed on line 19 (page 1) are within the 10 percent limitation imposed on corporations. Therefore, the $1,820 amount is allowed in full.

—Lines 1 through 6 of Part I (page 2) are used for tax computation purposes. The § 11(b) tax on taxable income of $34,642 (see line 26 of page 1) is $5,486 [$3,750 (15% of $25,000) + $1,736 (18% of $9,643)] and is entered on line 27 of page 1. Because $6,000 was prepaid, the overpayment of $514 can either be claimed as a refund or be credited towards the 1986 estimated tax (line 32 of page 1).

—Part III (page 2), although not designated as such, serves the same function as the Schedule M–1 to Form 1120 previously illustrated in Example 28 by reconciling net income per books with income per return (i. e., taxable income).

---

### Concept Summary

#### INCOME TAXES OF INDIVIDUALS AND CORPORATIONS COMPARED

|  | Individuals | Corporations |
|---|---|---|
| Computation of Gross Income | § 61. | § 61. |
| Computation of Taxable Income | § § 62, 63(b) through (i). | § 63(a). Concept of AGI has no relevance. |
| Deductions | Trade or business (§ 162); non-business (§ 212); some personal expenses (generally deductible as itemized deductions). | Trade or business (§ 162). |
| Charitable Contributions | Limited in any tax year to 50% of AGI; 30% for long-term capital gain property unless election is made to reduce fair market value of gift. | Limited in any tax year to 10% of taxable income computed without regard to the charitable contribution deduction, net operating loss, and dividends received deduction. |

| | Individuals | Corporations |
|---|---|---|
| | Contribution to private foundation—deduction for long-term capital gain property is fair market value less 40% of gain had the property been sold. | Contribution to private foundation—deduction for long-term capital gain property is fair market value less $28/46$ of gain had the property been sold. |
| | Inventory property—deduction is amount of the basis. | Inventory property—deduction is basis unless donee uses property in manner related to exempt purpose and solely for care of the ill, needy, or infants. In this case, deduction is basis plus one-half of appreciated value (not to exceed twice the basis). For contribution of scientific property to education organization, deduction is basis plus one-half of appreciated value (not to exceed twice the basis) if property is constructed by donor, donation is made within two years of construction, original user is donee, and property is used for research. |
| | Time of deduction—year in which payment is made. | Time of deduction—year in which payment is made unless accrual basis taxpayer. Accrual basis corporation can take deduction in year preceding payment if contribution was authorized by board of directors by end of year and contribution is paid by 15th day of third month of following year. |
| Casualty Losses | $100 floor on personal casualty and theft losses; nonbusiness casualty losses deductible only to extent losses exceed 10% of AGI. | Deductible in full. |
| Depreciation Recapture Under § 1250 | Recaptured to extent accelerated depreciation exceeds straight-line. | 20% of excess of amount that would be recaptured under § 1245 over amount recaptured under § 1250 is additional ordinary income. |
| Net Operating Loss | Adjusted for 60% net capital gain deduction, nonbusiness deductions over nonbusiness income, and personal exemptions. | Generally no adjustments. |
| Dividend Exclusion | $100 per taxpayer. | Generally 85% of dividends received. |
| Net Capital Gains | Only 40% of gain is taxed. | Taxed in full with other income unless taxpayer elects to tax total gain at alternative tax rate of 28%. |

|  | Individuals | Corporations |
|---|---|---|
| Capital Losses | Only $3,000 of capital loss per year can offset ordinary income; for long-term capital losses, $2 of loss is required to generate $1 deduction from ordinary income; loss is carried forward indefinitely to offset capital gains or ordinary income up to $3,000; carryovers remain long-term or short-term (as the case may be). | Can offset only capital gains; long-term losses are not reduced, since they cannot offset ordinary income; carried back three years and forward five; carryovers and carrybacks are short-term losses. |
| Tax Rates | Progressive (§ 1). | Only mildly progressive (§ 11). |
| Minimum Tax | Alternative tax applied only if it exceeds the regular tax; imposed at flat rate of 20% on amount of alternative minimum taxable income in excess of $30,000 ($40,000 for a joint return); alternative minimum taxable income is AGI plus tax preferences reduced by certain deductions. | Not an alternative tax; added to corporation's regular tax liability; tax is 15% on tax preferences in excess of greater of $10,000 or corporation's regular tax liability. |

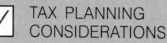

TAX PLANNING
CONSIDERATIONS

## CORPORATE VERSUS NONCORPORATE FORMS OF BUSINESS ORGANIZATION

The decision to use the corporate form in conducting a trade or business must be weighed carefully. Besides the nontax considerations attendant to the corporate form (i. e., limited liability, continuity of life, free transferability of interest, centralized management), tax ramifications will play an important role in any such decision. Close attention should be paid to the following:

1.  The regular corporate form means the imposition of the corporate income tax. Corporate-source income will be taxed twice—once as earned by the corporation and again when distributed to the shareholders. Since dividends are not deductible, a strong incentive exists in a closely-held corporation to structure corporate distributions in a deductible form. Thus, profits may be bailed out by the shareholders in the form of salaries, interest, or rents. Such procedures lead to a multitude of problems, one of which, the reclassification of debt as equity, is discussed in Chapter 3. The problems of unreasonable salaries and rents are covered in Chapter 4 in the discussion of constructive dividends.

2. Corporate source income loses its identity as it passes through the corporation to the shareholders. Thus, items possessing preferential tax treatment (e. g., interest on municipal bonds, long-term capital gains) are not taxed as such to the shareholders.

3. As noted in Chapter 4, it may be difficult for shareholders to recover some or all of their investment in the corporation without an ordinary income result, since most corporate distributions are treated as dividends to the extent of the corporation's earnings and profits.

4. Corporate losses cannot be passed through to the shareholders.

5. Long-term capital gains and losses generally receive more favorable tax treatment in the hands of noncorporate taxpayers.[33]

6. The liquidation of a corporation may well generate tax consequences to both the corporation and its shareholders (see Chapter 5).

7. On the positive side, the corporate form may be advantageous for shareholders in high individual tax brackets. With a current maximum corporate income tax rate of 46 percent, such shareholders would be motivated to avoid dividend distributions and retain profits within the corporation. An abuse of this approach, however, could lead to the imposition of the penalty tax on unreasonable accumulation of earnings or the special tax on personal holding companies (see Chapter 7).

8. The corporate form does provide the shareholders with the opportunity to be treated as employees for tax purposes if the shareholders, in fact, render services to the corporation. Such status makes a number of attractive tax-sheltered fringe benefits available. These include, but are not limited to, group term life insurance (§ 79), the $5,000 death gratuity [§ 101(b)(1)], accident and health plans (§ § 105 and 106), and meals and lodging (§ 119). These benefits are not available to partners and sole proprietors.

## THE ASSOCIATION ROUTE

Consideration 8 in the preceding section led to the popularity of the professional association. The major tax incentive involved was to cover the shareholder-employees under a qualified pension plan. Professionals, particularly physicians, who were not permitted to form regular corporations, either because of state law prohibitions or ethical restrictions, created organizations with sufficient corporate attributes to be classified as associations. The position of the IRS on the status of these professional associations (whether or not they should be treated as corporations for tax purposes) vacillated over a period of years.[34] After a series of judicial

---

**33.** Points 1, 4, and 5 could be resolved through a Subchapter S election (see Chapter 8), assuming the corporation qualifies for such an election. In part, the same can be said for point 2.

**34.** See, for example, Reg. § 301.7701–2(h), which took a negative approach.

losses,[35] however, the IRS has accepted their association status, assuming certain conditions are satisfied.[36]

Over recent years, the popularity of the association approach has diminished significantly. Changes in the tax law have curtailed the deferral opportunities of qualified pension and profit sharing plans available to employees. At the same time, improvements were made to H.R. 10 (i. e., Keogh) arrangements available to self-employed taxpayers. By placing the two types of plans on a parity with each other, therefore, one of the major incentives to achieve employee status through association status no longer exists.

## OPERATING THE CORPORATION

Tax planning to reduce corporate income taxes should occur before the end of the tax year. Effective planning can cause income to be shifted to the next tax year and can produce large deductions by incurring expenses before year-end. Attention should especially be focused on the following.

*Charitable Contributions.* Recall that accrual basis corporations may claim a deduction for charitable contributions in the year preceding payment if the contribution has been authorized by the board of directors by the end of the tax year and is paid on or before the fifteenth day of the third month of the following year. Even though the contribution may not ultimately be made, it might well be authorized. A deduction cannot be thrown back to the previous year (even if paid within the 2½ months) if it has not been authorized.

*Timing of Capital Gains and Losses.* The corporation should consider offsetting profits on the sale of capital assets by selling some of the depreciated securities in the corporate portfolio. In addition, any already realized capital losses should be carefully monitored. Recall that corporate taxpayers are not permitted to claim any net capital losses as deductions against ordinary income. Capital losses can be used only as an offset against capital gains. Further, net capital losses can only be carried back three years and forward five. Gains from the sales of capital assets should be timed to offset any capital losses. The expiration of the carryover period for any net capital losses should be watched carefully so that sales of appreciated securities occur before that date.

*Transferring Capital Assets to a Closely-Held Corporation.* Recall that the 60 percent capital gain deduction is not available to corporate taxpayers. For closely-held corporations having income in excess of $50,000, shareholders should not transfer capital assets to the corporation unless they have a substantial business reason for doing so. Income tax on the sale of capital assets is substantially lower at the individual shareholder level.

---

35. See, for example, *U. S. v. O'Neill,* 69–1 USTC ¶ 9372, 23 AFTR2d 69–1247, 410 F.2d 888 (CA–6, 1969), and *U. S. v. Empey,* 69–1 USTC ¶ 9158, 23 AFTR2d 69–425, 406 F.2d 157 (CA–10, 1969).
36. T.I.R. 1019; Rev.Rul. 70–101, 1970–1 C.B. 278; Rev.Rul. 70–455, 1970–2 C.B. 297; Rev.Rul. 72–468, 1972–2 C.B. 647; Rev.Rul. 73–596, 1973–2 C.B. 424; and Rev.Rul. 74–439, 1974–2 C.B. 405.

**Example 30.** A, an individual, has land she purchased five years ago that she has been holding for investment purposes. Her basis in the land is $60,000, and the fair market value is $160,000. If A transfers the land to her wholly owned corporation (which has income from other sources of $75,000) and the corporation sells the land, the income tax on the gain will be $28,000 ($100,000 gain × 28% alternative tax rate). The *maximum* tax on the sale should A sell the land is $20,000 ($100,000 gain less $60,000 capital gain deduction × 50% maximum tax rate for individuals).

*Net Operating Losses.* As noted in Example 20, in some situations the election to forgo a net operating loss carryback and utilize the carryforward option might generate greater tax savings. In this regard, one must take into account two considerations: (1), the time value of the tax refund that is lost by not using the carryback procedure and (2), the irrevocability of the election to forgo a net operating loss carryback. Thus, one cannot later choose to change if by chance the future high profits predicted in Example 20 do not materialize.

*Dividends Received Deduction.* Although the dividends received deduction normally is limited to the lesser of 85 percent of the qualifying dividends or 85 percent of taxable income, an exception is made when the full deduction yields a net operating loss. In close situations, therefore, the proper timing of income or deductions may yield a larger dividends received deduction.

**Example 31.** In the current year, T Corporation has the following income and expenses:

| | |
|---|---|
| Gross income from operations | $ 310,000 |
| Expenses from operations | 340,000 |
| Dividends received from domestic corporations | 200,000 |

The usual dividends received deduction of $170,000 (85% × $200,000) is limited to $144,500 [85% × $170,000 (taxable income)]. The full $170,000 cannot be claimed, because it does not generate or add to a net operating loss. (Taxable income of $170,000 less $170,000 does not result in a net operating loss.) However, if expenses are increased by only $1, the full $170,000 dividends received deduction could be claimed. There would then be a net operating loss of $1 ($310,000 − $340,001 + $200,000 − $170,000). Thus, the additional $1 of expense decreased taxable income from $25,500 ($170,000 − $144,500) to a net operating loss of $1, or a reduction in taxable income of $25,499.

*Organizational Expenditures.* To qualify for the 60-month amortization procedure of § 248, only organizational expenditures incurred in the first taxable year of the corporation can be considered. This rule could prove to be an unfortunate trap for corporations formed late in the year.

**Example 32.** T Corporation is formed in December 19X1. Qualified organizational expenditures are incurred as follows: $2,000 in December 19X1 and $3,000 in January 19X2. If T Corporation uses the calendar year for tax purposes, only $2,000 of the organizational expenditures can be written off over a period of 60 months.

The solution to the problem posed by Example 32 is for T Corporation to adopt a fiscal year that ends beyond January 31. All organizational expenditures will then have been incurred before the close of the first taxable year.

*Shareholder-Employee Payment of Corporate Expenses.*  In a closely-held corporate setting, shareholder-employees often pay corporate expenses (e. g., travel and entertainment) for which they are not reimbursed by the corporation. The IRS often disallows the deduction of these expenses by the shareholder-employee, as the payments are voluntary on the part of such shareholder-employee. If the deduction is more beneficial at the shareholder-employee level, a corporate policy against reimbursement of such expenses should be established. Proper planning in this regard would be to decide before the beginning of each tax year where the deduction would do the most good. Any corporate policy regarding reimbursement of such expenses could be modified on a year-to-year basis depending upon the varying circumstances.

## PROBLEM MATERIALS

### Discussion Questions

1. Briefly discuss the income tax consequences of the various forms of business organization in relation to the following:

   (a) The tax treatment of sole proprietorships.

   (b) Partnerships and the conduit concept.

   (c) Partnerships as reporting entities.

   (d) The similarities and dissimilarities between the tax treatment of partnerships, trusts, and estates.

   (e) The similarities between S corporations and partnerships.

   (f) The dissimilarities between S corporations and regular corporations.

   (g) The similarities and dissimilarities between the tax treatment of individuals and regular corporations.

2. What effect does state law have in determining whether an entity is to be treated as a corporation for Federal income tax purposes?

3. Under what circumstances may a corporation legally constituted under state law be disregarded for Federal income tax purposes?

4. Why might the IRS attempt to disregard a legally constituted corporate entity? Why might the shareholders attempt such?

5. Evaluate the disadvantages of using the corporate form in carrying on a trade or business in light of the following:

   (a) No deduction is permitted for dividend distributions.

   (b) The conduit concept does not apply.

6. Evaluate the advantages of using the corporate form in carrying on a trade or business in light of the following:

   (a) High individual income tax brackets of shareholders.

   (b) Employee status for tax purposes.

7. What is an association? How is it taxed?

8. Under what circumstances might the owners of a business wish to have the business classified as an association? Not to be so classified?

9. Compare the income tax treatment of corporations and individuals in the following respects:

   (a) Applicable tax rates. *28% max for ind 3-% for corps*

   (b) Adjusted gross income determination. *not relevant for corp*

   (c) The deduction for casualty losses.

   (d) Allowable tax credits.

   (e) Recapture of depreciation.

   (f) Dividends received from domestic corporations.

   (g) Net operating losses.

   (h) The minimum tax.

10. Compare the tax treatment of corporate and noncorporate taxpayers' capital gains and losses with respect to:

    (a) The net capital gain deduction.

    (b) The alternative tax.

    (c) A net long-term capital loss.

    (d) A net short-term capital loss.

    (e) Capital loss carrybacks.

    (f) Capital loss carryovers.

11. What is the justification for the dividends received deduction?

12. Under what circumstances may the dividends received deduction exceed 85% of the corporation's taxable income?

13. Compare the tax treatment of corporate and noncorporate taxpayers' charitable contributions with respect to:

    (a) The year of the deduction for an accrual basis taxpayer.

    (b) The percentage limitations on the maximum deduction allowed for any one year.

    (c) The amount of the deduction allowed for the donations of property.

14. In connection with organizational expenditures, comment on the following:

    (a) Those that qualify for amortization.

    (b) Those that do not qualify for amortization.

    (c) The period over which amortization can take place.

    (d) Expenses incurred but not paid by a cash basis corporation.

    (e) Expenses incurred by a corporation in its second year of operation.

    (f) The alternative if no election to amortize is made.

    (g) The timing of the election to amortize.

15. What are the conditions for filing a Form 1120-A?

16. What purpose is served by Schedule M-1 of Form 1120? By Schedule M-2?

## Problems

1. Using the legend provided, classify each of the following statements:

### Legend

I  Applies only to individual taxpayers

C  Applies only to corporate taxpayers

B  Applies to both individual and corporate taxpayers

N  Applies to neither individual nor corporate taxpayers

(a) A net capital loss can be carried back.

(b) Net long-term capital losses are carried forward as short-term capital losses.

(c) The net capital gain deduction is available.

(d) A $1,000 net short-term capital loss in the current year can be deducted against ordinary income only to the extent of $500.

(e) The alternative tax is 28% of the net capital gain.

(f) The carryforward period for net capital losses is five years.

(g) The applicable tax rates are progressive.

(h) The minimum tax does not apply.

(i) The investment tax credit applies.

(j) Net operating losses are not allowed to be carried back.

(k) The retirement income credit applies.

(l) The first $100 of qualified dividends received is excluded from gross income.

(m) The carryback period for excess charitable contributions is three years.

(n) Excess charitable contributions can be carried forward indefinitely.

(o) On the disposition of certain depreciable real estate, more ordinary income may result.

2. For taxable year 19X5, a corporation has gross profits of $250,000 from its sales, dividends of $90,000 from qualifying domestic corporations, and interest on municipal bonds of $9,000. Its business deductions total $60,000. Compute its tax liability for 19X5.

3. X Corporation had the following income and expenses in taxable year 19X5:

| | |
|---|---|
| Gross income from operations | $900,000 |
| Dividends from domestic corporations | 60,000 |
| Interest income | 30,000 |
| Expenses | 600,000 |

Compute its tax liability (ignore minimum tax computations).

4. Assume the same facts as Problem 3, except that X Corporation also has a long-term capital loss of $30,000. Compute its tax liability.

5. X Corporation acquired residential rental property on January 3, 1984, for $150,000. The property was depreciated using the accelerated method and a 15-year recovery period under ACRS. Depreciation in the amount of $33,000 was claimed. X Corporation sold the property on January 10, 1986, for $180,000. What is the gain on the sale, and how is it taxed?

6. Assume the property in Problem 5 was a commercial building and X Corporation used the straight-line method of depreciation with a 15-year recovery period under ACRS. What would be the gain on the sale, and how would it be taxed?

7. A corporation donated the following properties to various qualified charities during the current taxable year: inventory with a tax basis of $45,000 (fair market value of $60,000) to a university; land held (more than six months) for investment with a tax basis of $150,000 (fair market value of $210,000) to a church that promptly sold the property; land held (more than six months) for investment with a tax basis of $18,000 (fair market value of $60,000) to a private foundation. What is the corporation's charitable contribution deduction before applying the 10% limitation?

8. During 19X2, T Corporation (a calendar year taxpayer) had the following income and expenses:

| | |
|---|---:|
| Income from operations | $180,000 |
| Expenses from operations | 100,000 |
| Qualifying dividends from domestic corporations | 10,000 |
| Net operating loss carryback from 19X3 | 2,000 |

On June 3, 19X2, T Corporation made a contribution to a qualified charitable organization of $10,500 in cash (not included in any of the items listed above).

(a) Determine T Corporation's charitable contribution deduction for 19X2.

(b) What happens to any excess charitable contribution deduction not allowable for 19X2?

9. Pursuant to a resolution adopted by its board of directors, X Corporation, a calendar year accrual basis taxpayer, authorizes a $50,000 donation to City University (a qualified charitable organization) on December 20, 19X7. The donation is made on March 10, 19X8. Is the corporation correct in claiming a deduction (subject to statutory limitations) in 19X7? What if the donation were made on April 10, 19X8?

10. During 19X6 a corporation has $100,000 of gross income and $125,000 in allowable business deductions. Included in gross income is $30,000 in qualifying dividends from domestic corporations.

(a) Determine the corporation's net operating loss for 19X6.

(b) What happens to the loss if the corporation was newly created in 19X6?

(c) Newly created in 19X3?

11. A corporation has gross income from its business operations of $50,000. Its business deductions are $70,000. Dividends from domestic corporations total $10,000. What is the corporation's net operating loss?

12. In the current year a corporation had the following income and expenses:

| | |
|---|---:|
| Gross income from operations | $60,000 |
| Expenses from operations | 68,000 |
| Qualifying dividends from domestic corporations | 40,000 |

(a) Determine the corporation's dividends received deduction.

(b) Compute the deduction assuming the expenses from operations were only $64,000 (instead of $68,000).

13. P Corporation was formed on December 1, 19X2. Qualifying organizational expenses were incurred and paid as follows:

| | |
|---|---:|
| Incurred and paid in December 19X2 | $ 10,000 |
| Incurred in December 19X2 but paid in January 19X3 | 5,000 |
| Incurred and paid in February 19X3 | 3,000 |

Assume P Corporation makes a timely election under § 248 to amortize organizational expenditures over a period of 60 months. What amount may be amortized in the corporation's first tax year under each of the following assumptions:

(a) P Corporation adopts a calendar year and the cash basis of accounting for tax purposes.

(b) Same as (a), except that P Corporation does not adopt a calendar year but chooses, instead, a fiscal year of December 1–November 30.

(c) P Corporation adopts a calendar year and the accrual basis of accounting for tax purposes.

(d) Same as (c), except that P Corporation does not adopt a calendar year but chooses, instead, a fiscal year of December 1–November 30.

14. Determine the tax liability in each of the following situations:

| | X Corporation | Y Corporation | Z Corporation |
|---|---:|---:|---:|
| Gross income | $ 2,500,000 | $ 3,000,000 | $ 4,600,000 |
| Deductions | 1,300,000 | 1,700,000 | 2,500,000 |
| Net capital gain | –0– | 200,000 | –0– |

15. In 19X5 X Corporation has taxable income of $50,000, which includes a net long-term capital gain of $20,000. X had accelerated depreciation on real property of $16,000 in excess of what would have been permitted under the straight-line method. What is X Corporation's tax liability for 19X5?

16. Indicate in each of the following independent situations whether the corporation may file Form 1120–A:

| | A Corporation | B Corporation | C Corporation |
|---|---:|---:|---:|
| Sales of merchandise | $ 300,000 | $ 200,000 | $ 150,000 |
| Total assets | 100,000 | 180,000 | 200,000 |
| Total income (gross profit plus other income, including gains) | 240,000 | 245,000 | 190,000 |
| Member of controlled group | no | yes | no |
| Ownership in foreign corporation | no | no | no |
| Entitled to file Form 1120–A (Circle Y for yes or N for no) | Y N | Y N | Y N |

17. For 19X5, T Corporation, an accrual basis calendar year taxpayer, had net income per books of $154,250 and the following special transactions:

| | |
|---|---:|
| Life insurance proceeds received through the death of the corporation president | $ 100,000 |
| Premiums paid on the life insurance policy on the president | 10,000 |
| Prepaid rent received and properly taxed in 19X4 but credited as rent income in 19X5 | 15,000 |
| Rent income received in 19X5 ($10,000 is prepaid and relates to 19X6) | 25,000 |
| Interest income on tax-exempt bonds | 5,000 |
| Interest on loan to carry tax-exempt bonds | 3,000 |
| ACRS depreciation in excess of straight-line (straight-line was used for book purposes) | 4,000 |
| Capital loss in excess of capital gains | 6,000 |
| Federal income tax liability for 19X5 | 15,750 |

Using Schedule M–1 of Form 1120, compute T Corporation's taxable income for 19X5.

## Comprehensive Tax Return Problem

Novelco Corporation was formed on March 1, 1974, by Jim and Anne Adams to manufacture and assemble novelty items (mainly key chains and ballpoint pens). These items usually are customized with the client's name (and/or logo) for distribution as promotional material. Pertinent information regarding Novelco is summarized as follows:

—The business address is 5210 Union Street, Leesville, IL 60930.

—Employer identification number is 71-0395674; the principal business activity code is 3998.

—Jim and Anne Adams, brother and sister, each own one-half of the outstanding common stock, and no other class of stock is authorized. Every three years, they rotate the positions of president and vice-president. Currently, Anne is the president and Jim the vice-president. Both are full-time employees, and the corporation has no other officers. Each receives a salary of $50,000. Jim's Social Security number is 581-00-0836; Anne's is 581-00-2604.

—The corporation uses the accrual method of accounting and reports on a calendar year basis. The specific chargeoff method is used in handling bad debt losses, and inventories are determined under the lower of cost or market method with full absorption of cost. For book and tax purposes, the straight-line method of depreciation is used.

—During 1985, the corporation distributed a cash dividend of $60,000. Because a customer was injured on the business premises and has threatened legal action for personal damages, a reserve for contingencies is to be established in the amount of $20,000.

—In June 1985, the corporation received from the IRS a refund of $20,000 due to overpayment on its 1984 estimated income tax liability.

Selected portions of Novelco's profit and loss statement reflect the following debits and credits:

| Account | Debit | Credit |
|---|---|---|
| Gross sales | | $ 2,200,000 |
| Sales returns and allowances | $ 25,000 | |
| Cost of goods sold | 1,600,000 | |
| Dividends received from stock investments in U. S. corporations | | 20,000 |
| Interest income | | |
| Certificates of Deposit | $ 10,000 | |
| State bonds | 12,000 | 22,000 |
| Premiums on term life insurance (the policies are owned by the corporation and cover Jim and Anne Adams; the corporation is the designated beneficiary) | 12,000 | |
| Compensation of officers | 100,000 | |
| Salaries and wages—indirect | 60,000 | |
| Repairs | 3,000 | |
| Bad debts | 5,000 | |
| Rental expense | 11,000 | |
| Taxes (state, local, payroll—indirect) | 21,000 | |
| Interest expense— | | |
| Loan to purchase start bonds | $ 1,000 | |
| Other business loans and mortgages | 28,000 | 29,000 |
| Charitable contributions | 31,000 | |
| Depreciation—indirect | 4,000 | |
| Advertising in trade journals | 9,000 | |
| Other expenses (e. g., office expenses, sales commissions, legal and accounting fees) | 55,000 | |
| Long-term loss from the sale of stock held as an investment—no carryback was available | 3,900 | |

Information regarding the cost of goods sold is as follows:

| | |
|---|---|
| Beginning inventory (1/1/85) | $ 130,000 |
| Ending inventory (12/31/85) | 200,000 |
| Purchases (including subcontracted parts and raw materials) | 1,100,000 |
| Cost of labor—direct | 400,000 |
| Other costs [e. g., utilities, small tools, depreciation—direct ($13,000)] | 170,000 |

Net income per books (before any income tax accrual) is $273,100.

A comparative balance sheet for Novelco reveals the following information:

| Assets | January 1, 1985 | December 31, 1985 |
|---|---|---|
| Cash | $ 18,000 | $ 27,824 |
| Trade notes and accounts receivable | 110,000 | 125,000 |
| Inventories | 130,000 | 200,000 |
| State bonds | 120,000 | 140,000 |
| Certificates of deposit | 105,000 | 108,000 |
| Other current assets | 27,000 | 18,000 |
| Buildings and other depreciable assets | 280,000 | 304,000 |
| Accumulated depreciation | (88,000) | (105,000) |
| Land | 35,000 | 35,000 |
| Other assets | 15,000 | 17,000 |
| Total assets | $ 752,000 | $ 869,824 |

| Liabilities and Equity | January 1, 1985 | December 31, 1985 |
|---|---|---|
| Accounts payable | $   28,000 | $   24,000 |
| Other current liabilities | 13,000 | 11,000 |
| Mortgages | 180,000 | 168,000 |
| Capital stock | 200,000 | 200,000 |
| Retained earnings (appropriated and unappropriated) | 331,000 | 466,824 |
| Total liabilities and equity | $ 752,000 | $ 869,824 |

In early 1985, Novelco purchased a computer for $24,000 to maintain better control over its inventory. None of this five-year recovery period property was expensed, and Novelco decided to claim the maximum investment tax credit available. The depreciation attributable to the computer already has been accounted for in the cost of goods sold account.

During 1985, Novelco made estimated tax payments to the IRS of $100,000.

Prepare a Form 1120 for Novelco for tax year 1985.

## Research Problems

*Research Problem 1.* In 19X1, several unrelated individuals created Joya Trust with a transfer of undeveloped real estate located near a large metropolitan area. In return for the transfer, the grantors received beneficial interests in Joya that were of a stated value and freely transferable. Under the trust instrument, the trust was to last 25 years or until dissolution by the trustees, whichever occurred sooner. The trust was not to terminate upon the death of a trustee, and the trustees were empowered to appoint their own successors. The trustees were authorized to call annual meetings of the beneficiaries, but the votes of such beneficiaries were advisory only. Under applicable state law, the liability of the beneficiaries was limited to their investment in the trust.

Pursuant to authority granted by the trust instrument, Joya Trust arranged for the development of the real estate into recreational facilities (e. g., golf courses, tennis courts) and luxury housing units. When developed, the real estate was either sold or leased to the general public. Joya continued to manage the unsold and leased units, as well as the recreational facilities, until it was dissolved by action of its trustees in 19X9. During its existence, how should Joya Trust be treated for Federal income tax purposes? Why?

*Research Problem 2.* U and V are brothers and equal shareholders in X Corporation, a calendar year taxpayer. In 1984, and as employees, they incurred certain travel and entertainment expenditures on behalf of X Corporation. Because X Corporation was in a precarious financial condition, U and V decided not to seek reimbursement as to these expenditures. Instead, each brother deducted what he spent on his own individual return (Form 2106 for Form 1040). Upon audit of the returns filed by U and V For 1984, the IRS disallowed these expenditures. Do you agree? Why or why not?

# Corporations: Organization and Capital Structure 3

## CHAPTER OBJECTIVES

—Describe the tax consequences of incorporating a new or an existing business.

—Explain how to deal with subsequent property transfers to a controlled corporation.

—Describe the capital structure of a corporation and explain what it means for tax purposes.

—Discuss the advantages and disadvantages of preferring debt over an equity investment.

—Describe the nature and treatment of shareholder debt and stock losses.

—Describe the tax rules unique to multiple corporations that are controlled by the same shareholders.

—Establish some fundamental concepts relating to the consolidated return procedure.

Chapter 2 dealt with three principal areas fundamental to working with corporations: (1) the recognition of an entity as a corporation for Federal income tax purposes, (2) the tax rules applicable to the day-to-day operation of a corporation, and (3) the filing and reporting procedures governing corporations.

Chapter 3 addresses more sophisticated problems in dealing with corporations, summarized as follows:

—The tax consequences to the shareholders and the corporation upon the organization of the corporation.

—Once the corporation has been formed, the tax result that ensues when shareholders make later transfers of property.

—The capital structure of a corporation, including the treatment of capital contributions by nonshareholders and shareholders and the handling of investor losses suffered by shareholders.

—Selected problems that arise when dealing with related corporations. Here, some ground rules are established for dealing with consolidated returns.

## ORGANIZATION OF AND TRANSFERS TO CONTROLLED CORPORATIONS

### IN GENERAL

Absent special provisions in the Code, a transfer of property to a corporation in exchange for stock would be a sale or exchange of property and would constitute a taxable transaction. Gain or loss would be measured by the difference between the tax basis of the property transferred and the value of the stock received. Section 351 provides for the nonrecognition of gain or loss upon the transfer of property to a corporation solely in exchange for stock or securities if the persons transferring such property are in control of the corporation immediately after the transfer. The nonrecognition of gain or loss reflects the principle of continuity of the taxpayer's investment. There is no real change in the taxpayer's economic status. The investment in certain properties carries over to the investment in corporate stock or securities. The same principle governs the nonrecognition of gain or loss on like-kind exchanges under § 1031.[1] Gain is postponed until

---

1. Section 1031(a) covers the exchange of property held for productive use in a trade or business or for investment, but it specifically excludes "stock, bonds . . . or other securities."

a substantive change in the taxpayer's investment occurs (i. e., a sale to or a taxable exchange with outsiders). This approach can be justified under the wherewithal to pay concept discussed in Chapter 1.

Section 351(a) provides that gain or loss is not recognized upon the transfer by one or more persons of property to a corporation solely in exchange for stock or securities in that corporation if, immediately after the exchange, such person or persons are in control of the corporation to which the property was transferred. Section 351(b) provides that if property or money, other than stock or securities, is received by the transferors, gain will be recognized to the extent of the lesser of the gain realized or boot received (i. e., the amount of money and the fair market value of other property received). Loss is never recognized. The nonrecognition of gain or loss is accompanied by a carryover of basis.[2]

> **Example 1.**  A and B, individuals, form X Corporation. A transfers property with an adjusted basis of $30,000, fair market value of $60,000, for 50% of the stock. B transfers property with an adjusted basis of $40,000, fair market value of $60,000, for the remaining 50% of the stock. Gain is not recognized on the transfer because it qualifies under § 351. The basis of the stock to A is $30,000, while the basis of the stock to B is $40,000. X Corporation has a basis of $30,000 in the property transferred by A and a basis of $40,000 in the property transferred by B.

There are three requirements for nonrecognition of gain or loss: (1) a transfer of property for (2) stock or securities if (3) the transferors are in control of the transferee corporation.

## TRANSFER OF PROPERTY

Questions concerning exactly what constitutes property for purposes of § 351 have arisen. Services rendered are specifically excluded by the Code from the definition of property. With this exception, the definition of property is comprehensive. Unrealized receivables for a cash basis taxpayer are considered property, for example.[3] Secret processes and formulas, as well as secret information in the general nature of a patentable inventory, also qualify as property under § 351.[4]

## STOCK AND SECURITIES

If property is transferred to a corporation in exchange for any property other than stock and securities, the property constitutes boot and is taxable to the transferor shareholder to the extent of any realized gain. The Regulations state that stock rights and stock warrants are not included in the term "stock or securities."[5] Generally, however, the term "stock" needs

---

2.   §§ 358(a) and 362(a). See the discussion preceding Example 9.
3.   *Hempt Brothers, Inc. v. U. S.,* 74–1 USTC ¶ 9188, 33 AFTR2d 74–570, 490 F.2d 1172 (CA–3, 1974).
4.   Rev.Rul. 64–56, 1964–1 C.B. 133.
5.   Reg. § 1.351–1(a)(1)(ii).

no clarification. On the other hand, the definition of a "security" can be a problem. A security is an obligation of the corporation; however, courts have required that the definition of "security" be limited to long-term obligations and exclude short-term notes. Courts have held short-term notes to be the equivalent of cash.[6]

There is no definite length of time to maturity established to draw a line between long-term and short-term securities. Some courts would draw the line at five years; others at ten years. In *Camp Wolters Enterprises, Inc.*, the Court stated:

> The test as to whether notes are securities is not a mechanical determination of the time period of the note. Though time is an important factor, the controlling consideration is an overall evaluation of the nature of the debt, degree of participation and continuing interest in the business, the extent of proprietary interest compared with the similarity of the note to a cash payment, the purpose of the advances, etc.[7]

## CONTROL OF THE TRANSFEREE CORPORATION

To qualify as a nontaxable transaction under § 351, the transferor must be in control of the transferee corporation immediately after the exchange. "Control" for these purposes requires the person or persons transferring the property to own, immediately after the transfer, stock possessing at least 80 percent of the total combined voting power of all classes of stock entitled to vote and at least 80 percent of the total *number* of shares of all other classes of stock of the corporation [§ 368(c)]. Control can apply to a single person or to several individuals if they are all parties to an integrated transaction. If more than one person is involved, the Regulations affirm that the exchange does not necessarily require simultaneous exchanges by two or more persons, but they do comprehend situations in which the rights of the parties have been previously defined and the execution of the agreement proceeds ". . . with an expedition consistent with orderly procedure."[8]

> **Example 2.** A exchanges property, which cost him $60,000 but which has a fair market value of $100,000, for 70% of the stock of X Corporation. The other 30% is owned by B, who acquired it several years ago. The fair market value of the stock is $100,000. A realizes a taxable gain of $40,000 on the transfer. If A and B had transferred property to X Corporation in a simultaneous transaction or in separate transactions, both of which related to the execution of a previous agreement, with A receiving 70% of the stock and B receiving 30%, gain would not have been recognized to either party.

---

6.  *Turner v. Comm.*, 62–1 USTC ¶ 9488, 9 AFTR2d 1528, 303 F.2d 94 (CA–4, 1962). But compare *U. S. v. Mills, Jr.*, 68–2 USTC ¶ 9503, 22 AFTR2d 5302, 399 F.2d 944 (CA–5, 1968).
7.  22 T.C. 737 (1955), *aff'd.* in 56–1 USTC ¶ 9314, 49 AFTR 283, 230 F.2d 555 (CA–5, 1956).
8.  Reg. § 1.351–1(a)(1).

The Regulations confirm that stock or securities need not be issued to the transferring parties in proportion to the interest each held in the transferred property.[9] However, when stock and securities received are not proportionate to such interests, the transaction could produce a gift from one transferor to the other.

> **Example 3.** C and D organize a corporation with 500 shares of stock. C transfers property worth $10,000 for 100 shares, and D transfers property worth $5,000 for 400 shares. The transaction qualifies under § 351; however, if C did in fact make a gift to D, the transfer might be subject to a gift tax (see Chapter 11).

Section 351 treatment will be lost if stock is transferred to persons who did not contribute property, causing those who did to lack control immediately after the exchange. However, if a person performs services for the corporation in exchange for stock and also transfers some property, he or she is treated as a member of the transferring group although he or she is taxed on the value of the stock issued for services. To be a member of the group and aid in qualifying all transferors under the 80 percent test, the person contributing services must transfer property having more than a relatively small value in relation to the services he or she performed. The Regulations provide that stock or securities issued for property of relatively small value in comparison to the value of the stock and securities already owned, or to be received for services rendered, by the person transferring such property will not be treated as issued in return for property if the primary purpose of the transfer is to qualify the transaction under § 351 for concurrent transferors.[10]

> **Example 4.** A and B, individuals, transfer property to X Corporation, each in exchange for one-third of the stock. C, an individual, receives the other one-third of the stock for services rendered. The transaction will not qualify under § 351, because C is not a member of the group transferring property and A and B together received only 66⅔% of the stock. The post-transfer control requirement is not met. If C also transferred property, he would then be a member of the group, and the transaction would qualify under § 351. C would be taxed on the value of the stock issued for services, but the remainder of the transaction would be tax-free, assuming no boot was received. However, if the property transferred by C was of a relatively small value in comparison to the stock he received for his services, and the primary purpose for including the property was to cause the transaction to be tax-free for A and B, the exchange will not qualify under § 351. Gain or loss would be recognized by all parties.

Control is not lost if stock received by shareholders in a § 351 exchange is sold to persons who are not parties to the exchange shortly after

---

**9.**   Reg. § 1.351–1(b)(1).
**10.**   Refer to Footnote 5.

the transaction, unless the plan for ultimate sale of the stock existed before the exchange.[11]

Section 351 is mandatory and not elective. If a transaction falls within the provisions of § 351, neither gain nor loss is recognized on the transfer (except that gain is recognized to the extent of boot received), and there is a carryover of basis.

## ASSUMPTION OF LIABILITIES—§ 357

Absent § 357 of the Code, the transfer of mortgaged property to a controlled corporation could trigger gain to the extent of the mortgage whether the controlled corporation assumed the mortgage or took property subject to it. This is the case in nontaxable like-kind exchanges under § 1031. Liabilities assumed by the other party are considered the equivalent of cash and treated as boot. Section 357(a) provides, however, that the assumption of a liability by the acquiring corporation or the corporation taking property subject to a liability will not produce boot to the transferor shareholder in a § 351 transaction. Nevertheless, liabilities assumed by the transferee corporation are treated as "other property or money" as far as basis of stock received in the transfer is concerned. The basis of the stock received must be reduced by the amount of the liabilities assumed by the corporation [§ 358(d)].

> **Example 5.** C transfers property with an adjusted basis of $60,000, fair market value of $100,000, to X Corporation for 100% of the stock in X. The property is subject to a liability of $25,000 which X Corporation assumes. The exchange is tax-free under § § 351 and 357. However, under § 358(d), the basis to C of the stock in X Corporation is only $35,000 (basis of property transferred, $60,000, less amount of mortgage assumed, $25,000). The basis of the property to X Corporation is $60,000.

The rule of § 357(a) has two exceptions. Section 357(b) provides that if the principal purpose of the assumption of the liabilities is to avoid tax *or* if there is no bona fide business purpose behind the exchange, the liabilities, in total, will be treated as money received and taxed as boot. Further, § 357(c) provides that if the sum of the liabilities exceeds the adjusted basis of the properties transferred, the excess is taxable gain.

*Tax Avoidance or No Bona Fide Business Purpose Exception.* Section 357(b)(1)(A) generally poses few problems. A tax avoidance purpose for transferring liabilities to a controlled corporation would seem unlikely in view of the basis adjustment necessitated by § 358(d). Since the liabilities transferred reduce the basis of the stock or securities received for the property, any realized gain is merely deferred and not avoided. Such gain would materialize when and if the stock is disposed of in a taxable sale or exchange.

---

11. *Wilgard Realty Co. v. Comm.*, 42–1 USTC ¶ 9452, 29 AFTR 325, 127 F.2d 514 (CA–2, 1942). See also *Stewart v. Comm.*, 83–2 USTC ¶ 9573, 52 AFTR2d 83–5878, 714 F.2d 977 (CA–9, 1983).

Satisfying the bona fide business purpose will not be difficult if the liabilities were incurred in connection with the transferor's normal course of conducting his or her trade or business. But the bona fide business purpose requirement will cause difficulty if the liability is taken out shortly before the property is transferred and the proceeds therefrom are utilized for personal purposes.[12] This type of situation seems akin to a distribution of cash by the corporation which would, of course, be taxed as boot.

**Example 6.**  D transfers real estate (basis of $40,000 and fair market value of $90,000) to a controlled corporation in return for stock in such corporation. Shortly before the transfer, D mortgages the real estate and uses the $20,000 proceeds to meet personal obligations. Along with the real estate, the mortgage is transferred to the corporation. In this case, it would appear that the assumption of the mortgage lacks a bona fide business purpose within the meaning of § 357(b)(1)(B). Because the amount of the liability is considered boot, D has a taxable gain on the transfer of $20,000 [§ 351(b)].[13]

*Liabilities in Excess of Basis Exception.*  Unlike § 357(b), § 357(c) has posed numerous problems in § 351 transfers. Much litigation has centered around this section of the Code in recent years, particularly with respect to cash basis taxpayers who incorporate their businesses. Section 357(c) states that if the sum of liabilities assumed and the liabilities to which transferred property is subject exceeds the total of the adjusted bases of the properties transferred, the excess is taxable gain. Absent this provision, if liabilities exceed basis in property exchanged, a taxpayer would have a negative basis in the stock or securities received in the controlled corporation.[14] Section 357(c) alleviates the negative basis problem; the excess over basis is gain to the transferor.

**Example 7.**  A, an individual, transfers assets with an adjusted tax basis of $40,000 to a newly formed corporation in exchange for 100% of the stock. The corporation assumes liabilities on the transferred properties in the amount of $50,000. Absent § 357(c), A's basis in the stock of the new corporation would be a negative $10,000 (basis of property transferred, $40,000, plus gain recognized, $0, less boot received, $0, less liabilities assumed, $50,000). Section 357(c) causes A to recognize a gain of $10,000. The stock will have a zero basis in A's hands, and the negative basis problem is eliminated (basis of property transferred, $40,000, plus gain recognized, $10,000, less boot received, $0, less liabilities assumed, $50,000).

Accounts payable of a cash basis taxpayer that give rise to a deduction and amounts payable under § 736(a) (payments to a retiring partner or payments in liquidation of a deceased partner's interest) are not considered to be liabilities for purposes of § 357(c).

---

**12.**  See, for example, *Campbell, Jr. v. Wheeler,* 65–1 USTC ¶ 9294, 15 AFTR2d 578, 342 F.2d 837 (CA–5, 1965).
**13.**  The effect of the application of § 357(b) is to taint *all* liabilities transferred even though some may be supported by a bona fide business purpose.
**14.**  *Easson v. Comm.,* 33 T.C. 963 (1960), *rev'd.* in 61–2 USTC ¶ 9654, 8 AFTR2d 5448, 294 F.2d 653 (CA–9, 1961).

**Example 8.**  T, a cash basis individual, incorporates her sole proprietorship. In return for all of the stock of the new corporation, she transfers the following items:

|  | Adjusted Basis | Fair Market Value |
|---|---|---|
| Cash | $10,000 | $10,000 |
| Unrealized accounts receivable (i. e., amounts due to T but not yet paid to her) | 0 | 40,000 |
| Trade accounts payable | 0 | < 30,000 > |
| Note payable | < 5,000 > | < 5,000 > |

Unrealized accounts receivable and trade accounts payable have a zero basis, because under the cash method of accounting, no income is recognized until the receivables are collected and no deduction materializes until the payables are satisfied. The note payable has a basis, because it was issued for consideration received.

The accounts receivable and the trade accounts payable are disregarded. Thus, T has only transferred cash ($10,000) and a note payable ($5,000) and does not, therefore, have a § 357(c) problem of liabilities in excess of basis.

The definition of liabilities under § 357(c) excludes those obligations that would have been deductible to the transferor had he or she paid such obligations prior to the transfer. Consequently, T, in Example 8, would have no gain.

If both § 357(b) and (c) apply to the same transfer (i. e., the liability is not supported by a bona fide business purpose and also exceeds the basis of the properties transferred), § 357(b) predominates.[15] This could be of significance, because § 357(b) does not create gain on the transfer, as does § 357(c), but merely converts the liability to boot. Thus, the realized gain limitation continues to apply to § 357(b) transactions.

## BASIS DETERMINATION

Recall that § 351(a) postpones gain until a substantive change in the taxpayer's investment occurs. Postponement of the realized gain is accomplished through a carryover of basis pursuant to § § 358(a) and 362(a).

*Section 358(a).*  For a taxpayer transferring property to a corporation in a § 351 transaction, basis of stock or securities received in the transfer is the same as the basis the taxpayer had in the property transferred, increased by any gain recognized on the exchange and decreased by boot received.

*Section 362(a).*  The basis of properties received by the corporation is determined under § 362(a), which provides that basis to the corporation is the basis in the hands of the transferor increased by the amount of any gain recognized to the transferor shareholder.

---

15.   § 357(c)(2)(A).

**Example 9.** C and D form Y Corporation with the following investment: C transfers property (basis of $30,000 and fair market value of $70,000), and D transfers cash of $60,000. Each receives 50 shares of the Y Corporation stock, but C also receives $10,000 in cash. Assume each share of the Y Corporation stock is worth $1,200. Although C's realized gain is $40,000 [i. e., $60,000 (the value of 50 shares of Y Corporation stock) + $10,000 (cash received) − $30,000 (basis of the property transferred)], only $10,000 (the amount of the boot) is recognized. C's basis in the Y Corporation stock becomes $30,000 [i. e., $30,000 (basis of the property transferred) + $10,000 (gain recognized by C) − $10,000 (cash received)]. Y Corporation's basis in the property transferred by C is $40,000 [$30,000 (basis of the property to C) + $10,000 (gain recognized to C)]. D neither realizes nor recognizes gain or loss and will have a basis in the Y Corporation stock of $60,000.

**Example 10.** Assume the same facts as in Example 9, except that C's basis in the property transferred is $68,000 (instead of $30,000). Because recognized gain cannot exceed realized gain, the transfer generates only $2,000 of gain to C. The basis of the Y Corporation stock to C becomes $60,000 [i. e., $68,000 (basis of property transferred) + $2,000 (gain recognized) − $10,000 (cash received)]. Y Corporation's basis in the property received from C is $70,000 [i. e., $68,000 (basis of the property to C) + $2,000 (gain recognized by C)].

## RECAPTURE CONSIDERATIONS

*Recapture of Accelerated Cost Recovery (Depreciation).* In a pure § 351(a) nontaxable transfer (i. e., no boot involved) to a controlled corporation, the recapture of accelerated cost recovery rules do not apply.[16] Moreover, any recapture potential of the property carries over to the corporation as it steps into the shoes of the transferor-shareholder for purposes of basis determination.

**Example 11.** T transfers to a controlled corporation depreciable real estate (basis of $30,000 and a fair market value of $100,000) in return for additional stock. If sold by T, the property would have yielded a gain of $70,000, of which $20,000 would be recaptured as ordinary income under § 1250. If the transfer comes within § 351(a) because of the absence of boot, T has no recognized gain and no accelerated cost recovery to recapture. Should the corporation later dispose of the real estate in a taxable transaction, it will have to take into account the § 1250 recapture potential originating with T.

An interesting query is whether, upon a later sale by the corporation, § 291(a)(1) applies to cause more of the § 1250 recapture potential carryover to be ordinary income. Apparently not, as § 291(a)(1)(B) provides that the provisions of § 291(a)(1) do not apply to the disposition of any property to the extent § 1250(a) does not apply to the disposition by reason of § 1250(d). Section 1250(d) excepts transfers pursuant to § 351 from § 1250

---

16. § § 1245(b)(3) and 1250(d)(3).

coverage. To apply this exception only to the initial § 351 transfer would not cause the application of § 291(a)(1) in any case, as any gain recognized on the initial transfer that becomes § 1250 gain would be recognized only by the individuals. Consequently, for the exception to have meaning, the potential § 1250 carryover should also be exempt from coverage under § 291(a)(1).

*Recapture of the Investment Tax Credit.* Two problems arise with the transfer of § 38 property (i. e., property that yielded an investment tax credit on its acquisition). First, does the transfer to a controlled corporation trigger a recapture of the credit to the transferor-shareholder? Second, will a subsequent and premature disposition of the property by the transferee-corporation cause recapture, and from whom will the credit be recaptured?

In answer to the first question posed, § 47(b) precludes recapture with respect to a taxpayer who merely changes "the form of conducting the trade or business so long as the property is retained in such trade or business as § 38 property and the taxpayer retains a substantial interest in such trade or business." What is meant by the retention of a substantial interest in the business is not entirely clear. The Regulation in point does not offer much guidance when it suggests that the exchange of a five percent interest in a partnership for a five percent interest in a corporation constitutes the retention of a substantial interest.[17] But what about a 50 percent interest in a partnership for a 20 percent interest in a corporation? These are close judgment questions that eventually will have to be resolved by the courts.[18]

One should note that the recapture of the investment credit can operate independent of § 351. Thus, recapture of the credit can take place on a transfer of § 38 property to a controlled corporation even though no gain is recognized to the transferor under § 351(a). In this regard, the investment credit recapture rules differ from those applicable to depreciation and cost recovery. The recapture of depreciation and cost recovery comes into play only if the transfer results in recognized gain to the transferor.

Even if the recapture of the investment credit is avoided on the transfer of property to a controlled corporation, the transferor-shareholder does not cease to be vulnerable. Unlike the recapture of depreciation, the potential stays with the transferor-shareholder. Consequently, recapture can take place at the shareholder level if the corporation prematurely disposes of the property *or* if the shareholder terminates his or her substantial interest in the business through disposition of stock.[19]

**Example 12.** In 1982, T (an individual) purchased § 38 property for $12,000. T claimed an investment tax credit of $1,200 based on a recovery period of five years [see § 46(c)(7)]. In 1983, T forms X Corporation through the incorporation of his sole proprietorship. In return for all of the stock in the corporation, T transfers all of his assets (includ-

---

**17.** Reg. § 1.47–3(f)(2)(ii).

**18.** In *James Soares,* 50 T.C. 909 (1968), the Court found that the exchange of a 48% interest in a partnership for a 7.22% interest in a corporation was not the retention of a substantial interest in the business. Thus, recapture of the investment credit took place on the transfer to the corporation.

**19.** Reg. § 1.47–3(f)(5) and *W. F. Blevins,* 61 T.C. 547 (1974).

ing the § 38 property). In 1986, four years after T purchased the § 38 property, X Corporation sells it at a loss. Under these circumstances, T must recapture $240 of the credit previously claimed.[20] The fact that the property was sold at a loss by X Corporation makes no difference in the recapture of the investment tax credit. No recapture of the credit occurred upon the property's transfer to X Corporation because T retained a substantial interest in the business.

**Example 13.** Assume the same facts as in Example 12 except that X Corporation does not sell the § 38 property but continues to use it in its trade or business until the full five years have run. In 1986, however, T makes gifts to family members of 75% of the stock he holds in X Corporation. These gifts terminate T's substantial interest in the business, and T must recapture some of the investment tax credit previously claimed.

## TAX BENEFIT RULE

A taxpayer may have to take into income the recovery of an item previously expensed. Such income, however, will be limited to the amount of the deduction that actually produced a tax saving. The relevance of the tax benefit rule to transfers to controlled corporations under § 351 was first apparent in connection with accounts receivable and the reserve for bad debts.

**Example 14.** T, an accrual basis individual, incorporates her sole proprietorship. In return for all of the stock of the corporation, T transfers, among other assets, accounts receivable with a face amount of $100,000 and a reserve for bad debts of $10,000 (i. e., book value of $90,000). The addition to the reserve was previously deducted by T. The deduction resulted in a tax benefit to T of $10,000.

The IRS took the position that § 351 did not insulate the transfer from the tax benefit rule.[21] Since T had previously deducted the reserve for bad debts and such reserve was no longer necessary to her, the full $10,000 should be taken into income. In *Nash v. U. S.*, the Supreme Court disagreed.[22] Operating on the assumption that the stock T received must be worth only $90,000 (the book value of the receivables), the situation was compared to a sale. Because no gain would have resulted had the receivables been sold for $90,000, why should it matter that they were transferred to a controlled corporation under § 351?

The Supreme Court decision in *Nash,* however, does not imply that the tax benefit rule is inapplicable to transfers to controlled corporations when no gain is otherwise recognized under § 351(a). Returning to the facts in

---

**20.** Since the § 38 property was acquired after 1980, the rules contained in the Economic Recovery Tax Act (ERTA) of 1981 govern. Under ERTA, recapture is reduced by 2% for each full year the property is held prior to disposition (2% × 4 years = 8%, in this case). Hence, only 2% (10% minus 8%) of the credit is subject to recapture. Keep in mind, however, that pre-ERTA recapture rules apply to the disposition of § 38 property acquired before 1981.
**21.** Rev.Rul. 62–128, 1962–2 C.B. 139.
**22.** 70–1 USTC ¶ 9405, 25 AFTR2d 1177, 90 S.Ct. 1550 (USSC, 1970).

Example 14, suppose T was one of several transferors, and the value of the stock she received exceeded the book value of the receivables (i. e., $90,000). Could the excess be vulnerable to income recognition by virtue of the application of the tax benefit rule? The answer to this question has not been specifically passed upon by the courts.[23]

# CAPITAL STRUCTURE OF A CORPORATION

## CAPITAL CONTRIBUTIONS

The receipt of money or property in exchange for capital stock (including treasury stock) produces neither gain nor loss to the recipient corporation [§ 1032]. Gross income of a corporation also does not include shareholders' contributions of money or property to the capital of the corporation [§ 118]. Additional funds received from shareholders through voluntary pro rata payments are not income to the corporation even though there is no increase in the outstanding shares of stock of the corporation. Such payments represent an additional price paid for the shares held by the shareholders and are treated as additions to the operating capital of the corporation.[24]

Contributions by nonshareholders, such as land contributed to a corporation by a civic group or a governmental group to induce the corporation to locate in a particular community, are also excluded from the gross income of a corporation. This principle was established in 1925 in *Edwards v. Cuba Railroad Co.* In this decision, the Supreme Court held that subsidy payments from the Republic of Cuba to a New Jersey corporation that owned and operated a railroad in Cuba were not taxable income to the corporation.[25] The Court noted that the subsidy payments were not made for services rendered or to be rendered; the funds were used for capital expenditures. If property is transferred to a corporation by a nonshareholder for services rendered or for merchandise, the property or money does constitute taxable income to the corporation.[26]

The basis of property received by a corporation from a shareholder as a contribution to capital is the basis of the property in the hands of the shareholder increased by any gain recognized to the shareholder [§ 362(a)]. For property transferred to a corporation by a nonshareholder as a contribution to capital, the basis of the property is zero. If money is received by a corporation as a contribution to capital from a nonshareholder, the basis of any property acquired with the money during a 12-month period beginning on the day the contribution was received is reduced by the amount of the contribution. The excess of money received over the cost of new property is used to reduce the basis of other property held by the corporation [§ 362(c)]. The excess is applied in reduction of basis in the following order: (a) depre-

---

**23.** As will be seen in Chapter 5, the tax benefit rule is receiving wide application in the area of corporate liquidations.

**24.** Reg. § 1.118–1.

**25.** 1 USTC ¶ 139, 5 AFTR 5398, 45 S.Ct. 614 (USSC, 1925).

**26.** Reg. § 1.118–1. See also *Teleservice Co. of Wyoming Valley v. Comm.*, 27 T.C. 722 (1957), *aff'd.* in 58–1 USTC ¶ 9383, 1 AFTR2d 1249, 254 F.2d 105 (CA–3, 1958), *cert. den.* 78 S.Ct. 1360 (USSC, 1958), and *Hayutin v. Comm.*, 31 TCM 509, T.C.Memo. 1972–127, *aff'd.* in 75–1 USTC ¶ 9108, 35 AFTR2d 75–428, 508 F.2d 462 (CA–10, 1974).

ciable property, (b) property subject to amortization, (c) property subject to depletion, and (d) all other remaining properties. The reduction of the basis of property within each category is made in proportion to the relative bases of the properties.[27]

> **Example 15.** Assume a television company charges its customers an initial fee to hook up to a new television system installed in the area. These contributions will be used to finance the total cost of constructing the television facilities. The customers will then make monthly payments for the television service. Even though the initial payments were for capital expenditures, they still represent payments for services to be rendered by the television company, and as such, they are taxable income and not contributions to capital by nonshareholders.

> **Example 16.** A city donates land to X Corporation as an inducement for X to locate in the city. The receipt of the land does not represent taxable income. However, the land's basis to the corporation is zero. Assume the city also pays the corporation $10,000 in cash. The money is not taxable income to the corporation. However, when the corporation purchases property with the $10,000 (within the next 12 months), the basis of such property is reduced by $10,000.

## DEBT IN THE CAPITAL STRUCTURE

*Advantages of Debt.* In forming a corporation, shareholders should consider the relationship between debt and equity in the capital structure. Section 351 provides for nonrecognition of gain on a transfer for either stock or securities (i. e., long-term debt). Consequently, a shareholder can transfer property and receive both stock and long-term debt tax-free. The advantages of receiving long-term debt are numerous. Interest on debt is deductible by the corporation, whereas dividend payments are not. Further, the shareholders are not taxed on loan repayments made to them unless the repayments exceed basis. As long as a corporation has earnings and profits (see Chapter 4), an investment in stock cannot be withdrawn tax-free. Any withdrawals will be deemed to be taxable dividends to the extent of earnings and profits of the distributing corporation.

> **Example 17.** A, an individual, transfers assets with a tax basis of $100,000 to a newly formed corporation for 100% of the stock. The basis of the assets to the corporation is $100,000. In the first year of operations, the corporation has net income of $40,000. Such earnings are credited to the earnings and profits account of the corporation. If the corporation distributes $10,500 to A, the distribution will be a taxable dividend with no corresponding deduction to the corporation. Assume A transferred the assets for stock and debt in the amount of $50,000, payable in equal annual installments of $5,000 and bearing interest at the rate of 11%. The transfer would still be tax-free because the securities, the long-term debt, have a maturity date of 10 years. At the end of the year, the corporation would pay A $5,500 interest which

---

**27.** Reg. § 1.362–2(b).

would be tax deductible to it. The $5,000 principal repayment on the loan would not be taxed to A.

*Reclassification of Debt as Equity.* In certain instances, the IRS will contend that debt is really an equity interest and will deny the shareholders the tax advantages of debt financing. If the debt instrument has too many features of stock, it may be treated as a form of stock, and principal and interest payments will be considered dividends.

Though the form of the instrument will not assure debt treatment, the failure to observe certain formalities in the creation of the debt may lead to an assumption that the purported debt is, in fact, a form of stock. The debt should be in proper legal form, should bear a legitimate rate of interest, should have a definite maturity date, and should be repaid on a timely basis. Payments should not be contingent upon earnings. Further, the debt should not be subordinated to other liabilities, and proportionate holdings of stock and debt should be avoided.

Section 385 was added to the Internal Revenue Code in 1969. This section lists several factors that *may* be used to determine whether a debtor-creditor relationship or a shareholder-corporation relationship exists. The obvious thrust of § 385, however, is to turn the matter over to the U. S. Treasury Department to prescribe Regulations that would provide more definite guidelines as to when a corporation is or is not thinly capitalized. After a wondrous deliberation of more than a decade, such Regulations were proposed and, with significant modifications, scheduled to be completed in 1980. However, the effective date of such Regulations had been repeatedly postponed, causing further modification. The Treasury concluded that neither the final regulations, as published in December 1980, nor the proposed revisions, as published in January 1982, fully reflected the position of either the IRS or the Treasury on debt/equity matters; consequently, the final regulations and the proposed revisions have been withdrawn.[28] It is unlikely that the Treasury will adopt a new set of regulations.

## INVESTOR LOSSES

The choice between debt and equity financing entails a consideration of the tax treatment of worthless stock and securities versus the treatment of bad debts.

*Stock and Security Losses.* If stocks and bonds are capital assets in the hands of the holder, losses from their worthlessness will be governed by § 165(g)(1). Under this provision, a capital loss will materialize as of the last day of the taxable year in which the stocks or bonds become worthless. Because no deduction is allowed for a mere decline in value, the burden of proving complete worthlessness will be on the taxpayer claiming the loss.[29] Of course, an obvious way to recognize partial worthlessness would be to dispose of the stocks or bonds in a taxable sale or exchange.[30] But even

---

**28.** T.D. 7920, 1983–2 C.B. 69.

**29.** For an example of when this burden of proof was not met, see *Paris G. Singer,* 34 TCM, 337 T.C.Memo. 1975–63.

**30.** Reg. § 1.165–4(a).

then, the loss may be disallowed under § 267(a)(1) if the sale or exchange is to a related party.

When the stocks or bonds are not capital assets, worthlessness thereof would yield an ordinary loss under § 165(a).[31] Usually, however, stocks and bonds are held as investments and will be deemed capital assets. If, on the other hand, the stocks or bonds are an integral part of a taxpayer's trade or business, they are not capital assets. An obvious example would be stocks and bonds held by a broker for resale to customers in the normal course of business. Other possibilities are more subtle.

> **Example 18.** T Corporation manufactures a product from raw materials purchased from S Corporation. Because S Corporation also sells the materials to other concerns, T Corporation is sometimes unable to satisfy its needs. Consequently, to assure itself of a steady source of supply for its manufacturing operations, T Corporation acquires a controlling interest in S Corporation. Since the acquisition was not motivated by investment considerations, the S Corporation stock is not a capital asset in the hands of T Corporation. Thus, if the stock were to become worthless, the loss would be ordinary and not capital.[32]

Under certain circumstances involving stocks and bonds of affiliated corporations, an ordinary loss also would be allowed upon worthlessness. These conditions are set forth in § 165(g)(3). The possibility of an ordinary loss on the stock of small business corporations (i. e., § 1244) is discussed later in the chapter.

*Business vs. Nonbusiness Bad Debts.* In addition to the possible worthlessness of stocks and bonds, the financial demise of a corporation can lead to bad debt deductions. Such deductions can be either business bad debts or nonbusiness bad debts. The distinction between the two types of deductions becomes important for tax purposes in the following respects:

—Business bad debts are deducted as ordinary losses; nonbusiness bad debts are treated as short-term capital losses.[33] Thus, a business bad debt can generate a net operating loss while a nonbusiness bad debt cannot.[34]

—A deduction is allowed for the partial worthlessness of a business debt. Nonbusiness debts, however, can be written off only when they become entirely worthless.[35]

—Nonbusiness bad debt treatment is limited to noncorporate taxpayers. All of the bad debts of a corporation will qualify as business bad debts.[36]

---

31.  Reg. § 1.165–5(b).

32.  *Journal Co. v. U. S.,* 61–2 USTC ¶ 9605, 8 AFTR2d 5101, 195 F.Supp. 434 (D.Ct.Wis., 1961); *Electrical Fittings Corporation,* 33 T.C. 1026 (1960); *Smith and Welton, Inc. v. U. S.,* 58–2 USTC ¶ 9783, 2 AFTR2d 5872, 164 F.Supp. 605 (D.Ct.Va., 1958); and *Western Wine and Liquor Co.,* 18 T.C. 1090 (1952).

33.  Compare § 166(a) with § 166(d)(1)(B).

34.  Note the adjustments necessitated by § 172(d)(2).

35.  Compare § 166(a)(2) with § 166(d)(1)(A).

36.  § 166(d)(1).

But when is a debt business or nonbusiness? Unfortunately, since the Code sheds little light on the matter, the distinction has been left to the courts.[37] In a leading decision, the Supreme Court somewhat clarified the picture when it held that being an investor does not constitute, by itself, a trade or business.[38] Consequently, if an individual shareholder loans money to a corporation in his or her capacity as an investor, any resulting bad debt will be classified as nonbusiness. Nevertheless, the Court did not preclude the possibility of a shareholder-creditor incurring a business bad debt. If the loan was made in some capacity that does qualify as a trade or business, nonbusiness bad debt treatment can be avoided. For example, was the loan made to protect the shareholder's employment with the corporation? Employee status is a trade or business, and a loss on a loan made for this purpose will qualify for business bad debt treatment.[39] Shareholders may also receive business bad debt treatment if they are in the trade or business of loaning money or of buying, promoting, and selling corporations.

Suppose, however, the shareholder has multiple motives for making the loan. Again the Supreme Court was called upon to resolve the problem.[40] According to the Court the "dominant" or "primary" motive for making the loan should control the classification of the loss.

> **Example 19.**  T owns 48% of the stock of X Corporation, acquired several years ago at a cost of $100,000. T is also employed by the corporation at an annual salary of $40,000. At a time when X Corporation is experiencing financial problems, T loans it $50,000. Subsequently, the corporation becomes bankrupt, and both T's stock investment and his loans become worthless.

Granted that T's stock investment will be treated as a long-term capital loss (absent the application of § 1244 discussed below), but how will the bad debt be classified? If T can prove that the dominant or primary reason for making the loan was to protect his salary, a business bad debt deduction results. If not, it will be assumed that T was trying to protect his stock investment and nonbusiness bad debt treatment results. Factors to be considered in the resolution of this matter include the following:

—A comparison of the amount of stock investment with the trade or business benefit to be derived. In Example 19, this entails comparing the stock investment of $100,000 with the annual salary of $40,000. In this regard, the salary should be considered as a recurring item and not viewed in isolation. Obviously, $40,000 each year could mean a great deal to one who has no other means of support and who may have difficulty obtaining like employment elsewhere.

—A comparison of the amount of the loan with the stock investment and the trade or business benefit to be derived.

---

**37.**  For definitional purposes, § 166(d)(2) might be regarded as almost as worthless as the debt it purports to describe.

**38.**  *Whipple v. Comm.,* 63–1 USTC ¶ 9466, 11 AFTR2d 1454, 83 S.Ct. 1168 (USSC, 1963).

**39.**  *Trent v. Comm.,* 61–2 USTC ¶ 9506, 7 AFTR2d 1599, 291 F.2d 669 (CA–2, 1961).

**40.**  *U. S. v. Generes,* 72–1 USTC ¶ 9259, 29 AFTR2d 72–609, 92 S.Ct. 827 (USSC, 1972).

—The percentage of ownership held by the shareholder. A minority shareholder, for example, may be under more compulsion to loan the corporation money to protect his or her job than one who is in control of corporate policy.

In summary, it would be impossible to conclude whether the taxpayer in Example 19 suffered a business or nonbusiness bad debt without additional facts. Even with such facts, the guidelines are vague, as they must be when a taxpayer's intent or motivation is at issue. For this reason, this problem is the subject of frequent litigation.[41]

*Section 1244 Stock.* Section 1244 permits ordinary loss treatment up to a maximum of $50,000 per year ($100,000 if a joint return is filed) for losses on the sale or worthlessness of stock of so-called small business corporations. By placing shareholders on a more nearly equal basis with proprietors and partners as to the tax treatment of losses, the provision encourages investment of capital in small corporations. Gain on the sale of § 1244 stock remains capital; consequently, the shareholder has nothing to lose and everything to gain by complying with § 1244.

Only a small business corporation may issue qualifying § 1244 stock. The total amount of stock that can be offered under the plan to issue § 1244 stock cannot exceed $1,000,000. For these purposes, property received in exchange for stock is valued at its adjusted basis, reduced by any liabilities assumed by the corporation or to which the property is subject. Fair market value of the property is not considered. The $1,000,000 limitation is determined by property and money received for the stock as a contribution to capital and as paid-in capital on the date the stock is issued. Consequently, even though a corporation fails to meet these requirements when the stock is sold, the stock can still qualify as § 1244 stock if the requirements were met on the date the stock was issued.

The corporation must have derived more than 50 percent of its aggregate gross receipts from sources other than royalties, rents, dividends, interest, annuities, and sales and exchanges of stock or securities (only the gains are considered) for the corporation's most recent five tax years. This gross receipts requirement applies only if the corporation's receipts equal or exceed its deductions other than a net operating loss deduction or the dividends received deduction.

The amount of ordinary loss deductible in any one year on § 1244 stock is limited to $50,000 for a taxpayer filing a separate return and $100,000 for husband and wife filing a joint return. If the amount of the loss sustained in the taxable year exceeds these amounts, the remainder is considered a capital loss.

**Example 20.**  A taxpayer acquires § 1244 stock at a cost of $100,000. He sells the stock for $10,000 in one tax year. He has an ordinary loss (on a separate return) of $50,000 and a capital loss of $40,000. On a joint return the entire $90,000 loss would be ordinary.

Only the original holder of § 1244 stock, whether an individual or a partnership, qualifies for ordinary loss treatment. Should the stock be sold

---

**41.** See, for example, *W. Lee Knight,* 34 TCM 389, T.C.Memo. 1975–77; *Fred W. Marquart,* 35 TCM 572, T.C.Memo. 1975–117; and *Kelson v. U. S.,* 74–2 USTC ¶ 9714, 34 AFTR2d 74–6007, 503 F.2d 1291 (CA–10, 1974).

or donated, it loses its § 1244 status. If a partnership is involved, the individual must have been a partner at the time the partnership acquired the stock. Each partner's share of partnership tax attributes includes the share of the loss the partnership sustains on the stock.

Recall the advantages of issuing some debt to shareholders in exchange for capital contributions to a corporation. A disadvantage to debt occurs when compared to stock that qualifies under § 1244. Should the debt become worthless, the taxpayer will generally have a short-term capital loss rather than the ordinary loss (up to $50,000 per year, or $100,000 if a joint return is filed) for § 1244 stock.

If § 1244 stock is issued by a corporation in exchange for property that has an adjusted basis above its fair market value immediately before the exchange, the basis of the stock is reduced to the fair market value of the property on the date of the exchange for the purpose of determining ordinary loss upon a subsequent sale.

> **Example 21.** A taxpayer transfers property with a basis of $10,000 and a fair market value of $5,000 to a corporation in exchange for shares of § 1244 stock. Assuming the transfer qualifies under § 351, the basis of the stock would be $10,000, the same as the taxpayer's basis in the property. For purposes of § 1244, the basis is only $5,000. If the stock is later sold for $3,000, the total loss sustained is $7,000 ($10,000 − $3,000); however, only $2,000 is ordinary loss ($5,000 − $3,000). The remaining portion, $5,000, is capital loss.

If a shareholder contributes additional property or money to a corporation after he or she acquires § 1244 stock, the amount of ordinary loss upon a sale of the § 1244 stock is limited to his or her original contribution.

# PROBLEMS OF RELATED CORPORATIONS

When the same group of owners operate a business in the corporate form, there could be a distinct advantage to making use of multiple corporations. Consider, for example, a business that annually yields taxable income of $400,000. The corporate income tax on this amount would be $25,750 plus $138,000 [46% of $300,000 (the excess over $100,000)], or $163,750. If, however, this income could be divided equally among four corporations, the total tax would be $103,000 [$25,750 (the tax on $100,000) × 4 (the number of corporations)] for an overall savings of $60,750 ($163,750 − $103,000). As noted in Chapter 7, the use of multiple corporations (unless otherwise proscribed) could generate additional accumulated earnings tax credits (currently $250,000) to help avoid the tax on unreasonable accumulations of earnings.

## CONTROLLED GROUPS

To preclude the abuse with the use of multiple corporations, § 1561(a) requires special treatment for controlled groups of corporations. Controlled groups are limited to taxable income in each of the five brackets as though they were one corporation [§ 1561(a)(1)]. Referring to the illustration used above and presuming the controlled corporation rules apply, each of the four corporations would have only $6,250 (one-fourth of the first $25,000 of taxable income) subject to tax at 15 percent, $6,250 (one-fourth of the second $25,000 of taxable income) taxed at 18 percent, $6,250 (one-fourth of the third $25,000 of taxable income) taxed at 30 percent, and $6,250 (one-fourth of the fourth $25,000 of taxable income) taxed at 40 percent. This will be the required allocation unless all members of the controlled group consent to an apportionment plan providing for an unequal allocation of these amounts.

Section 1561(a)(2) requires similar procedures for the $250,000 accumulated earnings tax credit in a controlled group setting. In addition, members of a controlled group are treated as one taxpayer for purposes of the election to expense certain depreciable business assets under § 179. [A controlled group for purposes of § 179 has the same meaning as for § 1563(a), as discussed below, except that 50 percent is substituted for the 80 percent control prescribed by § 1563.] The $25,000 (plus 85 percent of income tax liability over $25,000) limitation on the amount of investment tax credit that can be claimed in a tax year is apportioned among the component members of a controlled group as defined in § 1563(a).

A controlled group of corporations includes parent-subsidiary corporations, brother-sister groups, combined groups, and certain insurance companies [§ 1563].

*Parent-Subsidiary Corporations.* A parent-subsidiary controlled group includes one or more corporations connected through stock ownership with a common parent corporation. A parent-subsidiary controlled group exists if (a) stock possessing at least 80 percent of the total combined voting power of all classes of stock entitled to vote or at least 80 percent of the total value of shares of all classes of stock of each of the corporations, except the common parent, is owned by one or more of the other corporations and (b) the common parent corporation owns stock possessing at least 80 percent of the total combined voting power of all classes of stock entitled to vote or at least 80 percent of the total value of shares of all classes of stock of at least one of the other corporations, excluding stock owned directly by such other corporations. (See Figure I and Figure II.)

**Figure I**

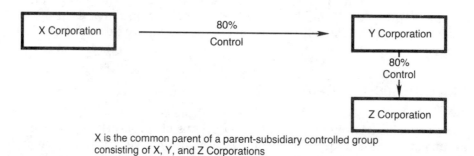

X is the common parent of a parent-subsidiary controlled group consisting of X, Y, and Z Corporations

**Figure II**

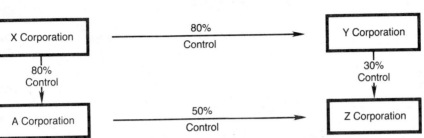

X is the common parent of a parent-subsidiary controlled group
consisting of X, Y, Z, and A Corporations.[42]

*Brother-Sister Corporations.* A brother-sister controlled group exists
if two or more corporations are owned by five or fewer persons (individuals,
estates, or trusts) who (a) possess stock representing at least 80 percent of
the total combined voting power of all classes of stock entitled to vote or at
least 80 percent of the total value of shares of all classes of stock of each
corporation and (b) have a common ownership of more than 50 percent of
the total combined voting power of all classes of stock entitled to vote or
more than 50 percent of the total value of shares of all classes of stock of
each corporation. The stock held by each such person is considered only to
the extent that such stock ownership is identical with respect to each corporation.

**Example 22.** The outstanding stock of Corporations W, X, Y, and Z,
each of which has only one class of stock outstanding, is owned by the
following unrelated individuals:

| Individuals | Corporations | | | | Identical Ownership |
|---|---|---|---|---|---|
| | W | X | Y | Z | |
| A | 40% | 30% | 60% | 60% | 30% |
| B | 50% | 20% | 30% | 20% | 20% |
| C | 10% | 30% | 10% | 10% | 10% |
| D | | 20% | | 10% | |
| Total | 100% | 100% | 100% | 100% | 60% |

Five or fewer individuals (A, B, and C) with more than a 50% common
ownership own at least 80% of all classes of stock in W, X, Y, and Z.
They own 100% of W, 80% of X, 100% of Y, and 90% of Z. Consequently, W, X, Y, and Z are regarded as members of a brother-sister
controlled group.

**Example 23.** Changing the facts, assume the ownership is as follows:

| Individuals | Corporations | | | | Identical Ownership |
|---|---|---|---|---|---|
| | W | X | Y | Z | |
| A | 20% | 10% | 5% | 60% | 5% |
| B | 10% | 20% | 60% | 5% | 5% |
| C | 10% | 70% | 35% | 25% | 10% |
| D | 60% | | | 10% | |
| Total | 100% | 100% | 100% | 100% | 20% |

---

**42.** Reg. § 1.1563–1(a)(2)(b)(ii).

In this instance, the identical ownership is only 20%. Consequently, the corporations are not members of a brother-sister controlled group.

**Example 24.** The outstanding stock of Corporations X and Y, each of which has only one class of stock outstanding, is owned as follows:

| | Corporations | | Identical |
| Individuals | X | Y | Ownership |
|---|---|---|---|
| A | 55% | 100% | 55% |
| B | 45% | | |
| Total | 100% | 100% | 55% |

Although the 50% common ownership test would have been met, the 80% test would not, as there is no common ownership in Y Corporation. Are X and Y brother-sister corporations? No, according to the U. S. Supreme Court.

The Regulations [Reg. § 1.1563–1(a)(3)] took the position that persons in a shareholder group (as in Example 24) could hold stock singly or in combination. However, in *U. S. v. Vogel Fertilizer Co.*,[43] the U. S. Supreme Court sided with the taxpayer and declared Reg. § 1.1563–1(a)(3) to be an unwarranted interpretation of the Internal Revenue Code. The Treasury Department has issued proposed regulations that would amend the current regulations to comply with the conclusions reached in *Vogel*.[44]

*Combined Groups.* A group of three or more corporations form a combined group if each corporation is a member of either a parent-subsidiary controlled group of corporations or a brother-sister controlled group of corporations and if at least one of the corporations is the common parent of a parent-subsidiary controlled group and is also a member of a brother-sister controlled group.

**Example 25.** A, an individual, owns 80% of all classes of stock of X and Z Corporations. X Corporation, in turn, owns 80% of all classes of stock of Y Corporation. Z owns all the stock of W Corporation. X, Y, Z, and W are members of the same combined group. As a result, X, Y, Z, and W are limited to taxable income in each of the five tax brackets and the $250,000 accumulated earnings tax credit as though they were one corporation. This is also the case as to the election to expense certain depreciable business assets under § 179 and as to the $25,000 (plus 85% of income tax liability over $25,000) limitation on the amount of the investment tax credit that can be claimed in a tax year.

---

**43.** 82–1 USTC ¶ 9134, 49 AFTR2d 82–491, 102 S.Ct. 821 (USSC, 1982).
**44.** See Prop. Reg. § 1.1563–1(a)(3), 1982–2 C.B. 735.

## CONSOLIDATED RETURNS

Corporations that are members of a parent-subsidiary controlled group, as defined in § 1504(a) of the Code,[45] may file a consolidated income tax return for a taxable year. Each corporation that has been a member of the group during any part of the taxable year for which the consolidated return is to be filed must consent by filing Form 1122.[46] It may also consent by the actual filing of a consolidated return on Form 1120 with an affiliations schedule on Form 851 that includes all the member corporations. Once a consolidated return is filed, the controlled group must continue to file consolidated returns unless it has secured permission from the IRS to discontinue the filing of such returns.[47] Applications for discontinuance of such filing are made to the IRS by the ninetieth day preceding the return's due date. A corporation that ceases to be a member of a consolidated group must generally wait five years before it can again file on a consolidated basis.

The privilege of filing a consolidated return is based on the concept that the affiliated group constitutes a single taxable entity despite the existence of technically separate businesses. By filing a consolidated return, the corporations can eliminate intercompany profits and losses on the principle that tax liability should be based on transactions with outsiders rather than on intra-group affairs.

Filing a consolidated return has distinct advantages. Income of a profitable company is offset by losses of another. Capital losses of one corporation can offset capital gains of another. Without this possibility, net capital losses cannot be deducted currently, as noted previously. Further, there is no § 482 problem (allocation of income and deductions among related corporations, discussed in Chapter 6).

Filing a consolidated return has certain disadvantages. Losses on intercompany transactions must be deferred. One corporation might incur net § 1231 losses that must be offset with net § 1231 gains of another corporation. Accounting for consolidated taxable income and deferral of intercompany transactions can become perplexing.

The filing of consolidated returns is available only to parent-subsidiary controlled groups; it is not available to brother-sister corporations.

*Computation of Consolidated Income.* Sections 1501–1504 and 1552, and the regulations pursuant thereto, prescribing the manner of computing consolidated income, are quite complex. The rules to determine consolidated taxable income of the group are briefly summarized in the following

---

**45.** A controlled group for this purpose is one or more chains of includible corporations connected through stock ownership with a common parent but only if (1) the common parent owns stock that represents at least 80% of the total voting power *and* 80% of the total value of stock of at least one of the includible corporations and (2) stock representing at least 80% of the total voting power *and* 80% of the total value of stock in each of the includible corporations (except the common parent) is owned directly by one or more of the includible corporations.

**46.** § 1501 and Reg. § § 1.1502–75(a) and (b).

**47.** Reg. § 1.1502–75(c).

paragraph. However, the complicated accounting adjustments required to determine consolidated taxable income are beyond the scope of this text.

The consolidated return is filed using the parent corporation's taxable year with the parent being responsible for filing the return. Each subsidiary must adopt the parent's accounting period the first year its income is included in the consolidated return. Consolidated net taxable income is computed by aggregating the separate taxable incomes for each corporation in the controlled group with certain adjustments. Net operating losses, capital gains and losses, Section 1231 gains and losses, charitable contributions, unrealized profits and losses from intercompany transactions, and dividends paid and received are eliminated. These items then are aggregated separately, with required adjustments, to compute consolidated taxable income.

*Limitation of Net Operating Loss Deductions.* A net operating loss deduction for the controlled group may be used to offset consolidated income of the group with the following exceptions. If the loss year was a separate return limitation year (an SRLY), the loss may be carried over only against income of the loss corporation. An SRLY is any year in which a member of the group filed a separate return. However, a separate return year of a member is not an SRLY if such member corporation was a member of the affiliated group for each day of such year. The separate return year of a corporation that is the common parent of the group is not an SRLY unless the corporation, while nominally the common parent, is not treated as the parent because of a reverse acquisition. (A reverse acquisition occurs when shareholders in the acquired corporation obtain more than 50 percent of the stock ownership in the acquiring corporation as a result of the acquisition.) A loss corporation can acquire a profitable subsidiary and apply its loss carryovers against the profits of that corporation unless a consolidated return change of ownership (a CRCO) accompanied the acquisition or a reverse acquisition occurred. A CRCO is a change of control in the corporate group, measured as at least a 50 percent change in the ownership of the corporation's outstanding stock since the beginning of the present or prior taxable year. If there has been a CRCO, carryover losses may offset income only of the original group.

Section 382 (discussed in Chapter 6) applies to net operating loss carryovers by the controlled group. If the limitations of § 382 apply, the net operating loss carryovers are reduced accordingly. Section 269 can apply to disallow such carryovers altogether.

If an existing loss corporation acquires a profitable business by purchasing the assets, rather than through a reorganization, and does not change stock ownership, its prior losses can offset future profits.

*Built-in Deductions.* Certain "built-in deductions," acquired by a subsidiary in an SRLY but which are realized in a consolidated return year, are treated as sustained by the subsidiary prior to the consolidated return year. Such built-in deductions may then be deducted only against income of the subsidiary that sustained the deductions.

**Example 26.** Beta Corporation is the common parent of a controlled group. Beta purchased the stock of Alpha Corporation on December 30, 19X6. Alpha owned a capital asset with an adjusted basis of

$20,000 but with a fair market value of $10,000 on December 30, 19X6. The asset was sold in 19X7 for $9,000. If the group files a consolidated return for 19X7, $10,000 of the $11,000 loss is a built-in deduction, because it was economically accrued in an SRLY. This portion of the loss can be deducted only against the separate income of Alpha.

**Example 27.** Assume the asset in Example 26 was depreciable property. Depreciation deductions attributable to the $10,000 difference between basis and fair market value on December 30, 19X6, are treated as built-in deductions and are limited to deductions against separate income of Alpha.

The rules relating to build-in deductions do not apply once the assets of the acquired subsidiary have been held by the controlled group for more than 10 years or if the total adjusted basis of all assets of the acquired subsidiary (other than cash, certain marketable securities, and goodwill) do not exceed the fair market value of all such assets by more than 15 percent.[48] Built-in deductions will be completely eliminated if the corporation was acquired because of such deductions.[49]

*Intercompany Transactions.* Intercompany transactions are divided into deferred intercompany transactions and transactions that are not deferred. Those transactions that are not deferred are taken into income and expense by the separate corporations in the same tax year so that there is a "wash" for purposes of computing consolidated taxable income. The deferred intercompany transactions are placed in a suspense account, and profits and losses are deferred until either the assets are sold to a taxpayer outside the controlled group or one of the parties to the transaction leaves the controlled group.

*Summary of Steps in Calculating Consolidated Taxable Income.* Briefly, the steps in calculating consolidated taxable income are as follows:

1. Combine the separately computed taxable income for each member of the controlled group.

2. Eliminate from the combined taxable income of the group any intercompany dividends and any built-in deductions. (Dividends paid to minority shareholders are not eliminated.)

3. Eliminate from the combined taxable income of the group, and then adjust to reflect a consolidated figure, the following items:

   (a) Any NOL deduction for each affiliate. [Any NOL deduction for an affiliate is subject to the SRLY and CRCO limitation rules. In addition, § § 382 and 269 are applicable to a recently acquired subsidiary to cause a possible disallowance of all or part of the loss carryover. (See Chapter 6.)]

   (b) Capital gains and losses for each affiliate.

   (c) Section 1231 gains and losses for each affiliate.

---

**48.** Reg. § 1.1502–15(a)(4).
**49.** Reg. § § 1.269–3(a) and (c).

(d) Charitable contribution deductions for each affiliate. [The consolidated charitable contribution deduction is limited to five percent of the adjusted consolidated taxable income (consolidated taxable income computed without regard to the dividends received deduction and any consolidated NOL or capital loss carrybacks).]

4. Transfer from combined taxable income certain intercompany transactions. [Intercompany transactions such as sales or exchanges of property or the performance of services where the amount of the expenditure for such services is capitalized (or any other expenditure where the amount of the expenditure is capitalized) among members of the controlled group are transferred to a deferred account.]

(a) Intercompany gains or losses on such deferred transactions are postponed until the property is sold to a third party.

(b) Generally, noncapitalized intercompany transactions are not deferred.

(c) The group may elect not to defer gain or loss on any otherwise deferred intercompany transactions.

**Example 28.** X, Y, and Z Corporations are members of a controlled group that has elected to file a consolidated return. In the current taxable year, the corporations have separate taxable income as follows: X, $50,000 taxable income from operations plus a § 1231 gain of $60,000; Y, $50,000 taxable income representing $80,000 taxable income from operations minus a § 1231 loss of $30,000; Z, taxable income from operations of $200,000. Consolidated taxable income for the group would be $330,000 plus a net § 1231 gain of $30,000, computed as follows: $300,000 (combined separately computed taxable income for X, Y, and Z Corporations) + $30,000 (§ 1231 loss deducted by Y in arriving at its separate taxable income) + net § 1231 gain of $30,000 [$60,000 (§1231 gain for X) − $30,000 (§ 1231 loss for Y)]. Tax liability for the group would be $139,950, computed as follows:

| | |
|---|---:|
| Tax on first $100,000 | $ 25,750 |
| Tax on $230,000 at 46% | 105,800 |
| Tax on net § 1231 gain ($30,000 at 28%) | 8,400 |
| | $ 139,950 |

Note that taxable income in this example would be less if the corporations had filed separate tax returns. Total combined tax liability would be $134,550 (or $5,400 less), computed as follows:

Tax liability for X

| | |
|---|---:|
| 15% of $25,000 | $ 3,750 |
| 18% of $25,000 | 4,500 |
| 28% of § 1231 gain of $60,000 | 16,800 |
| | $ 25,050 |

Tax liability for Y
(Because X, Y, and Z are affiliated corporations, they are limited to taxable income in each of the five tax brackets as though they were one corporation. Unless all members of the group consent to an apportionment plan providing for an unequal allocation of the five bracket amounts, the five brackets are divided equally among members of the group. Assume the members have consented to an unequal apportionment as set out in this example. An equal allocation of the tax brackets would produce the same total tax liability for the three corporations as the unequal apportionment used in this example.)

| | |
|---|---:|
| 30% of $25,000 | $ 7,500 |
| 40% of $25,000 | 10,000 |
| | $ 17,500 |

Tax liability for Z

| | |
|---|---:|
| 46% of $200,000 | $ 92,000 |

Combined tax liability

| | |
|---|---:|
| Tax liability for X | $ 25,050 |
| Tax liability for Y | 17,500 |
| Tax liability for Z | 92,000 |
| | $ 134,550 |

The difference in tax liability of $5,400 represents an additional gain of $30,000 taxed at 28% when separate returns are filed as compared to that gain being taxed at 46% when a consolidated return is filed (the $60,000 § 1231 gain must be offset by the § 1231 loss of $30,000 on a consolidated return). Gain of $30,000 × 18% (the difference between 46% and 28%) equals $5,400.

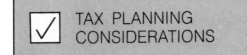

## TAX PLANNING CONSIDERATIONS

### WORKING WITH § 351

Effective tax planning with transfers of property to corporations involves a clear understanding of § 351 and its related Code provisions. The most important question in planning is simply: Does compliance with the requirements of § 351 yield the desired tax result?

*Utilizing § 351.* In using § 351(a), one should insure that all parties transferring property (which includes cash) receive control of the corporation. Although simultaneous transfers are not necessary, a long period of time between transfers could be vulnerable if the transfers are not properly documented as part of a single plan.

**Example 29.** C, D, and E decide to form the X Corporation with the following investment: cash of $100,000 from C, real estate worth $100,000 (basis of $20,000) from D, and a patent worth $100,000 (basis of zero) from E. In return for this investment, each party is to receive one-third of the corporation's authorized stock of 300 shares. On June 1, 19X4, after the corporate charter is granted, C transfers cash of $100,000 in return for 100 shares. Two months later, D transfers the real estate for another 100 shares. On December 3, 19X4, E transfers the patent for the remaining 100 shares.

Taken in isolation, the transfers by D and E would result in recognized gain to each. Section 351 would not be applicable, because neither D nor E achieves the required 80 percent control. If, however, the parties are in a position to prove that all transfers were part of the same plan, C's transfer can be counted and the 80 percent requirement is satisfied. To do this the parties should document and preserve evidence of their intentions. Also, it would be helpful to have some reasonable explanation for the delay in D's and E's transfers.

To meet the requirements of § 351, mere momentary control on the part of the transferor may not suffice if loss of control is compelled by a prearranged agreement.[50]

**Example 30.** For many years T operated a business as a sole proprietor employing R as manager. To dissuade R from quitting and going out on her own, T promised her a 30% interest in the business. To fulfill this promise, T transfers the business to newly formed X Corporation in return for all its stock. Immediately thereafter, T transfers 30% of the stock to R. Section 351 probably would not apply to the transfer by T to X Corporation; it appears that T was under an obligation to relinquish control. If this is not the case, and such loss of control was by voluntary act on the part of T, momentary control would suffice.[51]

Be sure that later transfers of property to an existing corporation satisfy the control requirement if recognition of gain is to be avoided. In this connection, a transferor's interest cannot be counted if the stock or securities received are of relatively small value in comparison to the value of those already owned and the primary purpose of the transfer is to qualify other transferors for § 351 treatment.[52] For purposes of issuing advance rulings, the IRS follows a policy of treating the amount transferred as *not* being relatively small in value if such amount is equal to, or in excess of, 10 percent of the fair market value of the stock and securities already owned by such person.[53]

**Example 31.** At a point when R Corporation has 800 shares outstanding (owned equally by T and her son) and worth $1,000 each, it

---

**50.** Rev.Rul. 54–96, 1954–1 C.B. 111.

**51.** Compare *Fahs v. Florida Machine and Foundry Co.*, 48–2 USTC ¶ 9329, 36 AFTR 1151, 168 F.2d 957 (CA–5, 1948), with *John C. O'Connor*, 16 TCM 213, T.C.Memo. 1957–50, *aff'd.* in 58–2 USTC ¶ 9913, 2 AFTR2d 6011, 260 F.2d 358 (CA–6, 1958).

**52.** Reg. § 1.351–1(a)(1)(ii). Refer to Example 4 of this chapter.

**53.** Rev.Proc. 77–37, 1977–2 C.B. 568.

issues an additional 200 shares to T in exchange for land (basis of $20,000 and fair market value of $200,000). Presuming the son makes no contribution, T's transfer does not meet the requirements of § 351. Since the son's ownership interest cannot be counted (he was not a transferor), T must satisfy the control requirement on her own. In this regard, she falls short, since she ended up with 600 shares [400 shares (originally owned) + 200 shares (newly received)] out of 1,000 shares now outstanding for only a 60% interest.[54] Thus, T must recognize a gain of $180,000 on the transfer.

**Example 32.** To make the transfer in Example 31 fall under § 351, what needs to be done? One possibility would be to include the son as a transferor so that his ownership interest can be counted in meeting the control requirement. In using the IRS guidelines to avoid the "relatively small in value" hurdle, this would entail an investment on the part of the son (for additional stock) of at least $40,000 in cash or property [10% × $400,000 (fair market value of the shares already owned)]. If this approach is taken, § 351 will apply to T and none of her realized gain of $180,000 will be recognized.

To keep the matter in perspective, be in a position to recognize when § 351 is not relevant.

**Example 33.** Assume the same facts as in Example 31, except that T receives no additional shares in R Corporation in exchange for the transfer of the land. Because T has made a contribution to capital, compliance with § 351 is of no consequence. No gain will be recognized by T due to such contribution, although a basis adjustment is in order as to her original 400 shares.[55] Other tax consequences, however, may materialize.[56]

*Avoiding § 351.* Because § 351(a) provides for the nonrecognition of gain on transfers to controlled corporations, it is often regarded as a relief provision favoring taxpayers. There could be situations, however, where the avoidance of § 351(a) produces a more advantageous tax result. The transferors might prefer to recognize gain on the transfer of property if they cannot be particularly harmed by the gain, either because they are in low tax brackets or because the gain will receive preferential long-term capital gain treatment. Keep in mind that the basis of the property to the corporation will be affected by the applicability or inapplicability of § 351(a).

**Example 34.** C and D form the X Corporation with a $20,000 cash investment. Shortly thereafter, they "sell" to the corporation a patent

---

**54.** The stock attribution rules of § 318 (see Chapter 4) do not apply to § 351 transfers. Consequently, the shares held by the son are not treated as being constructively owned by the mother.

**55.** If R Corporation is a foreign corporation, the result (in terms of recognition of gain) may well be different. See § 367(c)(2).

**56.** Because the son has benefited from T's capital contribution (i. e., his shares are, as a result, worth more), a gift has taken place. It could be, therefore, that T's capital contribution could lead to the imposition of a gift tax liability. In this connection, see Chapter 11.

they have developed (basis of zero) for $2,000,000, such sum payable in interest-bearing notes extending over an eight-year period. C and D elect to report the gain on the sale of the patent under the installment method (§ 453).

What have C and D tried to accomplish by structuring the transfer as a purported sale? First, the $2,000,000 gain recognized probably will be long-term capital gain.[57] Even better, the election of the installment method avoids the bunching of such gain and permits C and D to spread recognition thereof over the eight-year payout period. Second, X Corporation receives a basis in the patent of $2,000,000. Since a patent is an amortizable asset, the step-up in basis may be written off over its estimated useful life. Third, the interest element of the notes permits C and D to bail out corporate profits over the next eight years in a form deductible to the corporation. It is hoped that deductible interest would then become a substitute for nondeductible dividends.

What could go wrong with the intended tax consequences?

1.  The IRS could attempt to collapse the "sale" by taking the approach that the transfer really falls under § 351(a).[58] As such, the shareholders recognize no gain and their zero basis in the patent carries over to the corporation [§ 362(b)].

2.  The IRS could argue that the notes issued by X Corporation are really a form of stock and such debt should be reclassified as equity. If the argument succeeds, the corporation's interest payments on the notes become nondeductible dividends. Even worse, any principal payments on the notes also would be taxed to C and D as dividends to the extent of X Corporation's earnings and profits (see Chapter 4).

3.  Since a patent is depreciable property, § 1239 might apply to convert long-term capital gain (or § 1231 gain) into ordinary income. For § 1239 to become operative, however, either C *or* D must own 80 percent or more in value of the outstanding stock in X Corporation. In meeting the 80 percent test, the stock ownership of C and D is subject to the constructive ownership rules of § 318 (except that members of an individual's family include only the individual and his or her spouse).

In reaching the § 351(a) result (refer to point 1), it becomes necessary to conclude that C and D received *solely* stock or securities in X Corporation in return for the property transferred. But would the notes be classified as securities? The maturity period of the notes (i. e., eight years), although not controlling, is important. As noted previously, however, what

---

57.  Long-term capital gain would materialize from the general tax concepts applicable to the sale or exchange of capital assets. This presumes the patent is a capital asset in the hands of C and D, held for the required holding period, and a sale or exchange has taken place. The special provision of § 1235, normally relied on in the disposition of patent transfers, need not be utilized. At any rate, its use in this case is precluded by the related-person provision of § 1235(d).

58.  *U. S. v. Hertwig*, 68–2 USTC ¶ 9495, 22 AFTR2d 5249, 398 F.2d 452 (CA–5, 1968); *Robert W. Adams*, 58 T.C. 41 (1972); and *D'Angelo Associates, Inc.*, 70 T.C. 121 (1978).

is or is not a security is still unclear when maturity periods of 5 to 10 years are involved. If it can be assumed that the notes are not securities or stock (refer to point 2), the taxpayers would accomplish essentially the same desired tax result through § 351(b). The notes now become other property (boot), and the shareholders recognize a capital gain to the extent of the fair market value of such notes. The basis of the patent to the corporation becomes the basis in the hands of the transferors (i. e., zero) *plus* the gain recognized by the corporation's transferors.

In summary, the procedures followed in Example 34 appear highly susceptible to challenge by the IRS. The following modifications would be helpful in reducing the tax risk involved:

—Disassociating the sale of the patent from the formation of the corporation. Certainly, some time span should separate the two events. Perhaps the patent could have been leased to the corporation for a period of time, with the later sale proving to be the solution to the initial unsatisfactory arrangement.

—Shortening the maturity period of the notes. Consequently, even if the sale is tied to the § 351 formation, the chance of boot treatment under § 351(b) is improved.

—Capitalizing the corporation with more equity and less debt. Lessening the debt-to-equity ratio reduces the hazards of stock reclassification.

Another reason why a particular transferor might wish to avoid § 351 concerns possible loss recognition. Recall that § 351(a) refers to the nonrecognition of both gains and losses. In a boot situation, § 351(b)(2) specifically states: "No loss to such recipient shall be recognized." The course of action for a transferor who wishes to recognize loss on the transfer of property with a basis in excess of fair market value could be any of several alternatives:

—Sell the property to the corporation for its stock. As previously noted, this procedure may be collapsed by the IRS. If the sale is disregarded, the transferor ends up under § 351(a) with a realized, but unrecognized, loss.

—Sell the property to the corporation for other property or boot. Because the transferor receives no stock or securities, § 351 is inapplicable.

—Transfer the property to the corporation in return for securities. Surprisingly, the IRS has held that § 351 does not apply to a transferor who receives only securities and no stock.[59] In both this and the previous alternatives, one would have to watch for the possible disallowance of the loss under § 267.

Suppose, however, the loss property is to be transferred to the corporation and no loss is recognized by the transferor due to § 351(a). This could

---

59. Rev.Rul. 73–472, 1973–2 C.B. 115. But compare Rev.Rul. 73–473, 1973–2 C.B. 115.

present an interesting problem in terms of assessing the economic realities involved:

**Example 35.** E and F form the X Corporation with the following investment: property by E (basis of $40,000 and fair market value of $50,000) and property by F (basis of $60,000 and fair market value of $50,000). Each receives 50% of the X Corporation stock. Has F acted wisely in settling for only 50% of the stock? At first blush, it would appear so, since E and F each invested property of the same value ($50,000). But what about the tax considerations? Due to the basis carryover of § 362(b), the corporation now has a basis of $40,000 in E's property and $60,000 in F's property. In essence, then, E has shifted a possible $10,000 gain to the corporation, while F has transferred a $10,000 potential loss. (The higher basis in F's property has value to the corporation either in the form of higher depreciation deductions or less gain on a later sale.) With this in mind, an equitable allocation of the X Corporation stock would call for F to receive a greater percentage interest than E.

## RELATED CORPORATIONS

*Controlled Groups.* Recall that § 1561 was designed to prevent the abuse of operating a business as multiple corporations in order to obtain lower tax brackets and multiple minimum accumulated earnings tax credits. Corporations in which substantially all the stock is held by five or fewer persons are subject to the provisions of § 1561. Therefore, if ownership of voting stock is divided so that control of each corporation lies with the different individuals rather than with the individuals having a common control of all the corporations, the prohibitions of § 1561 can be avoided.

**Example 36.** A, B, and C, individuals, have voting stock in Corporations X, Y, and Z as follows:

| Shareholder | X | Y | Z | Common Ownership |
|---|---|---|---|---|
| A | 40 | 30 | 30 | 30 |
| B | 40 | 20 | 30 | 20 |
| C | 20 | 50 | 40 | 20 |
| Total | 100 | 100 | 100 | 70 |

Because the total combined ownership is more than 50% and the three individuals own at least 80% of the combined voting power, X, Y, and Z are treated as a controlled group and are subject to § 1561. Thus, Corporations X, Y, and Z are limited to taxable income in each of the five tax brackets and to the $250,000 accumulated earnings tax credit as though they were one corporation. Assume, however, that voting stock is divided differently so that each of the individuals—A, B, and C— control one of the corporations rather than having common control of all the corporations.

**Example 37.** A, B, and C hold voting stock in Corporations X, Y, and Z in the following percentages:

| Shareholder | X | Y | Z | Common Ownership |
|---|---|---|---|---|
| A | 80 | 10 | 10 | 10 |
| B | 10 | 80 | 10 | 10 |
| C | 10 | 10 | 80 | 10 |
| Total | 100 | 100 | 100 | 30 |

Now, the total combined ownership is less than 50%. Consequently, the corporations are not treated as a controlled group, since the prohibitions of § 1561 are not applicable.

The differences in ownership in the corporations could be alleviated somewhat by issuing nonvoting preferred stock to those shareholders with the 10 percent ownership. (Nonvoting stock is not considered to be stock for purposes of § 1563.)

*Consolidated Returns.* Effective tax planning for affiliated corporations (recall that brother-sister controlled groups cannot file consolidated returns) requires a determination of whether to file a consolidated return for the group. Because of the complex accounting required to compute consolidated taxable income, computations should be made initially to determine whether the tax savings from filing a consolidated return will be significant enough to warrant making the election. An incorrect decision can cause problems; once a consolidated return is filed, the affiliated group must continue to file such a return until it has secured permission from the IRS to discontinue doing so.

The principal advantage of filing a consolidated return is that the losses of one corporation may be used to offset the income of other corporations.

**Example 38.** In the current taxable year, X Corporation has taxable income from operations in the amount of $50,000 and has incurred a short-term capital gain of $10,000 and a long-term capital gain of $20,000. Its tax liability would be $16,850 [$3,750 (15% of $25,000) + $4,500 (18% of $25,000) + $3,000 (30% of $10,000) + $5,600 (28% of long-term capital gain of $20,000).] X owns 80% of the voting stock of Y Corporation, which had a tax loss from operations in the current taxable year of $30,000 plus a net short-term capital loss of $40,000. Y Corporation would have no tax liability filing a separate return. If X and Y file a consolidated return, tax liability would be only $3,000 [15% of $20,000 ($50,000 income from operations for X less $30,000 loss from operations for Y)]. The net short-term capital loss of $40,000 incurred by Y would offset the capital gains of $30,000 incurred by X. Consequently, there would be a tax savings of $13,850 ($16,850 income tax liability for X if a separate return is filed less $3,000 liability on a consolidated return).

Filing a consolidated return can have disadvantages. Although gain on intercompany transactions is deferred when a consolidated return is filed, intercompany losses are also deferred. In addition, the accounting for deferred transactions can become quite complex. (Because of the accounting complexity, an affiliated group may elect not to defer such gains and losses.) The possibility also exists that aggregate tax liability might be greater than separate tax liability should one member of the group have net § 1231 losses while another has § 1231 gains. (Refer to Example 28.) The accounting problems relating to built-in deductions and SRLY and CRCO limitations can be extensive.

Although the advantages of filing consolidated returns can be substantial, the filing of a consolidated return does eliminate the flexibility of corporate planning on a separate return basis. With the additional concern that filing a consolidated return can be disadvantageous, the election to file such a return should not be made if the tax advantages in doing so are small.

## PROBLEM MATERIALS

### Discussion Questions

1. In terms of justification and effect, Code § 351 (i. e., transfer to corporation controlled by transferor) and Code § 1031 (i. e., like-kind exchanges) are much alike. Explain.

2. F and S (father and son) form a corporation with a transfer of property valued at $200,000 and $100,000, respectively. In return for this property, F and S each receive 50% of the corporation's stock. Explain the tax consequences of these transfers as to

   (a) F.

   (b) S.

3. What does the term "property" include for purposes of § 351?

4. In arriving at the basis of stock received by a shareholder in a § 351 transfer, describe the effect of the following:

   (a) The shareholder receives other property (boot) in addition to stock.

   (b) Along with the property, the shareholder transfers a liability to the corporation.

   (c) The shareholder's basis in the property transferred to the corporation.

5. How does a corporation determine its basis in property received pursuant to a § 351 transfer?

6. What are "securities" for purposes of § 351? What difference does it make if debt instruments do or do not qualify as securities?

7. What is the control requirement of § 351? Describe the effect of the following in satisfying this requirement:

   (a) A shareholder renders services to the corporation for stock.

   (b) A shareholder both renders services and transfers property to the corporation for stock.

   (c) A shareholder has only momentary control after the transfer.

   (d) A long period of time elapses between the transfers of property by different shareholders.

8. Assuming a § 351(a) nontaxable transfer, explain the tax effect, if any, of the following transactions:

    (a) The transfer of depreciable property with recapture potential under § 1245 or § 1250.

    (b) The later sale of such property by the corporation.

    (c) The transfer of property upon which an investment tax credit has previously been claimed by the transferor.

    (d) The later sale of such property by the corporation.

9. At a point when X Corporation has been in existence for six years, shareholder T transfers real estate (adjusted basis of $20,000 and fair market value of $100,000) to the corporation for additional stock. At the same time, P, the other shareholder, purchases one share of stock for cash. After the two transfers, the percentage of stock ownership is as follows: 79% by T and 21% by P.

    (a) What were the parties trying to accomplish?

    (b) Will it work? Explain.

    (c) Would the result change if T and P are father and son?

10. Assume the same facts as in Question 9, except that T receives nothing from X Corporation for the transfer of the real estate to the corporation. Does this change the tax result as to T?

11. Before incorporating her apartment rental business, B takes out second mortgages on several of the units. B uses the mortgage funds to make capital improvements to her personal residence. Along with all of the rental units, B transfers the mortgages to the newly formed corporation in return for all of its stock. Discuss the tax consequences to B of the procedures followed.

12. K's sole proprietorship includes assets that, if sold, would yield a gain of $100,000. It also includes assets that would yield a loss of $30,000. K incorporates his business using only the gain assets. Two days later, K sells the loss assets to the newly formed corporation.

    (a) What was K trying to accomplish?

    (b) Will it work? Explain.

13. The recapture of the investment tax credit can operate independent of § 351. Explain.

14. In structuring the capitalization of a corporation, what are the advantages of utilizing debt as opposed to equity?

15. What factors are taken into account in determining whether or not a corporation is thinly capitalized?

16. Describe the tax effect to the corporation and its shareholders when the corporation is deemed to be thinly capitalized.

17. Presuming § 1244 does not apply, what is the tax treatment of stock that has become worthless?

18. Under what circumstances, if any, may a shareholder deduct a business bad debt on a loan he or she has made to the corporation?

19. T, an unmarried individual taxpayer, had invested $75,000 in the stock of X Corporation, which recently declared bankruptcy. Although T is distressed over the loss of her investment, she is somewhat consoled by the fact that the $75,000 will be an ordinary (rather than a capital) loss. Is T fully apprised of the tax result? Why or why not?

20. Several years ago, M purchased stock in Y Corporation for $40,000. Such stock has a current value of $5,000. Consider the following alternatives:

   (a) Without selling the stock, M deducts $35,000 for partial worthlessness of the Y Corporation investment.

   (b) M sells the stock to his son for $5,000 and deducts a $35,000 long-term capital loss.

   (c) M sells the stock to a third party and deducts a $35,000 long-term capital loss.

   (d) M sells the stock to a third party and deducts a $35,000 ordinary loss.

21. How does treatment as a controlled group of corporations work to the disadvantage of the corporate group?

22. What is the difference between a brother-sister controlled group and a parent-subsidiary controlled group?

23. Assume an individual, A, owns 80% of all classes of stock of two corporations, X and Y. X Corporation, in turn, owns all the stock of Z Corporation, and Y Corporation owns 80% of the stock of W Corporation. Would X, Y, Z, and W Corporations be members of a combined group? Explain.

24. What groups of corporations may file consolidated returns?

25. What are the advantages and disadvantages of filing a consolidated return?

26. Assume a parent corporation uses the calendar year as its taxable year. It owns 80% of all classes of stock in two subsidiary corporations that use a fiscal year for their tax years. The corporations wish to file a consolidated return. What tax year should be used?

27. When may a net operating loss for a controlled group be used to offset consolidated taxable income?

28. What is a built-in deduction of a controlled group?

29. What is the significance of a deferred intercompany transaction?

## Problems

1. X Corporation receives 30 acres of land and $10,000 cash from Plainland City to locate its office and plant in this community. The 30 acres of land are worth $50,000. X Corporation uses the $10,000 in cash to purchase equipment. What are the tax consequences to X Corporation upon the receipt of the land and cash from Plainland City?

2. X Corporation owns 80% of the total combined voting power of all classes of stock entitled to vote in Y Corporation. Y Corporation owns 40% of the stock in Z Corporation. X Corporation owns 80% of W Corporation, while the latter owns 30% of Z Corporation. Which corporations are part of a controlled group?

3. An individual, A, owns 50% of X Corporation. X Corporation owns 85% of all classes of stock in Y Corporation. Another individual, B, owns 20% of X Corporation and 60% of W Corporation. A owns 20% of W Corporation. C, another individual, owns 30% of X Corporation and 20% of W Corporation. Which, if any, of the above corporations are members of a controlled group?

4. The outstanding stock in X and Y Corporations, each of which has only one class of stock outstanding, is owned by the following unrelated individuals:

| | Corporations | |
|---|---|---|
| Shareholders | X | Y |
| A | 20 | 16 |
| B | 5 | 54 |
| C | 75 | 30 |
| Total | 100 | 100 |

(a) Determine if a brother-sister controlled group exists.

(b) Assume that B owns no stock in X Corporation and C owns 80 shares. Would a brother-sister controlled group exist? Why or why not?

5.    J and B form Y Corporation with the following investment:

| | Property Transferred | | Number of |
|---|---|---|---|
| | Basis to Transferor | Fair Market Value | Shares Issued |
| From J— | | | |
|    Land & building | $ 70,000 | $ 300,000 | |
|    Mortgage on land | | | 50 |
|      & building | 100,000 | | |
| From B— | | | |
|    Cash | 25,000 | 25,000 | |
|    Machinery | 50,000 | 75,000 | 50 |
|    Equipment | 80,000 | 100,000 | |

The mortgage is assumed by Y Corporation.

(a) How much gain, if any, must J recognize?

(b) What will be J's basis in the Y Corporation stock?

(c) What will be Y Corporation's basis in the land and building?

(d) How much gain, if any, must B recognize?

(e) What will be B's basis in the Y Corporation stock?

(f) What will be Y Corporation's basis in the machinery and equipment?

6.    C, D, E, and F (all individuals) form the X Corporation with the following investment:

| | Property Transferred | | Number of |
|---|---|---|---|
| | Basis to Transferor | Fair Market Value | Shares Issued |
| From C— | | | |
|    Cash | $ 30,000 | $ 30,000 | |
|    Unrealized accounts | | | 60 |
|      receivable | 0 | 30,000 | |
| From D— | | | |
|    Land & building | 70,000 | 150,000 | |
|    Mortgage on land | | | 50 |
|      & building | 100,000 | 100,000 | |
| From E— | | | |
|    Equipment | 95,000 | 80,000 | 70* |
| From F— | | | |
|    Personal services | | | |
|      rendered to X | | | |
|      Corporation | 0 | 20,000 | 20 |

*E receives $10,000 in cash in addition to the 70 shares.

The mortgage transferred by D is assumed by X Corporation. Assume the value of each share of X Corporation stock is $1,000.

(a) What, if any, is C's recognized gain or loss? *30 (on receivables) realized but not recognized*

(b) What basis will C have in the X Corporation stock? *0*

(c) What basis will X Corporation have in the unrealized accounts receivable? *0*

(d) How much gain or loss must D recognize? *debt in excess of basis recognize (100 – 70) = 30 (realized gain is $80)*

(e) What basis will D have in the X Corporation stock? *70 basis + 30 gain – 100 boot (debt assumed) = $0*

(f) What basis will X Corporation have in the land and building? *$70 + $30 = $100*

(g) How much gain or loss must E recognize? *none – can't recognize loss. Realized loss (despite boot) is $15*

(h) What basis will E have in the X Corporation stock? *95 – 10 = $85*

(i) What basis will X Corporation have in the equipment? *$95 = adj basis*

(j) How much income, if any, must F recognize? *$20,000*

(k) What basis will F have in the X Corporation stock? *$20,000*

7. A, B, C, and D form X Corporation with the following investments:

|  | Property Transferred |  | Number of Shares Issued |
|---|---|---|---|
|  | Basis to Transferor | Fair Market Value |  |
| From A— |  |  |  |
| Inventory | $ 10,000 | $ 30,000 | 30 |
| From B— |  |  |  |
| Equipment ($10,000 of depreciation taken by B in prior years) | 15,000 | 33,000 | 30* |
| From C— |  |  |  |
| Secret process | 5,000 | 30,000 | 30 |
| From D— |  |  |  |
| Cash | 10,000 | 10,000 | 10 |

*B receives $3,000 in cash in addition to the 30 shares.

Assume the value of each share of X Corporation stock is $1,000.

(a) What, if any, is A's recognized gain or loss? *Real 20,000   Basis = 10,000   Recog 0*

(b) What basis will A have in the X Corporation stock? *10,000*

(c) What basis will X Corporation have in the inventory? *10,000*

(d) How much gain or loss must B recognize? How is the gain or loss treated? *$3,000 Gain long term*

(e) What basis will B have in the X Corporation stock? *15,000 +/– 3,000 = 15,000*

(f) What basis will X Corporation have in the equipment? *18,000*

(g) What, if any, is C's recognized gain or loss? *Real 25,000   Recog. 0*

(h) What basis will C have in the X Corporation stock? *5,000*

(i) What basis will X Corporation have in the secret process? *5,000*

(j) How much income, if any, must D recognize? *0*

(k) What basis will D have in the X Corporation stock? *$10,000*

8.  A and B organize X Corporation by transferring the following property:

| | Property Transferred | | Number of |
| | Basis to<br>Transferor | Fair Market<br>Value | Shares<br>Issues |
| --- | --- | --- | --- |
| From A— | | | |
|   Unimproved land | $ 10,000 | $ 100,000 | 50 |
|   Mortgage on land | 50,000 | 50,000 | |
| From B— | | | |
|   Receivables | 60,000 | 50,000 | 50 |

Assume the value of each share of X Corporation stock is $1,000.

(a) What, if any, is A's recognized gain or loss?

(b) What basis will A have in the X Corporation stock?

(c) What basis will X Corporation have in the land?

(d) What, if any, is B's recognized gain or loss?

(e) What basis will B have in the X Corporation stock?

(f) What basis will X Corporation have in the receivables?

9.  T organized X Corporation and transferred land with a basis of $200,000, value of $600,000, and subject to a mortgage of $150,000. A month before incorporation, T borrowed $100,000 for personal purposes and gave the bank a lien on the land. X Corporation issued stock worth $350,000 to T and assumed the loans in the amount of $150,000 and $100,000. What are the tax consequences of the incorporation—

(a) To T?

(b) To X Corporation?

10. Indicate whether the following statements are true or false:

(a) If both § 357(b) and § 357(c) apply, the latter will control.

(b) For § 357(b) to apply, the transfer of the liability must be for the purpose of tax avoidance *and* lack a bona fide business purpose.

(c) Section 357(c) will not apply if there is no realized gain on the transfer.

(d) The application of § 357(b) to a transfer to a controlled corporation would not affect the basis of the stock received by the transferor.

(e) T transfers property (upon which an investment tax credit has previously been claimed) to a controlled corporation. A later sale of the property by the corporation could trigger recapture of the credit to T.

(f) Same as (e). A later sale of the stock by T could trigger recapture of the credit to T.

(g) T transfers depreciable property to a controlled corporation. The property possesses a recapture potential under § 1245. A later sale of the property by the corporation could trigger recapture of depreciation to T.

(h) T transfers accounts receivable (face amount of $50,000) and a reserve for bad debts of $5,000 for stock in a controlled corporation worth $45,000. Under these circumstances, the tax benefit rule will not cause any recognition of gain to T.

(i) P Corporation owns 80% of X Corporation and 90% of Y Corporation. X owns 30% of Z Corporation, and Y owns 50% of Z Corporation. Z owns 85% of W

Corporation and 90% of A Corporation. A owns 80% of B Corporation and 85% of C Corporation. P, X, Y, Z, W, A, B, and C Corporations are all members of a controlled group and may file a consolidated return.

11. T forms the X Corporation with an investment of $200,000 for which he receives $20,000 in stock and $180,000 in 8% interest-bearing bonds maturing in nine years. Several years later, T loans the corporation an additional $50,000 on open account. X Corporation subsequently becomes insolvent and is adjudged bankrupt. During the corporation's existence, T was paid an annual salary of $40,000. How might T's losses be treated for tax purposes?

12. X Corporation owns 100% of Y Corporation. In the current taxable year, X Corporation had taxable income from operations of $60,000 and incurred a § 1231 gain of $30,000 and a net long-term capital gain of $10,000. Y had taxable income from operations of $80,000 in the current taxable year plus a short-term capital loss of $5,000 and a § 1231 loss of $15,000.

(a) Compute tax liability for X and Y Corporations if a consolidated income tax return is filed.

(b) Compute tax liability for X Corporation and for Y Corporation if separate returns are filed. Assume X and Y Corporation have consented to an apportionment plan that would allocate the lowest corporate tax brackets to X Corporation, with Y Corporation taxed in the remaining brackets.

(c) Should X and Y Corporations file a consolidated return?

13. Assume the following transactions occurred in calendar year 19X6 for Corporations X, Y, and Z. X owns 100% of Y Corporation, and Y Corporation owns 100% of Z Corporation.

| Corporation | § 1231 Gain or Loss | Deferred Gain or Loss | Capital Gain or Loss Short-term | Long-term |
|---|---|---|---|---|
| X | $    3,000 | –0– | $ 5,000 | $ 10,000 |
| Y | 2,000 | $ 20,000 | 4,000 | (8,000) |
| Z | (9,000) | –0– | (6,000) | (12,000) |

Income (loss) from business operations was as follows:

| | | |
|---|---|---|
| X | $ 110,000 | |
| Y | 58,000 | (includes deferred gain of $20,000) |
| Z | (40,000) | |

Compute consolidated taxable income for X, Y, and Z Corporations.

14. T, an individual taxpayer who files a joint return with her spouse, acquired § 1244 stock at a cost of $200,000 two year ago. She sells the stock for $20,000 in the current tax year. How will the loss be treated for tax purposes?

15. T, an individual, transfers property with a basis of $40,000 and a fair market value of $20,000 to X Corporation in exchange for shares of §1244 stock. (Assume the transfer qualifies under § 351.)

(a) What is the basis of the stock to T?

(b) What is the basis of the stock for purposes of § 1244 to T?

(c) If T sells the stock for $10,000 two years later, how will the loss be treated for tax purposes?

16. A city donates land to X Corporation as an inducement for X to locate in the city. The land is worth $100,000. The city also donates $50,000 in cash to X.

    (a) What income, if any, must X recognize as a result of the transfer of land and cash to it by the city?

    (b) What basis will X have in the land?

    (c) If X purchases property with the $50,000 cash, what basis will X have in the property?

17. In 19X2, T, an individual, purchased § 38 property for $20,000. T claimed an investment tax credit of $2,000, based on a recovery period of five years. In 19X3, T transfers all of her assets (including the § 38 property) to X Corporation for all the stock in X. In 19X4, two years after T purchased the § 38 property, X Corporation sells the § 38 property. What, if any, tax results are there to T as a result of the sale by X Corporation?

18. T, an individual, transfers assets with a tax basis of $400,000 to a newly formed corporation for 100% of the stock. In the first year of operations, the corporation has net taxable income of $90,000. If the corporation distributes $74,000 to T, how will the distribution be treated for tax purposes—

    (a) To T?

    (b) To the corporation?

19. Assume in Problem 18 that T transferred the assets for stock in the amount of $200,000 and debt in the amount of $200,000, payable in equal annual installments of $50,000 plus interest at the rate of 12%. Assume again that the corporation has net taxable income of $90,000. If the corporation distributes $74,000 to T as payment on the debt, how will the distribution be treated for tax purposes—

    (a) To T?

    (b) To the corporation?

20. X Corporation is the common parent of a controlled group. X purchased stock of Y Corporation on December 20, 19X4. Y Corporation owned a capital asset with an adjusted basis of $50,000, fair market value of $10,000, on December 20, 19X4. The asset was sold in 19X6 for $5,000. The controlled group filed a consolidated return for 19X6. What amount of the loss on the sale of the asset can be used to offset capital gains on a consolidated basis?

21. Assume the asset in Problem 20 was not sold until 12 years after the purchase of the stock in Y Corporation. How much of the loss can be used to offset consolidated income?

## Research Problems

*Research Problem 1.* A cash basis partnership is incorporated. The newly formed corporation elects the cash method of accounting. The partnership transfers $30,000 of accounts receivable along with equipment, land, and cash. The corporation also agrees to pay accounts payable of the partnership in the amount of $40,000. The corporation files its return for its first year of operation and does not report the $30,000 received on accounts receivable of the partnership as income. It does deduct the $40,000 it paid on the partnership's accounts payable. The IRS disallows the deductions totaling $40,000 and increases the corporation's taxable income by $30,000, which represents the collection of partnership accounts receivable. What is the result?

*Research Problem 2.* A, a wealthy farmer, wants to take advantage of gift tax exclusions and give some of his property to his children. He decides to incorporate his farm operation in order to donate the property to his children more easily in the form of shares of stock. He transfers his property to a newly formed corporation for 100% of the stock. He gives 30% of the stock to his children immediately upon receipt. The IRS asserts, upon audit, that A is to be taxed on the initial transfer of property to the corporation because he failed to gain control of 80% of the stock. What is the result?

*Research Problem 3.* T incorporates her retail clothing business. She transfers all her business assets, total bases of $100,000, fair market value of $95,000, along with business liabilities of $10,000 and a personal note in the amount of $15,000 (representing money borrowed from the bank six months before incorporation to finance improvements on her home) to the corporation for 100% of its stock. What are the tax consequences of the transfer?

*Research Problem 4.* A and B, two doctors, form W, a professional association, to engage in the practice of medicine. W purchases X-ray equipment to be used in the business. A and B later form Y, an S corporation, to perform X-ray services for W. All the stock in Y is transferred by A and B to their children. W transferred the X-ray equipment to Y, with Y executing a note payable to W for the equipment. Y then hires an X-ray technician to perform the X-ray services for W. The X-ray equipment and the X-ray technician's office are located in the building owned by W. W does all the billing for X-ray services and then remits a percentage of its collections to Y. Y then pays the technician for his services, pays rent to W for use of the building, and pays W on the note it executed for payment of the X-ray equipment. During the tax year, Y had a profit that the children of A and B reported on their individual income tax returns. Upon audit, the IRS assessed a deficiency against W, asserting that all income and expenses of Y must be attributed to W, because Y was a sham corporation. The IRS also assessed a deficiency against A and B, stating that all distributions from Y to A's and B's children are constructive dividends to A and B from W Corporation. What are the results?

*Partial list of research aids:*

§ § 61 and 482.

*Edwin D. Davis,* 64 T.C. 1034 (1975).

*Engineering Sales, Inc. v. U. S.,* 75–1 USTC ¶ 9347, 35 AFTR2d 75–1122, 510 F.2d 565 (CA–5, 1975).

*Research Problem 5.* T owned and operated a farm producing cotton and grain sorghum. T transferred all the farm assets except the land and a portion of the equipment to a newly formed corporation for 100% of the stock. Before incorporation, T had paid farm expenses of $30,000 incurred in connection with planting the crops. T deducted the $30,000 on his individual income tax return; however, income from the crops was reported by the corporation, because the crops were harvested and sold after incorporation. Upon audit, the IRS disallowed the $30,000 deduction to T, reallocating it to the corporation under § 482. T challenges the reallocation. What is the result?

*Research Problem 6.* T purchased 100 shares of stock in X Corporation at a cost of $20,000, relying on a magazine advertisement regarding X Corporation and on information furnished by his friend, F, who owned some stock in X Corporation. T then purchased another 200 shares in X Corporation from F at a cost of $40,000. During the tax year, X Corporation became bankrupt, and T lost his entire investment. T deducted the $60,000 in full as a theft loss rather than reporting it as a capital loss, contending that the president of X Corporation and his friend, F, had defrauded him and other investors in that they knew the claims they made about X Corporation were erroneous. T, thus, claimed that the money was stolen from him. Is T correct in reporting the loss as a theft loss?

*Partial list of research aids:*

*Perry A. Nichols,* 43 T.C. 842 (1965).

*Research Problem 7.* T, a partner in a law firm, had represented a large corporation as its general counsel. This contact had brought large legal fees to the law firm. The corporation found itself in need of additional new financing and proposed a plan whereby substantial blocks of stock would be sold to a company that would loan additional funds to the corporation. T feared that the sale of the stock would cause a change in management of the corporation and that the legal work for the corporation would be transferred to another law firm. As a result, to protect his firm's retainer fee with the corporation, T purchased a large number of shares in the corporation for himself, paying a total of $100,000 for the shares. In 19X2, the corporation found itself in further financial difficulties, and the stock in the corporation became worthless. T deducted the $100,000 he paid for the then worthless stock in 19X2 as an ordinary loss. In 19X4, T's return was audited. The IRS contends that the $100,000 is a capital loss because the stock was a capital asset.

(a) What argument can be made in defense of T's position?

(b) How successful will it be?

*Partial list of research aids:*

*John A. Kuhnen,* 42 TCM 1438, T.C.Memo. 1981–600.

# Corporate Distributions Not in Complete Liquidation

# 4

## CHAPTER OBJECTIVES

—Distinguish between corporation distributions not in complete liquidation and those in complete liquidation of the corporation.
—Explain the concept of earnings and profits and its importance in measuring dividend income.
—Discuss the tax consequences of a property dividend to the recipient shareholder and to the corporation making the distribution.
—Differentiate between taxable and nontaxable stock dividends.
—Describe the various stock redemptions that qualify for sale or exchange treatment and thereby avoid dividend treatment.
—Review the tax rules governing the distribution of stock and securities of a controlled corporation.

A working knowledge of the rules pertaining to corporate distributions is essential for anyone dealing with the tax problems of corporations and their shareholders. The form of such distributions is important because it can produce varying tax results to shareholders. Dividends are taxed as ordinary income to the recipient shareholder (however, stock dividends may not be taxed at all); stock redemptions (qualifying under § 302) generally receive capital gain or loss treatment; corporate spin-offs or split-offs under § 355 do not represent a taxable event to the shareholders.

# DIVIDEND DISTRIBUTIONS

## TAXABLE DIVIDENDS—IN GENERAL

Distributions by a corporation to its shareholders are presumed to be dividends unless the parties can prove otherwise. Section 316 makes such distributions, whether in the form of cash or other property, ordinary dividend income to a shareholder to the extent of the distribution's pro rata share of earnings and profits (E & P) of the distributing corporation accumulated since February 28, 1913, or to the extent of corporate earnings and profits (E & P) for the current year.

Under § 301(c), the portion of a corporate distribution that is not taxed as a dividend (because of insufficient E & P) will be nontaxable to the extent of the shareholder's basis in the stock and will reduce that basis accordingly. The excess of the distribution over the shareholder's basis is treated as a capital gain if the stock is a capital asset.

> **Example 1.** As of January 1, 19X1, X Corporation (a calendar year taxpayer) has accumulated E & P of $30,000. In 19X1, the corporation distributes $40,000 to its *equal* shareholders, C and D. Only $30,000 of the $40,000 distribution is a taxable dividend. Suppose C's basis in his stock is $8,000, while D's basis is $4,000. Under these conditions, C must recognize a taxable dividend of $15,000 and reduce the basis of the stock from $8,000 to $3,000. The $20,000 D receives from X Corporation will be accounted for as follows: a taxable dividend of $15,000, a reduction in stock basis from $4,000 to zero, and a capital gain of $1,000.

Since earnings and profits (E & P) is the key to dividend treatment of corporate distributions, its importance cannot be emphasized enough.

## EARNINGS AND PROFITS (E & P)—§ 312

The term "earnings and profits" is not defined by the Code. Although § 312 lists certain transactions that affect E & P, it stops short of a complete definition. E & P does possess similarities to the accounting concept of retained earnings (i. e., earnings retained in the business); however, E & P and retained earnings are often not the same. For example, a stock dividend is treated for financial accounting purposes as a capitalization of retained earnings (i. e., it is debited to the retained earnings account and credited to a capital stock account), but it does not decrease E & P. Similarly, the elimination of a deficit in a "quasi-reorganization" increases retained earnings but does not increase E & P.

To fully understand the concept of E & P, it is helpful to keep several observations in mind. First, E & P might well be described as the factor that fixes the upper limit on the amount of dividend income shareholders would have to recognize as a result of a distribution by the corporation. In this sense, E & P represents the corporation's economic ability to pay a dividend without impairing its capital. Therefore, the effect of a specific transaction on the E & P account may be determined simply by considering whether or not the transaction increases or decreases the corporation's capacity to pay a dividend.

> **Example 2.** A corporation sells property (basis of $10,000) to its sole shareholder for $8,000. Due to § 267 (i. e., disallowance of losses on sales between related parties), the $2,000 loss cannot be deducted in arriving at the corporation's taxable income for the year. But since the overall economic effect of the transaction is a decrease in the corporation's assets by $2,000, the loss will reduce the current E & P for the year of sale.

> **Example 3.** A corporation pays a $10,000 premium on a keyman life insurance policy (i. e., the corporation is the owner and beneficiary of the policy) covering the life of its president. As a result of the payment, the cash surrender value of the policy is increased by $7,000. None of the $10,000 premium would be deductible for tax purposes, but current E & P would be reduced by $3,000.

> **Example 4.** A corporation collects $100,000 on a keyman life insurance policy. At the time the policy matured on the death of the insured-employee, it possessed a cash surrender value of $30,000. None of the $100,000 will be included in the corporation's taxable income [see § 101(a)], but $70,000 would be added to the current E & P account.

> **Example 5.** During 19X1, a corporation makes charitable contributions, $12,000 of which cannot be deducted in arriving at the taxable income for the year because of the 10% limitation of § 170(b)(2). However, pursuant to § 170(d)(2), the $12,000 is carried over to 19X2 and fully deducted in that year. The excess charitable contribution would reduce the corporation's current E & P for 19X1 by $12,000 and increase its current E & P for 19X2, when the deduction is allowed, by a like amount. The increase in E & P in 19X2 is necessitated by the fact

that the charitable contribution carryover reduces the taxable income for that year (the starting point for computing E & P) and already has been taken into account in determining the E & P for 19X1.

*Computation of E & P.* Barring certain important exceptions, E & P is increased by earnings for the taxable year computed in the same manner as is used in determining taxable income. If the corporation uses the cash method of accounting in computing taxable income, it must also use the cash method to determine the changes in E & P.[1]

E & P is increased for all items of income. Interest on municipal bonds, for example, though not taxed to the corporation, would increase the corporation's E & P.[2] Gains and losses from property transactions generally affect the determination of E & P only to the extent they are recognized for tax purposes (but refer to Example 2). Thus, a gain on an involuntary conversion not recognized by the corporation because the insurance proceeds are reinvested in property that is similar or related in service or use to the property converted (§ 1033) would not affect E & P. But the E & P account can be affected by both deductible and nondeductible items. Consequently, excess capital losses, expenses incurred to produce tax-exempt income, and Federal income taxes all reduce E & P, although such items do not enter into the calculation of taxable income.

The E & P account can be reduced only by cost depletion, even though the corporation may be using percentage (i. e., statutory) depletion for income tax purposes.[3] E & P cannot be reduced for accelerated depreciation for tax years beginning after June 30, 1972.[4] However, if a depreciation method such as units of production or machine hours is used, the adjustment to E & P can be determined on this basis.[5] If an accelerated method of computing depreciation, such as declining-balance or sum-of-the-years' digits, is used, the adjustment to E & P must be determined under the straight-line method. Later, when the asset is sold, the increase or decrease in E & P is computed by using the adjusted basis of the asset for E & P purposes.[6]

For cost recovery computed under ACRS and as to assets placed in service after 1980, a corporation must compute earnings and profits using the straight-line recovery method over recovery periods that are longer than those used under ACRS. The extended recovery periods that must be used to compute earnings and profits are 5 years for 3-year property, 12 years for 5-year property, 25 years for 10-year property, 35 years for 15-year public utility property, and 40 years for 18- and 19-year real property.[7]

---

1. Reg. § 1.312–6(a).
2. Reg. § 1.312–6(b).
3. Reg. § 1.312–6(c)(1).
4. § 312(k).
5. Reg. § 1.312–15(a)(2).
6. § 312(f)(1) and Reg. § 1.312–7(c)(2) (Ex. 3).
7. § 312(k)(3). This provision was amended by the Deficit Reduction Act of 1984 for real property placed in service in tax years beginning after September 30, 1984. The recovery period for real property was changed from 15 years to 18 years as to property placed in service after March 15, 1984, and on or before May 8, 1985, and to 19 years after May 8, 1985. The change was made to reflect more accurately the useful life of real property.

**Example 6.** On January 2, 1985, X Corporation purchased a machine for $30,000 that was then depreciated under ACRS. The asset was sold on January 2, 1987, for $27,000. For purposes of determining taxable income and E & P, cost recovery claimed on the machine and the machine's adjusted basis are summarized as follows:

|  | Cost Recovery | Adjusted Basis |
|---|---|---|
| Taxable Income | | |
| 1985: $30,000 × 15% | $ 4,500 | $ 25,500 |
| 1986: $30,000 × 22% | 6,600 | 18,900 |
| E & P | | |
| 1985: $30,000 ÷ 12-year recovery period ÷ ½ (half year for first year of service) | $ 1,250 | $ 28,750 |
| 1986: $30,000 ÷ 12-year recovery period | 2,500 | 26,250 |

Gain on the sale for purposes of determining taxable income and increase (decrease) in E & P is computed as follows:[8]

|  | Taxable Income | E & P |
|---|---|---|
| $27,000 − $18,900 (adjusted basis) | $ 8,100 | |
| $27,000 − $26,250 (adjusted basis) | | $ 750 |

The Deficit Reduction Act of 1984 made a number of changes in the computation of E & P so that E & P would more properly reflect a corporation's economic income. The changes will make it more difficult for corporations to make distributions to their shareholders that will represent a return of capital. The ultimate impact, therefore, will be to increase exposure to dividend income for shareholders.[9]

Pursuant to § 312(n)(4), E & P will be increased for gain realized by the distributing corporation (regardless of whether such gain is recognized) for a distribution of appreciated property as a property dividend or as a stock redemption.

A corporation's E & P for the year in which it sells property on the installment basis will be increased by the amount of any deferred gain. This is accomplished by treating all principal payments as having been received in the year of sale.[10]

---

**8.** E & P will be further reduced by income taxes on the sale plus the recapture of investment credit.

**9.** Accumulated E & P for taxable years of corporations beginning before September 30, 1984, will continue to be governed by prior rules. Thus, the changes will not affect the calculation of accumulated E & P up to the effective date of the 1984 Act.

**10.** Under prior law, gains from installment sales were not included in E & P until recognized for purposes of computing taxable income for the year. Thus, gain deferred for purposes of computing taxable income was also deferred for purposes of computing E & P. The new rule for computing E & P based on gains from installment sales applies to sales occurring after September 30, 1984, in taxable years ending after such date.

**Example 7.** In 1986, X Corporation, a calendar year taxpayer, sells unimproved real estate (basis of $100,000) for $500,000. Under the terms of the sale, X Corporation will receive two annual payments, beginning in 1987, of $250,000 each with interest of 12%. X Corporation does not elect out of the installment method. Although X Corporation's taxable income for 1986 will not reflect any of the gain from the sale, the corporation must increase E & P for 1986 by $400,000 (the deferred profit component).

A corporation that accounts for income and expenses attributable to a long-term contract on the completed contract method of accounting must use the percentage of completion basis in arriving at E & P.[11]

Intangible drilling costs [allowable as a deduction under § 263(c)] and mineral exploration and development costs [allowable under § 616(a) or § 617] are required to be capitalized for purposes of computing E & P. Once capitalized, these expenditures can be charged to E & P over a specified period: 60 months for intangible drilling costs and 120 months for mine exploration and development costs.[12]

*Summary of E & P Adjustments.* Recall that E & P serves as a measure of the earnings of the corporation that are treated as available for distribution as taxable dividends to the shareholders. Although E & P is initially increased by the corporation's taxable income, certain adjustments must be made to taxable income with respect to various transactions in determining the corporation's current E & P. Those adjustments are reviewed in the Concept Summary on the following page.

Other items that affect E & P, such as property dividends and stock redemptions, are covered later in the chapter and are not incorporated in the Concept Summary.

*The Source of the Distribution.* In determining the source of a dividend distribution, a dividend is deemed to have been made first from current E & P and then from E & P accumulated since February 28, 1913.[13]

**Example 8.** As of January 1, 19X1, Y Corporation has a deficit in accumulated E & P of $30,000. For tax year 19X1 it has current E & P of $10,000. In 19X1 the corporation distributed $5,000 to its shareholders. The $5,000 distribution will be treated as a taxable dividend, since it is deemed to have been made from current E & P. This will be the case even though Y Corporation will still have a deficit in its accumulated E & P at the end of 19X1.

---

11. Under prior law, income from long-term contracts accounted for under the completed contract method of accounting was included in E & P when such income was recognized for tax purposes, generally in the year in which the contract was completed. The new provision is applicable to contracts entered into after September 30, 1984, in taxable years ending after such date.

12. Under prior law, these costs were charged against E & P in the same manner as they were treated for purposes of computing taxable income. The new provision is applicable to amounts paid or accrued in taxable years beginning after September 30, 1984.

13. Reg. § 1.316–2(a).

━━━━━━━━━━━━━━━━ Concept Summary ━━━━━━━━━━━━━━━━

### E & P ADJUSTMENTS

| Nature of the Transaction | Effect on Taxable Income in Arriving at Current E & P |
|---|---|
| Tax-exempt income | Add |
| Federal income taxes | Subtract |
| Loss on sale between related parties | Subtract |
| Payment of premiums on life insurance policy on life of corporate officer | Subtract |
| Collection of proceeds of life insurance policy on life of corporate officer | Add |
| Excess charitable contribution (over 10% limitation) | Subtract |
| Deduction of excess charitable contribution in succeeding taxable year (increase E & P because deduction reduces taxable income while E & P was reduced in a prior year) | Add |
| Realized gain (not recognized) on an involuntary conversion | No effect |
| Percentage depletion (only cost depletion can reduce E & P) | Add |
| Accelerated depreciation (E & P is reduced only by straight-line, units of production or machine hours depreciation) | Add |
| Deferred gain on installment sale | |
| Before DRA of 1984 | No effect |
| After DRA of 1984 (all gain is added to E & P in year of sale) | Add |
| Long-term contract reported on completed contract method | |
| Before DRA of 1984 | No effect |
| After DRA of 1984 (use percentage of completion method) | Add |
| Intangible drilling costs deducted currently | |
| Before DRA of 1984 | No effect |
| After DRA of 1984 (reduce E & P in future years by amortizing costs over 60 months) | Add |
| Mining exploration and development costs | |
| Before DRA of 1984 | No effect |
| After DRA of 1984 (reduce E & P in future years by amortizing costs over 120 months) | Add |

If distributions made during the year exceed the current year's E & P, the portion of each distribution deemed to have been made from current E & P is that percentage that the total E & P for the year bears to the total distributions for that year.[14] This can make a difference if any of the shareholders sell their stock during the year and total distributions exceed current E & P.

**Example 9.** As of January 1, 19X1, Z Corporation has two *equal* shareholders, E and F, and accumulated E & P of $10,000. Current E & P for 19X1 amounts to $30,000. On August 1, 19X1, E sells all of his stock to G. Distributions during 19X1 are as follows: $40,000 to E and F ($20,000 to each) on July 1 and $40,000 to F and G ($20,000 to each)

---

14. Reg. § 1.316–2(b).

on December 1. The allocation result is summarized as follows:

|  | Source of Distribution | |
|---|---|---|
|  | Current E & P | Accumulated E & P |
| July 1 distribution ($40,000) | $ 15,000 | $ 10,000 |
| December 1 distribution ($40,000) | 15,000 | — |

The end result, in terms of tax consequences to the shareholders, is as follows:

|  | Shareholder | | |
|---|---|---|---|
|  | E | F | G |
| July distribution ($40,000) | | | |
| Dividend income— | | | |
| From current E & P ($15,000) | $ 7,500 | $ 7,500 | $ 0 |
| From accumulated E & P ($10,000) | 5,000 | 5,000 | 0 |
| Return of capital ($15,000) | 7,500 | 7,500 | 0 |
| December distribution ($40,000) | | | |
| Dividend income— | | | |
| From current E & P ($15,000) | 0 | 7,500 | 7,500 |
| From accumulated E & P ($0) | 0 | 0 | 0 |
| Return of capital ($25,000) | 0 | 12,500 | 12,500 |
| Total dividend income | $ 12,500 | $ 20,000 | $ 7,500 |
| Nontaxable return of capital (presuming sufficient basis in the stock investment) | $ 7,500 | $ 20,000 | $ 12,500 |

Note that the current E & P was allocated between both distributions, while the accumulated E & P was applied to and exhausted by the first distribution.[15]

*Distinguishing Between Current and Accumulated E & P.* Accumulated E & P can be defined as the total of all previous years' current E & P as computed on the first day of each taxable year in accordance with the tax law in effect during that year. The factors that affect the computation of the current E & P for any one year have been discussed previously. Why must the distinction be drawn between current and accumulated E & P when it is clear that distributions are taxable if and to the extent that current *and* accumulated E & P exist?

1. When there exists a deficit in accumulated E & P and a positive current E & P, distributions will be regarded as dividends to the extent of the current E & P. Refer to Example 8.

2. Current E & P is allocated on a pro rata basis to the distributions made during the year; accumulated E & P is applied (to the extent necessary) in chronological order beginning with the earliest distributions. Refer to Example 9.

---

**15.** Reg. § 1.316–2(c), Example.

3.  Unless and until the parties can show otherwise, it is presumed that any distribution is covered by current E & P.

4.  When there exists a deficit in current E & P (i. e., a current loss develops) and a positive balance in accumulated E & P, the accounts are netted at the date of distribution. If the resulting balance is zero or a deficit, the distribution is a return of capital. If a positive balance results, the distribution will represent a dividend to such extent. Any loss is allocated ratably during the year unless the parties can show otherwise.[16]

Distinctions 3 and 4 are illustrated as follows::

> **Example 10.** Q Corporation uses a fiscal year of July 1 through June 30 for tax purposes; T, Q Corporation's only shareholder, uses a calendar year. As of July 1, 19X4, Q Corporation had a zero balance in its accumulated E & P account. For fiscal year 19X4–19X5 the corporation suffered a $5,000 operating loss. On August 1, 19X4, Q Corporation distributes $10,000 to T. The distribution represents dividend income to T and must be reported as such when she files her income tax return for calendar year 19X4 on or before April 15, 19X5. Because T cannot prove until June 30, 19X5, that the corporation had a deficit for fiscal 19X4–19X5, she must assume the $10,000 distribution was fully covered by current E & P. When T learns of the deficit, she can, of course, file an amended return for 19X4 showing the $10,000 as a return of capital.

> **Example 11.** As of January 1, 19X5, R Corporation (a calendar year taxpayer) had accumulated E & P of $10,000. During 19X5 the corporation incurred a $15,000 net loss from operations that accrued ratably throughout the year. On July 1, 19X5, R Corporation distributes $6,000 in cash to H, its sole shareholder. The balance of both accumulated and current E & P as of July 1, 19X5, must be determined and netted because of the deficit in current E & P. The balance at this date would be $2,500 [$10,000 (accumulated E & P) − $7,500 (one-half of the current deficit of $15,000)]. Of the $6,000 distribution, $2,500 would be taxed as a dividend and $3,500 would represent a return of capital.

## PROPERTY DIVIDENDS

When a corporation distributes property rather than cash to a noncorporate shareholder, the amount distributed is measured by the fair market value of the property on the date of distribution. Section 301(c) is applicable to such distributions. Thus, the portion of the distribution covered by existing E & P is a dividend, and any excess is treated as a return of capital. If the fair market value of the property distributed exceeds the corporation's E & P and the shareholder's basis in the stock investment, a capital gain would result. If the shareholder is another corporation, the amount distributed is the lesser of (a) the fair market value of the property

---

16.   Reg. § 1.316–2(b).

or (b) the adjusted basis of the property in the hands of the distributing corporation immediately before the distribution, increased by the amount of gain recognized to the distributing corporation.[17] However, pursuant to § 311(d)(1), which requires recognition of gain to a corporation declaring and making a dividend distribution of appreciated property after June 13, 1984, the corporation must recognize such gain just as though the property had been sold at the time of the distribution. Consequently, as a practical matter, the amount distributed to a corporate shareholder would also be the fair market value of the property. For both noncorporate and corporate shareholders, the amount distributed is reduced by any liabilities to which the distributed property is subject immediately before and immediately after the distribution and by any liabilities of the corporation assumed by the shareholder in connection with the distribution.[18]

If the distribution is to a noncorporate shareholder, the basis assumed in the distributed property is the fair market value of the property on the date of the distribution. In the case of a corporate shareholder, the basis of the property received is the lesser of (a) the property's fair market value or (b) the adjusted basis of such property in the hands of the distributing corporation, increased by any gain recognized by the distributing corporation.[19] Effectively, then, because of § 311(d)(1), the basis to the corporate shareholder will also be the fair market value of the property on the date of distribution—the same as that for a noncorporate shareholder.

> **Example 12.** P Corporation has E & P of $60,000. It distributes land with a fair market value of $50,000 (adjusted basis of $30,000) to its sole shareholder, T. The land is subject to a liability of $10,000, which T assumes. T would have a taxable dividend of $40,000 [$50,000 (fair market value) − $10,000 (liability)]. The basis of the land to T is $50,000.

> **Example 13.** Ten percent of X Corporation is owned by Y Corporation. X Corporation has ample E & P to cover any distributions made during the year. One such distribution made to Y Corporation consists of a vacant lot with adjusted basis of $5,000 and a fair market value of $3,000. Y Corporation has a taxable dividend of $3,000, and its basis in the lot becomes $3,000.

Depreciated property is usually not a suitable subject for distribution as a property dividend. Note what has happened in Example 13. The loss of $2,000 (adjusted basis $5,000, fair market value $3,000), in effect, disappears. If, instead, the lot had first been sold and the $3,000 proceeds distributed, the loss would have been preserved for X Corporation.

## CONSTRUCTIVE DIVIDENDS

A distribution by a corporation to its shareholders can be treated as a dividend for Federal income tax purposes even though it is not formally

---

17. § 301(b).
18. § 301(b)(2).
19. § 301(d).

declared or designated as a dividend or issued pro rata to all share-holders.[20] Nor must the distribution satisfy the legal requirements of a dividend as set forth by applicable state law. The key factor determining dividend status is a measurable economic benefit conveyed to the share-holder. This benefit, often described as a constructive dividend, is distin-guishable from actual corporate distributions of cash and property in form only.

Constructive dividend situations usually arise in the context of the closely-held corporation. Here, the dealings between the parties are less structured, and frequently, formalities are not preserved. The constructive dividend serves as a substitute for actual distributions and is intended to accomplish some tax objective not available through the use of direct divi-dends. The shareholders may attempt to bail out corporate profits in a form deductible to the corporation (see, for example, items 6 through 9 below). Recall that dividend distributions do not provide the distributing corpora-tion with an income tax deduction, although they do reduce E & P. Alter-natively, the shareholders may be seeking benefits for themselves while avoiding the recognition of income (see, for example, items 1 through 6 below). Constructive dividends are, in reality, disguised dividends.

Do not conclude, however, that all constructive dividends are deliber-ate attempts to avoid actual and formal dividends. Often, constructive divi-dends are inadvertent; and consequently, a dividend result may come as a surprise to the parties (see, for example, item 1 below). For this reason, if for none other, an awareness of the various constructive dividend situa-tions is essential to protect the parties from unanticipated tax conse-quences. The types of constructive dividends most frequently encountered are summarized as follows:

1. Personal use by a shareholder of corporate-owned property (e. g., company-owned automobiles, airplanes, yachts, fishing camps, hunting lodges).[21] The measure of dividend income to the share-holder would be the fair rental value of the property for the period of its personal use.[22]

2. A bargain sale of corporate property to the shareholders. The mea-sure of the constructive dividend is the difference between amounts paid for the property and the property's fair market value on the date of sale.[23] Such questionable situations might be avoided by appraising the property on or about the date of sale. The appraised value becomes the price to be paid by the share-holders.

---

**20.**   See *Lincoln National Bank v. Burnet,* 3 USTC ¶ 1030, 12 AFTR 149, 63 F.2d 131 (CA–DC, 1933), and *Lengsfield v. Comm.,* 57–1 USTC ¶ 9437, 50 AFTR 1683, 241 F.2d 508 (CA–5, 1957).

**21.**   See, for example, *Ray R. Tanner,* 45 TCM 1419, T.C.Memo. 1983–230, and *Parker Tree Farms, Inc.,* 46 TCM 493, T.C.Memo. 1983–357.

**22.**   This result presumes the ownership of the property to be in the corporation. If not, and the ownership can be attributed to the shareholder, the measure of the constructive dividend would be the cost of the property. In this regard, bare legal title at the corporate level may not suffice. See, for example, *Raymond F. Daly,* 37 TCM 15, T.C.Memo. 1978–5.

**23.**   Reg. § 1.301–1(j). In *Claud E. Lynch,* 45 TCM 1125, T.C.Memo. 1983–173, the arm's length standard was not satisfied.

3. A bargain rental of corporate property to the shareholders. The measure of the constructive dividend would be the excess of the property's fair rental value over the rent actually paid. As in item 2, the importance of appraisal data to avoid any questionable situations should be readily apparent.

4. The satisfaction by the corporation of a shareholder's personal obligation to a third party.[24] The obligation involved need not be legally binding on the shareholder, but may, in fact, be a moral obligation.[25] Forgiveness by the corporation of shareholder indebtedness can create an identical problem.[26]

5. Advances by a corporation to a shareholder that are not bona fide (i. e., real) loans.[27] Whether an advance qualifies as a bona fide loan is a question of fact to be determined in light of the particular circumstances.

6. Interest-free (or below-market) loans by a corporation to a shareholder.[28]

7. Interest and principal payments made by a corporation where debt is reclassified as equity (refer to Chapter 3).[29]

8. Excessive rentals paid by a corporation for the use of shareholder property.[30]

9. Compensation paid to shareholder-employees that is deemed unreasonable.[31]

As noted in item 9, excessive salary payments to shareholder-employees are usually termed "unreasonable compensation." The excess over reasonable compensation is frequently deemed a constructive dividend and therefore not deductible by the corporation. In determining the reasonableness of salary payments, factors to be considered are the employee's qualifications; a comparison of salaries with dividend distributions; the prevailing rates of compensation for comparable positions in comparable business concerns; the nature and scope of the employee's work; the size and complexity of the business; a comparison of salaries paid to both gross

---

24. See, for example, *William D. Garner*, 35 TCM 1592, T.C.Memo. 1976–349.

25. *Montgomery Engineering Co. v. U. S.*, 64–2 USTC ¶ 9618, 13 AFTR2d 1747, 230 F.Supp. 838 (D.Ct.N.J., 1964); *aff'd.* in 65–1 USTC ¶ 9368, 15 AFTR2d 746, 344 F.2d 966 (CA–3, 1965).

26. Reg. § 1.301–1(m).

27. See, for example, *Richard B. Busch, Jr.*, 45 TCM 772, T.C.Memo. 1983–98.

28. See § 7872, added by the Deficit Reduction Act of 1984. These provisions generally apply to term loans made after June 6, 1984, and to demand loans outstanding on or after June 6, 1984. Demand loans outstanding on June 6, 1984, but paid off by 60 days after date of enactment (July 18, 1984) will not be subject to this rule.

29. See, for example, *Charles O. Finley & Co., Inc.*, 44 TCM 225, T.C.Memo. 1982–354; *Philip E. Bauer*, 45 TCM 910, T.C.Memo. 1983–120; *Towne Square, Inc.*, 45 TCM 478, T.C.Memo. 1983–10; and *Smithco Engineering, Inc.*, 47 TCM 966, T.C.Memo. 1984–43. However, compare *Electronic Modules Corporation v. U. S.*, 83–1 USTC ¶ 9113, 51 AFTR2d 83–614, 695 F.2d 1367 (CA-Fed. Cir., 1983), wherein the taxpayer was successful.

30. See, for example, *Scott C. Rethorst*, 31 TCM 1101, T.C.Memo. 1972–222; *aff'd.* in 75–1 USTC ¶ 9111, 35 AFTR2d 75–394, 509 F.2d 623 (CA–9, 1975).

31. See, for example, *Roth Properties Co. v. Comm.*, 75–1 USTC ¶ 9337, 35 AFTR2d 75–1093, 511 F.2d 527 (CA–6, 1975).

and net income; the salary policy of the taxpayer with respect to all employees; and, in the case of a small corporation with a limited number of officers, the amount of compensation paid the particular employee in previous years.[32]

Advances to shareholders that are not bona fide loans are also deemed to be constructive dividends as noted in item 5. Factors considered in determining whether an advance qualifies as a bona fide loan include whether the advance is on open account or is evidenced by a written instrument; whether the shareholder furnished collateral or other security for the advance; how long the advance has been outstanding; whether any payments have been made, excluding dividend sources; the shareholder's financial capability to repay the advance; the shareholder's use of the funds (e. g., payment of routine bills versus nonrecurring, extraordinary expenses); the regularity of such advances; and the dividend-paying history of the corporation.

If a corporation succeeds in getting past the hurdle of proving that an advance to a shareholder is a bona fide loan so that the advance is not deemed to be a constructive dividend as noted in item 5, the shareholder will still have a constructive dividend in the amount of the forgone interest as noted in item 6. However, the shareholder will also have a corresponding interest deduction. The problem relates to the corporation. The imputed interest element, which is a constructive dividend to the shareholder, is interest income to the corporation; however, because it is deemed to be a constructive dividend to the shareholder, there is no corresponding deduction to the corporation.

Constructive distributions possess the same tax attributes as actual distributions.[33] Thus, an individual shareholder would be entitled to the exclusion provided by § 116 and a corporate shareholder to the dividends received deduction of § 243. The constructive distribution would be a taxable dividend only to the extent of the corporation's current and accumulated E & P. As usual, the task of proving that the distribution constitutes a return of capital because of inadequate E & P rests with the taxpayer.[34]

## CONSEQUENCES TO THE CORPORATION OF A PROPERTY DIVIDEND

A property distribution by a corporation to its shareholders poses two questions. Does the distribution result in recognized gain to the corporation making the distribution? What effect will the distribution have on the corporation's E & P? The answers to these questions are discussed in the following subsections.

*Tax Effect on the Distributing Corporation.* Before the Deficit Reduction Act of 1984, no gain or loss was recognized to a corporation when it distributed appreciated or depreciated property as a dividend to its

---

32. *Mayson Manufacturing Co. v. Comm.,* 49–2 USTC ¶ 9467, 38 AFTR 1028, 178 F.2d 115 (CA–6, 1949).

33. *Simon v. Comm.,* 57–2 USTC ¶ 9989, 52 AFTR 698, 248 F.2d 869 (CA–8, 1957).

34. *DiZenzo v. Comm.,* 65–2 USTC ¶ 9518, 16 AFTR2d 5107, 348 F.2d 122 (CA–2, 1965).

shareholders.[35] Sections 311(b) and (c), 453(B), 1245(a), 1250(a), and 1252(a) provide exceptions to this rule.

The Deficit Reduction Act of 1984 amended § 311(d) so that § 311(d) is also now an exception to the nonrecognition provisions of § 311(a). Section 311(d) provides that gain (but not loss) will be recognized, with some exceptions, to the distributing corporation upon a distribution (nonliquidating) of appreciated property (other than a corporate obligation). Gain is recognized under § 311(d) as if the property had been sold by the corporation at its fair market value and the cash then distributed to the shareholders. However, the exceptions of § § 311(b) and (c) are to be applied before the provisions of § 311(d). A review of these modifications follows.

1. *LIFO Property.* Under § 311(b), a corporation distributing inventory determined under the LIFO method must recognize gain to the extent the cost of such goods, arrived at under the FIFO method, exceeds the cost of the goods using the LIFO method.

**Example 14.** Z Corporation distributes 100 units of product A to its shareholders. Product A is inventoried under the LIFO method and carries a cost basis of $1,300. Had the inventory been determined under the FIFO method, cost basis would have been $2,400. Under § 311(b), Z Corporation must recognize gain of $1,100 (i. e., $2,400 − $1,300) on the distribution.

2. *Property Subject to a Liability in Excess of Basis.* Section 311(c) requires the recognition of gain upon the distribution of property as a dividend if the property is subject to a liability that exceeds its adjusted basis. Gain is recognized to the extent of this excess. If the shareholder does not assume the liability, the gain recognized cannot be greater than the excess of the fair market value of the property over the property's adjusted basis.[36]

**Example 15.** X Corporation distributes to its sole shareholder and founder land used in the active conduct of its business with an adjusted basis of $10,000. Section 311(d) is not applicable for reasons discussed following Example 20. The land has a fair market value of $30,000 and is subject to a liability of $15,000. Under § 311(c), X Corporation has a gain of $5,000 on the distribution. If the fair market value of the land is only $13,000 and the shareholder does not assume the liability, the gain recognized would be limited to $3,000.

3. *Installment Obligations.* When a corporation distributes an installment obligation to its shareholders, gain is recognized to the distributing corporation under § 453B in an amount equal to the difference between the basis of the obligation and the fair market value on the date of distribution. The basis of an installment obligation is the face amount less the portion of the obligation that would be income if satisfied in full.

**Example 16.** R Corporation has installment notes with a face amount of $20,000 from the sale of property on the installment method

**35.** § 311(a).
**36.** § 311(c)(3) and Reg. § 1.311–1(d).

(gross profit percentage being 40%). The corporation distributes the notes as a dividend when the fair market value of the notes is $19,000. R Corporation must report gain in the amount of $7,000 computed as follows:

| | | |
|---|---:|---:|
| Fair market value of notes | | $ 19,000 |
| Face amount of notes | $ 20,000 | |
| Amount of income to be reported if the notes were satisfied in full (i.e., 40% × $20,000) | 8,000 | |
| Basis of notes | | 12,000 |
| Gain recognized on distribution | | $  7,000 |

4. *Depreciable Property.*  If depreciable property is distributed by a corporation to its shareholders, the distributing corporation must recognize gain to the extent of depreciation recapture under § § 1245 and 1250. Further, the distribution of farm property may cause the distributing corporation to recognize gain pursuant to § 1252.

**Example 17.**  V Corporation distributes to its shareholders depreciable real estate with an adjusted basis of $60,000 and a fair market value of $80,000. If the property had been sold by the corporation, gain of $20,000 would have resulted, $15,000 of which would have been recaptured under § 1250 and § 291(a) as ordinary income. V Corporation recognizes $15,000 of ordinary income on the distribution of the depreciable property.

Recapture occurs if property on which an investment credit has been taken is subsequently distributed as a dividend before the useful life chosen for investment tax credit purposes has expired.[37]

**Example 18.**  On January 10, 1986, W Corporation distributes to its sole shareholder machinery (basis of $6,000 and fair market value of $5,000). The property was acquired four years ago (i. e., in 1982) at a cost of $12,000. In the year of acquisition, the corporation claimed an investment tax credit of $1,200 (i. e., 10% × $12,000) based on a class life of five years. Code § 47 will require W Corporation to recapture $240 of the credit previously taken as additional tax liability.[38] Section 1245 is not applicable in this case, because recapture of depreciation occurs only if there is a realized *gain* on the disposition of the property.

5. *Appreciated Property.*  The Deficit Reduction Act of 1984 amended § 311(d)(1) so that, with a few exceptions, gain will be recognized to a distributing corporation should it distribute appreciated property either as

---

**37.**  § 47(a)(1).

**38.**  Property with a five-year recovery period under ACRS is allowed a 10% investment credit; however, the credit is recaptured in the amount of 20% for each year held less than the five years. Here, because the asset was held for four years, the recapture is only 20%, or $240. Each full year an asset is held before disposition reduces recapture by 2%; hence, for an asset held four years, the correct investment credit should have been only 8%.

a dividend or as a stock redemption. (Losses are not recognized.) Before the 1984 Act, as a general rule, gains were not recognized on dividend distributions. However, Congress believed that there is no compelling reason why a distribution of a property dividend should permit a corporation to escape taxation on any appreciated property. Under present § 311(d)(1), a corporation will generally recognize gain on appreciated property distributed as a dividend just as though the corporation had sold the property for its fair market value on the date of the distribution and had thereafter distributed the cash as a dividend.[39]

Sections 311(b) and 311(c) are applied before § 311(d).[40] Consequently, if a corporation distributes LIFO inventory, § 311(b) would be applied first and then § 311(d).

**Example 19.** X corporation distributes LIFO inventory to an individual shareholder. The inventory has a LIFO basis of $10,000 but a FIFO basis of $12,500. The fair market value of the property is $12,000. Under § 311(b), X must recognize gain of $2,500 [§ 311(d) would produce a gain of only $2,000].

**Example 20.** Assume the same facts as in Example 19, except that the inventory has a fair market value of $14,000. In this case, § 311(d) would cause a gain to the corporation of $4,000.

Gain is not recognized under § 311(d) for property dividends distributed to noncorporate shareholders to the extent the distribution is a qualified dividend on qualified stock. This is a dividend distribution to a noncorporate shareholder who has held stock representing at least 10 percent in value of the corporation's outstanding stock for at least five years preceding the date of distribution or has held the stock for the period during which the distributing corporation has been in existence, if that is less than five years.[41] The property dividend cannot be inventory property or receivables and must have been used by the corporation in the active conduct of its business.[42]

6. *Assignment of Income Doctrine.* An additional exception to the provisions of § 311(a) exists that can cause gain to the distributing corporation. This exception, created by the courts, is based on the assignment of income doctrine.

The Regulations state that proceeds of the sale of property made by a shareholder after receiving such property from a corporation ". . . may be imputed to the corporation if, in substance, the corporation made the sale."[43] In *U. S. v. Lynch,* the Court held that a distribution of corporate inventory with the expectation of immediate sale by the distributee-shareholders caused the sale and consequent income to be attributed to the cor-

---

**39.** The new provisions apply to distributions declared after June 13, 1984.
**40.** § 311(d)(1)(B).
**41.** § 311(e)(1). The constructive ownership rules of § 318 apply in determining stock ownership, with the addition of brothers and sisters and their spouses.
**42.** § 311(e)(3).
**43.** Reg. § 1.311–1(a).

poration.[44] However, in *Hines v. U. S.,* the Fifth Court of Appeals held there was no imputation to the corporation on a sale by its shareholders because the corporation did not negotiate the sale or participate therein after the distribution.[45] The Court said, ". . . only if the corporation in fact participated in the sale transaction, by negotiation, prior agreement, post-distribution activities, or participated in any other manner, would the corporation be charged with earning the income."

Consequently, property distributed by a corporation, which in effect represents an anticipatory assignment of income, will trigger additional tax liability to the corporation.[46] In *Comm. v. First State Bank of Stratford,*[47] a bank declared a dividend in kind consisting of certain notes that had been charged off as wholly worthless and deducted as bad debts by the corporation. The shareholders collected a number of notes. The Court held that the subsequent collection of the notes must be treated as realization of income by the bank under the anticipatory assignment of income rule. Income was recognized by the corporation when the notes were collected and not upon their distribution.

*Effect of Corporate Distributions on E & P.* In the event of a corporate distribution, the E & P account is reduced by the amount of money distributed or by the adjusted basis of property distributed less the amount of any liability to which the property distributed was subject or which the shareholder assumed with respect to the property distribution.[48] As noted previously, E & P is increased by gain realized, regardless of whether gain is recognized, for distributions of appreciated property as a property dividend or as a stock redemption.

> **Example 21.** M Corporation distributes property (not inventory or receivables) to a 5% shareholder, T (an individual). The property had a fair market value of $20,000 and an adjusted basis of $15,000. M Corporation would have a gain under § 311(d) of $5,000, which would be added to its E & P. The basis of the property would then be $20,000, and M's E & P would be reduced by $20,000. T would have dividend income of $20,000. [If T owned more than 10% of the value of M stock for at least five years (or during the period of M's existence, if that is less than five years) and if the property was used in the active conduct of M's business, M Corporation would not have income upon the distribution. Although M's E & P account would be increased by $5,000, the E & P account would be reduced by only $15,000 (the adjusted basis of the property). T would still report dividend income of $20,000.]

> **Example 22.** Assume the same facts as in Example 21 with these exceptions: The fair market value of the property is $15,000, and the adjusted basis of the property in the hands of M Corporation is $20,000. Because losses are not recognized under § 311(d), the E & P

---

**44.**    51–2 USTC ¶ 9507, 41 AFTR 407, 192 F.2d 718 (CA–9, 1951), *cert. den.,* 72 S.Ct. 770 (USSC, 1952). See also *Bush Brothers & Co.,* 73 T.C. 424 (1979); *aff'd* in 82–1 USTC ¶ 9129, 49 AFTR2d 82–481, 668 F.2d 252 (CA–6, 1982).

**45.**    73–1 USTC ¶ 9403, 31 AFTR2d 73–1215, 477 F.2d 1063 (CA–5, 1973).

**46.**    Reg. § 1.311–1(a).

**47.**    48–2 USTC ¶ 9317, 36 AFTR 1183, 168 F.2d 1004 (CA–5, 1948).

**48.**    § § 312(a) and (c).

account will be reduced by $20,000, and T must report dividend income of $15,000.

**Example 23.** Assume the same facts as in Example 22 with this addition: the property is subject to a liability of $5,000. E & P would now be reduced by $15,000 [$20,000 (adjusted basis) − $5,000 (mortgage)].

Under no circumstances can a distribution, whether cash or property, either generate or add to a deficit in E & P. Deficits can arise only through corporate losses.

## STOCK DIVIDENDS AND STOCK RIGHTS

*Stock Dividends—§ 305.* Because no change occurs in a shareholder's proportionate interest in a corporation upon receipt of a stock dividend, such distributions were initially accorded tax-free treatment.[49] Subsequently, the test for taxability of a stock dividend was based on change in the proportionate interest of a shareholder following the distribution. The 1954 Code simply stated that stock dividends would not be taxable unless (a) the shareholder could elect to receive either stock or property or (b) the stock dividends were in discharge of preference dividends. In response, corporations devised various methods to distribute stock dividends that would change the shareholder's interest and still qualify as tax-free.[50]

The current provisions of § 305 are based on the proportionate interest concept. To summarize the provisions of § 305, stock dividends are not taxable if they are pro rata distributions of stock, or stock rights, on common stock. Section 305(b) contains five exceptions to the general rule that stock dividends are nontaxable: (1) distributions payable either in stock or property; (2) distributions resulting in the receipt of the property by some shareholders and an increase in the proportionate interest of other shareholders in the assets or E & P of the distributing corporation; (3) distributions that result in the receipt of preferred stock by some common shareholders and the receipt of common stock by other shareholders; (4) distributions on preferred stock other than an increase in the conversion ratio of convertible preferred stock made solely to take account of a stock dividend or stock split with respect to stock into which the preferred is convertible; and (5) distributions of convertible preferred stock, unless it can be shown that the distribution will not result in a disproportionate distribution. Because holders of convertible securities are considered shareholders, payment of interest on convertible debentures will cause stock dividends paid on common stock to be taxable unless an adjustment is made on the conversion ratio or conversion price to reflect the stock dividend.[51] Note that the exceptions to nontaxability of stock dividends deal with various disproportionate distribution situations. If stock dividends are not taxable, there is no reduction in the corporation's E & P.[52] If

---

**49.** See *Eisner v. Macomber,* 1 USTC ¶ 32, 3 AFTR 3020, 40 S.Ct. 189 (USSC, 1920).

**50.** See "Stock Dividends," Senate Report 91–552, 1969–3 C.B. 519.

**51.** See Reg. § 1.305–3(d) for illustrations on how to compute required adjustments on conversion ratios or prices.

**52.** § 312(d)(1).

the stock dividends are taxable, the distribution is treated by the distributing corporation in the same manner as any other taxable property dividend.

If stock dividends are taxable, basis to the shareholder-distributee is fair market value, and the holding period starts on the date of receipt. If a stock dividend is not taxable, § 307 requires that the basis of the stock on which the dividend is distributed be reallocated. If the dividend shares are identical to these formerly held shares, basis in the old stock is reallocated by dividing the taxpayer's cost in the old stock by the total number of shares. If the dividend stock is not identical to the underlying shares (a stock dividend of preferred on common, for example), basis is determined by allocating cost of the formerly held shares between the old and new stock according to the fair market value of each. Holding period will include the holding period of the formerly held stock.[53]

> **Example 24.** A, an individual, bought 1,000 shares of stock two years ago for $10,000. In the current tax year, A received 10 shares of common stock as a nontaxable stock dividend. A's basis of $10,000 would be divided by 1,010; consequently, each share of stock would have a basis of $9.90 instead of the pre-dividend $10 basis.

> **Example 25.** Assume A received, instead, a nontaxable preferred stock dividend of 100 shares. The preferred stock has a fair market value of $1,000, and the common stock, on which the preferred is distributed, has a fair market value of $19,000. After the receipt of the stock dividend, the basis of the common stock is $9,500, and the basis of the preferred is $500, computed as follows:

| | |
|---|---:|
| Fair market value of common | $19,000 |
| Fair market value of preferred | 1,000 |
| | $20,000 |
| Basis of common: 19/20 × $10,000 | $ 9,500 |
| Basis of preferred: 1/20 × $10,000 | $   500 |

*Exception as to Public Utility Stock.* Section 305(e) provided that certain qualifying distributions of dividends in public utility stock made after December 31, 1981, and before January 1, 1986, would be excluded from gross income up to $750 per year ($1,500 for married filing jointly). The purpose of this exception was to encourage reinvesting of dividends in public utility stock. However, because § 305(e) is inapplicable to distributions made after December 31, 1985, current distribution of such dividends will be taxed under the general provisions of § 305.

*Stock Rights.* The rules for determining taxability of stock rights are identical to those determining taxability of stock dividends. If the rights are taxable, the recipient has income to the extent of the fair market value of the rights. The fair market value then becomes the shareholder-distributee's basis in the rights.[54] If the rights are exercised, the holding period

---

53. § 1223(5).
54. Reg. § 1.305–1(b).

for the new stock is the date the rights (whether taxable or nontaxable) are exercised. The basis of the new stock is the basis of the rights plus the amount of any other consideration given.

If stock rights are not taxable and the value of the rights is less than 15 percent of the value of the old stock, the basis of the rights is zero unless the shareholder elects to have some of the basis in the formerly held stock allocated to the rights.[55] If the fair market value of the rights is 15 percent of the value of the old stock and the rights are exercised or sold, the shareholder must allocate some of the basis in the formerly held stock to the rights. When the value is less than 15 percent of the value of the stock and the shareholder makes an election to allocate basis to the rights, such an election is made in the form of a statement attached to the shareholder's return for the year in which the rights are received.[56]

> **Example 26.** A corporation with common stock outstanding declares a nontaxable dividend payable in rights to subscribe to common stock. Each right entitles the holder to purchase one share of stock for $90. One right is issued for every two shares of stock owned. T owns 400 shares of stock purchased two years ago for $15,000. At the time of the distribution of the rights, the market value of the common stock is $100 per share and the market value of the rights is $8 per right. T receives 200 rights. He exercises 100 rights and sells the remaining 100 rights three months later for $9 per right. T need not allocate the cost of the original stock to the rights, because the value of the rights is less than 15% of the value of the stock ($1,600 ÷ $40,000 = 4%).
>
> If T does not allocate his original stock basis to the rights, his basis in the new stock will be $9,000 ($90 × 100). Sale of the rights would produce long-term capital gain of $900 ($9 × 100). The holding period of the rights starts with the date the original 400 shares of stock were acquired. The holding period of the new stock begins on the date the stock was purchased.
>
> If T elects to allocate basis to the rights, his basis in the rights would be $577, computed as follows: $1,600 (value of rights) ÷ $41,600 (value of rights and stock) × $15,000 = $577. His basis in the stock would be $14,423 [($40,000 ÷ $41,600) × $15,000 = $14,423]. When he exercises the rights, his basis in the new stock would be $9,288.50 [$9,000 (cost) + $288.50 (basis in 100 rights)]. Sale of the rights would produce a long-term capital gain of $611.50 [$900 (selling price) − $288.50 (basis in the remaining 100 rights)].

## STOCK REDEMPTIONS— EXCHANGE TREATMENT

To have a long-term capital gain, a capital asset held for more than six months must be sold or *exchanged* for consideration in excess of basis. Section 317 defines a stock redemption as an *exchange* between a corpora-

---

**55.** § 307(b)(1).
**56.** Reg. § 1.307-2.

tion and its shareholder of that corporation's stock for property. Putting these two rules together provides a shareholder with an opportunity to obtain favorable long-term capital gain treatment from a corporate distribution. The problem, however, comes with structuring the distribution so that it qualifies under one of the types of stock redemptions stipulated in the Code as being entitled to *exchange* treatment. Failure to qualify means the distribution will be treated as a dividend with ordinary income consequences. In this regard, it does not matter whether the parties intended a stock redemption to take place or whether the transfer is considered a stock redemption under applicable state law.

## HISTORICAL BACKGROUND AND OVERVIEW

Before the 1954 Code, stock redemptions that constituted ordinary taxable dividends were distinguished from those qualifying for capital gain treatment by the so-called dividend equivalency rule. When a redemption was essentially equivalent to a dividend, it would not qualify as a stock redemption; the entire amount received by the shareholder would be subject to taxation as ordinary income to the extent of the corporation's E & P.

> **Example 27.** A, an individual, owns 100% of the stock of X Corporation. X Corporation has E & P of $50,000. A sells one-half of his shares to the corporation for $50,000. His basis in one-half of the stock is $10,000, and he has held the stock for five years. If the sale of the stock to X Corporation qualified as a stock redemption, A would have a long-term capital gain of $40,000. However, such a distribution is essentially equivalent to a dividend. A's percentage of ownership of the corporation has not changed. Consequently, he is deemed to have received a taxable dividend of $50,000.

Under the 1954 Code, the following major types of stock redemptions qualify for exchange treatment and will, as a result, avoid dividend income consequences:

—Distributions not essentially equivalent to a dividend [§ 302(b)(1)].

—Distributions substantially disproportionate in terms of shareholder effect [§ 302(b)(2)].

—Distributions in complete termination of a shareholder's interest [§ 302(b)(3)].

—Distributions in partial liquidation of a corporation, but only to a noncorporate shareholder when (a) the distribution is not essentially equivalent to a dividend or (b) an active business is terminated [§ 302(b)(4)].

—Distributions to pay a shareholder's death taxes [§ 303].

## STOCK ATTRIBUTION RULES

To deter the use of certain qualifying stock redemptions as a means of achieving capital gains in related-party situations, § 318 imposes constructive ownership of stock (i. e., stock attribution) rules. In testing for a stock redemption, therefore, a shareholder may have to take into account the stock owned by others who fall within the definition of related parties. Related parties include immediate family, specifically, spouses, children, grandchildren, and parents. Attribution also takes place *from* and *to* partnerships, estates, trusts, and corporations (50 percent or more ownership required in the case of corporations).

> **Example 28.** T, an individual, owns 30% of the stock in X Corporation, the other 70% being held by her children. For purposes of § 318, T is treated as owning 100% of the stock in X Corporation. She owns 30% directly and, because of the family attribution rules, 70% indirectly.

> **Example 29.** C, an individual, owns 50% of the stock in Y Corporation. The other 50% is owned by a partnership in which C has a 20% interest. C is deemed to own 60% of Y Corporation: 50% directly and, because of the partnership interest, 10% indirectly.

The stock attribution rules of § 318 do not apply to stock redemptions to pay death taxes [§ 303]. Under certain conditions, the *family* attribution rules (refer to Example 28) do not apply to stock redemptions in complete termination of a shareholder's interest [§ 302(b)(3)].

## NOT ESSENTIALLY EQUIVALENT TO A DIVIDEND STOCK REDEMPTIONS—§ 302(b)(1)

Section 302(b)(1) provides that a redemption will be treated as a distribution in part or full payment in exchange for the stock if it is "not essentially equivalent to a dividend." A distribution is not essentially equivalent to a dividend when there has been a meaningful reduction of the shareholder's proportionate interest in the redeeming corporation. The facts and circumstances of each case will determine whether a distribution in redemption of stock is essentially equivalent to a dividend within the meaning of § 302(b)(1).[57] Courts have considered a decrease in the redeeming shareholder's voting control to be the most significant indicator of a meaningful reduction.[58] Other factors considered are reductions in the rights of redeeming shareholders to share in corporate earnings or to receive corporate assets upon liquidation.[59]

> **Example 30.** A, an individual, owns 58% of the common stock of Y Corporation. After a redemption of part of A's stock, A owns 51% of the stock of Y Corporation. A would continue to have dominant voting rights in Y; thus, the redemption would be treated as "essentially equivalent to a dividend," and A would have ordinary income on the entire amount of the distribution.

> **Example 31.** X Corporation redeems 2% of the stock of B, a minority shareholder. Before the redemption, B owned 10% of X Corporation. In this case, the redemption may qualify as "not essentially equivalent to a dividend." B experienced a reduction in her voting rights, her right

---

**57.** Reg. § 1.302–2(b). See *Mary G. Roebling,* 77 T.C. 30 (1981).
**58.** See *Jack Paparo,* 71 T.C. 692 (1979), and *Blanche S. Benjamin,* 66 T.C. 1084 (1976).
**59.** See *Grabowski Trust,* 58 T.C. 650 (1972).

to participate in current earnings and accumulated surplus, and her right to share in net assets upon liquidation.

There are few objective tests to determine when a redemption is or is not essentially equivalent to a dividend. This provision was specifically added to provide for redemptions of preferred stock.[60] Often, such stock is called in by the corporation without the shareholders exercising any control over the redemption. Some courts interpreted § 302(b)(1) to mean a redemption would be granted capital gain treatment if there was a business purpose for the redemption and there was no tax avoidance scheme to bail out dividends at favorable tax rates.[61] The real question was whether the stock attribution rules of § 318(a) applied to this provision. However, some courts appeared to be less concerned with the application of § 318(a) and more concerned with the presence of a business purpose for the redemption.

The question of the applicability of § 318 was presumably settled by the Supreme Court in *U. S. v. Davis*.[62] In *Davis*, taxpayer and his wife owned one-half of the common stock of a corporation. Taxpayer made an additional contribution of $25,000 for 1,000 shares of preferred stock, purchasing the preferred stock to increase the company's working capital so that it might qualify for a government loan. It was understood that the corporation would redeem the preferred stock after the loan was repaid. In the interim, taxpayer acquired the remaining common stock in the corporation and transferred it to his son and daughter. After the loan was fully repaid, the corporation redeemed taxpayer's preferred stock for $25,000. Taxpayer did not report the $25,000 on his personal income tax return, concluding it was a stock redemption under § 302 and did not exceed his stock basis. The IRS contended that the redemption was essentially equivalent to a dividend and was taxable as ordinary income under §§ 301 and 316. The Court of Appeals held that the redemption was not essentially equivalent to a dividend within the meaning of § 302(b)(1) because the redemption was a final step in a course of action that had a legitimate business purpose. The Supreme Court reversed the Court of Appeals, noting that under § 318(a) taxpayer constructively owned all the stock of the corporation. The Court further stated that § 318(a) applies to § 302(b)(1); consequently, taxpayer was deemed the owner of all the common stock either directly or indirectly. The Court concluded that a sole shareholder who causes part of his or her shares to be redeemed by the corporation can never qualify the redemption for capital gain treatment under § 302(b)(1). Such a redemption is always essentially equivalent to a dividend. The Court stated that to qualify for a stock redemption under § 302(b)(1), there must be ". . . a meaningful reduction of the shareholder's proportionate interest in the corporation." Two judges dissented, stating the majority opinion ". . . effectively cancels section 302(b)(1) from the Code."

In a more recent decision, *Davis* was limited in its application. In *Robin Haft Trust,* the First Court of Appeals refused to apply § 318(a) to

---

**60.**   See S.Rept.No.1622, 83d Cong., 2d Sess., at 44.

**61.**   See, for example, *Kerr v. Comm.*, 64–1 USTC ¶ 9186, 13 AFTR2d 386, 326 F.2d 225 (CA–9, 1964).

**62.**   70–1 USTC ¶ 9289, 25 AFTR2d 70–827, 90 S.Ct. 1041 (USSC, 1970).

deny capital gain treatment to a stock redemption when there was family discord.[63] The Court's contention was that the language "meaningful reduction" of a shareholder's proportionate interest in a corporation ". . . certainly seems to permit, if it does not mandate, an examination of the facts and circumstances to determine the effect of the transaction transcending a mere mechanical application of the attribution rules." The IRS has announced that it will not follow the *Robin Haft Trust* decision.[64] The Fifth Court of Appeals is in accord with the position of the IRS. In *David Metzger Trust*,[65] the Court stated that the IRS is correct in refusing to take family discord into account in applying the attribution rules.[66]

If a redemption is treated as an ordinary dividend, the shareholder's basis in the stock redeemed attaches to the remaining stock. According to the Regulations, this basis would attach to other stock held by the taxpayer (or to stock he or she owns constructively).[67]

> **Example 32.** Husband and wife each own 50 shares in X Corporation, representing 100% of the stock of X. All the stock was purchased for $50,000. Husband transfers one-half of his stock to his wife. Later, the corporation redeems husband's remaining one-half. Assuming the rules governing the complete termination of a shareholder's interest under § 302(b)(3) would not apply, such a redemption would be treated as a taxable dividend. Husband's basis in the remaining stock, $12,500, would attach to his wife's stock so that she would have a basis of $50,000 in the 75 shares she currently owns in X Corporation.

## SUBSTANTIALLY DISPROPORTIONATE REDEMPTIONS—§ 302(b)(2)

A redemption of stock qualifies for capital gain treatment under § 302(b)(2) if two conditions are met. (1) The distribution must be substantially disproportionate. To be substantially disproportionate, the shareholder must own, after the distribution, less than 80 percent of total interest in the corporation prior to his or her redemption. For example, if a shareholder has a 60 percent ownership in a corporation that redeems part of the stock, the redemption is substantially disproportionate only if the percentage of ownership after the redemption is less than 48 percent (80 percent of 60 percent). (2) The shareholder must own, after the distribution, less than 50 percent of the total combined voting power of all classes of stock entitled to vote.

In determining the percentage of ownership of the shareholder, it must be remembered that the constructive ownership rules of § 318(a) apply.

---

**63.** 75-1 USTC ¶ 9209, 35 AFTR2d 75-650, 510 F.2d 43 (CA-1, 1975).

**64.** See Rev.Rul. 80-26, 1980-1 C.B. 67.

**65.** 82-2 USTC ¶ 9718, 51 AFTR2d 83-376, 693 F.2d 459 (CA-5, 1982).

**66.** For other recent applications of the meaningful reduction test, see Rev.Rul. 75-502, 1975-2 C.B. 111; Rev.Rul. 75-512, 1975-2 C.B. 112; Rev.Rul. 76-385, 1976-2 C.B. 92; Rev.Rul. 77-218, 1977-1 C.B. 81; Rev.Rul. 78-401, 1978-2 C.B. 127; and Rev.Rul. 81-289, 1981-2 C.B. 82.

**67.** Reg. § 1.302-2(c).

**Example 33.** A, B, and C, unrelated individuals, own 30 shares, 30 shares, and 40 shares, respectively, in X Corporation. X Corporation has E & P of $200,000. The corporation redeems 20 shares of C's stock for $30,000. C paid $200 a share for the stock two years ago. After the redemption, C has a 25% interest in the corporation [20 shares of a total of 80 shares (100 − 20)]. This represents less than 80% of his original ownership (40% × 80% = 32%) and less than 50% of the total voting power. Consequently, the distribution qualifies as a stock redemption. C has a long-term capital gain of $26,000 [$30,000 − $4,000 (20 shares × $200)].

**Example 34.** Given the situation in Example 33, assume, in addition, that B and C are father and son. The redemption described previously would not qualify for capital gain treatment. C is deemed to own the stock of B so that after the redemption, he would have 50 shares of a total of 80 shares, more than 50% ownership. He would also fail the 80% test. Before the redemption, C is deemed a 70% owner (40 shares owned by him and 30 shares owned by B, his son). After the redemption, he is deemed a 62.5% owner (20 shares owned directly by him and 30 shares owned by B from a total of 80 shares). C has a taxable dividend of $30,000.

## COMPLETE TERMINATION OF A SHAREHOLDER'S INTEREST REDEMPTIONS—§ 302(b)(3)

If a shareholder terminates his or her entire stock ownership in a corporation through a stock redemption, the redemption will qualify for capital gain treatment. Such a complete termination would obviously meet the substantially disproportionate rules of § 302(b)(2). The difference in the two provisions is that the constructive ownership rules of § 318(a)(1) do not apply to § 302(b)(3) if (1) the former shareholder has no interest, other than that of a creditor, in the corporation after the redemption (including an interest as an officer, director, or employee) for at least 10 years, and (2) the former shareholder files an agreement to notify the IRS of any acquisition within the 10-year period and to retain all necessary records pertaining to the redemption during this time period. A shareholder can reacquire an interest in the corporation by bequest or inheritance, but in no other manner. The required agreement should be in the form of a separate statement signed by the shareholder and attached to the return for the year in which the redemption occurred. The agreement should recite that the shareholder agrees to notify the appropriate District Director within 30 days of a reacquisition of an interest in the corporation occurring within 10 years from the redemption.

A redeemed estate or trust may waive family attribution if, after the redemption, neither the entity nor its beneficiaries hold an interest in the corporation or acquire such an interest within the 10-year period and all parties involved file an agreement to be jointly and severally liable for any taxes due if a reacquisition occurs.[68]

---

**68.** § 302(c)(2)(C).

**Example 35.** In 1986, D, a 40% shareholder in X Corporation, dies; his will designates W as his sole beneficiary. The remaining interest in X Corporation is held as follows: 35% by X (D's son) and 25% by E (a key employee). After the executor of D's estate redeems all that is permissible under § 303 [i. e., the sum total of death taxes and administrative expenses (see discussion on next page)], a 10% interest remains in the estate. The remaining 10% interest can be redeemed under § 302(b)(3) if both the entity (D's estate) and the beneficiary (W) terminate all interest in the corporation and do not reacquire an interest within a 10-year period, and if the parties (D's estate and W) agree to be jointly and severally liable for any taxes due in the event of a reacquisition.

## REDEMPTIONS IN PARTIAL LIQUIDATIONS—§ 302(b)(4)

Recall that sale or exchange treatment for each of the previously discussed types of stock redemptions [§ § 302(b)(1), (2), and (3)] was dependent on shareholder—not corporate—considerations. The application of § 302(b)(4) is determined by corporate conditions.

Section 302(b)(4) permits sale or exchange treatment as to noncorporate shareholders[69] for partial liquidations, defined in § 302(e) to include either of the following:

—A distribution not essentially equivalent to a dividend.

—A distribution pursuant to the termination of an active business.

To qualify as a partial liquidation, however, any distributions must be made within the taxable year in which the plan is adopted or within the succeeding taxable year. The not essentially equivalent to a dividend approach is a carryover from prior § 346(a)(2) and is to be determined at the corporate level. Presumably, it encompasses prior case law, which basically required a genuine contraction of the business of the corporation.[70] In one of these cases, *Joseph W. Imler,* a corporation owned five buildings including one with seven stories.[71] Part of the large building was rented, and part was used directly in the corporation's business. A fire destroyed the two top floors, and the company recovered insurance proceeds. For business reasons, the company did not rebuild the two floors. Some of the shareholders' stock was purchased with excess funds collected as insurance proceeds from the fire. The Court held that the distribution qualified as a partial liquidation.

The genuine contraction of a corporate business concept has been difficult to apply, because it has no objective tests. The IRS has ruled that

---

**69.** Section 302(b)(4) applies to transfers after August 31, 1982; transfers before this date were governed by prior § 346, which applied to both corporate and noncorporate shareholders.

**70.** Section 302 now presents a true paradox for the reader. First, there is the not essentially equivalent to a dividend of § 302(b)(1), which is tested at the shareholder level. Second, there is the not essentially equivalent to a dividend of § 302(e), which looks to the effect of the distribution on the corporation. Thus, identical terminology in the same Code Section carries different meanings.

**71.** 11 T.C. 836 (1948).

proceeds from the sale of excess inventory distributed to shareholders in exchange for a part of their stock will not qualify.[72] Because of the subjectiveness of the genuine contraction of a corporate business test, it should not be relied upon without a favorable ruling from the IRS.

The requirements are objective with respect to the complete termination of a business test. If a corporation has more than one trade or business, both of which have been in existence for more than five years, and terminates one while continuing the other, the proceeds from the sale of the one trade or business can be distributed at capital gain rates to the shareholders so long as the trade or business was not acquired in a taxable transaction within such period. (The five-year requirement prevents the bailout of E & P by the acquisition and distribution of another business within a short period of time.) This type of distribution resembles a complete liquidation in which shareholders automatically receive capital gain treatment. Consequently, shareholders should receive the same tax benefits from a partial liquidation.

> **Example 36.** X Corporation has been selling a single product to its customers. It loses its major customer, and a severe drop in sales results. The corporation reduces its inventory investment and has substantial cash on hand. It redeems 20% of its outstanding stock as a liquidating dividend. A, an individual shareholder, receives $10,000 for stock that cost $5,000 two years ago. The distribution will not qualify under § 302; there was only one business activity, and the distribution is not a disproportionate redemption. Consequently, the $10,000 is a taxable dividend to A to the extent of his share of the corporation's E & P. (Such a distribution would not qualify as a genuine contraction of a corporate business, because it is simply a reduction of excess inventory.)

> **Example 37.** In 19X0, X Corporation, the owner and operator of a wholesale grocery business, acquired a freight-hauling concern. The acquisition was by purchase and therefore constituted a taxable transaction. In 19X3, the freight-hauling concern is distributed in kind on a pro rata basis to all of the shareholders of X Corporation. The distribution does not satisfy the requirements of § 302(e)(3) for two reasons. First, the business distributed had not been conducted for five years. Second, it was acquired by X Corporation in a taxable transaction. Since the distribution was pro rata among the shareholders, none of the regular types of stock redemptions [i. e., § 302(b)(1), (2), or (3)] should come into play. All other alternatives having been exhausted, X Corporation's distribution must fall into the classification of a dividend distribution.

## REDEMPTIONS TO PAY DEATH TAXES—§ 303

Section 303 provides an executor the opportunity to redeem stock in a closely-held corporation at capital gain rates when the stock represents a

---

**72.** Rev.Rul. 60–322, 1960–2 C.B. 118. In Rev.Rul. 79–184, 1979–1 C.B. 143, the IRS held that a distribution of the proceeds from the sale of stock of a wholly owned subsidiary to shareholders in redemption of their stock in the parent corporation was not a contraction of business operations. Consequently, it did not qualify as a partial liquidation.

substantial amount of the gross estate of the shareholder-decedent. The redemption is effected to provide the estate with liquidity. Stock in a closely-held corporation is generally not readily marketable; however, it could be redeemed if § 302 would not cause ordinary dividend treatment. Section 303, to an extent, alleviates this problem.

Section 303 is, in effect, an exception to § 302(b). If a stock redemption qualifies under § 303, the rules of § 302(b) do not apply. The redemption will qualify for capital gain treatment regardless of whether it is substantially disproportionate or not essentially equivalent to a dividend. Section 303 applies when a distribution is made with respect to stock of a corporation, the value of which stock, in the gross estate of a decedent, is in excess of 35 percent of the value of the adjusted gross estate of the decedent. (For a definition of "gross estate" and "adjusted gross estate" see the Glossary of Tax Terms in Appendix C.) In determining the 35 percent requirement, stock of two or more corporations is treated as the stock of a single corporation if 20 percent or more in value of the outstanding stock of each corporation is included in the decedent's gross estate.[73]

> **Example 38.** The adjusted gross estate of a decedent is $300,000. The gross estate includes stock in X and Y Corporations valued at $100,000 and $80,000, respectively. Unless the two corporations can be treated as a single corporation, § 303 will not apply to a redemption of the stock. Assume the decedent owned all the stock of X Corporation and 80% of the stock of Y. Section 303 would then apply, because 20% or more of the value of the outstanding stock of both corporations would be included in the decedent's estate. The 35% test would be met when the stock is treated as that of a single corporation.

Section 303 could provide a double benefit. If the stock has appreciated in value, such appreciation would not be taxed, because the value of the stock on the date of death (or the alternate valuation date when elected) becomes the income tax basis to the estate or heirs (see the discussion of § 1014 in Chapter 12).

> **Example 39.** The adjusted gross estate of D, decedent, was $600,000. The death taxes and funeral and administrative expenses of the estate totaled $200,000. Included in the estate was stock in X Corporation, a closely-held corporation, valued at $240,000. D had acquired the stock 10 years ago at a cost of $60,000. X Corporation redeems $200,000 of the stock from D's estate. The redemption would qualify under § 303; thus, it would not represent a dividend to D's estate. In addition, § 1014 would apply to give the stock a step-up in basis. Consequently, there would be no tax on the redemption.

The use of § 303 is subject to time limitations. Section 303 applies only to redemptions made within 90 days after the expiration of the period of limitations for the assessment of the Federal estate tax. If a petition for a redetermination of an estate tax deficiency is timely filed with the U. S. Tax Court, the applicable period for a § 303 redemption is extended to 60

---

73.  § 303(b)(2)(B).

days after the decision of the Court becomes final.[74] The latter extension of time applies only to bona fide contests in the Tax Court. It does not apply to a petition initiated solely for the purpose of extending the time period under § 303.[75] However, if deferred payment of estate taxes is elected under § 6166, the time for redemption is extended to the time permitted for the payment of the estate tax installments.

Section 303 could apply to the heirs of the decedent as well as to the decedent's executor or administrator. For example, if stock is given by a decedent within three years of death and is included in the gross estate (see Chapter 11), § 303 might be applicable to a redemption of such stock if its percentage requirements are met.

Section 303 applies only to the extent of the sum of the estate, inheritance, legacy, and succession taxes imposed by reason of the decedent's death and to the extent of the amount of funeral and administration expenses allowable as deductions to the estate.[76] Prior to the Tax Reform Act of 1976, there was no requirement that the estate have a liquidity problem or that the proceeds of the redemption be used specifically to pay these taxes and expenses. However, for persons dying after December 31, 1976, stock that can qualify for capital gain treatment must be redeemed from a shareholder whose interest in the estate is reduced by the payment of these taxes and expenses.

## EFFECT ON THE CORPORATION REDEEMING ITS STOCK

Having considered the different types of stock redemptions that will receive exchange treatment and result in capital gain or loss to the shareholder, what is the tax effect to the corporation redeeming its stock? If the corporation uses property to carry out the redemption, the possibility exists that it might have to recognize gain on the distribution. Furthermore, one needs to determine what effect, if any, the redemption will have on the corporation's E & P. These matters are discussed in the following paragraphs.

*Recognition of Gain to the Corporation.* Under § 311(a), as noted previously, the corporation recognizes no gain or loss upon the distribution of property to its shareholders. Section 311 provides exceptions with respect to LIFO inventory property, property subject to a liability in excess of its basis, and certain appreciated property. The recapture rules of § § 1245, 1250, and 1252 and the assignment of income doctrine provide further exceptions. With respect to a stock redemption using appreciated property (other than a corporate obligation), § 311(d) provides that the distributing corporation recognizes gain to the extent of the appreciation. This provision applies even if the distribution does not qualify a shareholder for capital gain treatment.

> **Example 40.**  R Corporation uses land (adjusted basis of $10,000 and fair market value of $30,000) to redeem some of the stock of a share-

74.  § 303(b)(1).
75.  Reg. § 1.303–2(e).
76.  § 303(a).

holder that is worth $30,000. R Corporation must recognize a gain of $20,000 as a result of the redemption. This is true even though the shareholder may have dividend income of $30,000, because the requirements of § 302 are not met.

There are limited exceptions to § 311(d). Some important exceptions are that § 311(d) does not apply to distributions in redemption of stock to pay death taxes (§ 303) and to distributions under § 302(b)(4) if the distribution was made to a noncorporate shareholder who had held at least 10 percent in value of the outstanding stock of the distributing corporation for the preceding five years or, if less than five years, for the period of the corporation's existence.

*Effect on Earnings and Profits.* The E & P account of a corporation is reduced as a result of a stock redemption in an amount not in excess of the ratable share of the E & P of the distributing corporation attributable to the stock redeemed.[77] In an early case, *Helvering v. Jarvis,* the Fourth Court of Appeals established the rule that the amount chargeable to the capital account is figured by multiplying the balance in the capital account by the ratio between the redeemed shares and the total shares outstanding before redemption.[78] After some controversy,[79] the IRS agreed to follow the *Jarvis* approach.[80] However, the Deficit Reduction Act of 1984 rescinded the *Jarvis* method. Section 312(n)(8) now provides that the E & P account of the distributing corporation must be reduced in proportion to the amount of the corporation's outstanding stock that is redeemed. In no case may this adjustment exceed the amount of the redemption.

> **Example 41.** X Corporation has 100 shares of stock outstanding. It redeems 30 shares for $100,000 at a time when it has paid-in capital of $120,000 and E & P of $150,000. The charge to E & P would be 30% of the amount in the E & P account ($45,000), and the remainder of the redemption price ($55,000) would be a reduction of the capital account. [Under the *Jarvis* approach, the charge to the capital account would be 30% of the amount in the account ($36,000), and the remainder of the redemption price ($64,000) would be a reduction of E & P.]

# STOCK REDEMPTIONS— NO EXCHANGE TREATMENT

Stock redemptions that do not fall under any of the four major types provided for in the Code will, of course, be treated as dividend distributions to the extent of E & P. Resourceful taxpayers, however, found two ways to circumvent the redemption provisions. Both involved structuring as a sale of the stock what was, in effect, a stock redemption or a dividend distribution. The widespread use of these approaches to obtain capital gain treatment led to the enactment of § 306 dealing with preferred stock bailouts and § 304 dealing with transfers of stock to related corporations.

---

**77.**  § 312(n)(8).

**78.**  41–2 USTC ¶ 9752, 28 AFTR 404, 123 F.2d 742 (CA–4, 1941).

**79.**  Rev.Rul. 70–531, 1970–2 C.B. 76.

**80.**  Rev.Rul. 79–376, 1979–2 C.B. 133.

## PREFERRED STOCK BAILOUTS—§ 306

*The Problem.* Suppose a shareholder would like to bail out corporate profits at long-term capital gain rather than ordinary income rates. Several possibilities exist:

—A sale of stock to the corporation that qualifies as a stock redemption under the four types provided for by § 302 or the one type allowed under § 303.

—A complete liquidation of the corporation under § 331.

—A sale of stock to third parties.

As noted previously, a stock redemption under § 302 may be difficult to carry out successfully in the case of a family corporation unless the shareholder completely terminates his or her interest in the corporation. A redemption of stock under § 303 would not be available until after the death of a shareholder. Partial liquidations are limited to peculiar circumstances and may be hard to arrange. Also, complete liquidations may not be feasible in the case of going concerns with good present and future profit potential. Lastly, the sale of stock to third parties may not be desirable if a shareholder wishes to maintain voting power in the corporation at its present level.

Clever taxpayers devised the following scheme to bail out corporate profits:[81]

*First,* the corporation issues a nontaxable preferred stock dividend on common stock [§ 305(a)]. The preferred stock is nonvoting.

*Second,* the shareholder assigns to the preferred stock an appropriate portion of the basis of the common stock [§ 307(a)].

*Third,* the shareholder sells the preferred stock to a third party for its fair market value. If the stock is a capital asset, the spread between the selling price and the assigned basis will be a capital gain. The holding period of the common stock can be counted [§ 1223(5)] to determine the nature of the gain—either short- or long-term capital gain.

*Fourth,* the third party holds the preferred stock for a suitable period of time (at least more than six months) and then returns it to the corporation for redemption at a premium. If the requirements of § 302(b)(3) are met (i. e., complete termination of a shareholder's interest), the difference between the purchase price and the redemption proceeds (i. e., the premium) will be taxed as a long-term capital gain.

Notice what has been accomplished. The original shareholder obtains the bailout of corporate profits at capital gain rates. No diminution in the control of the corporation occurs; the voting common stock has remained intact throughout. The third party purchaser of the preferred stock is, of course, rewarded for its cooperation by the premium paid upon the ultimate redemption of the stock.

*The Solution of § 306.* Because of the obvious tax avoidance possibilities of the preferred stock bailout approach, Congress enacted Code § 306.

---

**81.** *Chamberlin v. Comm.,* 53–2 USTC ¶ 9576, 44 AFTR 494, 207 F.2d 462 (CA–6, 1953), *cert. den.,* 74 S.Ct. 516 (USSC, 1954).

In essence, § 306 produces the following tax consequences:

—The shareholder will have ordinary income on the sale (but not the receipt) of the preferred stock to a third party to the extent that the fair market value of the preferred stock (on the date of distribution) would have been a dividend had the corporation distributed cash in lieu of stock [§ 306(a)(1)]. But such income is *not a dividend* and therefore has no effect on the issuing corporation's E & P.[82] In this respect, § 306 leads to a harsher result than a taxable dividend distribution.

—No loss is recognized on any sale of the preferred stock by the shareholder.

—If the shareholder does not sell the preferred stock to a third party but chooses, instead, to have it redeemed by the issuing corporation, the redemption proceeds will constitute dividend income to the extent of the corporation's E & P on the date of the redemption [§ 306(a)(2)].

**Example 42.** As of January 1, 19X9, Z Corporation has E & P of $150,000. T, the sole shareholder of Z Corporation, owns all of Z's common stock (100 shares) with a basis of $60,000. On January 1, 19X9, Z Corporation declares and pays a preferred stock dividend [nontaxable under § 305(a)] of 100 shares. After the dividend, the fair market value of one share of common is $2,000 and the fair market value of one share of preferred is $1,000. On January 2, 19X9, T sells the 100 shares of preferred to V for $100,000. Section 306 produces the following results:

—After the distribution and before the sale, the preferred stock will have a basis to T of $20,000 [($100,000 ÷ $300,000) × $60,000 (the original basis of the common stock)].

—The sale of the preferred stock generates $100,000 of ordinary income to T. This would have been the amount of dividend income T would recognize had cash instead of preferred stock been distributed.

—The $20,000 basis allocated to the preferred stock is not lost but should be returned to the common stock account.

—Z Corporation's E & P account remains unaffected by either the stock distribution or its subsequent sale.

**Example 43.** Assume the same facts as in Example 42 with this exception: Z Corporation's E & P was only $50,000 on the date the preferred stock was distributed. Under these circumstances, the $100,000 sale proceeds would be accounted for as follows: $50,000 ordinary income under § 306, $20,000 applied against the basis of the preferred stock, and $30,000 capital gain. Whether the capital gain was long-term or short-term would depend upon the holding period of the underlying common stock.

---

**82.**  Reg. § 1.306–1(b)(1).

*What Is § 306 Stock?*   Section 306 stock is stock other than common that (a) is received as a nontaxable stock dividend, (b) is received tax-free in a corporate reorganization or separation to the extent that either the effect of the transaction was substantially the same as the receipt of a stock dividend or the stock was received in exchange for § 306 stock, or (c) has a basis determined by reference to the basis of § 306 stock [§ 306(c)]. Stock rights are treated as stock for these purposes. Stock acquired through the exercise of such rights is treated as § 306 stock to the extent of the fair market value of the rights at the time of their distribution.

> **Example 44.**  D makes a gift of § 306 stock to her son, S. The transfer will not trigger ordinary income to D because no gain is recognized on a gift [§ 306(b)(3)], but the stock will be § 306 stock in the hands of S [§ 306(c)(1)(C)]. One might say that the § 306 ordinary income "taint" is transferred from D to S.

If a corporation has no E & P on the date of distribution of a nontaxable preferred stock dividend, the stock will not be § 306 stock.

> **Example 45.**  T transfers cash to a newly created corporation in return for all of its stock (1,000 shares of common and 500 shares of preferred). The preferred stock will not be § 306 stock; it was not issued as a nontaxable stock dividend [i. e., pursuant to § 305(a)]. But even if the stock were so issued, it would escape the § 306 taint because no E & P existed at the time of issuance [§ 306(c)(2)].

*Exceptions to § 306.*   Section 306(b) specifically excepts the following transactions from the general rule of § 306(a):

1. Sale by a shareholder of *all* (i. e., both common and preferred) of the stock interest to an unrelated third party. To determine what is a related or an unrelated party, refer to the constructive ownership of stock rules of § 318(a).

2. Redemption by a shareholder of *all* (i. e., both common and preferred) of the stock by the corporation, if such redemption qualifies under § 302(b)(3) (i. e., complete termination of a shareholder's interest).

3. Turning in stock to the corporation pursuant to a complete liquidation or a qualified partial liquidation under § 302(b)(4).

4. A disposition of stock on which gain or loss is not recognized. For the gift possibility, refer to Example 44. Other possibilities include a transfer of § 306 stock to a controlled corporation pursuant to § 351 (refer to Chapter 3) or a transfer by death. (However, as for transfers occurring after August 31, 1982, § 306 does apply to an otherwise qualified § 351 tax-free incorporation if the transferee corporation was formed or availed of to avoid the anti-bailout provisions. As to transactions occurring after August 31, 1982, § 318 attribution rules are applied to determine whether the receipt of § 306 stock in a reorganization or in a transaction falling under § 355 or § 351 is substantially the same as a dividend.) As noted in Example 44, the § 306 ordinary income taint does not disappear in gift situations but carries over to the transferee (or the property

received in exchange for the § 306 stock). Death of a shareholder is an exception; the preferred stock passes to the estate or heirs free of any taint.

5.  The transfer was not in pursuance of a plan having as one of its principal purposes the avoidance of the Federal income tax. What this means in actual practice is not entirely clear.[83] The Regulation in point refers to isolated dispositions of preferred stock by minority shareholders or a sale by a shareholder of all the preferred stock subsequent to a disposition of all the common stock.[84]

Most of the preceding exceptions can be understood by recalling the basic objective of the preferred stock bailout scheme—to bail out corporate profits at capital gain rates with no loss of control. One can hardly accomplish such an objective if, for example, *all* of the stock is sold to a third party or redeemed by the corporation (refer to exceptions 1 and 2).

## REDEMPTIONS THROUGH USE OF RELATED CORPORATIONS—§ 304

Without § 304, the rules of § 302 (detailing when a stock redemption is treated as a taxable dividend) could be circumvented if a shareholder had a controlling interest in more than one corporation. For example, a shareholder could sell the stock in X Corporation to Y Corporation and receive capital gain treatment regardless of whether the proportionate interest in X Corporation changed substantially as a result of the sale. Section 304 closes this loophole. When a shareholder sells stock of one corporation to a related corporation, the sale is treated as a redemption subject to § § 302 and 303.

Section 304 applies to a corporation's acquisition from a shareholder of stock of another corporation in exchange for property when the shareholder has at least a 50 percent ownership in both corporations. Section 317(a) defines "property" to mean money, securities, and any other property, except that stock (or rights to acquire stock) in the corporation making the distribution is specifically excluded. This means, then, that most tax-free corporate reorganizations involving the exchange of stock for stock would generally avoid the consequences of § 304.[85]

Control for the purpose of § 304 is defined as the ownership of stock possessing at least 50 percent of the total combined voting power of all classes of stock entitled to vote, or at least 50 percent of the total value of all classes of stock. Section 304 also applies if an individual has a 50 percent interest in a corporation that, in turn, has control (as defined above) of another corporation. For purposes of determining the 50 percent control, the constructive ownership rules of § 318(a) apply.[86]

---

**83.** *Fireoved v. U. S.,* 72–2 USTC ¶ 9485, 30 AFTR2d 72–5043, 462 F.2d 1281 (CA–3, 1972), and S.Rept. No.1622, 83d Cong., 2d Sess.
**84.** Reg. § 1.306–2(b)(3).
**85.** However, there might be a problem when a subsidiary distributes stock of the parent.
**86.** § 304(c)(2).

*Transfers Involving Brother-Sister Corporations.* If an individual controls two corporations[87] and transfers stock in one corporation to the other for property, the exchange is treated as a redemption of the stock of the *acquiring* corporation. The stock received by the acquiring corporation is treated as a contribution to its capital. Basis of the stock is the basis the shareholder had in the stock plus any gain recognized to the shareholder on the transfer. Assuming the exchange is treated as a dividend under § 302, the individual's basis in the stock of the acquiring corporation is increased by the basis of the stock he or she surrendered. In applying the provisions of § 302(b) to the exchange, reference is made to the shareholder's ownership of stock in the issuing corporation and not to his or her ownership of stock in the acquiring corporation.[88] The amount of dividend income is determined as if the property were distributed by the acquiring corporation to the extent of its E & P and then by the issuing corporation to the extent of its E & P.[89]

> **Example 46.** A owns 100 shares of X Corporation stock and 200 shares of Y Corporation stock, representing 50% ownership in both corporations. A sells 20 shares of stock in X Corporation to Y Corporation for $30,000. X Corporation has E & P of $100,000; Y Corporation has E & P of $20,000. The stock was purchased by A two years ago for $5,000. Section 304 applies to the transaction; therefore, the sale is treated as a redemption of the stock of Y Corporation. If the redemption qualifies under § 302(b), A will receive capital gain treatment. If not, the transaction will be considered a dividend subject to § 301. To determine ownership before and after the redemption, reference is made to A's ownership in X Corporation. After the sale, A owns 90 shares in X Corporation [100 shares originally owned − 20 shares transferred to Y Corporation + 10 shares (constructive ownership of one-half of the shares transferred to Y Corporation)]. [Because A owns 50% of Y Corporation, he is deemed to own 50% of the stock Y Corporation owns by virtue of § 318(a).] Of the 200 shares outstanding in X Corporation, A owns 90 shares, a 45% interest in X Corporation. This does not satisfy the 80% ownership test of § 302(b)(2); A, following the sale, does not own less than 80% of his interest in X Corporation before the sale. Consequently, the $30,000 received from Y Corporation is treated as a dividend under § 301 to the extent of A's share of the E & P of Y Corporation and then to the extent of the E & P of X Corporation. Thus, the entire $30,000 would be a taxable dividend. The $5,000 basis A had in the X Corporation stock that he sold to Y Corporation attaches to his basis in the Y Corporation stock. The basis of the X Corporation stock to Y Corporation is $5,000. [The not essentially equivalent to a dividend provision of § 302(b)(1) is assumed to be inapplicable.]

> **Example 47.** Assume A sells 60 of his shares in X Corporation to Y Corporation for $90,000. His basis in the 60 shares is $15,000. After

---

87. Control being determined under § 304 for these purposes.
88. See Reg. § 1.304–2(a).
89. § 304(b)(2).

the sale, A owns 70 shares in X Corporation (100 − 60 + 30 shares owned constructively). This represents a 35% ownership in X Corporation. It satisfies both the 50% ownership and the 80% ownership tests; consequently, A is entitled to capital gain treatment on the sale. A has a long-term capital gain of $75,000. The basis of the stock in X Corporation received by Y Corporation is $90,000 [$15,000 (A's basis) + $75,000 (gain recognized)]. A's basis in the Y Corporation stock remains the same.

*Parent-Subsidiary Situations.* If a subsidiary corporation acquires stock in its parent from a shareholder owning at least 50 percent of the parent corporation, § 304 applies to the transaction. However, the acquisition is treated as though the parent had *redeemed* its own stock.[90] The transaction is construed as a distribution from the subsidiary to the parent and a subsequent distribution from the parent to the individual shareholder.[91] The transfer is treated as a redemption of the parent corporation stock (rather than that of the acquiring corporation as would be the case in transactions involving brother-sister corporations). If the transaction does not qualify as a stock redemption, the shareholder's basis in the stock sold to the subsidiary attaches to the remaining stock owned in the parent.

**Example 48.** A, an individual, owns 50% of X Corporation, which, in turn, owns 50% of Y Corporation. X Corporation has 200 shares of stock outstanding, 100 of which are owned by B (no relationship to A). A sells 20 of his 100 shares to Y Corporation for $40,000. He purchased the 20 shares two years ago for $10,000. After the sale, A is considered to own 84 shares in X Corporation (100 − 20 + 4 shares owned constructively through Y Corporation). Y Corporation acquired 20 shares, of which 50% are constructively owned by X Corporation (10 shares). Of these 10 shares, 40% are now owned constructively by A (4 shares). A's 84 shares represent a 42% ownership in X Corporation, which does not meet the 80% ownership test of § 302(b)(2); consequently, the $40,000 is treated as a dividend to A to the extent of the E & P of Y Corporation and then to the extent of the E & P of X Corporation. The cost of the 20 shares, $10,000, attaches to A's basis in his remaining shares in X Corporation. X Corporation is deemed to have received a dividend from Y Corporation in the amount of $40,000.

# DISTRIBUTION OF STOCK AND SECURITIES OF A CONTROLLED CORPORATION

If a corporation has control [80 percent control as defined in § 368(c)] of another corporation, stock in the subsidiary corporation can be distributed to the shareholders of the parent corporation tax-free if the requirements of § 355 are met. When a subsidiary is newly formed to perfect a corporate division, § 355 applies through § 368(a)(1)(D) (i. e., a corporate divisive reorganization provision discussed in Chapter 6). However, when a subsid-

---

**90.** Reg. § 1.304–3(a).
**91.** § 304(b)(2).

iary already exists, § 355 alone applies. Section 355 is discussed further in Chapter 6 in connection with the corporate reorganization provisions; however, it is mentioned here, because applied alone, it involves a transaction resembling a dividend or a stock redemption.

Section 355 applies only (a) to distributions that involve all the stock of the subsidiary, or a sufficient amount to give control [as defined in § 368(c)] to the shareholders of the parent, and (b) when both the parent and the subsidiary, following the distribution, are engaged in a trade or business in which they had been so engaged for at least five years prior to the distribution. The distribution can take the form of a spin-off, a split-off, or a split-up.

A spin-off is a distribution of subsidiary stock to the shareholders of the parent corporation giving them control of that subsidiary. The shareholders of the parent do not surrender any of their stock for the subsidiary stock. This distribution resembles an ordinary dividend distribution. A split-off is identical to a spin-off except that the shareholders in the parent corporation exchange some of their parent corporation stock for the subsidiary stock. It more nearly resembles a stock redemption. A split-up is the distribution of the stock of two subsidiaries to shareholders of the parent in complete liquidation of the parent.

Section 355 requires that both the controlled corporation and the parent corporation be engaged in the active conduct of a trade or business for at least five years prior to the distribution. This requirement also appears in § 302(b)(4) with respect to partial liquidations.[92] If a corporation discontinues a trade or business that it has conducted for at least five years, it can distribute the assets pertaining to such business to the shareholders in exchange for their stock as a partial liquidation, but the shareholders must recognize capital gain. In the distributions of stock of a controlled corporation, pursuant to § 355, the shareholder recognizes no gain or loss.

What constitutes an active trade or business is often the subject of litigation. The Regulations take the position that the holding of stock, securities, land, or other property, including casual sales of such properties, is not an active trade or business.[93] The problem of defining an active trade or business is discussed in more detail in Chapter 6 in connection with the application of § 355 to a divisive reorganization.

> **Example 49.**  X Corporation has operated an active business for the past 10 years. It also owns all the stock of Y Corporation, which has been engaged in an active business for eight years. X Corporation distributes all the stock of Y Corporation to its shareholders. Both corporations continue to operate their separate businesses. Assuming a business reason exists for the distribution, the distribution qualifies under § 355, and the receipt of the Y Corporation stock is tax-free to the shareholders of X Corporation. This is a spin-off.

A shareholder can receive only stock or securities tax-free. If other property is received, it is considered boot and is subject to taxation under

---

**92.**   The five-year requirement was added to both § § 302(b)(4) and 355 to deter the bailout of E & P by the acquisition and distribution of another business within a short span of time.
**93.**   Reg. § 1.355–1(c)(1).

§ 356. To further qualify the exchange, it is tax-free only if securities are surrendered in a principal amount that is the same as the principal amount of the securities received. If the principal amount of the securities received is greater than the principal amount of the securities surrendered, or if no securities are surrendered, the shareholder has boot to the extent of the fair market value of the excess principal amount measured on the date of the exchange.

> **Example 50.** T, an individual, exchanges stock in X Corporation (the parent corporation) for stock and securities in Y Corporation (the subsidiary corporation) pursuant to § 355. The exchange is a tax-free split-off except to the extent of the securities received. The securities in Y have a principal amount of $1,000 and a fair market value of $950 on the date of the exchange. T has boot of $950.

> **Example 51.** Assume in Example 50 that T also surrenders securities in X for the securities in Y. The securities in X have a principal amount of $600. T has boot of $380, the fair market value of the excess principal of $400 [($950 ÷ $1000) × $400 = $380].

A distribution under § 355 must not be used principally as a device for the distribution of the E & P of either the distributing corporation or the controlled corporation. If the stock or securities of the controlled corporation are sold shortly after the exchange, the sale is evidence that the transaction was used as a device to distribute E & P.[94] There must also be a business purpose for a distribution made pursuant to § 355. The reason for this requirement is to limit § 355 to distributions incident to any readjustment of corporate structure ". . . as is required by business exigencies and which, in general, effect only a readjustment of continuing interests in property under modified corporate forms."[95] Problems with the antitrust laws would be an example of a business reason justifying the distribution of a subsidiary's stock to the parent's shareholders.

Every taxpayer who receives a distribution of stock or securities of a corporation controlled by a second corporation in which is held stock or securities must attach to the return for the year in which the distribution is received a detailed statement giving appropriate information to show the application of § 355. The statement must include a description of the stock and securities surrendered (if any) and received and the names and addresses of all the corporations involved in the transaction.[96]

The basis of stock received by a shareholder pursuant to § 355 is determined by §§ 358(b) and (c). Basis of the stock held before the exchange is allocated among the stock of all classes held immediately after the transaction in proportion to the fair market value of the stock of each class.[97] The rule is the same regardless of whether a spin-off, split-off, or split-up is involved. Regarding a spin-off (i.e., wherein stock is received in the subsidiary without the shareholder's surrendering stock in the parent), § 358(c)

---

**94.** Reg. § 1.355–2(b).
**95.** Reg. § 1.355–2(c).
**96.** Reg. § 1.355–5(b). See Rev. Proc. 81–41, 1981–2 C.B. 605, for a checklist of information to be included in a request for a ruling under § 355.
**97.** Reg. § 1.358–2(a)(2).

states that such a distribution is nonetheless treated as an exchange. A portion of the basis in the old stock is allocated to the new shares.

E & P of the distributing corporation is decreased by a distribution of stock in its subsidiary. The decrease is the lesser of (a) an amount determined by multiplying the distributing corporation's E & P by a fraction, the numerator of which is the fair market value of the subsidiary's stock and the denominator of which is the fair market value of all the parent corporation's assets, or (b) the net worth of the subsidiary. If this decrease is more than the E & P of the subsidiary, the E & P account of the subsidiary is increased to equal this decrease. If the subsidiary's E & P exceeds the decrease in the E & P of the parent, the subsidiary's E & P account will remain the same.[98]

If a distribution pursuant to § 355 fails to meet the requirements of this Section, such a distribution would become taxable. If a spin-off is involved, the stock distributed to the parent corporation's shareholders would be treated as an ordinary dividend. If a split-off is involved, the distribution would be treated as a stock redemption subject to the provisions of § 302 to determine whether it qualified for capital gain treatment or whether it would be treated as an ordinary dividend. If a split-up is involved, the transaction would be treated as a complete liquidation of the parent corporation.

---

**═══ Concept Summary ═══**

1.  Without a special provision, corporate distributions are taxed as dividend income to the recipient shareholder to the extent of his or her share of the distributing corporation's E & P accumulated since February 28, 1913, or to the extent of a pro rata share of current E & P. Any excess is treated as a return of capital to the extent of the shareholder's basis in the stock and, thereafter, as capital gain. See § § 301 and 316.

2.  With regard to noncorporate shareholders, property distributions are considered dividends (taxed as noted in item 1) in the amount of their fair market value. Although § 301(b) provides that corporate shareholders are taxed on the lesser of (a) the fair market value or (b) the adjusted basis of such property in the hands of the distributing corporation increased by the amount of any gain recognized to the distributing corporation, because § 311(d)(1) requires the distributing corporation to recognize gain on most distributions of appreciated property, for all practical purposes, a corporate shareholder is also taxed on the fair market value. The amount deemed distributed is reduced by any liabilities to which the property distributed is subject immediately before and immediately after the distribution and any liability of the corporation assumed by the shareholder in connection with the distribution. The shareholder's basis in such property is, for noncorpo-

---

**98.**  Reg. § 1.312–10.

rate shareholders, the fair market value and, for corporate shareholders, the lesser of (a) the fair market value or (b) the adjusted basis of such property in the hands of the distributing corporation increased by any gain recognized to the distributing corporation, which, again, is generally also the fair market value.

3.   Earnings and profits of a corporation are increased by corporate earnings for the taxable year computed in the same manner as the corporation computes its taxable income. As a general rule, the account is increased for all items of income, whether taxed or not, and reduced by all items of expense, whether deductible or not. See § 312. The Deficit Reduction Act of 1984 made a number of changes in the computation of E & P so that E & P will more accurately reflect a corporation's economic income. Refer to the Concept Summary on page 4-6 of this chapter for a summary of the effect of certain transactions on taxable income and current E & P.

4.   Section 311(a) provides that a corporation does not recognize gain or loss on corporate distributions. However, exceptions exist if a corporation distributes LIFO inventory that would have a higher cost if valued under the FIFO method [§ 311(b)] and property that is subject to a mortgage in excess of its tax basis to the distributing corporation [§ 311(c)]. In addition, § 311(d) provides an important exception for the distribution of appreciated property. Gain, but not loss, is recognized as though the property had been sold by the corporation at its fair market value. Exceptions to § 311(d) exist for property that (1) is not inventory or receivables, (2) was used by the corporation in the active conduct of its business, and (3) was distributed to noncorporate shareholders owning at least 10 percent in value of the outstanding stock of the distributing corporation for at least five years (or from the corporation's inception if that is less than five years). Exceptions to § 311(a) exist as to installment obligations, depreciable property subject to depreciation recapture rules under § § 1245 and 1250, and farm property subject to recapture under § 1252. In addition, the assignment of income doctrine makes unrealized income taxable to the distributing corporation. There is also a recapture of investment credit on property subject to such credit that is distributed before its useful life—determined for the purpose of claiming an investment credit—has expired.

5.   As a general rule, stock dividends or stock rights (representing stock in the distributing corporation) are not taxed. There are five exceptions: (1) distributions payable either in stock or property; (2) distributions that have the result of the receipt of property by some shareholders and an increase in the proportionate interest of other shareholders in the assets or E & P of the distributing corporation; (3) distributions that result in the receipt of preferred stock by some common shareholders and the receipt of common stock by other shareholders; (4) distributions on preferred stock other than an increase in the conversion ratio of convertible preferred stock made solely to take account of a stock dividend or stock split with respect to stock into which the preferred is convertible; and (5) distributions of convertible pre-

ferred stock, unless it can be shown that the distribution will not result in a disproportionate distribution. Changes in conversion ratios, changes in redemption prices, and differences between issue price and redemption price are taxable dividends. See § 305.

6.   Stock redemptions that qualify under § 302(b) are given capital gain treatment. Section 302(b) requires that such distributions either be substantially disproportionate, be not essentially equivalent to a dividend, or be a distribution to a noncorporate shareholder in a qualified partial liquidation. In making a determination of substantially disproportionate or not essentially equivalent to a dividend under § § 302(b)(1), (2), and (3), the rules of § 318(a) determining the constructive ownership of stock apply, unless the shareholder redeems all of his or her interest in the corporation and does not reacquire (other than by bequest or inheritance) any interest (except as a creditor) for 10 years after the redemption.

7.   Redemptions that are qualified partial liquidations must be made to noncorporate shareholders. A qualified partial liquidation occurs when the distribution is not essentially equivalent to a dividend (i. e., there is a genuine contraction of a corporate business) or when a corporation has had two or more trades or businesses for at least five years and discontinues one of the businesses, distributing all the assets of such business to its shareholders. It must continue the other business or businesses. Any distributions must be made within the taxable year in which the plan is adopted or within the succeeding taxable year. See § 302(b)(4).

8.   If stock included in a decedent's estate represents more than 35 percent of the adjusted taxable estate, it may upon redemption qualify for capital gain treatment separate and apart from § 302(b). Section 303 provides automatic capital gain treatment on the redemption of such stock.

9.   A corporation is taxed on the appreciation of property distributed in redemption of its stock with certain limited exceptions noted in § 311(d).

10.   A distribution of preferred stock as a nontaxable stock dividend to common shareholders is subject to special treatment outlined in § 306. The proceeds of a sale of § 306 stock or the redemption of such stock results in ordinary income to the extent of the distributing corporation's E & P (a) on the date of the distribution in the case of a *sale* of such stock or (b) on the date of the redemption in the case of the *redemption* of such stock. There are exceptions to § 306. If a corporation has no E & P on the date of distribution, § 306 will not apply. Further, it does not apply to redemptions of stock in partial or complete liquidations, distributions on which gain or loss is not recognized under some other provision (such as § 351 or § 355), and dispositions and redemptions that do not have the avoidance of Federal income tax as a principal purpose.

11.   The sale of stock in a controlled corporation (50 percent control) to another corporation controlled by the shareholder (also 50 percent control) is deemed a stock redemption and must be tested by

§ 302(b) or § 303 to determine if the shareholder will receive capital gain treatment or ordinary dividend treatment. See § 304.

12. The E & P account of the distributing corporation is reduced in a stock redemption in proportion to the amount of the corporation's outstanding stock that is redeemed.

13. Distributions of stock in a subsidiary corporation (80 percent controlled by the parent) are not taxed to the shareholders if the distribution is pursuant to § 355. To qualify under § 355, stock representing this "control" must be distributed to the parent's shareholders. Both the parent and subsidiary must continue a trade or business after the distribution. Further, each must have actively conducted this trade or business for at least five years prior to the redemption. The distribution must be motivated by a sound business purpose and not by a scheme to avoid Federal taxes.

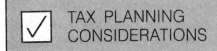

## TAX PLANNING CONSIDERATIONS

### CORPORATE DISTRIBUTIONS

In connection with the preceding discussion of corporate distributions, the following points might well need reinforcement:

—Because E & P is the measure of dividend income, its periodic determination is essential to corporate planning. Thus, an E & P account should be established and maintained, particularly if the possibility exists that a corporate distribution might represent a return of capital.

—Accumulated E & P is the sum of all past years' current E & P. No statute of limitations exists on the computation of E & P. The IRS could, for example, redetermine a corporation's current E & P for a tax year long since passed. Such a change would obviously affect accumulated E & P and would have a direct impact on the taxability of current distributions to shareholders.

—Taxpayers should be aware that manipulating distributions to avoid or minimize dividend exposure is possible.

**Example 52.** Q Corporation has accumulated E & P of $100,000 as of January 1, 19X5. During 19X5, it expects to have earnings from operations of $80,000 and to make a cash distribution of $60,000. Q Corporation also expects to sell a particular asset for a loss of $100,000. Thus, it anticipates incurring a deficit of $20,000 for the year. The best approach would be to recognize the loss as soon as possible and, immediately therefter, make the cash distribution to its shareholders. Suppose these two steps took place on January 1, 19X5. Because the current E & P for 19X5 will have a deficit, the accumulated E & P account must be brought up to date (refer to Example 11 in this chapter). Thus, at the time of the distribution, the combined E & P balance is zero [i. e., $100,000 (beginning balance in accumulated E & P) − $100,000 (existing deficit in current E & P)], and the $60,000 distribution to the shareholders constitutes a return of capital. (Note: Current deficits are allocated pro rata throughout the year unless the parties can prove otherwise. Here they can.)

**Example 53.** After several unprofitable years, Y Corporation has a deficit in accumulated E & P of $100,000 as of January 1, 19X5. Starting in 19X5, Y Corporation expects to generate annual E & P of $50,000 for the next four years and would like to distribute this amount to its shareholders. The corporation's cash position (for dividend purposes) will correspond to the current E & P generated. Compare the following possibilities:

    I.   On December 31 of 19X5, 19X6, 19X7, and 19X8, Y Corporation distributes a cash dividend of $50,000.

    II.  On December 31 of 19X6 and 19X8, Y Corporation distributes a cash dividend of $100,000.

Alternative I leads to an overall result of $200,000 in dividend income, since each $50,000 distribution is fully covered by current E & P. Alternative II, however, results in only $100,000 of dividend income to the shareholders. The remaining $100,000 is a return of capital. Why? At the time Y Corporation made its first distribution of $100,000 on December 31, 19X6, it had a deficit of $50,000 in accumulated E & P (the original deficit of $100,000 is reduced by the $50,000 of current E & P from 19X5). Consequently, the $100,000 distribution yields a $50,000 dividend (the current E & P for 19X6) and $50,000 as a return of capital. As of January 1, 19X7, Y Corporation's accumulated E & P now has a deficit balance of $50,000 (a distribution cannot increase a deficit in E & P). Add in $50,000 of current E & P from 19X7, and the balance as of January 1, 19X8, is zero. Thus, the second distribution of $100,000 made on December 31, 19X8, also yields $50,000 of dividends (the current E & P for 19X8) and $50,000 as a return of capital.

## CONSTRUCTIVE DIVIDENDS

Tax planning can be particularly effective in avoiding constructive dividend situations.

    —Shareholders should try to structure their dealings with the corporation on an arm's length basis. For example, reasonable rent should be paid for the use of corporate property, or a fair price should be paid for its purchase. Needless to say, the parties should make every effort to support the amount involved with appraisal data or market information obtained from reliable sources at or close to the time of the transaction.

—Dealings between shareholders and a closely-held corporation should be formalized as much as possible. In the case of loans to shareholders, for example, the parties should provide for an adequate rate of interest, written evidence of the debt, and a realistic repayment schedule that is not only arranged, but also followed.

—If corporate profits are to be bailed out by the shareholders in a form deductible to the corporation, a balanced mix of the different alternatives could lessen the risk of disallowance by the IRS. Rent for the use of shareholder property, interest on amounts borrowed from shareholders, or salaries for services rendered by shareholders are all feasible substitutes for dividend distributions. But overdoing any one approach may well attract the attention of the IRS. Too much interest, for example, might mean the corporation is thinly capitalized and, therefore, some of the debt really represents equity investment.

—Much can be done to protect against the disallowance of corporate deductions for compensation that is determined to be unreasonable in amount. Example 54 is an illustration, all too common in a family corporation, of what *not* to do.

> **Example 54.** Z Corporation is wholly owned by T. Corporate employees and annual salaries include Mrs. T ($8,000), T, Jr. ($4,000), T ($50,000), and E ($20,000). The operation of Z Corporation is shared about equally between T and E (an unrelated party). Mrs. T (T's wife) performed significant services for the corporation during the corporation's formative years but now merely attends the annual meeting of the board of directors. T, Jr. (T's son) is a full-time student and occasionally signs papers for the corporation in his capacity as treasurer. Z Corporation has not distributed a dividend for 10 years, although it has accumulated substantial E & P. What is wrong with this situation?
>
> > —Mrs. T's salary seems vulnerable unless one can prove that some or all of the $8,000 annual salary is payment for services rendered to the corporation in prior years (i. e., she was underpaid for those years).[99]
> >
> > —T, Jr.'s salary is also vulnerable; he does not appear to earn the $4,000 paid to him by the corporation. True, neither T, Jr. nor Mrs. T is a shareholder, but each one's relationship to T is enough of a tie-in to raise the unreasonable compensation issue.
> >
> > —T's salary appears susceptible to challenge. Why, for instance, is he receiving $30,000 more than E when it appears each shares equally in the operation of the corporation?

---

**99.** See, for example, *R. J. Nicoll Co.*, 59 T.C. 37 (1972).

—No dividends have been distributed by Z Corporation for 10 years, although the corporation is capable of doing so.

## STOCK REDEMPTIONS

Several observations come to mind in connection with tax planning for stock redemptions.

—The § 302(b)(1) variety (i. e., not essentially equivalent to a dividend) provides minimal utility and should be relied upon only as a last resort. Instead, the redemption should be structured to fit one of the safe harbors of either § 302(b)(2) (i. e., substantially disproportionate), § 302(b)(3) (i. e., complete termination), or § 303 (i. e., to pay death taxes).

—In the case of a family corporation in which all of the shareholders are related to each other, the only hope of a successful redemption might lie in the use of § 302(b)(3) or § 303. But in using § 302(b)(3), be careful that the family stock attribution rules are avoided. Here, strict compliance with § 302(c)(2) (i. e., the withdrawing shareholder does not continue as an employee of the corporation, etc., and does not reacquire an interest in the corporation within ten years) is crucial.

—The alternative to a successful stock redemption or partial liquidation is, of course, dividend treatment of the distribution under § 301. But do not conclude that a dividend is always undesirable from a tax standpoint. Suppose the distributing corporation has little, if any, E & P. Or the distributee-shareholder is another corporation. In this latter regard, dividend treatment might well be preferred due to the availability of the 85 percent dividends received deduction.

—When using the § 303 redemption, the amount to be sheltered from dividend treatment is the sum of death taxes and certain estate administration expenses. Nevertheless, a redemption in excess of the limitation will not destroy the applicability of § 303. Even better, any such excess (if properly structured) might qualify under § 302. Thus, § 302 can be used to pick up where § 303 left off.

—The timing and sequence of a redemption should be carefully handled.

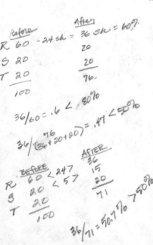

**Example 55.** P Corporation's stock is held as follows: R (60 shares), S (20 shares), and T (20 shares). R, S, and T are all individuals and are not related to each other. In early 19X1, the corporation redeems 24 of R's shares. Shortly thereafter, it redeems five of S's shares. Does R's redemption qualify as substantially disproportionate? Taken in isolation, it would appear to meet the requirements of § 302(b)(2)—the 80% and 50% tests have been satisfied. Yet, if the IRS takes into account the later redemption of S's shares, R has not satisfied the 50% test; he still owns $36/71$ of the corporation after both redemptions.[100] Some time lag between the two redemptions, therefore, would have placed R in a better position to argue against collapsing the series of redemptions into one.

| PROBLEM MATERIALS |
|---|

## Discussion Questions

1. What is meant by the term "earnings and profits"?

2. Why is it important to distinguish between "current" and "accumulated" E & P?

3. Describe the effect of a distribution in a year when the distributing corporation has—

   (a) A deficit in accumulated E & P and a positive amount in current E & P.

   (b) A positive amount in accumulated E & P and a deficit in current E & P.

   (c) A deficit in both current and accumulated E & P.

   (d) A positive amount in both current and accumulated E & P.

4. In 19X0, a corporation determined its current E & P to be $100,000. In 19X5, it makes a distribution to its shareholders of $200,000. The IRS contends that the current E & P of the corporation for 19X0 really was $150,000. Can the IRS successfully make this contention? What difference would the additional $50,000 in E & P make?

5. How does the assignment of income doctrine affect corporate distributions?

6. If a corporation is chartered in a state that prohibits the payment of dividends that impair "paid-in capital," is it possible for the corporation to pay a dividend that is a return of capital for tax purposes and yet comply with state law? Discuss.

7. A corporation with no E & P distributes a property dividend. Can it be said that the shareholders need not recognize any dividend income? Explain.

8. T, an individual shareholder, receives a distribution from X Corporation and treats it as a return of capital. Upon audit by the IRS, he tells the agent: "Show me that X Corporation had adequate E & P to cover the distribution, and I will report the distribution as dividend income." Please comment.

9. A corporation distributed property (adjusted basis of $100,000 and fair market value of $80,000) to its shareholders.

   (a) Has the corporation acted wisely? Why or why not?

   (b) Would it matter whether or not some of the shareholders are other corporations?

10. The suggestion is made that any distributions to shareholders by a calendar-year corporation should take place on January 1 before the corporation has developed any current E & P. Assess the validity of this suggestion.

11. X Corporation sells its plant and equipment to its shareholders. Shortly thereafter, X Corporation enters into a long-term lease for the use of these assets. In connection with the possible tax ramifications of these transactions, consider the following:

   (a) The sale of the assets for less than their adjusted basis to X Corporation.

   (b) The amount of rent X Corporation has agreed to pay.

12. Under what circumstances does the distributing corporation recognize income when it distributes appreciated property as a dividend to its shareholders? What if property is distributed as a stock redemption?

13. What are constructive dividends?

14. Why is it important that an advance from a corporation to a shareholder be categorized as a bona fide loan? With regard to the resolution of this issue,

comment on the relevance of the following factors:

(a) The corporation has never paid a dividend.

(b) The advance is on open account.

(c) The advance provides for 2% interest.

(d) No date is specified for the repayment of the advance.

(e) The advance was used by the shareholder to pay personal bills.

(f) The advance is repaid by the shareholder immediately after the transaction was questioned by the IRS on audit of the corporate income tax return.

15. How can shareholders bail out corporate profits in such a manner as to provide the corporation with a deduction? What are the risks involved?

16. Whether compensation paid to a corporate employee is reasonable is a question of fact to be determined from the surrounding circumstances. How would the resolution of this problem be affected by each of the following factors:

(a) The employee is not a shareholder but is related to the sole owner of the corporate-employer.

(b) The employee-shareholder never completed high school.

(c) The employee-shareholder is a full-time college student.

(d) The employee-shareholder was underpaid for her services during the formative period of the corporate-employer.

(e) The corporate-employer pays a nominal dividend each year.

(f) Year-end bonuses are paid to all shareholder-employees.

17. When are stock dividends taxable?

18. How are nontaxable stock rights handled for tax purposes? Taxable stock rights?

19. What is a preferred stock bailout?

20. T, a 30% shareholder in X Corporation, sells one-half of his preferred stock and one-half of his common stock to a third party.

(a) Is there any danger that § 306 could apply to the sale of the preferred stock?

(b) Why or why not?

21. It has been said that the operation of § 306 to a sale of preferred stock could have a harsher tax effect than if the corporation had distributed a taxable dividend in the first place. Explain.

22. What problems exist with respect to a corporation's redemption of its preferred stock?

23. Can a shareholder incur ordinary gain on a stock redemption that is not treated as a dividend? Explain.

24. Can a shareholder incur a loss on a stock redemption? Explain.

25. It has been said that a shareholder in a family corporation may have difficulty effectively utilizing § 302(b)(2) (i. e., substantially disproportionate) as a means of carrying out a stock redemption. Why? What other alternatives are available?

26. A corporation distributes $100,000 to a shareholder in complete redemption of the shareholder's stock. Can the corporation reduce its E & P by this amount? Explain.

27. Under what circumstances does § 303 apply to a stock redemption? What is the tax effect of the application of § 303?

28. "A § 303 stock redemption usually results in no gain or loss being recognized by the estate." Evaluate this statement.

(e) Sale of equipment to 100%
owned corporation
(adjusted basis was
$120,000 and selling price
was $50,000)         _____         _____

7. X Corporation advances $60,000 as an interest-free loan to its shareholder, A (an individual). X Corporation can prove the advance is a bona fide loan. What are the tax consequences of the loan to—

(a) X Corporation?

(b) A?

8. X Corporation distributes property (not inventory or receivables) used in the active conduct of its business to A, an individual, as a property dividend. A has owned her stock in X Corporation for the past six years. The property has a basis of $25,000 and a fair market value of $50,000. What are the tax consequences to X Corporation and to A if:

(a) A owns 8% of the value of the X Corporation stock?

(b) A owns 50% of the value of the X Corporation stock?

9. What are the tax consequences to X Corporation and to A if instead of a property dividend, the distribution in Problem 8 were a stock redemption qualifying under § 302(b)(3)? A has a basis in her stock in X Corporation of $20,000.

10. A paid $30,000 for 15 shares of stock in XY Corporation five years ago. In November 19X4, she received a nontaxable stock dividend of five additional shares in XY Corporation. She sells the five shares in March 19X5 for $10,000. What is her gain, and how is it taxed?

11. AB Corporation declares a nontaxable dividend payable in rights to subscribe to common stock. One right and $60 entitles the holder to subscribe to one share of stock. One right is issued for each share of stock owned. T, a shareholder, owns 100 shares of stock that she purchased two years ago for $3,000. At the date of distribution of the rights, the market value of the stock was $80 and the market value of the rights was $20 per right. T received 100 rights. She exercises 60 rights and purchases 60 additional shares of stock. She sells the remaining 40 rights for $750. What are the tax consequences of these transactions to T?

12. V Corporation has 1,000 shares of common stock outstanding. The shares are owned by unrelated shareholders as follows: H, 400 shares; I, 400 shares; and J, 200 shares. The corporation redeems 100 shares of the stock owned by J for $45,000. J paid $100 per share for her stock two years ago. The E & P of V Corporation was $100,000 on the date of redemption. What is the tax effect to J of the redemption?

13. In Problem 12, assume H is the father of J. How would this affect the tax status of the redemption? What if H were her brother instead of her father?

14. B owns 250 shares of stock in X Corporation and 200 shares of stock in Y Corporation, representing an 80% interest in both corporations. B sells 20 shares of Y stock to X Corporation for $20,000. The Y stock was acquired 10 years ago; the tax basis to B of these 20 shares is $2,000. B's share of the E & P of X Corporation is $10,000 on the date of sale; his share of the E & P of Y Corporation is $15,000. What are the tax consequences of this transaction?

15. T, an individual shareholder in P Corporation, exchanges stock in P (the parent corporation) for all the stock and some securities in S Corporation. The transaction meets the requirement of § 355. The stock in P that T exchanged had a fair market value of $120,000 and a tax basis of $80,000. The stock he received in S had a fair market value of $100,000; the securities had a fair market value of

$20,000 and a principal amount of $22,000. What gain, if any, is recognized by T?

16. The R & D Corporation had E & P of $45,000 when it made a current distribution of inventories with a cost of $60,000 (FIFO method) and a fair market value of $105,000.

   (a) Determine a sole noncorporate shareholder's taxable income from the distribution.

   (b) Determine a sole corporate shareholder's taxable income from the distribution.

17. Complete the following schedule for each case:

| | Accumulated E & P Beginning of Year | Current E & P | Cash Distributions (all on last day of year) | Amount Taxable | Return of Capital |
|---|---|---|---|---|---|
| (a) | $ 30,000 | ($ 10,000) | $ 40,000 | $ 20000 | $ 20000 |
| (b) | (40,000) | 20,000 | 30,000 | 20000 | RDC |
| (c) | 90,000 | 50,000 | 110,000 | 110,000 | — |
| (d) | 80,000 | (15,000) | 90,000 | 65000 | RoC |

   (e) Same as (d) except the distribution of $90,000 is made on June 30 and the corporation uses the calendar year for tax purposes [handwritten: $80 - 7.5 = 73,500$ ... $22,500$ ... $17,500$]

18. Complete the following schedule for each case:

| | Accumulated E & P Beginning of Year | Current E & P | Cash Distributions (all on last day of year) | Amount Taxable | Return of Capital |
|---|---|---|---|---|---|
| (a) | $150,000 | $45,000 | $75,000 | $ 75,000 | $ — |
| (b) | 15,000 | 37,500 [52,500] | 63,000 | 52,500 | 10,500 |
| (c) | (135,000) | 60,000 [75,000] | 45,000 | 45,000 | — |
| (d) | 52,500 | (45,000) [7500] | 37,500 | 7500 | 30,000 |

   (e) Same as (d) except the distribution of $37,500 is made on June 30 and the corporation uses the calendar year for tax purposes. [handwritten: $52,500 - 22,500 = 30,000$ ... $30,000$ ... $7500$]

19. The stock of the BC Corporation is owned as follows:

| | |
|---|---|
| Mr. B, Sr. | 25% |
| Mr. C, Sr. (B's brother) | 25% |
| T Corporation (100% of the stock is owned by Mr. C, Sr.) | 10% |
| Mrs. B (B, Sr.'s wife) | 10% |
| Mr. B, Jr. | 10% |
| Mr. C, Jr. | 15% |
| Mrs. C (C, Sr.'s wife) | 5% |

   What would be the effects of the following redemptions on the shareholders? (Work each problem independently based on the above ownership.)

   (a) One-half of Mrs. B's shares are redeemed for $60,000 in cash. Mrs. B's basis in the redeemed shares is $20,000.

   (b) One-half of T Corporation's stock is redeemed by a distribution of land with a value of $60,000 and a basis to the corporation of $8,000. T Corporation's basis in the redeemed stock was $20,000.

(c) All of Mr. B, Sr.'s stock is redeemed for $200,000 cash. His basis in the stock was $100,000.

(d) Following Mr. C, Sr.'s death, one-half of his stock (held by his estate) was redeemed to pay death taxes. The redemption price was $180,000, his cost was $50,000, and the value of the stock on the date of his death was $140,000.

20. On December 31, 19X5, prior to a stock redemption, the TB Corporation had accumulated E & P of $50,000 and paid-in capital from the 1,000 shares outstanding of $150,000. One-half of the stock was purchased by the corporation on that date for $75,000 cash in a redemption that was not equivalent to a dividend. In 19X6, the corporation had current E & P of $25,000 and distributed $50,000 in cash to the shareholders on December 31. How much taxable income did the shareholders realize from the $50,000 distribution?

21. X Corporation sells property, adjusted basis of $200,000, fair market value of $180,000, to its sole shareholder for $160,000. How much loss can the corporation deduct as a result of this transaction? What is the effect on the corporation's E & P for the year of sale?

22. X Corporation collects $150,000 on a keyman life insurance policy. The policy possessed a cash surrender value of $20,000 at date of death. What is the effect of this collection on the corporation's taxable income and on its E & P?

23. A corporation distributes LIFO inventory to its shareholders. Basis of the inventory is $16,000. Had the inventory cost been determined under FIFO, the basis would be $24,000. Market value of the inventory is $32,000. What is the effect of this distribution on the corporation's taxable income and on its E & P?

24. AB Corporation distributes to its shareholders realty not used in the active conduct in its business with an adjusted basis of $5,000 and fair market value of $10,000. The realty is subject to a liability of $7,500. What is the effect of this distribution on taxable income of the corporation?

25. XY Corporation distributes to a 5% shareholder equipment with an adjusted basis of $5,028 and fair market value of $7,000. The property was acquired two years ago at a cost of $8,000. In the year of acquisition, the corporation claimed an investment tax credit of $800 (10% of $8,000) based on an estimated useful life of five years. What are the tax consequences to XY Corporation on this transaction?

26. X Corporation has 500 shares of stock outstanding. It redeems 50 shares for $90,000 when it has paid-in capital of $300,000 and E & P of $400,000. What is the reduction in the E & P of X Corporation as a result of the redemption?

27. X and Y are the sole shareholders of AB Corporation, which has E & P of $200,000. X and Y both have a basis in their 100 shares in AB of $30,000. AB issued a 9% preferred stock dividend on the common shares of X and Y in 19X4. X and Y each received 50 shares of preferred stock with a par value of $1,000 per share. Fair market value of one share of common is $2,000, and fair market value of one share of preferred is $1,000.

(a) What are the tax consequences of the distribution to X and Y?

(b) What are the tax consequences to X if she later sells her preferred stock to Z for $60,000? Z is unrelated to X.

(c) What are the tax consequences to Y if he subsequently sells all his stock (both common and preferred) to W for $300,000? W is unrelated to Y.

(d) What are the tax consequences to X if she makes a gift to her daughter, D, of the preferred stock?

(e) What are the tax consequences to X and his son, S, if X dies and bequeaths his stock to S, who later sells the preferred stock to Z for $70,000. The preferred stock had a fair market value of $65,000 on the date of X's death.

28. The adjusted gross estate of D, decedent, is $800,000. The gross estate includes stock in A and B Corporations valued at $180,000 and $200,000, respectively. D owned 30% of A stock and 50% of B stock. Death taxes and funeral and administrative expenses for D's estate were $200,000. D had a basis of $30,000 in the A stock and $50,000 in the B stock. What are the tax consequences to D's estate if A Corporation redeems one-half of D's stock for $90,000 and B Corporation redeems one-half of D's stock for $100,000?

29. S owns 100 shares of W Corporation and 50 shares of Z Corporation, representing 100% ownership of W and 50% ownership of Z. S sells 25 shares of Z Corporation to W Corporation for $60,000. S purchased the stock in Z Corporation five years ago at a cost of $1,000 per share. What are the tax consequences of the sale, assuming W Corporation has E & P of $50,000 and Z Corporation has E & P of $300,000?

30. T, an individual, owns 50% of A Corporation, which in turn owns 50% of B Corporation. T sells 40 of his 100 shares in A Corporation to B Corporation for $50,000. T purchased the 40 shares three years ago for $15,000. What are the tax consequences of the sale assuming A Corporation has E & P of $60,000 and B Corporation has E & P of $40,000?

31. X Corporation operates an active business and owns all of the stock of Y Corporation, which also is engaged in the active conduct of a business. Both X and Y have been actively engaged in business for over five years. X Corporation distributes all the stock of Y Corporation to its shareholders pursuant to an antitrust decree. Both X and Y continue to operate their separate businesses. What are the tax consequences of the distribution to A, an individual shareholder, who receives stock in Y Corporation worth $30,000? A does not surrender any of her stock in X Corporation. What are the tax consequences to A if Y Corporation had been in existence for only two years before the distribution?

## Research Problems

*Research Problem 1.* The stock of X Corporation is held 10% by Y and 90% by Z. W would like to purchase all of this stock but has the cash to pay for only 60%. X Corporation has enough cash on hand to redeem 40% of its shares. Consider and evaluate, in terms of X Corporation, Y, Z, and W, the following alternatives:

(a) X Corporation redeems from Z 40% of the shares. W purchases the remaining 50% held by Z and the 10% owned by Y.

(b) W borrows enough money from a bank to purchase all of Y's and Z's shares. Later, W has X Corporation redeem 40% of the shares purchased to pay off the bank loan.

(c) X Corporation redeems all of Y's shares. W purchases 60% of the shares held by Z. X Corporation then redeems the remainder of Z's 30% interest.

(d) X Corporation distributes 90% of its cash to Z and 10% to Y. This reduces the value of the stock to a level where W's cash is adequate to purchase all of Z's and Y's shares.

*Partial list of research aids:*

*Television Industries, Inc. v. Comm.,* 60–2 USTC ¶ 9795, 6 AFTR2d 5864, 284 F.2d 322 (CA–2, 1960).

*Zenz v. Quinlivan,* 54–2 USTC ¶ 9445, 45 AFTR 1672, 213 F.2d 914 (CA–6, 1954).

*U. S. v. Carey,* 61–1 USTC ¶ 9428, 7 AFTR2d 1301, 289 F.2d 531 (CA–8, 1961).

*Research Problem 2.*   T is the president and majority shareholder of X Corporation. During 1980, T was paid a salary of $50,000 and received a year-end bonus of $200,000. Upon audit in 1981 of X Corporation, $150,000 of the amount paid to T was disallowed by the IRS as being unreasonable. Pursuant to a repayment agreement, T reimbursed X Corporation for the $150,000 in 1982. On his 1980 return, T had included the $150,000 in gross income. On his 1982 return, he deducted none of the repayment but elected the option set forth in § 1341(a)(5). Thus, T claimed a credit for the amount of tax that was generated by the inclusion of the $150,000 in his 1980 return. Upon audit of his 1982 return in 1983, the IRS did not accept the credit approach but did permit a deduction of $150,000 for 1982. Because T was in a higher tax bracket in 1980, a deficiency resulted for 1982. T comes to you for advice. Should he challenge the tax deficiency for tax year 1982?

*Research Problem 3.*   J, the principal shareholder of X Corporation, diverted sums totaling $60,000 from the corporation during tax year 19X3. Upon audit of J's return, the IRS contended these sums were taxable income to J under § 61 of the Code. J disagrees, stating that such sums represent constructive dividends and are taxable only to the extent of X Corporation's E & P, which J argues had a deficit in 19X2. The IRS contends that should § 61 not apply, the $60,000 would still be taxable income because X Corporation had income in 19X3. X Corporation is on the cash basis. It had a deficit in its E & P account as of January 1, 19X3. However, it had E & P in 19X3 of $65,000. Its income tax liability for 19X3 was $31,500. The IRS argues that $31,500 cannot be a charge against current E & P, because the tax was not paid until 19X4 and the corporation was on the cash basis. Consequently, the $60,000 would be taxable income to J in 19X3, regardless of whether it is income under § 61 or under § 301. J comes to you for advice. What advice would you give him?

*Research Problem 4.*   Y Corporation has life insurance policies on all its officers. It pays the insurance premiums and has all incidents of ownership in the policies. The corporate officers realized that though the proceeds of such policies would not be taxable to the corporation upon the death of a corporate officer, such proceeds would increase the corporation's E & P so that payments from such proceeds to the surviving spouses of the officers would represent taxable dividends to them. Consequently, at the insistence of the corporate officers, the board of directors of Y Corporation changed the beneficiaries of such policies, making the beneficiary of each policy the surviving spouse of the corporate officer. In 19X4, an officer died, and his widow received $100,000 from a policy on his life purchased by Y Corporation. The IRS's position is that the $100,000 received by the widow constituted a taxable dividend to her. The widow asks you for advice. What advice would you give her?

*Research Problem 5.*   A owns 40% of X Corporation; his father owns the remaining 60%. A also owns 70% of Y Corporation, with the remaining 30% being owned by his wife. A terminates his entire interest in X Corporation through a stock redemption that he reports as a long-term capital gain pursuant to § 302(b)(3). Three years later, Y Corporation enters into a contract with X Corporation whereby Y Corporation is given exclusive management authority over X Corporation's operations. Upon audit, the IRS disallowed long-term capital gain treatment on the stock redemption in X Corporation contending that A acquired an interest in X within 10 years from the date of the redemption because of Y's management contract with X. What is the result?

*Research Problem 6.*   X Corporation is controlled by H. As part of a property settlement incident to a divorce between H and W, X Corporation agrees to redeem the shares held by W (H's ex-wife). Because of cash-flow problems, the stock is to be redeemed in annual increments over a period from 1981 to 1986. Although the agreement is mandatory in its terms, no redemptions were carried out in 1981 or 1982; however, redemptions were effected in 1983. W reports the gain on the redemption of her stock as a capital gain under § 302(b)(1) in 1983. The IRS contends the redemption in 1983 is a dividend, as there has not been a "meaningful reduction" in W's stock interests. W contends that although the redemption in 1983 does not represent a meaningful reduction, when the redemptions are taken as a whole, the effect of all the redemptions does satisfy the meaningful reduction test. What is the result?

*Research Problem 7.*   The stock of Y Corporation was owned equally by 20 individuals. It became necessary for Y to borrow money to purchase inventory and to pay its operating expenses. Y Corporation was able to obtain loans for three years but only on the condition that individuals with substantial net worth guarantee the loans. Three of Y's shareholders agreed to guarantee the loans. They were paid a fee for the guaranty in the amount of 5% of the average outstanding indebtedness, prorated among the guarantors in proportion to the sum each personally guaranteed. Y Corporation deducted these fees, $30,000 in 1981 and $35,000 in 1982. Upon audit of Y's return in 1984, the IRS disallowed the deductions, reclassifying them as dividends. What is the result if Y challenges the tax deficiency?

# Corporations: Distributions in Complete Liquidation

# 5

## CHAPTER OBJECTIVES

—Contrast property dividends and stock redemptions with distributions in complete liquidation of a corporation.

—Review the tax effect of a complete liquidation on the corporation being liquidated.

—Discuss the various options that may be available to the shareholders as to the type of liquidation utilized.

—Explain the tax consequences to the shareholders when the corporation is collapsible.

—Recognize the tax planning opportunities available to minimize the income tax result in the complete liquidation of a corporation.

When a stock redemption is transacted, the assumption usually is that the corporation will continue as a separate entity. With complete liquidation, however, corporate existence terminates. In view of the difference in the result, the tax rules governing this type of distribution are not the same. This chapter reviews the tax impact of a complete liquidation on the corporation making the distributions and on the shareholders receiving such distributions.

# COMPLETE LIQUIDATIONS—AN OVERVIEW

Since the income tax provisions applicable to corporate liquidations are somewhat complex, an introductory summary will be helpful in sorting out the various applicable rules. Following the summary, distributions in liquidation are compared with those relating to stock redemptions and dividends (discussed in Chapter 4).

## SUMMARY OF THE TAX CONSEQUENCES

A complete liquidation of a corporation has tax ramifications for both the corporation being liquidated and the shareholders who receive distributions in complete liquidation of their stock investments. The tax effects of a liquidation on both the corporation and the shareholders are briefly summarized.

*Effect on the Corporation.* Two major tax provisions govern the tax effect of a complete liquidation on the corporation being liquidated.

—Under § 336 no gain or loss is recognized to a corporation distributing assets directly to its shareholders in return for their stock. Referred to as the "in kind" type of distribution, it is distinguishable from the situation where the corporation first sells the assets, then distributes the sale proceeds to its shareholders. The general rule providing for no gain or loss on in kind distributions is subject to numerous exceptions. The corporation may have to recognize gain (or make a direct addition to its tax liability) if the assets distributed consist of installment notes receivable, assets subject to the recapture of depreciation or the investment tax credit, or LIFO inventory. Further exceptions include the possible application of the tax benefit rule and the anticipatory assignment of income doctrine.

—Under § 337 no gain or loss is recognized to a corporation that sells property and, within a 12-month period, distributes all of its assets in complete liquidation. Known as the 12-month liquidation, it covers only the sale of property. As defined in § 337(b), "property" generally does not include installment notes receivable, accounts receivable, and inventory. The same exceptions relating to distributions in kind under § 336 (e. g., recapture of depreciation) apply to the 12-month liquidation. In such cases, the sale of property is not protected from the recognition of gain (or a direct addition to tax liability).

Sections 336 and 337 can apply to the same liquidation. Consequently, distributions in kind would be covered by § 336, while sales by the corporation would fall under the 12-month liquidation of § 337. However, § 337 is not applicable to redemptions that are qualified partial liquidations (refer to Chapter 4), the liquidation of a collapsible corporation, the one-month liquidation of § 333, and for most liquidations of a subsidiary corporation under § 332.

*Effect on the Shareholder.*   The tax treatment of a shareholder receiving a distribution in complete liquidation is subject to a general rule and three exceptions.

—The *general rule* of § 331 applies *exchange* treatment to the shareholder. Gain or loss will be recognized measured by the difference between the fair market value of the assets received from the corporation and the adjusted basis of the stock surrendered. When the stock is a capital asset, any gain or loss will be capital. The shareholder's basis in the assets received from the corporation will be the assets' fair market value on the date of distribution [§ 334(a)]. The general rule of § 331, therefore, follows the same approach taken with stock redemptions that qualify for exchange treatment (refer to Chapter 4).

—Section 341 converts any long-term capital gain the shareholder might otherwise have under the general rule into ordinary income if the corporation being liquidated is collapsible.

—Section 333 (known as the one-month liquidation) limits the shareholder's recognized gain to the greater of the proportionate share of the corporation's E & P or its cash *and* securities acquired since 1953. In no event, however, can more gain be recognized than is realized. A noncorporate shareholder must classify such gain as dividend income to the extent of a ratable share of E & P. Any excess recognized gain (where the corporation's cash plus post-1953 securities exceeds its E & P) is capital gain. All of a corporate shareholder's gain will be capital. The basis of property received pursuant to a § 333 liquidation will be the basis of the stock given up less the cash received plus the gain recognized by the shareholder [§ 334(c)]. The one-month liquidation is optional with the shareholders. If elected, the tax consequences described replace those applicable under the general rule of § 331.

—Section 332 is not elective (unless the liquidation falls under § 338, discussed below). When a parent corporation liquidates its subsidiary corporation, no gain or loss is recognized to the parent. This provision applies only when the parent owns 80 percent or more of the stock of the subsidiary. The basis to the parent of the assets received from the subsidiary is the same basis the assets had in the hands of the subsidiary [§ 334(b)(1)].

—Section 338 provides that when an acquiring corporation purchases at least 80 percent of the stock of another corporation, it may elect to be treated as the purchaser of the assets of the acquired corporation if it makes an election by the 15th day of the ninth month beginning after the month in which the purchase of the 80 percent or more of the acquired corporation's shares and voting power occurred. The subsidiary corporation need not be liquidated by the parent, but if it is, § 332 will apply to the liquidation so that no gain or loss will be recognized to the parent. The parent's basis in the assets of the subsidiary will be the cost of the stock to the parent. (If the subsidiary is not liquidated, it is treated as having sold its assets to the parent under § 337.)

*Comparative Illustrations.* The following examples compare the tax effect of the different types of liquidations.

**Example 1.** X Corporation has as its only asset unimproved land (adjusted basis of $100,000 and fair market value of $150,000). T, an individual, owns all of the outstanding stock in X Corporation, such stock having an adjusted basis of $80,000. X Corporation distributes the land to T in complete cancellation of all its outstanding stock. At the time of its liquidation, X Corporation's E & P is $30,000.

*Effect on the Corporation.* No gain is recognized by X Corporation, since the land is distributed in kind to T (§ 336). The same result materializes if the corporation sells the land and distributes the proceeds, and the requirements of the 12-month liquidation (§ 337) are satisfied.

*Effect on the Shareholder.* Pursuant to the general rule of § 331, T must recognize a gain of $70,000 [$150,000 (fair market value of the land) − $80,000 (adjusted basis of the stock)]. If the stock is a capital asset, the gain would be capital. T's basis in the land becomes $150,000, the land's fair market value on the date of the distribution [§ 334(a)].

**Example 2.** Assume the same facts as in Example 1 except that T elects to have the one-month liquidation of § 333 apply.

*Effect on the Corporation.* No gain is recognized by X Corporation, since the land is distributed in kind to T (§ 336). Because the 12-month liquidation of § 337 is not available for the one-month liquidation of § 333, a sale of the land by the corporation would yield a recognizable gain of $50,000 [$150,000 (sale proceeds) − $100,000 (adjusted basis of the land)].[1]

*Effect on the Shareholder.* Under § 333, T must recognize dividend income of $30,000, the greater of the corporation's E & P ($30,000) or its cash ($0) plus post-1953 securities ($0). By the application of § 334(c), T's

---

1. The gain of $50,000 less the corporate income tax it generates would be added to X Corporation's E & P (refer to Chapter 4). Under § 333, this forces T to recognize additional dividend income on the liquidation.

basis in the land becomes $110,000 [$80,000 (adjusted basis in the stock) − $0 (cash received) + $30,000 (gain recognized)].

**Example 3.** Assume the same facts as in Example 1 except that T is a corporation rather than an individual. Since T Corporation now is a parent and X Corporation is a subsidiary, the liquidation of X Corporation must fall under § 332.

*Effect on the Corporation.* No gain is recognized by X Corporation, since the land is distributed in kind to T Corporation (§ 336). Because the 12-month liquidation of § 337 generally is not available for the parent-subsidiary type of liquidation of § 332, a sale of the land by X Corporation would yield a recognizable gain of $50,000.

*Effect on the Shareholder.* In the liquidation of a subsidiary by a parent, no gain or loss is recognized by the parent corporation (§ 332). Under § 334(b)(1), T Corporation's basis becomes $100,000—the subsidiary's basis in the land carried over to the parent corporation. Assume, however, that T Corporation purchased at least 80 percent of X's stock for $80,000 and made a timely election pursuant to § 338 to treat the transaction as a purchase of the assets of X Corporation. T's basis in the land would then be $80,000.

## LIQUIDATIONS, STOCK REDEMPTIONS, AND DIVIDEND DISTRIBUTIONS—A COMPARISON OF THE EFFECTS UPON SHAREHOLDERS

Liquidations and stock redemptions parallel each other insofar as the E & P of the distributing corporation is concerned. Except for one type of liquidation (i. e., the one-month election of § 333), the E & P of the corporation undergoing liquidation has no tax impact on the gain or loss to be recognized by the shareholders. Such is the case because § 301 (governing dividend distributions) is specifically made inapplicable to complete liquidations.[2]

**Example 4.** Z Corporation, with E & P of $40,000, makes a cash distribution of $50,000 to its sole shareholder. Assume the shareholder's basis in the Z Corporation stock is $20,000 and it is held as an investment. If the distribution is not in complete liquidation or if it does not qualify as a stock redemption, the shareholder must recognize dividend income of $40,000 (i. e., the amount of Z Corporation's E & P) and must treat the remaining $10,000 of the distribution as a return of capital. On the other hand, if the distribution is pursuant to a complete liquidation or qualifies for exchange treatment as a stock redemption, the shareholder will have a recognized capital gain of $30,000 [$50,000 (the amount of the distribution) − $20,000 (the basis in the stock)]. In the latter case, note that Z Corporation's E & P is of no consequence to the tax result.

In the event the distribution results in a *loss* to the shareholder, there could be an important distinction between stock redemptions and liquida-

---

2.  § 331(b).

tions. The distinction could arise because § 267 (i. e., disallowance of losses between related parties) is applicable to stock redemptions but not to liquidations.

> **Example 5.** The stock of P Corporation is owned equally by three brothers, R, S, and T. At a point when T's basis in his stock investment is $40,000, the corporation distributes $30,000 to him in cancellation of all his shares. If the distribution is a stock redemption, the $10,000 realized loss is not recognized due to the application of § 267(a).[3] T and P Corporation are related parties because T is deemed to own more than 50% in value of the corporation's outstanding stock [§ 267(b)(2)]. Although T's direct ownership is limited to 33⅓%, through his brothers he owns indirectly another 66⅔% for a total of 100% [§ § 267(c)(2) and (4)]. Had the distribution qualified as a complete liquidation, T's $10,000 realized loss would be recognizable.

With reference to the basis of noncash property received from the corporation, the rules governing liquidations and stock redemptions are identical.

Section 334(a) specifies that the basis of such property distributed pursuant to a complete liquidation under § 331 shall be the fair market value on the date of distribution.

# EFFECT ON THE DISTRIBUTING CORPORATION

The tax consequences to the corporation in the process of liquidation are governed by § § 336 and 337. Section 336 covers distributions of corporate property in kind (i. e., the property is distributed as is), while § 337 deals with sales of corporate property with the distribution of the proceeds thereof to the shareholders. These Code provisions are not mutually exclusive, and both can, and frequently will, apply to the same liquidation.

## DISTRIBUTIONS IN KIND UNDER § 336

Section 336 provides that no gain or loss will be recognized to the distributing corporation upon the distribution of its property in complete liquidation. As usual, the general rule is subject to exceptions.

—Gain results from the distribution of installment notes receivable. The measure of the gain will be the difference between the fair market value of the note on the date of distribution and the adjusted basis in the hands of the corporation [§ § 336 and 453B(a)].

—Gain results on the distribution of LIFO inventory. The measure of the gain is the excess of the cost of the inventory using the FIFO method over the cost using LIFO [§ 336(b)].

—To the extent of any depreciation that would have been recaptured had the property been sold by the corporation, ordinary income will result [§ § 1245(d), 1250(i), and 291(a)].

---

3. *McCarthy v. Conley, Jr.,* 65–1 USTC ¶ 9262, 15 AFTR2d 447, 341 F.2d 948 (CA–2, 1965).

—Since the distribution will be treated as a disposition, recapture of some or all of any investment credit previously claimed by the distributing corporation may be in order [§ 47(a)]. Unlike the recapture of depreciation that produces ordinary income, the recapture of the investment credit means a direct addition to the tax liability of the corporation.

—Under certain conditions (see the discussion of § 337 in the following section) the *Court Holding Company*[4] concept could apply to attribute to the corporation the sale by the shareholders of property distributed to them. Thus, the sale could be attributed to the corporation if all or most of the negotiations were completed at the corporate level. As a result, the corporation would be forced to recognize as gain the difference between the selling price and its adjusted basis in the property.

—The corporation will have to take into income any assets distributed to the shareholders for which it has previously claimed a deduction. This matter, formerly in doubt, has been resolved by the U. S. Supreme Court.[5]

—The distributing corporation may have to recognize income under any one of several nebulous concepts of tax law. One such concept, the anticipatory assignment of income doctrine (discussed later in this chapter and in Chapter 4), could be applied. The authority of the IRS to make adjustments to a taxpayer's method of accounting in order to clearly reflect income [§ 446(b)] might be exercised to generate income to the corporation.

> **Example 6.**  U Corporation is a construction company reporting its income from operations on the completed contract method of accounting (i. e., no income is recognized until the contract is completed). Prior to the completion of a particularly lucrative construction contract, U Corporation liquidates and distributes its assets (including its construction contracts) to its shareholders in complete liquidation. Such avoidance of income recognition on the uncompleted construction contracts clearly does not reflect U Corporation's earnings, and the IRS may try to place U Corporation on a percentage of completion method of accounting (i. e., recognition of income proportionate to the percentage of contract completed).[6]

---

4.  *Comm. v. Court Holding Co.*, 45–1 USTC ¶ 9215, 33 AFTR 593, 65 S.Ct. 707 (USSC, 1945).

5.  See Rev.Rul. 74–396, 1974–2 C.B. 106, and Rev.Rul. 78–278, 1978–2 C.B. 134, for the position of the IRS on this issue. In *Bliss Dairy, Inc. v. Comm.*, 81–1 USTC ¶ 9429, 47 AFTR2d 81–1547, 645 F.2d 19 (CA–9, 1981), the Ninth Court of Appeals refused to apply the tax benefit rule to a distribution of assets under § 336. A contrary result, and one that is compatible with the position of the IRS, was reached in *Tennessee-Carolina Transportation, Inc. v. Comm.*, 78–2 USTC ¶ 9671, 42 AFTR2d 78–5716, 582 F.2d 378 (CA–6, 1978). This conflict in the Courts of Appeals was resolved when the U. S. Supreme Court reversed *Bliss Dairy, Inc.* in 83–1 USTC ¶ 9229, 51 AFTR2d 83–874, 103 S.Ct. 1134 (1983).

6.  The classic cases in this area are *Jud Plumbing & Heating Co. v. Comm.*, 46–1 USTC ¶ 9177, 34 AFTR 1025, 153 F.2d 681 (CA–5, 1946), and *Standard Paving Co. v. Comm.*, 51–2 USTC ¶ 9376, 40 AFTR 1022, 190 F.2d 330 (CA–10, 1951).

The preceding rules parallel those applicable to corporations using property to effect a *redemption* of stock (refer to Chapter 4). There are, however, several important differences. For example, § 311(d) applies to *most* stock redemptions (and to dividend distributions) but not to corporate liquidations. Consequently, the use of appreciated property to carry out a stock redemption (or a dividend distribution) could trigger gain to the distributing corporation.

> **Example 7.** V Corporation distributes unimproved land (basis of $20,000 and fair market value of $60,000) to one of its shareholders. If the distribution is made pursuant to a stock redemption (or a property dividend) and the exceptions of § 311(d)(2) do not apply, V Corporation must recognize a gain of $40,000. The distribution would not result in any gain to V Corporation if it was made pursuant to a complete liquidation.

Another difference arises when the subject matter of the distribution is property with a liability in excess of basis. Here, stock redemptions are treated no differently than regular dividend distributions, and the distributing corporation is susceptible to the recognition of gain under § 311(c). Such is not the case, however, when the distribution is made pursuant to a complete liquidation.[7]

## SALES BY THE LIQUIDATING CORPORATION— THE 12-MONTH LIQUIDATION OF § 337

As was true of § 336, § 337 deals with the effect on the corporation of a liquidation. Section 337 was added to the Code to provide a solution to the uncertainty created by two Supreme Court cases, *Commissioner v. Court Holding Company* and *U. S. v. Cumberland Public Service Company.*[8]

In *Commissioner v. Court Holding Company,* a corporation was organized solely to buy and hold an apartment building. While the corporation had title to the apartment building, negotiations for sale of the building took place. Because the corporation's attorney advised the parties that a large corporate tax would have to be paid on the sale, the corporation liquidated and transferred the building to its shareholders, a husband and wife. The shareholders then sold the building. Justice Black wrote the opinion of the Supreme Court which held that gain on the sale of the building must be attributed to the corporation. The executed sale was, in substance, a sale by the corporation. Five years later, in *U. S. v. Cumberland Public Service Company,* Justice Black again wrote the opinion of the Supreme Court, this time stating that gain would not be attributed to the corporation in a fact situation not substantially different from that in *Court Holding Company.*

In the *Cumberland Public Service* case, a closely-held corporation offered to sell all its stock to a cooperative. The cooperative refused to buy the stock, but countered with an offer to buy the assets of the corporation. To avoid paying a corporate tax on the sale, the corporation liquidated, and

---

7.  Reg. § 1.311–1(a).
8.  *U. S. v. Cumberland Public Service Co.,* 50–1 USTC ¶ 9129, 38 AFTR 978, 70 S.Ct. 280 (USSC, 1950). Refer to Footnote 4 for the citation to *Comm. v. Court Holding Co.*

the shareholders sold the assets to the cooperative. Justice Black concluded that because the corporation did not make the sale, it owed no tax. He distinguished the *Court Holding Company* decision on the grounds that findings of fact by the Tax Court in that case established that the sale had been made by the corporation.

The *Court Holding Company* and the *Cumberland Public Service* cases presented different tax treatment for a corporation that sold its assets and then liquidated than for a corporation that liquidated first, with the shareholders then effecting the sale. Further, it created a tax trap for the unwary who might arrange for the sale of corporate assets prior to liquidation. The tax consequences of sales made in the course of liquidation depended primarily upon the formal manner in which the transaction was arranged. Section 337 was added to the Code in 1954 to provide a definitive rule that would eliminate these uncertainties.[9]

Section 337 states that if a corporation distributes all its assets in complete liquidation within 12 months after the adoption of a plan of liquidation, no gain or loss will be recognized on the sale of property by the corporation during the 12-month period. As a result, the tax treatment for a corporation selling its assets and then liquidating is no different from that of the corporation that liquidates first, with the shareholders later selling the assets. The problem is that § 337 applies only to complete liquidations. Further, liquidations pursuant to the one-month type of § 333 and the liquidations of most subsidiary corporations pursuant to § 332 are not covered by § 337 [§ 337 (c)(1) and (2)]. The decisions in *Court Holding Company* and *Cumberland Public Service* would presumably still apply to these transactions.[10] Other limitations exist in applying § 337. By its own terms, § 337 is not applicable to some sales.

*Definition of "Property" Under § 337.* Section 337 applies to the sale of property by the liquidating corporation; consequently, the definition of the term "property" has presented a problem for some courts. Section 337(b) excepts from the term (a) inventory or property held by the corporation primarily for sale to customers in the ordinary course of its trade or business, (b) installment obligations acquired upon the sale of inventory items, and (c) installment obligations acquired with respect to property sold or exchanged before the date of the adoption of a plan of liquidation. However, § 337(b)(2) does permit inventory to be included as "property" if "substantially all" of the inventory is sold in bulk to one person in one transaction. However, with respect to LIFO inventory, even though sold in bulk, § 337(f) requires that the LIFO recapture amount (i. e., the excess of inventory costed under FIFO over inventory costed under LIFO) be recognized as gain on disposition.

In *Pridemark, Inc. v. Commissioner,* the Court stated that the term "property" used in § 337 was taken almost verbatim from the definition of capital assets found in § 1221; consequently, only the sale of capital assets

---

**9.**   S.Rept. 83d Cong., 2d Sess. 1954, *U. S. Code Congressional and Administrative News,* Vol. 3, West Publishing Co., p. 4896.

**10.**   In *Aaron Cohen,* 63 T.C. 527 (1975), the Court held *Court Holding Company* applicable to a § 333 liquidation. Because the contract of sale was entered into prior to the liquidation, gain on such sale was attributable to the corporation.

during the year of liquidation is exempted from taxation at the corporate level.[11] In the *Pridemark, Inc. v. Commissioner* case, the corporation used the accrual accounting method; however, it had not accrued income on certain uncompleted contracts. Income was accrued only when deliveries were begun. These contracts were sold by the corporation. The Court held that gain from the sale was attributed to the corporation as ordinary income because the uncompleted contracts were not capital assets. This same theory was applied to the taxpayer's advantage in *Coast Coil Company* in which certain accounts receivable of an accrual basis corporation were sold by the corporation at a loss prior to liquidation.[12] As an accrual basis taxpayer, the corporation had previously reported the accounts receivable as ordinary income. The Court held that the corporation could recognize a loss on the sale because the accounts receivable were not capital assets and thus not subject to § 337.

This concept was applied in a slightly different fashion in *Central Building and Loan Association*.[13] There, the liquidating corporation sold notes receivable that included accrued interest. The Court held that the collection of interest was not a "sale or exchange" of property and hence was income to the liquidating corporation.

The theory of limiting § 337 to the sale or exchange of capital assets is not sound. Section 1231 assets (i. e., depreciable assets and real estate used in the trade or business and held for more than six months) are covered by § 337; further, depreciable assets not held for more than six months and copyrights, letters, and other assets described in § 1221(3) would be covered. Inventory sold in bulk to one person is included. In a later case, the Tax Court stated its opinion that limiting the term "property" to capital assets was not warranted by legislative history behind § 337.[14] The Court held that no gain was recognized to a liquidating corporation on the sale of mortgage servicing contracts; the contracts were "property" under § 337, even though they were not capital assets.

*Anticipatory Assignment of Income Doctrine.* The assignment of income doctrine may be used to attribute income to a liquidating corporation despite § 337 and often is imposed simultaneously with a decision that "property" has not been sold so as to avoid recognition of gain under § 337. In *Pridemark, Inc. v. Commissioner,* the Court attributed income on uncompleted contracts to the liquidating corporation under the anticipatory assignment of income doctrine as well as the theory that "property" had not been distributed.[15] In *Central Building and Loan Association*, the accrued interest on notes receivable was also attributed to the liquidating corporation under the assignment of income doctrine.[16] The *Coast Coil Company* case noted the assignment of income doctrine, in that instance to

---

11. 65–1 USTC ¶ 9388, 15 AFTR2d 853, 345 F.2d 35 (CA–4, 1965).

12. 50 T.C. 528 (1968) *aff'd.* in 70–1 USTC ¶ 9270, 25 AFTR2d 70–787, 422 F.2d 402 (CA–9, 1970).

13. 34 T.C. 447 (1960).

14. *John T. Stewart III Trust,* 63 T.C. 683 (1975). Also see, Rev.Rul. 77–190, 1977–1 C.B. 88, wherein the IRS agreed that the term "property" is not limited to capital assets.

15. *Supra,* Footnote 11.

16. *Supra,* Footnote 13.

permit a loss on the sale of accounts receivable by an accrual basis corporation.[17]

In *John T. Stewart III Trust*,[18] the Tax Court stated its opinion that the assignment of income doctrine applies only to that portion of profits *earned* by the liquidating corporation through partial performance of a contract.

> **Example 8.** X Corporation is on the cash basis. It adopts a plan of complete liquidation and distributes to shareholders unrealized receivables and a contract on which payment had not been made. The assignment of income doctrine would undoubtedly be employed to tax income from subsequent collections to the liquidating corporation. However, with regard to the contract, if the corporation had not performed the stated requirements, taxpayers could rely on *John T. Stewart III Trust*. Profits would not have been *earned* by the liquidating corporation, and therefore, the assignment of income doctrine would not apply.

*Tax Benefit Rule.*   Income is recognized by a liquidating corporation, despite § 337, under the so-called tax benefit rule. If a corporation sells supplies it previously expensed, the corporation must recognize the proceeds from the sale of the supplies as income to the extent prior years' deductions produced a tax benefit to the corporation.[19]

> **Example 9.** Pursuant to a complete liquidation under § 337, P Corporation sells rental uniforms for $100,000. Such uniforms were expensed as acquired and therefore had a zero basis to the corporation at the time of the sale. To the extent P Corporation was able to obtain a tax benefit from the deduction for uniform purchases, it has income from the sale. The measure of the income is not the corporate income tax actually saved through the deduction but the amount deducted that reduced taxes. In no event, however, would P Corporation have to recognize income in excess of $100,000.[20]

The tax benefit rule has been applied to the allowance for bad debts. The IRS had taken the position that a corporation has income to the extent of the bad debt reserve account when it sells its accounts receivable regardless of the amount realized from the sale.[21] The IRS now has modified its position in the light of the Supreme Court decision in *Nash v. U. S.* (refer to Chapter 3).[22] The IRS will attribute income to the corporation only if the

---

**17.**  *Supra,* Footnote 12.
**18.**  *Supra,* Footnote 14. See also, *Midland Ross Corp v. U. S.*, 73–2 USTC ¶ 9678, 32 AFTR2d 73–5850, 485 F.2d 110 (CA–6, 1972), and *Storz v. Comm.*, 78–2 USTC ¶ 9587, 42 AFTR2d 78–5464, 583 F.2d 972 (CA–8 1978), *rev'g.* 68 T.C. 84 (1977).
**19.**  See *Comm. v. Anders*, 69–2 USTC ¶ 9478, 24 AFTR2d 69–5133, 414 F.2d 1283 (CA–10, 1969), *cert. den.*, 90 S.Ct. 431 (USSC, 1969); *Connery v. U. S.*, 72–1 USTC ¶ 9441, 29 AFTR2d 72–1188, 460 F.2d 1130 (CA–3, 1972).
**20.**  *Estate of David B. Munter*, 63 T.C. 663 (1975).
**21.**  Rev.Rul. 57–482, 1957–2 C.B. 49.
**22.**  The current position of the IRS is stated in Rev.Rul. 78–279, 1978–2 C.B. 135. Cases involving the application of the tax benefit rule to the sales of accounts receivable pursuant to plans of complete liquidation include *Bird Management, Inc.*, 48 T.C. 586 (1967), and *Citizens Acceptance Corp. v. U. S.*, 72–2 USTC ¶ 9510, 29 AFTR2d 72–1441, 462 F.2d 751 (CA–3, 1972).

receivables are sold for more than book value (i. e., face amount less the balance in the reserve).

**Example 10.** Q Corporation, an accrual basis taxpayer, adopts a plan of complete liquidation under § 337. Its accounts receivable (face amount of $100,000 with a reserve for bad debts of $10,000) are sold for $95,000. Subject to the tax benefit rule, the sale results in $5,000 of income to Q Corporation.

*Recapture Rules.* Sections 291(a), 1245, 1250, and 1252 do not except the nonrecognition provisions of § 337 from their recapture rules; consequently, these sections override § 337. Income is recognized by a liquidating corporation to the extent there would be a recapture of depreciation should depreciable assets be sold at their fair market values. Further, those assets that would produce a loss upon a sale cannot be offset against those producing a gain.

Because § 337 is subordinate to § 47, there is also investment credit recapture should a liquidating corporation dispose of § 38 assets prematurely.

*Straddle Sales.* Although the avowed purpose of § 337 is to protect a corporation from recognizing a gain on the sale of property during the liquidation period, a price must be paid for such treatment. The price is found in the language of § 337(a), which also disallows the recognition of any loss from the sale of property covered therein. To circumvent this result (i. e., nonrecognition of both gains and losses), the straddle sale approach was devised. Quite simply, it involves selling the *loss* assets *before* the plan of liquidation is adopted (§ 337 would be inapplicable) and selling the *gain* assets *after* the plan is adopted (§ 337 would be applicable). Consequently, the corporation could recognize its losses and avoid recognition of its gains.

**Example 11.** R Corporation owns Asset A (adjusted basis of $30,000 and fair market value of $20,000) and Asset B (adjusted basis of $20,000 and fair market value of $30,000). Both assets qualify as property for the purposes of § 337. On June 1, 19X1, Asset A is sold for $20,000. On July 1, 19X1, R Corporation adopts a plan of complete liquidation. Shortly thereafter, Asset B is sold for $30,000. What has been accomplished for tax purposes? Presuming the straddle sale approach is effective (i. e., Asset A is sold prior to the adoption of a plan of liquidation), R Corporation may recognize a loss of $10,000. The realized gain of $10,000 on the sale of Asset B is not recognized because its sale is effected after § 337 becomes applicable.

**Example 12.** Assume the same facts as in Example 11 except that both Assets A and B are sold after July 1, 19X1. Since the sales occur after the plan of liquidation was adopted, neither gain nor loss will be recognized. This treatment results because of the applicability of § 337 to both sales.

The key to the success of the straddle sale approach (Example 11) is an exact determination of when the plan of liquidation was adopted. Ordinarily, the controlling date is the date of adoption by the shareholders of a resolution authorizing the distribution of all the assets of the corporation in complete liquidation.[23] But could the IRS successfully contend that the plan was really adopted when the corporation decided to first sell its loss assets?[24] Such being the case, both losses and gains would go unrecognized if the liquidation took place within 12 months from the date of adoption of the "informal" plan.

Although courts have not been hesitant to find an informal plan of complete liquidation when no formal plan was adopted,[25] the presence of a formal plan appears to control.[26] Consequently, the straddle sale approach has been recognized when the parties have been careful to adopt a formal plan *after* the sale of the loss assets.[27]

*Expenses of Liquidation.* The expenses involved in liquidating a corporation fall into two major categories:

—General liquidation expenses. Examples include the legal and accounting cost of drafting a plan of liquidation or the cost of revocation of the corporate charter.

—Specific liquidation expenses relating to the disposition or sale of corporate assets. Examples include a brokerage commission for the sale of real estate or a legal fee to clear title and effect a transfer of property in kind to a shareholder.

General liquidation expenses are deductible to the corporation as business expenses under § 162. Specific liquidation expenses are deductible when they relate to distributions in kind under § 336 or to the sale of assets outside the scope of § 337. If associated with the sale of assets under § 337, the expenses must be offset against the selling price.[28] Such treatment, in effect, disallows any deduction. The offset decreases realized gain or increases realized loss, neither of which can be recognized.

**Example 13.** During its liquidation, R Corporation incurs the following expenses:

| | |
|---|---|
| General liquidation expenses | $ 12,000 |
| Legal expenses to effect a distribution (in kind under § 336) | 200 |
| Sales commissions to dispose of inventory (not covered under § 337) | 3,000 |
| Brokerage fee on sale of real estate (covered under § 337) | 8,000 |

---

**23.** Reg. § 1.337–2(b) does provide for the recognition of *both* gains and losses when the corporation sells "substantially all" of its property *prior* to the adoption of a plan of complete liquidation. In other cases, however, the date of the adoption of the plan of liquidation shall be determined from all of the facts and circumstances.
**24.** Rev.Rul. 57–140, 1957–1 C.B. 118.
**25.** *Alameda Realty Corporation,* 42 T.C. 273 (1964), and *Jessie B. Mitchell,* 31 TCM 1077, T.C.Memo. 1972–219.
**26.** But see *Harold O. Wales,* 50 T.C. 399 (1968), dealing with § 333 liquidations.
**27.** *Virginia Ice and Freezing Corp.,* 30 T.C. 1251 (1958), and *City Bank of Washington,* 38 T.C. 713 (1962).
**28.** *U. S. v. Morton,* 68–1 USTC ¶ 9143, 21 AFTR2d 368, 387 F.2d 441 (CA–8, 1968); *Of Course, Inc. v. Comm.,* 74–2 USTC ¶ 9546, 34 AFTR2d 74–5348, 499 F.2d 754 (CA–4, 1974); and *John T. Stewart III Trust,* 63 T.C. 683 (1975).

R Corporation can deduct only $15,200 (i. e., $12,000 + $200 + $3,000). The $8,000 brokerage fee must be applied against the selling price of the real estate.

*Involuntary Conversions.* If a corporation has its major asset or assets destroyed in a casualty (e. g., fire, storm), the shareholders may want to discontinue the business and liquidate the corporation. But what if the anticipated insurance recovery from the destruction of the asset(s) will generate a large realized gain? Can the recognition of any such gain be avoided through the use of § 337? Absent the adoption of a plan of complete liquidation prior to the casualty (an unlikely or suspicious possibility), § 337 was held by the Supreme Court to be not applicable to the gain.[29]

Because the decision reached by the Supreme Court could lead to harsh results by making § 337 unavailable to many involuntary conversions, subsection (e) was added to § 337. Under this provision, an involuntary conversion occurring within 60 days preceding the adoption of the plan will be deemed to fall within the 12-month period following such adoption. Thus, the shelter of § 337 can be obtained if the parties act within 60 days of the conversion.

*Assets Retained to Pay Claims.* Section 337 requires the distribution of all corporate assets within 12 months from the adoption of a plan of liquidation; however, assets may be retained to pay claims.[30] These assets must be reasonable in amount in relation to the specific liabilities involved and must be set apart for the purpose of paying such liabilities. Assets may be retained to pay contingent liabilities and expenses of liquidation.[31]

If assets are retained to pay debts owed to shareholders, caution should be exercised. In *John Town, Inc.,* assets were retained to pay notes held by the corporation's sole shareholder.[32] Because the notes were considered to be hybrid stock (i. e., the corporation was thinly capitalized), the Court held that the corporation did not meet the 12-month distribution requirement. Consequently, the nonrecognition provisions of § 337 did not apply.

*Installment Sales.* As previously noted, § 336 (dealing with distributions in kind in liquidation) excepts the disposition of installment obligations pursuant to § 453B from its nonrecognition provisions. Similarly, § 337(b) provides that installment obligations acquired from the sale or exchange of inventory and installment obligations acquired *before* the date of adoption of a plan of liquidation from the sale of property other than inventory are not included in the term "property" for the purposes of non-

---

29. *Central Tablet Manufacturing Co. v. U. S.,* 74–2 USTC ¶ 9511, 34 AFTR2d 74–5200, 94 S.Ct. 2516 (USSC, 1974). The rationale behind the decision was based on when the gain from the involuntary conversion is realized. If the gain is realized when the casualty occurs, the result reached by the Court, a subsequent adoption of a plan of complete liquidation cannot avoid its recognition. The taxpayers had argued that the gain is realized when the insurance recovery occurs and therefore followed in point of time the adoption of the plan.

30. If shareholders cannot be located, a distribution to a trustee or other person authorized by law to receive distributions for the benefit of such shareholders is considered a liquidating distribution. See Reg. § 1.337–2(b).

31. Reg. § 1.337–1 and Rev.Rul. 80–150, 1980–1 C.B. 316.

32. 46 T.C. 107 (1966), *aff'd.* in 67–1 USTC ¶ 9462, 19 AFTR2d 1389 (CA–7, 1967).

recognition treatment. Section 453B(d)(2)(B) states that if an installment obligation that would have produced no gain or loss to the corporation pursuant to § 337 is distributed by a corporation in the course of liquidation, gain or loss is not recognized. However, this rule does not apply to installment obligations arising from the sale of property subject to depreciation recapture.

Briefly, the provisions with respect to installment obligations are as follows: Installment obligations arising from (a) the sale of non-LIFO inventory property in bulk or (b) the sale of noninventory property (other than recapture property) *after* the date of adoption of a plan of liquidation are subject to the nonrecognition provisions.

> **Example 14.** On January 8, 19X1, V Corporation adopts a plan of complete liquidation. During the course of the liquidation (completed within 12 months), V Corporation distributes to its shareholders the following installment notes receivable:
>
> Note #1 received from the sale of corporate property in 19X0.
>
> Note #2 received from the bulk sale of non-LIFO inventory on March 20, 19X1.
>
> Note #3 received from the sale of nondepreciable property on June 1, 19X1.

Only the distribution of Note #1 will cause tax consequences to V Corporation. Since the bulk sale of the inventory and the sale of the nondepreciable property result in no recognized gain to the corporation (under § 337), the distribution of Note #2 and Note #3 is protected.

## FILING REQUIREMENTS FOR CORPORATE LIQUIDATIONS UNDER § 337

The Regulations require that a copy of the minutes of the shareholders' meeting in which the plan of liquidation was adopted be attached to the income tax return for the liquidating corporation.[33] In addition, a statement must be included listing the assets sold with dates of sale given. The statement should include computations of gain realized and gain not recognized pursuant to § 337. The date of the final liquidating distribution must be given, and a statement of any assets retained to pay liabilities and the nature of those liabilities is also required. An information return, Form 966, is filed with the IRS within 30 days after the adoption of the plan of liquidation. (Notification of this type is also required by some states.) Information returns (Form 1099-DIV, transmitted to each shareholder on or before January 31 of the year following the liquidation, and Form 1096, to the IRS by February 28) notify shareholders of their respective gains or losses.

## EFFECT ON THE SHAREHOLDER— THE GENERAL RULE

As noted at the beginning of this chapter, in terms of their effect on a shareholder, liquidations fall into one of four major classifications:

---

33.  Reg. § 1.337-6(a).

—The general rule of § 331 with basis determined under § 334(a).

—The liquidation of a subsidiary by a parent corporation. Here, § 332 applies and the basis is determined under § 334(b)(1).

—The liquidation of a subsidiary when the parent elects under § 338.

—The one-month liquidation of § 333 with basis determined under § 334(c).

## THE GENERAL RULE UNDER § 331

In the case of a complete liquidation, the general rule under § 331(a)(1) provides for exchange treatment. Since § 1001(c) requires the recognition of gain or loss on the sale or exchange of property, the end result is to treat the shareholder as having sold his or her stock to the corporation being liquidated. Thus, the difference between the liquidation proceeds and the adjusted basis of the stock (i. e., realized gain or loss), becomes the amount that is recognized. If the stock is a capital asset in the hands of the shareholder, capital gain or loss results.[34] As is usually true, the burden of proof is on the taxpayer to furnish evidence on the adjusted basis of the stock. In the absence of such evidence, therefore, the stock will be deemed to have a zero basis, and the full amount of the liquidation proceeds represents the amount of the gain to be recognized.[35]

Section 334(a) provides that under the general rule of § 331, the income tax basis to the shareholder of property received in a liquidation will be the property's fair market value on the date of distribution.

## SPECIAL RULE FOR CERTAIN INSTALLMENT OBLIGATIONS

The Installment Sales Revision Act of 1980[36] made significant changes when distributions in complete liquidation include installment obligations resulting from § 337 sales by the corporation. To understand these changes and why they came about, some discussion of the prior law is necessary.

*Prior Law.* Prior to the Installment Sales Revision Act, the presence of installment obligations in the liquidating distribution made no difference to the shareholder as to the tax result.

> **Example 15.** After a plan of complete liquidation has been adopted, X Corporation sells its only asset, unimproved land held as an investment that has appreciated in value, to P (an unrelated party) for $1,000,000. Under the terms of the sale, X Corporation receives cash of $250,000 and P's notes for the balance of $750,000. The notes are payable over 10 years ($75,000 per year) and carry a 12% rate of interest. Immediately after the sale, X Corporation distributes the cash and notes to S, an individual and sole shareholder. Assume that S has an

---

**34.** For insight as to what represents a capital asset, see § 1221 and *Corn Products Refining Co. v. Comm.*, 55–2 USTC ¶ 9746, 47 AFTR 1789, 76 S.Ct. 20 (USSC, 1955). But even if the stock is a capital asset, ordinary gain could result if the corporation is collapsible (see later in this chapter).

**35.** *John Calderazzo*, 34 TCM 1, T.C. Memo. 1975–1.

**36.** H.R. 6883 was signed by the President on October 19, 1980, and designated as P.L. 96–471.

adjusted basis in the X Corporation stock of $200,000 and that the installment notes possess a value equal to the face amount (i. e., $750,000). The tax result of these transactions is summarized as follows:

—No gain is recognized to X Corporation on the sale of the land [§ 337(a)].

—S must recognize a gain of $800,000 [$1,000,000 (liquidation proceeds) − $200,000 (adjusted basis in the stock)] in the year the cash and notes are distributed [§ 331(a)(1)].

—S's basis in the installment notes becomes $750,000 [§ 334(a)].

—Except for the interest element, subsequent collection of the notes will not result in further income to S.

Many shareholders attempted to ease the burden of the bunching of gain that resulted (e. g., $800,000 to S) through a sale of the stock to a related party (usually a trust) prior to the liquidation of the corporation. If such sale was accompanied by the issuance of installment notes, an election under § 453 allowed such gain to be deferred over the payout period.[37]

*Current Law.* Congress took note of the bunching-of-gain problem reflected by the result reached in Example 15 (as to S) and provided a form of relief. Under § 453(h), the shareholder's gain on the notes is deferred to the point of collection. Such treatment will require the shareholder to allocate his or her basis in the stock among the various assets received from the corporation.

**Example 16.** Assume the same facts as in Example 15 except that § 453(h) is applicable to the distribution. The tax effect of such distribution is summarized as follows:

—S must allocate the adjusted basis in the stock ($200,000) between the cash and the installment notes. Using the relative fair market value approach, 25% [$250,000 (amount of cash) ÷ $1,000,000 (total distribution)] of $200,000 (adjusted basis in the stock), or $50,000, is allocated to the cash, and 75% [$750,000 (amount of notes) ÷ $1,000,000 (total distribution)] of $200,000 (adjusted basis in the stock), or $150,000, is allocated to the notes.

—S must recognize $200,000 [$250,000 (cash received) − $50,000 (allocated basis of the cash)] in the year of the liquidation.

—Since S's gross profit on the notes is $600,000 [$750,000 (contract price) − $150,000 (allocated basis of the notes)], the gross profit percentage becomes 80% [$600,000 (gross profit) ÷ $750,000 (contract price)]. Thus, S must report a gain of $60,000 [$75,000 (amount of note) × 80% (gross profit percentage)] on the collection of each note over the next 10 years. Of course, the interest element would be accounted for separately.

---

37. See, for example, *Rushing v. Comm.,* 71–1 USTC ¶ 9339, 27 AFTR2d 71–1139, 441 F.2d 593 (CA–5, 1971), *aff'g.* 52 T.C. 888 (1969).

If distributions are received by the shareholder in more than one taxable year, basis reallocations may necessitate the filing of amended returns.[38]

Special rules apply if the installment obligations arise from sales between related parties.[39]

# EFFECT ON THE SHAREHOLDER— COMPLETE LIQUIDATION PURSUANT TO § 333

Section 333 is an exception to the general rule that a shareholder has a gain or loss upon a corporate liquidation.[40] It permits qualified shareholders to postpone some or all of the gain on a complete liquidation. If shareholders elect and the liquidation is completed within some one calendar month, § 333 postpones the recognition of gain on assets with substantial appreciation unrealized by the corporation on the date of liquidation. However, the shareholder does have recognized gain in an amount equal to the greater of (a) the shareholder's share of earnings and profits accumulated after February 28, 1913, or (b) amounts received by the shareholder consisting of money and stock and securities acquired by the corporation after 1953. In no event may recognized gain exceed realized gain. Only qualifying electing shareholders are entitled to the benefits of § 333.

## QUALIFYING ELECTING SHAREHOLDERS

A corporate shareholder owning 50 percent or more of the stock of a liquidating corporation cannot qualify under § 333. The remaining shareholders are divided into two groups: (a) noncorporate shareholders and (b) those corporate shareholders owning less than 50 percent of stock in the liquidating corporation.[41] Owners of stock possessing at least 80 percent of the total combined voting power of all classes of stock owned by shareholders in one of the above-mentioned groups must elect the provisions of § 333. If the 80 percent requirement is not met, the one-month liquidation treatment is not available to any member of that group. If owners of 80 percent of the stock in a particular group have elected § 333, and if a particular shareholder involved has also elected, such party becomes a qualifying electing shareholder.

Example 17. P Corporation's 100 shares of common stock are held as follows:

---

38. § 453(h)(2). For an example of such a possibility, see the Finance Committee Report on H.R. 6883 (reported with amendments on September 26, 1980).
39. §§ 453(h)(1)(C) and (D).
40. The predecessor to § 333 was enacted to permit and encourage the liquidation of personal holding companies in light of the imposition of the personal holding company tax (see Chapter 7). Intended as a temporary relief provision, it has, like many other Code Sections, become a permanent fixture.
41. Reg. § 1.333–2(a).

| Shareholder | Number of Shares Held |
|---|---|
| Q Corporation | 50 |
| R Corporation | 20 |
| S Corporation | 5 |
| T Corporation | 5 |
| A | 7 |
| B | 7 |
| C | 6 |

Under what circumstances, in the event P Corporation is liquidated, may § 333 be utilized by a particular shareholder? Because Q Corporation holds at least 50% of the stock, it cannot qualify for § 333, nor can it be considered in the election process. The remaining corporate shareholders (R, S, and T) collectively own 30 shares (20 + 5 + 5). Since 80% of 30 shares is 24 shares, the joint election of R Corporation (20 shares) with either S Corporation (5 shares) or T Corporation (5 shares) would make § 333 applicable to those corporate shareholders making the election. Turning to the noncorporate shareholders (A, B, and C) who hold a total of 20 shares (7 + 7 + 6), the minimum election requirement is 16 shares (80% × 20 shares). To reach this level, *all* noncorporate shareholders must agree to elect § 333. Note that combinations of any two noncorporate shareholders (A plus B, B plus C, or A plus C) will not generate the required 16 shares.

Shareholders not qualifying for or electing § 333 would come under the general rule of § 331, and their gain or loss would be determined by the difference between the fair market value of the liquidating distribution and the adjusted basis of the stock investment.

## MAKING THE ELECTION AND THE ONE-MONTH REQUIREMENT

An election to have liquidation proceeds taxed under § 333 is made on Form 964. The original and one copy of the form must be filed by the shareholder within 30 days after the adoption of a plan of liquidation.[42] If Form 964 is not filed within the 30-day period, the shareholder cannot utilize the provisions of § 333.[43] Once an election of § 333 is made, it cannot later be revoked. One Court, however was merciful when the shareholders showed that the decision to elect was based largely upon data that proved to be incorrect (i. e., the E & P of the liquidating corporation had been incorrectly determined).[44]

But even if the election is properly made and timely filed, § 333 will not apply unless the corporation is liquidated within one calendar month.[45]

---

**42.** § 333(d) and Reg. § 1.333–3.
**43.** See, for example, *Lee R. Dunavant,* 63 T.C. 316 (1974), and *Bachman v. U. S.,* 74–2 USTC ¶ 9763, 34 AFTR2d 74–6031 (D.Ct.Idaho, 1975).
**44.** *Meyer's Estate v. Comm.,* 53–1 USTC ¶ 9138, 42 AFTR 1005, 200 F.2d 592 (CA–5, 1952).
**45.** § 333(a)(2).

This requirement has led many to refer to the § 333 type of liquidation as the "one-month" liquidation. The one month chosen to carry out the liquidation need not be the same month in which the election was made. In this regard, it is easy to confuse the 30-day rule previously noted with the one-month requirement.

> **Example 18.** On June 1, 19X1, the shareholders of Y Corporation adopt a plan for complete liquidation. By June 28, 19X1, each shareholder executes and files a Form 964 electing § 333. The liquidation of Y Corporation commences on August 3, 19X1, and is concluded before the end of the month. Section 333 is applicable; both the 30-day and the one-month requirements have been satisfied.

The Regulations permit the corporation to retain cash beyond the month of liquidation if it will be necessary to pay unascertained and contingent liabilities—presuming such amount to be reasonable and the retention made in good faith. In addition, it is not necessary to actually dissolve the corporation under state law.[46]

## COMPUTATION OF GAIN UNDER § 333

As is the case under § 331, amounts received by shareholders electing under § 333 are treated as in full payment of their stock. Gain or loss is computed separately on each share of stock owned by a qualified electing shareholder.[47] The limited recognition of gain under § 333 applies only to *gain realized* on stock. Gain on some shares cannot be offset by losses on others. Losses are recognized in the year of liquidation. If a shareholder has only losses, he or she may still be required to file Form 964 so that the required 80 percent of shareholders in a particular group have elected. If the shareholder does not so file, the election may be lost for those shareholders who have gain.

Gain on each share of stock held by a qualified electing shareholder at the time of adoption of a plan of liquidation is recognized under § 333 only to the extent of the *greater* of (a) the shareholder's ratable portion of E & P of the corporation accumulated after February 28, 1913, computed as of the last day of the month of liquidation, without reduction for distributions made during that month and including all items of income and expense accrued to the date on which the transfer of all property under the liquidation is completed, or (b) the shareholder's ratable portion of the sum of cash and the fair market value of all stock or securities (acquired by the corporation after December 31, 1953) received by the shareholder. Dividend income to noncorporate shareholders is that portion of recognized gain not in excess of the shareholder's ratable share of E & P accumulated after February 28, 1913. The remainder of the gain is either short-term or long-term capital gain, depending on the length of time the stock has been held. A

---

46. Reg. § § 1.333–1(b)(1) and (2).
47. Reg. § 1.333–4(a).

qualified electing corporate shareholder has no dividend income; all recognized gain is capital gain.[48]

**Example 19.** The following *independent* cases illustrate the possible tax consequences to a shareholder under a § 333 liquidation:

| | | Distributing Corporation* | | Shareholder's Realized Gain | Shareholder's Recognized Gain | |
|---|---|---|---|---|---|---|
| Case | Type of Shareholder | E & P | Cash plus Post-1953 Securities | | Capital | Dividend |
| A | Corporation | $ 10,000 | $ 10,000 | $ 5,000 | $ 5,000 | $ –0– |
| B | Corporation | 10,000 | 20,000 | 40,000 | 20,000 | –0– |
| C | Corporation | 20,000 | 10,000 | 30,000 | 20,000 | –0– |
| D | Individual | 10,000 | 10,000 | 5,000 | –0– | 5,000 |
| E | Individual | 10,000 | 20,000 | 40,000 | 10,000 | 10,000 |
| F | Individual | 20,000 | 10,000 | 30,000 | –0– | 20,000 |

* Represents the shareholder's pro rata portion of these items.

In Example 19, note that gain recognized for both corporate and noncorporate shareholders can never exceed realized gain (Cases A and D). Also, all recognized gain by a corporate shareholder must be capital gain (Cases A, B, and C). An individual has a capital gain only if his or her share of cash plus post-1953 securities exceeds his or her share of the corporation's E & P (contrast Cases E and F).

## BASIS OF PROPERTY RECEIVED PURSUANT TO § 333

Property received in a liquidation wherein there is limited recognized gain is the same as the basis of the shares redeemed decreased by the amount of any money received and increased by gain recognized and unsecured liabilities assumed by the shareholders. This amount is allocated to the various assets received on the basis of their net fair market values (net fair market value of an asset is fair market value less any specific mortgage or pledge to which it is subject). Basis of a particular asset, as determined in this manner, is increased for any liens on that asset.[49] If a lien applies to several properties, the amount of the lien is divided among the properties on the basis of the fair market value of each property.[50]

**Example 20.** At the time of its liquidation in the current year, Z Corporation has E & P of $40,000 and the following assets and liabilities:

---

**48.** § 333(f) and Reg. § 1.333–4(b). The reason corporate shareholders are forced into capital gain treatment is easily explained. If this type of shareholder were permitted dividend treatment as to a pro rata share of the distributing corporation's E & P (as is the case with noncorporate shareholders), the tax impact would be mitigated through the application of the 85% dividends received deduction of § 243. Capital gain treatment therefore leads to a harsher tax effect on a corporate shareholder.

**49.** Reg. § 1.334–2.

**50.** For an excellent explanation of how basis is determined and allocated to property received in a § 333 liquidation, see *Ralph R. Garrow*, 43 T.C. 890 (1965), *aff'd.* in 66–2 USTC ¶ 9761, 18 AFTR2d 5981, 368 F.2d 809 (CA–9, 1966).

|  | Basis to Z Corporation | Fair Market Value |
|---|---|---|
| Cash | $ 30,000 | $ 30,000 |
| Xerox Corporation stock (held as an investment since 1968) | 40,000 | 30,000 |
| Unimproved land | 10,000 | 90,000 |
| Notes payable to outsiders | 10,000 | 20,000 |

All assets and liabilities are distributed to T, an individual and the sole shareholder. The notes payable do not relate to any specific asset but are secured by the general credit of the corporation. At the time of the liquidation, T's basis in the Z Corporation stock is $20,000. Assume the liquidation falls under § 333.

—T has a recognized gain of $60,000. Realized gain of $110,000 is computed as follows: $130,000 (fair market value of all the assets received *less* the notes payable) − $20,000 (T's basis in the Z Corporation stock). T's recognized gain is the greater of $40,000 (E & P) *or* $60,000 [$30,000 (cash) + $30,000 (post-1953 securities)] not to exceed his realized gain of $110,000.

—Of the $60,000 of recognized gain, $20,000 is capital gain and $40,000 is dividend income. Under § 333(e), capital gain is limited to the excess of $60,000 [$30,000 (cash) + $30,000 (post-1953 securities)] over $40,000 (E & P). Because $40,000 of the $60,000 recognized is dividend income (limited to E & P), only $20,000 is treated as a capital gain.

—Total basis to be allocated is $70,000 determined as follows: $20,000 (T's basis in the Z Corporation stock) + $60,000 (gain recognized by T) + $20,000 (liabilities assumed) − $30,000 (cash received). The amount allocated to the unimproved land is computed as follows:

$$\frac{\$90,000 \text{ (FMV of the land)}}{\$90,000 \text{ (FMV of the land)} + \$30,000 \text{ (FMV of the Xerox stock)}} \times \frac{\$70,000 \text{ (total basis}}{\text{to be allocated)}} = \frac{\$52,500 \text{ (basis}}{\text{in the land)}}$$

A similar computation, but with the numerator of the fraction changed from $90,000 to $30,000, allocates a basis of $17,500 to the Xerox Corporation stock.

**Example 21.** Assume the same facts as in Example 20 except that notes payable constitute a specific lien against the unimproved land.

—T's recognized gain and the nature of such gain remains the same (see above).

—The basis to be allocated among all assets is $50,000 determined as follows: $20,000 (T's basis in the Z Corporation stock) + $60,000 (gain recognized by T) − $30,000 (cash received). The amount allocated to the Xerox stock becomes \$15,000 [(\$30,000/\$100,000) × \$50,000]. In the case of the land, however, start with \$35,000 [(\$70,000/\$100,000) × \$50,000] and add \$20,000 (the specific lien) for a total of \$55,000. Since the liability relates to the land, it affects only the basis of that asset. Also, note that the numerator of the second fraction (i. e., \$70,000) and the denominator of both fractions (i. e., \$100,000) consider the value of the land net of the liability.

## EFFECT ON THE DISTRIBUTING CORPORATION

Code § 333 provides for a specified tax result for an electing shareholder. As such, it does not carry any direct tax consequences to the corporation being liquidated. There is, however, one important indirect effect on the corporation. When § 333 is utilized by any shareholder, § 337 becomes unavailable to the corporation.[51] Thus, gains and losses from the sale of corporate assets during the liquidation period become fully recognizable. From a planning standpoint, therefore, corporations undergoing liquidation should avoid sales of gain property and distribute such assets in kind to the shareholders under § 336. The tax consequences to the corporation resulting from a distribution in kind under § 336 were reviewed earlier in the chapter.

Besides the possible recognition of gain at the corporate level, another reason exists to avoid sales of property in connection with § 333 liquidations. Recall that one of the criteria determining the tax consequences to the electing shareholder is the E & P of the distributing corporation. Hence, sales by the corporation of gain property (through their effect on E & P) might well increase the dividend income to be recognized by a noncorporate shareholder or the capital gain by a corporate shareholder. In this connection, the *Court Holding Company* doctrine could pose a real danger.[52] If, for example, later sales by the shareholders of distributed property are attributed to the corporation, a double tax impact could materialize—tax to the liquidating corporation on any gain recognized plus a tax to the shareholders on any E & P so generated.[53]

## LIQUIDATION OF A SUBSIDIARY

Section 332, like the one-month liquidation of § 333, is an exception to the general rule that the shareholder recognizes gain or loss on a corporate liquidation. If a parent corporation liquidates a subsidiary corporation in which it owns at least 80 percent of the voting stock, no gain or loss is recognized under § 332. Section 333 differs from § 332 in that some gain may be recognized under § 333.

The requirements for application of § 332 are (a) the parent must own at least 80 percent of the voting stock of the subsidiary and at least 80

---

51. § 337(c)(1)(B).
52. *Supra,* Footnote 4.
53. This is precisely the result reached in *Aaron Cohen,* 63 T.C. 527 (1975). Further, the taxpayers were not allowed, in light of what happened, to revoke their § 333 election.

percent of all other classes of stock except nonvoting preferred, (b) the subsidiary must distribute all its property in complete redemption of all its stock within the taxable year or within three years from the close of the tax year in which a plan was adopted and the first distribution occurred, and (c) the subsidiary must be solvent.[54] If these requirements are met, § 332 becomes mandatory.

When a series of distributions occurs in the liquidation of a subsidiary corporation, the parent corporation must own the required amount of stock (80 percent) on the date of adoption of a plan of liquidation and at all times until all property has been distributed.[55] If the parent fails to qualify at any time, the provisions for nonrecognition of gain or loss do not apply to any distribution.[56] If a liquidation is not completed within one taxable year, for each taxable year that falls wholly or partly within the period of liquidation, the parent corporation shall file with its income tax return a waiver of the statute of limitations on assessment. The parent corporation may be forced to file a bond with the District Director to insure prompt payment of taxes should § 332 not apply.[57]

For the taxable year in which the plan of liquidation is adopted and for all taxable years within the period of liquidation, the parent corporation must file with its return a statement of all facts pertaining to the liquidation including a copy of the plan, a list of all properties received showing cost and fair market value, a statement of indebtedness of the subsidiary corporation to the parent, and a statement of ownership of all classes of stock of the liquidating corporation.[58]

## INDEBTEDNESS OF SUBSIDIARY TO PARENT

If a subsidiary satisfies a debt owed to the parent with appreciated property, it must recognize gain on the transaction unless § 332 applies. When § 332 is applicable, gain or loss is not recognized by the subsidiary upon the transfer of properties to the parent, even though some properties are transferred to satisfy the subsidiary's indebtedness to the parent.[59]

> **Example 22.** S Corporation owes its parent, P Corporation, $20,000. It satisfies the obligation by transferring land (worth $20,000 with a tax basis of $8,000). Normally, S Corporation would recognize a gain of $12,000 on the transaction. However, if the transfer is made pursuant to a liquidation under § 332, S Corporation would not recognize a gain.

Realized gain or loss is recognized by the parent corporation on the satisfaction of indebtedness, even though property is received during liquidation of the subsidiary. The special provision noted above does not apply to the parent corporation.

---

54. Reg. § § 1.332–2(a) and (b).
55. As is true with § 333 (the one-month liquidation) and § 337 (the 12-month liquidation), the date of the adoption of a plan of complete liquidation could be crucial in determining whether § 332 applies. See, for example, *George L. Riggs, Inc.*, 64 T.C. 474 (1975).
56. Reg. § 1.332–2(a).
57. Reg. § 1.332–4(a).
58. Reg. § 1.332–6.
59. § 332(c) and Reg. § 1.332–7.

**Example 23.** P Corporation purchased bonds of its subsidiary S at a discount. Upon liquidation of the subsidiary pursuant to § 332, P received payment in the face amount of the bonds. The transaction has no tax effect on S Corporation; however, P Corporation must recognize gain in the amount of the difference between its basis in the bonds and the amount received in payment.

If a parent corporation does not receive at least partial payment for its stock in a subsidiary corporation upon liquidation of the subsidiary, § 332 will not apply.[60] The parent corporation would then have a bad debt deduction for the difference between the value of any properties received from the subsidiary and its basis in the subsidiary debt.

Section 332 does not apply to the liquidation of an insolvent subsidiary corporation. If the subsidiary is insolvent, the parent corporation would have a loss deduction for its worthless stock in the subsidiary. The loss would be ordinary if more than 90 percent of the gross receipts for all tax years of the subsidiary were from sources other than passive sources.[61] Otherwise, the loss would be a capital loss.

**Example 24.** P Corporation paid $100,000 for all the stock of S Corporation 15 years ago. At present, S has a deficit of $600,000 in E & P. If P liquidates S, § 332 would not apply, because S is insolvent. P Corporation would have a loss deduction for its worthless stock in S Corporation. If more than 90 percent of the gross receipts of S Corporation for all tax years were from sources other than passive sources, the loss would be ordinary. Otherwise, it would be a capital loss. Assume P also loaned S Corporation $50,000. Since the assets are not sufficient to pay the liabilities, P would also have a loss on the note. Upon liquidation, the basis of the assets of S to P would be the fair market value. P's loss would be measured by the fair market value of S's assets less the liabilities payable to third parties less P's basis in the S stock and note.

## BASIS OF PROPERTY RECEIVED BY THE PARENT CORPORATION

*The General Rule of § 334(b)(1).*   Unless a parent corporation elects under § 338, property received by the parent corporation in a complete liquidation of its subsidiary under § 332 has the same basis it had in the hands of the subsidiary.[62] The parent's basis in stock of the liquidated subsidiary disappears. This is true even though some of the property was transferred to the parent in satisfaction of debt owed the parent by the subsidiary.

**Example 25.** P, the parent corporation, has a basis of $20,000 in stock in S Corporation, a subsidiary in which it owns 85% of all classes of stock. P Corporation purchased the stock of S Corporation 10 years ago. In the current year, P Corporation liquidates S Corporation and

---

60.   Reg. § 1.332–2(b).
61.   See § 165(g) and Reg. § 1.165–5.
62.   § 334(b)(1) and Reg. § 1.334–1(b).

acquires assets worth $50,000 with a tax basis to S Corporation of $40,000. P Corporation would have a basis of $40,000 in the assets, with a potential gain upon sale of $10,000. P Corporation's original $20,000 basis in S Corporation stock disappears.

**Example 26.** P Corporation has a basis of $60,000 in stock in S Corporation, a subsidiary acquired 10 years ago. It liquidates S Corporation and receives assets worth $50,000 with a tax basis to S Corporation of $40,000. P Corporation again has a basis of $40,000 in the assets it acquired from S Corporation. If it sells the assets, it will have a gain of $10,000 in spite of the fact that its basis in S Corporation stock was $60,000. P Corporation's loss will never be recognized.

Because the parent corporation takes the subsidiary's basis in its assets, the carryover rules of § 381 apply (see Chapter 6). The parent would acquire a net operating loss of the subsidiary, any investment credit carryover, capital loss carryover, and a carryover of E & P of the subsidiary. Section 381 applies to most tax-free reorganizations and to a tax-free liquidation under § 332 if the subsidiary's bases in its assets carry over to the parent.

*The Election of § 338.* Under the general rule of § 332(b)(1), several problems developed when a subsidiary was liquidated shortly after acquisition by a parent corporation.

1. When the basis of the subsidiary's assets was in excess of the purchase price of the stock, the parent received a step-up in basis in such assets at no tax cost. If, for example, the parent paid $100,000 for the subsidiary's stock and the basis of the assets transferred to the parent was $150,000, the parent enjoys a $50,000 benefit without any gain recognition. The $50,000 increase in basis of the subsidiary's assets could lead to additional depreciation deductions and either more loss or less gain upon the later disposition of the assets by the parent.

2. If the basis of the subsidiary's assets was below the purchase price of the stock, the parent suffered a step-down in basis in such assets with no attendant tax benefit. Return to Example 26. If the situation is changed slightly—the subsidiary's stock is not held for 10 years, but the subsidiary is liquidated shortly after acquisition—the basic inequity of the "no loss" situation is apparent.[63]

In the landmark decision of *Kimbell-Diamond Milling Co. v. Comm.*,[64] the courts finally resolved these problems. When a parent corporation liquidates a subsidiary shortly after the acquisition of its stock, the parent is really purchasing the assets of the subsidiary. Consequently, the bases of

---

**63.** There could be any number of reasons why one corporation would pay more for the stock in another corporation than the latter's basis in its assets. For one, the basis of assets has no necessary correlation to the fair market values. For another, the acquiring corporation may not have any choice in the matter if it really wants the assets. The shareholders in the acquired corporation may prefer to sell their stock rather than the assets of the corporation. Tax consequences, undoubtedly, would have some bearing on such a decision.

**64.** 14 T.C. 74 (1950), *aff'd.* in 51–1 USTC ¶ 9201, 40 AFTR 328, 187 F.2d 718 (CA–5, 1951), *cert. den.* 72 S.Ct. 50 (USSC, 1951).

such assets should be the cost of the stock. Known as the "single transaction" approach, the basis determination is not made under the general rule of § 334(b)(1). Since the Court's decision left in doubt precisely when the single transaction approach should apply, Congress enacted § 334(b)(2) to give assets acquired by a parent corporation upon liquidation of its subsidiary the same basis that the parent held in the stock of the subsidiary. For the exception of § 334(b)(2) to apply, the parent had to "purchase" at least 80 percent of the total combined voting power of all classes of stock (except nonvoting preferred) within a 12-month period, and within two years after the date on which the 80 percent of the stock was "purchased," the parent had to liquidate the subsidiary.

Because of abuses,[65] § 334(b)(2) was repealed by the Tax Equity and Fiscal Responsibility Act of 1982 and § 338 was substituted. Section 338 provides that for acquisitions after August 31, 1982, an acquiring corporation must, by the fifteenth day of the ninth month beginning after the month in which the acquisition occurs, make an irrevocable election whether or not to treat the acquisition as a purchase of the assets of the acquired corporation. If the parent elects under § 338, the purchasing corporation will have a basis in the subsidiary's assets equal to its basis in the subsidiary's stock. The subsidiary need not be liquidated. A purchasing corporation makes a qualified stock purchase if it acquires at least 80 percent of the voting power and at least 80 percent of the total shares (other than shares of nonvoting preferred stock) of the acquired corporation within a 12-month period beginning with the first purchase of stock.[66] An acquisition of stock by any member of an affiliated group, including the purchasing corporation, is considered to be an acquisition by the purchasing corporation.

Under § 338, the acquired corporation is deemed to have sold its assets for an amount equal to the purchasing corporation's "grossed-up" basis in the subsidiary's stock adjusted for liabilities of the subsidiary corporation. The grossed-up basis is the basis in the subsidiary stock multiplied by a fraction having 100 percent as its numerator and the percentage of value of the subsidiary's stock held by the purchasing corporation on the acquisition date as its denominator.[67] This amount is allocated among the subsidiary's assets as provided in regulations to be prescribed by the Treasury.

Section 337 applies to the deemed purchase of assets (under the rationale that the assets are involved in a complete liquidation) so that no gain or loss is recognized. However, there will be other tax consequences, such as immediate recapture of depreciation and investment credit, LIFO inventory adjustments, and application of the tax benefit rule. The subsidiary corporation will be treated as a new corporation as of the beginning of the

---

**65.** Corporations could delay the § 332 liquidation election for two years after the acquisition of the subsidiary and could liquidate over a three-year period, thus providing a five-year liquidation span. In addition, in the event several subsidiary corporations were purchased, the parent could pick and choose which it wished to liquidate. The choice, of course, was dictated by the recapture element and the desirability of preserving certain tax attributes.

**66.** The stock must be acquired in a taxable transaction (e. g., § 351 and other nonrecognition provisions do not apply).

**67.** § 338(b)(4).

day after the acquisition date; consequently, all tax attributes of the subsidiary are terminated. This, of course, precludes any of the tax consequences from being reflected on the parent corporation's consolidated return. Such recapture income will be reported on the return filed by the subsidiary for its taxable year ending on the acquisition date.

If less than 100 percent of the stock is purchased, the nonrecognition provisions of § 337 are limited to the acquiring company's percentage ownership. However, if the acquired corporation is liquidated during a one-year period beginning on the acquisition date of at least 80 percent of the acquired corporation and if § 333 does not apply to the liquidation, § 337 will again apply to the entire deemed sale.[68] In addition, if stock of the minority interest is obtained by the acquired corporation in a complete redemption of the minority stock that qualifies under § 302(b)(3), § 336 applies to the distribution as though the distribution were a complete liquidation.[69]

> **Example 27.** S Corporation has a basis of $800,000 in its assets, and its liabilities total $500,000. It has E & P of $200,000 and assets worth $2,000,000. P purchases 80% of the stock of S on March 10, 1986, for $1,200,000 [($2,000,000 less liabilities of $500,000) × 80%]. Because the purchase price of the S stock exceeds S's basis in the stock's assets, and to eliminate S's E & P, P should elect by December 15, 1986, to treat the acquisition as a purchase of the assets of S under § 338. S need not be liquidated for § 338 to apply. S will be deemed to have sold its assets for an amount equal to the grossed-up basis in the S stock. The basis of the S stock will be multiplied by a fraction, with 100% the numerator and 80% the denominator. Thus, the selling price of S's assets is deemed to be $1,500,000 [(100/80) × $1,200,000] adjusted for liabilities of S of $500,000, or $2,000,000. Selling price of $2,000,000 less basis of S's assets of $800,000 produces a gain of $1,200,000.

Because P did not purchase 100% of the stock of S, different tax results occur depending on whether or not S is liquidated. If S is not liquidated, it is treated as a new corporation as of March 11, 1986. The basis of S's assets would be $2,000,000, and the E & P would be eliminated. However, § 337 would be limited to P's 80% ownership; thus, 20% of the gain, or $240,000, must be recognized by S. This is ignoring the depreciation recapture or any gain because of LIFO inventory adjustments and the tax benefit rule.

If S is liquidated within a year after P's purchase of 80% of S's stock, § 337 will apply to provide nonrecognition of the entire $1,200,000 gain. However, the recapture of depreciation and investment credit rules apply, and LIFO inventory adjustments and the tax benefit rule will produce some gain to S. Once S is liquidated, P would have a basis of $1,600,000 in S's assets, representing 80% of S's assets. S's E & P would not carry over to P.

---

**68.** § 338(c)(1).
**69.** § 338(c)(2).

A consistency requirement under § 338 insures that the acquiring corporation does not pick and choose which of the acquired subsidiary corporations are to be covered by the § 338 election. For a one-year period before and after the acquisition of the subsidiary (the consistency period), the parent is deemed to have made an election under § 338 if it makes a direct purchase of assets from the subsidiary or from an affiliate of the subsidiary during that period.[70] (Exceptions exist, such as for asset purchases in the ordinary course of a business.)

> **Example 28.**  On June 15, 1986, P Corporation purchases all of the stock of T Corporation. Shortly thereafter, P Corporation purchases all of the assets of S Corporation, a subsidiary of T Corporation. P Corporation will be deemed to have made the election as to T Corporation.

In addition, during the consistency period, tax treatment of acquisitions of stock of two or more other companies that are members of an affiliated group must be consistent.[71]

> **Example 29.**  On June 1, 1986, P Corporation purchases all of the stock in T Corporation and makes a timely election under § 338. If T Corporation owns all the stock in S Corporation, the § 338 election also applies to S Corporation. This is so even though P Corporation never made an election as to S Corporation. On the other hand, if P Corporation does not make an election as to T Corporation, it cannot make the election as to S Corporation.

*A Comparison of § § 334(b)(1) and 338.*  Under the general rule of § 334(b)(1), a subsidiary's basis in its assets carries over to the parent corporation upon liquidation. The recapture rules of § § 1245, 1250, and 1252 do not apply to liquidations of subsidiary corporations when basis is determined under § 334(b)(1). Nor does § 47's provision for investment credit recapture apply. These sections except such liquidations from their provisions.[72] Consequently, a subsidiary liquidation pursuant to § § 332 and 334(b)(1) is completely tax-free.

On the other hand, a liquidation pursuant to § 338, while tax-free to the parent, does produce taxable income to the subsidiary under the recapture rules of § § 1245, 1250, and 1252.[73] The subsidiary also must recognize the recapture amount on LIFO inventory. Section 47, dealing with the recapture of the investment tax credit, also applies. Whether or not the tax benefit rule and the assignment of income doctrine apply to the subsidiary is not clear. In Revenue Ruling 74–396, the IRS held that the unused portion of previously expensed supplies would be income to the liquidated subsidiary in a complete liquidation, excluding liquidations in which basis is carried over pursuant to § 334(b)(1).[74]

---

70.  § 338(e).
71.  § 338(f).
72.  See, for example, § § 1245(b)(3), 1250(d)(3), and 47(b)(2).
73.  See, for example, *Lucar-Naylor Egg Ranches v. U. S.,* 75–1 USTC ¶ 9300, 35 AFTR2d 75–942, and 75–1 USTC ¶ 9329 (D.Ct.Calif., 1975).
74.  *Supra,* Footnote 5. However, in *Bliss Dairy, Inc. v. Comm.,* the Ninth Court of Appeals reaffirmed its position in *South Lake Farms, Inc.,* that the tax benefit rule is not relevant in a § 336 distribution in kind. The Supreme Court has reversed *Bliss Dairy, Inc.* and upheld the IRS.

If a liquidation under § 332 qualifies under § 338 and a timely election is made, the holding period of the property received by the parent corporation begins on the date the parent acquired the subsidiary's stock. If the corporation is not liquidated, the holding period of the assets to the subsidiary would start anew on the acquisition date, because the subsidiary is treated as having sold the assets as of that date and is treated as a new corporation that purchased all of the assets as of that date.[75] In a liquidation under § 334(b)(1), the holding period of the subsidiary carries over to the parent.

# EFFECT ON THE SHAREHOLDER— COLLAPSIBLE CORPORATIONS UNDER § 341

## THE PROBLEM

The tax avoidance objective that § 341 seeks to preclude is easily demonstrated by the use of an illustration.

> **Example 30.** C (a motion picture producer), D (a leading actor), and E (a leading actress) organize the M Corporation to film a motion picture. Each invests $50,000 and each receives one-third of the stock, and M Corporation borrows $300,000 to cover the estimated $450,000 cost of production. Since C, D, and E receive only modest compensation for their services, the estimated cost of production is considerably less than normal. After the film is completed, a preview is held. Based on reviews of the critics, the film is appraised at a value of $900,000. M Corporation is liquidated, and the film is distributed in kind to its shareholders. The film is subsequently released by the shareholders; over the next several years it earns $900,000 in royalty income.

What have the parties expected to accomplish?

—The corporation realizes none of the $900,000 in royalty income.[76]

—The corporation recognizes no gain on the liquidation because of § 336 (a distribution in kind in liquidation).

—The shareholders recognize a capital gain of $450,000 on the liquidation of the corporation.[77] The gain is determined under the gen-

---

75. § 338(a).

76. The corporation would appear to be vulnerable to the contention that it has made an anticipatory assignment of income (see the discussion earlier in the chapter). Thus, the income from the film might well be imputed to M Corporation. Strangely enough, the few cases passing on this contention refused to hold for the IRS. See *Herbert v. Riddell*, 52–1 USTC ¶ 9209, 41 AFTR 961, 103 F.Supp. 369 (D.Ct.Calif., 1952), and *Pat O'Brien*, 25 T.C. 376 (1955).

77. Because C, D, and E were paid only "modest" salaries for the services they rendered to M Corporation, it would not be illogical to conclude that some of the capital gain represents additional compensation to be taxed as ordinary income. Again, the IRS generally proved unsuccessful with this approach in the collapsible corporation area. See, for example, *Comm. v. Gross*, 23 T.C. 756 (1955), aff'd. in 56–2 USTC ¶ 9861, 50 AFTR 68, 236 F.2d 612 (CA–2, 1956).

eral rule of § 331 and represents the difference between $900,000 (the fair market value of the film) and $450,000 [$150,000 (shareholders' basis in the stock) + $300,000 (corporate liabilities assumed)].

—Under § 334(a), the shareholders receive a $900,000 basis in the film (its fair market value on the date of distribution).

—None of the $900,000 of royalties received from the showing of the film will be recognized as income to the shareholders. Because the shareholders will use the cost recovery approach as to the royalty income, the $900,000 basis must first be absorbed. In the event more or less than $900,000 ultimately is recovered, gain or loss will be recognized accordingly.

The shareholders hope to obtain a step-up in basis at capital gain rates. More important, the corporation is "collapsed" before it realizes any income, thereby neutralizing the double tax attendant to conducting a business in the corporate form.

Although it started with the motion picture industry, the collapsible corporation approach worked equally well with construction projects. Once the project is completed, and before any sales are made, the corporation is liquidated and its assets distributed in kind under § 336. The shareholders then proceed to sell the units, offsetting the sale proceeds against their new basis.

## THE STATUTORY SOLUTION

Section 117(m) of the 1939 Code, the predecessor of the present § 341, converted long-term capital gain into ordinary income if the distributing corporation was collapsible. Returning to Example 30, C, D, and E would each recognize ordinary income of $150,000 (for a total of $450,000) on the liquidation of M Corporation. But § 341 goes beyond the classic liquidation situation and covers two additional possibilities. First, a corporate distribution not in liquidation could convert long-term capital gain into ordinary income. Second, similar conversion occurs upon the sale of stock by a shareholder to another party.

**Example 31.** Assume the same facts as in Example 30 except that M Corporation is not liquidated. Prior to the release of the film, the corporation distributes to each of its shareholders excess borrowed funds of $60,000 (for a total of $180,000) not needed for production. Because the distribution occurs before M Corporation has generated any E & P, no dividend results. Under usual rules, each shareholder would report a $10,000 capital gain. The remaining $50,000 constitutes a return of capital [see § 301(c) and Chapter 4]. Section 341(a)(3) would transform the $10,000 of long-term capital gain into ordinary income if the distributing corporation is collapsible.

**Example 32.** Assume the same facts as in Example 30 except that C sells his stock for $200,000 after the film is completed and prior to M Corporation's liquidation. Section 341(a)(1) would convert any long-term capital gain from the sale to ordinary income if M Corporation is collapsible.

Section 341 does not generate gain—it merely transforms long-term capital gain into ordinary income. Consequently, nontaxable exchanges involving collapsible corporation stock (e. g., transfers to controlled corporations under § 351 or corporate reorganizations under § § 354 and 355— see Chapters 3 and 6) would not be affected. Section 341 is inapplicable to short-term capital gains and to losses.

## DEFINITION OF A COLLAPSIBLE CORPORATION

A collapsible corporation is defined by § 341(b) as a corporation

—*formed* or *availed of* principally

—for the *manufacture, construction,* or *production* of so-called § 341 property

—with a *view* to the *sale* of that corporation's stock or to a *liquidation*

—*before* the corporation realizes a *substantial part* of the income from § 341 property.

Section 341 property is defined as inventory property, property held by the corporation primarily for sale to customers in the ordinary course of its trade or business, unrealized receivables or fees, and § 1231 property (depreciable property and real estate used in a trade or business), all of which has been held for a period of less than three years.

## LIMITATIONS ON § 341

*The View Limitation.* The collapsible corporation result can be avoided if the *view* (or motive) to collapse arose after the manufacture, construction, or production of the property has been completed.[78] But such view to collapse must not have been entertained (or reasonably anticipated) by those in control of corporate policy at any time during the production process.[79] If this approach is to succeed, the withdrawing shareholder should be ready to provide and substantiate a good reason for doing so. Examples of post-production reasons include illness of an active shareholder, a shareholder's unexpected need for funds to start or expand another business, and a conflict among shareholders as to corporate policy.[80]

> **Example 33.** Z Corporation is formed by R, S, and T (all individuals) to construct and sell a shopping center. Each shareholder invests $200,000, and the remainder of the necessary construction funds are obtained by the corporation through mortgage financing. One year later, after the shopping center is built but before any of the units are sold, a severe dispute develops between R and the other shareholders. As a consequence of the dispute, R sells his stock to U for $500,000. R would appear to be in a good position to contend that his $300,000 long-term capital gain should not be converted to ordinary income (i. e., § 341 is inapplicable to him).

---

**78.** Reg. § § 1.341–2(a)(2) and (3).

**79.** See, for example, *Computer Sciences Corp.,* 63 T.C. 327 (1974), and *F. T. S. Associates,* 58 T.C. 207 (1972).

**80.** See, for example, *Joseph M. Crowe,* 62 T.C. 121 (1974).

The danger in relying on the approach taken in Example 33 is the difficulty in proving when the view to collapse first arose. Further, under some circumstances, it may be difficult to ascertain exactly when the manufacture, construction, or production was completed by the corporation.

*Realization of a Substantial Part of Future Income.* A corporation will not be collapsible if it realizes two-thirds of the taxable income from § 341 assets prior to sale or liquidation.[81]

*Other Limitations.* The harsh provisions of § 341 can also be avoided by certain other exceptions described in § 341.[82] These escape provisions are based on the theory that in certain instances, tax avoidance is not involved, and consequently, § 341 should not apply. Further discussion of these exceptions is beyond the scope of this text.

TAX PLANNING
CONSIDERATIONS

## EFFECT ON THE CORPORATION

The effect of a liquidation on the distributing corporation is governed by § 336 (distributions in kind) and § 337 (sales during the 12-month period). These two provisions may be combined to achieve a minimum tax effect.

> **Example 34.** X Corporation is in the process of complete liquidation and has met all of the requirements of § 337. It possesses 2,000 units of appreciated inventory (non-LIFO), 500 of which the shareholders would like distributed to them. The other 1,500 units are to be sold to a third party. Can the distribution and sale be accomplished tax-free? Yes, if the proper order is observed. First, the corporation should distribute the 500 units to its shareholders. The in-kind distribution would be nontaxable under § 336. Second, the remaining 1,500 units can be sold in one transaction and to one person. As such, this disposition of the remaining inventory qualifies as a bulk sale, the gain from which is not recognized by virtue of § 337(b)(2).

Because the determination of whether a transfer of inventory qualifies as a bulk sale is made at the time of its sale and not tied to previous dispositions, the possibility of loss sales should not be overlooked.

> **Example 35.** Y Corporation is in the process of complete liquidation and has satisfied all the requirements of § 337. It owns 3,000 units of inventory (non-LIFO), half of which have appreciated in value over their basis. The other 1,500 units would yield a loss if sold. If all the inventory units are sold to one person in one transaction, neither gain

---

**81.** § 341(b)(1)(A). Before the Deficit Reduction Act of 1984, a corporation would not be collapsible if it realized one-third of the income from § 341 assets prior to sale or liquidation. This rule was based on a court decision, *Comm. v. Kelley,* 61–2 USTC ¶ 9603, 8 AFTR2d 5232, 293 F.2d 904 (CA–5, 1961). The amendment to § 341(b)(1)(A) requiring that two-thirds of the taxable income from § 341 assets be realized is effective for sales, exchanges, and distributions occurring after July 18, 1984.

**82.** See § 341(d), (e), and (f).

nor loss is recognizable. Instead, why not sell the loss units first, followed by the sale of the gain units? The loss will be recognized because inventory (unless sold in bulk) does not qualify as property for purposes of the nonrecognition provisions of § 337. But since the gain sale is a bulk sale, § 337 applies to prevent the gain from being recognized. To insure against the possibility that the IRS might try to merge both sales as one transaction, each sale should be kept separate and distinct. Selling the inventory to different purchasers would help.[83]

Another possibility exists in utilizing the bulk sale of inventory provisions of § 337. The Code directs nonrecognition of gain or loss treatment in the case of a bulk sale of inventory "attributable to a trade or business of the corporation." It is possible, therefore, to have a bulk sale of one type of inventory and not of another.

**Example 36.** Z Corporation is engaged in the construction of homes for resale and also operates a retail outlet from which it sells home appliances to the general public. After the adoption of a plan of complete liquidation, the corporation sells its inventory of finished homes to various buyers. The inventory of home appliances, however, is sold to another corporation engaged in the same retailing business. The sale of the homes would result in recognized gain or loss to Z Corporation; however, the sale of the home appliances would not. In the latter case, it is assumed Z Corporation has met the requirements of § 337 and that the inventory is not determined under the LIFO method.

Other points to be considered in planning the desired tax result for a corporation in its liquidation are summarized as follows:

—A sale of accounts receivable for more than book value will trigger recapture of some or all of the reserve for bad debts due to the application of the tax benefit rule. Consequently, care should be taken in making an appropriate allocation to accounts receivable when these items are sold with other assets to the same purchaser. The same approach should be taken with property that possesses recapture of depreciation potential under § § 1245 and 1250. Proper allocation of the purchase price can reduce the recognized gain from the sale of such assets and therefore limit the amount that has to be recaptured as ordinary income.[84]

—With respect to attorney's fees incurred during liquidation, a proper allocation of such fees to general liquidation expenses, to the sale of property outside the scope of § 337, or to a distribution of property in kind under § 336 will cause such fees to be deductible to the corporation as a business expense under § 162. If the fees are associated with the sale of assets under § 337, they will be required to be offset against the selling price and as a result will not be allowed as deductions.

---

**83.** The course of action followed in Example 35 differs from the straddle sale approach (refer to Example 11 in this chapter) in one important respect. In the straddle sale, the loss property is disposed of *before* the plan of liquidation is adopted.
**84.** *Dorothy G. Armstrong*, 36 TCM 137, T.C.Memo. 1977–30.

—In making nontaxable distributions in kind under § 336, watch for the possible application of *Court Holding Company*. Particularly if the shareholders sell the property immediately after its receipt to the same parties who previously negotiated the sale with the corporation, the sale might be attributed to the corporation. In some cases, § 337 could neutralize the corporation's imputed gain if the distribution and sale occur within the 12-month liquidation period. It would not, however, if the asset distributed does not constitute property within the definition of § 337.

—For major asset corporations that suffer an involuntary conversion, the 60-day grace period of § 337(e) does not solve all timing problems. First of all, 60 days is not a long period of time. It is not inconceivable that 60 days may pass without the parties recognizing the need to adopt a plan of complete liquidation under § 337. Second, it is not always clear in this kind of situation what direction the parties ultimately will take. It may be, for example, that the use of § 1033 is preferable, since it avoids gain at both the corporation and shareholder levels. Nevertheless, compliance with the requirements of § 1033 can prove troublesome. Not only do all of the insurance (or condemnation) proceeds have to be reinvested within a specified period of time, but the replacement usually must be in property that is "similar or related in service or use." Such property may be difficult to find. Or if the insurance claim is contested, how much needs to be reinvested to avoid any recognition of gain? All of these variables could make the decision as to whether to liquidate (and make use of § 337) or continue in business (and make use of § 1033) a protracted one. The parties, however, can buy time by making use of the § 337(e) grace period and adopting a plan of complete liquidation. This keeps the § 337 option open. Bear in mind that the adoption of the plan does not require that the liquidation actually be carried out.

—In the case of straddle sales, be sure a *formal* plan of liquidation is adopted *after* the sale. The complete absence of a formal plan may enable the IRS to infer the adoption of an informal plan prior to the sale of the loss assets. This would disallow all gains and losses if the complete liquidation occurs within 12 months, or if not within 12 months, it could make all gains and losses taxable.

—Although the use of § 337 usually is advantageous to the taxpayer, in some situations it may prove to be an unwise choice. Suppose, for example, a plan is adopted and the amount of losses realized from the sales of corporate property exceeds the realized gains. Can anything be done to make § 337 inoperative so as to permit the recognition of both losses and gains? The obvious way to avoid § 337 would be to violate the 12-month rule by delaying the final liquidating distributions to the shareholders.[85]

---

85.  Rev.Rul. 77–150, 1977–1 C.B. 88.

## EFFECT ON THE SHAREHOLDER

Under the general rule of § 331, shareholders will have recognized gain or loss measured by the difference between the liquidation proceeds and the basis of the stock given up. In cases of a large gain, a shareholder may wish to consider shifting it to others. One approach is to give the stock to family members or donate it to charity. Whether this procedure will be successful depends on the timing of the transfer. If the donee of the stock is not in a position to prevent the liquidation of the corporation, the donor will be deemed to have made an anticipatory assignment of income. As a result, the gain will still be taxed to the donor. Hence, advance planning becomes crucial in arriving at the desired tax result.

Recall that § 453(h) provides some relief from the general rule of § 331 that all gain is to be recognized by the shareholder upon the shareholder's receipt of the liquidation proceeds. If the payment for the sale of § 337 corporate assets after a plan of liquidation has been adopted is by installment notes, the shareholders receiving such notes as liquidation distributions may report the gain on the installment method. Hence, some gain can be deferred to the point of collection of such notes.

One important decision that must be made is the type of liquidation most favorable to the shareholders. Section 333 (i. e., the one-month type), an elective provision, should be weighed very carefully.

—Large amounts of E & P at the corporate level may generate dividend income to the individual shareholder or capital gain to the corporate shareholder. Remember that sales by the corporation of gain property during the liquidation process could aggravate the problem further because of their effect on E & P.

—Even if little or no gain is recognized by the shareholder on a § 333 liquidation, the key to the choice of this election may lie with what happens to the property after distribution and how the property is classified in the hands of the shareholder.

**Example 37.** T, the sole shareholder of V Corporation, receives inventory (value of $80,000) and land (value of $20,000) in complete liquidation. T's basis in the V Corporation stock investment is $10,000. The inventory will be a noncapital asset to T because he is engaged in the same trade or business as the corporation.

In all probability, T would be ill-advised to elect § 333, even if no gain resulted from the liquidation. Under § 334(c) his basis in the inventory would be $8,000 [($80,000/$100,000) × $10,000 (the basis in the stock)]. A post-liquidation sale of the inventory for $80,000 would result in ordinary income of $72,000 [$80,000 (sales price) − $8,000 (allocated basis)]. If § 333 is not elected and the general rule of § 331 takes effect, T's basis in the inventory becomes $80,000 [§ 334(a).]. Thus, T substitutes $90,000 of capital gain [$100,000 (fair market value of all assets received) − $10,000 (the basis in the stock)] for $72,000 of ordinary income. Also, his basis in the land is $20,000 as opposed to the $2,000 [($20,000/$100,000) × $10,000] it would have been had § 333 been elected.

**Example 38.** Assume the same facts as in Example 37 except that V Corporation's only asset is land (value of $100,000) that T intends to hold as an investment. Presuming no gain results to T if § 333 is utilized, the election appears highly attractive. True, T's basis now becomes $10,000 (i. e., his basis in the stock). But because T does not intend to immediately dispose of the land, his low basis is of little consequence. Further, any gain on a later sale of the land investment would be capital. The alternative (use of the general rule of § 331) does provide a basis of $100,000 but would force T to recognize a gain of $90,000 [$100,000 (value of the land) − $10,000 (basis in the stock)] upon liquidation. Utilizing § 333 carries the advantage of postponing the recognition of gain without changing its classification (i. e., capital *vs.* ordinary).

In the event § 333 is to be used, close attention should be paid to the applicable procedural rules for making the election and carrying out the liquidation. Strict compliance with the 30-day and one-month requirements is essential.

Unlike § 333, the use of § 332 for the liquidation of a subsidiary is not elective. Nevertheless, some flexibility may be available.

—Whether § 332 applies depends on the 80 percent stock ownership test. Given some substance to the transaction, § 332 may well be avoided if a parent corporation reduces its stock ownership in the subsidiary below this percentage. On the other hand, the opposite approach may be desirable. A parent could make § 332 applicable by acquiring enough additional stock in the subsidiary to meet the 80 percent test.

—Once § 332 becomes operative, less latitude is present in determining the parent's basis in the subsidiary's assets. If § 334(b)(1) applies, the subsidiary's basis carries over to the parent. If § 338 applies and a timely election is made, the parent's basis becomes the cost of the stock. (If the subsidiary is not liquidated, the basis of the assets to the subsidiary is the parent's cost of the stock.) Presumably, § 338 can be avoided by failing to make a timely election.

—If a timely election is made under § 338, the parent corporation's basis in the stock of the subsidiary is allocated among the assets of the subsidiary under regulations to be issued by the IRS.[86]

**Example 39.** XY Corporation has operated a retail supply business at two different outlets for the past 10 years. Each of its two shareholders, A and B, manages one of the two outlets. A and B have had differences of opinion and wish to discontinue operation of XY Corporation.

Example 39 presents an opportunity to review several possibilities as to termination of the business.

1. If B wishes to discontinue operating in the corporate form but A wishes to continue, B could exchange all of his stock in XY Corporation for the assets of the outlet he operates. This would qualify

---

86.   § 338(b)(3).

as a complete termination of his interest under § 302(b)(3) and as a partial liquidation under § 302(b)(4). B would recognize a capital gain or loss measured by the difference between the fair market value of the business and his basis in the XY stock surrendered. As noted in Chapter 4, some gain may be recognized by XY because of the redemption; however, § 311(d) probably would be inapplicable, since the redemption is a qualified partial liquidation. A would have complete control of XY Corporation and could continue to operate in the corporate form.

2. If both shareholders are indifferent about whether the business should continue to operate in the corporate form, some thought should be given to a complete liquidation of XY Corporation. The liquidation could be carried out by making a distribution in kind of the assets of each outlet to the shareholder operating that outlet. As was true with reference to the stock redemption alternative, the shareholders would recognize a capital gain or loss measured by the difference between the fair market value of the property received and the basis of the stock given up. The various methods of handling the liquidation (previously noted) to avoid as much gain as possible at the corporate level should be considered. In addition, the possible utilization of § 333 by the shareholders might be an alternative.

3. If A and B wish to sell the business and discontinue operations altogether, a sale of the stock in XY Corporation is preferable. In this instance, each shareholder would have a capital gain measured by the difference in the selling price of his stock and his basis in that stock. Gain at the corporate level would be avoided.

4. Although an individual buyer or buyers of the corporate stock may be difficult to find (individual buyers would prefer to buy the assets of the corporation in order to obtain a step-up in basis in the corporate assets and to eliminate any E & P), A and B may be able to sell their stock to a corporate buyer. A corporate purchaser can obtain a step-up in basis in the corporate assets and also eliminate E & P by a timely election under § 338.

5. Assuming a buyer of the stock cannot be found, gain on the complete sale of the assets of XY Corporation can be postponed if XY sells the assets on the installment basis and distributes the installment notes to A and B. Although XY Corporation would be subject to some gain under § § 1245 and 1250 and under the tax benefit rule, it could escape gain on inventory items by selling all the assets to one buyer. A and B will be able to defer their gain on the liquidation to the point of collection of the installment notes.

The collapsible corporation provision of § 341 is a trap for the unwary. Even for those taxpayers who are aware of its implications, there may be honest doubt as to whether a corporation is collapsible or not. Although the Code now provides that a corporation will not be collapsible if two-thirds of the taxable income to be derived from § 341 assets is realized before a sale or liquidation,[87] it may be difficult to measure accurately the total taxable

---

87. § 341(b)(1)(A).

income to be derived from the property.[88] Unfortunately, the IRS generally will not issue private rulings on proposed transactions involving § 341.[89]

The various ways of avoiding collapsible corporation treatment have already been discussed. Suppose, however, the impact of § 341 cannot be avoided. Several approaches could mitigate the harshness of the tax result.

—The shareholder could sell the collapsible corporation stock on an installment basis. Consequently, ordinary income would be spread over more than one accounting period.

—The shareholder could give the collapsible corporation stock to family members in lower income tax brackets. Thereby, the overall tax effect of the later realization of ordinary income would be reduced.

—The death of a shareholder could neutralize some or all of the ordinary income element of § 341. Through an increase in the income tax basis of the stock to the estate or heirs, there would be a reduction of any gain realized on a late sale of the stock. Recall that § 341 does not generate gain but merely serves to convert long-term capital gain to ordinary income. The effect of death on the income tax basis of property is treated in Chapter 12 in connection with § 1014.

## PROBLEM MATERIALS

### Discussion Questions

1. Compare stock redemptions and liquidations with other corporate distributions in terms of the following:

   (a) Recognition of gain to the shareholder.

   (b) Recognition of gain by the distributing corporation.

   (c) Effect on the distributing corporation's E & P.

2. Compare stock redemptions with liquidations in terms of the following:

   (a) Possible application of § 311 to the distributing corporation.

   (b) Possible disallowance of a loss (i. e., § 267) to a shareholder.

3. Presuming the general rule of § 331 applies, would it make any difference to the shareholder whether he or she receives cash or property distributions from the corporation being liquidated? Explain.

4. What problem led to the enactment of § 337 (the 12-month liquidation)?

5. Can the same liquidation involve the application of both § 336 and § 337? Explain.

---

**88.** An underestimate may well destroy the base chosen for tax planning purposes. See, for example, *Manassas Airport Industrial Park, Inc. v. Comm.*, 77–2 USTC ¶ 9494, 40 AFTR2d 77–5444, 557 F.2d 1113 (CA–4, 1977), *aff'g.* 66 T.C. 566 (1976).

**89.** See Rev.Proc. 82–60, 1982–2 C.B. 848. However, in limited circumstances, the IRS will entertain ruling requests when the following conditions are met: (1) the corporation has been in existence for at least 20 years, or it has already realized a substantial portion of its taxable income from its § 341 assets; (2) the shareholder's interest in the corporation has not exceeded 10% during the last 20 years or during the period in which the corporation realized a substantial part of its taxable income from § 341 assets; and (3) the corporation conducted substantially the same trade or business throughout the appropriate period. See Rev.Proc. 83–85, 1983–2 C.B. 604.

*If installment recvble created before plan of organization,*
*must recognize gain unless its a bulk sale of inventory*

6. Why is § 337 termed the 12-month liquidation?

7. What is the definition of property under § 337? Why is this definition important?

8. How would the liquidating corporation be taxed on the sale of the following assets under § 337:

   (a) Inventory.

   (b) Depreciable property.

   (c) Property upon which an investment tax credit has previously been claimed.

   (d) Trade accounts receivable.

9. (a) What is a straddle sale?

   (b) What are its advantages?

   (c) What danger, if any, exists that it might not be successful?

10. What constitutes a plan of liquidation for purposes of § 337?

11. Discuss the tax treatment of liquidation expenses in connection with the following: *§337*

   (a) General liquidation expenses. *reduces sales price of asset to*

   (b) Expenses relating to a distribution of assets in kind. *- assoc with dist*

   (c) Expenses relating to a sale of property, the gain from which is not recognized under § 337. *offset*

   (d) Expenses relating to a sale of assets, the gain from which is recognized by the corporation. *- Not a LIQUIDATION since recognized. Deduct as cost of sale.*

12. Suppose a corporation has its major asset destroyed by fire. Under what circumstances might any gain resulting from the insurance proceeds be nonrecognizable under § 337? *If file plan w/in 60 days of invol. conversion involuntary conversion*

13. Under what conditions, if any, may a corporation retain assets beyond a 12-month period from the adoption of a plan of complete liquidation without losing the benefits of § 337?

14. Would a corporation have to recognize gain on a distribution of installment notes receivable to its shareholders in complete liquidation? In this context, consider the following:

   (a) The notes were received by the corporation from the sale of its property prior to the adoption of a plan of liquidation. *Recognize when distributed*

   (b) The notes were received by the corporation from the bulk sale of its inventory after the adoption of a plan of complete liquidation.

15. Why is a § 333 liquidation referred to as a one-month liquidation?

16. Under what conditions might a § 333 liquidation be advantageous? Disadvantageous? *If E&P is relatively low (or post 1953 cash + securities); then §333 good but if E&P high, not helpful*

17. Under what circumstances may an individual shareholder elect § 333? A corporate shareholder? *If ≥ 80% of qualified shareholders elect (owned 50% w/in last 5 yrs) Corp shareholder owning ≥ 50% - not qualified*

18. If some shareholders elect § 333, what tax consequences ensue to those who do not?

19. With regard to § 333, distinguish between the 30-day and the one-month requirements.

20. In determining the amount and classification of gain to the shareholders under § 333, comment on the effect of the following:

   (a) The E & P of the corporation being liquidated.

   (b) The type of shareholder involved (i. e., corporate or noncorporate).

*know when applicable + advantages*
*Know who's eligible for §333*
*+ how to figure T.I. + P*

(c) The shareholder's *realized* gain.

(d) The amount of the liquidating corporation's cash plus post-1953 securities.

21. In arriving at the basis of property received pursuant to a § 333 liquidation, what impact would the following have:

    (a) The shareholder's recognized gain.

    (b) The shareholder's basis in the stock investment.

    (c) The cash received by the shareholder.

    (d) The shareholder's assumption of a general liability of the corporation.

    (e) The shareholder's assumption of a liability of the corporation that relates to a specific asset received in the distribution.

22. When the individual shareholders of T Corporation decide to liquidate under § 333, it is determined that there is no current or accumulated E & P. Does this mean that no dividend income will result? Explain.

23. A corporation whose shareholders have elected § 333 will be prone not to sell its assets but instead to make distributions in kind under § 336. Is this a valid supposition? Why or why not?

24. On January 3, 1986, the shareholders of X Corporation decide on a complete liquidation. Although they would like to elect § 333, some doubt exists that X Corporation could wind up its affairs by January 31, 1986. Please comment.

25. In terms of the applicability of § 332, describe the effect of each of the following factors:

    (a) The adoption of a plan of complete liquidation.

    (b) The period of time in which the corporation must liquidate.

    (c) The amount of stock held by the parent corporation.

    (d) The solvency of the subsidiary being liquidated.

26. Under § 332, how is the satisfaction by a subsidiary of a debt owed to its parent treated for tax purposes?

27. Could a liquidation of one corporation involve § § 331, 332, and 333? Explain.

28. Describe the problem that led to the enactment of § 338.

29. What are the requirements for the application of § 338?

30. Under what circumstances could the application of § 338 be beneficial to the parent corporation? Detrimental?

31. Compare § § 334(b)(1) and 338 with respect to the following:

    (a) Carryover to the parent of the subsidiary's corporate attributes.

    (b) Recognition by the subsidiary of gain or loss on distributions to its parent.

32. Briefly describe the hoped-for tax results taxpayers were trying to achieve through the use of the collapsible corporation approach.

33. How can § 341 affect a sale by a shareholder of his or her stock to a third party? A distribution not in liquidation by the corporation to its shareholders?

34. What is meant by the statement: "Section 341 does not generate gain"?

35. (a) What is meant by the *view* to collapse?

    (b) Who must have this view?

    (c) Under what conditions might the absence of such view avoid collapsible corporation treatment?

36. When can the realization of some income at the corporate level avoid the collapsible corporation rules?

37. C Corporation is formed to construct and sell a residential housing subdivision. After the units are built (estimated value of $1,500,000) and $1,000,000 of the units are sold, C Corporation is liquidated. After liquidation, the shareholders are able to eventually realize $700,000 on the unsold units. Is there any vulnerability to § 341 (collapsible corporation) treatment? Explain.

38. Will the application of § 331 to a liquidation always result in capital gain or loss being recognized by a shareholder? Why or why not?

39. "The E & P of the corporation being liquidated will disappear."

    (a) Do you agree with this statement?

    (b) Why or why not?

40. Is it possible to have a complete liquidation where the existence of the corporation being liquidated is not terminated? Elaborate.

*Consequences to A: She recv's FMV so has gain of 90*
*to T corp: under 3116) 90 under redemption*
*0 to liquidation*
*§336 applies*

## Problems

1. T Corporation, with E & P of $50,000, distributes unimproved land with a basis of $60,000 and a fair market value of $150,000 to its shareholder, A. A has a $30,000 basis in her 1,000 shares in T Corporation. What are the tax consequences to T if the distribution is made pursuant to a complete liquidation of T? What are the tax consequences to T if the distribution is made pursuant to a redemption of A's stock wherein A owned 80% of T before the redemption and 75% after? What are the tax consequences to A under both alternatives?

*KNOW*

*150 FMV*
*60 Basis*
*90*

2. On July 31, 19X4, X Corporation, an accrual basis taxpayer, adopts a plan of liquidation. Assuming the liquidation does not come under § 333 or § 332 and is carried out within 12 months, determine the gain (or loss) and income (or expense) the corporation must recognize from the following transactions:

    (a) Small tools and supplies with a basis of zero (the cost had been previously expensed) and fair market value of $25,000 are distributed to X's shareholders. *Tax benefit rule implied (zero basis says they were written off before)*
    *Recognize gain of $25,000 (or up to amt written off)*

    (b) X's accounts receivable with a basis of $80,000 and a bad debt provision of $5,000 (face value of $85,000) are distributed to X's shareholders. Fair market value of the receivables is $75,000. *Don't recognize loss under §337.* *have already recognized income*
    *75,000 FMV*
    *80000 Basis*
    *<5000 loss>*

    (c) Machinery with a basis of $40,000 is sold for $30,000 on March 1, 19X4. *<10000 loss> recognized but IRS may allege sale* *Before Plan of liquidation*

    (d) Equipment with a basis of $50,000 is sold for $45,000 on August 10, 19X4. *<5000 loss> under §337 so not recognized*

    (e) Land with a basis of $60,000 is sold for $135,000 on November 1, 19X4. Commission on the sale was $5,000, and $1,000 was paid to an attorney to handle the sale. *135-5-1-60 = Gain realized* *not recognized*

    (f) X has inventory with a basis of $70,000. It sells the inventory to several customers in different transactions at a total selling price of $30,000. *inventory isn't property unless in bulk sale.* *not a bulk sale so have a loss - not covered under §337 - So recognize loss.*

    (g) Assume for (g) only that one of X's shareholders properly elects under § 333. X sells its inventory in bulk to one person in one transaction for $120,000. The inventory has a basis of $80,000. *$120-80 = 40,000 gain recognized* *337 thus doesn't apply*

    (h) Assume for (h) only that X is a cash basis taxpayer. X distributes unrealized receivables with a face value of $100,000 to its shareholder, A, on December 15, 19X4. *A has recv'd an unrealized revble - has zero basis & will recognize income as he collects. Could be interpreted as assignment of income.*

3. On June 1, 19X2, T Corporation adopts a plan of complete liquidation under § 337. Assuming the liquidation is carried out within the 12-month period, determine the gain (or loss) and income (or expense) that the corporation must recognize from each of the following transactions:

    (a) On January 15, 19X2, T Corporation sells some of its inventory (basis of $40,000, FMV of $32,000) to one of its customers.

(b) On July 1, 19X2, T Corporation sells to outsiders some machinery acquired four years ago (original cost of $50,000 and adjusted basis of $10,000) for $30,000.

(c) On August 3, 19X2, T Corporation distributes installment notes receivable (basis of $30,000) to its shareholders. The installment notes resulted from a sale in 19X1 of unimproved land and possess a present value of $54,000, face amount of $60,000.

(d) On August 5, 19X2, T Corporation sells its remaining non-LIFO inventory (basis of $10,000) to one of its customers for $25,000.

(e) On September 1, 19X2, T Corporation pays an attorney $600 to have its corporate charter revoked.

4. X Corporation distributes appreciated LIFO inventory (basis of $50,000) to A, its shareholder, as part of a complete liquidation (plan of liquidation was adopted January 2, 1986). The basis of the inventory under the FIFO method of inventory valuation would have been $80,000. What gain, if any, must X Corporation recognize on the distribution?

5. After a plan of complete liquidation has been adopted, W Corporation sells its only asset, unimproved land, to T (an unrelated party) for $500,000. Under the terms of the sale, W Corporation receives cash of $100,000 and T's note in the amount of $400,000. The note is payable in five years ($80,000 per year) and carries an interest rate of 13%. Immediately after the sale, W Corporation distributes the cash and notes to S, an individual and sole shareholder. Assume that S has an adjusted basis in the W Corporation stock of $100,000 and that the installment notes possess a value equal to the face amount. What are the tax results to S if the choice is to defer as much gain as possible on the transaction?

6. A, an individual and the sole shareholder of YZ Corporation, has a basis in her stock of $80,000. The corporation's only asset is an apartment building valued at $150,000 with an adjusted basis of $50,000. Potential § 1250 depreciation recapture is $30,000. Section 1245 recapture would have been $50,000. YZ sells the building for $150,000 and distributes the cash to A. What is the taxable gain to—

(a) YZ Corporation?

(b) A?

7. A, an individual, has 40 shares of stock in X Corporation, 20 of which were acquired in 1981 at a cost of $25,000 and 20 of which were acquired on January 10, 1986, at a cost of $10,000. X Corporation liquidates on July 1, 1986, and distributes $1,000 per share to its shareholders in complete liquidation. How will A be taxed on the distribution?

8. X Corporation is liquidated in 19X6 by A, an individual and its sole shareholder, when its E & P is $30,000. Pursuant to the liquidation, A receives the following items:

|  | Basis to X Corporation | Fair Market Value |
| --- | --- | --- |
| Cash | $ 10,000 | $ 10,000 |
| Accounts receivable | 10,000 | 10,000 |
| Land | 80,000 | 130,000 |
| Mortgage payable | (60,000) | N/A |
| Stock (acquired in 19X2) | 10,000 | 40,000 |

On the date of liquidation, A has a basis in his X Corporation stock of $20,000. The land is transferred to A subject to the mortgage. Assume the liquidation takes place under § 333.

(a) What is A's realized gain?

(b) What is A's recognized gain?

(c) How much of the recognized gain is capital gain?

(d) What will be X Corporation's recognized gain?

(e) What basis will A have in the stock?

(f) What basis will A have in the land?

(g) What basis will A have in the accounts receivable?

9. Answer the following questions with respect to an election under § 333:

    (a) Y Corporation adopts a plan of complete liquidation on March 1, 19X5. On March 15, 19X5, A and B, the only shareholders of Y, file written elections as required by § 333. Y Corporation is liquidated on August 31, 19X5, with the liquidation beginning on August 10, 19X5. Do A and B qualify for the provisions of § 333?

    (b) Y Corporation adopts its plan of liquidation on March 1, 19X5, and A and B file their written elections to come under § 333 on April 15, 19X5. The liquidation begins on May 1, 19X5, and concludes on May 20, 19X5. Do A and B qualify for the provisions of § 333?

    (c) Y Corporation has total assets with a basis of $100,000, fair market value of $200,000, consisting of cash of $10,000, marketable securities of $15,000, and land of $75,000. It has E & P of $9,000 and no liabilities. Y Corporation stock is owned by the following shareholders (basis in parentheses): 60% by X Corporation ($55,000); 15% by Z Corporation ($14,000); 10% by A, an individual ($9,000); 10% by B, an individual ($9,000); and 5% by C, an individual ($4,000). What consents will be required to qualify a liquidation of Y under § 333?

    (d) Assume all necessary consents were filed in (c). What would be the tax consequences to each of the shareholders upon Y's liquidation?

10. X Corporation has three equal shareholders, A, B, and C. C is a corporation; A and B are individuals. Each shareholder acquired the stock in X Corporation five years ago at a cost of $50,000. X liquidates with all of the shareholders electing under § 333. X has E & P of $60,000, cash of $75,000, stock and securities acquired after 1953 valued at $90,000, and land valued at $240,000. The assets are distributed in kind to A, B, and C—with each receiving a one-third interest in each asset—in a distribution meeting the requirements of § 333.

    (a) What gain must A, B, and C report, and how is the gain taxed?

    (b) What is the basis of the land to each shareholder?

11. The shareholders of R Corporation are as follows:

| Corporate Shareholders | Noncorporate Shareholders |
|---|---|
| X–40 shares | A–20 shares |
| Y–60 shares | B–20 shares |
| Z–30 shares | C–40 shares |
|  | D–30 shares |

How many shareholders must elect the provisions of § 333 before the section will apply to any shareholder?

12. Z Corporation adopts a plan of liquidation in 1986. Its shares are owned as follows: J, 100 shares; K, 100 shares; and P Corporation, 100 shares. The financial statement of Z Corporation is as follows:

*Assets*

|  | Basis to Z Corporation | Fair Market Value |
|---|---|---|
| Cash | $ 60,000 | $ 60,000 |
| Inventory | 100,000 | 90,000 |
| Machinery (depreciation allowed of $40,000) | 160,000 | 210,000 |
| Land | 200,000 | 240,000 |
|  | $ 520,000 | $ 600,000 |

*Liabilities and Shareholders' Equity*

|  | | |
|---|---|---|
| Accounts payable | $ 140,000 | $ 140,000 |
| Shareholders' equity— |  |  |
| Common stock | 300,000 | 460,000 |
| Retained earnings | 80,000 |  |
|  | $ 520,000 | $ 600,000 |

E & P equals retained earnings on the date of adoption of the plan of liquidation. There are no immediate plans for selling the machinery and land. What plan of liquidation should be followed, and what steps should be taken to perfect the liquidation for tax purposes?

13. X Corporation has been in existence for several years. A, an individual and X's sole shareholder, wants to liquidate the corporation. X Corporation has the following assets and no liabilities:

|  | Basis to X Corporation | Fair Market Value |
|---|---|---|
| Non-LIFO Inventory | $ 20,000 | $ 35,000 |
| Equipment ($30,000 of depreciation taken) | 15,000 | 60,000 |
| Supplies | –0– | 5,000 |
| Land | 30,000 | 120,000 |
| Installment notes with a face value of $80,000 (received from sale of inventory last year) | 20,000 | 70,000 |

A has a $30,000 basis in her stock investment. Compare the tax results to X Corporation and to A if—

(a) The assets of X Corporation are distributed to A, who continues to operate the business as a sole proprietorship.

(b) X Corporation sells the assets for fair market value and distributes the cash to A.

14. S Corporation is owned 90% by P Corporation. The parent is contemplating a liquidation of S Corporation and the acquisition of its assets. P purchased the stock of S a month ago on January 1, 19X6, for $200,000. The financial statement of S Corporation as of January 1, 19X6, is as follows:

*Assets*

|  | Basis to S Corporation | Fair Market Value |
|---|---|---|
| Cash | $ 20,000 | $ 20,000 |
| Inventory | 40,000 | 30,000 ⟨10 000⟩ |
| Accounts receivable | 80,000 | 50,000 ⟨30 000⟩ |
| Equipment | 200,000 | 160,000 ⟨40,000⟩ |
| Land | 260,000 | 140,000 ⟨120 000⟩ |
|  | $ 600,000 | $ 400,000 ⟨200000⟩ |

*Liabilities and Shareholders' Equity*

|  | | |
|---|---|---|
| Accounts payable | $ 60,000 | $ 60,000 |
| Mortgages payable | 100,000 | 100,000 |
| Common stock | 500,000 | 240,000 |
| Retained earnings | (60,000) | |
|  | $ 600,000 | $ 400,000 |

The management of P Corporation asks your advice on the feasibility of an election under § 338. How will you advise your client?

15.  At the time of its liquidation under § 332, S Corporation had the following assets and liabilities:

|  | Basis to S Corporation | Fair Market Value |
|---|---|---|
| Cash | $ 240,000 | $ 240,000 |
| Marketable securities | 180,000 | 480,000 |
| Unimproved land | 300,000 | 600,000 |
| Unsecured bank loan | (60,000) | (60,000) |
| Mortgage on land | (180,000) | (180,000) |

P Corporation, the sole shareholder of S Corporation, has a basis in its stock investment of $720,000. At the time of its liquidation, S Corporation's E & P was $960,000.

(a) How much gain (or loss) will S Corporation recognize if it distributes all of its assets and liabilities to P Corporation?

(b) How much gain (or loss) will P Corporation recognize?

(c) If § 334(b)(1) applies, what will be P Corporation's basis in the marketable securities it receives from S Corporation?

(d) What will be its basis in the unimproved land?

16.  P Corporation paid $900,000 for all the stock of S Corporation 10 years ago. S Corporation's balance sheet is as follows:

*Assets*

|  | |
|---|---|
| Cash | $ 22,500 |
| Inventory | 67,500 |
| Accounts receivable | 45,000 |
| Equipment | 180,000 |
| Land | 225,000 |
|  | $ 540,000 |

*Liabilities and Shareholders' Equity*

| | |
|---|---:|
| Accounts payable | $   360,000 |
| Payable to P Corporation | 540,000 |
| Common stock | 900,000 |
| Deficit | (1,260,000) |
| | $   540,000 |

What are the tax consequences to P Corporation if it liquidates S Corporation?

17. S Corporation is owned by W, who is interested in selling either his stock in S Corporation or its assets. The financial statement of S Corporation as of December 31, 19X5, is as follows:

*Assets*

| | Basis to S Corporation | Fair Market Value |
|---|---:|---:|
| Cash | $   7,500 | $   7,500 |
| Accounts receivable | 5,000 | 5,000 |
| Inventory | 7,500 | 12,500 |
| Equipment (depreciation allowed of $20,000) | 25,000 | 50,000 |
| Land | 50,000 | 100,000 |
| | $ 95,000 | $ 175,000 |

*Liabilities and Shareholders' Equity*

| | | |
|---|---:|---:|
| Accounts payable | $ 20,000 | $   20,000 |
| Mortgages payable | 25,000 | 25,000 |
| Common stock | 12,500 | 130,000 |
| Retained earnings | 37,500 | |
| | $ 95,000 | $ 175,000 |

P Corporation is interested in purchasing S Corporation. Should P Corporation purchase the stock for $130,000 or the assets for $175,000? If stock is purchased for $130,000, what steps should P Corporation take to secure maximum tax benefits?

18. Does § 341 apply to the following transactions? Why or why not?

(a) R Corporation acquired farmland and engaged in farming for several years. At a time when the farmland had substantially increased in value, R was liquidated and the farmland was distributed to R's shareholders.

(b) R Corporation acquired several sections of land that it held primarily for sale. At a time when the land had substantially increased in value, R was liquidated and the land was distributed to R's shareholders.

(c) The only asset of T Corporation is a building T constructed. Because of a severe recession, the building is valued at only $200,000. Its cost was $250,000. T has liabilities of $150,000. T is liquidated in the current tax year, and the building and T's liabilities are distributed to A, T's sole shareholder. A has a basis of $100,000 in his stock in T.

(d) C Corporation realized 10% of the profit from the sale of several houses it had constructed. The profit was reported by C in the previous tax year. In the current tax year, C is liquidated and the houses are distributed to C's shareholder, T. The houses are valued at $500,000. T's basis in her stock in C is $150,000.

(e) S Corporation is engaged in the construction business. B, a shareholder of S, is forced to sell his shares in S because of a dispute between him and the other shareholders of S. B makes a profit of $60,000 on the sale of his S stock.

19. S Corporation has a basis of $450,000 (fair market value of $1,000,000) in its assets and has E & P of $80,000. Its liabilities total $100,000. No gain or loss would be recognized on the sale of these assets if they were sold under a liquidation in which § 337 was applicable. P Corporation purchases 20% of all the stock of S Corporation for $180,000 on March 1, 1986; 15% on September 20, 1986, for $135,000; and 60% on December 1, 1986, for $540,000, or a total consideration of $855,000.

(a) Is P entitled to make an election under § 338?

(b) Assume P may make an election under § 338. Should P do so? When must P make such an election?

(c) What are the tax consequences to S Corporation and to P Corporation if P Corporation makes a valid election under § 338 but does not liquidate S?

(d) What tax result if S Corporation is liquidated four months after a valid § 338 election? A, an individual who holds the 5% minority interest in S Corporation, has a $10,000 basis in his stock in S. What tax result to A upon the liquidation?

20. T and S formed the TS Corporation in 19X0. T transferred assets worth $100,000 with an adjusted basis of $50,000 to TS for 1,000 shares of common stock of TS with a par value of $50 per share. S, T's son, transferred cash of $50,000 to TS for 1,000 shares of common stock of TS. TS Corporation made substantial profits from 19X0 to present and had an E & P of $400,000 on December 31, 19X5, the close of its tax year. XY Corporation purchased all the stock of TS on January 10, 19X6, at a cost of $550,000. What steps should XY take to obtain the maximum tax benefits? Explain.

21. S Corporation is wholly owned by A, an individual, who has a basis in the S stock of $50,000. S Corporation has the following assets and no liabilities:

| | Basis to S Corporation | Fair Market Value |
|---|---|---|
| Inventory | $ 50,000 | $ 80,000 |
| Equipment (§ 1245 depreciation recapture potential of $100,000) | 40,000 | 150,000 |
| Building (no recapture potential) | 30,000 | 200,000 |

P Corporation wants to buy the assets of S Corporation or the stock in S. What are the tax results to S Corporation, to P Corporation, and to A under the following circumstances:

(a) P purchases the S stock for $430,000 and makes an election under § 338.

(b) S Corporation adopts a plan of complete liquidation, sells all its assets to P Corporation, and distributes the cash of $430,000 to A.

(c) Which alternative is preferable to P Corporation?

22. S Corporation has a basis of $700,000 in its assets, fair market value of $1,500,000; its liabilities total $500,000. S has E & P of $150,000. P Corporation

purchases 85% of the stock of S Corporation on June 10, 1986, for $850,000. P makes a proper election to treat the acquisition as a purchase of the assets of S Corporation under § 338. S is not liquidated.

(a) What will be the tax basis of the assets of S Corporation?

(b) What, if any, gain must S Corporation recognize upon the transaction (ignore depreciation and investment credit recapture, LIFO adjustments, and application of the tax benefit rule)?

(c) What will be the E & P of S Corporation after P's purchase of 85% of the S stock?

## Research Problems

*Research Problem 1.* Prior to the liquidation of X Corporation, T, one of the shareholders, sells her stock (basis of $50,000) to a newly created T Trust for the stock's fair market value of $400,000. Under the sales agreement, T Trust is to pay $40,000 in the year of sale and $36,000 in each of the next 10 years. Interest of 10% is provided for on the notes T Trust issues for the deferred balance of $360,000. Shortly, after the sale, X Corporation liquidates and distributes to T Trust cash and property worth $400,000 in exchange for its stock.

The trust department of a local bank is the trustee of T Trust, and T's son and grandchildren are the designated holders of the life estate and remainder interests. (Note: See the Glossary of Tax Terms in Appendix C for a definition of these terms.)

(a) What is T trying to accomplish by the creation and use of T Trust?

(b) Will it work?

*Research Problem 2.* After adopting a plan of complete liquidation, X Corporation makes a bulk sale of its inventory, the gain from which is not recognized under § 337. On its final income tax return (i. e., Form 1120) for the year of liquidation, X Corporation reports a final inventory of zero but does not adjust the purchases account for the cost of the inventory sold in bulk. What is X Corporation trying to accomplish? What defense, if any, might the IRS raise?

*Partial list of research aids:*

*Winer v. Comm.*, 67–1 USTC ¶ 9169, 19 AFTR2d 423, 371 F.2d 684 (CA– 1, 1967).

*Research Problem 3.* For the past 10 years, B Corporation has operated a minor league baseball club. It derives its revenue from the sale of baseball player contracts to other clubs and from the gate receipts of baseball games. Because a major league club is scheduled to move into the same area, the shareholders of B Corporation adopt a plan of complete liquidation. After the plan is adopted, and within the 12-month period, B Corporation sells at a gain all of its baseball player contracts to different minor and major league clubs.

(a) What arguments could be made that the gain is not taxed to the corporation because of § 337?

(b) What defense might the IRS raise to make § 337 inapplicable to the baseball player contracts?

(c) Can you think of alternatives (other than the sale of the contracts to different parties) that would have avoided this problem?

*Partial list of research aids:*

*Hollywood Baseball Association*, 49 T.C. 338 (1968), *aff'd.* in 70–1 USTC ¶ 9521, 25 AFTR2d 70–788, 423 F.2d 494 (CA–9, 1970).

*Research Problem 4.* Pursuant to an offer made by A Corporation to purchase the assets of both P Corporation and S Corporation, a wholly owned subsidiary of P

Corporation, the two corporations simultaneously adopted plans of liquidation. The sales of assets by the corporations would have produced substantial gain to both corporations. However, because of § 337, the corporations recognized gain only with respect to § § 1245 and 1250 depreciation recapture. The shareholders of P Corporation reported capital gain upon the liquidation pursuant to § 331. Upon audit, the IRS asserted a deficiency with respect to gain on the sale of S Corporation's assets. According to the IRS, the liquidation of S Corporation was covered by § 332; consequently, § 337 was inapplicable under § 337(c)(2). Former management of S Corporation is asking your advice as to whether § 337 would apply to cause nonrecognition of gain on the sale of assets by S Corporation. What would you advise?

*Research Problem 5.* For 10 years, X Corporation had been engaged in the business of building and operating apartment buildings. The shareholders of X (A, B, and C) developed animosity towards one another and decided it would be in their best interests if X Corporation were dissolved.

A, B, and C held a meeting on January 10, 1984, at which time they drafted a written agreement summarizing their plans to liquidate. The agreement read, "Simultaneously with the execution of this agreement, X Corporation has adopted a plan of liquidation under the provisions of § 333 of the Internal Revenue Code."

After the agreement was executed, the shareholders held a special meeting on February 15, 1984, at which they passed a corporate resolution formally adopting a plan of liquidation. On March 11, 1984, A, B, and C filed elections (Form 964) to be taxed under § 333. Later it was discovered that an error had been made in the calculation of the E & P of X Corporation and that an election under § 333 would be disadvantageous. Consequently, the shareholders reported their gain as a long-term capital gain under § 331.

State law does not require a meeting of the shareholders to adopt a plan of liquidation so long as the shareholders have consented in writing to the liquidation. The shareholders' position is that their election under § 333 was ineffective in that it was made more then 30 days after the effective date of adoption of the plan of liquidation. Their contention is that the plan of liquidation was adopted on January 10, 1984. Thus, an election filed on March 11, 1984, would not be timely.

Upon audit of the returns of A, B, and C in 1985, the IRS asserted a deficiency against each contending that the proceeds from the liquidation must be taxed under § 333; thus, the shareholders had substantial ordinary income. The IRS contends that the plan of liquidation was adopted on February 15, 1984. Therefore, the elections made on March 11, 1984, were timely and binding.

(a) What argument can be made in defense of the shareholders' position?

(b) How successful will it be?

*Partial list of research aids:*

*Harold Wales,* 50 T.C. 399 (1968).

# Corporations: Reorganizations  6

## CHAPTER OBJECTIVES

—Explain the utility for tax purposes of a corporate reorganization.

—Describe the statutory requirements for the different types of reorganizations.

—Discuss the various administrative and judicial criteria for the different types of reorganizations.

—Become familiar with certain planning procedures available to insulate corporate reorganizations from adverse income tax consequences.

A corporate combination, usually referred to as a "reorganization," can be either a taxable or a nontaxable transaction. Assuming a business combination is taxable, § 1001 of the Code provides that the seller's gain or loss is measured by the difference between the amount realized and the basis of property surrendered. The purchaser's basis for the property received is the amount paid for such property, and the holding period begins on the date of purchase.

There are certain exchanges specifically excepted from tax recognition by the Code. For example, § 1031 provides that no gain or loss shall be recognized if property held for productive use or for investment is exchanged solely for ". . . property of a like kind . . ." Section 1033, if elected by the taxpayer, provides for partial or complete nonrecognition of gain if property destroyed, seized, or stolen is compulsorily or involuntarily converted into similar property. Further, § 351 provides for nonrecognition of gain upon the transfer of property to a controlled corporation. Finally, § § 361 and 368 provide for nonrecognition of gain in certain corporate reorganizations. The Regulations state the underlying assumption behind such nonrecognition of gain or loss—

> . . . the new property is substantially a continuation of the old investment still unliquidated; and, in the case of reorganizations, . . . the new enterprise, the new corporate structure, and the new property are substantially continuations of the old still unliquidated.[1]

## SUMMARY OF THE DIFFERENT TYPES OF REORGANIZATIONS

Section 368(a) of the Code specifies seven reorganizations that will qualify as nontaxable exchanges. It is important that the planner of a nontaxable business combination determine well in advance that the proposed transaction falls specifically within one of these seven described types. If the transaction fails to qualify, it will not be granted special tax treatment. In certain situations, the parties contemplating a corporate reorganization should obtain a letter ruling from the IRS that the proposed combination qualifies as a tax-free reorganization under § 368.

Section 368(a)(1) states that the term "reorganization" means:

(A) A statutory merger or consolidation.

(B) The acquisition by one corporation, in exchange solely for all or a part of its voting stock (or in exchange solely for all or a part of the

---

1. Reg. § 1.1011–2(c).

voting stock of a corporation that is in control of the acquiring corporation), of stock of another corporation if, immediately after the acquisition, the acquiring corporation has control of such other corporation (whether or not such acquiring corporation had control immediately before the acquisition).

(C) The acquisition by one corporation, in exchange solely for all or a part of its voting stock (or in exchange solely for all or a part of the voting stock of a corporation that is in control of the acquiring corporation), of substantially all of the properties of another corporation. But in determining whether the exchange is solely for stock, the assumption by the acquiring corporation of a liability of the other or the fact that property acquired is subject to a liability shall be disregarded.

(D) A transfer by a corporation of all or a part of its assets to another corporation if, immediately after the transfer, the transferor or one or more of the shareholders (including persons who were shareholders immediately before the transfer), or any combination thereof, is in control of the corporation to which the assets are transferred; but only if, in pursuance of the plan, stock or securities of the corporation to which the assets are transferred are distributed in a transaction that qualifies under § 354, § 355, or § 356.

(E) A recapitalization.

(F) A mere change in identity, form, or place of organization, however effected.

(G) A transfer by a corporation of all or a part of its assets to another corporation in a bankruptcy or receivership proceeding but only if in pursuance of the plan, stock and securities of the transferee corporation are distributed in a transaction that qualifies under § 354, § 355, or § 356.

These seven different types of tax-free reorganizations are designated by the letters identifying each: "Type A," "Type B," "Type C," "Type D," "Type E," "Type F," and "Type G" reorganizations. Basically, excepting the recapitalization (E), the change in form (F), and the insolvent corporation (G) provisions, a tax-free reorganization is (a) a statutory merger or consolidation, (b) an exchange of stock for voting stock, (c) an exchange of assets for voting stock, or (d) a divisive reorganization (the so-called spin-off, split-off, or split-up).

# GENERAL CONSEQUENCES OF TAX-FREE REORGANIZATIONS

Generally, no gain or loss is recognized to the security holders of the various corporations involved in a tax-free reorganization in the exchange of their stock and securities,[2] except when they receive cash or other consideration in addition to stock and securities.[3] As far as securities (long-term

---

**2.** The term "securities" includes bonds and long-term notes. Short-term notes are not considered to be securities. The problem of drawing a line between short-term and long-term notes was discussed in Chapter 3. Some courts include notes with a five-year maturity date as long-term; others, ten years.

**3.** § 358(a).

debt) are concerned, however, gain is not recognized if securities are surrendered in the same principal amount (or a greater principal amount) as the principal amount of the securities received.

If additional consideration is received, gain is recognized but not in excess of the sum of money and the fair market value of other property received.[4] If the distribution has the effect of the distribution of a dividend, any recognized gain is a taxable dividend to the extent of the shareholder's share of the corporation's earnings and profits. The remainder is treated as an exchange of property.[5] Loss is never recognized. The tax basis of stock and securities received by a shareholder pursuant to a tax-free reorganization will be the same as the basis of those surrendered, decreased by the amount of boot received and increased by the amount of gain and dividend income, if any, recognized on the transaction.[6]

> **Example 1.** A, an individual, exchanges stock he owns in X Corporation for stock in Y Corporation plus $2,000 cash. The exchange is pursuant to a tax-free reorganization of both corporations. A paid $10,000 for the stock in X two years ago. The stock in Y possesses a fair market value of $12,000. A has a realized gain of $4,000 ($12,000 + $2,000 − $10,000), which is recognized to the extent of the boot received, $2,000. Assume the distribution has the effect of a dividend. If A's share of earnings and profits in X is $1,000, that amount would be a taxable dividend. The remaining $1,000 would be treated as a gain from the exchange of property. A's basis in the Y stock would be $10,000 [$10,000 (basis in stock surrendered) − $2,000 (boot received) + $2,000 (gain and dividend income recognized)].

> **Example 2.** Assume A's basis in the X stock was $15,000. A would have a realized loss of $1,000 on the exchange, none of which would be recognized. His basis in the Y stock would be $13,000 [$15,000 (basis in stock surrendered) − $2,000 (boot received)].

Because there is a substituted basis in tax-free reorganizations, the unrecognized gain or loss will be recognized when the new stock or securities are disposed of in a taxable transaction.

No gain or loss is recognized to the acquired corporation on the exchange of property pursuant to a tax-free reorganization.[7] If the acquired corporation receives cash or other property in the exchange, as well as stock or securities in the acquiring corporation, gain is recognized to the corporation on such other property only if the corporation fails to distribute the "other property" to its shareholders. If the acquired corporation distributes boot received in a tax-free reorganization, the shareholders, and not the corporation, are taxed on any recognized gain occasioned by the receipt of boot.[8]

---

**4.** § 356(a)(1).
**5.** § 356(a)(2).
**6.** § 358.
**7.** § 361(a).
**8.** § 361(b). If the acquired corporation has sufficient earnings and profits and the shareholders receive pro rata distributions as boot, the boot is treated as a dividend and taxed as ordinary income and not as capital gain. See *Shimberg v. U. S.,* 78–2 USTC ¶ 9607, 42 AFTR2d 78–5575, 577 F.2d 283 (CA–5, 1978).

Gain or loss also is not recognized by the acquiring corporation.[9] Property received from the acquired corporation retains the basis it had in the hands of the acquired corporation, increased by the amount of gain recognized to the acquired corporation on the transfer.[10]

If a corporate exchange qualifies as a tax-free reorganization under one of the seven types mentioned, the tax consequences described are automatic regardless of the intent of the parties involved.

# TYPES OF TAX-FREE REORGANIZATIONS

## TYPE A

Although the terms are not analogous, "Type A" reorganizations include both mergers and consolidations. A "merger" has been defined as the union of two or more corporations in which one of the corporations retains its corporate existence and absorbs the other or others. These other corporations lose their corporate existence by operation of law.[11] A "consolidation," on the other hand, is effected when a new corporation is created to take the place of two or more constituent corporations which, consequently, lose their corporate existence by operation of law.[12]

> **Example 3.** Beta Corporation acquires all the properties of Alpha Corporation in exchange for 5,000 shares of stock in Beta Corporation. The Beta stock is distributed to Alpha's shareholders in complete liquidation of Alpha Corporation. This transaction qualifies as an "A" reorganization (assuming the requirements of state law are met). It is a statutory merger.

> **Example 4.** Alpha and Beta Corporations are consolidated under state law into a new corporation, Zeta Corporation. Zeta stock is distributed to the shareholders of Alpha and Beta in complete liquidation of each. This is an "A" reorganization, a consolidation.

The "Type A" reorganization is illustrated in Figure I.

*Advantages and Disadvantages.* The "A" reorganization allows greater flexibility than is present in other types of reorganizations because there is no requirement that consideration be voting stock. (This is a requirement for both the "B" and "C" reorganizations.) Further, the "A" reorganization allows money or property to change hands without disqualifying the business combination as a tax-free reorganization. The money or property will constitute boot, and some gain may be recognized; however, the receipt of this boot will not destroy the tax-free treatment of receiving stock as consideration. If consideration other than stock is to be used, the tax planners must be careful that they do not run afoul of the continuity of interest test. This test, promulgated by the courts, requires

---

**9.**  § 361(a).
**10.**  § 362(b).
**11.**  *Von Weise et al. v. Comm.,* 4 USTC ¶ 1238, 13 AFTR 708, 69 F.2d 439 (CA–8, 1934), *cert. den.,* 54 S.Ct. 866 (USSC, 1934).
**12.**  *Cortland Specialty Co. v. Comm.,* 3 USTC ¶ 980, 11 AFTR 857, 60 F.2d 937 (CA–2, 1932), *cert. den.,* 53 S.Ct. 316 (USSC, 1933).

**Figure I**

A COMPARISON OF THE TAX-FREE REORGANIZATIONS
"A" REORGANIZATION

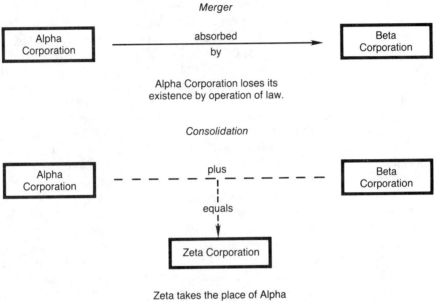

*Merger*

Alpha Corporation    absorbed by   →   Beta Corporation

Alpha Corporation loses its
existence by operation of law.

*Consolidation*

Alpha Corporation    plus    Beta Corporation

equals

Zeta Corporation

Zeta takes the place of Alpha
and Beta Corporations, which lose
their corporate existence by operation of law.

that at least 50 percent of the consideration used in a reorganization must be stock or the reorganization will be treated as a taxable transaction.

There are definite disadvantages to be considered before a "Type A" reorganization is activated. The "Type A" reorganization is statutory; therefore, compliance with applicable state law is a requirement to perfect the acquisition. In almost all states, shareholders of all corporations participating in a merger or consolidation are granted the right to dissent and have their shares appraised and bought. The problems in meeting the demands of objecting shareholders can become so cumbersome that the planners may be forced to abandon the "Type A" reorganization. In addition, because a majority of the shareholders of all corporations involved must approve the transaction, all of the problems inherent in shareholder meetings are brought to the fore. These problems are, of course, magnified if the stock of either of the corporations is widely held.

Another disadvantage of the "Type A" reorganization is the required assumption by the acquiring corporation of *all* liabilities of the acquired corporation. The surviving corporation assumes these liabilities of the acquired corporation as a matter of law. Though the legal procedure required to transfer assets and liabilities is not complex when a merger or consolidation occurs, the fact that all liabilities (including unknown and contingent liabilities) pass to the transferee corporation as a matter of law is a distinct disadvantage.

*The Use of a Subsidiary in a "Type A" Reorganization.* Many of the problems of compliance with state law in the "Type A" reorganization can be reduced if a subsidiary becomes the acquiring corporation. When a subsidiary acquires the assets of another corporation and gives its own voting stock as consideration, any problem regarding the validity of the stock transfer, for the most part, ends. However, the parent corporation might want the shareholders of the acquired corporation to hold its (the parent's) stock rather than that of the subsidiary to enable the parent to retain control over the subsidiary. The parent does not want to be the acquiring corporation, because it does not want to assume the liabilities of the acquired corporation. (If the subsidiary becomes the acquiring corporation, it will assume the liabilities of the acquired corporation, and the assets of the parent will be protected.) Further, a major problem of the "Type A" reorganization—securing the approval of a majority of the shareholders of the acquiring corporation—is removed because the parent corporation is the majority shareholder.[13] Consequently, only the approval of the board of directors of the parent corporation need be obtained. This also eliminates the possibility that the parent's shareholders might exercise their right to dissent. For these reasons, the use of a subsidiary corporation to effect the "A" reorganization should not be overlooked.

Under the 1939 Code, if a subsidiary corporation was involved in a reorganization, the parent corporation was not considered a party to the reorganization.[14] Thus, a shareholder who received stock in the parent was taxed on the stock received. The 1954 Code ended the possibility of just such an occurrence in either a "Type B" or "Type C" reorganization by specifically stating that a parent corporation can be a party to such a reorganization.[15]

Further, in 1968, a provision was added to the 1954 Code that provided that the exchange of a parent's stock by a subsidiary in a statutory merger (which occurs after October 22, 1968) can still qualify the reorganization as a tax-free "A" reorganization if (1) no subsidiary stock is used and (2) the exchange would have been an "A" reorganization had the merger been into the parent.[16]

In 1971, § 368(a)(2)(E) was added to the Code to allow a so-called reverse merger. To qualify as a tax-free reorganization under this provision, the surviving corporation must hold, in addition to its own properties, substantially all of the properties of the merged corporation. Further, the former shareholders of the surviving corporation must receive voting stock of the controlling corporation in exchange for control (80 percent) of the surviving corporation. The appearance of the terms "substantially all" of the properties, "voting stock" of the controlling corporation, and "control"[17]

---

**13.** The approval of a majority of the shareholders of the acquired corporation would still be required, of course.

**14.** *Groman v. Comm.*, 36–2 USTC ¶ 9523, 18 AFTR 643, 86 F.2d 670 (CA–7, 1936), *aff'd.* in 37–2 USTC ¶ 9533, 19 AFTR 1214, 58 S.Ct. 108 (USSC, 1937), and *Helvering v. Bashford*, 37–1 USTC ¶ 9069, 18 AFTR 826, 87 F.2d 827 (CA–3, 1937), *rev'd.* in 38–1 USTC ¶ 9019, 19 AFTR 1240, 58 S.Ct. 307 (USSC, 1938).

**15.** For example, with reference to the "C" reorganization, § 368(a)(1)(C) states ". . . (or in exchange solely for all or a part of the voting stock of a corporation which is in control of the acquiring corporation) . . ."

**16.** § 368(a)(2)(D).

**17.** Control is defined to mean 80% of the total combined voting power and 80% of the total number of all other classes of stock of the surviving corporation. See H.R. 91–1778, Tax Treatment of Certain Statutory Mergers, 91st Cong., 2d Sess. (1971).

presents problems in attempting to correlate this provision with the ordinary "A" reorganization in which a great degree of flexibility is permitted as far as consideration is concerned.

The following examples demonstrate the use of a subsidiary in an "A" reorganization.

> **Example 5.** Beta Corporation is a subsidiary of Parent Corporation. It also holds some stock in Parent. Beta transfers the Parent stock it owns to the shareholders of Alpha Corporation for substantially all the assets of Alpha. Alpha is liquidated. This is an "A" reorganization using parent company stock. If Parent Corporation is the only shareholder of Beta, the merger can be effected by securing approval of Parent's board of directors. The vote of Parent's shareholders is not required; thus, considerable time and expense are avoided. Further, Parent's assets are protected from Alpha Corporation's creditors.

> **Example 6.** In a "reverse" merger, Alpha Corporation, rather than Beta Corporation, would survive. Further, the stock in Parent Corporation must be voting stock only. The shareholders of Alpha must surrender their stock representing 80% control of Alpha to Parent for its voting stock. Beta Corporation would transfer all its assets to Alpha and be liquidated. Alpha Corporation then becomes the subsidiary of Parent Corporation.

The use of a subsidiary in an "A" reorganization and a reverse merger are illustrated in Figure II.

A disadvantage of the reverse merger is the requirement that voting stock of the parent corporation be used and that at least 80 percent of the stock of the acquired corporation be obtained. These requirements severely limit the flexibility present in the regular "A" reorganization. Indeed, the provision is drafted to correspond more closely with a "Type B" reorganization than with a "Type A."

Though §§ 368(a)(2)(D) and 368(a)(2)(E), which permit the use of a subsidiary in an "A" reorganization, appear to have opened new "planning possibilities"[18] in corporate reorganizations, there are certain state law requirements that must be considered before a conclusion can be made that the new amendments have removed some of the disadvantages of the "A" reorganization. The "A" reorganization, as previously noted, is a statutory reorganization. The statutes of the state of each corporation involved in the merger must be examined to determine whether the use of a parent corporation's stock is permitted in a statutory merger.

There are other problems to consider in the use of a subsidiary. Assume the parent corporation exchanges its stock for stock in the subsidiary before the reorganization. Does the parent increase its basis in the subsidiary's stock? The basis of the parent's stock to the parent is zero; consequently, the parent could not increase the basis of the subsidiary's stock unless the receipt can be tied to the subsidiary's later acquisition of assets in the reorganization. If it can, the parent's basis in the subsidiary's

---

**18.** Walsh and Gerard, "Planning Possibilities in Using Parent's Stock in a Corporate Acquisition," 30 *Journal of Taxation* (March 1969), p. 168.

### Figure II
### USE OF A SUBSIDIARY IN THE "A" REORGANIZATION

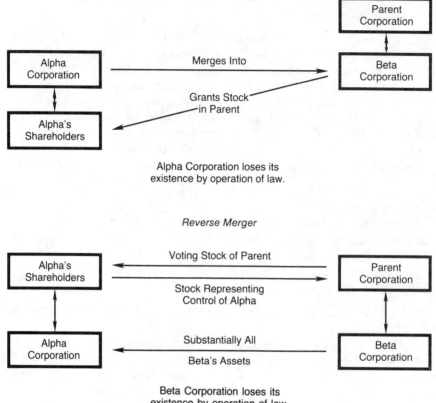

Alpha Corporation loses its
existence by operation of law.

*Reverse Merger*

Beta Corporation loses its
existence by operation of law.
Alpha becomes subsidiary of Parent.

stock is equal to the acquired corporation's basis in the assets less the
acquired corporation's liabilities. The concept behind this assumption is
that the assets of the acquired corporation are treated as having been first
acquired by the parent and then transferred to the subsidiary for the subsidiary stock. What if the parent transfers its stock to the subsidiary in a
separate transaction before the subsidiary acquires the assets of another
corporation? Would it receive an increase in its basis in the subsidiary's
stock after the reorganization? This question remains unanswered.

## TYPE B

A "Type B" reorganization involves the acquisition by a corporation of the
stock of another corporation solely in exchange for its voting stock. Immediately after the acquisition, the acquiring corporation must be in control
of the acquired corporation. This is, in simple terms, a transaction in the
form of an exchange of stock for voting stock. Voting stock must be the sole
consideration; this requirement is strictly construed.

**Example 7.** Alpha Corporation exchanges 20% of its voting stock for stock representing 80% of all classes of stock in Beta Corporation. The exchange qualifies as a "B" reorganization. Alpha becomes the parent of Beta. It should be noted that this type of reorganization precludes the use of boot; consequently, gain would never be recognized in a "B" reorganization.

**Example 8.** If, in the above example, Alpha Corporation exchanges nonvoting preferred stock or bonds in addition to voting stock, the transaction would not qualify as a "B" reorganization.

The "Type B" reorganization is illustrated in Figure III.

### Figure III
### "B" REORGANIZATION

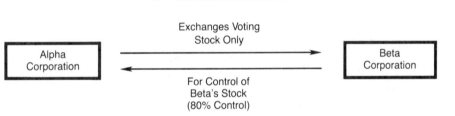

Exchanges Voting
Stock Only

For Control of
Beta's Stock
(80% Control)

Alpha Corporation becomes the parent
and Beta Corporation, the subsidiary.

*The Eighty Percent Control Requirement.* Stock may be acquired from the shareholders or directly from the corporation. If A Corporation has 100 shares outstanding, for example, B Corporation must acquire, in exchange for its voting stock, at least 80 of those shares. It could also acquire 400 newly issued shares directly from A Corporation. It would then own 400 shares of 500 outstanding shares, an 80 percent ownership.

The control level that must be reached by the parent, or acquiring corporation, is at least 80 percent of the total combined voting power of all classes of stock entitled to vote and at least 80 percent of the total number of shares of all other classes of stock of the corporation. This requirement does not mean that the acquiring corporation must actually "acquire" 80 percent of the acquired corporation, but rather that, after the acquisition, it must have an 80 percent ownership. As a consequence, certain problems arise. Alpha Corporation, in Example 7, might have earlier acquired 30 percent of Beta Corporation for cash. It now acquires another 50 percent through the issuance of voting stock. It is possible that the transaction will not be tax-free, because if both transactions are a continuing effort to gain control, Alpha Corporation has attained such control of Beta through the use of both cash and stock. However, the Regulations state that the acquisition of stock of another corporation by the acquiring corporation solely for its voting stock can be tax-free even though the acquiring corporation already owns stock of the other corporation.[19] Suppose, for example, ten years ago Alpha Corporation acquired 30 percent of Beta Corporation's stock for cash. In the current year, another 50 percent is acquired, but this time the acquisition is made through the use of Beta Corporation's voting stock. Under these circumstances, it seems unlikely that the two acquisitions were part of the same plan to gain control of Beta Corporation. Even though some of the shares were acquired with cash, the requirements of a "B" reorganization are still satisfied.

> **Example 9.** Beta has assets of $400,000 and liabilities of $100,000. Its common stock consists of 2,000 shares with a par value of $100 per share. It has no other classes of stock and has E & P of $100,000. Beta's assets are worth $500,000. Should Alpha acquire the assets and liabilities of Beta in a tax-free "A" reorganization, Alpha would have a basis of $400,000 in Beta's assets. [Property received from an acquired corporation has a carryover basis to the acquiring corporation. Basis in the hands of the acquired corporation carries over to the acquiring corporation. See § 362(b).] If Alpha acquires Beta by exchanging with Beta's shareholders 30% of its voting stock (worth $320,000) for 1,600 shares of Beta stock, the reorganization would qualify as a "B" reorganization. Beta would become the subsidiary of Alpha. Alpha's basis in the Beta stock would be the basis Beta's shareholders had in the stock. [Section 362(b) would again apply.] However, Beta's shareholders would have a substituted basis in the Alpha stock (their basis in the Alpha stock will have the basis they had in the Beta stock). (Basis for the shareholders of Beta is determined under § 358, which provides for a substituted basis rather than a carryover basis as under § 362.)

*The Use of a Subsidiary in a "Type B" Reorganization.* In the "Type B" reorganization, as in the "Type A," voting stock of the acquiring corporation's parent may be used. The following example demonstrates the use of a subsidiary in a "B" reorganization.

> **Example 10.** P Corporation is the parent of Alpha Corporation. Alpha Corporation also owns some stock in P. It exchanges stock (voting stock only) in P for control of the stock in Beta Corporation. This qualifies as a "B" reorganization. Beta would become the subsidiary of Alpha Corporation.

The use of a parent's stock by a subsidiary in a "Type B" reorganization is illustrated in Figure IV.

*The "Solely for Voting Stock" Requirement.* The "B" reorganization is limited in that the *sole* consideration must be voting stock. The "solely for voting stock" requirement originally applied to both the "B" and the "C"

---

**19.** Reg. § 1.368–2(c). Stock previously acquired for cash will not disqualify an exchange as a "B" reorganization if the stock acquisition standing alone constitutes a "B" reorganization. See *C. E. Graham Reeves,* 71 T.C. 727 (1979). However, the IRS recently held that the acquisition of 90% of the stock of a corporation for voting stock would not qualify as a "B" reorganization where a subsidiary of the acquiring corporation acquired the remaining 10% of the stock for cash. The IRS held that the acquisition of the 10% interest by the subsidiary was part of a prearranged plan to acquire the corporation. See Rev.Rul. 85–139, I.R.B. No. 36, 6.

### Figure IV

## USE OF A SUBSIDIARY IN A "B" REORGANIZATION

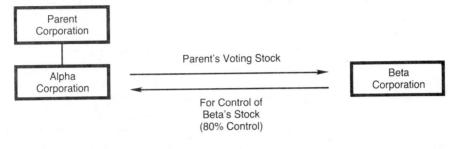

Beta Corporation becomes the
subsidiary of Alpha Corporation.

reorganizations and was first introduced in the Revenue Act of 1934.[20] Before that time, there was no specific requirement as to type of consideration. (This absence of any restriction on consideration was the reason for the judicially created doctrine of continuity of interest, discussed later in the chapter.)

The Supreme Court's rationalization for the inclusion of the "solely for voting stock" requirement in the 1934 Revenue Act can be found in *Helvering v. Southwest Consolidated Corporation*.[21] The Court asserted that this requirement was added to the reorganization statutes to assure that such statutes were not being used as a convenient method of "selling the business tax-free." The Court stated: "'Solely' leaves no leeway. Voting stock plus some other consideration does not meet statutory requirement." This rigid interpretation of "solely for voting stock" still applies to the "B" reorganization and is one of its greatest disadvantages.

"Voting stock" includes stock of any class that has a normal right to vote.[22] Hence, voting preferred stock qualifies. Court decisions indicate that rights or warrants to purchase additional voting stock do not qualify as voting stock.[23] The courts have stated that these are merely options to purchase stock; consequently, such options do not sustain rights intrinsic in the voting stock. The IRS has ruled that convertible debentures, also, do not constitute voting stock. According to the IRS, they are similar to warrants.[24] Stock whose voting rights are conditioned on future events will not qualify as voting stock. In Rev.Rul. 72–72, the IRS stated that an issue of common stock with voting rights withheld for a five-year period will not satisfy the voting stock requirement.[25] According to the IRS, such an ar-

---

**20.** § 112(g)(1)(B).

**21.** 41–1 USTC ¶ 9402, 27 AFTR 160, 119 F.2d 567 (CA–5, 1941), *rev'd.* in 42–1 USTC ¶ 9248, 28 AFTR 573, 62 S.Ct. 546 (USSC, 1942).

**22.** See, for example, *Erie Lighting Co. v. Comm.*, 38–1 USTC ¶ 9030, 20 AFTR 609, 93 F.2d 883 (CA–1, 1938).

**23.** *LeVant v. Comm.*, 67–1 USTC ¶ 9387, 19 AFTR2d 1308, 376 F.2d 434 (CA–7, 1967); *Comm. v. Baan*, 67–2 USTC ¶ 9556, 20 AFTR2d 5268, 382 F.2d 485 (CA–9, 1967); and *Gordon v. Comm.*, 70–1 USTC ¶ 9279, 25 AFTR2d 70–820, 424 F.2d 378 (CA–2, 1970), *cert. den.* 91 S.Ct. 63 (USSC, 1970).

**24.** Rev.Rul. 69–91, 1969–1 C.B. 106.

**25.** Rev.Rul. 72–72, 1972–1 C.B. 104.

rangement is identical to issuing nonvoting common stock that will automatically convert to voting common stock after five years.

Absent the voting stock problem, the stock for voting stock acquisition has the advantage of simplicity. Because, generally, the shareholders of the acquired corporation act individually in transferring their stock, the affairs of the corporation itself are not directly involved. Consequently, no formal action is required of the shareholders of the acquired corporation, at least not in their capacity as shareholders. Further, no formal action is required of the shareholders of the acquiring corporation (assuming there are sufficient treasury or unissued shares to effect the transaction without any formal shareholder action to increase authorized shares).[26] Thus, much of the shareholder problem presented in the "Type A" reorganization is eliminated. However, there can be disadvantages to a "B" reorganization. Assuming the acquiring corporation does not obtain a 100 percent control of the acquired corporation, problems may arise with respect to the minority interest remaining in the acquired corporation.

## TYPE C

The "Type C" reorganization involves the acquisition by the acquiring corporation of substantially all the assets of the acquired corporation solely in exchange for voting stock. It is basically an exchange of assets for voting stock.

For plans of reorganization adopted after July 18, 1984, a transaction will not qualify as a "C" reorganization unless the acquired corporation distributes the stock, securities, and other properties it receives in the reorganization, as well as any of its own properties.[27]

> **Example 11.** Alpha Corporation transfers voting stock representing a 30% interest in the corporation to Beta Corporation for "substantially all" the assets of Beta. After the exchange, Beta's only assets are the voting stock in Alpha Corporation. This exchange qualifies as a "C" reorganization if Beta distributes the voting stock to its shareholders.

The "Type C" reorganization is illustrated in Figure V.

*"Type A" and "Type C" Reorganizations Compared.* The "Type C" reorganization has almost the same consequences as the "Type A," but the rule with respect to consideration is more exacting for the "Type C." On the other hand, the "C" reorganization is preferable to the "A" in many circumstances. In the "C" reorganization, unlike the "A," the acquiring corporation assumes only those liabilities it chooses to assume. It is normally not liable for unknown or contingent liabilities.[28] Further, in the "C" reorgani-

---

26. Though shareholders in the "B" reorganization normally do not act through the corporation, this is subject to legal or other restrictions on transfers of shares. See Fox, *Business Organizations,* Vol. 13 (Albany, N.Y.: Matthew Bender, 1975), § 4.03, for a more detailed discussion.

27. § 368(a)(1)(G).

28. This assumes, of course, that the price paid for the assets is adequate, that the acquiring corporation has complied with the state's bulk sales statute, and that no cash or notes have been paid directly to the shareholders of the acquired corporation.

### Figure V
### "C" REORGANIZATION

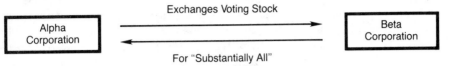

Alpha Corporation becomes the parent
and Beta Corporation, the subsidiary.

zation, in some states only the approval of the shareholders in the acquired corporation is required. This considerably diminishes the magnitude of the problem involved in the "A" reorganization. In addition, dissenters' rights are generally given only to the shareholders of the acquired corporation in a "C" reorganization, whereas these rights must be recognized in both the acquired and the acquiring corporation in a statutory merger or consolidation.

The "C" reorganization can also be effected by the use of a subsidiary, as demonstrated in the following examples.

**Example 12.** Parent Corporation is in control of Alpha Corporation. Alpha also owns some stock in Parent. It transfers the Parent stock (voting stock) to Beta Corporation for "substantially all" the assets of Beta. Beta is then liquidated. The transaction qualifies as a "C" reorganization.

**Example 13.** The acquiring corporation could be the parent corporation even though the subsidiary ultimately acquires the assets of the acquired corporation. Parent Corporation could acquire the assets of Beta for its voting stock and then transfer the assets to Alpha Corporation.

The use by a subsidiary corporation of its parent's stock in carrying out a "Type C" reorganization is illustrated in Figure VI.

### Figure VI
### USE OF A SUBSIDIARY IN A "C" REORGANIZATION

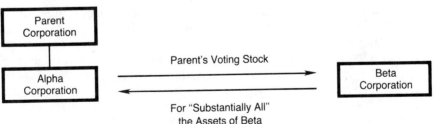

After the reorganization, Beta Corporation's
only asset would be Alpha's voting stock. When Beta is
liquidated, Alpha's stock will pass to Beta's shareholders.

*Consideration in the "Type C" Reorganization.* Consideration in the "C" reorganization normally would consist of voting stock, as in the "B" reorganization. However, there are exceptions to this rule. Section 368(a)(2)(B) provides that cash and other property will not destroy the tax-free status of the reorganization if at least 80 percent of the fair market value of all the property of the acquired corporation is obtained by the use of voting stock. In addition, an assumption of the liabilities of the acquired corporation is disregarded in determining whether the transaction is solely for voting stock.[29] The "C" reorganization is given a slight degree of freedom in reference to consideration, whereas the "B" is not. However, in making the statutory computation that "other property" does not exceed 20 percent of the fair market value of the property transferred, liabilities assumed by the acquiring corporation are, if the corporation receives other consideration, treated as "other property." As a practical matter, because liabilities assumed by the acquiring corporation normally exceed 20 percent of the fair market value of the assets acquired, the provision relaxing the requirement of "solely" for voting stock in the "C" reorganization is limited in its application. The following examples illustrate this problem.

> **Example 14.** Beta Corporation transfers assets with a fair market value of $200,000 to Alpha Corporation for voting stock valued at $160,000 and cash of $40,000. No liabilities are assumed. Beta uses the $40,000 to pay its liabilities, distributes the stock to its shareholders, and liquidates. The transaction qualifies as a "C" reorganization because "other property" received is exactly 20% of $200,000.

> **Example 15.** Assume in Example 14 that Beta's assets have a basis of $100,000. Beta would have a gain on the exchange of $40,000 because of the receipt of cash of $40,000. Beta's basis in the voting stock in Alpha would be $100,000 (its $100,000 basis in its assets plus the $40,000 gain recognized minus the $40,000 boot received). Alpha's basis in the Beta assets will be $140,000 (Beta's basis of $100,000 plus the $40,000 gain recognized to Beta). (Recall that basis for the acquiring corporation is determined under § 362, which provides for a carryover basis rather than a substituted basis as under § 358. Basis in property received by the acquiring corporation is the same basis as in the hands of the acquired corporation increased for any gain recognized to the acquired corporation on the transfer.)

> **Example 16.** Assume Beta has no liabilities. It liquidates and distributes the Alpha stock plus the $40,000 cash to X and Y, its shareholders. X has a basis of $60,000 in the Beta stock, and Y has a basis of $90,000 in the Beta stock. Now § 358 applies to determine basis. The $40,000 gain will be reported by X and Y. If each has a 50% ownership in Beta, each will have a gain of $20,000. Basis in the Alpha stock will be $60,000 for X ($60,000 basis in the Beta stock plus $20,000 gain recognized minus $20,000 boot received) and $90,000 for Y ($90,000 basis in the Beta stock plus $20,000 gain recognized minus $20,000

---

**29.** § 368(a)(1)(C).

boot received). Alpha's basis in the Beta property will be only $100,000, since Beta did not recognize any gain on the transfer.

**Example 17.** Assume in Example 14 that Beta transferred assets for stock valued at $140,000, cash of $40,000, and the assumption of $20,000 of its liabilities by Alpha. Liabilities would be counted as "other property" because Beta also received cash. "Other property" amounts to $60,000, which exceeds 20% of the fair market value of Beta Corporation's assets. The transaction does not qualify as a "C" reorganization.

**Example 18.** Assume Alpha Corporation gives Beta Corporation voting stock worth $120,000 and assumes $80,000 of Beta Corporation's liabilities. The transaction would qualify as a "C" reorganization. Liabilities assumed by the acquiring corporation are disregarded if no additional consideration (other than stock) is used.

*Asset Transfers.* The "C" reorganization requires that "substantially all" of the assets of the acquired corporation be transferred. There are numerous problems in determining whether the "substantially all" requirement has been met. There is no statutory definition of "substantially all." If a favorable ruling is to be obtained from the Internal Revenue Service, assets representing at least 90 percent of the fair market value of the net assets and at least 70 percent of the fair market value of the gross assets held by the acquired corporation must be transferred.[30] Smaller percentages than this rule of thumb adopted by the IRS may still qualify; however, the parties would have to rely on case law inasmuch as a favorable ruling could not be obtained.[31]

The results of a statutory merger and an asset acquisition, the "C" reorganization, are almost identical if the acquired corporation is liquidated in a "C" reorganization. In both situations, the acquiring corporation will receive the assets of the acquired. Because all the properties of the acquired corporation must be distributed, the acquired corporation generally is liquidated in a "C" reorganization, and the shareholders of the acquired will receive stock in the acquiring corporation. However, the methods used to achieve these almost identical results, as well as the legal consequences of the two, are considerably different. These differences make the choice of the preferable form of acquisition highly pertinent.

## TYPE D

The first three types of tax-free corporate reorganizations were designed for corporate combinations. The "D" reorganization differs from these in that it is a mechanism for corporate division. The "D" reorganization involves the transfer of all or part of the assets of one corporation to another corporation when the transferor, or one or more of its shareholders (or any combination thereof), is in control of the transferee corporation. The trans-

---

30. Rev.Proc. 74–26, 1974–2 C.B. 478, superseded by Rev.Proc. 77–37, 1977–2 C.B. 568.
31. See, for example, *Comm. v. First National Bank of Altoona, Pa.,* 39–2 USTC ¶ 9568, 23 AFTR 119, 104 F.2d 865 (CA–3, 1939), and *National Bank of Commerce of Norfolk v. U. S.,* 58–1 USTC ¶ 9278, 1 AFTR2d 894, 158 F.Supp. 887 (D.Ct.Va., 1958).

action must meet the requirements of § 354, § 355, or § 356 of the Internal Revenue Code. Section 354 requires that substantially all of the property of one corporation be transferred to the second corporation. All property received in the exchange by the transferor corporation must be distributed to the transferor's shareholders. If assets remain in the transferor corporation, the requirements of § 354 are not met. Section 355 requires that upon the transfer of a part of the assets of one corporation for control of another corporation, stock and securities received by the transferor corporation be distributed to its shareholders. Further, the requirements, noted in Chapter 4, that both corporations be actively engaged in a trade or business after the exchange, that only assets of an active trade or business be transferred, and that there be a business purpose for the exchange must be met. Section 356 applies only when a distribution pursuant to § 354 or § 355 involves property other than qualifying stock or securities. The "other property" becomes boot and is taxed pursuant to § 356.

The "D" reorganization can be a corporate combination. Section 354 applies to a transfer of all or substantially all of the assets of one corporation to another corporation for control (50 percent) of the second corporation. This transaction can also meet the requirements of a "C" reorganization. If a transaction can be both a "C" and a "D" reorganization, § 368(a)(2)(A) provides that it be treated as a "D" reorganization. This will insure that the distribution of stock or securities be made pursuant to § 354 or § 355. This type of "D" reorganization is essentially a transfer of parent corporation assets to the subsidiary. The parent is liquidated, with all the stock in the subsidiary being distributed to the parent's shareholders.

> **Example 19.** Alpha Corporation transfers all its assets to a newly formed corporation, Beta, for all of Beta's stock. The Beta stock is then transferred to Alpha's shareholders, and Alpha is liquidated. The transaction qualifies as a "D" reorganization. It is equivalent to an "E" or an "F" reorganization. In essence, it is a new corporate shell around an old body.

Control in a "D" reorganization has different meanings depending upon whether the reorganization is a corporate combination or a corporate division. If it is a corporate combination, control is ownership of at least 50 percent of the total voting stock *or* 50 percent of the total *value* of all classes of stock.[32] If the reorganization is a corporate division, control is ownership of at least 80 percent of the total voting stock *and* at least 80 percent of the total *number* of shares of all other classes of stock.[33]

*Spin-Offs, Split-Offs, and Split-Ups.* The more typical "D" reorganization involves a corporate division. One corporation transfers a part of its assets to another corporation for stock in that corporation. To qualify as a tax-free reorganization, the transferor corporation must obtain stock representing control (80 percent) in the transferee corporation and must distribute that stock to its shareholders pursuant to § 355. Section 355, which

---

**32.** § 368(c)(2). This provision was added to the Code by the Deficit Reduction Act of 1984 for plans of reorganization adopted after July 18, 1984. For plans adopted on or before this date, the control requirement is the same as for corporate divisions.
**33.** § 368(c)(1).

was discussed in Chapter 4, permits stock to be received tax-free by shareholders in a qualifying spin-off, split-off, or split-up. Consequently, the stock received in the new corporation must be distributed to the shareholders of the transferor corporation either as a spin-off, wherein the shareholders do not surrender any stock in the distributing corporation, or as a split-off, wherein the shareholders do surrender stock in the distributing corporation. A split-up involves the transfer of the assets of one corporation to two or more new corporations. Stock in the new corporations is distributed to the transferor's shareholders. The transferor corporation is liquidated. The spin-off, split-off, and split-up are illustrated in Figure VII.

Shareholders of a corporation may wish to divide the corporate assets and split up the business of a corporation for several reasons. Antitrust problems may arise; the shareholders may have differences of opinion; family planning may enter the picture. The old corporation could be liquidated with the assets distributed to the various shareholders. Those wishing to continue the business in corporate form could then establish a new corporation. Assets can be transferred to a controlled corporation tax-free under § 351. However, there are problems upon liquidation of the old corporation. Shareholders will normally recognize gain upon the liquidation. Further, recapture provisions under § § 1245, 1250, and 1252 generate tax at the corporate level. Recapture of the investment tax credit under § 47 is also a factor. Consequently, this route may not be the best. A stock redemption under § 302, either a substantially disproportionate distribution or a "qualified partial liquidation," is a possibility. Again, however, a capital gains tax must be paid. The better alternative is to effect a split-up under § 368(a)(1)(D) and distribute stock and securities in the new corporation pursuant to § 355.

> **Example 20.** A and B, individuals, are the sole shareholders of Alpha Corporation. Alpha Corporation was organized 10 years ago and has been actively engaged in the manufacturing business. Alpha manufactures two major products, Product 1 and Product 2. Considerable friction has developed between A and B, who wish to divide the business. A wants the assets used for the manufacture of Product 1, and B wants to continue the manufacture of Product 2. Two new corporations are formed, Beta and Zeta Corporations. All of the assets relating to the manufacture of Product 1 are transferred to Beta Corporation; the remaining assets are transferred to Zeta Corporation. The stock in Beta is transferred to A for his stock in Alpha, while the stock in Zeta is transferred to B for his stock in Alpha. Alpha is liquidated. The transaction qualifies as a "D" reorganization. Neither gain nor loss is recognized to either A or B upon the exchange of their stock in Alpha for stock in the new corporations by virtue of § 355. Gain or loss is not recognized to Alpha Corporation under § 361. Beta and Zeta Corporations receive the assets of Alpha tax-free under § 1032 (i. e., no gain or loss is recognized to a corporation on the receipt of money or other property in exchange for its stock).

> **Example 21.** A owns 200 shares of R Corporation stock with a basis of $40,000 (value of $60,000). In a "D" reorganization (a spin-off), she receives a distribution of 50 shares of S Corporation stock valued at

### Figure VII
## "D" REORGANIZATION

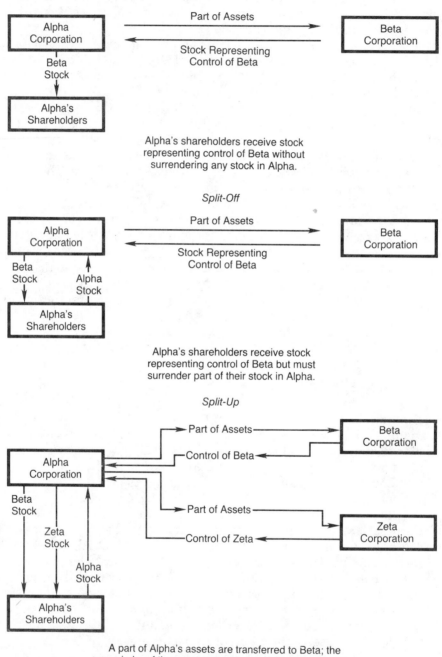

*Spin-Off*

Alpha's shareholders receive stock
representing control of Beta without
surrendering any stock in Alpha.

*Split-Off*

Alpha's shareholders receive stock
representing control of Beta but must
surrender part of their stock in Alpha.

*Split-Up*

A part of Alpha's assets are transferred to Beta; the
remainder of the assets are transferred to Zeta. Stock in
Beta and Zeta is transferred to Alpha's shareholders
for their stock in Alpha, and Alpha is liquidated.

$20,000. A surrenders none of her R stock. The basis she had in her R stock is allocated to the R stock and S stock on the basis of the fair market value of each. Thus, $20,000/$80,000 of the $40,000 basis, or $10,000, will be allocated to the S stock, and $60,000/$80,000 of the $40,000 basis, or $30,000, will be allocated to the R stock.

**Example 22.** Assume that a split-off occurred. A surrendered 100 shares of R stock for 50 shares of S stock. Again, her basis of $40,000 will be allocated among the R and S stock on the basis of the fair market value of each. The fair market value of the retained R stock is $30,000; thus, $30,000/$50,000 of the $40,000, or $24,000, will be allocated to the R stock A retained, and $20,000/$50,000 of the $40,000, or $16,000, will be allocated to the S stock.

*Requirements of § 355.* The "D" reorganization requires that the provisions of § 355 be met if the transfer is to be considered tax-free. All the requirements of § 355 discussed in Chapter 4 come into play. Stock representing control [control being 80 percent as defined in § 368(c)(1)] must be distributed to the shareholders of the transferor corporation. The assets transferred (plus those retained) must represent an active business that has been owned and conducted by the transferor corporation for at least five years prior to the transfer.

**Example 23.** Alpha Corporation has been engaged in the manufacture of certain products. It also owns investment securities. It transfers the investment securities to a newly formed corporation and distributes the stock of the new corporation to its shareholders. The transaction does not qualify as a "D" reorganization. The holding of investment securities does not constitute a trade or business. The shareholders of Alpha Corporation will be taxed on the receipt of the stock.

**Example 24.** Assume Alpha Corporation has a separate research department. It transfers the research department to a new corporation and distributes the stock of the new corporation to its shareholders. The activities of the research department do not constitute a trade or business; consequently, the transaction does not qualify as a "D" reorganization.

**Example 25.** Alpha Corporation manufactures a single product, but it has had two plants for the past 10 years. It transfers one plant and related activities to a new corporation and distributes the stock of the new corporation to its shareholders. The activities of each plant constitute a trade or business; consequently, the transaction qualifies as a "D" reorganization.

**Example 26.** Assume one of the plants in Example 25 has been in existence for only two years. Alpha Corporation transfers one plant and related activities to a new corporation and distributes the stock of the new corporation to its shareholders. Though the activities of each plant constitute a trade or business, one has not been in existence for at least five years; consequently, the transaction does not qualify as a "D" reorganization. (It does not matter which plant is transferred, since both—the one transferred and the one retained—must have been in existence for at least five years before the transfer.)

As noted in Chapter 4, § 355 requires a business purpose for the transfer and the absence of a tax avoidance scheme. However, there is no requirement that the distribution of stock and securities be pro rata if all the other requirements of § 355 are satisfied.[34]

> **Example 27.** A and B, individuals, own all the stock of Alpha Corporation, which has operated two active businesses for the past ten years. Alpha transfers the assets representing one business to a newly formed corporation, Beta Corporation. The stock of Beta is distributed only to B in exchange for a part of his stock in Alpha Corporation. The transaction qualifies as a "D" reorganization.

The Regulations[35] state that a "single" trade or business cannot be divided or separated and consequently effect a tax-free distribution of stock in the newly formed corporation. However, in *E. P. Coady* the Court stated that there is no language either in the statute or in Committee Reports denying tax-free treatment under § 355 to a transaction solely on the grounds it represents an attempt to divide a single trade or business.[36] Consequently, the Court held the Regulations invalid in this respect. In the *Coady* case, the corporation involved had been actively engaged in the construction business. Differences arose between the two shareholders. As a result, a new corporation was organized to which one-half the assets of the old corporation were transferred in exchange for all the stock of the new corporation. The stock of the new corporation was distributed to one of the shareholders of the old corporation in exchange for all his stock in the old corporation. Both corporations continued actively in the construction business.

In *W. W. Marett,* the Court applied the rule in *Coady* to permit the division of a single business when a spin-off, rather than a split-off as in *Coady,* was involved.[37] The Internal Revenue Service has acquiesced in both the *Coady* and the *Marett* decisions.[38]

## TYPE E

The "Type E" reorganization is a recapitalization—a major change in the character and amount of outstanding capital stock or paid-in capital of a corporation. The transaction is significant only as far as shareholders who

---

**34.** Reg. § 1.355–3(a). In Rev.Rul. 85–127, I.R.B. No. 33, 8, the IRS ruled that a transfer of three-fifths of the stock of a newly formed corporation (to which a part of the assets of the transferor corporation had been transferred) for one shareholder's surrender of all his stock in the transferor corporation with the other two-fifths transferred to the other shareholder, who surrendered no stock in the transferor corporation, satisfied the requirements of § 355. The distribution of three-fifths of the stock of the newly formed corporation in order to retain the shareholder as a key employee was a legitimate business purpose.

**35.** Reg. § 1.355–1(a).

**36.** 33 T.C. 771 (1960), *aff'd.* in 61–1 USTC ¶ 9415, 7 AFTR2d 1322, 289 F.2d 490 (CA–6, 1961).

**37.** 63–2 USTC ¶ 9567, 11 AFTR2d 1542 (D.Ct.Ga. 1963), *aff'd.* in 63–2 USTC ¶ 9806, 12 AFTR2d 5900, 325 F.2d 28 (CA–5, 1963).

**38.** Rev.Rul. 64–147, 1964–1 C.B. 136.

exchange stock or securities are concerned; the corporation itself receives no property and, consequently, should have no tax problems.

The Regulations give several examples of recapitalizations.[39] (1) A corporation with $100,000 par value bonds outstanding will, instead of liquidating the bonds for cash, discharge them by issuing preferred shares to the bondholders. (2) There is surrendered to a corporation for cancellation 25 percent of its preferred stock in exchange for no par value common stock. (3) A corporation issues preferred stock, previously authorized but unissued, for outstanding common stock. (4) An exchange is made of a corporation's outstanding preferred stock that possesses certain priorities with reference to the amount and time of payment of dividends and the distribution of the corporate assets upon liquidation for a new issue of the corporation's common stock having no such rights.

Assume an exchange is made of a corporation's outstanding preferred stock with dividends in arrears for other stock of the corporation. This constitutes a "Type E" reorganization. However, if there is an increase in the proportionate interest of the preferred shareholders in the assets or earnings and profits of the corporation, § 305 will trigger dividend income to the shareholders. An amount equal to the lesser of (a) the amount by which the fair market value or liquidation preference, whichever is greater, of the stock received in the exchange exceeds the issue price of the preferred stock surrendered, or (b) the amount of the dividends in arrears that is treated as a taxable dividend under § 305(b)(4).

As an example, the "E" reorganization can be employed when an elderly shareholder wishes to relinquish control of the corporation and exchanges his or her common voting stock for preferred stock. In Rev.Rul. 74–269, the IRS held that the exchange of all the father's stock in a corporation owned one-half by the father and one-half by his sons for newly issued nonvoting cumulative preferred stock was an "E" reorganization.[40] The IRS stated that any difference in values between stock received and stock surrendered could, for example, be treated as compensation or a gift.

In the exchange of bonds for stock, the question of the treatment of original issue discount arises. In Rev.Rul. 75–39, the IRS stated its opinion that no original issue discount is recognized as the result of an exchange of debentures for common and preferred stock in an "E" reorganization.[41] According to the IRS, § 1232 (now § 1271),[42] which requires part of any gain "realized" to be treated as ordinary income when original issue discount is involved, applies only to "recognized" gain.

If a shareholder exchanges his or her stock for bonds in the corporation, the former shareholder is in receipt of boot, taxable under § 356,

---

**39.** Reg. § 1.368–2(e).
**40.** 1974–1 C.B. 87. The preferred stock would not be § 306 stock to the father if the father received only preferred stock. However, if the father received some common, the preferred would be § 306 stock (unless the corporation had no E & P at the time of the distribution). See Rev.Rul. 59–84, 1959–1 C.B. 71, and Rev.Rul. 82–191, 1982–2 C.B. 78.
**41.** Rev.Rul. 75–39, 1975–1 C.B. 272.
**42.** The Deficit Reduction Act of 1984 recodified the rules relating to original issue discount and extended them to certain other obligations. Section 1232 was repealed and §§ 1271–1275 were added to the Code.

unless bonds are also surrendered either in the same amount as or in a greater principal amount than the bonds received.

## TYPE F

The "Type F" reorganization is "a . . . mere change in identity, form or place of organization, however effected."[43] The IRS has ruled that if a reorganization qualifies as an "A," "C," or "D" reorganization and, at the same time, as an "F" reorganization, "Type F" reorganization treatment will predominate.[44]

> **Example 28.** X Corporation changes its name to Y Corporation. This is an "F" reorganization.

> **Example 29.** X Corporation, a corporation organized in New Mexico, incorporates Y Corporation in Texas and transfers all its assets to Y in exchange for all Y's stock. X is to be liquidated. Its shareholders surrender all their X stock for a pro rata distribution of the Y stock. This transaction can be an "A," a "C," or a "D" reorganization. It also satisfies the requirements of an "F" reorganization; consequently, it will be treated as an "F" reorganization.

The surviving corporation in an "F" reorganization is actually the same corporation as its predecessor. Consequently, the tax characteristics of the predecessor carry over to the successor. Because such a reorganization is a mere change in identity or form, net operating losses can be carried back as well as forward.

In the past, courts had applied the "F" reorganization provision to a combination of a number of operating companies if there was uninterrupted business continuity and substantially the same ownership before and after the reorganization. This permitted post-reorganization losses to be carried back to prior taxable years of the transferor-merged corporation.[45] However, § 368(a)(1)(F) was amended so that the "F" reorganization is restricted to a single operating corporation.[46] Consequently, net operating losses of a surviving corporation in a multiple reorganization can generate only a loss that can be carried forward.

An "F" reorganization will not jeopardize the status of § 1244 stock, nor will it terminate a valid Subchapter S election.[47] This is true because there can be no significant change in stock ownership in the "F" reorganization.[48]

## TYPE G

The Bankruptcy Act of 1980 created the "G" reorganization, which is a transfer of all or a part of the assets of a debtor corporation in a bank-

---

**43.** § 368(a)(1)(F).

**44.** Rev.Rul. 57–276, 1957–1 C.B. 126.

**45.** See, for example, *Estate of Stauffer,* 68–2 USTC ¶ 9634, 22 AFTR2d 5771, 403 F.2d 611 (CA–9, 1968).

**46.** A reorganization that involves more than a single operating corporation will be considered under the other applicable reorganization provisions.

**47.** See Reg. § 1.1244(d)–3(d)(1) and Rev.Rul. 64–250, 1964–2 C.B. 333.

**48.** Rev.Rul. 66–284, 1966–2 C.B. 115.

ruptcy, receivership, foreclosure, or similar proceeding in a Federal or state court to an acquiring corporation wherein stock or securities of the acquiring corporation are distributed in a transaction that qualifies under § 354, § 355, or § 356. The debtor corporation's creditors must receive voting stock of the acquiring corporation equal to 80 percent or more of the total fair market value of the debt of the debtor corporation.

# JUDICIAL CONDITIONS

A discussion of the reorganization concept must consider certain basic conditions that pervade the entire field of corporate reorganizations. Various judicially created doctrines—sound business purpose, continuity of interest, and continuity of business enterprise—have become basic requirements for the tax-free status of corporate reorganizations. In addition, the courts have formulated the so-called step transaction doctrine to determine tax status of a reorganization effected through a series of related transactions. There is also a further requirement that a plan of reorganization exist before tax-free status will be granted an exchange. In essence, these requirements have prescribed additional requirements for tax-free status of corporate reorganizations.

## SOUND BUSINESS PURPOSE

The courts have established the rule that even though the reorganization statutes have been literally followed, a transaction will not be tax-free unless it exhibits a bona fide business purpose. This rule was developed in 1935 by the landmark case of *Gregory v. Helvering.*[49]

In the *Gregory* case, Mrs. Gregory owned all of the stock in United Mortgage Corporation (subsequently referred to as UMC). Along with its operating assets, UMC held as an investment some appreciated stock in Monitor Corporation. Mrs. Gregory wanted to obtain the Monitor Corporation stock to sell it and keep the proceeds. Obviously, the problem the parties faced was how to carry out this objective with a minimum of tax consequences. A direct distribution of the stock to Mrs. Gregory would have resulted in dividend income to the extent of the lesser of the stock's fair market value or UMC's earnings and profits (refer to Chapter 4). Would the redemption of part of Mrs. Gregory's stock in UMC by using Monitor Corporation stock have produced preferential capital gains? Since Mrs. Gregory was the sole shareholder in UMC, such distribution would have been treated as a dividend under the predecessor of § 302 (refer to Chapter 4). A complete liquidation of UMC probably would have given Mrs. Gregory the stock in Monitor Corporation with a step-up in basis (to its fair market value) at preferential capital gain rates (refer to Chapter 5). Apparently, the parties did not wish to take such a drastic step.

In view of the shortcomings of these alternatives, Mrs. Gregory and her tax advisers came up with the following approach. First, UMC formed Averill Corporation. In return for a transfer of the Monitor Corporation stock, UMC received all of the stock in Averill Corporation. Second, immediately after the transfer, UMC distributed the Averill Corporation stock

---

**49.** 35–1 USTC ¶ 9043, 14 AFTR 1191, 55 S.Ct. 266 (USSC, 1935).

to Mrs. Gregory. Third, Mrs. Gregory assigned an allocable portion of her basis in the UMC stock to the Averill stock. As a further tax consequence, the holding period of the Averill stock now included that of the UMC stock. Fourth, three days after it was formed, Averill Corporation was liquidated. Pursuant to the liquidation, Mrs. Gregory surrendered all of her Averill stock in exchange for all of that corporation's assets (i. e., the Monitor Corporation stock). The spread between the fair market value of the Monitor Corporation stock and the basis allocated to the Averill Corporation stock represented long-term capital gain to Mrs. Gregory (refer to Chapter 5). Mrs. Gregory immediately sold the Monitor Corporation stock for its fair market value and retained the sale proceeds. Since the basis in the Monitor Corporation stock had been stepped up through the liquidation of Averill, no gain or loss on the sale was recognized by Mrs. Gregory (refer to Chapter 5).

The taxpayer argued, and rightly so, that the approach taken in the first three steps met the literal definition of a nontaxable reorganization as it then existed. The Supreme Court, however, was not willing to stop with the satisfaction of the applicable statutory requirements. The Court noted that the creation and liquidation of Averill Corporation served no business purpose. It was, instead, a mere device through which Mrs. Gregory could hope to avoid dividend income consequences. Since the substance of the transaction was a direct distribution by UMC of the Monitor stock to Mrs. Gregory, she should be taxed accordingly and the various intervening steps disregarded. In rendering the opinion of the Court, Justice Sutherland stated:

> Putting aside, then, the question of motive in respect of taxation altogether, and fixing the character of the proceeding by what actually occurred, what do we find? Simply an operation having no business or corporate purpose—a mere device which put on the form of a corporate reorganization as a disguise for concealing its real character, and the sole object and accomplishment of which was the consummation of a preconceived plan, not to reorganize a business or any part of a business, but to transfer a parcel of corporate shares to the petitioner . . . the transaction upon its face lies outside the plain intent of the statute. To hold otherwise would be to exalt artifice above reality and to deprive the statutory provision in question of all serious purpose.

A new doctrine was established in the *Gregory* case,[50] and with it, some degree of uncertainty and doubt as to the final tax status of a corporate reorganization was introduced.[51] The Regulations have followed the courts in recognizing the business purpose requirement.[52]

The test of business purpose, and whether it may reflect the shareholder's purpose as opposed to that of the corporation's, is not well-defined. In

---

**50.** Cited in Footnote 49.
**51.** The *Gregory* case became a precedent for all transactions that might be shams devised merely for tax avoidance purposes. It brought about the principle of substance over form. The Internal Revenue Service and the courts will look through the form of a transaction to determine what really took place. There must be a sound business purpose in all business transactions.
**52.** See Reg. § 1.368–1(c).

*Bazley v. Commissioner,* the Court implied that the benefit to the corporation must be direct and substantial.[53] However, in more recent cases, courts have conceded that it is sometimes impossible to draw a line between the purpose of the corporation and the purpose of the shareholders.[54]

Cases indicate the business purpose doctrine does not operate in reverse. It is normally the revenue agent who asserts lack of business purpose to deny tax-free status to a corporate reorganization. Occasionally, however, the taxpayer wanted the transaction to be taxable in order to receive a step-up in basis in assets or to recognize a loss. In some cases taxpayers have attempted to employ the business purpose doctrine to prevent the transaction from being considered a reorganization. In those instances, however, the courts have required the taxpayers to abide by the form of the transaction and have upheld the contention of the IRS that such transaction was a reorganization.[55] One reason for giving the IRS this benefit is that the taxpayer is initially in command of tax consequences. Generally, "business purpose" is devised in the offices of the taxpayer's attorneys; consequently, taxpayers should not be allowed to benefit from the option of producing or failing to produce documentation of a sufficient purpose.[56]

## CONTINUITY OF INTEREST

The continuity of interest doctrine is founded in the basic philosophy of the tax-free reorganization (i. e., if a shareholder or corporation has substantially the same investment after a corporate exchange as before, there should be no tax imposed upon the transaction). Under the Revenue Act of 1921, a reorganization was defined as follows:

> A merger or consolidation (including the acquisition by one corporation of at least a majority of the voting stock and at least a majority of the total number of shares of all other classes of stock of another corpo-

---

53. 47–1 USTC ¶ 9288, 35 AFTR 1190, 67 S.Ct. 1489 (USSC, 1947).

54. See *Estate of Moses L. Parshelsky,* 62–1 USTC ¶ 9460, 9 AFTR2d 1382, 303 F.2d 14 (CA–2, 1962), and *Lewis v. Comm.,* 49–2 USTC ¶ 9377, 38 AFTR 377, 176 F.2d 646 (CA–1, 1949).

55. In *Survaunt v. Comm.,* 47–2 USTC ¶ 9344, 35 AFTR 1557, 162 F.2d 753 (CA–8, 1947), the Court found a legitimate business purpose for a reorganization despite taxpayer's contention there was none. The Court stated that a new corporation took title to assets of the old corporation and continued to carry on the same identical corporate business; hence, a reorganization. The Court stated that a personal, as opposed to a corporate, reason for the arrangement would not change the result, citing *Lyon, Inc. v. Comm.,* 42–1 USTC ¶ 9418, 29 AFTR 205, 127 F.2d 210 (CA–6, 1942) as authority. In the *Lyon* decision, the Court stated that the taxing authorities may not consider a corporation a reality or a mere fiction, whichever view produces the greater revenue. According to the Court such a view ". . . would not conform to a long held concept of due process nor contribute to public confidence in the fairness of government in tax transactions with its citizens." Nonetheless, the Court in the *Lyon* decision found a business purpose for the transaction. The Court stated that when a corporation lacking in economic reason ". . . is so transformed and vitalized that a new economic enterprise has come into being with purpose, function and reason for permanent existence, then we think it is the product of a reorganization . . ."

56. See Michaelson, "Business Purpose and Tax-Free Reorganizations," 41 *Yale Law Journal* (January 1952), p. 14, and Chirelstein, "Learned Hand's Contribution to the Law of Tax Avoidance," 77 *Yale Law Journal* (January 1968), p. 440.

ration, or of substantially all the properties of another corporation), a recapitalization, or a mere change in identity, form, or place of organization of a corporation, however effected.[57]

Under Congressional definition, a purchase by one corporation of a majority of the shares of all classes of stock of another corporation or of substantially all of the properties of another corporation was a reorganization, even if it was for cash. However, if the transaction was for cash, nonrecognition of gain would not follow because of other provisions in the Revenue Act. On the other hand, short-term notes could be used and would be considered securities to satisfy provisions upon which the benefits of nonrecognition of gain depended. Consequently, short-term notes were often given in sales transactions. With this came charges that the reorganization provisions were avenues for tax avoidance.[58]

The Revenue Act of 1924 removed some of the more obvious loopholes of the 1921 Act; however, the lack of controls with respect to consideration remained. As a result, the courts created the continuity of interest test to close loopholes in the statutory formula.

The use of short-term notes was first disallowed in 1932 in *Cortland Specialty Co. v. Commissioner.*[59] In the *Cortland* case, substantially all of the assets of one corporation were acquired for cash and notes, payable within 14 months. The Court ruled that promissory notes would not qualify as securities and stated that the Revenue Act, while giving the widest room for all kinds of changes of corporate structures, "... does not abandon the primary requisite that there must be some continuity of interest on the part of the transferor corporation or its stockholders in order to secure exemption." In the following year, a similar situation reached the courts and was decided in the same manner. In *Pinellas Ice & Cold Storage v. Commissioner,* taxpayer transferred 99 percent of its assets to another corporation in exchange for cash and notes due within five months.[60] Justice McReynolds stated that before a corporate reorganization will qualify for tax-free status "... the seller must acquire an interest in the affairs of the purchasing company more definite than that incident to ownership of its short-term purchase money notes." The *Pinellas* decision has often been cited as authority for the concept that a tax-free exchange must not resemble a sale.

In *LeTulle v. Scofield,* a corporation transferred all its assets to another corporation for cash and bonds of the transferee corporation.[61] The Supreme Court held that the transaction was not a tax-free reorganization. If the only interest the transferor retained was a creditor interest—even

---

57. § 202(c)(2), Revenue Act of 1921.
58. Prevention of Tax Avoidance, Preliminary Report of Subcommittee of Committee on Ways and Means, 73rd Cong., 2d Sess. (1934); J. S. Seidman, *Seidman's Legislative History of Income Tax Laws* (Englewood Cliffs, N.J.: Prentice-Hall, Inc., 1938), p. 332.
59. 3 USTC ¶ 980, 11 AFTR 857, 60 F.2d 937 (CA–2, 1932), *cert. den.* 53 S.Ct. 316 (USSC, 1933).
60. 3 USTC ¶ 1023, 11 AFTR 1112, 53 S.Ct. 257 (USSC, 1933).
61. 40–1 USTC ¶ 9150, 23 AFTR 789, 60 S.Ct. 313 (USSC, 1940). See also *Roebling v. Comm.,* 44–2 USTC ¶ 9388, 32 AFTR 1083, 143 F.2d 810 (CA–3, 1944), *cert. den.* 65 S.Ct. 131 (USSC, 1944).

though a long-term interest secured by a mortgage on the properties transferred—it was still insufficient to satisfy the continuity of interest test.

The Internal Revenue Service has attempted to define exactly how much equity shareholders of the acquired corporation must receive in the acquiring corporation to satisfy the continuity of interest test. For purposes of issuing an advance ruling, the IRS will deem the continuity of interest test to be met if shareholders of the acquired corporation, in the aggregate, receive stock in the acquiring corporation equal in value to at least 50 percent of all formerly outstanding stock of the acquired corporation.[62] Not all shareholders of the acquired corporation need to have a proprietary interest in the surviving corporation; the requirement is applied to the total consideration given in the acquisition. The requirement would be met if one or more of the acquired corporation's shareholders retain a sufficient proprietary interest in the continuing corporation.

> **Example 30.**  Alpha Corporation with 50 shareholders merges into Beta Corporation pursuant to state statute. Under the plan of merger, the shareholders of Alpha can elect to receive either cash or stock in Beta. Thirty of the shareholders (holding 40% of Alpha's outstanding stock) elect to receive cash, while the remaining 20 shareholders of Alpha (holding 60% of the stock) elect to receive stock in Beta. This plan satisfies the continuity of interest test. The shareholders receiving cash would, of course, be taxed on the transaction; however, those receiving stock would not.

> **Example 31.**  A and B, individuals, each hold 50% of the stock of Alpha Corporation. Alpha merges into Beta Corporation. A receives cash for his stock in Alpha, while B receives stock in Beta. This should also qualify as a tax-free merger. B receives stock in Beta equal in value to at least 50% percent of the formerly outstanding stock in Alpha. A will be taxed on the transaction, but B will not.

The continuity of interest requirement presents complications principally for the "A" reorganization. The other reorganization provisions have statutory limitations on consideration that surpass the requirements of the continuity of interest test as defined by the IRS; consequently, this test generally presents no problem.

---

**62.**  Rev.Proc. 74–26, 1974–2 C.B. 478, § 3.02, updated by Rev.Proc. 77–37, 1977–2 C.B. 568. In *Paulsen v. Commissioner,* 85–1 USTC ¶ 9116, 55 AFTR2d 85–482, 105 S.Ct. 627 (1985), the Supreme Court ruled that shareholders had a gain on the exchange of their stock pursuant to a merger between a state savings and loan association and a Federal savings and loan association. The shareholders exchanged their guaranty stock in the state savings and loan association for passbook savings accounts and Certificates of Deposits in the Federal savings and loan association. The savings accounts and Certificates of Deposits were the only form of equity in the Federal savings and loan association, and they entitled the holder to dividends and the right to vote. However, the Supreme Court held that the equity interest in the Federal savings and loan association was much smaller than in the stock association. The shareholders had exchanged stock for essentially cash with an insubstantial equity interest. Consequently, the Court held that the exchange did not satisfy the continuity of interest test.

## CONTINUITY OF BUSINESS ENTERPRISE

The Regulations make reference to a "continuity of business enterprise under the modified form" as a prerequisite for a tax-free reorganization.[63] This requirement is an expansion of the sound business purpose principle as established in *Gregory v. Helvering*.[64] However, it is a separate test. Originally, it was interpreted to mean that the acquiring corporation must conduct business activities of the same type as did the acquired corporation.[65] Amendments to the Regulations provide that this test is satisfied only if the transferee continues the historic business of the transferor or, if the business is not continued, uses a significant portion of the assets of the transferor in the transferee's business.[66]

## STEP TRANSACTION

The court-imposed step transaction doctrine is employed to determine whether a reorganization is tax-free when a series of related transactions are involved. The courts look at the conditions before and after the change in ownership and, assuming the series of transactions are related, will consider all such transactions to be one for tax purposes. In *American Bantam Car Co.*, the Court proffered a test for determining whether a series of steps is to be treated as a single indivisible transaction.[67] The Court stated that such a test is one of mutual interdependence: "Were the steps so interdependent that the legal relations created by one transaction would have been fruitless without a completion of the series?"

The step transaction presents complications for reorganizations when "unwanted" assets are involved. If the acquired corporation attempts to dispose of its unwanted assets prior to a reorganization, the doctrine might be utilized to defeat tax-free status of the reorganization on the contention that substantially all of the properties were not transferred. The "substantially all" requirement is present in the "C" reorganization, the "D" reorganization, and the subsidiary "A" reorganization. Assuming application of the step transaction is sustained, a prior nontaxable disposition of unwanted assets and a later reorganization would be treated as a single transaction; consequently, the acquiring corporation would have failed to acquire substantially all of the acquired corporation's assets.

The case of *Helvering v. Elkhorn Coal Company* illustrates the difficulty of disposing of unwanted assets in a "C" reorganization.[68] In that case, Mill Creek Company wanted to acquire certain, but not all, of the assets of Elkhorn, the old company. A direct conveyance of the desired property to Mill Creek would not have been a tax-free reorganization because the unwanted assets were a substantial portion of Elkhorn's total

---

63.  Reg. § 1.368–1(b).
64.  Cited in Footnote 49.
65.  See Rev.Rul. 56–330, 1956–2 C.B. 204.
66.  Reg. § 1.368–1(d).
67.  11 T.C. 397 (1948), *aff'd.* in 49–2 USTC ¶ 9471, 38 AFTR 820, 177 F.2d 513 (CA–3, 1949), *cert. den.* 70 S.Ct. 622 (USSC, 1950).
68.  38–1 USTC ¶ 9238, 20 AFTR 1301, 95 F.2d 732 (CA–4, 1938), *cert. den.* 59 S.Ct. 65 (USSC, 1938).

assets. A valid "Type C" reorganization would not have been possible, because substantially all of the assets would not have been conveyed. Elkhorn organized a new corporation to which it transferred the unwanted assets for all the stock of the new company and distributed this stock to its shareholders. Elkhorn then transferred its remaining assets to Mill Creek. Elkhorn was dissolved. Taxpayer claimed that the first transfer was tax-free under § 351 as a transfer to a corporation in exchange for at least 80 percent of the new company's stock. It contended that the later transfer by Elkhorn of its remaining property to Mill Creek in return for stock was a tax-free reorganization. The IRS agreed that the first transfer was tax-free; however, it stated that there was a single plan embracing all the transfers. Accordingly, they should be treated as made at substantially the same time. According to the IRS, the first transfer was equivalent to a retention of assets by Elkhorn. If the unwanted assets had remained in Elkhorn, the transfer of assets to Mill Creek would not have met the "substantially all" test. The Court agreed with the IRS. It considered the transfer of unwanted assets to the new corporation to be an attempt by the parties to take advantage of the statute by placing Elkhorn in a position to transfer substantially all of its assets. This was held to be tax avoidance.

The *Elkhorn* case involved two nontaxable events. If unwanted assets are sold to an unrelated purchaser in a taxable transaction, the *Elkhorn* case might have no application. Further, a dividend distribution to shareholders of the transferor corporation should not affect the tax-free nature of a subsequent reorganization. On the other hand, if a transfer to shareholders is in connection with a stock redemption wherein the shareholders receive capital gain treatment, there might again be a question as to the tax-free status of a subsequent reorganization.

In *Commissioner v. Gordon* the Supreme Court refused to apply the step transaction doctrine to a spin-off despite taxpayer's assertion that two transactions should be one.[69] In the *Gordon* case, the Court upheld the IRS's contention that the step transaction did not apply. Normally, the IRS attempts to disallow the nontaxable status of a reorganization by asserting the application of the step transaction doctrine. In upholding the contention of the IRS that the doctrine would not apply, the Supreme Court also limited future applicability of the doctrine. The Court stated:

> It would be wholly inconsistent . . . to hold that the essential character of a transaction, and its tax impact, should remain not only undeterminable but unfixed for an indefinite and unlimited period in the future, awaiting events that might or might not happen. This requirement that the character of a transaction be determinable does not mean that the entire transaction must necessarily occur within a tax year. It does, however, mean that if one transaction is to be characterized as a "first step" there must be a binding commitment to take the later steps.

The "binding commitment" to take later steps for the first transaction to be characterized as a "first step" places a limitation on the "mutual interdependence" test prescribed by the Court in *American Bantam Car*. Taxpay-

---

**69.** 68–1 USTC ¶ 9383, 21 AFTR2d 1329, 88 S.Ct. 1517 (USSC, 1968).

ers can possibly find an outlet in *Gordon* for future transfers of unwanted assets should the IRS assert the step transaction doctrine to defeat the tax-free status of a subsequent reorganization.

The IRS generally views any transaction occurring within one year of the reorganization as part of the acquisition, assuming there is no proof the transaction was, in fact, unrelated. However, in Revenue Ruling 69–48 the doctrine was applied to transactions 22 months apart.[70] The doctrine can bring the continuity of interest test into prominence in a "B" or "C" reorganization should shareholders of the transferor corporation immediately dispose of stock received in the transferee corporation. In the case of an "A" reorganization, the application of the doctrine can cause an otherwise tax-free reorganization to be deemed a purchase. This is possible if the shareholders do not retain their equity interests for a reasonable period of time.

## LIQUIDATION-REINCORPORATION

As noted in Chapter 5, gain on a distribution to shareholders is capital gain in a complete liquidation pursuant to § 331. Further, assets received in a liquidation receive a step-up in basis, and the accumulated earnings and profits account of the distributing corporation is closed. Under § 351, assets can be transferred to a new, controlled corporation tax-free. The tax benefits of these two Code Sections make the liquidation of a corporation with high earnings and profits appealing. The assets will have a step-up in basis from the liquidation. This step-up in basis can then be transferred to a new, controlled corporation. The cash in the old corporation will have been removed at capital gain rates because of the liquidation.

The Regulations address the problem of a liquidation-reincorporation. According to Regulation § 1.331–1(c), a liquidation followed by a transfer to another corporation, or a liquidation preceded by such a transfer, may have the effect of a dividend distribution. Regulation § 1.301–1(l) states that a distribution to shareholders is a dividend distribution, even though taking place at the same time as certain other transactions, if it is in substance a separate transaction. The Regulation mentions, as examples, distributions to shareholders in connection with a recapitalization, a reincorporation, or a merger of one corporation with a newly organized corporation possessing little or no property. These provisions in the Regulations are an attempt to eliminate the tax advantages of liquidation-reincorporations.

The Internal Revenue Service often relies on the reorganization provisions to prevent tax advantages inherent in liquidation-reincorporations. The IRS has attempted to classify a liquidation-reincorporation as either a "Type E" or a "Type F" reorganization on the theory that the shareholders' proportionate interests in the new corporation are the same as in the old.[71] The IRS has also attempted to bring such transactions within the provisions of the "D" reorganization. If a liquidation followed by a reincor-

---

70.   1969–1 C.B. 106.
71.   Rev.Rul. 61–156, 1961–2 C.B. 2, and *Davant v. Comm.*, 66–2 USTC ¶ 9618, 18 AFTR2d 5523, 366 F.2d 874 (CA–5, 1966), *cert. den.* 87 S.Ct. 1370 (USSC, 1967).

poration can be validly labeled a reorganization, there is no step-up in basis in any of the assets. Further, accumulated earnings and profits carry over to the new corporation pursuant to § 381. Any assets retained by shareholders of the liquidated corporation constitute boot and are taxed to the shareholders as such. If the distributions are pro rata, § 356 would cause such distributions to be treated as ordinary dividends to the extent of earnings and profits of the distributing corporation.

In the past, for a liquidation-reincorporation to qualify as a "D" reorganization, the shareholders of the liquidated corporation had to have an 80 percent control of the newly formed corporation.[72] This control requirement often prevented the IRS from successfully contending that a liquidation-reincorporation constituted a "D" reorganization. Because § 304, which is designed to prevent the bailout of E & P at capital gains rates, has a 50 percent control requirement, the Deficit Reduction Act of 1984 changed the control test for "D" reorganizations that are corporate combinations to conform to that of § 304. Thus, the transferor corporation or its shareholders are treated as having control of the transferee corporation if the transferor corporation or its shareholders own stock possessing at least 50 percent of the total combined voting stock or 50 percent of the total value of all classes of stock. In addition, the constructive ownership rules of § 318(a) apply in determing control. Thus, more liquidation-reincorporation transactions will be treated as "D" reorganizations.

If the business of the liquidated corporation is not continued by the new corporation, the IRS's assertion that the liquidation-reincorporation is in reality a reorganization can more easily be rebutted. In *Pridemark v. Commissioner,* the Court stated that there is a "complete liquidation" of the first corporation if the newly formed corporation does not resume the business of the liquidated corporation.[73]

> **Example 32.** X Corporation has assets with a fair market value of $100,000 and a tax basis of $60,000. X is liquidated. A, the sole shareholder of X, has a basis of $20,000 in his stock in X. A retains $10,000 cash and transfers the remaining assets received in the liquidation to a newly formed corporation, Y, for all the stock in Y. If the first transaction qualifies as a liquidation pursuant to § 331, A would have a capital gain of $80,000. There would be no tax on the transfer of the assets to Y, and Y would have a basis of $90,000 in assets received. A would have a $90,000 basis in his stock in Y. If the IRS successfully contends the transaction is a "D" reorganization, the $10,000 cash would be an ordinary dividend to A to the extent of the earnings and profits of X. The assets acquired by Y would have a basis of $50,000, and the earnings and profits of X (less the $10,000 dividend distributed to A) would carry over to Y. A would have a basis of $20,000 in his stock in Y.

---

**72.** *Joseph C. Gallagher,* 39 T.C. 144 (1962), and *Herman Berghash,* 43 T.C. 743 (1965), *aff'd.* in 66–1 USTC ¶ 9446, 17 AFTR2d 1163, 361 F.2d 257 (CA–2, 1966); and *Atlas Tool Co. v. Comm.,* 80–1 USTC ¶ 9177, 45 AFTR2d 80–643, 614 F.2d 860 (CA–3, 1980).

**73.** 65–1 USTC ¶ 9388, 15 AFTR2d 853, 345 F.2d 35 (CA–4, 1965).

# OTHER CONSIDERATIONS

## PLAN OF REORGANIZATION AND PARTIES THERETO

Section 361 states that a "party to a reorganization" recognizes neither gain nor loss if it exchanges property under a "plan of reorganization" for stock or securities in another corporation also a "party to the reorganization." Section 354 provides that gain or loss will not be recognized if stock or securities in a corporation that is a "party to the reorganization" are exchanged solely for stock or securities in the same corporation or in another corporation also a "party to the reorganization." Section 368 does not mention "plan of reorganization," and the term is not defined in the Code. The Regulations state that "plan of reorganization" has reference to a consummated transaction specifically defined as a reorganization under § 368.[74] The Regulations take the position that the term limits, rather than enlarges, the definition of "reorganization." Only those exchanges or distributions that are directly a part of transactions described in § 368 produce nonrecognition of gain or loss.

The connotation placed upon "plan of reorganization" is essentially the same concept applicable to the step transaction doctrine. Acts would normally be included in the "plan" if their consummation was contemplated when the first step was commenced and if their absence would have resulted in none of the acts being performed.[75] Both the requirement that the transaction be "pursuant to a plan of reorganization" and the step transaction doctrine refer to a series of steps or acts.

The requirement that there be a "plan of reorganization" implies that a formal, written document is essential. The Regulations, in fact, refer to the adoption of a plan of reorganization.[76] Though the courts have not required a written plan, nonetheless, it is preferable that the parties execute a formal document. Such a document serves to delineate the rights of all parties and to enumerate the required steps to perfect the exchange.

The "parties to reorganization" are defined in § § 368(b)(1) and (2). Parties to a reorganization include a corporation resulting from the reorganization, both corporations in an acquisition by one corporation of stock or properties of another, and the parent of the acquiring corporation when parent stock is exchanged for property in "A," "B," or "C" reorganization.

> **Example 33.** A parent corporation, Alpha, uses stock of its subsidiary, Beta, as consideration for the acquisition of assets in Zeta Corporation. The transaction will not qualify as a tax-free reorganization, because Beta is not a "party to the reorganization." (Refer back to Figures II, IV, and VI. Parent stock can be exchanged by a subsidiary in a reorganization, but a parent that is a party to a reorganization cannot use subsidiary stock to effect a reorganization. The parent must use its own stock.)

---

74. Reg. § 1.368–2(g).
75. *Hortense A. Menefee*, 46 B.T.A. 865 (1941).
76. Reg. § 1.368–3(a).

## ASSUMPTION OF LIABILITIES

Because a corporate reorganization normally results in a continuation of the business activities of the previous corporations, liabilities are seldom liquidated. The acquiring corporation will either assume liabilities of the acquired organization or take property subject to liabilities. In a regular sale or purchase of properties, the assumption of liabilities by the purchaser is part of the selling price.[77] As noted in Chapter 3, in some nonrecognition transactions assumption of liabilities is considered boot and, hence, taxable. This is not true in a § 351 transaction because of § 357. Also, in a tax-free reorganization pursuant to §§ 357 and 368(a)(1)(C), assumed liabilities are, for the most part, disregarded in computing taxable gain to the transferor corporation. At first glance, then, assumption of liabilities in a corporate reorganization would seem to present few problems. However, there are troublesome areas.

Section 357(c), which, irrespective of § 357(a), provides that liabilities in excess of basis are taxable gain, was discussed in Chapter 3 in connection with a § 351 transaction. This provision supposedly has no effect on tax-free reorganizations other than the "D" reorganization. Section 357(c) specifically states that it is applicable to exchanges ". . . to which § 351 applies, or to which § 361 applies by reason of a plan of reorganization within the meaning of § 368(a)(1)(D) . . ." The "D" reorganization, alone, would be affected. However, § 368(a)(2)(A) provides that if a transaction qualifies both as an acquisition of assets for stock under § 368(a)(1)(C) and as a transfer to a controlled corporation under § 368(a)(1)(D), it is treated as a § 368(a)(1)(D) transaction. Consequently, taxpayers might be misled as to the application of § 357(c).

Section 368(a)(1), which discusses the acquisition of another corporation's properties solely in exchange for all or a part of the acquirer's voting stock, specifically states that the assumption of a liability of the acquired corporation will be disregarded. Congress added this provision to the predecessor of § 368(a)(1)(C) to eliminate any "solely for voting stock" problem in the "C" reorganization. However, § 368(a)(1)(B) contains no similar provision. Thus, any assumption of a liability by the transferor corporation in a "B" reorganization presumably will violate the "solely for voting stock" requirement. Normally, however, the assumption of liabilities is not present in a "B" reorganization inasmuch as "Type B" is simply a change in stock ownership.

# CARRYOVER OF
# CORPORATE TAX ATTRIBUTES

## IN GENERAL

The determination of the tax features of an acquired corporation to be carried over to the acquiring or successor corporation is a significant problem in a corporate acquisition and in the liquidation of a subsidiary corpo-

---

**77.** *Crane v. Comm.*, 47–1 USTC ¶ 9217, 35 AFTR 776, 67 S.Ct. 1047 (USSC, 1947).

ration. Some tax features of an acquired corporation (the carryover of losses, tax credits, and deficits) will be welcomed by a successor corporation. Others may prove less welcome. It is immaterial whether the acquiring corporation desires the carryover of certain tax attributes of its acquired predecessor inasmuch as the carryover rules, if applicable, are mandatory. Thus, the carryover rules should be carefully considered in every corporate acquisition; they may, in fact, determine the form of the acquisition. This is particularly true in the liquidation of a subsidiary pursuant to § 332. The carryover rules apply in the liquidation of a controlled subsidiary under § 332 if the basis of the transferred assets carries over to the parent. If basis of assets is determined pursuant to the single transaction approach of § 338, the carryover rules do not apply.

## THEORY OF CARRYOVERS

Before the advent of § 381, case law determined the aggregate tax benefits of an acquired corporation that could be carried over to the successor. With respect to net operating losses, general theory held that only the corporation sustaining the loss could take the deduction. Because of this theory, the form of a corporate acquisition largely determined whether a tax loss could be carried over to the acquiring corporation. If a statutory merger or consolidation occurred, the courts permitted the carryover of the predecessor corporation's deductions. Because there was an amalgamation of assets and liabilities of the two corporations through operation of law, a carryover was justified. On the other hand, carryovers were not permitted in other forms of corporate acquisitions.[78]

With respect to the carryover of earnings and profits of a predecessor corporation, the courts held that although a credit balance in earnings and profits of the acquired corporation would carry over to the successor corporation, a deficit would not.[79] This rule was supposedly grounded on the desire to prevent escape of earnings and profits from taxation. However, in one Court of Appeals case, the carryover of a deficit to a successor corporation that had no accumulated earnings and profits on the date of the reorganization was permitted.[80] The Court held that a deficit of the predecessor corporation could be used to reduce earnings and profits acquired after the date of the reorganization. This reasoning of the Court of Appeals was later criticized by the Tax Court.[81]

The Supreme Court brought added confusion into the carryover area in its 1957 decision in *Libson Shops v. Koehler*.[82] Seventeen corporations, all owned by the same shareholders in the same proportion, merged into one corporation that subsequently conducted the entire business as a sin-

---

**78.** *New Colonial Ice Co. v. Helvering,* 4 USTC ¶ 1292, 13 AFTR 1180, 54 S.Ct. 788 (USSC, 1934).

**79.** *Comm. v. Sansome,* 3 USTC ¶ 978, 11 AFTR 854, 60 F.2d 931 (CA–2, 1931), *cert. den.* 53 S.Ct. 291 (USSC, 1932), and *Comm. v. Phipps,* 49–1 USTC ¶ 9204, 37 AFTR 827, 69 S.Ct. 616 (USSC, 1949).

**80.** *U. S. v. Snider,* 55–1 USTC ¶ 9523, 47 AFTR 1368, 224 F.2d 165 (CA–1, 1955).

**81.** *Frelbro Corp.,* 36 T.C. 864 (1961), *rev'd.* in 63–1 USTC ¶ 9388, 11 AFTR2d 1216, 315 F.2d 784 (CA–2, 1963).

**82.** 57–1 USTC ¶ 9691, 51 AFTR 43, 77 S.Ct. 990 (USSC, 1957).

gle enterprise. Prior to the merger, three corporations had suffered net operating losses. These losses were claimed by the successor corporation on its income tax return. The Supreme Court stated that the corporation claiming the loss must be the same taxable entity that sustained the loss, thereby disallowing a carryover.

Though the *Libson* case was decided under the 1939 Code, it presented problems in determining its relationship to the 1954 Code. The decision has been cited as authority for the proposition that carryover privileges are not available unless there is a continuity of business enterprise. However, some recent cases have ruled that by enacting the 1954 Code, Congress destroyed any precedent value of the decision in *Libson Shops*.[83] Other cases still follow the doctrine.[84]

The IRS has indicated that it will apply the *Libson* decision doctrine in any loss carryover not within the scope of § 381. The Senate Finance Committee, in drafting the Tax Reform Act of 1976, specifically stated that *Libson Shops* will no longer apply.[85]

Although § 381 now determines which tax benefits of an acquired corporation can be carried over to the successor, it does not apply to all transactions. In instances where it does not apply, the vague and confusing case law presumably is still applicable.

## ALLOWANCE OF CARRYOVERS

The inconsistency of the case law was rectified, to an extent, when Congress enacted § 381 as a part of the 1954 Code. Section 381 provides for the carryover of various specific tax attributes from one corporation to another in certain tax-free liquidations and reorganizations. It permits the successor corporation ". . . to step into the 'tax shoes' of its predecessor corporation."[86]

Though § 381 presumably solves the problem of carryovers in many instances, it does not apply to all tax items nor does it apply to all transactions. Section 381(c) lists the tax features of an acquired corporation that can be carried over to a successor corporation. Section 381 does not apply to any other items. Further, only the following transactions are covered: the "A," the "C," the "F," the nondivisive "D" and "G" reorganizations, and the liquidation of a controlled subsidiary under § 332 wherein the subsidiary's basis in its assets carries over to the parent. As to other tax items and transactions, the tax practitioner still faces confusing and contradictory case law.

*Net Operating Loss Carryovers.* A net operating loss carryover, as determined under § 172, is permitted as a deduction of the successor corpo-

---

**83.**   *Exel Corp. v. U. S.,* 71–2 USTC ¶ 9731, 28 AFTR2d 71–5992, 451 F.2d 80 (CA–8, 1971); *Maxwell Hardware Co. v. Comm.,* 65–1 USTC ¶ 9332, 15 AFTR2d 692, 343 F.2d 713 (CA–9, 1965); and *Frederick Steel Co. v. Comm.,* 67–1 USTC ¶ 9279, 19 AFTR2d 820, 375 F.2d 351 (CA–6, 1967), *cert. den.* 88 S.Ct. 219 (USSC, 1967).

**84.**   *Home Construction Corp. of America v. U. S.,* 71–1 USTC ¶ 9267, 27 AFTR2d 71–837, 439 F.2d 1165 (CA–5, 1971).

**85.**   1976–3 (Vol. 3) C.B. 206. .

**86.**   S.Rept. 1622, 83d Cong., 2d Sess. (1954).

ration under § 381(c)(1). However, there are limitations on the amount of the carryover. Sections 381(c)(1)(B) and 382(b) limit the aggregate deduction the successor corporation can obtain from net operating losses of the predecessor corporation or corporations, while § 269 will deny the deduction altogether if there exists a tax avoidance scheme.

Under § 381(c)(1)(B), the amount of a net operating loss that can be carried to the first tax year ending after the transfer date is limited to a percentage representing the remaining days in that tax year. For example, if two corporations merged on July 1, 19X5, only a portion of a net operating loss of the acquired corporation could be used to offset income for tax year 19X5. The amount would be limited to one-half of the taxable income of the acquiring corporation. This limitation applies only for the purpose of computing the net operating loss deduction of the successor corporation for the successor's first taxable year ending after the date of the transfer. The limitation does not apply for purposes of determining the portion of any net operating loss that may be carried to any taxable year of the successor corporation after the first taxable year.

> **Example 34.** Alpha Corporation merges into Beta Corporation on December 16, 19X5. Alpha Corporation had a net operating loss of $73,000, while Beta Corporation has taxable income for 19X5 of $100,000. Only $4,110 ($100,000 × 15/365 = $4,110) of the $73,000 net operating loss can be used to offset Beta's taxable income for 19X5. Beta would have taxable income of $95,890 ($100,000 − $4,110) for 19X5. The remainder of the loss carryover from Alpha Corporation, $68,890, would be carried forward to offset Beta's 19X6 taxable income.
>
> If the merger had taken place on December 31, 19X5, there would have been no net operating loss deduction for 19X5 ($100,000 × 0/365 = $0). The entire loss of $73,000 would be carried to 19X6.

The taxable years to which a net operating loss can be carried back or forward are prescribed by § 172(b)(1), which contains the general rules for net operating losses.[87]

Timing is important if a net operating loss carryover is possible. Section 381(b)(1) states that the taxable year of the transferor corporation will end on the date of distribution or transfer (except in the case of an "F" reorganization).[88] Section 381(c)(1)(A) states that the net operating loss carryovers are carried to the first taxable year of the acquiring corporation ending after the date of the transfer, subject to the limitation noted above. If the transfer should not be completed by the last day of the taxable year of both corporations, the application of the first rule will produce a short taxable year for the loss corporation (it will end on the date of transfer),

---

**87.** See Reg. § 1.381(c)(1)–1(e)(3) for the application of this Section to corporate reorganizations.

**88.** In the "F" reorganization, the transferor corporation's year does not end on the transfer date. Carryovers are considered as though there had been no reorganization. A net operating loss could, thus, be carried back as well as forward. (This assumes that a single corporation is involved in the merger, as the "F" reorganization no longer is applicable in the case of multiple corporations.)

which will be counted as a full year for purposes of the 15-year carryover period. The portion of the taxable year of the acquiring corporation commencing on the date of transfer will count as a full year in computing the carryover period. Thus, a full year could be lost. For example, a transferor corporation's net operating loss for 1986 would be spread over only 14 years if it is merged into a calendar year transferee corporation on any day in 1986 other than December 31. Two taxable years would occur in 1986 so that the carryover would apply to years 1986 through 2000.

Section 382 imposes limitations on the carryover of a net operating loss of an acquired corporation. Section 382(a) applies to a "purchase" of stock, whereas § 382(b) applies to reorganizations. Section 382(a) provides that the net operating loss carryover of an acquired corporation is reduced if there has been a change of more than 60 percent in the ownership of the corporation's outstanding stock since the beginning of the present or prior taxable year.[89] The so-called purchase rule, effective January 1, 1986, requires that ownership of stock of the 15 principal shareholders at the end of the year be compared to their ownership at the beginning of the current year and at the beginning of each of the two prior years to determine if the 60 percentage point change has occurred. (An increase of 60 percentage points is not the same as an increase of 60 percent.[90]) The two-year "lookback" will not be applied except to taxable years beginning on or after January 1, 1986. If the 60 percentage point change is met, a net operating loss carryover will be reduced as follows: For each percentage point in excess of 60, up to and including 80, the reduction is $3\frac{1}{2}$; and for each percentage point above 80, the carryover loss is reduced $1\frac{1}{2}$. For an 85 percentage point change in ownership, a net operating loss would be reduced $77\frac{1}{2}$ percent [$3\frac{1}{2} \times 20$ percentage points $(60 - 80$ range$) = 70\%$. Then $1\frac{1}{2} \times 5$ percentage points $= 7\frac{1}{2}\%$, and $70\% + 7\frac{1}{2}\% = 77\frac{1}{2}\%$.].

Section 382(b) applies to limit the amount of the net operating loss carryover in all reorganizations when shareholders of the loss corporation own less than 40 percent of the fair market value of outstanding common stock in the acquiring corporation immediately after the reorganization.[91] If shareholders of the loss corporation own stock in the acquiring corporation before the reorganization, this stock is not considered in computing

---

89. For stock ownership changes occurring before January 1, 1986, a 50 percentage point change is required before § 382(a) is applicable. The provision applies to a purchase of stock through which one or more of the ten principal shareholders obtained a percentage of the total value of the outstanding stock that was at least 50 percentage points above the interest held at the beginning of the present or prior taxable year. In addition, the loss elimination occurs only if the acquired corporation fails to continue to carry on substantially the same trade or business as that conducted before the change. The Tax Reform Act of 1976 substantially revised § 382. The changes were originally to become effective as of July 1, 1978. However, because of problems with the 1976 Act, the effective date of the changes has been constantly postponed. The Revenue Act of 1978 postponed the effective date of the changes to July 1, 1980. P.L. 96–167 changed the effective date to July 1, 1982. P.L. 97–119 then postponed the changes to July 1, 1984. The Deficit Reduction Act of 1984 has changed the effective date to January 1, 1986, to provide additional time for further study.

90. Reg. § 1.382(a)–1(d)(1). For example, a shareholder who owns 4% of the fair market value of the stock of a corporation and increases his or her ownership to 6% has had a 50% increase in ownership, but only a 2 percentage point increase.

91. Twenty percent for reorganization plans adopted prior to January 1, 1986.

the 40 percent requirement.[92] Should the shareholders of the loss corporation own less than 40 percent of the stock of the successor corporation, the loss carryover is reduced proportionately. This limitation is applicable whether the loss corporation is the successor or predecessor. The percent of reduction in the amount of allowed deduction pursuant to § 382(b) is determined as follows:[93] If there is at least a 20 percent stock ownership, the net operating loss will be reduced by $3\frac{1}{2}$ multiplied by the number of percentage points less than 40 that the loss corporation's shareholders receive. If there is less than 20 percent ownership, the net operating loss is reduced by 70 percent plus $1\frac{1}{2}$ multiplied by the number of percentage points less than 20. For example, in a 15 percent ownership, the loss would be reduced by $77\frac{1}{2}$ percent. [The number of percentage points less than 20 = 5 (20 − 15). Then, 5 percentage points $\times$ $1\frac{1}{2}$ = $7\frac{1}{2}$% and 70% + $7\frac{1}{2}$% = $77\frac{1}{2}$%.]

> **Example 35.** Alpha Corporation acquires the assets of Beta Corporation, the loss corporation. Beta has a net operating loss of $100,000. Immediately after the acquisition, the shareholders of Beta own 12% of the fair market value of the stock of Alpha. The 12% figure reduces the net operating loss of Beta Corporation (to be carried over) by $82,000, or 82%, computed as follows: 20 − 12 = 8 percentage points less than 20. Then, 8 $\times$ $1\frac{1}{2}$% = 12%, and 70% + 12% = 82%.

The purpose of § 382(b) is ". . . to ensure that the net operating loss carryovers from a corporation a party to a reorganization will be allowed in full only when the shareholders of the loss corporation have a substantial continuing interest in the acquiring corporation."[94]

*Earnings and Profits.* In *Commissioner v. Sansome,* the Court held that the earnings and profits of an acquired corporation carries over to a successor corporation. In *Commissioner v. Phipps,* however, the successor corporation was not permitted to apply a deficit in the acquired corporation's earnings and profits against its own earnings and profits.[95] There was confusion in applying these general rules. Section 381(c)(2) clarifies these rules with respect to the carryover of earnings and profits of a predecessor corporation. Earnings and profits of a predecessor corporation is deemed to have been received by the successor corporation as of the date of the distribution or transfer. A deficit, on the other hand, may be used to offset earnings and profits accumulated by the successor corporation only after the date of the transfer. Thus, both earnings and profits and deficits carry over, but deficits reduce earnings and profits only after the date of transfer.

If one corporation has accumulated earnings and profits and the other has a deficit, the deficit can be used only to offset earnings and profits accumulated after the date of the transfer. If this is the case, the acquiring corporation will be considered as maintaining two separate earnings and profits accounts after the date of transfer, the first containing the total accumulated earnings and profits as of the date of the transfer and the

---

92. See Reg. § 1.382(b)–1(a)(2).
93. § 382(b)(2).
94. Reg. § 1.382(b)–1(c).
95. For the citations to *Comm. v. Sansome* and *Comm. v. Phipps,* refer to Footnote 79.

second containing total deficits as of such date.[96] The deficit in one account may not be used to reduce accumulated earnings and profits in the other account.

*Capital Loss Carryovers.* Section 381(c)(3) prescribes the same limitations for the carryover of capital losses of the predecessor corporation as those imposed on the carryover of net operating losses. The taxable year of the acquiring corporation to which a capital loss is carried is the first taxable year ending after the date of transfer. The capital loss carryover is a short-term capital loss to the acquiring corporation, and the amount deductible in the year of transfer is limited to a percent of the net capital gains of the successor corporation computed with reference to the number of days remaining in the tax year.

> **Example 36.** Beta Corporation, the acquired corporation, has a capital loss in the amount of $30,000. Beta transfers all its assets to Alpha Corporation on July 1, 19X6. Alpha Corporation files its return on the basis of a calendar year. Alpha Corporation has net capital gains (computed without regard to any capital loss carryovers) for 19X6 of $40,000. The amount of capital loss carryover for 19X6 would be $20,000 ($40,000 × ½).

Section 382(b), which limits the carryover of a net operating loss of a predecessor corporation if the shareholders of the loss corporation own less than 40 percent of the fair market value of the outstanding common stock of the acquiring corporation immediately after the reorganization, is, pursuant to § 383, applicable to the capital loss carryover. The limitation is computed in the same manner as the limitation on a net operating loss. If the shareholders of the loss corporation own less than 40 percent of the stock of the successor corporation,[97] the loss carryover is reduced proportionately. Thus, if the shareholders own 10 percent of the successor corporation, 85 percent of the capital loss would be denied the successor corporation.

*Method of Accounting.* Section 381(c)(4) provides that the acquiring corporation must use the method of accounting used by the acquired corporation on the date of transfer unless different methods were employed by the acquired and the acquiring corporations. If different methods were used, the Code requires the acquiring corporation to use different methods if the business of the acquired corporation is operated as a separate and distinct business after the reorganization.[98]

*Other Carryovers.* Numerous other carryover items are prescribed by § 381. The successor corporation would determine depreciation on acquired assets in the same manner as did the predecessor corporation. Should installment obligations pass to a transferee corporation in a reorganization, the transferee corporation would also report income from such obligations on the installment method. Should there be an involuntary conversion, the successor corporation is treated as the predecessor. The successor corpora-

---

**96.** Reg. § 1.381(c)(2)–1(a)(5).
**97.** Twenty percent if the plan of reorganization was adopted before January 1, 1986.
**98.** Reg. § 1.381(c)(4)–1(c)(4).

tion also stands in the "tax shoes" of the predecessor with respect to unused investment credits and recapture of the investment tax credit should there be early dispositions. Section 383 limits the amount of unused investment tax credits (as well as foreign tax credits and other credits) that may be carried over if the shareholders of the acquired corporation own, immediately after the transfer, less than 40 percent of the fair market value of the stock of the acquiring corporation.[99] (The limitation under § 383 is applied to these credits in the same manner as it is applied to capital loss carryovers.)

Though the carryover items under § 381 are numerous, those remaining have limited applicability and are not discussed in this text.

## DISALLOWANCE OF CARRYOVERS

Irrespective of § 381, § 269 can be utilized by the Internal Revenue Service to disallow the carryover of tax benefits if a tax avoidance scheme is apparent. Section 269 states that if a corporation acquires property of another corporation primarily to evade or avoid Federal income tax by securing the benefit of a deduction, credit, or other allowance that the acquiring corporation would not otherwise enjoy, the deduction, credit, or other allowance will be disallowed. Whether or not the principal purpose is the evasion or avoidance of taxes becomes a question of fact. If the business of the loss corporation is promptly discontinued after a corporate reorganization, § 269 will undoubtedly be asserted by the IRS in an attempt to disallow the loss carryover.

Section 269 may be applied to disallow a net operating loss carryover even though such carryover might be limited pursuant to § 382.[100]

> **Example 37.** Alpha Corporation, which has a net operating loss of $100,000, is merged into Beta Corporation. Beta Corporation acquires Alpha for the principal purpose of utilizing the net operating loss. After the merger, the former shareholders of Alpha own 10% of the fair market value of the stock in Beta. Pursuant to § 382, only $15,000 of the net operating loss could be used by Beta; however, pursuant to § 269, none of it can be used by Beta. (Note: If the plan of reorganization was adopted before January 1, 1986, the $15,000 referred to above would be $50,000.)

---

> ✓    TAX PLANNING
>         CONSIDERATIONS

---

## ASSESSING THE POSSIBLE ALTERNATIVES

The various types of corporate reorganizations should not be considered in isolation. Often the parties involved can achieve the desired tax result through more than one type of reorganization.

---

**99.** Twenty percent if the plan of reorganization was adopted before January 1, 1986.
**100.** Reg. § 1.269–6.

**Example 38.** X Corporation operates two businesses, each of which has been in existence for five years. One business is a manufacturing operation; the other is a wholesale distributorship. Z Corporation wishes to acquire only the former business and does not, therefore, want to purchase all the assets of X Corporation. X Corporation has a net operating loss, a deficit in earnings and profits, and a basis in its assets in excess of their fair market value.

What course of action might be advisable to transfer the manufacturing operation from X to Z with the least, if any, tax consequences? Compare the following three possibilities:

1. X Corporation transfers the manufacturing operation to Z Corporation in return for some of the latter's stock.

2. X Corporation forms Y Corporation to which it transfers the wholesale distributorship in return for all of Y's stock. The Y stock is then distributed to X's shareholders. This portion of the arrangement represents a nontaxable spin-off. X Corporation now transfers the manufacturing operation to Z Corporation in exchange for some of the latter's stock.

3. The nontaxable spin-off described in possibility 2 is followed by Z Corporation's acquisition of all the X Corporation stock in exchange for some of Z's stock. The end result, of course, is that X Corporation becomes a subsidiary of Z Corporation.

Possibility 1 probably would not fit within the definition of a "Type C" reorganization because substantially all of the assets were not transferred by X Corporation in return for Z Corporation stock. Although the manufacturing operation (i. e., the "wanted" assets) was transferred, the wholesale distributorship (i. e., "unwanted" assets) was not.

Possibility 2 suffers from these same shortcomings. If the spin-off is disregarded, the transaction becomes an unsuccessful attempt to carry out a "Type C" reorganization (i. e., possibility 1). Disregarding the spin-off would be the natural result of following the step transaction doctrine as applied in the *Elkhorn* decision.[101]

Possibility 3 follows a different approach. Though starting with the spin-off of the "unwanted" assets, the "wanted" assets are obtained by Z Corporation through the purchase of the X stock. Taken by itself, this last step satisfies the stock for stock requirement of a "B" reorganization. If, however, the step transaction doctrine is applied and the spin-off is disregarded, the Y Corporation stock distributed to X's shareholders might be considered as property *other than voting stock* in Z Corporation. The IRS has not chosen to take this position and will recognize the nontaxability of a spin-off of "unwanted" assets followed by a "B" reorganization.[102]

## RESOLVING SHAREHOLDER DISPUTES

The utility of a split-off under the "Type D" reorganization should not be overlooked as a means of resolving shareholder disputes.

---

**101.** Cited in Footnote 68.
**102.** Rev.Rul. 70–434, 1970–2 C.B. 83.

**Example 39.** Alpha Corporation was organized 10 years ago and since that time has operated retail and wholesale businesses. Alpha's two shareholders, R and S, each manage one of the businesses. Due to a difference of opinion between R and S over corporate policy, R and S decide to separate the two businesses.

Presuming R and S plan to continue operating each business in the corporate form, the obvious way to avoid any tax consequences on the division would be to pursue a "Type D" reorganization. Alpha Corporation could form Beta Corporation by transferring to it one of the businesses, say the wholesale operation, in return for all the Beta stock. Next the Beta stock would be distributed to the manager of the wholesale business, R, in exchange for all of his stock in Alpha Corporation. After the nontaxable split-off, S has the retail business through his sole ownership in Alpha Corporation, and R has control of the wholesale operation through the ownership of Beta Corporation.

## REORGANIZATIONS COMPARED WITH
## STOCK REDEMPTIONS AND LIQUIDATIONS

Example 39 presents an opportunity to review certain other possibilities discussed in previous chapters.

1. If, for example, one of the shareholders, say S, wishes to continue operating in the corporate form while the other does not, the stock redemption approach should be considered (refer to Chapter 4). Thus, R could exchange all of his stock in Alpha Corporation for the wholesale business. This would qualify as a complete termination of a shareholder's interest under § 302(b)(3) and as a partial liquidation under § 302(b)(4). R would recognize a capital gain or loss measured by the difference between the fair market value of the wholesale business and his basis in the Alpha stock surrendered. As noted in Chapter 4, some gain may be recognized by Alpha Corporation because of the redemption. Section 311(d) (i. e., gain recognition to the corporation upon the use of appreciated property to redeem stock) probably would be inapplicable, since the redemption completely terminates the shareholder's interest and the redemption is a qualified partial liquidation. Under these circumstances, S would have sole control of Alpha Corporation and, thereby, the retail business.

2. If both shareholders are indifferent about whether the businesses should continue to operate in the corporate form, some thought should be given to a complete liquidation of Alpha Corporation. The liquidation could be carried out by making a distribution in kind of the wholesale business to R and of the retail business to S. As was true with reference to the stock redemption alternative, the shareholders would recognize a capital gain or loss measured by the difference between the fair market value of the property received and the basis of the stock given up (refer to Chapter 5).

Much can be said for the stock redemption and liquidation approaches if the corporate assets are appreciated in value over their tax bases. Because the shareholder(s) will take fair market value as their tax basis in any property distributed, a so-called fresh start is achieved. The price to be paid for such step-up in basis is, of course, the capital gain the shareholder(s) must recognize on the distribution. On the other hand, if the primary concern of the shareholder(s) is to postpone the recognition of *any* gain on the division of the businesses, the "Type D" reorganization becomes the preferable alternative. In a purely tax-free exchange, moreover, there will be no change in income tax basis. Thus, S's basis in the Alpha Corporation stock remains the same, while R's basis in the Alpha stock surrendered carries over to the new Beta Corporation stock received. At the corporate level, Alpha will retain the same basis it had in the retail business and Beta Corporation will assume Alpha's basis in the wholesale operation.

*Carryover Considerations.* The tax differences between corporate reorganizations and liquidations become pronounced in other respects.

> **Example 40.** P Corporation is desirous of acquiring the assets of S Corporation. These assets have a basis to S Corporation of $300,000 and a fair market value of $200,000. Further, S Corporation has incurred losses in its operations during the past several years and possesses unabsorbed net operating losses. P Corporation plans to continue the business conducted by S, hoping to do so on a profitable basis.

To carry out the acquisition planned by P Corporation, one must assess the tax consequences of various available alternatives. In this connection, consider the following:

1. Using cash and/or other property, P Corporation purchases the assets directly from S Corporation. Following the purchase, S Corporation liquidates and distributes the cash and/or property to its shareholders.

2. P Corporation purchases all of the stock in S Corporation from its shareholders. Shortly thereafter, P liquidates S.

3. Utilizing a "Type A" reorganization, S Corporation merges into P Corporation. In exchange for their stock, the shareholders of S Corporation receive stock in P Corporation.

4. Under a "Type C" reorganization, S Corporation transfers all of its assets to P Corporation in return for the latter's voting stock. S then distributes the P stock to its shareholders.

A satisfactory resolution must center around the preservation of S Corporation's favorable tax attributes—the high basis in the assets and the net operating loss carryovers. In this regard, alternative 1 is highly unsatisfactory. The purchase price (probably $200,000) becomes the basis of the assets in the hands of P Corporation. Further, any unused net operating losses will disappear upon the liquidation of S Corporation. It is true, however, that S Corporation will have a realized loss of $100,000 [$300,000 (basis in the assets) − $200,000 (sale proceeds)] from the sale of its assets. Even so, the realized loss may generate little, if any, tax savings to S Corporation because of either of two possibilities. First, the realized loss would not be recognizable if the sale took place after the adoption of a plan of complete liquidation and the requirements of § 337 (i. e., the 12-month liquidation) are otherwise met (refer to Chapter 5). Second, even if the loss is recognizable, it means little, absent offsetting gains. In view of S Corporation's past history (i. e., unabsorbed net operating loss carryovers), it appears doubtful that such gains would be present in the year of sale.

Alternative 2 suffers from the same shortcomings as alternative 1. When the liquidation of a subsidiary under § 332 occurs, the basis of property received by the parent corporation is determined under either § 334(b)(1) or § 338 (assuming it applies and a timely election is made). In this case, if the parent elects under § 338, the assumed cost of the S Corporation stock ($200,000) becomes P's basis in the assets received from S (refer to Chapter 5). Consequently, the $100,000 built-in loss S Corporation had in its assets disappears and benefits neither P nor S. Likewise, S Corporation's unused net operating loss carryovers disappear.

If an election under § 338 is not made, the general rule of § 334(b)(1) applies for basis determination purposes. Thus, S Corporation's basis in its assets carries over to P Corporation. In this regard, what P Corporation paid for the S stock becomes irrelevant. Other tax attributes of S Corporation (e. g., net operating losses) will, under certain circumstances, carry over to P Corporation. There are certain tax risks, however. Section 269 (dealing with the disallowance of any deduction or credit when the acquisition was made to evade or avoid income tax) could present a problem. Section 269(b) specifically applies to a liquidation within two years after the acquisition date of a qualified stock purchase when an election is not made under § 338. Section 269(b)(1)(D) provides that if the principal purpose of the liquidation is the avoidance of income tax by securing the benefit of a deduction, credit, or other allowance, the items involved may be disallowed.

Alternatives 3 and 4 should accomplish the same tax result as not electing under § 338 but with less tax risk. Presuming P Corporation can establish a business purpose for the "Type A" or "Type C" reorganization, § 269 can be avoided.

## THE ROLE OF THE INDIVIDUAL RULING

Before leaving the area of corporate reorganizations, one further point needs emphasis. When feasible, the parties contemplating a corporate reorganization should apply for and obtain from the IRS an individual ruling concerning the income tax effect of the transaction(s). Assuming the parties carry out the transfers as proposed in the ruling request, a favorable ruling provides, in effect, an insurance policy leading to the desired tax result. If the tax implications are significant, as they often are with corporate reorganizations, the advantage of obtaining prior IRS approval should be apparent. The pros and cons of individual rulings and the procedures by which they are obtained are discussed in Chapter 14.

## PROBLEM MATERIALS

### Discussion Questions

1. What is the theory underlying nonrecognition of gain or loss in a corporate reorganization?

2. Briefly explain the seven forms of corporate reorganizations that qualify for non-recognition treatment.

3. What is the continuity of interest test? *no chnge in ownership*
*at least 50% of consideration must be stock*

4. What are the advantages of effecting a business combination through a "Type A" reorganization?

5. What problems exist in effecting a business combination through a "Type A" reorganization?

6. How can the use of a subsidiary corporation in a "Type A" reorganization solve some of its inherent problems?

7. How does the step transaction doctrine affect the tax consequences of corporate combinations? *Pre-reorganization xfers*

8. What is the liquidation-reincorporation doctrine?

9. How does the business purpose requirement affect a tax-free reorganization?

10. In what instances will a "Type C" reorganization be more beneficial than a "Type A" reorganization?

11. How does the receipt of boot affect the tax-free status of a corporate reorganization?

12. When is the receipt of bonds tax-free in a "Type E" reorganization?

13. Why can a "Type F" reorganization give the surviving corporation more tax benefits in certain instances than can an "A" or a "C" reorganization?

14. Do capital loss carryovers survive in a tax-free reorganization? Investment tax credit carryovers?

15. Does the assumption of liabilities of an acquired corporation by the acquiring corporation trigger gain recognition to the acquired corporation?

16. What is a reverse merger?

17. What is the difference between a spin-off pursuant to § 355 and a spin-off coupled with a "Type D" reorganization?

18. In what instances is a "Type D" reorganization accompanied by transfer of only part of the assets of the transferor corporation beneficial?

19. Can a corporation divide a single trade or business and qualify the transaction for tax-free status as a "Type D" reorganization? *Yes under Cody & Marcett*

20. What reorganizations are not covered by the carryover provisions of § 381?

21. What is the status of a net operating loss carryover if the assets of the loss corporation are purchased by another corporation?

22. Will a deficit in earnings and profits of an acquired corporation carry over to offset earnings and profits of the acquiring corporation? *No*

23. X Corporation transfers all its assets to a newly formed corporation, Y, for all of Y's stock. The Y stock is exchanged with X's shareholders for all their stock in X. X is then liquidated. Does the exchange qualify as a tax-free reorganization? Explain. *Acquisitive D cnea hor ✓ yes - type F or C*

24. X Corporation is interested in acquiring the assets of Y Corporation. Y has a basis of $400,000 in its assets (fair market value of Y's assets is $250,000). Y has incurred substantial losses in the last few years and has a $175,000 net operating loss carryover. X believes it could make some changes in operations and could make Y a successful corporation. What is the best alternative for tax purposes in acquiring either the assets or the stock of Y Corporation?

## Problems

1. What type of reorganization is effected in the following transactions:

   (a) A Corporation acquires all the properties of B Corporation in exchange for 2,000 shares of stock in A. The A stock is distributed to the shareholders of B. B is then liquidated.

   (b) S Corporation exchanges voting stock in P, its parent, for 90% of the stock in A Corporation.

   (c) A and B Corporations transfer all their assets to C, a new corporation. C stock is distributed to shareholders of A and B; A and B are then liquidated.

   (d) A Corporation transfers voting stock representing a 10% interest to B Corporation for 90% of all classes of its stock.

   (e) S Corporation, a subsidiary of P Corporation, transfers P stock to the shareholders of X Corporation for substantially all the assets of X. X is liquidated.

   (f) S Corporation transfers voting stock in P Corporation, its parent, to A Corporation for substantially all of A's assets. A then distributes the P stock to its shareholders.

   (g) S Corporation transfers all its assets to X Corporation. P, the parent of S, transfers its voting stock to the shareholders of X for 80% control of X Corporation. S Corporation is liquidated.

   (h) A Corporation transfers assets worth $150,000 to B Corporation for voting stock worth $100,000, the assumption of liabilities in the amount of $25,000, and cash of $25,000.

   (i) A Corporation has been actively engaged in two businesses for the past 10 years. It transfers assets of one business to a newly formed corporation and distributes stock in the new corporation, representing control of such corporation, to the shareholders of A.

   (j) A Corporation manufactures a single product but has two plants. One plant was established three years ago; the other has been in existence since the corporation was organized eight years ago. A transfers the older plant to a new corporation and distributes stock in the new corporation to one-half its shareholders in exchange for all their A stock.

   (k) Common shares in A Corporation are owned by father and son. The father exchanges his common stock in A for newly issued nonvoting cumulative preferred stock.

   (l) A, a New York corporation, incorporates B in Delaware and transfers all its assets to B in exchange for B's stock. A is subsequently liquidated.

   (m) A parent corporation exchanges stock in its subsidiary for substantially all the assets of X Corporation.

2. (a) K, a shareholder of X Corporation, exchanges her X Corporation stock for stock in Y Corporation. The exchange is pursuant to a tax-free reorganization of X and Y. K paid $80,000 for her stock in X Corporation five years ago. The X stock is worth $160,000, and the stock K receives in Y is worth $140,000. What is K's basis in the Y Corporation stock?

   (b) Assume K receives $20,000 cash in addition to the Y stock. What are the tax consequences to K, and what basis does she have in the Y Corporation stock?

3. Pursuant to a plan of reorganization, X Corporation's shareholders deposit all their stock in X with X Corporation; X then exchanges its shareholders' stock with Y Corporation for 30% of the voting stock of Y. X Corporation delivers the Y stock to its shareholders.

(a) What are the tax results of the transaction?

(b) Assume Y also transferred 10% of its nonvoting preferred stock to X, with X then delivering the preferred stock as well as the voting stock to its shareholders. What is the tax result?

4. P Corporation transfers part of its voting stock to Y Corporation's only shareholders, A and B. A and B then transfer all their stock in Y to S Corporation, a subsidiary of P. Does this qualify as a tax-free reorganization? Why or why not?

5. X Corporation transfers assets with a tax basis of $100,000, fair market value of $150,000, to Y Corporation for voting stock in Y worth $130,000 and $20,000 cash. X uses the $20,000 to pay its liabilities in the amount of $20,000, distributes the Y stock to its shareholder, and is liquidated. What are the tax consequences of the transfer? What are the basis of the assets to Y and the basis of the Y Corporation stock to X?

6. Assume the same facts as Problem 5 except the consideration given by Y consists of voting stock worth $100,000 and the assumption of $50,000 of X Corporation's liabilities. What are the tax consequences and the bases of assets and stock transferred?

7. X Corporation transfers 30% of its voting stock to Y Corporation for Y's assets worth $2,000,000. X also assumes liabilities of Y in the amount of $500,000. Y transfers the X stock to its shareholders for their Y stock. Y Corporation is then liquidated. Does this qualify as a tax-free reorganization? Suppose X transferred its voting stock plus $500,000 cash for Y's assets worth $2,000,000. Y distributes the cash and voting stock to its shareholders and is liquidated. Does this qualify as a tax-free reorganization?

8. X Corporation has 1,000 shares of $100 par value preferred stock and 2,000 shares of $100 par value common stock outstanding. A, a highly valued employee of X, owns 200 shares of preferred stock and 400 shares of common, or 20% of each. B owns the remaining shares, or 80% of each. To retain A in the corporation, B agrees to surrender 1,000 of his shares of common stock for 1,000 shares of preferred stock to give A a 40% ownership in X. Will this transaction qualify as a tax-free reorganization? Why or why not? What are some possible tax problems that could arise?

9. P Corporation owns 100% of the stock in S Corporation. S owns 10% of P's voting stock and 30% of all classes of stock in X Corporation. P wants to acquire control of X in a tax-free transaction. How can this be done?

10. A Corporation transfers assets with a fair market value of $900,000 to B Corporation for voting stock in B worth $700,000 and the assumption of A Corporation's liabilities in the amount of $200,000. The liabilities consist of accounts payable, $40,000; mortgage payable, $156,000; and reorganization expenses, $4,000. Does the transaction qualify as a tax-free reorganization?

11. X Corporation merges into Y Corporation on June 30, 19X5. Both corporations have a calendar year. X has a net operating loss of $180,000. Y's taxable income for 19X5 is $240,000. How much of the loss can be used to offset Y's 19X5 taxable income?

12. X Corporation has a deficit in earnings and profits of $60,000. It acquires the assets of Y Corporation in 19X5 in a statutory merger. Y has earnings and profits of $300,000. After the merger, X distributes $180,000 to its shareholders. How will the $180,000 be treated for tax purposes?

13. X Corporation uses the cash method of accounting for computing taxable income for its service business. In 19X5, X acquires the assets of Y Corporation in a statutory merger. Y has been using the accrual method of accounting for its

retail boat business. X continues both the retail and service operations after the merger as separate businesses. What accounting method must be used to compute taxable income?

14. A Corporation is merged into B Corporation in a statutory merger. A Corporation had 4,000 shares of common stock, with a fair market value of $100 a share, outstanding. One of A's shareholders exchanges his A stock (100 shares) for which he paid $70 per share for ten 6% debenture bonds in B Corporation (face value *and* fair market value of $1,000 per bond). What are the tax consequences to the shareholder?

15. Assume the shareholder in Problem 14 exchanges his stock for 100 shares of stock in X Corporation. B Corporation was holding the X stock as an investment. The stock was worth $90 per share.

16. X Corporation acquires the assets of Y Corporation in a statutory merger. Y Corporation has a net operating loss of $400,000. Immediately after the transfer, the shareholders of Y own 15% of the fair market value of X's stock. How much of Y's net operating loss can be used by X?

17. A, an individual, exchanges stock she owns in Y Corporation for stock in X Corporation and, in addition, receives $8,000 cash. The exchange is pursuant to a tax-free reorganization of both corporations. A paid $60,000 five years ago for the stock in Y Corporation. The stock in X Corporation possesses a fair market value of $80,000. A's share of E & P of Y Corporation is $6,000. How will A treat this transaction for tax purposes?

18. Assume the same facts as in Problem 17 except that A paid $100,000 (instead of $60,000) for her stock in Y Corporation. How would A treat the transaction for tax purposes?

19. X Corporation transfers assets with a fair market value of $50,000 to Y Corporation and receives voting stock valued at $40,000 and cash of $10,000. No liabilities are assumed. X distributes the cash and the stock in Y to its shareholders and is liquidated. Does this transaction qualify as a tax-free reorganization?

20. X Corporation transfers assets with a fair market value of $200,000 to Y Corporation and receives voting stock valued at $140,000 and cash of $40,000, and Y Corporation assumes $20,000 of X Corporation's liabilities. X distributes the cash and stock in Y and is liquidated. Would this transaction qualify as a "C" reorganization?

21. A and B formed XY Corporation in January 19X3 by each investing $50,000 in cash and receiving 5,000 shares of $10 par value common stock in XY. XY acquired operating assets with the $100,000 cash and continued in business until December 31, 19X5, at which time the basis in its assets was $80,000. XY Corporation had a net operating loss carryover of $20,000 as of the end of that tax year. On December 31, 19X5, XY transferred all its assets to C Corporation for $100,000 worth of stock in C and $20,000 cash. XY then distributed the C stock and $20,000 cash to its shareholders, A and B, in exchange for A's and B's stock in XY. XY was liquidated. A received $60,000 worth of C stock, and B received $40,000 of stock and the $20,000 cash. The C stock transferred to XY represented a 20% ownership in C. What are the tax consequences of the transaction to C, XY, A, and B?

22. T Corporation has assets with a basis of $500,000 and liabilities of $150,000. Its common stock consists of 10,000 shares at a par value of $10 per share. T has E & P of $250,000 and assets worth $800,000. W Corporation exchanges with T's shareholders 1,000 shares of its voting stock (worth $520,000) for 8,000 shares of common stock in T. What are the tax results of the exchange?

23. T Corporation has assets with a basis of $200,000. T transfers the assets (worth $400,000) to W Corporation for voting stock valued at $320,000, cash of $30,000, and the assumption of $50,000 of T's liabilities. T distributes the voting stock in W and the cash of $30,000 to A, its sole shareholder, and liquidates. A had a basis of $80,000 in his stock in T. What are the tax consequences of the transfer to T, W, and A?

24. A had 100 shares of stock in X Corporation with a basis of $100 per share and a fair market value of $200 per share. Pursuant to a tax-free split-off, A received 50 shares of Y Corporation in exchange for 25 shares in X Corporation. The Y stock was worth $100 per share. What are the tax consequences of the exchange to A?

25. T, an individual, is a 10% shareholder in X Corporation. X Corporation, with E & P of $150,000 and assets worth $750,000, is merged into Y Corporation. T receives cash of $5,000, common stock in Y Corporation worth $60,000, and preferred stock in Y worth $10,000. T's basis in her X Corporation stock was $14,000. Assuming that the merger qualifies as an "A" reorganization, what are the tax consequences—

    (a) To T?

    (b) To X Corporation?

    (c) To Y Corporation?

26. Alpha Corporation has assets with a basis of $200,000 and a fair market value of $300,000, liabilities of $40,000, and E & P of $160,000. Beta Corporation, with E & P of $100,000, acquires all the assets of Alpha Corporation in a "C" reorganization. Beta transfers cash of $40,000 and voting stock worth $260,000 to Alpha in exchange for all of Alpha's assets. Alpha uses the cash to pay off its liabilities, distributes the voting stock in Beta to its two shareholders, A and B, and liquidates. A and B have an aggregate basis of $30,000 in their Alpha stock. What are the tax consequences—

    (a) To A and B?

    (b) To Alpha Corporation?

    (c) To Beta Corporation?

27. X Corporation is owned 100% by A, an individual, who purchased the stock in X 10 years ago at a cost of $20,000. X Corporation has assets with a basis of $110,000, fair market value of $220,000, no liabilities, and E & P of $160,000. X Corporation is liquidated in the current tax year. A retains $90,000 of the cash distributed upon X Corporation's liquidation and transfers the remaining assets, worth $130,000, to Y, a newly formed corporation, for 100% of the stock in Y Corporation. What are the tax consequences—

    (a) To A?

    (b) To Y?

28. X Corporation has a deficit in E & P of $100,000 and a net operating loss of $50,000. On December 30, 19X5, Y Corporation acquires all the assets of X Corporation in an "A" reorganization, transferring 10% of its stock to the shareholders of X Corporation. Y has E & P of $60,000. In tax year 19X6, Y Corporation has taxable income of $40,000 and distributes $50,000 to its shareholders.

    (a) How much, if any, of the net operating loss of X Corporation can be used by Y Corporation to offset its taxable income of $40,000?

    (b) How would the $50,000 distribution be treated for tax purposes?

## Research Problems

*Research Problem 1.* N Insurance Company acquired S Insurance Company in a tax-free reorganization. S Insurance Company had a net operating loss carryover of $200,000. S Insurance Company acquired stock in N Insurance Company as consideration for the transfer of its assets to N. It did not liquidate and retained the stock in N as its principal asset. N Insurance Company deducted S Insurance Company's net operating loss carryover on its income tax return. The IRS disallowed the deduction under Reg. § 1.382(b)–1(a)(2). The Regulation states that shareholders of a loss corporation do not own stock in the acquiring corporation for purposes of determining the amount of a net operating loss of the acquired corporation that can be carried over to the acquiring corporation, unless there is an actual distribution of that stock to the individual shareholders. N Insurance Company contends that it is entitled to all the loss carryover because the stock it transferred to S represented 50% of the value of all its outstanding stock and it had no control over the disposition of that stock by S Insurance Company. N Insurance Company seeks your advice. What would you advise the corporation?

*Research Problem 2.* C Corporation redeemed all the stock of a group of shareholders who owned 45% of its outstanding stock. It then transferred all its assets to a newly formed corporation, D. D stock was transferred to its shareholders, the former controlling group (55%) of C, for their stock in C. C Corporation officers contend the transfer was a "Type D" reorganization. Two short-year tax returns were filed for the tax year of the reorganization. C filed a return for the period from the beginning of its tax year, January 1, to the date of dissolution, April 30. D filed from the period beginning February 1, the date of incorporation, to December 31. The Internal Revenue Service contends the transfer is a "Type F" reorganization; therefore, short-year returns for two different corporations cannot be filed. What is your opinion?

*Research Problem 3.* The former shareholders of R Corporation exchanged all their shares in R for voting stock in M Corporation. The agreement provided that a sufficient number of shares in M, valued at $20 per share, would be issued to the shareholders of R to equal the value of R shares. In the event the purchase price was not evenly divisible by shares at $20 per share, the difference would be paid in cash. The value of shares was not so divisible; therefore, each shareholder was paid an additional $40 in lieu of fractional shares. The shareholders of R did not report any gain on their income tax returns with respect to the stock exchange. The IRS contends there is a taxable gain to each shareholder based on the difference between the fair market value of shares in M plus the $40 cash and the tax basis of the stock in R. The IRS is of the opinion the exchange is not nontaxable; it is an exchange for stock and cash and, hence, does not qualify as a "Type B" reorganization. The shareholders seek your advice. What would you advise?

*Research Problem 4.* L Corporation sustained losses in the amount of $1,000,000 in the business of selling home appliances. L entered into an agreement with the controlling shareholders of the corporation. The shareholders agreed to provide the capital to add a subdivision for the sale of automobiles. The shareholders were involved in the sale of automobiles in a partnership. They transferred the assets of the partnership to the corporation in return for nonvoting preferred stock. It was agreed that if the automobile dealership was discontinued by the corporation, the preferred stock would be redeemed using 90% of the assets of the automobile business. The corporation operated the automobile dealership at substantial profits and later discontinued the home appliance business. The net operating losses from the appliance business were deducted as loss carryovers. Upon audit, the Internal Revenue Service disallowed a deduction of the net operating losses under the authority of

§ § 382(a) and 269 of the Internal Revenue Code and the decision of the Supreme Court in *Libson Shops, Inc. v. Koehler*, 57–1 USTC ¶ 9691, 51 AFTR 43, 77 S.Ct. 990 (USSC, 1957). The corporate officers seek your advice.

*Research Problem 5.* X Corporation and Y Corporation are brother-sister corporations and are engaged in similar activities, although X Corporation is much smaller than Y Corporation. X Corporation holds a valuable franchise issued by W Corporation. W Corporation is acquired by Z Corporation. Z Corporation then informs X Corporation that X Corporation has too small a capitalization to hold the franchise. Z Corporation proposes to transfer the franchise to a larger corporation but would agree to accept Y Corporation as a qualified holder. Consequently, X Corporation, with approval of its shareholders, transfers the franchise to Y Corporation and then adopts a plan of complete liquidation, since X's major source of income no longer exists. X Corporation then sells its remaining assets to Y Corporation and distributes the sale proceeds to its shareholders. X Corporation is then formally dissolved, and the shareholders of X treat their distribution as one in complete liquidation and recognize a long-term capital gain on the transaction. Upon audit, the IRS disallows the long-term capital gain and substitutes dividend income stating that the transactions, when viewed as a whole, constituted a "D" type of reorganization. The shareholders of X Corporation seek your advice.

*Research Problem 6.* T Corporation had a large net operating loss. A, an individual who was the sole shareholder and president of W Corporation, purchased all the stock of T on January 10, 19X4. On December 15, 19X4, W adopted a plan to merge T and W. After the merger on January 5, 19X5, T was liquidated. W Corporation offset the net operating loss of T against its income from operations in 19X5. Upon audit of W's return, the IRS disallowed the carryover of T's loss to W. A seeks your advice. A's argument is that she was the sole shareholder of both T and W on the date of the merger; thus, the provisions of § 382 provide that all the loss of T can be carried over to W. What would you advise A?

*Research Problem 7.* A and B, individuals, each own 20% of the voting stock of X Corporation. A owns 40% of Y Corporation, and B owns 60% of Y. On December 30, 19X4, X Corporation transferred all its assets to Y Corporation in consideration of the transfer of an additional 40 shares in Y Corporation to A and an additional 60 shares in Y Corporation to B. Y Corporation used X Corporation's bases in its assets for purposes of calculating its depreciation deduction on those assets for tax year 19X5 and deducted a net operating loss of X Corporation on its 19X5 return, contending that the transfer between X Corporation and Y Corporation was a "D" reorganization. As a result, the bases of X's assets and X's net operating loss carried over to Y Corporation pursuant to § 381. Upon audit of Y Corporation's return for 19X5, the IRS disallowed a carryover of X Corporation's bases in its assets and X's net operating loss, contending that the transfer between X and Y Corporations was a sale of X's assets to Y. According to the IRS, the transfer did not qualify as a "D" reorganization, because the requirements of § 354(b)(1) were not met. The IRS contended that the stock of Y Corporation must have been received by X Corporation and then distributed to X Corporation's shareholders. The corporate officers of Y Corporation contend that this would have been a mere formality. They seek your advice regarding the audit.

*Partial list of research aids:*

*South Texas Rice Warehouse Co.,* 43 T.C. 540 (1965).

*Rose v. U. S.,* 81–1 USTC ¶ 9271, 47 AFTR2d 81–1070, 640 F.2d 1039 (CA–9, 1981).

# Corporate Accumulations 7

## CHAPTER OBJECTIVES

—Explain the purpose of the accumulated earnings tax and the personal holding company tax.

—Define the "reasonable needs of the business" and its role in avoiding the accumulated earnings tax.

—Explain the mechanics of the accumulated earnings tax.

—Define the requirements for personal holding company status.

—Discuss the mechanics of the personal holding company tax.

—Compare the accumulated earnings tax with the personal holding company tax and show how each of these taxes can be avoided or controlled.

Chapter 8 discusses one major technique for minimization of the tax liability of closely-held corporations: the S corporation election. However, some of the corporations that fall into the closely-held category either may not qualify for the election or may find it unattractive. For these other taxpayers, how can corporate earnings be transmitted to the shareholders while at the same time insuring a deduction for the corporation? One method is to reduce the amount of equity capital invested in a controlled corporation by increasing the debt obligations. In other words, convert dividends into interest payments deductible by the corporation. This method has limits. The Internal Revenue Service may contend that the capital structure is unrealistic and the debt is not *bona fide*. For these reasons the IRS will disallow the corporate deduction for interest expense (refer to Chapter 3).

An alternative possibility is to convert the earnings of the closely-held corporation into compensation to the officers, generally the major shareholders. The compensation is a deductible expense. If it were not for the reasonableness requirement, officer-shareholders could withdraw all corporate profits as salaries and thereby eliminate the corporate tax (refer to Chapter 4). However, the reasonableness requirement prevents a corporation from deducting as salaries what are, in fact, nondeductible dividends.

Another approach entails the lease of shareholder-owned property to the corporation. The corporation (the lessee) deducts the lease payment from gross income and saves taxes at the corporate level. Although the shareholders must recognize the rental payments as ordinary income, there is an overall tax savings because the corporation obtains deductions for what are essentially dividend payments. However, the IRS may classify such payments as "disguised dividends" and disallow the rental deductions (refer to Chapter 4).

A fourth method is simply to accumulate the earnings at the corporate level. Congress took steps to stem such accumulations as early as the first income tax law enacted under the Sixteenth Amendment. Today, in addition to the usual corporate income tax, an extra tax is imposed on earnings accumulated beyond the reasonable needs of the business. Also, a penalty tax may be imposed on undistributed personal holding company income.

This chapter demonstrates how the accumulation of earnings can be employed without leading to adverse tax consequences—the imposition of additional taxes.

# PENALTY TAX ON UNREASONABLE ACCUMULATIONS

One method of optimizing the distribution of earnings in a corporation is to accumulate the earnings until the most advantageous time to distribute them to shareholders is reached. If the board of directors is aware of the tax problems of the shareholders, it can channel earnings into their pockets with a minimum of tax cost by using any of several mechanisms. The corporation can distribute dividends only in years when the major shareholders are in lower tax brackets. Alternatively, dividend distributions might be curtailed causing the value of the stock to increase, in a manner similar to that of a savings account, as the retained earnings (and the earnings and profits account) increase. Later, the shareholders can sell their stock at an amount that reflects the increased retained earnings and incur tax at the favorable capital gain rates. Third, the corporation could be liquidated. In this case, the retained earnings would be transmitted to the shareholders tax-free or at the cost of only one capital gains tax. Or fourth, the shareholders can choose to retain their shares. Upon death, the estate or heirs would receive a step-up in basis equal to the fair market value of the stock on date of death or, if elected, on the alternate valuation date. As a result, the increment in value represented by the step-up in basis would be largely attributable to the earnings retained by the corporation and would not be subject to income taxation.

However, there are problems involved in any situation in which corporate earnings are accumulated. As previously mentioned, a penalty tax may be imposed on accumulated taxable earnings, or a personal holding company tax may be levied on certain accumulated passive income. Consider first the accumulated earnings tax. Accumulation can be accomplished; however, the tax law is framed to discourage the retention of earnings that are unrelated to the business needs of the company. Earnings retained in the business to avoid the imposition of the tax that would have been imposed on distributions to the shareholder are subject to a penalty tax.

## THE ELEMENT OF INTENT

Although the penalty tax is normally applied against closely-held corporations, a corporation is not exempt from the tax merely because its stock is widely held.[1] For example, in a Second Court of Appeals decision the tax was imposed upon a widely-held corporation with over 1,500 shareholders. However, a much smaller group of shareholders actually controlled the corporation.[2] As a practical matter the IRS may have difficulty establishing the required tax avoidance purpose in the case of a widely-held corporation in which no small group has legal or effective control of the corporation.

The key to imposition of the tax is not the number of the shareholders in the corporation, but whether a shareholder group controls corporate

---

1. § 532(c).
2. *Trico Products v. Comm.*, 43–2 USTC ¶ 9540, 31 AFTR 394, 137 F.2d 424 (CA–2, 1943).

policy. If such a group does exist and withholds dividends to protect its own tax position, a § 531 problem might materialize.

When a corporation is formed or availed of to shield its shareholders from individual taxes by accumulating rather than distributing earnings and profits, the "bad" purpose for accumulating earnings is considered to exist under § 532(a). This subjective test, in effect, asks: "Did the corporation and/or shareholder(s) *intend* to retain the earnings in order to avoid the tax on dividends?" According to the Supreme Court, this tax avoidance motive need *not* be the dominant or controlling purpose for accumulating the earnings to trigger application of the penalty tax; it need only be a contributing factor to the retention of earnings.[3] If a corporation accumulates funds beyond its reasonable needs, such action is determinative of the existence of a "bad" purpose, unless the contrary can be proven by the preponderance of the evidence.[4] The fact that the business is a mere holding or investment company is *prima facie* evidence of this tax avoidance purpose.[5]

## IMPOSITION OF THE TAX
## AND THE ACCUMULATED EARNINGS CREDIT

The tax is imposed in addition to the regular corporate tax and the 15 percent minimum tax. The rates are 27½ percent on the first $100,000 of accumulated taxable income and 38½ percent on all accumulated taxable income in excess of $100,000.

Most corporations are allowed a minimum $250,000 credit against accumulated taxable income, even though it might be accumulating earnings beyond its reasonable business needs. However, certain personal service corporations in health, law, engineering, architecture, accounting, actuarial science, performing arts, and consulting are limited to a $150,000 accumulated earnings credit. Moreover, a non-service corporation (other than a holding or investment company) may retain more than $250,000 ($150,000 for a service organization) of accumulated earnings if the company can justify that the accumulation is necessary to meet the "reasonable needs of the business."[6]

The accumulated earnings credit is the greater of the following:

1. The current earnings and profits for the tax year that are needed to meet the reasonable needs of the business (see the discussion below) less the net long-term capital gain for the year (net of any tax thereon). In determining the reasonable needs for any one year, the accumulated earnings and profits of past years must be taken into account.

2. The amount by which $250,000 exceeds the accumulated earnings and profits of the corporation at the close of the preceding tax year (designated the "minimum credit").

---

3.   *U. S. v. The Donruss Co.*, 69–1 USTC ¶ 9167, 23 AFTR2d 69–418, 89 S.Ct. 501 (USSC, 1969).

4.   § 533(a).

5.   § 533(b). See, for example, *H. C. Cockrell Warehouse Corp.*, 71 T.C. 1036 (1979).

6.   §§ 535(c) and 537; see also Reg. § 1.537–1.

**Example 1.** T Corporation, a calendar year manufacturing concern, has accumulated E & P of $120,000 as of December 31, 19X3. For 19X4 it has no capital gains and current E & P of $140,000. A realistic estimate places T Corporation's reasonable needs of the business for 19X4 at $200,000. Under item 1, T Corporation's accumulated earnings credit based on the reasonable needs of the business would be $80,000 [$200,000 (reasonable needs of the business) − $120,000 (accumulated E & P)]. Pursuant to item 2, the minimum accumulated earnings credit would be $130,000 [$250,000 (minimum credit allowed for nonservice corporations) − $120,000 (accumulated E & P as of the close of the preceding tax year)]. Thus, the credit becomes $130,000 (i. e., the greater of $80,000 or $130,000).

Several observations should be made about the accumulated earnings credit. First, the minimum credit of $250,000 is of no consequence as long as the prior year's ending balance in accumulated E & P is $250,000 or more. Second, when the credit is based on reasonable needs, the credit is the amount that exceeds accumulated E & P. Third, a taxpayer must choose between the reasonable needs credit (item 1) or the minimum credit (item 2). Combining the two in the same year is not permissible. Fourth, although the § 531 tax is not imposed on accumulated E & P, the amount of the credit depends upon the balance of this account as of the end of the preceding year.

## REASONABLE NEEDS OF THE BUSINESS

It has been firmly established that if a corporation's funds are invested in assets essential to the needs of the business, the IRS will have a difficult time imposing the accumulated earnings tax. "Thus, the size of the accumulated earnings and profits or surplus is not the crucial factor; rather it is the reasonableness and nature of the surplus."[7] What are the reasonable business needs of a corporation? This is precisely the point upon which difficulty arises and which creates controversy with the IRS.

*Justifiable Needs—In General.* The reasonable needs of a business include the business's reasonably anticipated needs.[8] These anticipated needs must be specific, definite, and feasible. A number of court decisions illustrate that indefinite plans referred to only briefly in corporate minutes merely provide a false feeling of security for the taxpayer.[9]

The Regulations list some legitimate reasons that could indicate that the earnings of a corporation are being accumulated to meet the reasonable needs of the business. Earnings may be allowed to accumulate to provide for *bona fide* expansion of the business enterprise or replacement of plant and facilities as well as to acquire a business enterprise through the purchase of stock or assets. Provision for the retirement of *bona fide* in-

---

**7.** *Smoot Sand & Gravel Corp. v. Comm.*, 60–1 USTC ¶ 9241, 5 AFTR2d 626, 274 F.2d 495 (CA–4, 1960).

**8.** § 537(a)(1).

**9.** *Fine Realty, Inc. v. U. S.*, 62–2 USTC ¶ 9758, 10 AFTR2d 5751, 209 F.Supp. 286 (D.Ct.Minn., 1962); *Young's Rubber Corp.*, 21 TCM 1593, T.C.Memo. 1962–300; *Motor Fuel Carriers, Inc. v. U. S.*, 65–2 USTC ¶ 9454, 15 AFTR2d 1153, 244 F.Supp. 380 (D.Ct.Fla., 1965).

debtedness created in connection with the trade or business (e. g., the establishment of a sinking fund for the retirement of bonds issued by the corporation) is a legitimate reason for accumulating earnings under ordinary circumstances. Providing necessary working capital for the business (e. g., to acquire inventories) and providing for investment or loans to suppliers or customers (if necessary to maintain the business of the corporation) are valid grounds for accumulating earnings.[10] Funds may be retained for self-insurance[11] and realistic business contingencies (e. g., lawsuits, patent infringement).[12] Accumulations to avoid an unfavorable competitive position[13] and to carry keyman life insurance policies[14] are justifiable.

The reasonable business needs of a company also include the post-death § 303 redemption requirements of a corporation.[15] Accumulations for such purposes are limited to the amount needed (or reasonably anticipated to be needed) to effect a redemption of stock included in the gross estate of the decedent-shareholder.[16] This amount may not exceed the sum of the death taxes and funeral and administrative expenses allowable under § § 2053 and 2106.[17]

The Revenue Act of 1978 amends § 537(b) to provide that reasonable accumulations to pay future product liability losses shall represent a reasonable anticipated need of the business. Guidelines for the application of this change are to be prescribed by the IRS in the form of Regulations.

*Justifiable Needs—Working Capital Requirements in Inventory Situations.* For many years the penalty tax on accumulated earnings was based upon the concept of retained earnings. The courts generally looked at retained earnings alone to determine whether there was an unreasonable accumulation. However, a corporation may have a large retained earnings balance and yet possess no liquid assets with which to pay dividends. Therefore, the emphasis should more appropriately be placed upon the liquidity of a corporation. Does the business have liquid assets *not* needed that could be used to pay dividends? It was not, however, until 1960 that the courts began to use this liquidity approach.[18]

Gradually the courts began to develop a test based on the normal operating cycle of a business. Initially, a standard of one year's operating expenses was adopted as the appropriate benchmark.[19] Subsequently, the reasonable needs of the business were divided into two categories:

---

10.  Reg. § 1.537–2(b).

11.  *Halby Chemicals Co., Inc. v. U. S.,* 67–2 USTC ¶ 9500, 19 AFTR2d 1589 (Ct.Cls., 1967).

12.  *Dielectric Materials Co.,* 57 T.C. 587 (1972).

13.  *North Valley Metabolic Laboratories,* 34 TCM 400, T.C.Memo, 1975–79.

14.  *Emeloid Co. v. Comm.,* 51–1 USTC ¶ 66,013, 40 AFTR 674, 189 F.2d 230 (CA–3, 1951). Keyman life insurance is a policy on the life of a key employee that is owned by and made payable to the employer. Such insurance would enable the employer to recoup some of the economic loss that could materialize upon the untimely death of the key employee.

15.  The § 303 redemption to pay death taxes and administration expenses of a deceased shareholder was discussed in Chapter 4.

16.  § 537(a)(2) and (b)(1).

17.  § 303(a).

18.  See *Smoot Sand & Gravel Corp. v. Comm.,* cited in Footnote 7.

19.  *Sterling Distributors, Inc. v. U. S.,* 63–1 USTC ¶ 9288, 11 AFTR2d 767, 313 F.2d 803 (CA–5, 1963).

1. Working capital needed for day-to-day operations.

2. Expenditures of a noncurrent nature (extraordinary expenses).

The operating cycle of a business is the average time interval between the acquisition of materials (or services) entering the business and the final realization of cash. The courts seized upon the operating cycle because it had the advantage of objectivity for purposes of determining working capital. There are two distinct cycles in a normal business:

1. Purchase of inventory → the production process → finished goods inventory
2. Sale of merchandise → accounts receivable → cash collection

A systematic operating cycle formula was developed in *Bardahl Manufacturing Co.* and *Bardahl International Corp.*[20] Thus, the technique became known as the *Bardahl* formula.

The standard method now used to determine the reasonable working capital needs for a corporation can be outlined as follows:[21]

$$\text{Inventory Cycle} = \frac{\text{Average[22] Inventory}}{\text{Cost of Goods Sold}}$$

*Plus*

$$\text{Accounts Receivable Cycle} = \frac{\text{Average Accounts Receivable}}{\text{Net Sales}}$$

*Minus*

$$\text{Accounts Payable Cycle} = \frac{\text{Average Accounts Payable[23]}}{\text{Purchases}}$$

*Equals*

A Decimal Percentage

The decimal percentage derived above, when multiplied by the cost of goods sold plus general, administrative, and selling expenses (not includ-

---

**20.** *Bardahl Manufacturing Co.*, 24 TCM 1030, T.C.Memo. 1965–200; *Bardahl International Corp.*, 25 TCM 935, T.C.Memo. 1966–182. See also *Apollo Industries, Inc. v. Comm.*, 66–1 USTC ¶ 9294, 17 AFTR2d 518, 358 F.2d 867 (CA–1, 1966).

**21.** These formulas assume that working capital needs are computed on a yearly basis; however, this may not provide the most favorable result. A business that experiences seasonally based high and low cycles illustrates this point. For example, a construction company can justify a greater working capital need if computations are based on a cycle that includes the winter months only and not an annual average. See *Audits of Construction Contracts*, AICPA, 1965, p. 25. In the same vein, an incorporated CPA firm would choose a cycle during the non-busy season.

**22.** Both of the original Bardahl decisions used the so-called peak cycle approach, whereby the inventory and accounts receivable figures are the amounts for the month end during which the total amount in inventory and accounts receivable were the greatest. In fact, the *Bardahl International* decision specifically rejected the average cycle approach. However, some courts have rejected the peak cycle approach. See, for example, *W. L. Mead, Inc.*, 34 TCM 924, T.C.Memo. 1975–215. A peak cycle approach probably should be used where the business of the corporation is seasonal [see *Magic Mart, Inc.*, 51 T.C. 775 (1969)].

**23.** The accounts payable cycle was developed in *Kingsbury Investments, Inc.*, 28 TCM 1082, T.C.Memo. 1969–205. See also, *W. L. Mead, Inc.*, 34 TCM 924, T.C.Memo. 1975–215.

ing Federal income taxes and depreciation),[24] equals the working capital needs of the business.

If the statistically computed working capital needs plus any extraordinary expenses are more than the current year's net working capital, no penalty tax is imposed. Working capital is the excess of current assets over current liabilities. This amount is the relatively liquid portion of the total business capital that is a buffer for meeting obligations within the normal operating cycle of the business.

However, if working capital needs plus any extraordinary expenses are less than the current year's net working capital, the possibility of the imposition of a penalty tax does exist.[25]

In *Bardahl Manufacturing Corp.* the costs and expenses used in the formula were those of the following year, whereas in *Bardahl International Corp.*, costs and expenses of the current year were used. Use of the subsequent year's expected costs seems to be the more equitable position.

The IRS normally takes the position that the operating cycle should be reduced by the accounts payable cycle, since the payment of such expenses may be postponed by various credit arrangements that will reduce the operating capital requirements. However, a number of court decisions have omitted such a reduction. In any case, a corporate tax planner should not have to rely on creditors to avoid the accumulated earnings penalty tax. The corporation with the most acute working capital problem will probably have a large accounts payable balance. If the previously outlined formula for determining reasonable working capital needs is used, a large accounts payable balance will result in a sizable reduction in the maximum working capital allowable before the tax is imposed. For tax planning purposes, a corporation should hold accounts payable at a reduced level.

*Justifiable Needs—Working Capital Requirements in Noninventory Situations.* In 1972 the government applied the mathematical *Bardahl* formula to determine the working capital needs of an engineering firm (a noninventory company). Regrettably, the Court did not show the government's *Bardahl* calculations. In *Simons-Eastern Co. v. U. S.*, the government calculated, under the *Bardahl* formula, total excess earnings retained for the years 1966, 1967, and 1968 of $464,219.13, $725,246.33, and $738,150.26, respectively.[26] On the other hand, the taxpayer used a human resource accounting (HRA) approach and asserted that the service organization should be allowed a cycle of six months which would have resulted in less excess accumulated earnings.

The taxpayer's use of the HRA approach is actually based on its contention that the strength of the business, and its only asset, is its highly

---

**24.** In *W. L. Mead, Inc.*, cited in Footnote 23, the Tax Court allowed depreciation to be included in the expenses of a service firm with no inventory. Likewise, in *Doug-Long, Inc.*, 72 T.C. 158 (1979), the Tax Court allowed a truck stop to include quarterly estimated tax payments in operating expenses.

**25.** *Electric Regulator Corp. v. Comm.*, 64–2, USTC ¶ 9705, 14 AFTR2d 5447, 336 F.2d 339 (CA–2, 1964) used "quick assets."

**26.** 73–1 USTC ¶ 9279, 31 AFTR2d 73–640, 354 F.Supp. 1003 (D.Ct.Ga., 1972). See also, *Delaware Trucking Co., Inc.*, 32 TCM 105, T.C.Memo. 1973–29, and *Magic Mart, Inc.* cited in Footnote 22.

educated, skilled technicians. These individuals must be available first to attract clients and second to execute their projects efficiently. The taxpayer held that it would be foolish to abruptly discharge these highly paid specialists, recruited and trained at considerable expense, because of a business decline that might, in fact, prove to be of brief duration. Thus, the taxpayer urged the Court to accept an operating cycle of six months (e. g., an operating reserve of six times the monthly professional and technical payroll). The Court accepted neither the IRS's nor the taxpayer's position:

> As seen, the plaintiff is strictly a service organization and this makes a manufacturing formula inappropriate for rigid application. Moreover, "it has no magic" and the soundest approach seems to call for an examination of the particular needs of the business in question. Neither the taxpayer nor the government is bound by the rigidity of the mathematical precision of *Bardahl* nor of a set period.[27]

Instead, the Court added to the IRS's *Bardahl*-calculated operating reserve the reasonable professional and technical payroll for an additional period of two months (or 60 days). The Court felt that this extra amount would ". . . allow sufficient reserve for one cycle of full operation plus a reasonable period, i. e., 60 days, of curtailed operation to recapture business or, in the alternative, to face up to hard decisions on reducing the scope of the entire operation or abandoning it."[28] Further, the Court expressed its opinion that a multiple of reasonable professional and technical salaries is a useful method for determining the amount to be included in an operating reserve. However, the Court did not indicate why it selected two months as the magic number. It can be anticipated that the courts will continue to evolve a *Bardahl*-like formula for noninventory corporations.

*No Justifiable Needs.* Certain situations do *not* call for the accumulation of earnings. For example, accumulating earnings to make loans to shareholders[29] or brother-sister corporations is not considered within the reasonable needs of the business.[30] Accumulations to retire stock without curtailment of the business and for unrealistic business hazards (e. g., depression of the U. S. economy) are invalid reasons for accumulating funds,[31] as are accumulations made to carry out investments in properties or securities unrelated to the corporation's activity.[32]

> **Example 2.** For a period of years, M, Inc., a trucking company, has considered the purchase of various vehicles and other facilities directly related to its business. It has, during the same time, also invested in oil and gas drilling projects (mostly wildcats). Despite substantial accumulated earnings, the corporation made no distributions of dividends during the same period of years. The Claims Courts

---

27. *Supra,* Footnote 26.
28. *Supra,* Footnote 26.
29. Reg. § § 1.537–2(c)(1), (2), and (3).
30. See *Young's Rubber Corp.* cited in Footnote 9.
31. *Turnbull, Inc. v. Comm.,* 67–1 USTC ¶ 9221, 19 AFTR2d 609, 373 F.2d 91 (CA–5, 1967), and Reg. § 1.537–2(c)(5).
32. Reg. § 1.537–2(c)(4).

imposed the penalty tax, because the plan to acquire vehicles and facilities was not supported by documents in existence or prepared during the taxable years at issue. Furthermore, accumulations to further the oil and gas investments were unjustified. (The company was not in the oil and gas business, and the corporation was only a minority investor.)[33]

*Measuring the Accumulation.*  Should the cost or fair market value of assets be used to determine whether a corporation has accumulated earnings and profits beyond its reasonable needs? This issue remains unclear. The Supreme Court has indicated that fair market value is to be used when dealing with marketable securities.[34] Although the Court admitted that the concept of earnings and profits does not include unrealized appreciation, it asserted that to determine if accumulated earnings are reasonable the current asset ratio must be considered. Thus, the Court looked to the economic realities of the situation and held that fair market value is to be used with respect to readily marketable securities. The Court's opinion did not address the proper basis for valuation of assets other than marketable securities; however, the IRS may assert that this rule should be extended to include other assets. Therefore, tax advisers and corporate personnel should regularly check all security holdings to guard against accumulations caused by the appreciation of investments.

> **Example 3.**  C Company had accumulated earnings and profits of approximately $2,000,000. Five years ago, the company invested $150,000 in various stocks and bonds. At the end of the current tax year, the fair market value of these securities approximated $2,500,000. Two of C Company's shareholders, father and son, owned 75% of the stock. If these securities are valued at cost, current assets minus current liabilities are deemed to be equal to the reasonable needs of the business. However, if the marketable securities are valued at their $2,500,000 fair market value, the value of the liquid assets would greatly exceed the corporation's reasonable needs. Under the Supreme Court's economic reality test, the fair market value must be used; consequently, the corporation would be subject to the § 531 penalty tax.

## MECHANICS OF THE PENALTY TAX

The taxable base of the accumulated earnings tax is a company's accumulated taxable income (ATI). Taxable income of the corporation is modified as follows:[35]

$$\text{ATI} = \text{taxable income} \pm \text{certain adjustments} - \text{the dividends}$$
$$\text{paid deduction} - \text{the accumulated earnings credit}$$

---

**33.**  *Cataphote Corp. of Miss. v. U. S.*, 75–2 USTC ¶ 9753, 36 AFTR2d 75–5990 (Ct.Cls., 1975).

**34.**  *Ivan Allen Co. v. U. S.*, 75–2 USTC ¶ 9557, 36 AFTR2d 75–5200, 95 S.Ct. 2501 (USSC, 1975).

**35.**  § 535(a).

The "certain adjustments" include the following items (for a corporation not a mere holding or investment company):

As deductions—

  (1)  Corporate income tax accrued (§ 11).

  (2)  Charitable contributions in excess of 10 percent of adjusted taxable income.

  (3)  Capital loss adjustment.[36]

  (4)  Excess of net long-term capital gain over net short-term capital loss (diminished by the capital gain tax).[37]

And as additions—

  (1)  Capital loss carryovers and carrybacks.

  (2)  Net operating loss deduction.

  (3)  The 85 percent dividends received deduction.

Note that item 4, in effect, allows a corporation to accumulate any capital gains without a penalty tax.

> **Example 4.** A service corporation was organized in 19X5 to shelter any income from its sole shareholder. Its taxable income for 19X5 was $210,000. No dividends were paid during the year (or in the first two and one-half months of the second year). Even in the absence of any reasonable needs of the business that would justify an accumulation of funds, the company would not be subject to the accumulated earnings tax in 19X5. Assuming a corporate tax of $76,350, the taxable income would be reduced to $133,650. Since there is an accumulated earnings credit of $150,000 available to this service company, $16,350 is treated as an accumulated earnings credit carryover.

> **Example 5.** During 19X6, the corporation in Example 4 again has $210,000 of taxable income, resulting in a corporate tax of $76,350. No dividends were paid during the year (or in the first two and one-half months of the following year). The accumulated earnings credit carryover of $16,350 does not cover the taxable income less tax liability ($210,000 − $76,350). The accumulated taxable income (ATI) of $117,300 ($133,650 − $16,350) would result in a § 531 tax of $34,160.50 [($100,000 × .275) + ($17,300 × .385)].

Payment of dividends reduces the amount of accumulated taxable income subject to the penalty tax. The dividends paid deduction includes those dividends paid during the tax year that the shareholders must report as ordinary income *and* any dividends paid within two and one-half months after the close of the tax year.[38] Further, a shareholder may file a consent statement to treat as a dividend the amount specified in such con-

---

**36.** Effective after July 18, 1984, the capital loss adjustment is calculated by reducing the capital loss by the greater of (a) the nonrecaptured capital gain deduction or (b) the corporation's accumulated earnings and profits as of the close of the preceding tax year. § 535(b)(5)(B). Items 3 and 4 are either/or deductions, since a corporation would not have both in the same year.

**37.** Net capital gains must be reduced by net capital losses from earlier years after July 18, 1984. § 535(b)(7)(A).

**38.** § § 535(a), 561(a), and 563(a).

sent. A consent dividend is taxed to the shareholder even though it is not actually distributed. However, the consent dividend is treated as a contribution to the capital of the corporation (i. e., paid-in capital) by the shareholder.[39]

**Example 6.** A nonservice closely-held corporation has the following financial transactions for calendar year 1986:

| | |
|---|---:|
| Taxable income | $ 300,000 |
| Tax liability | 117,750 |
| Excess charitable contributions | 22,000 |
| Short-term capital loss adjustment | (40,000) |
| Dividends received | 100,000 |
| Research and development expenses | 46,000 |
| Dividends paid in 1986 | 40,000 |
| Accumulated earnings (1/1/86) | 220,000 |

Presuming the corporation is subject to the § 531 tax and has *no* reasonable business needs that would justify its accumulations, the accumulated taxable income is calculated as follows:

| | | |
|---|---:|---:|
| Taxable income | | $ 300,000 |
| Plus: 85% dividends received deduction | | 85,000 |
| | | $ 385,000 |
| Less: Tax liability | $ 117,750 | |
|     Excess charitable contributions | 22,000 | |
|     Net short-term capital loss adjustment | 40,000 | |
|     Dividends paid | 40,000 | |
|     Accumulated earnings credit | | |
|       carryover ($250,000 − $220,000) | 30,000 | 249,750 |
| Accumulated taxable income | | $ 135,250 |

Thus, the accumulated earnings penalty tax for 1986 would be $41,071.25 [($100,000 × 27½%) + ($35,250 × 38½%)].

**Example 7.** In Example 6, assume that the reasonable needs of the business of § 535(c) amount to $270,000 in 1986. The current year's accumulated earnings would be reduced by $50,000, rather than the $30,000, of accumulated earnings credit carryover. Thus, accumulated taxable income would be $115,250, and the penalty tax would be $33,371.25. Note that the first $220,000 of accumulated earnings *cannot* be omitted in determining whether taxable income for the current year is reasonably needed by the enterprise.

# PERSONAL HOLDING COMPANY PENALTY TAX

The personal holding company (PHC) tax was enacted to discourage the sheltering of certain types of passive income in corporations owned by high tax bracket individuals. These "incorporated pocketbooks" were frequently

---

**39.** § 565(a) and (c)(2). The consent dividend procedure would be appropriate if the corporation is not in a position to make a cash or property distribution to its shareholders.

found in the entertainment and construction industries. For example, a taxpayer could shelter the income from securities in a corporation, which would pay no dividends, and allow the corporation's stock to increase in value. Thus, as with the accumulated earnings tax, the purpose of the PHC tax is to force the distribution of corporate earnings to the shareholders. However, in any one year the IRS cannot impose both the PHC tax and the accumulated earnings tax.[40]

> **Example 8.** A great deal of tax savings could be achieved by incorporating a "pocketbook" if § 541 did not exist. Assume that investments that yield $50,000 a year are transferred to a corporation by a 50% income tax bracket shareholder. A tax savings of $16,750 would occur each year if no dividends were paid to the shareholder. With no corporation, there would be a total tax liability of $25,000, but with a corporation the tax liability would be only $8,250 in 1986 [($25,000 × .15) + ($25,000 × .18)]. Further, if the yield of $50,000 were in the form of dividends, the corporate tax would be even less because of the dividends received deduction.

Whether a corporation will be included within the statutory definition of a personal holding company for any particular year depends upon the facts and circumstances in evidence during that year.[41] Therefore, personal holding company status may be conferred even in the absence of any such active intent on the part of the corporation. For example, in *Weiss v. U. S.*,[42] a manufacturing operation adopted a plan of complete liquidation under § 337, sold its business, and invested the proceeds of the sale in U.S. Treasury bills and certificates of deposits.[43] During the liquidating corporation's last tax year, 100 percent of its adjusted ordinary gross income was interest income. Since the corporation was owned by one shareholder, the corporation was a PHC, even though in the process of liquidation.

Certain types of corporations are expressly excluded from PHC status in § 542(c):

—Tax-exempt organizations under § 501(a).

—Banks and domestic building and loan associations.

—Life insurance companies.

—Surety companies.

—Foreign personal holding companies.

—Lending or finance companies.

—Foreign corporations.

—Small business investment companies.

---

**40.** § 532(b)(1) and Reg. § 1.541–1(a).

**41.** *Affiliated Enterprises, Inc. v. Comm.*, 44–1 USTC ¶ 9178, 32 AFTR 153, 140 F.2d 647 (CA–10, 1944).

**42.** 75–2 USTC ¶ 9538, 36 AFTR2d 75–5186 (D.Ct.Ohio, 1975). See also, *O'Sullivan Rubber Co. v. Comm.*, 41–2 USTC ¶ 9521, 27 AFTR 529, 120 F.2d 845 (CA–2, 1941).

**43.** Section 337 often permits a corporation to avoid the recognition of gain upon the sale of its assets if such sales are effected within a 12-month period and are pursuant to a plan of complete liquidation. Refer to Chapter 5.

Absent these exceptions, the business world could not perform necessary activities without a high rate of taxation. For example, a legitimate finance company should not be burdened by the personal holding company tax, because it is performing a valuable business function of loaning money, whereas an incorporated pocketbook's major purpose is to shelter the investment income from the higher individual tax rates.

## DEFINITION OF A PERSONAL HOLDING COMPANY

Two tests are incorporated within the PHC provisions:

—Was more than 50 percent of the *value* of the outstanding stock owned by five or fewer individuals at any time during the *last half* of the taxable year?

—Is a substantial portion (60 percent or more) of the corporate income (adjusted ordinary gross income) composed of passive types of income such as dividends, interest, rents, royalties, or certain personal service income?

If the answer to both of these questions is affirmative, the corporation is classified as a PHC. Once classified as a PHC, the corporation is required to pay a 50 percent penalty tax in addition to the regular corporate income tax.

*Stock Ownership Test.* To meet the stock ownership test, more than 50 percent *in value* of the outstanding stock must be owned, directly or indirectly, by or for not more than five individuals sometime during the last half of the tax year. Thus, if the corporation has nine or fewer shareholders, it automatically meets this test. If 10 unrelated individuals own an *equal* portion of the value of the outstanding stock, the stock ownership requirement would not be met. However, if these 10 individuals do not hold equal value, the test would be met.

Note that this ownership test is based on fair market value and not on the number of shares outstanding. Fair market value is determined in light of all the circumstances and is based on the company's net worth, earning and dividend paying capacity, appreciation of assets, and other relevant factors. If there are two or more classes of stock outstanding, the total value of all the stock should be allocated among the various classes according to the relative value of each class.[44]

In determining the stock ownership of an individual, very broad constructive ownership rules are applicable. Under § 544, the following attribution rules determine indirect ownership:

1.  Any stock owned by a corporation, partnership, trust, or estate is considered to be owned proportionately by its shareholders, partners, or beneficiaries.

2.  The stock owned by the members of an individual's family (brothers, sisters, spouse, ancestors, and lineal descendants) or by the individual's partner is considered to be owned by such individual.

---

44. Reg. § 1.542–3(c).

3. If an individual has an option to purchase stock, such stock is regarded as owned by that person.[45]

4. Convertible securities are treated as outstanding stock.

**Example 9.** A and B, two individuals, are the equal beneficiaries of a trust that owns the entire capital stock of M Corporation. M Corporation owns all of the stock of N Corporation. Here all of the stock of M Corporation and N Corporation is considered to be owned equally by A and B by reason of indirect ownership under § 544(a)(1).

**Example 10.** X Corporation during the last half of the tax year had 1,000 shares of outstanding stock, 499 of which were held by various individuals having no relationship to one another and none of whom were partners. The remaining 501 shares were held by seven shareholders as follows:

| | |
|---|---|
| H | 100 |
| H's spouse | 50 |
| H's brother | 20 |
| H's sister | 70 |
| H's father | 120 |
| H's son | 80 |
| H's daughter | 61 |

Under the family attribution rules of § 544(a)(2), H is considered to own 501 shares of X for purposes of determining stock ownership in a personal holding company.

Attribution rules 2, 3, and 4 are applicable only for the purpose of classifying a corporation as a personal holding company and cannot be used to avoid the application of the PHC provisions. Basically, these broad constructive ownership rules make it difficult for a closely-held corporation to avoid application of the stock ownership test. For example, convertible securities would be treated as outstanding stock only if the effect of the inclusion is to make the corporation a personal holding company (and not to expand the total amount of stock in order to avoid PHC classification).

*Gross Income Test.* The gross income test is met if 60 percent or more of the corporation's *adjusted ordinary gross income* (AOGI) is composed of certain passive income items (i. e., PHC income). Adjusted ordinary gross income is calculated by subtracting the following from gross income (as defined by § 61):

—Gains from the sale or disposition of capital assets.

—Section 1231 gains.

—Expenditures attributable to income from rents and mineral royalties (such as depreciation, property taxes, interest expense, and rental payments).[46]

The deduction of the first two items from gross income results in the intermediate concept *ordinary gross income* (OGI), the use of which is noted

45. For examples of how these constructive ownership rules operate, see Reg. § § 1.544–2, –3(a), and –4.
46. § § 543(b)(1) and (2).

subsequently. The starting point, gross income, is not necessarily synonymous with gross receipts. In fact, for transactions in stocks, securities, and commodities, the term "gross income" includes only the excess of gains over any losses.[47]

Personal holding company income (see Figure I) includes income from dividends;[48] interest; royalties; annuities; rents; mineral, oil, and gas royalties; copyright royalties; produced film rents; and amounts from certain personal service contracts. Any amount from personal service contracts is classified as PHC income only if (a) some person other than the corporation has the right to designate, by name or by description, the individual who is to perform the services and (b) the person so designated owns, directly or indirectly, 25 percent or more in value of the outstanding stock of the corporation at some time during the taxable year.[49] See Example 27 later in the chapter.

**Figure I**

PERSONAL HOLDING COMPANY INCOME

| Types of PHCI | Statutory Location | Examples in This Chapter |
|---|---|---|
| Dividends | § 543(a)(1) | 11,12,13,15,18,19 |
| Interest | § 543(a)(1) | 11,12,28 |
| Royalties (other than oil, gas, mineral, and copyright) | § 543(a)(1) | |
| Annuities | § 543(a)(1) | |
| Rents | § 543(a)(2) | 11,12,13,14,18,28 |
| Mineral, oil, and gas royalties | § 543(a)(3) | 15 |
| Copyright royalties | § 543(a)(4) | |
| Produced film rents | § 543(a)(5) | |
| Corporate property used by shareholders | § 543(a)(6) | |
| Personal service contract income | § 543(a)(7) | 27 |
| Subchapter J income | § 543(a)(8) | |

**Example 11.** M Corporation has four shareholders, and its adjusted ordinary gross income (AOGI) is $95,000, composed of gross income from a merchandising operation of $40,000, interest income of $15,000, dividend income of $25,000, and adjusted income from rents of $15,000. Total passive income is $55,000 ($15,000 + $25,000 + $15,000). Since 60% of AOGI (i.e., $57,000) is greater than the passive income ($55,000), this corporation is not a personal holding company.

**Example 12.** Assume in Example 11 that the corporation received $21,000 in interest income rather than $15,000. Total passive income is now $61,000 ($21,000 + $25,000 + $15,000). Since 60% of AOGI (i. e., $60,600) is less than passive income of $61,000, this corporation is a personal holding company.

---

**47.** Reg. § 1.542–2.
**48.** The Deficit Reduction Act of 1984 made dividends as a result of § 304(b)(4) to be personal holding company income. What is interesting is that the change was made retroactive to August 31, 1982. Refer to Chapter 4 for a discussion of § 304(b)(4).
**49.** § 543(a)(7). For an application of the 'right to designate,' see *Thomas P. Byrnes, Inc.*, 73 T.C. 416 (1979).

Rental income is normally classified as PHC income, but it can be excluded from that category if two tests are met. The first test is met if a corporation's adjusted income from rents is 50 percent or more of the corporation's AOGI. The second test is satisfied if the total dividends paid for the tax year, dividends considered as paid on the last day of the tax year, and consent dividends are equal to or greater than the amount by which the nonrent PHC income exceeds 10 percent of ordinary gross income.[50] Of course, the taxpayer wishes to meet both tests so that the rent income can be excluded from PHC income for purposes of the gross income test referred to above. (See Figure IV later in the chapter.)

With respect to this 50 percent test, "adjusted income from rents" is defined as gross income from rents reduced by the deductions allowable under § 543(b)(3). These deductions are depreciation, property taxes, interest, and rent. Generally, compensation is not included in the term "rents" and is not an allowable deduction. The final amount included in AOGI as adjusted income from rents cannot be less than zero.

**Example 13.** Assume that Z Corporation has rental income of $10,000 and the following business deductions:

| | |
|---|---|
| Depreciation on rental property | $ 1,000 |
| Interest on mortgage | 2,500 |
| Real property taxes | 1,500 |
| Salaries and other business expenses (§ 162) | 3,000 |

The adjusted income from rents included in AOGI is $5,000 (i. e., $10,000 − $1,000 − $2,500 − $1,500). Salaries and other § 162 expenses do not affect the calculation of AOGI.

A company deriving its income primarily from rental activities can avoid PHC status by merely distributing as dividends the amount of nonrental PHC income that exceeds 10 percent of its ordinary gross income.

**Example 14.** During the tax year, N Corporation receives $15,000 in rental income, $4,000 in dividends, and a $1,000 long-term capital gain. Corporate deductions for depreciation, interest, and real estate taxes allocable to the rental income amount to $10,000. The company paid a total of $2,500 in dividends to its eight shareholders. The company's OGI would be $19,000 [($15,000 + $4,000 + $1,000 = $20,000) − $1,000], and AOGI would be $9,000 ($19,000 − $10,000). Since adjusted rental income of $5,000 ($15,000 − $10,000) exceeds $4,500, 50% of AOGI ($9,000), this corporation meets the 50% test. Nonrental PHC income is $4,000 and 10% of OGI is only $1,900. Therefore, dividends of at least $2,100 ($4,000 − $1,900) must be paid to meet the 10% test. Since $2,500 in dividends are paid, N Corporation meets the 10% test; the rental income is not classified as PHC income.

Similar to rental income, adjusted income from mineral, oil, and gas royalties can be excluded from PHC income classification if three tests are

---

**50.** § 543(a)(2).

met.[51] First, adjusted income from such royalties must constitute 50 percent or more of AOGI. Second, nonroyalty PHC income may not exceed 10 percent of OGI. Note that this 10 percent test is not accompanied by the dividend escape clause previously described in relation to rental income; therefore, corporations receiving income from mineral, oil, or gas royalties must be careful to minimize nonroyalty PHC income. Furthermore, adjusted income from rents and copyright royalties is considered to be nonroyalty PHC income whether or not treated as such by §§ 543(a)(2) and (4). Third, the company's business expenses under § 162 (other than compensation paid to shareholders) must be at least 15 percent of AOGI.

> **Example 15.** P Corporation has gross income of $4,000, which consists of gross income from oil royalties in the amount of $2,500, $400 of dividends, and $1,100 from the sale of merchandise. The total amount of the deductions for depletion, interest, and property and severance taxes allocable to the gross income from oil royalties equals $1,000. Deductions allowable under § 162 amount to $450. P Corporation's AOGI equals $3,000 ($4,000 − $1,000), and its adjusted income from oil royalties is $1,500 ($2,500 − $1,000). Since the adjusted income from oil royalties constitutes 50% or more of the AOGI, test one is met. Non-royalty PHC is $400 (composed solely of the $400 of dividends). Such amount is not more than 10% of OGI; therefore, the second test is satisfied. Since the $450 of § 162 expenses equals 15% of AOGI ($3,000), the third requirement is satisfied. P Corporation's adjusted income from oil royalties does not constitute PHC income.

## CALCULATION OF THE PHC TAX

To this point, the discussion has focused on the determination of personal holding company status. If an entity is classified as a PHC, a new set of computations is relevant in determining the amount upon which the 50 percent tax is imposed. This tax base is called undistributed PHC income (UPHC income). Basically, this amount is taxable income, subject to certain adjustments, *minus* the dividends paid deduction.

The starting point is corporate taxable income as determined for regular tax purposes. To this amount the following adjustments must be made:

—The normal Federal income tax accrual (other than the PHC tax and the accumulated earnings tax) for the tax year is deductible. The deduction is determined under the accrual method even though the corporation may actually use the cash receipts and disbursements method. Any contested, unpaid tax is not considered accrued until the issue is resolved.[52]

—Excess charitable contributions beyond the corporate limitation of 10 percent of taxable income can be deducted up to the 20 percent or 30 percent or 50 percent limitations imposed upon individuals.[53]

---

**51.** § 543(a)(3).

**52.** Reg. § 1.545–2(a)(1)(i).

**53.** Reg. § 1.545–2(b)(2)(ii).

—The excess of long-term capital gain over short-term capital loss (net of tax) is deducted from taxable income.[54] Thus, long-term capital gains can be accumulated in a corporation and are not subject to the PHC tax.

—The dividends received deduction and other special deductions allowed by § § 241 through 250 (other than the organizational expense deduction) are not available. Such amounts must be added back to taxable income to determine the penalty tax base.[55]

—Any net operating loss, except for the preceding year, must be added back.[56]

—Under certain conditions, business expenses and depreciation attributable to nonbusiness property owned by the corporation that exceed the income derived from such property must be added back to taxable income to determine UPHC income.[57]

The above adjustments to taxable income result in a figure called *adjusted taxable income* (ATI).

*Dividends Paid Deduction.* Since the purpose of the PHC penalty tax is to force a corporation to pay dividends, five types of dividends paid deductions reduce the amount subject to the 50 percent penalty tax. (See Figure II later in the chapter.) First, dividends actually paid during the tax year ordinarily reduce UPHC income.[58] However, such distributions must be pro rata. They must exhibit no preference to any shares of stock over shares of the same class or to any class of stock over other classes outstanding.[59] This prohibition is especially harsh when portions of an employee-shareholder's salary are declared unreasonable and classified as a disguised or constructive dividend.[60] In the case of a property dividend, the dividends paid deduction is limited to the adjusted basis of the property (not the property's fair market value) in the hands of the distributing corporation at the time of the distribution.[61]

> **Example 16.** Three individuals are equal shareholders in a personal holding company. A property dividend with an adjusted basis of $20,000 (FMV of $30,000) is paid to the three shareholders in the following proportion: 25%, 35%, and 40%. This is not a pro rata distribution; therefore, the dividends are not deductible from UPHC income.

A two and one-half month grace period following the close of the tax year exists. Dividends paid during this period may be treated as paid during the tax year just closed. However, the amount allowed as a deduction from UPHC income cannot exceed either (1) the UPHC income for the tax

---

**54.**  § 545(b)(5) and *Litchfield Securities Corp. v. U. S.,* 64–1 USTC ¶ 9106, 12 AFTR2d 6042, 325 F.2d 667 (CA–2, 1963).

**55.**  § 545(b)(3).

**56.**  § 545(b)(4).

**57.**  § 545(b)(6).

**58.**  § § 561(a)(1) and 562.

**59.**  § 562(c).

**60.**  Refer to Chapter 4 and *Henry Schwartz Corp.,* 60 T.C. 728 (1973).

**61.**  Reg. § 1.562–1(a). *Fulman v. U. S.,* 78–1 USTC ¶ 9247, 41 AFTR2d 78–698, 98 S.Ct. 841 (USSC, 1978).

year or (2) 20 percent of the total dividends distributed during the tax year.[62] Reasonable cause may not be used to overcome the 20 percent limitation even if the taxpayer relied upon incorrect advice given by an accountant.[63]

The consent dividend procedure involves a hypothetical distribution of the corporate income taxed to the shareholders. Since the consent dividend is taxable, a dividends paid deduction is allowed. The shareholder's basis in his or her stock is increased by the consent dividend (i. e., a contribution to capital), and a subsequent actual distribution of the consent dividend might be taxed. The consent election is filed by the shareholders at any time not later than the due date of the corporate tax return.[64] The consent dividend is considered distributed by the corporation on the last day of the tax year and is included in the gross income of the shareholder in the tax year in which or with which the tax year of the corporation ends.[65] The obvious disadvantage of this special election is that the shareholders must pay taxes on dividends they do not actually receive. However, if cash is not available for dividend distributions, the consent dividend route is a logical alternative.

> **Example 17.** Q Corporation, a calendar year taxpayer solely owned by T, is a PHC. Dividends of $30,000 must be paid to avoid the PHC tax, but the company has a poor cash position. T elects the consent dividend treatment under § 565, and he is taxed on $30,000 of dividends. The shareholder's basis in Q Corporation stock is increased by $30,000 as a result of this special election. Thus, the corporation does not incur the PHC tax, but T is taxed even though he receives no cash from the corporation with which to pay such tax.

Even after a corporation has been classified as a PHC, a belated dividend distribution made in a subsequent tax year can avoid the PHC penalty tax. This deficiency dividend provision allows the payment of a dividend within 90 days after the determination of the PHC tax deficiency for a prior tax year. A determination occurs when a decision of a court is final, a closing agreement under § 7121 is signed, or a written agreement is signed between the taxpayer and a District Director.[66] Note that the dividend distribution cannot be made before the determination or after the running of the 90-day time period.[67] Furthermore, the deficiency dividend procedure does not relieve the taxpayer of interest, additional amounts, or assessable penalties computed with respect to the PHC tax.[68]

---

**62.** § § 563(b) and 543(a)(2)(B)(ii).

**63.** *Kenneth Farmer Darrow,* 64 T.C. 217 (1975).

**64.** Reg. § 1.565–1(b)(3).

**65.** Reg. § 1.565–1(b)(1).

**66.** Reg. § 1.547–2(b).

**67.** See *Leck Co., Inc. v. U. S.,* 73–2 USTC ¶ 9694, 32 AFTR2d 73–5891 (D.Ct.Minn., 1973), in which the taxpayer made distributions prior to the determination of the PHC tax liability and was denied deficiency dividend treatment. However, see *Hanco Distributing, Inc. v. U. S.,* 73–2 USTC ¶ 9632, 32 AFTR2d 73–5485 (D.Ct.Utah, 1973). In this case, the taxpayer was allowed deficiency treatment, although the letter of the law was, by mistake, not followed.

**68.** § 547(a).

A dividend carryover from two prior years may be available to reduce the adjusted taxable income of a PHC. When the dividends paid by a company in its prior years exceed the company's adjusted taxable income for such years, the excess amount may be deducted in the current year. See § 564(b) for the manner of computing this dividend carryover and Figure II for a summary of dividends paid deductions.

**Figure II**

DIVIDENDS PAID DEDUCTION

| Type of Dividend | Availability | Timing | Statutory Location | Effect on Shareholders |
|---|---|---|---|---|
| Current year | Both § 531 and § 541 | By end of year. | § 561(a)(1) | Reduction in ATI and UPHC. |
| Two and one-half month grace period* | Both | On or before the 15th day of the 3rd month after end of year. | § § 563(a) and (b) | Reduction in ATI and UPHC. |
| Consent dividend | Both | Not later than due date of corporate tax return. | § 565(a) | Treated as a dividend as of end of tax year and given back as a contribution to capital. |
| Dividend carryover | PHC | Not later than due date of the corporate tax return. | § 564 | Reduction in UPHCI. |
| Deficiency dividend | PHC | Within 90 days after determination of PHC tax deficiency. | § 547 | Treated as if dividend paid in offending year. No impact on interest and penalties. |

*Under the § 531 tax, dividends paid within the first two and one-half months of the succeeding year must be carried back to the preceding year. In the case of the § 541 tax, the carryback is optional—some or all of the dividends can be deducted in the year paid. The 20% limit on carrybacks applicable to § 541 [see § 563(a)] does not cover § 531 situations.

*Personal Holding Company Planning Model.* Some of the complex personal holding company provisions may be developed into a flow chart format. Figure III and Figure IV provide a personal holding company planning model and the rules for the rent exclusion test, respectively.

*Computation Illustrated.* After the appropriate adjustments have been made to corporate taxable income and the sum of the dividends paid has been subtracted, the resulting figure is undistributed PHC income (UPHC income). The undistributed PHC income is multiplied by the 50

**Figure III\***
## PERSONAL HOLDING COMPANY PLANNING MODEL

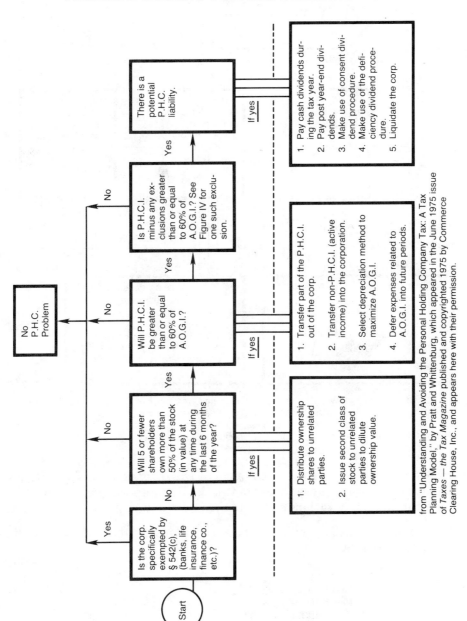

from "Understanding and Avoiding the Personal Holding Company Tax: A Tax Planning Model," by Pratt and Whittenburg, which appeared in the June 1975 issue of *Taxes — the Tax Magazine* published and copyrighted 1975 by Commerce Clearing House, Inc., and appears here with their permission.

**Figure IV\***
RENT EXCLUSION TEST

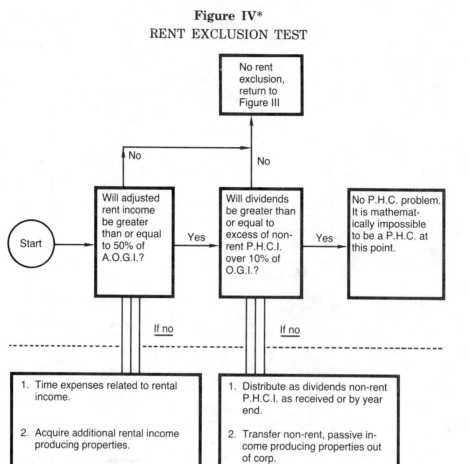

\* from "Understanding and Avoiding the Personal Holding Company Tax: A Tax Planning Model," by Pratt and Whittenburg, which appeared in the June 1975 issue of *Taxes — the Tax Magazine* published and copyrighted 1975 by Commerce Clearing House, Inc., and appears here with their permission.

percent tax rate to obtain the PHC tax. The tax revenue from the PHC tax may be small, but the mere threat of this confiscatory tax prompts owners to monitor their corporations and take the necessary steps to avoid the tax.

**Example 18.** X Corporation had the following items of income and expense in 1986:

| | |
|---|---:|
| Dividend income | $ 40,000 |
| Rent income | 150,000 |
| Depreciation expense | 40,000 |
| Mortgage interest | 30,000 |
| Real estate taxes | 30,000 |
| Salaries | 20,000 |
| Dividends paid (three shareholders) | 20,000 |
| Corporate income tax liability (§ 11) | 5,730 |

Ordinary gross income would be $190,000 ($40,000 + $150,000), and AOGI would be $90,000 ($190,000 − $40,000 − $30,000 − $30,000). Taxable income is $36,000, computed as follows:

| | | | |
|---|---|---:|---:|
| Rent income | | | $ 150,000 |
| Dividend income | | | 40,000 |
| | | | $ 190,000 |
| Less: | Depreciation expense | $40,000 | |
| | Mortgage interest | 30,000 | |
| | Real estate taxes | 30,000 | |
| | Salaries | 20,000 | 120,000 |
| | | | $ 70,000 |
| Less: | Dividends received deduction | | |
| | ($40,000 × 85%) | | 34,000 |
| Taxable income | | | $ 36,000 |

The adjusted income from rents is $50,000 ($150,000 − $100,000). The corporation does meet the 50% rental income test, since $50,000 is greater than 50% of AOGI ($90,000 × 50% = $45,000). But the corporation did not pay at least $21,000 of dividends (nonrental PHC income $40,000 − $19,000 = $21,000); therefore, the 10% rental income test is not met, and the rental income is classified as PHC income. Since all income is passive, this corporation is a PHC. The PHC tax of $22,135 would be calculated as follows:

| | | |
|---|---|---:|
| Taxable income | | $ 36,000 |
| Plus: | Dividends received deduction | |
| | ($40,000 × 85%) | 34,000 |
| | | $ 70,000 |
| Less: | § 11 tax | 5,730 |
| | | $ 64,270 |
| Less: | Dividends paid | 20,000 |
| Undistributed PHCI | | $ 44,270 |
| | | × .50 |
| PHC tax liability | | $ 22,135 |

**Example 19.** Assume in Example 18 that $22,000 of dividends are paid to the shareholders (instead of $20,000). In this case, the rental income is not PHC income because the 10% test is met ($22,000 is equal to or greater than the nonrental PHC income in excess of 10% of OGI). Thus, an increase of at least $2,000 in the dividends paid in Example 18 avoids the $22,135 PHC tax liability.

# COMPARISON OF SECTIONS 531 AND 541

A review of several important distinctions between the penalty tax on the unreasonable accumulation of earnings (§ 531) and the tax on personal holding companies (§ 541) will set the stage for the presentation of tax planning considerations applicable to the § 541 tax.

—Unlike § 531, there is no element of intent necessary for the imposition of the § 541 tax.[69] This makes § 541 a real trap for the unwary.

—The imposition of the § 541 tax is not affected by the past history of the corporation. Thus, it could be just as applicable to a newly formed corporation as to one that has been in existence for many years. Obviously, such is not the case with the § 531 tax; past accumulations have a direct bearing on the determination of the accumulated earnings credit. In this sense, younger corporations are less vulnerable to the § 531 tax, since complete insulation generally is guaranteed until accumulations exceed $250,000.

—Although one could conclude that both taxes pose threats for closely-held corporations, the stock ownership test of § 542(a)(2) makes this very explicit with regard to the § 541 tax. However, publicly held corporations can be subject to the § 531 tax if corporate policy is dominated by certain shareholders who are using the corporate form to avoid income taxes on dividends through the accumulation of corporate profits.[70]

—Sufficient dividend distributions can negate both taxes. In the case of § 531, however, such dividends must be distributed on a timely basis. Both taxes allow a two and one-half month grace period and provide for the consent dividend procedure.[71] Only the § 541 tax allows the deficiency dividend procedure.

—Differences in reporting procedures arise because the § 541 tax is a self-assessed tax; the § 531 tax is not. For example, if a corporation is a personal holding company, it must file a Schedule PH along with its Form 1120 (the corporate income tax return) for the year involved. Failure to file the Schedule PH can result in the imposition of interest and penalties and also brings into play a special six-year statute of limitations for the assessment of the § 541 tax.[72] On the other hand, the § 531 tax is assessed by the IRS and consequently requires no reporting procedures on the part of the corporate taxpayer.

---

**69.** In light of the Supreme Court decision in *Donruss* (refer to Footnote 3 and the text thereto), one wonders what role, if any, intent will play in the future in aiding taxpayers to avoid the § 531 tax. In this connection, see the dissenting opinion in this decision issued by Justice Harlan.

**70.** § 531(c).

**71.** Under the § 531 tax, dividends paid within the first two and one-half months of the succeeding year *must* be carried back to the preceding year. In the case of the § 541 tax, the carryback is optional—some or all of the dividends can be deducted in the year paid. The 20% limit on carrybacks applicable to § 541 [see § 563(a)] does not cover § 531 situations.

**72.** § 6501(f). See also Chapter 14.

| ✓ | TAX PLANNING CONSIDERATIONS |
|---|---|

## THE § 531 TAX

*Justifying the Accumulations.* The key defense against imposition of the § 531 tax is a successful assertion that the accumulations are necessary to meet the reasonable needs of the business. Several points should be kept in mind:

—To the extent possible, the justification for the accumulation should be documented. If, for example, the corporation plans to acquire additional physical facilities for use in its trade or business, the minutes of the board of directors' meetings should reflect the decision. Furthermore, such documentation should take place during the period of accumulation. This may require some foresight on the part of the taxpayer, but meaningful planning to avoid a tax problem should not be based on what happens after the issue has been raised by an agent as the result of an audit. In the case of a profitable closely-held corporation that accumulates some or all of its profits, the parties might well operate under the assumption that § 531 is always a potential issue. Recognition of a tax problem at an early stage is the first step in a satisfactory resolution.

—Keep in mind that multiple reasons for making an accumulation are not only permissible but invariably advisable. Suppose, for example, a manufacturing corporation plans to expand its plant. It would not be wise to stop with the cost of such expansion as the only justification for all accumulations. What about further justification based on the corporation's working capital requirements as determined under the *Bardahl* formula or some variation thereof? Other reasons for making the accumulation may well be present and should be recognized.

—The reasons for the accumulation should be sincere and, once established, pursued to the extent feasible.

**Example 20.** In 19X0 the board of directors of S Corporation decide to accumulate $1,000,000 to fund the replacement of S's plant. Five years pass, and no steps are taken to initiate construction.

**Example 21.** In 19X0 the board of directors of Y Corporation decide to accumulate $1,000,000 to fund the replacement of Y's plant. In the ensuing five-year period, the following steps are taken: a site selection committee is appointed (19X1); a site is chosen (19X2); the site (i. e., land) is purchased (19X3); an architect is retained, and plans are drawn up for the new plant (19X4); bids are requested and submitted for the construction of the new plant (19X5).

Compare Examples 20 and 21. Quite obviously Y Corporation is in a much better position to justify the accumulation. Even though the plant has not yet been replaced some five years after the accumulations began, the progress toward its ultimate construction speaks for itself. On the other hand, S Corporation may be hard-pressed to prove the sincerity of its objective for the accumulations in light of its failure to follow through on the projected replacement.

—The amount of the accumulation should be realistic under the circumstances.

**Example 22.** W Corporation plans to replace certain machinery at an estimated cost of $500,000. The original machinery was purchased for $300,000 and, because of $250,000 in depreciation deducted for tax purposes, possesses a present book value of $50,000. How much of an accumulation can be justified for the replacement to avoid the § 531 tax? At first blush, one might consider $500,000 as the appropriate amount, since this represents the estimated replacement cost of the machinery. But what about the $250,000 in depreciation that W Corporation has already deducted? If it is counted again as part of a reasonable accumulation, a double tax benefit results. Only $250,000 [i. e., $50,000 (the unrecovered cost of the old machinery) + $200,000 (the additional outlay necessary)] can be justified as the appropriate amount for an accumulation.[73]

**Example 23.** During the current year, a competitor files a $2,000,000 patent infringement suit against Z Corporation. Competent legal counsel advises Z Corporation that the suit is groundless. Under such conditions, the corporation can hardly justify accumulating $2,000,000 because of the pending lawsuit.

—Since the § 531 tax is imposed on an annual basis, justification for accumulations may vary from year to year.[74]

**Example 24.** For calendar years 19X1 and 19X2, R Corporation was able to justify large accumulations due to a pending additional income tax assessment. In early 19X3 the assessment is settled and paid. After the settlement, R Corporation can no longer consider the assessment as a reasonable anticipated need of the business.

*Danger of Loans to Shareholders.* The presence of loans made by a corporation to its shareholders often raises the § 531 issue. If this same corporation has a poor dividend-paying record, it becomes particularly vulnerable. When one recalls that the avowed goal of the § 531 tax is to force certain corporations to distribute dividends, the focus becomes clear. If a corporation can spare funds for loans to shareholders, it certainly has the capacity to pay dividends. Unfortunately, the presence of such loans can cause other tax problems for the parties.

---

**73.** *Battelstein Investment Co. v. U. S.,* 71–1 USTC ¶ 9227, 27 AFTR2d 71–713, 442 F.2d 87 (CA–5, 1971).
**74.** Compare *Hardin's Bakeries, Inc. v. Martin, Jr.,* 67–1 USTC ¶ 9253, 19 AFTR2d 647, 293 F.Supp. 1129 (D.Ct.Miss., 1967), with *Hardin v. U. S.,* 70–2 USTC ¶ 9676, 26 AFTR2d 70–5852 (D.Ct.Miss., 1970), aff'd., rev'd., rem'd. by 72–1 USTC ¶ 9464, 29 AFTR2d 72–1446, 461 F.2d 865 (CA–5, 1972).

**Example 25.** During the year in question, Q Corporation made advances of $120,000 to its sole shareholder, T. Although prosperous and maintaining substantial accumulations, Q Corporation has never paid a dividend. Under these circumstances, the IRS could move in either of two directions. The Service could assess the § 531 tax against Q Corporation for its unreasonable accumulation of earnings. Alternatively, the IRS could argue that the advances were not bona fide loans but, instead, taxable dividends.[75] Such a dual approach places the taxpayers in a somewhat difficult position. If, for example, they contend that the advance was a bona fide loan, T avoids dividend income but Q Corporation becomes vulnerable to the imposition of the § 531 tax.[76] On the other hand, a concession that the advance was not a loan hurts T but helps Q Corporation avoid the penalty tax.

*Role of Dividends.* The relationship between dividend distribution and the § 531 tax needs further clarification. It would be helpful to pose and answer several questions. First, can the payment of enough dividends completely avoid the § 531 tax? The answer must be in the affirmative because of the operation of § 535. Recall that this provision defines accumulated taxable income as *taxable income* [adjusted by § 535(b)] *minus the sum of the dividends paid deduction* (defined in § 561) *and the accumulated earnings credit* [defined in § 535(c)]. Since the § 531 tax is imposed on accumulated taxable income, no tax would be due if the dividends paid and the accumulated earnings credit are large enough to offset taxable income. Sufficient dividends, therefore, will avoid the tax.[77] Second, can the payment of *some* dividends completely avoid the § 531 tax? As the question is worded, the answer must be *no.* Theoretically, even significant dividend distributions will not insulate a corporation from the tax.[78] From a practical standpoint, however, the payment of dividends indicates that the corporation is not being used exclusively to shield its shareholders from tax consequences. To the extent this reflects the good faith of the parties and the lack of tax avoidance motivation, it is a factor the IRS will consider with regard to the § 531 issue.

*Role of the S Corporation Election.* An S corporation election will circumvent the application of the § 531 tax.[79] However, the protection only covers the period of S corporation status and is not retroactive to years during which the entity was a regular corporation.

**Example 26.** P Corporation, a calendar year taxpayer, makes a timely and proper election under Subchapter S effective for tax year 19X8. Since its formation in 19X0, P Corporation has accumulated significant earnings and has never paid a dividend. The election pro-

---

75. Refer to the discussion of constructive dividends in Chapter 4.
76. *Ray v. U. S.,* 69–1 USTC ¶ 9334, 23 AFTR2d 69–1141, 409 F.2d 1322 (CA–6, 1969).
77. Such dividends must, however, be taxable to the shareholders. Nontaxable stock dividends issued under § 305(a) do not affect the dividends paid deduction.
78. In *Henry Van Hummell, Inc.* v. *Comm.,* 66–2 USTC ¶ 9610, 18 AFTR2d 5500, 364 F.2d 746 (CA–10, 1966), the § 531 tax was imposed even though the corporation paid out over 60% of its taxable income as dividends.
79. See Chapter 8.

tects the corporation from the imposition of the § 531 tax for year 19X8 and for whatever subsequent years it remains in effect. It would not, however, preclude the IRS from assessing the tax on P Corporation for those years open under the statute of limitations in which it qualified as a regular corporation.[80]

## AVOIDING THE § 541 TAX

The classification of a corporation as a personal holding company requires the satisfaction of *both* the stock ownership and the gross income tests. Obviously, then, failure to meet either of these two tests will avoid PHC status and the § 541 tax.

—The stock ownership test of § 542(a)(2) can be handled through a dispersion of stock ownership. Success might not be achieved, however, unless the tax planner watches the application of the stock attribution rules of § 544.

—Remember the following relationship when working with the gross income test:

$$\frac{\text{PHC income}}{\text{AOGI}} = 60\% \text{ or more}$$

Decreasing the numerator (PHC income) or increasing the denominator (AOGI) of the fraction will reduce the resulting percentage. Keeping the resulting percentage below 60 percent precludes classification as a personal holding company. To control PHC income, investments in low-yield growth securities are preferable to those that generate heavy interest or dividend income. Capital gains from the sale of such securities will not affect personal holding company status, since they are not included in either the numerator or the denominator of the fraction. Investments in tax-exempt securities are also attractive because the interest income therefrom, like capital gains, carries no effect in applying the gross income test.

—Income from personal service contracts may, under certain conditions, constitute PHC income.

**Example 27.** B, C, and D (all attorneys) are equal shareholders in X Company, a professional association engaged in the practice of law. E, a new client, retains X Company to pursue a legal claim. Under the terms of the retainer agreement, E designates B as the attorney who will perform the legal services. The suit is successful, and 30% of the judgment E recovers is paid to X Company as a fee. Since the parties have met all of the requirements of § 543(a)(7), the fee received by X Company is PHC income.[81]

---

80. The use of an S corporation election to avoid § 531 or § 541 would be of doubtful value. Since under S corporation status all corporate profits (whether or not distributed) are taxed to the shareholders, a similar result can be achieved by simply operating as a regular corporation and distributing actual and consent dividends.
81. The example presumes X Company will be treated as a corporation for Federal tax purposes. As noted in Chapter 2, this is the usual result of professional association status.

The result reached in Example 27 could have been avoided had B not been specifically designated in the retainer agreement as the party to perform the services.

—Rent income may or may not be PHC income. The relative amount of rent income is the key consideration. If

$$\frac{\text{Adjusted income from rents}}{\text{AOGI}} = 50\% \text{ or more}$$

and nonrent PHC income less 10 percent of OGI is distributed as a dividend, rent income will not be PHC income. Maximizing adjusted income from rents clearly will improve the situation for taxpayers. Since adjusted income from rents represents gross rents less expenses attributable thereto, a conservative approach in determining such expenses would be helpful. The taxpayer should be encouraged to minimize depreciation (e. g., choose straight-line over accelerated cost recovery method). This approach to the handling of expenses attributable to rental property has to be confusing to many taxpayers because it contradicts what is normally done to reduce income tax consequences.

—In some cases it may be possible to reduce personal holding company exposure by readjusting corporate structures.

**Example 28.** P Corporation carries on two principal activities: a rental business (approximately 49% of total gross receipts) and a finance operation (approximately 51% of total gross receipts). As presently constituted, P Corporation could well be classified as a personal holding company. (One cannot be sure without applying the stock ownership tests.) The gross income test is probably satisfied, since interest income from the finance operation and rents from the rental business are PHC income.[82] The separation of these two activities into multiple corporations would solve the problem.[83] The rents no longer are PHC income due to the 50% or more test of § 543(a)(2); the finance operation would be an excepted corporation to which the personal holding company tax does not apply.[84]

In the same vein, business combinations (e. g., mergers and consolidations) or the filing of a consolidated return by an affiliated group of corporations could be used to dilute the PHC income of one corporation with the income from operations of another to avoid meeting the gross income test.

Corporations in the process of liquidation could be particularly susceptible to the personal holding company tax for two reasons. Operating income may be low because the corporation is in the process of winding up its business. If passive investment income remains at the level maintained during periods of normal operations or perhaps increases, the corporation

---

**82.** See, for example, *Hilldun Corp.* v. *Comm.*, 69–1 USTC ¶ 9319, 23 AFTR2d 69–1090, 408 F.2d 1117 (CA–2, 1969).

**83.** The separation could be carried out as a nontaxable reorganization. Refer to Chapter 6.

**84.** Pursuant to § 542(c)(6), a lending or finance company is excepted under certain circumstances.

might satisfy the gross income test.[85] In addition, the parties may never realize that the corporation was a personal holding company until it has been completely liquidated. At this point, the tax can no longer be neutralized through the issuance of a deficiency dividend.[86] The apparent solution to the problem is to recognize the vulnerability of the corporation and keep it on the safe side of the gross income test. Good control can be obtained over the situation if the earlier corporate distributions in liquidation include those assets that generate PHC income.

Personal holding company status need not carry tragic tax consequences if the parties are aware of the issue and take appropriate steps. Since the tax is imposed on undistributed personal holding company income, properly timed dividend distributions will neutralize the tax and avoid interest and penalties. Also, as long as a corporation holds PHC status, the § 531 tax cannot be imposed.

> **Example 29.** X Corporation is owned entirely by two sisters, R and S (ages 86 and 88, respectively). X Corporation's major assets comprise investments in low-yield and high-growth securities, unimproved real estate, and tax-exempt bonds, all of which have a realizable value of $500,000. The basis of the stock in X Corporation to each sister is $50,000.

The liquidation of X Corporation (a frequent solution to undesired PHC status) would be disastrous to the two sisters. As noted in the discussion of § 331 in Chapter 5, such liquidation would result in the recognition of a capital gain of $400,000.[87] In this case, therefore, it would be preferable to live with personal holding company status. Considering the nature of the assets held by X Corporation, this may not be difficult to do. Keep in mind that the interest from the tax-exempt bonds is not PHC income. Should X Corporation wish to sell any of its investments, the long-term capital gain that would result is not PHC income. The PHC tax on any other income (i. e., the dividends from the securities) can be controlled through enough dividend distributions to reduce undistributed PHCI to zero. Furthermore, as long as X Corporation remains a PHC, it is insulated from the § 531 tax (the imposition of which would be highly probable in this case).

The liquidation of X Corporation should await the deaths of R and S and consequently should be carried out by their estates or heirs.[88] By virtue of the application of § 1014 (see Chapter 12), the income tax basis in the stock would be stepped up to its fair market value on the date of death and much, if not all, of the capital gain potential presently existing would be eliminated.

---

**85.** Investment or PHC income might increase if the corporation, pending complete dissolution, invested some or all of the proceeds from the sale of its operating assets.

**86.** *Michael C. Callan,* 54 T.C. 1514 (1970), and *L.C. Bohart Plumbing & Heating Co., Inc.,* 64 T.C. 602 (1975).

**87.** Although long-term capital gains are entitled to a 60% deduction, the bunching effect has to be taken into account. Also, a large amount of capital gain triggers the imposition of the alternative minimum tax.

**88.** A redemption of stock to pay death taxes and administration expenses might well be a viable alternative to a liquidation of the corporation. Refer to the discussion of § 303 in Chapter 4.

## PROBLEM MATERIALS

### Discussion Questions

1. List some valid business reasons for accumulating funds in a closely-held corporation.

2. Explain the purpose(s) underlying the creation of the accumulated earnings penalty tax and the personal holding company tax.

3. Explain the consent dividend provision of § 565.

4. A merger of two corporations could result in the imposition of the § 531 tax upon the surviving corporation. Is this possible? Explain.

5. Explain the *Bardahl* formula. How could it be improved?

6. Why may a corporation not wish to include Federal income taxes into the calculation of the *Bardahl* formula (i. e., the accounts payable turnover)?

7. Why is it desirable for a closely-held corporation to maintain a good dividends record (i. e., pay some dividends each year)?

8. May a holding or investment company accumulate more than $250,000 of earnings if the company can justify that such excess is necessary to meet the reasonable needs of the business?

9. How can human resource accounting be used in an accumulated earnings situation?

10. A holding company's only income item during 19X6 is a $300,000 long-term capital gain. Calculate any accumulated earnings penalty tax.

11. Can the IRS impose both the PHC tax and the accumulated earnings tax upon a construction company?

12. ATI = taxable income ± certain adjustments + the dividends paid deduction − the accumulated earnings credit. Please comment.

13. In making the "certain adjustments" (refer to Question 12) necessary in arriving at ATI, which of the following items should be added (+), should be subtracted (−), or will have no effect (NE) on taxable income:

    (a) A nontaxable stock dividend distributed by the corporation to its shareholders.

    (b) Corporate income tax incurred and paid.

    (c) Charitable contributions paid in the amount of 10% of taxable income.

    (d) A net operating loss carried over from a prior year that was deducted.

    (e) The 85% dividends received deduction.

14. If a corporation has a § 11 tax of 46% and also incurs an accumulated earnings tax of 27.5%, what is the aggregate tax rate? An accumulated earnings tax of 38.5%?

15. Ms. J (a widow) and Mr. K (a bachelor) are both shareholders in H Corporation (closely-held). If they elope during the year, what possible effect, if any, could it have on H Corporation's vulnerability to the § 541 tax?

16. M Corporation is a consulting firm. Its entire outstanding stock is owned by three individuals. M Corporation entered into a contract with T Corporation to perform certain consulting services in consideration of which T was to pay M $65,000. The individual who was to perform the services was not designated by name or description in the contract, and no one but M had the right to designate such person. Does the $65,000 constitute personal holding company income?

17. N is a U. S. corporation wholly owned by B, a nonresident alien individual. Ninety-two percent of N's gross income consists of interest from loans to U. S. individuals and corporations. The remainder of N's gross income is derived from buying, selling, and leasing U. S. real property. In 1986, N's entire gross income consists of rents and interest received from sources within the United States. N is neither a lending nor a finance company under § 542(c)(6). Does the exception in § 542(c)(7) protect this corporation from the personal holding company penalty tax? (Hint: See Rev.Rul. 85–140, I.R.B. No. 36, 9)

18. Which of the following income items could be personal holding company income:

    (a) Dividends.

    (b) Interest.

    (c) Rental income.

    (d) Sales of merchandise.

    (e) Annuities.

    (f) Mineral royalties.

    (g) Copyright royalties.

    (h) Produced film rents.

    (i) Gain from sale of securities.

19. D, a shareholder in H Corporation, dies, and under his will the stock passes to his children. If H Corporation is a personal holding company, what effect, if any, will D's death have on the continuation of this status?

20. How is AOGI calculated?

21. Diagram (or flow chart) the rent exclusion tests for purposes of the PHC tax.

22. The election to capitalize (rather than to depreciate) certain expenses to rental property could make a difference in determining whether or not the corporate lessor is a personal holding company. How could this be so?

23. If the 50% test as to rents is satisfied, the § 541 tax cannot be imposed upon the corporation. Do you agree? Why or why not?

24. General Motors Corporation has no difficulty avoiding either the § 531 tax or the § 541 tax. Explain.

25. Four individuals start a software company in 1984 and lose $1,000,000 the first year. They do not sell a product but usually license products to their customers. In 1985, the company breaks even, but in 1986 the company makes a profit of $1,000,000. Discuss.

26. The payment of enough dividends can avoid either the § 531 or the § 541 tax. Explain.

27. Explain the deficiency dividend election.

28. If a corporation has a § 11 tax of 46% and also incurs a PHC tax, what is the aggregate tax rate?

29. Relate the following points to the avoidance of the § 531 tax:

    (a) Documentation of justification for the accumulation.

    (b) Multiple justifications for the accumulation.

    (c) Follow-up on the established justification for the accumulation.

    (d) Loans by the corporation to its shareholders.

    (e) The corporation's record of substantial dividend payments.

    (f) An S corporation election.

30. Relate the following points to the avoidance of the § 541 tax:
    (a) Sale of stock to outsiders.
    (b) An increase in AOGI.
    (c) A decrease in PHC income.
    (d) Long-term capital gains recognized by the corporation.
    (e) Corporate investment in tax-exempt bonds.
    (f) Income from personal service contracts.
    (g) The choice of straight-line depreciation for rental property owned by the corporation.
    (h) A merger of several corporations.
    (i) The liquidation of a corporation.

31. Compare the § 531 tax to the § 541 tax on the basis of the following items:
    (a) The element of intent.
    (b) Applicability of the tax to a newly created corporation.
    (c) Applicability of the tax to a publicly held corporation.
    (d) The two and one-half month rule with respect to the dividends paid deduction.
    (e) The availability of the deficiency dividend procedure.
    (f) Procedures for reporting and paying the tax.

## Problems

1. A nonservice corporation has accumulated earnings and profits of $225,000 as of December 31, 19X4. The company has earnings for the taxable year 19X5 of $100,000 and has a dividends paid deduction under § 561 of $30,000. The corporation determines that the earnings for the tax year that may be retained for the reasonable needs of the business amount to $55,000, and it is entitled to a $5,000 § 535(b)(6) deduction. Calculate the accumulated earnings credit for the tax year ending December 31, 19X5.

2. A calendar year medical services corporation has accumulated earnings and profits of $90,000 on January 1, 19X4. For the calendar year of 19X4, the corporation has taxable income of $100,000 with an income tax liability of $25,750. This corporation has no reasonable needs that justify an accumulation of its earnings and profits. Calculate the amount vulnerable to the accumulated earnings penalty tax.

3. In 19X5 Corporation M, a retail company, retained $60,000 for its reasonable business needs. The company had a long-term capital gain of $20,000 and a net short-term capital loss of $15,000, with a resulting capital gain tax of $1,400. The accumulated earnings and profits at the end of 19X4 was $260,000. On January 25, 19X5, a taxable dividend of $80,000 was paid. Calculate the accumulated earnings credit for 19X5.

4. A manufacturing corporation had accumulated earnings and profits on January 1, 19X4, of $250,000. Its taxable income for the year 19X4 was $75,000, on which it owed accrued income taxes of $15,750. The corporation paid no dividends during the year. There were no other adjustments to determine accumulated taxable income. Assume that the Claims Court determined that the corporation is subject to the accumulated earnings tax and that the reasonable needs of the business required retained earnings in the total amount of $256,500. Determine the amount subject to the accumulated earnings tax and explain why.

5. A construction corporation is accumulating a significant amount of earnings and profits. Although the corporation is closely-held, it is not a personal holding company. The following facts relate to the tax year 19X4:

   —Taxable income, $450,000.

   —Dividend income from a qualified domestic corporation, $30,000.

   —Dividends paid in 19X4, $70,000.

   —Consent dividends, $35,000.

   —Dividends paid on 2/1/X5, $5,000.

   —Accumulated earnings credit, $10,000.

   —Excess charitable contributions of $9,000 (i.e., the portion in excess of the amount allowed as a deduction in computing the § 11 tax).

   —Net capital loss adjustment of $3,000.

   Compute both the corporate income tax and any accumulated earnings tax.

6. The following facts relate to a closely-held legal services corporation's 1986 tax year:

   | | |
   |---|---:|
   | Net taxable income | $ 400,000 |
   | Federal income taxes | 163,750 |
   | Excess charitable contributions | 20,000 |
   | Capital loss adjustment | 20,000 |
   | Dividends received | 120,000 |
   | Dividends paid | 60,000 |
   | Accumulated earnings, 1/1/86 | 130,000 |

   (a) Assume that this is not a personal holding company. Calculate any accumulated earnings tax.

   (b) Can the deficiency dividend procedure be applicable to the accumulated earnings tax?

7. Which of the following purposes can be used by a corporation to justify accumulations to meet the reasonable needs of the business:

   (a) X Corporation creates a reserve for a depression that might occur in 1988.

   (b) P Corporation has an extraordinarily high working-capital need.

   (c) Q Corporation, a manufacturing company, invests in several oil and gas drilling funds.

   (d) N, a hotel, is being sued because of a structural accident that injured 32 people.

   (e) M Corporation is considering establishing a sinking fund to retire some bonds.

   (f) Z Corporation carries six keyman life insurance policies.

   (g) T Corporation makes loans to R Corporation, an unrelated party who is having financial problems and who is a key customer.

   (h) B Corporation agrees to retire 20% of its outstanding stock without curtailment of its business.

8. A wholly owned motor freight corporation has permitted its earnings to accumulate. The company has no inventory but wishes to use the *Bardahl* formula to determine the amount of operating capital required for a business cycle. The following facts are relevant:

| | |
|---|---:|
| Yearly revenues | $ 3,300,000 |
| Average accounts receivable | 300,000 |
| Yearly expenses | 3,500,000 |
| Average accounts payable | 213,000 |

(a) Determine the turnover rate of average accounts receivable.

(b) Determine the number of days in the accounts receivable cycle.

(c) Determine the expenses for one accounts receivable cycle.

(d) Determine the number of days in the accounts payable cycle.

(e) Determine the nondeferred expenses for the accounts receivable cycle.

(f) Determine the operating capital needed for one business cycle.

(g) Explain why the time allowed a taxpayer for the payment of accounts payable should be taken into consideration in applying the *Bardahl* formula.

9. Indicate in each of the following independent situations whether or not the corporation involved has any accumulated taxable income and, if so, the amount (assume the corporation is not a mere holding or investment company):

| | F<br>Corporation | G<br>Corporation |
|---|---:|---:|
| Taxable income | $ 150,000 | $ 500,000 |
| Accrued Federal income taxes | 48,750 | 218,150 |
| Capital loss adjustment | 1000 | |
| Net LTCG | | 42,000 |
| Tax on LTCG | | 11,760 |
| Contributions in excess of 10% | 10,000 | |
| NOL deduction | 24,000 | |
| 85% dividends received deduction | | 40,000 |
| Dividends paid deduction | 4,000 | 8,000 |
| Accumulated earnings credit | 135,000 | 102,000 |

10. March is the longest operating cycle for U Corporation, which has reasonable business needs of $30,000 in addition to the working capital required for one operating cycle. Certain additional information is provided as follows:

| | |
|---|---:|
| Accounts receivable—March | 120,000 |
| Inventory—March | 160,000 |
| Accounts payable—March | 101,000 |
| Cost of goods sold | 1,000,000 |
| Other expenses (less depreciation) | 100,000 |
| Depreciation | 90,000 |
| Sales | 2,000,000 |
| Dividends paid | 7,000 |
| Accumulated earnings (beginning) | 180,000 |
| Accrued Federal income taxes | 228,000 |

Determine the operating cycle needs of U Corporation without considering accrued Federal income taxes as an operating expense.

11. S Corporation is having accumulated earnings problems but has no accounts receivable. T, the corporation's accountant, provides you with the following information:

Year-end balances:

| | | |
|---|---|---|
| Current assets | | |
| Cash | | $ 25,000 |
| Inventory (average) | | 72,000 |
| | | $ 97,000 |
| Current liabilities | | 17,000 |
| Working capital available | | $ 80,000 |

Income statement:

| | | |
|---|---|---|
| Gross sales | | $ 330,000 |
| Less: Sales returns and allowances | | 30,000 |
| | | $ 300,000 |
| Less: Cost of goods sold | $ 170,000 | |
| Sales and administrative | | |
| expenses | 45,000 | |
| Depreciation | 20,000 | |
| Income taxes | 15,000 | 250,000 |
| Net income | | $ 50,000 |

Calculate the working capital *required* for the corporation if purchases total $140,000.

12. The stock of P Corporation is owned as follows:

| | |
|---|---|
| S Corporation (wholly owned by K) | 100 shares |
| K's wife | 100 shares |
| K's partner | 100 shares |
| K's wife's sister | 100 shares |
| A | 50 shares |
| B | 30 shares |
| C | 20 shares |
| Unrelated individuals with 10 or fewer shares | 500 shares |
| Total | 1000 shares |

Do five or fewer individuals own more than 50% of P Corporation?

13. N Corporation, at some time during the last half of the taxable year, had 1,800 shares of outstanding stock, 450 of which were held by various individuals having no relationship to one another and none of whom were partners. The remaining 1,350 shares were held by 51 shareholders as follows:

| Relationship | | Shares | | Shares | | Shares | | Shares | | Shares |
|---|---|---|---|---|---|---|---|---|---|---|
| An individual . | A | 100 | B | 20 | C | 20 | D | 20 | E | 20 |
| His father .... | AF | 10 | BF | 10 | CF | 10 | DF | 10 | EF | 10 |
| His wife ..... | AW | 10 | BW | 40 | CW | 40 | DW | 40 | EW | 40 |
| His brother .. | AB | 10 | BB | 10 | CB | 10 | DB | 10 | EB | 10 |
| His son...... | AS | 10 | BS | 40 | CS | 40 | DS | 40 | ES | 40 |
| His daughter by former marriage (son's half-sister) . | ASHS | 10 | BSHS | 40 | CSHS | 40 | DSHS | 40 | ESHS | 40 |

| Relationship | Shares | | Shares | | Shares | | Shares | | Shares | |
|---|---|---|---|---|---|---|---|---|---|---|
| His brother's wife ....... | ABW | 10 | BBW | 10 | CBW | 10 | DBW | 160 | EBW | 10 |
| His wife's father ..... | AWF | 10 | BWF | 10 | CWF | 110 | DWF | 10 | EWF | 10 |
| His wife's brother .... | AWB | 10 | BWB | 10 | CWB | 10 | DWB | 10 | EWB | 10 |
| His wife's brother's wife ....... | AWBW | 10 | BWBW | 10 | CWBW | 10 | DWBW | 10 | EWBW | 110 |
| His partner .... | AP | 10 | — | — | — | — | — | — | — | — |

Is the stock ownership test of § 544 met for determining whether this corporation is a personal holding company?

14. A corporation has gross income of $20,000, which consists of $11,000 of rental income and $9,000 of dividend income. The corporation has $3,000 of rental income adjustments and pays $8,000 of dividends to its nine shareholders.

    (a) Calculate adjusted income from rents.

    (b) Calculate AOGI.

    (c) Is the so-called 50% test met? Show calculations.

    (d) Is the 10% rental income test met? Show calculations.

    (e) Is the corporation a personal holding company?

15. Assume one change in the situation in Problem 14. Rental income adjustments are decreased from $3,000 to $2,000. Answer the same questions as in Problem 14.

16. A corporation has interest income of $20,000, rental income of $60,000, and income from an operating business (not PHC income) of $30,000. Expenses in the amount of $15,000 relate directly to the rental income. Assume there are nine shareholders and the 10% test is met. Is this corporation a PHC? Explain.

17. A corporation has $10,000 of dividend income, $40,000 of gross income from rents, and $30,000 of personal service income (not PHC income). Expenses in the amount of $30,000 relate directly to the rental income. Assume there are eight shareholders and the 10% test is met. Is this corporation a PHC? Explain.

18. A corporation has gross income of $20,000, which consists of gross income from rent of $15,000, dividends of $1,500, a capital gain from the sale of securities of $1,000, and $2,500 from the sale of merchandise. Deductions directly related to the rent income total $10,000.

    (a) Calculate OGI.

    (b) Calculate AOGI.

    (c) Calculate adjusted income from rents.

    (d) Does the rental income constitute PHC income? Explain.

    (e) Is this corporation a PHC (assuming there are four shareholders)?

19. Assume the same facts as in Problem 18 except that divided income is $2,500 (rather than $1,500) and the corporation pays $500 of dividends to its shareholders. Answer the questions included in Problem 18.

20. T is the sole owner of a corporation. The following information is relevant to the corporation's tax year just ended:

| | |
|---|---:|
| Capital gain | $ 20,000 |
| Dividend income | 30,000 |
| Rental income | 130,000 |
| Rental expenses | 40,000 |
| Section 162 business expenses | 15,000 |
| Dividends paid | 12,000 |

(a) Calculate OGI.

(b) Calculate AOGI.

(c) Calculate adjusted income from rents.

(d) Calculate nonrental PHC income.

(e) Does this corporation meet the 50% rental income test? Explain.

(f) Does this corporation meet the 10% rental income test? Explain.

(g) Is this company a PHC?

(h) Would your answers change if $15,000 of dividends are paid?

21.  X Corporation has the following financial data for the tax year 19X4:

| | |
|---|---:|
| Rental income | $ 430,000 |
| Dividend income | 2,900 |
| Interest income | 50,000 |
| Operating income | 9,000 |
| Depreciation (rental warehouses) | 100,000 |
| Mortgage interest | 125,000 |
| Real estate taxes | 35,000 |
| Officers' salaries | 85,000 |
| Dividends paid | 2,000 |

(a) Calculate OGI.

(b) Calculate AOGI.

(c) Does X Corporation meet the rental test of § 543(a)(2)(A)?

(d) Does X Corporation meet the 10% dividend test of § 543(a)(2)(B)?

(e) How much in dividends could X Corporation pay within the two and one-half month grace period during 19X5?

(f) If the 19X4 corporate income tax return has not been filed, what would you suggest for X Corporation?

22.  Using the legend provided, classify each of the following statements accordingly:

*Legend*

A = relates only to the tax on unreasonable accumulation of earnings (i. e., the § 531 tax)

P = relates only to the personal holding company tax (i. e., the § 541 tax)

B = relates to both the § 531 tax and the § 541 tax

N = relates to neither the § 531 tax nor the § 541 tax

(a) The tax is applied to adjusted taxable income of the corporation.

(b) The tax is a self-assessed tax.

(c) An accumulation of funds for reasonable business purposes will help avoid the tax.

(d) A consent dividend mechanism can be used to avoid the tax.

(e) If the stock of the corporation is equally held by ten unrelated individuals, the tax cannot be imposed.

(f) Any charitable deduction in excess of the 10% limitation is allowed as a deduction before the tax is imposed.

(g) Gains from the sale or disposition of capital assets are not subject to the tax.

(h) A sufficient amount of rental income will cause the tax not to be imposed.

(i) A life insurance company would not be subject to the tax.

(j) A corporation with only dividend income would avoid the tax.

23. Determine whether the following factors or events will increase (+), decrease (−), or have no affect (NA) on the working capital needs of a corporation when calculating the *Bardahl* formula:

(a) Decrease in depreciation deduction.

(b) Use of peak inventory figure rather than average inventory.

(c) An increase in the annual cost of goods sold.

(d) Purchase of a tract of land for a future parking lot.

(e) Use of average receivables rather than peak receivables.

(f) An increase in annual net sales.

(g) An increase in accounts payable.

(h) An increase in the annual expenses.

(i) Gain on the sale of treasury stock.

24. The personal holding company tax is computed on an amount called undistributed personal holding company (UPHC) income. To arrive at UPHC income, certain adjustments are made to taxable income. Determine whether the following independent items are positive (+), negative (−), or no adjustment (NA):

(a) Federal income taxes on the accrual basis.

(b) Tax-free interest from Municipal Bonds.

(c) Charitable deductions in excess of 10%.

(d) Net capital gain minus any taxes.

(e) Dividends paid during the taxable year.

(f) 100% dividends received deduction.

(g) NOL carryforward from two tax years ago.

(h) Consent dividends under § 565.

25. Indicate in each of the following independent situations whether or not the corporation involved is a personal holding company (assume the stock ownership test is met):

|  | A Corporation | B Corporation | C Corporation | D Corporation |
|---|---|---|---|---|
| Sales of merchandise | $  8,000 | $    0 | $    0 | $  2,500 |
| Capital gains | 0 | 0 | 0 | 1,000 |
| Dividend income | 15,000 | 5,000 | 1,000 | 2,500 |
| Gross rental income | 10,000 | 5,000 | 9,000 | 15,000 |
| Expenses related to rents | 8,000 | 2,500 | 8,000 | 10,000 |
| Dividends paid | 0 | 0 | 0 | 500 |
| Personal holding company? (Circle Y for yes or N for no) | Y  N | Y  N | Y  N | Y  N |

26. Indicate in each of the following independent situations whether or not the corporation involved is a PHC (assume the stock ownership test is met):

|  | E Corporation | F Corporation | G Corporation | H Corporation |
|---|---|---|---|---|
| Sales of merchandise | $ 0 | $ 3,000 | $ 0 | $ 0 |
| Capital gains | 0 | 0 | 1,000 | 0 |
| Interest income | 20,000 | 4,800 | 2,000 | 60,000 |
| Gross rental income | 80,000 | 1,200 | 20,000 | 50,000 |
| Expenses related to rents | 60,000 | 1,000 | 10,000 | 0 |
| Dividends paid | 12,000 | 0 | 0 | 20,000 |
| Personal holding company? (Circle Y for yes or N for no) | Y  N | Y  N | Y  N | Y  N |

27. Calculate in each of the following independent situations the personal holding company tax liability:

|  | X Corporation | Y Corporation |
|---|---|---|
| Taxable income | $ 140,000 | $ 580,000 |
| Dividends received deduction | 37,000 | 70,000 |
| Contributions in excess of 10% | 4,000 | 10,000 |
| Federal income taxes | 33,850 | 240,000 |
| Net capital gain | 70,000 | 40,000 |
| Capital gain tax | 19,600 | 11,200 |
| NOL under § 172 |  | 12,000 |
| Current year dividends | 11,000 | 110,000 |
| Consent dividends |  | 25,000 |
| Two and one-half month dividends | 3,000 |  |

## Comprehensive Tax Return Problem

J and P are equal owners of Q, Inc. (79-8275912), a holding company in Greenville, N.C. In preparing to file Schedule PH (Form 1120) for this corporation, you gather the following data:

| | |
|---|---|
| Taxable income (line 28, Form 1120) | $ 530,000 |
| Dividends received | 200,000 |
| Interest income | 250,000 |
| Royalties from a patent | 126,000 |
| Annuities | 40,000 |
| Copyright royalties | 60,000 |
| Contributions in excess of 10% | 2,000 |
| Organization expenses | 25,000 |
| Federal tax liability accrued | 203,750 |
| NOL carryforward | 40,000 |
| Net capital gain | 110,000 |
| Dividends paid within 2½ months after end of year | 30,000 |
| Dividends paid during the year (after March 15) | 40,000 |
| Consent dividends | 60,000 |
| Dividends carryover | 20,000 |

From the preceding information, prepare Schedule PH. If any information is missing, make realistic assumptions.

## Research Problems

*Research Problem 1.* P Corporation, a closely-held corporation, owns all of the stock of S Corporation, with which it does not file a consolidated return. As of January 1, 19X0, P Corporation has a deficit in accumulated earnings and profits and anticipates no current earnings and profits for tax year 19X0. On the other hand, S Corporation has $700,000 in accumulated earnings and profits and expects current earnings and profits of at least $200,000. On July 1, 19X0, P Corporation borrows $200,000, from a local bank, using the stock in S Corporation as collateral for the loan. Shortly thereafter, P Corporation distributes the loan proceeds to its shareholders. S Corporation, although profitable in its past and current activities, has never paid a dividend.

(a) What are the hoped-for tax consequences of the loan and the distribution of the proceeds?

(b) What could go wrong in terms of what the taxpayers were trying to accomplish?

*Research Problem 2.* Dr. B owns 90% of the stock of Dental Services, Inc. Dr. B performs medical services under an employment contract with the corporation. He is the only dentist employed and is the only officer of the corporation actively engaged in the production of income. Dental Services, Inc. furnishes office space and equipment and employs a dental hygienist and a receptionist to assist Dr. B.

(a) Various patients receive dental care from Dr. B. Does Dental Services have personal holding company income under § 543(a)(7)?

(b) Suppose Patient J secures an absolute binding promise from Dr. B that the dentist will personally perform a root canal operation and that the dentist has no right to substitute another dentist. Would your answer change?

*Research Problem 3.* X owns 100% of both A and B Corporations. A Corporation's accumulated earnings for 1983, 1984, 1985, and 1986 were reflected almost entirely in liquid assets, which were used to obtain bonding on the construction work of the sister corporation, B. A Corporation itself undertook no construction work as a general contractor and paid no dividends during the three-year period. Both corporations entered into an indemnity agreement under which both would be liable to the bonding company for any loss suffered by the bonding company from the issuance of a bond to either of the corporations. A Corporation was merged into B Corporation in early January 1985. Assume that A Corporation would be subject to the accumulated earnings tax if the reasonable business needs of B Corporation are not considered. Would A Corporation be subject to the accumulated earnings tax in 1983, 1984, 1985, and 1986?

*Research Problem 4.* Y is the majority owner of B Corporation and S Corporation. B Corporation made interest-free loans to S Corporation during 1986. If a legitimate rate of interest had been charged, the interest income would cause B Corporation to be a personal holding company. As an adviser to this brother-sister group, discuss any possible tax risks.

*Research Problem 5.* During early 1987, P Corporation's controller discovers that the corporation is a personal holding company for 1986. He decides to use the deficiency dividend procedure under § 547 for avoiding the PHC tax. The company is short of cash. Can a consent dividend qualify for deficiency dividend treatment? Should the controller make a full disclosure of the liability for the PHC tax on the 1986 corporate tax return by filing a Schedule PH?

*Research Problem 6.* P Corporation owns 90% of S Corporation. X, an individual, owns all of the stock of P Corporation. During 1986, a cash distribution is made by S Corporation (the subsidiary) to shareholder X in exchange for P stock (the parent). Assume that this distribution is considered a distribution in redemption of P stock under § 304(a)(2). Can § 304(a)(2) generate dividend income to P (the parent) for PHC purposes?

*Research Problem 7.* V and S are equal shareholders of P Corporation. In 19X5 the corporation received gross rent of $5,000 from a 30-unit apartment building it owned. The company incurred depreciation, interest, and property tax expenses in the amount of $900 that were attributable to the building. The company also received $500 rent from a duplex it leased to V and S. The company incurred depreciation, interest, and property tax expenditures in the amount of $200 (attributable to the duplex). The company also had $3,000 gross income from a bookstore it owned and operated, and the company received dividend income of $1,000 from R Corporation. Discuss.

# S Corporations 8

## CHAPTER OBJECTIVES

—Provide an in-depth discussion of the rules governing S status.
—Describe those corporations that qualify for the S election.
—Discuss how the election must be made and, once made, how it can be lost.
—Explain the effect of the S election on the corporation and its shareholders.
—Describe the situations where S status is desirable or undesirable.

# GENERAL CONSIDERATIONS

Subchapter S[1] of the Internal Revenue Code of 1954 allows for the unique treatment of certain corporations for Federal income tax purposes. At the outset, it is important to stress that an S corporation is, in terms of legal characteristics under state law, no different from any other corporation. The election of S status, therefore, merely makes the operational provisions of § § 1361–1379 applicable as to the Federal income tax.

## ADVANTAGES OF THE CORPORATE FORM

Operating a business in the corporate form entails numerous tax and nontax advantages. Among the more important nontax advantages are the attributes of continuity of existence, free transferability of ownership interests, and limited liability. The corporation, possessing continuity of existence, will survive the withdrawal or death of any of its owners (i. e., shareholders). Thus, the corporation normally will continue to exist until such time as the shareholders decide upon its liquidation. Free transferability of ownership interests permits shareholders to dispose of stock in whatever manner they desire. This flexibility can be crucial in a family setting in which an individual wishes to shift some of the income from the business to related parties in lower income tax brackets. As noted in Chapter 9, this may be impossible to accomplish if the business is being operated in the partnership form. Often, the key nontax advantage the corporate form offers is the limited liability characteristic. If a corporation fails, a shareholder's loss is limited to the amount of the stock investment. When one contrasts this result with what could happen in a partnership setting, where all of a partner's personal assets may be at the mercy of the partnership's creditors, the disparity in treatment becomes quite clear.

## DISADVANTAGES OF THE CORPORATE FORM

Operating a business in the corporate form carries several distinct tax disadvantages. First, the system of double taxation materializes. Profits are taxed to the corporation as earned and to the shareholders when distributed as dividends. Second, losses suffered at the corporate level cannot be passed through to the shareholders. Such losses remain locked within

---

1. The Subchapter S Revision Act of 1982 labels a Subchapter S corporation as an "S corporation." It also designates regular corporations (i. e., those that have not elected S status) as "C corporations." C corporations are those that are governed by Subchapter C of the Code (§ § 301–386).

the corporation and are unavailable to the shareholders.[2] This last disadvantage would be of considerable importance in the formation of a new business where losses in the early years are often anticipated. In such situations, the owners of a business would like to receive the immediate tax advantage of such losses.

## SUBCHAPTER S IN PERSPECTIVE

Because of the tax disadvantages just noted, there is considerable support for the proposition that many persons have been deterred from using corporations, although they may have had good reasons (e. g., limited liability) for preferring this form of operation. In the interest of preventing tax considerations from interfering with the exercise of sound business judgment (i. e., whether to operate a business in the corporate form), Congress in 1958 enacted Subchapter S of the Code.[3]

Subchapter S (§ § 1361 through 1379) permits certain corporations to avoid the corporate income tax and enables them to pass through operating losses to their shareholders. It represents an attempt to achieve a measure of tax neutrality in resolving the difficult problem of whether a business should be conducted as a sole proprietorship, partnership, or corporation.

In dealing with the provisions of Subchapter S, certain observations should be kept in mind.

1. S corporation status is an elective provision. Failure to make the election will mean that the rules applicable to the taxation of corporations (i. e., Subchapter C status) and shareholders will apply (refer to Chapter 2).

2. S corporations are regular corporations in the legal sense. The S election encompasses only the Federal income tax consequences of electing corporations. In fact, many states do not recognize the S election, and in such cases, such corporations are subject to the state corporate income tax and whatever other state corporate taxes are imposed.

3. S corporations are not treated by Federal income tax law as either partnerships or regular corporations. The tax treatment is almost like partnership taxation, but it involves a unique set of tax rules.

4. Because Subchapter S is a relief provision, strict compliance with the applicable Code provisions generally has been required by both the IRS and the courts. Slight deviation from the various governing requirements may therefore lead to an undesirable and often unexpected tax result (e. g., the loss of the S election).

---

**2.** The losses might eventually materialize upon the sale of the stock or during the liquidation of the corporation. Such losses, however, probably would be capital and not ordinary.
**3.** The same justification applies to § 351, which permits tax-free incorporation of a new or existing business. Refer to Chapter 3.

5. The S election is available only to small business corporations as defined in § 1361.[4]

# QUALIFICATION

## DEFINITION OF A SMALL BUSINESS CORPORATION

A small business corporation:[5]

—Is a domestic corporation.

—Is not an "ineligible corporation."

—Has no more than 35 shareholders.

—Has as its shareholders only individuals, estates, and certain trusts.

—Issues only one class of stock.

—Does not have a nonresident alien shareholder.

*Ineligible Corporation Limitation.* In addition to being a domestic corporation, a small business corporation cannot be a member of an affiliated group, as defined in § 1504. Thus, an S corporation cannot own 80 percent or more of the stock of another corporation. Under certain conditions, however, a corporation can establish one or more inactive affiliates, looking to the possibility that such companies may be needed in the future. The "affiliated group" prohibition does not apply as long as the affiliated corporations do not engage in business or produce gross income.[6]

**Example 1.** T Corporation is formed in Texas to develop and promote a new fast-food franchise system designated "Texas Chicken Delight." If successful in Texas, the shareholders of T Corporation plan to expand the operation to New Mexico, Oklahoma, Arkansas, and Louisiana. With this in mind and with a view toward protecting the name and product identification of the parent corporation, T Corporation forms subsidiaries in each of these states. Although T Corporation, together with its subsidiaries, is now a member of an affiliated group, it can qualify as a small business corporation as long as the subsidiaries remain inactive and generate no gross income. If any of the subsidiaries begin conducting business, T Corporation can no longer maintain its S election.

---

**4.** Somewhat confusing is the fact that the Code contains several definitions of small business corporation, each pertinent to a different tax consequence. For example, compare the definition in § 1361 with the one in § 1244(c)(2), which relates to ordinary loss treatment for stock losses. These provisions, however, are not mutually exclusive. Thus, a corporation can be a small business corporation for both purposes as long as it satisfies both definitions.
**5.** § 1361(b)(1). Note that the definition of "small" for purposes of Subchapter S relates to the number of shareholders and not to the size of the corporation. This approach is to be sharply contrasted with § 1244, which looks to the capitalization of the corporation. Section 1244 is discussed in Chapter 3.
**6.** § 1361(c)(6).

*Number of Shareholders Limitation.* An electing corporation is limited to 35 shareholders. This number corresponds to the private placement exemption under Federal securities law. In testing for the 35 shareholder limitation, husband and wife are to be treated as one shareholder as long as they remain married. Further, the estate of a husband or wife along with the surviving spouse is treated as one shareholder.[7]

**Example 2.** H and W (husband and wife) jointly own 10 shares in S Corporation, with the remaining 90 shares outstanding owned by 34 other persons. H and W are divorced, and pursuant to the property settlement approved by the court, the 10 shares held by H and W are divided between them (five to each). Before the divorce settlement, S Corporation had only 35 shareholders. After the settlement, it has 36 shareholders and can no longer qualify as a small business corporation.

*Type of Shareholder Limitation.* To be a small business corporation, all the corporation's shareholders must be either individuals, estates, or certain trusts.[8] Stated differently, none of the shareholders may be partnerships, corporations, or nonqualifying trusts. The justification for this limitation is related to the 35 shareholder restriction. If, for example, a partnership with 40 partners was qualified to be a shareholder, could it not be said that there would be at least 40 owners of the corporation. If this were permitted, the 35 shareholder restriction could be easily circumvented by indirect ownership. Keep in mind that an S corporation can be a partner in a partnership or can own stock of another corporation or all the stock of an inactive subsidiary corporation.

The tax law permits a voting trust arrangement.[9] The utility of such an arrangement is illustrated in Example 3.

**Example 3.** A, B, and C (three individuals) each own one-third of the stock of an S corporation. Because they cannot agree on major corporate policy, all transfer the voting rights of their stock to a specially created "voting trust" with an independent third party as trustee. The trustee now has all of the voting power of the stock, and he or she can establish and follow a consistent management policy for the corporation without the interference of A, B, or C.

Other exceptions exist that mitigate the rule that a trust cannot be a shareholder in an S corporation. Since these exceptions are of limited applicability, they are not discussed in the text.

*Nonresident Alien Prohibition.* A corporation will not qualify as a small business corporation if it has as one of its shareholders a nonresident alien.[10] In a community property jurisdiction where one of the spouses is married to a nonresident alien, this rule could provide a trap for the un-

---

7. § 1361(c)(1).
8. § 1361(b)(1)(B).
9. § 1361(c)(2)(A)(iv).
10. § 1361(b)(1)(C).

wary.[11] A resident alien or a nonresident U. S. citizen would be a permissible S corporation shareholder.

*One Class of Stock Limitation.* There must be only one class of stock issued and outstanding.[12] Congress apparently felt that the capital structure of a small business corporation should be kept simple. Allowing more than one class of stock (e. g., common and preferred) would complicate the pass-through to the shareholders of various corporate tax attributes. Authorized and unissued stock or treasury stock of another class will not disqualify the corporation. Likewise, unexercised stock options, warrants, and convertible debentures do not constitute a second class of stock.

The second-class-of-stock prohibition has not always been a clear-cut issue. Originally the IRS strongly argued that debt reclassified as equity (refer to Chapter 3) could create a second class of stock.[13] Presuming a corporation to be thinly capitalized, some or all of its debt is considered to represent shareholder's equity. Since debt is different from regular stock, so the IRS argued, the corporation could have unequal classes of stock.[14] After numerous court defeats,[15] the IRS finally announced that it will no longer litigate this issue, pending a change in its Regulations.[16]

For many years, differences in voting rights among shares of common stock would create a second class of stock.[17] However, for taxable years beginning after December 31, 1982, differences in voting rights among shares of common stock are permitted.[18]

An instrument that is straight debt is not treated as a second class of stock and cannot disqualify an S election.[19] A straight debt instrument means a written unconditional promise to pay on demand or on a specified date a sum certain in money so long as the interest rate and payment date

---

**11.** See, for example, *Ward v. U. S.,* 81–2 USTC ¶ 9519, 48 AFTR2d 81–5337, 661 F.2d 226 (Ct. Cls., 1981), where the Court found that the stock was owned as community property. Since the taxpayer-shareholder (a U. S. citizen) was married to a citizen and resident of Mexico, the nonresident alien prohibition was violated. If the taxpayer-shareholder had held the stock as his separate property, the S election would have been valid.

**12.** § 1361(b)(1)(D).

**13.** Reg. § 1.1371-1(g).

**14.** In 1966 the IRS conceded that a corporation would not have two classes of stock if the debt was held by the shareholders in substantially the same proportion as the shareholding.

**15.** See, for example, *Portage Plastics Co., Inc. v. Comm.,* 73–1 USTC ¶ 9261, 31 AFTR2d 73–864, 486 F.2d 632 (CA–7, 1973).

**16.** TIR 1248 (July 27, 1973). The thin capitalization rationale is based on the preference of debt over equity as a means of bailing out the profits of a closely-held corporation (i. e., deductible interest as opposed to nondeductible dividends). Using this device as a deliberate tax avoidance means seems highly unlikely in the case of an S corporation, because the corporation generally pays no tax and therefore does not gain by obtaining an interest deduction.

**17.** Rev.Rul. 71–522, 1971–2 C.B. 316, and *Pollack v. Comm.,* 68–1 USTC ¶ 9318, 21 AFTR2d 68–1056, 392 F.2d 509 (CA–5, 1968). However, there is existing judicial support for the proposition that disproportionate voting rights among the shareholders would not constitute a second class of stock if they were not part of the original capital structure of the corporation and arose later because of honest disagreement among the shareholders. See, for example, *Parker Oil Co.,* 58 T.C. 985 (1972).

**18.** § 1361(c)(4).

**19.** § 1361(c)(5)(A).

are fixed. These items are fixed if they are not contingent on the profits of the corporation, the discretion of the corporation, or other similar factors. However, the fact that the interest rate is dependent upon the prime rate or a similar measure not related to the debtor corporation does not disqualify the instrument from being treated under this safe harbor rule. For this rule to apply, the instrument must not be convertible into stock and must be held by a person eligible to hold S corporation stock.

Since a safe harbor debt instrument may still be treated as stock under general tax principles, Congress instructed the Treasury to prescribe regulations relating to their treatment in an S corporation setting. These legislative regulations are to prevent tax avoidance and preclude unfair, harsh results to taxpayers.

The classification of an instrument outside the safe harbor rules as debt or stock is to be made under the usual tax law classification principles.

## MAKING THE ELECTION

If the corporation satisfies the definition of a small business corporation, the next step to achieving S status is a valid election. In this regard, the key factors are who must make the election and when the election must be made.

*Who Must Elect.* The election is made by filing Form 2553, and all shareholders must consent thereto.[20] For this purpose, both husband and wife must file consents if their stock is held as joint tenants, tenants in common, tenants by the entirety, or community property. Since the husband and wife are generally considered as one shareholder for purposes of the 35 shareholder limitation (see above), this inconsistency in treatment has led to considerable taxpayer grief—particularly in community property states where the spouses may not realize that their stock is jointly owned as a community asset.[21]

The consent of a minor shareholder can be made by the minor or legal or natural guardian (e. g., parent). If the stock is held under a state Uniform Gifts to Minors Act, the custodian of the stock may consent for the minor, but only if the custodian is also the minor's legal or natural guardian. The minor would not be required to issue a new consent when coming of age and the custodianship terminates.[22]

*When the Election Must Be Made.* To be effective for the following year, the election can be made any time during the current year. To be effective for the current year, however, the election must be made on or before the fifteenth day of the third month of such current year. An elec-

---

**20.**  § 1362(a)(2). But see Example 7 for a situation where a nonshareholder may have to consent.

**21.**  The confusion arising from community property ownership situations led to the enactment of special legislation to provide relief during the first few years following the passage of Subchapter S. However, the confusion still exists. See, for example, *Clemens v. Comm.*, 72–1 USTC ¶ 9167, 29 AFTR2d 72–390, 453 F.2d 869 (CA–9, 1971).

**22.**  Rev.Rul. 66–116, 1966–1 C.B. 198; Rev.Rul. 68–227, 1968–1 C.B. 381; and Rev.Rul. 71–287, 1971–2 C.B. 317.

tion can be effective for a short tax year of less than two months and fifteen days even if not made until the following tax year.[23]

**Example 4.** In 1985, X Corporation, a calendar year C corporation, wants to become an S corporation beginning January 1, 1986. An election made any time during 1985 will accomplish this objective. If, however, the election is made in 1986, it must be made on or before March 15, 1986. An election after March 15, 1986, will not make X Corporation an S corporation until 1987.

No statutory authority exists for obtaining an extension of time for filing an election or consent, but permission may be obtained for extension of time to file a consent if a timely election is filed, reasonable cause is given, and interests of the government are not jeopardized.

An election cannot be made for an entity not yet in existence.[24] In the case of a newly created corporation, the question may arise as to when the 2½-month election period begins to run. Reg. § 1.1372–2(b)(1) specifies that the first month begins at the earliest occurrence of any of the following events: (1) when the corporation has shareholders, (2) when it acquires assets, or (3) when it begins doing business.[25]

**Example 5.** Several individuals acquire assets on behalf of T Corporation on June 29, 19X4, and begin doing business on July 3, 19X4. They subscribe to shares of stock, file articles of incorporation for T Corporation, and become shareholders on July 7, 19X4. The S election must be filed no later than 2½ months from June 29, 19X4 (i. e., on or before September 12) to be effective for 19X4.

Even if the 2½-month rule is met, a current election will not be valid until the following year under either of the following conditions:

—The eligibility requirements were not met during any part of the taxable year before the date of election.

—Persons who were shareholders during any part of the taxable year before the election date but were not shareholders when the election was made did not consent.[26]

These rules prevent the allocation of income or losses to preelection shareholders who either were ineligible to hold S corporation stock or did not consent to the election.

**Example 6.** As of January 15, 19X4, the stock of X Corporation (a calendar year C corporation) was held equally by three shareholders: U and V, individuals, and Z Corporation. On that date, Z Corporation sells its interest to U and V. On March 14, 19X4, U and V make the S election by filing Form 2553. X Corporation cannot become an S corporation until 19X5. Because it had another corporation as a share-

---

**23.** § 1362(b).

**24.** See, for example, *T. H. Campbell & Bros., Inc.*, 34 TCM 695, T.C.Memo. 1975.

**25.** For support of Reg. § 1.1372–(2)(b)(1) see, for example, *Thomas E. Bone*, 52 T.C. 913 (1969), and *Nick A. Artukovich*, 61 T.C. 101 (1973).

**26.** § 1362(b)(2).

holder, X Corporation was not a small business corporation during all of the taxable year before the election date.

**Example 7.** Assume the same facts as in Example 6 except that all of the shareholders are individuals. Again, X Corporation cannot become an S corporation until 19X5. Although the election was timely filed, Z did not consent thereto. Had all of the shareholders (i. e., U, V, and Z) during the year signed Form 2553, S status would have taken effect as of January 1, 19X4.

Once an election is made, it does not have to be renewed and remains in effect unless otherwise lost.

## LOSS OF THE ELECTION

An S election can be lost in any of the following ways:

—A new shareholder owning more than one-half of the stock affirmatively refuses to consent to the election.

—Shareholders owning a majority of shares (voting and nonvoting) voluntarily revoke the election.

—The number of shareholders exceeds the maximum allowable limitation.

—A class of stock other than voting or nonvoting common stock is created.

—There is an acquisition of a subsidiary other than certain nonoperating subsidiaries.

—The corporation fails the passive investment income limitation.

—A nonresident alien becomes a shareholder.

Some of these possibilities are explored under separate subheadings in the pages to follow.

*Affirmative Refusal.* After 1982,[27] a new shareholder of an S corporation after the initial election does not have the power to terminate the election by affirmatively refusing to consent to the election unless the new shareholder owns more than one-half of the stock.[28] A new minority shareholder, therefore, is now bound by the initial election.

*Voluntary Revocation.* Section 1362(d)(1) permits a voluntary revocation of the election if shareholders owning a majority of shares consent. A revocation filed up to and including the fifteenth day of the third month of the tax year is effective for the entire tax year, unless a prospective effective date is specified. A revocation made after the fifteenth day of the third month of the tax year is effective on the first day of the following tax year (unless a prospective date is specified, in which case the termination is effective as of the specified date).

---

27. For tax years beginning after December 31, 1976, and before January 1, 1983, a new shareholder could affirmatively refuse to consent to a Subchapter S election on or before the sixtieth day after the day on which the stock was acquired and thereby terminate the election.

28. § 1362(d)(1)(B).

**Example 8.** The shareholders of T Corporation, a calendar year S corporation, elect to revoke the election on January 5, 19X6. Assuming the election is duly executed and timely filed, T Corporation will become a regular corporation for calendar year 19X6. If, on the other hand, the election is not made until June 19X6, T Corporation will not become a regular corporation until calendar year 19X7.

A revocation that designates a prospective effective date results in the splitting of the year into a short S corporation taxable year and a short C corporation taxable year. The day *before* the day on which the revocation occurs is treated as the last day of a short S corporation taxable year, and the day on which the revocation occurs is treated as the first day of the short regular corporate taxable year (i. e., Subchapter C treatment). The corporation should allocate the income or loss for the entire year on a pro rata basis; there is no requirement that the books of the corporation be closed as of the revocation date.[29]

**Example 9.** Assume the same facts as in Example 8, except that the corporation elects the prospective date of July 1, 19X6, as the revocation date. June 30, 19X6, will be treated as the last day of the short S corporation taxable year. The short regular corporate taxable year will run from July 1, 19X6, to December 31, 19X6. Any income or loss for the entire year shall be allocated among the short years on a prorated basis.

Rather than a pro rata allocation, the corporation can elect with the consent of all individuals who were shareholders at any time during the S short year to report the income or loss on each return (Form 1120S and Form 1120) on the basis of income or loss shown on the corporate permanent records (including working papers). Under the alternative method, items are attributed to the short S corporation and C corporation years according to the time they were incurred (as reflected in the records).[30] That is, the items are assigned to each short taxable year under the normal tax accounting rules. In fact, if 50 percent or more of the S corporation's stock is sold or exchanged in an S termination year, items have to be allocated according to the normal accounting rules (even when no election is made).

*Cessation of Small Business Corporation Status.* A corporation not only must be a small business corporation to make the S election, but also must continue to qualify as such to keep the election. In other words, meeting the definition of a small business corporation is a continuing requirement for maintaining the S status. Disqualification is an involuntary termination, and the loss of the election applies as of the date on which the event occurs.[31]

**Example 10.** T Corporation has been a calendar year S corporation for three years. On August 13, 19X2, one of its 35 shareholders sells

---

**29.**  § § 1362(e)(1) and (2).
**30.**  § 1362(e)(3).
**31.**  § 1362(d)(2)(B). For years before 1983, the loss of the election applied to the entire tax year in which the disqualification occurred.

*some* of his stock to an outsider. T Corporation now has 36 shareholders, and it ceases to be a small business corporation. For calendar year 19X2, T Corporation will be treated as an S corporation through August 12, 19X2, and as a regular corporation from August 13 through December 31, 19X2.

*Passive Investment Income Limitations.*  Before 1982, the law provided for an involuntary termination of the election in the event the corporation had gross receipts consisting of more than 20 percent in passive investment income. After 1981, an S corporation that has no Subchapter C accumulated earnings and profits at the end of the tax year is no longer covered by a passive investment income limitation. Such a corporation can have any amount of passive income.

There is a passive investment income limitation for corporations with accumulated earnings and profits from years in which the corporation was a regular C corporation. If such a corporation has passive income in excess of 25 percent of gross receipts for three consecutive taxable years, the S election is terminated as of the beginning of the following taxable year.[32]

> **Example 11.**  For 1984, 1985, and 1986, B Corporation, a calendar year S corporation, has had passive income in excess of 25% of the gross receipts. If B Corporation has accumulated earnings and profits from years in which it was a regular C corporation, the election is terminated beginning January 1, 1987.

According to § 1362(d)(3)(B), the harmful earnings and profits are generated only in years in which an S election was not in effect. Since everything is reflected in basis adjustment, an S corporation cannot generate earnings and profits. However, C corporation earnings and profits could be acquired by an S corporation from a regular corporation where earnings and profits carry over under § 381 (refer to Chapter 6).

Although the definition of passive investment income appears to parallel that of personal holding company income (refer to Chapter 7), the two are not identical. For example, long-term capital gain from the sale of securities would be passive investment income but would not be personal holding company income. Also, there are no relief provisions for rent income similar to the personal holding company rules. Other differences exist.

The inclusion of gains from the sale of securities within the definition of passive investment income generally has made it difficult, if not impossible, for corporations dealing in security transactions to achieve S status.[33] The same was true for finance companies before 1983, since interest was passive investment income and loan repayments are not (under the Regulations) includible in gross receipts.[34] However, for tax years after

---

**32.**   § 1362(d)(3)(A)(ii).

**33.**   See for example, *Buhler Mortgage Co., Inc.,* 51 T.C. 971 (1969), *aff'd.* in 71–2 USTC ¶ 9558, 28 AFTR2d 71–5252, 443 F.2d 1362 (CA–9, 1971), and *Zychinski v. Comm.,* 74–2 USTC ¶ 9834, 34 AFTR2d 74–6249, 506 F.2d 637 (CA–8, 1974).

**34.**   See, for example, *Marshall v. Comm.,* 75–1 USTC ¶ 9160, 35 AFTR2d 75–526, 510 F.2d 259 (CA–10, 1975). But compare *Puckett v. Comm.,* 75–2 USTC ¶ 9841, 36 AFTR2d 75–6332, 522 F.2d 1385 (CA–5, 1975).

1982 the law was amended to exclude from passive income any interest on deferred payment sales of property held for sale to customers (described in § 1221) as well as interest income from the conduct of a finance or lending business as defined in § 542(c)(6).[35]

Rents present a unique problem. Although classified by the Code as passive investment income, Reg. § 1.1372–4(b)(5)(vi) states that rents will not fall into this category if the corporation (landlord) renders significant, not just regular, services to the occupant (tenant).

**Example 12.** T Corporation owns and operates an apartment building. Although the corporation provides utilities for the building, maintains the lobby in the building, and furnishes trash collection for the tenants, this does not constitute the rendition of significant services for the occupants.[36] Thus, the rents paid by the tenants of the building represent passive investment income to T Corporation.

**Example 13.** Assume the fact situation as in Example 12, with one addition—T Corporation also furnishes maid service to its tenants. Now the services rendered are significant, in that they go beyond what one might normally expect the landlord of an apartment building to provide.[37] Under these changed circumstances, the rental income is no longer passive investment income.

*Reelection After Termination.* After the election has been terminated, § 1362(g) enforces a five-year waiting period before a new election can be made. The Code does, however, allow for the IRS to make exceptions to this rule and to permit an earlier reelection by the corporation. If the election is inadvertently terminated, the IRS can waive the effect of the terminating event for any period if the corporation timely corrects the event and if the corporation and shareholders agree to be treated as if the election had been in effect for such period.[38] No five-year waiting period is required to make a new S election when the prior election was revoked in a pre-1983 taxable year.

The Senate Finance Committee expects the IRS to be reasonable in granting waivers so that corporations whose S eligibility requirements have been inadvertently lost do not suffer the tax consequences of a termination if no tax avoidance would result from continued S corporation treatment. The Committee indicated that it would be appropriate to waive the terminating event when the one class of stock requirement is inadvertently breached but no tax avoidance has resulted. The waiver may be made retroactive for all years or retroactive for the period in which the entity again became eligible for S treatment.[39]

---

**35.** § 1362(d)(3)(D).

**36.** *Bramlette Building Corp., Inc.,* 52 T.C. 200 (1969), *aff'd.* in 70–1 USTC ¶ 9361, 25 AFTR2d 70–1061, 424 F.2d 751 (CA–5, 1970), and *City Markets, Inc. v. Comm.,* 70–2 USTC ¶ 9691, 26 AFTR2d 70–5760, 433 F.2d 1240 (CA–6, 1970).

**37.** For various rulings clarifying the meaning of "significant" see, for example, Rev.Rul. 65–91, 1965–1 C.B. 431; Rev.Rul. 65–83, 1965–1 C.B. 430; Rev.Rul. 65–40, 1965–1 C.B. 429; Rev.Rul. 64–232, 1964–2 C.B. 334; and Rev.Rul. 61–112, 1961–1 C.B. 399.

**38.** § 1362(f).

**39.** Sen. Fin. Com. Rep. No. 97640 on H.R. 6055 "Subchapter S Revision Act of 1982," September 8, 1982.

# OPERATIONAL RULES

An S corporation is largely a tax-reporting rather than a taxpaying entity. In this respect, the entity is taxed much like a partnership. Under the conduit concept, the taxable income of an S corporation flows through to its shareholders whether or not it is distributed in the form of actual dividends. Likewise, losses of the entity are allocated to the shareholders who report them on their individual tax returns. Other corporate transactions that flow through under the conduit concept include net long-term capital gains and losses, charitable contributions, tax-exempt interest, foreign tax credits, and investment tax credits. Parallel to the partnership rules under § 702, each shareholder of an S corporation takes into account separately his or her pro rata share of certain items of income, deductions, and credits. Under § 1366(b), the character of any item of income, expense, gain, loss, or credit is determined at the corporate level. These tax items pass through as such to each shareholder based on the prorated number of days during the relevant S year that each held stock in the corporation.

## COMPUTATION OF TAXABLE INCOME

After 1982, Subchapter S taxable income or loss generally is determined according to the tax rules applicable to partnerships in § 703, except that the amortization of organization expenditures under § 248 is an allowable deduction.[40] Thus, Subchapter S taxable income or loss is arrived at according to the tax rules applicable to individuals. Although an S corporation generally is not a taxable entity, § 1363(b)(1) requires that Subchapter S taxable income be separately computed.

Certain deductions not allowable for a partnership are not allowable for an S corporation, including the zero bracket amount, personal exemptions, alimony deductions, personal moving expenses, and expenses for the care of certain dependents. Furthermore, provisions of the Code governing the computation of taxable income applicable only to corporations, such as the dividends received deduction (i. e., § 243) or the special rules regarding corporate tax preferences (i. e., § 291), do not apply.[41]

In general, items are divided into (1) nonseparately computed income or losses and (2) separated income, losses, deductions, and credits that could affect the tax liability of any shareholders. In essence, the residue of nonseparate items are lumped together into an undifferentiated amount that constitutes Subchapter S § 1366(a)(1)(B) taxable income or loss. Each shareholder receives a pro rata portion of this amount. Under § 1366(a)(1), for a shareholder who dies during the year, the share of the pro rata items up to the date of death must be reported on his or her final individual income tax return. Elections generally are made at the corporate level, except for those elections that the partners of a partnership may make separately (e. g., foreign tax credit election).

---

**40.** § 1363(b).
**41.** § 703(a)(2).

The following items are separately stated, and each shareholder takes into account his or her pro rata share (i. e., it is passed through):[42]

—Tax-exempt income.[43]

—Long-term and short-term capital gains and losses.

—Section 1231 gains and losses.

—Charitable contributions.

—Foreign tax credits.

—Basis of § 38 new and used property, used for calculating the investment tax credit or immediate expensing under § 179.

—Dividends qualifying for exclusion under § 116.

—Depletion.

—Foreign income or losses.

—Wagering gains or losses [§ 165(d)].

—Nonbusiness income or loss (§ 212).

—Recoveries of prior taxes, bad debts, and delinquency amounts (§ 111).

—Soil and water conservation expenditures [§ 263(a)(1)(C)].

—Intangible drilling costs [§ 263(c)].

—Mining exploration expenditures (§ 617).

—Amortization of reforestation expenditures (§ 194).

—Investment interest, income, and expenses covered under § 163(d).

**Example 14.** The following is the income statement for the B Company, an S corporation:

| | | | |
|---|---|---:|---:|
| Sales | | | $ 40,000 |
| Less cost of sales | | | 23,000 |
| Gross profit on sales | | | $ 17,000 |
| Less: | | | |
| | Interest expense | $ 1,200 | |
| | Charitable contributions | 400 | |
| | Advertising expenses | 1,500 | |
| | Other operating expenses | 2,000 | 5,100 |
| | | | $ 11,900 |
| Add: | Tax-exempt income | $    300 | |
| | Dividend income | 200 | |
| | Long-term capital gain | 500 | |
| | | $ 1,000 | |
| Less: | Short-term capital loss | (150) | 850 |
| Net income per books | | | $ 12,750 |

---

**42.** § § 1366(a) and (b).

**43.** Tax-exempt income passes through to the shareholders and increases their tax bases. A subsequent distribution does not result in taxation of the tax-exempt income.

Subchapter S taxable income for B Company is calculated as follows, using net income for book purposes as a point of departure:

| | | | |
|---|---|---:|---:|
| Net income per books | | | $ 12,750 |
| Separated items: | | | |
| Deduct: Tax-exempt interest | $ 300 | | |
| Dividend income | 200 | | |
| Long-term capital gain | 500 | | |
| | | (1,000) | |
| Add: Charitable contributions | $ 400 | | |
| Short-term capital loss | 150 | 550 | |
| Net | | | (450) |
| Subchapter S taxable income | | | $ 12,300 |

The $12,300 of Subchapter S taxable income, as well as the separated items, should be divided among the shareholders based upon their stock ownership.

## TAX TREATMENT TO SHAREHOLDERS OF CASH AND PROPERTY DISTRIBUTIONS

The amount of any distribution to a shareholder is equal to the amount of the cash plus the fair market value of any property distributed. Either of two sets of distribution rules applies, depending upon whether the electing corporation has accumulated earnings and profits.

A distribution by an S corporation having no accumulated earnings and profits is not includible in gross income to the extent that it does not exceed the shareholder's adjusted basis in stock. When the amount of the distribution exceeds the adjusted basis of the stock, such excess is treated as a gain from the sale or exchange of property (i. e., capital gain in most cases, unless the corporation is collapsible).[44]

> **Example 15.** P, Inc., a calendar year S corporation has no accumulated earnings and profits at the end of 19X2 or 19X3. J, an individual shareholder, receives a cash dividend during 19X4 of $12,200 from P, Inc. J's basis in his stock is $9,700. J shall recognize a capital gain from the cash distribution of $2,500, the excess of the distribution over the stock basis ($12,200 − $9,700). The remaining $9,700 is tax-free and reduces J's basis to zero.

An S corporation is to maintain an accumulated adjustments account (AAA). Essentially, the AAA is a cumulative total of undistributed net income items for S corporation taxable years beginning after 1982. The AAA is adjusted in a similar fashion to the shareholder's stock basis, except there is no adjustment for tax-exempt income and related expenses. The AAA is a corporate account, whereas the shareholder basis in the shareholder's stock investment is calculated at the shareholder level. Unlike stock, therefore, the AAA can have a negative balance. The AAA is determined at the end of the year of a distribution rather than at the time such distribution is made. A pro rata portion of each distribution is treated

---

44. § 1368(b). For a treatment of collapsible corporations, refer to Chapter 5.

as made out of the AAA when more than one distribution occurs in the same year. The AAA is decreased proportionately for the percentage of stock redeemed in a § 302(a) or § 333 transaction.[45]

The treatment of a distribution by an S corporation with accumulated earnings and profits is summarized as follows:[46]

1.  Tax-free up to the amount in the AAA.

2.  Any previously taxed income (PTI) in the corporation under the prior set of rules follows next on a tax-free basis. However, PTI probably cannot be distributed in property other than in cash [according to Reg. § 1.1375–4(b) under prior law].

3.  A distribution in excess of the sum of the AAA and any PTI is treated as a dividend to the extent of accumulated earnings and profits. Accordingly, such amount is subject to the § 116 dividend exclusion. With the consent of all of its shareholders, an S corporation can elect to have a distribution treated as made from accumulated earnings and profits rather than from the AAA. Otherwise, no adjustments are made to accumulated earnings and profits during S years except for distributions taxed as dividends; investment tax credit recapture applicable to the corporation; and adjustments from redemptions, liquidations, reorganizations, and divisions. For example, accumulated earnings and profits can be acquired in a reorganization under § 381(c)(2).

4.  Any residual amount is applied against the shareholder's remaining basis in his or her stock.[47] Such amount is considered to be a return of capital, which is not taxable and does not qualify for the dividend exclusion. To the extent a property distribution is treated as a return of basis, the basis is reduced by the fair market value of the asset.

5.  Distributions that exceed the shareholder's tax basis for the stock are taxable as capital gains (with no dividend exclusion) unless the corporation is collapsible.

These rules apply to a shareholder regardless of the manner in which the stock is acquired.

> **Example 16.** T, a calendar year S corporation, distributes a $1,200 cash dividend to its only shareholder, X, on December 31, 19X4. The shareholder's basis in his stock is $100 on December 31, 19X3, and the corporation has no accumulated earnings and profits. For 19X4, T Corporation had $1,000 of earnings from operations, $500 of deductions, and tax-exempt income of $500.
>
> X must report $1,000 of income and $500 of deductions. The tax-exempt income retains its character and is not taxed to the shareholder. X's stock basis is increased by the $500 tax-exempt income and the $1,000 taxable income and decreased by the $500 of deductions.

---

**45.** § § 1368(c)(1) and (e)(1). Before 1983, a similar account was called previously taxed income (PTI).

**46.** § 1368(c).

**47.** § 1368(c)(3).

---

**Concept Summary**

## CLASSIFICATION PRIORITIES FOR DIVIDENDS
## PAID BY AN S CORPORATION[a]

| Dividends Paid Where Subchapter C Earnings and Profits Exist | Dividends Paid Where No Subchapter C Earnings and Profits Exist |
|---|---|
| 1. Tax-free to the extent of accumulated adjustment account.[b] | 1. Nontaxable to the extent of adjusted basis in stock. |
| 2. Any PTI from pre-1983 tax years can be distributed tax-free. | 2. Excess treated as gain from the sale or exchange of property (i. e., capital gain in most cases).[c] |
| 3. Excess distribution is an ordinary dividend from accumulated earnings and profits.[d] | |
| 4. Next distribution is tax-free reduction in basis of stock. | |
| 5. Any excess distribution treated as gain from the sale or exchange of stock (i. e., capital gain in most cases).[c] | |

(a) A distribution of appreciated property by an electing corporation results in a gain that is allocated to and reported by the shareholders.
(b) For the first 2½ months in 1983, any almost-PTI can be distributed tax-free.
(c) Collapsible treatment under § 341 may cause ordinary income treatment.
(d) An election is available to pay out accumulated earnings and profits before the AAA [§ 1368(e)(3)].

---

The results of current operations affect the shareholder's basis before the application of the distribution rule.

Immediately before the cash dividend, X's stock basis is $1,100. Thus, $1,100 of the dividend is tax-free (i. e., a tax-free recovery of basis), but X has a $100 gain from the sale or exchange of stock. X, therefore, will have a basis in the stock of zero as of December 31, 19X4. (Refer to the Concept Summary, second column.)

**Example 17.** Assume the same facts as in Example 16, except that T Corporation had Subchapter C earnings and profits of $750. X has an AAA of $500 ($1,000 − $500), which does not include the tax-exempt income. X's basis in the stock immediately before the distribution would be $1,100, since under § 1367(a)(1)(A) X's basis is increased by the tax-exempt income. Therefore, X is not taxed on the first $500, which is a recovery of the AAA. The next $700 is taxable from the accumulated earnings and profits account. (Refer to the first column of the Concept Summary.) X will have a final basis in the stock of $600 ($1,100 − $500). Although the taxable portion of the distribution does not reduce basis in the stock, the nontaxable AAA distribution does.

Schedule M on page 4 of Form 1120S (reproduced below) contains a column labeled "Other adjustments account." Essentially this account is used to make the balance sheet balance and includes items not included in the calculation of the AAA, such as tax-exempt income and any related nondeductible expenses. Since this account is below the earnings and profits tier, distributions from this "plug" account are unimportant. Once the earnings and profits account reaches zero, distributions fall under the two-tier system: (1) nontaxable to the extent of basis and (2) capital gain. The instructions to Form 1120S indicate that there is no need for an other adjustments account when there is no accumulated earnings and profits.

**Example 18.** During 1986, S Corporation had the following transactions:

| | |
|---|---:|
| Accumulated adjustments account, beginning of year | $ 8,500 |
| Prior-taxed income, beginning of year | 6,250 |
| Ordinary income (line 24) | 25,000 |
| Tax-exempt interest | 4,000 |
| Life insurance proceeds | 5,000 |
| Payroll penalty expense | 2,000 |
| Charitable contributions | 3,000 |
| Unreasonable compensation | 5,000 |
| Expenses related to tax-exempt interest | 2,000 |
| Distributions to shareholders | 16,000 |

S Corporation's Schedule M for the current year appears as follows:

| Schedule M | Analysis of Shareholders' Undistributed Taxable Income Previously Taxed, Accumulated Adjustments Account, and Other Adjustments Account (If Schedule L, column (d), amounts for lines 25, 26, or 27 are not the same as corresponding amounts on line 9 of Schedule M, attach a schedule explaining any differences. See instructions.) | | |
|---|---|---|---|
| | Shareholders' undistributed taxable income previously taxed | Accumulated adjustments account | Other adjustments account |
| 1 Balance at beginning of year . . . . . . | $6,250 | $ 8,500 | 0 |
| 2 Ordinary income from page 1, line 24 . . . | | 25,000 | |
| 3 Other additions . . . . . . . . . . | | 0 | $9,000** |
| 4 Total of lines 1, 2, and 3 . . . . . . . | 0 | 33,500 | 9,000 |
| 5 Distributions other than dividend distributions | 0 | 16,000 | 0 |
| 6 Loss from page 1, line 24 . . . . . . . | | 0 | |
| 7 Other reductions . . . . . . . . . | | 10,000* | 2,000 |
| 8 Add lines 5, 6, and 7 . . . . . . . . | 0 | 26,000 | 2,000 |
| 9 Balance at end of tax year—Subtract line 8 from line 4 . . . . . . . . . . . | 6,250 | 7,500 | 7,000 |

```
*Payroll penalty expense    $2,000    **Tax-exempt interest      $4,000
 Charitable contributions    3,000      Life insurance proceeds   5,000
 Unreasonable compensation   5,000
```

Any distribution of cash by the corporation with respect to the stock during a post-termination transition period of approximately one year is applied against and reduces the adjusted basis of the stock to the extent that the amount of the distribution does not exceed the accumulated adjustments account.[48] Thus, a terminated S corporation should make a cash distribution during the one-year period following termination to the extent of all previously undistributed net income items for all S tax years.

> **Example 19.** P, a calendar year S corporation during 19X3, voluntarily elects to terminate the S election effective January 1, 19X4. As of the end of 19X3, Q, the sole shareholder, has an AAA of $1,300. Code § 1371(e) allows Q to receive a nontaxable distribution of cash during a post-termination transition period of approximately one year to the extent of Q's AAA. Thus, a cash dividend of $1,300 during 19X4 would be nontaxable to Q but would reduce the adjusted basis of Q's stock.

A former S corporation may elect not to have the post-termination rules apply. Thus, with the consent of all of its shareholders to whom distributions are made during the post-termination transition period, the new C corporation might pay dividends (rather than AAA distributions) to avoid a possible accumulated earnings or personal holding company tax.

If a corporation was an S corporation in a taxable year before January 1, 1983, both § § 1375(d) and (f) of the prior law are applicable with respect to undistributed taxable income (UTI) for any tax year beginning before January 1, 1983.[49] Thus, previously taxed income can be distributed tax-free to the shareholder who included it in income. Further, a distribution of UTI within the 2½-month grace period of the first tax year subject to the new law is considered a tax-free distribution of the UTI for the prior year.

> **Example 20.** In 19X4, X Corporation, a calendar year S corporation, has a post-1982 accumulated adjustments account of $5,500. In addition, it has accumulated earnings and profits from pre-1983 years of $4,500. T, the sole shareholder, receives in 19X4 a $19,000 cash distribution from X Corporation. If T's basis in his stock investment is $13,900, the distribution will be treated as follows:

|  |  |
|---|---:|
| Nontaxable accumulated adjustments account | $ 5,500 |
| Taxable dividend | 4,500 |
| Nontaxable return of capital | 8,400 |
| Capital gain | 600 |
| Total amount of the distribution | $ 19,000 |

## CORPORATE TREATMENT OF CERTAIN PROPERTY DISTRIBUTIONS

After 1982, a gain is recognized by an S corporation on any distribution of appreciated property (other than in a complete liquidation) in the same manner as if the asset had been sold to the shareholder at its fair market value.[50] The corporate gain is passed through to the shareholders. There is an important reason for this rule. Otherwise, property could be distributed

---

**48.** § § 1371(e) and 1377(b).

**49.** § 1379(c).

**50.** § 1363(d).

tax-free (other than for certain recapture) and later sold without income recognition to the shareholder because of the stepped-up basis equal to fair market value.[51] A loss will not be recognized on assets that are worth less than basis. Furthermore, when depreciated property is distributed, the shareholder receives a basis in the asset equal to the asset's fair market value. Thus, the potential loss disappears. The character of the gain—capital gain or ordinary income—will depend upon the type of asset being distributed.

> **Example 21.** Q Corporation, an S corporation, distributes a tract of land held as an investment to T, a majority shareholder. The land was purchased for $22,000 many years ago but is currently worth $82,000. Under § 1363(d), Q Corporation must recognize a gain of $60,000.

Several exceptions exist to the recognition of gain at the corporate level on the distribution of appreciated property. First, an S corporation will recognize a gain on a distribution in a complete liquidation only to the extent that it would be recognized by a C corporation (e. g., recapture of depreciation). Second, the nonrecognition of gain rules of a 12-month liquidation under § 337 apply to an S corporation. Third, distributions in a tax-free reorganization or divisive transaction are protected by § § 354, 355, and 356. However, an S corporation is not protected by the partial liquidation rules for noncorporate shareholders.

## THE SHAREHOLDER'S TAX BASIS

The initial tax basis of stock in an S corporation is calculated similarly to the basis of stock in a regular corporation, dependent upon the manner in which shares are acquired (e. g., gift, inheritance, purchase). Once the initial tax basis is determined, various transactions during the life of the corporation affect the shareholder's basis in the stock.

A shareholder's basis is increased by further stock purchases and capital contributions. Operations during the year also cause the following upward adjustments to basis:[52]

—Nonseparately stated computed income

—Separately stated income items (i. e., nontaxable income).

—Depletion in excess of basis in the property.

The following items cause a downward adjustment to basis (but not below zero):[53]

—Nonseparately stated computed loss.

—Separately stated loss and deduction items.

—Distributions not reported as income by the shareholder (i. e., an AAA distribution) or gain from the sale or exchange of property under § 1368.

---

**51.** There is a similar rule when a corporation uses appreciated property to carry out certain stock redemptions and partial liquidations. Refer to the discussion of § 311(d) in Chapter 4.

**52.** § 1367(a)(1).

**53.** § 1367(a)(2).

—Nondeductible expenses of the corporation not chargeable to capital.

—Shareholder's deduction for depletion under § 611 with respect to oil and gas wells.

A shareholder's basis in the stock can never be reduced below zero, and any excess decrease is applied to reduce (but not below zero) the shareholder's basis in any indebtedness of the electing corporation.[54] Once the basis of any debt is reduced, it is later increased (only up to the original amount) by subsequent net income items. The adjustment is made *before* any increase to the basis in the stock but only to the extent that the debt basis was reduced in a taxable year *after* 1983.[55]

**Example 22.** T, a sole shareholder, has a $7,000 stock basis and a $2,000 loan basis in a calendar year S corporation at the beginning of 19X5. Subchapter S net income during 19X5 is $8,200. There is a short-term capital loss of $2,300 and $2,000 of tax-exempt interest income. A total of $15,000 is distributed to T on November 15, 19X5. T's basis in his stock is zero, and his loan basis is $1,900 ($2,000 − $100) at the end of 19X5:

| | |
|---|---:|
| Beginning basis in the stock | $ 7,000 |
| Income | 8,200 |
| Short-term capital loss | (2,300) |
| Tax-exempt interest income | 2,000 |
| | $ 14,900 |
| Less distribution | −14,900 |
| Final basis in the stock | $ —0— |

Because stock basis cannot be reduced below zero, the $100 excess distribution reduces the loan basis.

## NET OPERATING LOSS

One major advantage of an S election is the ability to pass through any net operating loss (NOL) of the corporation directly to its shareholders. Under § 1366(a)(1)(A), such a loss is deductible by the shareholders for the year in which the corporation's tax year ends. The corporation is not entitled to the NOL. The loss is deducted in arriving at adjusted gross income (i. e., it is a deduction *for* AGI). A shareholder's basis in the stock is reduced to the extent of any pass-through of the net operating loss. Further, a shareholder's AAA is reduced by the net loss allocated to the shareholder. Apparently, the AAA is reduced only by the amount *actually* deductible during the tax year.[56]

Net operating losses are allocated among shareholders in the same manner as is income. NOLs are allocated on a daily basis to all shareholders who owned stock during the tax year.[57] Presumably, transferred shares

---

54.  § 1367(b)(2)(A).
55.  § 1367(b)(2)(B).
56.  § 1368 (e)(1)(A).
57.  § 1377(a)(1).

are considered to be held by the transferee (not the transferor) on the date of the transfer.[58]

> **Example 23.** An S corporation has a $20,000 NOL for the current year. The stock was at all times during the tax year owned by the same 10 shareholders, each of whom owned 10% of the stock. Each shareholder is entitled to deduct $2,000 from gross income for the tax year in which the corporate tax year ends.

An S corporation's NOL pass-through cannot exceed a shareholder's adjusted basis in the stock plus the basis of any loans made by the shareholder to the corporation. If a taxpayer is unable to prove the tax basis, the NOL pass-through can be denied.[59] In essence, a shareholder's stock basis or indebtedness basis cannot go below zero. As noted previously, once a shareholder's adjusted stock basis has been eliminated by an NOL, any excess net operating loss is used to reduce the shareholder's basis for any loans made to the corporation (but never below zero). The basis for loans is established by the actual advances made to the corporation and not by indirect loans.[60]

The fact that a shareholder has guaranteed a loan made to the corporation by a third party has no effect upon the shareholder's loan basis, unless payments actually have been made as a result of that guarantee.[61] If the corporation defaults on an indebtedness and the shareholder makes good on the guarantee, the shareholder's indebtedness basis is increased by such extent.[62] A subsequent increase in basis has no influence on results of a prior year in which an NOL exceeded a shareholder's adjusted basis.

A shareholder's share of an NOL may be greater than both the basis in the stock and the basis of the indebtedness. A shareholder is entitled to carry forward a loss to the extent that the loss for the year exceeds both the stock basis and the loan basis. Any loss carried forward may be deducted *only* by the same shareholder if and when the basis in the stock of and loans to the corporation is restored.[63] Any loss carryover remaining at the end of a one-year post-termination transition period is lost forever.[64] The post-termination transition period is the later of (1) one year after the effective date of the termination of the S election or the due date for the last S return (whichever is later) or (2) 120 days after the determination that the corporation's S election had terminated for a previous year. Thus, if a shareholder has a loss carryover, he or she should increase the stock/loan basis and flow through the loss before disposing of the stock.

Net operating losses from regular-corporation years cannot be utilized at the corporate level, nor can they be passed through to the shareholders. Further, the running of the carryforward period continues during S status.[65] Consequently, it may not be appropriate for a corporation that

---

**58.** Reg. § 1.1374–1(b)(3).
**59.** See *Donald J. Sauvigne,* 30 TCM 123, T.C.Memo. 1971–30.
**60.** *Ruth M. Prashker,* 59 T.C. 172 (1972).
**61.** See, for example, *B. James Parson,* 33 TCM 789, T.C.Memo. 1974–183.
**62.** Rev.Rul. 70–50, 1970–1 C.B. 178.
**63.** § 1366(d).
**64.** § 1377(b).
**65.** § 1371(b).

has unused net operating losses to make this election. When a corporation is expecting losses in the future, an election should be made before the loss year.

Under § 1367(b)(3), any corporate losses and deductions for the tax year are passed through to the shareholder and in turn reduce the shareholder's debt basis before determining any nonbusiness bad debt deduction (due to the shareholder's debt becoming worthless). In essence, if debt owed to a shareholder becomes worthless during a tax year, the shareholder's share of the S corporation's losses for that tax year is deductible to the extent of the pre-worthlessness debt basis.

The NOL provisions create a need for sound tax planning during the last election year and the post-termination transition period. If it appears that the S corporation is going to sustain a net operating loss or use up any loss carryover, each shareholder's basis should be analyzed to determine if it can absorb the share of the loss. If basis is insufficient to absorb the loss, further investments should be considered before the end of the post-termination transition year. Such investment can be accomplished through additional stock purchases from the corporation or from other shareholders to increase basis. This action will insure full benefit from the net operating loss or loss carryover.

> **Example 24.** A calendar year C corporation has a net operating loss in 19X5 of $20,000. A valid S election is made in 19X6, and there is another $20,000 NOL in that year. The stock of the corporation was at all times during 19X6 owned by the same 10 shareholders, each of whom owned 10% of the stock. T, one of the 10 shareholders, has an adjusted basis at the beginning of 19X6 of $1,800. None of the 19X5 NOL may be carried forward into the S year. Although T's share of the 19X6 NOL is $2,000, the deduction for the loss is limited to $1,800 in 19X6 with a $200 carryover.

If a loan's basis has been reduced and is not restored, income will result when the loan is repaid. If the corporation issued a note as evidence of the debt, repayment constitutes an amount received in exchange for a capital asset, and the amount that exceeds the shareholder's basis is entitled to capital gain treatment.[66] However, if the loan is made on open account, the repayment constitutes ordinary income to the extent that it exceeds the shareholder's basis for the loan. Each repayment must be prorated between the gain portion and the repayment of the debt.[67] Thus, a note should be given to obtain capital gain treatment for the income that results from a loan's repayment.

## TAX TREATMENT OF LONG-TERM CAPITAL GAINS

Although an S corporation generally is a tax-reporting rather than a tax-paying entity, certain long-term capital gains may be taxed under § 1374(a). The effect of § 1374 is to hinder the use of Subchapter S on a

---

**66.** *Joe M. Smith,* 48 T.C. 872 (1967), *aff'd.* and *rev'd.* in 70–1 USTC ¶ 9327, 25 AFTR2d 70–936, 424 F.2d 219 (CA–9, 1970), and Rev.Rul. 64–162, 1964–1 C.B. 304.
**67.** Rev.Rul. 68–537, 1968–2 C.B. 372.

one-shot basis to avoid the tax on corporate capital gains. Before passage of this corporate capital gains tax, a regular corporation could "save" its capital asset sales for several years, elect S corporation status, sell the capital assets, and pass such gains to the shareholders to avoid the capital gains tax at the corporate level.

**Example 25.** A corporation operates several years as a C corporation but postpones most of its capital asset dispositions. During the current year, the corporation elects S status and disposes of all of its accumulated capital assets. Without § 1374, any capital gains would pass through to the shareholders, avoiding the corporate tax. Next year the S election could be terminated, and the corporation could begin accumulating its capital asset transactions until the next time it makes the one-shot election.

*Tax Consequences at the Corporation Level.* Under § 1374(a), an S corporation is taxed on capital gains if it meets all of the following requirements. First, the taxable income of the corporation must exceed $25,000. Second, the excess of the net long-term capital gain (LTCG) over the net short-term capital loss must exceed $25,000. Third, this amount must exceed 50 percent of the corporation's taxable income for the year.

However, the corporation may fall within the above requirements and still avoid the special tax at the corporate level because of two exceptions to these rules. Under § 1374(c), the tax does not apply to those corporations that have had valid elections in effect for the three previous tax years. Moreover, a new corporation in existence for less than four tax years can avoid the tax if it has operated under Subchapter S since it was founded. After 1982, an S corporation and a predecessor S corporation are treated as one corporation for purposes of determining whether either of these exceptions applies. Thus, the corporation that has elected S status for sound business reasons generally will find its pattern of taxation unaffected by the realization of capital gains.

The alternative corporate capital gains rate is applied only to those gains that exceed $25,000. Pursuant to § 1374(b), the total tax will be no more than the amount that would result from applying the standard corporate rates to the taxable income of the corporation were it not an S corporation. Taxable income is determined under § 63(a) without regard to the net operating loss and the special deductions in § § 241 through 250 (except for the organization expenditures provided for in § 248).[68]

Any tax applied at the corporate level reduces the amount of the long-term capital gain to be passed through to the shareholders.[69]

**Example 26.** An S corporation has four equal shareholders and does not meet the 3-year exception. For the year, it has taxable income of $90,000. The corporation also has a $100,000 net long-term capital gain taxable under § 1374. The capital gains tax at the corporate level

---

**68.** § 1374(d). These special deductions include various types of dividends received deductions, deduction of bond premium on repurchase, and payments to the National Railroad Passenger Corporation.
**69.** § 1366(f)(2).

is $21,000, which is 28% of $75,000. The first $25,000 of net long-term capital gain is exempt from this tax. Since the amount that will be treated as long-term capital gain by the shareholders is reduced by any tax paid at the corporate level, the amount that can be treated as long-term capital gain by each shareholder is $19,750. This amount is computed by subtracting the tax ($21,000) from $100,000 and dividing the amount into four equal parts. Thus, each shareholder would include $19,750 in personal long-term capital gains.

Section 1374 attempts to prevent one abuse of the S corporation: A C corporation may not avoid the capital gains tax at the corporate level by making a temporary S election. However, where capital gains are taxed at the corporate level, the overall tax may be less under S status than it would be for a C corporation.

If an S corporation is subject to the capital gains tax, it may also be subject to the 15 percent minimum tax. After 1978, an S corporation is treated as a corporation for purposes of the minimum tax. For an S corporation, the tax is levied only against the capital gains preference item (that is subject to a corporate tax) after subtracting an exemption. The remainder is taxed at the applicable rate. For years after December 31, 1975, the exemption is the greater of $10,000 or the regular income tax for the year.[70] Note that only the capital gains preference item is taxed by the minimum tax at the S corporation level.[71]

Any capital gain subject to the passive investment income tax of § 1375 (see the following section) is not subject to the § 1374 penalty tax.[72] Section 1231 gains are not aggregated with capital gains at the corporate level but pass through separately.

*Tax Consequences at the Shareholder Level.* A net long-term capital gain retains its character when passed through to the shareholders. After 1982, net capital gains are no longer offset by ordinary losses at the corporate level.

> **Example 27.** An S corporation has three equal shareholders and realizes a net long-term capital gain of $9,000 for the current tax year. In the same year, the corporation has taxable income and current earnings and profits in excess of $9,000. If no distributions are made, each shareholder must include $3,000 in gross income as a long-term capital gain. (This result assumes that the capital gains tax preference tax does not apply at the corporate level.)

> **Example 28.** During 19X5, S Corporation has a $20,000 ordinary loss and a net long-term capital gain of $30,000. T, the sole shareholder, must report a long-term capital gain of $30,000 and a $20,000 Subchapter S ordinary loss at the shareholder level.

The amount includible in the gross income of a shareholder as a pass-through item is treated as a long-term capital gain to the extent of the

---

70. § 56(c).
71. § 58(d).
72. § 1375(c)(2).

shareholder's pro rata share of the S corporation's net long-term capital gain for the year of distribution. The corporate net long-term capital gain is reduced by any capital gain special tax imposed by § 1374. Under § 1371(c), the earnings and profits of an S corporation are not reduced by any amount except for certain adjustments for redemptions, liquidations, reorganizations, and divisive transactions and the portion of a distribution treated as a dividend under § 1368(c)(2).

> **Example 29.** An S corporation with one shareholder, T, has a net long-term capital gain of $48,000 and Subchapter S taxable income of $3,000. The corporation has no accumulated earnings and profits and has an accumulated adjustments account of $12,200. During 19X5, it made cash distributions of $56,000 to T. The corporation paid a $6,440 capital gains tax. T would treat $41,560 as a long-term capital gain ($48,000 − $6,440), $3,000 as ordinary income, and $11,440 as a tax-free distribution from the accumulated adjustments account if sufficient basis exists.

## PASSIVE INVESTMENT INCOME PENALTY TAX

A tax is imposed on the excess passive income of S corporations with accumulated earnings and profits from Subchapter C years.[73] The tax rate is 46 percent (the highest corporate rate) on that portion of the corporation's net passive income that bears the same ratio to the total net passive income for the tax year as the excess gross passive income bears to the total gross passive income for the year. However, the amount subject to the tax may not exceed the taxable income of the corporation.[74]

Passive investment income means gross receipts derived from royalties, rents, dividends, interest, annuities, and sales and exchanges of stocks and securities.[75] To prevent the churning of assets, only the net gain from the disposition of capital assets (other than stocks and securities) is taken into account in computing gross receipts. Net passive income means passive income reduced by any deductions directly connected with the production of such income. Nonrefundable credits are not allowable against the § 1375 tax, and any gain subject to tax is exempt from the capital gains tax under § 1374. Any tax due to the application of § 1375 reduces the amount the shareholders must take into income.

An S corporation's excess net passive income (ENPI) can be calculated from the following formula:

$$\begin{array}{c}\text{Excess net} \\ \text{passive income}\end{array} = \frac{\begin{array}{c}\text{Passive investment income} \\ \text{in excess of 25\% of} \\ \text{gross receipts for the year}\end{array}}{\begin{array}{c}\text{Passive investment} \\ \text{income for the year}\end{array}} \times \begin{array}{c}\text{Net passive} \\ \text{investment income} \\ \text{for the year}\end{array}$$

---

**73.** § 1375(a).
**74.** § 1375(b).
**75.** § 1362(d)(3)(D)(i).

The excess net passive income cannot exceed the corporate taxable income for the year without considering any net operating loss deduction under § 172 or the special deductions allowed by § § 241–250 (except the organization expense deduction in § 248).

**Example 30.** At the end of 19X4, S Corporation, an electing corporation, has gross receipts totaling $264,000 (of which $110,000 is passive investment income). Expenditures directly connected to the production of the passive investment income total $30,000. Therefore, S Corporation has net passive investment income of $80,000 ($110,000 − $30,000), and the amount by which its passive investment income for tax year 19X4 exceeds 25% of its gross receipts is $44,000 ($110,000 passive investment income less $66,000). Excess net passive income is $32,000, calculated as follows:

$$\text{ENPI} = \frac{\$44,000}{\$110,000} \times \$80,000 = \$32,000$$

S Corporation's passive investment income tax for 19X4, therefore, is $14,720 ($32,000 × 46%).

An S corporation may elect to terminate its election rather than pay the § 1375 penalty tax. However, if this choice is made and S status is lost, a new S election cannot be made for five years without the consent of the IRS.

## FRINGE BENEFIT RULES

Since 1983, a number of fringe benefits are not available to any shareholder owning more than two percent of the stock of an S corporation. The constructive ownership rules of § 318 (refer to Chapter 4) are applicable in determining the two percent ownership test.[76] Thus, such a shareholder-employee is not regarded as an employee for purposes of the following benefits:

—Group term life insurance (§ 79).

—The $5,000 death benefit exclusion [§ 101(b)].

—The exclusion from income of amounts paid for an accident and health plan (§ 105).

—The exclusion from income of amounts paid by an employer to an accident and health plan (§ 106).

—Exclusion from income of meals and lodging furnished for the convenience of the employer (§ 119).

—Workers' compensation payments on behalf of the shareholder-employee.[77]

**Example 31.** P Corporation, an S corporation, pays for the medical care of two shareholder-employees during 19X4. T, an individual owning 2% of the stock, receives $1,700. S, an individual owning 20% of

---

76. § § 1372(a) and (b).
77. Rev.Rul. 72–596, 1972–2 C.B. 395.

the stock, receives $3,100. The $1,700 would be deducted as a business expense by P Corporation. The $3,100 paid on behalf of S is not deductible by the corporation because of the ownership of more than 2% of the stock. S can deduct the $3,100 only to the extent that personal medical expenses are allowable as an itemized deduction under § 213.

An S corporation in existence as of September 28, 1982, may continue any existing fringe benefits on such date until the first tax year after December 31, 1987. The S election must continue in effect, and there must not be a 50 percent change of ownership.

For tax years after 1983, the regular corporate rules for retirement plans apply to S corporations. Thus, contributions to a defined contribution plan are limited to the smaller of $30,000 or 25 percent of compensation. The limitation on maximum accrued benefits of a defined benefit plan is the smaller of $90,000 or 100 percent of compensation. Although more restrictive top-heavy rules may apply to S corporations, many of the structural differences favoring a regular corporate plan are eliminated.

## OTHER OPERATIONAL RULES

*Choice of Tax Year.* After October 20, 1982, a corporation that makes an S election is required to use either a calendar year or some other accounting period for which the corporation establishes a business purpose to the satisfaction of the IRS.[78] (A 52- to 53-week taxable year is an example of an acceptable accounting period to the IRS.) A corporation with an S election in effect on October 20, 1982, may continue its current tax year so long as 50 percent or more of the outstanding stock in such corporation on that date continues to be owned by the same shareholders.[79] Transfers of stock by reason of death, by gift from a family member, and between parties to an intrafamily buy-sell agreement (in effect on September 28, 1982) are not considered changes in ownership with respect to this transitional rule.

The IRS allows an S corporation to adopt, retain, or change to an accounting period other than a permitted calendar year in the following circumstances:

—Where shareholders holding more than one-half of the shares of the stock (as of the first day of the tax year to which the request relates) have the same tax year or are concurrently changing to the tax year the corporation adopts, retains, or changes to.

—Where shareholders holding more than one-half of the shares of the stock (as of the first day of the tax year to which the request relates) have a tax year or are concurrently changing to a tax year that results in a deferment of income to each of the shareholders of three months or less.

—Where the tax year adopted, retained, or changed to coincides with the S corporation's natural business year.[80]

---

78.   § § 1378(a) and (b).
79.   § 1378(c).
80.   Rev.Proc. 83–25, 83–1 C.B. 689.

*Investment Tax Credit.* An S election is treated as a mere change in the form of conducting a trade or business for purposes of the investment tax credit recapture. However, an S corporation still continues to be liable for any investment tax credit recapture for Subchapter C taxable years upon early disposition of property.[81] Any corporate tax as a result of the recapture of an investment tax credit (ITC) reduces the earnings and profits of the corporation.

The amount of the qualified investment credit property purchased by the S corporation (and not the investment tax credit itself) passes through to the shareholders on a pro rata basis.[82] Any premature disposition of the property results in investment tax credit recapture at the shareholder level.

An S corporation is required to inform shareholders on their annual K-1s of their share of the original cost basis of any property disposed of, along with the length of time the § 38 property was held by the corporation. Certain events, such as death of shareholders, § 351 transfers, certain § 333 liquidations, and termination of an S election, do not result in § 38 recapture. However, if the C corporation prematurely disposes of the assets, the applicable tax on recapture is reported by the shareholders who received the original investment tax credit. Under § 48(q)(6), the stock basis of a shareholder is adjusted to correspond with the adjustment to the basis of the property at the corporate level when the investment tax credit is allowable or recapturable.

Since the investment in qualified property passes through to the shareholders, recapture falls upon them when the corporation prematurely disposes of the property (or ceases to use it as § 38 property).[83] Recapture may also be required of any shareholder who prematurely disposes (by sale or otherwise) of too much of the stock. According to Regulation § 1.47–4(a)(ii), which has been judicially tested, any change in the shareholder's proportionate ownership below 66⅔ percent and 33⅓ percent of original investment triggers proportionate recapture at the shareholder level.[84] The purchaser of the stock is *not* allowed to claim the investment tax credit on the amount of the purchase price of the stock allocated to the § 38 property. Since the S corporation is still the user of the § 38 property, although inequitable, no ITC is available to the purchaser of the stock.

> **Example 32.** In 19X4, a C corporation purchases § 38 property upon which it properly claims an investment credit. On January 1, 19X5, the C corporation becomes an S corporation; under present law, there is no recapture as a result of the election. Near the end of 19X5, the company sells the property. The corporation will be subject to any recapture tax as a result of the disposition. Any earnings and profits account would be decreased by the recapture amount.

---

**81.** § 1371(d).

**82.** § 1366(a)(1)(A).

**83.** Reg. § 1.47–4(a)(1).

**84.** *Charbonnet v. U. S.,* 72–1 USTC ¶ 9266, 29 AFTR2d 72–633, 455 F.2d 1195 (CA–5, 1972).

**Example 33.** Suppose the corporation in Example 32 purchased the § 38 property during 19X5 (when the S election was in effect). The qualified investment in this property—not the investment tax credit—passes through to the shareholders. This qualified investment is apportioned among the shareholders in the same manner as other pass-through items. If the property is disposed of too soon, the shareholders are considered to have made the premature disposition. Thus, Reg. § 1.47–4(a) reflects that the shareholders are liable for any investment tax credit recapture on a premature disposition of the property by the S corporation.

*Oil and Gas Producers.* Oil and gas producers probably will not wish to choose S status. The election by a C corporation of Subchapter S is treated as a transfer of oil and gas properties under § 613A(c)(13)(C). Therefore, as of the date of the election, neither the shareholders nor the electing corporation will be allowed to claim percentage depletion on production from proven oil or gas wells. A shareholder is considered the producer of oil for purposes of the windfall profit tax.

*Miscellaneous Rules.* A summary of other points that should be mentioned to complete the discussion of the possible effects of various Code provisions on S corporations follows:

—An S corporation may own stock in another corporation, but an S corporation may not have a corporate shareholder. An S corporation is not eligible for a dividends received deduction under § 243; any dividends received are passed through to the shareholders as a separately computed tax item under § 1366(a)(1).

—It is still beneficial for an S corporation to issue § 1244 stock.

—Excess investment interest of the corporation passes through to the shareholders. Like other items, such pass-through is allocated on a pro rata basis.[85]

—The hobby loss provisions of § 183 are applicable to S corporations. Although § 183 was enacted by the Tax Reform Act of 1969, prior case law precluded the pass-through of losses to the shareholders when the corporation was not deemed to be engaged in a trade or business.[86]

—An S corporation may create accumulated earnings and profits in certain transactions involving redemptions, liquidations, reorganizations, and divisive reorganizations.

—An S corporation is not subject to the 10 percent of taxable income limitation applicable to charitable contributions made by a C corporation under § 170(b)(2).

—If an S corporation is collapsible under § 341, certain capital gain on distributions may be treated as ordinary income (see Chapter 5).

—So-called at-risk provisions generally apply to S corporation shareholders in taxable years beginning after December 31, 1982. Essen-

---

**85.** § 163(d)(4)(C).
**86.** See, for example, *Arthur H. Eppler,* 58 T.C. 691 (1972).

tially, the amount at risk is determined separately for each shareholder, and the amount of the losses of the corporation that are passed through and deductible by the shareholders are not affected by the amount the S corporation has at risk. A shareholder usually is considered at risk with respect to an activity to the extent of cash and the adjusted basis of other property contributed to the electing corporation, any amount borrowed for use in the activity with respect to which the taxpayer has personal liability for payment from personal assets, and the net fair market value of personal assets that secure nonrecourse borrowing.[87]

—The new safe harbor rules for purposes of assuring that a transaction will be characterized as a lease do not apply to S corporations.[88]

—Foreign taxes paid by an electing corporation will pass through to the shareholders and should be claimed as either a deduction or a credit (subject to the applicable limitations).[89] However, an electing corporation is not eligible for the foreign tax credit with respect to taxes paid by a foreign corporation in which the S corporation is a shareholder.

—Any family member who renders services or furnishes capital to an electing corporation must be paid reasonable compensation or the IRS can make adjustments to reflect the value of such services or capital.[90] This rule may make it more difficult for related parties to shift Subchapter S taxable income to children or other family members.

—The percentage or cost depletion allowance is computed separately by each shareholder. Each shareholder is treated as having produced his or her pro rata share of the production of the electing corporation, and each is allocated a respective share of the adjusted basis of the electing corporation as to oil or gas property held by the corporation.[91]

—An S corporation is placed on the cash method of accounting for purposes of deducting business expenses and interest owed to a cash basis related party (including a shareholder who owns at least two percent of the stock in the corporation).[92] Thus, the timing of the shareholder's income and the corporate deduction must match.

—The $125,000 investment tax credit limitation on used property applies at both the corporate and the shareholder levels.

—No carryovers are allowable from a C corporation year to an S corporation year. However, the intervening S tax years count as elapsed years for purposes of determining when the carryover expires.

---

**87.** The at-risk rules and their significance for income tax purposes are discussed in Chapter 10.
**88.** § 168(f)(8)(B)(i)(I).
**89.** § 1373(a).
**90.** § 1366(e).
**91.** § 613A(c)(13).
**92.** §§ 267(b) and (f).

—Since few adjustments are allowed to the accumulated earnings and profits account during S tax years, no catch-up adjustments can be made to offset timing differences between earnings and profits and taxable income during prior C tax years. Permanent timing differences may develop in transactions occurring in C tax years involving the LIFO inventory method, intangible drilling costs, and construction period charges (refer to Chapter 4).

> ☑ TAX PLANNING
> CONSIDERATIONS

## DETERMINING WHEN THE ELECTION IS ADVISABLE

Effective tax planning with S corporations begins with determining whether the election is appropriate. In this context, one should consider the following factors:

—Are losses from the business anticipated? If so, the election may be highly attractive because these losses pass through to the shareholders.

—What are the tax brackets of the shareholders? If the shareholders are in high individual income tax brackets, it may be desirable to avoid S corporation status and have profits taxed to the corporation at lower rates (e. g., 15 percent or 18 percent). When the immediate pass-through of Subchapter S taxable income is avoided, profits of the corporation may later be bailed out by the shareholders at capital gain rates through stock redemptions, liquidating distributions, or sales of stock to others; received as dividend distributions in low tax bracket years; or negated by a partial or complete step-up in basis upon the death of the shareholder.[93] On the other hand, if the shareholders are in low individual income tax brackets, the pass-through of corporate profits does not impact so forcefully, and avoidance of the corporate income tax becomes the paramount consideration. Under these circumstances, the S election could be highly attractive. Bear in mind, however, that an S corporation usually escapes Federal taxes but may not be immune from state and local taxes imposed on corporations.

—Closely allied to the above is the possible pass-through to the shareholders of any qualified investment that the corporation may be allowed on the acquisition of § 38 property. Such pass-through would occur if the corporation has elected S corporation status.

—Does a C corporation anticipate significant long-term capital gains or § 1231 gains in the next taxable year? Assuming the corporation does, it might consider the one-shot election approach, whereby S corporation status would be in effect for only the year of recognition of these gains. After the year of recognition, the corporation could either voluntarily revoke the election or arrange to have the elec-

---

**93.** See the discussion of § 1014 in Chapter 12.

tion terminate through involuntary means. Although some of these gains might be taxed to the corporation by virtue of § 1374 or § 1375, the overall tax consequence probably would be less severe than if the election had not been made.[94]

**Example 34.** Assume a C corporation is considering selling capital assets that will result in a net long-term capital gain of $100,000. If the corporation has other income of at least $100,000, the § 1375 penalty tax does not apply. If the sole shareholder is in the 30% tax bracket, a one-shot election would result in a $4,900 tax savings:

|  | C Corporation | S Corporation |
|---|---|---|
| Corporate tax | $ 28,000 | $ 21,000 |
| Amount distributed | 72,000 | 79,000 |
| Shareholder tax (30%) | 21,600 | 23,700 |
| Total taxes | $ 49,600 | $ 44,700 |

—Does a C corporation have a net operating loss carryover from a prior year? Keep in mind that such loss cannot be used in an S year. Even worse, S years count in the 15-year carryover limitation. But even if the S election is made, one might consider losing the election before the carryover limitation expires. This would permit utilization of the loss by what is now a C corporation.

Keep in mind that except for the operational rules contained in §§ 1361–1379, an S corporation will fall within many of the other provisions in the Code generally applicable to all corporations. In the case of a stock redemption, for example, one would look to the rules set forth in §§ 302, 303, and 304 (refer to Chapter 4). Likewise, the liquidation of an S corporation would involve §§ 336 and 337 as to the effect on the corporation and §§ 331 and 333 as to the effect on the shareholder (refer to Chapter 5). An S corporation may not use § 332 to liquidate an inactive subsidiary, because § 1371(a)(2) treats an S corporation as an individual when acting in a shareholder capacity. This same reasoning forecloses the use of a § 338 election as to a purchasing corporation.

## MAKING A PROPER ELECTION

Once the parties have decided the election is appropriate, it becomes essential to insure that the election is properly made.

—Make sure all shareholders consent thereto. If any doubt exists concerning the shareholder status of an individual, it would be wise to have such party issue a consent anyway.[95] Not enough consents will be fatal; the same cannot be said for too many consents.

---

94. The loss of the election probably would bring into play the five-year waiting period of § 1362(g) before a new election could be made. Under such circumstances, it is doubtful that the IRS would be willing to waive this waiting period. See, for example, Rev.Rul. 78–307, 1978–2 C.B. 222. There is, therefore, a definite constraint on how often the one-shot election can be utilized.

95. See *William B. Wilson*, 34 TCM 463, T.C.Memo. 1975–92.

—Be sure that the election is timely and properly filed. Along this line, either hand carry the election to an IRS office or send it by certified or registered mail. Needless to say, a copy of the election should become part of the corporation's permanent files.

—Regarding the above, be careful to ascertain when the fifteenth day of the third month period begins to run for a newly formed corporation. Remember that an election made too soon (i. e., before the corporation is in existence) is worse than one made too late. If serious doubt exists concerning when this period begins, more than one election might be considered a practical means of guaranteeing the desired result.

## PRESERVING THE ELECTION

Recall, however, how an election can be lost. To preserve an election, the following points should be kept in mind:

—As a starting place, all parties concerned should be made aware of the various transactions that lead to the loss of an election.

—Watch for possible disqualification as a small business corporation. For example, the divorce of a shareholder, accompanied by a property settlement, could violate the 35-shareholder limitation. Or the death of a shareholder could result in a nonqualifying trust becoming a shareholder. The latter circumstance might well be avoided by utilizing a buy and sell agreement binding the deceased shareholder's estate to turn in the stock to the corporation for redemption or, as an alternative, to sell it to the surviving shareholders.[96]

—Make sure a new majority shareholder (including the estate of a deceased shareholder) does not file a refusal to continue the election.

—Watch for the passive investment income limitation of § 1375(a). Avoid a consecutive third year with excess passive income if a corporation has accumulated earnings and profits. In this connection, assets that produce passive investment income (e. g., stocks and bonds, certain rent properties) might well be retained by the shareholders in their individual capacities and thereby kept out of the corporation.

—Do not transfer stock to a nonresident alien.

—Do not create an active affiliate.

## PLANNING THE OPERATION OF THE CORPORATION

Operating an S corporation to achieve optimum tax savings for all parties involved requires a great deal of care and, most important, an understanding of the applicable tax rules.

—Although the accumulated adjustments account (AAA) is used primarily by an S corporation with accumulated earnings and profits from a Subchapter C year, all S corporations should maintain an

---

**96.** See the discussion in Chapter 12 for the treatment of buy and sell agreements.

accurate record of the AAA. Because there is a grace period for distributing the AAA after termination of the S election, the parties must be in a position to determine the balance of the account.

—Under the new rules, it is advisable to avoid accumulated earnings and profits. There is the ever present danger of terminating the election because of excess passive investment income in three consecutive years. Further, there is the § 1375 penalty tax on excess passive net income. Thus, try to eliminate such accumulated earnings and profits through a dividend distribution or liquidation of the corporation with a subsequent reincorporation. If the accumulated earnings and profits account is small, to eliminate the problem, all the shareholders may consent under § 1368(e)(3) to have distributions treated as made first from accumulated earnings and profits rather than from the AAA.

—If excess passive income is a problem, try to put the passive income into the first two years and hold the passive income in the third year below the 25 percent mark. Or get rid of the earnings and profits before the end of the third year. The bypass election under § 1368(e)(3) may be used to avoid a termination under § 1362(d)(3) or the penalty tax under § 1375 because of excess passive investment income. This election allows the corporation to distribute all of the accumulated earnings and profits before the end of the year.

—The AAA bypass election under § 1368(e)(3) may be used to avoid the accumulated earnings tax or personal holding company tax in the year preceding the first tax year under Subchapter S. Because distributions of the AAA are not treated as dividends as described in § 562(a), the bypass election allows the accumulated earnings and profits to be distributed instead.

—Be careful of a 50 percent change in stock ownership. In such a case, a fiscal year corporation must change to a calendar year. Further, "grandfather" fringe benefits in existence on September 28, 1982, will fall under partnership treatment.

—Do not issue a fatal second class of stock. Issue straight debt to avoid creating a second class of stock. Establish an instrument with a written unconditional promise to pay on demand or on a specific date a sum certain in money with a fixed interest rate and payment date.

—Section 1368(e)(1)(A) indicates that a net loss allocated to a shareholder reduces the AAA. This required adjustment should encourage an electing corporation to make annual distributions of net income to avoid the reduction of an AAA by a future net loss.

—A net loss in excess of tax basis may be carried forward and deducted only by the same shareholder in succeeding years. Thus, before disposing of the stock, increase the basis of such stock/loan to flow through the loss. The next shareholder does not obtain the carryover loss.

—Any unused carryover loss in existence on termination of the S election may be deducted only in the next tax year and is limited to the individual's *stock* basis (not loan basis) in the post-termination year.[97] The shareholder may wish to purchase more stock to increase the tax basis in order to absorb the loss.

—There are still some differences in cash and property distributions. Old previously taxed income in an electing corporation can be distributed only in cash according to prior authority. Also, a distribution of appreciated property by an S corporation may result in a gain allocated to and reported by the shareholders.

—The amount of salary that a shareholder-employee of an S corporation is paid can have varying tax consequences and should be considered carefully. Larger amounts might be advantageous if the maximum contribution allowed under the retirement plan has not been reached. Smaller amounts may be beneficial if the parties are trying to shift taxable income to lower-bracket shareholders, to lessen payroll taxes,[98] to curtail a reduction of Social Security benefits, or to reduce losses that do not pass through because of the basis limitation. Many of the problems that do arise in this area can be solved with advanced planning. Most often, such planning involves making before-the-fact projections of the tax positions of the parties involved.

—The IRS does have the power to require that reasonable compensation be paid to family members who render services or provide capital to the S corporation. Section 1366(e) allows the IRS to make adjustments in the items taken into account by family-member shareholders to reflect the value of services (or capital) provided by such parties.

—Try, as best as possible, to time the acquisition by the corporation of § 38 property to provide maximum benefit to the shareholders on the pass-through of the qualified investment. Allocated amounts of § 38 property are passed through to shareholders in their taxable year in which or with which the S corporate year ends. Thus, if an S corporation has a fiscal year different from the shareholders, accelerated purchases of § 38 property in the earlier part of the fiscal year may be necessary to avoid delaying the tax benefit for a shareholder to a year later than the year placed into service. Also, be careful of recapture situations that might be triggered through a premature disposition of § 38 property or by a shareholder's disposition of the stock.

—An S corporation may use the installment method under § 453 and control the tax on capital gains.[99] If a corporation anticipates a capital gain in excess of $25,000, it may elect to spread the gain over a number of years or, at least, beyond the third electing year. This manner of circumventing the capital gain tax can be most fruitful when §§ 1245 and 1250 assets are involved. Under both Reg. §§ 1.1245–6(d) and 1.1250–1(c)(6), all ordinary income is recog-

---

**97.** § 1366(d)(3).
**98.** In this regard, see Rev.Rul. 74–44, 1974–1 C.B. 287.
**99.** Rev.Rul. 65–292, 1965–2 C.B. 319.

nized first; thus, the S corporation can recognize the ordinary income first and save the § 1231 gains for years after the third electing year.

—If the shareholders of an S corporation decide to terminate the election through involuntary means, make sure that the disqualifying act possesses substance. When the intent of the parties is obvious and the act represents a technical noncompliance rather than a real change, the IRS may be able to disregard it and keep the parties in S status.[100]

## PROBLEM MATERIALS

### Discussion Questions

1. What are the major advantages and disadvantages of an S election?

2. Which of the following items could be considered to be disadvantageous (or potential hazards) for S elections:

    (a) The 85% dividends received deduction is lost.

    (b) Foreign tax credit is not available.

    (c) Net operating loss at the corporate level cannot be utilized.

    (d) Constructive dividends are not actually distributed.

    (e) A locked-in AAA occurs after termination.

    (f) An AAA is a personal right that cannot be transferred.

    (g) Basis in stock is increased by constructive dividends.

    (h) A trust is treated as a shareholder.

    (i) Salaries of certain shareholders are not high enough.

3. What happens to net operating losses incurred in preelection years when an S corporation terminates its election?

4. What is the tax effect on its shareholders when an S corporation that has an accumulated adjustments account terminates its election and makes subsequent distributions?

5. An S corporation has taxable income of $10,000 for its first electing tax year, 19X9, and accumulated earnings and profits through 19X8 of $20,000 (prior to the election). During 19X9, the corporation pays a $16,000 cash dividend to its sole shareholder who has a $6,500 stock basis. What amount qualifies for the dividend exclusion?

6. X, Inc. (a calendar year corporation), has a $25,000 net operating loss for 19X5. On January 10, 19X6, the president contacts you for advice as to the practicality of an S election for 19X6. Apparently the president is expecting another $30,000 net operating loss this year. Discuss the possibility and effect of the election.

7. K is considering creating an S corporation for her interior decorating business. She has a friend who has an S corporation with a January 31 fiscal year. She wishes to set up a similar fiscal year. Please advise K.

8. Y's basis in his S corporation is $5,500, but he anticipates that his share of the net operating loss for this year will be $7,400. The tax year is not closed. Advise Y.

---

**100.** See *Clarence L. Hook*, 58 T.C. 267 (1972).

9.  On February 23, 19X4, the two 50% shareholders of a calendar year corporation decide to elect to be an S corporation. One of the shareholders had purchased her stock from a previous shareholder on January 18, 19X4. Discuss any potential problems.

10. Q is the sole owner of a calendar year S corporation that manufactures solar water heaters. On March 9, Q realizes that the corporation is going to make a very large profit. Discuss how Q can terminate his corporation's S election.

11. Which, if any, of the following will prevent a corporation from making a valid S corporation election:

    (a) There are 26 shareholders.

    (b) One shareholder is a resident alien.

    (c) One of the shareholders is a partnership.

    (d) There is a net operating loss during the year.

    (e) One-half of the common stock does not have voting rights.

    (f) One of the shareholders is an estate.

    (g) One of the shareholders is a minor.

12. In 1986, an S corporation distributes land worth $88,000 to a 50% shareholder. The land cost $22,000 three years ago. Discuss any tax impact on the corporation as well as on the shareholder from this distribution. The corporation has no accumulated earnings and profits, and the stock basis is $102,000.

13. A termination of the calendar year S corporation election is effective as of the first day of the following tax year in which of the following situations:

    (a) A partnership becomes a shareholder on April 2.

    (b) There is a failure of the passive investment income limitation.

    (c) A new 45% shareholder affirmatively refuses to consent to the S election.

    (d) Shareholders owning 57% of the outstanding stock file a formal revocation on February 23.

    (e) A fatal second class of stock is issued on March 3.

    (f) The electing corporation becomes a member of an affiliated group on March 10.

14. T, a shareholder-employee, owns 11% of an S corporation that was incorporated in 1983. Which of the following items are deductible by this corporation if paid on behalf of T in 1986:

    (a) Salary of $22,000.

    (b) $370 paid for an accident and health plan under §§ 105 and 106.

    (c) Bonus of $9,050.

    (d) Premiums of $625 on the cost of $45,000 of group term life insurance.

    (e) $2,075 of meals and lodging furnished to T for the convenience of the corporation.

    (f) $5,000 of employee death benefits paid to T's beneficiary (wife) on his death in November.

15. Which of the following income items are considered generally to be passive investment income as defined in § 1362(d)(3)(D):

    (a) Royalties from a book.

    (b) Mineral royalties.

    (c) Long-term capital gain from the sale of land held as an investment.

(d) Annuity income.

(e) Section 1245 gain from the sale of an automobile.

(f) Section 1231 gain from the sale of real estate.

(g) Receipts received from the liquidation of a 60%-owned subsidiary.

(h) Dividend income from a domestic corporation.

(i) Dividend income from a foreign corporation.

(j) Rent income from an apartment unit.

(k) Interest income.

(l) Long-term capital gain from the sale of stock held as an investment.

16. An S corporation recently had its S election involuntarily terminated. Does the corporation have to wait five years before making a new election?

17. One of your clients is considering electing S corporation status. T, Inc., is a six-year old company with two equal shareholders who paid $30,000 each for their stock. In 1986, T, Inc., has a $35,000 NOL carryforward. Estimated income is $40,000 for 1986 and approximately $25,000 for each of the next three years. Assume that the two shareholders are in the 45% and 40% tax brackets. Should T, Inc., make an S election for 1986?

## Problems

1. A calendar year S corporation has no accumulated earnings and profits in 19X3. The corporation makes a cash dividend of $90,000 to Q, an individual shareholder. Q's accumulated adjustments account is $40,000, and the adjusted basis in his stock is $70,000. Determine how this distribution should be taxed.

2. In Problem 1, assume the same facts except that Q's share of accumulated earnings and profits is $10,000. Would your answer change?

3. At the end of 19X4, an S corporation has gross receipts of $190,000 and gross income of $170,000. The corporation has accumulated earnings and profits of $22,000 and taxable income of $35,000. It has passive investment income of $100,000, with $30,000 of expenses directly related to the production of passive investment income. Calculate the excess net passive income (ENPI) and any § 1375 penalty tax.

4. P owned 10% of the outstanding stock of a calendar year S corporation. P sold all of his stock to Q on July 1, 19X5. At the end of 19X5, the total AAA was $800,000 before considering any distributions, and the amount in the accumulated earnings and profits account was $800,000. The S corporation made a distribution of $600,000 to the shareholders on April 1, 19X5, which included a distribution of $60,000 to P. On October 1, 19X5, another distribution of $600,000 was made to the shareholders, including $60,000 to Q. Determine what amount is taxable to P and Q.

5. A corporation has a net operating loss in 19X4 of $20,000. A valid S election is made in 19X5, and again there is a $20,000 NOL. The stock of the corporation was at all times during 19X5 owned by the same 10 shareholders, each of whom owned 10% of the stock. If R, one of the 10 shareholders, has an adjusted basis at the beginning of 19X5 of $1,600, what amount, if any, may she deduct on her individual tax return for 19X5? Assume the corporation uses a calendar year for tax purposes.

6. For 19X4, a C corporation elects S corporation status. The only income in 19X4 is a $100,000 capital gain from the sale of stock. How much tax must the corporation pay in 19X4?

7. Assuming the same facts in Problem 6, how much tax does the sole shareholder have to pay in 19X4, assuming he has no other capital transactions and is in the 50% tax bracket?

8. Assume the same facts as in Problems 6 and 7. If the corporation had elected S treatment four years earlier, what would the total tax for the corporation and the sole shareholder be in 19X4?

9. M owns stock in an S corporation. The corporation sustains a net operating loss during 19X9, and M's share of the loss is $45,000. Her adjusted basis in the stock is $24,000, but she has a loan outstanding to the corporation in the amount of $3,000. What amount, if any, is she entitled to deduct with respect to the NOL?

10. A calendar year S corporation owes $90,000 to P, a calendar year shareholder. At the end of 19X4, P's stock basis in the S corporation was zero and the debt basis was $70,000. In 19X5 the S corporation becomes bankrupt, and the debt to P becomes worthless. P's share of the S corporation's ordinary losses for 19X5 is $40,000, which is passed through and used by P in computing his 19X5 taxable income. These same losses reduce P's debt basis to $30,000. Determine any losses P may recognize.

11. An S corporation's profit and loss statement for 19X4 shows net profits of $75,000 (i. e., book income). The corporation has three equal shareholders. From supplemental data, you obtain the following information about the corporation for 19X4:

| | |
|---|---:|
| Advertising expense | $ 7,000 |
| Tax-exempt income | 1,500 |
| Dividends received | 9,000 |
| Section 1231 gain | 6,000 |
| Section 1245 gain | 20,000 |
| Recovery of bad debts | 3,500 |
| Capital losses | 6,000 |
| Salary to owners (each) | 8,000 |
| Cost of goods sold | 82,000 |

(a) Compute Subchapter S § 1366(a)(1)(B) taxable income or (loss).

(b) What would be one of the shareholders' portion of § 1366(a)(1)(B) taxable income or (loss)?

(c) If one of the shareholders and his wife have $10,000 of personal dividends, what would be their taxable dividends if they file a joint return.

12. The tax return of an S corporation shows a net loss of $8,700 [i. e., § 1366(a)(1)(B) loss] for 19X4. G, an individual, owns 30% of the stock during the entire year. While auditing the corporate books, you obtain the following information for 19X4:

| | |
|---|---:|
| Salaries paid to the three owners | $ 42,000 |
| Charitable contributions | 6,000 |
| Tax-exempt interest | 1,500 |
| Dividends received ($4,000 was from a foreign company) | 9,000 |
| Section 1231 losses | 3,000 |
| Section 1245 gain | 15,000 |
| Recoveries of prior property taxes | 3,000 |
| Cost of goods sold | 64,000 |
| Capital losses | 4,500 |
| Selling expenses | 4,200 |
| Long-term capital gains | 15,000 |

(a) Compute book income or (loss).

(b) If G's tax basis in his stock is $2,200 at year-end, what amount may he deduct in 19X4 on his individual tax return?

13. The tax return of an S corporation shows taxable income of $70,000 [i. e., a § 1366(a)(1)(B) gain] for 19X4. P, an individual, owns all of the stock during the year. The corporate books show the following information for 19X4:

| | |
|---|---:|
| P's beginning stock basis | $ 2,000 |
| Cash dividends to P | 30,000 |
| Tax-exempt interest | 3,000 |
| Net sales | 182,000 |
| Section 1245 gain | 10,000 |
| Section 1231 loss | 8,000 |
| Charitable contributions | 7,000 |
| Cost of goods sold | 72,000 |
| Capital loss | 5,000 |
| Overhead expenses | 12,000 |
| Long-term capital gain | 9,000 |
| Political contributions | 2,000 |
| P's loan to S corporation | 12,000 |
| P's additional stock purchases | 4,000 |
| P's beginning AAA | 13,000 |

(a) Compute P's stock basis at the end of 19X4.

(b) Compute P's ending AAA account.

14. At the beginning of 19X4, T, the sole shareholder of a calendar year S corporation, has a stock basis of $6,300. From supplemental data, you obtain the following information about the corporation for 19X4:

| | |
|---|---:|
| Tax-exempt insurance proceeds | $ 10,000 |
| Long-term capital gain | 8,000 |
| Section 1231 gain | 4,000 |
| Section 1366(a)(1)(B) taxable income | 23,000 |
| Distribution to T | 11,000 |
| Charitable contributions | 1,000 |
| Section 1250 gain | 4,000 |
| Dividends received | 6,000 |
| Short-term capital loss | 3,000 |
| Long-term capital loss | 2,000 |

Calculate T's ending stock basis.

15. B owns 50% of the stock in an S corporation. This corporation sustains a $12,000 net operating loss and a $2,000 capital loss during 19X9. B's adjusted basis in the stock is $2,000, but she has a loan outstanding to the corporation for $3,000. What amount, if any, is she entitled to deduct with respect to these losses on her Form 1040 for 19X9?

16. An S corporation had a net operating loss of $36,500 in 19X8 (not a leap year). E and B were the equal and only shareholders of the corporation from January 1 to January 21, 19X8. On January 21,19X8, E sold his stock to B for $41,000. At the beginning of 19X8, both E and B had a basis of $40,000 in the stock of the corporation. (Note: On the date of the sale, stock is regarded as being held by the transferee.)

(a) What amount, if any, of the NOL will pass through to E?

(b) What amount of the NOL will pass through to B?

(c) What gain, if any, will be taxable to E on the sale of his stock?

17. Z purchased all the stock of S Corporation on March 1, 19X8, for $200,000. Throughout 19X8 and 19X9, the corporation was an S corporation. During 19X8, the corporation did not make any distributions and reported a profit of $20,450, of which $5,000 was attributable to the period before Z acquired the stock.

Because of illness, Z sold his stock in S Corporation on October 20, 19X9. The corporation operated at a loss of $13,860 during 19X9 but did make a $4,000 dividend distribution on July 1, 19X9. Four thousand dollars of the loss was sustained after Z sold his stock. (Assume no special election is made.)

(a) What amount, if any, of the corporation's income must Z include in his gross income for 19X8? (Assume a non-leap year.)

(b) Determine the amount, if any, of the corporation's net operating loss for 19X9 that Z may deduct.

(c) Calculate Z's gain (or loss) if he sells his entire interest in S Corporation for $225,000.

18. In the following independent statements, indicate whether the transaction will increase (+), decrease (−), or have no effect (NE) on the adjusted basis of a shareholder's stock in an S corporation:

(a) Tax-exempt income.

(b) Long-term capital gain.

(c) Net operating loss.

(d) Section 1231 gain.

(e) Excess of percentage depletion over the basis of the property.

(f) Section 1366(a)(1)(B) income.

(g) Nontaxable return-of-capital distribution by the corporation.

(h) Charitable contributions.

(i) Business gift in excess of $25.

(j) Section 1245 gain.

(k) Dividends received by the S corporation.

(l) Short-term capital loss.

(m) Recovery of a bad debt.

(n) Long-term capital loss.

19. An S corporation reports its income on a calendar year basis. On April 1, 19X3, the corporation issues a second class of stock which terminates the election. Through March 31, the corporate records show that the corporation has $42,000 of income, $22,000 of deductions, and $18,000 of tax credits. On December 31, 19X3, the tax records indicate that the corporation has earned $340,000 of income and has deductions of $180,000 and tax credits of $43,000. Assume no special elections are made.

(a) What amounts would the sole shareholder show on his individual return in 19X3?

(b) Compute the taxable income for the C corporation.

20. A calendar year S corporation purchases $200,000 of new § 38 property with a five-year cost recovery. A owns 50% of the stock for the entire year. B sells his 50% of the stock to C on November 1, 19X5. Calculate the division of the § 38 property among the shareholders.

21. B is the sole shareholder in S, Inc., an S corporation. B also operates a sole proprietorship. During the year ending December 31, 19X5, S, Inc., purchases $145,000 of used § 38 property. The proprietorship additionally acquires $25,000 of used § 38 property. How much used qualified investment credit property may B benefit from on his 19X5 return?

22. In December 19X6, and pursuant to a qualified partial liquidation, an S corporation distributes property valued at $90,000 (with an adjusted basis of $30,000) to its only shareholder, D.

(a) What amount, if any, is taxable to the corporation?

(b) Assume the adjusted basis of the property is $100,000 instead of $30,000. What amount is taxable?

23. Using the following legend, classify the transaction as a plus (+) or minus (−) in Schedule M on page 4 of Form 1120S:

    LEGEND

    PTI  = Shareholders' undistributed taxable income previously taxed
    AAA = Accumulated adjustments account
    OAA = Other adjustments account
    NA   = No impact directly on Schedule M

    (a) Receipt of tax-exempt interest income.

    (b) Unreasonable compensation determined.

    (c) Ordinary income (line 21).

    (d) Distribution of nontaxable income (PTI) from 1981.

    (e) Nontaxable life insurance proceeds.

    (f) Expenses related to tax-exempt securities.

    (g) Charitable contributions.

    (h) Gifts in excess of $25.

    (i) Nondeductible fines.

    (j) Organizational expenses.

24. During 1984, N, an individual, loans $100,000 to his solely owned S corporation. During 1985, his basis in the debt is reduced to $60,000 because N recognized $40,000 of losses from the S corporation on his personal tax return. In March 1986, the corporation repays $50,000 of the loan to the shareholder. How much income, if any, does N recognize in 1986? [See Rev.Rul. 68–537.]

25. X, an individual, owns 50% of an S corporation's stock with a basis of $40,000. X receives a corporate distribution of appreciated property with a fair market value of $18,000 (adjusted basis of $4,000). Calculate X's stock basis *after* the property distribution.

26. An S corporation's only asset is an appreciated apartment complex with an adjusted basis of $200,000. The current fair market value of the complex is $1,000,000; depreciation recapture is $240,000. The only shareholder, Q, has a $30,000 basis in her stock. The S corporation adopts a plan of liquidation under § 337, and the apartment complex is sold for $1,000,000. Assume an individual capital gain rate of 20%, an ordinary income rate of 50%, and an S corporation capital gain rate of 28%. Calculate the total taxes payable by Q and the S corporation.

27. B, Inc., a calendar year S corporation is owned 60% by P and 40% by Q. On January 1, 1985, the corporation places into service equipment with a cost basis of $100,000 (five-year recovery property).

    (a) What happens to the two shareholders in 1985 with respect to the investment tax credit?

    (b) Assume that on January 18, 1987, Q sells his 40% interest in B, Inc., to M, an individual. What tax result to Q and M?

    (c) Assume that on January 15, 1987, the S election is terminated. What tax result?

    (d) Assume that the corporation is liquidated under § 337 early in January 1986, with P receiving cash of $120,000 and Q receiving all of the other assets worth $80,000. What happens?

    (e) Suppose that on January 3, 1987, P dies. What happens?

## Comprehensive Tax Return Problem

John Martin (234-10-5214) and Stan Mitchell (244-58-8695) are 55% and 45% owners of Ram, Inc. (74-8265910), a textile manufacturing company located in Kannapolis, N.C. The company's first S election was on January 1, 1975. The following information was taken from the income statement for 1985:

| | |
|---|---:|
| Other income | $ 380 |
| Interest income | 267 |
| Gross sales | 1,376,214 |
| Beginning inventory (1985) | 7,607 |
| Direct labor | 303,102 |
| Direct materials used | 278,143 |
| Other direct costs | 149,356 |
| Ending inventory (1985) | 13,467 |
| Taxes | 39,235 |
| Contributions to United Fund | 445 |
| Contribution to Senator Brown's campaign | 5,000 |
| Fines (illegal) | 34 |
| Life insurance premiums (the corporation is the beneficiary) | 98 |
| Compensation to shareholder/officers (proportionate to ownership) | 34,934 |
| Salaries and wages | 62,103 |
| Interest | 17,222 |
| Repairs | 16,106 |
| Depreciation | 16,154 |
| Advertising | 3,246 |
| Pension plan contributions | 6,000 |
| Employee benefit program | 2,875 |
| Other deductions | 63,784 |
| Net income | 384,884 |

A comparative balance sheet appears as follows:

| | Beginning of the Year | End of the Year |
|---|---:|---:|
| Cash | $ 47,840 | $ 61,242 |
| Accounts receivable | 134,685 | 194,721 |
| Inventories | 7,607 | 13,467 |
| Prepaid expenses | 10,333 | 7,582 |
| Loans to shareholders | 313 | 727 |
| Buildings and trucks | 138,203 | 244,348 |
| Accumulated depreciation | (84,235) | (100,389) |
| Land | 1,809 | 16,513 |
| Life insurance | 11,566 | 18,344 |
| | $ 268,121 | $ 456,555 |
| Accounts payable | 52,404 | 82,963 |
| Notes payable (less than one year) | 5,122 | 8,989 |
| Loans from shareholders | 155,751 | 191,967 |
| Notes payable (more than one year) | 21,821 | 33,835 |
| Loan on life insurance | 5,312 | 16,206 |
| Capital stock | 1,003 | 1,003 |
| Paid-in capital | 9,559 | 9,559 |
| Retained earnings (unappropriated) | (8,314) | (8,314) |
| Prior taxed income | 41,585 | 41,585 |
| Accumulated adjustments account | –0– | ? |
| Other adjustments account | –0– | ? |
| Treasury stock | (16,122) | (16,122) |
| | $ 268,121 | $ 456,555 |

The accounting firm provides the following additional information:

| | |
|---|---:|
| Property qualifying for investment credit (light-duty truck) | $ 16,000 |
| Dividends paid to shareholders | 290,000 |

From the preceding information, prepare Form 1120S and Schedule K-1 for John Martin. If any information is missing, make realistic assumptions.

## Research Problems

*Research Problem 1.* In 1970, S Corporation is formed by T to engage in a new venture. Under its charter granted by the state of incorporation, S Corporation is authorized to issue both common and preferred stock. However, only common stock is issued to T. At the time of incorporation, a Form 2553 is properly executed and timely filed with the IRS.

After several years of operating losses and when it appears that S Corporation might generate a modest profit, the preferred stock is issued to T as a stock dividend. In the years following the dividend, S Corporation enjoys substantial taxable income, none of which is distributed as dividends. As a result of the undistributed profits, T is able to sell his preferred stock to an unrelated third party for $100,000 on April 14, 1984. In 1985, S Corporation redeems all of its outstanding preferred stock for $120,000.

Comment on these transactions in connection with the following:

(a) The tax status of S Corporation from 1970 to present.

(b) The tax consequences to T during this period.

(c) The tax consequences to the third party upon the redemption of the preferred stock.

From a tax planning standpoint, assess the wisdom of the procedures that were carried out.

*Research Problem 2.* On March 14, 19X5, a client walks into your office and indicates that his S corporation has $115,000 of previously taxed income. Upon further questioning, you learn that the corporation has accumulated earnings and profits of $76,000. Your new client wants to know how to get this PTI out of his solely owned corporation. Subsequent investigation indicates that his stock basis is $98,000 and his accumulated adjustments account has a balance of $71,000.

*Research Problem 3.* During 19X9, S's share of his S corporation's net operating loss is $7,000. At the end of the year, the adjusted basis of his stock in the corporation is $2,500. In addition, he has loaned $2,000 to the corporation. During the next year, his share of taxable income is $800 before he sells his stock, and the corporation repays S the $2,000 loan. Discuss all tax considerations.

*Partial list of research aids:*

Code § 1366(d).

*Byrne v. Comm.,* 66–2 USTC ¶ 9483, 17 AFTR2d 1272, 361 F.2d 939 (CA–7, 1966).

*Sam Novell,* 29 TCM 92, T.C.Memo. 1970–31.

*Research Problem 4.* F Corporation was organized by T in 1979 and shortly thereafter purchased all of the assets of P Corporation. Among the assets transferred were a race track and all of the stock of R Corporation (a wholly owned subsidiary of P Corporation). R Corporation had been formed by P Corporation in 1963, and its sole asset consisted of land near the race track but in another county. Other transactions involving these entities are summarized in chronological order as follows:

—Between 1967 and 1975, R Corporation and P Corporation entered into a lease for the use of the land as a parking lot for the race track. There was some evidence that P Corporation paid to R Corporation some rents under the lease arrangement.

—During 1976, R Corporation granted an easement over its land to a pipeline transmission company.

—In 1977, the directors of R Corporation executed a mortgage on the land to secure a loan to P Corporation. The instrument named both R Corporation and P Corporation as mortgagors.

—In 1980, R Corporation granted another easement over its land, this time to a utility. The consideration for the easement, however, was paid to F Corporation.

—R Corporation filed corporate income tax returns for 1979, 1980, and 1981. It reported no income and no expenses; the forms bore the notation "CORPORATION INACTIVE."

—During the years at issue, R Corporation had no office, bank account, or employees. It negotiated no leases with and received no rent from F Corporation. The latter paid all of the upkeep expenses of the land, as well as the real estate taxes and other carrying charges associated with it.

After making a timely election under Subchapter S, T deducted on his individual tax returns for 1980 and 1981 F Corporation's net operating losses. Discuss the propriety of these losses in light of the affiliated group restriction.

*Research Problem 5.* Taxpayer P is the sole shareholder of a C corporation. The corporation was formed several years ago and operates an apartment complex. P is considering making an S election. The apartment complex furnishes the following services and facilities for the tenants:

—A swimming pool including patio, outdoor furniture, rest rooms, and large beach umbrellas.

—A laundry room.

—A recreation room equipped with kitchen appliances and furniture that is available for parties and meetings.

—Individual storage compartments separate from the apartments.

—Apartments with full electric kitchen, dishwasher, carpeting, and draperies.

—Redecoration of each apartment every three years.

—Message service.

—Individual parking spaces.

—Cable television service.

—Full-time maintenance for any kind of day-to-day repairs and odd jobs.

—Normal services such as utility hookups.

—Maintenance of a qualification fee at a nearby golf course to provide future tenants with the option to join the club.

Advise this taxpayer about making the S election with respect to the passive investment income requirements in § 1362(d)(3). As to C status, what about § 543(a)(2)?

*Research Problem 6.* On February 10, 19X5, a calendar year S corporation mistakenly issues a second class of stock, thereby terminating the S election. During 19X5, the corporation had nonseparately computed income of $200,000, nonseparately computed deductions of $60,000, tax-exempt income of $20,000, and tax credits of $30,000. The corporate records indicate that through February 9, 19X5, the S corporation earned $20,000 of nonseparately computed income, incurred $5,000 of nonseparately computed deductions, and had no tax-exempt income or tax credits. Discuss the annualization procedure for this corporation, including the special election provided for in § 1362(e)(3).

*Research Problem 7.* A calendar year S corporation is equally owned by A and B during the first half of 1985. B sells all of his stock to C on July 2, 1985. Up to the date of the sale, the corporation had incurred a $70,000 operating loss. After the stock sale, the corporation had $20,000 of income from operations. Discuss the alternatives available to the three shareholders.

*Research Problem 8.* On July 19, 1986, several taxpayers as primary applicants and B as a secondary applicant apply for a loan of $725,000 from a local bank. On August 12, 1986, the taxpayers agree to buy some farm land and several pieces of farm equipment for $775,000. The next day a warranty deed is issued by the sellers showing consideration of $775,000. The farm land is transferred to X, an S corporation organized by B. On August 19, 1986, B and X sign a variable interest rate loan for $700,000 on which they agree to be jointly and severally liable. This note is secured by a mortgage for the land owned by X. B and his spouse sign the mortgage and other loan documents on behalf of X Corporation. On August 23, 1986, the taxpayers sign the articles of incorporation that were filed with the state in which X was incorporated. In organizing the S corporation (X), the assets and liabilities are transferred under § 351. The $700,000 bank loan is included in the transfer. Do the shareholders receive an adjusted basis increase as a result of a third-party loan?

# Partnerships: Formation and Operation  9

## CHAPTER OBJECTIVES

—Define a partnership.
—Discuss the tax ramifications of forming and operating a partnership.
—Explain how nonliquidating distributions to the partners are handled.
—Provide insight as to when the partnership form of doing business is advisable.

# OVERVIEW

Before enactment of the Internal Revenue Code of 1954, taxpayers operating a business in partnership form were faced with a high degree of uncertainty as to the tax consequences of their activities. This uncertainty was attributable to the lack of statutory rules governing the tax effects of transactions between partners and their partnership. The absence of clarifying provisions in the 1939 Code[1] resulted in a reliance on case law in tax planning for partners and partnerships, and the paucity of relevant cases contributed to the need for specific legislation.

Subchapter K of the 1954 Code contains the basic statutory rules governing the tax consequences of transactions between partners and their partnerships. Passage of these provisions (§ § 701 through 761) has, for the most part, rendered much of the pre-1954 case law inapplicable. However, many of the statutory rules of Subchapter K and the general approach taken in drafting the partnership provisions can be traced to judicial decisions rendered before 1954. Unfortunately, the limited number of cases decided within the past three decades offers little guidance for such unsettled questions as the following:

1.  What is the waiting period for a partnership allocation and distribution to be made to a partner who contributed property to avoid the disguised sales rules?

2.  When is a substantial interest retained in property contributed for a partnership interest so that recapture of investment tax credits can be avoided?

3.  Are suspended pass-through losses available to a transferee partner whose partnership interest is acquired by gift?

For these and other unsettled questions, taxpayers and advisers must rely heavily upon the specific statutory language of Subchapter K and related Treasury authority for guidance.

## TAXATION OF PARTNERSHIP INCOME

Unlike corporations, estates, and trusts, partnerships are not considered separate tax entities for purposes of determining and paying Federal income taxes. Instead, partnership members are subject to tax on their dis-

---

1.  Although Supplement F of the 1939 Code contained nine sections dealing with the taxation of partners and partnerships, the lack of detail in these provisions and the increasing complexities of the business environment made these statutory guidelines inadequate for tax planning purposes.

tributive share of partnership income, even if an actual distribution is not made.[2] Thus, the partnership tax return (Form 1065) serves only as an information device to determine the character and amount of each partner's distributive share of partnership income and expense.[3] Although a partnership is not considered a separate tax entity for purposes of determining and paying Federal income taxes, it is treated as such for other tax purposes. Also, a partnership is treated as a separate legal entity under civil law with the right to own property and transact business in its own name.[4]

The unique treatment of partners and partnerships under Subchapter K can be traced to two general concepts that evolved long before enactment of the 1954 Code: the *entity concept* and the *aggregate* or *conduit concept.* Both concepts have been applied in civil and common law, and their influence can be seen in practically every related statutory rule. With some rules directed toward the entity concept, others based solely on the conduit concept, and still others containing a mixture of both, an individual studying the partnership provisions for the first time might find the rules difficult to grasp. However, by concentrating on the basic purpose underlying each rule, one can better understand each rule's rationale and general approach.

*Entity Concept.* The entity concept treats partners and partnerships as distinct separate units and gives the partnership its own tax "personality." The right to select its own tax year (subject to certain limitations), ACRS method (statutory percentage rate or straight-line), and accounting method is a direct reflection of this concept. This concept can be found in the statutory rules requiring a partnership to file an information tax return and treating partners as separate and distinct parties from the partnership in certain transactions between them.

*Aggregate or Conduit Concept.* From the perspective of the aggregate or conduit concept, the partnership is merely a channel through which income, credits, deductions, etc., flow to the partners for tax consideration. Under this concept, a partnership is considered as nothing more than a collection of taxpayers joined in an agency relationship with each other. Imposition of the income tax on individual partners rather than the partnership and the disallowance of certain deductions and tax credits reflect the influence of this concept.

*Combined Concepts.* Many sections of the Code contain a blend of both the entity and aggregate concepts, such as the statutory provisions concerning the formation, operation, and liquidation of a partnership.

---

**2.** Section 701 contains the statutory rule that partners are liable for income tax in their separate or individual capacities. The partnership itself cannot be subject to the income tax on its earnings.

**3.** § 6031.

**4.** See, for instance, the Uniform Partnership Act and the Uniform Limited Partnership Act, which have been adopted by most states and govern the legal conduct of businesses operating in partnership form.

## WHAT IS A PARTNERSHIP?

The Uniform Partnership Act defines a partnership as "an association of two or more persons to carry on as co-owners a business for profit."[5] Similarly, a common law definition considers a partnership to be the contractual relationship between two or more persons who join together to carry on a trade or business, each contributing money, property, labor, or skill, and all with the expectation of sharing in the profits and losses of the business. The definition of a partnership for Federal income tax purposes is much broader than the state law definition.

Sections 761(a) and 7701(a)(2) of the Code define a partnership as a syndicate, group, pool, joint venture, or other unincorporated organization through or by means of which any business, financial operation, or venture is carried on, and which is not classified as a corporation, trust, or estate. This definition of a partnership, carried over from the 1939 Code, provides adequate guidance in the classification of many typical partnerships. However, certain types of unincorporated businesses have been classified as corporations for Federal income tax purposes.[6] If the organization exhibits the characteristics of an *association* developed by the Supreme Court[7] and contained in Treasury Regulations,[8] it will be classified as a corporation regardless of its owners' intent. Thus, classification as a partnership for tax purposes can be more complex than the basic definition might indicate.[9]

Avoiding the corporate classification does not automatically qualify an organization for partnership status. For instance, a joint undertaking to share the expenses of constructing and maintaining a ditch to drain surface water from properties does not qualify the owners as partners.[10] Likewise, mere co-ownership of property that is maintained, kept in repair, and rented or leased does not constitute a partnership. If tenants in common of farm property lease the land to a farmer for cash or a share of the crops, they do not necessarily create a partnership. The Regulations provide that tenants in common may be partners if they actively carry on a trade, business, financial operation, or venture and divide the profits.[11] Thus, a partnership would exist if the co-owners of an apartment building leased space and, in addition, provided services to the occupants either directly or through an agent.[12]

---

5. § 6(1), Uniform Partnership Act.
6. Refer to Chapter 2.
7. *Morrissey v. Comm.*, 36–1 USTC ¶ 9020, 16 AFTR 1274, 56 S.Ct. 289 (USSC, 1935).
8. Reg. § 301.7701–2(a).
9. See W. S. McKee, W. F. Nelson, and R. L. Whitmire, *Federal Taxation of Partnerships and Partners* (Boston, Mass.: Warren, Gorham & Lamont, Inc., 1977 with updates), Chapter 3, for an excellent analysis of the criteria used in determining the existence of a partnership for Federal tax purposes.
10. Reg. § 1.761–1(a) and Reg. § 301.7701–3(a).
11. Reg. § 301.7701–3(a).
12. Reg. § 1.761–1(a) and Reg. § 301.7701–3(a).

## EXCLUSION FROM PARTNERSHIP TREATMENT

Under § 761(a) certain unincorporated organizations may be excluded, completely or partially, from treatment as partnerships for Federal income tax purposes. The exclusion applies to organizations availed of (1) for investment purposes rather than the active conduct of a business, (2) for the joint production, extraction, or use of property but not for the purpose of selling services or products produced or extracted, or (3) by dealers in securities for a short period for purposes of underwriting, selling, or distributing a particular security issue. All members of the organization must agree to the election and be able to compute their income without the necessity of computing partnership taxable income.[13] It is important to note that such an election does not preclude the organization from being considered a partnership for other purposes of the Internal Revenue Code.[14]

## WHO IS A PARTNER?

Section 761(b) defines a partner as one who is a member of a partnership. Unlike the S corporate shareholder restrictions, there are no limitations on who may own a partnership interest.[15] For instance, an individual, estate, trust, corporation or another partnership can be a partner in the same partnership. However, certain problems can arise when a minor child is a member of a family partnership or when a corporation is the general partner in a limited partnership. These problems are discussed in Chapter 10 under SPECIAL PARTNERSHIP PROBLEMS—Family Partnerships and Limited Partnerships.

# PARTNERSHIP FORMATION

The general provisions applicable to partnership formation are contained in § § 721 through 723. Like their counterparts in the corporate area, these statutes provide for tax-free partnership formations and admission of new partners and for the rules used to determine the basis of a partner's interest and of transferred property. Standing alone they do not, in all situations, assure the nonrecognition of gain or loss upon formation of a partnership. Therefore, other provisions that supplement these rules must be examined. The depreciation recapture provisions of § § 1245 and 1250 are structured to provide for tax-free transfers of depreciable property to a partnership.[16] Section 47(b) provides that recapture of investment tax credits is not required by the contributing partner if the contributed prop-

---

13. See Reg. § 1.761–2(a) for a discussion of investing partnerships and operating agreements. Both may be excluded from application of the partnership provisions of Subchapter K. Reg. § 1.761–2(b) outlines the manner of electing a complete or partial exclusion.
14. See *Olin Bryant,* 46 T.C. 848 (1966), *aff'd.* in 68–2 USTC ¶ 9521, 22 AFTR2d 5375, 399 F.2d 800 (CA–5, 1968), where a joint venture had elected to be excluded from Subchapter K but was still considered a partnership for purposes of the investment tax credit provisions. Also see, *Madison Gas & Electric Co.,* 72 T.C. 521 (1979), where the co-ventures in a nuclear power plant were disallowed deductions for certain start-up costs. The Court considered the costs to be capital expenditures of a new tax entity (a partnership) and thus not deductible.
15. See § 1361(b)(1) for restrictions imposed upon shareholders of an S corporation.
16. § § 1245(b)(3) and 1250(d)(3).

erty continues to qualify as § 38 property and the partner retains a substantial interest in the partnership.[17] Sometimes these supplemental provisions contain interacting rules that trigger gain recognition when property is contributed, such as those found in § 752 on debt treatment and in § 731 on the extent of gain or loss recognition from distributions (real or fictional).

## CONTRIBUTIONS TO PARTNERSHIP

The aggregate concept is reflected in the general rule of § 721 that indicates that no gain or loss is recognized to a partnership or any of its partners upon the contribution of property in exchange for a partnership interest. In addition to initial formation transfers, this rule applies to all subsequent contributions of property. Thus, the partners of an existing partnership can be insulated from gain or loss recognition upon the admission of a new partner if the partnership interest is in exchange for a property contribution. Although cash and most other contributions of tangible or intangible properties are covered by the general rule of § 721, circumstances exist where § 721 is inapplicable.

*Consideration Received for Transfers.* When a partner transfers cash or other property to a partnership and the partnership directly or indirectly transfers cash or other property to the partner (or another partner), the transfers when viewed together may be characterized as a sale rather than as a contribution under § 721 and an unrelated distribution under § 731. When this characterization takes place, the transfers are treated as occurring between the partner acting in his or her capacity as a nonpartner and the partnership.[18] To receive contribution treatment, the partner transferring the cash or other property must receive an appropriate interest in the partnership and the partnership must not make inappropriate transfers to the partner (or another partner). Care is advised in planning such transfers if the desired results are to be obtained, especially in planning for the lead or lag time between the property contribution date and the partnership allocation and distribution dates.

*Services Rendered or To Be Rendered.* Another situation where the general rule is inapplicable involves the exchange of a partnership interest for services rendered or to be rendered to the partnership. The partnership interest received in exchange for services can be a *capital interest,* a *profits interest,* or both. The Regulations provide that the fair market value of any part of an interest in partnership capital transferred to a partner for services shall be considered as compensation for such services.[19] The recipient must recognize the amount so determined as ordinary income in the year

---

**17.** See *W. F. Blevins,* 61 T.C. 547 (1974), and *James Soares,* 50 T.C. 909 (1968), for applications of the substantial interest test of § 47(b).

**18.** Section 707(a)(2)(B), effective for transfers after March 31, 1984, is intended to counteract the effect of *John H. Otey,* 70 T.C. 312 (1978), aff'd. in 80–2 USTC ¶ 9817, 47 AFTR2d 81–301, 634 F.2d 1046 (CA–6, 1980). Although this provision has about the same impact as existing Reg. § 1.721–1(a), Congress authorized the IRS to issue statutory (rather than interpretive) regulations to carry out its intent.

**19.** Reg. § 1.721–1(b)(1). See also *F. G. McDougal,* 62 T.C. 720 (1974), *acq.* 1975–1 C.B. 2.

actually or constructively received.[20] If a profits interest in a partnership is received for *future services*, the Regulations[21] imply that the recipient will not be taxed immediately. Instead, the service partner will report a share of partnership profits annually as they are determined. However, if the profits interest is received for *past services* and the interest has a determinable fair market value, the recipient may be taxed immediately on the receipt of such interest.[22]

**Example 1.** In the current tax year, C receives a 20% capital and profits interest in the AB Partnership for services previously rendered to the partnership. At the time of transfer, the partnership had assets with a $50,000 fair market value, an adjusted basis of $30,000, and no liabilities. Section 721 does not apply to this transaction. Thus, C includes $10,000 (the fair market value of the capital interest received) as ordinary income in the current tax year. Additionally, C's share of partnership profits in future tax years is included in ordinary income as reported by the partnership, unless the value of the profits interest can be determined immediately (which is not ordinarily the case).

If the services received by the AB Partnership in Example 1 are related to a direct or indirect allocation and distribution to C and the performance of the services, allocation, and distribution when viewed together are characterized as occurring between C acting as a nonpartner and the AB Partnership, the allocation and distribution are not to a "partner."[23] When this characterization takes place, the value of the services may be deductible to the partnership under § 162 as a trade or business expense, provided the requirements of deductibility are met. If such requirements are not met, the value of such services should be capitalized under § 263.

**Example 2.** From the viewpoints of A and B in Example 1, the partnership transferred assets with a fair market value of $10,000 (20% of $50,000) and an adjusted basis of $6,000 (20% of $30,000) in payment for services received. These transferred assets were recontributed by C for a partnership interest. The difference of $4,000 ($10,000 less $6,000) is a recognizable gain, the character of which is generally determined by the nature of the assets to the partnership.

*Profits Assumption for Text.* It should be noted that although a partner may have different capital and profit interest percentages, it is possible that such interests are equal. One should assume that all future reference to a capital interest percentage implies an equal profits interest percentage unless otherwise specified.

---

20. See *Sol Diamond,* 56 T.C. 530 (1971), *aff'd.* in 74–1 USTC ¶ 9306, 33 AFTR2d 74–852, 492 F.2d 286 (CA–7, 1974), for a unique determination of the value of a partnership profits interest given in exchange for services rendered to a partnership.
21. See § 83 and the Regulations thereunder.
22. See the parenthetical distinction made in Reg. § 1.721–1(b)(1).
23. § 707(a)(2)(A), effective for transfers after February 29, 1984, is intended to prevent an indirect deduction of payments for services received for a partnership interest (via a partnership allocation and distribution) that should be capitalized under § 263. Note that this section is not limited to payments for services that should be capitalized. To be certain its intent is followed, Congress authorized the IRS to issue related statutory regulations.

*Collapsible Transactions.* The nonrecognition provision of § 721 will not apply if the partnership is used solely to effect a tax-free exchange of properties. For example, assume that two partners in the same partnership have appreciated properties they wish to exchange free of tax. Assume further that the properties involved cannot qualify under any other non-recognition provision of the Code (e. g., a like-kind exchange under § 1031). Each partner contributes his or her appreciated property to the partnership. Shortly thereafter, each receives what is hoped to be a nontaxable distribution of the property contributed by the other. Under these circumstances, the IRS may collapse the transactions into a single taxable exchange. It is also possible that the transfers will be treated as occurring between the partnership and the partners acting in nonpartner capacities under the disguised sales rules.[24]

*Diversification of Investments.* Section 721(b) was added to the Code by the Tax Reform Act of 1976 to provide another exception to the general rule of nonrecognition of gain on the contribution of property to a partnership. The contributing partner is required to recognize any gain realized on the transfer of property to a partnership that would be treated as an investment company (within the meaning of § 351) if the partnership were incorporated. A partnership will be considered an investment company if, after the transfer, more than 80 percent of the value of its assets (excluding cash and nonconvertible debt obligations) is held for investment and consists of readily marketable stocks or securities. The purpose of this provision is to prevent investors from using the partnership form to diversify their investment portfolios or exchange stocks or securities on a tax-free basis. Similar action was taken by Congress in 1967 to prevent use of the nonrecognition provision of § 351 to accomplish the same result in tax-free transfers to controlled corporations [see § 351(e)].

*Liabilities in Excess of Basis.* Finally, § 721 may be inapplicable in the case of contributions of property subject to a liability in excess of basis. The interaction of § § 752(b) and 731 may require recognition of gain in this situation. See Example 7 for an illustration of such a case.

## BASIS OF PARTNERSHIP INTEREST

The tax basis of a partnership interest (sometimes referred to as "outside basis") acquired in a nontaxable transfer of property to a partnership is determined under § 722. Generally, the contributing partner's interest equals the sum of money contributed plus the adjusted basis of any other property transferred. However, if gain is recognized under § 721(b), the partner's basis must be increased accordingly. Note that the basis of a partner's interest may or may not equal the partner's capital account per books.

*Accounting for Contributed Property.* When property is contributed to a partnership for a capital interest, generally it is recorded for financial accounting purposes at its fair market value with a corresponding offset to the partner's capital account. It should be noted that some partnerships

---

**24.** § 707(a)(2)(B).

maintain their accounting books on a tax basis.[25] Unless otherwise stated, the following examples assume that all property contributions are recorded at fair market value.

**Example 3.** In return for having rendered services and contributed property (basis of $50,000, fair market value of $80,000) to the KLM Partnership, A receives a 25% capital interest valued at $100,000. The contribution of property is nontaxable under § 721. However, the receipt of a partnership interest for services results in compensation to A of $20,000 (value of partnership interest of $100,000 less value of property contributed of $80,000). A's tax basis in the KLM Partnership is $70,000 (basis of the property contributed of $50,000 plus ordinary income recognized of $20,000). For financial accounting purposes, A's capital account immediately after acquisition of the partnership interest is $100,000.

**Example 4.** U and W form an equal partnership with a cash contribution of $30,000 from U and a land contribution (adjusted basis of $18,000 and fair market value of $30,000) from W. Although the books of the UW Partnership reflect a credit of $30,000 in each partner's capital account, only U will have a tax basis of $30,000. W's tax basis will be $18,000, the tax basis of the contributed property. Immediately after formation, the partnership books and tax basis are as follows:

|  | Per Books | Tax Basis |
|---|---|---|
| Cash | $ 30,000 | $ 30,000 |
| Property | 30,000 | 18,000 |
| Total | $ 60,000 | $ 48,000 |

|  | Capital Accounts | Interest Basis |
|---|---|---|
| U | $ 30,000 | $ 30,000 |
| W | 30,000 | 18,000 |
| Total | $ 60,000 | $ 48,000 |

If the UW Partnership sells the land for $30,000 shortly after formation, no gain results for financial accounting purposes ($30,000 selling price less $30,000 fair market value basis). However, for tax purposes the sale results in a $12,000 gain ($30,000 selling price less $18,000 contributed basis). Although U and W generally report profits and losses equally, under § 704(c) all of the unrealized appreciation at the contribution date ($12,000) is reported by W, the partner who

---

**25.** Regulation § 1.704–1(b)(2)(iv)(b) requires the capital accounts of partners to be increased by the fair market value of contributed property (net of related liabilities) so that substantial economic effect is achieved for partnership allocations.

contributed the land. If the land was sold for a gain of more than $12,000, W would report the first $12,000 and the remainder would be split equally.

*Contributed Property With Debt.* When property subject to a liability is contributed to a partnership or if the partnership assumes any of the transferor partner's liabilities, the basis of the partnership interest must be reduced by the amount of the liabilities assumed by the other partners.[26] Debt on property that is not assumed directly is treated as assumed by the transferee partnership to the extent of the property's fair market value.[27] Thus, any debt on contributed property that is not assumed directly (to the extent of the property's fair market value) and any debt assumed directly by the partnership must be considered when determining the basis of a partner's interest.[28] Correspondingly, the noncontributing partners increase their basis by that portion of the liabilities assumed directly or indirectly on the transfer. Generally, each partner's loss-sharing ratio is used to determine the amount of liabilities assumed. Absent some specific reference to the contrary, it is assumed that the partners share losses in the same ratio as they share profits.[29] These adjustments to the basis of a partnership interest result from the application of § 752. Under § 752(a), an increase in a partner's share of partnership liabilities is treated as a contribution of money by the partner to the partnership. Likewise, § 752(b) requires that a decrease in a partner's share of partnership liabilities be considered a distribution of money by the partnership.

> **Example 5.** X, Y, and Z form the XYZ Partnership with the following contributions: cash of $50,000 from X for a 50% interest in capital and profits, cash of $25,000 from Y for a 25% interest, and property valued at $33,000 from Z for a 25% interest. The property contributed by Z has an adjusted basis of $15,000 and is subject to a mortgage of $8,000, which is assumed by the partnership. Z's interest in the XYZ Partnership is $9,000, determined as follows:

---

**26.** Reg. § 1.722–1.

**27.** § 752(c) and Reg. § 1.752–1(c).

**28.** Amended § 704(c), effective for property and debt contributions after March 31, 1984, is intended to prevent debt contributed by a cash basis partner to a cash basis partnership from being treated as debt under § 752 for interest basis purposes. The full effect of this provision is currently unknown. In addition, it is possible that the contributed property, debt, and deemed distribution as a result of the debt will fall under the disguised sales rules of § 707(a)(2)(B). S. Rept. No. 169, 98th Cong., 2d Sess. 230 (1984), indicates that the Committee does not intend to change the tax treatment of partners under § § 721, 731, and 752 when property and debt are contributed to a partnership in a nonabusive situation. It is hoped that the new statutory regulations will continue the practice of increasing the interest basis of a partner who contributes property and debt in nonabusive situations. The remainder of this chapter assumes that this practice will be continued.

**29.** In the case of a limited partnership, only the general partner(s) would be entitled to this treatment. However, if the debt involved was a nonrecourse liability (i. e., where none of the partners are personally liable), all of the partners (including limited partners) are treated as sharing such a liability under § 752(c) in the same proportion as they share profits. Chapter 10 contains a section on limited partnerships that discusses nonrecourse liabilities.

|  |  |
|---|---:|
| Adjusted basis of Z's contributed property—§ 722 | $ 15,000 |
| Increase in Z's share of partnership debt (25% of $8,000)—§ 752(a) | 2,000 |
| Subtotal | $ 17,000 |
| Decrease in Z's individual debt—§ 752(b) | 8,000 |
| Basis of Z's interest in the XYZ Partnership | $ 9,000 |

The same result will occur if the basis of the contributed property is decreased by the portion of Z's debt assumed by X and Y ($15,000 less 75% of $8,000). Using this net approach, the increase in Z's share of the partnership debt is not added to the basis of the contributed property when determining Z's interest.[30]

**Example 6.** Assuming the same facts as in Example 5, X and Y will have a basis in their partnership interest of $54,000 and $27,000, respectively.

|  | X | Y |
|---|---:|---:|
| Cash contribution | $ 50,000 | $ 25,000 |
| Plus portion of mortgage assumed and treated as an additional cash contribution: |  |  |
| (50% of $8,000) | 4,000 |  |
| (25% of $8,000) |  | 2,000 |
| Basis of interest in XYZ Partnership | $ 54,000 | $ 27,000 |

The basis of a contributing partner's interest may be reduced to zero if the property transferred is subject to a liability in excess of the property's basis. It should be noted that the basis of a partnership interest under §§ 705(a)(2) and 733, like the basis of any other kind of property, never can be negative. Thus, if the portion of the liability assumed by the noncontributing partners exceeds the contributing partner's basis, *recognizable* gain will result.[31] Further, § 731 provides that such a gain shall be considered as a gain from the sale of a partnership interest, and under § 741, the gain would be considered a capital gain.[32] However, ordinary income may result if the transferred property was subject to depreciation recapture.[33]

---

30. Reg. § 1.752–1(c).
31. Reg. § 1.752–1(c).
32. See W. S. McKee, W. F. Nelson, and R. L. Whitmire, *Federal Taxation of Partnerships and Partners* (Boston, Mass.: Warren, Gorham & Lamont, Inc., 1977 with updates), § 4.03(1)(c), and Arthur B. Willis, John S. Pennell, and Phillip F. Postlewaite, *Partnership Taxation,* Third Edition (Colorado Springs, Colo.: McGraw-Hill Book Company, 1982 with updates), §§ 24.02 and 112.05.
33. Reg. § 1.1245–4(c)(4) (Ex. 3).

**Example 7.** Assume the same facts as in Example 5, except that the property contributed by Z is land held for investment with a fair market value of $49,000 that is subject to a mortgage of $24,000 (instead of $8,000). Z's interest would be zero, and a $3,000 gain must be recognized:

| | |
|---|---|
| Adjusted basis of the land to Z | $ 15,000 |
| Less portion of mortgage assumed by X and Y and treated as a distribution of money to Z (75% of $24,000) | 18,000 |
| Realized gain | ($ 3,000) |

The $3,000 in excess of Z's outside basis is treated as a capital gain from the sale or exchange of a partnership interest under § 731(a). Further, under § 1223(1), the holding period of the contributed property must be used to determine whether the gain is a long-term capital gain. [Note that the interaction of § § 752(b) and 731 negates the nonrecognition provision of § 721.]

If the $3,000 gain recognized by partner Z in Example 7 appears to be harsh treatment, consider the tax consequences if the property had been contributed to a corporation. Under § 357(c), the entire excess of the liability over Z's basis in the property (i. e., $9,000) would have resulted in a taxable gain. The use of the partnership form in this instance results in a tax benefit to Z.

*Contributed ITC Property.* What happens if the property contributed for a partnership interest is § 38 property on which the investment tax credit (ITC) was claimed by the contributing partner and the appropriate time period to avoid recapture has not lapsed? Section 47(b) provides that the ITC is not recaptured "by reason of a mere change in the form of conducting the trade or business so long as the property is retained in such trade or business as section 38 property and the taxpayer retains a substantial interest in such trade or business." In addition, the basis of the property in whole or in part must be determined by reference to the basis of such property in the transferor's hands, and substantial assets necessary to operate the same trade or business are transferred with the § 38 property. If the trade or business is not the same as before the transfer, it appears the ITC would be recaptured.

The transferor is considered to have retained a substantial interest in the trade or business only if immediately after the change in form and until the potential for recapture has expired the transferor's interest in the same trade or business is equal to or greater than the interest before the transfer or is substantial in relation to the total interests of all persons.[34] If the sole owner of ITC property contributes the property to a partnership for a 50 percent interest, the retained interest is considered substantial in

---

**34.** Reg. § 1.47–3(f)(2), H. Rept. No. 1447 and S. Rept. No. 1881, 87th Cong., 2d Sess. (1962), and W. *Frank Blevins,* 61 T.C. 547 (1974).

relation to the other partners.[35] However, when ITC property was transferred to a partnership for a 48 percent interest and six months later the partnership interest was transferred to a corporation for a 7.22 percent interest, the Tax Court held that the exchange of the 48 percent partnership interest for the 7.22 percent corporate interest did not qualify as retention of a substantial interest.[36] Thus, the ITC recapture rules were triggered. The property contributed for the 48 percent partnership interest was not challenged in this case. Since so little authority exists on what constitutes the retention of a substantial interest in the same trade or business, caution is advised if the ITC recapture rules are to be avoided.

*Basis and Holding Period.* The basis of a partnership interest acquired other than by the contribution of property must be determined under provisions of the Code outside Subchapter K.[37] For instance, if a partnership interest is acquired by purchase, its basis will be determined under § 1012. Likewise, if the interest is acquired by gift or inheritance, its basis will be determined under § 1015 and § 1014, respectively. Generally, the holding period of a partner's interest acquired by a noncash property contribution includes the holding period of the contributed property. However, if the contributed property is neither a capital asset nor a § 1231 asset in the hands of the transferor (e. g., inventory or property held for sale to customers), the holding period starts on the day the interest is acquired. The holding period of an interest acquired by a cash contribution or by purchase is determined under the general holding period rules. The holding period of an interest acquired by gift or by inheritance is determined under related rules.

After its initial determination, the basis of a partner's interest is subject to continuous fluctuations. It will be *increased* by additional contributions and the sum of current and prior years' distributive share of the following:

—Taxable income of the partnership, including capital gains.

—Tax-exempt income of the partnership.

—The excess of the deductions for depletion over the basis of the partnership's property subject to depletion.[38]

Similarly, the basis of a partner's interest will be *decreased*, but not below zero, by the partner's limited depletion deduction for partnership oil and gas property [i. e., limited by § 613A(c)(7)(D) to the partner's proportionate share of the partnership's adjusted basis in oil and gas property] and by the sum of the current and prior years' distributive share of the following:

—Partnership losses, including capital losses.

—Partnership expenditures that are not deductible in computing taxable income or loss and are not capital expenditures (e. g., interest and expenses incurred to produce tax-exempt income, personal living expenses of partners, and contributions to public charities).[39]

---

**35.** Reg. § 1.47–3(f)(6) (Ex. 5).

**36.** *James Soares,* 50 T.C. 909 (1968).

**37.** § 742.

**38.** § 705(a) and Reg. § 1.705–1(a)(2).

**39.** § 705(a) and Reg. § 1.705–1(a)(3).

*Impact of Partnership Debt.* Changes in partnership liabilities (including trade accounts payable and bank loans) also affect the basis of a partner's interest. For instance, a partner's basis is *increased* by the pro rata share of liabilities incurred by the partnership[40] and is *decreased* by the pro rata share of decreases in partnership liabilities.[41] The impact of changes in a partnership's liabilities on its partners' respective bases reflects the aggregate concept of partnership taxation. If the partnership is viewed as a common pool of assets to which each partner contributes, any changes in this pool will have a corresponding impact on the partners' interest in those assets. Thus, when the acquisition of partnership assets is financed by creditors, the partners are generally treated as if they each borrowed proportionate amounts of money and contributed them to the partnership, which then used the money to purchase the assets. Exceptions exist when determining the at-risk basis of a partner's interest under § 465. If partnership assets are used to satisfy creditor obligations, the partners are treated as if they constructively received a distribution of money from the partnership and then satisfied the obligations. Consequently, as the partnership's pool of assets increases or decreases, the partners' bases in the partnership increase or decrease simultaneously.

*Alternative Basis Rule.* Section 705(b) provides an *alternative rule* for determining the basis of a partner's interest if the basis determination rules previously cited cannot be applied practically or if, in the opinion of the IRS, it is reasonable to conclude from a consideration of all facts that the result produced will not vary substantially from the regular approach.[42] Under the alternative rule, the adjusted basis of a partner's interest can be determined by reference to a partner's share of the adjusted basis of partnership property that would be distributable upon termination. Note that the term "inside basis" is sometimes used to refer to the partnership's basis in the assets and each partner's proportionate share of such basis. In using the alternative rule, certain adjustments may be required to reflect significant discrepancies in the adjusted basis of partnership property arising as a result of contributed property, transfers of partnership interests, or distributions of property to the partners.

**Example 8.** R, S, and T are equal partners in the RST Partnership, which owns various properties with an adjusted basis of $24,000. Since each partner's share in this adjusted basis is one-third, each would have an adjusted interest basis under the alternative rule of $8,000.[43]

**Example 9.** Assume the same facts as in Example 8, except that R's interest is sold to U for $10,000 at a time when the fair market value of the partnership property is $30,000. U's one-third interest in the partnership (outside basis) is $10,000. However, reference to the total adjusted basis of partnership property would yield only $8,000 for U's

---

**40.** Reg. § 1.752–1(a).
**41.** Reg. § 1.752–1(b).
**42.** Reg. § 1.705–1(b). But see *Coloman v. Comm.*, 76–2 USTC ¶ 9581, 38 AFTR2d 76–5523, 540 F.2d 427 (CA–9, 1976), where the taxpayer was denied the use of the alternative rule when he had no satisfactory evidence as to the partnership's adjusted basis of its property.
**43.** Reg. § 1.705–1(b) (Ex. 1).

one-third interest (inside basis). Therefore, U is allowed a basis adjustment of $2,000 under the alternative rule.[44]

## BASIS AND NATURE OF CONTRIBUTED PROPERTY

Section 723 states that the basis of property contributed to a partnership shall be the adjusted basis of such property to the contributing partner at the time of contribution, increased by the amount of gain recognized by the contributing partner under § 721(b) as a result of the transfer.

*Historical Perspective.* The Tax Reform Act of 1976 added § 721(b) as an exception to the existing rule that no gain or loss is recognized to the partnership or partners on a contribution of property for a partnership interest. This exception prohibited the nonrecognition rule of § 721(a) from applying to a transfer of property to a partnership that would be treated as an investment company under § 351 if incorporated. The 1976 Act modified § 723 to provide that the adjusted basis of contributed property was to be increased by the gain recognized by the contributing partner. Although the addition to § 723 was aimed at the exception under § 721(b), no such limitation was stated in § 723. As a result of this limiting omission and the clear language of § 723, many individuals concluded that the basis of contributed property should be increased by any gain recognized by the contributing partner. However, Congress via the Deficit Reduction Act of 1984 retroactively corrected the limiting omission to the effective date of the Tax Reform Act of 1976 (February 17, 1976) by inserting the words "under section 721(b)" in § 723. Partnerships that have increased the basis of contributed property for any non-§ 721 recognized gain will have to retroactively reverse such increase. If the property is no longer held or the property is depreciable or is ACRS property, retroactive adjustment problems may be encountered by the partnership and its partners.

> **Example 10.** K and L form an equal partnership with a contribution of land valued at $100,000 from K and a contribution of equipment valued at $150,000 from L. K's basis in the land is $30,000. The equipment contributed by L has an adjusted basis of $20,000 and is subject to a mortgage of $50,000, which is assumed by the partnership. K's interest basis is $55,000 ($30,000 basis in the contributed land increased by 50% of the $50,000 mortgage on the equipment). Under § 722 and Reg. § 1.722–1 (Ex. 2), L's interest basis is zero ($20,000 basis in the contributed equipment decreased, but not below zero, by 50% of the $50,000 mortgage on the equipment treated as assumed by K). Also, §§ 705(a)(2) and 733 clearly indicate that the basis of a partner's interest as a result of a distribution cannot be reduced below zero. In addition, L will have a taxable gain of $5,000, because the debt share treated as assumed by K exceeded L's contributed basis by this amount. Note that L's gain will be ordinary income to the extent of any § 1245 depreciation recapture potential associated with the transferred equipment.

---

44.   Reg. § 1.705–1(b) (Ex. 2).

The partnership has a $30,000 basis in the land and a $20,000 basis in the equipment. Before the Deficit Reduction Act of 1984, it was thought that a partnership could increase its basis in contributed property by *any* gain recognized by the contributor. Congress clarified this situation in 1984 by amending § 723 to clearly indicate that an increase in the basis of contributed property can be made only if a gain to the contributing partner is recognized under § 721(b) at the time of contribution.

If the partnership increased the basis of the equipment by the gain recognized by L and claimed depreciation or ACRS deductions on this increased amount, several adjustments may be necessary. First, the basis increase should be reversed and depreciation or ACRS deductions recomputed. For closed tax years, claimed depreciation or ACRS deductions should be handled under the allowed or allowable rule of § 1016. For open tax years, related deductions will have to be reduced. If the equipment was disposed of by the partnership in an open tax year, related gain or loss will have to be recomputed. If the disposition took place in a closed tax year, no adjustments are necessary.

*Holding Period.* The partnership's holding period for contributed property includes the period the property was held by the contributing partner, since the property's basis is determined by reference to the contributing partner's basis.[45]

*Depreciation Method and Period.* Although the contributing partner's property basis and holding period carry over to the partnership, the transfer of certain depreciable property could result in unfavorable tax consequences to the partnership. For instance, a partnership will not be allowed to immediately expense any part of the cost of § 179 property whose basis is determined by reference to the transferor partner.[46] Although the Economic Recovery Tax Act of 1981 (ERTA) provided this particular limitation, a similar limitation was imposed under prior law for old § 179 additional first-year (bonus) depreciation.[47] Additionally, ERTA added § 168(f)(10) to the Code to prevent a partnership from using an accelerated cost recovery method or period that differs from that of the transferor partner. Similar rules existed under prior law that prohibited a partnership from using accelerated depreciation methods if the contributing partner was considered the original user of the property.[48] Thus, if the loss of immediate expensing or cost recovery deductions would be detrimental to the contributing partner, consideration should be given to retaining ownership of the property and leasing the property to the partnership until the beneficial deductions are exhausted.

*Receivables, Inventory, and Capital Loss Property.* The Deficit Reduction Act of 1984 added § 724 to the Code for certain property contributed to a partnership after March 31, 1984. Section 724(a) indicates that any gain

---

45. § 1223(2) and Reg. § 1.723–1.
46. § 179(d)(2)(C).
47. Reg. § 1.179–3(c)(1)(iii).
48. Reg. § § 1.167(c)–1(a)(6) and 1.167(j)–1(a)(2)(ii).

or loss recognized by the partnership on the disposition of contributed receivables that were unrealized in the contributing partner's hands immediately before the contribution date shall be treated as ordinary. The definition of unrealized receivables is contained in § 751(c), modified so that any reference to a partnership means the contributing partner. These receivables include such things as the right to receive payment for goods or services delivered or to be delivered to the extent that they were not previously included in the partner's income.

New § 724(b) indicates that any gain or loss by the partnership on the disposition of contributed inventory during the five-year period starting on the contribution date that was inventory in the contributor's hands immediately before the contribution shall be treated as ordinary. Inventory for this provision is generally defined in § 751(d). It includes all property that is not a capital asset or a § 1231 asset. However, property that fails the test of a § 1231 asset strictly because of its holding period is excluded from the definition of inventory for purposes of § 724(b).

When capital loss property is contributed to a partnership, § 724(c) indicates that any loss recognized by the partnership on the property's disposition during the five-year period starting on the contribution date shall be treated as a capital loss to the extent of any unrealized loss at the contribution date. This provision is aimed at taxpayers who try to convert a capital loss into an ordinary loss by contributing real estate to a real estate partnership who holds the property as inventory.

Congress was concerned that the provisions of § 724 might be circumvented via nontaxable exchanges. With the exception of C stock received in a nontaxable § 351 exchange, § 724(d)(3)(A) indicates that substitute basis property received in a nontaxable exchange for property subject to § 724 is also subject to these provisions.

## ORGANIZATION AND SYNDICATION COSTS

Section 709(a) provides the general rule that amounts paid or incurred to organize a partnership or to promote the sale of (or to sell) a partnership interest are not deductible by the partnership. However, § 709(b) provides an exception that permits a ratable amortization of some of these costs.

*Organization Costs.* Under § 709(b), organization costs paid or incurred in taxable years beginning after December 31, 1976, may, at the irrevocable election of the partnership, be amortized ratably over a period of not less than 60 months starting with the month in which the partnership began business. Note that signing of the partnership agreement may not be the point in time when the partnership began business. The election must be made by the due date (including extensions) of the partnership return for the year it began business by detailing items and taking the deduction.[49] Although an amended return may be used to add qualified expenditures not included on the original election return, generally it may not be used to make the election.

---

**49.** Reg. § 1.709–1(c).

Section 709 (b)(2) defines organizational costs as expenditures that are (1) incident to the creation of the partnership; (2) chargeable to a capital account; and (3) of a character which, if incident to the creation of a partnership having an ascertainable life, would be amortized over such a life. These expenditures include filing, accounting, and legal fees incident to the partnership's organization. To be deductible, such expenditures must be incurred within the period that starts a reasonable time before the partnership begins business and ends with the due date (without extensions) of the tax return for that year. In addition, cash method partnerships are not allowed to deduct *in the year incurred* a portion of such expenditures that are paid after that year's end. The portion of such expenditures that would have been deductible in a prior year, if paid before that year's end, is deductible in the year of payment. The following items are not part of organization costs: expenses associated with acquiring assets for or transferring assets to the partnership, expenses associated with the admission or removal of partners other than at the time the partnership is first organized, expenses associated with a contract relating to the operation of the partnership trade or business (even where the contract is between the partnership and one of its members), and syndication costs.

*Syndication Costs.* Unlike the allowed treatment of organization costs, § 709(a) requires syndication costs to be capitalized with no amortization allowed. This provision applies to all such costs paid or incurred for tax years beginning after December 31, 1975. Syndication costs are those expenditures incurred in connection with promoting and marketing interests in partnerships [e. g., brokerage fees; registration fees; related legal fees for the underwriter, placement agent, and issuer (the general partner or partnership) for securities advice and for advice pertaining to the adequacy of tax disclosures in the prospectus or placement memo for securities law purposes; accounting fees related to offering materials; and printing costs of prospectus, placement memo, and materials for selling and promotion].[50] Note that fees incurred for tax advice regarding how the partnership is to operate and projections or forecasts that are used to plan operations and structure transactions are not syndication costs and should be deductible as § 709 organizational costs or as § 195 start-up expenditures. In either case, they would be amortizable over a period of 60 months or more.

# PARTNERSHIP OPERATION

The statutory provisions that govern the operation of a partnership are contained in Code § § 701 through 708. The rules govern who is taxed on partnership's income, how such income is determined, and how and when it is reported. Also included are the rules governing the determination of a partner's interest basis and the effect of transactions between a partnership and partners.

---

**50.** Reg. § 1.709–2(b).

## MEASURING AND REPORTING PARTNERSHIP INCOME

Although a partnership is not subject to Federal income taxation,[51] it must determine its taxable income and file an income tax return for information purposes.[52]

*Tax Return and Schedule K–1.* The principal purpose of the partnership return (Form 1065) is to provide information necessary for determining the character and amount of each partner's distributive share of partnership income, expenses, and credits (an application of the aggregate or conduit concept of partnerships). Usually one general partner must sign the return. If a receiver, trustee in bankruptcy, or assignee controls the partnership property or business, that person must sign the return. The return is due on the fifteenth day of the fourth month following the close of the partnership's taxable year.[53] Concurrent with this filing, the partnership is required to provide each partner with a Schedule K–1, which indicates each partner's distributive share of all items of income, deductions, and credits and enables the partners to timely file their own personal income tax returns.

Under § 6222, each partner's share of partnership items as defined in § 6231(a)(3) must be reported on the partner's individual tax return in the same manner as presented on Schedule K–1, Form 1065, or the IRS must be notified of any inconsistent treatment at the time of such reporting. A partnership with ten or fewer partners, all of whom are either estates or natural persons (other than nonresident aliens), where each partner's share of partnership items is the same for all items is automatically excluded from this rule. By election, the partnership may have this reporting rule apply.

*Failure To File Penalty.* To encourage compliance, § 6698 imposes a penalty on the partnership of $50 per month (or fraction thereof), but not to exceed five months, for failure to file a complete and timely information return without reasonable cause.[54] The monthly penalty is assessed for each partner in the partnership during any part of the taxable year. Thus, if a partnership with 20 partners failed to file Form 1065 for its taxable year (without reasonable cause), the partnership could be liable for a penalty of $5,000 ($50 × 20 × 5). More important, every general partner of the partnership would be personally liable for the entire penalty.

*Elections.* In addition to the reporting function, Form 1065 is used to make various elections. With few exceptions, the partnership must make the elections affecting the computation of its taxable income. For instance, selection of the method of accounting, an election not to use the install-

---

**51.** Section 701 provides that a partnership shall not be subject to the income tax. Instead, the income tax is imposed on the partners in their separate or individual capacities. This is a reflection of the conduit concept discussed previously. It should be noted, however, that a partnership is subject to other Federal tax provisions. For instance, a partnership is required to pay the employer's share of Social Security taxes and unemployment taxes, and it must withhold income taxes on its employees' salaries or wages.

**52.** § 6031.

**53.** Reg. § 301.6031–1(e)(2).

**54.** Section 6698 was added to the Code by the Revenue Act of 1978 and is effective for returns for taxable years beginning after December 31, 1978.

ment method of reporting sales, or the option to expense intangible drilling and development costs must be made by the partnership and will apply to all partners in all partnership transactions.[55] The electing capacity of the partnership is an expression of the entity concept.

*Measurement and Reporting Process.* The measurement and reporting of partnership income requires a two-step approach. First, § 702(a) requires that certain transactions be segregated and reported separately on the partnership return (and on each partner's Schedule K–1):

1. Gains and losses from sales or exchanges of capital assets not meeting the long-term holding period requirement (short-term capital gains and losses).

2. Gains and losses from sales or exchanges of capital assets meeting the long-term holding period requirement (long-term capital gains and losses).

3. Gains and losses from sales or involuntary conversions of real or depreciable property used in the business meeting the long-term holding period requirement (i. e., § 1231 gains or losses).

4. Charitable contributions as defined in § 170(c).

5. Dividends qualifying for exclusion under § 116 or deduction under Part VIII, Subchapter B, of the Code.

6. Taxes paid or accrued to foreign countries and to possessions of the United States that can be claimed as a credit.

7. Other items of income, gain, loss, deduction, or credit to the extent provided by the Regulations.

8. Taxable income or loss, exclusive of the preceding items.

The Regulations expand the list of category 7 items to be segregated and reported separately:

—Recovery of tax benefit items (§ 111).

—Gains and losses from wagering transactions [§ 165(d)].

—Soil and water conservation expenditures (§ 175).

—Nonbusiness expenses (§ 212).

—Medical and dental expenses (§ 213).

—Alimony payments (§ 215).

—Amounts representing taxes and interest paid to cooperative housing corporations (§ 216).

—Intangible drilling and development costs [§ 263(c)].

—Exploration expenditures (§ § 615 and 617).

—Income, gain, or loss to the partnership arising from a distribution of unrealized receivables [§ 751(b)].

—Partially tax-exempt interest on obligations of the United States or its instrumentalities.

---

**55.** Reg. § 1.703–1(b)(1).

—Any items of income, gain, loss, deduction, or credit subject to a special allocation under the partnership agreement that differ from the allocation of partnership taxable income or loss generally.[56]

In addition, the Regulations require the partners to take into account separately their distributive share of any partnership item that would result in an income tax liability for a partner different from that which would result if the item were not taken into account separately.[57] Thus, the partners must take into account separately such things as their share of all partnership items that would be considered tax preference items for purposes of the minimum tax, their share of any investment tax credits, and their share of any § 179 immediate expensing amounts.

The reason for the required segregation and direct allocation to the individual partners of the preceding items is rooted in the aggregate or conduit concept. This first stage of measuring and reporting partnership income is necessary because the items subject to this treatment affect the computation of various exclusions, deductions, and credits at the partner level. Thus, these items must pass through to the individual partners without loss of identity.

The second stage of the measurement and reporting process deals with all partnership items not segregated or directly allocated as previously described.[58] All items not separately stated under § 702(a) are netted at the partnership level. In this process, the taxable income of a partnership is computed in the same manner as the taxable income of an individual taxpayer, except that a partnership is not allowed the following deductions:[59]

—The deduction for personal exemptions.

—The deduction for taxes paid to foreign countries or possessions of the United States.

—The deduction for charitable contributions.

—The deduction for net operating losses.

—The additional itemized deductions allowed individuals in §§ 211 through 220.

—The deduction for depletion under § 611 with respect to oil and gas interests.

The result of this second measuring stage is the partnership's ordinary income or loss that is reported on the first page (line 24) of Form 1065. This amount and each of the items that must be segregated and listed separately are reported on Schedule K of Form 1065 and then allocated and reported on a Schedule K-1 for each partner. The partners must then report their distributive share of these items on their own tax return, regardless of whether or not an actual distribution is made.

*Return Illustrated.* Completed page 1 of Form 1065, Schedule K, and page 1 of Schedule K-1 are reproduced here for the equal XY Partnership for the current year. XY received consulting fees of $50,000 and paid items listed on page 9-24:

---

**56.** Reg. §§ 1.702–1(a)(7) and (8)(i).
**57.** Reg. § 1.702–1(a)(8)(ii).
**58.** § 702(a)(8).
**59.** § 703(a).

| Form **1065** | U.S. Partnership Return of Income | OMB No. 1545-0099 |
|---|---|---|
| Department of the Treasury Internal Revenue Service | ▶ For Paperwork Reduction Act Notice, see Form 1065 Instructions.<br>For calendar year 1985, or fiscal year beginning _____, 1985, and ending _____, 19___ | 19**85** |

| A  Principal business activity | Use IRS label. Otherwise, please print or type. | Name<br>XY Partnership | D  Employer identification number<br>22-6872310 |
|---|---|---|---|
| B  Principal product or service | | Number and street<br>700 University Avenue | E  Date business started<br>1-1-84 |
| C  Business code number | | City or town, state, and ZIP code<br>Madison, Wisconsin 53705 | F  Enter total assets at end of tax year<br>$ 1,000 -- |

| | | | Yes | No |
|---|---|---|---|---|
| G  Check method of accounting: | (1) ☒ Cash | N  Was there a distribution of property or a transfer of a partnership interest during the tax year? If "Yes," see page 5 of the Instructions concerning an election to adjust the basis of the partnership's assets under section 754. | | X |
| | (2) ☐ Accrual  (3) ☐ Other | | | |
| H  Check applicable boxes: | (1) ☒ Final return | O  At any time during the tax year, did the partnership have an interest in or a signature or other authority over a bank account, securities account, or other financial account in a foreign country (see page 5 of Instructions)? If "Yes," write the name of the foreign country ▶ | | X |
| | (2) ☐ Change in address  (3) ☐ Amended return | | | |
| I  Number of partners in this partnership ▶ 2 | | | | |
| J  Is this partnership a limited partnership (see page 3 of Instructions)? | X (No) | P  Was the partnership the grantor of, or transferor to, a foreign trust which existed during the current tax year, whether or not the partnership or any partner has any beneficial interest in it? If "Yes," you may have to file Forms 3520, 3520-A, or 926 (see page 5 of Instructions). | | X |
| K  Is this partnership a partner in another partnership? | X (No) | | | |
| L  Are any partners in this partnership also partnerships? | X (No) | Q  Check this box if the partnership has filed or is required to file Form 8264, Application for Registration of a Tax Shelter. ☐ | | |
| M  Does the partnership meet **all** the requirements shown on page 5 of the Instructions under **Question M** | X | | | |

| Income | | | |
|---|---|---|---|
| 1a | Gross receipts or sales $ _____  1b  Minus returns and allowances $ _____  Balance ▶ | 1c | 50,000 -- |
| 2 | Cost of goods sold and/or operations (Schedule A, line 7) | 2 | |
| 3 | Gross profit (subtract line 2 from line 1c) | 3 | |
| 4 | Ordinary income (loss) from other partnerships and fiduciaries | 4 | |
| 5 | Taxable interest and nonqualifying dividends | 5 | |
| 6a | Gross rents $ _____  6b  Minus rental expenses (attach schedule) $ _____ | | |
| c | Balance net rental income (loss) ▶ | 6c | |
| 7 | Net income (loss) from royalties (attach schedule) | 7 | |
| 8 | Net farm profit (loss) (attach Schedule F (Form 1040)) | 8 | |
| 9 | Net gain (loss) (Form 4797, line 17) | 9 | |
| 10 | Other income (loss) | 10 | |
| 11 | **TOTAL** income (loss) (combine lines 3 through 10) | 11 | 50,000 -- |

| Deductions | | | |
|---|---|---|---|
| 12a | Salaries and wages (other than to partners) $ _____  12b  Minus jobs credit $ _____  Balance ▶ | 12c | |
| 13 | Guaranteed payments to partners (see page 7 of Instructions) | 13 | |
| 14 | Rent | 14 | 20,000 -- |
| 15a | Total deductible interest expense not claimed elsewhere on return (see page 7 of Instructions).  [15a] | | |
| b | Minus interest expense required to be passed through to partners on Schedule K-1(1065), lines 10, 15a (2), and 15a(3)  [15b] | | |
| c | Balance ▶ | 15c | |
| 16 | Taxes | 16 | |
| 17 | Bad debts (see page 7 of Instructions) | 17 | |
| 18 | Repairs | 18 | |
| 19a | Depreciation from Form 4562 (attach Form 4562) $ _____  19b  Minus depreciation claimed on Schedule A and elsewhere on return $ _____  Balance ▶ | 19c | |
| 20 | Depletion (**Do not deduct oil and gas depletion.** See page 8 of Instructions.) | 20 | |
| 21a | Retirement plans, etc. (see page 8 of Instructions) | 21a | |
| b | Employee benefit programs (see page 8 of Instructions) | 21b | |
| 22 | Other deductions (attach schedule) | 22 | 2,450 -- |
| 23 | **TOTAL** deductions (add amounts in column for lines 12c through 22) | 23 | 22,450 -- |
| 24 | Ordinary income (loss) (subtract line 23 from line 11) | 24 | 27,550 -- |

**Please Sign Here**

Under penalties of perjury, I declare that I have examined this return, including accompanying schedules and statements, and to the best of my knowledge and belief it is true, correct, and complete. Declaration of preparer (other than taxpayer) is based on all information of which preparer has any knowledge.

▶ Franklin C. Xenia     ▶ 4-1-86
Signature of general partner     Date

| Paid Preparer's Use Only | Preparer's signature ▶ Jay L. Bing | Date 4-1-86 | Check if self-employed ▶ ☒ | Preparer's social security no. ▶ 282 12 1236 |
|---|---|---|---|---|
| | Firm's name (or yours, if self-employed) and address ▶ Jay L. Bing<br>190 Capital Square, Madison, WI | | E.I. No. ▶ 38 8226910<br>ZIP code ▶ 55703 | |

**SCHEDULE K (Form 1065)**
Department of the Treasury
Internal Revenue Service

**Partners' Shares of Income, Credits, Deductions, etc.**

▶ File this form if there are more than ten Schedules K–1 (Form 1065) to be filed with Form 1065.
▶ Attach to Form 1065. ▶ See Instructions for Schedule K (Form 1065) in the Instructions for Form 1065.

OMB No. 1545–0099

**1985**

| Name of partnership | Employer identification number |
|---|---|
| XY Partnership | 22-6872310 |

| | | (a) Distributive share items | (b) Total amount | |
|---|---|---|---|---|
| **Income (Loss)** | 1 | Ordinary income (loss) (page 1, line 24) . . . . . . . . . . . . . . . | *1 | 27,550 -- |
| | 2 | Guaranteed payments . . . . . . . . . . . . . . . . . . . . | 2 | |
| | 3 | Dividends qualifying for exclusion . . . . . . . . . . . . . . . | 3 | |
| | 4 | Net short-term capital gain (loss) (Schedule D, line 4) . . . . . . . . | *4 | |
| | 5 | Net long-term capital gain (loss) (Schedule D, line 9) . . . . . . . . | *5 | |
| | 6 | Net gain (loss) under section 1231 (other than due to casualty or theft) . . . . | *6 | |
| | 7 | Other (attach schedule) . . . . . . . . . . . . . . . . . . | 7 | |
| **Deduc- tions** | 8 | Charitable contributions (attach list) . . . . . . . . . . . . . . | 8 | 200 -- |
| | 9 | Expense deduction for recovery property (section 179) from Form 4562 . . . . . . | *9 | |
| | 10 | Other (attach schedule) . . . . . . . . . . . . . . . . . . | 10 | |
| **Credits** | 11 | Credit for income tax withheld . . . . . . . . . . . . . . . | 11 | |
| | 12 | Other (attach schedule) . . . . . . . . . . . . . . . . . . | *12 | |
| **Self- Employ- ment** | 13a | Net earnings (loss) from self-employment . . . . . . . . . . . . . | 13a | |
| | b | Gross farming or fishing income . . . . . . . . . . . . . . . | 13b | |
| | c | Gross non-farm income . . . . . . . . . . . . . . . . . . | 13c | |
| **Tax Preference Items** | 14a | Accelerated depreciation on nonrecovery real property or 15–year or 18–year real property | 14a | |
| | b | Accelerated depreciation on leased personal property or leased recovery property other than 15–year or 18–year real property . . . . . . . . . . . . . | 14b | |
| | c | Depletion (other than oil and gas) . . . . . . . . . . . . . . | 14c | |
| | d | (1) Gross income from oil, gas, and geothermal properties . . . . . . . | 14d(1) | |
| | | (2) Deductions allocable to oil, gas, and geothermal properties . . . . . . | 14d(2) | |
| | e | (1) Qualified investment income included on page 1, Form 1065 . . . . . . | 14e(1) | |
| | | (2) Qualified investment expenses included on page 1, Form 1065 . . . . . . | 14e(2) | |
| | f | Other (attach schedule) . . . . . . . . . . . . . . . . . . | 14f | |
| **Investment Interest** | 15a | Interest expense on: | | |
| | | (1) Investment debts incurred before 12/17/69 . . . . . . . . . . | 15a(1) | |
| | | (2) Investment debts incurred before 9/11/75, but after 12/16/69 . . . . . . | 15a(2) | |
| | | (3) Investment debts incurred after 9/10/75 . . . . . . . . . . . | 15a(3) | |
| | b | (1) Investment income included on page 1, Form 1065 . . . . . . . . | 15b(1) | |
| | | (2) Investment expenses included on page 1, Form 1065 . . . . . . . . | 15b(2) | |
| | c | (1) Income from "net lease property" . . . . . . . . . . . . . | 15c(1) | |
| | | (2) Expenses from "net lease property" . . . . . . . . . . . . . | 15c(2) | |
| **Foreign Taxes** | 16a | Type of income _____ | | |
| | b | Foreign country or U.S. possession* _____ | | |
| | c | Total gross income from sources outside the U.S. (attach schedule) . . . . . . | *16c | |
| | d | Total applicable deductions and losses (attach schedule) . . . . . . . | 16d | |
| | e | Total foreign taxes (check one): ▶ ☐ Paid ☐ Accrued . . . . . . | 16e | |
| | f | Reduction in taxes available for credit (attach schedule) . . . . . . . | 16f | |
| | g | Other (attach schedule) . . . . . . . . . . . . . . . . . . | 16g | |
| **Other** | 17 | Other items and amounts not included in lines 1 through 16g that are required to be reported separately to partners. See instructions. **Caution:** *Attach a schedule that lists these items and amounts* . . . . . . . . . . . . . . . . . . . | | |

*You are not required to complete lines 1, 6, 9, 12 (see instructions), 16b, and 16c on Schedule K (Form 1065). Completion of these lines is optional because the amounts which would appear in column b appear elsewhere on Form 1065 or on other IRS forms or IRS schedules attached to Form 1065. Lines 4 and 5 must be completed only if any partner has a specially allocated capital gain (loss). (See instructions for line item.)

**For Paperwork Reduction Act Notice, see Form 1065 Instructions.**      Schedule K (Form 1065) 1985

**SCHEDULE K-1 (Form 1065)**
Department of the Treasury
Internal Revenue Service

**Partner's Share of Income, Credits, Deductions, etc.**
For calendar year 1985 or fiscal year
beginning _____, 1985, and ending _____, 19___

OMB No. 1545-0099

**1985**

Partner's identifying number ▶ 317-03-9876     Partnership's identifying number ▶ 22-6872310

| Partner's name, address, and ZIP code | Partnership's name, address, and ZIP code |
|---|---|
| Franklin C. Xenia<br>3407 Pelham Drive<br>Madison, Wisconsin 53713 | XY Partnership<br>700 University Avenue<br>Madison, Wisconsin 53703 |

**A** Is partner a general partner (see page 3 of Instructions for Form 1065)? . . . . . . . . . . [X] Yes [ ] No

**B** Partner's share of liabilities (see page 10 of Instructions for Form 1065):
Nonrecourse . . . . . . . . . $ -0-
Other . . . . . . . . . $ -0-

**C** What type of entity is this partner? ▶ Individual

**D** Enter partner's percentage of:

| | (i) Before decrease or termination | (ii) End of year |
|---|---|---|
| Profit sharing . . . . . . . . . | _____ % | 50 % |
| Loss sharing . . . . . . . . . | _____ % | 50 % |
| Ownership of capital . . . . . | _____ % | 50 % |

**E** IRS Center where partnership filed return ▶ Kansas City
**F** Tax Shelter Registration Number ▶

**G** Reconciliation of partner's capital account:

| (a) Capital account at beginning of year | (b) Capital contributed during year | (c) Ordinary income (loss) from line 1 below | (d) Income not included in column (c), plus nontaxable income | (e) Losses not included in column (c), plus unallowable deductions | (f) Withdrawals and distributions | (g) Capital account at end of year |
|---|---|---|---|---|---|---|
| 500 | | 13,775 | | 100 | 13,700 | 475 |

| | | (a) Distributive share item | (b) Amount | (c) 1040 filers enter the amount in column (b) on: |
|---|---|---|---|---|
| **Income (Loss)** | 1 | Ordinary income (loss) . . . . . . . . . . . . . | 13,775 | Sch. E, Part II, col. (e) or (f) |
| | 2 | Guaranteed payments . . . . . . . . . . . . | | Sch. E, Part II, column (f) |
| | 3 | Dividends qualifying for exclusion . . . . . . | | Sch. B, Part II, line 4 |
| | 4 | Net short-term capital gain (loss). . . . . . . | | Sch. D, line 4, col. (f) or (g) |
| | 5 | Net long-term capital gain (loss) . . . . . . . | | Sch. D, line 12, col. (f) or (g) |
| | 6 | Net gain (loss) under section 1231 (other than due to casualty or theft) | | Form 4797, line 1 |
| | 7 | Other (attach schedule) . . . . . . . . . . | | (Enter on applicable lines of your return) |
| **Deductions** | 8 | Charitable contributions . . . . . . . . . . . | 100 | See Form 1040 instructions |
| | 9 | Expense deduction for recovery property (section 179) . . . . . | | (See Partner's Instructions for Schedule K-1 (Form 1065)) |
| | 10 | Other (attach schedule) . . . . . . . . . . | | (Enter on applicable lines of your return) |
| **Credits** | 11 | Credit for income tax withheld . . . . . . . . | | See Form 1040 instructions, line 57 for Backup Withholding |
| | 12 | Other (attach schedule) . . . . . . . . . . | | (Enter on applicable lines of your return) |
| **Self-employment** | 13 a | Net earnings (loss) from self-employment . . . . . . . . | | Sch. SE, Part I |
| | b | Gross farming or fishing income . . . . . . . | | (See Partner's Instructions for Schedule K-1 (Form 1065)) |
| | c | Gross nonfarm income . . . . . . . . . . . | | |
| **Tax Preference Items** | 14 a | Accelerated depreciation on nonrecovery real property or 15-year or 18-year real property. . . . . . . . . . . . . . . | | Form 6251, line 4c |
| | b | Accelerated depreciation on leased personal property or leased recovery property other than 15-year or 18-year real property . . . . . . . . . | | Form 6251, line 4d |
| | c | Depletion (other than oil and gas) . . . . . . . . | | Form 6251, line 4i |
| | d | (1) Gross income from oil, gas, and geothermal properties . . . . | | See Form 6251 instructions |
| | | (2) Deductions allocable to oil, gas, and geothermal properties . . | | See Form 6251 instructions |
| | e | (1) Qualified investment income included in Schedule K-1, line 1 . . | | (See Partner's Instructions for Schedule K-1 (Form 1065)) |
| | | (2) Qualified investment expenses included in Schedule K-1, line 1 | | |
| | f | Other (attach schedule) . . . . . . . . . . . | | |

For Paperwork Reduction Act Notice, see Form 1065 Instructions.        Schedule K-1 (Form 1065) 1985

| | |
|---|---:|
| Rents for office space and equipment | $20,000 |
| Electricity | 1,500 |
| Supplies | 950 |
| Contribution to United Way | 200 |

In comparing Schedules K and K–1, note that each line on Schedule K is reflected on Schedule K–1. Schedule K–1 also provides instructions for partners filing as individual taxpayers as to the tax return form and place to report their respective shares of items.

*Impact of Withdrawals.* It is important to note that actual withdrawals of a partner during the year do not affect the partnership's income measurement and reporting process but are treated as distributions made on the last day of the partnership's tax year.[60] Furthermore, when partner withdrawals exceed the partners' shares of partnership income, the partners may be required to recognize the excess as income unless repayment is required. If repayment is required, the excess drawings would be treated as a loan rather than a current distribution.[61] Distributions are discussed under PARTNERSHIP DISTRIBUTIONS.

## ALLOCATING PARTNERSHIP INCOME

Under § 704(a), a partner's distributive share of partnership items is determined by the partnership agreement. Under § 704(b), the partnership agreement may provide different ratios for sharing items of income, gain, loss, deductions, or credits among the individual partners. Before the Tax Reform Act of 1976, many commentators thought the varying interests of partners during the year could be ignored and such items could be retroactively allocated to partners according to their partnership interests at year-end. Retroactive allocations also were thought to apply to partners admitted during the year. The IRS[62] and the Committee Reports underlying the Tax Reform Act of 1976 make it clear that the varying interests of partners in a partnership during the year must be considered when allocating such items. After the Tax Reform Act of 1976, many individuals tried to effect retroactive allocations via cash basis and tiered partnerships. The Deficit Reduction Act of 1984 eliminated this opportunity. Now, § 706(d)(2)(A) indicates that cash basis items must be allocated first to each day in the partnership's tax year, then to partners in proportion to their interests in the partnership at the close of each day.

Allocable cash basis items include interest, taxes, service payments, lease and rental payments, and other items specified in statutory regulations to be issued. As for undesignated items, § 706(d)(1) indicates that such items are to be allocated to partners after considering the partners' varying interests during the partnership year. To be issued statutory regulations will likely use a mid-month convention to determine how to make this allocation for newly admitted partners. In addition, § 704(b) states that a partner's distributive share of income, gain, loss, deduction, or credit

---

60. Reg. § 1.731–1(a)(1)(ii).
61. Reg. § 1.731–1(c)(2).
62. Rev.Rul. 77–310, 1977–2 C.B. 217.

shall be determined in accordance with the partner's interest in the partnership (determined by taking into account all of the facts and circumstances) if either of the following occurs:

1. The partnership agreement does not provide as to the partner's distributive share of such items *or*

2. The allocation to a partner of such items under the agreement does not have *substantial economic effect.*

The Regulations provide that the manner in which profits or losses are actually recorded on the partnership books (i. e., their division between the partners' accounts) generally determines the profit- and loss-sharing ratios in the absence of a partnership agreement.[63] Additionally, in determining whether an allocation has substantial economic effect, the Regulations[64] and case law[65] suggest that the allocation must affect the dollar amount of a partner's share of income or loss independent of the tax consequences. Regulation § 1.704–1(b)(2) indicates that a two-part analysis is required to determine if an allocation has substantial economic effect: (1) economic effect test and (2) substantiality test.

Although each test for substantial economic effect has several parts, only the main elements are summarized here. To meet the economic effect test, an allocation must:

1. Be consistent with the economic arrangement of the partners so that the partner receiving the allocation also receives the economic benefit or bears the economic risk or burden.

2. Affect the dollar amount received by the partners to the same extent as the allocation.

To meet the substantiality test, there must be a reasonable possibility that the allocation will affect substantially the dollar amount to be received by the partners independent of the tax consequences.

> **Example 11.** A and B form a general partnership, with each contributing $40,000 of cash. The AB Partnership purchases an item of tangible personal property for $80,000 and immediately places it in service. The partnership agreement provides the following:
>
> —A and B will have equal cash flows and will share equally in taxable income and loss (computed before cost recovery deductions).
>
> —All cost recovery deductions are to be allocated to A.
>
> —All allocations are to be reflected in the partners' capital accounts, maintained according to Regulation § 1.704–1(b)(2)(iv).
>
> —Each partner is entitled to equal distributions upon liquidation regardless of the partners' capital account balances.

---

**63.** Reg. § 1.704–1(b)(1).

**64.** Reg. § 1.704–1(b)(2).

**65.** See *Stanley C. Orrisch,* 55 T.C. 395 (1971), *aff'd.* in 31 AFTR2d 73–1069 (CA–9, 1973), and *Martin Magaziner,* 37 TCM 873, T.C.Memo. 1978–205. For an excellent discussion of the substantial economic effect test, see Solomon, "Current Planning for Partnership Start-up, Including Special Allocations, Retroactive Allocations and Guaranteed Payments," *37th N.Y.U. Tax Institute,* Vol. 1 (1979), pp. 13–1 to 13–77.

During the first year of operations, the partnership recognizes no taxable income or loss before cost recovery deductions of $20,000. Since the partners made equal contributions to the partnership, share equally in taxable income or loss (exclusive of cost recovery deductions), will have equal cash flows, and will share equally in any liquidation proceeds, it must be concluded that the economic arrangement between them is to share equally the risk of potential decreases in the value of the property and that the partners' interests are equal. The fact that A and B are entitled to equal distributions on liquidation indicates that A does not bear the full risk of the $20,000 of cost recovery deductions. Thus, the special allocation to A will be disregarded, because it lacks economic effect, and the cost recovery deductions will be reallocated equally to A and B.

**Example 12.** Assume the same facts as in Example 11, except that the partnership agreement provides that liquidation proceeds will be distributed in accordance with the partners' capital accounts if the partnership is liquidated within the first five years of existence. Assume that the agreement provides that after the first five years of existence, liquidation proceeds are to be distributed equally. Since the capital accounts do not govern the liquidation proceeds during the entire life of the partnership, the special allocation of cost recovery deductions has no economic effect. Such deduction must be allocated equally between the partners.

**Example 13.** Assume the same facts as in Example 11, except that liquidation proceeds throughout the life of the partnership are to be distributed in accordance with the partners' capital accounts and that following liquidation no partner is required by either the partnership agreement or by state law to refund any capital account deficit for distribution to partners with positive balances or for payment to creditors. If the property is sold at the end of Year 1 for $60,000 and the partnership is liquidated, A would receive $20,000 and B would receive $40,000. Note that there was no gain or loss on the sale of the property (selling price of $60,000 less adjusted basis of $60,000). Since neither partner had a deficit capital account before the liquidating distribution, the allocation of $20,000 of cost recovery deduction to A has substantial economic effect.

**Example 14.** Assume the same facts as in Example 13. Assume also that in Year 2 the cost recovery deductions are $20,000 and the property is sold at the end of the year for $35,000. Here, the sale of the property produces a $5,000 loss (selling price of $35,000 less adjusted basis of $40,000). The capital accounts of the partners at the end of Year 2 are determined as follows:

|  | A | B |
|---|---|---|
| Balances at formation | $ 40,000 | $ 40,000 |
| Year 1 cost recovery deductions | (20,000) | –0– |
| Balances at end of Year 1 | $ 20,000 | $ 40,000 |
| Year 2 cost recovery deductions | (20,000) | –0– |
| Loss on sale | (2,500) | (2,500) |
| Balances at end of Year 2 | $ (2,500) | $ 37,500 |

Since B bears the entire economic burden of the $5,000 loss, the entire $5,000 loss will be reallocated to B. If a deficit capital account restoration agreement had been in effect, all portions of the special allocation of cost recovery deductions would have substantial economic effect, and no reallocation would be necessary.

*Required Allocations.* A special allocation that results in the shifting of tax benefits to partners who could take full advantage of selected items would be subject to close IRS scrutiny. However, Congress provided for required allocations of income, gain, loss, and deduction with respect to contributed property via the Deficit Reduction Act of 1984 to mitigate the inequities that might arise due to the differing nature of property contributed to a partnership by individual partners.[66]

Section 704(c) provides that the IRS will prescribe Regulations so that income, gain, loss, and deduction with respect to property contributed to a partnership can be shared among the partners in a manner that will take into account the discrepancy between the basis of the property to the partnership and the fair market value at the time of contribution. The Joint Committee Report accompanying the Deficit Reduction Act of 1984 indicated that the old regulations under repealed § 704(c)(2) may be relied on until new regulations are proposed. Under these regulations, the amount allocated to the partners cannot exceed the total of the amount properly allowable to the partnership.[67] In addition, the Joint Committee was concerned that the allocation of depreciation under the new statutory regulations might become burdensome for small operating partnerships. It indicated that the new regulations should provide some degree of flexibility for these partnerships in allocating depreciation in nonabusive situations. Example 15, which is based on the old regulations, illustrates the complexity of the depreciation problem under the new provision.

> **Example 15.** A and B form an equal partnership on January 1 of the current year and immediately start operations. A contributes cash of $95,000, and B contributes land and an office building with adjusted bases of $5,000 and $60,000 and fair market values of $5,000 and $90,000, respectively. Immediately after formation, A and B each have an effective $47,500 fair market value interest in the cash and $2,500 and $45,000 FMV interests in the land and building, respectively. The building's full basis ($90,000 for financial accounting and $60,000 for taxes) is recovered by the straight-line method over 18 years, using the one-half month convention for the month the property is placed in service and the disposition month.
>
> At the start of the third year, the land and building are sold for $97,000 (land $5,000 and building $92,000). From a financial accounting viewpoint, A and B each realize a gain of $6,000 on the sale (one-half the difference between the selling price of $97,000 and the land's and building's unrecovered bases at the sale date of $85,000). For taxes, all of A's fair market value interest in the land ($2,500) and building ($45,000) is included in the partnership's tax basis. The re-

---

66. § 704(c).
67. Reg. § 1.704–1(c)(2)(i).

maining $17,500 of tax basis belongs to B. This amount, when combined with B's unrealized appreciation on the building of $30,000, equals B's fair market value interest of $47,500.

For financial accounting, A and B each receive an annual deduction for recovery of the building's basis of $2,500 (one-half of $90,000 divided by 18 years). For taxes, A receives a recovery deduction of $2,500 ($45,000 fair market interest divided by 18 years) and B receives an $833 recovery deduction ($15,000 fair market interest divided by 18 years). Although B cannot claim a recovery deduction for the $30,000 of unrealized appreciation, the amount must be reduced using the same method and period used for determining the recovery deductions (straight-line and 18 years). When the land and building are sold for $97,000, A has a taxable gain of $6,000 and B has a taxable gain of $32,667.

|  | Total | A | B |
|---|---|---|---|
| Selling price | $97,000 | $48,500 | $48,500 |
| Basis | $65,000 | $47,500 | $17,500 |
| Less: Recovery deductions | 6,667 | 5,000 | 1,667 |
| Adjusted basis | $58,333 | $42,500 | $15,833 |
| Taxable gain | $38,667 | $ 6,000 | $32,667 |

A and B could have computed their taxable gains as follows:

| | | |
|---|---|---|
| Selling price | | $97,000 |
| Less: Adjusted basis | | 58,333 |
| Taxable gain | | $38,667 |
| B's unrealized appreciation at the contribution date | $30,000 | |
| Less: ($30,000/18) x 2 | 3,333 | 26,667 |
| Remaining gain split equally | | $12,000 |

Thus, A's gain is $6,000 and B's gain is $32,667 (one-half of the $12,000 plus $26,667).

If the adjusted basis of the building contributed by B in Example 15 were less than $45,000, a complex tax reimbursement agreement would be necessary to bring about equity between the partners. Such an agreement would have to consider the time value of money and the additional taxes A would have to pay annually because of lost recovery deductions. For example, instead of an adjusted basis of $60,000 at the contribution date, assume the building's basis was $18,000. Although A's fair market value interest in the building is $45,000, recovery deductions are allowed only on $18,000 under the ceiling limitation of Regulation § 1.704–1(c)(2)(i). Thus, A would lose $1,500 of recovery deductions annually (the difference between $45,000 divided by 18 years and $18,000 divided by 18 years). The amount of additional taxes paid by A would depend on A's marginal tax rate each year. It should be noted that the Committee Reports accompanying the Deficit Reduction Act of 1984 suggest that the ceiling limitation in the Regulation be amended to permit an allocation to the contributing partner of a sufficient amount of gain on the disposition of the property in excess of the adjusted built-in gain at the time of contribution.

Another problem is created if the market value of the building declines at a rate greater than the recovery deduction rate and the building is sold at a later date for a gain. A's portion of the decline in economic value cannot be deducted. Under the ceiling limitation of Regulation § 1.704–1(c)(2)(i), no loss is allocated to A and all of the gain is allocated to B. To avoid such a problem, B could sell a half interest in the building to A at the fair market value before the contribution date and recognize a gain on the property's sale. A and B could then contribute their halves of the building to the partnership and, under Regulation § 1.704–1(c)(3), use their respective bases to determine depreciation deductions and gain or loss on disposal. If B does not want to recognize an immediate gain from the sale of a half interest in the building, but A and B still want to form a partnership, an easy and equitable solution to the problem seems impossible.

## BASIS ADJUSTMENTS AND LIMITATIONS ON LOSSES

Once the basis of a contributing partner's interest is determined, it is subject to continuous fluctuation. It is increased by such things as further contributions, the sum of current and prior years' distributive share of partnership income not withdrawn, any income retained by the partnership that was exempt from tax, and the excess of the deductions for depletion over the basis of the property subject to depletion. Likewise, it is decreased by such things as the amount of money and the adjusted basis of property distributed to the partner by the partnership, the sum of current and prior years' distributive share of deductible partnership losses, and the partner's share of nondeductible partnership expenditures that are not capital expenditures (e. g., charitable contributions and investment interest expenses). However, note again that a partner's basis can never be reduced below zero.[68]

*Partnership Liabilities.* The basis of a partner's interest must be adjusted for changes in partnership liabilities. Recall that any increase in a partner's share of partnership liabilities is treated as a contribution of money to the partnership and thus increases the basis of the partner's interest.[69] Similarly, any decrease in a partner's share of partnership liabilities is treated as a distribution of money and decreases the basis of the partner's interest.[70] Such adjustments are automatic and will occur regardless of the partnership's method of accounting (i. e., cash, accrual, or hybrid method). Note that exceptions exist when determining the at-risk basis of a partner's interest under § 465. The impact of § § 705, 733, and 752(d) and partnership liabilities on a partner's interest basis are illustrated in the following examples.

---

**68.** § § 705(a)(2) and 733.

**69.** § 752(a).

**70.** § 752(b).

**Example 16.** A and B are equal partners in the AB Partnership. To purchase a parcel of real estate to be used as a potential office site, the partnership borrows $50,000 from a local savings and loan association. As a result of the loan, A's and B's partnership interests are each increased by $25,000.

**Example 17.** Assume the same facts as in Example 16, except that the AB Partnership repays $20,000 of the loan. The repayment decreases A's and B's partnership interests by $10,000 each.

**Example 18.** Assume the same facts as in Example 16, except that the partnership decides not to use the real estate after all. Instead, the property is distributed to A. At the time of distribution, the property has an adjusted basis and fair market value of $50,000 and is subject to a mortgage of $30,000. As a result of the distribution, A's interest is decreased by $35,000 as follows:

| | |
|---|---:|
| Decrease in an amount equal to the adjusted basis of property distributed | $ 50,000 |
| Decrease as a result of the reduction in A's share of partnership liabilities (½ of $30,000) | 15,000 |
| Increase as a result of the assumption of a partnership liability | (30,000) |
| Net decrease | $ 35,000 |

**Example 19.** Assume the same facts as in Example 18. What effect will the distribution of the real estate to A have on B's interest? B's interest is decreased by $15,000, since the distribution decreased B's share of partnership liabilities.

*Loss Limitations.* Section 704(d) limits the amount of partnership losses a partner can deduct. Specifically, a partner's deduction of partnership losses (including capital losses) is limited to the adjusted basis of the partner's interest at the end of the partnership year before considering any losses for that year. Distributions during the year are taken into account before losses are applied against basis. Losses that cannot be deducted by a partner because of the § 704(d) limitation are suspended and carried over for use when the partner has a sufficient year-end interest basis to absorb them.[71]

The limitation of § 704(d) is similar to the limitation on losses provided by § 1366(d) in the case of an S corporation. However, a shareholder's interest basis does not include a pro rata share of all debt of an S corporation. Only debt due to a shareholder is included in the shareholder's interest basis. Thus, a partnership offers greater leveraging opportunities than

---

**71.** Such losses are generally personal to the partner who incurred them. However, one commentator has indicated that the losses should be available to a transferee partner whose interest is acquired by gift. See W. S. McKee, W. F. Nelson, and R. L. Whitmire, *Federal Taxation of Partnerships and Partners* (Boston, Mass.: Warren, Gorham & Lamont, Inc., 1977 with updates), § 10.10[3], [c].

does an S corporation. Partnership and S corporation losses in excess of interest basis are suspended and carried forward for use against future increases in interest basis. Such increases might result from additional capital contributions, additional liabilities, or future income. Before 1983, losses in excess of a Subchapter S shareholder's interest basis were lost forever.

> **Example 20.** C and D do business as the CD Partnership, sharing profits and losses equally. All parties use the calendar year. At the start of the current year, C's partnership interest is $25,000. The partnership sustained an operating loss of $80,000 in the current year and earned a profit of $70,000 in the next year. For the current year, only $25,000 of C's $40,000 distributive share of the partnership loss (one-half of $80,000 loss) can be deducted. As a result, the basis of C's partnership interest is zero as of January 1 of the next year, and C must carry forward the remaining $15,000 of partnership losses.

> **Example 21.** Assume the same facts as in Example 20. Since the partnership earned a profit of $70,000 for the next calendar year, C will report partnership income of $20,000 ($35,000 distributive share of income less the $15,000 carryover loss). The adjusted basis of C's partnership interest now becomes $20,000.[72]

It should be noted that C's entire $40,000 share of the current year partnership loss could have been deducted in the current year if C had contributed an additional $15,000 or more in capital by December 31. Likewise, if the partnership had incurred additional debt of $30,000 or more by the end of the current year, C's basis would have been increased to permit the entire share of the distributive loss to be deducted in that year.[73] Thus, if partnership losses are projected for a given year, careful tax planning can insure the deductibility of a partner's distributive share of such losses.

*Allocation of Pass-throughs.* If ordinary losses, short-term and long-term capital losses, § 1231 losses, etc., exist and the amount of interest basis needed to absorb the partner's aggregate share is insufficient, the amount of each item used on the partner's individual tax return is limited.

> **Example 22.** E and Z are equal partners in the EZ Partnership. For the current year, the partnership had an ordinary loss from operations of $20,000, a long-term capital gain of $2,000, and a short-term capital loss of $8,000. Z's distributive share of these items is $10,000 of the operating loss, $1,000 of the long-term capital gain, and $4,000 of the short-term capital loss. The partnership had no other transactions for the current year. At the start of the current year, Z's interest basis in the partnership was $6,000. How much of each loss can Z claim as a deduction in the current year? First, Z's interest basis at the end of the current year before considering the partnership losses must be determined. Then, Z's deductible share of each loss must be computed.

---

**72.** Reg. § 1.704–1(d)(4) (Ex. 1).
**73.** See Example (2), Reg. § 1.704–1(d)(4). Also note that the business purpose test might be applied to any tax-motivated year-end borrowing by the partnership.

At the end of the current year before considering the losses, Z's interest basis is $7,000 (start-of-the-year interest basis of $6,000 plus Z's $1,000 share of the long-term capital gain). Z's aggregate share of the losses for the year is $14,000 ($10,000 of ordinary loss and $4,000 of short-term capital loss), and Z's interest basis of $7,000 must be apportioned to the individual losses in the ratios of 10:14 and 4:14. Thus, Z can deduct $5,000 of the ordinary loss (10/14 of $7,000) and $2,000 of the short-term capital loss (4/14 of $7,000). The remainder of these losses is carried forward until Z has a sufficient year-end interest basis before considering these and future losses to absorb them. If Z is an individual, the short-term capital loss is first offset against Z's short-term capital gains and then against Z's long-term capital gains. Any remaining short-term capital loss is then offset against Z's ordinary income, subject to the usual offset rules.

*At-Risk Provisions.*  The Tax Reform Act of 1976 introduced statutory provision § 465 and amended § 704(d) to limit losses that a partner may deduct to the partner's interest *at risk* in the partnership at the end of the taxable year. The Revenue Act of 1978 made subsequent changes in both of these statutes to expand the application of the at-risk limitations. The Deficit Reduction Act of 1984 amended the at-risk rules so that all activities by a partnership with respect to § 1245 property that is leased and placed in service during any taxable year are treated as a single activity. The provisions are directed toward nonrecourse debt and are discussed in Chapter 10 under SPECIAL PARTNERSHIP PROBLEMS—Limited Partnerships. It is important to note that general partnerships with nonrecourse debt are subject to these same limitations.

## TAXABLE YEARS OF PARTNER AND PARTNERSHIP

Selecting the proper tax year for a partnership and understanding how and when a partner's and partnership's tax years automatically close are important from a tax planning standpoint.

*Selecting the Tax Year.*  In computing a partner's taxable income for a specific year, § 706(a) requires that each partner's distributive share of partnership income and guaranteed payments for the partnership year that ends with or within the partner's taxable year be included. Generally, the guaranteed payments are includible in the partner's income only for the appropriate partnership year in which the partnership deducted them as paid or accrued *under the partnership's method of accounting.*[74] A calendar year partner's distributive share of income for the partnership year that ends with January 31 of the current year is reported on the partner's current year income tax return. Guaranteed payments are discussed under PARTNERSHIP OPERATIONS—Transactions Between Partner and Partnership.

Under § 706(a), theoretically there can be an effective deferral of a partner's share of partnership income of up to 11 months. This deferral is possible, because drawings against a partner's distributive share of part-

---

74.   Reg. § 1.707–1(c).

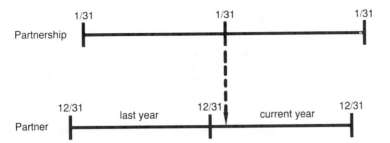

nership income are treated as made on the last day of the partnership's taxable year. In fact, distributions made after January 31 of the current year will not be reported by the calendar year partners until the partners file their tax returns for next year. Practically, it is difficult to obtain this 11 months' deferral with a new partnership. Section 706(b) and the Regulations generally provide that the IRS must consent to any adoption or change of a partnership taxable year.[75] There are two principal exceptions to this rule:

1. Without consent, a partnership must adopt the same taxable year as all of its principal partners (partners with a five percent or greater interest in capital or profits). Additionally, an existing partnership may change to the same taxable year as all of its principal partners or to the same taxable year that all of its principal partners are concurrently adopting.

2. If not all of the principal partners are on the same taxable year, a partnership may initially adopt a calendar year.

When consent is required, it is generally conditional upon finding a business purpose for the adoption or change. However, the IRS normally will give its consent if the effective income deferral does not exceed three months.[76] The tax effect of the deferral, however, will be spread over ten years. The excess of income over expenses for the period immediately following the short tax year (but not to exceed three months) is added to the income of this short year. One-tenth of the excess may then be deducted, beginning in this short tax year, over a ten-year period. If expenses for the period immediately following the short tax year (but not to exceed three months) are equal to or greater than the income for this period, no adjustments are made in the short tax year or the following nine years.

**Example 23.** O, D, and E are equal partners in the calendar year ODE Partnership. The partnership's ordinary income for the current calendar year is $12,000, earned at a quarterly rate of $3,000. The partnership has obtained permission from the IRS to change to a fiscal year ending September 30 of the current calendar year. For the short period (January 1 through September 30), the partnership reports $9,000 of ordinary income plus the $3,000 of income earned during the period October 1 through December 31. For the short period ending September 30 of the current calendar year, the ODE Partnership can

---

**75.** Reg. § 1.706–1(b).
**76.** Rev.Proc. 72–51, 1972–2 C.B. 832.

take a deduction of $300 (¹⁄₁₀ of the $3,000). For the next calendar year, the ODE Partnership earned ordinary income of $16,000 at the rate of $4,000 per quarter. Thus, for its first full fiscal year ending September 30, it reports ordinary income of $15,000. This amount includes the same $3,000 previously reported with the short period return, plus the $12,000 earned during the last three quarters of this fiscal year. For this first full fiscal year and the following eight subsequent fiscal years, the ODE Partnership can deduct $300 as an adjustment for the double reporting.

Although the double reporting of income appears damaging under the preceding rules, such is not necessarily the case. First, using the ODE Partnership (in Example 23) as a departure point and assuming all partners are on the calendar year, the reporting by the partners of ODE's income for the first three fiscal months of each year (October 1 through December 31) is deferred 12 additional months for as long as ODE retains a September 30 fiscal year. Second, the amount of combined income for ODE's short fiscal year and first full fiscal year may be smaller than ODE's combined income for the current and next (second) calendar years.

**Example 24.** Assume the same facts as in Example 23. Assume also that ODE's income for the second calendar year is $18,000 earned at a quarterly rate of $4,500. ODE's combined income for its short and first full fiscal years is $2,100 less than its combined income for the first two calendar years.

| First calendar year = $ 12,000 | | Second calendar year = $ 18,000 | |
|---|---|---|---|
| Short Fiscal Year | | First Full Fiscal Year | |
| | Income | | Income |
| 1/1–9/30 (first year) | $  9,000 | 10/1–12/31 (first year) | $  3,000 |
| 10/1–12/31 (first year) | 3,000 | 1/1–9/30 (second year) | 13,500 |
| Total | $ 12,000 | Total | $ 16,500 |
| Less: 1/10 of $3,000 | 300 | Less: 1/10 of $3,000 | 300 |
| Total | $ 11,700 | Total | $ 16,200 |

| | |
|---|---|
| ODE's combined income for first two calendar years ($12,000 + $18,000) | $ 30,000 |
| ODE's combined income for short and first full fiscal years ($11,700 + $16,200) | 27,900 |
| Difference | $  2,100 |

Under § 443, a partnership that changes its tax year should file its return for a short period without annualizing taxable income. The partnership must attach to the return either a copy of the letter from the IRS granting permission to change or a statement indicating that the partnership is changing its tax year to the tax year of all its principal partners or to the tax year to which all its principal partners are concurrently changing.[77] However, a principal partner may not change to a taxable year

---

77.   Reg. § 1.706–1(b)(5)(ii)(a).

other than that of the partnership unless it is established to the satisfaction of the IRS that there is a valid business purpose for such change.[78]

*Close of the Tax Year.* Once established, when does a partnership's tax year close? The taxable year of a partnership closes upon termination of the partnership. However, a partnership's tax year generally does not close upon the death of a partner; the entry of a new partner; or the liquidation, sale, or exchange of an existing partnership interest.[79] In the case of the sale or liquidation of an entire interest, the partnership's tax year will close as to that partner's disposing of the partnership interest.[80] However, generally this rule does not apply in the event the disposition involves less than an entire interest.[81] Additionally, the taxable year of the partnership will close as to a deceased partner if the partnership agreement so provides. Close of the partnership's taxable year with respect to a deceased partner usually should be avoided because of the bunching of income (partnership income from more than 12 months included in one taxable year of a partner) that will be reported on the decedent's final income tax return.

The termination of a partnership will, of course, close the partnership's tax year. In addition to the clear-cut situation involving outright liquidation or other dissolution of the partnership, § 708(b)(1) states that an existing partnership will be considered as terminated if either of the following occurs:

1. No part of any business, financial operation, or venture of the partnership continues to be carried on by any of the partners in a partnership.

2. Within a 12-month period there is a sale or exchange of 50 percent or more of the total interest in partnership capital and profits.[82]

The consequences of some of the rules previously discussed are illustrated by the following examples.

**Example 25.** Partner R died on November 20 of the last calendar year with a one-third interest in the RST Partnership. The partnership uses a fiscal year ending September 30; R used a calendar year. The partnership agreement does not contain a provision for termination or a special accounting upon the death of a partner. Under these circumstances, the partnership's tax year does not close with R's

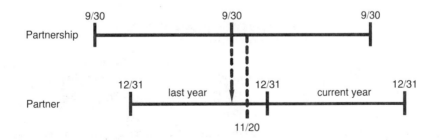

---

**78.** § 706(b)(2).
**79.** § 706(c)(1).
**80.** § 706(c)(2)(A).
**81.** § 706(c)(2)(B).
**82.** § 708(b)(1)(A) and (B).

death. Instead, income from the fiscal year ending September 30 of the current calendar year will be taxed to R's estate or other successor in interest. Income from the fiscal year ending September 30 of the last calendar year must be reported on R's final income tax return covering the period from January 1 to November 20.[83]

**Example 26.** Assume the same facts as in Example 25, except that the partnership agreement provides for the termination of a partner's interest as of the date of death with a special accounting to be rendered at that time. Although R's death will not affect the surviving partners, it will close the partnership's tax year as to R. Thus, R's final income tax return for the last calendar year must include R's share of partnership income both for the fiscal year ending September 30 of the last calendar year and for the period from October 1 to R's death.

**Example 27.** Assume the same facts as in Example 25, except that on November 20 of the last calendar year R's entire partnership interest is sold to a third party. Again, the partnership's tax year will not close with respect to the remaining partners. However, R's share of partnership income for the fiscal year ending September 30 of the last calendar year and for the short period ending on the sale date must be reported on R's tax return for the last year.[84]

**Example 28.** Assume the same facts as in Example 27, except that R's entire interest represents 60% of the partnership rather than a one-third interest. The result of the disposition of this 60% interest does not change as to R, but the same is not true for the remaining partners. Since an interest of 50% or more in the partnership has changed hands, § 708(b)(1) (B) requires that the partnership's tax year be closed as of November 20 of the last calendar year for all partners; the RST Partnership is considered to be terminated with that date.

## TRANSACTIONS BETWEEN PARTNER AND PARTNERSHIP

The entity theory of a partnership has been adopted in the general rule governing transactions between a partner and the partnership. Thus, under § 707(a) a partner engaging in a transaction with the partnership can be regarded as a nonpartner or outsider. Applications of this rule include the following:

1.  Loans of money or property by the partnership to the partner or by the partner to the partnership.

2.  The sale of property by a partner to the partnership or the purchase of property by the partner from the partnership.

3.  The rendition of services by the partnership to the partner or by the partner to the partnership.[85]

Transactions between a partner and the partnership are subject to close scrutiny. Through § § 267(a)(1), (a)(2), and (e), an accrual basis part-

---

**83.**  Reg. § § 1.706–1(c)(2)(ii) and (iii).
**84.**  Reg. § 1.706–1(c)(2)(i) and (ii).
**85.**  Reg. § 1.707–1(a).

nership that makes expense and interest payments to related cash basis payees can deduct such payments only when the payees include them in gross income. Such payments are not disallowed; they are only deferred. Note that § 707(a) payments generally are covered by these provisions. Although losses from sales or exchanges between related parties are also covered by § 267(a)(1) regardless of the method of accounting used, losses from sales or exchanges between a partner and a partnership or between two partnerships are not covered by § 267(a)(1). Such losses are covered by § 707(b). In addition, guaranteed payments to partners under § 707(c) and certain expenses and interest paid or accrued by a partnership owning low-income housing to any qualified five-percent or less partner[86] are not covered by § 267(a)(1). Furthermore, § 707(b) requires ordinary rather than capital gain treatment for certain transactions between partners and a partnership.

Related parties for purposes of § 267 are quite extensive and include any person, as well as any person related to this person under § § 267(b) or 707(b)(1), who owns directly or indirectly any capital or profits interest in the following:

1. The partnership.
2. A partnership in which the first partnership owns directly or indirectly any capital or profits interest.

In lieu of the attribution rules of § 267(c)(3), interests owned directly or indirectly by or for a C corporation are considered as owned by the shareholders who own directly or indirectly five percent or more in value of the corporation's stock. Finally, related parties under § 267(b)(10) include a corporation and a partnership in which the same person owns more than 50 percent in value of the corporation's stock (a controlled corporation) *and also owns* more than a 50 percent interest in the partnership's capital or profits (a controlled partnership).

*Deferred expenses.* Under § § 267(e) and 267(a)(2), an accrual basis partnership cannot take an immediate deduction for interest and other expenses accrued to a cash basis partner but must defer the deduction until the partner includes such amounts in gross income. Certain expenses and interest of partnerships owning low-income housing that are paid or incurred to a five-percent or less partner and guaranteed payments to partners under § 707(c) are excluded from this deferral.

**Example 29.** The BOQ Partnership uses the accrual method of accounting. At the start of last year Q, a cash basis individual who owns a 30% interest in BOQ's capital and profits, loaned BOQ $5,000 at 12%, compounded annually, for business purposes. At the end of last year, BOQ had accrued and unpaid interest on this loan of $600. On December 31 of the current year, Q received a $1,272 check from BOQ. The accompanying remittance advice indicated that the check included $600 for last year's interest (12% × $5,000) and $672 for the current year's interest (12% × $5,600). Both parties use the calendar year. Q includes the $1,272 in gross income of the current year, and

---

**86.** § 267(e)(5)(C).

BOQ deducts the full $1,272 as interest expense for the current year. BOQ could not deduct the $600 of interest due to Q last year, since Q did not include it in last year's gross income.

*Losses Disallowed.* Under § 707(b)(1), losses from the sale or exchange of property will be disallowed if they arise in either of the following cases:

1. Between a partnership and a partner whose direct or indirect interest in the capital or profits of the partnership is more than 50 percent.

2. Between two partnerships in which the same persons own more than a 50 percent interest in the capital or profits.

If one of the purchasers later sells the property, any gain realized will be recognized only to the extent that it exceeds the loss previously disallowed.[87] The offset of the disallowed loss is available only to the original transferee who acquired the property by purchase or exchange.[88] Although the disallowed loss may be used by the transferee to offset any subsequent gain on the property's disposal, it cannot be used to increase or create a loss.

> **Example 30.** R owns a 35% interest in the capital and profits of the RST Partnership. On September 1 of the current year, R sells property with an adjusted basis of $50,000 to the partnership for its fair market value of $35,000. Assuming R is not related to any partners (within the meaning of § 267), a recognized loss of $15,000 is to be reported.

> **Example 31.** Assume the same facts as in Example 30, except that R's brother owns a 40% interest in the capital and profits of the partnership. Section 707(b)(3) provides that the constructive ownership of a partnership interest is to be determined by § 267. Under § 267, constructive ownership takes place between brothers and sisters; thus, R is deemed to own a 75% interest in the partnership (35% direct ownership plus the 40% interest owned by R's brother). Consequently, § 707(b)(1)(A) is applicable, and R's $15,000 loss is disallowed.

> **Example 32.** Assume the same facts as in Example 31. If the RST Partnership later sells the property for $40,000, none of the $5,000 (sale price of $40,000 less adjusted basis to partnership of $35,000) gain will be recognized. Section 267(d) permits the partnership to offset any subsequent gain by the loss previously disallowed. The unused $10,000 of R's disallowed loss disappears.

*Conversion of Capital Gain.* Under § 707(b)(2), gains are treated as ordinary income in a sale or exchange of property directly or indirectly between a partner and partnership or between two partnerships if more than 80 percent of the capital or profits interest in the partnership or partnerships is owned directly or indirectly by the same person or persons. This rule does not apply, however, if the property in the hands of the transferee

---

87. Reg. § 1.707–1(b)(1)(ii).
88. Reg. § 1.267(d)–1(a)(3).

(purchaser) immediately after the transfer is a capital asset.[89] Note that § 707(b)(2) converts capital gain into ordinary income if the ownership and nature tests are met. It does not convert ordinary income into capital gain.

In evaluating the 50 percent test for losses or the 80 percent test for gains, the following rules are applicable:

1. Any interest owned directly or indirectly by or for a corporation, partnership, estate, or trust is considered to be owned proportionately by or for its shareholders, partners, or beneficiaries.

2. An individual is considered as owning the interest owned directly or indirectly by or for family members.

3. The family of an individual includes only brothers and sisters (whether by the whole or half blood), spouse, ancestors, and lineal descendants.

4. An interest constructively owned by a person under rule 1 is treated, for applying rules 1 and 2, as actually owned by that person. However, an interest constructively owned by an individual under rule 2 is not treated as owned by him or her for purposes of again applying rule 2 to make another the constructive owner of the interest.[90]

*Guaranteed Payments.* Payments made by a partnership to one of its partners for services rendered or for the use of capital to the extent they are determined without regard to the income of the partnership are treated by the partnership in the same manner as payments made to a person who is not a partner.[91] Referred to as *guaranteed payments* under § 707(c), such payments generally are deductible by the partnership as a business expense and must be reported as ordinary income by the receiving partner. Their deductibility distinguishes guaranteed payments from a partner's distributive share of income that is not deductible by the partnership. The Tax Reform Act of 1976 amended § 707(c) to clarify an earlier misconception that guaranteed payments automatically were deductible by the partnership.[92] Specifically, revised § 707(c) states that a guaranteed payment is deductible by a partnership if it is not a capital expenditure under § 263 and if it meets the tests of § 162(a) as an ordinary and necessary business expense.

> **Example 33.** Under the terms of the LMN Partnership agreement, N is entitled to a fixed annual salary of $18,000 without regard to partnership income. L, M, and N share profits and losses equally. After deducting the guaranteed payment, the partnership has $36,000 of ordinary income. N reports $30,000 of ordinary income for the partnership tax year that ends with or within N's tax year ($18,000 guar-

---

**89.** § 707(b)(2).
**90.** Reg. § 1.707–1(b)(3). See examples of constructive ownership in Reg. § 1.267(c)–1(b).
**91.** But see *Edward T. Pratt,* 64 T.C. 203 (1975), for a broad interpretation of the phrase "without regard to the income of the partnership."
**92.** *Jackson E. Cagle, Jr.,* 63 T.C. 86 (1974), *aff'd.* in 76–2 USTC ¶ 9672, 38 AFTR2d 76–5834, 539 F.2d 409 (CA–5, 1976).

anteed payment plus his one-third distributive share of partnership income of $12,000).[93]

*Minimum Guaranteed Payment.* If a partner is to receive a percentage of partnership income with a stipulated minimum payment, the guaranteed payment is the amount by which the minimum guarantee exceeds the partner's share of partnership income before taking into account the minimum guaranteed amount.

**Example 34.** In this example, assume the partnership does not have any separately stated items. Under the partnership agreement, M is to receive 40% of partnership income, but in no event less than $10,000. In the current year, the partnership has income of $15,000 before considering M's guaranteed payment. M's share is $6,000 (40% of $15,000). Thus, the guaranteed payment that may be deducted by the partnership is $4,000 (excess of $10,000 minimum guarantee over $6,000 share of partnership income before considering the guaranteed payment). M's ordinary income from the partnership is $10,000, and the remaining $5,000 of income is reported by the other partners in proportion to their profit shares under the agreement. Note that M's share of partnership income after deducting the guaranteed payment is 54.55% [$6,000 ÷ ($15,000 − $4,000)].[94]

*Losses and Guaranteed Payments.* When the partnership agreement provides for a guaranteed payment and such payment results in a partnership loss, the partner must report the full guaranteed payment and separately account for the distributive share of the loss. This reporting assumes the partnership agreement provides for the partner receiving the guaranteed payment to share in partnership losses resulting from such payments.

**Example 35.** Partner T in the STP Partnership is to receive a payment of $20,000 for services plus 20% of the partnership income or loss. After deducting the $20,000 payment to T, the partnership has a loss of $10,000. Of this amount, $2,000 (20% of $10,000) is T's distributive share which, subject to the limitation imposed by § 704(d), is to be reported on T's tax return. In addition, T must report the guaranteed payment of $20,000 as ordinary income.[95]

**Example 36.** Assume the same facts as in Example 35, except that instead of a $10,000 loss, the partnership has $40,000 of capital gains and no deductions or income items other than the $20,000 paid to T as a guaranteed payment. Since the items of partnership income or loss must be segregated under § 702(a), the partnership has a $20,000 ordinary loss and $40,000 in capital gains. T's 20% distributive share of these items is a $4,000 ordinary loss and an $8,000 capital gain. Additionally, T must report the $20,000 guaranteed payment as ordinary income.[96]

---

**93.** See Reg. § 1.707–1(c) (Ex. 1).
**94.** Reg. § 1.707–1(c) (Ex. 2) and Rev.Rul. 69–180, 1969–1 C.B. 183.
**95.** Reg. § 1.707–1(c) (Ex. 3).
**96.** Reg. § 1.707–1(c) (Ex. 4).

*Partners as Employees.* It should be noted that a partner generally may not qualify as a partnership employee for tax purposes. For example, a partner receiving guaranteed payments will not be regarded as an employee of the partnership for the purposes of withholding taxes or for qualified pension and profit sharing plans.[97]

# PARTNERSHIP DISTRIBUTIONS

There are three basic types of distributions from a partnership, and a different set of rules governs the income tax consequences of each: (1) distributions of cash and other property that will not result in the liquidation of the distributee partner's interest (i. e., a current distribution), (2) liquidating distributions of money and other property, and (3) distributions that affect the partner's proportionate interests in § 751 property of the partnership (disproportionate distributions). The tax consequences of the last two types are discussed in Chapter 10 under LIQUIDATING AND DISPROPORTIONATE PARTNERSHIP DISTRIBUTIONS.

## NONLIQUIDATING DISTRIBUTIONS

The statutory provisions that govern the treatment of nonliquidating distributions of cash and other partnership property are contained in §§ 731 through 733 of the Code. Section 731 controls the extent of gain or loss recognition on partnership distributions. Sections 732 and 733 provide the rules for determining basis of property received in a distribution and the effect of distributions upon the distributee partner's interest.

Section 731(b) states that no gain or loss shall be recognized by a partnership on the distribution of money or other property to a partner. Similarly, § 731(a) provides the general rule that no gain or loss is recognized by a partner receiving such distributions. However, gain is recognized when *money* received in a distribution exceeds the basis of the partner's interest immediately preceding the distribution. Thus, distributions of property other than money will never result in gain or loss recognition to the partner unless they involve disproportionate distributions of § 751 property. Any gain recognized is treated as being from the *sale* or *exchange* of a partnership interest. The character of such gain would be determined under § 741, discussed in Chapter 10 under SALE OF A PARTNERSHIP INTEREST.

Section 733 provides that nonliquidating distributions from a partnership will reduce the distributee partner's basis in the partnership interest (but not below zero) by (1) the sum of money distributed and (2) the basis to such partner of distributed property other than money. Additionally, § 732 provides that the basis of property (other than money) distributed to a partner in a nonliquidating distribution is the adjusted basis to the partnership immediately before the distribution.[98] However, the basis of the

---

**97.** Reg. § 1.707–1(c).
**98.** § 732(a)(1).

property may not exceed the adjusted basis of the partner's interest in the partnership reduced by any money received in the same transaction.[99]

When the bases of distributed properties are limited by the basis of the partner's interest, an allocation of basis must be made under § 732(c). The manner of allocation is discussed in Chapter 10 under LIQUIDATING AND DISPROPORTIONATE PARTNERSHIP DISTRIBUTIONS. However, when no § 751 property or inventory is involved, the "remaining" basis of the partner's interest is allocated to the properties in the ratio of their adjusted bases to the partnership.[100] Section 735(b) states that the holding period of the property received as a distribution includes that of the partnership.

> **Example 37.** D, a partner in the DEF Partnership, receives a nonliquidating distribution of land, which has a basis to the partnership of $5,000, and cash of $3,000. If D's adjusted basis before the distribution is $7,000, no gain is recognized. However, the land has a basis of $4,000, and D's basis is reduced to zero. Note that the cash received reduced D's basis first. The $4,000 remaining basis was then allocated to the land.

> **Example 38.** Assume the same facts as in Example 37, except that the cash distribution amounted to $9,000. Under these circumstances, D recognizes a gain of $2,000. Under § 731(a), the gain is considered to be from the sale or exchange of a partnership interest. Additionally, the basis of the land in D's hands and the basis of D's partnership interest are both reduced to zero.[101]

> **Example 39.** R receives a nonliquidating distribution from the RST Partnership when the basis of R's interest is $30,000. The distribution consists of $5,000 of cash and land with an adjusted basis to the partnership of $15,000 and a fair market value of $20,000. R's basis in the land is $15,000, and R's partnership interest is reduced to $10,000.[102]

What happens when § 38 property on which the investment tax credit (ITC) was claimed is distributed in a nonliquidating distribution before the appropriate time period to avoid recapture has lapsed? If the partner receiving the ITC property had contributed it to the partnership and avoided recapture on the contribution, this partner might avoid recapture on the distribution under the "mere change in the form of conducting the trade or business." Apparently the ITC recapture rules would not be triggered if (1) the property is retained in the same trade or business, (2) substantial assets necessary to operate the trade or business are distributed with the § 38 property, (3) the basis of the § 38 property is determined in whole or part by reference to the partnership's basis, and (4) the distributee retains a substantial interest in such trade or business.[103] If the distributed property was purchased by the partnership and the ITC claimed, it seems clear that

---

**99.**  § 732(a)(2).
**100.**  § 732(c)(2).
**101.**  Reg. § 1.731–1(a)(1)(i).
**102.**  Reg. § 1.732(a) (Ex. 1).
**103.**  Refer to earlier discussion in the chapter under "Contributions to Partnership."

the partners not receiving the § 38 property would have to recapture their related shares of the ITC. Assuming the distributee partner meets the tests under § 47(b) concerning a "mere change in the form of conducting the trade or business," apparently this partner's share of the ITC would not have to be recaptured.[104]

| ✓ | TAX PLANNING CONSIDERATIONS |
|---|---|

The principal factors contributing to the popularity of the partnership form of conducting a business are the ease with which a partnership can be formed and the flexibility allowed under the Federal income tax law for allocating items of income, loss, deductions, or credits among the partners. The partnership form is not free of uncertain tax consequences. Conflicting concepts of partnership taxation and the lack of judicial interpretations of the partnership provisions of the Code require careful and continuous planning to insure expected income tax results.

### SELECTING THE PARTNERSHIP FORM

The decision to use the partnership form in conducting a trade or business should be made only after a careful consideration of both tax and nontax differences among alternative forms of business organization. Nontax considerations such as the need to raise more capital or the desire to share the burden of losses generally eliminate sole proprietorships as alternatives. Thus, when two or more persons are faced with the decision of selecting a form of doing business together, the comparison will be between a partnership and a corporation. The major differences between these alternative business forms are as follows:

—Unlike corporations, partnerships generally involve unlimited liability, lack continuity of life, and have restrictions on the free transferability of ownership interests. The free transferability of a partnership interest may not exist if, under local law, the partnership is dissolved when an interest is transferred or if the general partners must accept a transferee as a partner before such status is conferred. However, in some cases, although the general partners may not formally approve a transferee as a partner, informal approval may take place via the general partners' actions or inactions. When the nontax considerations mentioned above are important, the corporate form may be preferable.

—Unlike partnerships, corporations are taxable entities separate and apart from their owners. Thus, unless S corporation status is elected (refer to Chapter 8), any corporate-source income will be taxed twice.

---

**104.** Reg. § 1.47–3(f)(6) (Ex. 3 and Ex. 4).

—Corporate income loses its identity when distributed to shareholders. Consequently, income eligible for preferential tax treatment at the corporate level (e. g., tax-exempt interest) does not receive preferential treatment at the shareholders' level, unless an S election is made.

—Corporate losses cannot be passed through to shareholders unless S corporation status is elected. Even then, the shareholders may not have enough interest basis in the corporation to permit claiming all of the losses. Recall that although an S corporation shareholder's interest includes debt due *to* the shareholder, it does not include other corporate liabilities. Therefore, if the business is highly leveraged (i. e., financed by debt as opposed to equity capital) and losses are expected in the early years, the partnership form may be preferable.

—The sale of corporate stock usually results in capital gain or loss. The sale of a partnership interest can result in both ordinary income and capital gain or loss. This distinction is clarified in Chapter 10 under SALE OF A PARTNERSHIP INTEREST.

—As a separate entity, a corporation is free to select any fiscal year for tax purposes. Consequently, there is the possibility of up to 11 months of income tax deferral by establishing a February 1 to January 31 fiscal tax year. Recall that partnerships can offer a three-month deferral only if IRS permission is obtained. A new S corporation formed on or after October 20, 1982, must use a calendar year unless it can convince the IRS that it has a legitimate business purpose for adopting a different tax year.

—Corporate ownership allows more flexibility for income splitting among family members through gifts of ownership interests. As discussed in Chapter 10, under SPECIAL PARTNERSHIP PROBLEMS—Family Partnerships, such partnerships are carefully scrutinized by the IRS to prevent the assignment of income among family members.

—Partners report their distributive share of partnership income for the partnership tax year that ends with or within the partner's tax year. The method of accounting used by the partnership for measuring income (i. e., cash, hybrid, or accrual) controls. Cash basis shareholders generally report salaries, interest, rents, or dividends from the corporation when received. Thus, any income accumulated by a corporation is not taxed to shareholders (unless it is an S corporation) until distributed. Partners are taxed on their respective shares of partnership income whether or not distributed.

—As discussed in Chapter 7, the corporate form may be advantageous for noncorporate shareholders (individuals) at or near the highest individual tax bracket. Such shareholders might attempt to avoid the individual tax rates by diverting a portion of their income to a closely-held corporation for tax and retention when the corporation is taxed at a lower rate. Recall that an abuse of this approach could lead to the imposition of the penalty tax on unreasonable accumulation of earnings or the penalty tax on personal holding companies.

—Before the Tax Equity and Fiscal Responsibility Act of 1982 (TEFRA), perhaps the most significant tax differences between partnerships and corporations existed in the area of tax-sheltered fringe benefits. Recall that the corporate form provides shareholders with the opportunity to be treated as *employees* for tax purposes if they actually render services to the corporation. Such status made a number of attractive tax-sheltered fringe benefits available. These included, but were not limited to, the following: group term life insurance [§ 79], the $5,000 death gratuity [§ 101(b)(1)], accident and health plans [§ § 105 and 106], meals and lodging [§ 119], and qualified pension and profit sharing plans [§ § 401–404]. These benefits could be substantial and were not available to the partners of a partnership. After 1983, most of the differences between corporate and self-employed pension plans were eliminated, discrimination rules became applicable to group term life insurance, and tax-free death benefits under § 101(b)(3)(B) became available to self-employed individuals.

A comparison of the several tax attributes of partnerships, S corporations, and regular corporations is presented in Figure I.

## FORMATION AND OPERATION

In connection with the formation and operation of a partnership, the following points merit close attention:

—If a joint venture is formed solely for investment purposes, for the joint production, extraction, or use of property, or for purposes of underwriting, selling, or distributing a particular security issue by dealers, consideration should be given to electing exclusion from the partnership provisions of Subchapter K. In many situations, taxpayers may be uncertain as to whether they have formed a partnership and could be treated as such for income tax purposes. If the partnership form is undesirable and the possibility exists that the organization may be a partnership for tax purposes, the election procedures under § 761 should be followed.

—If any part of an interest in partnership capital is transferred for services, the recipient must treat the fair market value of such interest as compensation for income tax purposes. Each partner surrendering a portion of the partnership's capital interest must report the transfer as a sale of a partnership interest and recognize gain or loss accordingly. If these results are not desirable, the service partner can be given a higher future profits interest in lieu of an immediate capital interest in the partnership.

—Recall that the contribution of property to a partnership subject to a liability in excess of its basis may result in gain recognition to the contributing partner. If the contributed property were subject to depreciation recapture, ordinary income would result. Also note that unless the partnership is considered the original user of depreciable property, it will not be allowed to deviate from the contributing partner's recovery period or method elected for such property under the ACRS rules. In situations such as these, thought should

**Figure I**

TAX ATTRIBUTES OF DIFFERENT FORMS OF BUSINESS
(Assume Partners and Shareholders Are All Individuals)

|  | Partnership | S Corporation* | Regular Corporation** |
|---|---|---|---|
| Restrictions on type or number of owners | None. | Only individuals, estates, and certain trusts can be owners. Maximum number of shareholders limited to 35. | None. |
| Incidence of tax | Entity not subject to tax. Partners in their separate capacity subject to tax on their distributive share of income. | Except for certain capital gains, related preference tax, and violations of passive investment income tests when accumulated earnings and profits are present from Subchapter C tax years, entity not subject to income tax. Shareholders are subject to tax on income attributable to their stock ownership. C corporations that claim an investment tax credit and elect S status remain liable for any ITC recapture potential. | Income subject to double taxation. Entity subject to tax, and shareholder subject to tax on any corporate dividends received. |
| Maximum tax rate | 50% at partner level. | 50% at shareholder level. | 46% at corporate level plus 50% on any corporate dividends. |
| Choice of tax year | Selection generally restricted to coincide with tax year of principal partners or calendar year. | Restricted to a calendar year unless IRS approves a different year for business purposes. | Unrestricted selection allowed at time of filing first tax return. |
| Timing of taxation | Partners report their share of income in their tax year with or within which the partnership's tax year ends. Partners in their separate capacity may be subject to declaration and payment of estimated taxes. | Shareholders report their share of income in their tax year with or within which the corporation's tax year ends. Generally, the corporation uses a calendar year; but see "Choice of tax year" immediately above. Shareholders may be subject to declaration and payment of estimated taxes. | Corporation subject to tax at close of its tax year. May be subject to declaration and payment of estimated taxes. Dividends will be subject to tax at the shareholder level in the tax year received. |
| Basis for allocating income to owners | Profit and loss sharing agreement. May provide for special allocations of income and deductions among partners. Cash basis items of multi-tiered and cash basis partnerships are allocated on a daily basis. Other partnership items are allocated after considering varying interests of partners. | Pro rata share based on stock ownership. Shareholder's pro rata share is determined on a daily basis according to the number of shares of stock held on each day of the corporation's tax year. | Not applicable. |

*Refer to Chapter 8 for details on S corporations.
**Refer to Chapters 2 to 6 for details on regular corporations.

**Figure I (con't)**

| | Partnership | S Corporation* | Regular Corporation** |
|---|---|---|---|
| Character of income taxed to owners | Conduit—retains source characteristics. | Conduit—retains source characteristics. | All source characteristics are lost when income is distributed to owners. |
| Basis for allocating a net operating loss to owners | Profit and loss sharing agreement. Cash basis items of multi-tiered and cash basis partnerships are allocated on a daily basis. Other partnership items are allocated after considering varying interests of partners. | Prorated among shareholders on a daily basis. | Not applicable. |
| Limitation on losses deductible by owners | Partner's investment plus share of liabilities. At-risk rules apply to liabilities. Indefinite carryover for excess loss. | Shareholder's investment plus loans made by shareholder to corporation. At-risk rules apply to liabilities. Indefinite carryover for excess loss. | Not applicable. |
| Tax consequences of earnings retained by entity | Taxed to partners when earned and increases their respective basis in partnership interest. | Taxed to shareholders when earned and increases their respective basis in stock. | Taxed to corporation as earned and may be subject to penalty tax if accumulated unreasonably. |
| Nonliquidating distributions to owners | Not taxable unless money received exceeds recipient partner's basis in partnership interest. Existence of § 751 assets may cause tax problems. See Chapter 10. | Generally not taxable unless the distribution exceeds the shareholder's investment plus loans made by shareholder to corporation. Existence of accumulated earnings and profits could cause some distributions to be dividends. | Taxable in year of receipt if covered by earnings and profits or if exceeds basis in stock. |
| Splitting of income among family members | Difficult—IRS will not recognize a family member as a partner unless certain requirements are met. See Chapter 10. | Rather easy—gift of stock will transfer tax on a pro rata share of income to the donee. However, IRS can make adjustments to reflect adequate compensation for services. | Same as an S corporation except that donees will be subject to tax only on earnings actually or constructively distributed to them. Other than unreasonable compensation, IRS generally cannot make adjustments to reflect adequate compensation for services and capital. |
| Organizational costs | Amortizable over 60 months. | Same as partnership. | Same as partnership. |
| Charitable contributions | Conduit—partners are subject to deduction limitations in their own capacity. | Conduit—shareholders are subject to deduction limitations in their own capacity. | Limited to 10% of taxable income before certain deductions. |
| Tax preference items | Conduit—passed through to partners who must account for such items in their separate capacity. | Conduit—passed through to shareholders, except for certain capital gains that are subject to minimum tax at corporate level. | Subject to minimum tax at corporate level. |
| Capital gains | Conduit—partners must account for their respective shares. | Conduit, with certain exceptions—shareholders must account for their respective shares. | Taxed at corporate level. |

*Refer to Chapter 8 for details on S corporations.
**Refer to Chapters 2 to 6 for details on regular corporations.

### Figure I (con't)

| | | | |
|---|---|---|---|
| Capital losses | Conduit—partners must account for their respective shares. | Conduit, with certain exceptions—shareholders must account for their respective shares. | Carryback three years and carryover five years, deductible only to extent of capital gains. |
| § 1231 gains and losses | Conduit—partners must account for their respective shares. | Conduit, with certain exceptions—shareholders must account for their respective shares. | Taxable or deductible at corporate level only. Five-year lookback rule for § 1231 losses. |
| Foreign tax credits | Conduit—passed through to partners. | Generally a conduit—passed through to shareholders. | Available at corporate level only. |
| Investment tax credits | Conduit—passed through to partners. | Conduit—passed through to shareholders. | Available at corporate level only. |

*Refer to Chapter 8 for details on S corporations.

**Refer to Chapters 2 to 6 for details on regular corporations.

be given to retaining ownership of the property and leasing it to the partnership.

—Although the Code does not require a written partnership agreement, many of the statutory provisions governing the tax consequences to partners and their partnerships refer to such an agreement. Remember, for instance, that § 704(a) provides for the determination of a partner's distributive share of income, gain, loss, deduction, or credit in accordance with the partnership agreement. Consequently, if taxpayers operating a business in partnership form want a measure of certainty as to the tax consequences of their activities, a carefully drafted partnership agreement is crucial. If such an agreement contains the obligations, rights, and powers of the partners, it should prove invaluable in settling controversies among partners and providing some degree of certainty as to the tax consequences of the partners' actions.

—Taxpayers also should be alert to the potential advantages and pitfalls of special allocation agreements. If one or more partners assume all of the economic risks associated with the formative years of the partnership, it seems logical that these partners should be entitled to the tax benefits. A special allocation agreement can be used to assign all losses to these partners until such time as they have recouped their investment. Recall, however, that such arrangements are subject to careful IRS scrutiny and must have substantial economic effect. As a result, great care should be exercised in drafting such agreements, and adequate documentation should be drawn up and preserved to insure the desired tax results.

—Caution should be exercised when sales or exchanges are contemplated between a partnership and a partner if that partner is a related party under § 707(b). Losses from such transactions will be disallowed, and certain gains may be treated as ordinary income (rather than as capital gain).

Tax planning considerations for partnership distributions are contained in Chapter 10.

## PROBLEM MATERIALS

### Discussion Questions

1. Distinguish between the entity concept and the aggregate or conduit concept of a partnership.

2. What is a partnership for Federal income tax purposes?

3. Under what circumstances can organizations elect to be excluded from the partnership tax provisions? Why would an organization wish to be excluded?

4. Compare the nonrecognition of gain or loss provision on contributions to a partnership with the similar provision found in corporate formation (§ 351). What are the major differences and similarities?

5. Under what circumstance does the receipt of a partnership interest result in ordinary income recognition? What is the effect of such an event on the partnership and the other partners?

6. How is a contributing partner's interest basis determined?

7. If appreciated property is contributed to a partnership in exchange for a partnership interest, what basis does the partnership take in such property?

8. How is the holding period of a partnership interest determined? The partnership's holding period in contributed property?

9. What effect does the contribution of property subject to a liability have on the contributing partner's interest basis? What is the effect on the bases of the other partners' interests?

10. What is the effect to the partner of a contribution of property subject to a liability in excess of the partner's basis in the property? To the partnership?

11. What transactions or events will cause a partner's interest to continuously fluctuate?

12. Why is a partnership required to file an information return (Form 1065)?

13. Describe the two-step approach used to determine partnership income. Why is this computation necessary?

14. Under what circumstances can an allocation of income or expense to a partner differ from the general profit- and loss-sharing ratios? Under what circumstances would such an allocation be justified? What could go wrong?

15. To what extent can partners deduct their distributive share of partnership losses? What happens to any unused losses?

16. When can a partnership have a taxable year different from its principal partners? When must partners report their share of partnership income?

17. Under what circumstances will a partnership's tax year close?

18. When may a partner engage in a transaction with the partnership without tax difficulties? What could go wrong?

19. What are guaranteed payments? When might such payments be used?

20. When will a nonliquidating distribution result in a gain to the recipient partner? How is the recipient partner's basis in any property received determined? How is the recipient partner's basis in the partnership determined after the distribution?

## Problems

1. L and K form an equal partnership with a cash contribution of $60,000 from L and a property contribution (adjusted basis of $30,000 and a fair market value of $60,000) from K.

   (a) How much gain, if any, must L recognize on the transfer? Must K recognize any gain?

   (b) What is L's basis in the partnership?

   (c) What is K's basis in the partnership?

   (d) What basis will the partnership have in the property transferred by K?

2. Z provides services to the XY Partnership in exchange for a one-third interest in capital and profits. The services, which are deductible under § 162 of the Code (i. e., trade or business expenses), were completed at the start of the current year. The XY Partnership made the interest transfers at the start of the current year, and the partners agreed that the partnership would be known as the XYZ Partnership. The partners and the partnership are on the calendar year basis and use the cash method of reporting taxable income. Immediately before the interest transfers, the balance sheet of the XY Partnership appeared as follows:

|  | Basis | FMV |  |  | Basis | FMV |
|---|---|---|---|---|---|---|
| Land | $60,000 | $180,000 | Capital—X | | $30,000 | $ 90,000 |
| | | | Capital—Y | | 30,000 | 90,000 |
| | $60,000 | $180,000 | | | $60,000 | $180,000 |

   (a) How much income, if any, must Z recognize in the current year from receipt of the partnership interests, and how is it reported for tax purposes?

   (b) What is Z's interest basis in the partnership immediately after the transfers take place?

   (c) How much income, if any, must the partnership recognize from the transfers, and how is it reported for tax purposes?

   (d) Prepare a balance sheet of the XYZ Partnership at the end of the current year, assuming no other transactions took place during the year and the fair market value of the land did not change during the year.

   (e) At the start of the next year, the XYZ Partnership sells the land for its $180,000 fair market value. How much is the gain on the sale, and how will it be reported for tax purposes?

3. In return for the rendition of services to the partnership and the contribution of property (basis of $4,000 and fair market value of $25,000) to the PA Partnership, E receives a 30% capital interest valued at $35,000.

   (a) How much income must E recognize?

   (b) What is E's basis in the partnership?

   (c) What are the potential tax consequences to the other partners and the PA Partnership?

4. If the property described in Problem 3 is sold by the partnership:

   (a) For $17,000, how much of the gain must be recognized by E?

   (b) For $33,000, how much of the gain will be allocated to E?

5. L, B, and R form the LBR Partnership on January 1 of the current year. In return for a 30% capital interest, L transfers property (basis of $24,000, fair market value of $37,500) subject to a liability of $15,000. The liability is assumed by the partnership. B transfers property (basis of $37,500, fair market value of $22,500)

for a 30% capital interest, and R transfers cash of $30,000 for the remaining 40% interest.

(a) How much gain must L recognize on the transfer?

(b) What is L's basis in the partnership?

(c) How much loss may B recognize on the transfer?

(d) What is B's basis in the partnership?

(e) What is R's basis in the partnership?

(f) What basis will the LBR Partnership have in the property transferred by L?

(g) What is the partnership's basis in the property transferred by B?

6. Assume the same facts as in Problem 5, except that the property contributed by L has a fair market value of $67,500 and is subject to a mortgage of $45,000.

(a) How much gain must L recognize on the transfer?

(b) What is L's basis in the partnership?

(c) What is B's basis in the partnership?

(d) What is R's basis in the partnership?

(e) What basis will the LBR Partnership have in the property transferred by L?

(f) If the partnership borrows $200,000 to purchase an office building, what effect, if any, will this have on each partner's basis in the partnership? What effect will the loan *repayment* have on each partner's basis?

7. Q, R, and T form an equal partnership on January 1 of the current year. Q contributes cash of $5,000 and a panel truck with a fair market value of $12,000 that he had purchased on July 1 of last year for $15,000 as a personal use recreational vehicle. R contributes cash of $5,000 and land with a fair market value of $12,000 that he had purchased four months earlier for use as an employees' parking lot in his sole proprietorship. After purchasing the land for $11,600 and placing it in service, he discovered that most of his employees rode the bus to work. T, who is in the business of buying and selling computers, contributes $5,000 and a computer with a cost of $10,000 and a fair market value of $12,000. With some of the cash, QRT rents a fully equipped pizza parlor in a building next to the land contributed by R and goes into the pizza business. The land is used as a customer parking lot, the panel truck is used to deliver pizzas, and the computer is used for accounting work. QRT claims neither investment tax credits under § 46 nor immediate expensing under § 179 and uses straight-line method and minimum time period for cost recovery deductions. At the start of year three, QRT sells the noncash items to unrelated parties: delivery truck for $5,100, land for $12,200, and computer for $8,200.

(a) What is the starting date of each partner's interest in QRT?

(b) How much is the gain or loss on the sale of each item?

(c) What is the nature of each gain or loss?

(d) How is each gain or loss divided among the partners?

8. As of January 1 of the last year, the basis of D's 25% capital interest in the DEF Partnership was $24,000. D and the partnership use the calendar year for tax purposes. The partnership incurred an operating loss of $100,000 for the last year and a profit of $8,000 for the current year.

(a) How much loss, if any, may D recognize for the last year?

(b) How much net reportable income must D recognize for the current year?

(c) What is the basis of D's interest as of January 1 of the current year?

(d) What basis will D have in the partnership as of January 1 of the next year?

(e) What year-end tax planning would you suggest to ensure that partners can deduct their share of partnership losses?

9. LM and KM are equal partners in the calendar year M & M Partnership. For the current year, the partnership had an operating loss of $60,000, a long-term capital loss of $4,000, and a short-term capital gain of $9,000. The partnership had no other transactions for the current year. At the start of the current year, LM's interest basis in the M & M Partnership was $28,000 and KM's was $19,500.

(a) How much short-term capital gain must LM report on her tax return for the current year?

(b) How much short-term capital gain must KM report on her tax return for the current year?

(c) How much of the operating loss and the long-term capital loss must LM report on her tax return for the current year?

(d) How much of the operating loss and the long-term capital loss must KM report on her tax return for the current year?

(e) What is the basis of LM's partnership interest at the start of the next calendar year? Of KM's interest at the start of the next calendar year?

10. The S-Q Partnership has operated for several years on a calendar year basis. It recently received IRS permission to switch to a fiscal year ending with October 31 to conform to its tax and natural business years. For the current calendar year, its operating income was $24,000, earned at the rate of $2,000 per month. For the next calendar year, it earned operating income at the rate of $3,000 per month for all 12 months. Assuming no other partnership transactions and the partnership's first fiscal year ends October 31 of the current calendar year:

(a) What is the aggregate taxable income reportable by the partnership for the short fiscal year?

(b) What is the aggregate taxable income reportable by the partnership for its first full fiscal year ending October 31 of the next calendar year?

11. The Four Lakes Partnership is owned by four sisters (25% interest each). One sister sells investment property to the partnership for its fair market value of $54,000 (basis $72,000).

(a) How much loss, if any, may this sister recognize?

(b) If the partnership later sells the property for $81,000, how much gain must it recognize?

(c) If the sister's basis in the investment property was $20,000, instead of $40,000, how much, if any, capital gain would she recognize on the sale?

12. Under a partnership agreement, Q, the owner of a 30% interest in the QPD partnership, is entitled to a 30% interest in partnership profits. In no event will Q receive less than $100,000. For the current year, the partnership had ordinary income of $200,000 before any adjustment for the minimum payment to Q. As of January 1 of the current year, Q's interest was $30,000. On January 1 of the next year, the partnership distributed the $100,000 promised to Q. All parties use the calendar year for tax purposes. The partnership uses the accrual method of accounting, and Q uses the cash method.

(a) How much income must Q recognize for the current year?

(b) What is the nature of Q's income?

(c) What will be Q's partnership interest as of December 31 of the current year, assuming the partnership agreement indicates that all unpaid guaranteed payments at year-end are to be treated as a capital contribution by the partner to whom due?

(d) Assuming that partners P and D each own a 35% interest in capital and profits of the partnership, how much income must each report for the current year, and what is its nature?

13. N, an equal partner in the MN Partnership, is to receive a payment of $20,000 for services plus 50% of the partnership's profits or losses. After deducting the $20,000 payment to N, the partnership has a loss of $12,000.

(a) How much, if any, of the $12,000 partnership loss will be allocated to N?

(b) What is the net income from the partnership that N must report on his personal income tax return?

14. X, who has a partnership interest of $23,000, receives a nonliquidating distribution that consists of cash of $3,000, land parcel A with an adjusted basis of $4,000 and a fair market value of $5,000, and land parcel B with an adjusted basis of $8,000 and a fair market value of $15,000.

(a) How much gain, if any, must X recognize on the distribution?

(b) What basis will X have in the distributed land parcels?

(c) What is X's partnership interest after the distribution?

15. Assume the same facts as in Problem 14, except that the cash distribution amounts to $13,000 instead of $3,000.

(a) How much gain, if any, must X recognize on the distribution?

(b) What basis will X have in the land parcels?

(c) What is X's partnership interest after the distribution?

16. FM and FT are equal partners in the calendar year F & F Partnership. FM uses a fiscal year ending June 30, and FT uses a calendar year. FM is paid an annual calendar year salary of $50,000. For the last calendar year, the F & F Partnership's taxable income was $40,000. For the current calendar year, the partnership's taxable income is $50,000.

(a) What is the aggregate amount of income from the partnership that must be reported by FM for his tax year that ends within the current calendar year?

(b) What is the aggregate amount of income from the partnership that must be reported by FT for the current calendar year?

(c) If FM's annual salary is increased to $60,000 starting on January 1 of the current calendar year and the taxable income of the partnership for the last year and the current year are the same (i. e., $40,000 and $50,000), what is the aggregate amount of income from the partnership that must be reported by FM for his tax year that ends within the current calendar year?

17. On October 1 of the last calendar year, T is invited to join the partnership of PFK & Associates, a local certified public accounting firm. In exchange for a cash contribution of $10,000 to the partnership, T receives a 5% interest in capital and profits. Prior to admission, T was employed as one of the partnership's salaried managers and received $2,500 monthly as compensation. As a new partner, T is entitled to monthly cash drawings of $4,000. The partnership has an October 1 to September 30 fiscal year for tax purposes and reports profits of $800,000 and $1,000,000, respectively, for its fiscal years ending September 30 of the current and next calendar years.

(a) Assuming partner T is a cash basis calendar year taxpayer who withdraws $4,000 per month, how much income from the partnership must he report for the last calendar year?

(b) For the current calendar year?

18. Assume that PFK & Associates partnership described in Problem 17 purchased $100,000 of new equipment on December 1 of the last calendar year, and the property was to be treated as ACRS (accelerated cost recovery system) recovery property with a five-year class life.

    (a) What is the maximum amount of investment tax credit available to T?

    (b) If the partnership elects to treat $5,000 of the investment in the new equipment as a § 179 deduction, what effect will it have on T's share of the investment tax credit? What will be T's share of the qualifying investment in § 179 property?

    (c) On which personal income tax returns of T must each of the above items be reported?

19. For each of the following independent statements, indicate whether the tax attribute is applicable to partnerships (P), S corporations (S), both business forms (B), or neither business form (N). (*Hint:* Refer to Chapter 8 regarding S corporations and to Figure I in this chapter.)

    _____ (a) Flow-through to owners of net operating losses.

    _____ (b) Flow-through to owners of capital losses.

    _____ (c) Unrestricted selection of taxable year.

    _____ (d) An increase in the organization's trade accounts payable will increase the tax basis of the owner's interests.

    _____ (e) An owner's share of losses in excess of tax basis can be carried forward indefinitely.

    _____ (f) A nonliquidating distribution of money or other property is generally not taxable to the owners.

    _____ (g) Income retained in the business will not be taxed to the owners until distributed to them.

    _____ (h) Organizational costs can be amortized over a 60-month period.

20. For each of the following independent statements, indicate whether the tax attribute is applicable to nonelecting (regular) corporations (C), partnerships (P), both business forms (B), or neither business form (N):

    _____ (a) Restrictions are placed on the type and number of owners.

    _____ (b) Business income will be taxable to the owners rather than to the entity.

    _____ (c) Distributions of earnings to the owners will result in a tax deduction to the entity.

    _____ (d) The source characteristics of an entity's income flow through to the owners.

    _____ (e) Capital gains are subject to tax at the entity level.

    _____ (f) Organizational costs can be amortized over a period of 60 months or more.

    _____ (g) Investment tax credits are passed through to the owners.

21. The books and records of the BWCA Partnership for its current calendar year disclosed the following items of income and expense:

| | |
|---|---:|
| Sales (net) | $625,000 |
| Cost of goods sold | 230,000 |
| Dividends from American Motors, Inc. | 10,000 |
| Interest on City of Milwaukee bonds | 3,000 |
| Gain on sale of equipment held two years | 2,500* |
| Salaries to partners | 32,000 |
| Interest on partners' capital account | 16,000 |
| Interest on bank loan | 2,750 |
| Contribution to Camp Fire, Inc. | 200 |
| Rental of office space | 6,000 |

*Depreciation on the equipment since acquisition was $2,000.

(a) What was the aggregate amount of "gross income" flow from the partnership to the partners for the current year?

(b) What was the taxable income of the partnership for the current year?

22. E and Z are equal partners in the EZ Partnership. At the beginning of the current year, E's capital account has a balance of $10,000 and the partnership has debts of $30,000 payable to unrelated parties. The following information about EZ's operations for the current year is obtained from the partnership's records:

| | |
|---|---:|
| Taxable income under § 702(8) | $ 40,000 |
| Tax-exempt interest income | 5,000 |
| Dividends from unrelated corporations | 8,000 |
| § 1245 gain | 4,000 |
| § 1231 gain | 6,200 |
| Long-term capital gain | 500 |
| Long-term capital loss | 100 |
| Short-term capital loss | 250 |
| Charitable contribution to Girl Scouts | 800 |
| Cash distribution to E | 10,000 |

Assume none of the property was contributed by the partners and year-end partnership debt payable to unrelated parties is $24,000.

(a) What is E's interest basis at the beginning of the year?

(b) What is E's interest basis at the end of the current year?

(c) If EZ were an S corporation, what would E's interest basis be at the end of the year, assuming the capital account balance at the beginning of the year for E represents E's stock account and equals her beginning interest basis in the corporation?

## Comprehensive Tax Return Problem

James R. Wesley (297-19-9261), Rita B. Healthy (284-74-7832), Susan C. Yourez (257-62-3544), and Frank T. Bizzano (219-75-3822) are equal partners in WHYB, a small business management advisory partnership. The partnership uses the cash basis and calendar year and began operations on January 1 two years before the start of the current year. Since that time, it has experienced a 30% growth rate each year. Its current address is 2937 Skyline Speedway, Bloomington, IN 47401. During the current year, each partner withdrew $40,000. The following information was taken from the partnership's income statement for the current year:

| | |
|---|---:|
| Receipts | |
|     Fees collected | $ 275,000 |
|     Tax-exempt interest | 1,600 |
| Payments | |
|     Advertising | 5,000 |
|     Contribution to Boy Scouts | 800 |
|     Employee salaries | 42,000 |
|     Equipment rental | 6,000 |
|     Office rent | 24,000 |
|     Salary to James R. Wesley | 12,000 |
|     Taxes | 4,600 |
|     Utilities | 3,700 |
|     Insurance premiums | 2,200 |

Last year's Form 1065 and related K–1 Schedules disclosed the following:

—Maximum write-off for organizational expenses was $220.

—Each partner's capital account at year-end was $3,971.

—Cash balance at year-end was $15,224.

*Required:*

(a) Prepare Form 1065 and Schedule K for the WHYB Partnership for the current year. Do not supply answers to questions where appropriate information is not furnished.

(b) Prepare Schedule K–1 for James R. Wesley for the current year.

## Research Problems

*Research Problem 1.* FH, GR, and MO each own a 30% interest in the capital and profits of a farming partnership operating near Anaheim, California. The remaining 10% is owned by the QSY Trust. At formation, the partners considered the name National HRO Partnership, since they envisioned a nationwide circuitry of interconnected farms. After considerable discussion, the name HRO Partnership was selected.

HRO owns three farms, and each partner, exclusive of the trust, resides on one of them and manages the farm as if it were a separate and distinct business. The partnership has been in existence for three years and for tax purposes aggregates income and expenses of the three farms. During the first three years of operation, HRO purchased several assets on which the investment tax credit (ITC) was claimed and allocated to the four partners in accordance with their general profit-sharing ratios. Toward the end of last year, GR became upset about the way profits were shared and operations handled and, to put it mildly, "blew a fuse."

On January 1 of the current year, the partnership distributed substantially all of its assets to the partners. FH, GR, and MO received the farms they resided on and the related property used on the farm on which the ITC was claimed. The QSY Trust received only cash. After the distribution, the individual farms were operated as sole proprietorships with the received ITC property being used in the same way it was used before the breakup.

On its tax return for the current year, the QSY Trust plans to report an ITC recapture on the premature distribution of related property from HRO. GR has discussed the situation with FH and MO and has learned that neither of them plans to report any ITC as being recaptured on his current year tax return. When asked as to the reason no ITC recapture will be reported, FH and MO each responded "on the advice of counsel." GR is confused and uncertain as to whether he is receiving static from the QSY trustee or from FH and MO. He thinks that different reportings may be appropriate considering (1) the types of reporting entities involved and (2) the types of distributions to the partners. He contacts you, his tax adviser, to determine appropriate answers to the following questions regarding the necessary tax reporting of ITC recapture in the current year as a result of the HRO property distributions:

(a) To what extent must GR report any ITC recapture?

(b) To what extent must FH and MO report any ITC recapture?

(c) To what extent must the QSY Trust report any ITC recapture?

*Partial list of research aids:*

Reg. § § 1.47–3(f) and 1.47–6(a)(2).

*Baker* v. *U. S.,* 75–2 USTC ¶ 9559, 36 AFTR2d 75–5193, 398 F. Supp 1143 (D.Ct. Texas, 1975).

*George Loewen,* 76 T.C. 90 (1981), *acq.* 1983–2 C.B. 1.

*James Soares,* 50 T.C. 909 (1968).

*Research Problem 2.* AM, FL, and RD were equal partners in the MLD Partnership, engaged in property management and development near Olentangy, Ohio. Two years ago RD, a cash basis taxpayer who had never been involved in property management and development, decided to take the plunge and invest in the ML Partnership (subsequently known as the MLD Partnership). RD invested $135,000 in cash for a one-third interest in the capital, profits, and losses under an amended partnership agreement that states:

. . . partners have no liability in excess of their capital investment.

The original partnership agreement (which was amended before RD's admission to the partnership) stated:

. . . the partners intend to conduct business as a general partnership.

For the first year that RD was a member of the partnership, MLD reported a loss of $408,000, of which RD's share was $136,000. RD reported a deductible loss from the partnership on his tax return for that calendar year of $135,000, the amount in his capital account and the basis of his partnership interest. In late November of last year, when RD learned that his share of the partnership's loss to date was approximately $199,000, he decided he had had enough splashing around in the puddle of property management and development. On December 1 of last year, RD and the MLD Partnership executed a sales agreement in which the partnership purchased RD's interest for $275,000, payable in 10 equal annual installments plus 10% interest on the unpaid balance, with the first payment to start on June 1 of the current year. The agreement specified that RD would pay the MLD Partnership in one lump sum the total share of partnership losses allocated to him in excess of his interest basis and capital account. At the time the agreement was signed, these excess losses amounted to $200,000. This payment to MLD was to be made by RD on or before the end of one year after the agreement was signed. MLD reported a negative capital balance for RD of $200,000 on its tax return for last year.

On May 15 of the current year, the sales agreement was amended to delete the installment payments and replace them with a 10% promissory note for $275,000 that MLD gave RD. On receipt of the note, RD immediately wrote across the face of the note, "Paid in Full," signed and dated the note, made a copy, and returned the note to AM. In addition, RD gave AM his personal check for $200,000 in full payment of his share of the partnership losses in excess of his interest basis and capital account at the time the sales agreement was signed.

RD has come to you, his tax adviser, and asked how the items just discussed should be reported on his tax return for the current year. He informs you that although he is in the 50% tax bracket and has acquired a lot of business sense over the past 20 years, on this series of transactions with MLD he really took a bath. He also informs you that he has been thinking about the reporting problem and wonders if it will be acceptable for him to report a $275,000 long-term capital gain on the sale of his partnership interest to MLD and a $200,000 deductible ordinary loss. For purposes of this problem, assume that there are no § 751 assets (i. e., the kind of assets that can convert a capital gain into ordinary income). What kind of tax advice should you give RD?

*Partial list of research aids:*

§ § 704(d) and 706(c)(2)(A)(i).

Reg. § 1.704–1(d)(1).

H. Rept. 1337 and S. Rept. 1622 to accompany H. Rept. 8300, 83d Cong. 2d Sess. (1954).

*Research Problem 3.* JM and WY are equal shareholders of M & W Salvage Yards, Incorporated, of Eureka, California. They have held their stock in the corporation continuously since the company's formation. The corporation has been very successful in recent years buying and selling scrap metals. JM and WY are currently working for the corporation and are receiving $80,000 each as compensation for their services. Although the reasonableness of their salaries was not questioned in a recent IRS audit, the corporation's accumulation of nearly $500,000 of earnings and profits was challenged. After many hours of discussions, JM, WY, and the examining agent concluded that the corporation must begin implementation of its expansion plans or make dividend distributions to avoid the penalty of the accumulated earnings tax in future years.

JM and WY decided that cash dividends were out of the question because of the corporation's need for all the cash currently available. Consequently, they immediately began evaluating the assets of the corporation that could be likely choices for property dividend distributions. One choice was a 10-acre tract of land located on Highway 101 and within a short distance of a major housing development north of San Francisco. The property had been purchased by the corporation in 1980 for $50,000 as a site for a future scrap yard. Two years ago it was decided that the 10-acre tract of land was not a good site for a scrap yard. Since then, the land has been held by the corporation as an investment. A local real estate broker estimates that the land is now worth approximately $300,000 and would be an ideal location for a small shopping center.

After careful deliberations, JM and WY concluded that they should arrange for the construction of a shopping center; lease space for a cleaners, convenience store, liquor store, and laundromat; and hire a local rental property management company to manage the property. Within two months, JM and WY had commissioned an architect, made arrangements for construction of the center, and negotiated a $750,000 loan from a creditor located in Crescent City, California. They estimate that the total cost of construction will be $900,000, and they anticipate tax losses (due primarily to large ACRS deductions) for the first six years of operation. These forecasted losses range from $150,000 for each of the first three years to a low of $50,000 in the sixth year. Beginning in the seventh year, they anticipate taxable income of $75,000, and by the tenth year, an annual taxable income in excess of $100,000.

JM and WY plan to contribute $75,000 each to the new venture and ask you for advice on the following remaining questions:

1. Whether their corporation should distribute the land to them as a taxable property dividend or contribute the property to the new venture in exchange for a share of profits and losses.

2. Whether the shopping center venture should be operated as a regular corporation, an S corporation, or a partnership.

In your response to their questions, indicate what additional information you might need to properly evaluate the alternatives.

# Partnerships: 10
## Transfer of Partnership Interests; Family and Limited Partnerships

## CHAPTER OBJECTIVES

—Explain the tax consequences that result from the sale or exchange of a partnership interest.
—Compare the disposition of interest by gift, by death, and by abandonment.
—Explain how the liquidation of a partnership is treated.
—Describe the special constraints that exist in a family partnership and in a limited partnership.

Under the entity approach, a partnership interest is treated as an *intangible asset* separate and apart from the assets of the partnership. When the entity approach is applicable, the tax consequences of a partnership interest transfer are similar to those of a corporate ownership interest transfer. However, under the aggregate or conduit concept of partnerships, a partnership interest would be considered an ownership interest in each partnership asset. When the aggregate approach is applicable, the tax consequences are quite different. Whether the entity or aggregate approach applies depends on both the type of transfer and the nature of the partnership's underlying assets. A further complexity arises when the optional adjustments to the bases of partnership interests occur prior to or as a result of such transfers.

Chapter 10 reviews the tax consequences of partnership interest transfers and the special problems confronted by family and limited partnerships.

## SALE OF A PARTNERSHIP INTEREST

As stated above, a partner's interest, much like a shareholder's corporate interest, can be sold or exchanged in whole or in part. Unlike a shareholder's corporate interest, a partnership interest would be considered an ownership interest in each partnership asset. As a result of applying both the entity and aggregate concepts, the gain or loss that results from a disposition of a partnership interest may be fragmented into capital gain or loss and ordinary income or loss.

### GENERAL RULE

Under § 741, a partnership interest is a capital asset, the sale or exchange of which results in capital gain or loss. Such gain or loss is measured by the difference between the amount realized and the selling partner's adjusted basis in the partnership.

*Liabilities.* In computing both the amount realized on the sale of a partner's interest and the adjusted basis of the sold interest, the selling partner takes into account partnership liabilities. The effect of changes in partnership liabilities was discussed in Chapter 9 under PARTNERSHIP FORMATION—Basis of Partnership Interest. However, § 752(d) provides that the amount of the selling partner's personal liabilities and share of partnership liabilities assumed by the purchasing partner must be included in computing the amount realized on the sale. Likewise, the purchasing partner includes any assumed indebtedness as a part of the consideration paid for the partnership interest.

**Example 1.** C originally invested $50,000 in cash for a one-third interest in the accrual basis CDE Partnership. During the aggregate period of membership, C's share of partnership income was $90,000. Over that same period, C withdrew $60,000. C's capital account balance is now $80,000, and partnership liabilities are $45,000, of which C's share is $15,000. Thus, C's inside and outside bases in the partnership are $95,000 ($80,000 capital account plus $15,000 share of partnership debts). C's partnership interest is sold to F for $110,000 cash, with F assuming C's share of partnership liabilities. The total amount realized by C is $125,000 ($110,000 cash received plus $15,000 of partnership debts transferred to F). C's gain on the sale is $30,000 ($125,000 realized less adjusted basis of $95,000).

**Example 2.** Assuming the same facts as in Example 1, what is F's outside basis in the DEF partnership? Since F did not contribute money or other property to the partnership, § 722 is not applicable to the determination of F's interest basis. Instead, F refers to § 1012, which indicates that the basis of property acquired by purchase is its cost. Thus, F's outside basis is $125,000 ($110,000 cash plus $15,000 of assumed partnership debts).

Several collateral effects that result from the sale or exchange of a partnership interest are discussed in the sections that follow.

*Variance in Basis.* Note that in Example 2, F's outside basis in the DEF partnership is $30,000 greater than F's proportionate share of the basis in underlying partnership assets (an amount equal to the basis used to measure C's gain on the sale). To correct this discrepancy, F may be entitled to a special basis adjustment under § 743(b). The requirements and procedures for making such an adjustment are discussed under OPTIONAL ADJUSTMENT TO BASIS OF PARTNERSHIP PROPERTY—Sale or Exchange of an Interest.

*Tax Years That Close.* Another collateral effect of the sale or exchange of a partnership interest is that a partnership's tax year closes as of the sale date for the partner disposing of an entire interest.[1] As a result, income bunching may take place because the selling partner's distributive share of partnership income for the closed tax year is reported in that partner's tax year that includes the sale date.

**Example 3.** Assume the same facts as in Example 1, except that the CDE Partnership had earned income of $12,000 as of the sale date of C's entire interest. Since the partnership's tax year closes with respect to C, $4,000 of partnership income is reported in C's tax year that includes the sale date. In addition, C's income share from the last partnership year that may have closed in C's tax year that includes the sale date is also reported. Note that C's capital account and inter-

---

1.  § 706(c)(2)(A).

est basis are both increased by $4,000, and gain on the sale is reduced correspondingly.

Additionally, the sale or exchange of a partnership interest may result in a termination of the entire partnership. Recall from Chapter 9 under PARTNERSHIP OPERATION—Taxable Years of Partner and Partnership—that under § 708(b), the sale or exchange of 50 percent or more of the total interest in partnership capital and profits within any 12-month period terminates the partnership. As a result of the termination, the partnership's tax year ends and income bunching may take place, because all partners are required to report their share of profits up to the date of termination. Also, any favorable fiscal year may be lost because the new partnership must make all new elections. Recall from the same Chapter 9 section that restrictions exist that may limit the tax year election and that the IRS is reluctant to approve a tax year when income subject to tax is to be deferred more than three months. Thus, great care should be exercised in effecting the disposition of a partner's interest if it represents a 50 percent or greater interest in capital and profits or if the sum of the transfers within any 12-month period is expected to do so.

> **Example 4.**  Assume the same facts as in Example 1, except that three months after C's interest is sold to F, D's one-third interest is sold to G. As a result of D's sale, two-thirds of the interest in capital and profits of the old CDE Partnership has been sold within a 12-month period and the DEF Partnership is deemed to have terminated under § 708 when D's interest is sold. D, E, and F must report their ratable share of partnership income or loss on termination. However, if three months after F acquired C's interest in the CDE partnership F then sold this interest to G (rather than D's sale to G), the DEF partnership would not terminate, because the same interest was sold.[2]

*ITC Recapture.*  Another collateral effect of the sale of a partner's interest involves the investment tax credit (ITC). The selling partner's share of the ITC that was passed through from the partnership may be recaptured in whole or in part, because the appropriate holding period for related property has not been met.[3] Under the aggregate concept of partnerships, the selling partner is treated as having sold an undivided interest in each partnership asset. If the selling partner's interest in the "general profits" of the partnership or in the particular item of property on which the ITC was claimed is reduced below two-thirds of the partner's interest determined at the time the property was placed in service, the selling partner is considered to have disposed of a like portion of the ITC property and the recapture rules are triggered. If subsequent to this reduction the selling partner's interest is further reduced to less than one-third of the partner's interest at the time the property was placed in service, additional recapture may take place.[4] An exception to these recapture

---

2.  Reg. § 1.708–1(b)(ii).
3.  § 47(a) and Reg. § 1.47–6(a)(2).
4.  Reg. § 1.47–6.

rules exists for a partnership interest transferred between corporate partners who are members of the same affiliated group filing a consolidated tax return.[5] Note that under § 48(q)(6)(A), an increase in the basis of ITC property to reflect a recaptured ITC flows through and affects the basis of the partner's interest. When the ITC was taken and the basis of property decreased, the partner's interest basis was also affected.

*Lost ITC.* Unfortunately, the purchasing partner is faced with the entity concept and may not be allowed to claim the ITC on the ratable share of assets purchased. Remember that § 48 disallows the ITC on property used after its acquisition by a person who used such property before the acquisition.[6]

When the relationship between the buyer of a partnership interest (or of partnership property) and the seller is such that losses are disallowed under § 267 or § 707(b), the buyer is denied the ITC. For example, assume that a partnership sells used property of the type that qualifies as ITC property to a 60 percent partner. Since losses on transactions between the parties are disallowed under § 707(b), the buyer will be denied the ITC on the used property. If a partnership interest is sold to a related party as defined in § 267, it would seem that the buyer would be denied the ITC on the used partnership property becauses losses on transactions between the parties would be denied under § 267. If the buyer of a partnership interest and the seller are not related as defined in § 267, the ITC may still be denied to the buyer if the continuing partners own more than a 50 percent interest in the partnership's capital or profits. However, when a § 267 relationship does not exist and the continuing partners own 50 percent or less of the partnership's capital or profits, it appears the ITC on the used partnership property that qualifies for the credit may be allowed.[7]

## EFFECT OF § 751 ASSETS

A major exception to the general rule of § 741 arises when a partnership interest is sold or exchanged and the partnership possesses certain assets, sometimes referred to as "hot assets." Section 751 provides that an amount realized from the sale of a partnership interest attributable to *unrealized receivables* or *substantially appreciated inventory* is treated as received from the sale of a noncapital asset. This treatment results in ordinary income. The principal purpose of this provision is to prevent the conversion of ordinary income into capital gain through the sale of a partnership interest. Section 751 also can apply to partnership distributions that have the effect of a "disposition" of ordinary income assets.

*Unrealized Receivables.* The term "unrealized receivables" includes any rights (contractual or otherwise) to receive payment, to the extent not

---

**5.** Reg. § 1.1502–3(f)(2)(i).

**6.** § 48(c)(1).

**7.** See *Edward A. Moradian,* 53 T.C. 207 (1969), *acq.* substituted for *nonacq.* in 1982–2 C.B. 2; *Holloman v. Comm.,* 77–1 USTC ¶ 9409, 39 AFTR2d 77–1482, 551 F.2d 987 (CA–5, 1977); Reg. § 1.48–3(a)(2)(i); and Rev.Rul. 82–213, 1982–2 C.B. 31.

previously included in income under the partnership's method of accounting, for the following:

1. Inventory delivered or to be delivered to the extent the proceeds would be treated as being from the sale or exchange of property other than a capital asset.

2. Services rendered or to be rendered.[8]

Sometimes the method of accounting, the nature of the property, or the property's holding period affects whether an item is includible in the term under the above requirements. Under the cash method of accounting, trade receivables from inventory sales and from services rendered (including related notes receivable) are included in the term, while under the accrual method they are not. The gain element in installment receivables from the sale of inventory by a dealer or from the sale of real or personal property used in a trade or business that does not meet the long-term holding period requirement is fully includible in the term under the installment method of accounting. However, the gain element in installment receivables from the sale of capital assets or § 1231 assets is excluded.

The term "unrealized receivables" includes, in addition to the above items, the recapture potential from the assumed disposition at fair market value of the following:

1. Mining property, to the extent of exploratory expenditures under § 617.

2. Stock of a Domestic International Sales Corporation (DISC), to the extent of accumulated DISC income under § 995.

3. Stock of certain foreign corporations, to the extent of accumulated earnings and profits under § 1248.

4. Real and personal property, to the extent of depreciation under § 1245 or § 1250.

5. Farm property held less than 10 years, to the extent of expenditures for soil, water, and land conservation under § 1252.

6. Franchises, trademarks, and trade names, to the extent the transferor retains a significant power, right, or interest under § 1253.

7. Oil, gas, and geothermal property, to the extent of intangible drilling and development costs under § 1254.

8. The ordinary income portion of market discount bonds under § 1278 and of short-term obligations under § 1283.

*Substantially Appreciated Inventory.* The term "substantially appreciated inventory" is defined in § 751(d) and includes virtually all partnership property except money, capital assets, and § 1231 property.[9] Specifically, the term includes (1) stock in trade or property held for sale to customers in the ordinary course of business, (2) any other property which on sale or exchange is neither a capital asset nor a § 1231 asset, (3) any other property which if sold or exchanged would result in a taxable § 1246

---

**8.** § 751(c).
**9.** Reg. § 1.751–1(d).

gain (relating to foreign investment company stock), and (4) any other property held by the partnership which if held by the selling or distributee partner would be considered to be property of the type described in the first three categories. Accounts and notes receivable of an accrual basis partnership are included in the definition of inventory under § 751(d), since they are neither capital assets nor § 1231 assets. Also note that the definition is broad enough to include all items considered to be unrealized receivables.[10] The disadvantage of including unrealized receivables in inventory can be seen when a determination is made as to whether it is substantially appreciated. Note that unrealized receivables are § 751 assets regardless of whether or not the inventory is substantially appreciated. Thus, by themselves, they are hot assets. In addition, because they may be included at a zero basis[11] in the tests to determine if the inventory is substantially appreciated, they greatly enhance the possibility of this occurring.

Inventory items are considered to be substantially appreciated if at the time of their sale or distribution their aggregate fair market value exceeds 120 percent of their total adjusted basis to the partnership *and* if their fair market value is more than 10 percent of the fair market value of all partnership property other than money.[12] In applying these tests, it is important to note that all inventory items are evaluated as a group rather than individually. Thus, if there is substantial appreciation of all inventory items taken collectively, each item will be treated as substantially appreciated even if a specific item has not appreciated.[13]

When making the 120 percent test for substantially appreciated inventory, the cost of the property without regard to special basis adjustments to partners generally is used as the adjusted basis. Also, the term "fair market value" has the same meaning as the term "market" under the § 471 Regulations.[14] Again, since unrealized receivables usually have a zero basis, the inclusion of such items in inventory is a significant factor in the test for substantial appreciation under § 751.

*Section 751 Applied.*   The application of § 751 to the sale of a partner's interest is illustrated in Examples 5 through 7. Section 751's effect upon certain partnership distributions is discussed under LIQUIDATING AND DISPROPORTIONATE PARTNERSHIP DISTRIBUTIONS.

**Example 5.**   C's interest in the equal ABC Partnership is sold to D for $15,000 cash. On the sale date, the partnership's cash basis balance sheet reflects the following:

---

10.   Reg. § 1.751–1(d)(2)(ii).
11.   Reg. § 1.751–1(c)(5).
12.   § 751(d)(1).
13.   Reg. § 1.751–1(d)(1).
14.   Reg. § 1.471–4 indicates that under ordinary circumstances, "market" means the bid price prevailing at the inventory date for the particular merchandise in the quantity usually purchased.

*Assets*

| | Adjusted Basis Per Books | Market Value |
|---|---|---|
| Cash | $ 10,000 | $ 10,000 |
| Accounts receivable (for services) | 0 | 30,000 |
| Other assets | 14,000 | 14,000 |
| Total | $ 24,000 | $ 54,000 |

*Liabilities and Capital*

| | | |
|---|---|---|
| Liabilities | $  9,000 | $   9,000 |
| Capital accounts | | |
| A | 5,000 | 15,000 |
| B | 5,000 | 15,000 |
| C | 5,000 | 15,000 |
| Total | $ 24,000 | $ 54,000 |

Section 751(a) applies to the sale because the partnership has unrealized receivables in the form of accounts receivable. The total amount realized by C is $18,000 ($15,000 cash price plus $3,000 of partnership liabilities assumed by D). C's one-third interest in partnership property includes $10,000 of market value in unrealized receivables. Consequently, $10,000 of the $18,000 realized must be considered as received in exchange for C's interest in the partnership's accounts receivable. The remaining $8,000 realized by C is considered to be in exchange for a capital asset. C's basis in the partnership is $8,000 ($5,000 capital account plus a $3,000 share of partnership liabilities). No portion of C's basis is attributable to the unrealized receivables, since the property has a zero basis in the hands of the partnership and such basis would have carried over under § 732 if C had received them in a distribution. Thus, the difference between the $10,000 realized for the receivables and C's zero basis in them is ordinary income. The entire $8,000 of C's basis in the partnership is treated as being in non-Section 751 property and is applied against the remaining $8,000 of consideration received from the sale ($18,000 realized less $10,000 allocated to the sale of § 751 assets). Consequently, C has no capital gain or loss. Instead, the entire $10,000 gain is ordinary income.[15]

**Example 6.** Assume the same facts as in Example 5, except that C's basis in partnership property (other than unrealized receivables) is $7,000 instead of $8,000. Under these circumstances, C has a capital gain of $1,000. However, if C's basis is $9,000, an unusual situation arises. In such a case, C must still report $10,000 of ordinary income from the sale of unrealized receivables. At the same time, C has a capital loss of $1,000 on the sale of non-Section 751 property. Note that

---

15. Reg. § 1.751–1(g) (Ex. 1).

the total gain on the sale of $9,000 ($18,000 realized less C's basis of $9,000) is fragmented into two parts—ordinary income and capital loss.

**Example 7.** K's one-third interest in the KLM Partnership is sold to P for $36,000 in cash. At the time of the sale, the balance sheet of the partnership, which uses the cash method of accounting, reflects the following:

*Assets*

|  | Adjusted Basis Per Books | Market Value |
|---|---|---|
| Cash | $ 3,000 | $ 3,000 |
| Notes receivable | 12,000 | 12,000 |
| Accounts receivable | 0 | 6,000 |
| Merchandise inventory | 30,000 | 60,000 |
| Depreciable assets | 15,000 | 24,000 |
| Investment in stocks and bonds | 12,000 | 15,000 |
| Total assets | $ 72,000 | $ 120,000 |

*Liabilities and Capital*

|  | Adjusted Basis Per Books | Market Value |
|---|---|---|
| Accounts payable | $ 4,500 | $ 4,500 |
| Notes payable | 7,500 | 7,500 |
| Capital accounts |  |  |
| K | 20,000 | 36,000 |
| L | 20,000 | 36,000 |
| M | 20,000 | 36,000 |
| Total | $ 72,000 | $ 120,000 |

In determining whether § 751 applies to the sale of K's interest, the partnership must have unrealized receivables *or* substantially appreciated inventory. Thus, each partnership asset must be categorized as either § 751 property or non-Section 751 property. In classifying each asset, note that the $6,000 of accounts receivable represents unrealized receivables. This alone gives rise to some ordinary income. Additionally, if any of the $9,000 excess of fair market value of depreciable assets over basis ($24,000 less $15,000) represents depreciation recapture potential under § 1245 or § 1250, it also represents unrealized receivables.

Assuming that $6,000 of this excess market value represents § 1245 recapture potential, the KLM partnership has a total of $12,000 in unrealized receivables with a zero basis. However, unrealized receivables are also included in inventory. As a result, the test for substantially appreciated inventory must be made. The classification of each asset is presented below. Note that the depreciable assets are reflected as § 1231 assets with a basis of $15,000 and a market value of $18,000. This treatment is required, since the remaining $6,000 of excess market value represents depreciation recapture classified as § 751 property.

| Non-Section 751 Property | Adjusted Basis Per Books | Market Value |
|---|---|---|
| Cash | $ 3,000 | $ 3,000 |
| Section 1231 assets | 15,000 | 18,000 |
| Investments in stocks and bonds | 12,000 | 15,000 |
| Total | $ 30,000 | $ 36,000 |

| Section 751 Property | | |
|---|---|---|
| Notes receivable | $ 12,000 | $ 12,000 |
| Unrealized receivables (accounts receivable and § 1245 recapture) | –0– | 12,000 |
| Merchandise inventory | 30,000 | 60,000 |
| Total | $ 42,000 | $ 84,000 |
| Grand totals | $ 72,000 | $ 120,000 |

In testing for substantially appreciated inventory, note that the fair market value of all assets other than cash is $117,000 ($120,000 total assets less $3,000 cash). Since the $84,000 fair market value of the inventory items (§ 751 property) exceeds 120% of the partnership's adjusted basis in these items [$50,400 ($42,000 × 120%)], the first test for substantially appreciated inventory has been met. Because the fair market value of these assets exceeds 10% of the market value of all partnership assets other than cash [$11,700 (10% × $117,000)], the second test is also met. Thus, the inventory items are "substantially appreciated." K allocates the amount realized on the sale between § 751 assets and non-Section 751 assets. The total amount realized on the sale is $40,000 ($36,000 cash price plus $4,000, K's one-third of the partnership's liabilities). The amount of K's basis in the partnership is $24,000 ($20,000 capital account plus $4,000 of partnership's liabilities). In fragmenting the sale, K allocates $28,000 of the amount realized to the § 751 assets (one-third of $84,000, the fair market value of such items). Since K's basis in the inventory items is $14,000 (one-third of $42,000, the basis of receivables and inventory), K will have ordinary income of $14,000 from the sale. The remaining $12,000 of consideration received from the sale ($40,000 realized less $28,000 applied to the § 751 assets) is allocated to the sale of K's interest in non-Section 751 assets. Since K's basis in these assets is $10,000 ($24,000 total basis less $14,000 assigned to § 751 assets), K has a $2,000 capital gain. This gain is attributable to K's $1,000 share of the appreciation in value of the § 1231 assets (one-third of $3,000) and the $1,000 share of the appreciation in value of the investments in stocks and bonds (one-third of $3,000).

Although the computations required in Example 7 are rigorous, the results represent the economic reality of the sale. A different presentation of the data may be helpful.

| | Total Amount Realized on Sale | Allocation of Amount Realized | |
| --- | --- | --- | --- |
| | | To Section 751 Assets | To Other Assets |
| Cash received | $ 36,000 | ⅓ of the fair market value of items in each category | |
| Liabilities transferred to P (⅓ of $12,000) | 4,000 | | |
| Total realized | $ 40,000 | $ 28,000 | $ 12,000 |

| | Total Basis in Partnership Interest | Allocation of Basis | |
| --- | --- | --- | --- |
| | | To Section 751 Assets | To Other Assets |
| Capital account | $ 20,000 | ⅓ of the adjusted basis of items in each category | |
| K's share of partnership liabilities (⅓ of $12,000) | 4,000 | | |
| Total basis | $ 24,000 | $ 14,000 | $ 10,000 |
| Gain realized | $ 16,000 | $ 14,000 | $ 2,000 |
| | | Ordinary Income | Capital Gain |

*Tiered Partnerships.* Before the Deficit Reduction Act of 1984, some individuals argued that when a partnership interest was sold or exchanged, only the assets of the partnership in which the interest was transferred were to be considered in determining the applicability of § 751. In an attempt to avoid § 751 treatment, tiered partnerships were formed. For example, parent partnership P would form and own an interest in subsidiary partnership S. All operations would be carried on by S, and S would own all the § 751 assets. (No § 751 assets would be owned by P.) When an interest in P was transferred, it was argued that § 751 was inapplicable because P did not own such assets. For sales, exchanges, and distributions after March 31, 1984, when a determination must be made as to the presence of § 751 assets, the Deficit Reduction Act of 1984 and related Committee Reports clarify the situation. Here, new § 751(f) indicates that a partnership will be treated as owning its proportionate share of *all* assets of any partnership in which it is a partner. Although this provision may work to the disadvantage of tiered partnerships, it can also work to their advantage. Recall the two tests for substantially appreciated inventory. Although some or all of the assets in a subsidiary partnership may pass both tests, when the parent's proportionate interest in these assets is combined with the parent's own assets, one or both tests may be failed.

*Tax Reporting.* After 1984, when a partnership owns § 751 property, partners who sell or exchange a partnership interest must promptly notify the partnership of such transfers.[16] After the notification is received, the partnership must file an information return with the IRS for the calendar year in which such transfers took place. The return will contain the names and addresses of the transferors and transferees and such other informa-

---

16.  § 6050K.

tion as may be prescribed by statutory regulations (to be issued). In addition, each person whose name is shown on the calendar year return is to be furnished the name and address of the partnership making the return and the information shown on the return with respect to such person. Failure to notify the partnership of such transfers or failure to file the information return and notify the parties involved will result in a $50 penalty for each failure. A penalty will not be assessed on the partnership if a transferor fails to notify the partnership of such a transfer.[17] Also, the penalty will not be assessed if it can be shown that a failure was due to a reasonable cause and not to willful neglect. The maximum penalty for all such failures in any one calendar year is $50,000.

In addition to the above reporting, the results of the sale or exchange must be reported on the transferor's tax return. The Regulations require the transferor to submit a statement that sets forth separately the following information:[18]

—Date of sale or exchange.

—Adjusted basis of partnership interest and portion thereof attributable to § 751 assets.

—Amount realized from sale or exchange and portion thereof attributable to § 751 assets.

Additional information is required if the transferor has a special basis adjustment under § 743(b) that reflects an adjusted basis in partnership assets different from the partner's proportionate share of the partnership's basis in such assets. Special basis adjustments are discussed under OPTIONAL ADJUSTMENT TO BASIS OF PARTNERSHIP PROPERTY— Sale or Exchange of an Interest.

# EXCHANGE OF A PARTNERSHIP INTEREST

Unlike a sale that results from a transfer of property solely for money, an exchange involves a reciprocal transfer of property. Even if the parties involved pay or receive cash in addition to the property transferred, the transaction will be deemed an exchange. Usually, the tax consequences of an exchange are the same as those of a sale. However, the distinction between sales and exchanges is important because certain exchanges qualify as nontaxable events. Exchanges of partnership interests that might qualify for nonrecognition treatment are discussed in the sections that follow.

## TRANSFERS TO CONTROLLED CORPORATIONS

Section 351(a) provides that gain or loss is not recognized on the transfer by one or more persons of property to a corporation solely in exchange for stock or securities in that corporation if immediately after the exchange, such person or persons are in control of the corporation to which the property was transferred.[19]

---

**17.** § 6678.
**18.** Reg. § 1.751–1(a)(3).
**19.** Refer to Chapter 3 for a complete discussion of § 351.

*Partner's Interest Basis.* If the conditions of § 351 are met, the transfer of a partnership interest to a corporation will be treated as a nontaxable exchange. Recall that § 357(c)(1) requires the transferor to recognize gain to the extent that any debt assumed by the corporation or debt to which the transferred property is subject exceeds the transferor's basis in the property transferred. Consequently, if the transferor's share of partnership liabilities exceeds the adjusted basis of the partnership interest at the time of the transfer, gain is recognized to the extent of such excess. Determining the character of such gain requires an allocation of basis and amount realized on the exchange similar to that presented in Example 7 in connection with a sale of a partnership interest.

It should be noted that § 357(c)(3) was added by the Revenue Act of 1978 and amended by the Technical Corrections Act of 1979 to allow taxpayers transferring debt to a corporation under § 351 after November 6, 1978, to exclude transferred liabilities the payment of which would (1) give rise to a deduction when paid or (2) be described in § 736(a). An exception to excluding transferred liabilities from § 357(c)(1) treatment is found in § 357(c)(3)(B). This provision indicates that liabilities that resulted in the creation of, or increase in, the basis of any property cannot be excluded. Additionally, the transfer of a partnership interest to a corporation has collateral effects similar to those associated with a sale. All items of partnership income or loss, deduction, or credit attributable to the transferred interest are apportioned between the transferor partner and the corporation. Moreover, if the partnership interest transferred represented 50 percent or more of the total interest in capital and profits, the partnership is terminated under § 708.

*Incorporation Methods.* If the partners of a partnership decide to incorporate their business, three methods exist to accomplish the desired change in form:

1. Each partner's interest is transferred to the corporation in exchange for stock under § 351. As a result, the partnership terminates under § 708(b)(1)(B), and the corporation owns all partnership assets.

2. The partnership transfers all of its assets to the corporation in exchange for stock and the assumption of partnership liabilities. The stock is then distributed to the partners in proportion to their partnership interests.

3. The partnership makes a pro rata distribution of all its assets and liabilities to its partners in complete liquidation. The partners then transfer their undivided interests in the assets and liabilities to the corporation in exchange for stock under § 351.

Before July 23, 1984, the IRS concluded that these incorporation methods all had the same income tax results where the partnership used the accrual method of accounting; the partnership had assets and liabilities consisting of cash, equipment, and accounts payable; and the liabilities did not exceed the adjusted basis of the assets. Thus, regardless of the incorporation approach taken, the transaction was treated as a transfer by the partnership of its assets and liabilities to the corporation and then as a liquidating distribution of the corporation's stock to the partners.[20] For incorporations after July 22, 1984, the IRS has concluded that although none of the three methods cause gain or loss to be recognized, they do cause different tax results.[21] Figure I summarizes these results.

Selecting the appropriate incorporation method is crucial. If the corporation plans to issue § 1244 stock, the "original stockholders," not the partnership, must be the partners. Otherwise, any § 1244 ordinary loss benefits will be forfeited when the partners become shareholders.[22] If an S election is to be made by the corporation after the partnership's assets are received, such an election will be invalid if the partnership is the shareholder.[23] If the corporation is already in existence and operates under an S election, the election will terminate if the partnership is a shareholder.[24] Consequently, when a partnership is to be incorporated with § 1244 stock or an S election is made, or if the partnership is to be incorporated into an existing S corporation, incorporation method 3 should be followed (i. e., the partnership should make a pro rata distribution of all of its assets and liabilities to its partners in a complete liquidation, and the partners should then transfer these items to the corporation in a § 351 exchange).

## LIKE-KIND EXCHANGES

Another attempt to achieve nonrecognition treatment involves the exchange of an interest in one partnership for an interest in another partnership. If the partnership interests exchanged could qualify as like-kind property under § 1031, no gain or loss would be recognized.

Before the Deficit Reduction Act of 1984, it was thought that under certain circumstances an interest in one partnership could be exchanged tax-free for an interest in another partnership under the like-kind exchange rules of § 1031. Amended provision § 1031(a)(2)(D), effective for exchanges after July 18, 1984, clearly indicates that § 1031 does not apply to an exchange of partnership interests. No limitation to this provision is contained in § 1031. However, the related Committee Reports accompanying the Deficit Reduction Act of 1984 indicate that this provision is applicable to an exchange of interests in different partnerships (not the same partnership). The meaning of this limiting statement is unclear. Additionally, in 1984 the IRS ruled that under certain circumstances a general partnership interest may be converted into a limited partnership interest in the same partnership without gain or loss recognition (or vice versa).[25] In the ruling, the IRS held that the conversion was not a sale or exchange.

---

**20.** Rev.Rul. 70–239, 1970–1 C.B. 74.

**21.** Rev.Rul. 84–111, 1984–2 C.B. 88.

**22.** Refer to Chapter 3 for a discussion of § 1244 stock. Also, see *Jerome Prizant,* 30 TCM 817, T.C.Memo. 1977–196.

**23.** Reg. § 1.1371–1(e).

**24.** Refer to Chapter 8 for a discussion of the tax consequences of a termination of Subchapter S status.

**25.** Rev.Rul. 84–52, 1984–1 C.B. 157.

**Figure I**

PARTNERSHIP INCORPORATION:
SUMMARY OF REVENUE RULING 84–111

| Method | To | Basis | Holding Period |
|---|---|---|---|
| 1 | Corporation | Basis of assets equals interest bases of partners allocated by rules of § 732(c), discussed under **LIQUIDATING AND DISPROPORTIONATE PARTNERSHIP DISTRIBUTIONS**— Liquidating Distributions of Property. | Holding period of each asset includes holding period by partnership. |
| | Each Partner | Basis of stock equals basis of partner's interest reduced by debt assumed by corporation. | Holding period of stock includes holding period of partner's interest, except that holding period of stock received for § 751 assets that are neither capital assets nor § 1231 assets starts the day after exchange date. |
| 2 | Corporation | Basis of each asset equals the basis to partnership immediately before transfer. | Holding period of each asset includes partnership's holding period. |
| | Partnership | Basis of stock equals basis of assets transferred reduced by debt assumed by corporation. | Holding period of stock to the extent received for capital assets and § 1231 assets includes partnership's holding period. Holding period of stock received for noncapital and non-§ 1231 assets starts the day after exchange date. |
| | Each Partner | Basis of stock equals partner's interest in partnership just before transfer reduced by debt assumed by corporation. | Holding period of stock includes partnership's holding period for stock. |
| 3 | Corporation | Basis of assets equals basis of assets to partners received in liquidating distribution. | Holding period of assets equals the partners' holding period in assets received in liquidating distribution. |

| Each Partner | Basis of assets received in liquidating distribution equals basis of partner's interest reduced by money received. Net effect of debt is zero. | Holding period of assets includes partnership's holding period. |
| --- | --- | --- |
| | Basis of stock equals basis of assets received in liquidating distribution reduced by debt assumed by corporation. | Holding period of stock to the extent received for capital assets and § 1231 assets includes partner's holding period. Holding period of stock received for noncapital and non-§ 1231 assets starts the day after exchange date. |

# OTHER DISPOSITIONS OF PARTNERSHIP INTERESTS

A partner's interest may, in addition to being sold or exchanged, be transferred by gift, death, abandonment or forfeiture, or certain distributions. Termination and changes in partnership interests as a result of distributions are discussed under LIQUIDATING AND DISPROPORTIONATE PARTNERSHIP DISTRIBUTIONS. Dispositions of partnership interests resulting from gifts, death, and abandonment or forfeiture are discussed in the following sections.

## GIFT OF A PARTNERSHIP INTEREST

Generally, the gift of a partnership interest results in neither gain nor loss to the donor. The partnership interest is considered intangible property separate and apart from the partnership. The donee determines the basis and holding period of the acquired interest under the rules of § § 1015 and 1223. If the donor's entire interest in the partnership is transferred, all items of partnership income, loss, deduction, or credit attributable to the interest transferred are prorated between the donor and donee in accordance with § 706(d).

However, several exceptions exist to the general rule of treating gifts as nontaxable transfers. If the partnership uses the cash method of accounting and has accounts receivable at the time of transfer, the gift may be considered an anticipatory assignment of income by the donor. Similarly, if the partnership has installment notes receivable, the gift of an interest may be considered a disposition under § 453B.[26] In either case, the IRS may be successful in treating the gift of a partnership interest as a taxable event. Additionally, if the donor's share of partnership liabilities exceeds the donor's basis in the partnership, the gift will be treated as part gift and part sale.[27] Because of these possibilities, the donor should exercise caution in transferring a partnership interest by gift.

---

26. Rev.Rul. 60–352, 1960–2 C.B. 208.
27. Rev.Rul. 75–194, 1975–1 C.B. 180.

## DEATH OF A PARTNER

Many of the tax issues associated with the death of a partner were discussed in Chapter 9 under PARTNERSHIP OPERATION—Taxable Years of Partner and Partnership. Recall that unless the partnership agreement provides for the termination of a partner's interest as of the date of death, the partnership's tax year does not close with respect to the interest transferred to a deceased partner's estate or other successor in interest. Furthermore, the transfer of a partnership interest as a result of death is not considered a sale or exchange under Regulation § 1.708–1(b)(1)(ii). Even if the deceased partner's interest is 50 percent or more of the total interest in partnership capital and profits, § 708(b)(1) does not operate to terminate the entire partnership. Moreover, the death of a partner does not trigger recapture of the investment tax credit under § 47(b)(1) or result in a taxable disposition of installment obligations under § 453B(c). However, other problems must be considered when a partnership interest is transferred as a result of a partner's death.

The deceased partner's estate or other successor in interest may be precluded from continuing as a member of the partnership or may wish to dispose of the partnership interest. In certain professional partnerships, local law prohibits an estate or other successor in interest from continuing as a partner beyond a certain time period. In other cases, the remaining partners may wish to buy out or liquidate the deceased partner's interest in the partnership. In such situations, usually there is a provision in the partnership agreement specifying a valuation method and the manner in which the deceased partner's interest will be terminated.

If the remaining partners choose to purchase the deceased partner's interest, the estate or other successor in interest must determine the basis of the partnership interest under § 1014. The purchasing partners may be entitled to a special basis adjustment under § 743 for their respective shares of the interest acquired. If the partnership interest is to be liquidated, decisions regarding the form and time of liquidating distributions must be made. If the estate or other successor in interest is to continue as a partnership member, a special basis adjustment may be available under § 743 to reflect the difference between the fair market value of its share of partnership assets and the partnership's basis in these assets.

## ABANDONMENT OR FORFEITURE
## OF A PARTNERSHIP INTEREST

Historically, an abandonment or forfeiture of a partnership interest is a rare event. However, the proliferation of economically unsound tax-shelter partnerships has led to a growing number of such dispositions. The abandonment or forfeiture of a partnership interest results in an ordinary loss deduction when the partner's share of partnership debt is zero or when such debt is nonexistent.[28] Although a partnership interest is a capital asset, the abandonment loss is an ordinary loss because an abandonment is not a sale or exchange. However, if the partner has a share of the partner-

---

28. *Gaius G. Gannon,* 16 T.C. 1134 (1951), *acq.,* and *Palmer Hutcheson,* 17 T.C. (1951), *acq.* However, partnership debt was not a problem in these cases.

ship debt the abandonment is treated as a sale or exchange through the operation of the constructive distribution rules.[29]

> **Example 8.**  X owns a $20,000 interest in the equal XYZ Partnership, which has liabilities (all of a nonrecourse type) of $90,000. XYZ is involved in real estate development. Rather than continue in an economically unsound venture, X withdraws from the partnership, receiving nothing from the partnership or the remaining partners. Under § 752(b), the decrease in X's share of the liabilities of $30,000 is regarded as a distribution of money to X by the partnership. Furthermore, under § 731(a) the distribution of money in excess of the distributee partner's interest is treated as a gain from the sale or exchange of that interest. As a result, X is required to recognize a gain of $10,000 ($30,000 − $20,000) on the deemed sale. Moreover, if the partnership has any § 751 assets, a portion of the gain is ordinary income.

# LIQUIDATING AND DISPROPORTIONATE PARTNERSHIP DISTRIBUTIONS

Recall that three types of distributions from a partnership exist. Nonliquidating distributions of money and other property were treated in Chapter 9. Distributions that result in the liquidation of a partner's interest or that affect the distributee partner's proportionate interest in § 751 property are discussed in the sections that follow. However, the general rules covering nonliquidating partnership distributions need to be reviewed to provide a frame of reference for the subsequent discussion of liquidating and disproportionate distributions.

## REVIEW OF NONLIQUIDATING DISTRIBUTIONS

The statutory provisions that govern the treatment of nonliquidating distributions of cash and other partnership property are contained in § § 731 through 733 of the Code. Section 731 controls the extent of gain or loss recognition on partnership distributions. Sections 732 and 733 provide the rules for determining basis of property received in a distribution and the effect of distributions upon the distributee's partnership interest.

Section 731(b) states that no gain or loss shall be recognized by a partnership on the distribution of money or other property to a partner. Similarly, § 731(a) states the general rule that no gain or loss is recognized by a partner receiving such distributions. Specifically, loss is never recognized, and gain is recognized only if *money* received in a distribution exceeds the basis of the partner's interest immediately preceding the distribution. Thus, distributions of property other than money will not result in the recognition of gain or loss to the partner unless they involve disproportionate distributions of § 751 property. Any gain recognized is treated as gain from the *sale* or *exchange* of a partnership interest. However, the character of such gain is determined under rules previously discussed governing the sale of a partnership interest.

---

**29.**  *Edward H. Pietz,* 59 T.C. 207 (1972), and *Milledge L. Middleton,* 77 T.C. 310 (1981), *aff'd per curiam* in 82–2 USTC ¶ 9713, 51 AFTR2d 83–353, 693 F.2d 124 (CA–11, 1982).

Section 733 provides that nonliquidating distributions from a partnership reduce the distributee partner's interest (but not below zero) by (1) the sum of money distributed and (2) the basis to such partner of distributed property other than money. Additionally, § 732 provides that the basis of property (other than money) distributed to a partner in a nonliquidating distribution is the property's adjusted basis to the partnership immediately before the distribution.[30] However, the basis of the property may not exceed the adjusted basis of the partner's interest reduced by any money received in the same transaction.[31]

When the basis of properties distributed is limited by the partner's interest, an allocation of basis must be made under § 732(c). The manner of allocation is discussed in the section dealing with liquidating distributions. However, when unrealized receivables or inventory is not involved, the remaining basis of the partner's interest is allocated to the properties in the ratio of their adjusted bases to the partnership.[32] Section 735(b) states that the holding period of the property received as a distribution includes that of the partnership. Examples 37 to 39 in Chapter 9 illustrate these rules.

In the previous discussion of dispositions of partnership interests, it was noted that some distributions can have the effect of a sale or exchange of § 751 property (ordinary income assets). Also, it was observed that in such cases, § 751 is made applicable to insure recognition of all ordinary income. When a partner's proportionate share of § 751 assets is received in a distribution, § 751 is not applicable and the rules outlined above generally control the tax consequences of the distribution.

Although a proportionate distribution of § 751 assets may not immediately result in income recognition, any subsequent disposition of unrealized receivables by the distributee partner triggers ordinary gain or loss recognition.[33] Similarly, a subsequent sale or exchange of inventory items triggers ordinary gain or loss recognition if the partner sells or exchanges such items within five years of the distribution date.[34] Even if the partner holds an inventory item for five years before the item's disposition, ordinary gain or loss still results if the inventory item is not a capital asset in the partner's hands.[35] This rule applies to all inventory items defined in § 751(d)(2) without regard to whether they were substantially appreciated within the meaning of § 751(d)(1).

**Example 9.** B receives a proportionate share of inventory items (basis of $16,000) in a nonliquidating distribution from the partnership. Fourteen months later, B sells the property for $20,000. Even though the inventory is a capital asset in B's hands and the long-term holding period is met, the $4,000 recognized gain is taxed as ordinary income. If the five-year holding period of § 735(a)(2) had been met, the $4,000 gain would be a long-term capital gain.

---

**30.**   § 732(a)(1).
**31.**   § 732(a)(2).
**32.**   § 732(c)(2).
**33.**   § 735(a)(1).
**34.**   § 735(a)(2).
**35.**   Reg. § 1.735–1(a)(2).

## GENERAL NATURE OF LIQUIDATING DISTRIBUTIONS

Distributions in liquidation of partnership interests have a multiple character. First, they are similar to all partnership distributions and generally are treated as a tax-free return of capital. Unlike corporate shareholders, partners may be able to withdraw their investment without tax consequences. Under the general rule, unrealized appreciation or depreciation in the market value of distributed partnership property is not recognized. Consequently, the basis of such property is determined by reference to its basis in the hands of the partnership and the basis of the distributee partner's interest prior to the distribution. Second, depending upon how the transaction is structured, a liquidating distribution may have the same effect as the sale of a partnership interest. Here, the parties may be required to recognize gain or loss; otherwise, such gain or loss might escape recognition when only cash is distributed. Third, there are two overriding considerations: All income and expense (or loss) should be recognized at some time, and ordinary income should not be converted into capital gain.

Finally, as a result of the Deficit Reduction Act of 1984, § 761(e) was inserted into the Code. This provision indicates that for purposes of § § 708 and 743 and any other provision specified in the statutory regulations (to be issued), a distribution is treated as an exchange. Although the related Committee Reports discuss distributions of partnership interests by corporations and partnerships, no such limitation is mentioned in the new provision. Does this provision apply to redemptions of partnership interests via liquidating distributions? If the answer is yes and a redeemed interest constitutes 50 percent or more of the total interest in capital and profits, the partnership terminates under § 708. If the redeemed interest does not constitute such an interest, but, when combined with other interests that are sold, exchanged, or redeemed within a 12-month period it does constitute such an interest, the partnership terminates. The new § 761(e) statutory regulations (to be issued) should be examined carefully to determine whether redemptions of partnership interests are considered a § 761(e) distribution.

Liquidating distributions can take several forms. A partner's interest can be liquidated by a series of cash payments or a lump-sum distribution in kind. The cash payments may be based on the partnership's annual income or may be a guaranteed payment. Distributions in kind may be a lump sum or one of a series in liquidation of a partnership interest. Since the statutory rules differ with respect to liquidating distributions of money and distributions of other property, the money distributions are given separate treatment.

## LIQUIDATING DISTRIBUTIONS OF MONEY

The character and treatment of liquidating distributions of money are governed by § 736 of the Code. Money payments are allocated between amounts paid for the partner's interest in partnership property under § 736(b) and other payments under § 736(a).[36] It is important to note that

---

36. Reg. § 1.736–1(a)(2).

the allocation generally is made in accordance with the partnership agreement.

*Section 736(a) Payments.* Cash payments for goodwill in excess of the partner's share of the goodwill's basis to the partnership that have not been specifically provided for in the partnership agreement and payments for unrealized receivables are ordinary income to the receiving partner under § 736(a). Such payments are treated as income distributions if determined by reference to the partnership income or as guaranteed payments under § 707(c) if not so determined. The receiving partner includes the payments in gross income for the related partnership year that ends with or within the partner's year.[37] To the partnership, such payments are taken as a reduction in the amount of partnership income available to continuing partners or as a deduction from gross income to arrive at the partnership's taxable income.[38]

The allowance of a deduction under § 707(c) or a reduction in partnership income available to continuing partners for amounts paid for a partnership interest seems anomalous. However, such treatment is consistent with the overall statutory scheme, since under the general rule, the partnership is not able to increase its basis in the unrealized receivables and goodwill. As a result, ordinary income is earned on all unrealized receivables as they are realized or collected. For example, § 1245 depreciation recapture potential is undiminished and results in ordinary income to the partnership when and if the related asset is sold or exchanged.

*Section 736(b) Payments.* Cash payments for a partner's interest in partnership property are essentially the same as current (nonliquidating) distributions. Under § 736(b)(2), such payments do not include the following:

—Payments for unrealized receivables.

—Payments for goodwill in excess of the partner's share of the goodwill's basis to the partnership that have not been specifically provided for in the partnership agreement.

Note that if the partnership agreement provides for goodwill payments to a partner in excess of the partner's share of the partnership basis, such payments are treated as a capital gain. Liquidating cash payments under § 736(b) are generally considered a return of capital to the extent of the partner's basis in the partnership, and gain is recognized to the extent of any excess. However, if substantially appreciated inventory as defined in § 751(d) is present, ordinary income is created. The recipient of § 736(b) payments takes the payments into account in the year received.[39]

---

**37.** Reg. § 1.736–1(a)(5).

**38.** For an interesting and unlikely to be repeated result of a partnership liquidation, see *C. F. Phillips,* 40 T.C. 157 (1963), and *H. C. Miller v. U. S.,* 67–2 USTC ¶ 9685, 20 AFTR2d 5569 (Ct.Cl., 1967). In these related cases, the retiring partner (Phillips) was allowed to treat all the liquidating payments as § 736(b) payments in exchange for his partnership interest even though there was no partnership agreement as to such classification. The remaining partner (Miller) was allowed to treat the payments he made as § 736(a) payments and thus deduct them. This contrary treatment resulted from the partners taking their cases to different courts.

**39.** Reg. § 1.736–1(a)(5).

*Liabilities.* In making computations under § 736, due consideration must be given to partnership liabilities. A partner's interest generally includes a share of partnership liabilities. Liabilities forgiven or assumed by another party (or by the partnership) are treated as cash withdrawals. Normally, the amount included in the partner's basis for liabilities is the same as the amount considered withdrawn, and the two amounts "wash." When a partner's share of partnership liabilities exceeds the basis of the partner's interest, gain recognized can exceed the cash actually received. This can occur when loan proceeds have been withdrawn by the partners or when cumulative partnership losses have exceeded the partner's capital investment (exclusive of debts).

*Lump-sum Payment.* Examples 10 and 11 illustrate the application of § 736 when a lump-sum cash payment is made to eliminate a partner's entire partnership interest and when liabilities are present.

**Example 10.** At the time T decides to withdraw from the ACT Partnership, the partnership's balance sheet for tax purposes contains the following:

| *Assets* | Adjusted Basis Per Books | Market Value |
|---|---|---|
| Cash | $ 60,000 | $ 60,000 |
| Equipment | 30,000 | 24,000 |
| Building | 90,000 | 120,000 |
| Total | $ 180,000 | $ 204,000 |

| *Liabilities and Capital* | | |
|---|---|---|
| Mortgage payable | $ 60,000 | $ 60,000 |
| Capital accounts | | |
| A | 40,000 | 48,000 |
| C | 40,000 | 48,000 |
| T | 40,000 | 48,000 |
| Total | $ 180,000 | $ 204,000 |

Assume T's entire interest in the partnership is liquidated by a lump-sum cash distribution of $48,000 and the assumption of T's share of partnership liabilities by the remaining partners. T's realized gain is computed as follows:

| | |
|---|---|
| Amount realized | |
| Cash | $ 48,000 |
| Liabilities assumed by other partners (⅓ of $60,000) and treated as money distributed | 20,000 |
| Total realized | $ 68,000 |
| Less: Basis of partnership interest | |
| Capital account of $40,000 plus ⅓ of partnership liabilities | 60,000 |
| Gain realized | $ 8,000 |

Assuming no depreciation recapture potential exists for the equipment or building, no § 751 property is involved in the liquidation. Thus, T's $8,000 gain would be treated as a capital gain from the sale of a partnership interest. If there was any recapture potential, however, it would be considered an unrealized receivable under § 751. In such a case, the amount attributable to T's interest therein would be treated as ordinary income under § 736(a).

**Example 11.** Assume the same facts as in Example 10, except that $15,000 of § 1250 recapture potential exists on the building and T's share is $5,000. Of the total amount realized by T, $5,000 is treated as a § 707(c) guaranteed payment deductible by the partnership. The amount treated as received for T's interest in partnership property is $63,000, and the capital gain realized is $3,000. Under the general rule, the basis of the building to the partnership is still $90,000, and the recapture potential remains at $15,000. However, the partnership may elect to adjust its basis in the remaining assets to reflect the gain recognized by the withdrawing partner.

*Series of Payments.* When liquidating cash distributions are spread over a number of years, it is necessary to allocate the total amounts paid between § 736(a) and § 736(b) payments. If the partners have dealt at arm's length and specifically agreed to the allocation and timing of each class of payment, such an agreement normally controls for tax purposes.[40]

**Example 12.** Partner X retires from the equal XYZ Partnership at a time when partnership debt is $90,000. It has been agreed among all partners that X's interest in partnership assets, exclusive of unrealized receivables and goodwill, is worth $105,000. To totally liquidate X's interest, it is further agreed that X will be paid $15,000 in cash per year for 10 years and the remaining partners will assume X's share of partnership liabilities for a total consideration of $180,000 (cash of $150,000, plus $30,000 debt assumption). If the partners agree that the assumption of X's share of liabilities and the first $75,000 of cash payments made by the partnership are to be treated as consideration for X's interest in partnership assets (exclusive of unrealized receivables and goodwill), this agreement controls for tax purposes. For the first five years, the $105,000 of payments (including the assumption of partnership debts) is treated as liquidating distributions under § 736(b). X realizes gain subject to the provisions of §§ 731, 741, and 751, and the partnership is not entitled to deduct any of these payments. However, in each of the next five years, X recognizes ordinary income of $15,000, and the partnership deducts the same amount as a guaranteed payment under § 707(c).

If the partners do not enter into a specific agreement as to the timing of payments for the two classes, a pro rata part of each payment is treated as a § 736(b) payment and the balance is treated as a § 736(a) payment. Further, if there is a deficiency in any year of *required* § 736(b) payments,

---

**40.** Reg. § 1.736–1(b)(5)(iii).

payments in the subsequent year are considered payments of this deficiency.[41]

> **Example 13.** Assume the same facts as in Example 12, except that the partners agree to a value of $120,000 (instead of $105,000) for X's interest in partnership assets, exclusive of unrealized receivables and goodwill. Further assume that there is no specific agreement as to the timing of the payments for each class, except that the liabilities are assumed immediately. In this situation, all payments are allocated between § 736(a) and § 736(b). This allocation is made for the cash payments as well as the assumption of X's share of liabilities. Thus, two-thirds ($120,000/$180,000) of each payment is treated as a distribution under § 736(b) and the balance as a guaranteed payment under § 736(a). For the cash payments, $10,000 is treated as a § 736(b) payment and $5,000 is treated as a § 736(a) payment. If only $7,000 is paid in one year, instead of the required $15,000, the entire sum is treated as a § 736(b) payment. If $19,000 is paid in the subsequent year, $13,000 is treated as a § 736(b) payment ($10,000 for the current year plus the $3,000 deficiency for the prior year). The remaining $6,000 is treated as a § 736(a) payment.

*Contingent Payments.* If the total liquidating payments are contingent, then absent a specific agreement to the contrary, all payments are considered as payments for an interest in partnership property under § 736(b) until the total value of such interest has been paid.[42] As in the previous example, if the partners agree on the value of the retiring partner's interest in partnership property, the agreement normally controls for tax purposes.

> **Example 14.** Assume the same facts as in Example 13, except that instead of receiving $15,000 per year, X receives 20% of partnership profits for a period of 10 years. Assume further that the cash amounts paid under the agreement are as follows:
>
> | | |
> |---|---|
> | Year 1—$20,000 | Year 6—$ 4,000 |
> | Year 2—$35,000 | Year 7—$ 9,000 |
> | Year 3—$15,000 | Year 8—$18,000 |
> | Year 4—$10,000 | Year 9—$31,000 |
> | Year 5—$23,000 | Year 10—$26,000 |
>
> Assuming that the agreed value of X's interest in partnership assets other than unrealized receivables and goodwill was $120,000 less the liabilities assumed of $30,000, all payments made for the first four years, plus $10,000 paid in year 5, are § 736(b) payments. All amounts paid in years 6 through 10, plus $13,000 paid in year 5, are treated as ordinary income under § 736(a).

As stated earlier, § 736(b) payments generally are treated in the same manner as current (nonliquidating) cash distributions. Thus, they reduce

---

41. Reg. §§ 1.736–1(b)(5)(i) and (7) (Ex. 1).
42. Reg. §§ 1.736–1(a)(1)(ii) and (b)(5)(ii).

the liquidating partner's basis dollar for dollar and result in income (gain) only to the extent of the excess. Such excess is treated as capital gain except to the extent it is attributable to substantially appreciated inventory. Keep in mind, however, that liquidating payments for a withdrawing partner's share of unrealized receivables must be treated as ordinary income.

> **Example 15.**  Assume the same facts as in Example 14. Further assume that X's basis in the partnership is $95,000. Since the payments are not fixed or stated in amount, X must use the cost recovery method of accounting for the liquidating payments. Thus, the $20,000 of cash received and relief of $30,000 in liabilities in year one, plus the $35,000 received in year 2, and $10,000 of the $15,000 received in year 3 are treated as a return of capital. This is the same treatment as that given to current cash distributions. Further, assuming none of the gain is attributable to substantially appreciated inventory, X recognizes capital gain of $5,000, $10,000, and $10,000 in years 3, 4, and 5. [Total § 736(b) payments of $120,000 less basis of $95,000, with resulting capital gain of $25,000.]

As an alternative to the cost recovery method described above, the Regulations allow a withdrawing partner to recognize the gain from a partnership interest in much the same manner as though it were an installment sale.[43] Note, however, that such treatment is allowed only if the total of § 736(b) payments is a fixed sum *and* the partner elects such treatment for the first taxable year in which such payments are received.

> **Example 16.**  Assume the same facts as in Example 15, except that the basis of X's interest is $60,000, X makes the special election provided by the Regulations, and the total § 736(b) payments to be received are $120,000. X treats 50% of each payment as gain and the remaining 50% as a return of capital. This election could also be made for the § 736(b) payments in the circumstances described in Examples 13 and 14.

## LIQUIDATING DISTRIBUTIONS OF PROPERTY

In some situations, partnerships find it impractical or undesirable to liquidate a retiring partner's interest solely by cash distributions. Instead, some or all of the withdrawing partner's interest is liquidated through other property distributions. If the partnership does not have § 751 property or if the distributions do not change the proportionate ownership of such property, the tax treatment of liquidating property distributions is essentially the same as current (nonliquidating) distributions. However, a major difference in the tax treatment of the two distributions exists (i. e., losses are recognized under certain circumstances in liquidating distributions).

*Basis of Distributed Property.*  Section 732(b) provides that cash distributions reduce the withdrawing partner's basis dollar for dollar and are taken into account before subsequent or contemporaneous distributions of

---

**43.**  Reg. § 1.736–1(b)(6).

other property. Additionally, § 732(c) indicates that the partner's remaining basis after reduction by cash distributions is first allocated to the distributed unrealized receivables and inventory (whether or not substantially appreciated) in an amount equal to the partnership's adjusted basis in such property. If the partnership's bases in the receivables and inventory exceed the partner's remaining interest, it is allocated to such properties in the ratio of their adjusted bases to the partnership. Next, if the withdrawing partner has any basis remaining in the partnership after reductions for cash distributions and unrealized receivables and inventory, the remainder is allocated to any other properties received in the ratio of the adjusted bases of these other properties to the partnership.

*Gain or Loss Recognition.* Gain is recognized only when the cash received exceeds the partner's interest. Loss is recognized only if the sum of the cash received plus the basis of distributed unrealized receivables and inventory is less than the adjusted basis of the partner's interest prior to the liquidating distribution and no other property is distributed.

*Application of Rules.* Each of the above rules is illustrated in the following examples. In each example, assume that the amounts distributed are in complete liquidation of the partner's interest in partnership property and that they equal the value of that interest.

**Example 17.** When T's partnership interest is $25,000, T receives cash of $15,000 and a proportionate share of inventory and buildings in a liquidating distribution. The inventory has a basis of $20,000 and a fair market value of $30,000 in the hands of the partnership. The building's basis is $8,000 and its fair market value $12,000. The building was depreciated under the straight-line method; thus, no recapture potential exists. Under these circumstances, T does not recognize a gain or loss. After reducing T's basis by the cash received, the remaining $10,000 is allocated to the inventory. Thus, the basis of the inventory in T's hands is $10,000, and the basis of the building is zero. Note that $10,000 of the inventory's original basis in the hands of the partnership appears to have been *lost* in the liquidating distribution. As discussed under OPTIONAL ADJUSTMENT TO BASIS OF PARTNERSHIP PROPERTY, the partnership may be able to "save" this portion of the inventory's basis by making an election to adjust the basis of its remaining inventory.

**Example 18.** Assume the same facts as in Example 17, except that there was no inventory and T received two buildings (neither building being subject to depreciation recapture). Assume further that Building 1 had a basis of $6,000 and Building 2 a basis of $9,000 to the partnership. Again, no gain or loss is recognized. Instead, the $10,000 basis of T's interest remaining after reduction for the cash received is simply allocated to the buildings in the ratio of their bases to the partnership. Thus, T's basis in Building 1 is $4,000 ($6/15 \times$ $10,000) and in Building 2 is $6,000 ($9/15 \times$ $10,000). The $5,000 of partnership basis in the buildings that could not be passed on to T may be *lost* in the distribution.

**Example 19.** When R's basis is $15,000, R receives a liquidating distribution of $7,000 cash and a proportionate share of inventory having a partnership basis of $3,000 and a fair market value of $10,000. Since R cannot allocate to the inventory more than $3,000 of the $8,000 remaining basis after reduction for cash, R recognizes a $5,000 capital loss on the liquidation, and the basis of the inventory is $3,000.

**Example 20.** Assume the same facts as in Example 19, except that R receives $19,000 of cash in addition to the inventory. Under these circumstances, R recognizes a capital gain of $4,000 (cash of $19,000 less $15,000 basis), and the inventory takes a zero basis.

Recall from Review of Nonliquidating Distributions at the beginning of this section that § 735 applies to the inventory distributed in the preceding examples. Thus, gain realized by the withdrawing partner on the subsequent disposition of the inventory is ordinary income unless the disposition occurs more than five years after the distribution. Presumably, anyone who receives the inventory from the withdrawing partner as a gift or by reason of death is not bound by the five-year holding period requirement. Also, it should be remembered that the withdrawing partner's holding period of all other property received in a liquidating distribution includes the partnership's related holding period.

## DISPROPORTIONATE DISTRIBUTIONS

Both the aggregate and entity concepts of partnerships are illustrated in the tax consequences of disproportionate distributions. A disproportionate distribution occurs when either less than or more than the partner's proportionate share of the partnership's unrealized receivables and substantially appreciated inventory (§ 751 property) is received. Recall that absent a special allocation agreement that has economic substance under § 704(b) or a required allocation under § 704(c), each partner has an interest in each asset of the partnership (the aggregate concept). Although § 741 provides that a partnership interest is a capital asset, remember that gain on the disposition of an interest attributable to unrealized receivables and substantially appreciated inventory (§ 751 property) is treated as ordinary income. Also remember that although proportionate distributions (either current or liquidating) of such property are subject to the general rules previously discussed, special rules apply to disproportionate distributions. Specifically, § 751(b) provides that to the extent (1) a partner receives § 751 property in exchange for the partner's interest in other property *or* (2) a partner receives other property in exchange for the partner's interest in § 751 property, the distribution is treated as a taxable exchange of properties between the partner and the partnership (the entity concept).

*Purpose Behind § 751(b).* Section 751(b) was placed in the Code to prevent an arbitrary allocation of ordinary income and capital gain items among partners. For example, substantially appreciated inventory (§ 751 property with ordinary income potential) might be distributed to a partner in a low tax bracket. At the same time, property with capital gain potential (non-Section 751 property) might be retained by the partnership primarily to benefit partners in a high tax bracket. This example is, in fact, a disproportionate distribution.

*Confusing Viewpoints.* Does § 736 apply to disproportionate distributions of in-kind property that terminate a partner's entire interest? On this point, the Code and Regulations lack certainty, and leading commentators have been unable to agree on their meaning. The discussion that follows does not assume such an application.[44]

*Transactions: Real and Fictional.* To understand the tax consequences of a disproportionate distribution of § 751 assets that terminates a partner's entire interest, it should be noted that two distributions must be considered: a real distribution and a fictional nonliquidating (current) distribution that precedes the real one. After the real distribution, the § 751 assets could be held exclusively by the leaving partner, by the partnership, or by both parties in some ratio disproportionate to their market value interests in such property before the distribution. If the ownership ratio in the § 751 assets is the same before and after the real distribution, the disproportionate rules of § 751 do not apply. If none of the § 751 assets are held by the leaving partner after the real distribution, the fictional distribution includes only this partner's share of these assets. If all of the § 751 assets are held by the leaving partner after the real distribution, the fictional distribution includes a portion of this partner's share of the non-Section 751 assets. This portion generally equals at market value the remaining partners' share of the § 751 assets. If the leaving partner does not hold all of the § 751 assets after the real distribution but holds § 751 assets in a ratio that exceeds such partner's share of assets before the distribution, the excess share received must be determined. The fair market value of this excess share of the § 751 assets received in the real distribution equals at-market value the leaving partner's share of the non-Section 751 assets received in the fictional distribution.

After the fictional distribution, the leaving partner fictionally sells (and the remaining partnership fictionally buys) all of the assets received in the fictional distribution and takes payment in some or all of the assets included in the real distribution. The partners can agree which assets are exchanged for an interest in § 751 assets. When the fictional distribution takes place, the leaving partner's interest is reduced by the distributed adjusted basis of the related assets to the partnership. When the fictional sale takes place, the leaving partner generally recognizes income and takes a basis in the assets received in payment equal to the market value paid. The nature (character) of the income recognized depends on the nature of the assets given up. Generally, this nature is determined at the partnership level. After the fictional distribution and sale, the remaining portion of the real distribution (which includes those assets or share of assets excluded from the fictional transactions) is taxed under § § 731 and 732. When the § 751 assets are included in the real distribution, § 735(a)

---

**44.** See Grover A. Cleveland, "Retirement Payments to Partners: Timing of Recognition of Income," *The Journal of Taxation* (August 1982), pp. 86–90, for an excellent discussion of the interplay between § § 736 and 751, the confusion caused by related Regulations, and the mixed positions taken by leading commentators.

generally maintains the ordinary income element of the leaving partner's share of these assets. In addition, § 732(c)(1) prevents a step-up in basis of the leaving partner's share of the § 751 assets.

*Disproportionate Distributions Illustrated.* The tax consequences of disproportionate distributions of § 751 assets are illustrated in the following examples.

**Example 21.** Partnership LMN has the following balance sheet:

*Assets*

|  | Adjusted Basis Per Books | Market Value |
|---|---|---|
| Trade accounts receivable | $ –0– | $ 18,000 |
| Other assets | 18,000 | 36,000 |
| Total | $ 18,000 | $ 54,000 |

*Liabilities and Capital*

| Capital accounts | | |
|---|---|---|
| L | $  6,000 | $18,000 |
| M | 6,000 | 18,000 |
| N | 6,000 | 18,000 |
| Total | $ 18,000 | $ 54,000 |

Assume that in liquidation of M's entire interest, the partnership distributes $6,000 of receivables and other assets with a fair market value of $12,000. Since M's exact share of all assets is received, the rules of § § 731 and 732 apply and the rules of § 751 do not apply. No gain or loss is recognized by M or by the partnership. The receivables have a zero basis in M's hands, and the other assets have a basis of $6,000 (the same as in the hands of the partnership).

**Example 22.** Now assume LMN distributes $18,000 worth of other assets in liquidation of M's entire interest. This is a *disproportionate distribution* subject to the provisions of § 751. M's share of the accounts receivable is treated as being distributed. M is then treated as having sold these receivables to the remaining partnership for an additional $6,000 of other property. The partnership is considered to have exchanged $6,000 of other property for M's interest in the receivables. M recognizes ordinary income of $6,000 ($6,000 fair market value of the excess share of other assets received − zero basis of M's share of accounts receivable surrendered). M takes a basis of $12,000 in other property received.

| | |
|---|---|
| M's interest before the distribution | $  6,000 |
| Less: Partnership's basis in receivables in fictional distribution (⅓ of $ —0—) | —0— |
| Basis of non-Section 751 assets excluded from the fictional transactions | $  6,000 |
| Plus: Fictional price paid to acquire non-Section 751 assets | 6,000 |
| Basis of all non-Section 751 assets received by M | $ 12,000 |

The partnership recognizes a gain of $3,000 on the exchange of other property ($6,000 fair market value of the excess share of accounts receivable retained by the partnership − $3,000 basis of the portion of other assets exchanged) and after the distribution holds receivables with a basis of $6,000 and other assets with a basis of $9,000. The nature of the gain depends on the nature of the assets given up. The capital accounts of L and N are $7,500 each. In addition, the partnership holds $12,000 of other receivables with a basis of zero. The impact of the liquidation on M's interest and on L's and N's interests could be analyzed as follows:

| M's Proportionate Share | Assets FMV | FMV Received | Fictional Dist. Basis | Fictional Sale FMV | Gain (Loss) |
|---|---|---|---|---|---|
| Trade accounts receivable | $ 6,000 | $ —0— | $ —0— | $ 6,000 | $ 6,000* |
| Other assets | 12,000 | 18,000 | —0— | —0— | N/A |
| | $ 18,000 | $ 18,000 | | $ 6,000 | |

*Ordinary income to M under § 751.

| L's & N's Proportionate Shares | Assets FMV | FMV Received | Fictional Paid Basis | Fictional Paid FMV | Gain (Loss) |
|---|---|---|---|---|---|
| Trade accounts receivable | $ 12,000 | $ 18,000 | $ —0— | $ —0— | $ N/A |
| Other assets | 24,000 | 18,000 | 3,000 | 6,000 | 3,000** |
| | $ 36,000 | $ 36,000 | | $ 6,000 | |

**Nature of gain depends on the nature of assets given up.

**Example 23.** Now assume the partnership distributes $18,000 of receivables in liquidation of M's entire interest. This is also a § 751 distribution. M is considered to have received a distribution of non-Section 751 assets equal to the market value of the remaining partners' share of the § 751 assets. Then M is considered to have exchanged the non-Section 751 assets for an additional $12,000 worth of receivables. M recognizes a gain of $6,000 on the exchange ($12,000 fair market value of the excess share of accounts receivable received − $6,000 basis of the other assets surrendered) and after the distribution has $12,000 worth of receivables with a basis of $12,000, plus an additional $6,000 of receivables with a basis of zero.

| | |
|---|---|
| M's interest before the distribution | $ 6,000 |
| Less: Partnership's basis in non-Section 751 assets in fictional distribution [⅔ of remaining partners' market value share of § 751 assets, matched with an equal amount of non-Section 751 assets in the distribution, reduced to partnership's basis—50% of (⅔ × $18,000)] | 6,000 |
| Basis of § 751 assets excluded from the fictional transactions | —0— |
| Plus: Fictional price paid to acquire § 751 assets | 12,000 |
| Basis of all § 751 assets acquired by M | $ 12,000 |

The partnership is considered to have exchanged $12,000 of receivables for M's interest in other property. It recognizes ordinary income of $12,000 ($12,000 fair market value of excess share of other assets retained by the partnership – zero basis of accounts receivable distributed in excess of M's share) and after the distribution has $36,000 of other property with an adjusted basis of $24,000 (original basis of $18,000 plus $6,000 gain recognized by M). The capital accounts of L and N are $12,000 each.

*Income Event.* In evaluating Examples 22 and 23, note that it is not the *receipt* of property that triggers the recognition of income but rather the exchange. Thus, in disproportionate distributions, the receipt of § 751 property requires recognition of gain or loss attributable to an interest relinquished in other property. Similarly, the receipt of other property requires the recognition of income attributable to relinquished § 751 property. Further, the partner normally receives the property interest the partnership is considered to have exchanged, while the partnership retains the property interest the partner is considered to have exchanged.

*Exceptions.* Section 751(b)(2)(A) provides an exception to the general rule of § 751. A distribution to a partner of property that the partner contributed to the partnership is not considered a § 751 distribution, notwithstanding that the distribution is otherwise disproportionate. Additionally, § 751(b)(2)(B) provides that § 751 does not apply to distributions described in § 736(a). Recall that such liquidating distributions are treated as a distribution of profit or as a guaranteed payment and are already subject to ordinary income treatment.

> **Example 24.** Assume the same facts as in Example 22, except that the $18,000 worth of other property distributed to M was originally contributed by M. In this case, § 751 does not apply; and under §§ 731 and 732, neither M nor the partnership recognizes gain or loss. M has a basis of $6,000 in the property distributed. The partnership holds $18,000 of receivables with a basis of zero and other property worth $18,000 with a basis of $9,000. The capital accounts of L and N are $6,000 each. Note that in this case there has been a "loss" of basis of $3,000 to the partnership without tax benefit ($18,000 original basis – $6,000 basis to withdrawing partner M – $9,000 basis left with the partnership).

# OPTIONAL ADJUSTMENT TO BASIS OF PARTNERSHIP PROPERTY

Except to the extent that § 751 applies, the basis of property in the hands of a continuing partnership is not adjusted as a result of the transfer of a partnership interest or on account of current or liquidating distributions. In some situations, this rule produces inequitable results. For example, consider a partnership that owns a building with a basis of $300,000 and a fair market value of $900,000. Assume an individual buys a one-third interest in the partnership for $300,000 (an amount equal to one-third of the value of the building). Although the price paid for the interest was based on fair market value, the building's depreciation continues to be determined on the partnership's related basis of $300,000, of which the new partner's share is only $100,000.

In other situations, an effective loss of basis without tax benefit results. Consider again Example 24. L and N have effectively exchanged property with a basis of $9,000 for a partnership interest with a basis of $6,000. Since no gain or loss is recognized, $3,000 of basis is *lost*. However, the bases of the remaining partners' (L and N) interests are not diminished; each retains a balance of $6,000. Partnership income may be overstated, since it reflects depreciation on $9,000 of other assets instead of the true investment of L and N of $12,000. This point would be clearer if the partnership had liquidated M's interest for a cash payment of $18,000. The partnership would have effectively paid the full fair market value for M's interest of $6,000 in receivables and $12,000 in other property. Nevertheless, under the general rule, the basis of the receivables is zero and the basis of the other property is $18,000.

The general rules also can produce *inequitable* benefits. For example, a partner who purchases a one-third interest in a partnership owning a building with a fair market value of $300,000 and an adjusted basis of $600,000 obtains the benefits of a *double* depreciation deduction. Likewise, a partnership that redeems a partner's interest for a cash payment less than the retired partner's share of the adjusted basis of the partnership assets does not reduce the basis of those assets. To prevent or alleviate these results, § 754 permits partnerships to make a special election under which the basis of partnership assets may be adjusted following either a sale or exchange of an interest or a distribution of partnership property.

## SALE OR EXCHANGE OF AN INTEREST

If an election under § 754 is in effect and if a partner's interest is sold or exchanged, the partner dies, or a § 761(e) distribution is made, § 743(b) provides that the partnership shall effect one of the following:

1.  *Increase* the adjusted basis of partnership property by:

| | |
|---|---|
| Transferee's interest basis in partnership | $ XXX |
| Less: Transferee's share of adjusted basis of all partnership property | XXX |
| Increase | $ XXX |

2.  *Decrease* the adjusted basis of partnership property by:

| | |
|---|---|
| Transferee's share of adjusted basis of all partnership property | $ XXX |
| Less: Transferee's interest basis in partnership | XXX |
| Decrease | $ XXX |

The amount of the increase or decrease constitutes an adjustment affecting the basis of partnership property with respect to the transferee partner only. Thus, for purposes of depreciation, depletion, gain or loss, and distributions, the transferee partner has a special basis for those partnership properties that are adjusted under § 743(b). This special basis is the partner's share of the common partnership basis (i. e., the adjusted basis of such properties to the partnership without regard to any special basis adjustment of any transferee) *plus or minus* any special basis adjustments. A partner's share of the adjusted basis of partnership property is equal to the sum of the partner's interest in partnership capital, surplus, and partnership liabilities. Generally, if a partner's interest in partnership capital and profits is one-third, the partner's share of the adjusted basis of partnership property is one-third.[45]

**Example 25.** R is a member of the RST Partnership, and all partners have equal interests in capital and profits. The partnership has made a § 754 election. R's interest is sold to U for $66,000 plus R's share of the partnership debt. The balance sheet of the partnership at the date of the sale shows the following:

*Assets*

|  | Adjusted Basis Per Books | Market Value |
|---|---|---|
| Cash | $ 15,000 | $ 15,000 |
| Accounts receivable | 30,000 | 30,000 |
| Inventory | 60,000 | 63,000 |
| Depreciable assets | 60,000 | 120,000 |
| Total | $ 165,000 | $ 228,000 |

*Liabilities and Capital*

|  | | |
|---|---|---|
| Liabilities | $ 30,000 | $ 30,000 |
| Capital accounts | | |
| R | 45,000 | 66,000 |
| S | 45,000 | 66,000 |
| T | 45,000 | 66,000 |
| Total | $ 165,000 | $ 228,000 |

The amount of the adjustment under § 743(b) is the difference between the basis of the transferee's interest in the partnership and the transferee's share of the adjusted basis of partnership property. Under § 742, the basis of U's interest is $76,000 (the cash paid for R's interest of $66,000 plus U's $10,000 share of partnership liabilities). U's share of the adjusted basis of partnership property is $55,000 (i. e., $45,000 plus $10,000). The amount of the adjustment (to be added to the basis of partnership property) is $21,000:

| | |
|---|---|
| Transferee's interest basis in partnership | $ 76,000 |
| Less: Transferee's share of adjusted basis of all partnership property | 55,000 |
| Increase | $ 21,000 |

---

**45.**   Reg. § 1.743–1(b)(1).

This amount is allocated to partnership property in accordance with the rules set forth in § 755 and the Regulations thereunder.[46]

Under LIQUIDATING AND DISPROPORTIONATE PARTNERSHIP DISTRIBUTIONS—General Nature of Liquidating Distributions—it was noted that as a result of the Deficit Reduction Act of 1984, § 761(e) was inserted into the Code. This provision was aimed at distributions of partnership interests in tiered partnerships by corporations and partnerships. When such an event takes place, § 761(e) treats the distribution as an exchange for purposes of § § 708 and 743 and any other provision specified in statutory regulations (to be issued). Does this provision apply to redemptions of partnership interests, or is it limited to distributions of partnership interests? Although the limitation is mentioned in the Committee Reports, no such limitation is found in the provision itself. The new § 761(e) statutory regulations (when issued) should be checked carefully to see if they provide clarity to the situation. Example 30 illustrates the need for a § 743 adjustment when a partnership interest is distributed, and Example 31 shows how such adjustment takes place.

## PARTNERSHIP DISTRIBUTIONS

If an election under § 754 is in effect, the basis of partnership property is increased upon a distribution to a partner under § 734 by the following:

—The amount of any gain recognized by a distributee partner, and

—The excess of the adjusted basis of any property distributed in the hands of the partnership immediately before the distribution over the adjusted basis of that property in the hands of the distributee.

Conversely, the basis of partnership property is decreased by the following:

—Any loss recognized by a distributee partner, and

—In the case of a liquidating distribution, the excess of the adjusted basis of any property distributed in the hands of the distributee over the basis of such property in the hands of the partnership immediately before the distribution.

**Example 26.** T has a partnership basis of $30,000 and receives a § 736(b) payment of $75,000 which terminates T's interest. Gain of $45,000 is recognized, and the partnership increases the basis of its property by such amount if the partnership has a § 754 election in effect.

**Example 27.** Assume the same facts as in Example 26, except that T receives only $10,000. The loss recognized by T under § 731(a)(2) is $20,000, and the partnership reduces the basis of its remaining property by this amount if the partnership has a § 754 election in effect.

**Example 28.** R has a partnership basis of $50,000 and receives a building having an adjusted basis to the partnership of $120,000,

---

**46.** Reg. § 1.743–1(b)(1) (Ex. 1).

which terminates R's interest. The building's basis in R's hands is $50,000 [§ 732(b)]. If a § 754 election is in effect, the partnership increases the basis of its remaining property by $70,000:

| | |
|---|---|
| Partnership's adjusted basis in distributed property | $ 120,000 |
| Less: distributee's basis in distributed property | 50,000 |
| Total | $ 70,000 |

**Example 29.** Assume the same facts as in Example 28, except that the partnership's basis in the building was $40,000. R's basis in the building is still $50,000, and the partnership reduces the basis of its remaining property by $10,000:

| | |
|---|---|
| Distributee's basis in distributed property | $ 50,000 |
| Less: Partnership's adjusted basis in distributed property | 40,000 |
| Total | $ 10,000 |

The amount of any required adjustment is allocated to the partnership property in the manner prescribed by § 755 and the Regulations thereunder.

## MAKING THE ELECTION

An election can be made under § 754 for any year in which a transfer or distribution occurs by attaching a statement to a timely filed partnership return (including extensions). If made, the election applies to transfers of interest governed by § 743 [i. e., sales, exchanges, death of a partner, and § 761(e) distributions] and distributions governed by § 734. The election cannot be made to apply to only one section or the other. Note, however, that adjustments can be made only in the case of distributions described in § 731 or § 736(b). No adjustment will be made for § 736(a) payments treated as profit distributions or guaranteed payments.[47]

An election is binding for the year for which made and for all subsequent years unless the IRS consents to its revocation. Permission to revoke is generally granted for good business reasons, such as a change in the nature of the business or an increase in the frequency of transfers of interest. Permission is not granted if it appears the primary purpose is to avoid downward adjustments to basis otherwise required under the election.[48]

Before the Deficit Reduction Act of 1984, it was possible in tiered partnerships to utilize advantageously a § 754 election and the related basis adjustment rules of § 734. The following example illustrates this technique:

**Example 30.** The AB Partnership, which had a § 754 election in effect, owned two assets:

---

**47.** Reg. § 1.754–1(b).
**48.** Reg. § 1.754–1(c).

|  | Adjusted Basis | FMV |
|---|---|---|
| Land 1 | $ –0– | $ 100 |
| Land 2 | 100 | 100 |
| Total assets | $ 100 | $ 200 |

Partner A, who had a controlling interest in AB, had a zero interest basis. To reinvest the proceeds in more productive assets, AB wanted to sell Land 1 and Land 2 without recognizing a gain. To accomplish its objectives, AB formed the CD Partnership and contributed Land 2 for a 99% interest in capital and profits. Under § 723 the basis of Land 2 to CD was $100, and under § 722 the basis of AB's interest in CD was $100. CD did not make a § 754 election. AB then distributed its investment in CD to A in a nonliquidating distribution. Since A's interest basis in AB was zero, A took a zero basis in CD under § 732. As long as A's interest in CD is retained, the zero basis in CD has no effect. Since AB had a § 754 election in effect, it had a special basis adjustment increase of $100 for Land 1. At this point, AB sold Land 1 for $100 without recognizing a gain [$100 selling price less (zero common basis plus $100 special basis adjustment)]. It then reinvested the $100 in another asset that was more productive. A later had CD sell Land 2 for the fair market value of $100 without recognizing a gain and reinvest the proceeds in a more productive asset. What was the net effect of these transactions? In essence, the investment in both land parcels was shifted without gain recognition.

The Deficit Reduction Act of 1984 (DRA) eliminated this opportunity for manipulation through an added sentence at the end of § 734(b) and the insertion of new provision § 761(e). The sentence at the end of § 734(b) indicates that a special basis adjustment for the distributing partnership's assets under § 734(b)(1)(B) shall not take place if the distributed property is an interest in another partnership that does not have a § 754 election in effect. Without the insertion of new provision § 761(e), a § 754 election by the partnership whose interest is distributed would have no effect. In other words, the partnership whose interest is distributed would not have a special basis adjustment for its assets under § 743 because there was no sale, exchange, or partner's death. New provision § 761(e) solves this problem. It indicates that distributions are to be treated as exchanges for purposes of § 743. As mentioned earlier, the Committee Reports accompanying DRA indicate that § 761(e) is applicable when an interest in a partnership is distributed.

**Example 31.** Assume the same facts as in Example 30 with the following exceptions: (1) DRA has been enacted, and (2) CD has made a proper election under § 754. Under § 743(b)(2), A has a special basis adjustment decrease in CD's Land 2 of $99 (the difference between A's $99 share of the basis in this asset and A's zero interest basis in CD). When CD sells Land 2, A will receive a gain of $99 [$100 selling price less ($100 common basis minus $99 special basis adjustment)].

# SPECIAL PARTNERSHIP PROBLEMS

In addition to the topical areas discussed thus far, two problem areas remain: family partnerships and limited partnerships. These areas can present substantial problems for taxpayers and their advisers. Unfortunately, time and space limitations preclude an in-depth treatment of each. However, the topics are briefly discussed in the following sections.[49]

## FAMILY PARTNERSHIPS

Under § 704(e), family partnerships require special treatment because of the close association of partners. Distributive shares of partnership income may be channeled to low tax bracket partners (e. g., children) who perform little, if any, real service for the partnership.

*Family Members.* The family, for purposes of § 704(e), includes only husband and wife, ancestors, lineal descendants, and any trusts for the primary benefit of such persons. Note that brothers and sisters are not included.[50] A family member will be recognized as a partner in either of the following cases:

—Capital is a material income-producing factor, and the family member's capital interest is acquired in a bona fide transaction (even if by gift or purchase from another family member), in which ownership, dominion, and control are received.[51]

—Capital is not a material income-producing factor, but the family member contributes substantial or vital services.[52]

*Capital.* If a substantial portion of the partnership's gross income results from the use of capital, such as substantial inventories or investments in plant, machinery, or equipment, it is considered to be a material income-producing factor. If most of the partnership's capital results from borrowings, however, the anticipated allocation of partnership profits might be disallowed.

In a 1974 decision, the Tax Court dealt with a unique interpretation of what constituted *capital* for purposes of the test of capital as a material income-producing factor.[53] The case involved a corporate general partner (owned 79.5 percent by an individual) and five trusts as limited partners (each of which had been established by this same individual). The corporation contributed $556, while each of the trusts contributed $1,000 to the

---

49. For an excellent discussion of the problems associated with the transfer of a partnership interest for services, see Cowan, "Receipt of a Partnership Interest for Services," *32nd. N.Y.U. Tax Institute,* Vol. 2 (1974), p. 1501. For a more in-depth discussion of family and limited partnerships, see Arthur B. Willis, John S. Pennell, and Philip F. Postlewaite, *Partnership Taxation,* Third Edition (Colorado Springs, Colorado: McGraw-Hill Book Co., 1982 with updates), Chapters 17–18.

50.  § 704(e)(3).

51.  § 704(e)(1). Also see *Ginsberg v. Commissioner,* 74–2 USTC ¶ 9660, 34 AFTR2d 74–5760, 502 F.2d 965 (CA–6, 1974), *aff'g.* 32 TCM 1019, T.C.Memo. 1973–220, where the donor retained such control that the donee's ownership interest was deemed illusory. As a result, the donor was considered the partner for tax purposes.

52.  Reg. § 1.704–1(e).

53.  *Carriage Square, Inc.,* 69 T.C. 119 (1977).

capital of the partnership. The partnership agreement provided that the partners were to participate in profits or losses in proportion to their capital contributions. The partnership borrowed substantial amounts of capital, principally as a result of loan guarantees from the individual owning stock in the corporate partner and also the grantor of the five trusts. In reviewing the allocation of more than $300,000 of profits over the first three years of partnership operations, the Court concluded that borrowed capital was not capital of the partnership for purposes of the test of capital as a material income-producing factor. As a result, the allocation of more than 90 percent of the partnership's profits to the trusts was disallowed, and the Court concluded that the arrangement was not a partnership.

Ordinarily, capital is not a material income-producing factor if the income of the business consists principally of fees, commissions, or other compensation for personal services performed by members or employees of the partnership.[54] To alleviate the uncertainty of whether capital is a material income-producing factor in family partnerships, many taxpayers and their advisers might be inclined to request an individual ruling from the IRS. Unfortunately, the IRS has indicated it will not rule on this issue.[55]

A capital interest in a partnership is an interest in the partnership's assets distributable to the owner of the capital interest upon withdrawal from, or liquidation of, the partnership. Thus, the mere right to share in earnings and profits is not a capital interest in the partnership.[56]

*Gift of Capital Interest.* If a family member acquires a capital interest by gift in a family partnership in which capital is a material income-producing factor, limitations exist on the amount of income that may be allocated to this interest. First, the donor of the interest must be allowed an amount of partnership income that represents reasonable compensation for services to the partnership.[57] Then, the remaining income is generally divided among the partners according to their agreement for sharing partnership profits or losses. However, the portion of the remaining income allocated to the donee may not be greater than the amount allocated to the donor in proportion to their respective capital interests.[58] Further, an interest purchased by one family member from another is considered to be created by gift for the purpose of reallocation.[59]

> **Example 32.** A partnership in which a 50% interest was transferred by sale between a parent and child (considered a gift) had a profit of $90,000 in the current year. Capital is a material income-producing factor. The parent performed services valued at $20,000. The child performed no services. Under these circumstances, $20,000 must be allocated to the parent as compensation. Of the remaining $70,000 of income attributable to capital, at least 50%, or $35,000, must be allocated to the parent. The child's share cannot exceed $35,000.

---

54. Reg. § 1.704–1(e)(1)(iv).
55. Rev.Proc. 86–3, I.R.B. No. 1, 26.
56. Reg. § 1.704–1(e)(1)(v).
57. § 704(e)(2).
58. Reg. § 1.704–1(e)(3)(i)(a).
59. § 704(e)(3).

## LIMITED PARTNERSHIPS

Limited partnerships have been used as a tax shelter in such activities as oil drilling ventures, real estate development, cattle feeding, and motion picture production to provide investors with tax advantages (i. e., pass-through of losses and capital gain treatment) while limiting liability to original investment.[60]

*Historical Perspective.*  Before 1976, nonrecourse financing was vigorously used by limited partnerships to permit loss deductions far in excess of the partners' original investment. Such deductions were possible because the Regulations permitted all partners of a limited partnership to share nonrecourse liabilities under § 752(c) for basis purposes in the same proportion as they shared profits.[61] Many of these arrangements were promoted as providing investors in the venture's early years with positive cash flows and tax deductions in multiples of two to three times the dollar amounts initially invested.

When an investment proved profitable, the limited partners were faced with reporting their respective shares of partnership profits which, rather than being distributed in cash, were used to retire the partnership's nonrecourse debt. To offset the tax consequences of reporting "illusory income," investors sought additional shelters. If an investment proved to be economically unsound, investors either abandoned or forfeited their limited partnership interests or made a gift of them to any willing (and perhaps unknowing) donee. Allegedly, many dispositions of limited partnership interests went unreported or undetected because of inadequate tax reporting and the strained audit capability of the IRS.

Congressional reaction to the extensive use of limited partnerships as a shelter device resulted in modifications to the Internal Revenue Code. The Tax Reform Act of 1976 introduced two major changes that affected limited partnerships. First, § 704(d) was amended to provide that losses from a partnership that could be deducted by a partner would be limited to the basis of the partner's interest determined without regard to nonrecourse liabilities incurred after 1976. This provision did not apply to partnerships whose principal activity was investing in real estate (other than mineral property) or to any activity covered by § 465. Second, § 465 was inserted into the Code for tax years beginning after 1975 to restrict loss deductions for certain taxpayers (individuals, personal holding companies, and S corporations) from four specified activities to the extent of their at-risk investment. Like amended § 704(d), this provision operated to prohibit a partner from deducting losses against that portion of the partner's interest basis represented by nonrecourse debt. The four specified activities were as follows:

1.  Holding, producing, or distributing motion pictures or videotapes.

2.  Farming, except farming activities involving trees other than fruit or nut trees.

---

**60.**  Although a similar result may be achieved by forming a corporation followed by an S election, the shareholder limit imposed by § 1361(b)(1) may restrict the amount of capital that can be raised through this approach.

**61.**  Reg. § 1.752–1(e).

3. Equipment leasing.

4. Exploring for or exploiting oil and gas resources.

Under either set of at-risk rules, losses not allowed as deductions in the current tax year could be carried forward until the taxpayer had sufficient capital at risk in the activity to absorb them. Additionally, the activity list was expanded via the Energy Tax Act of 1978 to include exploring for or exploiting § 613(e) geothermal deposits.

Immediately after enactment of the Tax Reform Act of 1976, taxpayers and their advisers sought ways to circumvent the at-risk rules by either avoiding the partnership form or not engaging in any of the specified activities. As a result, master recordings, books, monographs, and coal were used as tax shelters. The IRS countered these shifts by issuing numerous rulings setting forth its opposition[62] and by requesting legislation to strengthen the at-risk rules to prevent further erosion of the tax base. Congressional response was reflected in the Revenue Act of 1978.

*Contemporary At-Risk Rules.* For tax years beginning after 1978, the Revenue Act of 1978 repealed § 704(d) and expanded the at-risk rules of § 465 to cover all taxpayers, including regular corporations when closely-held,[63] and (with two specific exceptions) all activities engaged in by a taxpayer in carrying on a trade or business or for the production of income.[64] The two exceptions are the holding of real property (other than mineral property) and the leasing of § 1245 equipment by certain closely-held corporations.[65] Since the § 704(d) provision restricting loss deductions was now covered by § 465, it was repealed for tax years beginning after 1978.

A corporation is considered to be closely-held if five or fewer individuals own more than 50 percent of the stock. The stock ownership rules of § 542(a)(2), using the attribution rules of § 318, are applied in determining if a corporation is closely-held. A closely-held corporation engaged in equipment leasing may qualify for a specific exemption. If 50 percent or more of its gross receipts for the tax year are from equipment-leasing activities, the closely-held corporation is not subject to § 465.[66] However, if losses are disallowed for a given tax year because the corporation does not meet the requirement for exclusion, such losses can be deducted in any subsequent tax year in which the requirement is met.

Another change introduced by the Revenue Act of 1978 deals with a special recapture rule applicable to previously allowed losses.[67] If a taxpayer's amount at risk under § 465 at the end of any tax year is less than zero, the taxpayer is required to include the excess in gross income for that year. The taxpayer is entitled to treat the amount so included as a deduction

---

**62.** See, for example, Rev.Rul. 77–397, 77–398, and 77–401 (1977–2 C.B. 178, 179, and 215, respectively). These are only three of nine rulings issued by the IRS on October 31, 1977, aimed at tax shelters. Because of the date of their issuance, these pronouncements have been termed the "Halloween Rulings."

**63.** § 465(a)(1).

**64.** § 465(c).

**65.** § § 465(c)(3)(D) and (c)(4).

**66.** § 465(c)(4)(A).

**67.** § 465(e).

allocable to that activity for the first succeeding taxable year. Negative amounts at risk can occur as a result of distributions and conversion of recourse to nonrecourse debt. It is important to note that the special recapture rule is not applicable to negative amounts at risk resulting from losses allowed before 1979. Thus, if the taxpayer's capital at risk at the close of the last tax year beginning before 1979 was less than zero, the recapture rule is applied as if the amount at risk were zero on that date.[68]

The following examples illustrate some of the at-risk rules:

**Example 33.** T invests $10,000 cash in the GT Limited Partnership in the current year for a 10% limited liability interest in capital and profits. Shortly thereafter, the partnership acquires real estate subject to a nonrecourse mortgage of $150,000. T's share of losses from the first year of operations is $23,000. Even though T has only $10,000 of capital at risk in the activity, T's partnership interest is increased by $15,000 under Regulation § 1.752–1(e) (10% share of the $150,000 debt) and T is allowed to claim the full share of the losses. Note that real estate activities are exempt from the at-risk rules.

**Example 34.** Assume the same facts as in Example 33, except that the partnership acquired the distribution rights to a motion picture (rather than real estate) with a nonrecourse mortgage. T's deduction for the loss is limited to $10,000 of capital at risk in the venture. The $13,000 of excess losses would have to be carried forward to a tax year in which T has more capital at risk to be deducted.

**Example 35.** U invests $5,000 in the CC Limited Partnership in the current year for an interest in capital and profits as a general partner. Shortly thereafter, the partnership acquires the master recording of a well-known vocal artist for $50,000 cash and a $200,000 *recourse* mortgage. U's share of the recourse debt is $10,000, and his basis in the partnership is $15,000 ($5,000 cash investment plus $10,000 share of the recourse debt). U's share of partnership losses in the first year of operations (due principally to depreciation of a master disc) is $11,000. Under these circumstances, U is entitled to deduct $11,000 of partnership losses, because the at-risk rules of § 465 do not apply.

**Example 36.** Assume the same facts as in Example 35. After deducting the share of losses from the partnership's first year of operations, U's basis in the partnership interest is $4,000 ($15,000 − $11,000). If the recourse debt is converted into nonrecourse debt in the second year of partnership operations, U is required to recapture $6,000 of excess losses claimed in the earlier year. This amount represents the negative amount of capital U has at risk in the activity ($5,000 − $11,000). However, U can carry these losses forward to subsequent years.

The next major piece of at-risk legislation to have an impact on tax shelters was the Economic Recovery Tax Act of 1981 (ERTA). Through ERTA, Congress enacted at-risk rules for investment tax credit property

---

**68.** § 465(e)(2).

placed in service after February 18, 1981. These rules are applicable to the same taxpayers and activities found in § 465. A credit is allowed for the portion of qualified ITC property to the extent invested amounts are at risk. All invested amounts borrowed, including nonrecourse debt, from a qualified person or a Federal, state, or local government (or related instrumentality) are considered to be at risk if the taxpayer at all times has a 20 percent at-risk investment in the property and the amount was not borrowed from a related person. A qualified person is an insurance company, a pension trust, a § 128(c)(2) lending institution, or any other person regularly engaged in the business of lending money. The Deficit Reduction Act of 1984 moved the definition of a related party from § 267(b) to § 168(e)(4).

*Guaranteed Nonrecourse Debt.* Congress was concerned about the ability of general partners to guarantee nonrecourse debt without altering its character. In *Raphan*[69] the U. S. Claims Court indicated that the guarantee of nonrecourse debt by a general partner was really the guarantee of the partner acting in a nonpartner capacity. Thus, the liability remained nonrecourse, and all partners under § 752 would share in the debt for interest basis purposes. As a result, all partners were allowed to increase their deductible losses from partnership operations. Through the Deficit Reduction Act of 1984, Congress instructed the Treasury not to follow *Raphan* and to update and revise its regulation under § 752 to take account of current commercial practices and arrangements, such as assumptions, guarantees, indemnities, and similar arrangements.

*Corporate General Partner.* Another problem confronting limited partnerships is the required assumption of unlimited liability by the general partner or partners. A variation of the limited partnership that is used to solve this problem is to make the general partner a corporation. Whether such an arrangement is recognized for tax purposes depends upon the application of Rev.Proc. 72–13.[70] A limited partnership with a corporation as the sole general partner is recognized as such if the following requirements are met:

1. The limited partners do not own directly or indirectly, individually, or in the aggregate, over 20 percent of the corporate general partner's stock, including the stock of any of its affiliates.

2. If the corporate general partner has an interest in only one limited partnership and total contributions to that partnership are under $2,500,000, the net worth of such partner at all times must be at least 15 percent of that total or $250,000, whichever is less. If total contributions are $2,500,000 or more, the net worth of such a partner must at all times be at least 10 percent of total contributions. Net worth for this purpose excludes such partner's interest in the limited partnership and accounts and notes receivable from and payable to the limited partnership.

---

**69.** *Raphan v. U. S.,* 83–2 USTC ¶ 9613, 52 AFTR2d 83–5987, 3 Cl.Ct. 457 (Cls.Ct., 1983), *affd. in part, rev'd. in part,* in 85–1 USTC ¶ 9297, 85 AFTR2d 85–1154, 759 F.2d 879 (Fed. Cir., 1985).
**70.** 1972–1 C.B. 735.

3. If the corporate general partner has an interest in more than one limited partnership, the above net worth requirements are applied separately for each limited partnership, and such partner must at all times have (exclusive of any interest in, and notes and accounts receivable from and payable to, any limited partnership in which such partner has any interest) a net worth at least equal to the sum of the amounts required under item 2 for each separate limited partnership.

4. The current fair market value of corporate assets must be used for purposes of computing the net worth of the corporate general partner (items 2 and 3).

5. The purchase of a limited partnership interest by a limited partner does not entail either a mandatory or discretionary purchase or an option to purchase any type of security of the corporate general partner or its affiliate.

6. The organization and operation of the limited partnership must be in accordance with the applicable state statute relating to limited partnerships.

Because of the tax-shelter advantages of limited partnerships, the IRS has attempted to restrict and even eliminate their use in certain areas. Since limited partnerships have many characteristics similar to those of

---

## Concept Summary

1. A partner's partnership interest is a capital asset and generally results in a capital gain or loss on disposal.

2. The basis of a partner's partnership interest includes a share of the partnership debt. Generally, the debt share is determined by the partner's loss sharing ratio. When the debt is *recourse* of a limited partnership, only the general partners share in it. If the debt is *nonrecourse,* the general and limited partnerships share in it according to their profit sharing ratios.

3. The interest bases of the selling and buying partners include an appropriate share of the partnership debt. Thus, the selling price and purchase price also include such a debt share.

4. The sale of a partnership interest may trigger investment tax credit (ITC) recapture, and the buying partner may be denied a used property ITC if one of several relationships between the buyer and seller is present.

5. When hot assets are present, ordinary income may be recognized on the disposal of a partner's interest or when partnership property is distributed to a partner. The term "hot assets" refers to unrealized receivables and substantially appreciated inventory.

6. Unrealized receivables include amounts earned by a cash basis taxpayer from services rendered or to be rendered and inventory delivered or to be delivered to the extent the proceeds would be treated as being from the sale or exchange of property other than a capital asset. In addition, unrealized receivables include the fair market portion of the depreciation recapture potential under §§ 1245 and 1250 that would result if the underlying asset were sold. The basis of this recapture potential is zero.

7. Substantially appreciated inventory includes virtually all property except money, capital assets, and § 1231 property. Inventory is considered to be substantially appreciated if at the time of its sale or distribution its aggregate fair market value exceeds 120 percent of its adjusted basis and if its fair market value is more than 10 percent of the fair market value of all partnership property exclusive of cash. This definition encompasses unrealized receivables.

8. When determining if a partnership has hot assets, the partnership is treated as owning a proportionate share of all the assets of any partnership in which it is a partner.

9. If a partnership has hot assets and a distribution causes the interests of the partners in these assets to change (i. e., a disproportionate distribution takes place), ordinary income is recognized. Sometimes this income is recognized by the partnership, and at other times it is recognized by the distributee partner.

10. The partnership recognizes ordinary income from the disproportionate distribution of hot assets when the partners who did not receive these assets have their fair market value interests in them reduced. The distributee partner recognizes ordinary income when his or her fair market value interest in these assets is reduced.

11. When a partnership is incorporated, it is important to select the appropriate incorporation method to prevent potential disastrous results. If the corporation plans to issue § 1244 stock, the original shareholders and not the partnership must be the partners. If an S corporation election is to be made, the election will be invalid if the partnership is a shareholder.

12. If a partner's interest is liquidated by a distribution of money, cash payments in excess of the partner's share of the recorded goodwill basis is generally ordinary income. Such payments are treated as an income distribution if determined by reference to the partnership income or as a guaranteed payment if not so determined. If the partnership agreement calls for goodwill payments in excess of the partner's share of its recorded basis, such payments are generally treated as a capital gain to the extent of the excess.

13. Cash payments for a partner's interest in partnership property essentially are treated as current (nonliquidating) distributions. Such payments do not include payments for the partner's interest in the partnership's goodwill (to the extent not provided for in the partnership agreement) or in unrealized receivables. If substantially appreciated inventory is present, ordinary income is created.

14. The like-kind exchange rules of § 1031 do not apply to the exchange of partnership interests in different partnerships.

15. When a partnership interest is sold and the outside basis of the incoming partner's interest does not equal that partner's inside basis, or if a distribution of partnership assets is made and the basis of the assets to the distributee is not a carryover basis but is determined by reference to the partner's outside interest basis, a special basis adjustment is possible. To obtain this adjustment, the partnership must either make or have in effect an election under § 754 of the Code. The special basis adjustment is made under the rules of § 734 when a distribution is involved and under § 743 when a sale is involved.

corporations, the IRS has considered some to be corporations for Federal income tax purposes.[71] Thus, if investors want the tax benefits of the partnership form, it is crucial that the requirements of Rev.Proc. 72–13 be fulfilled. One means of assuring that a limited partnership is recognized as

---

**71.** See, however, *Phillip G. Larson,* 66 T.C. 159, *acq.* in 1979–1 C.B. 1, and *Zuckman v. U. S.,* 75–2 USTC ¶ 9778, 36 AFTR2d 75–6193, 524 F.2d 729 (Ct.Cls., 1975). In each of these cases, the IRS tried unsuccessfully to treat a limited partnership with a corporate general partner as an association and thereby taxable as a corporation. See also Rev.Rul. 79–106, 1979–1 C.B. 448.

such for tax purposes is to obtain an advance ruling from the IRS. It should be noted, however, that such ruling requests are subject to tight restrictions.[72]

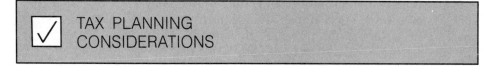

TAX PLANNING
CONSIDERATIONS

# SALES AND EXCHANGES OF PARTNERSHIP INTERESTS

## DELAYING ORDINARY INCOME ON THE SALE OF A PARTNERSHIP INTEREST

Several unexpected tax consequences that can be associated with the sale or other disposition of a partnership interest merit review. First, § 741 treats a partnership interest as a capital asset, the sale or exchange of which results in the recognition of capital gain or loss. This provision represents an application of the entity concept of partnerships. Remember, however, that under § 751 any gain attributable to the transferor partner's share of unrealized receivables or substantially appreciated inventory items will be treated as ordinary income. Consequently, a partner planning to dispose of a partnership interest in a taxable transaction might consider either an installment sale or a pro rata distribution of the partner's share of § 751 assets, followed by a sale of the remaining interest in the partnership. Although the subsequent disposition of the § 751 assets usually results in ordinary income, the partner can spread the income tax consequences over more than one tax year.

## BUNCHING OF INCOME

The sale or exchange of a partner's entire interest in a partnership may also result in an unexpected bunching of income. Keep in mind that the partnership's tax year closes as of the date of the transfer, and as a result, the transferor partner's distributive share of partnership income may have to be reported as of that date. Proper timing of the sale or exchange could alleviate the bunching problem. However, the sale or exchange also may result in a complete termination of the partnership. Such an event could have devastating effects on both the transferor partner and the remaining partners. If the transaction results in the sale or exchange of 50 percent or more of the total interest in partnership capital and profits within any 12-month period, the partnership is deemed to terminate under § 708. This possibility could be avoided by prohibiting any potential terminating sales or exchanges under the partnership agreement. Remember that unless § 761(e) applies, the liquidation of a partner's interest does not constitute a sale or exchange under § 708.

---

**72.** See Rev.Proc. 74–17, 1974–1 C.B. 438, for the additional requirements imposed on the limited partnership with a sole corporate general partner in requesting an advance ruling. See also Rev.Proc. 75–16, 1975–1 C.B. 676, which provides a checklist of information required with such ruling requests. See also Rev.Proc. 86–3, I.R.B. No. 1, 26, in which the IRS indicates that it will not issue advance rulings or determination letters regarding special allocation arrangements.

## BASIS ADJUSTMENT FOR TRANSFEREE PARTNERS

If a partnership interest is acquired by purchase, the partner may want to condition such acquisition on the partnership's promise to make an election under § 754. Such an election would adjust the basis in the partner's ratable share of partnership assets to reflect the difference between the purchase price and the selling partner's share of the basis in partnership assets. Failure to do so could result in the loss of future depreciation deductions as well as the conversion of ordinary losses into capital losses.

## AVOIDING PROBLEMS ON EXCHANGES OF INTERESTS

Another point to remember is that tax-free transfers of partnership interests are difficult to achieve. If a partner plans to transfer a partnership interest to a controlled corporation, § 357(c) may result in gain recognition because the transferor partner's share of liabilities exceeds the adjusted basis of the partner's interest. Also, according to § 1031(a)(2)(D), the like-kind exchange rules do not apply to an exchange of partnership interests. No limitation to this provision is contained in § 1031. The related Deficit Reduction Act of 1984 Committee Reports indicate that the provision is applicable to exchanges of interests in different partnerships (not the same partnership). The IRS has ruled in 1984 that under certain circumstances a general partnership interest may be converted into a limited interest (or vice versa) without gain or loss being recognized. The ruling indicates that the conversion is not a sale or exchange.

## TIMING OTHER DISPOSITIONS OF PARTNERSHIP INTERESTS

The disposition of a partnership interest by gift or abandonment or forfeiture may also result in unexpected recognition of gain. If the partner's share of partnership liabilities (recourse as well as nonrecourse) exceeds the adjusted basis of the partnership interest, the operation of §§ 752 and 731 cause such transfers to be treated as taxable sales. The only relief from these provisions is to time the disposition to occur in a tax year in which the partner has other losses to offset the gain that results.

## DEATH AND THE PARTNERSHIP AGREEMENT

A limited possibility exists to effectively plan for the disposition of a partnership interest as a result of death. The bunching of income in the deceased partner's final tax year can be avoided or accomplished by means of the partnership agreement. More important, the remaining partners can avoid unnecessary and unpleasant problems of dealing with the deceased partner's successor in interest by a well-planned and carefully drafted partnership agreement. If the successor in interest continues as a member of the partnership, an election under § 754 should be considered. This would enable the transferee's basis in the partnership's assets to be adjusted under § 743 to reflect the difference in the deceased partner's basis in the interest and the successor's basis in the partnership interest (as determined under § 1014).

# PLANNING PARTNERSHIP DISTRIBUTIONS

In planning for any partnership distributions, taxpayers should be alert to the following rules:

—Gain must be recognized by the distributee receiving *either* current *or* proportionate liquidating distributions *only* to the extent that any money distributed exceeds the partner's basis in the partnership.

—Loss is never recognized on current distributions. However, the distributee may recognize a loss on a liquidating distribution if *only* money, and/or inventory, and/or unrealized receivables are distributed, *and* only then if the basis of this property is less than the withdrawing partner's basis in the partnership interest.

—Gain or loss recognized by the distributee is a capital gain or loss in both current and liquidating distributions *except* when a portion of the gain must be treated as ordinary income to the extent it is attributable to unrealized receivables or substantially appreciated inventories.

—The distributee's basis in property received in a current distribution is the basis of the property to the partnership *except* that it cannot exceed the partner's basis in the partnership interest reduced by any money received in the same distribution.

—The basis of property received in a liquidating distribution is dependent upon the type of property distributed. The distributee partner's basis in inventory and unrealized receivables is the same basis the property had to the partnership but cannot exceed the partner's basis in the partnership reduced by any money distributed. Any other property distributed is assigned the withdrawing partner's remaining basis in the partnership.

—If a partner receives inventory or unrealized receivables in either a current or liquidating distribution, ordinary income results when a disposition of such property occurs. Recall that if the inventory items are held for at least five years before being sold, capital gain treatment might be achieved.

—Gain or loss cannot be recognized by a partnership on either current or liquidating distributions except on a disproportionate distribution of § 751 property.

—The holding period of property received in either a current or liquidating distribution includes the holding period of the partnership.

—For purposes of § 708 (relating to the continuation of a partnership) and § 743 (relating to the optional adjustment to the basis of partnership property), the distribution of a partnership interest by a corporation or a partnership is treated as an exchange. In certain circumstances, such a distribution would cause the partnership to terminate with income bunching and the loss of a valuable fiscal year election.

## VALUATION PROBLEMS

It is important to note that the value of a partner's interest or any partnership assets agreed upon by all partners is considered to be correct by both the IRS and the courts. Thus, in planning the sale or liquidation of a partnership interest, it is advisable to document the results of the bargaining process. Also, to avoid valuation problems on liquidation, it would be extremely helpful to have some formula or agreed-upon procedure incorporated in the partnership agreement.

# OTHER PARTNERSHIP INTERESTS

Taxpayers planning to operate a family business in partnership form should give careful thought to the requirements of § 704(e) and the Regulations thereunder. The following elements are essential for the recognition of the family partnership:

—A genuine intent of the parties to conduct the business as a partnership.

—Contribution of capital or vital services by each partner to the partnership.

Taxpayers considering a tax-sheltered investment opportunity should seek professional advice concerning the economic soundness of the proposal as well as the potential legal and tax consequences of ownership. Projections as to the soundness of the investment, future direction of the economy, financial forecasts, insurance requirements, legal advice, and tax consultation will be costly. In some cases the cost of expert advice might exceed any expected tax savings yielded by the investment.

As a final note, the continuation of a successful business in partnership form must be constantly reevaluated. If any of the partners wish to bring members of the family into the business, the problems inherent in family partnerships must be considered. Generally, it is easier to assign income to children by the gift of corporate stock than by the gift of a partnership interest. Additionally, the flexibility and tax benefits of the partnership form must be examined in comparison with the limited liability and tax benefits of the corporate form. The progressive individual tax rates and the renewed interest in eliminating the double taxation on corporate income suggest the need for constant appraisal of the taxpayer's choice of conducting a business in partnership form.

## PROBLEM MATERIALS

### Discussion Questions

1. What is the nature of a partnership interest under the entity concept of partnerships? Under the aggregate or conduit concept?

2. What is the character of a gain or loss recognized on the sale or exchange of a partnership interest?

3. What are unrealized receivables of a partnership? Substantially appreciated inventory items?

4. Discuss the possible collateral effects of a sale or exchange of a partnership interest.

5. Under what circumstances will the transfer of a partnership interest to a controlled corporation for stock result in taxable gain?

6. Describe the alternative methods of incorporating a partnership. Which method is recognized by the IRS?

7. What are the collateral effects of incorporating a partnership?

8. Discuss the problems involved in attempting a nontaxable like-kind exchange of partnership interests.

9. Under what circumstances will the gift of a partnership interest result in a taxable sale?

10. What are the anticipated income tax results of an abandonment or forfeiture of a partnership interest? What can go wrong?

11. Discuss the various types of distributions from a partnership and the tax consequences of each.

12. Distinguish between a sale of a partnership interest and a liquidation. Specifically, discuss the tax consequences of a sale of a partnership interest to the selling partner, the purchaser, and the partnership itself. What type of liquidation could be used to avoid immediate gain recognition by the withdrawing partner?

13. Distinguish between § 736(a) payments and § 736(b) payments. What are the tax consequences of such payments to the remaining partners and the partnership?

14. If liquidating payments are to be spread over a number of years, how are the payments to be allocated between § § 736(a) and (b)?

15. Under what circumstances is a loss recognized by a withdrawing partner whose entire interest is liquidated in a proportionate distribution of assets?

16. Distinguish between the basis adjustments allowed under § § 734 and 743. Why are such adjustments allowed? When could an unfavorable result occur?

17. What is a family partnership? Under what circumstances can a family member be a partner in such a partnership? What income allocation is required?

18. What is a limited partnership? What types of related tax shelters have been developed? What could go wrong?

19. Discuss the applicability of § 465 to limited partnerships.

20. What is the special recapture rule of § 465? Under what circumstances will it become applicable?

## Problems

1. At the end of the current year, K, an equal partner in the four-person KLOM Partnership, has an interest basis of $18,000 in the partnership, including a $40,000 share of partnership debt. On December 1 of last year, the partnership purchased and immediately placed in service five-year ACRS property qualifying for $24,000 of investment tax credits and $5,000 of rapid expensing under § 179, which it elected to take. K last year properly claimed a 25% share of the ITCs and the § 179 amount. At the end of the current year, K's share of the partnership's § 1245 recapture potential (including K's share of the § 179 expensed amount) is $12,000. For simplicity, assume that the partnership did not have any taxable income or loss in the current year and that all parties use the

calendar year. Describe the income tax consequences to K in each of the following situations that take place at the end of the current year:

(a) K sells the partnership interest to T for $25,000 cash and the assumption of the appropriate share of partnership liabilities.

(b) K exchanges the 25% partnership interest for a 25% limited partnership interest in the continuing KLOM Partnership valued at $30,000. L, O, and M remain general partners, each with a 25% interest in partnership capital and profits.

(c) Faced with the possibility of having to contribute an additional $50,000 to the partnership to keep it operating, K abandons the partnership interest and the remaining partners assume K's share of existing partnership liabilities.

(d) K dies after a lengthy illness on December 31 of the current year. K's widow becomes the immediate successor in interest.

2. Briefly discuss the changes that would have to be made to the responses given in Problem 1 if the KLOM Partnership had $88,000 of unrealized receivables at the end of the current year, including any recapture potential under § 1245 of the Code.

3. L, a partner in the cash basis LAM Partnership, has a 30% interest in partnership profits and losses. The partnership's balance sheet at the end of the current year is as follows:

| | Basis | FMV | | Basis | FMV |
|---|---|---|---|---|---|
| Cash | $ 25,000 | $ 25,000 | L, Capital | $ 54,000 | $ 135,000 |
| Receivables | —0— | 240,000 | A, Capital | 63,000 | 157,500 |
| Land | 155,000 | 185,000 | M, Capital | 63,000 | 157,500 |
| Totals | $ 180,000 | $ 450,000 | Totals | $ 180,000 | $ 450,000 |

Assume that L sells her interest in the LAM Partnership to J at the end of the current year for cash of $135,000.

(a) How much income must L report on her tax return for the current year from the sale, and what is its nature?

(b) If the partnership did not make a § 754 election or have one in effect, what is the type and amount of income that J must report in the next year when the receivables are collected? Assume no other transactions in the next year.

(c) If the partnership did make a § 754 election, what is the type and amount of income that J must report in the next year when (assuming no other transactions in the next year):
1. The receivables are collected?
2. The land (which is used in the LAM Partnership's business) is sold for $205,000?

4. X's interest in the equal HEX Partnership is sold to Y for $47,000 cash and the assumption of X's share of partnership liabilities. On the sale date, the partnership's cash basis balance sheet reflects the following:

*Assets*

| | Adjusted Basis Per Books | Market Value |
|---|---|---|
| Cash | $ 27,000 | $ 27,000 |
| Accounts receivable | —0— | 90,000 |
| Section 1231 assets | 33,000 | 33,000 |
| Total | $ 60,000 | $ 150,000 |

*Liabilities and Capital*

| | | |
|---|---:|---:|
| Note payable | $ 9,000 | $ 9,000 |
| Capital accounts | | |
| H | 17,000 | 47,000 |
| E | 17,000 | 47,000 |
| X | 17,000 | 47,000 |
| Total | $ 60,000 | $ 150,000 |

(a) What is the total amount realized by X on the sale?

(b) How much, if any, ordinary income must X recognize on the sale?

(c) How much capital gain to X?

(d) What will be Y's basis in the partnership interest acquired?

(e) If the partnership makes an election under § 754 to adjust the bases of the partnership assets to reflect the sale, what adjustment must be made?

5. Assume in Problem 4 that X's partnership interest is not sold to an outsider. Instead, the partnership makes a proportionate liquidating distribution to X, and the remaining partners assume X's share of the liabilities. X receives cash of $6,000, accounts receivable of $30,000, and a § 1231 asset worth $11,000.

(a) How much gain or loss must X recognize?

(b) What basis will X have in the accounts receivable?

(c) What basis will X have in the § 1231 asset?

6. Suppose that X's partnership interest in Problem 5 is terminated with a distribution of $47,000 of accounts receivable instead of the proportionate distribution described.

(a) How much gain or loss, if any, must X recognize?

(b) What basis will X have in the receivables?

(c) How much gain or loss, if any, must the partnership recognize on the distribution? Will this be ordinary or capital gain or loss?

(d) What basis will the partnership have in the § 1231 assets as a result of the distribution?

7. Suppose that X in Problem 6 receives cash of $14,000 and all the § 1231 assets worth $33,000 instead of the accounts receivable in a disproportionate distribution in termination of X's entire interest.

(a) How much gain or loss, if any, must X recognize? Will it be ordinary or capital gain or loss?

(b) What basis will X have in the § 1231 assets after the distribution?

(c) How much gain or loss, if any, must the partnership recognize on the distribution?

(d) What basis will the partnership have in the accounts receivable as a result of the distribution?

8. D's 25% interest in the CADE Partnership is sold to G for $15,000 cash and assumption of partnership liabilities. At the date of the sale, the partnership's cash basis balance sheet reflects the following:

*Assets*

| | Adjusted Basis Per Books | Market Value |
|---|---:|---:|
| Cash | $ 10,000 | $ 10,000 |
| Accounts receivable | 0 | 20,000 |
| Depreciable assets | 16,000 | 24,000 |
| Capital assets | 14,000 | 18,000 |
| Total | $ 40,000 | $ 72,000 |

*Liabilities and Capital*

| | | |
|---|---|---|
| Notes payable | $ 12,000 | $ 12,000 |
| Capital accounts | | |
| C | 7,000 | 15,000 |
| A | 7,000 | 15,000 |
| D | 7,000 | 15,000 |
| E | 7,000 | 15,000 |
| Total | $ 40,000 | $ 72,000 |

(a) What is the total amount realized by D on the sale?

(b) If there is $4,000 of § 1245 depreciation recapture potential associated with the partnership's assets, how much ordinary income must D recognize on the sale?

(c) How much capital gain to D?

(d) What will be G's basis in the partnership interest acquired?

(e) Assuming that a § 754 election is in effect at the time of the sale, what effect will it have on G's basis in the partnership interest acquired?

9. In addition to assuming the facts in Problem 8, assume that E's partnership interest is sold to G after D's interest is sold to G.

(a) What effect, if any, will this transaction have on the existing partnership?

(b) What unfavorable tax consequences could result from E's sale?

(c) If the partnership did not intend to make an election under § 754 and it did not have one in effect at the date of G's acquisition, what effect will these facts have on G's basis in the partnership interest acquired?

10. QSO is an equally owned partnership with the following balance sheet at the end of the current year:

*Assets*

| | Adjusted Basis Per Books | Market Value |
|---|---|---|
| Cash | $ 21,000 | $ 21,000 |
| Investment in QRV Partnership | 90,000 | 180,000 |
| Total | $ 111,000 | $ 201,000 |

*Liabilities and Capital*

| | | |
|---|---|---|
| Note payable | $ 18,000 | $ 18,000 |
| Capital accounts | | |
| Q | 31,000 | 61,000 |
| S | 31,000 | 61,000 |
| O | 31,000 | 61,000 |
| Total | $ 111,000 | $ 201,000 |

The balance sheet of the QRV Partnership at the end of the current year is as follows:

*Assets*

| | Adjusted Basis Per Books | Market Value |
|---|---|---|
| Cash | $ 40,000 | $ 40,000 |
| Unrealized receivables | —0— | 65,000 |
| Inventory held for sale | 60,000 | 95,000 |
| Total | $ 100,000 | $ 200,000 |

*Liabilities and Capital*

| Capital accounts | | |
|---|---|---|
| QSO (90% share) | 90,000 | 180,000 |
| X (5% share) | 5,000 | 10,000 |
| Z (5% share) | 5,000 | 10,000 |
| Total | $ 100,000 | $ 200,000 |

At the end of the current year, Q's interest in the QSO Partnership is sold to R for $61,000 in cash plus the assumption of Q's liability share.

(a) How much does Q realize on the sale?

(b) What is the basis of R's interest in the RSO Partnership?

(c) How much of a gain or loss does Q recognize from the sale, and what is its nature?

(d) If QSO and QRV both have § 754 elections in effect, what kind of special basis adjustments are available?

(e) If QSO has a § 754 election in effect but QRV does not, what kind of special basis adjustments are available?

11.  The basis of L's partnership interest is $17,080. L receives a pro rata liquidation distribution consisting of $9,760 cash and L's share of inventory having a basis of $12,200 to the partnership and a fair market value of $18,300.

(a) How much gain or loss, if any, must L recognize as a result of the distribution?

(b) What basis will L have in the inventory?

(c) If the inventory is sold two years later for $18,000, what are the tax consequences to L?

(d) As a result of the liquidating distribution, what are the tax consequences to the partnership?

12.  Assume the same facts as in Problem 11, except that L's basis in the partnership is $24,400 instead of $17,080.

(a) How much gain or loss, if any, must L recognize on the distribution?

(b) What basis will L have in the inventory?

(c) What are the tax consequences to the partnership?

13.  D's partnership basis is $64,500. In a pro rata distribution in liquidation of the partnership, D receives $12,900 cash and two parcels of land having bases of $17,200 and $12,900 to the partnership. Each parcel of land was held by the partnership for investment, and the parcels had fair market values of $32,250 and $43,000.

(a) How much gain or loss, if any, must D recognize on the distribution?

(b) What basis will D have in each parcel?

(c) If the land had been held as inventory by the partnership, what effect, if any, would it have on the responses to parts (a) and (b)?

14.  Assume the same facts as in Problem 13 except that D received $21,500 cash and an old truck having a basis of $430 to the partnership and a fair market value of $215.

(a) How much loss, if any, may D recognize on the distribution?

(b) What basis will D have in the truck?

(c) Suppose D's son drives the truck to school for one year before selling it for $100. How much loss may D recognize on the sale of the truck? What tax planning procedure could have prevented this result?

15. S is an equal partner in the SW&J Partnership and has an interest basis of $225,000 at the end of the partnership's current year. S receives the following distribution from the partnership in complete termination of his interest: cash of $112,500 and two pieces of property with partnership bases and fair market values as follows:

|  | Partnership Basis | | FMV | |
|  | Amount | Fraction | Amount | Fraction |
|---|---|---|---|---|
| Land A | $ 90,000 | ⅔ | $ 135,000 | ⅗ |
| Land B | 45,000 | ⅓ | 90,000 | ⅖ |
| Totals | $ 135,000 | | $ 225,000 | |

Assume both pieces of property were used in the partnership in connection with its business and that § 751 assets are not present.

(a) How much income is recognized by S on the liquidating distribution, and what is its nature?

(b) What is the basis of Land A and of Land B to S?

(c) If S had received cash of $67,500 (instead of $112,500) and the two land parcels, what would be the basis of Land A and of Land B to S?

(d) If S had received cash of $230,000 (instead of $112,500 or $67,500) and the two land parcels, what would be the basis of Land A and of Land B to S?

(e) For (d), if the partnership had previously made a § 754 election, what would be the aggregate amount of the adjustment under § 734 and its direction (i. e., upward or downward adjustment of basis)?

16. At the time J decides to retire from the JET Partnership, JET's balance sheet for tax purposes contains the following:

|  | *Assets* | |
|  | Adjusted Basis Per Books | Market Value |
|---|---|---|
| Cash | $ 193,500 | $ 193,500 |
| Section 1231 assets | 64,500 | 64,500 |
| Investment in land | 77,400 | 193,500 |
| Total assets | $ 335,400 | $ 451,500 |

|  | *Liabilities and Capital* | |
|---|---|---|
| Mortgage payable | $ 64,500 | $ 64,500 |
| Capital accounts | | |
| J | 90,300 | 129,000 |
| E | 90,300 | 129,000 |
| T | 90,300 | 129,000 |
| Total | $ 335,400 | $ 451,500 |

It has been agreed by all partners that J's interest in the partnership assets, exclusive of goodwill, is worth $129,000. To totally liquidate J's interest, it is further agreed that J will be paid $64,500 per year for three years and J's share of partnership liabilities will be assumed immediately by the remaining partners.

(a) How should the total payments be allocated between § 736(a) and § 736(b) payments?

(b) What are the tax consequences to J for the current and next two years?

(c) What are the tax consequences to the partnership of each of the three payments?

17. Assume the same facts as in Problem 16, except that instead of receiving $64,500 per year for three years, J is to receive 30% of partnership profits for five years. The amounts paid to J are as follows:

Year 1—$43,000     Year 4—$30,100
Year 2—$34,400     Year 5—$64,500
Year 3—$51,600

(a) What are the tax consequences to J of each of the five payments?

(b) What are the tax consequences to the partnership upon making each of the payments?

18. In each of the following proportionate liquidating distributions, determine the amount and character of any gain or loss to be recognized by each partner and the basis of each asset (other than cash) received. Additionally, indicate the amount of any optional basis adjustments available to the distributing partnership if a § 754 election is in effect.

(a) R has a partnership basis of $18,000 and receives a distribution of $25,000 in cash.

(b) S has a partnership basis of $9,000 and receives $3,000 cash and a capital asset with a basis to the partnership of $4,000 and a fair market value of $12,000.

(c) T has a partnership basis of $15,000 and receives $4,000 cash, inventory with a basis to the partnership of $8,000, and a capital asset with a partnership basis of $10,000. The inventory and capital asset have fair market values of $5,000 and $7,000, respectively.

19. P and C, parent and child, operate a local apparel shop as a partnership. The PC Partnership earned a profit of $20,000 in the current year. C's equal partnership interest was acquired by purchase from the parent. Assume that capital is a material income-producing factor and that P manages the day-to-day operations of the shop without any help from C. Further assume that $8,000 is reasonable compensation for P's services.

(a) How much of the partnership income must be allocated to P?

(b) What is the maximum amount of partnership income that can be allocated to C?

20. T invests $25,000 cash in the CP Limited Partnership for a 5% limited liability interest in capital and profits. Shortly thereafter, the partnership acquires a completed 10-story office building for a cash down payment of $500,000 and subject to a nonrecourse mortgage of $1,500,000.

(a) What is T's basis in the limited partnership after the acquisition of the office building?

(b) Assuming that T's share of the partnership losses for the first year of operation is $35,000, how much of the loss is T allowed to recognize?

(c) What is T's basis in the partnership after deducting T's allowed loss?

21. S has an equal interest in the profits and losses of the SIE Partnership. During the current year, S agrees to retire from the partnership just before the current year ends and receive the following cash payments for his entire partnership interest: $30,600 just before the end of the current year and payments aggregating $68,000 over the following two years. The partners agree that the partnership's goodwill is worth $30,600 at the instant of S's retirement and that the payments to S for his partnership interest cover his share of the goodwill. The closing balance sheet of the partnership *just before* the first cash payment to S is as follows:

| | Books | FMV | | Books | FMV |
|---|---|---|---|---|---|
| Cash | $ 44,200 | $ 44,200 | Debt | $ 10,200 | $ 10,200 |
| Unrealized receivables | —0— | 102,000 | Capital, S | 34,000 | 71,400 |
| Capital and § 1231 assets | 68,000 | 78,200 | Capital, I | 34,000 | 71,400 |
| | | | Capital, E | 34,000 | 71,400 |
| Totals | $ 112,200 | $ 224,400 | Totals | $ 112,200 | $ 224,400 |

In addition, before the current year ends, the remaining partners agree to assume S's share of partnership debt existing just before the first payment.

(a) What is the basis of S's partnership interest just before the first payment?

(b) What is S's aggregate interest in § 736(b) property just before the first payment?

(c) In the aggregate, how much in the way of § 736(a) payments will be received by S?

(d) Assuming no other partnership provisions regarding S's retirement, how will S be taxed on all retirement amounts for the current year?

(e) In (d), could S do anything to change the way the retirement amounts are taxed?

22. L has an 80% profit and loss interest in the QSL Partnership and a zero interest basis. The balance sheet of QSL at the end of the current year is as follows:

*Assets*

| | Adjusted Basis Per Books | Market Value |
|---|---|---|
| Cash | $ 10,000 | $ 10,000 |
| Investment in XYZ Partnership | 1,000 | 1,000 |
| Land on 73rd Street | —0— | 1,000 |
| Total | $ 11,000 | $ 12,000 |

*Capital*

| | | |
|---|---|---|
| Capital accounts | | |
| Q | $ 5,500 | $ 5,600 |
| S | 5,500 | 5,600 |
| L | —0— | 800 |
| Total | $ 11,000 | $ 12,000 |

The balance sheet of the XYZ Partnership at the end of the current year is as follows:

|  | Assets | |
|---|---|---|
|  | Adjusted Basis Per Books | Market Value |
| Cash | $ 111 | $ 111 |
| Land on 54th Street | 1,000 | 1,000 |
| Total | $ 1,111 | $ 1,111 |

|  | Capital | |
|---|---|---|
| Capital accounts |  |  |
| QSL (99% share) | $ 1,000 | $ 1,000 |
| M (1% share) | 55 | 55 |
| N (1% share) | 56 | 56 |
| Total | $ 1,111 | $ 1,111 |

The XYZ Partnership was formed when QSL contributed the land on 54th Street for a 99% interest and M and N each received a 1% interest for contributions of $55 and $56, respectively.

(a) If QSL distributes its investment in XYZ to L at the end of the current year, what is L's basis in XYZ?

(b) Assume QSL had a § 754 election in effect and XYZ did not. If QSL, immediately after distributing its interest in XYZ to L, sold the land on 73rd Street for $1,000, how much gain (if any) would be recognized?

(c) After the transactions in (b), what would be the basis of the land on 54th Street to XYZ?

(d) What will be the result if at a later date L has XYZ sell the land on 54th Street for $1,000?

(e) Would your answer in (b) be different if QSL and XYZ each had a § 754 election in effect when the XYZ interest was distributed to L? If so, how would it differ?

## Research Problems

*Research Problem 1.* Five years ago, an enterprising group of young real estate developers, with a substantial list of financial successes in residential apartments and shopping centers in the northwest continental United States, organized Harpervalley Development Formations (HDF), a general real estate development and management partnership located in Harpervalley, Oregon. At that time, these men and women together had invested $25,000 in HDF, and the partnership had acquired an option to buy some choice land on the southwest side of Harpervalley, adjacent to Interstate Highway 90 near the airport. The partners planned to sell another $475,000 of general partnership units in HDF and secure about $5,000,000 of nonrecourse financing. The funds would be used to purchase the optioned land and construct a showcase apartment-shopping center complex with appropriate landscaping. JP, the leading sparkplug behind HDF, had made an impressive loan presentation request to the board of directors of the Ranchers Insurance Group (RIG). BM, then president of RIG, was fairly certain the board would approve the $5,000,000 loan to HDF on a nonrecourse basis with the land (to be purchased) and the apartment-shopping center complex (to be constructed) pledged as collateral.

At a cocktail party at his country club the Saturday evening before the RIG board was to approve the loan to HDF, BM mentioned to his childhood sweetheart, SA, that HDF planned to construct an apartment-shopping center complex on the southwest side of the city. He suggested that SA consider making an investment in HDF and hinted that RIG would likely be a heavy participant. SA, an attractive widow, about 50, with two married children, had made her own fortune in the stock market before marrying JA, a wealthy rancher in the valley area. She told BM, whose advice she valued highly, that she had discussed the project with JP the prior weekend over dinner and was seriously considering such an investment. On Monday morning, SA telephoned JP and informed him that she had placed her check in the mail to him along with the necessary signed papers to make her a general partner in HDF. On Wednesday of the same week, the RIG board approved the loan. HDF immediately purchased the optioned land and constructed the apartment-shopping center complex. After all the general partnership units in HDF were sold, SA's $100,000 investment provided her with a 20% interest in capital, profits, and losses.

Although SA had not received any cash flow from the HDF Partnership during the past four years, she did receive the following share of partnership losses, which she deducted on her tax returns to offset substantial amounts of other income:

| Year | Loss |
|------|------|
| 1 | $ 20,000 |
| 2 | 40,000 |
| 3 | 40,000 |
| 4 | 100,000 |

Toward the middle part of last year, the economy took a deep downturn. Several of the mines and factories in the area closed down, and many local ranchers had to lay off a substantial number of their workhands. These events had a drastic effect on the revenues and operations of the HDF apartment-shopping center complex.

By late October of the current year, it was evident that the partnership would be unable to make the loan and interest payment due to RIG on January 15 of next year. A meeting of the partners was called for November 5, at which time the complete situation was explained. None of the local partners wanted HDF to default on the loan to RIG. It was decided that the management group of HDF would try to find a buyer for all partnership interests who would be willing to assume the loan to RIG. On November 30, each partner received a letter indicating that a potential buyer had been located. This potential buyer was in the process of having the properties appraised. On December 20, each partner received a letter indicating that the appraisals had been completed and that the average of the three independent appraisals was $3,000,000, with a variance between the high and low appraisals of $30,000. The letter also announced that there would be a partners' meeting on December 30 of the current year, at which time the full offer from the potential buyer would be disclosed and each partner's share of the loss for the year would be announced.

At the December 30 meeting, SA learned that her share of the current year's operating loss was $200,000 (her share of the loss for the fifth year of operations). RE, a real estate investor from Denver, was introduced. JP indicated that RE would be willing to assume the debt to RIG and reimburse each partner for his or her share of the selling expenses, which included the finder's fee paid to locate RE. SA's share of these expenses would be $500. JP indicated the importance of making a quick decision, because the next payment to RIG was due on January 15. JP indicated that if the payment was not made on time, HDF would be in default on the unpaid loan principal of $4,500,000 plus interest. After much discussion, it was decided to accept RE's offer. On December 31, the transfer contract was signed and each partner received a check from RE as reimbursement for the selling expenses. SA received a check for $500 and a statement confirming that her share of the operating loss for the year was $200,000.

SA has contacted you, a local CPA, to determine how the above facts should be presented on her tax return for the current year. From these facts you are to determine:

(a)   The basis of SA's interest in the HDF Partnership on December 31, the disposal date, ignoring any interest due for the use of money.

(b)   The amount of investment gain or loss from the disposal of SA's interest in HDF. Your answer should contain some general comments regarding the nature of the gain or loss.

(c)   The proper presentation for the $200,000 share of the current year loss.

*Partial list of research aids:*

§ § 61, 704, 752, and 1001.

Reg. § § 1.61–12 and 1.752–1.

*Gavins S. Millar,* 67 T.C. 656 (1977).

*Peninsula Properties Co., LTD,* 47 B.T.A. 84 (1942).

*Unique Art Manufacturing Co., Inc.,* 8 T.C. 1341 (1947).

*Research Problem 2.* RD was a 25% partner in the Pleasant View Partnership, which was organized 17 years ago to construct and manage an apartment building in Indianapolis, Indiana. Three years ago, RD and his partners disagreed on some management policies and RD decided to retire from the partnership and move to Florida. The partners agreed on the value of RD's partnership interest and agreed that it would be liquidated by the immediate assumption of RD's share of the partnership's debt and a series of cash payments over the year of retirement and the next nine years.

In the year of RD's retirement and in each of the next two years, RD received a check from the partnership in liquidation of his partnership interest of $8,000. In the current year, he received the fourth $8,000 check from the partnership on December 15. However, on July 10 in the current year, RD received another check for $5,000 from the partnership. The letter that accompanied the $5,000 check indicated that the garage at the back of the apartment rental property was destroyed by a fire, that no automobiles of tenants were in the garage at the time of the fire, and that the check represented RD's share of the insurance proceeds. The letter also indicated that RD's share of the garage's adjusted basis at the date of the fire was $2,000, that the garage had been depreciated by the straight-line method, and that the remaining partners had decided not to replace the garage.

RD was pleased when he received the $5,000 check, since he had recently been talking to the tenants of an apartment building he owned and managed in Sarasota, Florida, about plans for constructing a garage on the property in which they could rent space to house their cars. With the $5,000 and some other money, RD had a garage constructed on the property that was placed in service on September 25 of the current year.

Since RD's tax return for the current year will be due in a few months, RD has contracted with you to determine if he will be able to make an election under § 1033 to defer gain recognition from the proceeds he received from the garage fire in Indianapolis. He informs you that the garage destroyed in the fire was in existence at the date of his retirement from the Pleasant View Partnership and that all appropriate documentation is available for your examination, including a letter from his former partners that grants him the right to retain all tax elections he had in the partnership at the date of his retirement. Will RD be able to make an appropriate election under § 1033 to defer any income recognition on the $5,000 received from the garage fire?

*Research Problem 3.* SSH, a calendar year corporation located on the southwest side of Lincoln, Nebraska, near William Jennings Bryan's home, is owned by six calendar year shareholders. The shareholders of SSH are sole proprietors of businesses in a shopping mart, which is also located on the southwest side of Lincoln. SSH rents office space from the shopping mart owners and has assets consisting of a small amount of cash, a few pieces of office equipment, and six 15% limited partner interests in the capital and profits of RP. RP is a January 31 fiscal year limited partnership that owns and operates residential property on the west side of Lincoln near the airport. RP took accelerated depreciation and statutory percentage accelerated cost recovery deductions in excess of related straight-line amounts on its real property. As a result of these deductions, RP had operating losses.

On November 15 of the current year, SSH adopted a plan of complete liquidation and on December 5 sold its office equipment to an unrealted party for book value. On December 31 of the current year, SSH made its one and only liquidating distribution, distributing to each shareholder in exchange for its stock an equal amount of cash and a 15% interest in RP. After the distribution, 90% of RP is owned by the former shareholders of SSH. The other 10% interest is owned by the same taxpayers who helped form the partnership several years ago.

The former treasurer of SSH, who was also a shareholder in SSH, has contracted with you to determine the answers to the following questions and report back to her before the tax returns for SSH and RP are due:

(a) Must SSH report ordinary income under § 1250 for the excess depreciation taken by RP when it (SSH) distributed the six 15% interests in RP in a § 336 liquidating distribution?

(b) Was RP terminated when the six 15% interests in it were distributed to SSH shareholders?

# The Federal Gift and Estate Taxes 11

## CHAPTER OBJECTIVES

—Illustrate the mechanics of the unified transfer tax.
—Establish what persons are subject to this tax.
—Review the formulas for the Federal gift and estate taxes.
—Set forth what transfers are subject to the Federal gift or estate tax.
—Describe the exclusions and the deductions available in arriving at a taxable gift or a taxable estate.
—Illustrate the computation of the Federal gift or estate tax by making use of all available credits.
—Explain the objective of a program of lifetime giving.
—Show how the gift and estate taxes can be reduced.

# TRANSFER TAXES—IN GENERAL

Until now, the text has dealt primarily with the various applications of the Federal income tax. Also important in the Federal tax structure are various excise taxes that cover transfers of property. Sometimes designated as transaction taxes, excise taxes are based on the value of the property transferred and not on the income derived therefrom. Two such taxes—the Federal estate tax and the Federal gift tax—are the central focus of Chapters 11 and 12.

Before the enactment of the Tax Reform Act of 1976, Federal law imposed a tax on the gratuitous transfer of property in one of two ways. If the transfer was during the owner's life, it was subject to the Federal gift tax. If, however, the property passed by virtue of the death of the owner, the Federal estate tax applied. Both taxes were governed by different rules including a separate set of tax rates. Because Congress felt that lifetime transfers of wealth should be encouraged, the gift tax rates were lower than the estate tax rates.

The Tax Reform Act of 1976 made significant changes to the approach taken by the Federal estate and gift taxes. Basically, much of the distinction between life and death transfers was eliminated. Instead of these transfers being subject to two separate tax rate schedules, the Act substituted a unified transfer tax to cover all gratuitous transfers. Thus, gifts are subject to a gift tax at the same rates as those applicable to transfers at death. In addition, current law eliminates the prior exemptions allowed under each tax and replaces them with a unified tax credit.

## NATURE OF THE TAXES

The Federal gift tax is imposed on the right to transfer property by one person (i. e., the donor) to another (i. e., the donee) for less than full and adequate consideration. The tax is payable by the donor.[1] If, however, the donor fails to pay the tax when due, the donee may be held liable for the tax to the extent of the value of the property received.[2] The gift tax is to be determined by using the fair market value of the property as of the date of the gift.

---

1. § 2502(c).
2. § 6324(b).

The Federal estate tax[3] dates from 1916 and, as is true with the origin of many taxes, was enacted to generate additional revenue in anticipation of this country's entry into World War I. The tax is designed to tax transfers at death, although it may have some application to lifetime transfers that become complete upon the death of the donor or to certain gifts when made within three years of death. The tax is, in several respects, unlike the typical inheritance tax imposed by many states and some local jurisdictions. First, the Federal death tax is imposed on the decedent's entire estate. It is a tax on the right to pass property at death. Inheritance taxes are taxes on the right to receive property at death and are therefore levied on the beneficiaries.[4] Second, the relationship of the beneficiaries to the decedent usually has a direct bearing on the inheritance tax determination. In general, the more closely related the parties, the larger the exemption and the lower the applicable rates.[5] Except for one instance, the Federal death tax accords no difference in treatment based on the relationship of a decedent to his or her beneficiaries.[6]

The Federal gift tax, enacted later, was designed to improve upon the effectivenesss of the income and estate taxes. Apparently, Congress felt that one should not be able to give away property, thereby shifting the income tax consequences to others and further avoiding estate taxes on the death of the transferor, without incurring some tax liability. The answer, then, was the Federal gift tax, which covered inter vivos (i. e., lifetime) transfers.

*Persons Subject to the Tax.* To determine whether a transfer is subject to the Federal gift tax, one must first ascertain if the donor is a citizen or resident of the United States. If the donor is not a citizen or a resident, it becomes important to determine whether the property involved in the gift was situated within the United States.

The Federal gift tax is applied to all transfers by gift of property wherever situated by individuals who, at the time of the gift, were citizens or residents of the United States.[7] The term "United States" includes only the 50 states and the District of Columbia; it does not include U. S. possessions or territories. For a U. S. citizen, the place of residence at the time of the gift is immaterial.

For individuals who are neither citizens nor residents of the United States, the Federal gift tax is applied only to gifts of property situated

---

**3.** The constitutionality of the Federal estate tax was upheld in *New York Trust Co. v. Eisner,* 1 USTC ¶ 49, 3 AFTR 3110, 41 S.Ct. 506 (USSC, 1921).

**4.** As a practical matter, the inheritance tax will usually be paid by the executor or administrator of the estate. The executor has the legal responsibility under state law of collecting and paying over the tax. The amount involved, however, will have been deducted from the shares paid or to be paid each beneficiary.

**5.** For example, one state's inheritance tax provides an exemption of $50,000 for surviving spouses, with rates ranging from 5% to 10% on the taxable portion. This is to be contrasted with an exemption of only $1,000 for strangers (persons unrelated to the deceased), with rates ranging from 14% to 18% on the taxable portion. Other exemptions and rates fall in between these extremes to cover beneficiaries variously related to the decedent.

**6.** The one exception would be the marital deduction for qualifying transfers of property from the decedent to the surviving spouse.

**7.** Reg. § 25.2501–1(a)(1).

within the United States.[8] A gift of intangible personal property (e. g., stocks and bonds) usually is not subject to the Federal gift tax when made by nonresident aliens.[9]

A gift by a corporation is considered a gift by its individual shareholders. A gift to a corporation is generally considered a gift to its individual shareholders, except that in certain cases, a gift to a charitable, public, political, or similar organization may be regarded as a gift to the organization as a single entity.[10]

The Federal death tax is applied to the entire estate of a decedent who, at the time of his or her death, was a resident or citizen of the United States.[11] If the decedent was a U. S. citizen, the residence at death makes no difference for this purpose.

If the decedent was neither a resident nor a citizen of the United States at the time of death, the Federal estate tax will nevertheless be imposed on the value of any property situated within the United States. In such case, the tax determination is controlled by a separate subchapter of the Internal Revenue Code.[12] In certain instances, these tax consequences outlined in the Internal Revenue Code may have been modified by death tax conventions (i. e., treaties) between the United States and various foreign countries.[13] Further coverage of this area is beyond the scope of this text; the discussion to follow is limited to the tax treatment of decedents who were residents or citizens of the United States at the time of death.[14]

*Formula for the Gift Tax.* Like the income tax, which uses taxable income (and not gross income) as a tax base, the gift tax rates do not usually apply to the full amount of the gift. Deductions and the annual exclusion may be allowed to arrive at an amount called the *taxable gift*. However, unlike the income tax, which does not take into account taxable income from prior years, *prior taxable gifts* must be added in arriving at the tax base to which the unified transfer tax is applied. Otherwise, the donor could start over again each year with a new set of progressive rates.

> **Example 1.** D makes taxable gifts of $500,000 in 1985 and $500,000 in 1986. Presuming no other taxable gifts and *disregarding the effect of*

---

**8.** § 2511(a).

**9.** § § 2501(a)(2) and (3). But see § 2511(b) and Reg. § § 25.2511–3(b)(2), (3), and (4) for exceptions.

**10.** Reg. § § 25.0–1(b) and 25.2511–1(h)(1). But note the exemption from the Federal gift tax for certain transfers to political organizations discussed later.

**11.** § 2001(a). The term "United States" includes only the 50 states and the District of Columbia; it does not include U. S. possessions or territories. § 7701(a)(9).

**12.** Subchapter B (§ § 2101 through 2108) covers the estate tax treatment of decedents who are neither residents nor citizens. Subchapter A (§ § 2001 through 2056) covers the estate tax treatment of those who are either residents or citizens.

**13.** At present, the United States has death tax conventions with the following countries: Australia, Austria, Canada, Finland, France, Greece, Ireland, Italy, Japan, Netherlands, Norway, Republic of South Africa, Switzerland, and the United Kingdom. At the time of this writing, a death tax treaty with West Germany was pending ratification by the U. S. Senate. The United States has gift tax conventions with Australia, France, Japan, and the United Kingdom.

**14.** Further information concerning Subchapter B (§ § 2101 through 2108) can be obtained by reading the Code Sections involved (and the Treasury Regulations thereunder). See also the Instructions to Form 706NA, U. S. Estate Tax Return of Nonresident not a citizen of the U. S.

*the unified tax credit,* D must pay a tax of $155,800 (see Appendix A, page A-8) on the 1985 transfer and a tax of $345,800 on the 1986 transfer (using a tax base of $1,000,000). Had not the 1985 taxable gift been included in the tax base for the 1986 gift, the tax would have been $155,800. One can easily see that the correct tax liability of $345,800 is more than twice $155,800.

Because the gift tax is cumulative in effect, a credit is allowed against the gift taxes paid (or deemed paid) on prior taxable gifts included in the tax base.[15]

**Example 2.** Assume the same facts as in Example 1. D will be allowed a credit of $155,800 against the gift tax of $345,800. Thus, D's gift tax liability for 1986 becomes $190,000 ($345,800 − $155,800).

The formula for the gift tax is summarized below. [Note: Section (§) references are to the portion of the Internal Revenue Code involved.]

| | | |
|---|---:|---:|
| Determine whether the transfers are or are not covered by referring to § § 2511 through 2519; list the fair market value of only the covered transfers | | $ xxx,xxx |
| Determine the deductions allowed by § 2522 (charitable), § 2523 (marital) | $ xx,xxx | |
| Claim the annual exclusion (per donee) under § 2503(b), if available | 10,000[16] | xx,xxx |
| Taxable gifts [as defined by § 2503(a)] for the current period | | $ xx,xxx |
| Add: Taxable gifts from prior years | | xx,xxx |
| Total of current and past taxable gifts | | $ xx,xxx |
| Compute the gift tax on the total of current and past taxable gifts by using the rates found in Appendix A | | $ x,xxx |
| Subtract: The gift tax paid or deemed paid on past taxable gifts and the unified tax credit | | xxx |
| Gift tax due on transfers during the current period | | $ xxx |

*Formula for the Federal Estate Tax.* The Federal unified transfer tax at death, commonly referred to as the Federal estate tax, is summarized below. [Note: Section (§) references are to the portion of the Internal Revenue Code involved.]

---

15. The deemed paid credit is explained later in the chapter.
16. The annual exclusion before 1982 was $3,000. The change to $10,000 was made by the Economic Recovery Tax Act of 1981 to allow larger gifts to be exempt from the Federal gift tax. Such change has to be commended in light of the inflationary trend in the economy. In the case of gifts of jointly owned property (e. g., joint tenancies, tenancies by the entirety, tenancies in common, community property) or of gifts by one spouse when the election to split gifts under § 2513 is made, the maximum annual exclusion would be $20,000 per donee.

| | | |
|---|---:|---:|
| Gross estate (§ § 2031–2046) | | $ xxx,xxx |
| Subtract: | | |
|    Expenses, indebtedness, and | | |
|       taxes (§ 2053) | $ xx | |
|    Losses (§ 2054) | xx | |
|    Charitable bequests (§ 2055) | xx | |
|    Marital deduction (§ 2056) | xx | x,xxx |
| Taxable estate (§ 2051) | | $ xx,xxx |
| Add: Post-1976 taxable gifts | | |
|    [§ 2001(b)] | | x,xxx |
| Tax base | | $ xxx,xxx |
| Tentative tax on total transfers | | |
|    [§ 2001(c)] | | $ xx,xxx |
| Subtract: | | |
|    Unified transfer tax on post-1976 | | |
|       taxable gifts (i. e., gift taxes paid) | $ xx | |
|    Other tax credits (including the | | |
|       unified tax credit) [§ § 2010–2016] | xx | x,xxx |
| Estate tax due | | $ xxx |

The gross estate is determined by using the fair market value of the property on the date of the decedent's death (or on the alternate valuation date if applicable). Valuation considerations are discussed in Chapter 12.

The reason for adding post-1976 taxable gifts to the taxable estate to arrive at the tax base goes back to the scheme of the unified transfer tax. Starting in 1977, all transfers, whether lifetime or by death, are to be treated the same. Consequently, taxable gifts made after 1976 must be accounted for upon the death of the donor. Note, however, that the double tax effect of including these gifts is mitigated by allowing a credit against the estate tax for the gift taxes previously paid.

*Role of the Unified Tax Credit.* Before the unified transfer tax, the gift tax allowed a $30,000 specific exemption for the lifetime of the donor. A comparable $60,000 exemption was allowed for estate tax purposes. The justification for these exemptions was to allow donors and decedents to transfer modest amounts of wealth without being subject to the gift and estate taxes. Unfortunately, inflation took its toll, and more taxpayers were being subject to these transfer taxes than Congress felt was appropriate. The congressional solution, therefore, was to rescind the exemptions and replace them with the unified tax credit.[17]

To curtail revenue loss, the credit was phased in as follows.[18]

---

17. § § 2010 and 2505.
18. The original phase-in (Tax Reform Act of 1976) was scheduled to level off at $47,000 in 1981. Due to the continuing inflationary trend in the economy, the phase-in with a stairstep increase in the amount of the credit was extended to 1987 (Economic Recovery Tax Act of 1981).

| Year of Death | Amount of Credit | Amount of Exemption Equivalent |
|---|---|---|
| 1977 | $ 30,000[19] | $ 120,667 |
| 1978 | 34,000 | 134,000 |
| 1979 | 38,000 | 147,333 |
| 1980 | 42,500 | 161,563 |
| 1981 | 47,000 | 175,625 |
| 1982 | 62,800 | 225,000 |
| 1983 | 79,300 | 275,000 |
| 1984 | 96,300 | 325,000 |
| 1985 | 121,800 | 400,000 |
| 1986 | 155,800 | 500,000 |
| 1987 & thereafter | 192,800 | 600,000 |

The exemption equivalent is the amount of the transfer that will pass free of the gift or estate tax by virtue of the credit.

**Example 3.** In 1986, D makes a taxable gift of $500,000. Presuming she has made no prior taxable gifts, D will not owe any gift tax. Under the tax rate schedules (see Appendix A, page A-8), the tax on $500,000 is $155,800, which is the exact amount of the credit allowed.[20]

The Tax Reform Act of 1976, allowed donors one last chance to use the $30,000 specific exemption on lifetime gifts. If, however, such use occurred on gifts made after September 8, 1976 (and before January 1, 1977),[21] the unified tax credit must be reduced by 20 percent of the exemption so utilized.[22]

**Example 4.** Net of the annual exclusion, D, a widow, made gifts of $10,000 in June 1976 and $20,000 in December 1976. Assume D has never used any of her specific exemption and chooses to use the full $30,000 to cover the 1976 gifts. Under these circumstances, the unified tax credit will be reduced by $4,000 (i. e., 20% × $20,000). Note that the use of the specific exemption on transfers made before September 9, 1976, will have no effect on the credit.

# THE FEDERAL GIFT TAX

## GENERAL CONSIDERATIONS

*Requirements for a Gift.* For a gift to be complete under state law, the following elements must be present:

—A donor competent to make the gift.

—A donee capable of receiving and possessing the property.

---

19. The amount of the credit for gift tax purposes was $6,000 for the period from January 1, 1977, through June 30, 1977. Otherwise, the credit for gift and estate tax purposes has been the same.
20. The rate schedules are contained in § 2001(c).
21. After 1976, the specific exemption no longer is available.
22. § § 2010(c) and 2505(c). The adjustment to the credit because of the use of the specific exemption applies whether the gift or estate tax is involved.

—Donative intent on behalf of the donor.

—Actual or constructive delivery of the property to the donee or the donee's representative.

—Acceptance of the gift by the donee.

What transfers are or are not gifts under state law is important in applying the Federal gift tax. But state law does not always control in this matter. For example, with reference to the element of donative intent, the Regulations make it quite clear that this is not an essential factor in the application of the Federal gift tax to the transfer.[23]

> **Example 5.** B (age 24) consents to marry D (age 62) if D transfers $200,000 of his property to her. The arrangement is set forth in a prenuptial agreement, D makes the transfer, and B and D are married. D lacked donative intent, and in most states no gift has been made from D to B. Nevertheless, the transfer would be subject to the Federal gift tax.

The key to the result reached in Example 5 and to the status of other types of transfers is whether full and adequate consideration in money or money's worth was given for the property transferred.[24] Although such consideration is present in Example 5 (i. e., property for marriage) for purposes of state law, Reg. § 25.2512–8 reads: "A consideration not reducible to a value in money or money's worth, as love and affection, promise of marriage, etc., is to be wholly disregarded, and the entire value of the property transferred constitutes the amount of the gift."

*Incomplete Transfers.* The Federal gift tax does not apply to transfers that are incomplete. Thus, if the transferor retains the right to reclaim the property or, for all intents and purposes, has not really parted with the possession of the property, a taxable event has not taken place.

> **Example 6.** D creates a trust, income payable to S for life, remainder to R.[25] Under the terms of the trust instrument, D can revoke the trust at any time and repossess trust corpus and income therefrom. No gift takes place on the creation of the trust; D has not ceased to have dominion and control over the property.

> **Example 7.** Assume the same facts as in Example 6, except that one year after the transfer, D relinquishes his right to terminate the trust. At this point, the transfer becomes complete and the Federal gift tax applies.[26]

*Business versus Personal Setting.* In a business setting, full and adequate consideration in money or money's worth is apt to exist. Reg. § 25.2512–8 provides that "a sale, exchange, or other transfer of property

---

**23.** § 25.2511–1(g)(1).

**24.** § 2512(b).

**25.** The holder of a life estate (called a life tenant) has the right to the use of the property (including the right to the income therefrom) for his or her life. On the death of the life tenant, the property passes to the designated remainderperson (called the remainder interest).

**26.** Reg. § 25.2511–2(f).

made in the ordinary course of business (a transaction that is bona fide, at arm's length, and free of any donative intent) will be considered as made for an adequate and full consideration in money or money's worth." If the parties are acting in a personal setting, however, a gift usually is the result.

> **Example 8.** D loans money to S in connection with a business venture. About a year later, D forgives part of the loan. D probably has not made a gift to S if D and S are unrelated parties.[27]

> **Example 9.** Assume the same facts as in Example 8, except that D and S are father and son and no business venture is involved. If the loan itself was not, in fact, a disguised gift, the later forgiveness will probably be treated as a gift.[28]

Do not conclude, however, that the presence of *some* consideration may be enough to preclude Federal gift tax consequences. Again, the answer may rest on whether the transfer occurred in a business setting.

> **Example 10.** D sells S some real estate for $40,000. Unknown to D, the property contains valuable mineral deposits and is really worth $100,000. D may have made a bad business deal, but he has not made a gift to S of $60,000.

> **Example 11.** Assume the same facts as in Example 10, except that D and S are father and son. In addition, D is very much aware of the fact that the property is worth $100,000. D has made a gift to S of $60,000.

*Certain Excluded Transfers.* Transfers to political organizations [as defined in § 527(e)(1)] made after May 7, 1974, are exempt from the application of the Federal gift tax.[29] This change in the Code made unnecessary the previous practice whereby candidates for public office established multiple campaign committees to maximize the number of annual exclusions available to their contributors. As noted later, an annual exclusion of $10,000 (previously $3,000) for each donee passes free of the Federal gift tax.

The Federal gift tax does not apply to tuition payments made to an educational organization (e. g., a college) on another's behalf. Nor does it apply to amounts paid on another's behalf for medical care.[30] In this regard, perhaps, the law is realistic, since most donors would not likely recognize these items as being transfers subject to the gift tax.

*Lifetime versus Death Transfers.* Be careful to distinguish between lifetime (i. e., inter vivos) and death (i. e., testamentary) transfers.

---

**27.** The forgiveness could, however, result in taxable income to S under § 61(a)(12).

**28.** Loans between relatives are highly suspect and, on many occasions, have been treated as gifts. The issue usually arises when the creditor tries to claim a bad debt loss and the IRS contends that a bona fide debt never existed. A potential gift tax problem exists if the loan is recognized and no interest (or a below-market rate) is provided for. The problem of gift loans is discussed later in the chapter.

**29.** § 2501(a)(5).

**30.** § 2503(e).

**Example 12.** D buys a U. S. savings bond, which he registers as follows: "D, payable to S upon D's death." No gift is made when D buys the bond; S has received only a mere expectancy (i. e., to obtain ownership of the bond at D's death). Anytime before his death, D may redeem or otherwise dispose of the bond and thereby cut off S's interest. On D's death, no gift is made, because the bond passes to S by testamentary disposition.[31]

**Example 13.** D purchases an insurance policy on his own life (face value of $100,000) and designates S as the beneficiary. Until his death, D remains the owner of the policy and pays all premiums thereon. In accordance with the reasoning set forth in Example 12, no gift to S is made either when the policy is purchased or when D pays any of the premiums thereon. On D's death, the $100,000 proceeds pass to S as a testamentary and not as an inter vivos transfer.[32]

## TRANSFERS SUBJECT TO THE GIFT TAX

Whether or not a transfer will constitute one subject to the Federal gift tax will depend upon the application of § § 2511 through 2519 and the Regulations thereunder.

*Gift Loans.* To understand recent legislation enacted by Congress, an illustration is helpful.

**Example 14.** Before his daughter (D) leaves for college, F loans her $300,000. D signs a note that provides for repayment in five years. The loan, however, contains no interest element, and neither F nor D expects any interest to be paid. Following F's advice, D invests the loan proceeds in income-producing securities. During her five years in college, D uses the income from the investments to pay for college costs and other living expenses. On the maturity date of the note, D repays the $300,000 she owes F.

Regarding the factual situation presented in Example 14, what were the parties trying to accomplish? Presuming the loan is recognized as valid, D and F would hope for the following results:

1. No gift has taken place as to the loan proceeds.

2. No gift has taken place as to the interest element. Although D enjoys the use of the loan funds interest-free, until recently no court had held that this was a benefit subject to the Federal gift tax.[33]

---

31. It will be included in D's gross estate under § 2033 (property in which the decedent had an interest).
32. The proceeds would be included in D's gross estate under § 2042(2).
33. The result reached in *Lester Crown,* 67 T.C. 1060 (1977), was thought to be valid until repudiated in *Dickman v. Comm.,* 84–1 USTC ¶ 9240, 53 AFTR2d 84–1608, 104 S.Ct. 1086 (USSC, 1984). In *Dickman,* the Supreme Court found that the interest element was subject to the Federal gift tax.

3. The income from the invested loan proceeds will be taxed to D. This will save income taxes for the family unit if one assumes that D is in a lower tax bracket than F.

4. No income will result to F as to the forgone interest element. Again, this result was based on a very solid judicial foundation.[34]

In the Deficit Reduction Act of 1984, Congress resolved to rectify what it considered to be an abusive situation (i. e., Example 14). In a gift loan arrangement, the following consequences now ensue:

—F will have made a gift to D of the interest element. The amount of the gift will be determined by the difference between the amount of interest charged (in this case, none) and the market rate (as determined by the yield on certain U. S. government securities). (Compare result 2.)

—The interest element must be included in F's gross income and will be subject to the Federal income tax. (Compare result 4.)

—D will be allowed an income tax deduction as to the interest element. This will benefit D only if she is in a position to itemize her deductions *from* adjusted gross income.

Section 7872(f)(3) defines a gift loan as "any below-market loan where the foregoing [*sic*] of interest is in the nature of a gift." Unless tax avoidance was one of the principal purposes of the loan, special limitations apply if the gift loan does not exceed $100,000. In such a case, the interest element shall not exceed the borrower's net investment income.[35] Furthermore, if such net investment income does not exceed $1,000, it shall be treated as zero. Under the $1,000 *de minimis* rule, therefore, the interest element is to be disregarded.

*Certain Property Settlements (§ 2516).* Normally, the settlement of certain marital rights is not regarded as being for consideration in money or money's worth and is therefore subject to the Federal gift tax.[36] As a special exception to this general approach, Congress saw fit to enact § 2516. Under this provision, transfers of property interests made under the terms of a written agreement between spouses in settlement of their marital or property rights are deemed to be for adequate consideration and are thereby exempt from the Federal gift tax if a final decree of divorce is obtained within the three-year period beginning on the date one year before such agreement is entered into. Likewise excluded are transfers to provide a reasonable allowance for the support of minor children (including legally adopted children) of a marriage. The agreement need not be approved by the divorce decree.

*Disclaimers (§ 2518).* A disclaimer is a refusal by a person to accept property that is designated to pass to him or her. The effect of the disclaimer is to pass the property to someone else.

---

34. See, for example, *J. Simpson Dean,* 35 T.C. 1083 (1961), which negated imputed income as to the borrower.

35. Net investment income has the same meaning given to the term by § 163(d)(3). Generally, net investment income is investment income (e. g., interest, dividends, rents) less related expenses.

36. See Reg. § 25.2512–8 and Example 5 in this chapter.

**Example 15.** D dies intestate (i. e., without a will) and is survived by a son, S, and a grandson, GS.[37] At the time of his death, D owned real estate which, under the applicable state law of intestate succession, passes to the closest lineal descendant, S in this case. If, however, S disclaims his interest in the real estate, state law provides that the property would pass to the next lineal descendant, GS in this case. At the time of D's death, S has considerable property of his own although GS has none.

Why might S want to consider issuing a disclaimer as to his inheritance and have the property pass directly from D to GS? By so doing, an extra transfer tax might be avoided. If the disclaimer does not take place, (i. e., S accepts the inheritance) and the property eventually passes to GS (either by gift or by death), the later transfer will be subject to the application of either the gift tax or the estate tax.

For many years, whether or not a disclaimer was effective to avoid a Federal transfer tax depended on the application of state law. To illustrate by using the facts of Example 15, if state law determined that a disclaimer by S after D's death still meant that the real estate was deemed to have passed through S, the Federal gift tax would apply. In essence, S would be treated as if he had inherited the property from D and then given it to GS. As state law was not always consistent in this regard and sometimes was not even known, the application or nonapplication of Federal transfer taxes could depend on where the parties lived. To remedy this situation and provide some measure of uniformity to the area of disclaimers, § § 2046 and 2518 were added to the Code by the Tax Reform Act of 1976.

In the case of the gift tax, meeting the requirements of § 2518 would treat a timely lifetime disclaimer by S (refer to Example 15) as if the property went directly from D to GS. Since it is not regarded as having passed through S (regardless of what state law holds), it will not be subject to the Federal gift tax.

Section 2518(c)(1) also permits the avoidance of the Federal gift tax in cases of a partial disclaimer of an undivided interest.

**Example 16.** Assume the same facts as in Example 15, except that S wishes to retain one-half of the real estate for himself. If S makes a timely disclaimer of an undivided one-half interest in the property, the Federal gift tax will not apply as to the portion passing to GS.

*Other Transfers Subject to Gift Tax.* Other transfers that may carry gift tax consequences (e. g., the exercise of a power of appointment, the creation of joint ownership) are discussed and illustrated in connection with the Federal estate tax.

---

**37.** All states provide for an order of distribution in the event someone dies without a will. After the surviving spouse who receives some or all of the estate, the preference is usually in the following order: down to lineal descendants (e. g., children, grandchildren), up to lineal ascendants (e. g., parents, grandparents), and out to collateral relations (e. g., brothers, sisters, aunts, and uncles).

## ANNUAL EXCLUSION

*In General.*    The first $10,000 of gifts made to any one person during any calendar year (except gifts of future interests in property) is excluded in determining the total amount of gifts for the year.[38] The annual exclusion is applied to all gifts of a present interest made during the calendar year in the order in which made until the $10,000 exclusion per donee is exhausted. For a gift in trust, each beneficiary of the trust is treated as a separate person for purposes of the exclusion.

A future interest may be defined as one that will come into being (as to use, possession, or enjoyment) at some future date. Examples of future interests would include such possessory rights, whether vested or contingent, as remainder and reversionary interests that are commonly encountered when property is transferred to a trust. On the other hand, a present interest is an unrestricted right to the immediate use, possession, or enjoyment of property or of the income therefrom.

> **Example 17.**    During the current year, D makes the following cash gifts: $8,000 to R and $12,000 to S. D may claim an annual exclusion of $8,000 with respect to R and $10,000 with respect to S.[39]

> **Example 18.**    By a lifetime gift, D transfers property to a trust with a life estate (with income payable annually) to R and remainder upon R's death to S. D has made two gifts: one to R of a life estate and one to S of a remainder interest.[40] The life estate is a present interest; therefore, it qualifies for the annual exclusion. The remainder interest granted to S is a future interest and does not qualify for the exclusion. Note that S's interest does not come into being until some future date (i. e., on the death of R).

Although Example 18 indicates that the gift of an income interest is a present interest, this may not always prove to be the case. If a possibility exists that the income beneficiary may not receive the immediate enjoyment of the property, the transfer is one of a future interest.

> **Example 19.**    Assume the same facts as in Example 18 except that the income from the trust need not be payable annually to R but may, at the trustee's discretion, be accumulated and added to corpus. Since R's right to receive the income from the trust is conditioned on the trustee's discretion, it is not a present interest and no annual exclusion will be allowed. The mere possibility of diversion is enough; it would not matter if the trustee never exercised his or her discretion to accumulate and did, in fact, distribute the trust income to R annually.

*Trust for Minors.*    Code § 2503(c) offers an important exception to the future interest rules discussed above. Under this provision, a transfer for the benefit of a person who has not attained the age of 21 years on the date of the gift may be considered a gift of a present interest even though the

---

**38.**   § 2503(b).
**39.**   The $2,000 passing to S in excess of the $10,000 annual exclusion might not have generated any gift tax liability to D by virtue of the unified tax credit under § 2505.
**40.**   The valuation of each of these gifts is treated in Chapter 12.

minor is not given the unrestricted right to the immediate use, possession, or enjoyment of the property. For the § 2503(c) exception to apply, the following conditions must be satisfied:

—Both the property and its income may be expended by or for the benefit of the minor before he or she attains the age of 21.

—Any portion of the property or its income not expended by the minor's attainment of age 21 shall pass to the minor at that time.

—If the minor dies before attaining the age of 21, the property and its income will be payable either to his or her estate or as he or she may appoint under a general power of appointment.[41]

Thus, the § 2503(c) exception would allow a trustee to accumulate income on behalf of a minor beneficiary without converting the income interest to a future interest.

**Example 20.** D places property in trust, income payable to S until he reaches 21, remainder to S or S's estate. Under the terms of the trust instrument, the trustee is empowered to accumulate the trust income or apply it towards S's benefit. In either event, the accumulated income and corpus must be paid to S whenever he reaches 21 years of age or to whomever S designates in his will if he dies before reaching such age. The conditions of § 2503(c) are satisfied; therefore, D's transfer qualifies for the annual exclusion. S's interest is a present interest.

## DEDUCTIONS

In arriving at taxable gifts, a deduction is allowed for transfers to certain qualified charitable organizations. On transfers between spouses, a marital deduction may be available. Since both the charitable and marital deductions apply in determining the Federal estate tax, these deductions are discussed later in the chapter.

## COMPUTING THE FEDERAL GIFT TAX

*The Unified Transfer Tax Rate Schedule.* The top rates of the unified transfer tax rate schedule originally reached as high as 70 percent (see Appendix A, page A-5). To be consistent with the top rates applicable under the Federal income tax, under the Economic Recovery Tax Act of 1981, the maximum unified transfer tax rates were slated to be reduced to 50 percent during a phase-in period extending from 1982 through 1985. The Deficit Reduction Act of 1984 postponed the phase-in reduction to 50 percent until 1988 (see Appendix A, page A-9). Thus, the top rate will remain at 55 percent through 1987 (see Appendix A, page A-8).

Keep in mind that the unified transfer tax rate schedule applies to all transfers (by gift or death) after 1976. Different rate schedules apply for pre-1977 gifts (see Appendix A, page A-11) and pre-1977 deaths (see Appendix A, page A-10).

---

41. See later in the chapter for the definition of a general power of appointment.

*The Deemed Paid Adjustment.* Reviewing the formula for the gift tax (earlier in the chapter), note that the tax base for a current gift includes *all* past taxable gifts. The effect of such inclusion is to force the current taxable gift into a higher bracket due to the progressive nature of the unified transfer tax rates (refer to Example 1). To mitigate such double taxation, however, the donor is allowed a credit for any gift tax previously paid (refer to Example 2).

To limit the donor to a credit for the gift tax *actually paid* on pre-1977 taxable gifts would be unfair. Pre-1977 taxable gifts were subject to a lower set of rates (see Appendix A, page A-11) than those contained in the unified transfer tax rate schedule. As a consequence, the donor is allowed a "deemed paid" credit on pre-1977 taxable gifts. This is the amount that would have been due under the unified transfer tax rate schedule had it been applicable. Post-1976 taxable gifts do not need the deemed paid adjustment, since the same rate schedule is involved in all gifts.

**Example 21.** In early 1976, T made taxable gifts of $600,000, upon which a Federal gift tax of $135,525 (see Appendix A, page A-11) was paid. Assume T makes further taxable gifts of $600,000 in 1986. The unified transfer tax on the 1986 gifts would be determined as follows:

| | | |
|---|---:|---:|
| Taxable gifts made in 1986 | | $ 600,000 |
| Add: Taxable gifts made in 1976 | | 600,000 |
| Total of current and past taxable gifts | | $ 1,200,000 |
| Unified transfer tax on total taxable gifts per Appendix A, page A-8 [$345,800 + (41% × $200,000)] | | $ 427,800 |
| Subtract: | | |
| The deemed paid tax on pre-1977 taxable gifts per Appendix A, page A-8 [$155,800 + (37% × $100,000)] | $ 192,800 | |
| The unified tax credit for 1986 | 155,800 | 348,600 |
| Gift tax due on the 1986 taxable gift | | $ 79,200 |

Note that the gift tax actually paid on the 1976 transfer was $135,525. Nevertheless, the deemed paid credit allowed T on the gift was $192,800, considerably more than what was paid.

*The Election to Split Gifts by Married Persons.* To understand the reason for the gift-splitting election of § 2513, consider the following situations:

**Example 22.** H and W are husband and wife and reside in Michigan, a common law state.[42] H has been the only breadwinner in the family, and W has no significant amount of property of her own. Neither has made any prior taxable gifts or has used the $30,000 specific exemp-

---

**42.** The following states have the community property system in effect: Louisiana, Texas, New Mexico, Arizona, California, Washington, Idaho, Nevada and Wisconsin (effective January 1, 1986). All other states follow the common law system in ascertaining the rights of spouses to property acquired after marriage.

tion previously available for pre-1977 gifts. In 1986, H makes a gift to S of $1,020,000. Presuming the election to split gifts did not exist, H's gift tax is as follows:

| | |
|---|---:|
| Amount of gift | $ 1,020,000 |
| Subtract: The annual exclusion | 10,000 |
| Taxable gift | $ 1,010,000 |
| Gift tax on $1,010,000 per Appendix A, page A-8 [$345,800 + (41% × $10,000)] | $ 349,900 |
| Subtract: The unified tax credit for 1986 | 155,800 |
| Gift tax due on the 1986 taxable gift | $ 194,100 |

**Example 23.** Assume the same facts as in Example 22, except that H and W always have resided in California. Even though H is the sole breadwinner, the gift to S probably involves community property.[43] If this is the case, the gift tax is worked out as follows:

| | H | W |
|---|---:|---:|
| Amount of the gift (50% × $1,020,000) | $ 510,000 | $ 510,000 |
| Subtract: The annual exclusion | 10,000 | 10,000 |
| Taxable gifts | $ 500,000 | $ 500,000 |
| Gift tax on $500,000 per Appendix A, page A-8 | $ 155,800 | $ 155,800 |
| Subtract: The unified tax credit for 1986 | 155,800 | 155,800 |
| Gift tax due on the 1986 taxable gifts | $   –0– | $   –0– |

By comparing the results of Examples 22 and 23, it should be quite apparent to the reader that married donors residing in community property jurisdictions possessed a significant gift tax advantage over those residing in common law states. To rectify this inequity, the Revenue Act of 1948 incorporated into the Code the predecessor to § 2513. Under this Section, a gift made by a person to someone other than his or her spouse may be considered, for Federal gift tax purposes, as having been made one-half by each spouse. Returning to Example 22, this means H and W could treat the gift passing to S as being made one-half by each of them, in spite of the fact that the cash may have belonged to H. Consequently, the parties were able to achieve the same tax result as that outlined in Example 23.

To split gifts, the spouses must be legally married to each other at the time of the gift. If they are divorced later in the calendar year, they may still split the gift if neither marries anyone else during that year. They both must signify on their separate gift tax returns their consent to have all gifts made in that calendar year split between them. In addition, both must be citizens or residents of the United States on the date of the gift. A gift from one spouse to the other spouse cannot be split. Such a gift might, however, be eligible for the marital deduction allowed by § 2523.

The § 2513 election to split gifts would not be necessary when husband and wife transfer community property to a third party. It would, however,

---

43. Income from personal services generally is community property.

be available if the subject of the gift consisted of the separate property of one of the spouses.[44] The election, then, is not limited to residents of common law states.

## PROCEDURAL MATTERS

Having determined what transfers are subject to the Federal gift tax and the various deductions and exclusions available to the donor, consideration should be accorded to the procedural aspects of the tax. The sections to follow discuss the return itself, the due dates for filing and paying the tax, and other related matters.

*The Federal Gift Tax Return.* For transfers by gift after 1981, a Form 709 (U. S. Gift Tax Return) must be filed whenever the gifts for any one calendar year exceed the annual exclusion or involve a gift of a future interest. Regardless of amount, however, transfers between spouses that are offset by the unlimited marital deduction do not require the filing of a Form 709.[45]

> **Example 24.** In 1986, D makes five gifts, each in the amount of $10,000, to his five children. If the gifts do not involve future interests, a Form 709 need not be filed to report the transfers.

> **Example 25.** During 1986, M makes a gift of $20,000 cash of her separate property to her daughter. To double the amount of the annual exclusion allowed, F (M's husband) is willing to split the gift. Since the § 2513 election can be made only on a gift tax return, a form needs to be filed. This is the case in spite of the fact that no gift tax will be due as a result of the transfer. Useful for this purpose is Form 709–A (U. S. Short Form Gift Tax Return) available to simplify the gift-splitting procedure.

Presuming a gift tax return is due, it must be filed on or before the fifteenth day of the April following the year of the gift.[46] As is the case with other Federal taxes, when the due date falls on Saturday, Sunday, or a legal holiday, the date for filing the return is the next business day. Note that the filing requirements for Form 709 have no correlation to the accounting year used by a donor for Federal income tax purposes. Thus, a fiscal year taxpayer would have to follow the April 15 rule as to any reportable gifts.

*Extensions of Time and Payment of Tax.* If sufficient reason is shown, the Internal Revenue Service Centers are authorized to grant reasonable extensions of time for filing of the return.[47] Unless the donor is abroad, no extension in excess of six months may be granted. The application must be made before the due date of the return and must contain a full report of the causes for the delay. For a calendar year taxpayer, an extension of time for

---

**44.** Separate property is property acquired before marriage and property acquired after marriage by gift or inheritance.

**45.** § 6019(2).

**46.** § 6075(b)(1).

**47.** § 6081.

---

**Concept Summary**

1. The Federal gift tax applies to all gratuitous transfers of property made by U. S. citizens or residents. In this regard, it does not matter where the property is located.
2. In the eyes of the IRS, a gratuitous transfer is one not supported by full and adequate consideration in money or money's worth. If the parties are acting in a business setting, such consideration usually will exist. If, however, purported sales are between family members, such transfers are suspect of a gift element.
3. If a lender loans money to another and intends some or all of the interest element to be a gift, this arrangement is categorized as a gift loan. To the extent that the interest provided for is less that the market rate, three tax consequences ensue. First, a gift has taken place between the lender and the borrower as to the interest element. Second, income may result to the lender. Third, an income tax deduction may be available to the borrower.
4. Property settlements can escape the gift tax if a divorce occurs within a prescribed period of time.
5. A disclaimer is a refusal by a person to accept property designated to pass to that person. The effect of a disclaimer is to pass the property to someone else. If certain conditions are satisfied, the issuance of a disclaimer will not be subject to the Federal gift tax.
6. Except for gifts of future interests, a donor will be allowed an annual exclusion of $10,000. The future interest limitation does not apply as to certain trusts created for minors.
7. By making the election to split a gift, a married couple will be treated as two donors. Such an election doubles the annual exclusion and makes available the unified tax credit to the nonowner spouse.
8. The election to split gifts would not be necessary if the property is jointly owned by the spouses. Such would be the case if the property is part of the couple's community.
9. In determining the tax base for computing the gift tax, all prior taxable gifts must be added to current taxable gifts. Thus, the gift tax is cumulative in nature.
10. Gifts are reported on Form 709 or Form 709–A. The return is due on the fifteenth day of the fourth month following the year of the gift.

---

filing an income tax return also extends the time for filing the Form 709.[48] An extension of time to file the return does not extend the time for payment of the tax.

The tax shown on the gift tax return is to be paid by the donor at the time and place fixed for the filing of the return.[49] A reasonable extension of time, not to exceed six months (unless the donor is abroad), may be granted by the Service Center, at the request of the donor, for the payment of the tax shown on the return.[50]

Interest must be paid on any amount of tax that is not paid on or before the last date prescribed for the payment of the tax.[51] In addition, a penalty of one-half of one percent per month of the unpaid balance (up to a maxi-

---

**48.** § 6075(b)(2).
**49.** § 6151.
**50.** § 6161(a)(1).
**51.** § 6601.

mum of 25 percent) will be imposed unless the failure to pay was for reasonable cause. A penalty is also imposed for failure to file a gift tax return.[52]

# THE FEDERAL ESTATE TAX

The discussion of the estate tax that follows is developed to coincide with the pattern of the formula appearing earlier in the chapter. In brief, the formula for the estate tax is summarized as follows:

$$
\begin{array}{l}
\text{Gross estate} \\
- \text{ Deductions allowed} \\
\hline
\text{Taxable estate} \\
+ \text{ Post-1976 taxable gifts} \\
\hline
\text{Tax base} \\
\hline\hline
\text{Tentative tax on total transfers} \\
- \text{ Tax credits} \\
\hline
\text{Estate tax due} \\
\hline\hline
\end{array}
$$

The key components in the formula are the gross estate, the taxable estate, the tax base, and the credits allowed against the tentative tax.

## GROSS ESTATE

Simply stated, the gross estate comprises all property subject to the Federal estate tax. This in turn depends on the provisions of the Internal Revenue Code as supplemented by IRS pronouncements and the judicial interpretations of Federal courts.

Contrasted with the gross estate is the concept of the probate estate. Controlled by state (rather than Federal) law, the probate estate consists of all of a decedent's property subject to administration by the executor or administrator of the estate operating under the supervision of a local court of appropriate jurisdiction (usually designated as a probate court).[53] The probate estate is frequently smaller than the gross estate, because it contains only property owned by the decedent at the time of death and passing to heirs under a will or under the law of intestacy (i. e., the order of distribution for those dying without a will). As noted later, such items as the proceeds of many life insurance policies become part of the gross estate but are not included in the probate estate.

*Property Owned by the Decedent (§ 2033).*  Property owned by the decedent at the time of death will be includible in the gross estate. The nature of the property or the use to which it was put during the

---

**52.**  § § 6651(a)(1) and (2).

**53.**  An executor (or executrix) is the decedent's personal representative as appointed under the decedent's will. An administrator (or administratrix) is appointed by the local probate court of appropriate jurisdiction, usually because the decedent failed to appoint an executor in his or her will (or such designated person refused to serve) or the decedent died without a will.

decedent-owner's lifetime has no significance as far as the death tax is concerned. Thus, personal effects (clothing, etc.), stocks, bonds, furniture, jewelry, works of art, bank accounts, and interests in businesses conducted as sole proprietorships and partnerships are all included in the deceased owner's gross estate. In other words, no distinction is made between tangible or intangible, depreciable or nondepreciable, business or personal assets.

The application of § 2033 can be illustrated as follows:

**Example 26.** D dies owning some City of Denver bonds. The fair market value of the bonds plus any interest accrued to the date of D's death is includible in D's gross estate. Although interest on municipals is normally not taxable under the Federal income tax, it is, nevertheless, property owned by D at the time of his death.

**Example 27.** D dies on April 8, 19X4, at a time when she owns stock in X Corporation and in Y Corporation. On March 1, 19X4, both corporations authorized a cash dividend payable on May 1, 19X4. In the case of X Corporation, the dividend was payable to shareholders of record as of April 1, 19X4, while Y Corporation's date of record is April 10, 19X4. D's gross estate includes the following: the stock in X Corporation, the stock in Y Corporation, and the dividend on the X Corporation stock. It does not include the dividend on the Y Corporation stock.

**Example 28.** D dies holding some promissory notes issued to him by his son. In his will D forgives these notes, relieving the son of any obligation to make payments thereon. The fair market value of these notes will be included in D's gross estate.

**Example 29.** D died while employed by Z Corporation. Pursuant to an informal but nonbinding company policy, Z Corporation awards one-half of D's annual salary to his widow as a death benefit. Presuming that D had no vested interest in and that the widow had no enforceable right to the payment, none of it will be includible in his gross estate.[54]

*Dower and Curtesy Interests (§ 2034).* In its common law (nonstatutory) form, dower generally gave a surviving widow a life estate in a portion of her husband's estate (usually the real estate he owned) with the remainder passing to their children. Most states have modified and codified these common law rules, and variations between jurisdictions are not unusual. In some states, for example, a widow's statutory share of her deceased husband's property may mean outright ownership in a percentage of both his real estate and personal property. Curtesy is a similar right held by the husband in his wife's property taking effect in the event he survives her. Most states have abolished the common law curtesy concept and have, in some cases, substituted a modified statutory version.

Dower and curtesy rights are incomplete interests and may never materialize. Thus, if a wife predeceases her husband her dower interest in her husband's property is lost. This result is to be contrasted with the situation

---

**54.** *Barr's Estate,* 40 T.C. 164 (1963).

existing in community property jurisdictions. A deceased spouse's interest in the community is considered complete and is not lost by death. Thus, if a wife predeceases her husband, one-half of their community property passes to her heirs (or as she otherwise designates in her will).

The distinction between dower (and curtesy) and community property becomes very important for Federal estate tax purposes. Code § 2034 makes it quite clear that anything passing from the deceased spouse to the surviving spouse in the form of dower (or curtesy) shall be included in the gross estate of the deceased spouse. On the other hand, neither § 2033 nor § 2034 forces the surviving spouse's share of the community into the gross estate of the deceased spouse; that interest is not incomplete but was his or hers before death.

These rules are illustrated in the following examples.

**Example 30.** D dies without a will leaving an estate of $600,000. Under state law, W (D's widow) is entitled to one-third of D's property. The $200,000 W receives will be included in D's gross estate.[55] (Note: If W predeceased D, her dower interest would be defeated, and neither her probate nor gross estate would include any of D's property.)

**Example 31.** D and W are husband and wife, have always lived in Texas (a community property state), and at the time of D's death held community property of $1,000,000. Only $500,000 of this property (D's share of the community) will be included in D's gross estate.[56] [Note: If W predeceased D, $500,000 of the community property (her share) would be included in her gross estate.]

*Adjustments for Gifts Made Within Three Years of Death (§ 2035).* For many years the tax law provided that the value of property given by a decedent within three years of death should be included in his or her gross estate. The rule, moreover, made sense under a system where the gift and estate taxes were separate from each other and one (the gift tax) provided for a lower set of rates. Under this type of structure, a provision was needed to preclude the tax avoidance that would result from a deathbed transfer. Otherwise a decedent could enjoy the ownership of property almost up to the point of death and, by making the last-minute gift, bypass the higher estate tax rates. Congress arbitrarily settled on a three-year period during which such gifts would be vulnerable to inclusion in the donor's gross estate at their fair market value on date of death (or alternate valuation date if applicable).

A further possibility for avoidance was the estate tax savings that could be accomplished on any gift tax that was paid as a result of the transfer. Because such funds were no longer held at death, they would not be included in the gross estate. Congress precluded this approach in the Tax Reform Act of 1976 by requiring the "gross-up" procedure. Under this approach, any gifts brought back into the gross estate must include the gift

---

55. Depending on the nature of the interest W receives in the $200,000, this amount could qualify D's estate for a marital deduction under § 2056. This possibility is discussed at greater length later in the chapter. For the time being, however, the focus is on what is or is not included as part of the decedent's gross estate.
56. The inclusion comes under § 2033 (property owned by the decedent).

tax paid thereon. Any such gift tax, however, would be allowed as a credit against the estate tax of the donor-decedent.

If one operates on the assumption that no difference exists between the rates applicable to lifetime and death transfers (i. e., the same rate schedule applies), as is presently the case with the unified transfer tax scheme, why force inclusion in the gross estate of gifts made within a three-year period prior to the donor's death? Such inclusion only compelled the parties to revalue the property, since it was the fair market value of the property on the date of the donor's death (or alternate valuation date if applicable) and not the value of the property on the date of the gift that measured what was added to the gross estate. Congress recognized these problems and in the Economic Recovery Tax Act of 1981 significantly revamped the approach of § 2035.

For donors dying after 1981, the following modifications of § 2035 were made:

—Except as noted below, gifts made within three years of death are treated the same as any other post-1976 taxable gifts. Consequently, they are added to the *taxable estate* in arriving at the tax base for applying the unified transfer tax at death (see the formula for the Federal estate tax discussed earlier). This means the property will not have to be revalued because it is the fair market value on the date of the gift (not on the date of death) that will control.

—The gross-up approach, however, is retained. Thus, any gift tax paid on gifts made within three years of death must be added to the *gross estate*.

**Example 32.** In 1984, D makes a taxable gift of property in the amount of $50,000, upon which he pays a gift tax of $6,000. At the time of his death in 1986, the property is worth $75,000. As to the transfer, D's gross estate must include $6,000 (the gross-up of the gift tax) and $50,000 must be added to D's taxable estate in arriving at the tax base.

The pre-ERTA three-year rule has been retained for transfers of property interests that would have been included in the gross estate by virtue of the application of § 2036 (transfers with a retained life estate), § 2037 (transfers taking effect at death), § 2038 (revocable transfers), and § 2042 (proceeds of life insurance).[57]

**Example 33.** In 1984, D transferred an insurance policy on her life (worth $9,000 with a maturity value of $40,000) to S, the designated beneficiary. Due to the $10,000 annual exclusion, D incurred no gift tax on the transfer. Upon D's death in 1986, S receives the $40,000 in insurance proceeds. D's gross estate must include $40,000 concerning the policy.

The three-year rule also applies in testing for qualification under § 303 (stock redemptions to pay death taxes and administration expenses),

---

57. § 2035(d)(2). Sections 2036, 2038, and 2042 are discussed later in the chapter.

§ 2032A (special valuation procedures), and § 6166 (extensions of time to pay death taxes).[58]

*Transfers with a Retained Life Estate (§ 2036).* Code § § 2036 through 2038 were enacted on the premise that the estate tax can be avoided on lifetime transfers only if the decedent does not retain control over the property. The logic of this approach is somewhat difficult to dispute—one should not be able to escape the tax consequences of property transfers at death while at the same time remaining in a position during life to enjoy some or all of the fruits of ownership.

Code § 2036 requires inclusion of the value of any property transferred by the deceased during lifetime for less than adequate consideration (in money or money's worth) if there was retained either of the following:

1. The possession or enjoyment of, or the right to the income from, the property.

2. The right, either alone or in conjunction with any person, to designate the persons who shall possess or enjoy the property or the income therefrom.

"The possession or enjoyment of, or the right to the income from, the property," as it appears in § 2036(a)(1), is considered to have been retained by or reserved to the decedent to the extent that such income, etc., is to be applied toward the discharge of a legal obligation of the decedent. The term "legal obligation" includes a legal obligation of the decedent to support a dependent during the decedent's lifetime.[59]

The practical application of § 2036 can best be explained by turning to two illustrations.

> **Example 34.** F's will passes all of his property to a trust, income to D for his life (i. e., D is given a life estate), and upon D's death, corpus (i. e., the principal) goes to R (i. e., R is granted a remainder interest). On D's death, none of the trust property will be included in his gross estate. Although D held a life estate, § 2036 is inapplicable, because D was not the transferor (F was) of the property.[60]

> **Example 35.** By deed D transfers the remainder interest in her ranch to S, retaining for herself the right to continue occupying the property until death. Upon D's death, the fair market value of the ranch will be included in D's gross estate under § 2036(a)(1).[61]

*Revocable Transfers (§ 2038).* Another type of lifetime transfer that is drawn into a decedent's gross estate is covered by § 2038. Under this Section, the gross estate includes the value of property interests transferred

---

**58.** § § 2035(d)(3) and (4). Sections 303, 2032A, and 6166 are discussed in Chapter 12 in connection with valuation and liquidity problems.

**59.** Reg. § 20.2036–1(b)(2).

**60.** Section 2033 (property owned by the decedent) would compel inclusion in D's gross estate of any income distributions he was entitled to receive at the time of his death.

**61.** D is further subject to the gift tax. The amount of the gift would be the fair market value of the ranch on the date of the gift less the portion applicable to D's retained life estate [as determined under the tables contained in Reg. § § 20.2031–7(f) and 25.2512–5(f)—see Appendix A, page A–16]. Any gift tax incurred would be eligible for the estate tax credit allowed under § 2012.

by the decedent (except to the extent that the transfer was made for adequate and full consideration in money or money's worth) if the enjoyment of the property transferred was subject, at the date of his death, to any power of the decedent to alter, amend, revoke, or terminate the transfer. This includes the power to change the beneficiaries or the power to accelerate or increase any beneficiary's enjoyment of the property.

The capacity in which the decedent could exercise the power is immaterial. If the decedent gave property in trust, making himself or herself the trustee with the power to revoke the trust, the property would be included in his or her gross estate. If the decedent named another person as trustee with the power to revoke, but reserved the power to later appoint himself or herself trustee, the property would also be included in his or her gross estate. If, however, the power to alter, amend, revoke, or terminate was held at all times solely by a person other than the decedent and the decedent reserved no right to assume these powers, the property is not included in the decedent's gross estate under § 2038.

The Code and the Regulations make it quite clear that inclusion in the gross estate under § 2038 is not avoided by relinquishing a power within three years of death.[62]

In the event § 2038 applies, the amount includible in the gross estate is only the portion of the property transferred that is subject, at the decedent's death, to the decedent's power to alter, amend, revoke, or terminate.

The preceding rules can be illustrated as follows.

**Example 36.** D transfers securities to S under the state's Uniform Gifts to Minors Act designating himself as the custodian. Under the Act, the custodian has the authority to terminate the custodianship at any time and distribute the proceeds to the minor. D dies four years later and before the custodianship is terminated.[63]

Although the transfer is effective for income tax purposes, it runs afoul of § 2038. Under this Section, the fair market value of the securities on the date of D's death will be included in D's gross estate for Federal estate tax purposes.[64]

**Example 37.** Assume the same facts as in Example 36, except that D dissolves the custodianship (thereby turning the securities over to S) within three years of death. The fair market value of the securities on the date of D's death will be includible in D's gross estate.[65]

**Example 38.** Assume the same facts as in Example 36, except that S becomes of age and the custodianship terminates prior to D's death. Nothing will be included in D's gross estate upon D's death.

---

**62.** § 2038(a)(1) and Reg. § 20.2038–1(e)(1).

**63.** The Uniform Gifts to Minors Act permits the ownership of securities to be transferred to a minor with someone designated as the custodian. The custodian has the right to sell the securities, collect any income therefrom, and otherwise act on behalf of the minor without court supervision. The custodianship arrangement is convenient and inexpensive. Under most state laws, the custodianship terminates when the minor reaches age 21.

**64.** Rev.Rul. 57-366, 1957–2 C.B. 618. See also *Dorothy Struit,* 54 T.C. 580 (1970), *aff'd.* in 71–2 USTC ¶ 12,815, 28 AFTR2d 71-6289, 452 F.2d 190 (CA–7, 1971).

**65.** § 2035(d)(2).

**Example 39.** G transfers securities to S under the state's Uniform Gifts to Minors Act designating D as the custodian. Nothing relating to these securities will be included in D's gross estate upon D's death during the term of the custodianship. Code § 2038 is not applicable, because D was not the transferor. G's death during the custodianship should cause no estate tax consequences; G has retained no interest or control over the property transferred.

In the area of incomplete transfers (i. e., § § 2036 and 2038) there is much overlap in terms of application. It is not unusual, therefore, to find that either or both of these Sections apply to a particular transfer.

*Annuities (§ 2039).* Annuities can be divided by their origin into commercial and noncommercial contracts. The noncommercial annuities are those issued by private parties and, in some cases, charitable organizations that do not regularly engage in such activities. Although both varieties have much in common, noncommercial annuities present special income tax problems and are not treated further in this discussion.

Reg. § 20.2039–1(b)(1) defines an annuity as representing "one or more payments extending over any period of time." According to this Regulation, the payments may be equal or unequal, conditional or unconditional, periodic or sporadic. Most commercial contracts fall into one of four general patterns:

1. *Straight-life annuity.* The insurance company promises to make periodic payments to X, the annuitant, during his or her life. Upon X's death, the company has no further obligation under the contract.

2. *Joint and survivor annuity.* The insurance company promises to make periodic payments to X and Y during their lives with the payments to continue, usually in a diminished amount, for the life of the survivor.

3. *Self and survivor annuity.* The company agrees to make periodic payments to X during his or her life and, upon X's death, to continue these payments for the life of a designated beneficiary. This and the preceding type of annuity are most frequently used by married couples.

4. *Refund feature.* The company agrees to return to the annuitant's estate or other designated beneficiary a portion of the investment in the contract in the event of the annuitant's premature death.

In the case of a straight-life annuity contract, nothing will be included in the gross estate of the annuitant at death. Code § 2033 (i. e., property in which the decedent had an interest) does not apply, because the annuitant's interest in the contract is terminated by death. Code § 2036 (i. e., transfers with a retained life estate) does not cover the situation; a transfer that is a "bona fide sale, for an adequate and full consideration in money or money's worth" is specifically excluded from § 2036 treatment. The purchase of a commercial annuity is presumed to entail adequate and full consideration unless some evidence exists to indicate that the parties were not acting at arm's length.

**Example 40.** D purchases a straight-life annuity that will pay him $1,000 a month when he reaches age 65. D dies at age 70. Except for the payments he received prior to his death, nothing relating to this annuity will affect D's gross estate.[66]

In the case of a survivorship annuity (classifications 2 and 3), the estate tax consequences under § 2039(a) are usually triggered by the death of the first annuitant. The amount included in the gross estate is the cost from the same company of a comparable annuity covering the survivor at his or her attained age on the date of the deceased annuitant's death.[67]

**Example 41.** Assume the same facts as in Example 40, except that the annuity contract provides for W to be paid $500 a month for life as a survivorship feature. W is 62 years of age when D dies. Under these circumstances, D's gross estate will include the cost of a comparable contract that would provide an annuity of $500 per month for the life of a person (male or female, as the case may be) age 62.

Full inclusion in the gross estate of the survivorship element is subject to the important exception of § 2039(b). Under this provision, the amount includible is to be based on the proportion of the deceased annuitant's contribution to the total cost of the contract. This can be expressed by the following formula:

$$\frac{\text{Decedent's contribution to purchase price}}{\text{Total purchase price of the annuity}} \times \begin{array}{c}\text{Value of the}\\\text{annuity (or refund)}\\\text{at decedent's death}\end{array} = \begin{array}{c}\text{Amount includible in}\\\text{the deceased annuitant's}\\\text{gross estate}\end{array}$$

**Example 42.** Assume the same facts as in Example 41 except that D and W are husband and wife and have always lived in a community property state. The premiums on the contract were paid with community funds. Because W contributed one-half of the cost of the contract, only one-half of the amount determined under Example 41 would be included in D's gross estate.[68]

For persons dying before 1985, an exclusion from the gross estate of up to $100,000 was allowed as to certain pension benefits. The exclusion covered distributions from qualified pension and profit sharing plans that were attributable to an employer's contributions.[69] Also covered were distributions from Individual Retirement Accounts (IRAs), Keogh (H.R. 10) plans, and tax-sheltered annuities. The exclusion was allowed only if the following conditions were satisfied:

---

**66.** D's income tax consequences before death would be governed ty § 72. Based on the exclusion ratio under § 72(b), a portion of each payment would be nontaxable.

**67.** Reg. § 20.2031–8(a)(3).

**68.** The result reached in Example 42 is not unique to community property jurisdictions. For example, the outcome would have been the same in a noncommunity property state if W had furnished one-half of the consideration from her own funds.

**69.** A qualified plan is one that meets the requirements of § 401(a).

—The benefit was not payable to the estate.

—If the benefit was payable in a lump-sum form, the beneficiary had to forgo the advantages of the 10-year averaging provisions of § 402(a).[70]

The Deficit Reduction Act of 1984 repealed the exclusion for persons dying after 1984. The reasons for the repeal were twofold. First, the exclusion often was not needed when the surviving spouse was the recipient of the pension benefit. Inclusion in the gross estate would be offset by an additional marital deduction. Second, allocation problems resulted if the distribution exceeded $100,000 and multiple beneficiaries were involved.

*Joint Interests (§ 2040 and § 2511).* Assume that D and Y own an undivided, but equal, interest in a piece of property. Such joint ownership could fall into any one of four categories: joint tenancy, tenancy by the entirety, tenancy in common, or community property.

If D and Y hold ownership as joint tenants, the right of survivorship exists.[71] If D predeceases Y, D's rights terminate and Y becomes the sole owner of the property. During his or her lifetime, a joint tenant usually possesses the right of severance—the right to have the property partitioned or to sell his or her interest to another. In the event of severance (either partition or sale), the right of survivorship ceases. If, for example, D sells his interest in a joint tenancy to Z, the joint tenancy terminates and Y and Z now hold the property as tenants in common.

A tenancy by the entirety is, basically, a joint tenancy between husband and wife. One important difference, however, is the absence of the right of severance, except by divorce. D, for example, may transfer his interest to Y, but he cannot sell to another or secure a partition of the property.

Acting together, husband and wife can terminate the tenancy by transferring their interest to a third party. Thus, D and Y may join together to sell their interest to Z.

Under the tenancy in common and community property arrangements, the rights of each owner extend beyond the owner's death. Thus, if D predeceases Y, one-half, or whatever interest he holds in the property, is included in his *probate* estate and passes to his heirs or other appointees. At least in the case of a tenancy in common, a tenant possesses the right to secure a partition of the property or to otherwise dispose of the interest. As to community property, however, partitions or other dispositions are not so easily accomplished, and state law should be checked carefully in this regard.

The Federal estate tax treatment of tenancies in common or of community property follows the logical approach of taxing only that portion of the property included in the deceased owner's probate estate. Thus, if D, X, and

---

**70.** Distributions from noncontributory qualified plans will be subject to the Federal income tax. Section 402(a) mitigates the bunching effect of a lump-sum distribution by providing a special averaging procedure.

**71.** Under the laws of some states, a joint tenancy will not exist unless the parties have specifically provided for the right of survivorship. In case of doubt, it is usually assumed that the parties did not intend the harsh result of a joint tenancy (i. e., survivor takes all), and a tenancy in common is presumed.

Z are tenants in common in a tract of land, each owning an equal interest, and D dies, only one-third of the value of the property is included in the gross estate. This one-third interest is also the same amount that will pass to D's heirs or appointees.

> **Example 43.** D, X, and Z acquire a tract of land, ownership listed as tenants in common, each party furnishing $20,000 of the $60,000 purchase price. At a point when the property is worth $90,000, D dies. If D's undivided interest in the property is 33⅓%, the gross estate *and* probate estate includes $30,000.[72]

In the case of certain joint tenancies, the tax consequences are different. All of the property is included in the deceased co-owner's gross estate unless it can be proven that the surviving co-owners contributed to the cost of the property.[73] If a contribution can be shown, the amount to be excluded is calculated by the following formula:

$$\frac{\text{Surviving co-owner's contribution}}{\text{Total cost of the property}} \times \text{Fair market value of the property}$$

In computing a survivor's contribution, any funds received as a gift *from the deceased co-owner* and applied to the cost of the property cannot be counted. However, that income or gain from gift assets can be so counted.

If the co-owners receive the property as a gift *from another,* each co-owner will be deemed to have contributed to the cost of his or her own interest.

The preceding rules can be illustrated as follows.

> **Example 44.** D and Y (father and son) acquire a tract of land, ownership listed as joint tenancy with right of survivorship, D furnishing $40,000 and Y $20,000 of the $60,000 purchase price. Of the $20,000 provided by Y, $10,000 had previously been received as a gift from D. At a point when the property is worth $90,000, D dies. Because only $10,000 of Y's contribution can be counted (the other $10,000 was received as a gift from D), Y has only furnished ⅙ (i. e., $10,000/$60,000) of the cost. Thus, D's gross estate must include ⅚ of $90,000, or $75,000.[74] D's death makes Y the immediate owner of the property by virtue of the right of survivorship; therefore, none of the property will be part of D's probate estate.

> **Example 45.** F transfers property to D and Y as a gift listing ownership as joint tenancy with the right of survivorship. Upon D's death,

---

72. Unless the parties provided otherwise, each tenant would be deemed to own an interest equal to the portion of the original consideration he or she furnished. On the other hand, the parties could have provided, for example, that D would receive an undivided half interest in the property although he contributed only one-third of the purchase price. In such case, X and Z have made a gift to D when the tenancy was created, and D's gross estate and probate estate would each include $45,000.

73. § 2040.

74. This presumes Y can prove that he did in fact make the $10,000 contribution. In the absence of such proof, the full value of the property will be included in D's gross estate.

one-half of the value of the property will be included in the gross estate. Since the property was received as a gift and the donees are equal owners, each will be considered as having furnished one-half of the consideration.

Before the Economic Recovery Tax Act of 1981, married persons who held property in joint tenancy or tenancy by the entirety were subject to a myriad of rules, some being similar to those already discussed in connection with joint ownership between nonspouses. Several reasons convinced Congress to modify these rules for situations where the property is held jointly (with the right of survivorship) between husband and wife. The reasons are summarized as follows:

—Simplification of the tax law was important in that most joint ownership arrangements involve husband and wife.

—Prior law placed an undue burden on the surviving spouse to prove his or her contribution to the cost of the property (refer to Example 44, but assume that D and Y are husband and wife).

—In view of the unlimited marital deduction (see later in the chapter), both for estate and gift tax purposes, the old rules possessed little continuing validity.

Code § 2040(b) as amended provides for an automatic-inclusion rule upon the death of the first joint-owner spouse to die after 1981. Regardless of the amount of the contribution furnished by each spouse, one-half of the value of the property will be included in the gross estate of the spouse that predeceases.

**Example 46.** In 1982, H purchases real estate for $100,000 using his separate funds and listing title as "H and W, joint tenants with the right of survivorship." H predeceases W four years later when the property is worth $300,000. If H and W are husband and wife, H's gross estate must include $150,000 (½ of $300,000) as to the property.

**Example 47.** Assume the same facts as in Example 46, except that it is W (instead of H) who dies first. Presuming the date of death value to be $300,000, W's gross estate must include $150,000 as to the property. In this regard, it is of no consequence that W did not contribute to the cost of the real estate.[75]

Whether or not a gift results when property is transferred into some form of joint ownership will depend on the consideration furnished by each of the contributing parties for the ownership interest thereby acquired.

**Example 48.** D and S purchase real estate as tenants in common, each furnishing $20,000 of the $40,000 cost. If each is an equal owner in the property, no gift has occurred.

---

75. In both Examples 46 and 47, inclusion in the gross estate of the first spouse to die will be neutralized by the unlimited marital deduction allowed for estate tax purposes (see the discussion of § 2056 later in the chapter). Recall that under the right of survivorship feature, the surviving joint tenant obtains full ownership of the property. The marital deduction generally is allowed for property passing from one spouse to another.

**Example 49.** Assume the same facts as in Example 48, except that of the $40,000 purchase price, D furnishes $30,000 and S only $10,000. If each is an equal owner in the property, D has made a gift to S of $10,000.

**Example 50.** M purchases real estate for $240,000, the title to the property being listed as follows: "M, D, and S as joint tenants with the right of survivorship." If under state law the mother (M), the daughter (D), and the son (S) are deemed to be equal owners in the property and each has the right of severance, M will be treated as having made gifts of $80,000 to D and $80,000 to S.

Several principal exceptions exist to the general rule that the creation of a joint ownership with disproportionate interests resulting from unequal consideration will trigger gift treatment. First, if the transfer involves a joint bank account, there is no gift at the time of the contribution.[76] If a gift occurs, it will be when the noncontributing party withdraws the funds provided by the other joint tenant. Second, the same rule applies to the purchase of U. S. savings bonds. Again, any gift tax consequences will be postponed until such time as the noncontributing party appropriates some or all of the proceeds for his or her individual use.

**Example 51.** D deposits $20,000 in a bank account under the names of D and S as joint tenants. Both D and S have the right to withdraw funds from the account without the other's consent or joinder. D has not made a gift to S when the account is established.

**Example 52.** Assume the same facts as in Example 51. At some later date, S withdraws $5,000 from the account for her own use. At this point, D has made a gift to S of $5,000.

**Example 53.** D purchases a U. S. savings bond that he registers in the names of D and S. After D dies, S redeems the bond. No gift takes place when D buys the bond. In addition, S's redemption is not treated as a gift, because the bond passed to her by testamentary disposition (i. e., S acquired the bond by virtue of surviving D) and not through a lifetime transfer.[77]

*Powers of Appointment (§ 2041 and § 2514).* A power of appointment is a power to determine who shall own or enjoy, presently or in the future, the property subject to the power. It must be created by another; therefore, it does not include a power created or retained by the decedent when he or she transferred his or her own property. The term "power of appointment" includes all powers that are in substance and effect powers of appointment regardless of the terminology used in a particular instrument and regardless of local property law. If, for example, a trust instrument provides that the income beneficiary may appropriate or consume the principal of the trust, this right is a power of appointment over the principal even though it may not be designated as such.

---

**76.** Reg. § 25.2511–1(h)(4).
**77.** The fair market value of the bond would be included in D's gross estate under § 2040.

Powers of appointment fall into one of two classifications: general and special. A general power of appointment is one in which the decedent could have appointed himself, his creditors, his estate, or the creditors of his estate. On the other hand, a special power enables the holder to appoint to others but *not* to himself, his creditors, his estate, or the creditors of his estate. Assume, for example, that D has the power to designate how the principal of the trust will be distributed among X, Y, and Z. At this point, D's power is only a special power of appointment. If D were further given the right to appoint the principal to himself, what was a special then becomes a general power of appointment.

Three things can happen to a power of appointment: exercise, lapse, or release. To exercise the power would be to appoint the property to one or all of the parties designated. A lapse occurs upon failure to exercise a power. Thus, if a holder, D, failed to indicate how the principal of a trust will be distributed among X, Y, and Z, D's power of appointment would lapse and the principal would pass in accordance with the terms of the trust instrument. A release occurs if the holder relinquishes a power of appointment. A release should be distinguished from a disclaimer. In the former situation, the act follows after the acceptance of the power. If the designated holder decides he or she does not want the power, he or she may disclaim (i. e., refuse) and avoid the tax consequences attendant to a release. To constitute a disclaimer, the refusal must be made on a timely basis, be unequivocal, and be effective under applicable law.

The transfer tax consequences of powers of appointment can be summarized as follows:

1. No tax implications come about through the exercise, lapse, or release of a special power of appointment.

2. Only the exercise of a general power of appointment created before October 22, 1942, would result in a gift or cause inclusion in the holder's gross estate. The lapse or release of such powers during life or upon the death of the holder causes no tax consequences.

3. The exercise, lapse, or release of a general power of appointment created after October 21, 1942, during life or upon the death of the holder will cause the fair market value of the property (or income interest) subject to the power to be a gift or to be included in the holder's gross estate.

4. In connection with (3), a lapse of a general power is subject to gift or estate taxation only to the extent that the value of the property that could have been appointed exceeds the greater of either $5,000 or five percent of the aggregate value of the property out of which the appointment could have been satisfied.

5. In connection with (3), a holder is not considered to have had a general power of appointment if the power was exercisable only with the consent or joinder of the creator of the power or a person having a substantial adverse interest in the property subject to the power. For this purpose, the trustee administering a trust in his or

her fiduciary capacity does not, by that fact alone, have an adverse interest in the trust.[78]

6.   In connection with (3), a holder is not considered to have had a general power of appointment if he or she had a right to consume or invade for his or her own benefit, as long as such right is limited by an ascertainable standard relating to his or her health, education, support, or maintenance. A power to use the property for the "comfort, welfare, or happiness" of the holder is not an ascertainable standard and therefore is a general power of appointment.

These rules can be illustrated as follows (assume all powers were created after October 21, 1942).

> **Example 54.**  F, D's father, leaves his property in trust, life estate to D and remainder to whichever of D's children D decides to appoint under his will. D's power is not a general power of appointment, because he cannot exercise it in favor of himself, his creditors, his estate, or the creditors of his estate. Thus, regardless of whether or not D exercises the power, none of the trust property subject to the power will be included in his gross estate.

> **Example 55.**  Assume the same facts as in Example 54. In addition to the testamentary power to designate the beneficiary of the remainder interest, D is given a power to direct the trustee to pay to D from time to time so much of corpus as he might request "for his support." Although D now has a power that he can exercise in favor of himself, it is not a general power of appointment, because it is limited to an ascertainable standard. Thus, none of the property subject to these powers will be subject to the gift tax or be included in D's gross estate at D's death.[79]

*Life Insurance (§ 2042).*  Under § 2042, the gross estate includes the proceeds of life insurance on the decedent's life if (1) they are receivable by the estate, (2) they are receivable by another for the benefit of the estate, or (3) the decedent possessed an incident of ownership in the policy.

Life insurance on the life of another owned by a decedent at the time of his or her death would be included in his or her gross estate under § 2033 (i. e., property in which the decedent had an interest) and not under § 2042. The amount includible is the replacement value of the policy.[80] Under these circumstances, inclusion of the face amount of the policy would be inappropriate; the policy has not yet matured.

> **Example 56.**  At the time of his death, D owned a life insurance policy on the life of S, face amount of $100,000 and replacement value of

---

**78.**  See Reg. § 20.2041–3(c)(2) for examples of what constitutes a substantial adverse interest.

**79.**  The result would have been different if D's power of invasion were, say, "for his comfort and happiness." In such case, the power would not be limited by an ascertainable standard and would constitute a general power of appointment. As to the gift tax rules, see § 2514(c)(1).

**80.**  Reg. § 20.2031–8(a)(1).

$25,000, with W as the designated beneficiary. Since the policy has not matured at D's death, § 2042 is inapplicable. However, § 2033 (i. e., property in which the decedent had an interest) would compel the inclusion of $25,000 (the replacement value) in D's gross estate.[81]

The term "life insurance" includes whole life policies, term insurance, group life insurance, travel and accident insurance, endowment contracts (before being paid up), and death benefits paid by fraternal societies operating under the lodge system.[82]

As just noted, proceeds of insurance on the life of the decedent receivable by the executor or administrator or payable to the decedent's estate are included in the gross estate. It is not necessary that the estate be specifically named as the beneficiary. For example, if the proceeds of the policy are receivable by an individual beneficiary and are subject to an obligation, legally binding upon the beneficiary, to pay taxes, debts, and other charges enforceable against the estate, the proceeds will be included in the decedent's gross estate to the extent of the beneficiary's obligation. If the proceeds of an insurance policy made payable to a decedent's estate are community assets and, under state law, one-half belongs to the surviving spouse, only one-half of the proceeds will be considered as receivable by or for the benefit of the decedent's estate.

Proceeds of insurance on the life of the decedent not receivable by or for the benefit of the estate are includible if the decedent possessed at his or her death any of the incidents of ownership in the policy, exercisable either alone or in conjunction with any other person, even if acting as trustee. In this connection, the term "incidents of ownership" not only means the ownership of the policy in a technical legal sense. Generally speaking, the term has reference to the right of the insured or his or her estate to the economic benefits of the policy. Thus, it also includes the power to change beneficiaries, to revoke an assignment, to pledge the policy for a loan, or to surrender or cancel the policy.[83]

> **Example 57.** At the time of death, D was the insured under a policy (face amount of $100,000) owned by S with W as the designated beneficiary. The policy originally was taken out by D five years ago and immediately transferred as a gift to S. Under the assignment, D transferred all rights in the policy except the right to change beneficiaries. D died without having exercised this right, and the policy proceeds are paid to W. Under § 2042(2), the retention of an incident of ownership in the policy (e. g., the right to change beneficiaries) by D forces $100,000 to be included in the gross estate.

A group life insurance policy taken out by the decedent's employer on the life of the decedent is included in the employee's gross estate if the decedent had the right to change beneficiaries, to cancel the policy, or to exercise similar control over the policy. On the other hand, an irrevocable

---

**81.** If the policy were owned by D and W as community property, only $12,500 would be included in D's gross estate.
**82.** Reg. § 20.2042–1(a)(1). As to travel and accident insurance, see *Comm. v. Estate of Noel*, 65–1 USTC ¶ 12,311, 15 AFTR2d 1397, 85 S.Ct. 1238 (USSC, 1965).
**83.** Reg. § 20.2042–1(c)(2).

assignment by the employee-insured of all rights under the policy will be recognized for tax purposes under certain conditions. First, such assignment must be permitted under state law and under the terms of the insurance contract. Second, the employee must have possessed the right to convert the group policy into an individual insurance policy upon the termination of his or her employment.[84]

Assuming that the deceased-insured holds the incidents of ownership in a policy, how much will be includible in the gross estate if the insurance policy is a community asset? Only one-half of the proceeds become part of the deceased spouse's gross estate.

In determining whether or not a policy is community property or what portion of it might be so classified, state law controls. In this regard there appear to be two general views followed. Under the inception of title approach, the key to classification depends on when the policy was originally purchased.[85] If purchased prior to marriage, the policy will be separate property regardless of how many premiums were paid after marriage with community funds. However, in the event the noninsured spouse is not the beneficiary of the policy, he or she may be entitled to reimbursement from the deceased-insured spouse's estate for one-half of the premiums paid with community funds.

In some community property jurisdictions, the classification of a policy follows the tracing approach: the nature of the funds used to pay premiums controls.[86] Thus, if a policy was paid for 20 percent with separate funds and 80 percent with community funds, 20 percent of it will be separate property and 80 percent will be community property. At what point in time the policy was purchased should make no difference. Conceivably, a policy purchased after marriage with the premiums paid exclusively with separate funds would be classified entirely as separate property.

The mere purchase of a life insurance contract with the designation of someone else as the beneficiary thereunder does not constitute a gift. As long as the purchaser still owns the policy, nothing has really passed to the beneficiary. Even on the death of the insured-owner no gift takes place; the proceeds going to the beneficiary constitute a testamentary and not a lifetime transfer. But consider the following possibility:

> **Example 58.** D purchases an insurance policy on his own life which he transfers to S. D retains no interest in the policy (such as the power to change beneficiaries or to revest in himself or his estate the economic benefits of the policy). Under these circumstances, D has made a gift to S. Furthermore, if D continues to pay the premiums on the transferred policy, each payment will constitute a separate gift.

Under certain conditions, the death of the insured might represent a gift to the beneficiary of part or all of the proceeds. This may prove true when the owner of the policy is not the insured.

---

84. Rev.Rul. 68–334, 1968–1 C.B. 403.
85. The inception of title approach is followed in at least three states: Louisiana, Texas, and New Mexico.
86. This appears to be the rule in California and Washington.

**Example 59.** D owns an insurance policy on the life of S with T as the designated beneficiary. Up until the time of S's death, D retained the right to change the beneficiary of the policy. The proceeds paid to T by the insurance company by reason of S's death constitute a gift from D to T.[87]

**Example 60.** H and W live in a community property state. With community funds H purchases an insurance policy on his own life with a face amount of $100,000 and designates S as the revocable beneficiary. On H's death the proceeds of the policy are paid to S. If under state law H's death makes the transfer by W complete, W has made a gift to S of $50,000. Since the policy was held as community property, W was deemed to be the owner of only one-half of the policy.[88]

*Effect on the Gross Estate of Certain Generation-Skipping Transfers.* Before the Tax Reform Act of 1976, the trust device could be used with maximum effect as a means of skipping a generation of transfer taxes.

**Example 61.** D's will specifies that $1,000,000 of her estate is to be placed in trust, life estate to S (D's son) and remainder to GS (D's grandson). Five years later when S dies, the value of the trust is $2,250,000.

**Example 62.** Assume the same facts as in Example 61, except that the property passes outright (i. e., no trust arrangement is involved) to S. Five years later when S dies, the property (still owned by him) is worth $2,250,000. Under S's will, the property passes to GS.

The contrast between Examples 61 and 62 materialized upon the death of S. In Example 61 none of the trust assets would have been included in S's gross estate. Although S held a life estate, § 2036 would not come into play, since he was not the grantor of the trust. In Example 62, however, full inclusion is warranted by virtue of the application of § 2033 (i. e., property in which the decedent had an interest). Thus, the use of the trust device in Example 61 allowed the parties to skip a generation of transfer taxes (i. e., an estate tax on S's death).

Because of the possibility that substantial wealth could escape transfer taxes by using the approach of Example 61, § 2601 was enacted to impose a tax on certain generation-skipping transfers. The basic approach of the change is to treat the second generation from the grantor as having made a taxable disposition when the property passes to the third generation.[89]

**Example 63.** Assume the same facts as in Example 61, except that § 2601 applies to the arrangement. Upon S's death, the Federal estate tax will be imposed on the $2,250,000 as if it had passed from S (the second generation) to GS (the third generation).[90]

---

87. *Goodman v. Comm.*, 46–1 USTC ¶ 10,275, 34 AFTR 1534, 156 F.2d 218 (CA–2, 1946).
88. One-half of the proceeds of the policy ($50,000) would be included in H's gross estate under § 2042.
89. Under § 2612, the second generation in termed a "deemed transferor."
90. Although the discussion has utilized the lineal descendant type of situation (e. g., grandmother, son, grandson), the tax on generation-skipping transfers is not so limited. For a definition of what represents a generation-skipping transfer, see § 2611.

In determining the amount of the tax, the value of the trust must be added to the tax base of the estate of the second-generation beneficiary. Thus, the amount of the tax is the difference between the estate tax on the aggregate and the estate tax on the individually owned assets of the beneficiary.[91] Although the computation procedure treats the trust assets as if they had passed through the estate of the beneficiary, the actual generation-skipping tax is paid from the assets of the trust.[92]

**Example 64.** Assume the same facts as in Example 63, but with the further provision that S leaves a taxable estate of $1,000,000 and has not made any post-1976 taxable gifts. Disregarding the effect of any tax credits (including the unified tax credit), the generation-skipping tax is calculated as follows:

| | |
|---|---:|
| S's taxable estate | $ 1,000,000 |
| Add the value of the trust less the $250,000 adjustment (see below) | 2,000,000 |
| Tax base | $ 3,000,000 |
| Aggregate estate tax on $3,000,000 (see Appendix A) | $ 1,290,800 |
| Less the estate tax on S's taxable estate of $1,000,000 (see Appendix A) | 345,800 |
| Tax on the generation-skipping portion | $ 945,000 |

This transfer tax is not applicable to the first $250,000 passed to the grantor's grandchildren by each of the grantor's children.[93]

**Example 65.** D places property in trust, income payable to her children, R and S, for life, remainder to her grandchildren. When the remainder interest materializes (i. e., on the death of R and of S), R has two children and S has none. A maximum of $250,000 can be excluded, since S has no children.

**Example 66.** Assume the same facts as in Example 65, except that S is survived by a child (i. e., D's grandchild). The exclusion from the generation-skipping transfer tax now becomes $500,000 [$250,000 (the amount passing to R's children) + $250,000 (the amount passing to S's child)].

## TAXABLE ESTATE

After the gross estate has been determined, the next step is to arrive at the taxable estate. By virtue of § 2051, the taxable estate is the gross estate less the following: expenses, indebtedness, and taxes (§ 2053); losses (§ 2054); charitable transfers (§ 2055); and the marital deduction (§ 2056). As previously noted, the charitable and marital deductions also carry gift tax ramifications.

*Expenses, Indebtedness, and Taxes (§ 2053).* A deduction is allowed for funeral expenses; expenses incurred in administering property; claims

---

91. § 2602.
92. § 2603.
93. § § 2613(a)(4), (b)(5), and (6).

against the estate; and unpaid mortgages and other charges against property, the value of which is included in the gross estate without reduction for the mortgage or other indebtedness.

Expenses incurred in administering community property are deductible only in proportion to the deceased spouse's interest in the community.[94]

Administration expenses include commissions of the executor or administrator, attorney's fees of the estate, accountant's fees, court costs, and certain selling expenses for disposition of estate property.

Claims against the estate include property taxes accrued prior to the decedent's death, unpaid income taxes on income received by the decedent in his or her lifetime, and unpaid gift taxes on gifts made by the decedent in his or her lifetime.

Amounts that may be deducted as claims against the estate are only for enforceable personal obligations of the decedent at the time of his or her death. Deductions for claims founded on promises or agreements are limited to the extent that the liabilities were contracted in good faith and for adequate and full consideration in money or money's worth. However, a pledge or subscription in favor of a public, charitable, religious, or educational organization is deductible to the extent that it would have constituted an allowable deduction had it been a bequest.[95]

Deductible funeral expenses include the cost of interment, the burial plot or vault, a gravestone, perpetual care of the grave site, and the transportation expense of the person bringing the body to the place of burial. If the decedent had, prior to death, acquired cemetery lots for himself or herself and his or her family, no deduction will be allowed, but such lots will not be included in his or her gross estate under § 2033 (i. e., property in which the decedent had an interest).

*Losses (§ 2054).* Section 2054 permits an estate tax deduction for losses from casualty or theft incurred during the period of settlement of the estate. As is true with casualty or theft losses for income tax purposes, any anticipated insurance recovery must be taken into account in arriving at the amount of the deductible loss. If the casualty occurs to property after it has been distributed to an heir, the loss belongs to the heir and not to the estate. If the casualty occurs prior to the decedent's death, it should be claimed on the appropriate Form 1040. The fair market value of the property (if any) on the date of death plus any insurance recovery would be included in the gross estate.

As is true of certain administration expenses, a casualty or theft loss of estate property can be claimed as an income tax deduction on the fiduciary return of the estate (Form 1041). But the double deduction prohibition of § 642(g) applies; claiming the income tax deduction requires a waiver of the estate tax deduction.

*Transfers to Charity (§ 2055 and § 2522).* A deduction is allowed for the value of property in the decedent's gross estate that was transferred by

---

**94.** *U. S. v. Stapf,* 63–2 USTC ¶ 12,192, 12 AFTR2d 6326, 84 S.Ct. 248 (USSC, 1963).

**95.** § 2053(c)(1)(A) and Reg. § 20.2053–5.

the decedent through testamentary disposition to (or for the use of) any of the following:

1.  The United States or any political subdivision therein.

2.  Any corporation or association organized and operated exclusively for religious, charitable, scientific, literary, or educational purposes, as long as no benefit inures to any private individual and no substantial activity is undertaken to carry on propaganda or otherwise attempt to influence legislation or participate in any political campaign on behalf of any candidate for public office.

3.  A trustee or trustees of a fraternal society, order, or association operating under the lodge system if the transferred property is to be used exclusively for religious, charitable, scientific, literary, or educational purposes, and no substantial activity is undertaken to carry on propaganda or otherwise attempt to influence legislation or participate in any political campaign on behalf of any candidate for public office.

4.  Any veteran's organization incorporated by an Act of Congress (or any of its subdivisions) as long as no benefit inures to any private individual.

The organizations just described are identical to the ones that qualify for the Federal gift tax deduction under § 2522. With the following two exceptions, they are also the same organizations that will qualify a donee for an income tax deduction under § 170:

—Certain nonprofit cemetery associations qualify for income tax but not death and gift tax purposes.

—Foreign charities may qualify under the estate and gift tax but not under the income tax.

No deduction will be allowed unless the charitable bequest is specified by a provision in the decedent's will or the transfer was made before death and the property is subsequently included in the gross estate. Generally speaking, a deduction does not materialize when an individual dies intestate (i. e., without a will). The bequest to charity must be mandatory as to the amount involved and cannot be based on the discretion of another. It is, however, permissible to allow another, such as the executor of the estate, the choice of which charity will receive the specified donation. Likewise, a bequest may be expressed as an alternative and still be effective if the noncharitable beneficiary disclaims (i. e., refuses) the intervening interest before the due date for the filing of the death tax return (i. e., nine months after the decedent's death plus any extensions of time granted for filing).

*Marital Deduction (§ 2056 and § 2523).* The marital deduction originated with the Revenue Act of 1948 as part of the same legislation that permitted married persons to secure the income-splitting advantages of filing joint income tax returns. The purpose of these statutory changes was to eliminate the major tax variations that could develop between taxpayers residing in community property and in common law states. The marital deduction was designed to provide equity in the estate and gift tax areas.

In a community property state, for example, no marital deduction generally was allowed, since the surviving spouse already owned one-half of the community and such portion was not included in the deceased spouse's gross estate. In a common law state, however, most if not all of the assets often belonged to the breadwinner of the family. Upon such person predeceasing, all of these assets were included in his or her gross estate. [Recall that a dower or curtesy interest (regarding a surviving spouse's right to some of the deceased spouse's property) does not reduce the gross estate.] To equalize the situation, therefore, a marital deduction, usually equal to one-half of all separate assets, was allowed upon the death of the first spouse.

In the Economic Recovery Tax Act of 1981, Congress decided to dispense with these historical justifications and to recognize husband and wife as a single economic unit. Consistent with the approach taken under the income tax, spouses are to be considered as one for transfer tax purposes. By making the marital deduction unlimited in amount, neither the gift tax nor the estate tax will be imposed on outright interspousal transfers of property. Unlike prior law, the new unlimited marital deduction even includes one spouse's share of the community property transferred to the other spouse.

Under § 2056, the marital deduction is allowed only for property included in the deceased spouse's gross estate and which passes or has passed to the surviving spouse. Property that passes from the decedent to the surviving spouse includes any interest received as (1) the decedent's legatee, devisee, heir, or donee; (2) the decedent's surviving tenant by the entirety or joint tenant; (3) the appointee under the decedent's exercise (or lapse or release) of a general power of appointment; or (4) the beneficiary of insurance on the life of the decedent.

> **Example 67.** At the time of his death in the current year, D owned an insurance policy on his own life (face amount of $100,000) with W (his wife) as the designated beneficiary. D and W also owned real estate (worth $250,000) as tenants by the entirety (D having furnished all of the purchase price). As to these transfers, $225,000 ($100,000 + $125,000) would be included in D's gross estate, and this amount represents the property that passes to W for purposes of the marital deduction.[96]

Under certain conditions, disclaimers of property by the surviving spouse in favor of some other heir will affect the amount that passes and therefore qualifies for the marital deduction. Thus, if W is entitled to $400,000 of H's property but disclaims $100,000 in favor of S, the residuary legatee under the will, the $100,000 will pass from H to S and not from H to W. Disclaimers by some other heir in favor of the surviving spouse may have a similar effect. Suppose W, as residuary legatee, will receive $300,000 under H's will, but the will also provides that S is to receive a

---

**96.** Inclusion in the gross estate would fall under § 2042 (i. e., proceeds of life insurance) and § 2040 (i. e., joint interests). Although D provided the full purchase price for the real estate, § 2040(b) requires inclusion of only one-half of the value of the property when one spouse predeceases the other.

specific bequest of $100,000. If S issues a timely disclaimer in favor of W, the amount passing from H to W for purposes of the marital deduction will be increased from $300,000 to $400,000.

When a property interest passes to the surviving spouse, subject to a mortgage or other encumbrance, or when an obligation is imposed upon the surviving spouse in connection with the passing of a property interest, only the net value of the interest after reduction by the amount of the mortgage or other encumbrance qualifies for the marital deduction. However, if the executor is required, under the terms of the decedent's will or under local law, to discharge the mortgage or other encumbrance out of other assets of the estate or to reimburse the surviving spouse, the payment or reimbursement constitutes an additional interest passing to the surviving spouse.

Federal estate taxes or other death taxes that are paid out of the surviving spouse's share of the gross estate are not included in the value of property passing to the surviving spouse. Therefore, it is usually preferable for the deceased spouse's will to provide that death taxes be paid out of the portion of the estate that does not qualify for the marital deduction.

Certain interests in property passing from the deceased spouse to the surviving spouse are referred to as "terminable interests." Such an interest is one that will terminate or fail after the passage of time, upon the happening of some contingency, or upon the failure of some event to occur. Examples are life estates, annuities, estates for terms of years, and patents. A terminable interest will not qualify for the marital deduction if another interest in the same property passed from the deceased spouse to some other person for less than adequate and full consideration in money or money's worth, and by reason of its passing, such other person or his or her heirs may enjoy part of the property after the termination of the surviving spouse's interest.[97]

> **Example 68.** H's will places his property in trust, life estate to W, remainder to S or his heirs. The interest passing from H to W does not qualify for the marital deduction; it will terminate on W's death, and S or his heirs will thereafter possess or enjoy the property.

> **Example 69.** Assume the same facts as in Example 68, except that the trust was created by H during his life. No marital deduction is available for gift tax purposes for the same reason given in Example 68.[98]

> **Example 70.** During his life, H purchased a joint and survivor annuity providing for payments to himself for life and then to W for life should she survive. All payments cease on the death of H or W, whoever dies last. If H dies first, the value of the survivorship annuity included in his gross estate under § 2039(a) and passing to W will qualify for the marital deduction. Although W's interest in the annu-

---

97. § § 2056(b)(1) and 2523(b)(1).

98. Both Examples 68 and 69 contain the possibility of a qualified terminable interest property (QTIP) election discussed later in this section.

ity will terminate on her death, it is not a terminable interest; no other person may possess or enjoy the property after her death.

The justification for the terminable interest rule can be illustrated by examining more closely the possible result of Examples 68 and 69. Without the rule, H could have passed property to W at no cost because of the marital deduction. Yet, on W's death, none of this property would have been included in W's gross estate.[99] Apparently, then, the marital deduction should not be available in situations where the surviving spouse can enjoy the property and still pass it to another without tax consequences. The marital deduction merely postpones the transfer tax on the death of the first spouse; it operates to shift any such tax to the surviving spouse.

The terminable interest rule takes another form when one considers the exception of § 2056(b)(5).[100] Under this provision a property interest passing from the deceased spouse to the surviving spouse will qualify for the marital deduction (and not be considered a terminable interest) under the following conditions:

1.  The survivor is entitled for life to all of the income from the entire interest.

2.  Such income is payable annually or at more frequent intervals.

3.  The survivor has the power, exercisable in favor of himself or herself (or his or her estate) to appoint the entire interest.

4.  Such power is exercisable by him or her alone and in all events (although it may be limited to exercise either during life or by will).

5.  No part of the interest is subject to a power in any other person to appoint to anyone other than the surviving spouse.

Note that conditions 3 and 4 require the surviving spouse to be the holder of a general power of appointment over the property. The exercise, release, or lapse of the power during the survivor's life or at death would be subject to either the gift or the death tax.[101] Thus, if Examples 68 and 69 were modified to satisfy the preceding conditions, the life estate passing from H to W would not be a terminable interest and would qualify for the marital deduction.

As previously noted, the purpose of the terminable interest rule is to ensure that property not taxed to the transferor-spouse (due to the marital deduction) will be subject to the gift tax or the estate tax upon disposition by the transferee-spouse.

Consistent with the objective of the terminable interest rule, the Economic Recovery Tax Act of 1981 provides an alternative means for obtaining the marital deduction. Effective for gifts and estates of decedents dying after 1981, the marital deduction will be allowed for transfers of qualified

---

**99.** Section 2036 (i. e., transfers with a retained life estate) would not apply to W; W was not the original transferor of the property.

**100.** The gift tax counterpart to § 2056(b)(5) is § 2523(e).

**101.** § § 2514 and 2041.

terminable interest property (commonly referred to as QTIP). This is defined as property:

—That passes from one spouse to another by gift or at death.

—For which the transferee-spouse has a qualifying income interest for life.

In the case of a donee or a surviving spouse, a qualifying income interest for life exists under the following conditions:

—Such person is entitled for life to all of the income from the property (or a specific portion thereof), payable at annual or more frequent intervals.

—No person (including the spouse) has a power to appoint any part of the property to any person other than the surviving spouse during his or her life.[102]

If these conditions are met, an election can be made to claim a marital deduction as to the qualified terminable interest property. For estate tax purposes, the election is made by the executor of the estate on Form 706 (the Federal estate tax return). For gift tax purposes, the election is made by the donor spouse on Form 709 (the Federal gift tax return). The election is irrevocable.

If the election is made, a transfer tax will be imposed upon the qualified terminable interest property when the transferee-spouse disposes of it by gift or upon death. If the disposition occurs during life, the gift tax applies measured by the fair market value of the property as of that time.[103] If no lifetime disposition takes place, the fair market value of the property on the date of death (or alternate valuation date if applicable) will be included in the gross estate of the transferee-spouse.[104]

> **Example 71.** In 1986, H dies and provides in his will that certain assets (fair market value of $400,000) are to be transferred to a trust under which W (H's wife) is granted a life estate with the remainder passing to their children upon her death. Presuming all of the above requirements are satisfied and H's executor so elects, H's estate will receive a marital deduction of $400,000.

> **Example 72.** Assume the same facts as in Example 71, with the further stipulation that W dies in 1990 when the trust assets are worth $900,000. This amount must be included in W's gross estate.

Because the estate tax will be imposed on assets not physically included in the probate estate, the new law provides for a shifting of the liability attributable thereto to the heirs. The amount that can be shifted is to be determined by comparing the estate tax liability both with and without the inclusion of the qualified terminable interest property. This right of recovery can be negated by a provision in the deceased spouse's will.[105]

---

**102.** §§ 2523(f) and 2056(b)(7).

**103.** § 2519.

**104.** § 2044.

**105.** § 2207A(a).

## COMPUTING THE FEDERAL ESTATE TAX

Once the taxable estate has been determined, post-1976 taxable gifts are added to arrive at the tax base. Note that pre-1977 taxable gifts do not enter into the computation of the tax base.

> **Example 73.** D dies in 1986 leaving a taxable estate of $800,000. During her life, D made taxable gifts as follows: $50,000 in 1975 and $100,000 in 1982. For estate tax purposes, the Federal estate tax base becomes $900,000 determined as follows: $800,000 (taxable estate) + $100,000 (taxable gift made in 1982).

With the unified transfer tax rate schedule contained in § 2001(c), the tentative tax on the tax base then is computed. Using the facts in Example 73, the tax on $900,000 is $306,800 [$248,300 + (39% × $150,000)]—see Appendix A, page A-8.

From the tentative estate tax, subtract all available estate tax credits to arrive at the estate tax (if any) that is due.

## ESTATE TAX CREDITS

*Unified Tax Credit (§ 2010).* From previous discussion of this credit, recall that the amount of the credit allowed depends upon the year of the transfer. Returning to Example 73, the credit allowed on the gift in 1982 would be $62,800. Since the exemption equivalent of this amount is $225,000 (refer to the table preceding Example 3 of this chapter), no gift tax is due on this transfer. On D's death in 1986, however, the unified tax credit is $155,800, which is less than the tentative tax of $306,800 (refer to the discussion following Example 73). Disregarding the effect of any other estate tax credits, D's estate owes a tax of $151,000 [$306,800 (tentative tax on a tax base of $900,000) − $155,800 (unified tax credit for 1986)].

Also recall that an adjustment to the unified tax credit will be necessary if any portion of the specific exemption was utilized on gifts made after September 8, 1976, and before January 1, 1977. In this regard, refer to Example 4.

*Credit for State Death Taxes (§ 2011).* Section 2011 allows a limited credit for the amount of any death, inheritance, legacy, or succession tax actually paid to any state (or to the District of Columbia) attributable to any property included in the gross estate. Like the credit for foreign death taxes paid, this provision mitigates the harshness of subjecting the same property to multiple death taxes.

The credit allowed is limited to the lesser of the amount of tax actually paid or the amount provided for in a table contained in § 2011(b). (See Appendix A, page A-12.) No credit is available if the adjusted taxable estate is $40,000 or less.[106]

> **Example 74.** D's adjusted taxable estate is $38,000, and the state of appropriate jurisdiction imposes a death tax of $1,500 on this amount. None of the $1,500 paid qualifies for the death tax credit.

---

106. Under § 2011(b), the adjusted taxable estate means the taxable estate reduced by $60,000.

**Example 75.** D's adjusted taxable estate is $140,000, and the state of appropriate jurisdiction imposes a death tax of $3,000 on this amount. Of the $3,000 paid in state death taxes, only $1,200 would be deductible in view of the table contained in § 2011(b).

As noted in Examples 74 and 75, it may be entirely possible that the credit allowed by § 2011 proves to be less than the amount of state death taxes paid. The reverse is, of course, possible but usually not the case. Most states insure that the minimum tax payable to the jurisdiction is at least equal to the credit allowed by the table contained in § 2011(b). Sometimes this result is accomplished by a "sponge" tax superimposed on the regular inheritance tax. Thus, if the regular inheritance tax yielded $2,500, but the maximum credit allowed by the table is $3,200, a sponge tax would impose an additional $700 in state death taxes. In other states, the whole state death tax liability depends entirely upon the amount allowed for Federal death tax purposes as the credit under § 2011(b). Thus, in the previous illustration, the state death tax would be an automatic $3,200.

*Credit for Gift Taxes (§ 2012).* A credit is allowed under § 2012 against the estate tax for any Federal gift tax paid on a gift of property subsequently included in the donor-decedent's gross estate.

**Example 76.** In 1965, D transfers a remainder interest in a farm to her children, retaining for herself a life estate. As a result of the transfer, D incurred and paid a Federal gift tax of $45,000. D dies in 1986 when the property is worth $400,000. Since the application of § 2036 (retention of a life estate) forces the inclusion of the farm in D's gross estate, a double tax effect results. To mitigate this effect, § 2012 allows D's estate a credit for some or all of the $45,000 in gift taxes previously paid.

The adjustments that might be necessary in working out the amount of the credit could become somewhat complicated and are not discussed further.[107]

Under the Tax Reform Act of 1976, only taxable gifts made after 1976 will be added to the donor's taxable estate in arriving at the base for the application of the unified transfer tax at death. To the extent these gifts have exceeded the unified transfer tax credit and have generated a tax, such tax should be credited against the transfer tax due at death.

*Credit for Tax on Prior Transfers (§ 2013).* Suppose, for example, D owns some property that he passes at death to S. Shortly thereafter, S dies and passes the property to R. Assuming both estates are subject to the Federal estate tax, one can easily imagine the multiple effect involved in successive death situations. To mitigate the possible multiple taxation that might result, § 2013 provides relief in the form of a credit for a death tax on prior transfers.[108] Thus, to return to the preceding hypothetical case, S's

---

**107.** They are illustrated and explained in the instructions to Form 706 and in Reg. § 20.2012–1.

**108.** The double estate tax effect might not be complete if S were D's spouse and some or all of the property passing from D to S qualified D's estate for a marital deduction. For this reason, § 2013(d)(3) requires an adjustment to determine the credit for tax on prior transfers in the event the marital deduction is a factor.

estate may be able to claim as an estate tax credit some of the taxes paid by D's estate.

The credit is limited to the lesser of the following amounts:

1.  The amount of the Federal estate tax attributable to the transferred property in the transferor's estate.

2.  The amount of the Federal estate tax attributable to the transferred property in the decedent's estate.

To apply the preceding limitations, certain adjustments must be made that are not covered in this work.[109] One must note, however, that it is not necessary for the transferred property to be identified in the present decedent's estate or for it to be in existence at the time of the present decedent's death. It is sufficient that the transfer of property was subjected to the Federal estate tax in the estate of the transferor and that the transferor died within the prescribed period of time.

If the transferor died within two years before or two years after the present decedent's death, the credit is allowed in full (subject to the preceding limitations). If the transferor died more than two years before the decedent, the credit is a certain percentage: 80 percent if the transferor died within the third or fourth year preceding the decedent's death, 60 percent if within the fifth or sixth year, 40 percent if within the seventh or eighth year, and 20 percent if within the ninth or tenth year.

> **Example 77.** Pursuant to D's will, S inherits property. One year later S dies. Assume the estate tax attributable to the inclusion of the property in D's gross estate was $15,000 and that attributable to the inclusion of the property in S's gross estate is $12,000. Under these circumstances, S's estate may claim a credit against its estate tax of $12,000 (refer to limitation 2).

> **Example 78.** Assume the same facts as in Example 77, except that S dies three years after D's death. The applicable credit is now 80% of $12,000, or $9,600.

*Credit for Foreign Death Taxes (§ 2014).*   Under § 2014, a credit is allowed against the estate tax for any estate, inheritance, legacy, or succession tax actually paid to any foreign country. For purposes of this provision, the term "foreign country" not only means states in the international sense but also refers to possessions or political subdivisions of foreign states and to possessions of the United States.

The credit is allowed for death taxes paid (1) with respect to property situated within the foreign country to which the tax is paid, (2) with respect to property included in the decedent's gross estate, and (3) with respect to the decedent's estate. No credit is allowed for interest or penalties paid in connection with foreign death taxes.

The credit is limited to the lesser of the following amounts:

1.  The amount of the foreign death tax attributable to the property situated in the country imposing the tax and included in the decedent's gross estate for Federal estate tax purposes.

---

109.   See the instructions to Form 706 and Reg. § § 20.2013–2 and –3.

2.  The amount of the Federal estate tax attributable to particular property situated in a foreign country, subject to death tax in that country, and included in the decedent's gross estate for Federal estate tax purposes.

Both of these limitations may require certain adjustments to arrive at the amount of the allowable credit. Such adjustments are illustrated in the Regulations and are not discussed in this text.[110] In addition to the credit for foreign death taxes under the provisions of Federal estate tax law, similar credits are allowable under death tax conventions with a number of foreign countries.[111] If a credit is allowed either under the provisions of law or under the provisions of a convention, that credit that is most beneficial to the estate is allowed.

## PROCEDURAL MATTERS

A Federal estate tax return, if required, is due nine months after the date of the decedent's death.[112] This time limit applies to all estates regardless of the nationality or residence of the decedent. Not infrequently, however, an executor will request and obtain from the IRS an extension of time for filing Form 706 (estate tax return).[113]

In the case of the estate of a citizen or resident of the United States dying after 1976, Form 706 must be filed by the executor or administrator under the following conditions:[114]

| Year of Death | Gross Estate in Excess of |
| --- | --- |
| 1977 | $ 120,000 |
| 1978 | 134,000 |
| 1979 | 147,000 |
| 1980 | 161,000 |
| 1981 | 175,000 |
| 1982 | 225,000 |
| 1983 | 275,000 |
| 1984 | 325,000 |
| 1985 | 400,000 |
| 1986 | 500,000 |
| 1987 & thereafter | 600,000 |

The preceding filing requirements may be lower when the decedent has made taxable gifts after 1976 or has utilized any of the $30,000 specific gift tax exemption after September 8, 1976.

**Example 79.** D dies in 1986 leaving a gross estate of $495,000. If D has never made any post-1976 taxable gifts or used the specific gift tax

---

110. Reg. § § 20.2014–2 and –3.
111. For the list of countries with which the United States has death tax conventions, refer to Footnote 13.
112. § 6075(a).
113. § 6081.
114. § 6018(a).

exemption after September 8, 1976, Form 706 need not be filed by his estate.

**Example 80.** Assume the same facts as in Example 79, except that D made a taxable gift of $20,000 in 1980. Since the filing requirement now becomes $480,000 [$500,000 (the regular filing requirement for 1986) − $20,000 (the post-1976 taxable gift)], Form 706 must be filed by D's estate.

Form 706 must be filed with the IRS Service Center serving the district in which the decedent lived at the time of death. The return must be accompanied by various documents relevant to the determination of tax liability. Among items that must be included are statements on Form 712 to be obtained from the insurance companies involved for each insurance policy listed on the return.

Penalties are provided for willful failure to make and file a timely return and for willful attempts to evade or defeat payment of tax.[115]

---

## Concept Summary

1. Both the Federal gift and estate taxes are excise taxes on the transfer of wealth.
2. The starting point for applying the Federal estate tax is to determine what assets are subject to tax. Such assets comprise a decedent's gross estate. The gross estate must be distinguished from the probate estate, since the later classification includes those assets subject to administration by the executor of the estate.
3. Although the gross estate generally will not include any gifts made by the decedent within three years of death, it will include any gift tax paid on such transfers.
4. Based on the premise that one should not continue to enjoy or control property and not have it subject to the estate tax, certain incomplete transfers are subject to inclusion in the gross estate.
5. Upon the death of a joint tenant, the full value of the property will be included in the gross estate unless the survivor(s) made a contribution towards the cost of the property. Spouses are subject to a special rule that calls for automatic inclusion of one-half of the value of the property in the gross estate of the first tenant to die. As to joint tenancies (or tenancies by the entirety) between husband and wife, therefore, it makes no difference who furnished the original consideration. The creation of joint ownership will be subject to the gift tax when a tenant receives a lesser interest in the property than is warranted by the consideration furnished.
6. A power of appointment is the right to determine who shall own or enjoy, presently or in the future, the property subject to the power. The exercise, lapse, or release of a general power of appointment during the life of the holder will be subject to the gift tax. If the exercise, lapse, or release occurs at death, the property subject to the power will be included in the holder's gross estate. If, however, a special power of appointment is involved, no gift or estate tax consequences will result. Barring certain exceptions, a special power cannot be used to benefit the holder or his or her estate.
7. If the decedent is the insured, life insurance proceeds will be included in the gross estate if either of two conditions is satisfied. First, the proceeds are payable to the estate or for the benefit of the estate. Second, the decedent possessed incidents of ownership (e. g., the right to change beneficiaries) over the policy. A transfer of an unmatured life insurance policy is subject to the gift tax. A gift also occurs when a policy matures and the owner of the policy is not the insured or the beneficiary.

---

115. See, for example, § § 6651, 6653, 6672, and 7203.

8. In moving from the gross estate to the taxable estate, certain deductions are allowed. Under § 2053, deductions are permitted for various administration expenses (e. g., executor's commissions, funeral costs), debts of the decedent, and certain unpaid taxes. Casualty and theft losses incurred during the administration of an estate also can be deducted in arriving at the taxable estate.

9. Charitable transfers are deductible if the designated organization holds qualified status with the IRS at the time of the gift or upon death.

10. Transfers to a spouse qualify for the gift or estate tax marital deduction. Except as noted in (11), such transfers are subject to the terminable interest limitation.

11. The terminable interest limitation will not apply if the transferee spouse is given a general power of appointment over the property or the QTIP election is made. In the case of a lifetime transfer, the donor spouse makes the QTIP election. In the case of a testamentary transfer, however, the executor of the estate of the deceased spouse has the election responsibility.

12. The tax base for determining the estate tax is the taxable estate plus all post-1976 taxable gifts. From the tax so derived, subtract all available credits.

13. Of prime importance in the tax credit area is the unified tax credit. For 1986, the unified tax credit is $155,800 (exemption equivalent of $500,000). The final phase-in of the credit is scheduled to occur in 1987, when the credit rises to $192,800 (an exemption equivalent of $600,000).

14. Other Federal estate tax credits include credits for state death taxes, gift taxes, tax on prior transfers, and foreign death taxes.

15. If due, a Fedeal estate tax return (Form 706) must be filed within nine months of the date of the decedent's death. The IRS grants extensions for those estates that encounter difficulty in complying with this deadline.

## TAX PLANNING CONSIDERATIONS

# THE FEDERAL GIFT TAX

Before 1977, two sets of tax rates applicable to transfers for insufficient consideration existed. Since the gift tax rates were lower than the estate tax rates, this, by itself, placed a premium on lifetime giving as a means of reducing the overall tax burden. After 1976, however, the estate tax savings from a lifetime gift usually will be limited to the appreciation on the property that develops after the transfer is made. This result materializes because transfers by gift and by death are now subject to the same set of rates [i. e., the uniform transfer tax of § 2001(c)]. Also, taxable gifts made after 1976 must be added to the taxable estate in arriving at the amount of the estate tax.

As to taxable gifts that generate a tax, consideration must be given to the time value to the donor of the gift taxes paid. Since the donor loses the use of these funds, the expected interval between a gift (the imposition of the gift tax) and death (the imposition of the death tax) might make the gift less attractive from an economic standpoint. On the plus side, however, is the estate tax savings that would result from any gift tax paid. Since these funds are no longer in the gross estate of the donor (except for gifts within three years of death), the estate tax thereon is avoided.

Gifts made after 1976 do, nevertheless, possess distinct advantages. First, and often most important, income from the property will generally be shifted to the donee. If the donee is in a lower bracket than the donor, the family unit will save on income taxes. Second, the proper spacing of gifts can further cut down the Federal gift tax by maximizing the number of annual exclusions available. Third, all states but one impose some type of death tax, but only a minority impose a gift tax. Thus, a gift might completely avoid a state transfer tax.

In minimizing gift tax liability in lifetime giving, the optimum use of the annual exclusion can have significant results. Important in this regard are the following observations:

1. Because the annual exclusion is available every year, space the gifts over as many years as possible. To carry out this objective, start the program of lifetime giving as soon as is feasible. As an illustration, a donor could give as much as $100,000 to a donee if equally spaced over a 10-year period without using any of the unified transfer tax credit and incurring any gift tax.

2. To the extent consistent with the wishes of the donor, maximize the number of donees. For example, a donor could give $500,000 to five donees over a 10-year period ($100,000 apiece) without using any of the unified transfer tax credit and incurring any gift tax.

3. For the married donor, make use of the election to split gifts under § 2513. As an example, a married couple can give $1,000,000 to five donees over a 10-year period (i. e., $20,000 per donee each year) without using any of their unified transfer tax credit and incurring any gift tax.

4. Watch out for gifts of future interests. As noted earlier in the chapter, the annual exclusion is available only for gifts of a present interest.

Income tax considerations in lifetime giving are discussed under TAX PLANNING CONSIDERATIONS in Chapter 12.

# THE FEDERAL ESTATE TAX

## CONTROLLING THE AMOUNT OF THE GROSS ESTATE

Presuming an estate tax problem is anticipated, the starting point for planning purposes would be to reduce the size of the potential gross estate. Aside from initiating a program of lifetime giving, several other possibilities exist.

*Incomplete Transfers.* If property is to be excluded from a donee's gross estate by means of a lifetime transfer, the consequences of transfers deemed incomplete for estate tax purposes must be recognized. In general, transfers are considered incomplete if the transferor continues to exercise control over the property or to enjoy its use.

**Example 81.** In 19X0, M transfers title to her personal residence to D, her daughter. Until the time of her death in the current year, M continues to live in the residence.

In Example 81, the residence will be included in the gross estate of the donor (i. e., M) if an express or implied agreement exists between the donor and the donee for continued occupancy of the property.[116] This result is dictated by § 2036(a)(1); the transferor did not surrender the right to possession or enjoyment of the property.

If no express or implied agreement exists between the parties, may one be inferred by virtue of the fact that the transferor does not vacate the premises after the gift but continues to live there until his or her death? In this regard, the situation described in Example 81 could be precarious, to say the least.

An implied agreement will probably be found in Example 81 unless the parties can produce some strong proof to show otherwise. An affirmative answer to any of the following questions would be helpful, though not controlling, in excluding the residence from M's gross estate:

—Did M report the transfer on a gift tax return and, if appropriate, pay a Federal gift tax thereon?

—Did M pay a reasonable rental to D for her continued occupancy of the premises?

—Did D, as any owner might be expected to do, absorb the cost of maintaining the property?

—If the property was income-producing (e. g., a farm or ranch), did D collect and report the income therefrom?[117]

*Life Insurance.* If the insured wants to keep the proceeds of a life insurance policy out of his or her gross estate, no incidents of ownership can be retained. All too often, a policy is transferred but the transferor has unsuspectingly retained some incident of ownership that may cause inclusion in the gross estate. The only way to prevent this from happening is to carefully examine the policy itself. Needless to say, only through this review procedure can one be assured that all incidents of ownership have been released.

*Generation-Skipping Transfers.* Because of the period of time that may pass before the death of the second generation, planning to stay within the $250,000 exclusion for lineal descendant situations may be very difficult.

**Example 82.** In 1986, D places $250,000 worth of securities in trust, income payable to his son, S, for life, remainder to S's children. At the time of S's death 15 years later, the securities have increased in value to $1,000,000. Of the $1,000,000 that is deemed transferred from S (i. e., the second generation) to the children (i. e., D's grandchildren and the third generation), only $250,000 is excluded. The balance of $750,000 will be subject to the generation-skipping transfer tax.

---

**116.** See, for example, *Guynn v. U. S.,* 71–1 USTC ¶ 12,742, 27 AFTR2d 71–1653, 437 F.2d 1148 (CA–4, 1971).
**117.** Compare, for example, *Estate of Ethel R. Kerdolff,* 57 T.C. 643 (1972) with *Estate of Roy D. Barlow,* 55 T.C. 666 (1971).

The rules applying the generation-skipping tax do not cover irrevocable trusts in existence as of June 11, 1976, or those created by a will in existence on the same date if the decedent died prior to January 1, 1983.

Furthermore, the rules cover only situations involving trust, or trust equivalent, arrangements and where a beneficial interest passes from a second to a third generation.

**Example 83.** Pursuant to a will, D leaves property to her grandchildren. Since the transfer was directly to the grandchildren and D's children had no beneficial interest in the property, there is no generation-skipping tax imposed. Note that D has, in effect, skipped a transfer tax on a generation in bypassing the children and leaving the property directly to the grandchildren.

**Example 84.** H creates a trust, income payable to W, his wife, for life and, on her death, remainder to their children. No tax will be imposed on W's death, since a wife is deemed to be of the same generation as her husband. There exists, therefore, no generation skipping.

## PROPER HANDLING OF ESTATE TAX DEDUCTIONS

Estate taxes can be saved either by reducing the size of the gross estate or by increasing the total allowable deductions. Thus, the lower the taxable estate, the less the amount of estate tax generated. Planning in the deduction area generally involves the following considerations:

—Making proper use of the marital deduction.

—Working effectively with the charitable deduction.

—Handling other deductions and losses allowed under § § 2053 and 2054 properly.

*The Marital Deduction in Perspective.* When planning for the estate tax marital deduction, both tax and nontax factors have to be taken into account. In the tax area, two major goals exist that guide planning. They are the equalization and the deferral approaches described as follows:

—Attempt to equalize the estates of both spouses. Clearly, for example, the estate tax on $2,000,000 is more than double the estate tax on $1,000,000 [compare $780,800 with $691,600 ($345,800 × 2)].

—Try to postpone estate taxation as long as possible. On a $1,000,000 amount, for example, what is the time value of $345,800 in estate taxes deferred for a period of, say, 10 years?

Planning prior to the Economic Recovery Tax Act of 1981 generally represented a compromise between the equalization and the deferral approaches. In part, the equalization route was motivated by several provisions in the tax law. First, the maximum marital deduction was limited to 50 percent of the adjusted gross estate. Consequently, any amount in excess of the 50 percent limit passing to the surviving spouse did not qualify for the marital deduction. Second, the unified tax credit for 1981 and thereafter was scheduled to level off at $47,000. As a result, a surviving spouse who died after 1981 was supposed to have only a $47,000 credit available. Third, and for larger estates, the maximum marginal estate tax bracket could reach as high as 70 percent.

The changes made by the Economic Recovery Tax Act of 1981 have had a noticeable impact on the stress previously placed on the equalization approach. To begin with, the new unlimited marital deduction enables the planner to avoid entirely the estate tax upon the death of the first spouse. Although too much property to the surviving spouse violates the equalization goal, if the surviving spouse lives long enough, the unified tax credit reaches the maximum phase-in amount of $192,800 (for 1987 and thereafter). Also, for persons dying after 1988, the top bracket of the unified transfer tax is due to be lowered to 50 percent. All of these scheduled changes, therefore, add impetus to the deferral approach. This means, of course, making optimum use of the marital deduction by passing enough property to the surviving spouse to eliminate the estate tax of the first spouse to die.

But tax planning must remain flexible and be tailored to the individual circumstances of the parties involved. Before the equalization approach is cast aside, therefore, consider the following variables:

—Both spouses are of advanced age and/or in poor health and neither is expected to survive the other for a prolonged period of time. For example, one cannot plan on a $192,800 unified tax credit if the surviving spouse is not expected to live until 1987.

—The spouse that is expected to survive has considerable assets of his or her own. To illustrate, a spouse that passes a $250,000 estate to the survivor who already has assets of $1,000,000 is trading a 32 percent bracket for a later 43 percent bracket.

—Because of appreciation, property worth $250,000 today when it passes to the surviving spouse may be worth $1,000,000 five years later when the survivor dies.

—The possibility always exists that the phase-in of the increase in the unified tax credit and/or the lowering of the marginal top bracket rate to 50 percent may not take place. Predicting what Congress will or will not do is, to say the least, dangerous. In the estate and gift tax areas, moreover, the Tax Reform Act of 1976 and the Economic Recovery Tax Act of 1981 provide a track record of radical changes. It would be ludicrous to say that further changes could not occur in the future.

*The Marital Deduction—Sophistication of the Deferral Approach.* When the saving of estate taxes for the family unit is the sole consideration, the equalization and deferral approaches can be combined with maximum effect.

**Example 85.** At the time of his death in 1986, H had never made any post-1976 taxable gifts or used his specific exemption on any pre-1977 gifts. Under H's will, his disposable estate of $1,000,000 passes to W, his surviving spouse.[118]

**Example 86.** Assume the same facts as in Example 85, except that H's will provides as follows: $500,000 to the children and the remainder (i. e., $500,000) to W.

---

118. For this purpose, disposable estate means the gross estate less administration and other expenses and debts.

From a tax standpoint, which is the better plan? Although no estate tax results from either arrangement, Example 85 represents overkill in terms of the marital deduction. Why place an additional $500,000 in W's potential estate when it can pass free of tax to the children through the application of the $155,800 unified tax credit available for 1985?[119] Clearly, then, the arrangement in Example 86 is to be preferred, as it avoids unnecessary concentration of wealth in W's estate.

On occasion the disclaimer procedure can be used to maximize the deferral approach.

> **Example 87.**  At the time of his death in 1986, H had never made any post-1976 gifts or used his specific exemption on pre-1977 gifts. Under H's will, his disposable estate of $1,500,000 passes as follows: $600,000 to S (H's adult son) and the remainder ($900,000) to W (H's surviving spouse). Shortly after H's death, S issues a disclaimer as to $100,000 of his $600,000 bequest. Such amount, therefore, passes to W as the remainderperson under H's will.

Because the unified tax credit for 1986 is $155,800 (with an exemption equivalent of $500,000), S's disclaimer avoids an estate tax on $100,000. The end result is to increase the marital deduction by $100,000 and eliminate *any* estate tax upon H's death.[120]

*Effectively Working With the Charitable Deduction.*  As a general guide to obtain overall tax savings, lifetime charitable transfers are to be preferred over testamentary dispositions. For example, an individual who gave $10,000 to a qualified charity during his or her life would secure an income tax deduction, avoid any gift tax, and reduce the gross estate by the amount of the gift. By way of contrast, if the $10,000 had been willed to charity, no income tax deduction would be available and the amount of the gift would be includible in the decedent's gross estate (though later deducted for estate tax purposes). In short, the lifetime transfer provides a double tax benefit (i. e., income tax deduction plus reduced estate taxes) at no gift tax cost; the testamentary transfer merely neutralizes the effect of the inclusion of the property in the gross estate (i. e., inclusion under § 2033 and then deduction under § 2055).

To insure that an estate tax deduction will be allowed for a charitable contribution, the designated recipient must fall within the classifications set forth in § 2055. The status of the organization on the date the transfer becomes effective, and not on the date the will authorizing the transfer was executed, controls.

> **Example 88.**  In 19X2, D drew up and executed a will in which he provided for $100,000 to pass to the XYZ Academy, a nonprofit educational organization described in § 2055(a)(2) and, at that time, approved by the IRS as a qualified recipient. In 19X4, the qualified status of the XYZ Academy was revoked for practicing racial discrimi-

---

**119.**  The exemption equivalent of a credit of $155,800 is $500,000.

**120.**  In drafting the will, it must have been assumed that H would live beyond 1986. In such case, the credit tops off at $192,800 (an exemption equivalent of $600,000), and no disclaimer would have been needed.

nation in the enrollment of its student body.[121] D dies in 19X9 and the executor of his estate, being compelled to satisfy the provisions of the will, transfers $100,000 to the XYZ Academy.

Even though D may have been unaware of the action taken by the IRS in 19X4, no charitable deduction will be allowed his estate; the recipient was no longer qualified on the date of his death. Of course, it may be that D, even if he had known about the probable loss of the charitable deduction, would still have wished the bequest carried out as originally conceived. If not, it is easy to say that the error was of D's own making because of his failure over this period of years to have his estate planning situation reviewed.

A possible way to circumvent the quandary posed by Example 88 (other than changing D's will prior to his death) would be to express the charitable bequest in more flexible terms. The transfer to the XYZ Academy could have been conditioned on this organization's continued status as a qualified recipient at the time of D's death. Or D's will may grant his executor the authority to substitute a different, but comparable, charitable organization *that is qualified* in the event the disqualification of the named group occurs.

On occasion, a charitable bequest may be dependent on the issuance of a disclaimer by a noncharitable heir. These situations frequently arise when special types of property or collections, which the decedent may feel a noncharitable heir should have a choice of receiving, are involved. If the charitable organization is the residuary legatee under a decedent's will, a disclaimer by a specific legatee passes the property by operation of the will to the holder of the residual interest and qualifies the estate for a charitable deduction under § 2055. Any exercise of such disclaimers in favor of charitable organizations should be carefully considered; another course may be more advantageous taxwise.

**Example 89.** D specified in his will that his valuable art collection is to pass to his son or, if the son refuses, to a designated and qualified art museum. At the time the will was drawn, D was aware of the fact that his son was not interested in owning the art collection. If, after D's death, the son issues a timely disclaimer, the art collection will pass to the designated museum, and D's estate will be allowed a charitable deduction for its death tax value.

**Example 90.** D's will specifies that one-half of his disposable estate is to pass to his wife and the remainder of his property to a designated and qualified charitable organization. If the wife issues a timely disclaimer after D's death, all of the property will pass to the charity and will qualify for the § 2055 charitable deduction.

---

**121.** Most of the organizations that are qualified recipients (which would permit the donor a charitable deduction) are listed in IRS Publication 78. This compilation, revised and supplemented from time to time, is designed to cover § 170 transfers (i. e., the income tax deduction situation). Publication 78 will, with the exceptions noted in this chapter, also apply to § 2055 (estate tax deduction) and § 2522 (gift tax deduction) transfers.

Has the son acted wisely if he issued the disclaimer in favor of the museum (refer to Example 89)? Although such a disclaimer would provide D's estate with a deduction for the value of the art collection, consider the income tax deduction alternative. If the son accepts the bequest, he can still dispose of the collection (and fulfill his father's philanthropic objectives) through lifetime donation to the museum and, at the same time, obtain for himself an income tax deduction under § 170. Whether this will save taxes for the family unit depends on a comparison of the father's estate tax bracket with the estimated income tax bracket of the son. If the value of the collection runs afoul of the percentage limitations of § 170(b)(1), the donations could be spread over more than one year. If this is done, and to protect against the contingency of the son's dying before donation of the entire collection, the son could neutralize any potential death tax consequences by providing in his will for the undonated balance to pass to the museum.

The use of a disclaimer in Example 90 would be sheer folly. It would not reduce D's estate tax; it would merely substitute a charitable deduction for the marital deduction. Whether the wife issues a disclaimer or not, no estate taxes will be due. The wife would be well-advised to accept her legacy and, if she is so inclined, to make lifetime gifts of it to a qualified charity. In so doing, she generates an income tax deduction for herself.

*Proper Handling of Other Deductions and Losses Under Code § § 2053 and 2054.* Many § 2053 and § 2054 deductions and losses may be claimed either as estate tax deductions or as income tax deductions of the estate on its fiduciary return (Form 1041), but a choice must be made.[122] In such a case, the deduction for income tax purposes will not be allowed unless the estate tax deduction is waived. It is possible for these deductions to be apportioned between the two returns. Certain expenses exist that do not follow this general rule. These variations are summarized as follows:

1. An expense deductible for estate tax purposes may not qualify as an income tax deduction. An example might be interest expense incurred to carry tax-exempt bonds that is disallowed for income tax purposes under § 265(2). If this expense is not claimed under § 2053 for estate tax purposes, it will be completely lost.

2. Medical expenses incurred by the decedent but unpaid at the time of his or her death are covered by a special rule. If paid out of the estate during a one-year period beginning with the day after death, these expenses may be claimed as an income tax deduction in the year incurred or as an estate tax deduction, but not both.[123] Thus, the choice is between the decedent's appropriate Form 1040 or the estate's estate tax return.[124] Note that the estate's income tax return (Form 1041) is not involved.

3. Expenses in respect of a decedent fall into a special classification. Generally, they are expenses of a cash basis taxpayer, accrued at

---

**122.** § 642(g) and Reg. § 20.2053–1(d).
**123.** § 213(c).
**124.** Such expenses may be split (i. e., divided in any way between Form 1040 and the estate tax return).

the time of his or her death but not deductible on the final Form 1040 by reason of the method of accounting.[125] Such deductions are allowed both for income tax and estate tax purposes. The deductions are available for income tax purposes to whoever is liable for and makes the payment. They include business and nonbusiness expenses (§ § 162 and 212), interest (§ 163), taxes (§ 164), and a possible credit for foreign taxes (§ 27). A deduction for depletion is allowed to the recipient of the income to which it relates.

4. Brokerage commissions and other expenses relating to the sale of estate property can be offset against the sale price of the property in computing taxable income of the estate or can be deducted on the estate tax return. A choice will have to be made whether these expenses will be claimed as income tax or estate tax deductions.

The preceding rules can be illustrated by the following examples:

**Example 91.** The executor of D's estate is paid a proper commission (authorized under local law and approved by the probate court of appropriate jurisdiction) of $10,000 from estate assets. Such commission expense can be claimed on the estate tax return (Form 706) or on the income tax return of the estate (Form 1041) or split in any way between the two returns. However, no more than $10,000 can be claimed.

**Example 92.** The executor of D's estate pays $5,000 in burial expenses (authorized under local law and approved by the probate court of appropriate jurisdiction) from estate assets. The $5,000 expense should be claimed on the estate tax return; it is not an item properly deductible for income tax purposes.

**Example 93.** At the time of his death, D (a cash basis taxpayer) owed a local bank $10,000 on a loan due in several months. On the due date of the loan, the executor of D's estate pays the bank $10,800, which represents the principal amount of the loan ($10,000), interest accrued prior to D's death ($700), and interest accrued after D's death ($100). The amount deductible on the estate tax return (Form 706) is $10,700.[126] Because the interest accrued prior to D's death is an expense in respect of a decedent, it can also be claimed as an income tax deduction by whoever pays it. Since the interest was paid by the estate, it should be claimed on the estate's income tax return (Form 1041) along with the $100 of interest expense accrued after D's death.

When a choice is available in the handling of § § 2053 and 2054 expenses and losses, any decision must take into account different tax implications. A number of questions first have to be asked and satisfactorily resolved. Is the executor of the estate also the residuary legatee? If so, it

---

**125.** § 691(b).

**126.** The loan and interest accrued before death are deductible as a claim against the estate under § 2053(a)(3). This does not include any interest accrued after death. In this regard, it would not matter if the executor elected the alternate valuation date (see Chapter 12) for the estate. See Reg. § 20.2053–4 and Rev.Rul. 77–461, 1977–2 C.B. 324. Compare *Estate of Jane deP. Webster,* 65 T.C. 968 (1976).

would usually be rather pointless for him or her to claim any commissions due for serving in the capacity of executor. Although it would generate a § 2053 deduction (on Form 706) or an income tax deduction on the fiduciary return of the estate (on Form 1041), claiming the commission results in taxable income to the executor. If the commission is not claimed, the amount involved should pass through to the executor tax-free by virtue of his or her rights as residuary legatee.[127]

## PROBLEM MATERIALS

### Discussion Questions

1. The unified transfer tax adopts a new approach to the taxation of life and death transfers after 1976. Explain.

2. Why can the unified transfer tax be categorized as an excise tax? In this regard, how does it differ from an income tax?

3. Upon whom is the Federal gift tax imposed? Suppose such party is unable to pay the tax?

4. What are the major differences between the Federal estate tax and the typical inheritance tax levied by many states?

5. T, a resident and citizen of Canada, owns real estate located in Rochester, New York.

   (a) Would T be subject to the U. S. gift tax if she transferred this property as a gift to her Canadian son?

   (b) Would T be subject to the U. S. estate tax if she died and left the property to her Canadian son?

6. Explain what is meant by the statement that the Federal gift tax rates are cumulative in nature?

7. What effect, if any, do prior gifts made by a decedent have on the determination of the decedent's estate tax liability?

8. What effect, if any, does prior utilization of the $30,000 specific exemption have on the unified tax credit currently available?

9. What is meant by the exemption equivalent of the unified tax credit?

10. Reg. § 25.2512–8 states: "A consideration not reducible to a value in money or money's worth, as love and affection, promise of marriage, etc., is to be wholly disregarded, and the entire value of the property transferred constitutes the amount of the gift."

    (a) What does this Regulation mean?

    (b) When might it apply?

11. X sells property to Y for $50,000. If the property is really worth $100,000, has X made a gift to Y? What additional facts would you want to know before answering this question?

---

**127.** Section 102(a) specifies that a "bequest, devise, or inheritance" is excludible from gross income.

12. In connection with gift loans, comment on the following points:

    (a) Since any interest element recognized by the lender as income can be deducted by the borrower, the income tax effect is neutralized for the family unit.

    (b) The borrower's net investment income for the year is less than $1,000.

    (c) The gift loan involved only $95,000.

    (d) The lender charged the borrower interest of 4%.

13. In the absence of § 2516, why would certain property settlements incident to a divorce be subject to the Federal gift tax?

14. In connection with § 2518 dealing with disclaimers, comment on the following:

    (a) The role of state law.

    (b) The avoidance of a Federal gift tax or the Federal estate tax.

    (c) The disclaimer of only a partial interest.

15. What is the justification for the annual exclusion? In what manner does it resemble the gift tax treatment of the following:

    (a) Tuition payments to an educational organization on behalf of another.

    (b) Medical care payments on behalf of another.

16. What purpose is served by the § 2503(c) trust for minors?

17. In connection with the gift-splitting provision of § 2513, comment on the following:

    (a) What it was designed to accomplish.

    (b) How the election is made.

    (c) Its utility in a community property jurisdiction.

18. D makes the following taxable gifts: $200,000 in 1975 and $350,000 in 1986. On the 1975 gift, D incurred and paid a Federal gift tax of $40,000. How should the gift tax be determined on the 1986 gift?

19. In connection with the filing of a Federal gift tax return, comment on the following:

    (a) No Federal gift tax is due.

    (b) The § 2513 election to split gifts is to be used.

    (c) A gift of a future interest is involved.

    (d) The donor uses a fiscal year for Federal income tax purposes.

    (e) The donor obtained from the IRS an extension of time for filing his or her Federal income tax return.

20. Distinguish between the following:

    (a) The gross estate and the taxable estate.

    (b) The gross estate and the probate estate.

21. Distinguish between the following:

    (a) Dower and curtesy and the surviving spouse's statutory share of the deceased spouse's property.

    (b) Dower and curtesy (or its statutory version) and the surviving spouse's share of his or her community property.

    What difference do these distinctions carry for Federal estate tax purposes?

22. After 1982, no taxable gifts made within three years of death will be included in the gross estate of the donor. Evaluate the soundness of this statement.

23.  D transfers a remainder interest in her resident to her adult son and continues to occupy the premises until her death five years later. Will the property be included in D's probate estate? Gross estate?

24.  Using community property, H creates a trust, life estate to W (H's wife), remainder to their children upon W's death.

  (a) Is there any estate tax effect upon H's death four years later?

  (b) Is there any estate tax effect upon W's death five years later?

25.  The elimination of the $100,000 estate tax exclusion for distributions from a qualified pension plan will not generate any additional estate tax because of the application of the marital deduction. Do you agree with this observation? Why or why not?

26.  It has been said that community property is much like a tenancy in common. Do you agree? Why or why not?

27.  At the time of X's death, X was a joint tenant with Y in a parcel of real estate. With regard to the inclusion in X's gross estate under § 2040, comment on the following independent assumptions:

  (a) The property was received by X and Y as a gift from D.

  (b) Y provided all of the purchase price of the property.

  (c) Y's contribution was received as a gift from X.

  (d) X's contribution was derived from income generated by property received by X as a gift from Y.

28.  Under what circumstances will the creation of a joint tenancy not constitute a gift when one of the tenants furnishes more of the consideration than the other (others)?

29.  If the holder can use the power to appoint some of the property for his or her benefit, it is a general power of appointment. Do you agree? Why or why not?

30.  T owns a policy on the life of S, with D as the designated beneficiary. Upon S's death, the insurance proceeds are paid to D.

  (a) Are any of the proceeds included in S's gross estate?

  (b) Does S's death generate any tax consequences to T?

31.  What are expenses in respect of a decedent? How are they treated for tax purposes?

32.  W, the surviving spouse of H, is the executrix of H's estate. Also, W is designated by H's will as the remainderperson of H's estate. In deciding whether W should claim or waive any commissions she might be entitled to for serving as executrix, what tax factors should be considered?

33.  Unpaid medical expenses of a decedent are handled for tax purposes in the same manner as funeral expenses. Do you agree or disagree with this statement? Explain.

34.  For tax purposes, what difference does it make whether a casualty loss occurs before or after the death of the owner of the property?

35.  In terms of the QTIP (qualified terminable interest property) election, comment on the following:

  (a) Who makes the election.

  (b) What the election accomplishes.

  (c) The tax effect of the election upon the death of the surviving spouse.

36. Explain the difference between the equalization and deferral approaches to the estate tax marital deduction. In this regard, have changes in the tax law modified tax planning with the marital deduction?

37. In the case of married persons, the real danger of an estate tax burden materializes upon the death of the surviving spouse. Do you agree or disagree with this observation? Why?

## Problems

1. In each of the following independent situations, indicate whether the transfer by D is, or could be, subject to the Federal gift tax:

    (a) D makes a contribution to an influential political figure.

    (b) D makes a contribution to B Corporation, of which he is not a shareholder.

    (c) In consideration of his upcoming marriage to B, D establishes a savings account in B's name.

    (d) Same as (c). After their marriage, D establishes a joint checking account in the names of "D and B."

    (e) Same as (d). One year after the checking account is established, B withdraws all of the funds.

    (f) D exercises a special power of appointment in favor of B.

    (g) D enters into an agreement with B whereby he will transfer property to her in full satisfaction of her marital rights. One month after the agreement, the transfer occurs. Later D and B are divorced.

    (h) D purchases U. S. savings bonds, listing ownership as "D and B." Several years later, and after D's death, B redeems the bonds.

2. In each of the following independent situations, indicate whether the transfer by D is, or could be, subject to the Federal gift tax:

    (a) D purchases real estate and lists title as "D and B as joint tenants." D and B are brothers.

    (b) Same as (a), except that D and B are husband and wife.

    (c) D creates a revocable trust with B as the designated beneficiary.

    (d) Same as (c). One year after creating the trust, D releases all power to revoke the trust.

    (e) D takes out an insurance policy on his life, designating B as the beneficiary.

    (f) Same as (e). Two years later, D dies and the policy proceeds are paid to B.

    (g) D takes out an insurance policy on the life of W and designates B as the beneficiary. Shortly thereafter, W dies and the policy proceeds are paid to B.

    (h) D pays for B's college tuition.

3. In 1976, R purchased real estate for $300,000, listing ownership as follows: "R and S, equal tenants in common." R predeceases S in 1986 when the property is worth $500,000. Before 1976, R had not made any taxable gifts or utilized the $30,000 specific exemption. Assume R and S are brothers.

    (a) Determine R's gift tax consequences, if any, in 1976.

    (b) How much, if any, of the property should be included in R's gross estate?

4. In 1982, T purchased real estate for $250,000, listing title to the property as follows: "T and U, joint tenants with the right of survivorship." Under applicable state law, both parties possess the right of severance. U predeceases T in 1986, when the real estate is worth $400,000. Assume T and U are brothers and that

neither has made any other taxable gifts or utilized his $30,000 specific exemption.

    (a) Determine T's gift tax consequences, if any, in 1982.

    (b) How much, if any, of the property should be included in U's gross estate?

5.   Assume the same facts as in Problem 4, except that T and U are husband and wife (rather than brothers).

    (a) Determine T's gift tax consequences, if any, in 1982.

    (b) How much, if any, of the property should be included in U's gross estate? Will any such inclusion generate an estate tax liability? Explain.

6.   In January 1986, H and W enter into a property settlement under which H agrees to pay $500,000 to W in return for the release of her marital rights. At the time the agreement is signed, H pays W $100,000 as a first installment. Although the parties intended to obtain a divorce, H dies in July 1986 before legal proceedings have been instituted. After H's death, the executor of H's estate pays to W the $400,000 remaining balance due under the property settlement.

    (a) What are the gift tax consequences of the $100,000 payment made upon the signing of the agreement? Why?

    (b) What are the estate tax consequences of the $400,000 paid to W from estate assets after H's death? Why?

7.   In 1986, M makes a gift to her daughter of securities worth $600,000. M has never made any prior taxable gifts or utilized her $30,000 specific exemption. F (M's husband), however, made a taxable gift of $500,000 in early 1976 upon which he paid a gift tax of $109,275. At the time of F's gift, F was not married to M.

    (a) Determine M's gift tax liability on the 1986 transfer, assuming the parties chose not to make the election to split gifts under § 2513.

    (b) What would the liability be if the election to split the gift were made?

8.   Before her death in 1986, D (a widow) made the following transfers:

    —A gift of real estate (basis of $50,000 and fair market value of $200,000) to S (D's son). The gift was made in 1984 and resulted in a Federal gift tax of $10,000, which D paid. On the date of D's death, the property is worth $220,000.

    —A gift of an insurance policy on D's life to B (the designated beneficiary). The policy was worth $10,000 but had a maturity value of $50,000. The gift was made in 1985 and resulted in no Federal gift tax liability.

    —A gift of stock (basis of $40,000 and fair market value of $100,000) to R. The gift was made in 1980 and resulted in no Federal gift tax liability. On the date of D's death, the stock was worth $300,000.

Presuming the alternate valuation date is not elected, how much should be included in D's gross estate as to these transfers?

9.   D dies on July 7, 19X4, at a time when he owns stock in Z Corporation and W Corporation. On June 1, 19X4, both corporations authorized cash dividends payable on August 1, 19X4, For Z Corporation, the dividend was payable to shareholders of record as of July 1, 19X4, while W Corporation's date of record was July 10, 19X4. After D's death, the executor of the estate received dividends in the following amounts: $6,000 from Z Corporation and $8,000 from W Corporation. D also owned some City of Minneapolis tax-exempt bonds. As of July 7, 19X4, the accrued interest on the bonds was $7,500. On December 1, 19X4, the executor of the estate received $10,000 in interest ($2,500 accrued since D's

death) from the bonds. Concerning the dividends and interest, how much should be included in D's gross estate?

10. G would like to make a lifetime transfer in trust of $300,000 to his son, S, and accomplish the following objectives:

—Avoid any death tax on the deaths of G, S, and W (S's wife).

—Give S the right to determine what portion of the remainder should be allocated between W and their children, A and B.

—Give S some additional security by allowing him to reach corpus should the need materialize.

—Prevent S from squandering all of corpus to the detriment of W, A, or B.

In light of § 2041, what do you suggest?

11. In each of the following independent situations, determine how much should be included in D's gross estate under § 2042 as to the various life insurance policies involved. Assume that none of the policies are community property.

(a) At the time of his death, D owned a paid-up policy on the life of B, with S as the designated beneficiary. The policy had a replacement cost of $80,000 and a maturity value of $300,000.

(b) W owns a policy on the life of D ($300,000 maturity value) with D's estate as the designated beneficiary. Upon D's death, the insurance company pays $300,000 to D's estate.

(c) Four years before his death, D transferred a policy on his life ($300,000 maturity value) to S as a gift. D retained the power to change beneficiaries. At the time of the transfer, the designated beneficiary was S. Because D had never exercised his right to change beneficiaries, the insurance company pays S $300,000 upon D's death.

(d) Same as (c), except that D releases the power to change beneficiaries one year before his death.

12. In 1984, G creates a trust, life estate to S (G's son), remainder to GS (G's grandson), with securities worth $600,000. G dies in 1986, and S dies in 1995. At the time of his death, S had a taxable estate of his own of $1,200,000, and the value of the trust is $2,500,000.

(a) Will any of the trust be included in G's gross estate? Why?

(b) How will the estate tax be determined on S's death?

13. Comment on how each of the following independent situations should be handled for estate tax purposes:

(a) Before her death in 1986, D issued a note payable to her daughter in the amount of $100,000 for which no consideration was ever received by D. After D's death, the daughter files a claim against the estate and collects $100,000 on the note.

(b) At the time of her death, D (a widow) owned 10 cemetery lots (each worth $5,000), which she had purchased many years before for herself and her family.

(c) At the time of his death, D was delinquent in the payment of back Federal income taxes. Such taxes are paid by D's executor from assets of the estate.

14. Before his death in 1986, D donates stock held as an investment (basis of $8,000 and fair market value of $15,000) to his church. Under the same circumstances, E transfers an equal amount of property, except that such donation occurs pursuant to E's will. Assume that both taxpayers were in a 50% bracket for income

tax purposes and that their estates will be subject to a top death tax rate of 40%. Which taxpayer is in a better tax position? Why?

15. Four different persons (D, E, F, and G) die in 1986, each leaving a disposable estate of $1,000,000 and none having made any post-1976 taxable gifts. Each decedent leaves a surviving spouse and a will dictating the disposition of his or her property. From a tax standpoint, evaluate the following various testamentary schemes:

    (a) Under D's will, the full disposable estate passes to a qualified charity.

    (b) Under E's will, the full disposable estate passes to the surviving spouse.

    (c) Under F's will, the disposable estate is to be divided between the surviving spouse and a qualified charitable organization.

    (d) Under G's will, $500,000 passes to the children and the balance goes to the surviving spouse.

16. In 1986, H places in trust $500,000 worth of securities. Under the terms of the trust instrument, W (H's wife) is granted a life estate, and on W's death, the remainder interest passes to H and W's children (as W determines in her will). Upon W's death 18 years later, the trust assets are valued at $2,000,000.

    (a) How much, if any, marital deduction will be allowed on the gift made in 1986.

    (b) How much, if any, of the trust will be included in W's gross estate upon W's death?

17. Assume the same facts as in Problem 16, except that H made the qualified terminable interest property election when the trust was created. Further assume that W has no choice as to which of her children will receive the remainder interest upon her death.

    (a) How much, if any, marital deduction will be allowed on the gift made in 1986?

    (b) How much, if any, of the trust will be subject to the Federal estate tax upon W's later death?

18. Assume the filing requirement for 1986 is a gross estate in excess of $500,000. What would the filing requirement be for a decedent who had the following transactions before his or her death in 1986?

    —Utilized $10,000 of the $30,000 specific gift tax exemption on a gift made in June 1976.

    —Used the balance of the $30,000 specific gift tax exemption on a gift made in October 1976.

    —Made a taxable gift of $100,000 in November 1976.

    —Made a taxable gift of $100,000 in 1978.

## Comprehensive Tax Return Problem

During 1985, Robert and Susan Brown (Social Security Nos. 463-04-7964 and 466-36-4596) resided at 4321 Mt. Vernon Place, Altview, VA 23284. In their 25 years of marriage, the Browns have always lived in common law states. Robert Brown practices internal medicine, and Susan Brown is a partner in a well-known architectural firm in Richmond, Virginia. Both practices have been highly successful.

During 1985, the Browns made the following transfers (without adjustment for the annual exclusion or the marital deduction):

|  | Robert Brown | Susan Brown |
|---|---|---|
| Cash gift to Susan Brown. | $ 50,000 | |
| Payment to Oxford University for David Brown's (22-year-old son) tuition. | 16,000 | $ 2,000 |
| Payment to Clinical Associates for psychiatric treatment rendered to Mildred Hogan. Mildred is Robert Brown's aunt and suffers from severe depression. For income tax purposes, she does not qualify as the Browns' dependent. | 13,000 | |
| Gift to David Brown of securities owned by Susan Brown. The securities had a basis to Susan Brown of $18,000 and a fair market value on the date of the gift of $100,000. | | 100,000 |
| Cash gift to Lea Brown (21-year-old daughter). | 30,000 | 20,000 |
| Cash gift to Mary Smith (the Browns' housekeeper). | | 4,000 |
| Cash gift to Bonnie Davis (Susan Brown's sister) to enable her to cover certain personal debts. | 9,000 | 11,000 |
| A savings account established for James Brown (14-year-old son) under the Virginia Uniform Gifts to Minors Act. Robert Brown is designated as the custodian of the account. | 30,000 | 30,000 |

In past years, the Browns have made the following taxable gifts:

| Year | Robert Brown | Susan Brown |
|---|---|---|
| 1976 | $ 30,000 | $ 30,000 |
| 1978 | 100,000 | — |
| 1979 | 50,000 | 20,000 |
| 1981 | 100,000 | 100,000 |
| 1982 | 80,000 | — |
| 1983 | 150,000 | 50,000 |
| 1984 | 100,000 | — |

The gifts made by the Browns in 1976 occurred in December. Since both parties chose to make use of their specific exemption, the gift tax return filed for 1976 resulted in no taxable gifts and no gift tax liability. As to all past gifts, the Browns have elected to use the gift-splitting provisions of § 2513.

*Required:*

(a) Determine how much, if any, Federal gift tax will have been paid on the pre-1985 taxable gifts Robert and Susan Brown have made.

(b) Complete Forms 709 (U. S. Federal gift tax return) for the gifts made in 1985.

## Research Problems

*Research Problem 1.* During the current year, D establishes a trust with 500 shares of D Corporation stock. Under the terms of the trust instrument, income from the stock is to be paid to or accumulated for S, D's son, until he reaches age 21. At this point the trust is to terminate if S, by written request, so decides. If not, the trust will continue until S reaches age 30. Upon termination of the trust, all income and principal are to be paid to S. In the event S dies during the term of the trust, all accumulated income and principal are to be paid to S's estate or to whomever S may direct under a general power of appointment. Although the designated trustee, a local bank, is empowered to expend trust income for S's benefit, the trustee does not possess the right to dispose of the stock without D's consent.

After the transfer, the outstanding stock of D Corporation (5,000 shares of common) is held as follows: 500 shares by the trust and 4,500 shares by D. For the 10 years preceding the gift, no dividends were paid on the D Corporation stock.

(a) Would D be allowed an annual exclusion for the gift in trust to S? Explain.

(b) Assuming D dies while the trust was still in effect, could the trust be included in D's gross estate? Explain.

*Partial list of research aids:*

Code § § 2035, 2036, 2038, and 2503.

*Stark* v. *U. S.,* 73–1 USTC ¶ 12,921, 31 AFTR2d 1457, 477 F.2d 131 (CA–8, 1973).

Rev.Rul. 74–43, 1974–1 C.B. 285.

*Estate of Arthur A. Chalmers,* 31 TCM 792, T.C.Memo. 1972–158.

*Research Problem 2.* On October 1, 1976, H makes a gift of $66,000 to his son. In reporting the gift, W (H's wife) made the election under § 2513. As a result, no gift tax was due. W dies in 1986, and in completing Form 706, her executor claims a unified tax credit of $155,800.

(a) Why was no gift tax due on the 1976 gift?

(b) Did the executor of W's estate act correctly in claiming a unified tax credit of $155,800 on Form 706? Why or why not?

*Research Problem 3.* Before her death in 1986, D entered into the following transactions:

(a) In 1981 she borrowed $35,000 from a bank, which sum she promptly loaned to her controlled corporation. The executor of D's estate repaid the bank loan but never attempted to collect the amount due D from the corporation.

(b) In 1978 D promised her sister, S, a bequest of $200,000 if S would move in with her and care for her during an illness (which eventually proved to be terminal). D never kept her promise, as her will was silent on any bequest to S. After D's death, S sued the estate and eventually recovered $120,000 for breach of contract.

(c) One of the assets in D's estate was a palatial residence that passed to R under a specific provision of the will. R did not want the residence preferring, instead, cash. Per R's instructions, the residence was sold. Expenses incurred in connection with the sale were claimed as § 2053 expenses on Form 706 filed by D's estate.

(d) Before her death, D incurred and paid certain medical expenses but did not have the opportunity to file a claim for partial reimbursement from her insurance company. After her death, the claim was filed by D's executor, and the reimbursement was paid to the estate.

Discuss the estate and income tax ramifications of each of these transactions.

*Partial list of research aids:*

Code § § 61(a)(1) and (12), 111, 213, 691, 2033, and 2053.

*Estate of Allie W. Pittard,* 69 T.C. 391 (1977).

*Estate of Myron M. Miller,* 37 TCM 1547, T.C.Memo. 1978–374.

*Joseph F. Kenefic,* 36 TCM 1226, T.C.Memo. 1977–310.

*Hibernia Bank* v. *U. S.,* 78–2 USTC ¶ 13,261, 42 AFTR2d 78–6510, 581 F.2d 741 (CA–9, 1978).

Rev.Rul. 78–292, 1978–2 C.B. 233.

*Research Problem 4.* On August 1, 19X3, H transfers securities in X Corporation to his son, S, under the Florida Uniform Gifts to Minors Act. Under the transfer, W (H's wife and mother of S) is designated as the custodian of the stock. On September 3, 19X3, W transfers securities in X Corporation to her son, S, under the Florida Uniform Gifts to Minors Act. Under the transfer, H is designated as the custodian of the stock. H dies in 19X4 as a result of an accident. Will any of the securities in X Corporation be included in H's gross estate?

*Partial list of research aids:*

*Exchange Bank and Trust Co.* v. *U. S.,* 82–2 USTC ¶ 13,505, 51 AFTR2d 83–1317, 694 F.2d 1261 (CA–Fed. Cir., 1982).

*Estate of Herbert Levy,* 46 TCM 910, T.C.Memo. 1983–453.

# Valuation and Liquidity Problems 12

## CHAPTER OBJECTIVES

—Emphasize the importance of the valuation process to the estate and gift tax areas.

—Review the rules governing the valuation of different assets and business interests.

—Explain the purpose of the alternate valuation date and the rules governing its use.

—Explain the purpose of the special use valuation method and its utility as a tax-saving procedure.

—Summarize the income tax basis considerations of property acquired by gift or by inheritance.

—Recognize and plan for the problem of estate liquidity.

—Review the different provisions of the law whereby the payment of estate taxes can be extended beyond their normal due date.

# IMPORTANCE OF VALUATION

One essential element in working with the tax law concerns the satisfactory resolution of the valuation problem. Recall that the gift tax is predicated on the fair market value of the property on the date of the transfer. In the case of the Federal estate tax, it is the fair market value on the date of the owner's death or alternate valuation date (if available and elected) that controls. Even more subtle are the income tax considerations inherent in this problem.

> **Example 1.** D would like to give to S an unimproved tract of land that he inherited from his grandmother 20 years ago. Rather apparent is the importance of the value of the property on the date of the gift; this is the starting point in determining the gift tax implications of the transfer. A less obvious but equally important consideration is the determination of S's income tax basis in the property. To determine S's basis one must know D's adjusted basis in the property.[1] Since D inherited the property, § 1014 controls, and his basis will be the land's fair market value as of 20 years ago.

The fair market value of the land transferred in Example 1 is important in at least two respects: D's gift tax consequences and S's income tax basis upon the later disposition of the property in a taxable sale or exchange. Not mentioned, but nevertheless consequential, would be the effect the fair market value of the land had on the death taxes paid by the grandmother's estate.

In the sections to follow, the question of valuation is discussed together with its tax implications.

# THE VALUATION PROCESS

## VALUATION IN GENERAL

Although the Internal Revenue Code refers to "value" and even "fair market value," these terms are not considered at length.[2] Code § 2031(b) comes closest to a definition when it treats the problem of stocks and securities for

---

1. Section 1015 determines the income tax basis to the donee of property acquired as a gift. These rules are discussed later in the chapter.
2. See, for example, § § 1001(b), 2031(a), and 2512(a). The exception might be the special use valuation procedures enacted by the Tax Reform Act of 1976. Under § § 2032A(e)(7) and (8), certain valuation procedures are set forth for valuing farms and interests in closely-held businesses.

which no sales price information (i. e., the usual case with closely-held corporations) is available. In such situations, "the value thereof shall be determined by taking into consideration, in addition to all other factors, the value of stock or securities of corporations engaged in the same or similar line of business which are listed on an exchange."

Reg. § 20.2031–1(b) is more specific in defining fair market value as "the price at which property would change hands between a willing buyer and a willing seller, neither being under any compulsion to buy or to sell and both having reasonable knowledge of relevant facts." The same Regulation makes it clear that the fair market value of an item of property is not to be determined by a forced sale price. Nor is the fair market value to be determined by the sale price of the item in a market other than that in which such item is most commonly sold to the public, taking into account the item's location whenever appropriate. Thus, for property that generally is obtained by the public in a retail market, the fair market value of such property is the price at which such property (or comparable items) would be sold at retail.

> **Example 2.** At the time of his death, D owned three automobiles. These automobiles must be included in D's gross estate at their fair market value on the date of D's death or on the alternate valuation date (if available and elected). To arrive at the fair market value of these automobiles, look to the price for which automobiles of approximately the same description, make, model, age, condition, etc., could be purchased by a member of the general public. The price for which these automobiles would be purchased by a dealer in used automobiles would be inappropriate, because an automobile is an item generally obtainable by the public in a retail market.[3]

If tangible personalty[4] is sold as a result of an advertisement in the classified section of a newspaper and the property is of a type often sold in this manner, or if the property is sold at a public auction, the price for which it is sold will be presumed to be the retail sales price of the item at the time of the sale. This price also will be presumed to be the retail sales price on the applicable valuation date if the sale is made within a reasonable period following the valuation date and there is no substantial change in market conditions or other circumstances affecting the value of similar items.[5]

## VALUATION OF PARTICULAR TYPES OF PROPERTY

Before turning to a consideration of how tax planning can aid in resolving the valuation problem, some discussion of the rules applicable in valuing particular types of property interests is in order.

*Stocks and Bonds.* If there is a market for stocks and bonds on a stock exchange, in an over-the-counter market, or otherwise, the mean between

---

**3.** Reg. § § 20.2031–1(b) and 25.2512–1.
**4.** Tangible personalty would include all property except real estate and intangible property. For this purpose, intangible property includes stocks and bonds.
**5.** Rev.Proc. 65–19, 1965–2 C.B. 1002.

the highest and lowest quoted selling prices on the valuation date is the fair market value per unit. If there were no sales on the valuation date but there were sales on dates within a reasonable period before and after the valuation date, the fair market value is determined by taking a weighted average of the means between the highest and the lowest sales prices on the nearest date before and the nearest date after the valuation date. The average is to be weighted *inversely* by the respective number of trading days between the selling dates and the valuation date.[6]

**Example 3.** D makes a gift to S of shares of stock in X Corporation. The transactions closest to the date of the gift that involve this stock took place two trading days before the date of the gift at a mean selling price of $10 and three trading days after the gift at a mean selling price of $15. The $12 fair market value of each share of X Corporation stock is determined by the following computation:

$$\frac{(3 \times \$10) + (2 \times \$15)}{5} = \$12$$

If no transactions occurred within a reasonable period before and after the valuation date, the fair market value may be determined by taking a weighted average of the means between the bona fide bid and asked prices on the nearest trading dates before and after the valuation date, if both such dates are within a reasonable period of time.[7]

If no actual sales prices or bona fide bid and asked prices are available on a date within a reasonable period before the valuation date but are available on a date within a reasonable period after the valuation date, or vice versa, the mean between the highest and lowest available sales prices or bid and asked prices on that date may be taken as the value.[8]

If selling prices or bid and asked prices are not available, as is typically the case with securities of a closely-held corporation, fair market value is to be determined by taking the following into account:

1. In the case of bonds, the soundness of the security, the interest yield, the date of maturity, and other relevant factors.

2. In the case of shares of stock, the corporation's net worth, prospective earning power, dividend-paying capacity, and other relevant factors.

Some of the "other relevant factors" referred to above are the goodwill of the business, the economic outlook in the particular industry, the company's position in the industry, and the value of securities of other corporations engaged in the same or similar lines of business.[9] The ramifications of these concepts as applied to the valuation of stock in a closely-held corporation are discussed later in the chapter.

Shares in an open-end investment company (i. e., mutual fund) are

---

**6.** Reg. §§ 20.2031–2(b) and 25.2512–2(b).
**7.** Reg. §§ 20.2031–2(c) and 25.2512–2(c).
**8.** Reg. §§ 20.2031–2(d) and 25.2512–2(d).
**9.** Reg. §§ 20.2031–2(f) and 25.2512–2(f). See also Rev.Rul. 59–60, 1959–1 C.B. 237, which discusses the subject at greater length than do the Regulations.

valued at the redemption, or bid, price of the security. The IRS formerly took the position that the public offering, or asked, price should be used until the U. S. Supreme Court held to the contrary.[10]

*Interest in Businesses.* The fair market value of any interest in a business, whether a sole proprietorship or partnership, is the net amount that a willing purchaser would pay for the interest of a willing seller, neither being under any compulsion to buy or sell and both having reasonable knowledge of the relevant facts.

The relevant facts to be considered in valuing the business are (1) a fair appraisal of the assets of the business; (2) the demonstrated earning capacity of the business; and (3) certain other factors used in arriving at the valuation of corporate stock, to the extent applicable to the particular situation. Special attention should be given to the determination of an adequate value for the goodwill of the business if no bona fide purchase agreement exists.[11]

*Notes Receivable.* The fair market value of notes, secured or unsecured, is presumed to be the amount of unpaid principal plus interest accrued to the valuation date, unless the parties (e. g., executor, donor) establish a lower value or prove the notes are worthless. Factors such as a low interest rate and a distant maturity date would be relevant in showing that a note is worth less than its face amount. The key to proving that a note is entirely or partially worthless would be the financial condition of the obligor and the absence of any value as to property pledged or mortgaged as security for the obligation.[12]

> **Example 4.** At the time of his death, D held a note (face amount of $5,000) issued by his son, S. Although S is solvent, he does not have to satisfy the obligation because D forgives the note in his will. Presuming the note is payable on demand, it must be included in D's gross estate at $5,000 plus accrued interest. If not immediately due and/or the interest provided for is under the current rate, a discount may be in order, and the fair market value of the note would be less than $5,000. The burden of proof to demonstrate that less than the fair market value of the note should be included in the gross estate is on the executor.

*Insurance Policies and Annuity Contracts.* The value of a life insurance policy on the life of a person other than the decedent or the value of an annuity contract issued by a company regularly engaged in the selling of contracts of that character is the cost of a comparable contract.[13]

> **Example 5.** D purchased from an insurance company a joint and survivor annuity contract. Under the contract's terms, D is to receive

---

**10.** *U. S. v. Cartwright,* 73–1 USTC ¶ 12,926, 31 AFTR2d 73–1461, 93 S.Ct. 1713 (USSC, 1973). The difference in the two prices represents the marketing cost of such shares.

**11.** Reg. § § 20.2031–3 and 25.2512–3. But see the special use valuation procedures of § 2032A(e)(8) discussed later in the chapter.

**12.** Reg. § § 20.2031–4 and 25.2512–4.

**13.** Reg. § § 20.2031–8(a)(1) and 25.2512–6(a).

payments of $9,600 per year for his life. Upon D's death, D's wife (W) is to receive $7,200 annually for her life. Ten years after the purchase of the annuity, and when W is 40 years of age, D dies. The value of the annuity contract on the date of D's death [and the amount includible in D's gross estate under § 2039(a)] will be the amount the insurance company would charge for an annuity providing for the payment of $7,200 annually for the life of a female 40 years of age.

**Example 6.** At the time of his death, D owns an insurance policy (face amount of $100,000) on the life of his son, S. The policy is one on which no further payments need be made (e. g., single premium policy or a paid-up policy). The value of the policy on the date of D's death (and the amount includible in D's gross estate under § 2033 as property in which the decedent had an interest)[14] will be the amount the insurance company would charge for a single premium contract (face amount of $100,000) on the life of a person the same age as S.

The valuation of an insurance policy by determining the amount charged for a comparable policy is not readily ascertainable when, on the date of valuation, the contract has been in force for some time and further premium payments are to be made. In such a case, the value may be approximated by adding to the interpolated terminal reserve the proportionate part of the gross premium last paid before the valuation date that covers the period extending beyond that date.[15]

The valuation of annuities issued by parties not regularly engaged in the sale of annuities requires the use of special tables issued by the IRS. Which table must be used depends on whether the valuation date occurs before 1971, after 1970 and before December 1, 1983, or after November 30, 1983. These three sets of tables reflect an attempt on the part of the IRS to adjust for the increase in interest rates that has taken place over the years.[16] The two most recent sets of tables are reproduced in Appendix A.

**Example 7.** Under the terms of F's will, D (F's son) is entitled to receive an annuity of $20,000 payable annually for life. When D is 50 years old, he assigns the annuity to S as a gift. If the assignment was made in 1982, column 2 of Table A(1), Reg. § 20.2031–10(f), yields a factor of 11.3329 (male, age 50). Multiplying 11.3329 by the annual payment of $20,000 yields a fair market value of $226,658. Thus, when D assigns his annuity to S, he has made a gift of $226,658.

**Example 8.** Assume the same facts as in Example 7, except that the assignment by D occurred in 1986. Turning to column 2 of Table A,

---

**14.** The policy is not includible in D's gross estate under § 2042, because it has not matured. Refer to Chapter 11.

**15.** The terminal reserve of a life insurance policy generally will approximate the policy's cash surrender value. For an illustration on how to arrive at the "interpolated terminal reserve," see Reg. § 20.2031–8(a)(3) (Ex. 3).

**16.** Effective for transfers after November 30, 1983, the tables issued by the IRS are based on a factor of 10%. For transfers after 1970 and before December 1, 1983, the factor was 6%; and 3½% was used for pre-1971 transfers.

Reg. § 25.2512–5(f), the factor is now 8.4743 for a person age 50. Thus, the fair market value of the annuity is 8.4743 × $20,000, or $169,486.[17]

If the annuity is payable other than annually (i. e., at the end of each year) or if it is dependent on the lives of two or more persons, other tables must be used.[18]

*Life Estates, Terms for Years, Reversions, and Remainders.* As was true with noncommercial annuities, the valuation of life estates, income interests for a term of years, reversions, and remainders involves the use of tables. Again, it is important to ascertain when the transfer occurred. The two most recent tables are reproduced in Appendix A.

**Example 9.** D transfers $100,000 in trust, life estate to W, remainder to S on W's death. At the time of the gift, W is a female, age 35. If the gift took place on November 30, 1983, Table A(2) of Reg. § 25.2512–9(f) yields a factor of 0.87593 (column 3) for a female, age 35.[19] [Note: The factor for a remainder interest is 0.12407 (column 4).] Thus, D has made a gift of $87,593 (i. e., 0.87593 × $100,000) to W and a gift of $12,407 (i. e., 0.12407 × $100,000) to S.[20]

**Example 10.** Assume the same facts as in Example 9, except that the transfer occurs in 1986. Referring to Table A of Reg. § 25.2512–5(f), a life estate for a person age 35 shows a factor of 0.93868 [column (3)]; the factor for a remainder interest is 0.06132 [column (4)]. Consequently, D has made a gift of $93,868 (i. e., 0.93868 × $100,000) to W and a gift of $6,132 (i. e., 0.06132 × $100,000) to S. Note that the value of the life estate ($93,868) when added to the value of the remainder interest ($6,132) equals the total amount of the gift ($100,000).

**Example 11.** In 1986, D transfers by gift $100,000 worth of securities. The securities were placed in trust, income payable to M for 11 years, reversion to D or his estate. Based on Table B of Reg. § 25.2512–5(f), the appropriate factor is 0.649506 [see column (3), term certain

---

**17.** The Regulations contain identical tables for estate tax situations. For transfers after November 30, 1983, see Reg. § 20.2031–7(f). For transfers after 1970 and before December 1, 1983, see Reg. § 20.2031–10(f).

**18.** If the valuation date occurs before 1971, see T.D. 6334 (1958–2 C.B. 627) as amended by T.D. 7077 (1970–2 C.B. 183).

**19.** The pre-1971 and the current tables are unisex (i. e., no distinction is made between male and female). The tables applicable to transfers after 1970 and before December 1, 1983, do make a distinction between the sexes.

**20.** What is the significance of the division of a gift into several distinct parts? Such a division becomes important in determining the applicability of the annual exclusion under § 2503(b) and the marital deduction under § 2523. Under the facts of Example 9, an annual exclusion probably would be allowed with respect to the gift to W and would not be allowed with respect to the interest passing to S (because of the future interest limitation). If W is D's wife, no marital deduction would be allowed, because the life estate she receives is a terminable interest. (Note: The qualified terminable interest exception discussed in Chapter 11 applies only to gifts between spouses occurring after 1981.)

for 11 years)]. Thus, D has made a gift to M of $64,950.60 (i. e., 0.649506 × $100,000).

## THE ALTERNATE VALUATION DATE

Under certain conditions, requiring the use of the date of death value for estate tax purposes could work a real hardship on the estate. Suppose, for example, the gross estate contained property that significantly decreased in value after the owner died but before the administration of his or her estate could be wound up and all charges against it satisfied. As happened during the Great Depression, it is entirely possible that the death tax liability alone (based on the date of death value) could wipe out the assets of an estate. In recognition of such a possibility, Congress enacted the predecessor of § 2032. Under this provision, the executor of the estate is given the option to value property included as of an alternate date that falls after the date of death but before the due date of the return.

Although the alternate valuation date was designed to reduce the amount of the gross estate, in practice the opposite effect was sometimes desirable. Based on the rule that the valuation used for estate tax purposes becomes the income tax basis of the property, a higher value could lead to potential income tax savings for the heirs. This would produce a very attractive result when the higher value yielded little, if any, estate tax liability.

> **Example 12.** D dies in 1986 leaving a disposable estate valued at $1,000,000. During his life D had never made any post-1976 taxable gifts or used his specific exemption of $30,000. Under D's will, $500,000 of the estate is to pass to his children, while the remainder goes to his surviving spouse, W. Because the estate has a large portfolio of marketable securities and the stock market rose after D's death, the disposable estate jumped to $1,200,000 in six months.

Electing the alternate valuation date in Example 12 would be a win-win situation. The election does not increase estate taxes, because the additional $200,000 in value is neutralized by the marital deduction. The only result is positive, since the election gives W $200,000 more in income tax basis.

Congress finally decided to eliminate the windfall that was possible in Example 12. The Deficit Reduction Act of 1984 amended § 2032 to permit the election only when the effect will be to reduce both the value of the gross estate *and* the Federal estate tax liability. Thus, the election of § 2032 in Example 12 no longer is possible for two reasons. First, the election would increase (rather than reduce) the value of the gross estate. Second, the election would not reduce the Federal estate tax liability. Due to the interplay of the unified tax credit exemption equivalent ($500,000 for 1986) and the marital deduction, the use of date of death or alternate valuation date does not carry any estate tax consequences. In either case, no estate tax is due.

Several observations can be made about the alternate valuation date that will aid in its understanding and application.

1. The choice of the alternate valuation date is elective with the executor or administrator of the estate. If no affirmative action is taken, the date of death value must be used.[21]

2. The election may be made on an estate tax return filed no more than one year late. Once made, the election is irrevocable.[22]

3. The election cannot be made for Federal tax purposes unless a Federal estate tax return must be filed.[23] The following schedule summarizes the filing requirements:[24]

| Year of Death | Filing Required When Gross Estate Exceeds— |
|---|---|
| Prior to 1977 | $ 60,000 |
| 1977 | 120,000 |
| 1978 | 134,000 |
| 1979 | 147,000 |
| 1980 | 161,000 |
| 1981 | 175,000 |
| 1982 | 225,000 |
| 1983 | 275,000 |
| 1984 | 325,000 |
| 1985 | 400,000 |
| 1986 | 500,000 |
| 1987 and later | 600,000 |

For the post-1976 period, the amounts listed above must be reduced by taxable gifts made after 1976. This adjustment is consistent with the scheme of the unified transfer tax at death. Recall that in determining the estate tax, post-1976 taxable gifts must be added to the taxable estate.

4. The election covers *all* assets included in the gross estate and cannot be applied to only a portion of the property.

5. The use of the alternate valuation date may require adjustment for changes in value due to a mere lapse of time.

6. The alternate valuation date is the earlier of six months following the date of death or when the property is "distributed, sold, exchanged, or otherwise disposed of."[25]

7. Generally, any income generated by the property after the owner's death must be accounted for separately and has no effect on the amount determined as of the alternate valuation date.

---

**21.** The election is made by checking the appropriate box on the Federal estate tax return and placing the alternate valuation date values in the corresponding column. Apparently, the failure to do the former is not disastrous as long as the alternate valuation date values are listed and used in completing the return.

**22.** § 2032(d). Before the effective date of the Deficit Reduction Act of 1984, the election had to be made on a timely filed estate tax return.

**23.** Depending upon the applicable state law, an alternate valuation date might be available for state death and income taxes.

**24.** § 6018.

**25.** § § 2032(a)(1) and (2) and Reg. § 20.2032–1(c).

These points may be illustrated as follows:

**Example 13.** D dies in January of 1986. Without obtaining an extension from the IRS, the executor of D's estate files the Federal estate tax return on February 3, 1987, and elects the alternate valuation date. On March 4, 1988, the executor files an amended return for the estate using the date of death valuation. Since the election of the alternate valuation date was valid (made within one year of the due date of the return), it is irrevocable. Therefore, the amended return switching to date of death valuation is not an acceptable procedure.

**Example 14.** At the time of her death in 1986, D had a gross estate of $490,000 which, six months later, was valued at $485,000. In 1980, however, D made a taxable gift of $20,000. Since the filing requirement for 1986 now becomes $480,000 ($500,000 − $20,000) instead of $500,000, the alternate valuation date can be elected.[26]

**Example 15.** D's gross estate includes the following property:

|  | Value on Date of Death | Value on Alternate Valuation Date |
|---|---|---|
| Land | $ 380,000 | $ 382,000 |
| Stock in X Corporation | 170,000 | 155,000 |
| Stock in Y Corporation | 190,000 | 198,000 |
| Total | $ 740,000 | $ 735,000 |

If D's estate elected the alternate valuation date, the value to be used would be $735,000. It would not be permissible for the estate to use the lower of the date of death or the alternate valuation date values for each individual asset. Thus, the estate *could not* choose the $380,000 value for the land, $155,000 for the X Corporation stock, and $190,000 for the Y Corporation stock (thereby reflecting a total of $725,000).

**Example 16.** On the date of death, D owned a patent (fair market value of $100,000) with a remaining life of 10 years. Six months later the patent possessed a fair market value of $90,000. Because some of the change in value of the patent must be due to the lapse of time (i. e., it has a remaining life of only nine and one-half years), the value of the patent on the alternate valuation date must be adjusted accordingly. Thus, dividing $90,000 by 0.95 (the ratio of the remaining life of the patent at the alternate date to the remaining life of the patent at the date of the decedent's death) yields a value of $94,736.84 on the alternate valuation date.[27]

---

**26.** It is not clear whether the election of the alternate valuation date would be wise in this case. Even though the gross estate would be $490,000 without the election, by the time this is reduced by any expenses allowable under § 2053 and the exemption equivalent of the unified tax credit is taken into account, how much, if any, estate tax would be due? Furthermore, using the date of death value would provide a higher income tax basis (i.e., $490,000 versus $485,000) for the assets of the estate.

**27.** Reg. § 20.2032–1(f)(2).

**Example 17.** At the time of his death, D held some stock in Z Corporation. In a will, D bequeathed the stock to S. The stock had a value as follows: $30,000 on the date of D's death, $28,000 four months later, and $27,000 six months after D's death. Four months after D's death, the executor satisfies the bequest by distributing the Z Corporation stock to S. If the estate elects the alternate valuation date, the stock should be included in the gross estate at $28,000. Although its value six months after D's death is $27,000, it was "distributed, sold, exchanged, or otherwise disposed of" before this date.

**Example 18.** At the time of D's death, one of D's assets was rental property worth $320,000 with accrued rents of $13,000. Six months later the property is worth $330,000, the rents of $13,000 have been paid, and an additional $18,000 has been accrued. Whether the alternate valuation date is or is not elected will make no difference in the treatment of the accrued rents. In either case, $13,000 will be included in D's gross estate; this is the amount accrued to the point of death.[28] The $18,000 accrued within the six-month period after death has no estate tax consequences.[29] Thus, the election of the alternate date means the inclusion in D's gross estate of $13,000 of accrued rents and rental property worth $330,000.

## THE SPECIAL USE VALUATION METHOD

For persons dying after 1976, § 2032A permits an executor to elect to value certain classes of real estate used in farming or in connection with a closely-held business at its "current" use rather than the usual "highest," "best," or "most suitable" use. The major objective of this provision was to provide a form of limited relief against the possibility that a portion of the family farm might have to be sold by the heirs to pay death taxes.

**Example 19.** At the time of his death, D owned a farm on the outskirts of a large city that was used for truck-farming purposes. For farming purposes, the property would have a value of $300,000 (i. e., the "current use" value).[30] As a potential site for a shopping center, however, the property is worth $800,000 (i. e., the "most suitable use" value). If D died prior to 1977, the farm would be included in his gross estate at $800,000. If D died after 1976, the executor of his estate could elect to include only $300,000 in the gross estate. The availability of the election presumes that the conditions set forth in § 2032A, and discussed below, are satisfied.

---

**28.** If D used the cash basis of accounting during life, the $13,000 would be income in respect of a decedent under § 691. As such, it would be subject to the income tax of the recipient. Under the accrual basis of accounting, the $13,000 would be taxed to D and reported on D's final Form 1040.

**29.** The $18,000 of rents accrued after D's death would be subject to the income tax. If taxed to the estate, it would be reported on Form 1041.

**30.** Sections 2032A(e)(7) and (8) set forth various methods of valuation to be applied in arriving at "current use" value.

The special use valuation election is available if *all* of the following conditions are satisfied:

1. At least 50 percent of the adjusted value of the gross estate consists of *real* or *personal* property devoted to a qualifying use (i. e., used for farming or used in a closely-held business) at the time of the owner's death.[31]

2. The *real* property devoted to a qualifying use comprises at least 25 percent of the adjusted value of the gross estate. For purposes of satisfying both the 50 percent test (condition 1) and the 25 percent test, the qualifying property is considered at its "most suitable use" value. Referring to Example 19, this means that the property would be treated as if it had a value of $800,000 (not $300,000). The adjusted value of the gross estate is the gross estate less certain unpaid mortgages and other indebtedness.

3. The qualifying property passes to a qualifying heir of the decedent. A qualifying heir includes certain family members as set forth in § 2032A(e)(2).

4. The *real* property has been owned by the decedent or the decedent's family for five out of the eight years ending on the date of the decedent's death and was devoted to qualifying use during such period of time.

5. The decedent or a member of the decedent's family has participated materially in the operation of the farm or business during the period specified under condition 4.[32]

Originally, the special use valuation procedure permitted a reduction in estate tax valuation of no more than $500,000. Under the Economic Recovery Tax Act of 1981, this amount has been increased as follows:[33]

| Year | Amount of Reduction |
|---|---|
| 1981 | $ 600,000 |
| 1982 | 700,000 |
| 1983 and later | 750,000 |

**Example 20.** At the time of his death in 1986, D owned a farm with a "most suitable use" value of $2,000,000 but a "current use" value of $1,000,000. Assuming the property qualifies under § 2032A and the special use valuation election is made, D's gross estate must include $1,250,000. Thus, for 1986, only $750,000 in value can be excluded under § 2032A.

The election of § 2032A will have an effect on the qualifying heir's income tax basis in the property. Referring to Example 20, the use of § 2032A means the heir will have an income tax basis of $1,250,000 in the

---

**31.** §§ 2032A(b)(1)(A) and (b)(2). For a definition of "farm" and "farming," see §§ 2032A(e)(4) and (5).

**32.** § 2032A(b)(1)(C)(ii). "Material participation" is defined in § 2032A(e)(6).

**33.** § 2032A(a)(2).

farm. Had § 2032A not been elected and had the "most suitable use" value been included in D's gross estate, the income tax basis would have become $2,000,000.

Section 2032A(c) provides that the benefits (i. e., estate tax savings) derived from the special use valuation method will be recaptured as additional estate tax liability if the heir disposes of the property or ceases to use it as qualifying use property within a period of 10 years from the date of the decedent's death.

**Example 21.** Assume the same facts as in Example 20. Further assume that by electing § 2032A, D's estate tax liability was reduced by $245,000. Three years after D's death, H (the qualifying heir) sells the farm for $3,000,000. At this point, the $245,000 additional estate tax liability that would have been imposed had § 2032A not been utilized becomes due.

Any additional tax liability due to the application of the recapture rules will be imposed upon the qualifying heir. In this connection, § 6324B gives the IRS security for compliance with the terms of § 2032A by placing a special lien on the qualifying property. The IRS may subordinate this special lien to third party creditors if it feels its interest would otherwise be adequately secured.

In a recapture situation, an upward adjustment in income tax basis can be elected by the heir.[34] The adjustment is the difference between the value of the property that would have been included in the gross estate had § 2032A not been elected and the amount actually included under § 2032A.

**Example 22.** Assume the same facts as in Example 21. If H chooses to do so, he can add $750,000 to the basis in the farm in determining the gain or loss to be recognized on its sale.

When a qualified heir makes the election to increase basis, he or she must pay interest on the amount of the estate tax that is recaptured. The interest is computed (at rates in effect during the period involved) commencing from nine months after the date of death to the due date of the recaptured estate tax.

# INCOME TAX CONSIDERATIONS IN VALUATION

Valuation is not only important for gift and estate tax determination but also crucial for income tax purposes. In the area of family tax planning, the focus generally is on the income tax basis a donee or an heir will receive as a result of lifetime or testamentary transfers.

## BASIS OF PROPERTY ACQUIRED BY GIFT—§ 1015

The income tax basis of property acquired by gift could depend on whether the donee sells the property for a gain or for a loss and, in certain cases, on when the gift occurred.

---

34.   § § 1016(c)(1) and (5).

—If the gift took place before 1921, the donee's basis for gain or loss will be the fair market value of the property on the date of the gift.[35]

—If the gift took place after 1920 and before 1977, the donee's basis for gain is the donor's adjusted basis plus any gift tax paid on the transfer (but not to exceed fair market value on the date of the gift). The basis for loss is the lower of the basis for gain or the fair market value of the property on the date of the gift.

—If the gift took place after 1976, the donee's basis for gain is the donor's adjusted basis plus only the gift tax attributable to the appreciation of the property to the point of the gift. The basis for loss is the lower of the basis for gain or the fair market value of the property on the date of the gift.[36]

These rules are illustrated by the following examples:

**Example 23.** In 1920, D received real estate as a gift from her grandfather. The property cost the grandfather $10,000 and was worth $25,000 on the date of the gift. D's income tax basis for gain or loss is $25,000.

**Example 24.** In 1975, D receives stock as a gift from M. The stock cost M $10,000 and had a fair market value of $50,000 on the date of the gift. As a result of the transfer, M paid a gift tax of $5,000. D's income tax basis for gain and for loss is $15,000 [$10,000 (M's basis) + $5,000 (gift tax paid by M)]. D does not have a different basis for loss, since the fair market value of the property on the date of the gift (i. e., $50,000) is not lower than the basis for gain (i. e., $15,000).

**Example 25.** Assume the same facts as in Example 24, except that the gift took place in 1986 (instead of 1975). D's income tax basis for gain is $14,000 determined as follows:

| | |
|---|---|
| M's adjusted basis on the date of the gift | $10,000 |
| Gift tax attributable to the $40,000 appreciation $\left(\dfrac{\$40,000}{\$50,000} \times \$5,000\right)$ | 4,000 |
| D's income tax basis for gain | $14,000 |

D's basis for loss would also be $14,000, based on the same reasoning set forth in Example 24.

The effect of the new rule, as illustrated in Example 25, is to deny a donee any increase in basis for the gift tax attributable to the donor's adjusted basis. In making the allocation, one has to assume that $1,000 of the gift tax paid related to M's $10,000 basis and $4,000 to the $40,000 appreciation in the property.

---

**35.** § 1015(c).
**36.** § § 1015(a) and (d).

## BASIS OF PROPERTY ACQUIRED BY DEATH—§ 1014

*General Rule.* Except as otherwise noted below, the income tax basis of property acquired from a decedent will be the fair market value on the date of death or, if elected, on the alternate valuation date. As to property that has appreciated in value from point of acquisition to date of death, this result causes a step-up in income tax basis for the estate or heir of the deceased owner. A step-up in basis, then, means that appreciation existing at death escapes the application of the Federal income tax.

> **Example 26.** At the time of his death in 1986, D owned real estate (adjusted basis of $100,000) worth $400,000 that he leaves to S. Presuming the alternate valuation date is not elected, S's income tax basis in the property becomes $400,000. Thus, a subsequent sale of the real estate by S for $400,000 would result in no gain or loss to S.

> **Example 27.** Assume the same facts as in Example 26, except that shortly before death, D sells the real estate for $400,000. Based on this assumption, D has a gain of $300,000 taxable under the income tax.

By contrasting Examples 26 and 27, one can easily see that the rules place a premium on holding appreciated property until death to take advantage of the step-up in basis result. The same cannot be said for property that has declined in value. Here there is the danger that death would cause a step-down in basis—a result to be avoided if a sale of the property would have generated a deductible income tax loss.

> **Example 28.** At the time of his death in 1986, D held stock with an adjusted basis of $50,000 and a fair market value of $30,000. Because only $30,000 is included in the gross estate, the basis of the stock to the estate or heir is this amount. Had D sold the stock prior to death, some or all of the $20,000 loss might have been salvaged.[37]

*Community Property.* Although there is usually no change in basis for property not part of a decedent's gross estate, a special exception applies to community property. In such situations, the surviving spouse's one-half of the community takes on the same basis as the half included in the deceased spouse's gross estate.[38] The reason for and the effect of this special rule can be illustrated as follows:

> **Example 29.** D and W were husband and wife and lived in a common law state. At the time of D's death in 1986, D owned assets (worth $800,000 with a basis to him of $100,000), which he bequeathed to W. Presuming the transfer qualifies under § 2056, D's estate is allowed a marital deduction of approximately $800,000. As the property passes through D's estate, W would receive a step-up in basis to $800,000.

---

**37.** Whether the sale would have helped D would depend on his capital gains position at the time of his death and whether he lived long enough to take advantage of the loss. If the stock is a capital asset, the loss could be offset against any realized capital gains, and any excess up to $3,000 per year could be applied against other income [§ 1211(b)]. Any unabsorbed capital losses existing at the time of death are lost except to the extent they might be utilized by a surviving spouse on a joint return for the year of the deceased spouse's death.
**38.** § 1014(b)(6).

**Example 30.** Assume the same facts as in Example 29, except that D and W had always lived in California (a community property state). If the $800,000 worth of property were community property, only one-half of this value would be included in D's gross estate. Because the other one-half does not pass through D's estate (i. e., it already belongs to W), is it fair to deny W a new basis therein? Therefore, allowing the surviving spouse's share of the community to take on a basis equal to that half included in the deceased spouse's gross estate merely equalizes the income tax result generally achieved in common law states with the use of the marital deduction. By giving W an income tax basis of $800,000 (i. e., $400,000 for H's half passing to her plus $400,000 for her half) and including only $400,000 in D's gross estate, the tax outcome is essentially the same as that outlined in Example 29.

*Step-Up in Basis and the One-Year Rule.* To understand the exception of § 1014(e), consider the following situation:

**Example 31.** H and W are husband and wife and reside in a common law state. When the parties learn that W has a terminal illness, H transfers property (basis of $50,000 and fair market value of $200,000) to W as a gift. W dies shortly thereafter, and under the provisions of W's will, the property returns to H.

If it were not for § 1014(e), what have the parties accomplished? No gift tax occurs on the transfer from H to W because of the application of the marital deduction (§ 2523). Upon W's death, the bequest from W to H does not generate any estate tax, because the inclusion of the property in W's gross estate is offset by the marital deduction (§ 2056). Through the application of the general rule of § 1014, H would end up with the same property, the basis of which has been stepped up to $200,000. Thus, this procedure would enable H to get a "free ride" as to an increase in income tax basis of $150,000.

When applicable, § 1014(e) forces H (the original donor) to assume the property with the same basis it had to W immediately prior to W's death. Since W's basis would have been determined under § 1015 (basis of property acquired by gift), W's basis would have been $50,000 (donor's adjusted basis) plus any gift tax adjustment (none in this case) and any capital additions made by the donee (none in this case), or $50,000. If § 1014(e) applies to Example 31, H ends up where he started (i. e., with $50,000) in terms of income tax basis.

For § 1014(e) to be operative, the following conditions must be satisfied:

—The decedent must have received appreciated property as a gift during the one-year period ending with his or her death. Under § 1014(e)(2)(A), appreciated property is defined as property whose fair market value on the date of its transfer exceeded the adjusted basis in the hands of the donor.

—The property is acquired from the decedent by the donor (or the donor's spouse).

—The property must have been acquired after August 13, 1981, by persons dying after 1981.

Although Example 31 concerns a transfer between spouses, the application of § 1014(e) is not so limited. The provision would apply with equal effect if, for example, the donor-heir were a son of the donee-decedent. In such cases, moreover, the technique used in Example 31 might prove to be more susceptible to the imposition of transfer taxes (viz., gift and estate taxes) because of the unavailability of the marital deduction.

## INCOME IN RESPECT OF A DECEDENT

Income in respect of a decedent can be defined as income earned by a decedent to the point of his or her death but not reportable on the final income tax return by virtue of the method of accounting used. Most frequently applicable to decedents using the cash basis of accounting, it will apply, for example, to an accrual basis taxpayer who held installment notes receivable at the time of death, the gain from which has been deferred under § 453.

For estate tax purposes, income in respect of a decedent will be included in the gross estate at its fair market value on the appropriate valuation date. For income tax purposes, however, the income tax basis of the decedent transfers over to the estate or heirs. There is neither a step-up nor step-down possibility as is true of property received by death.[39] Furthermore, the recipient of such income must classify it in the same manner (i. e., ordinary income, capital gain) as would have the decedent.[40]

> **Example 32.** D, a cash basis taxpayer, made some loans prior to death. At the time of her death, interest of $3,200 had accrued on these loans. This amount, plus the sum of $300 accrued after death, was collected by the executor of D's estate. Regardless of when D died, the $3,200 of interest is income in respect of a decedent and is includible in the gross estate. The $3,500 paid to the estate must be reported as interest income on the fiduciary return (i. e., Form 1041).

> **Example 33.** D, an accrual basis taxpayer, sold some undeveloped real estate held as an investment (basis of $40,000) for $100,000, receiving $30,000 in cash and an 8% interest-bearing note payable in two annual installments of $35,000 each. On a timely filed income tax return, D chose not to elect out from reporting the gain under the installment method.[41] D dies before the first installment is due and at a time when the note possesses a fair market value (without interest) of $68,000.[42] The note is collected (with accrued interest) as follows: $35,000 by the executor of D's estate three months after D's death and $35,000 by S (D's heir) one year and three months after D's death. The note is includible in D's gross estate at a value of $68,000 plus accrued

---

**39.** § 1014(c).
**40.** § 691(a)(3).
**41.** § 453(d). Installment sales treatment is automatic unless the seller affirmatively elects to recognize the gain in the year of the sale.
**42.** Although the face amount of the note is $70,000, the note's value at any one time depends on the factors previously discussed in this chapter. Probably the main reasons that the note in this case possesses a fair market value of only $68,000 on the date of D's death are the low rate of interest it carries and the fact that it is not immediately due and payable.

interest to date of death. Since the note represents income in respect of a decedent, the note's income tax basis remains the same as it was in the hands of D. Thus, when the estate collects the first installment of $35,000, it will recognize gain (for income tax purposes) of $21,000 based on a gross profit percentage of 60%.[43] The same gain must be recognized by S upon the collection of the remaining $35,000. Whether gain recognized by the estate and S will be ordinary or capital depends upon its character to D had he lived to collect the installments.[44]

Since denying a change in income tax basis for income in respect of a decedent, even though it is included in the gross estate, has the effect of subjecting the same asset to both income and death taxes, § 691(c) provides a limited form of relief. Under this provision, the recipient of income in respect of a decedent is allowed an income tax deduction for the Federal death tax attributable to the inclusion of the income interest in the gross estate. To illustrate, in Example 32 recall that $3,200 of interest was income in respect of a decedent, and such interest later was paid to D's estate. To oversimplify the solution, assume further the inclusion of $3,200 in the gross estate resulted in an additional Federal death tax of $640. On its income tax return (Form 1041) for the year in which the interest income is reported, the estate may claim an income tax deduction of $640.

## ESTATE LIQUIDITY

### RECOGNIZING THE PROBLEM

Even with effective predeath family tax planning directed toward a minimization of transfer taxes, the smooth administration of an estate necessitates a certain degree of liquidity. After all, probate costs will be incurred and, most important of all, death taxes must be satisfied. In the meantime, the surviving spouse and dependent beneficiaries may have to be supported. Without funds to satisfy these claims, estate assets may have to be sold at sacrifice prices, and most likely, the decedent's scheme of testamentary disposition will be defeated.

> **Example 34.** At the time of D's death, D's estate was made up almost entirely of a large ranch currently being operated by S, one of D's two sons. Because the ranch had been in the family for several generations and was a successful economic unit, it was D's hope that S would continue its operation and share the profits with R, D's other son. Unfortunately, R, on learning that his mother had died without a will, demanded and obtained a partition and sale of his share of the prop-

---

**43.** The gross profit percentage is computed by dividing the gross profit by the selling price. D's gross profit on the sale was the selling price of $100,000 less his adjusted basis of $40,000, or $60,000. Thus, $60,000 divided by $100,000 yields 60%. The gain of $21,000 is determined by multiplying the $35,000 payment received by 60%.

**44.** Because the real estate was unimproved (i. e., no recapture of depreciation on improvements is in order) and held as an investment at the time of sale, it would appear that the gain is capital.

erty.[45] Additional land was sold to pay for administration expenses and death taxes. After all of the sales had taken place, the portion remaining to S could not be operated profitably, and he subsequently was forced to give up the family ranch activity.

What type of predeath planning might have avoided the result reached in Example 34? Certainly D should have recognized and provided for the cash needs of the estate. Life insurance payable to her estate, although it adds to the estate tax liability, could have eased or solved the problem.[46] Furthermore, D made a serious error in dying without a will. A carefully drawn will could have precluded R's later course of action and perhaps kept much more of the ranch property intact.[47]

## EXTENSIONS OF TIME FOR PAYMENT OF DEATH TAXES

Being able to defer the payment of death taxes may be an invaluable option for an estate that lacks cash or "near-cash" assets (e. g., marketable securities). In this connection, three possibilities exist:

—The discretionary extension of time (§ 6161).

—The extension of time when the estate includes the value of a reversionary or remainder interest (§ 6163).

—The extension of time when the estate consists largely of an interest in a closely-held business (§ 6166).

Each of these aids to estate liquidity is discussed in the following sections.

*Discretionary Extension of Time to Pay Estate Taxes—§ 6161.* Currently, an executor or administrator may request an extension of time for paying the death tax for a period not to exceed 10 years from the date fixed for the payment. Such a request will be granted by the IRS whenever there is "reasonable cause." Reasonable cause is not limited to a showing of undue hardship. It includes cases in which the executor or administrator is unable to readily marshal liquid assets because they are located in several jurisdictions, or the estate is largely made up of assets in the form of payments to be received in the future (e. g., annuities, copyright royalties, contingent fees, or accounts receivable), or the assets that must be liquidated to pay the estate tax must be sold at a sacrifice or in a depressed market.

*Extension of Time When an Estate Includes the Value of a Reversionary or Remainder Interest—§ 6163.* If the gross estate includes a reversionary or remainder interest in property, the payment of the part of the tax attrib-

---

**45.** D dies intestate; it is therefore assumed that the two sons shared equally in her property under the appropriate state law of descent and distribution (i. e., intestate succession). If D was survived by a husband, the disposition of the property might have been different.

**46.** This presumes that D was insurable or that the cost of any such insurance would not be prohibitive.

**47.** The ranch could have been placed in trust, life estate to S and R, remainder to their children. With such an arrangement, R would have been unable to sell corpus. Also, D could have tried to arrange her estate so that it could qualify for the extension of time to pay death taxes under § 6166 (see the discussion later in the chapter).

utable to that interest may, at the election of the executor, be postponed until six months after that interest falls into possession. Once the initial postponement period has ended, a further extension of up to three years can be obtained upon the showing of reasonable cause by the executor of the estate.

Notice of the exercise of the election to postpone the payment of the tax attributable to a reversionary or remainder interest should be filed with the IRS before the date fixed for the payment of the tax.

> **Example 35.** In 1972, D transfers property in trust, income payable to M, D's mother, for her life, reversion to D or his estate.[48] In 1986, D predeceases M when M is 80 years of age and the fair market value of trust corpus is $100,000. D held a reversionary interest at the time of his death; therefore, the value of the $100,000 trust corpus (adjusted for M's intervening life estate) must be included in D's gross estate.[49] Thus, $100,000 × 0.56341, or $56,341, must be so included.[50] If D's executor chose to utilize the election permitted by § 6163, the payment of the death tax attributable to the $56,341 inclusion could be postponed until at least six months after M's life estate terminates (i. e., on her death).

The logic supporting the election provided for by § 6163 is easily explained. Without the election, D's estate would be forced to pay a death tax on property it does not have and will not have until the reversionary interest comes into its possession on M's death.

*Extension of Time When the Estate Consists Largely of an Interest in a Closely-Held Business—§ 6166.* By way of background, Congress always has been sympathetic to the plight of an estate that includes an interest in a closely-held business. The immediate imposition of the estate tax in such a situation may force the liquidation of the business at distress prices or, as an alternative, cause the interest to be sold to outside parties. Congress also was mindful of the fact that the extension of time to pay taxes under § 6161 (discussed above) was not a complete solution, since it largely was discretionary with the IRS.

A possible resolution of the problem is § 6166 which, if applicable, requires the IRS to accept a 15-year payout procedure [five-year deferral (except for the interest element) followed by 10-year installment payments of the estate tax]. One would hope that this delay would enable the business to generate enough income with which to buy out the deceased owner's interest without disruption of operations or other financial sacrifice.

To meet the requirements of § 6166, the decedent's interest in a farm or other closely-held business must be more than 35 percent of his or her adjusted gross estate.[51] The adjusted gross estate is the gross estate less the sum allowable as deductions under § 2053 (i. e., expenses, indebted-

---

**48.** The trust probably was created for income tax purposes because the income therefrom will not be taxed to D under § 673(c). Presumably, M is in a lower income tax bracket than D.

**49.** § 2033.

**50.** See Reg. § 20.2031–7(f), Table A, Remainder Column, for a person age 80 (see Appendix A).

**51.** § 6166(a)(1).

ness, and taxes) and § 2054 (i. e., casualty and theft losses during the administration of an estate).

An interest in a closely-held business includes the following:[52]

—A sole proprietorship.

—An interest in a partnership carrying on a trade or business where 20 percent of the capital interest in such partnership is included in the gross estate *or* the partnership has 15 or fewer partners.

—Stock in a corporation carrying on a trade or business if 20 percent or more in the value of the voting stock of such corporation is included in the gross estate *or* such corporation has 15 or fewer shareholders.

In meeting the requirements noted above, a decedent and his or her surviving spouse will be treated as one owner (i. e., shareholder or partner) if the interest is held as community property, tenants in common, joint tenants, or tenants by the entirety. Also, attribution from family members is allowed. In determining who is a family member, reference is made to § 267(c)(4).[53]

> **Example 36.** At the time of his death, D held a 15% capital interest in the XYZ Partnership. D's son holds another 10%. The XYZ Partnership had 16 partners including D and his son. As the son's interest is attributed to D, his estate is deemed to hold a 25% interest and the XYZ Partnership (for purposes of § 6166) has only 15 partners.

In satisfying the more than 35 percent test for basis qualification under § 6166 (see above), interests in more than one closely-held business can be aggregated when the decedent's gross estate includes 20 percent or more of the value of each such business.[54]

> **Example 37.** D's estate includes stock in X Corporation and Y Corporation, each of which qualifies as a closely-held business (see above). If the stock held in each corporation represents 20% or more of the total value outstanding, the stocks can be combined for purposes of the more than 35% test.

If the conditions of § 6166 are satisfied and the provision is elected, the following results transpire:

—No payments on the estate tax attributable to the inclusion of the interest in a closely-held business in the gross estate need be made for the first five years. After such five-year period, annual installments must be made over a period not longer than 10 years.

—From the outset, interest at the rate of four percent must be paid.[55] The rate is limited to the first $1,000,000 of estate tax value.

---

**52.** § 6166(b)(1).
**53.** § 267 deals with the disallowance of losses and expenses between related parties.
**54.** § 6166(c).
**55.** § 6601(j)(1).

—Acceleration of deferred payments may be triggered upon the happening of certain subsequent events (e. g., disposition of the interest, failure to make scheduled principal or interest payments).[56]

In qualifying for § 6166, the main objective would be to prune the potential estate of those assets that may cause the 35 percent test not to be satisfied. In this regard, lifetime gifts of such assets as marketable securities and life insurance should be considered.[57]

> ## ✓ TAX PLANNING CONSIDERATIONS

In addition to the points already discussed, much can be done to minimize taxes while resolving the issue of valuation. Most often, this involves the determination of a value that will withstand challenge by the IRS without unduly compromising the tax position of the family unit.

Closely tied to the valuation issue are the basis ramifications of § 1015 (basis of property acquired by gift) and § 1014 (basis of property acquired through inheritance). Income tax considerations, moreover, could well make the basis rules a key factor in the valuation process. In this regard, the planning potential rests with the difference between transfers by gift and transfers at death.

### GENERAL PLANNING CONSIDERATIONS

Somewhat basic but frequently overlooked are certain procedures that should be pursued in establishing a sound value for tax purposes. These procedures are summarized below:

1.  Obtain competent appraisal information. Needless to say, such information should be in writing.

2.  In obtaining appraisal data, be sure to choose the right expert for the job. Such assets as works of art, antique furniture, mineral deposits, and closely-held stock present special problems and require appraisal by persons with special expertise. Rest assured that the IRS also has access to highly qualified valuation experts.

3.  Obtain and preserve comparable sales information. It is never too early to start building a file on what is happening in the marketplace to property similar in nature and use. Such information may be difficult to reconstruct at some later time.

4.  Maintain a record of the cost of property transferred as a gift. The donee will, of course, need this information for income tax purposes if the property is disposed of in a taxable exchange. If the fair market value of the property on the date of the gift might be less than the donor's basis, the property should be appraised. Recall

---

**56.** § 6166(g).
**57.** A gift within three years of death will not be effective for this purpose due to the operation of § 2035(d)(4).

that the income tax basis of the property to the donee for purposes of loss determination is the lesser of the donor's adjusted basis or the fair market value on the date of the gift.

5. All interested parties (i. e., donees and heirs) should have access to relevant valuation data. At a minimum, donees should be given copies of gift tax returns and heirs copies of death tax returns.

*Transfers at Death and the Alternate Valuation Date.* In the event of transfers at death, the same appraisal data described above should also cover the alternate valuation date. Further, when considering election of the alternate valuation date, one must be on the lookout for significant changes in value since the decedent's death. Such changes may not be obvious and thus difficult to discern.

**Example 38.** On the date of D's death, D owned an insurance policy on the life of his wife, with their son as the designated beneficiary. The policy possessed a value of $30,000 on the date of D's death but carried a maturity value of $300,000. Four months after D's death, D's wife dies and the insurance company pays the $300,000 policy proceeds to the son. It could be disastrous from a tax standpoint if D's estate elected the alternate valuation date. D's gross estate must then include $300,000—the maturity value of the policy. If the alternate valuation date is not elected, only $30,000 need be included; this amount represents the date of death value of the policy.

*Special Use Valuation Procedure of § 2032A.* Because of the conditions imposed upon the application of the special valuation method, qualifying for its use may be difficult. Also, the maximum gross estate reduction through the use of the election is limited in amount. Unfortunately, the special valuation method is limited to estate tax situations and is not available to reduce the valuation of property transferred by gift.

Despite its shortcomings, the special use valuation will be highly advantageous under the proper circumstances. Such might be the case where there is substantial appreciation in "most suitable use" value over "current use" value and the heirs of the decedent wish to continue operating the qualifying business. In such situations, it might be ruinous to the business not to make the election and thereby avoid or reduce the transfer tax at death on the appreciation.

In planning for the future use of the special use valuation method, taxpayers should keep in mind both the 50 percent test and the 25 percent test relating to the value of qualifying assets included in the adjusted value of the gross estate. If difficulty is anticipated in satisfying these percentage requirements, lifetime gifts of nonqualifying property should be carried out. Be careful, however, of gifts made within three years of the donor's death. Although such gifts usually are no longer included in the gross estate of the donor for estate tax purposes, they are counted when testing for the percentage requirements of § 303 (redemption to pay death taxes and administration expenses—refer to Chapter 4), § 2032A, and § 6166 (extension of time to pay estate taxes in installments).

**Example 39.** In planning to meet the percentage requirements of § 2032A, D transfers by gift marketable securities worth $200,000. If

D dies within three years of the gift, the value of such securities must be included in her gross estate in applying the 50% and 25% tests of § 2032A. This "as if" approach, however, does not have the effect of making such securities subject to actual inclusion in the gross estate.

## LIFETIME GIFTS—INCOME TAX CONSIDERATIONS

*Income Tax Consequences to the Donor.* Presuming lifetime giving is desired, great care should be exercised in selecting the property to be given away. Of initial importance might be any income tax consequences to the donor generated by the gift.

> **Example 40.** Last year, D sold real estate (basis of $40,000) to P (an unrelated party) for $100,000 receiving $20,000 in cash and P's note for $80,000. On a timely filed return, D did not elect out of the installment method of reporting the gain on the sale. This year, when the note has a fair market value of $76,000, D gives it to his son, S. In addition to the gain of $12,000 (60% × $20,000) on the down payment, D must recognize $44,000 when he disposes of the note. This represents the difference between the fair market value of the note ($76,000) and D's unrecovered basis of $32,000 [$40,000 (original basis) − $8,000 (amount of basis applied against the down payment)]. The gift of an installment obligation is treated as a taxable disposition under § 453B(a).

If the obligor and obligee are related persons, the tax law provides for a different result. In such cases, the entire unreported gain will be taxed on what, in effect, is a cancellation of the obligation. Referring to Example 40, assume the original sale was to S (a related party) and not to P (an unrelated party). Under § 453B(f)(2), when D (the obligee) gives (or otherwise cancels) the note to S (the obligor), D must recognize a gain of $48,000 [60 percent (gross profit percentage) × $80,000 (face amount of the note)]. In defining related person, § 453(f)(1) makes reference to the attribution rules of § 318(a) (refer to Chapter 4 and the discussion of certain stock redemptions).

> **Example 41.** In 1984, D acquired for use in his trade or business some § 38 property, upon which was claimed an investment tax credit of $3,000 based on a cost of $30,000 and a recovery period of five years.[58] After using the property for one full year, D gives it to S. The premature disposition of the property will trigger recapture by D of $2,400 of the credit as additional income tax liability in the year of the gift.[59]

Would there be any difference to D had the transfers outlined in the above examples been testamentary? In other words, suppose the property had passed to S by virtue of D's death rather than by gift. The disposition of an installment note receivable (Example 40) or § 38 property (Example 41)

---

**58.** Under § 46(c)(7), the credit for § 38 property with a recovery period of five years is 10%.
**59.** § 47(a)(5)(B) reduces the recapture amount by 2% for each full year the property is held. Expressed differently, D must recapture 80% of the $3,000 previously claimed as a credit.

by death is not a taxable event under the income tax; therefore, the results would have been different.[60] But in Example 40, the unrealized gain, though not taxed to D, will not go unrecognized. As income in respect of a decedent it will be taxed to whoever collects the note. In Example 41, however, the investment credit recapture potential is removed by death. Thus, even if S sold the § 38 property right after D's death and before the five-year period had run, there would be no recapture of the credit.

*Income Tax Consequences to the Donee.* What about the income tax position of the donee? Certainly this must be an important factor in the donor's choice of property to transfer as a gift.

> **Example 42.** D makes a gift to S of depreciable tangible personalty (adjusted basis of $20,000 and a fair market value of $30,000) used in the trade or business. If D had sold the property for $30,000, he would have recognized a gain of $10,000, all of which would have been ordinary income under the recapture of depreciation provisions of § 1245. The gift does not generate income to D; such transfers are excepted from the usual recapture of depreciation rules by § 1245(b)(1).[61] The recapture potential of the property is, however, transferred to the donee. As a consequence, if S sold the property for $30,000 immediately after the gift, he must recognize a gain of $10,000, all of which would be recaptured as ordinary income.

> **Example 43.** D makes a gift to S of preferred stock in X Corporation (basis to D of $8,000, fair market value of $40,000). The stock was received by D as a nontaxable stock dividend on common stock and, if sold, would produce $40,000 of ordinary income as § 306 stock.[62] The gift will cause no income tax consequences to D, but S's tax position is quite another matter. The § 306 taint shifts to S.[63] If S ever disposes of the stock in a taxable transaction, the same ordinary income potential D held will materialize.

In both Examples 42 and 43, any gain, including the ordinary income element, would go unrecognized if the property was passed by death.[64] Any gain from after-death appreciation (Example 43) on the disposition of the stock would qualify for long-term capital gain treatment if such disposition

---

**60.** § § 453B(c) and 47(b)(1). If the installment obligation passes to the obligor (or is otherwise cancelled by the obligee's will), it will be treated as a transfer by the obligee's estate and will trigger recognition of gain to the estate. If the parties are related persons [within the meaning of § 318(a)], the face amount of the obligation will be deemed to be the obligation's fair market value. See § 691(a)(5).

**61.** With respect to depreciable real estate, see § 1250(d)(1) for a like exception.

**62.** The preferred stock bailout rule of § 306 was explained in Chapter 4. Under the factual situation presented in Example 43, the earnings and profits of X Corporation at the time the preferred stock was issued as a dividend must have been at least $40,000. Therefore, any basis D had allocated to the preferred from the common stock [under Code § 307(a)] cannot be used to offset gain but must be returned to the common stock account.

**63.** § 306(c)(1)(C) and Reg. § 1.306–3(e).

**64.** § 1245(b)(2) and Reg. § 1.306–3(e). Note that the income tax basis of the property to the estate or heirs will be determined under § 1014.

were pursuant to a § 303 stock redemption to pay death taxes and administration expenses (discussed in Chapter 4).

Just because a testamentary transfer might produce a more favorable income tax result does not mean this type of property is always unsuitable for gifts. The owner of the property (i. e., D) may be unable or unwilling to retain the property until death. If the property is to be disposed of prior to this time, shifting the income tax consequences to someone else (i. e., S) may be less costly from a tax standpoint to the family unit. Such might be the case if the donee (i. e., S) is in a lower tax bracket than the donor or has losses that will neutralize some or all of the gain on the later sale of the property.[65] On the other hand, the donee may not intend to sell the property. In this event, any built-in income tax potential should provide no real concern.

> **Example 44.** D owns a summer home in Arkansas which, because of its location and accessibility to recreational facilities, has been used for many years by the family for vacation purposes. The property has an adjusted basis of only $40,000 but has appreciated to a present value of $110,000. D would like to exclude the property from his gross estate but still keep it in the family. S, D's son, plans to continue vacationing at the summer home and would make it available to the rest of the family in the event the property became his.

There is much to be said in favor of a gift of the summer home to S. Although S's basis for income tax purposes will be only $40,000, this creates no real problem, because S does not plan to dispose of the property.

Example 44 raises another interesting point. Aside from the gift tax liability, what has D really lost by making the transfer? One would hope the donee-son will permit his father (D) to use the property for its intended recreational purpose. As long as such use is by invitation only and there exists no express or implied agreement requiring S to do so, the hoped-for estate tax result will be accomplished.[66]

*Other Considerations.* In addition to the preceding, other considerations that might affect the type of property to be given include the following:

> —Property that may be difficult to value for estate tax purposes. Though this substitutes one valuation problem for another, the gift tax valuation may be more easily resolved.

---

**65.** One must be wary of situations in which the sale by the donee was prearranged by the donor or the sale takes place shortly after the gift of the property. If this happens, the IRS may try to collapse the gift and argue that the sale really was made by the donor and not the donee. If its argument is successful, the income tax consequences will be attributed to the donor and not the donee.

**66.** After the transfer, the parties must be careful to treat S as the true owner of the summer home. If not, the IRS may contend that D has retained "the possession or enjoyment" of the property. If this were the case, the property would be includible in D's gross estate upon his death by virtue of § 2036(a)(1). Refer to the discussion of incomplete transfers in Chapter 11.

—Property located in other states and in foreign countries. Not only might this eliminate the possibility of multiple death taxes, but it could save on probate costs.[67]

—Property with a high income yield. This is predicated on the assumption that the donor can spare the income from the gift property and is in a high personal income tax bracket. In terms of the objective family tax planning, it should follow that the donee is in a lower income tax bracket than is the donor.

—The liquidity of the property. Because many estates encounter a problem of liquidity, at least some cash or near-cash assets (e. g., marketable securities) should be retained. Thus, an executor will not be forced to sell nonliquid assets at bargain prices in order to raise funds to meet pressing administration expenses.

## TRANSFERS BY DEATH—INCOME TAX CONSIDERATIONS

*General Guidelines.* In some cases, it may be advisable to maximize death tax values in order to achieve a higher income tax basis for the estate or heirs. The option may be available when there is conflict as to the true value of an asset. This might be the case with hard to value property such as real estate, intangibles, interests in closely-held businesses, antiques, and valuable collections. Here, the true value of assets may fall within a range, and upon the high and low even expert appraisers may disagree. Under such circumstances, the executor of an estate may be in a position to select a realistic value that is most beneficial for tax purposes to the parties involved.[68]

Whether or not it is wise to increase death tax values in order to add to income tax basis is a matter that must be considered carefully. Some of the variables that will enter any such decision follow:

1. The effect that the increase in death value will have on the income tax basis of the property.

2. The additional death taxes that will result from the increased valuation. In light of the unified tax credit, it may well be that many small or modest estates would incur little, if any, additional death taxes by a higher date of death valuation.

3. The planned disposition of the property by the estate or heirs. If, for example, no sale or other taxable disposition is envisioned, a higher income tax basis usually holds little attraction.[69]

4. The nature of any gain to be recognized by the estate or heirs. A higher basis means more if the property will generate ordinary income rather than long-term capital gain.

5. The income tax bracket of the estate or heirs.

---

67. Ancillary court proceedings may have to be instituted in the states or countries where the property is located to wind up the estate. Needless to mention, this means additional court costs, legal fees, etc.

68. Whether such value will be acceptable to the IRS is another problem.

69. But even though the property will not be disposed of in a taxable exchange, a high income tax basis could make good sense if the property is depreciable, depletable, or amortizable in the hands of the estate or heirs.

A direct correlation exists in terms of the effect that the increase in death value will have on income tax basis (see variable 1). Since the basis becomes whatever value was used for death tax purposes, every dollar of increased valuation means a dollar of additional basis.

*How Conclusive Is the Value Used for Estate Tax Purposes?* Suppose a value is used for estate tax purposes and reflected on the estate tax return. At some future date, an heir sells some of the property included in the gross estate and, in computing the basis for gain or loss, believes the value used for estate tax purposes was incorrect. Is there any chance of success in arguing for a different value and thereby changing the income tax basis? The answer is yes, but with definite reservations.

An heir's tax motivation for challenging a lower valuation used for estate tax purposes should be discernable. If it can be proven that the value at the time of death was in excess of that reported, less gain might result on the later sale of the property. Even better, a higher value on the date of death may not, in the absence of fraud on the part of the executor,[70] generate additional estate taxes because the statute of limitations on further assessments by the IRS has run.[71] Whether or not an heir's challenge will succeed depends on a consideration of the following factors:

1. The value reflected on the estate tax return and accepted by the IRS is presumed to be correct.[72] Thus, the heir has the burden of rebutting the presumption.

2. To rebut the presumption of correctness, it would be important to determine by what means the property was originally valued. Did the valuation result from a mere unilateral determination by the IRS or, on the other hand, was it the result of carefully considered compromise between the estate and the IRS? The presumption would be more difficult for the heir to overcome in the latter instance.

3. Did the heir have a hand in setting the original value? If so, the doctrine of estoppel might preclude disputing such value. Under this doctrine, the courts might hold that the heir is now trying to obtain unfair advantage. Thus, the heir used or influenced the use of a lower value for estate tax purposes (thereby saving estate taxes) and now wants a higher value for income tax purposes (thereby saving on recognized gain).[73] The doctrine of estoppel is appropriately used because the IRS is prevented by the statute of limitations from assessing the additional estate taxes that would

---

**70.** There is no statute of limitations on further assessments in the case of fraud. See § 6501(c)(1) and Chapter 14.

**71.** If the statute of limitations has not run, the heir might try for a higher income tax basis by having the estate tax valuation raised. However, this would necessitate the cooperation of the decedent's executor and the acceptance by the IRS of the new valuation.

**72.** Rev.Rul. 54–97, 1954–1 C.B. 113; *H. B. Levy,* 17 T.C. 728 (1951); and *Malcolm C. Davenport,* 6 T.C. 62 (1946).

**73.** In *William A. Beltzer,* 74–1 USTC ¶ 9373, 33 AFTR2d 74–1173, 495 F.2d 211 (CA–8, 1974) *aff'g.* 73–2 USTC ¶ 9512, 32 AFTR2d 73–5250 (D.Ct.Neb., 1973), the doctrine of estoppel was invoked against the taxpayer, since as the executor of the estate, he had been instrumental in setting the original value reported on the death tax return.

otherwise be payable if the proposed new value is allowed.[74] On the other hand, if the heir had no hand in the administration of the estate and took no part in determining the value used, it would appear that the heir should not be estopped when attempting to alter such value.

4.  Even if the heir can avoid the application of the doctrine of estoppel, justification for a new value must be produced. Perhaps there now exists some evidence of value unknown or not available to the executor of the estate when the property was originally valued. But was this evidence known to the parties involved in the original valuation and thereby taken into account? If not, was it foreseeable? Remember that the valuation process does not involve hindsight but should consider only the factors reasonably available on the appropriate valuation date.

## VALUATION PROBLEMS WITH A CLOSELY-HELD CORPORATION

A previous section of this chapter considered the criteria used to arrive at a value for stocks and bonds for which there is no recognized market.[75] Special attention is necessary, however, to certain concepts peculiar to this area that can carry a marked impact on value.

*Valuation Approaches.*  If a high value is to be avoided, the issue of goodwill has to be satisfactorily resolved. Particularly if the corporation's record of past earnings is higher than usual for the industry, the IRS is apt to claim the presence of goodwill as a corporate asset. As an indication of what this could mean, consider the following illustration:

**Example 45.**  At the time of death, D owned 70% of the stock of D Corporation, with the remaining 30% held by various family members. Over the past five years, D Corporation has had average net profits of $100,000, and on the date of D's death, the book value (i. e., corporate net worth) of the corporation's stock was $250,000. If the IRS determined 8% to be the appropriate rate of return, one approach to the valuation of D Corporation stock would yield the following result:

| | |
|---|---:|
| Average net profit for the past five years | $ 100,000 |
| 8% of the $250,000 book value | 20,000 |
| Excess earnings over 8% | $  80,000 |
| | |
| Value of goodwill (5 × $80,000) | $ 400,000 |
| Book value | 250,000 |
| Total value of the D Corporation stock | $ 650,000 |

---

**74.**  Sections 1311 through 1315 (Mitigation of Effect of Limitations and Other Provisions), which permit the statute of limitations to be disregarded under certain conditions, would not be applicable here because different taxpayers (the estate and the heir) and different taxes (the estate tax and the income tax) are involved.

**75.**  These criteria are set forth in Reg. § 20.2031–2(f) as supplemented by Rev.Rul. 59–60, 1959–1 C.B. 237.

Thus, the IRS might contend that the stock be included in D's gross estate at 70 percent of $650,000, or $455,000. If the estate wishes to argue for a lower valuation, relevant factors might include any of the following:

1. The average net profit figure for the past five years (i. e., $100,000) may not be representative. Perhaps it includes some extraordinary gains that normally do not occur or are extraneous to the business conducted by the corporation.[76] The figure may fail to take into account certain expenses that normally would be incurred but, for some justifiable reason, have been deferred.[77]

2. The appropriate rate of return for this type of business may not be 8 percent. If higher, there would be less goodwill because the business is not as profitable as it seems.

3. If D had been a key person in the operation of D Corporation, could it be possible that some or all of any goodwill developed by the business is attributed to his or her efforts? If so, is it not reasonable to assume that such goodwill might be seriously impaired by D's death?

Aside from the issue of goodwill, the valuation of closely-held stock should take other factors into account. For example, it would be relevant to consider the percentage of ownership involved. If the percentage represents a minority interest and the corporation has a poor dividend-paying record, a substantial discount might be in order.[78] The justification for such a discount would be the general inability of the holder of the minority interest to affect corporate policy, particularly with respect to the distribution of dividends. At the other extreme is an interest large enough to represent control, either actual or effective. Considered alone, a controlling interest would call for a higher valuation.[79]

A controlling interest, however, might be such that the disposition of the stock within a reasonable period of time after the valuation date could have a negative effect on any market for such shares. Known as the "blockage rule," this concept recognizes what may happen in terms of per unit value when a large block of shares is marketed at one time.[80] Most often, it is applied to stock for which there is a recognized market. The blockage rule will permit a discount from the amount at which smaller lots are selling on or about the valuation date.[81] The blockage rule could have a

---

**76.** An example might be a windfall profit for a particular year because of an unusual market situation. Or, suppose the corporation recognized a large gain from an appreciated investment held for many years.

**77.** In a family business during periods of expansion and development, it is not uncommon to find an unusually low salary structure. Profits might be considerably less if the owner-employees of the business were being paid the true worth of their services.

**78.** See, for example, *Jack D. Carr,* 49 TCM 507, T.C.Memo. 1985–19.

**79.** See, for example, *Helvering v. Safe Deposit and Trust Co. of Baltimore, Exr. (Estate of H. Walters),* 38–1 USTC ¶ 9240, 21 AFTR 12, 95 F.2d 806 (CA–4, 1938), *aff'g.* 35 B.T.A. 259 (1937), in which the court stated ". . . . the influence of the ownership of a large number of shares upon corporate control might give them a value in excess of prevailing market quotations. . . ." See also Reg. § 20.2031–2(e).

**80.** Reg. § 20.2031–2(e).

**81.** See, for example, *Estate of Robert Damon,* 49 T.C. 108 (1967).

bearing on the valuation of other assets, but its application appears better suited to stocks and securities.[82]

Because most stock in closely-held corporations does not have a recognized market, a discount for lack of marketability may be in order. The discount recognizes the costs that would have to be incurred in creating a market for such shares to effectuate their orderly disposition.[83] Such a discount could be significant when one considers typical underwriting expenses and other costs attendant to going public.

*Resolving the Valuation Problem for Stock in Closely-Held Corporations.* Since the valuation of closely-held stock is subject to so many variables, planning should be directed toward bringing about some measure of certainty.

> **Example 46.** D wants to transfer some of his stock in Z Corporation to a trust formed for his children. He also would like to make a substantial contribution to his alma mater, State University. At present, the stock of Z Corporation is owned entirely by D and has never been traded on any market or otherwise sold or exchanged. Z Corporation's past operations have proved profitable, and Z established a respectable record of dividend distributions. Based on the best available information and taking into account various adjustments (e. g., discount for lack of marketability), D feels each share of Z Corporation stock possesses a fair market value of $120.

Of course, it would be easy enough for D to make a gift of some of the stock to the trust set up for his children and use the $120 per share valuation. What assurance is there the IRS will accept this figure? If it does not and if it is successful in increasing the fair market value per share, D could end up with additional gift tax liability. Although D cannot guarantee this will not happen, he could hedge against any further gift tax liability. Concurrently with the gift of stock to the trust formed for his children, D could make an outright transfer of some of the shares to S.U., thereby generating an income tax deduction. D would base the income tax deduction on the same value used for gift tax purposes.[84] If the IRS later raises the value and assesses more gift tax, D could file an amended income tax return, claim a larger charitable contribution deduction, and obtain an offsetting income tax refund. To carry out this hedge, the amount of Z Corporation stock D would have to donate to S.U. would depend on a comparison of his gift tax and income tax brackets for the year of the transfers. It should be noted that no gift tax liability would be incurred for the stock transferred

---

82. In *Estate of David Smith,* 57 T.C. 650 (1972), the estate of the now-famous sculptor argued for the application of the blockage rule to 425 sculptures included in the gross estate.
83. See, for example, *Estate of Mark S. Gallo,* 50 TCM 470, T.C.Memo. 1985–363. In this case, the taxpayer also argued that a bad product image (i. e., the Thunderbird, Ripple, and Boone's Farm brands) would depress the value of the stock. Since the trend was towards better wines, association with cheaper products had a negative consumer impact.
84. The use of fair market value as the measure of the charitable contribution deduction presumes the Z Corporation stock, if sold by D, would yield long-term capital gain. See § 170(e).

to S.U. by virtue of the charitable deduction allowed for gift tax purposes by § 2522 (discussed in Chapter 11).

*The Buy and Sell Agreement and Valuation.* The main objective of a buy and sell agreement is to effectuate the orderly disposition of a business interest without running the risk of such interest falling into the hands of outsiders. Moreover, if properly designed and executed, a buy and sell agreement can ease the problems of estate liquidity and valuation.

Two types of buy and sell agreements exist: the entity and the cross-purchase arrangements. Under the entity type, the business itself (i. e., partnership or corporation) agrees to buy out the interest of the withdrawing owner (i. e., partner or shareholder). In the case of a corporation, this normally takes the form of a stock redemption plan set up to qualify for income tax purposes under either § 302(b) or § 303.[85] Under the cross-purchase type of buy and sell agreement, the surviving owners (i. e., partners or shareholders) agree to buy out the withdrawing owner (i. e., partner or shareholder).

> **Example 47.** R, S, and D are equal shareholders in T Corporation, and all three share in its management. In 19X1, all agree to turn in their stock to the corporation for redemption at $100 per share in the event any one of them withdraws (by death or otherwise) from the business. In 19X8, D dies and the estate redeems the stock from T Corporation at the agreed-upon price of $100 per share.

> **Example 48.** Assume the same facts as in Example 47, except the agreement is the cross-purchase type under which each shareholder promises to buy a share of the withdrawing shareholder's interest. In 19X8, D dies and the estate sells the stock in T Corporation to R and S for $100 per share.

Will the $100 per share paid to D's estate determine the amount to be included in D's gross estate? The answer is yes, subject to the following conditions:

1. The $100 per share price was reasonable when established. In this connection, one must look to the value of the stock when the agreement was made (i. e., 19X1) and not when executed (i. e., 19X8).

2. The decedent's estate was legally obligated to dispose of the stock at $100 per share.

3. The decedent was bound by the agreement as to lifetime transfers. Thus, had D decided to sell the stock prior to death, the stock would have to be offered first to T Corporation (Example 47) or to R and S (Example 48) for $100 per share.[86]

Meeting these conditions and establishing the $100 per share value for death tax purposes is, of course, an ideal way to solve an otherwise difficult valuation problem. Unless properly handled, however, the fixed price approach (e. g., $100 per share) might work an inequity to some of the par-

---

**85.** The taxpayer wishes to have the distribution treated as being in exchange for stock rather than as dividend. Refer to Chapter 4.

**86.** Reg. § 20.2031–2(h) and *Estate of Mabel G. Seltzer*, 50 TCM 1250, T.C.Memo. 1985–519.

ties. Although the price might have been reasonable when the agreement was drawn up, what if a substantial change in the value of the business interest takes place by the time the agreement becomes effective? Referring to Example 48, suppose the value of a share of T Corporation stock increases from $100 in 19X1 to $150 in 19X8. D's estate must sell the stock for $100; therefore, is there any doubt that R and S have obtained an unfair economic advantage? Of course, the possible inequity might be relieved by avoiding a fixed price commitment and substituting some type of formula that would better take into account business fluctuations (e. g., book value, capitalization of earnings). But even if the fixed price feature is to be retained, a sound approach would be to reset the price at periodic intervals. Thus, the agreement could require the parties to reevaluate the price every two years. A procedure could be established whereby the reevaluation will be carried out by qualified appraisers not possessing an interest in the business and mutually acceptable to the shareholders of T Corporation.

## PROBLEM MATERIALS

### Discussion Questions

1. In 1919, M made a gift to D (M's daughter) of the family sterling silver. In 1970, D made a gift of the same property to G (D's daughter). Because of unusual medical expenses, G is forced to sell the silver in 1986. In determining G's gain, what role does valuation play?

2. Discuss the relevance of the following in defining "fair market value" for Federal gift and estate tax purposes:

   (a) § 2031(b).

   (b) The definition contained in Reg. § 20.2031–1(b).

   (c) A forced sale price.

   (d) The location of the property being valued.

   (e) The sentimental value of the property being valued.

   (f) The wholesale price of the property.

   (g) Tangible personalty sold as a result of an advertisement in the classified section of a newspaper.

3. What factors should be considered in the valuation of bonds of a closely-held corporation when selling prices and bid and asked prices are not available? In the valuation of stock in a closely-held corporation under similar circumstances?

4. At the time of his death, D held some notes receivable (face amount of $20,000 and accrued interest of $4,000) issued by his son for sums borrowed from D. In his will, D forgives the loans but not the accrued interest thereon.

   (a) How should these items be handled for Federal estate tax purposes?

   (b) For Federal income tax purposes?

5. What factor controls in determining the value of shares in an open-end investment company (mutual funds)?

6. D creates a trust, life estate to W, remainder to S upon W's death.

   (a) Why is it necessary to value the life estate and the remainder interest separately?

(b) In this regard, would it matter if the transfer occurred in 1970? In 1982? In 1986? Explain.

7. Comment on the following relative to the valuation of life insurance and annuity policies:

   (a) The annuity contract is not issued by a company regularly engaged in the sale of annuity contracts.

   (b) The annuity contract is issued by a company regularly engaged in the sale of annuity contracts.

   (c) The life insurance policy being valued is paid-up.

   (d) The life insurance policy has been in force for some time, and further premium payments must be made to continue the policy.

   (e) The "interpolated terminal reserve" of the policy.

8. What is the justification for the alternate valuation date (i. e., § 2032)?

9. In connection with the alternate valuation date (§ 2032), comment on the following:

   (a) Its elective nature.

   (b) How the election is made.

   (c) Who makes the election.

   (d) When the election is available.

   (e) What assets the election covers.

   (f) Effect on changes in value caused by a mere lapse of time.

   (g) The treatment of income earned by property after the death of the decedent.

   (h) A disposition by an executor of estate property *within* six months from the date of the decedent's death.

10. In each of the following independent situations, determine whether or not the alternate valuation date can be elected:

| | | Fair Market Value of the Gross Estate | |
| | | | Alternate Valuation |
| Decedent | Year of Death | Date of Death | Date |
|---|---|---|---|
| A | 1987 | $ 595,000 | $ 580,000 |
| B | 1987 | 590,000 | 610,000 |
| C | 1986 | 510,000 | 490,000 |
| D | 1986 | 520,000 | 530,000 |

11. In Question 10, would your answer be different if A had made a taxable gift of $10,000 in 1976? A taxable gift of $10,000 in 1980?

12. In Question 10, why might C's estate not elect the alternate valuation date (presuming it is otherwise available)?

13. Contrast current use value with most suitable use value. Why might there be a difference between the two values?

14. What type of hardship does the special valuation method of § 2032A purport to ease?

15. Comment on the special valuation method in connection with the following:

   (a) The 50% test and the 25% test.

   (b) Qualifying property.

   (c) The five-out-of-eight-years requirement.

   (d) The qualifying heir.

(e) The $750,000 limitation.

(f) The recapture possibility.

16. Presuming the special valuation method is elected by an estate and the qualifying heir disposes of the property within a 10-year period, what will be the income tax basis of the property?

17. What are some of the shortcomings of the special valuation method?

18. Review the income tax basis rules applicable when a donee sells property received as a gift under the following conditions:

(a) The gift took place before 1921.

(b) The gift took place after 1920 and before 1977.

(c) The gift took place after 1976.

19. In 1948, F purchased a collection of rare coins and in 1972 gave the coins to S. S died in 1984, and the collection passed to G under S's will. In 1986, G sells the collection. In determining G's gain or loss for income tax purposes, is F's purchase price relevant? Why or why not?

20. What is meant by a step-up in basis as to property acquired from a decedent? A step-down in basis?

21. What effect, if any, will the death of a spouse have on the income tax basis of the surviving spouse's share of the community property? Explain.

22. S gives property to his widowed mother. Nine months after the gift, S's mother dies. Under her will, the same property returns to S. Comment on the tax ramifications of these transfers.

23. H gives property to his wife, W. Thirteen months after the gift, W dies. Under her will, the same property returns to H. What are the gift, estate, and income tax consequences?

24. Assume the same facts as in 23, except that W dies 10 months after the gift. Again, comment on the gift, estate, and income tax consequences.

25. Under § 691(c), the party who collects income in respect of a decedent is allowed an income tax credit for the estate tax attributable to the inclusion of the income in the gross estate. Is this a correct statement? Why or why not?

26. W, a widow, dies in 1986 without a will. At the time of her death, W owned a ranch that was being operated by her unmarried son, S. W's only other heir is her daughter D. D lives in the city, is married, and has four small children. S hopes to expand the ranch and improve the breeding stock of the herd.

(a) Do you anticipate any potential problems with these circumstances?

(b) Presuming some planning had preceded W's death, what might have been a more desirable testamentary scheme?

27. Code § 6163 permits an executor of an estate to request an extension of time for the payment of death taxes attributable to the value of a reversionary interest included in the gross estate.

(a) Why is this provision equitable?

(b) Give an example of its application.

(c) If § 6163 is applicable, how long is the extension that can be obtained?

28. Section 6166 commonly is referred to as the "5-year deferral, 10-year installment payment" provision. Explain.

29. In connection with § 6166, comment on the following:

(a) The more than 35% test.

(b) The definition of a closely-held business.

(c) The family attribution rules.

(d) The aggregation rules.

30. T, currently still alive, almost complies for her estate's election of § 6166. T is not concerned, however, because prior to her death she plans on giving away her life insurance policy. This, she believes, will allow her estate to meet the requirements of § 6166. Any comment?

31. Discuss the income tax consequences to the donor and the donee of gifts of the following types of property:

(a) Installment notes receivable.

(b) § 38 property.

(c) § § 1245 and 1250 property.

(d) § 306 stock.

32. Sometimes it may be advisable to resolve questionable estate tax valuation issues in favor of the higher possible values. Discuss this approach in light of the following factors:

(a) The estate tax bracket of the decedent.

(b) Whether the heirs plan to dispose of the property.

(c) The character of the asset in the hands of the heir (e. g., depreciable property, capital assets).

(d) The income tax bracket of the heir.

33. How conclusive is the valuation used for Federal income tax purposes in establishing the income tax basis of the property to the heirs?

34. Comment on the following points in relation to the valuation of stock in a closely-held corporation:

(a) The deceased shareholder was a key employee of the corporation.

(b) The past earnings of the corporation include large and nonrecurring gains.

(c) The deceased shareholder held only a minority interest in the corporation.

(d) The deceased shareholder held a controlling interest in the corporation.

(e) The cost the corporation would incur in going public.

35. During the same year in which a donor gives stock in a closely-held corporation to family members, donations of some of the stock are made to a qualified charitable organization. In terms of tax planning, what might be accomplished by such a procedure?

36. Under what circumstances will a price specified in a buy and sell agreement be effective in valuing the interest in a closely-held business for death tax purposes?

## Problems

1. On the date of D's death, D owned 500 shares of X Corporation common stock. Three days previously, the stock was traded in an over-the-counter market for $20 per share. Two days after D's death, the stock was traded in the same market at $17 per share. Based on this information alone and presuming the alternate valuation date is not elected, what value for the stock should be included in D's gross estate?

2. Under an annuity arrangement set up by a parent's will, A is entitled to receive $10,000 payable annually for life. When A is 55 years of age, she assigns the

annuity contract to her son as a gift. Using the appropriate valuation table from the Regulations (reproduced in Appendix A), determine the amount of the gift A has made to the son if the assignment to the son occurred in 1981. In 1986.

3. D transfers $200,000 in trust, life estate to W, remainder to S on W's death. At the time of the gift, W is a female, age 40. Determine the value of the gift to W under each of the following assumptions:

   (a) The transfer in trust occurred in 1982.

   (b) The transfer in trust occurred in 1986.

4. After 1983, D transfers by gift $100,000 worth of securities. These securities are placed in trust, income payable to M for 11 years, reversion to D or her estate. Value the gift made to M when the trust was created.

5. Assume the same facts as in Problem 4, except that the transfer to the trust took place in early 1983. Value the gift to M when the trust was created.

6. D (a male, age 70) creates a trust with securities worth $200,000. Under the terms of the trust instrument, the income from the trust is to be paid to D for his life, with corpus passing to S (D's son) upon D's death. D dies in 1990 when the value of the trust is $500,000 and S is age 40.

   (a) Value the gift to S if the trust was created in 1982.

   (b) Value the gift to S if the trust was created in 1986.

   (c) Upon D's death, how much, if any, of the trust will be included in D's gross estate (refer to Chapter 11)?

7. On the date of D's death, D owned a patent (fair market value of $200,000) with a remaining life of 12 years. Six months later, the patent possessed a fair market value of $180,000.

   (a) If the alternate valuation date is elected, at what value will the patent be included in D's gross estate?

   (b) Under (a), what would be the result if the patent is sold by the executor for $190,000 four months after D's death?

8. At the time of her death, D held rental property worth $200,000 on which rents of $6,000 had been accrued. Six months later, the property is worth $205,000. By this time, the rents of $6,000 have been paid and an additional $4,000 accrued. How much should be included in D's gross estate if the alternate valuation date is not elected? If the alternate valuation date is elected?

9. Comment on the following statements relating to § 2032A:

   (a) Section 2032A will apply even if the qualifying property is willed by the decedent to a nonfamily member.

   (b) If § 2032A applies, current use value (as opposed to most suitable use value) can be used for the qualifying property, but not to exceed a limit on the adjustment of $1,000,000.

   (c) The special use valuation method cannot be used in setting the valuation of a lifetime gift.

   (d) Full recapture of the benefit of the special use valuation method would not occur if the qualifying heir were to sell the property 10 years after the decedent's death.

   (e) Recapture occurs only if the qualifying property is sold.

   (f) In any recapture situation, an income tax basis adjustment is required.

   (g) Lifetime gifts of nonqualifying assets may help in satisfying the 50% and 35% requirements of § 2032A.

(h) In satisfying the 50% and 35% requirements, the qualifying property is to be valued at most suitable use value.

10. M gives stock to S at a time when the stock has a fair market value of $60,000. The stock was acquired by M 10 years prior to the gift at a cost of $20,000. Determine S's income tax basis for gain or loss under each of the following assumptions:

(a) The gift occurred before 1921.

(b) The gift occurred after 1920 but before 1977. M paid a gift tax of $4,500 on the transfer.

(c) The gift occurred after 1976. M paid a gift tax of $4,500 on the transfer.

11. In the current year, F gives stock to D at a time when it has a fair market value of $80,000. The stock was acquired by F four years ago at a cost of $100,000. As a result of the transfer, F incurred and paid a gift tax of $4,000. Determine D's gain or loss if the stock is sold later for:

(a) $75,000.

(b) $90,000.

(c) $105,000.

12. In 1980, M gives publicly traded stock to S at a time when the stock has a fair market value of $300,000. The stock was acquired by M 10 years ago at a cost of $100,000. As a result of the transfer, M incurred and paid a gift tax of $18,000. Determine S's gain or loss if S sells the stock in 1986 for:

(a) $200,000.

(b) $110,000.

(c) $330,000.

13. At the time of his death in 1986, H was married to W and both were residents of the State of Washington. Among their assets, H and W held community property with the following cost and value attributes:

|  | Adjusted Basis to H and W | Fair Market Value | |
| --- | --- | --- | --- |
|  |  | Date of Death | Alternate Valuation Date |
| Depreciable real estate | $ 50,000 | $ 200,000 | $ 220,000 |
| Stock in X Corporation | 300,000 | 600,000 | 550,000 |
| Stock in Y Corporation | 250,000 | 240,000 | 230,000 |

Under H's will, all property H owns passes to W.

(a) How much is included in H's gross estate if the date of death value is used?

(b) If the alternate valuation date is elected?

(c) What will be W's income tax basis in the property under (a)? Under (b)?

(d) Which choice would be preferable?

14. W dies in 1986 and is survived by H, her husband. Except for stock in Z Corporation which is bequeathed to a qualified charitable organization, W's will provides that all of her property shall pass to H. Relevant information concerning her

estate, including cost and value attributes, follows:

| | Adjusted Basis to W | Fair Market Value | |
|---|---|---|---|
| | | Date of Death | Alternate Valuation Date |
| Adjusted gross estate (including the stock in Z Corporation) | $ 300,000 | $ 900,000 | $ 850,000 |
| Stock in Z Corporation | 60,000 | 70,000 | 100,000 |

(a) Is the election of the alternate valuation date available?

(b) What will be H's income tax basis in the property he receives from W?

15. In March 1985, T gives to D the following securities:

| Item | Basis to T | Fair Market Value |
|---|---|---|
| Stock in R Corporation | $ 70,000 | $ 20,000 |
| Stock in S Corporation | 40,000 | 80,000 |

D dies in February 1986, at which time the securities have a fair market value as follows: $30,000 (R Corporation) and $90,000 (S Corporation). Assume that no gift tax resulted from the transfer, D's estate does not elect the alternate valuation date, and D's will passes the securities to T. What income tax basis will T have in the stock of R Corporation? Of S Corporation?

16. In April 1985, T gives D a house (basis of $50,000 and a fair market value of $150,000) to be used as her personal residence. As a result of the transfer, T incurs and pays a gift tax of $9,000. Prior to her death in March 1986, D installs a swimming pool in the backyard at a cost of $10,000. The residence is worth $170,000 on the date of D's death, and D's estate does not elect the alternate valuation date. Determine the income tax basis of the property to the heir based on the following assumptions:

(a) Under D's will, the residence passes to T.

(b) Under D's will, the residence passes to S (D's son).

17. Prior to his death, D sold a parcel of unimproved real estate held as an investment (basis of $30,000) for $90,000, receiving $10,000 in cash and a 12% interest-bearing note payable in five annual installments of $16,000 each. In reporting the gain from the sale, D did not elect out from the installment method (i. e., § 453). Before his death in the current year, D collected one installment of $16,000 (plus interest) as it came due. The remaining installments (plus interest) are collected by either D's estate or his heirs. The note possesses a fair market value of $60,000 on the date of D's death, and the alternate valuation date is not elected.

(a) Discuss D's income tax consequences in the year of sale.

(b) Discuss D's income tax consequences for the year in which D collected the first $16,000 installment.

(c) What are the death tax consequences upon D's death?

(d) What are the income tax consequences to the estate and heirs upon the collection of the remaining installments?

18. Indicate whether the following statements related to the extension of time when the estate consists largely of an interest in a closely-held business (§ 6166) are true or false:

    (a) No interest need be paid for the first five years.

    (b) The value of the farm or other closely-held business must be more than 35% of the gross estate.

    (c) Four percent is the rate charged on the delayed payments up to the first $1,000,000 of estate value.

    (d) If the interest consists of stock in a corporation, the corporation cannot have more than 15 shareholders.

    (e) The estate of a partner cannot qualify unless at least 20% of the capital interest in the partnership is included in the gross estate.

    (f) Annual installment payments of the deferred estate tax liability are to be made over a period of 15 years.

    (g) Acceleration of deferred payments will occur if the interest is disposed of prematurely.

    (h) In satisfying the more than 35% test, interests in more than one business cannot be aggregated.

19. On the date of D's death, D owned an insurance policy on the life of S that named G as the designated beneficiary. The policy has a value of $15,000 on the date of D's death, but carries a maturity value of $100,000. Five months after D's death, S dies and the insurance company pays the policy proceeds of $100,000 to G. How much is included in D's gross estate if the alternate valuation date is not elected? If D's estate elects the alternate valuation date?

20. Last year, D sold real estate (basis of $80,000) to P (an unrelated party) for $200,000, receiving $40,000 in cash and P's notes for the balance. The notes carry a 10% rate of interest and mature annually at $16,000 each year over a period of 10 years. D did not elect out of the installment method as to reporting the gain on this sale. Before any of the notes mature and when the notes have a total fair market value of $150,000, D gives them to S. Disregarding the interest element, what are D's income tax consequences as a result of the gift?

21. Assume the same facts as in Problem 20, except that P is D's son. Disregarding the interest element, what are D's income tax consequences as a result of the gift?

## Research Problems

*Research Problem 1.* In 1973, D transferred by gift to his grandchildren 3,000 shares of X Corporation (a family enterprise). The gift was reported on a timely filed Form 709 which listed the value of each share as being $20. Because of the election to split the gifts (§ 2513), the application of the annual exclusion [§ 2503(b)], and the specific exemption (former § 2521), no gift tax resulted from the transfer.

In 1983, D (now a widower) transfers an additional 6,000 shares of X Corporation to his grandchildren. On a timely filed Form 709, a value per share of $40 is used to determine the gift tax due. On audit of the return in 1986, the IRS assesses additional gift tax liability based on the following assumptions:

—The value of the stock in 1973 was $30 per share.

—The value of the stock in 1983 was $50 per share.

Presuming the IRS is correct in its determination of the true values of the stock and assuming the absence of fraud on the part of D or his wife, evaluate the following observations:

(a) Since the statute of limitations has expired on the 1973 gifts, no additional gift tax liability can be assessed on this transfer.

(b) The value of the X Corporation stock in 1973 should have no relevance to the determination of the gift tax liability on the 1983 transfer.

Suppose D and his wife chose not to use the full amount of their specific exemption on the first transfer, and as a result, the 1973 gift resulted in a tax of $100.

(c) Would this change in facts alter the validity of observation (b)?

(d) Could the nonuse of the unified tax credit (applicable to post-1976 taxable gifts) accomplish the same result?

*Research Problem 2.* For many years, the shares of X Corporation were held as follows:

| Owner | Number of Shares |
|-------|------------------|
| Mrs. T | 60 |
| Q | 20 |
| R | 20 |

Neither Q nor R is related to each other or to Mrs. T.

In late 1985, Mrs. T is contacted by a group of investors who want to acquire control of X Corporation. While preliminary negotiations are in progress for the sale of the stock, Mrs. T creates four irrevocable trusts, to each of which she transfers 15 shares of the stock. Mrs. T's son is designated as the trustee of all trusts, with a different grandchild named as the beneficiary of each trust.

In early 1986, the trusts created by Mrs. T sell the shares of X Corporation to the group of investors for $400 each. Shortly thereafter, the investors acquire the remaining shares held by Q and R for $250 each.

On a timely filed gift tax return, Mrs. T reports the transfers to the four trusts. The gift tax paid by Mrs. T is based on a value of $250 per share.

(a) Justify Mrs. T's position on the valuation of the stock for gift tax purposes.

(b) How could the IRS dispute this determination?

(c) Could Mrs. T suffer any income tax consequences from these transactions? Explain.

*Partial list of research aids:*

§ 644.

*Driver v. U. S.,*76–2 USTC ¶ 13,155, 38 AFTR2d 76–6315 (D.Ct.Wis., 1976).

*Blanchard v. U. S.,* 68–1 USTC ¶ 12,567, 23 AFTR2d 69–1803, 291 F.Supp. 348 (D.Ct.Iowa, 1968).

*Research Problem 3.* In 1977, D established a trust with 3,000 shares of X Corporation. Under the terms of the trust instrument, income is payable to S (D's son, age 20) for life, remainder to D or his estate. Although a local bank is designated as the independent trustee, such trustee is precluded from exchanging or selling the X Corporation stock. For each of the 10 years preceding the transfer in trust, X Corporation had paid an average dividend on its stock of 3%. Neither D nor the trustee has any control, directly or indirectly, over the management and operation of X Corporation. The stock of X Corporation is traded on the American Stock Exchange and was quoted at $50 per share when the transfer to the trust occurred and $80 per share on the date of D's death.

At the time of his death in 1986, D was receiving payments of $800 per month from a noncommercial annuity contract issued by his former employer. Under the terms of the contract, W (D's wife) is entitled to receive reduced payments of $400 per month for the rest of her life. At the point of D's death, W was age 45 and recuperating from recent surgery.

(a) What are the gift tax implications of D's transfer in trust in 1977?

(b) What are the estate tax implications as to the reversionary interest in the trust on D's death in 1986?

(c) What are the estate tax implications as to the annuity on D's death in 1986?

*Partial list of research aids:*

§§ 2033, 2039, and 6163.

Reg. §§ 20.2031–7(f) and 25.2512–9(f).

*Thomas E. Jones, Jr.,* 36 TCM 380, T.C.Memo. 1977–87.

Rev.Rul. 77–195, 1977–1 C.B. 295.

Rev.Rul. 66–307, 1966–2 C.B. 429.

*Research Problem 4.* On June 1, 19X5, D entered into a contract to sell real estate for $100,000 (adjusted basis of $20,000). The sale was conditioned on a rezoning of the property for commercial use. A $5,000 deposit placed in escrow by the purchaser was refundable in the event the rezoning was not accomplished. After considerable controversy, the application is approved on November 10, 19X5, and two days later, the sum of $95,000 is paid to D's estate in full satisfaction of the purchase price. D died unexpectedly on November 1, 19X5.

(a) Discuss the estate and income tax consequences of this set of facts if it is assumed that the sale of the real estate occurred after D's death.

(b) Before D's death.

(c) When do you think the sale occurred? Why?

*Partial list of research aids:*

Code §§ 691 and 1014.

*George W. Keck,* 49 T.C. 313 (1968) *rev'd.* in 69–2 USTC ¶ 9626, 24 AFTR2d 69–5554, 415 F.2d 531 (CA–6, 1969).

*Trust Company of Georgia v. Ross,* 68–1 USTC ¶ 9133, 21 AFTR2d 311, 392 F.2d 694 (CA–5, 1967).

*Research Problem 5.* At the time of his death, D left an estate that consisted of, among other assets, a farm and a hardware business. The farm had a special use valuation of $400,000 but a present use value of $60,000. By itself, the farm comprised 42% of the adjusted value of the gross estate. Combined with the hardware business, however, the relative value of both moved to 53%. The farm included real estate, but the hardware business did not, since it had been operated on leased premises. Thus, the value of the hardware business was entirely made up of personalty (e. g., inventory). Predicated on the assumption that the conditions of § 2032A were satisfied, the executor of D's estate valued the farm at $60,000 for estate tax purposes. Upon audit by the IRS, § 2032A was deemed inapplicable and the value of the farm was raised to $400,000. Which party is right, and why?

*Research Problem 6.* At the time of his death, D was a partner in a personal injury law firm. One of the cases D had pending involved a considerable amount of money, but there was doubt as to whether the client would be successful and, if so, as to how much the recovery would be. Nevertheless, the case was settled four months after D's death, and D's share of the contingent fee ultimately was paid to the estate.

Under such circumstances, would the election of § 2032 by the executor of D's estate be ill-advised? Why or why not?

*Research Problem 7.* D makes a gift of stock (basis of $187,866) to her son S. As a result of the transfer, a Federal gift tax of $954,383.77 is incurred. Pursuant to an understanding between the parties, the gift tax is paid by S. (Note: Such an arrangement is termed a "net gift.") Are there any income tax ramifications to D?

*Research Problem 8.* The stock of X Corporation is held equally by five individuals, including R and S. R makes a gift of his stock to P who, after seven months, sells it to another. S dies and passes his stock to Q. Three months after S's death, Q sells the stock to the same peron who purchased P's stock. Presuming X Corporation was collapsible (within the meaning of § 341) during all of these transactions, discuss the income tax consequences upon the following:

(a) R's gift to P.

(b) P's sale of the stock.

(c) S's death.

(d) Q's sale of the stock.

# Income Taxation of Trusts and Estates  13

## CHAPTER OBJECTIVES

—Present choices as to methods and periods of accounting.
—Set forth applicable tax rates, exemptions, and reporting requirements.
—Define recognition of income.
—Describe allowable deductions and credits.
—Explain taxation of beneficiaries.
—Present the special rules that apply to trusts that sell appreciated property received as a gift, that
  accumulate income, and over which the creator (grantor) of the trust retains certain rights.

# AN OVERVIEW OF SUBCHAPTER J

Chapters 11 and 12 discussed the transfer tax provisions of the Internal Revenue Code. Several of the valuable income and estate tax planning techniques considered therein involved the use of the trust entity. Moreover, the very nature of estate taxation necessarily entails the estate of the decedent. It is now appropriate to cover the income tax treatment of trusts and estates.

The income taxation of trusts and estates is governed by Subchapter J of the Internal Revenue Code, § § 641 through 692. Similarities will be apparent between Subchapter J and the income taxation of individuals (e. g., the definitions of gross income and deductible expenditures), partnerships (e. g., the conduit principle), and S corporations (e. g., the conduit principle and the trust as a separate taxable entity). Several important new concepts will be introduced, however, including the determination of distributable net income and the tier system of distributions to beneficiaries.

For income tax purposes, trusts and estates are divided into three categories:

1. Estates and ordinary trusts.
2. Grantor trusts.
3. Special trusts.

The primary concern of this chapter is the income taxation of estates and ordinary trusts. Grantor trusts are discussed to a limited extent in a later section of the chapter. Special trusts, such as alimony trusts[1] and pension and profit sharing trusts,[2] are beyond the scope of this text.

## WHAT IS A TRUST?

The Code does not contain a definition of a trust. However, the Regulations explain that the term "trust," as used in the Code, refers to an arrangement created by a will or by an *inter vivos* (lifetime) declaration, through which trustees take title to property for the purpose of protecting or conserving it for the beneficiaries.[3]

Typically, then, the creation of a trust involves at least three parties: the *grantor* (sometimes referred to as the settlor or donor), whose selected

---

1. § 682.
2. § 401.
3. Reg. § 301.7701–4(a).

assets are transferred to the trust entity; the *trustee,* who may be either an individual or a corporation and who is charged with the fiduciary duties associated with the trust agreement; and the *beneficiary,* whose rights to receive property from the trust are defined by applicable state law and by the trust document. In some situations, however, fewer than three persons may be involved, as specified by the trust agreement. For instance, an elderly individual who no longer can manage his or her own property (e. g., because of ill health) could create a trust under which he or she was both the grantor and the beneficiary so that a corporate trustee could be charged with management of the grantor's assets. In another situation, the grantor might designate himself or herself as the trustee of the trust assets. For example, a parent who wants to transfer selected assets to a minor child might use a trust entity to assure that the minor does not waste the property. By identifying himself or herself as the trustee, the parent would retain virtual control over the property that is transferred.

Under the general rules of Subchapter J, however, the trusts just described are not recognized for income tax purposes. When only one party is involved (i. e., when the same individual is grantor, trustee, and sole beneficiary of the trust), Subchapter J rules do not apply and the entity is ignored for income tax purposes. As discussed later in the chapter, if the grantor remains a direct or indirect beneficiary of the trust, or if he or she retains excessive administrative powers over the trust assets, the trust is classified as a *grantor trust* and some or all of the trust income is taxable to the grantor.[4]

## OTHER DEFINITIONS

When the grantor transfers title of selected assets to a trust, those assets become the *corpus* (body), or principal, of the trust. The trust corpus, in most situations, earns *income,* which may be distributed to the beneficiaries, or accumulated for the future, by the trustee as the trust instrument directs.

In the typical trust, the grantor creates two types of beneficiaries: one entitled to receive the accounting income of the trust and one who will receive the trust corpus that remains at the termination of the trust entity. Those beneficiaries in the former category hold an *income interest* in the trust, and those in the latter category hold a *remainder interest* in the trust's assets. If the grantor retains the remainder interest, such interest is known as a *reversionary interest* (i. e., the corpus reverts to the grantor when the trust entity terminates).

As identified by the trust document, the term of the trust may be for a specific number of years (i. e., for a *term certain*) or it may be until the occurrence of a specified event. For instance, a trust could be created that would exist (a) for the life of the income beneficiary—in this case, the income beneficiary is known as a *life tenant* in the trust corpus; (b) for the life of some other individual; (c) until the income or remainder beneficiary reaches the age of majority; or (d) until the beneficiary, or another individual, marries, receives a promotion, or reaches some specified age.

---

**4.** § § 673–677.

The trustee may be required to distribute the accounting income of the entity according to a distribution schedule specified in the agreement. However, the trustee can be given a greater degree of discretion with respect to the timing and nature of such distributions. If the trustee can determine, within guidelines that may be included in the trust document, either the timing of the income or corpus distributions or the specific beneficiaries who will receive them (from among those identified in the agreement), the trust is referred to as a *sprinkling trust* (i. e., the trustee can "sprinkle" the distributions among the various beneficiaries). As discussed in Chapters 11 and 12, family-wide income taxes can be reduced when such income is received by those who are subject to lower marginal income tax rates. Thus, if the trustee is given a sprinkling power, the income tax liability of the family unit can be manipulated via the trust agreement.

For purposes of certain provisions of Subchapter J, a trust must be classified as either a *simple trust* or a *complex trust*. A simple trust is one that (a) is required to distribute its entire trust accounting income to designated beneficiaries every year, (b) has no beneficiaries that are qualifying charitable organizations, and (c) makes no distributions of trust corpus during the year. A complex trust is any trust that is not a simple trust.[5] These criteria are applied to the trust every year. Thus, every trust will be classified as a complex trust in the year in which it terminates (i. e., because it will be distributing all of its corpus during that year).

## WHAT IS AN ESTATE?

An estate is created upon the death of every individual. This entity is charged to collect and conserve all of the individual's assets, satisfy all of his or her liabilities, and distribute the remaining assets to the heirs identified by state law or the will.

In the typical case, the creation of an estate involves at least three parties: the *decedent,* all of whose probate assets are transferred to the estate for disposition; the *executor* or *executrix* (the latter is a female), who is appointed under the decedent's valid will (or the *administrator* or *administratrix,* if no valid will exists); and the *beneficiaries* of the estate, who are to receive the corpus of the estate by bequest, devise, or inheritance. The executor (or executrix) or administrator (or administratrix) holds the fiduciary responsibility to operate the estate as directed by the will, applicable state law, and the probate court.

It is important to recognize that the assets that constitute the probate estate are not identical to those that constitute the gross estate for transfer tax purposes (refer to Chapter 11). Indeed, many of the gross estate assets do not enter the domain of the *probate estate* and thus are not subject to disposition by the executor or administrator. For instance, property held by the decedent as a joint tenant passes to the survivor(s) by operation of the applicable state's property law rather than through the probate estate. Proceeds of life insurance policies on the life of the decedent, over which the decedent held the incidents of ownership, are not under the control of

---

5. Reg. § 1.651(a)–1.

the executor or administrator. Rather, the designated beneficiaries of the policy receive the proceeds outright under the insurance contract.

An estate is a separate taxable entity. Thus, taxpayers may find it profitable, under certain circumstances, to prolong the estate's existence. This situation is likely to arise when the heirs are already in a high income tax bracket. Therefore, the heirs would prefer to have the income generated by the estate assets taxed at the estate's lower marginal income tax rates. However, the tax authorities have recognized this possibility of shifting income to lower-bracket taxpayers. The Regulations caution that if the administration of an estate is unduly prolonged, the estate will be considered terminated for Federal income tax purposes after the expiration of a reasonable period for the performance by the executor of all duties of administration.[6]

## NATURE OF TRUST AND ESTATE TAXATION

Estates and trusts are separate taxable entities, and their income taxation is governed by Subchapter J of the Internal Revenue Code. In general, the taxable income of a trust or an estate is taxed to the entity or to its beneficiaries to the extent that each has received the accounting income of the entity. Thus, Subchapter J creates a modified conduit principle relative to the income taxation of trusts, estates, and their beneficiaries: Whoever receives the accounting income of the entity, or some portion of it, is liable for the income tax thereon.

> **Example 1.** Beneficiary A receives 80% of the 19X4 accounting income of Trust Z. The trustee accumulated the other 20% of the income, at her discretion under the trust agreement, and added it to the trust corpus. A is liable for income tax on the 19X4 distribution only, while Trust Z is liable for the income tax on the accumulated portion of the income.

The modified conduit principle of Subchapter J is subject to several exceptions. For instance, some trusts may be treated as associations and therefore will be subject to the corporate income tax.[7] In addition, part or all of the income of certain trusts must be taxed to the grantor if he or she retains too much control over the trust property or income.[8]

### FILING REQUIREMENTS

The fiduciary is required to file a Form 1041 (U.S. Fiduciary Income Tax Return) in the following situations:

> —In the case of an estate, if its gross income for the year is $600 or more.

---

**6.** Reg. § 1.641(b)–3(a).
**7.** Refer to Chapter 2 for a discussion of associations taxed as corporations; see also *Morrissey v. Comm.,* 36–1 USTC ¶ 9020, 16 AFTR 1274, 56 S.Ct. 289 (USSC, 1936).
**8.** § § 673–678.

—In the case of a trust, if there is any taxable income or, when there is no taxable income, if there is gross income of $600 or more.

—In the case of either an estate or a trust, if there is a beneficiary who is a nonresident alien.[9]

Although the fiduciary is responsible for filing Form 1041 and paying any income tax due, he or she has no personal liability for the tax. In general, the IRS must look to the assets of the estate or the trust for the tax due. The fiduciary may become personally liable for such tax if excessive distributions of assets have been made (e. g., payment of debts, satisfaction of bequests) and therefore render the entity unable to pay the tax due.[10] An executor or administrator may obtain from the IRS a discharge from personal liability.[11] Taking advantage of this procedure would be highly advisable before making any substantial distributions of estate assets.

The fiduciary return is due no later than the fifteenth day of the fourth month following the close of the entity's taxable year. The return should be filed with the Internal Revenue Service Center for the region in which the fiduciary resides or has his or her principal place of business. If it chooses to do so, an estate may pay its tax in quarterly payments, one-fourth each on or before the fifteenth day of the fourth, seventh, tenth, and thirteenth months of (or after) the tax year.[12] A trust does not have this privilege, however, and the entire tax must be paid when its return is filed.

## ACCOUNTING PERIODS AND METHODS

An estate or trust may use any of the tax accounting methods available to individuals. The method of accounting used by the grantor of a trust or the decedent of an estate does not carry over to the entity. Once a method has been adopted, any change is subject to the same limitations applicable to other taxpayers.[13]

An estate or trust has the same election available to any new taxpayer regarding the choice of a tax year. Thus, the estate of a calendar year decedent dying on March 3 could select any fiscal year or report on a calendar year basis.[14] If the latter is selected, the estate's first taxable year would include the period from March 3 to December 31. More importantly, if the first or last tax years are short years (i. e., less than one calendar year), income for such years need not be annualized.[15] Finally, changes in accounting periods are subject to the same limitations applicable to other taxpayers.[16]

---

9. § 6012(a).
10. Reg. § 1.641(b)–2(a).
11. § 6905 and the Regulations thereunder.
12. § 6152(a)(2).
13. See § 446 and the Regulations thereunder.
14. § 441.
15. Reg. § 1.443–1(a)(2).
16. See § 442 and the Regulations thereunder.

## TAX RATE AND PERSONAL EXEMPTION

The tax rates that apply to an estate or trust are the same as those for married persons filing separately. However, the zero bracket amount available to married persons filing separately is not available to either an estate or a trust.[17] Estates and trusts also are precluded from using the Tax Table in determining the amount of income tax liability.[18]

In addition to the regular income tax, an estate or trust may be subject to the alternative minimum tax imposed on tax preference items.[19] Trusts also may be subject to a special tax imposed by § 644 on gains from the sale or exchange of certain appreciated property. The rules with respect to this special tax are discussed in more detail in later sections of the chapter.

Both trusts and estates are allowed a personal exemption in computing the fiduciary tax liability. All estates are allowed a personal exemption of $600. The exemption available to a trust, however, depends upon the type of trust involved. A trust that is required to distribute all of its income currently is allowed an exemption of $300. All other trusts are allowed an exemption of only $100 per year.[20]

Note that the classification of trusts as to the appropriate personal exemption is similar, but not identical, to the distinction between simple and complex trusts. The classification as a simple trust is more stringent.

> **Example 2.** Trust X is required to distribute all of its current accounting income to Ms. A. Trust Y is required to distribute all of its current accounting income, one-half to Mr. B and one-half to State University, a qualifying charitable organization. The trustee of Trust Z can, at her discretion, distribute the current accounting income or corpus of the trust to Dr. C. None of the trusts makes any corpus distributions during 19X4. All of the accounting income of Trust Z is distributed to Dr. C in 19X4.
>
> Trust X is a simple trust; it will receive a $300 personal exemption for 19X4. Trust Y is a complex trust; it will receive a $300 personal exemption for 19X4. Trust Z is a complex trust; it will receive a $100 personal exemption for 19X4.

# TAXABLE INCOME OF TRUSTS AND ESTATES

Generally, the taxable income of an estate or trust is computed in a manner similar to that used for an individual. Subchapter J does, however, present several important exceptions and special provisions that distinguish the computation of taxable income for such entities. Thus, a systematic approach to this taxable income calculation is necessary. Figure I illustrates the computation method followed in this chapter.

---

**17.** Compare the Tax Rate Schedules in § § 1(d) and 1(e). (They are reproduced in Appendix A.)

**18.** § 3(b)(3).

**19.** § 55.

**20.** § 642(b).

**Figure I**

ACCOUNTING INCOME, DISTRIBUTABLE NET INCOME,
AND THE TAXABLE INCOME OF THE ENTITY
AND ITS BENEFICIARIES

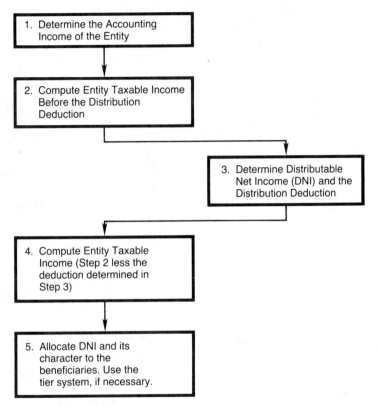

## ENTITY ACCOUNTING INCOME

The first step in determining the taxable income of a trust or estate is to compute the entity's accounting income for the period. Although this prerequisite is not apparent from a cursory reading of Subchapter J, a closer look at the Code reveals a number of references to the income of the entity.[21] Wherever the term "income" is used in Subchapter J without some modifier (e. g., *gross* income or *taxable* income), the statute is referring to the accounting income of the trust or estate for the appropriate tax year.

Thus, a definition of entity accounting income is critical to an understanding of the Subchapter J computation of fiduciary taxable income. Under state law, entity accounting income is the amount that the income beneficiary of the simple trust or estate is eligible to receive from the entity. Most importantly, the calculation of such accounting income is virtually under the control of the grantor or decedent (through a properly drafted trust agreement or will). If the document has been drafted at arm's length, a court will enforce a fiduciary's good-faith efforts to carry out the specified computation of accounting income.

---

21.   For example, see § § 651(a)(1), 652(a), and 661(a)(1).

By allocating specific items of income and expenditure either to the income beneficiaries or to corpus, the desires of the grantor or decedent are put into effect. For instance, the typical document allocates to income any receipts of interest, dividends, rents, and royalties; the net profits from a business owned by the trust or estate; and most stock dividends, especially those less than or equal to six percent of the underlying stock. Moreover, the document usually allocates to income a portion of the fiduciary's fees and investment commissions and the operating expenses of the entity's business interests. Conversely, the agreement or will typically allocates to corpus a portion of the fiduciary's fees and investment commissions, depreciation allowances relative to the business assets of the entity, casualty losses associated with the entity property, and the capital gains and losses relative to the trust's investment assets. Of course, the treatment of such items of income and expenditure for taxable income purposes does not determine the treatment of such items in computing entity accounting income.

Where the controlling document is silent as to the proper allocation to income or corpus of one or more of the entity's items of income or expenditure, state law prevails. Thus, such allocations are an important determinant of the benefits received from the entity by its beneficiaries and the timing of such benefits.

> **Example 3.** The A Trust is a simple trust. Mrs. B is its sole beneficiary. In 19X4, the trust earns $20,000 in taxable interest and $15,000 in tax-exempt interest. In addition, the trust recognizes an $8,000 long-term capital gain. The trustee assesses a fee of $11,000 for the year. If the trust agreement allocates fees and capital gains to corpus, trust accounting income is $35,000 for 19X4, and Mrs. B receives that amount. Thus, the income beneficiary receives no immediate benefit from the trust's capital gain, and she bears none of the financial burden of the fiduciary's fees.
>
> | | |
> |---|---:|
> | Interest income | $ 35,000 |
> | Long-term capital gain | ±   0* |
> | Fiduciary's fees | ±   0* |
> | Trust accounting income | $ 35,000 |
>
> *Allocable to corpus

**Example 4.** Assume the same facts as in Example 3, except that the trust agreement allocates the fiduciary's fees to income. The 19X4 trust accounting income is $24,000, and Mrs. B receives that amount.

> | | |
> |---|---:|
> | Interest income | $ 35,000 |
> | Long-term capital gain | ±   0* |
> | Fiduciary's fees | − 11,000 |
> | Trust accounting income | $ 24,000 |
>
> *Allocable to corpus

**Example 5.** Assume the same facts as in Example 3, except that the trust agreement allocates to income all capital gains and losses and one-half of the trustee's commissions. The 19X4 trust accounting income is $37,500, and Mrs. B receives that amount.

| | |
|---|---|
| Interest income | $ 35,000 |
| Long-term capital gain | + 8,000 |
| Fiduciary's fees | − 5,500* |
| Trust accounting income | $ 37,500 |

*One-half allocable to corpus

## GROSS INCOME

The gross income of an estate or trust is similar to that of an individual.[22] Section 641 provides that gross income includes the following:

1. Income that is to be distributed currently by the fiduciary to the beneficiaries.

2. Income accumulated or held for future distribution under the terms of the will or trust.

3. Income that, at the discretion of the fiduciary, may be either distributed to the beneficiaries or accumulated on their behalf.

4. Income received by estates of deceased persons during the period of administration or settlement of the estate.

Although all of the foregoing items may represent gross income to the estate or trust, bear in mind that an offsetting deduction may be allowed for item 1 and, to the extent paid or credited to the beneficiary, for items 3 and 4.

In determining the gain or loss to be recognized by an estate or trust upon the sale or other taxable disposition of assets, the rules for basis determination are similar to those that apply to other taxpayers. Thus, the basis of property to an estate received from a decedent is determined under § 1014 (refer to Chapter 12 for a more detailed discussion of basis determination). Property received as a gift (the usual case in most trust arrangements) is controlled by § 1015. Property purchased by the trust receives the grantor's basis, increased by any gain recognized by the grantor on the transfer.

*Property Distributions.* In general, no gain or loss is recognized by the entity upon its distribution of property to a beneficiary, pursuant to the provisions of the will or trust document. In this regard, the beneficiary of the distribution assigns to the distributed property a basis equal to that of the estate or trust. Moreover, the distribution absorbs distributable net income (DNI) and qualifies for a distribution deduction (both of which concepts are explained in subsequent sections of this chapter) to the extent of the lesser of the distributed asset's basis to the beneficiary or the asset's fair market value as of the distribution date.[23]

> **Example 6.** The H Trust distributes a painting, basis of $40,000 and fair market value of $90,000, to beneficiary K in 19X5. K's basis in the painting is $40,000. The distribution absorbs $40,000 of H's 19X5 DNI, and H may claim a $40,000 distribution deduction relative to the transaction.

---

**22.** Reg. § 1.641(a)–2.
**23.** § 643(d).

**Example 7.** Assume the same facts as in Example 6, except that H's basis in the painting is $100,000. K's basis in the painting is $100,000. The distribution absorbs $90,000 of H's 19X5 DNI, and H may claim a $90,000 distribution deduction.

With respect to distributions that occur after June 1, 1984, the trustee or executor can elect under § 643(d) to recognize gain or loss with respect to such distributed property. If such an election is made, the beneficiary's basis in the asset is equal to the asset's fair market value as of the distribution date. In addition, the distribution absorbs DNI and qualifies for a distribution deduction to the extent of the asset's fair market value. Note that Code § 267 can restrict a trust's deduction for such losses.

**Example 8.** The G Estate distributes an antique piano, basis to G of $10,000 and fair market value of $15,000, to beneficiary K in 19X5. The executor elects that G recognize the related $5,000 gain on the distribution. Accordingly, K's basis in the piano is $15,000 ($10,000 basis to G + $5,000 gain recognized). Absent such an election, G would recognize no gain, and K's basis in the piano would be $10,000.

**Example 9.** Assume the same facts as in Example 8, except that G's basis in the piano is $18,000. The executor elects that G recognize the related $3,000 loss on the distribution. Accordingly, K's basis in the piano is $15,000 ($18,000 − $3,000). Absent such an election, G would recognize no loss, and K's basis in the piano would be $18,000.

*Dividend Income.* The § 116 exclusion for qualifying dividends is available to an estate or trust to the extent that the dividends are retained by the entity.

**Example 10.** A trust receives $2,000 in taxable dividends from qualifying domestic corporations, $1,400 of which is distributed to its beneficiaries. The trust may claim a dividend exclusion of $30 [($600/$2,000) x $100]. The beneficiaries will be deemed to have received the dividends allocable to them on the *same date* as received by the estate or trust.[24]

However, the exclusion claimed by an estate or trust will not diminish the exclusion to which each beneficiary is entitled. Thus, if a married beneficiary receives dividends from an estate or trust and dividends from other sources amount to $200 or more, he or she is entitled to a full $200 exclusion, without regard to any exclusion claimed by the estate or trust.

*Income in Respect of a Decedent.* The gross income of a trust or estate includes income in respect of a decedent (IRD).[25] In the case of a cash basis decedent, IRD includes accrued salary, interest, rent, and other income items that were not constructively received prior to death. For both cash and accrual basis decedents, IRD includes death benefits from qualified retirement plans and deferred pay contracts, income from a partnership whose tax year does not end with the death of the deceased partner, subse-

---

**24.** § 116(c)(3).
**25.** Reg. § 1.691(a)–1(b). The concept of IRD was introduced in Chapter 11.

quent collection of installment notes receivable (reported under § 453), and subsequent realization of contingent claims.

The tax consequences of income in respect of a decedent can be summarized as follows:

1. The fair market value of the right to IRD on the appropriate valuation date is included in the decedent's gross estate.[26] Thus, it is subject to the Federal estate tax.[27]

2. The decedent's basis in the property carries over to the recipient (i. e., the estate or heirs). There is no step-up or step-down in the basis of IRD items.

3. Gain or loss is recognized to the recipient of the income, measured by the difference between the amount realized and the adjusted basis of the IRD in the hands of the decedent. The character of such gain or loss depends upon the treatment that it would have received had it been realized by the decedent prior to death. Thus, if the decedent would have realized capital gain, the recipient must do likewise.[28]

4. Expenses related to the IRD (such as interest, taxes, and depletion) that properly were not reported on the final income tax return of the decedent may be claimed by the recipient, if the obligation is associated with the IRD. These items are known as *expenses in respect of a decedent.* They are deductible for both Federal estate and income tax purposes.[29]

**Example 11.** K died on July 13, 19X7. On August 2, 19X7, K's estate received a check (before deductions) for $1,200 from K's former employer; this was K's compensation for the last pay period of his life. On November 23, 19X7, K's estate received a $45,000 distribution from the qualified profit sharing plan of K's employer, the full amount to which K was entitled under the plan. Both K and the estate are calendar year cash basis taxpayers.

The last salary payment and the profit sharing plan distribution constitute IRD to K's estate: K had earned such items during his lifetime, and the estate had an enforceable right to receive each of them after K's death. Consequently, K's gross estate includes $46,200 with respect to these two items. However, the income tax basis to the estate for these items is not stepped up (i. e., from zero to $1,200 and $45,000, respectively) upon distribution to the estate.

The estate must report gross income of $46,200 for tax year 19X7 with respect to the IRD items. Technically, the gain that is recognized upon the receipt of the IRD is $46,200 [$1,200 + $45,000 (amounts realized) − $0 (adjusted basis)].

---

**26.** § 2033.
**27.** To mitigate the effect of double taxation (i. e., imposition of both the death tax and income tax), § 691(c) allows the recipient an income tax deduction for the estate tax attributable to the income.
**28.** § 691(a)(3) and Reg. § 1.691(a)–3.
**29.** § 691(b).

Although this result (i.e., that the IRD is included both in K's gross estate and in the gross income of the estate for 19X7) may appear to be harsh, recall that it is similar to that which applies to all of a taxpayer's earned income: The amount is subject to income tax upon its receipt, and, to the extent that it is not consumed by the taxpayer before death, it constitutes an element of the gross estate.

> **Example 12.** Assume the same facts as in Example 11, except that K was an accrual basis taxpayer. IRD now includes only the $45,000 distribution from the qualified retirement plan. K's last paycheck was included in the gross income of his own last return (i. e., for the tax year 1/1/X7 through 7/13/X7). Since the $1,200 salary already was recognized properly under K's usual method of tax accounting, it does not constitute IRD: It is not gross income when it is received by the executor.

> **Example 13.** Assume the same facts as in Example 11. K's last paycheck was reduced by $165 for state income taxes that were withheld by the employer. The $165 tax payment is an expense in respect of a decedent, and it is allowed as a deduction *both* on K's estate tax return and on the estate's 19X7 income tax return.

## ORDINARY DEDUCTIONS

As a general rule, the taxable income of an estate or trust is similar to that of an individual. Thus, deductions are allowed for ordinary and necessary expenses paid or incurred in carrying on a trade or business;[30] for the production or collection of income; for the management, conservation, or maintenance of property; and in connection with the determination, collection, or refund of any tax.[31] Reasonable administration expenses, including fiduciary fees and litigation costs in connection with the duties of administration, also qualify for a deduction under § 212.

Expenses attributable to the production or collection of tax-exempt income are not deductible.[32] The amount of the disallowed deduction is found by using an apportionment formula, based upon the composition of the income elements of trust accounting income for the year of the deduction. This apportionment of the § 212 deduction is made without regard to the trust accounting income allocation of such expenses to income or to corpus. The deductibility of the fees is determined strictly by the Code (i. e., under § § 212 and 265), and the allocation of expenditures to income and to corpus is controlled by the trust agreement or will or by state law.

> **Example 14.** The S Trust operates a business and invests idle cash in marketable securities. Its sales proceeds for 19X4 are $180,000. Expenses for wages, cost of sales, and office administration are $80,000. Interest income recognized in 19X4 is $20,000 from taxable bonds and $50,000 from tax-exempt bonds. The trustee claims a

---

**30.** § 162.
**31.** § 212.
**32.** § 265.

$35,000 fee for his 19X4 activities. According to the trust agreement, $30,000 of this amount is allocated to the income beneficiaries and $5,000 is allocated to corpus.

The sales proceeds are included in the gross income of the trust under § 61. The costs associated with the business are deductible in full under § 162. The taxable income is included in S's gross income under § 61, but the tax-exempt income is excluded under § 103. The fiduciary's fees are deductible by S under § 212, but a portion of the deduction is lost because of the § 265 prohibition against deductions for expenses incurred in the generation of tax-exempt income. Trust accounting income for 19X4 is $140,000 [$180,000 sales + $70,000 interest income ($50,000 of which is tax-exempt) − $80,000 cost of sales − $30,000 allocable fiduciary fees]. Thus, 50/250 of the fees of $35,000 can be traced to tax-exempt income, and $7,000 of the fees is nondeductible.

Note that for purposes of this computation, only the income elements of the current trust accounting income are included in the denominator. Moreover, the allocation of portions of the fees to income and to corpus is irrelevant for this calculation.

| | |
|---|---:|
| Sales income | $ 180,000 |
| Cost of sales | − 80,000 |
| Interest income ($50,000 is exempt) | + 70,000 |
| Fiduciary's fees, as allocated | − 30,000 |
| Trust accounting income | $ 140,000 |

Computation of the disallowed deduction for fiduciary's fees:

$$\$35,000\text{* (total fees paid)} \times \frac{\$50,000\text{** (exempt income elements of trust accounting income)}}{\$250,000\text{** (all income elements of trust accounting income)}}$$

$$= \$7,000 \text{ (amount disallowed)}$$

*All of the fees, and not just those that are allocated to income, can be deductible by the trust under § 212.
**The numerator and denominator of this fraction are not reduced by expense items allocable to income (e. g., the cost of sales).

Under § 642(g), amounts deductible as administration expenses or losses for death tax purposes (under § § 2053 and 2054) cannot be claimed by the estate for income tax purposes unless the estate files a waiver of the death tax deduction. Although these expenses cannot be deducted twice, they may be allocated as the fiduciary sees fit between Forms 706 and 1041; they need not be claimed in their entirety on either return.[33] The prohibition against double deductions does not extend to expenses in respect of a decedent, which expenses are deductible both for estate tax purposes and on the income tax return of the recipient of the IRD.[34]

Trusts and estates are allowed cost recovery deductions. However, such deductions are required to be apportioned among all of the parties involved. An estate is allowed a deduction for depreciation, depletion, and amortization, to be apportioned among the estate and the heirs, legatees,

---

**33.** Reg. § 1.642(g)–2.
**34.** § 691(b).

and devisees on the basis of the estate's accounting income allocable to each.[35]

Similarly, the allowable cost recovery deductions for property held in trust must be apportioned among the trust accounting income beneficiaries and the trust on the basis of the current accounting income allocable to each.[36] If the trust instrument (or state law) requires or permits the trustee to maintain a reserve for depreciation, the deduction first is allocated to the trust to the extent that current accounting income is set aside for such reserve. Any part of the deduction in excess of this amount is apportioned among the income beneficiaries and the trust on the basis of the current trust accounting income allocable to each.[37]

> **Example 15.** L and M are the equal income beneficiaries of the N Trust. Under the terms of the trust agreement, the trustee has complete discretion as to the timing of the distributions from N's current accounting income. The trust agreement allocates all depreciation expense to income. In 19X4, the trustee distributes 40% of the current trust accounting income to L, and she distributes 40% of the income to M; thus, 20% of the 19X4 income is accumulated. The depreciation deduction allowable to N for 19X4 is $100,000. This deduction is allocated among the trust and its beneficiaries on the basis of the distribution of current accounting income: L and M can each claim a $40,000 deduction for 19X4, and the trust can deduct $20,000.

> **Example 16.** Assume the same facts as in Example 15, except that the trust agreement allocates all depreciation expense to corpus. L and M can each still claim a $40,000 depreciation deduction for 19X4, and N retains its $20,000 deduction. The Code assigns the depreciation deduction proportionately to the recipients of current entity accounting income. Allocation of depreciation to income or to corpus is irrelevant in determining which party properly can claim the deduction.

> **Example 17.** G creates a trust, with S and D as income beneficiaries, by the transfer of income-producing depreciable property. Under the terms of the trust instrument, the income from the trust is to be distributed to S and D annually in equal shares. The trustee is authorized to set aside income as a depreciation reserve. For the current year, depreciation expense on the trust property is $7,000, and the trustee allocates $5,000 of current trust accounting income as a depreciation reserve. The trust can claim a $5,000 depreciation deduction, and S and D are entitled to deduct $1,000 each.

The depreciation recapture provisions of the Code are applied in the event that property is sold or otherwise disposed of in a taxable transfer. In determining the recapture potential of such property, however, one must take into account any depreciation claimed by the original transferor when the entity assumes a substituted basis. Thus, on a sale by a trust of property received by transfer from the grantor, the amount of depreciation sub-

---

**35.**   Reg. § 1.167(h)–1(c) and Reg. § 1.611–1(c)(5).

**36.**   § § 167(h) and 611(b)(3).

**37.**   Reg. § 1.167(h)–1(b) and Reg. § 1.611–1(c)(4).

ject to recapture includes the depreciation claimed by the grantor prior to its transfer to the trust. However, depreciation recapture potential disappears at death; thus, when an entity receives depreciable property from a decedent, the recapture potential is reduced to zero.

## DEDUCTIONS FOR LOSSES

An estate or trust is allowed a deduction for casualty or theft losses that are not covered by insurance or other arrangement. Such losses may also be deductible by an estate for Federal death tax purposes under § 2054. As a result, an income tax deduction will not be allowed to an estate unless the death tax deduction is waived.[38]

The net operating loss deduction allowed under § 172 is available for estates and trusts. The carryback of a net operating loss may reduce the distributable net income of the trust or estate for the carryback year and therefore affect the amount taxed to the beneficiaries for that year. This permits the beneficiary to recompute his or her tax liability for such prior year and file a claim for a refund.[39] In computing a net operating loss, the estate or trust cannot take into account deductions for charitable contributions or for distributions to beneficiaries. Moreover, any of a trust's income or deductions that are assignable to the grantor (see the later discussion of grantor trusts) cannot be considered.[40]

Certain losses realized by an estate or trust also may be disallowed. The rules disallowing losses are not unique and apply to all taxpayers. Thus, the wash sales provisions of § 1091 disallow losses on the sale or other disposition of stock or securities when substantially identical stock or securities are acquired by the estate or trust within the prescribed 30-day period. Likewise, § 267 disallows certain losses, expenses, and interest with respect to transactions between related taxpayers. Under § 267(b), the term "related taxpayers" includes, in addition to other relationships, the following:

—A grantor and a fiduciary of any trust.

—A fiduciary of a trust and a fiduciary of another trust, if the same person is a grantor of both trusts.

—A fiduciary of a trust and a beneficiary of such trust.

—A fiduciary of a trust and a beneficiary of another trust, if the same person is a grantor of both trusts.

—A fiduciary of a trust and a corporation, more than 50 percent in value of the outstanding stock of which is owned, directly or indirectly, by or for the trust or by or for a person who is a grantor of the trust.

Except for the possibility of unused losses in the year of termination, the capital losses of an estate or trust cannot be deducted by a bene-

---

**38.** See Reg. § 1.642(g)–1 for the required statement waiving the estate tax deduction. Also, see Reg. § § 1.165–7(c) and 1.165–8(b) requiring that such a statement be filed to allow an income tax deduction for such losses.

**39.** See Rev.Rul. 61–20, 1961–1 C.B. 248.

**40.** Reg. § 1.642(d)–1.

ficiary.[41] They are deductible only on the fiduciary income tax return. The tax treatment of these losses is the same as that for individual taxpayers. Recall, however, that in the case of property acquired from a decedent, any loss on the disposition of such property will be deemed long-term under § 1223(11). For example, if an executor sells a capital asset five months after the decedent's death for less than the asset's basis, the estate recognizes a long-term capital loss.

## CHARITABLE CONTRIBUTIONS

An estate or complex trust is allowed a deduction for contributions to charitable organizations under the following conditions:

1.  The contribution must be made pursuant to the will or trust instrument.

2.  The recipient must be a qualified organization. For this purpose, qualified organizations include the same charities that qualify individual and corporate donors for the deduction, except that estates and trusts are permitted a deduction for contributions to certain foreign charitable organizations.

3.  Generally, the contribution must be paid in the tax year claimed, but a special rule permits a fiduciary to treat amounts paid in the year immediately following as a deduction for the preceding year.[42] This rule treats estates and complex trusts more liberally than it does either individuals or corporations. In the case of individuals, the year of payment always controls. Under § 170(a)(2), accrual basis corporations may, under certain conditions, claim a deduction for a pledge to a qualifying organization if the contribution is paid within two and one-half months of the end of the tax year.

4.  In addition, estates are allowed a deduction for amounts permanently set aside for charitable purposes, regardless of when the charity actually receives the contribution.[43]

Estates and complex trusts are not subject to a limitation on the extent of their deductible charitable contributions for the year (e. g., to a percentage of taxable or adjusted gross income), as are individuals and corporations. Nonetheless, two special rules may reduce the amount of the contribution that qualifies for a deduction by the entity.[44] First, the deduction is limited to amounts included in the gross income of the entity in the year of the contribution. A contribution is deemed to have been made proportionately from each of the income elements of entity accounting income. Thus, in the event that the entity has tax-exempt income, the contribution is deductible only to the extent that the income elements of entity accounting income for the year of the deduction are included in the entity's gross income. This rule is similar to that used to limit the § 212 deduction for

---

41. § 642(h).
42. § 642(c)(1) and Reg. § 1.642(c)–1(b).
43. This provision also is available to a few trusts. See § 642(c)(2).
44. Reg. § 1.642(c)–3(b) and (c).

fiduciary fees and other expenses incurred to generate tax-exempt income. However, if the will or trust agreement requires that the contribution be made from a specific type of income or from the current income from a specified asset, the document will control (i. e., the allocation of the contribution to taxable and tax-exempt income will not be required).

**Example 18.** The K Trust has gross rental income in 19X4 of $80,000, expenses attributable to the rents of $60,000, and tax-exempt interest from state bonds of $20,000. Under the trust agreement, the trustee is directed to pay 30% of the annual trust accounting income to the United Way, a qualifying organization. Under this provision, the trustee pays $12,000 to the charity in 19X5 (i. e., 30% × $40,000). The charitable contribution deduction allowed for 19X4 is $9,600 [($80,000/$100,000) × $12,000].

**Example 19.** Assume the same facts as Example 18, except that the trust instrument also requires that the contribution be paid from the net rental income. The agreement controls, and the allocation formula need not be applied. Thus, the entire $12,000 is allowed as a charitable deduction for 19X4.

A second limitation applies to estates and complex trusts that allocate long-term capital gains to corpus (as is usually the case). When a charitable contribution is made during a year in which the entity recognizes a net long-term capital gain, a portion of the contribution deduction is lost. The reduction is made because the entity receives tax-exempt income from the gain in the form of the 60 percent long-term capital gains deduction. Again, it is presumed that the contribution is made proportionately from each of the entity's receipts for the year. The contribution deduction is reduced, then, by 60 percent of the net long-term capital gain included in the total contribution. Thus, the amount of the capital gain presumed to be included in the total contribution is determined as follows:

$$\frac{\text{Net long-term capital gain}}{\text{Total gross income}} \times \text{Total contribution made}$$

**Example 20.** The V Trust has ordinary income of $90,000 and net long-term capital gains (allocable to corpus) of $60,000 in 19X4. Pursuant to the trust instrument, a charitable contribution of $30,000 is made. The amount of the capital gain included in the charitable contribution is $12,000 [($60,000/$150,000) × $30,000]. Since $7,200 of this amount (60% × $12,000) is disallowed, the charitable deduction is $22,800 ($30,000 − $7,200).

## DEDUCTION FOR DISTRIBUTIONS TO BENEFICIARIES

The modified conduit approach of Subchapter J is embodied in the deduction allowed to trusts and estates for the distributions made to beneficiaries during the year. When the beneficiary receives a distribution from the trust, some portion of that distribution may be subject to income tax on his or her own return. At the same time, the distributing entity is allowed a deduction for some or all of the distribution. Thus, the modified conduit principle of Subchapter J is implemented. A good analogy to this operation can be found in the taxability of corporate profits distributed to employees as taxable wages: The corporation is allowed a deduction for the payment, but the employee has received gross income in the form of compensation.

A critical value that is used in computing the amount of the entity's distribution deduction is *distributable net income* (DNI). DNI serves several functions, as it is defined in Subchapter J:

1. DNI is the maximum amount of the distribution on which the beneficiaries could be taxed.[45]

2. DNI is the maximum amount that can be used by the entity as a distribution deduction for the year.[46]

3. The makeup of DNI carries over to the beneficiaries (i. e., the items of income and expenses will retain their DNI character in the hands of the distributees).[47]

Subchapter J presents a circular definition, however, with respect to DNI. The DNI value is necessary to determine the entity's distribution deduction and therefore its taxable income for the year. However, the Code defines DNI as a modification of the entity's taxable income itself. Thus, using the systematic approach to determine the taxable income of the entity and of its beneficiaries, as enumerated in Figure I (earlier in the chapter), one first must compute *taxable income before the distribution deduction,* modify that amount to determine DNI and the distribution deduction, return to the calculation of *taxable income,* and apply the deduction that has been found.

*Taxable income before the distribution deduction* includes all of the entity's items of gross income, deductions, gains, losses, and exemptions for the year. Therefore, in computing this amount, one must (1) determine the appropriate personal exemption for the year, (2) claim any net long-term capital gains deduction available to the entity (i. e., because the controlling document allocates such gains to corpus), (3) allow the applicable dividend exclusion for such income retained by the estate or complex trust, and (4) account for all of the other gross income and deductions of the entity.

The next step in Figure I is the determination of *distributable net income,* computed by making the following adjustments specified to the entity's *taxable income before the distribution deduction:*[48]

1. Add back the personal exemption.

2. Add back the dividend exclusion.

3. Add back *net* tax-exempt interest. To arrive at this amount, reduce the total tax-exempt interest by any portion paid to or set aside for charitable purposes and by related expenses not deductible under § 265.

---

**45.** §§ 652(a) and 662(a).
**46.** §§ 651(b) and 661(c).
**47.** §§ 652(b) and 662(b).
**48.** These and other (less common) adjustments are detailed in § 643.

4. Add back the long-term capital gains deduction claimed by the entity (i. e., with respect to such gains allocated to corpus).

5. Subtract any net capital gains taxable to the entity (those that are allocable to corpus). In other words, the only net capital gains included in distributable net income are those attributable to income beneficiaries or to charitable contributions.

6. Add back the entity's *net* capital losses.

Since taxable income before the distribution deduction is computed by deducting all of the expenses of the entity (whether they were allocated to income or to corpus), distributable net income will be reduced by expenses that are allocated to corpus. The effect of this procedure is to reduce the taxable income of the income beneficiaries, even though the actual distributions to them exceed DNI, because the distributions are not reduced by expenses allocated to corpus. Aside from this shortcoming of Subchapter J, DNI offers a good approximation of the current-year economic income available for distribution to the entity's income beneficiaries.

Because distributable net income includes the net tax-exempt interest income of the entity, that amount must be removed from DNI in computing the distribution deduction. Thus, the deduction is the lesser of (1) the deductible portion of DNI or (2) the amount actually distributed to the beneficiaries during the year. With respect to estates and complex trusts, the amount actually distributed during the year may include discretionary distributions of income and distributions of corpus permissible under the will or trust instrument.

**Example 21.** The P Trust is required to distribute its current accounting income annually to its sole income beneficiary, Mr. B. Capital gains and losses and all other expenses are allocable to corpus. In 19X4, P incurs the following items:

| | |
|---|---|
| Dividend income | $25,000 |
| Taxable interest income | 15,000 |
| Tax-exempt interest income | 20,000 |
| Net long-term capital gains | 10,000 |
| Fiduciary's fees | 6,000 |

(1) The 19X4 trust accounting income is $60,000; this includes the tax-exempt interest income, but not the fees or the capital gains, pursuant to the trust document. B receives $60,000 from the trust for 19X4.

(2) Taxable income before the distribution deduction is computed as follows:

| | |
|---|---|
| Dividend income | $25,000 |
| Interest income | 15,000 |
| Net long-term capital gains | 10,000 |
| Long-term capital gains deduction | (6,000) |
| Fiduciary's fees (40/60) | (4,000) |
| Personal exemption | (300) |
| Total | $39,700 |

The tax-exempt interest is excluded under § 103. The trust is allowed a long-term capital gains deduction, because such gains are allocable to corpus under the trust instrument. Only a portion of the fees is deductible, because some of the fees are traceable to the tax-exempt income. The trust receives a $300 personal exemption, because it is required to distribute its annual trust accounting income.

(3) DNI and the distribution deduction are computed in the following manner:

| | | |
|---|---:|---:|
| Taxable income before the distribution deduction (from above) | | $39,700 |
| Add back: Personal exemption | | 300 |
| Long-term capital gains deduction of the trust | | 6,000 |
| Subtract: Net long-term capital gains of the trust | | (10,000) |
| Add: Net tax-exempt income— | | |
| Tax-exempt interest | $20,000 | |
| Less disallowed fees | (2,000) | 18,000 |
| Distributable net income | | $54,000 |
| | | |
| Distribution deduction (DNI $54,000 − Net tax-exempt income $18,000) | | $36,000 |

(4) Finally, return to the computation of the 19X4 taxable income of the P Trust. Simply, it is:

| | |
|---|---:|
| Taxable income before the distribution deduction | $39,700 |
| Minus: Distribution deduction | 36,000 |
| Taxable income, P Trust | $ 3,700 |

A simple test should be applied at this point to assure that the proper figure for the trust's taxable income has been determined. On what precisely is P to be taxed? P has distributed to Mr. B all of its gross income except the net long-term capital gains. After applying the 60% deduction, P has taxable income of $4,000. The $300 personal exemption further reduces taxable income to $3,700.

Note that the trust was not allowed to claim any of the $100 exclusion with respect to its dividend income. Since all of the dividend income was distributed to the beneficiary, the trust was precluded from taking any such exclusion. Of course, Mr. B will claim his own exclusion with respect to the distribution of the dividend.

**Example 22.** The Q Trust is required to distribute all of its current accounting income equally to its two beneficiaries, Ms. F and the Universal Church, a qualifying charitable organization. Capital gains and losses and depreciation expenses are allocable to the income beneficiaries. Fiduciary fees are allocable to corpus. In 19X4, Q incurs fiduciary fees of $18,000 and the following:

| (1) | Rental income | $100,000 |
| | Depreciation expense (rental income property) | − 15,000 |
| | Other expenses related to rental income | − 30,000 |
| | Net long-term capital gains | + 20,000 |
| | Accounting income, 19X4, Q Trust | $ 75,000 |

| (2) | Taxable rental income | $100,000 |
| | Depreciation deduction | 0 |
| | Rental expense deductions | (30,000) |
| | Net long-term capital gains | 20,000 |
| | Long-term capital gains deduction | 0 |
| | Fiduciary's fees | (18,000) |
| | Personal exemption | (300) |
| | Charitable contribution deduction | (37,500) |
| | Taxable income before the distribution deduction | $ 34,200 |

Since Q received no tax-exempt income, a deduction is allowed for the full amount of the fiduciary's fees. Q is a complex trust, but since it is required annually to distribute its full accounting income, a $300 exemption is allowed. The trust properly claims neither the net long-term capital gains deduction nor the depreciation deduction for the rental property. Capital gains are allocated to the income beneficiaries under Q's trust instrument, and a capital gains deduction is allowed to the entity only if such gains are allocable to corpus. The depreciation deduction is available only to the recipients of the entity's accounting income for the period. Thus, the deduction will be split equally between Ms. F and the church. Of course, such a deduction probably is of no direct value to the church, since the church is not subject to the income tax. The trust's charitable contribution deduction is based upon the $37,500 that the charity actually received (i. e., one-half of trust accounting income).

| (3) | Taxable income before the distribution deduction | $34,200 |
| | Add back: Personal exemption | 300 |
| | Distributable net income | $34,500 |
| | Distribution deduction | $34,500 |

The only adjustment necessary to compute DNI is the adding back of the trust's personal exemption. There is no tax-exempt income, and the net long-term capital gains are allocated to the income beneficiaries (i. e., not to corpus). Furthermore, Subchapter J requires no adjustment relative to the charitable contribution. Thus, DNI is computed only from the perspective of Ms. F, who also received $37,500 from the trust.

| (4) | Taxable income before the distribution deduction | $34,200 |
| | Minus: Distribution deduction | 34,500 |
| | Taxable income, Q Trust, 19X4 | $ (300) |

Perform the simple test (referred to above) to assure that the proper 19X4 taxable income for the Q trust has been computed. All of the trust's gross income has been distributed to Ms. F and the charity. As is the case with most trusts that distribute all of their annual income, the personal exemption is "wasted" by the Q Trust.

## TAX CREDITS

An estate or trust is allowed an investment tax credit to the extent that the credit is not allocable to the beneficiaries.[49] Similarly, any limitation on the credit for the purchase of qualifying used property is applied at both the entity and the beneficiary levels.[50] Recapture of the investment tax credit will apply to an estate or trust.[51] An estate or trust may claim the foreign tax credit allowed under § 901 to the extent that it is not allocable to the beneficiaries.[52] Although neither estates nor trusts are allowed the tax credits for political campaign contributions,[53] both are permitted to claim the targeted jobs credit[54] for wages paid to certain new employees.[55] Like the investment tax credit, all of these credits must be apportioned between the estate or trust and the beneficiaries on the basis of the income allocable to each.

# TAXATION OF BENEFICIARIES

The beneficiaries of an estate or trust receive taxable income from the entity under the modified conduit principle of Subchapter J. As just discussed, distributable net income determines the maximum amount that could be taxed to the beneficiaries for any tax year. In addition, the constitution of the elements of DNI carries over to the beneficiaries (e. g., net long-term capital gains retain their tax-favored character when they are distributed from the entity to the beneficiary).

The timing of any tax consequences to the beneficiary of a trust or estate presents little problem, except when the parties involved use different tax years. In such a situation involving a simple trust, the amount that a beneficiary is required to include in gross income is based upon the distributable net income of the trust for any taxable year or years of the trust ending with or within his or her taxable year.[56] A similar rule applies to estates and complex trusts.[57]

**Example 23.** A trust uses a fiscal year ending on March 31 for tax purposes. Its sole income beneficiary is a calendar year taxpayer. For

---

**49.** § 48(f).
**50.** § 48(f)(3).
**51.** See Reg. § 1.47–5(b) for examples.
**52.** § 642(a)(1).
**53.** § 642(a)(2).
**54.** § § 44B and 51.
**55.** § 52(e).
**56.** § 652(c).
**57.** § 662(c).

the calendar year 19X6, the beneficiary reports whatever income was assignable to her for the trust's fiscal year April 1, 19X5, to March 31, 19X6.[58]

## DISTRIBUTIONS BY SIMPLE TRUSTS

The amount taxable to the beneficiaries of a simple trust is limited by the trust's distributable net income. However, since DNI includes net tax-exempt income and tax-favored net long-term capital gains, the amount included in the gross income of the beneficiaries could be less than DNI. Moreover, when there is more than one income beneficiary, the elements of DNI must be apportioned ratably according to the amount required to be distributed currently to each.

> **Example 24.** For calendar year 19X6, a simple trust has ordinary income of $40,000, a long-term capital gain of $15,000 (allocable to corpus), and a trustee commission expense of $4,000 (payable from corpus). Its two income beneficiaries, A and B, are entitled to the trust's annual accounting income, based on shares of 75% and 25%, respectively. Although A receives $30,000 as his share (75% × trust accounting income of $40,000), he will be allocated DNI of only $27,000 (75% × $36,000). Likewise, B is entitled to receive $10,000 (25% × $40,000), but she will be allocated DNI of only $9,000 (25% × $36,000). The $15,000 capital gain is taxed to the trust.

## DISTRIBUTIONS BY ESTATES AND COMPLEX TRUSTS

A problem arises with respect to distributions from estates and complex trusts when there is more than one beneficiary who receives a distribution from the entity during the year and the controlling document does not require a distribution of the entire accounting income of the entity.

> **Example 25.** The trustee of the W Trust may distribute the income or corpus of the trust at his discretion in any proportion between the two beneficiaries of the trust, Ms. K and Dr. L. Under the trust instrument, Ms. K must receive $15,000 from the trust every year. In 19X4, the trust's accounting income is $50,000 and its distributable net income is $40,000. The trustee pays $35,000 to Ms. K and $25,000 to Dr. L for 19X4.

How is W's distributable net income to be divided between Ms. K and Dr. L? Several arbitrary methods of allocating the DNI between the beneficiaries can be devised, but Subchapter J resolves the problem by creating a two-tier system to govern the taxation of beneficiaries in such situations.[59] The tier system determines precisely which distributions will be included in the gross income of the beneficiaries in full, which will be included in part, and which will not be included at all.

---

**58.** If the trust were terminated as of December 31, 19X6, the beneficiary must include any trust income assignable to her for the short year. This could result in a bunching of income in 19X6.

**59.** § § 662(a)(1) and (2).

Income that is required to be distributed currently, whether or not it is distributed, is categorized as a *first-tier distribution*. All other amounts properly paid, credited, or required to be distributed are considered to be *second-tier distributions*.[60] First-tier distributions are taxed in full to the beneficiaries to the extent that distributable net income is sufficient to cover these distributions. If the first-tier distributions exceed distributable net income, however, each beneficiary is taxed only on a proportionate part of the DNI. Second-tier distributions are not taxed if the first-tier distributions exceed DNI. However, if both first- and second-tier distributions are made and the first-tier distributions do not exceed distributable net income, the second-tier distributions are taxed to the beneficiaries proportionately to the extent of the "remaining" DNI.

The following formula is used to allocate DNI among the appropriate beneficiaries when only first-tier distributions are made and those amounts exceed DNI:

$$\frac{\text{First-tier distributions to the beneficiary}}{\text{First-tier distributions to all noncharitable beneficiaries}} \times \begin{array}{c}\text{Distributable net}\\\text{income (without}\\\text{deduction for chari-}\\\text{table contributions)}\end{array} = \begin{array}{c}\text{Beneficiary's}\\\text{share of}\\\text{distributable}\\\text{net income}\end{array}$$

Note that in working with this formula, amounts that pass to charitable organizations are not considered.

When both first- and second-tier distributions are made and the first-tier distributions exceed distributable net income, this formula is applied to the first-tier distributions. Note, in this case, that none of the second-tier distributions are taxed, because all of the DNI has been allocated to the first-tier beneficiaries.

If both first and second-tier distributions are made and the first-tier distributions do not exceed the distributable net income, but the total of both first and second-tier distributions does exceed DNI, the second-tier beneficiaries must recognize income as follows:

$$\frac{\text{Second-tier distributions to the beneficiary}}{\text{Second-tier distributions to all beneficiaries}} \times \begin{array}{c}\text{Remaining distributable}\\\text{net income (after first-}\\\text{tier distributions and}\\\text{charitable contributions)}\end{array} = \begin{array}{c}\text{Beneficiary's}\\\text{share of}\\\text{distributable}\\\text{net income}\end{array}$$

Charitable contributions are taken into account at this point.

**Example 26.** The trustee of the G Trust is required to distribute $10,000 per year to both Mrs. H and Mr. U, the two beneficiaries of the entity. In addition, she is empowered to distribute other amounts of trust income or corpus at her sole discretion. In 19X4, the trust has accounting income of $60,000 and distributable net income of $50,000. However, the trustee distributes only the required $10,000 each to H and to U. The balance of the 19X4 income is accumulated, to be added to trust corpus.

---

**60.** Reg. § § 1.662(a)–2 and –3.

In this case, only first-tier distributions have been made, but the total amount of such distributions does not exceed DNI for the year. Although DNI is the maximum amount that must be included by the beneficiaries for the year, no more can be included in gross income by the beneficiaries than is distributed by the entity. Thus, H and U each may be subject to tax on $10,000 as their proportionate shares of G's DNI.

**Example 27.** Assume the same facts as in Example 26, except that distributable net income for 19X4 is $12,000. H and U each receive $10,000, but they cannot be taxed in total on more than DNI. Thus, each is taxed on $6,000 [DNI of $12,000 × ($10,000/$20,000 of the first-tier distributions)].

**Example 28.** Return to the facts described in Example 25. Ms. K receives a first-tier distribution of $15,000. Second-tier distributions include $20,000 to Ms. K and $25,000 to Dr. L. W's distributable net income is $40,000. The DNI is allocated between Ms. K and Dr. L as follows:

(1) First-tier distributions
     To Ms. K                 $15,000 DNI
     To Dr. L                 0
   Remaining DNI = $25,000

(2) Second-tier distributions
     To Ms. K                 $11,111 DNI (20/45 × $25,000)
     To Dr. L                 $13,889 DNI (25/45 × $25,000)

**Example 29.** Assume the same facts as in Example 28, except that accounting income is $80,000 and DNI is $70,000. The DNI is allocated between Ms. K and Dr. L as follows:

(1) First-tier distributions
     To Ms. K                 $15,000 DNI
     To Dr. L                 0
   Remaining DNI = $55,000

(2) Second-tier distributions
     To Ms. K                 $20,000 DNI
     To Dr. L                 $25,000 DNI

**Example 30.** Assume the same facts as in Example 28, except that accounting income is $18,000 and DNI is $12,000. The DNI is allocated between Ms. K and Dr. L as follows:

(1) First-tier distributions
     To Ms. K                 $12,000 DNI
       (i. e., limited to the DNI ceiling)
     To Dr. L                 0
   Remaining DNI = $0

(2) Second-tier distributions
     To Ms. K                 $0 DNI
     To Dr. L                 $0 DNI

**Example 31.** The Y Estate is required to distribute its current income as follows: 50% to A, 25% to B, and 25% to C (a qualifying charitable organization). During the current year, it has accounting income of $40,000 and distributable net income of $27,000, both without the deduction for charitable contributions. Pursuant to the trust instrument, the following amounts are paid out: $20,000 to A (50% × $40,000), $10,000 to B, and $10,000 to C. A must include $18,000 in gross income [($20,000/$30,000) × $27,000], and B must include $9,000 [($10,000/$30,000) × $27,000]. Note that the distribution to the charitable organization was not considered in allocating distributable net income to the first-tier beneficiaries (i. e., the denominator of the fraction is only $30,000).[61]

**Example 32.** The will that created the V Estate requires that $20,000 be distributed annually to Mrs. V. If any accounting income remains, it may be accumulated or it may be distributed to Miss V or to W College, a qualifying charitable organization. In addition, the executor of the estate may invade corpus for the benefit of Mrs. V, Miss V, or the college. In 19X4, the accounting income of the estate is $35,000 and DNI is $25,000, both computed before the charitable contribution deduction. The executor pays $30,000 to Mrs. V and $10,000 each to Miss V and to the college. The DNI is to be allocated among the beneficiaries as follows:

(1) First-tier distributions
| | |
|---|---|
| To Mrs. V | $20,000 DNI |
| To Miss V | 0 |
| To charity | 0 |
| Remaining DNI = $0 | |
| ($25,000 DNI − first-tier distributions $20,000) | |
| − charitable contributions $10,000) | |

The charitable contribution does not reduce the exposure to DNI for the first-tier distribution, but it is applied in computing the DNI that remains for the second-tier distributions.

(2) Second-tier distributions
| | |
|---|---|
| To Mrs. V | $0 DNI |
| To Miss V | $0 DNI |
| To charity | $0 DNI |

*Separate Share Rule.* For the sole purpose of determining the amount of distributable net income for a complex trust with more than one beneficiary, the substantially separate and independent shares of different beneficiaries in the trust are treated as *separate trusts*.[62] The reason for this special rule can be illustrated as follows:

**Example 33.** Under the terms of the trust instrument, the trustee has the discretion to distribute or accumulate income on behalf of G and H (in equal shares). The trustee also has the power to invade

**61.** Reg. § 1.662(a)–2(e) (Ex. 2).
**62.** Reg. § 1.663(c)–1(a).

corpus for the benefit of either beneficiary to the extent of that beneficiary's one-half interest in the trust. For the current year, the distributable net income of the trust is $10,000. Of this amount, $5,000 is distributed to G and $5,000 is accumulated on behalf of H. In addition, the trustee pays $20,000 from corpus to G. Without the separate share rule, G would be taxed on $10,000 (the full amount of the DNI). With the separate share rule, G is taxed on only $5,000 (his share of the DNI) and receives the $20,000 corpus distribution tax-free. The trust will be taxed on H's $5,000 share of the DNI that is accumulated.

The separate share rule is designed to prevent the inequity that otherwise would result if the corpus payment were treated under the regular rules applicable to second-tier beneficiaries. Referring to Example 33, the effect of the separate share rule is to produce a two-trust result: one trust for G and one for H, each with DNI of $5,000.

## CHARACTER OF INCOME

Consistent with the modified conduit principle of Subchapter J, various classes of income (e. g., dividends, long-term capital gains, tax-exempt interest) retain the same character for the beneficiaries that they had when they were received by the entity. However, if there are multiple beneficiaries *and* if all of the distributable net income is distributed, a problem arises with respect to the allocation of the various classes of income among the beneficiaries. Distributions are treated as consisting of the same proportion of each class of the items that enter into the computation of DNI as the total of each class bears to the total DNI of the entity. This allocation does not apply, however, if the terms of the governing instrument specifically allocate different classes of income to different beneficiaries or if local law requires such an allocation.[63] Expressed as a formula, this generally means the following:

$$\frac{\text{Beneficiary's total share of DNI distributed}}{\text{Total DNI distributed}} \times \begin{array}{c}\text{Total of DNI element}\\ \text{deemed distributed}\\ \text{(e. g., tax-exempt interest)}\end{array} = \begin{array}{c}\text{Beneficiary's share}\\ \text{of the DNI element}\end{array}$$

If the entity distributes only a part of its distributable net income, the amount of a particular class of distributable net income that is deemed distributed must first be determined. This is done as follows:

$$\frac{\text{Total distribution}}{\begin{array}{c}\text{Total distributable}\\ \text{net income}\end{array}} \times \begin{array}{c}\text{Total of a particular}\\ \text{class of distributable}\\ \text{net income}\end{array} = \begin{array}{c}\text{Total of the DNI element}\\ \text{deemed distributed}\\ \text{(e. g., tax-exempt interest)}\end{array}$$

**Example 34.** During the current year, a trust has distributable net income of $40,000, including the following: $10,000 of taxable interest,

---

63. Reg. § 1.662(b)–1.

$10,000 of tax-exempt interest, and $20,000 of dividends. The trustee distributes, at her discretion, $8,000 to M and $12,000 to N, both non-charitable beneficiaries. The amount of each element of distributable net income that is deemed distributed will be $5,000 of taxable interest [($20,000 total distributed/ $40,000 DNI) × $10,000 taxable interest in DNI], $5,000 of tax-exempt interest [($20,000/$40,000) × $10,000], and $10,000 of dividends [($20,000/$40,000) × $20,000]. M's share of this income is $8,000, made up of $2,000 of taxable interest [($8,000 DNI received by M/$20,000 total DNI distributed) × $5,000 taxable interest distributed], $2,000 of tax-exempt interest [($8,000/$20,000) × $5,000], and $4,000 of dividends [($8,000/$20,000) × $10,000]. The remaining amount of each income item deemed distributed is N's share: $3,000 of taxable interest, $3,000 of tax-exempt interest, and $6,000 of dividends.

**Example 35.** The P Trust incurs the following items in 19X8:

| | |
|---|---:|
| Taxable interest income | $100,000 |
| Taxable dividend income | 80,000 |
| Long-term capital gains (allocable to income) | 20,000 |
| Fiduciary's fees (allocable to corpus) | 10,000 |

The sole income beneficiary of the trust is guaranteed an annual $175,000 payment from the trustee. In addition, the trustee is empowered to distribute, at his discretion, any additional amounts of corpus and accumulated income as the beneficiary, Mr. A, requires. No such additional payments were made for 19X8. Both the trust and Mr. A are calendar year cash basis taxpayers. Results of the 19X8 trust activities are summarized in the following steps:

| | | |
|---|---|---:|
| (1) | Interest income | $100,000 |
| | Dividend income | + 80,000 |
| | Long-term capital gains | + 20,000 |
| | Fiduciary's fees | ± 0 |
| | Trust accounting income, 19X8 | $200,000 |
| | | |
| (2) | Interest income | $100,000 |
| | Dividend income | + 80,000 |
| | Dividend exclusion | − 13* |
| | Long-term capital gains | + 20,000 |
| | Long-term capital gains deduction | − 0 |
| | Fiduciary's fees | − 10,000 |
| | Personal exemption | − 100 |
| | Taxable income before the distribution deduction | $189,887 |

*Dividend deemed paid = $175,000 (distribution) × [$80,000 (dividend income)/$200,000 (income elements of trust accounting income)] = $70,000
Dividend deemed retained by P = $80,000 − $70,000 = $10,000
Dividend exclusion = $100 (maximum exclusion) × proportion of dividend retained by P [$10,000/$80,000] = $12.50

(3)   Taxable income before the
distribution deduction      $189,887

Add back:

     Personal exemption      +    100

     Dividend exclusion      +     13

Distributable net income      $190,000

Distribution deduction [lesser of
DNI ($190,000) or amount
distributed ($175,000)]      $175,000

(4)   Taxable income before the
distribution deduction      $189,887

     Distribution deduction      −175,000

     Trust taxable income      $ 14,887

(5)   The next step is to determine the character of the income that A received via his distribution from the P Trust. DNI is constituted of three elements: interest income, dividend income, and long-term capital gain. The $10,000 deduction for the fiduciary's fees is allocated among each of the three DNI elements, absent a provision in the trust instrument to the contrary. Since less than the full amount of DNI was distributed, compute the amount of each DNI element that A received. The constitution of DNI is determined as follows:

Interest income [$190,000 (DNI) × $100,000
     (DNI element)/$200,000 (total of DNI
     elements)]      $95,000

Dividend income [$190,000 × ($80,000/
     $200,000)]      76,000

Long-term capital gain [$190,000 ×
     ($20,000/$200,000)]      19,000

Next, determine the extent of the distribution of each of these items to A.

Interest income [$95,000 (DNI element) ×
     $175,000 (DNI distributed)/$190,000
     (total DNI)]      $87,500

Dividend income [$76,000 × ($175,000/
     $190,000)]      70,000

Long-term capital gain [$19,000 ×
     ($175,000/$190,000)]      17,500

Finally, compute the increase in Mr. A's 19X8 adjusted gross income that results from his $175,000 distribution from P.

Interest income (no exclusion is allowed)      $ 87,500

Dividend income (net of $100 exclusion)      69,900

Long-term capital gain ($17,500 × 40%)      7,000

Increase in 19X8 AGI      $164,400

Thus, although DNI is the maximum amount that could be included in the income beneficiary's own taxable income for any year, the character-of-income rules often operate to generate gross income for the beneficiary that is less than this amount.

*Special Allocations.* Under certain circumstances, the parties may modify the character-of-income allocation method set forth above. A modification will be permitted only to the extent that the allocation is required in the trust instrument and only to the extent that it has an economic effect independent of the income tax consequences of the allocation.[64] Recall that substantial economic effect also is required for special allocations of various items of income, deductions, or credits for partnerships [§ 704(b)].

> **Example 36.** Return to the facts described in Example 34. Assume that the beneficiaries are elderly individuals who have pooled their investment portfolios and avail themselves of the trustee's professional asset management skills. Suppose that the trustee has the discretion to allocate different classes of income to different beneficiaries and that she designates all of N's $12,000 distribution as being from the tax-exempt income. Such a designation *would not be recognized* for tax purposes; the allocation method of Example 34 must be used.
>
> Suppose, however, that the trust instrument stipulated that N was to receive all of the income from tax-exempt securities, because only N contributed the exempt securities to the trust corpus. Pursuant to this provision, the $10,000 of the nontaxable interest is paid to him. This allocation is recognized, and $10,000 of N's distribution is tax-exempt.

## LOSSES IN THE TERMINATION YEAR

The ordinary net operating and capital losses of a trust or estate do not flow through to the entity's beneficiaries, as would such losses from a partnership or an S corporation. However, in the year in which an entity terminates its existence, the beneficiaries do receive a direct benefit from the loss carryovers of the trust or estate.[65]

Net operating losses and net capital losses are subject to the same carryover rules that otherwise apply to an individual (i. e., net operating losses can be carried back three years and then carried forward 15 years; net capital losses can be carried forward only, and for an indefinite period by the entity). However, if the entity incurs a net operating loss in the last year of its existence, the excess of deductions over the entity's gross income will be allowed to the beneficiaries (i. e., it will flow through to them directly). This net loss will be available as a deduction *from* adjusted gross income in the beneficiary's tax year with or within which the entity's tax year ends, in proportion to the relative amount of corpus assets that each beneficiary receives upon the termination of the entity.

Moreover, any carryovers of the entity's other net operating and net capital losses flow through to the beneficiaries in the year of termination,

---

**64.** Reg. § 1.652(b)–2(b).
**65.** Reg. § § 1.642(h)–1 and –2.

in proportion to the relative amount of corpus assets that each beneficiary receives. The character of the loss carryforward is retained by the beneficiary, except that a carryover of a net capital loss to a corporate beneficiary always is deemed to be short-term. Beneficiaries who are individuals can use these carryforwards as deductions *for* adjusted gross income.

> **Example 37.** The E Trust terminates on December 31, 19X4. It had used a fiscal year ending July 31. For the termination year, the trust incurred a $15,000 net operating loss. In addition, the trust had an unused net operating loss carryforward of $23,000 from the year ending July 31, 19X1, and an unused net long-term capital loss carryforward of $10,000 from the year ending July 31, 19X3. D receives $60,000 of the trust corpus upon termination, and Z Corporation receives the remaining $40,000. D and Z are calendar year taxpayers.
>
> D can claim an itemized deduction of $9,000 [($60,000/$100,000) × $15,000] for the trust's net operating loss in the year of termination. In addition, she can claim a $13,800 deduction *for* adjusted gross income in 19X4 (60% × $23,000) for the other net operating loss carryforward of E, and she can use $6,000 of E's net long-term capital loss carryforward with her other 19X4 capital transactions.
>
> Z Corporation receives ordinary business deductions in 19X4 for E's net operating losses: $6,000 for the loss in the year of termination and $9,200 for the carryforward from fiscal 19X1. Moreover, Z can use the $4,000 carryforward of E's net capital losses to offset against its other 19X4 capital transactions, although the loss must be treated as short-term. With respect to both D and Z, the losses flow through in addition to the other tax consequences of E that they received on July 31, 19X4 (i. e., at the close of the usual tax year of the trust), under Subchapter J. Moreover, if the loss carryovers are not used by the beneficiaries in calendar year 19X4, the short year of termination will exhaust one of the years of the usual carryforward period (e. g., D can use E's net operating loss carryforward through 15 years).

## SPECIAL TAX COMPUTATION FOR TRUSTS

Congress enacted § 644 to discourage the transferring of appreciated property to a trust, which then would sell the property and thereby shift the gain on the appreciation of the asset to the trust's lower tax rates. This provision imposes a special tax on trusts that sell or exchange property at a gain within two years after the date of its transfer in trust by the transferor. The special tax applies, however, only if the fair market value of the property at the time of the initial transfer exceeded the adjusted basis of the property immediately after the transfer (i. e., after any applicable adjustment for gift taxes paid).

The tax imposed by § 644 is equal to the amount of additional income tax that the transferor would have been required to pay (including any alternative minimum tax) had the gain been included in his or her gross income for the tax year of the sale. Note, however, that the tax applies only to an amount known as *includible gain*. Such gain is the lesser of the following:

—The gain recognized by the trust on the sale or exchange of any property *or*

—The excess of the fair market value of such property at the time of the initial transfer in trust by the transferor over the adjusted basis of such property immediately after the transfer.[66]

The character of the gain includible by the trust is determined as if the property actually were sold or exchanged by the transferor. Whether the disposed-of property is a capital asset generally is determined by reference to its character in the hands of the transferor.[67]

Several situations exist wherein the tax will not be imposed.[68] For instance, the tax will be inapplicable to the sale or exchange of property (a) acquired by the trust from a decedent or (b) that occurs after the death of the transferor.

**Example 38.** On July 1, 19X8, G created an irrevocable trust with a transfer of 200 shares of Z Corporation stock. At the time of the transfer, the stock was a capital asset to G. It has a fair market value of $30,000; its basis to the trust was $20,000. On October 1, 19X8, the trust sold the stock for $35,000. Section 644 will apply, because the stock was sold at a gain within two years after its transfer in trust *and* its fair market value at the time of the initial transfer exceeded its adjusted basis to the trust immediately after the transfer. The trust must report a § 644 gain of $10,000 [i. e., the lesser of its gain recognized on the sale ($15,000) or the appreciation in the hands of G]. This $10,000 is taxed to the trust at G's 19X8 income tax rates on a net capital gain. The remaining $5,000 of the gain is taxed to the trust under the usual Subchapter J rules.

**Example 39.** Assume the same facts as in Example 38, except that the fair market value of the stock at the time of the transfer was $18,000. Section 644 will not apply to the subsequent sale by the trust, since the fair market value of the stock on that date was less than the stock's basis to the trust. Note also that the § 644 tax would not apply in Example 38 if the stock were sold either at a loss or more than two years after the date of its initial transfer to the trust.

## THE THROWBACK RULE

To understand the purpose and rationale of the throwback provision, one must review the general nature of taxation of trusts and their beneficiaries. The usual rule is that the income from trust assets will be taxed to the trust itself or to the beneficiary, but not to both. Generally, then, a beneficiary is not taxed on any distributions in excess of the trust's distributable net income. Thus, trustees of complex trusts might be tempted to arrange distributions in such a manner that would result in minimal income tax consequences to all of the parties involved. For instance, if the trust is

---

**66.** § 644(b) and (d)(2).
**67.** § 644(c).
**68.** § 644(e).

subject to a lower marginal income tax rate than are its beneficiaries, income could be accumulated at the trust level for several years before it is distributed to the beneficiaries. In this manner, the income that would be taxed to the beneficiaries in the year of distribution would be limited by the trust's DNI for that year. Further tax savings could be achieved by the use of multiple trusts, because the income during the accumulation period would be spread over more than one taxpaying entity, thereby avoiding the graduated tax rates.

To discourage the use of these tax minimization schemes, the Code has, since 1954, contained some type of *throwback rule*. Because of this rule, a beneficiary's tax on a distribution of income accumulated by a trust in a prior year will approximate the increase in the beneficiary's tax for such a prior year that would have resulted had the income been distributed in the year that it was earned by the trust. The tax as so computed, however, is levied for the actual year of the distribution. In essence, the purpose of the throwback rule is to place the beneficiaries of complex trusts in the same nominal tax position as would have existed had they received the distributions during the years in which the trust was accumulating the income.

A detailed description of the application of the throwback rule is beyond the scope of this text. However, some basic terms and concepts are presented in the following sections to familiarize the reader with the applicable statutory provisions and their purpose.

## BASIC TERMS

An understanding of the throwback rule requires the definition of two important terms: (1) *undistributed net income* and (2) *accumulation distributions*. Undistributed net income is defined in § 665(a) as the distributable net income of the trust reduced by first- and second-tier distributions and the income tax paid by the trust on any remaining undistributed DNI. An accumulation distribution is defined in § 665(b) as any distribution from a trust for a particular year in excess of the trust's DNI for the year.

The throwback rule applies only to complex trusts that do not distribute all current accounting income. Thus, the rule does not apply to estates or simple trusts. Moreover, the rule applies only in years when the complex trust makes an accumulation distribution. When this occurs, the distribution is "thrown back" to the earliest year in which the trust had any undistributed net income. The accumulation is thrown back to succeeding years sequentially until it is used up. Accumulation distributions made after 1973 may not be thrown back to years before 1969. Moreover, distributions of accounting income, capital gains that are allocable to corpus, and income accumulated prior to the beneficiary's attaining age 21 are not subject to the throwback procedure.[69]

Because of the effect of the throwback rule, the beneficiary may be required to pay an additional income tax in the year of the accumulation distribution. The tax due for this year will be the sum of the tax on the beneficiary's taxable income (without the accumulation distribution) and

---

**69.** § § 665(b) and (e).

the tax on the accumulation distribution.[70] The trust may not claim a refund (i. e., if the tax that it paid exceeded that which would have been paid by the beneficiary).[71] Finally, accumulation distributions to the same beneficiary, of at least $1,000 each, from multiple trusts will be treated as an accumulation distribution from a single trust.[72]

> **Example 40.** In 19X3, the T Trust was subject to a marginal Federal income tax rate of 19%, while its sole income beneficiary, O, was subject to 50% marginal rate. O encouraged the trustee to accumulate $7,500 of the trust's 19X3 DNI, which totaled $10,000. The balance of the DNI was distributed to O in 19X3. If T's tax on this accumulation, after credits, was $1,200, T's undistributed net income for 19X3 is $6,300 [$10,000 (DNI) − $2,500 (distribution of income) − $1,200 (taxes paid)].
>
> By 19X8, A's marginal rate had fallen to 23%, and A encouraged the trustee to distribute to him, in that year, an amount equal to the 19X8 DNI of $12,000 plus the $6,300 that had been accumulated, after taxes, in 19X3. When the trustee complied with O's wish, she made an accumulation distribution of $6,300.
>
> The tax on accumulation distributions is levied upon O in 19X8. O's additional tax will approximate what O would have paid in 19X3 had the trust distributed its full DNI in that year (i. e., the $6,300 accumulation distribution will be subject to approximately a 50% marginal tax rate and not to O's prevailing 23% rate). Although no interest or penalty is due with the tax on the accumulation distribution, the additional tax clearly discourages the manipulation of trust distributions to split taxable income among entities for tax avoidance purposes.

## TAX ON ACCUMULATION DISTRIBUTION

The tax imposed on the accumulation distribution is determined by adding a fraction of the distribution to the beneficiary's taxable income for three of the five immediately preceding tax years (excluding both the year of the highest taxable income and the year of the lowest taxable income).[73] The fraction is calculated by dividing the accumulation distribution by the number of years in which it was earned by the trust. Once the additional tax on the taxable income (adjusted for the fraction of the accumulation distribution) for the three years is determined, the beneficiary must calculate an average additional tax for each of the three years and multiply it by the number of years over which the trust earned the income. The result is the tax on the accumulation distribution.[74]

---

**70.**  § 668(a).

**71.**  § 666(e).

**72.**  § 667(c).

**73.**  § 667(b).

**74.**  For further details on calculating the partial tax, see Reg. § 1.669(b)–1A.

## THE SIXTY-FIVE DAY RULE

Amounts paid or credited to the beneficiaries in the first 65 days of the trust's tax year may be treated as paid on the last day of the preceding taxable year. Use of this provision offers the trustee some flexibility in timing distributions so that trust accumulations, and the resulting throwback procedures, can be avoided. This treatment is an election available to the trustee.[75]

# GRANTOR TRUSTS

A series of special statutory provisions contained in § § 671 through 679 of the Code applies when the grantor of the trust retains beneficial enjoyment or substantial control over the trust property or income. In such an event, the grantor is taxed on the trust income, and the trust is disregarded for income tax purposes. Of course, the person who is taxed on the income is allowed to claim, on his or her own return, any deductions or credits attributable to the income.[76] These special rules concern only the Federal income tax treatment of the trust. Another part of the Code deals with the Federal estate and gift tax consequences of such incomplete transfers (see Chapters 11 and 12). There is no complete correlation among the operation of these different Federal taxes. Clearly, however, such taxes restrict the grantor's ability to redirect the income recognized from trust corpus to the trust or its beneficiaries.

## REVERSIONARY TRUSTS

The income of a reversionary (or Clifford) trust will not be taxed to the grantor (i. e., it will be taxed under the usual rules applicable to trusts) if one of the following conditions is met: (1) the income interest of the trust is established for more than 10 years; (2) the income interest is based upon the life of the beneficiary; (3) the income interest is based upon the life of a third party, provided that the third party has a life expectancy of longer than 10 years.[77]

> **Example 41.** F creates a trust, income payable to S for 11 years, reversion to F. During the trust term, the income will be taxed to S. (If the duration of the income interest were only nine years, the income would be taxed to F, the grantor.)

> **Example 42.** F creates a trust, income payable to S for S's life, reversion to F. During S's life, the income will be taxed to him. In this situation, it does not matter how old S is or how long he is expected to live.

> **Example 43.** F creates a trust, income payable to S for the term of M's life, reversion to F. The income will be taxed to S until M's death, if

---

**75.** See Reg. § 1.663(b)–2 for the manner and timing of such an election.

**76.** § 671.

**77.** Reg. § 1.673(a)–1(c)

at the time the trust was created M had a life expectancy of longer than 10 years.

Under § 673, none of the income of a Clifford trust can become available for the benefit of the grantor if the trust is to be tax-effective. Thus, if the trustee is given the power to accumulate income, the accumulation eventually must be distributed to the beneficiary (i. e., it cannot pass to the grantor upon the termination of the trust). However, any capital gains allocable to corpus and recognized by the trust are taxed currently to the grantor.[78]

Creation of a reversionary trust is subject to the Federal gift tax. If the grantor dies before the income interest expires, the present value of the reversionary interest is included in his or her gross estate under § 2033; thus, a Federal estate tax could also result.

## POWERS RETAINED BY THE GRANTOR

Sections 674 through 677 contain other restrictions as to the extent of the powers over the trust that the grantor can retain without incurring grantor trust status upon the entity. Thus, a violation of any of these provisions means that the income of the trust will be taxed to the grantor (i. e., the usual Subchapter J rules will not apply to the trust).

Section 674 provides that the grantor will be treated as the owner of any portion of a trust (and therefore taxed on the income therefrom) if he or she retains (a) the beneficial enjoyment of corpus and/or (b) the power to dispose of the trust income without the approval or consent of any adverse party. An adverse party is any person having a substantial beneficial interest in the trust who would be adversely affected by the exercise or nonexercise of the power that the grantor possesses over the trust assets.[79] A nonadverse party is any person who is not an adverse party.

The rule stated above has exceptions. Section 674(b) stipulates several powers (regardless of who holds them) that will not cause income to be taxed to the grantor:

—To apply the income toward the support of the grantor's dependents (except to the extent that it actually is applied for this purpose).[80]

—To change the distribution of the income of a reversionary trust, if such power becomes effective more than 10 years after the trust is created.[81]

—To control the disposition of income by means of a will (i. e., upon the grantor's death).

—To allocate trust income or corpus among charitable beneficiaries.

—To invade corpus on behalf of a designated beneficiary.

—To postpone temporarily the payment of income to a beneficiary.

---

**78.**   Reg. § 1.673(a)–1(a)(2).
**79.**   § § 672(a) and (b). See Reg. § 1.672(a)–1 for examples of adverse party situations.
**80.**   § 677(b).
**81.**   § 673.

—To withhold income from a beneficiary during his or her minority or disability.

—To allocate receipts and disbursements between income and corpus.[82]

The retention by the grantor or a nonadverse party of certain administrative powers over the trust will cause the income therefrom to be taxed to the grantor under § 675. Such powers include powers to deal with trust income or corpus for less than full and adequate consideration and to borrow from the trust without providing adequate interest or security.[83]

The grantor of a trust will be taxed on the trust's income if he or she (or a nonadverse party) possesses the power to revoke the trust.[84] An exception is allowed, however, to protect the reversionary trust arrangement previously discussed.[85] Thus, a power to revoke that is exercisable only after more than 10 years will not result in the taxation of trust income to the grantor during the applicable period.

A grantor may be taxed on all or part of the income of a trust when, without the consent of any adverse party, the income is or, in the discretion of the grantor or a nonadverse party (or both), the income may be:

—Distributed to the grantor or the grantor's spouse.

—Held or accumulated for future distribution to the grantor or the grantor's spouse.

—Applied to the payment of premiums on insurance policies on the life of the grantor or the grantor's spouse.[86]

Moreover, trust income accumulated for the benefit of someone whom the grantor is *legally obligated* to support will be taxed to the grantor, but only to the extent that it actually is applied for such purpose.[87]

> **Example 44.** F creates an irrevocable trust in 19X6 for his children, with a transfer of income-producing property and an insurance policy on the life of M, F's wife. During the year, the trustee applies $3,000 of the trust income in payment of the premiums on the policy covering M's life. F is taxed on $3,000 of the trust's income in 19X6.

> **Example 45.** M creates an irrevocable accumulation trust. Her son, S, is the life beneficiary, remainder to any grandchildren. During the year, the trust income of $8,000 is applied as follows: $5,000 toward S's college tuition and other related educational expenses and $3,000 accumulated on S's behalf. If, under state law, M has an obligation to support S and this obligation includes providing a college education, M is taxed on the $5,000 that is so applied.

---

82. See Reg. § 1.674(b)–1 for a further discussion of these exceptions and for examples illustrating their applicability.
83. See Reg. § 1.675–1(b) for a further discussion of this matter.
84. § 676(a).
85. § 676(b).
86. § 677(a).
87. § 677(b).

═══════════════════ Concept Summary ═══════════════════

1. Estates and trusts are temporary entities, created to locate, maintain, and distribute assets and to satisfy liabilities, according to the wishes of the decedent or grantor as expressed in the will or trust document.

2. Generally, the estate or trust acts as a conduit of the taxable income that it receives. Thus, to the extent that such income is distributed by the entity, it is taxable to the beneficiary. Taxable income that is retained by the entity is taxable to the entity itself.

3. The estate or trust may select any acceptable tax accounting period or method. The tax rates that apply to such entities are the same as those for married individuals who file separate returns, although no zero bracket amount is allowed to the estate or trust.

4. The entity's accounting income first must be determined. Accounting conventions that are stated in the controlling document or, lacking such provisions, in state law allocate specific items of receipt and expenditure either to income or to corpus. Income beneficiaries typically receive payments from the entity that are equal to this accounting income amount.

5. The taxable income of the entity is computed using the computational scheme in Figure I. The entity usually recognizes income in respect of a decedent. It is allowed a pro rata portion of the dividend exclusion. Deductions for fiduciary's fees and for charitable contributions may be reduced if the entity received any tax-exempt income during the year. Depreciation deductions are assigned proportionately to the recipients of accounting income. Upon election, realized gain or loss on assets that properly are distributed in kind can be recognized by the entity.

6. A distribution deduction, computationally derived from distributable net income (DNI), is allowed to the entity. DNI is the maximum amount on which entity beneficiaries can be taxed. Moreover, the constitution of DNI is assigned to the recipients of the distributions.

7. Additional taxes are levied under Subchapter J to discourage (1) the transfer of appreciated assets to a lower-bracket estate or trust which quickly disposes of the assets in a taxable exchange; (2) the accumulation of trust income at the lower marginal tax rates of the entity followed by a subsequent distribution of the accumulation to beneficiaries; and (3) the retention of excessive administrative powers by the grantor of a trust when the gross income therefrom is taxed to a lower-bracket beneficiary.

☑ TAX PLANNING
CONSIDERATIONS

Many of the tax planning possibilities for estates and trusts have been discussed in Chapters 11 and 12. However, there are several specific tax planning possibilities that should help to minimize the income tax effects on estates and trusts and their beneficiaries. These items are discussed in the following sections in connection with postmortem tax planning and the use of trusts as income tax savings devices. A series of examples illustrating the interrelationship among income, gift, and estate taxes is included.

### INCOME TAX PLANNING FOR ESTATES

As a separate taxable entity, an estate can select its own tax year and accounting methods. The executor of an estate should consider selecting a fiscal year, because this will determine when beneficiaries must include income distributions from the estate in their own tax returns. Beneficiaries must include the income for their tax year with or within which the estate's tax year ends. Proper selection of the estate's tax year thus could result in a smoothing out of income and a reduction of the income taxes for all parties involved.

Caution should be taken in determining when the estate is to be terminated. If a fiscal year had been selected for the estate, a bunching of income to the beneficiaries could occur in the year in which the estate is closed. Although prolonging the termination of an estate can be effective for income tax planning, keep in mind that the IRS carefully examines the purpose of keeping the estate open. Since the unused losses of an estate will pass through to the beneficiaries, the estate should be closed when the beneficiaries can enjoy the maximum tax benefit of such losses.

The timing and amounts of income distributions to the beneficiaries also present important tax planning opportunities. If the executor can make discretionary income distributions, he or she should evaluate the relative income tax brackets of the estate and its beneficiaries. By timing such distributions properly, the overall income tax liability can be minimized. Care should be taken, however, to time such distributions in light of the estate's distributable net income.

> **Example 46.** For several years before his death on March 7, 19X1, D had entered into annual deferred compensation agreements with his employer. These agreements collectively called for the payment of $200,000 six months after D's retirement or death. To provide a maximum 12-month period within which to generate deductions to offset this large item of income in respect of a decedent, the executor or administrator of the estate should elect a fiscal year ending August 31. The election is made simply by filing the estate's first tax return for the short period of March 7, 19X1, to August 31, 19X1.

> **Example 47.** B, the sole beneficiary of an estate, is a calendar year cash basis taxpayer. If the estate elects a fiscal year ending January 31, all distributions during the period of February 1, 19X1, to December 31, 19X1, will be reported on B's tax return for calendar year 19X2 (due April 15, 19X3). Thus, any income taxes that result from a $50,000 distribution made by the estate on February 20, 19X1, will be deferred until April 15, 19X3.

> **Example 48.** Assume the same facts as in Example 47. If the estate is closed on December 15, 19X2, the distributable net income for both the fiscal year ending January 31, 19X2, and the final tax year ending December 15, 19X2, will be included in B's tax return for the calendar year 19X2. To avoid the effect of this bunching of income, the estate should not be closed until calendar year 19X3.

> **Example 49.** Assume the same facts as in Example 48, except that the estate has a substantial net operating loss for the period February 1, 19X2, to December 15, 19X2. If B is in a high marginal income tax bracket for calendar year 19X2, the estate should be closed in that year so that the excess deductions will be passed through to its beneficiary. However, if B anticipates being in a higher tax bracket in 19X3, the termination of the estate should be postponed.

**Example 50.** Review Examples 28 through 30 carefully. Note, for instance, the flexibility that is available to the executor or administrator with respect to the timing of second-tier distributions of income and corpus of the estate. To illustrate, if Dr. L is subject to a high marginal tax rate, distributions to her should be minimized, except in years when DNI is low. In this manner, her exposure to gross income from such distributions can be controlled so that most of the distributions that she receives will be free of income tax.

In general, those beneficiaries who are subject to high marginal tax rates should be made second-tier beneficiaries of the estate. Most likely, these individuals will have less of a need for an additional steady stream of (taxable) income, and the income tax savings with respect to these parties can be relatively large. Moreover, a special allocation of tax-favored types of income and expenses should be considered so that, for example, tax-exempt income can be directed more easily to those beneficiaries in higher marginal income tax brackets.

## INCOME TAX PLANNING WITH TRUSTS

The great variety of trusts provides the grantor, trustee, and beneficiaries with excellent opportunities for tax planning. One of the greatest advantages of trusts is the opportunity to shift income away from a higher-tax-bracket grantor to a lower-tax-bracket trust or its beneficiaries. The earlier discussion of short-term reversionary trusts should be examined carefully, however, because many such attempts have failed, resulting in unwanted income and capital gain that is taxed to the grantor.

Like an estate, a trust is a separate taxable entity that can select its own tax year and accounting methods. The same tax planning opportunities that are available to the executor of an estate are available to the trustee in selecting a fiscal year for the trust. In addition, the distributions from a trust are taxable to the trust's beneficiaries to the extent of the trust's distributable net income. Thus, if income distributions are discretionary, the trustee can time such distributions to minimize the income tax consequences to all parties. Remember, however, that the throwback rule applies to complex trusts. Consequently, the timing of distributions may prove to be of a more limited benefit than is available with respect to an estate, and it could result in a greater nominal tax than if the distributions had been made annually. The trustee of a complex trust should thus consider the 65-day rule, which permits the trust to treat distributions made within 65 days of the end of its tax year as if they were made on the last day of such year. Proper use of this provision could help the trustee in both minimizing the overall income tax consequences and avoiding the throwback rule for the beneficiaries.

## INTERRELATIONSHIP AMONG INCOME, GIFT, AND ESTATE TAXES

One of the greatest advantages of trusts is the opportunity to shift income away from a higher-tax-bracket grantor to a lower-tax-bracket trust or its beneficiaries. Unfortunately, this income tax planning opportunity cannot be undertaken without consideration of the corollary gift and estate tax consequences.

**Example 51.** G creates a trust for B, but he reserves the power to revoke the trust. The power is not relinquished by G before his death. A gift tax will not be imposed on this transfer in trust, because the gift is deemed to be incomplete: The grantor retained the right to revest beneficial title to the property in himself. However, income and estate taxes will not be avoided. G will be taxed on any income earned by the trust because of the retained power to revoke the trust. In addition, the value of all of the assets remaining in the trust at G's death will be included in the value of G's gross estate under § 2038, since the transfer in trust was revocable.

**Example 52.** G creates a trust for B, and he retains no control or reversionary interest over trust corpus or income. Since this transfer is a completed gift, it will be subject to the gift tax under § 2501. G can avoid both income and estate tax, however, because he has made an irrevocable transfer and has not retained any power over trust corpus or income.

**Example 53.** G creates a trust, income to be paid to B for 12 years, reversion to G or her estate. This transfer represents a gift of an income interest; thus, it will be subject to gift tax under § 2501. The transfer also will shift the income tax burden away from G during the 12-year term of the trust, because the trust meets the requirements of § 673(a). G will not avoid the estate tax on the assets transferred in trust, however. If she dies before the expiration of the reversionary period, the value of her reversion in the trust's assets still will be included in her gross estate under § 2033.

**Example 54.** G creates a trust, reserving for himself an income interest for his life, remainder to B. This transfer will not avoid any of the related taxes. First, since the transfer represents a gift of a remainder interest, it will be subject to gift tax under § 2501. The value of all assets remaining in the trust at G's death will be included in G's gross estate under § 2036(a)(1), since the transfer in trust represents a transfer with a retained life estate. Finally, G will be subject to income tax on all income earned by the trust during his lifetime under both §§ 674 and 677 because of the retained life estate.

**Example 55.** G transfers separate property to a trust, income to M for life, remainder to F. G includes in the trust agreement a provision that permits the trustee to designate someone else as the income beneficiary. The trustee is G's husband (a nonadverse party). This transfer will be subject to gift tax under § 2501, because it is a completed gift. G also will be subject to income tax on all of the trust income under § 677, because such income can be distributed to G or her spouse (the trustee) without the approval or consent of any adverse party. The estate tax will be avoided, however, because G did not retain any power or control over the assets transferred.

The usual tax objective of an inter vivos trust is to secure the results of Examples 52 or 53. In recent years, however, the popularity of the revocable trust (Example 51) has been increasing among those who do not have immediate income tax problems, who wish to avoid the cost and delay of probate proceedings, or who do not anticipate significant estate tax consequences. The usual advantage of the revocable trust is that, when a beneficial interest of a surviving spouse qualifies (i. e., no terminable interest is involved), the estate tax marital deduction is available.

Because of the unhappy tax situation, the results of Example 54 are usually unintended. They could be the result of planning, however, if the grantor has some specific objective in mind and is not concerned with tax consequences. Example 55 clearly indicates that there is no direct correlation between the income tax and the estate tax. Thus, it is entirely conceivable to make a transfer in trust that avoids the estate tax but does not shift the income tax burden away from the grantor.

The sometimes unexpected interplay among income, gift, and estate taxes illustrated above should suggest that taxpayers exercise caution in the creation of trusts. A hastily created trust to effect some short-term income tax savings could result in either an immediate gift tax or future estate taxes that exceed the anticipated income tax savings.

## DISTRIBUTIONS OF IN-KIND PROPERTY

The ability of the trustee or executor to elect to recognize the realized gain or loss relative to a distributed noncash asset allows the gain or loss to be allocated to the optimal taxpayer.

> **Example 56.** The Y Estate distributed some stock, basis of $40,000 and fair market value of $50,000, to beneficiary L in 1986. Y is subject to a 19% marginal income tax rate, and L is subject to a 43% marginal rate. The executor of Y should elect that the entity recognize the related $10,000 realized gain in 1986, thereby subjecting the gain to Y's lower marginal tax rate and reducing L's future capital gains income.

> **Example 57.** Assume the same facts as in Example 56, except that Y's basis in the stock is $56,000. The executor of Y should *not* elect that the entity recognize the related $6,000 loss, thereby shifting the $56,000 basis and the potential loss to L's higher marginal tax rates.

## PROBLEM MATERIALS

### Discussion Questions

1. What is the importance of the accounting income of a trust or estate in determining its taxable income?

2. When must an income tax return be filed for an estate? A trust? When could the fiduciary be held liable for the income tax due from an estate or trust?

3. What is the general scheme of the income taxation of trusts and estates? How does the modified conduit concept relate to this general approach?

4.  Under what circumstances could an estate or trust be taxed on a distribution of property to a beneficiary?

5.  What is income in respect of a decedent? What are the tax consequences to a recipient of income in respect of a decedent?

6.  How must an estate or trust treat its deductions for cost recovery? How does this treatment differ from the deductibility of administrative expenses or losses for estate tax purposes?

7.  What happens to the net operating loss carryovers of an estate or trust if the entity is terminated before the deductions can be taken? How can this provision be used as a tax planning opportunity?

8.  Discuss the income tax treatment of charitable contributions made by an estate or trust. How does this treatment differ from the requirements for charitable contribution deductions of individual taxpayers? What effect does a long-term capital gain have on the charitable contribution deduction for an estate or trust?

9.  What is distributable net income? Why is this amount significant in the income taxation of estates and trusts and their beneficiaries?

10. Distinguish between first- and second-tier distributions from estates and complex trusts. Discuss the tax consequences to the beneficiaries receiving such distributions.

11. What is the separate share rule? Why would this rule be of particular significance to a beneficiary who receives both first- and second-tier distributions?

12. How must the various classes of income be allocated among multiple beneficiaries of an estate or trust?

13. Under what circumstances would special allocations of particular classes of income to specific beneficiaries be recognized for income tax purposes?

14. What is the purpose of the special tax imposed on trusts by § 644? When is the tax applicable? How can it be avoided?

15. What is the throwback rule? When is it applicable? Why was such a rule adopted?

16. What is the 65-day rule, and under what circumstances can it be useful as a tax planning opportunity?

17. What is a reversionary trust? How can such a trust be established to insure that the income will not be taxed to the grantor?

18. What powers can be retained by the grantor of a trust without causing trust income to be taxed to the grantor?

19. Under what circumstances may the grantor be taxed on all or part of the income of a trust? How might state law help to avoid taxation to the grantor?

20. Discuss the tax planning opportunities presented by the ability of a trust or estate to select a particular tax year.

## Problems

1.  The F Estate received $20,000 in taxable dividends from domestic corporations during 19X9. It distributed $75,000 of its $100,000 accounting income for 19X9 to its sole beneficiary, G. F's 19X9 distributable net income was $80,000. The balance of F's income was accumulated and reinvested by the executor.

    (a) How much can F claim as a 19X9 dividend exclusion?

    (b) How much can G, a widow, claim as a 19X9 dividend exclusion?

2. The P Trust operates a welding business. Its 19X9 ACRS deductions properly amounted to $35,000. P's 19X9 accounting income was $150,000, of which $80,000 was distributed to first-tier beneficiary Q, $60,000 was distributed to second-tier beneficiary R, and $10,000 was accumulated by the trustee. R also received a $15,000 corpus distribution. P's distributable net income was $52,000. Identify the treatment of P's cost recovery deductions.

3. The J Trust incurred the following items in 19X9 using the cash basis of tax accounting:

| | |
|---|---|
| Taxable interest income | $40,000 |
| Tax-exempt interest income | 35,000 |
| Long-term capital gains | 25,000 |
| Fiduciary's fees | 10,000 |

The trustee distributed $12,000 to a qualified charitable organization in 19X10, designating such payment as from 19X9 accounting income. The trust instrument allocates capital gains and fiduciary fees to income. Compute J's 19X9 charitable contribution deduction.

4. Assume the same facts as in Problem 3, except that capital gains are allocated to corpus.

5. Assume the same facts as in Problem 4, except that the trust instrument directs that all charitable contributions be paid from J's taxable interest income.

6. The W Trust distributes $40,000 cash and a plot of land, basis of $15,000 and fair market value of $22,000, to its sole beneficiary, X. W's current-year distributable net income is $95,000. For each of the following independent cases, indicate (1) the amount of W's DNI deemed to be distributed to X, (2) W's distribution deduction for the land, and (3) X's basis in the land:

(a) No § 643(d) election is made.

(b) The trustee makes a § 643(d) election.

(c) Same as (a), except that W's basis in the land is $26,000.

(d) Same as (b), except that W's basis in the land is $26,000.

7. Assume the same facts as in Problem 6, except that W is an estate.

8. The X Trust had the following sources of income for the year 19X8:

| | |
|---|---|
| Dividends from a domestic corporation | $150,000 |
| Taxable interest | 75,000 |
| Long-term capital gains | 15,000 |
| Tax-exempt interest | 60,000 |
| Total | $300,000 |

The trustee's commission for the year amounted to $20,000.

(a) How much of the trustee's commission is allocable to tax-exempt income?

(b) Can such amount be deducted by the trust? See § 265 and Reg. § 1.643(a)–5(a).

(c) Is there any possibility that all of any tax return preparation fee may not be deductible by the trust?

9. The Q Estate uses a fiscal year ending August 31 for Federal income tax purposes. For the year ending August 31, 19X4, the estate had accounting income of $80,000 and distributable net income of $76,000. The estate has an unused net operating loss carryforward of $40,000 from 19X0. Its sole beneficiary, Mrs.

Q, recognized an unusually low amount of taxable income from her other 19X4 activities. The IRS is applying pressure to terminate the estate on December 31, 19X4. What would be the tax consequences of such a termination to the estate and to Mrs. Q? Should the executor attempt to keep the estate open into 19X5?

10. The LMN Trust is a simple trust that uses the calendar year for tax purposes. Its three income beneficiaries (L, M, and N) are entitled to the trust's annual accounting income in shares of one-third each. For calendar year 19X8, the trust has ordinary income of $60,000, a long-term capital gain of $18,000 (allocable to corpus), and a trustee commission expense of $6,000 (allocable to corpus).

    (a) How much income is each beneficiary entitled to receive?

    (b) What is the trust's distributable net income for 19X8?

    (c) What is the trust's 19X8 taxable income?

    (d) How much will be taxed to each of the beneficiaries?

11. Assume the same facts as in Problem 10, except that the trust instrument allocates the capital gain to income.

    (a) How much income is each beneficiary entitled to receive?

    (b) What is the trust's distributable net income for 19X8?

    (c) What is the trust's 19X8 taxable income?

    (d) How much will be taxed to each of the beneficiaries?

12. The SP Trust uses a fiscal year ending January 31 for income tax purposes. A, the trust's sole income beneficiary, is a calendar year taxpayer. The trust is required to distribute all of its income to A currently. For its fiscal year ending January 31, 19X8, the trust has distributable net income of $30,000. It recognizes a $40,000 capital gain (allocable to income) on July 1, 19X8. How much income will be taxed to A from the trust for the calendar year 19X8?

13. A trust is required to distribute $20,000 annually to its two income beneficiaries, A and B, in shares of 75% and 25%, respectively. If trust income is not sufficient to pay these amounts, the trustee is empowered to invade corpus to the extent necessary. During the current year, the trust has distributable net income of $12,000, and the trustee distributes $15,000 to A and $5,000 to B.

    (a) How much of the $15,000 distributed to A must be included in her gross income?

    (b) How much of the $5,000 distributed to B must be included in his gross income?

    (c) Are these distributions considered to be first-tier or second-tier distributions?

14. Under the terms of the trust instrument, the trustee has discretion to distribute or accumulate income on behalf of W, S, and D in equal shares. The trustee also is empowered to invade corpus for the benefit of any of the beneficiaries to the extent of their respective one-third interest in the trust. In 19X8, the trust has distributable net income of $48,000. Of this amount, $16,000 is distributed to W and $10,000 is distributed to S. The remaining $6,000 of S's share of DNI and D's entire $16,000 share are accumulated by the trust. Additionally, the trustee distributes $20,000 from corpus to W.

    (a) How much income is taxed to W?

    (b) To S?

    (c) To D?

    (d) To the trust?

15. During the current year, an estate has $60,000 of distributable net income composed of $30,000 in dividends, $20,000 in taxable interest, and $10,000 in tax-exempt interest. The trust's two noncharitable income beneficiaries, S and T, receive $20,000 each.

    (a) How much of each class of income will be deemed to have been distributed?

    (b) How much of each class of income is deemed to have been distributed to S? To T?

16. The trustee of the M Trust is empowered to distribute accounting income and corpus to the trust's equal beneficiaries, Mr. P and Dr. G. In 19X4, the trust incurs the following:

| | |
|---|---|
| Taxable interest income | $40,000 |
| Tax-exempt interest income | 60,000 |
| Long-term capital gains—allocable to corpus | 35,000 |
| Fiduciary's fees—allocable to corpus | 12,000 |

    The trustee distributed $25,000 to P and $28,000 to G in 19X4.

    (a) What is M's 19X4 trust accounting income?

    (b) What is M's 19X4 distributable net income?

    (c) What is the amount of taxable income recognized by P from these activities? By G? By M?

17. Ms. D contributes 100 shares of Y Corporation stock to an irrevocable trust on July 1, 19X4, income to her son, remainder to her grandson in 12 years. D's basis in the stock is $40,000; the fair market value of the stock at the date of the transfer is $300,000. On June 20, 19X6, the trust sells the stock on the open market for $175,000. What is the amount of gain or loss recognized by the trust on the sale? How is the tax computed, and who is liable for it? How would the recognized gain have been treated had the stock been sold for $415,000?

18. Z contributes 100 shares of T Corporation stock to an irrevocable trust on July 1, 19X4, income to his daughter, reversion in 11 years. The stock has a fair market value of $200,000 on the date of the gift. Z has exhausted his unified transfer tax credit prior to the creation of the trust but has not made any other lifetime taxable gifts. Under the terms of the trust agreement, net long-term capital gains are allocable to corpus. In 19X5, the trust recognizes $40,000 ordinary income, $10,000 tax-exempt income, and $18,000 net long-term capital gains. Z dies on July 1, 19X9. The trustee is a corporation that is unrelated to either Z or his daughter.

    (a) What are the gift tax consequences of the creation of the trust in 19X4?

    (b) What are the income tax consequences relative to the trust's 19X5 activities?

    (c) What are the implications of the trust for Z's Federal estate tax liability?

19. In each of the following independent cases, determine whether the grantor of the trust will be taxed on the trust income:

    (a) G transfers property in trust, income payable to W (his wife) for life, remainder to his grandson. G's son is designated as the trustee.

    (b) G transfers income-producing assets and a life insurance policy to a trust, life estate to his children, remainder to his grandchildren. The policy is on the life of G's wife, and the trustee (an independent trust company) is instructed to pay the premiums with income from the income-producing assets. The trust is designated as the beneficiary of the policy.

(c) G transfers property in trust. The trust income is payable to G's grandchildren, as W (G's wife) sees fit. W and an independent trust company are designated as trustees.

(d) G transfers property in trust, income payable to W (G's ex-wife), remainder to G or his estate upon W's death. The transfer was made in satisfaction of G's alimony obligation to W. An independent trust company is designated as the trustee.

(e) G transfers property in trust, income payable to M (G's 90-year-old mother) for her life and reversion to G or his estate. M dies four years after the trust is created. The trustee is an unrelated party.

(f) G transfers property in trust, income payable to C, a qualified charity, for five years, reversion to G or his estate. An independent trust company is designated as the trustee.

20. For each of the following independent statements, indicate whether the tax attribute is applicable only to estates (E), only to complex trusts (T), to both estates and complex trusts (B), or to neither (N):

(a) Unrestricted selection of taxable year.

(b) The entity's income tax liability may be paid in quarterly installments.

(c) The entity must file an income tax return if its gross income for the year is $600 or more.

(d) The entity must use the cash method of reporting its income and deductions.

(e) The entity is entitled to a personal exemption of $300.

(f) A special income tax may be imposed on gains from the sale or exchange of certain appreciated property.

(g) In the year of termination, the entity's net operating loss carryovers will be passed through to the beneficiaries.

(h) The entity's fiduciary is generally free to select the date of the entity's termination.

(i) The entity's deduction for charitable contributions is not subject to a percentage limitation.

(j) Distributions from the entity may be subject to the throwback rule.

21. S is the sole income beneficiary of a well-endowed trust. She believes that the trustee should be accumulating the trust accounting income that is being earned so that S can receive it after she retires and, presumably, when she will be subject to a lower marginal income tax rate. S presently is subject to a 45% marginal rate. Describe how the throwback rule inhibits the trustee from manipulating the timing of income distributions in this manner for each of the following independent cases:

(a) S is age 45.

(b) S is age 15.

(c) The trust allocates capital gains to income.

(d) The entity is the estate of S's father.

22. W wishes to transfer some of the income from his investment portfolio to his daughter, age 6. W wants the trust to be able to accumulate income on his daughter's behalf and to meet any excessive expenses associated with the daughter's prep school and private college education. Furthermore, W wants the trust to protect his daughter against his own premature death without increasing his Federal gross estate. Thus, W provides the trustee with the powers to pur-

chase insurance on his life and to meet tuition, fee, and book expenses of his daughter's education.

The trust is created in 19X0. A whole life insurance policy with five annual premium payments is purchased in that year. The trustee spends $10,000 for the daughter's college expenses in 19X12 (but in no other year). W dies in 19X18. Has the trust been tax-effective?

23. The O Trust has generated $40,000 in depreciation deductions for 19X9. Its accounting income for that year is $21,000. In computing this amount, pursuant to the trust document, depreciation was allocated to corpus. Accounting income was distributed at the trustee's discretion: $15,000 to Mr. H and $6,000 to Ms. J.

(a) Compute the depreciation deductions that H, J, and O may claim.

(b) Same as (a), except that depreciation was allocated to income.

(c) Same as (a), except that the trustee distributed $6,000 each to H and to J and retained the remaining accounting income.

(d) Same as (a), except that O is an estate (and not a trust).

24. For each of the following independent cases, describe a tax planning situation in which the tax adviser properly would suggest the following:

(a) A grantor trust be created.

(b) Trust accumulations be made, even though the tax on accumulation distributions will be levied on the eventual payments.

(c) A transfer of an appreciated asset to a trust be made, even though the § 644 tax will be levied on the entity.

## Comprehensive Tax Return Problem

Prepare the 1985 Fiduciary Income Tax Return (Form 1041) for the Kathryn Anne Thomas Trust. In addition, determine the amount and character of the income and expense items that each beneficiary must report for 1985 and prepare a Schedule K-1 for Harold Thomas.

The 1985 activities of the trust include the following:

| | |
|---|---:|
| Office building rental income | $600,000 |
| Rental expenses: | |
|   Management | 85,000 |
|   Utilities and maintenance | 375,000 |
|   Taxes and insurance | 115,000 |
|   Straight-line cost recovery | 200,000 |
| Taxable interest income | 100,000 |
| Tax-exempt interest income | 50,000 |
| Net long-term capital gains | 265,000 |
| Fiduciary's fees | 120,000 |

Under the terms of the trust instrument, depreciation, net capital gains and losses, and one-third of the fiduciary's fees are allocable to corpus. The trustee is required to distribute $100,000 to Harold every year. In 1985, the trustee distributed $100,000 to Harold and $20,000 to Patricia Thomas. No other distributions were made.

The trustee, Wisconsin State National Bank, is located at 3100 East Wisconsin Avenue, Milwaukee, WI 53201. Its employer identification number is 84-7602487.

Harold lives at 9880 East North Avenue, Shorewood, WI 53211. His identification number is 498-01-8058.

Patricia lives at 6772 East Oklahoma Avenue, St. Francis, WI 53204. Her identification number is 499-02-6531.

## Research Problems

*Research Problem 1.* Thanks to a recent speech that you gave to the Kiwanis Club, Y has been convinced of the tax-saving opportunities that are presented by the creation of trusts. He recognizes that a great deal of income can be shifted to the marginal income tax rates that apply to his three children, and he is willing to give up as much control over the trust corpus assets as is necessary to avoid a grantor trust classification.

Y is very enthusiastic about trusts—so much so, that he instructs you to place $30,000 each into 12 trusts for each of his children. These 36 trusts would be administered separately by you, as trustee, but they would differ only in the assets that are used to fund them and in the termination date specified in the trust instrument. Specifically, one of each child's 12 trusts is scheduled to terminate annually, commencing in 15 years. Can the proliferation of multiple trusts, given the same grantor, the same trustee, the same beneficiaries, but different corpus assets and termination dates, be accepted under prevailing tax law?

*Partial list of research aids:*

Code § 643(e).

*Estelle Morris Trusts,* 51 T.C. 20 (1968).

*Edward L. Stephenson Trust,* 81 T.C. 283 (1983).

*Research Problem 2.* In May 19X9, F creates a trust, income payable to his daughter (D), reversion to F or his estate, upon the earlier of D's death or 10 years and 1 month from the date of creation of the trust. The trust is funded with 1,000 shares of X Corporation common stock valued at $100,000 and having a basis to F of $20,000. Discuss the potential tax consequences to F for each of the following independent situations:

(a) To minimize the expenses of the trust, F designates himself trustee.

(b) On April 15, 19X9, dividends were declared on the X Corporation stock, payable to shareholders of record on June 1, 19X9.

(c) As a result of a broad decline in stock market prices during the summer months of 19X9, the independent trustee sells 500 shares of X Corporation stock for $45,000 and reinvests the proceeds in U.S. Treasury bills yielding 12% interest and maturing in one year.

(d) Two years after creation of the trust, and at the insistence of his daughter, F transfers 200 shares of Y Corporation common stock to the trust. The stock is worth $50,000 and has a dividend-paying record of at least 10% annually.

*Partial list of research aids:*

Code §§ 644, 673, 674, and 677.

Reg. §§ 1.676(b)–1 and 1.677(a)–1(f).

*M. G. Anton,* 34 T.C. 842 (1960).

*C. O. Bibby,* 44 T.C. 638 (1965).

*Research Problem 3.* Two physicians, P and M, practice in a partnership known as the P-M Clinic. They own the clinic as tenants in common. In November 19X6, they approach you with a plan to create reversionary trusts for their children. Each trust would have slightly more than a 10-year life, and each physician would transfer her undivided one-half interest in the clinic property into a trust for her children. A bank will serve as an independent trustee for each physician's grantor trust. On the day following the creation of the trusts, the P-M partnership is to enter into a lease agreement with the bank trustee for a period of 10 years. Their questions for your review and comments are as follows:

(a) Is this plan a viable income tax planning effort to get deductible contributions in the form of rent payments into a trust for the children?

(b) What could go wrong?

(c) Can you recommend a better plan?

*Partial list of research aids:*

*Perry v. U.S.,* 75–2 USTC ¶ 9629, 36 AFTR2d 75–5500, 520 F.2d 235 (CA–4, 1975).

*Mathews v. Comm.,* 75–2 USTC ¶ 9734, 36 AFTR2d 75–5965, 520 F.2d 323 (CA–5, 1975).

*Hudspeth v. Comm.,* 75–1 USTC ¶ 9224, 35 AFTR2d 75–676, 509 F.2d 1224 (CA–9, 1975).

*Research Problem 4.* Your client has come to you for some advice regarding gifts of property. She has just learned that she must undergo major surgery, and she would like to make certain gifts before entering the hospital. On your earlier advice, she had established a plan of lifetime giving for four prior years. Consider each of the following assets that she is considering to use as gifts to family and friends. In doing so, evaluate the income tax consequences of having such property pass through her estate to the designated legatee.

(a) She plans to give a cottage to her son to fulfill a promise made many years ago. The cottage has been owned by your client for the past 15 years and has a basis to her of $30,000 (fair market value of $20,000).

(b) Since she has $100,000 of long-term capital losses that she has been carrying forward for the past few years, she is considering making a gift of $200,000 in installment notes to her daughter. Her basis in the notes is $100,000, and the notes' current fair market value is $190,000.

(c) She has promised to make a special cash bequest of $25,000 to her grandson in her will. However, she does not anticipate having that much cash immediately available after her death. She requests your advice concerning the income tax consequences to the estate if the cash bequest is settled with some other property.

*Research Problem 5.* T has successfully operated a home appliance center in Springfield, Illinois, for the past eight years. The business has been conducted under the name of T's Appliance Center, Inc., and T is the sole shareholder. Until recently, the appliance center was located on rented premises owned by another local merchant. Last year, T purchased land located nearby and constructed a suitable building at a cost of $185,000. The building was completed on August 31, 1981. On the same date, T transferred the property to the "T Short-Term Irrevocable Trust," and his wife, W, was named the trustee. The trust instrument provided that the trust was to terminate 10 years and 10 days after the last contribution to it was made. All of the trust accounting income was to be paid annually to T and W's three children (ranging in age from two to eight years) or for their benefit, with all capital gains and losses being allocated to corpus. At the termination of the trust, all accrued but undistributed income was to be distributed to the children or to their appointees, and all trust corpus was to revert to T.

As trustee, W was given the power to invest, rent, sell, or exchange trust property and the power to loan trust property to any person with provision for reasonable interest and security. She immediately leased the building to T's Appliance Center, Inc., for 10 years at a monthly rental of $1,500. The lease terms were drafted in accordance with the advice of a local real estate broker as to a reasonable rent and lease period.

After noticing that the trust has accumulated over $30,000 of cash, T seeks your advice as to what interest rate and repayment terms should be required if he borrows the cash surplus from the trust. What would be your advice in light of § 675?

# Tax Administration and Practice  14

CHAPTER OUTLINE

CHAPTER OBJECTIVES

—Summarize the organization and structure of the IRS.
—Examine the various administrative pronouncements issued by the IRS and evaluate how they can be used in tax practice.
—Review the audit process, including how returns are selected for audit and the various types of audits conducted by the IRS.
—Explain how interest on a deficiency or a refund is determined and when it is due.
—Discuss the various penalties that can be imposed on acts of noncompliance by taxpayers.
—Review the rules governing the statute of limitations on assessments and on refunds.
—Summarize the statutory and nonstatutory prohibitions and guides for those engaged in tax practice.

# TAX ADMINISTRATION

To provide quality tax consulting services it is necessary to understand how the IRS is organized and how its various administrative groups function. For example, the taxpayer may object to a proposed deficiency assessment resulting from an IRS audit. The tax specialist must be familiar with IRS administrative appeal procedures to make a fully informed decision concerning appeal of the deficiency.

## ORGANIZATIONAL STRUCTURE

The responsibility for administering the tax laws rests with the Treasury Department. The Internal Revenue Service, as part of the Department of the Treasury, has been delegated the operational aspects of enforcing the tax law.

Key positions within the IRS organizational chart and the major responsibilities of these positions are summarized in Figures I and II. An organizational chart depicting the interrelationship of positions described by Figures I and II appears in Figure III.

## IRS PROCEDURE—INDIVIDUAL RULINGS

Rulings that are issued by the National Office represent a written statement of the position of the IRS concerning the tax consequences of a course of action contemplated by the taxpayer. Individual rulings do not have the force and effect of law, but they do provide guidance and support for taxpayers in similar transactions. The IRS will issue rulings only on uncompleted, actual (rather than hypothetical) transactions or on transactions that have been completed prior to the filing of the tax return for the year in question.

The IRS will not, in certain circumstances, issue a ruling. It will not rule in cases that essentially involve a question of fact.[1] For example, no ruling will be issued to determine whether compensation paid to employees is reasonable in amount and therefore allowable as a deduction.[2]

A ruling simply represents the current opinion of the IRS on the tax consequences of a particular transaction with a given set of facts. IRS rulings are not immutable. They are frequently declared obsolete or superseded by new revenue rulings in response to tax law changes. However,

---

1. Rev.Proc. 86–1, I.R.B. No. 1, 6.
2. Rev.Proc. 86–3, I.R.B. No. 1, 26.

**Figure I**

ORGANIZATION OF THE IRS NATIONAL OFFICE

*Duties*

| | |
|---|---|
| 1. Commissioner of Internal Revenue | The Commissioner is appointed by the President. His responsibilities are to establish policy, to supervise the activities of the entire IRS organization, and to act in an advisory capacity to the Treasury on legislative matters. |
| 2. Deputy Commissioner | The Deputy Commissioner provides overall coordination and direction, advises the Commissioner in planning and controlling IRS policies and programs, and provides line supervision over three (3) Associate Commissioners and seven (7) Regional Commissioners. |
| 3. Associate Commissioners (3) A. Operations | Advises the Commissioner on policy matters affecting operations and is responsible for the operating functions (among which are approval and examination of Employee Plans and Exempt Organizations, investigation of criminal fraud, examination of tax returns, collection of delinquent accounts, and the Tax Information program). Under the supervision of this Associate Commissioner are four (4) Assistant Commissioners. |
| B. Policy and Management | Advises on policy matters affecting agency administration and is responsible for the administrative functions (among which are tax forms and publications design, printing, and distribution; personnel and administration; training and employee development; management information systems; and fiscal management). Three (3) Assistant Commissioners are under the supervision of this Associate Commissioner. |
| C. Data Processing | Principal adviser on and serves as spokesperson for the data processing functions (among which are designing, developing, testing, and maintaining computer software used; processing of tax returns and information documents; accounting for all revenues collected by the Service; and maintaining master files of all taxpayer accounts). There are two (2) Assistant Commissioners under the supervision of this Associate Commissioner. |
| 4. Chief Counsel | The Chief Counsel defends the IRS in the Tax Court and participates with the Department of Justice in other tax litigation, reviews rulings, prepares proposed regulations, and is charged with the Corporation Tax Division, Individual Tax Division, and Appeals Division. |

revocation or modification of a ruling is usually not applied retroactively to the taxpayer who received the ruling if he or she acted in good faith in reliance upon the ruling and if the facts in the ruling request were in agreement with the completed transaction. The IRS may revoke any ruling if, upon subsequent audit, the agent finds a misstatement or omission of facts or substantial discrepancies between the facts in the ruling request

**Figure II**

ORGANIZATION OF THE IRS FIELD ORGANIZATION

*Duties*

| | |
|---|---|
| 1. Regional Commissioners (7) | 1. Establish regional standards, programs, and policies and have final settlement authority in the administrative appeal procedure for disputed tax deficiencies. |
| 2. District Directors (63) | 2. Establish primary contact with taxpayers; collect delinquent taxes; perform audit work, including the selection of taxpayers for audit; issue determination letter to taxpayers. |
| 3. Service Centers (10) | 3. Serve as primary centers for tax return processing work, including selection of returns for audit. |

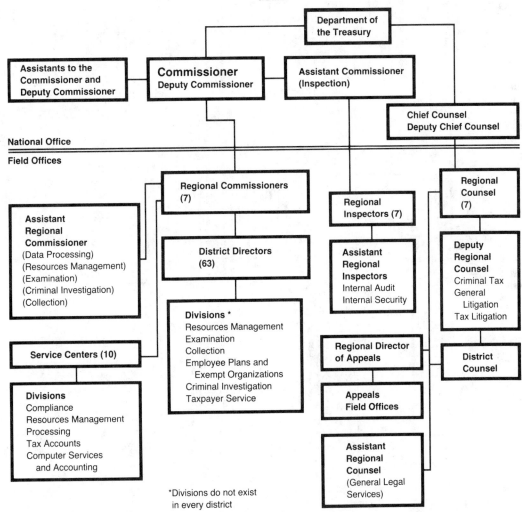

and the actual situation. A ruling may be relied upon only by the taxpayer who requested and received it.

Issuance of rulings benefits both the IRS and the taxpayer. The IRS ruling policy is an attempt to promote a uniform application of the tax

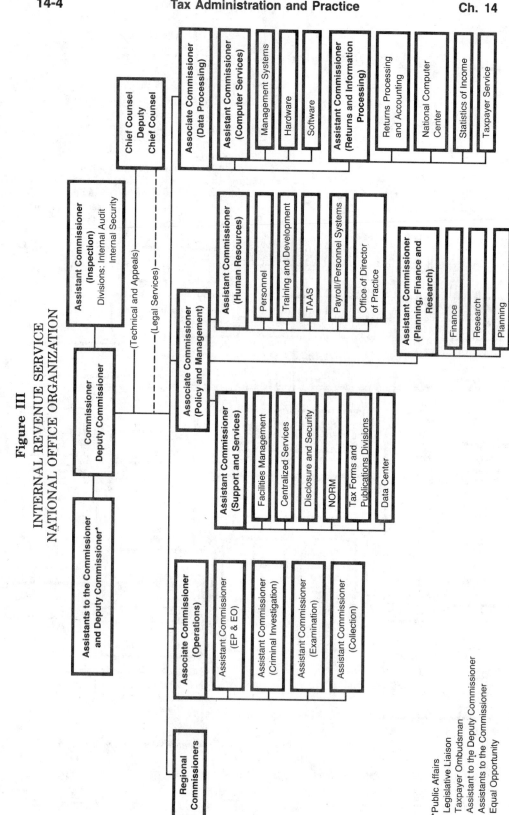

**Figure III**
**INTERNAL REVENUE SERVICE**
**NATIONAL OFFICE ORGANIZATION**

laws. In addition, other benefits may accrue to the government through the issuance of rulings. Rulings may reduce the volume of litigation or number of disputes with revenue agents that would otherwise result, and they give the IRS an awareness of the significant transactions being consummated by taxpayers. From the taxpayer's point of view, an advance ruling reduces the uncertainty of potential tax consequences resulting from a proposed course of action. Taxpayers frequently request a ruling prior to the consummation of a tax-free corporate reorganization because of the severe tax consequences that would result if the reorganization is subsequently deemed to be taxable. Liquidations, stock redemptions, and transfers to controlled corporations under § 351 are other sensitive areas in which taxpayers want confirmation.

Individual rulings that are of both sufficient importance and general interest may be published as Revenue Rulings (in anonymous form) and thus made available to all taxpayers. Prior to 1976, the position of the IRS was that unpublished (letter) rulings were confidential information and should not be made available to other taxpayers. This position was successfully challenged by taxpayers as being in violation of the Freedom of Information Act.[3] Due to this litigation, the Tax Reform Act of 1976 inserted new provisions regarding public disclosure of IRS written determinations.[4] In general, all unpublished letter rulings, determination letters, and technical advice memoranda are now open to public inspection once identifying details and certain confidential information have been deleted. Letter rulings and technical advice memoranda now are reprinted and published by Prentice-Hall and Commerce Clearing House. The general availability of such materials assists in the conduct of tax research and planning.

## IRS PROCEDURE—ADDITIONAL ISSUANCES

In addition to unpublished letter rulings and published rulings, the IRS also issues the following:

—Revenue procedures.

—Determination letters.

—Technical advices.

Determination letters are issued by the District Director for completed transactions when the issues involved are covered by judicial or statutory authority, regulations, or rulings. Determination letters are issued for various death, gift, income, excise, and employment tax matters.

**Example 1.** T Corporation recently opened a car clinic and has employed numerous mechanics. The corporation is not certain if the mechanics are to be treated as employees or as independent contractors for withholding and payroll tax purposes. T Corporation may request a determination letter from the appropriate District Director.

---

3. *Tax Analysts and Advocates v. Comm.*, 74–2 USTC ¶ 9635, 34 AFTR2d 74–5731, 505 F.2d 352 (CA–DC, 1974).
4. § 6110.

**Example 2.**  Assume the same facts as in Example 1. T Corporation would like to establish a pension plan that qualifies for the tax advantages of § § 401 through 404. To determine whether the plan qualifies, a determination letter can be requested and obtained from the IRS.

**Example 3.**  A group of physicians plans to form an association to construct and operate a hospital. The determination letter procedure is appropriate to ascertain the group's status—either subject to the Federal income tax or tax-exempt.

Technical advice is rendered by the National Office to the District Director and/or Regional Commissioner in response to the specific request of an agent, Appellate Conferee, or District Director. The taxpayer may ask that a request for technical advice be made if an issue in dispute is not treated by the law or precedent and/or published rulings or regulations. Technical advice also is appropriate when there is reason to believe that the tax law is not being administered consistently by the IRS. For example, a taxpayer may inquire why an agent proposes to disallow a certain expenditure when agents in other districts permit the deduction.

## THE AUDIT PROCESS

*Selection of Returns for Audit.*  The IRS uses the Discriminant Function System (DIF) as a starting point in the selection of tax returns for audit. This selection procedure utilizes mathematical formulas to select tax returns that are most likely to contain errors and yield substantial amounts of additional tax revenues upon audit. Despite the use of computer selection processes, the ultimate selection of returns for audit is still conducted by the classification staff within the Audit Division of the IRS.

The IRS does not openly disclose all of its audit selection techniques.[5] However, the following observations can be made regarding the probability of a return's selection for audit:

—Certain groups of taxpayers are subject to audit more frequently than others. These groups include individuals with gross income in excess of $50,000, self-employed individuals with substantial business income and deductions, and cash businesses where the potential for tax evasion is high.

**Example 4.**  T owns and operates a liquor store on a cash-and-carry basis. As all of T's sales are for cash, T might well be a prime candidate for an audit by the IRS. Obviously, cash transactions are easier to conceal than those made on credit.

—If a taxpayer has been audited in a past year and such audit led to the assessment of a substantial deficiency, a return visit by the IRS is to be expected.

---

**5.**  Under the Freedom of Information Act, taxpayers have sued the IRS to disclose the criteria used to develop standards for auditing tax returns. The status of these cases is still not clear. However, the tax law amended § 6103(b)(2) to provide that nothing in any Federal law shall be interpreted to require disclosure of standards used for the selection of returns for examination. This change is applicable to disclosures after July 19, 1981.

—An audit might materialize if information returns (e. g., Form W–2, Form 1099) are not in substantial agreement with the income reported on taxpayer's return.[6]

—If an individual's itemized deductions are in excess of norms established for various income levels, the probability of an audit is increased. Also, certain types of deductions (e. g., casualty and theft losses, office in the home, tax-sheltered investments) are sensitive areas, since the IRS realizes that many taxpayers will determine the amount of the deduction incorrectly or may not be entitled to the deduction at all.

—The filing of a refund claim by the taxpayer may prompt an audit of the return.

—Certain returns are selected on a random sample basis [known as the Taxpayer Compliance Measurement Program (TCMP)] to develop, update, and improve the DIF formulas (see above). TCMP is the long-range research effort of the IRS designed to measure and evaluate taxpayer compliance characteristics. TCMP audits are tedious and time-consuming, since the taxpayer generally is asked to verify most or all items on the tax return.

—Information is often obtained from other sources (e. g., other government agencies, news items, informants).

**Example 5.** T reports to the police that while he was out of town his home was burglarized and one of the items taken was a shoe box containing cash of $25,000. A representative of the IRS reading the newspaper account of the burglary might well wonder why someone would keep such a large amount of cash in a shoe box at home.

**Example 6.** After 15 years, B is discharged by her employer, Dr. F. Shortly thereafter, the IRS receives a letter from B informing it that Dr. F keeps two sets of books, one of which substantially understates his cash receipts.[7]

Many individual taxpayers mistakenly assume that if they do not hear from the IRS within a few weeks following the filing of the return or if they have received a refund check, no audit will be forthcoming. As a practical matter, most individual returns are examined within two years from the date of filing. If not, they generally remain unaudited. All large corporations are subject to annual audits; and in many instances, tax years will remain open for extended periods, since the taxpayer may agree to waive the statute of limitations pending settlement of unresolved issues.

*Verification and Audit Procedures.* The tax return is initially checked for mathematical accuracy. A check is also made for deductions, exclu-

---

6. Over the years, the IRS has been able to correlate an increasing number of information returns with the returns filed by taxpayers.

7. Section 7623 and Reg. § 301.7623–1 enable the IRS to pay rewards to persons who provide information that leads to the detection and punishment of those who violate the tax laws. Such rewards may not exceed 10% of the taxes, fines, and penalties recovered as a result of such information.

sions, etc., that are clearly erroneous. An obvious error would be the failure to comply with the five percent limitation on the deduction for medical expenses. In such cases, the Service Center merely sends the taxpayer revised computations and a bill for the corrected amount of tax if the error results in additional tax liability. Taxpayers usually are able to settle such matters through direct correspondence with the IRS without the necessity of a formal audit.

Office audits are conducted by a representative of the District Director's Office either in the office of the IRS or through correspondence. Individual returns with few or no items of business income are usually handled through the office audit procedure. In most instances, the taxpayer will be required merely to substantiate a deduction, credit, or item of income that appears on the return.

> **Example 7.**  An individual may have claimed medical expenses that are in excess of a normal amount for taxpayers on a comparable income level. The taxpayer will be asked to present documentation in the form of cancelled checks, invoices, etc., for the items in question. Note the substantiation procedure here that is absent from the mathematical check and simple error discovery process mentioned above.

The field audit procedure is commonly used for corporate returns and for returns of individuals engaged in business or professional activities. This type of audit generally entails a more complete examination of a taxpayer's transactions. By way of contrast, an office audit usually is directed towards fewer items and is therefore narrower in scope.

A field audit is conducted by IRS agents at the office or home of the taxpayer or at the office of the taxpayer's representative. It is common practice for tax firms to hold conferences with IRS agents in the firm's office during the field audit of a corporate client. The agent's work may be facilitated by a review of certain tax workpapers and discussions with the taxpayer's representative relative to items appearing on the tax return.

Upon a showing of good cause, a taxpayer may request and obtain a reassignment of his or her case from an office to a field audit. The inconvenience and expense involved in transporting records and other supporting data to the agent's office may constitute good cause for reassignment.

*Settlement with the Revenue Agent.*  Following the audit, the IRS agent may either accept the return as filed or recommend certain adjustments. The Revenue Agent's Report (RAR) is reviewed by the agent's group supervisor and the Review Staff within the IRS. In most instances, the agent's proposed adjustments are approved. However, it is not uncommon for the Review Staff or group supervisor to request additional information or to raise new issues.

Agents must adhere strictly to IRS policy as reflected in published rulings, Regulations, and other releases. The agent cannot settle an unresolved issue based upon the probability of winning the case in court. Usually, issues involving factual questions can be settled at the agent level, and it may be advantageous for both the taxpayer and the IRS to reach agreement at the earliest point in the settlement process. For example, it may be to the taxpayer's advantage to reach agreement at the agent level and avoid any further opportunity for the IRS to raise new issues.

A deficiency (an amount in excess of tax shown on the return or tax previously assessed) may be proposed at the agent level. The taxpayer might wish to pursue to a higher level the disputed issues upon which this deficiency is based. The taxpayer's progress through the appeal process is discussed in subsequent sections of this chapter.

If agreement is reached upon the proposed deficiency, Form 870 (Waiver of Restrictions on Assessment and Collection of Deficiency in Tax) is signed by the taxpayer. One advantage to the taxpayer of signing Form 870 at this point is that interest stops accumulating on the deficiency 30 days after the form is filed.[8] When this form is signed, the taxpayer effectively waives his or her right to the receipt of a statutory notice of deficiency (i. e., the 90-day letter) and to subsequent petition to the Tax Court. In addition, it is no longer possible for the taxpayer to go to the Appeals Division. The signing of Form 870 at the agent level generally closes the case. However, since Form 870 does not have the effect of a closing agreement, even after the taxpayer pays the deficiency, the taxpayer may subsequently sue for refund of the tax in a Federal District Court or in the Claims Court. Further, the IRS is not restricted by Form 870 and may assess additional deficiencies if deemed necessary.

Figure IV contains a flow chart representing the audit process from selection of return for audit to settlement at, or appeal from, the agent level.

### THE TAXPAYER APPEAL PROCESS

If agreement cannot be reached at the agent level, the taxpayer receives a copy of the Revenue Agent's Report and a transmittal letter, which is commonly referred to as the 30-day letter. The taxpayer is granted 30 days to request an administrative appeal. If an appeal is not requested, a statutory notice of deficiency will be issued (i. e., the 90-day letter).

If an appeal is desired, an appropriate request must be made to the Appeals Division. Such request must be accompanied by a written protest except in the following cases:

    —The proposed tax deficiency does not exceed $2,500 for any of the tax periods involved in the audit.

    —The deficiency resulted from a correspondence or office audit (i. e., not as a result of a field audit).

The Appeals Division is authorized to settle all tax disputes based on the hazards of litigation. Since the Appeals Division has final settlement authority until a statutory notice of deficiency (i. e., the 90-day letter) has been issued, the taxpayer may be able to obtain a percentage settlement. In addition, an overall favorable settlement may be reached through a "trading" of disputed issues. The Appeals Division occasionally may raise new issues if the grounds are substantial and of significant tax impact.

Both the Appeals Division and the taxpayer have the right to request technical advice from the National Office of the IRS. When technical advice is favorable to the taxpayer, the Appeals Division is bound by such

---

8. § 6601(c).

**Figure IV**

INCOME TAX APPEAL PROCEDURE OF THE
INTERNAL REVENUE SERVICE

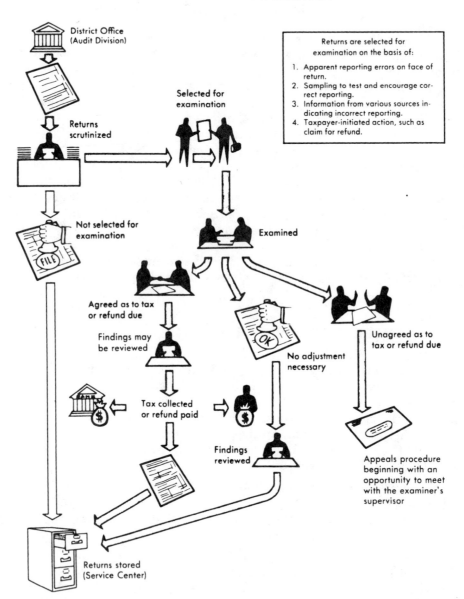

advice. If the technical advice, however, is favorable to the IRS, the Appeals Division may nevertheless settle the case based on the hazards of litigation.

In a hazard of litigation situation, the facts are known but the application of the law to such facts may be uncertain. Also, there could be some question about establishing the facts with clear certainty, as might be the case when the taxpayer or a witness is not expected to give convincing testimony. Another possibility might involve situations where the facts are so ambiguous that they could, by different interpretation, lead to contrary tax results.

> **Example 8.** At the time of the audit of T, the corporation that T controls had advances outstanding to T in the amount of $20,000. The IRS field agent held that these advances were constructive dividends to T (refer to the discussion in Chapter 4). Some facts point toward this result (e. g., the corporation is closely-held, T has made no repayments, and the loan balance has increased over several years). Other facts, however, appear to indicate that these advances are bona fide loans (e. g., the advances are evidenced by a written instrument with interest provided for, T has the independent means of repayment, and the corporation has a good dividend-paying record). The Appeals Division and taxpayer's representative assess the hazards of litigation as being 50% for each side. Thus, if T chose to take the issue to court, she would have an even chance of winning or losing her case. Based on this assessment, both sides agree to treat $10,000 of the advance as a dividend and $10,000 as a bona fide loan. The agreement enables T to avoid $10,000 of dividend income (i. e., the loan portion) and saves her the cost of litigating the issue.

By going to the Appeals Division, therefore, the taxpayer was able to obtain a satisfactory settlement otherwise unobtainable from the agent.

If agreement cannot be reached with the Appeals Division, the IRS issues a statutory notice of deficiency (90-day letter), which gives the taxpayer 90 days to file a petition with the Tax Court. (See Figure V for a review of the income tax appeal procedures, including the consideration of claims for refund.) After the case has been docketed in the Tax Court, the taxpayer has the opportunity to arrange for possible pretrial settlement with the Regional Counsel of the IRS. The Appeals Division settlement power is transferred to the Regional Counsel when the case is docketed for a Tax Court trial after the issuance of the statutory notice of deficiency.[9]

Taxpayers who file a petition with the U. S. Tax Court have the option of having their case heard before the informal Small Claims Division if the amount of the deficiency or claimed overpayment does not exceed $10,000.[10] If the Small Claims Division is used, neither party may appeal the case and the decisions of the Small Claims Division are not treated as precedents for other cases.

The economic costs of a settlement offer from the Appeals Division should be weighed against the costs of litigation and the probability of winning the case. Consideration should be given to the impact of such settlement upon the tax liability for future periods, in addition to the years under audit.

If a settlement is reached with the Appeals Division, the taxpayer is required to sign Form 870AD. The IRS considers this settlement to be binding upon both parties, absent fraud, malfeasance, concealment, or mis-

---

9. Rev.Proc. 78–9, 1978–1 C.B. 563.
10. § 7463(a).

## Figure V

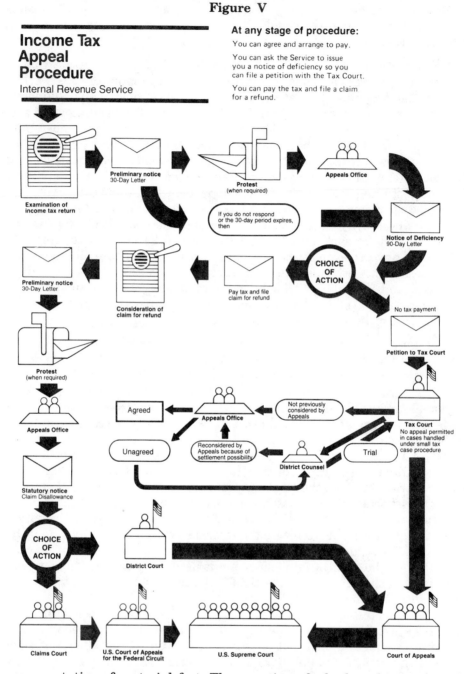

**Income Tax Appeal Procedure**
Internal Revenue Service

**At any stage of procedure:**

You can agree and arrange to pay.

You can ask the Service to issue you a notice of deficiency so you can file a petition with the Tax Court.

You can pay the tax and file a claim for a refund.

representation of material fact. The question of whether this settlement form is binding upon the taxpayer (whether settlement prevents the taxpayer from filing a subsequent refund claim and suit for refund) has been litigated with conflicting results.[11]

---

11. Compare *Stair v. U. S.*, 75–1 USTC ¶ 9463, 35 AFTR2d 75–1515, 516 F.2d 560 (CA–2, 1975), with *Unita Livestock Corp. v. U. S.*, 66–1 USTC ¶ 9193, 17 AFTR2d 254, 355 F.2d 761 (CA–10, 1966).

## INTEREST

An important consideration for the taxpayer during negotiations with the IRS is the interest that accrues upon overpayments, deficiency assessments, and unpaid taxes. A taxpayer can effectively stop the accrual of interest upon a deficiency assessment by signing Form 870 and paying the tax. This action can then be followed by a suit in a Federal District Court or the Claims Court for recovery of the amount of the tax payment. If the Tax Court is selected as a forum, the tax usually is not paid and interest continues to accrue.

*Determination of the Interest Rate.* In 1975, Congress began to recognize that the interest rate applicable to Federal tax underpayments and overpayments should be made more realistic in terms of what occurs in the business world. Accordingly, the Code was changed to authorize the IRS to adjust the percentage every two years to conform with commercial rates. A further amendment in 1981 changed the guidelines to provide for annual adjustments (as of each January 1) based on the average prime rate for the preceding September.

Legislation enacted in 1982 goes one step further by amending § 6621(b) to sanction semiannual adjustments as of January 1 and July 1 of each year. The adjustments are to be based on the average prime rate for the six months ending on the last day of the previous September or March, as the case may be. For 1986, the interest rate from January 1 through June 30 was set at 10 percent and from July 1 through December 31 at 9 percent. Prior interest rates are summarized in Figure VI.

Figure VI is not of mere historical interest. In cases of deficiency assessments or claims for refund, interest in computed in accordance with the rates in effect during the period involved.

**Example 9.** T, a calendar year taxpayer, is audited by the IRS in March 1986 and is assessed a deficiency for the return he timely filed for calendar year 1983. Since interest begins to run from the due date of the return (April 15, 1984, in T's case), the applicable rates are 11%, 13%, 11%, and 10%.

In the case of assessments where the statute of limitations is not applicable (e. g., no return was filed or fraud was involved—see later in the

## Figure VI
### PRIOR INTEREST RATES

| Applicable Period | Rate |
|---|---|
| July 1, 1985, thru December 31, 1985 | 11% |
| January 1, 1985, thru June 30, 1985 | 13 |
| July 1, 1983, thru December 31, 1984 | 11 |
| January 1, 1983, thru June 30, 1983 | 16 |
| February 1, 1982, thru December 31, 1982 | 20 |
| February 1, 1980, thru January 31, 1982 | 12 |
| February 1, 1978, thru January 31, 1980 | 6 |
| February 1, 1976, thru January 31, 1978 | 7 |
| July 1, 1975, thru January 31, 1976 | 9 |
| Prior to July of 1975 | 6 |

chapter), determining the interest element could prove to be a mathematical nightmare.

> **Example 10.** T, a calendar year taxpayer, did not file a gift tax return (Form 709) for a taxable gift made in 1974. On audit by the IRS in early 1986, she is assessed a deficiency. The interest computation on the deficiency would have to cover the full range of Figure VI.

*Computation of the Amount of Interest.* Prior law required that any interest on a deficiency or a refund be determined using the simple-interest method. For interest accruing after 1982, § 6622 requires that the amount be compounded daily. Depending on the interest rate applicable, the daily compounding approach conceivably could double the principal amount over a period of five years or so. Consequently, this change in the method of computing interest should not be taken lightly.

The IRS has prepared and made available tables through which the daily compounded amount can be determined. Such tables will ease the burden of those who prepare late returns where additional taxes are due.[12]

The old rule (i. e., the simple-interest method) continues to apply to the penalty on underpayments of estimated tax by individuals and corporations. However, the semiannual interest rate adjustments (discussed above) will have to be used in arriving at the amount of the underpayment-of-estimated-tax penalty.

*IRS Deficiency Assessments.* Under § 6601(c) interest usually accrues from the unextended due date of the return until 30 days after the taxpayer agrees to the deficiency by signing Form 870. If the taxpayer does not pay the amount shown on the IRS's "notice and demand" (tax bill) within 10 days, interest again accrues on the deficiency. However, no interest is imposed upon the portion of the tax bill that represents interest on the previous deficiency.

*Refund of Taxpayer's Overpayments.* If the overpayment is refunded to the taxpayer within 45 days after the date the return is filed or is due, no interest is allowed. Interest is authorized, however, when the taxpayer files an amended return or makes a claim for refund of prior year's tax (e. g., when net operating loss or investment credit carrybacks result in refunds of prior year's tax payments).

In the past and in the light of high interest rates of up to 20 percent (refer to Figure VI), it has proven advantageous for many taxpayers to delay filing various tax returns that lead to refunds. Thus, the IRS was placed in the unfortunate role of providing taxpayers with a high-yield savings account. Amendments to §§ 6601 and 6611 are intended to end this practice. The gist of the amendments is to preclude any interest accruing on a refund until such time as the IRS is properly notified of the refund.

Specifically the new law (applicable to returns filed 30 days after September 3, 1982) places taxpayers applying for refunds in the following described positions:

> —When a return is filed after the due date, interest on any overpayment accrues from the date of filing. However, no interest will be due if the IRS makes the refund within 45 days of the date of filing.

---

12. These tables can be found in Rev.Proc. 83–7, 1983–1 C.B. 583.

**Example 11.** T, a calendar year taxpayer, files her return for 1985 on December 2, 1986, such return reflecting an overwithholding of $2,500. On June 10, 1987, T receives a refund of her 1985 overpayment. Under these circumstances, the interest on T's refund begins to accrue on December 2, 1986.

**Example 12.** Assume the same facts as in Example 11, except that the refund is paid to T on January 10, 1987 (rather than June 10, 1987). No interest would be due on the refund, as it has been made within 45 days of the filing of the return.

—In no event will interest accrue on an overpayment unless the return that is filed is in "processible form." Generally, this means that the return must contain enough information to enable the IRS to identify the taxpayer and to determine the tax (and overpayment) involved.

—In the case of a carryback situation (e. g., net operating loss, capital loss, certain tax credits), interest on any refund will commence accruing on the due date of the return (disregarding extensions) for the year in which such carryback arises. Even then, however, no interest will accrue until a return is filed or, if filed, the IRS pays the refund within 45 days.

**Example 13.** X Corporation, a calendar year taxpayer, incurs a net operating loss during 1985 which it can carry back to tax year 1982 for a refund. On December 27, 1986, it files a Form 1139 (Corporate Application for Tentative Refund) claiming the refund. The earliest that interest can commence accruing in this situation is March 15, 1986, but since the return was not filed until December 27, 1986, the later date controls. If, however, the IRS pays the refund within 45 days of December 27, 1986, no interest is due.

## PENALTIES

A penalty is treated as an addition to the tax liability rather than a deductible interest expense.[13] Some taxpayers mistakenly believe that penalties are deductible and do not fully appreciate the consequences of actions that trigger the imposition of such penalties.

*Failure to File and Failure to Pay.* For a failure to file a tax return by the due date (including extensions), a penalty of five percent per month (up to a maximum of 25 percent) is imposed on the amount of tax shown as due on the return.[14]

For a failure to pay the tax due as shown on the return, a penalty of one-half of one percent per month (up to a maximum of 25 percent) is imposed on the amount of the tax. A comparable penalty is assessed if the taxpayer fails to pay a deficiency assessment within 10 days.

In all of these cases, a fraction of a month counts as a full month. Also note that these penalties relate to the net amount of the tax due.

---

13. § 6662.
14. § 6651(a).

**Example 14.** T, a calendar year taxpayer, has $18,000 withheld for income taxes by her employer during 1985. Her total tax liability for 1985 proves to be $20,000. Without obtaining an extension from the IRS, she files her Form 1040 in early August of 1986 and encloses a check for the balance due of $2,000. The failure to file and the failure to pay penalties apply to the $2,000.

During any month in which both the failure to file penalty and the failure to pay penalty apply, the failure to file penalty is reduced by the amount of the failure to pay penalty.[15]

**Example 15.** R files his tax return 10 days after the due date. Along with the return he remits a check for $3,000, which is the balance of the tax owed by R. Disregarding the interest element, R's total penalties are as follows:

| | | |
|---|---:|---:|
| Failure to pay penalty (½ of 1% × $3,000) | | $ 15 |
| Plus: | | |
| Failure to file penalty (5% × $3,000) | $ 150 | |
| Less failure to pay penalty for the same period | 15 | |
| Failure to file penalty | | 135 |
| Total penalties | | $ 150 |

In Example 15, note that the penalties for one full month are imposed even though R was delinquent by only 10 days. Unlike the method used to compute interest, any part of a month is treated as a whole month.

Because the existing penalty for failure to file may not serve as a significant enough deterrent when the tax due is small or the delay in filing is short, § 6651(a) was amended to provide for a minimum penalty. The minimum penalty is the *lesser* of $100 or the amount of tax still due.

The minimum penalty will apply only if the return is not filed within 60 days (with allowed extensions) of its due date. A showing of reasonable cause will excuse its imposition.

The new minimum penalty is not in addition to the regular failure to file penalty. It merely is in lieu of such penalty in the event that a higher amount is the result.

When the minimum failure to file penalty applies, the amount of the failure to file penalty (when applicable) is not reduced by the failure to pay penalty. Rather, both penalties apply concurrently, and the combined total is due and owing.

**Example 16.** T, a calendar year individual taxpayer, files her 1985 return 70 days after its due date. T did not obtain an extension of time for filing her return, and such return reflects additional income tax due of $300. The regular penalty for T's delinquency would have been $45 (as determined under the procedure used in Example 15 using three months). Through the application of the minimum penalty, T's failure to file penalty will be $100. To this must be added a failure to pay penalty of $4.50 [1.5% (0.5% per month for three months) × $300], for total penalties of $104.50.

---

**15.** § 6651(c)(1).

These penalties can be avoided upon a showing by the taxpayer that the failure to file and/or failure to pay was due to reasonable cause and not due to willful neglect. The Code is silent on what constitutes reasonable cause, and the Regulations do little to clarify this important concept.[16] Court decisions, however, do set some specific criteria, summarized as follows:

—The reliance by the taxpayer on the advice of a *competent* tax adviser given in good faith provided the facts are fully disclosed to the adviser and he or she considered the specific question represents reasonable cause.[17] No reasonable cause was found, however, where the taxpayer delegated the filing task to another even if such person was an accountant or an attorney.[18]

—Not qualifying as reasonable cause includes lack of information on the due date of the return,[19] illness that does not incapacitate a taxpayer from completing a return,[20] refusal of the taxpayer's spouse to cooperate for joint return purposes,[21] and ignorance or misunderstanding of the tax law.[22]

As previously noted, an extension of time granted by the IRS will avoid the failure to file penalty. It will not, however, exonerate the taxpayer from the failure to pay penalty. But if a taxpayer, for whatever reason, is not in a position to complete the return, how is he or she able to determine the tax liability? The Regulations mercifully provide some latitude in resolving this quandary. If the extension is of the "automatic," four-month variety sanctioned by Reg. § 1.6081–4, the penalty for failure to pay will not be imposed if the additional tax liability due is no greater than 10 percent of the tax shown on the return.[23]

**Example 17.** S, a calendar year taxpayer, is self-employed and during 1985 makes quarterly payments of estimated taxes of $40,000. In early April of 1986, she applies for and obtains a four-month extension for filing her 1985 income tax return. In late May of 1986, S completes her 1985 return and delivers it to the IRS along with a check covering the additional tax that is due of $3,900. Under these circumstances, S has circumvented both the failure to file and the failure to pay penalties. She will, however, owe interest on the $3,900 that was paid late.

When the 10 percent rule is not satisfied, the failure to pay penalty will be imposed on the *full* amount due.

---

**16.** Reg. § 301.6651–1(c)(1) likens reasonable cause to the exercise of "ordinary business care and prudence" on the part of the taxpayer.

**17.** *Estate of Norman Bradley,* 35 TCM 70, T.C.Memo. 1974–17.

**18.** *U. S. v. Boyle,* 85–1 USTC ¶ 13,602, 55 AFTR2d 85–1535, 105 S.Ct. 687 (USSC, 1985).

**19.** *Beck Chemical Equipment Co.,* 27 T.C. 840 (1957).

**20.** *Jacob Gassman,* 26 TCM 213, T.C.Memo. 1967–42, and *Babetta Schmidt,* 28 T.C. 367 (1957). Compare *Estate of Kirchner,* 46 B.T.A. 578 (1942).

**21.** *Electric and Neon, Inc.,* 56 T.C. 1324 (1971).

**22.** *Stevens Brothers Foundation, Inc.,* 39 T.C. 93 (1965).

**23.** Reg. § 301.6651–1(c)(3)(i). The Regulation is premised on the assumption that satisfying the 10% rule constitutes reasonable cause.

**Example 18.** Assume the same facts as in Example 17, except that S's additional tax liability proved to be $5,000 (rather than $3,900). In this event, a failure to pay penalty will be imposed on the full $5,000 that was paid late.

*Negligence Penalty.* A penalty for underpayment of a tax liability is imposed if the underpayment is attributable to negligence or intentional disregard of rules and regulations (but without intent to defraud).[24] The amount of the penalty is five percent of the underpayment.

The negligence penalty has been assessed when a taxpayer knowingly deducts personal expenditures as business expenses[25] or claims excessive business deductions that are not supported by adequate records or other substantiation.[26] The penalty will not be imposed, however, where an error is due to an honest misunderstanding of the facts or law that might occur with an average or reasonable person.

Because of concern on the part of Congress over noncompliance by some taxpayers, § 6653 was amended (effective for taxes due after 1981) to provide a nondeductible addition-to-tax penalty equal to 50 percent of the interest attributable to that portion of an underpayment resulting in the imposition of the negligence penalty.

**Example 19.** T underpaid his taxes for 1985 in the amount of $20,000, such underpayment being attributable to negligence. If the interest on the underpayment was $4,000, T's total negligence penalty is determined as follows:

| | |
|---|---|
| Regular negligence penalty (5 percent × $20,000) | $ 1,000 |
| Penalty imposed on the interest due as a result of the negligence (50 percent × $4,000) | 2,000 |
| Total negligence penalty | $ 3,000 |

*Fraud.* A 50 percent penalty is imposed on any underpayment resulting from fraud on the part of the taxpayer. Known as the civil fraud penalty, it attaches to the deficiency assessed by the IRS and not just to the items pertaining to the fraud. When applicable, however, the penalties for failure to file and for failure to pay do not come into play. Likewise, the negligence penalty of five percent cannot be imposed.[27]

In 1982 a new penalty was added in situations where civil fraud is involved. In addition to the regular penalty, culpable taxpayers now will be assessed 50 percent of any interest attributable to the fraud.

**Example 20.** T's tax deficiency of $30,000 is entirely attributable to civil fraud. Interest on this underpayment amounts to $12,000. Thus, T owes $63,000 [$30,000 (the deficiency) + $15,000 (the civil fraud

---

**24.** § 6653(a)(1).
**25.** *James J. Arditto,* 30 TCM 866, T.C.Memo. 1971–210.
**26.** *David Axelrod,* 56 T.C. 248 (1971).
**27.** Note the precise wording of § 6653(a) [i. e., "(but without intent to defraud)"].

penalty) + $12,000 (interest on the deficiency) + $6,000 (the new penalty)].[28]

In a fraud situation, the burden of proof is on the IRS to show by a "preponderance of the evidence" that the taxpayer had a specific intent to evade a tax.[29] Although the Code and the Regulations do not provide any assistance in ascertaining what constitutes civil fraud, it seems clear that mere negligence on the part of the taxpayer (however great) will not suffice. In this regard, consideration has to be given to the particular facts involved. Fraud has been found in cases where there have been manipulation of the books,[30] substantial omissions from income,[31] and erroneous deductions.[32]

In addition to civil fraud penalties, the Code contains numerous criminal sanctions that carry varying monetary fines and/or imprisonment.[33] The difference between civil and criminal fraud is one of degree. A characteristic of criminal fraud is the presence of willfulness on the part of the taxpayer. Thus, § 7201 dealing with attempts to evade or defeat a tax contains the following language:

> Any person who *willfully* attempts in any manner to evade or defeat any tax imposed by this title or the payment thereof shall, in addition to other penalties provided by law, be guilty of a felony and, upon conviction thereof, shall be fined not more than $100,000 ($500,000 in the case of a corporation), or imprisoned not more than five years, or both, together with the costs of prosecution. [Emphasis added.]

As to the burden of proof, the IRS must show that the taxpayer was guilty of willful evasion "beyond the shadow of any reasonable doubt." Recall that in the civil fraud area, the standard applied to measure culpability was "by a preponderance of the evidence."

*Substantial Understatements of Tax Liability.* Section 6661 is designed to strike at middle and high income taxpayers who play the so-called audit lottery, that is, those who take questionable and undisclosed positions on their tax returns in the hope that the return will not be selected for audit. Of course, a disclosure of such positions would have called attention to the return and increased the probability of audit.

A substantial understatement of a tax liability transpires when the understatement exceeds the larger of 10 percent of the tax due or $5,000. (Note: The monetary ceiling for corporations is $10,000.) The understatement to which the penalty applies is 10 percent of the difference between the amount of tax required to be shown on the return and the amount of tax actually shown on the return.

---

**28.** § 6653(b). The penalty becomes effective as to any tax the payment of which is required after September 3, 1982.

**29.** § 7454(a).

**30.** *Dogget v. Comm.,* 60–1 USTC ¶ 9342, 5 AFTR2d 1034, 275 F.2d 823 (CA–4, 1960).

**31.** *Harvey Brodsky,* 21 TCM 578, T.C.Memo. 1962–105.

**32.** *Lash v. Comm.,* 57–2 USTC ¶ 9725, 51 AFTR 492, 245 F.2d 20 (CA–1, 1957).

**33.** The more important of the criminal fraud provisions are found in § § 7201–7207.

The penalty can be avoided under any of the following circumstances:

—The taxpayer has "substantial authority" for such treatment.

—The relevant facts affecting the treatment are adequately disclosed in the return or in a statement attached thereto.

—The taxpayer has reasonable cause and acts in good faith.

The broad criteria utilized in § 6661 as a means of avoiding the penalty undoubtedly provide taxpayers with little, if any, concrete safe harbors. However, "substantial" is to be tested by looking to the taxpayer's position and not to the contrary authority.

There is the further quandary as to what will constitute adequate disclosure. Although "adequate disclosure" is not a new concept, it remains to be seen whether past interpretations will carry over to the § 6661 penalty area.

*Penalty for Overvaluation.* Section 6659 provides for a graduated addition to tax for certain income tax valuation or basis overstatements. The penalty applies only to the extent of any income tax underpayment of at least $1,000 that is attributable to such overvaluation (or basis overstatement) and only if the taxpayer is an individual, a closely-held corporation, or a personal service corporation.

When a valuation (or basis) overstatement exists, the following percentages are to be used to determine the applicable addition to tax:

| If the valuation claimed is the following percentage of the correct valuation | The applicable percentage is |
|---|---|
| At least 150% but not more than 200% | 10% |
| More than 200% but not more than 250% | 20% |
| More than 250% | 30% |

For tax returns filed before 1985, the penalty did not apply if the property involved had been held by the taxpayer for over five years. Likewise, the law did not distinguish between situations that dealt with contributions of property to charity and those that did not. The Deficit Reduction Act of 1984 eliminates the five-year exception and places charitable contributions into the 30 percent applicable percentage amount.

**Example 21.** In 1981, T purchased a painting for $10,000. In 1983 and when the painting is worth $20,000 (as later determined by the IRS), T donates the painting to an art museum. Based upon the appraisal of a cousin who is an amateur artist, T deducts $40,000 for the donation on a timely filed return for 1983.

**Example 22.** Assume the same facts as in Example 21 except that the donation occurred in 1984 (not 1983) and the timely filed return took place in 1985 (not in 1984). (Assume in both Examples 21 and 22 that T is in the 50% income tax bracket in the year of donation.)

In Example 21 the prior overvaluation rules apply, since the return was filed before 1985. Because the overvaluation was 200 percent [$40,000 (value used) compared to $20,000 (true value)], the applicable percentage is 10 percent. The penalty, therefore, is 10 percent of the underpayment of $5,000 [50% (tax bracket) × $10,000 (overvaluation) = $5,000 (resulting underpayment)], or $500.

As to the return filed after 1984, Example 22 comes under the new overvaluation rules. Because a charitable contribution is involved, the applicable percentage becomes 30 percent. Thus, the penalty is $1,500 [30% × $5,000 (underpayment)].

If the taxpayer can establish that there was a reasonable basis for the valuation claimed on the return, and the claim was made in good faith, the IRS can waive all or part of the penalty. It is doubtful that Examples 21 and 22 would constitute the type of situation where the IRS might choose to waive the penalty. For an item of art this valuable, relying on the appraisal of a relative who is an amateur artist does not seem to represent a good faith attempt at compliance.

*Penalty for Undervaluation.* Prior to the Deficit Reduction Act of 1984, there was no penalty for undervaluation. New § 6660 concerns the valuation of property used in determining the Federal gift tax (as reported on Form 709) and the Federal estate tax (as reported on Form 706). The penalty materializes when the tax underpayment is $1,000 or more due to undervaluation of assets transferred and applies to returns filed after 1984.

The following percentages are to be used to determine the applicable addition to tax:

| If the valuation claimed is the following percentage of the correct valuation | The applicable percentage is |
|---|---|
| 50% or more but not more than 66⅔% | 10% |
| 40% or more but less than 50% | 20% |
| Less than 40 percent | 30% |

The IRS is authorized to waive the penalty if the taxpayer can prove that a reasonable basis existed for the valuation used and that he or she acted in good faith.

*Penalty for Promoting Abusive Tax Shelters.* Section 6700 imposes a penalty upon those persons who organize (or aid in the organization of) or participate in the sale of certain abusive tax shelters. The penalty applies when the organizer or seller makes either of the following:

—A statement on tax benefits that he or she knows or has reason to know is false or fraudulent.

—A valuation error on services or property of more than 200 percent of the correct amount.

Originally, the penalty was the greater of $1,000 or 10 percent of the gross income derived from the activity (i. e., promoting or selling the abusive tax shelter). The Deficit Reduction Act of 1984, however, raised the 10 percent amount to 20 percent.

As to the overvaluation aspects of the penalty, the IRS may waive the penalty if the valuation used had a reasonable basis and was made in good faith.

*Failure to Pay Estimated Income Taxes.* A penalty is imposed for a failure to pay estimated income taxes. The penalty applies both to corporations and to individuals and is based on the rate of interest in effect.[34] For individuals, under changes made by the Deficit Reduction Act of 1984, each required installment payment of estimated tax is one-fourth of the lesser of (1) 80 percent of the tax shown on the current year return, (2) 100 percent of the preceding year's tax, or (3) 80 percent of tax determined by a special annualizing procedure. Different rules and percentages apply to corporations.

The penalty is levied on the amount of the underpayment for the period of underpayment. Payments of estimated tax are credited against unpaid installments in the order in which the installments are required to be paid. An equal part of withholding is deemed paid on each due date.

**Example 23.** The tax liability for T, an individual taxpayer, for 1985 is $12,000 and for the prior year was $15,000. T made four quarterly payments of $1,500 (including amounts withheld from wages) with the following results:

| Payment Due Date | Required Payment | Actual Payment | Payments Credited | | | |
|---|---|---|---|---|---|---|
| | | | 4/15/85 | 6/17/85 | 9/16/85 | 1/15/86 |
| 4/15/85 | $ 2,400 | $ 1,500 | $ 1,500 | $ 900 | | |
| 6/17/85 | 2,400 | 1,500 | | 600 | $ 1,500 | $ 300 |
| 9/16/85 | 2,400 | 1,500 | | | | 1,200 |
| 1/15/86 | 2,400 | 1,500 | | | | –0– |

T owes a penalty on $900 (the amount of underpayment) from April 15 to June 17 (period of underpayment), on $1,500 from June 17 to September 16, on $300 from June 17 to January 15, 1986, on $1,200 from September 16 to April 15, 1986, and on $2,400 from January 15 to April 15, 1986.

Prior law provided that individuals whose tax liability (over the amount withheld) was less than $100 were not required to file a declaration of estimated taxes. The $100 amount, which had remained constant for many years, was not realistic in view of the inflation that had taken place. Also it represented a compliance burden unnecessarily imposed on taxpayers, considering the relatively small amounts involved.

In 1981 Congress increased the tax liability threshold for payments of

---

**34.** § § 6654 and 6655. Section 6654(a) and § 6655(a) refer to the penalty as "an addition to the tax" (i. e., the income tax, self-employment tax). Since these so-called additions to the tax have the characteristics of penalties, they have been classified as such in the text. Unlike interest on an underpayment or a tax deficiency, additions to the tax and penalties are not deductible for income tax purposes.

estimated taxes from \$100 to \$500 over a four-year period.[35] The phase-in period and amount is as follows:

| Taxable Year Beginning in | Threshold Amount |
| --- | --- |
| 1982 | \$ 200 |
| 1983 | 300 |
| 1984 | 400 |
| 1985 and thereafter | 500 |

Consequently, individuals whose tax liability (in excess of withholdings) does not exceed the threshold amount would not be required to pay estimated tax, nor would they be penalized for underpayment of estimated tax.

*False Information with Respect to Withholding.* Prior to the Economic Recovery Tax Act of 1981, a civil penalty of \$50 could be imposed when the taxpayer claimed withholding allowances based on false information. The criminal penalty for willfully failing to supply information or for willfully supplying false or fraudulent information in connection with wage withholding was a fine of up to \$500 and/or up to one year of imprisonment.

Since the Federal income tax is predicated on a pay-as-you-go approach, taxpayers who do not comply with the withholding procedures could well place themselves in a position where they would be unable to pay the taxes due for a particular year. Faced with what appeared to be increasing noncompliance with these reporting requirements, Congress amended the Code to provide stiffer monetary penalties. Effective for acts and failure to act after 1981, the civil penalty is raised from \$50 to \$500, while the criminal penalty becomes \$1,000.[36] Consistent with the approach taken by Congress, the IRS amended its Regulations so as to require employers who receive from an employee a Form W–4 (Employee Withholding Allowance Certificate) that claims more than 14 exemptions to submit such form to the IRS.[37]

> **Example 24.** When first employed by X Corporation, T (a single person) completes a Form W–4 listing 19 exemptions. If the completion of this form occurred after 1981, T may be subject to a civil penalty of \$500 or, if the act is willful, a criminal penalty of up to \$1,000 and/or imprisonment of up to one year. In any event, X Corporation must apprise the IRS of the Form W–4 filed by T, since more than 14 exemptions have been claimed.

*Failure to Make Deposits of Taxes and Overstatements of Deposits.* When the business is not doing well or cash flow problems develop, there is a great temptation on the part of employers to "borrow" from Uncle Sam. One way this can be done is to fail to pay over to the IRS the amounts that have been withheld from the wages of employees for FICA and income tax purposes. Needless to say, the IRS does not appreciate being denied the use

---

**35.** § 6654(e)(1).
**36.** § § 6682 and 7205 as amended by the Economic Recovery Tax Act of 1981.
**37.** T.D. 7803 (1982–1 C.B. 155).

of such funds and has a number of weapons at its disposal to discourage the practice. Some of these penalties are summarized as follows:

—A penalty of five percent of any underdeposited amount not paid on or before the prescribed due date, unless it can be shown that the failure is due to reasonable cause and not due to willful neglect.[38]

—A penalty of 25 percent of any overstated deposit claim unless such overstatement is due to reasonable cause and not due to willful neglect.

—Various criminal penalties.[39]

—A 100 percent penalty if the employer's actions are willful.[40] The penalty is based on the amount of the tax evaded, not collected, or not accounted for or paid over. Since the penalty is assessable against the "responsible person" of the business, it could be that more than one party may be vulnerable (e. g., the president and treasurer of a corporation).[41]

In addition to these penalties, of course, the actual tax due must be remitted. An employer remains liable for the amount that should have been paid over even though the withholdings have not been taken out of the wages of its employees.[42]

## ADMINISTRATIVE POWERS OF THE IRS

*Examination of Records.* For the purpose of determining the correct amount of tax due, the Code authorizes the IRS to examine the taxpayer's books and records and to summon those persons responsible to appear before the IRS and, when they appear, to produce the necessary books and records.[43] Taxpayers are required to maintain certain recordkeeping procedures and retain those records that are necessary to facilitate the audit.[44] It should be noted that the files, workpapers, and other memoranda of a tax practitioner may be subpoenaed, since the courts have not extended to CPAs the privileged communication doctors and lawyers sometimes possess with respect to their clients.

*Assessment and Demand.* The Code permits the IRS to assess a deficiency and to demand payment for the tax.[45] However, no assessment or effort to collect the tax may be made until 90 days following the issuance of a statutory notice of a deficiency (i. e., the 90-day letter). The taxpayer is, therefore, given 90 days to file a petition to the U. S. Tax Court which effectively prevents the deficiency from being assessed or collected pending the outcome of the case.[46]

**38.** § 6656(a).
**39.** See, for example, § 7202 (willful failure to collect or pay over a tax).
**40.** § 6672.
**41.** Although the IRS might assess the penalty against more than one person, it cannot collect more than the 100% due.
**42.** § 3403.
**43.** § 7602.
**44.** § 6001.
**45.** § 6212.
**46.** § 6213.

Certain exceptions to this assessment procedure should be noted:

—The IRS may issue a deficiency assessment without waiting 90 days if mathematical errors in the return incorrectly state the tax at less than the true liability.

—If the IRS believes the assessment or collection of a deficiency is in jeopardy, it may assess the deficiency and demand immediate payment.[47] The taxpayer is able to stay the collection of the jeopardy assessment by filing a bond for the amount of the tax and interest.[48] This action will prevent the sale of any property that has been seized by the IRS.

Following assessment of the tax, the IRS will issue a notice and demand for payment.[49] The taxpayer is usually given 10 days following the notice and demand for payment to pay the tax. If the tax is not paid, the IRS can place a tax lien upon the taxpayer's property.[50] In addition, the taxpayer's property can be seized and sold in order to satisfy the claim.[51] However, in certain cases, the Code provides for an extension in the payment of a deficiency to prevent "undue hardship."[52]

If property is transferred and the tax is not paid, the subsequent owners of the property may be liable for the tax. This pursuit of the tax liability against succeeding owners is referred to as transferee liability. For example, if an estate is insolvent and unable to pay the estate tax, the executor or the beneficiaries may be liable for its payment.[53]

*Offers in Compromise and Closing Agreements.* The Code provides specific authority for the IRS to negotiate a compromise if there is doubt either in determining the amount of the actual liability or in the taxpayer's ability to pay the tax.[54] In Rev.Proc. 68–16 the IRS has enumerated situations in which closing agreements will be issued:[55]

1.  An executor or administrator requires a determination of the tax liability either to facilitate the distribution of estate assets or to relieve himself or herself of fiduciary responsibility.

2.  A liquidating corporation needs a determination of tax liability to proceed with the process of dissolution.

3.  A taxpayer wishes to close returns on an annual basis.

4.  Creditors demand evidence of the tax liability.

If the taxpayer is financially unable to pay the total amount of the tax, a Form 656 (Offer in Compromise) must be filed with the District Director or the IRS Service Center. The IRS investigates the claim by evaluating the taxpayer's financial ability to pay the tax. In some instances, the com-

---

47.  § 6861.
48.  § 6863(a).
49.  § 6303(a).
50.  § 6321.
51.  § 6331(b).
52.  § 6161(b).
53.  § 6901.
54.  § 7122 and Reg. § 301.7122–1(a).
55.  1968–1 C.B. 770, § 4.01.

promise settlement will include an agreement for final settlement of the tax through payments of a specified percentage of the taxpayer's future earnings. The District Director must obtain approval from the IRS Regional Counsel if the amount involved exceeds $500. This settlement procedure usually entails lengthy periods of negotiation with the IRS and is generally used only in extreme cases.

A closing agreement is binding on both the Government and the IRS, except upon a subsequent showing of fraud, malfeasance, or misrepresentation of a material fact.[56] The closing agreement may be added to Form 870 in reaching agreement upon the entire amount of tax due for a year under audit, used when disputed issues carry over to future years, and employed to dispose of a dispute involving a specific issue for a prior year or a proposed transaction involving future years. If, for example, the IRS is willing to make substantial concessions in the valuation of assets for death tax purposes, it may require a closing agreement from the recipient of the property to establish the tax basis of the assets for income tax purposes.

## THE STATUTE OF LIMITATIONS

A statute of limitations defines the period of time during which one party may pursue against another party a cause of action or other suit allowed under the governing law. Failure to satisfy any requirement provides the other party with an absolute defense should he or she see fit to invoke the statute. Inequity would result if there were no statute limiting action. Permitting the lapse of an extended period of time between the initiation of a claim and its pursuit could place the defense of such claim in jeopardy. Witnesses may have died or disappeared; records or other evidence may have been discarded or destroyed.

In terms of Federal tax consequences, it is important to distinguish between the statute of limitations on assessments by the IRS and the statute applicable to refund claims by a taxpayer.

*Assessment and the Statute of Limitations.* In general, any tax that is imposed must be assessed within three years of the filing of the return (or, if later, the due date of the return).[57] Some exceptions to this three-year limitation follow:

—If no return is filed or a fraudulent return is filed, assessments can be made at any time. There is, in effect, no statute of limitations.

—If a taxpayer omits an amount of gross income in excess of 25 percent of the gross income stated on the return, the statute of limitations is increased to six years. The courts have interpreted this extended period of limitations rule to include only those items affecting income and not the omission of items affecting cost of goods sold.[58] In addition, gross income includes capital gains in the *gross* income amount (i. e., not reduced by capital losses).

---

**56.** § 7121(b).

**57.** §§ 6501(a) and (b)(1).

**58.** *The Colony, Inc. v. Comm.*, 58–2 USTC ¶ 9593, 1 AFTR2d 1894, 78 S.Ct. 1033 (USSC, 1958).

**Example 25.** During 19X1, T (an individual taxpayer) had the following income transactions (all of which were duly reported on his timely filed return):

| | | |
|---|---:|---:|
| Gross receipts | | $ 480,000 |
| Less cost of goods sold | | (400,000) |
| Net business income | | $ 80,000 |
| Capital gains and losses— | | |
| Capital gain | $ 36,000 | |
| Capital loss | 12,000 | 24,000 |
| Total income | | $ 104,000 |

T retains your services in 19X5 as a tax consultant. It seems that he inadvertently omitted some income on his 19X1 return and he wishes to know if he is "safe" under the statute of limitations. The six-year statute of limitations would apply, putting T in a vulnerable position only if he omitted more than $129,000 on his 19X1 return [($480,000 + $36,000) × 25%].

—The statute of limitations may be extended by mutual consent of the District Director and the taxpayer.[59] This extension covers a definite period and is made by signing Form 872. The extension is frequently requested by the IRS when the lapse of the statutory period is imminent and the audit has not been completed. In some situations, the extensions may apply only to unresolved issues. This practice often is applied to audits of corporate taxpayers and explains why many corporations have "open years."

Special rules relating to assessment are applicable in the following situations:

—Taxpayers (corporations, estates, etc.) may request a prompt assessment of the tax.

—The period for assessment of the personal holding company tax is extended to six years after the return is filed only if certain filing requirements are met.

—If a partnership or trust files a tax return (a partnership or trust return) in good faith and a later determination renders it taxable as a corporation, such return is deemed to be the corporate return for purposes of the statute of limitations.

—The assessment period for capital loss, net operating loss, and investment credit carrybacks is generally related to the determination of tax in the year of the loss or unused credit rather than in the carryback years.

If the tax is assessed within the period of limitations, the IRS has six years from the date of assessment to collect the tax.[60] However, if the IRS issues a statutory notice of deficiency to the taxpayer, who then files a Tax Court petition, the statute is suspended on both the deficiency assessment

---

**59.** § 6501(c)(4).
**60.** § 6502(a).

and the period of collection until 60 days after the decision in the Tax Court becomes final.[61]

*Refund Claims and the Statute of Limitations.*   To receive a tax refund, the taxpayer is required to file a valid refund claim. The official form for filing a claim is Form 1040X for individuals and Form 1120X for corporations. A refund claim must follow certain procedural requirements. If it does not, the claim may be rejected with no consideration of its merit. These procedural requirements include the following:

—A separate claim must be filed for each taxable period.

—The grounds for the claim must be stated in sufficient detail.

—The statement of facts must be sufficient to permit IRS appraisal of the merits of the claim.[62]

The refund claim must be filed within three years of the filing of the tax return or within two years following the payment of the tax if this period expires on a later date.[63] In most instances the three-year period is relevant for determining running of the statute of limitations. To be allowed, a claim must be filed during this period.

Certain exceptions are incorporated in the Code that can inadvertently reduce the benefits of the refund claim.[64]

**Example 26.**  On March 10, 19X2, T filed his 19X1 income tax return reflecting a tax of $10,500. On July 11, 19X3, he filed an amended 19X1 return showing an additional $3,000 of tax which was then paid. On May 20, 19X5, he filed a claim for refund of $4,500. Assuming T is correct concerning the claim for refund, how much tax can he recover? The answer is only $3,000. Because the claim was not filed within the three-year period, T is limited to the amount he actually paid during the last two years. One might note that T would be entitled to interest on the $3,000 from July 11, 19X3 (the date of the overpayment), to a date not more than 30 days prior to the date of the refund check (subject to the 45-day rule discussed earlier in the chapter).

**Example 27.**  D had $10,000 withheld in 19X1. Because of heavy itemized deductions, D assumed she had no further tax to pay for the year. For this reason, and because of the exigencies of business, and without securing an extension, she did not file her 19X1 return until June 9, 19X2. Actually, the return showed a refund of $600, which D ultimately received. On May 3, 19X5, D filed a $4,000 claim for refund of her 19X1 taxes. How much, if any, of the $4,000 may D recover? None. Although the time limitation was met (i. e., the claim was filed within three years of the filing of the return), the amount limitation was not. A refund cannot exceed the amount paid within three years preceding the filing of the claim, and for this purpose, D's withholdings were deemed paid as of April 15, 19X2. Had D requested and obtained an extension covering the filing of her 19X1 return, the claim for refund would have been timely and taxes paid would have exceeded the refund claimed.

---

**61.**   § 6503(a)(1).
**62.**   Reg. § 301.6402–2.
**63.**   § § 6511(a) and 6513(a).
**64.**   § 6511(b).

Section 6511(d)(1) sets forth special rules for claims relating to bad debts and worthless securities. A seven-year period of limitations applies in lieu of the normal three-year rule. The extended period is provided in recognition of the inherent difficulty associated with identification of the exact year a bad debt or security becomes worthless.

Refund claims relative to capital or net operating loss carrybacks may be filed within three years after the time for filing the tax return (including extensions) for the year of the loss. The IRS will accelerate the processing of a refund from a net operating loss carryback if Form 1045 (applicable to individuals) or Form 1139 (applicable to corporations) is utilized. But this special procedure is available only if the form is filed within the year following the year of the loss. In other cases, a Form 1040X or Form 1120X should be used.

If the taxpayer's refund claim is rejected by the IRS, a suit for refund generally may be filed six months after the filing of the claim.[65] This suit is filed in a Federal District Court or in the Claims Court.

*Mitigation of the Statute of Limitations.* Sections 1311 through 1315 contain a set of complex rules designed to preclude either the IRS or a taxpayer from taking advantage of the statute of limitations when to do so would be inequitable. Simply stated, these sections prevent the use of the statute as a means of obtaining a double benefit by maintaining an inconsistent position.

> **Example 28.** In 19X1, T Corporation inadvertently claimed as a deduction a $10,000 expenditure that should have been charged to a capital account and depreciated over a period of 10 years. In 19X5, and after the statute of limitations has run on tax year 19X1, T Corporation cannot begin claiming depreciation on this asset. If it does, the IRS can force T Corporation to make an adjustment for 19X1, eliminating the inappropriate portion of the $10,000 deduction.

> **Example 29.** In 19X2, U Corporation makes a $20,000 distribution to its sole shareholder, V. On audit of V's income tax return for 19X2, the IRS deems the distribution to be fully covered by U Corporation's earnings and profits and forces V to recognize the $20,000 as dividend income. In 19X7, V sells his stock for $80,000 more than his investment therein. Can the IRS now claim that V has a gain of $100,000 because the 19X2 distribution really was a return of capital (thereby forcing V to reduce his stock basis and increase his gain by $20,000)? No. This would be the assumption of an inconsistent position by the IRS and would be inequitable to V.

# TAX PRACTICE

## THE TAX PRACTITIONER

*Definition.* What is a tax practitioner? What service does the practitioner perform? To begin defining the term "tax practitioner," one should consider whether the individual is qualified to practice before the IRS. Generally, practice before the IRS is limited to CPAs, attorneys, and per-

---

**65.** § 6532(a)(1).

sons who have been enrolled to practice before the IRS (termed "enrollees"). In most cases, enrollees are admitted to practice only if they take and successfully pass a special examination administered by the IRS. CPAs and attorneys are not required to take this examination and are automatically admitted to practice if they are in good standing with the appropriate licensing board regulating their profession.

Persons other than CPAs, attorneys, and enrollees may, however, be allowed to practice before the IRS in limited situations. Circular 230 (issued by the Treasury Department and entitled "Rules Governing the Practice of Attorneys and Agents Before the Internal Revenue Service") permits the following notable exceptions:

—A taxpayer may always represent himself or herself. A person also may represent a member of his or her immediate family if no compensation is received for such services.

—Regular full-time employees may represent their employers.

—Corporations may be represented by any of their bona fide officers.

—Partnerships may be represented by any of the partners.

—Trusts, receiverships, guardianships, or estates may be represented by their trustees, receivers, guardians, administrators, or executors.

—A taxpayer may be represented by whoever prepared the return for the year in question. However, such representation cannot proceed beyond the agent level.

**Example 30.**  T, an individual, is currently undergoing audit by the IRS for tax years 19X1 and 19X2. She prepared the 19X1 return herself but paid Z Company, a bookkeeping service, to prepare the 19X2 return. Z Company may represent T in matters concerning only 19X2. However, even with respect to 19X2, Z Company would be unable to represent T at an Appeals Division proceeding. T could, of course, represent herself, or she could retain a CPA, attorney, or enrollee to represent her in matters concerning both years under examination.

*Rules Governing Tax Practice.*  Circular 230 further prescribes the rules governing practice before the IRS. As applied to CPAs, attorneys, and enrollees the following are imposed:

—A requirement to make known to a client any error or omission he or she may have made on any return or other document submitted to the IRS.

—A duty to submit records or information lawfully requested by the IRS.

—An obligation to exercise due diligence as to accuracy in the preparation and filing of tax returns.

—A restriction against unreasonably delaying the prompt disposition of any matter before the IRS.

—A restriction against charging the client "an unconscionable fee" for representation before the IRS.

—A restriction against representing clients with conflicting interests.

Anyone can prepare a tax return or render tax advice, regardless of his or her educational background or level of competence. Likewise, there is nothing to preclude the "unlicensed" tax practitioner from advertising his or her specialty, from directly soliciting clients, or from otherwise violating any of the standards of conduct controlling CPAs, attorneys, or enrollees. Nevertheless, there do exist some restraints that govern all parties engaged in rendering tax advice or preparing tax returns for the general public.

—If the party holds himself or herself out to the general public as possessing tax expertise, he or she could be liable to the client if services are performed in a negligent manner. At a minimum, the measure of such damage would be any interest and penalties the client incurs because of the practitioner's failure to exercise due care.

—If someone agrees to perform a service (e. g., preparation of a tax return) and subsequently fails to do so, the aggrieved party may be in a position to obtain damages for breach of contract.

—The IRS requires all persons who prepare tax returns for a fee to sign as preparer of the return.[66] Failure to comply with this requirement could result in penalty assessment against the preparer.

—The Code prescribes various penalties for the deliberate filing of false or fraudulent returns. Such penalties are applicable to a tax practitioner who either was aware of the situation or actually perpetrated the false information or the fraud.[67]

—Code § 7216 prescribes penalties for tax practitioners who disclose to third parties information they have received from clients in connection with the preparation of tax returns or the rendering of tax advice.

**Example 31.** T operates a tax return preparation service. His brother-in-law, B, has just taken a job as a life insurance salesman. In order to help B find contacts, T furnishes B with a list of the names and addresses of all of his clients who report adjusted gross income of $10,000 or more. T is in violation of § 7216 and is subject to penalties.

—All non-attorney tax practitioners should avoid becoming engaged in activities that constitute the unauthorized practice of law. If they engage in this practice, action could be instituted against them in the appropriate state court by the local or state bar association. What actions constitute the unauthorized practice of law are undefined, and the issue remains an open question upon which reasonable minds can easily differ.

*Legislative Disclosure Requirement.* Due to widespread abuse in the commercial tax return preparation field, tax law includes provisions to regulate the conduct of parties who prepare tax returns and claims for

---

**66.** Reg. § 1.6065–1(b)(1). Rev.Rul. 84–3, 1984–1 C.B. 264, contains a series of examples as to when a person will be deemed to be a preparer of the return.

**67.** § 7206.

refund for compensation. The rules provide for disclosure requirements and ethical standards for income tax return preparers. Severe penalties are provided for noncompliance, and the IRS has the power to seek injunctive relief through court action to prohibit a preparer from engaging in certain unauthorized practices.[68]

For the 12-month period beginning on July 1 of *each* year, employers of tax return preparers are required to retain a record of the name, Social Security number, and place of work for each return preparer and make that record available for inspection upon request by the District Director.[69] A sole proprietor also must retain and make available such a record with respect to himself or herself. A $100 penalty may be assessed for failure to retain and make available such record, and a $5 penalty may be assessed for failure to set forth any item therein.[70] Certain individuals who prepare tax returns for others are exempted from the tax return preparer regulatory requirements (e. g., a fiduciary who prepares a tax return or refund claim for a beneficiary).[71]

*Other Legislative Penalties:* The following penalties also are provided under the Code:

1. A $100 penalty with respect to each return or claim for refund if the tax return preparer understates the taxpayer's liability and such understatement is due to the negligent or intentional disregard of rules and regulations.[72] The term "rules and regulations" includes the Code, Regulations, and published rulings.

   It should be noted that a preparer has not negligently or intentionally disregarded the rules and regulations if he or she in good faith and with a reasonable basis takes the position that a rule or regulation does not accurately reflect the Code.

2. A $1,000 ($10,000 for corporations) penalty per return or document is imposed against persons who aid in the preparation of returns or other documents that they know will result in understatement of tax liability. Aiding does not include clerical assistance in the preparation process. This penalty will not be imposed if the preparer penalty (refer to item 1) is invoked.[73]

3. A $500 per return penalty will be assessed on the preparer if the understatement of tax is due to a willful understatement of the taxpayer's tax liability. For example, a willful understatement occurs where a preparer disregards information furnished by the taxpayer in an attempt to wrongfully reduce the tax liability.

4. A $25 penalty is assessed against the preparer for failure to sign a return or furnish the preparer's identifying number and a $50 penalty is assessed for failure to retain a copy or list of taxpayers for whom returns or claims for refund have been prepared.

---

**68.** § 7407(a).
**69.** Reg. § 1.6060–1(a).
**70.** Reg. § 1.6695–1(e).
**71.** § 7701(a)(36)(B).
**72.** § 6694.
**73.** § 6701.

5.  A $25 penalty is assessed if the preparer fails to furnish a copy of the return or claim for refund to the taxpayer unless the failure is due to reasonable cause and not due to willful neglect.[74]

6.  A $500 penalty may be assessed if a preparer endorses or otherwise negotiates a check for refund of tax that is issued to the taxpayer.

*Guidelines for the Imposition of the Negligence Penalty.* In connection with preparer penalties under § 6694(a) (refer to item 1), Rev.Proc. 80–40 provides guidelines as to what constitutes the negligent disregard of rules and regulations.[75] These guidelines are illustrated in a series of revenue rulings and are discussed below.[76]

In determining whether the penalty under § 6694(a) is to be asserted, all of the relevant facts and circumstances of each case will be taken into account. One such factor is the nature of the error causing the understatement. Was the provision that was misapplied or not discovered so complex, uncommon, or highly technical that a competent preparer of tax returns of the type at issue might reasonably be unaware or mistaken as to its applicability? Would a general review of the return have disclosed the error to the preparer? An isolated mathematical or clerical error ordinarily reflects no more than mere inadvertence and will not result in the imposition of the penalty.

> **Example 32.** A taxpayer furnished T, the income tax return preparer, with all of the Forms 1099–INT (Statement for Recipients of Interest Income) that he had received. T failed to list the amount shown on one of the Forms 1099–INT on Schedule B of Form 1040. The omission was inadvertent and was the only error T made in preparing the return. Also, the error resulted in an understatement of tax liability that was not substantial. Under these circumstances, the negligence penalty will not be imposed on T.

> **Example 33.** Assume the same facts as in Example 32, except that T correctly listed all of the amounts shown on the Forms 1099–INT on Schedule B but made an error in totaling the separate amounts. Again, the error led to an understatement of tax liability that was not substantial. As was true with Example 32, the negligence penalty will not be imposed.

The results reached in Examples 32 and 33 would have been different if the error had been substantial or so conspicuous that it should have been discovered by the preparer.

The IRS also will consider the frequency of errors. A pattern of errors on a return is presumptive of negligence and generally will result in the assertion of the penalty even though no one error would have done so.

---

74. § 6695.
75. 1980–2 C.B. 774.
76. Rev.Rul. 80–262 (1980–2 C.B. 375), Rev.Rul. 80–263 (1980–2 C.B. 376), Rev.Rul. 80–264 (1980–2 C.B. 377), Rev.Rul. 80–265 (1980–2 C.B. 377), and Rev.Rul. 80–266 (1980–2 C.B. 378).

**Example 34.** Assume the same facts as in Example 32, except that T fails to list the amounts shown on two of the Forms 1099–INT. Also, as was true in Example 33, he makes an error in totaling the separate amounts. Further, T used the wrong Tax Table in determining the tax. Although the errors resulted in an understatement of tax liability that was not substantial, the negligence penalty will be imposed on T.

The IRS also will consider the materiality of errors. An error resulting in a material understatement may be greater indication of negligence than a similar error resulting in a less material understatement. But even where all of the relevant facts and circumstances suggest that the return was negligently prepared, the penalty under § 6694(a) generally will not be asserted if:

—The preparer's normal office practice indicates that the error in question rarely would occur.

—The normal office practice was followed in preparing the return in question.

Examples of normal office practice include a system to promote accuracy and consistency in the preparation of returns (e. g., a checklist), a method for obtaining the necessary information from the taxpayer, examining the prior year's return, and review procedures. The normal office practice of the preparer will not be relevant where the error is flagrant or either there is a pattern of errors on a particular return or an error is repeated on numerous returns.

**Example 35.** Due to an oversight, T, an income tax return preparer, failed to report a substantial minimum tax liability resulting from a net capital gain deduction shown on the client's 19X1 return. This was the only error on the return. To show that the normal office practice was to correctly apply the minimum tax provisions, T had a checklist reflecting that such tax had to be taken into account. Also, T's working papers indicated that the checklist had been reviewed. Considering T's knowledge, the internal procedures for review, and other facts and circumstances, the indications were that this error rarely would occur. In this type of situation, T will not be liable for the negligence penalty.

The penalty under § 6694(a) generally will not apply where a preparer in good faith relies without verification on information furnished by the client. Thus, the preparer is not required to audit, examine, or review books and records, business operations, or documents or other evidence in order to verify independently the client's information. However, the preparer may not ignore the implications of information either furnished by the taxpayer or which actually was known. Furthermore, the preparer shall make reasonable inquiries if the information furnished appears to be incorrect or incomplete.

**Example 36.** T prepared the Federal income tax returns for S and S Corporation (wholly owned by S) for tax year 19X1. T was not the auditor of S Corporation and had no knowledge of any loans by S to S Corporation. Although T deducted the interest paid by S Corporation to S on Form 1120, she did not report any interest income on S's Form

1040. The information provided by S Corporation to T did not reflect who received the interest payment, and the information furnished by S did not reveal the receipt of such payment. Under these conditions, T will not be subject to the negligence penalty.

**Example 37.** Assume the same facts as in Example 36, except that the information provided by S Corporation revealed that S was the payee of the interest. Here, the penalty applies.

Some provisions of the Code [e. g., § 274(d)] require the existence of specific facts and circumstances (e. g., the maintenance of specific documents) before a deduction may properly be claimed. In these cases, the preparer should make appropriate inquiries to determine the existence of such facts and circumstances before claiming a deduction.

**Example 38.** T prepared a tax return for a client in which he deducted business entertainment expenditures. T did not make any inquiries of the client concerning whether or not such expenditures satisfied the substantiation requirements of § 274(d). On later audit by the IRS it was revealed that no such substantiation existed and the deduction was disallowed. Although T was unaware of the true facts when the return was prepared, the negligence penalty will be imposed.

**Example 39.** Assume the same facts as in Example 38, except that T made the inquiry and was assured of the existence of the required substantiation by the client. Here, the negligence penalty will not apply to T.

## ETHICAL CONSIDERATIONS—"STATEMENTS ON RESPONSIBILITIES IN TAX PRACTICE"

Tax practitioners who are CPAs or attorneys must abide by the codes or canons of professional ethics applicable to their respective professions. The various codes and canons have much in common with and parallel the standards of conduct set forth in Circular 230. Tax practice is greatly affected by the prohibition against designation of a specialty. With some exceptions at the state bar association level, an attorney or a CPA cannot indicate on letterhead, business cards, or other approved listing that he or she specializes in tax matters or that his or her practice is limited to this field. From this standpoint, attorneys and CPAs are unlike physicians and dentists who have developed and effectively utilized an elaborate system of specialization.

In the belief that CPAs engaged in tax practice required further guidance in the resolution of ethical problems, the Tax Committee of the AICPA began issuing periodic statements on selected topics. The first of these "Statements on Responsibilities in Tax Practice" was released in 1964. Some of the statements that have been issued to date are summarized as follows:

—A CPA should sign as the preparer of a Federal tax return only if he or she is satisfied that reasonable effort has been made to provide appropriate answers to the questions on the return that are applicable to the taxpayer. When such questions are left unanswered, the reason for such omissions should be stated. The possibility that an answer to a question might prove disadvantageous to the taxpayer does not justify its omission. Likewise, it does not justify omitting the reason the question was not answered.

**Example 40.** T, a CPA, is in the process of completing the 19X8 tax return for a client, X Corporation. During the year, X Corporation made a $20,000 cash distribution to its shareholders. T knows that the distribution is not covered by current earnings and profits but is not sure of the corporation's accumulated earnings and profits. Corporate management has decided to treat the distribution as a return of capital but is unwilling at this time to incur the expense and inconvenience of asking T to determine the balance of the accumulated earnings account. While completing Form 1120, T encounters the following question: "During this taxable year, did you pay dividends (other than stock dividends and distributions in exchange for stock) in excess of your current and accumulated earnings and profits?" Under these circumstances, T cannot answer *yes* or *no* to the question. The reason for his failure to do so should be explained in a note attached to the return. It does not matter that such a note may trigger an audit of the transaction by the IRS.

—A CPA may sign a return containing a departure from the treatment of an item on a prior year's tax return that was made pursuant to an administrative proceeding with the IRS. The departure need not be disclosed on the return.

**Example 41.** Upon audit of T Corporation's income tax return for 19X4, the IRS disallowed $20,000 of the $100,000 salary paid to its president and sole shareholder on the grounds of unreasonable compensation [§ 162(a)(1)]. You are the CPA who has been engaged to prepare T Corporation's income tax return for 19X5. Again the corporation paid its president a salary of $100,000 and chose to deduct this amount. Because you are not bound in 19X5 by what the IRS deemed reasonable for 19X4, the full $100,000 can be claimed as a salary deduction.

—A CPA may prepare tax returns involving the use of estimates if such use is generally acceptable or if, under the circumstances, it is impractical to obtain exact data. When estimates are used, they should be presented in such a manner as to avoid the implication of greater accuracy than exists. The CPA should be satisfied that estimated amounts are not unreasonable under the circumstances.

**Example 42.** In connection with the preparation of his return for the past year, your client informs you that he estimates he donated $3,000 in cash to qualified charitable organizations, little of which is supported by receipts or other substantiation. Considering the nature of the client, you feel the $3,000 amount is reasonable. Under these conditions, the deduction can be claimed. You should, however, advise the client that some or all of these expenses could be disallowed by the IRS due to the absence of full substantiation. It would be improper, for example, to deduct only $2,999, as this implies greater accuracy than, in fact, exists.

—A CPA should promptly advise a client upon learning of an error in a previously filed return or upon learning of a client's failure to file a required return. The advice can be oral or written and should include a recommendation of the corrective measures, if any, to be taken. The error or other omission should not be disclosed to the IRS without the client's consent. If the past error is material and is not corrected by the client, the CPA may be unable to prepare the current year's tax return. Such might be true if the error has a carryover effect that precludes the correct determination of the tax liability for the current year.

**Example 43.** In connection with the preparation of a client's 19X5 income tax return, you discover the final inventory for 19X4 was materially understated. First, you should advise the client to file an amended return for 19X4 reflecting the correct amount in final inventory. Second, if the client refuses to make this adjustment, you should consider whether the error will preclude you from preparing a substantially correct return for 19X5. Because this will probably be the case (the final inventory for 19X4 becomes the beginning inventory for 19X5), you should withdraw from the engagement. If the error is corrected by the client, you may proceed with the preparation of the tax return for 19X5. You should, however, assure yourself that the error is not repeated.

—When the CPA is representing a client in an administrative proceeding with respect to a return in which there is an error known to the CPA that has resulted or may result in a material understatement of tax liability, he or she should request the client's agreement to disclose the error to the IRS. Lacking such agreement, the CPA may be compelled to withdraw from the engagement.

**Example 44.** While representing a client on an audit of her 19X5 income tax return, you discover that she inadvertently omitted a material amount of taxable income. First, you should advise the client that the omission be disclosed to the IRS. Second, if the client refuses to make the disclosure, you should consider withdrawing from the engagement. Whether you should or should not withdraw can generally be resolved by determining which alternative will least compromise the client's position. Withdrawal during the audit might trigger increased IRS scrutiny that would disclose the omission.

—In providing tax advice to a client, the CPA must use judgment to assure that the advice reflects professional competence and appropriately serves the client's needs. No standard format or guidelines can be established to cover all situations and circumstances involving written or oral advice by the CPA. The CPA may communicate with the client when subsequent developments affect advice previously provided with respect to significant matters. However, he or she cannot be expected to assume responsibility for initiating such communication, except while assisting a client in implementing procedures or plans associated with the advice provided. Of course, the CPA may undertake this obligation by specific agreement with his or her client.

**Example 45.** In 19X4, your client requests advice concerning the tax implications of a proposed transaction. You prepare a written summary concerning this matter, and the client follows this advice in consummating the transaction. The client carries out the same transaction in 19X5, again relying on your advice but without checking with you concerning the continuing soundness of the original advice. It turns out that the law has been changed, and the tax advice is no longer correct. Unless you originally agreed to inform the client of any tax law changes affecting this matter, you should not be held responsible for his continued reliance. However, to fully serve your client you should follow up in such situations.

—In preparing a return, the CPA ordinarily may rely on information furnished by the client. The CPA is not required to examine or review documents or other evidence supporting the client's information in order to sign the return as preparer. Although the examination of supporting data is not required, the CPA should encourage clients to provide such supporting data when appropriate. The CPA should make use of the client's returns for prior years whenever feasible. The implications of information known to the CPA cannot be ignored, and accordingly, the CPA is required to make reasonable inquiries when the information, as presented, appears to be incorrect or incomplete. If a CPA prepares a Federal tax return, the return should be signed by the CPA with no modification of the preparer's declaration.

**Example 46.** A CPA can normally take a client's word concerning the validity of dependency exemptions. But suppose a recently divorced client wants to claim his three children (of whom he does not have custody) as dependents. You must act in accordance with § 152(e)(2) in preparing the return, and this will require a waiver by the custodial parent. Without this waiver, you should not claim the dependency exemptions on your client's tax return.

**Example 47.** While preparing a client's income tax return for 19X4, you review his income tax return for 19X3. In comparing the dividend income reported on the 19X3 Schedule B with that received in 19X4, you note a significant decrease. Further investigation reveals the variation is due to a stock sale in 19X4 which, until now, was unknown to you. Thus, the review of the 19X3 return has unearthed a transaction that should be reported on the 19X4 return.

The foregoing statements merely represent guides to action and are not part of the AICPA's Code of Professional Ethics. But because the statements are representative of standards followed by members of the profession, a violation thereof might indicate a deviation from the standard of due care exercised by most CPAs. The standard of due care is at the heart of any suit charging negligence that is brought against a CPA.

☑ TAX PLANNING
CONSIDERATIONS

## STRATEGY IN SEEKING AN ADMINISTRATIVE RULING

*Determination Letters.*  In many instances, the request for an advance ruling or a determination letter from the IRS is a necessary or desirable planning strategy. The receipt of a favorable ruling or determination reduces the risk associated with a transaction when the tax results are in doubt. For example, the initiation or amendment of a pension or profit sharing plan should be accompanied by a determination letter from the District Director. Otherwise, on subsequent IRS review, the plan may not qualify and the tax deductibility of contributions to the plan will be disallowed. In some instances, the potential tax effects of a transaction are so numerous and of such consequence that to proceed without a ruling is unwise.

*Individual Rulings.*  It may, in some cases, not be necessary or desirable to request an advance ruling. For example, it is generally not desirable to request a ruling if the tax results are doubtful, but the company is committed to completion of the transaction in any event. If a ruling is requested and negotiations with the IRS indicate that an adverse determination will be forthcoming, it is usually possible to have the ruling request withdrawn. However, the National Office of the IRS may forward its findings, along with a copy of the ruling request, to the District Director. In determining the advisability of a ruling request, consideration should be given to the potential exposure of other items in the tax returns of all "open years."

A ruling request may delay the consummation of a transaction if the issues are novel or complex. Frequently, a ruling can be processed within three months, although in some instances a delay of a year or more may be encountered.

*Technical Advice.*  In the process of contesting a proposed deficiency with the Appeals Division, consideration should be given to a request for technical advice from the National Office of the IRS. If such advice is favorable to the taxpayer, it is binding on the Appeals Division. The request may be particularly appropriate when the practitioner feels that the agent or Appeals Division has been too literal in the interpretation of an IRS ruling.

## CONSIDERATIONS IN HANDLING AN IRS AUDIT

As a general rule, attempts should be made to settle disputes at the earliest possible stage of the administrative appeal process. New issues may be raised by IRS personnel if the case goes beyond the agent level. It is usually possible to limit the scope of the examination by furnishing pertinent information that is requested by the agent. Extraneous information or fortuitous comments may result in the opening of new issues and should therefore be avoided. Agents usually appreciate prompt and efficient response to inquiries, since their performance may in part be judged by their ability to close or settle assigned cases.

To the extent possible, it is advisable to conduct the investigation of field audits in the practitioner's office rather than in the client's office. This procedure permits greater control over the audit investigation and may facilitate the agent's review and prompt closure of the case.

Many practitioners feel that it is generally not advisable to have clients present at the scheduled conferences with the agent, since the client may give emotional or gratuitous comments that impair prompt settlement. If the client is not present, however, he or she should be advised of the status of negotiations. It should be clear that the client is the final authority with regard to any proposed settlement.

The tax practitioner's workpapers should include all research memoranda, and a list of resolved and unresolved issues should be continually updated during the course of the IRS audit. Occasionally, agents will request access to excessive amounts of accounting data for the purpose of engaging in a so-called fishing expedition. Providing blanket access to working papers should be avoided. Workpapers should be carefully reviewed to minimize opportunities for the agent to raise new issues not otherwise apparent. It is generally advisable to provide the agent with copies of specific workpapers upon request. An accountant's workpapers are not privileged and may therefore be subpoenaed by the IRS.

In unusual situations, a Special Agent may appear to gather evidence in the investigation of possible fraud. When this occurs, the taxpayer should be advised to seek legal counsel to determine the extent of his or her cooperation in providing information to the agent. Also, it is frequently desirable for the tax adviser to consult personal legal counsel in such situations. If the taxpayer receives a revenue agent's report (RAR), it generally indicates that the IRS has decided not to initiate criminal prosecution proceedings. The IRS usually does not take any action upon a tax deficiency until the criminal matter has been resolved.

## LITIGATION CONSIDERATIONS

During the process of settlement with the IRS, the taxpayer must assess the economic consequences arising from possible litigation. Specifically, it is necessary to weigh the probability of winning in court with the costs of settlement (i. e., legal and court costs). In some instances, taxpayers become overly emotional and do not give adequate consideration to the economic and psychological costs of litigation.

Signing of Form 870 or 870AD precludes the use of the Tax Court as a forum for future litigation. In such event, the taxpayer's only recourse is to pay the taxes and sue for a refund upon denial of a claim for refund. The Tax Court was established originally to permit taxpayers the opportunity to litigate issues without first paying the tax on the deficiency. Some taxpayers, however, prefer to litigate the case in the Federal District Court or the Claims Court, since the payment of tax effectively stops the running of interest on the deficiency.

In the selection of a proper tax forum, consideration should be given to the decisions of the various courts in related cases. The Tax Court will follow the decisions of Courts of Appeals if the court is one to which the taxpayer may appeal.[77] For example, if an individual is in the Fifth Court of Appeals that has issued a favorable opinion on the same issue that currently confronts the taxpayer, the Tax Court will follow this opinion with respect to the taxpayer's case, even if previous Tax Court decisions have been adverse.

If the issue involves a question in which equity is needed, strategy may dictate the choice of the Federal District Court (where a jury trial is obtainable) or the Claims Court, which has frequently given greater weight to equity considerations than to strict legal precedent.

## PENALTIES

As previously discussed, penalties are imposed upon a taxpayer's failure to file a return or pay a tax when due. These penalties can be avoided if the failure is due to reasonable cause and not due to willful neglect. Reasonable cause, however, has not been liberally interpreted by the courts and should not be relied upon in the routine type of situation.[78] A safer way to avoid the failure to file penalty would be to obtain from the IRS an extension of time for filing the return. Although an extension of time for filing does not normally excuse the failure to pay penalty, it will do so in the case of the automatic four-month variety if the 90 percent rule has been satisfied (refer to Example 17 in this chapter).

Since it is not deductible for income tax purposes, the penalty for failure to pay estimated taxes can become quite severe. Often trapped by this provision are employed taxpayers with outside income. Such persons may forget about such outside income and place undue reliance on the amount withheld from wages and salaries as being adequate to cover their liability. For such persons, not only does April 15 provide a real shock (i. e., in terms of the additional tax owed) but a penalty situation may have evolved. One possible way for an employee to mitigate this problem (presuming the employer is willing to cooperate) is described as follows:

> **Example 48.** T, a calendar year taxpayer, is employed by X Corporation and earns (after withholding) a monthly salary of $4,000 payable at the end of each month. T also receives income from outside sources (e. g., interest, dividends, consulting fees). After some quick calculations in early October of 1986, T determines that he has underestimated his tax liability for 1986 by $7,500 and will be subject to the penalty for the first two quarters of 1986 and part of the third quarter. T, therefore, completes a new Form W-4 in which he arbitrarily raises his income tax withholding by $2,500 a month. X Corporation accepts the Form W-4, and as a result, an extra $7,500 is paid to the IRS on T's account for the payroll period from October through December 1986.

The reason T avoids any penalties for the underpayment in Example 48 for the first three quarters is that withholding of taxes is allocated over the

---

77. *Jack E. Golsen,* 54 T.C. 742 (1970).
78. *Dustin v. Comm.,* 72-2 USTC ¶ 9610, 30 AFTR2d 72-5313, 467 F.2d 47 (CA-9, 1972), *aff'g.* 53 T.C. 491 (1969).

year involved. Thus, a portion of the additional $7,500 withheld in October–December is assigned to the January 1–April 15 period, the April 16–June 15 period, etc.[79] Had T merely paid the IRS an additional $7,500 in October, this would not have affected the penalty for the earlier quarters.

## STATUTE OF LIMITATIONS ON REFUND CLAIMS

*Avoiding the Statute of Limitations.*   A refund claim must be filed within the statutory period of limitations (usually within three years from the time the return was filed). The failure to file a refund claim within this period will prevent the recovery of previous overpayments of tax.

Suppose a matter is pending that, upon being resolved, could have an impact on a taxpayer's own situation. Although the taxpayer may not be personally involved in the controversy, a favorable outcome would result in a refund. By the time the issue is settled, however, any such claim might be barred by the statute of limitations. To prevent this from happening, the taxpayer should consider filing what is known as a "protective claim for refund." This will keep the statute of limitations from running until such time as the IRS acts upon the claim. The IRS will hold up on either approving or denying the claim until the pending matter is decided.

> **Example 49.**   For the past few years, T has been paying a special Federal excise tax on crude oil. Recently, a lower court held that this tax is unconstitutional. Because the amount of revenue at stake is considerable and large numbers of taxpayers are involved, the U. S. Supreme Court agrees to hear the appeal by the IRS. To freeze the running of the statute until the Supreme Court makes its decision, T files claims for refund for all open years in which she has paid the excise tax. Thus, T has protected herself from the statute of limitations in the event the tax is held to be unconstitutional. On the other hand, she loses nothing if the tax is found to be constitutional and her claim for refund is denied, since the tax has already been paid.

A protective claim for refund also may be advisable in situations where the controversy has not reached the litigation stage.

> **Example 50.**   X Corporation is a shareholder in Y Corporation. Over the years, X Corporation has made advances to Y Corporation, and such transactions have been treated as bona fide loans by the parties. Annually, therefore, Y Corporation has been deducting interest expense, and X Corporation has been recognizing interest income. Upon audit of Y Corporation, the IRS is threatening to disallow Y Corporation's interest expense deduction on the grounds that the advances were not loans but represented contributions to capital. Consequently, the purported interest payments are really nondeductible dividend distributions. Based on these facts, X Corporation might be well advised to file protective claims for refund for all open years. These claims would be predicated on the assumption that if dividends are the

---

**79.**   § 6654(e)(2).

ultimate result, X Corporation should be allowed the 85% dividends received deduction. Keep in mind that interest income is fully taxed, while dividends received by a corporate shareholder enjoy preferential treatment.

*Voluntary Extension of the Statute of Limitations.* If the IRS is unable to complete its audit within the period prior to the expiration of the statute of limitations, the taxpayer may be asked to agree to an extension of time for assessment by signing Form 872. It may be unwise to agree to this extension, since the IRS may subsequently assess a larger overall deficiency. Failure to agree to the extension of time, however, could force the IRS to issue a statutory notice of deficiency. This could cause the statutory notice to be unduly weighted against the taxpayer, since it may contain many adjustments that otherwise could have been resolved if the IRS had been permitted more time to consider the matter.

## PROBLEM MATERIALS

### Discussion Questions

1. Why is it necessary for a tax practitioner to be familiar with the IRS organization and its administrative appeal procedures?

2. Why does the IRS issue rulings solely on uncompleted actual transactions or upon transactions that have been completed prior to the filing of the tax return?

3. Under what circumstances will a ruling be revoked by the IRS and applied retroactively to the detriment of the taxpayer?

4. During the course of your research of a tax problem, you find that another company received a favorable unpublished (letter) ruling approximately two years ago based on facts similar to your situation. What degree of reliance may be placed upon this ruling?

5. Under what circumstances might the request for an advance ruling be considered a necessity? Are there situations in which a ruling should not be requested? Why?

6. In what situations might a taxpayer seek a determination letter?

7. What purpose does a request for technical advice serve?

8. What, if any, is the relationship between DIF and TCMP?

9. A taxpayer is fearful of filing a claim for refund for a prior year because he is convinced that the claim will cause an audit by the IRS of that year's return. Please comment.

10. In March of 1986, T receives a refund check from the IRS for the amount of overpayment she claimed when she filed her 1985 return in January. Does this mean that her 1985 return will not be audited? Explain.

11. Comment on the following:

    (a) An RAR.

    (b) Form 870.

    (c) The 30-day letter.

    (d) The 90-day letter.

12. If a taxpayer wishes to go to the Appeals Division of the IRS, when is a written protest required?

13. What is meant by the term "hazards of litigation"?

14. Can the IRS agent settle cases based on the hazards of litigation?

15. Is it possible or desirable to "trade" unresolved issues with the Appeals Division?

16. How may the running of interest on a deficiency assessment be stopped?

17. V, a calendar year taxpayer, files her 1985 income tax return on February 9, 1986, on which she claims a $1,200 refund. If V receives her refund check on May 2, 1986, will it include any interest? Explain.

18. In 1986, S's 1984 income tax return is audited by the IRS, and as a result, a deficiency is assessed. S is appalled by this development, since this means he will have to pay nondeductible interest from 1984 to the point of assessment. Is S under a misunderstanding on the tax rules concerning this matter? Explain.

19. Why may it be desirable to settle with the agent rather than to continue by appealing to a higher level within the IRS?

20. For the completion and filing of his 1985 income tax return, R retains the services of a CPA. Because of a particularly hectic tax season, the CPA does not complete and file the return until June of 1986. Does this exculpate R under the reasonable cause exception from the failure to file and pay penalties? Would it make any difference if R were entitled to a refund for 1985?

21. T, a self-employed, calendar year taxpayer, does not plan to prepay any of his taxes for the current year. Although he appreciates that an addition to tax exists for underpayments, since he is in the 50% bracket this means an after-tax outlay of only one-half of the penalty. Do you have any difficulty with T's assumptions?

22. What bearing should the interest rate currently in effect have on each of the following situations:

    (a) Whether a taxpayer litigates in the U. S. Tax Court or the Claims Court.

    (b) The penalty for underpayment of estimated taxes.

    (c) The negligence penalty.

23. Describe each of the following items:

    (a) A closing agreement.

    (b) An offer in compromise.

24. Frequently, tax litigation involves unresolved questions relating to several years prior to the current year. How is it possible for the IRS to assess a deficiency for these years, since the statute of limitations expires three years from the date of filing of the tax return?

25. In connection with the negligence penalty that might be imposed on the preparers of tax returns, comment on the significance of each of the following:

    (a) A substantial error.

    (b) An inconspicuous error.

    (c) A pattern of frequency of errors.

    (d) The preparer's normal office practice.

    (e) No verification by the preparer of information furnished by the client.

26. Certain individuals have stated that the preparation of a tax return by a qualified professional lends credibility to the return. Therefore, CPAs and attorneys should act in an impartial manner in the preparation of tax returns and should serve the overall enforcement needs of society for the administration of tax justice. Should a tax professional be an "umpire" or an "advocate"? Explain.

27. T, a vice-president of Z Corporation, prepared and filed the corporate Form 1120 for 19X3. This return is being audited by the IRS in 19X5.

    (a) May T represent Z Corporation during the audit?

    (b) Can such representation continue beyond the agent level (e. g., before the Appellate Division)?

28. In 19X2, S sold his business to B. Pursuant to an agreement between them, $40,000 of the selling price of $250,000 was allocated to the inventory of the business. In 19X4 and upon final audit of S's 19X2 income tax return, the IRS contends that the inventory should have been valued at $60,000. (This would have the effect of increasing S's ordinary income from the sale by $20,000.) What should B do under these circumstances?

29. During the course of an audit, the IRS agent requests a mutual extension of the statute of limitations for certain tax years. The agent states that this action is necessary to permit the completion of the audit. What are some of the pros and cons related to the signing of Form 872?

## Problem Materials

1. T, a calendar year taxpayer, does not file her 1985 return until June 3, 1986. At this point, she pays the $3,000 balance due on her 1985 tax liability of $30,000. T did not apply for and obtain any extension of time for filing the 1985 return. When questioned by the IRS on her delinquency, T asserts: "If I was too busy to file my regular tax return, I was too busy to request an extension."

    (a) Is T liable for any penalties for failure to file and for failure to pay?

    (b) If so, compute such penalties.

2. R, a calendar year taxpayer, was unable to file his 1985 income tax return on or before April 15, 1986. He did, however, apply for and obtain an automatic extension from the IRS. On May 10, 1986, R delivers his completed return to the IRS and remits the $5,000 balance due on his 1985 tax liability of $41,000.

    (a) Determine R's penalty for failure to file.

    (b) For failure to pay.

    (c) Would it make any difference as to your answers to (a) and (b) if R's tax liability for 1985 were $51,000 (instead of $41,000)? Explain.

3. S, a calendar year individual taxpayer, files his 1985 return 65 days after its due date. S did not obtain an extension for filing his return, and such return reflects additional income tax due of $500. Based on this information and disregarding the interest factor, how much more does S owe the IRS?

4. Assume the same facts as in Problem 3, except that the additional income tax due was $80 (rather than $500). Based on these new facts and disregarding the interest element, how much more does S owe the IRS?

5. R, a calendar year individual taxpayer, files her 1984 return on January 10, 1986. R did not obtain an extension for filing her return, and such return reflects additional income tax due of $3,800.

    (a) What are R's penalties for failure to file and to pay?

    (b) Would your answer to (a) change if R, before the due date of the return, had retained a CPA to prepare the return and it was the CPA's negligence that caused the delay?

6. U underpaid his taxes for 1985 in the amount of $10,000, such underpayment being attributable to negligence. If the interest on the underpayment was $2,200, what is U's total negligence penalty?

7.  Assume the same facts as in Problem 6, except that the entire underpayment was attributable to civil fraud. How much does U owe the IRS?

8.  In 1983, T made a charitable contribution of property which he valued at $20,000. This amount was claimed by T as a deduction on his 1983 income tax return filed in 1984. What is T's overvaluation penalty if the real value of this donated property is $8,000? (Assume T is in a 50% income tax bracket.)

9.  Assume the same facts as in Problem 8, except that the charitable contribution occurred in 1985 and was deducted on a return filed in 1986. What is T's overvaluation penalty?

10. In 19X0, T Corporation purchased 10% of the stock in X Corporation for $100,000. In 19X2, X Corporation made a cash distribution to its shareholders of $500,000 ($50,000 of which was received by T Corporation). As all parties were convinced that X Corporation had no earnings and profits at the time of the distribution, no dividend income was recognized by any of the shareholders. After the statute of limitations had expired, the IRS correctly determined that the distribution was fully covered by earnings and profits and should have been reported by the shareholders as dividend income. In 19X8, T Corporation sells its stock investment in X Corporation for $250,000.

    (a) How much gain should T Corporation recognize as a result of the sale?

    (b) If T Corporation recognizes a gain of $150,000 as a result of the sale, does the IRS have any recourse?

11. The 1986 tax liability for R, a self-employed individual taxpayer, is $36,000. For 1985, R paid a tax of $45,000. R made four quarterly payments of $5,000 each towards his 1986 tax liability.

    (a) Presuming the quarterly payments were timely, what amount and for what period will that amount be subject to the failure to pay estimated tax penalty?

    (b) Would your answer to (a) change if the tax liability for 1985 had been $20,000 (instead of $45,000)? Why?

12. When T accepted employment in 1985 with X Corporation he completed a Form W–4 listing 14 exemptions. Since T was single and had no dependents, he misrepresented his situation on Form W–4.

    (a) What penalties, if any, might the IRS impose upon T?

    (b) Presuming X Corporation is unaware of T's true situation, does it have any responsibility concerning this matter?

13. What is the applicable statute of limitations in each of the following independent situations:

    (a) No return was filed by the taxpayer.

    (b) A corporation is determined to have been a personal holding company for the year in question.

    (c) For 19X0, the XYZ Associates filed a Form 1065 (i. e., a partnership return). In 19X5, the IRS determined that the organization was not a partnership in 19X0 but was, in fact, a corporation.

    (d) In 19X0, T incurred a bad debt loss that she failed to claim.

    (e) On his 19X0 return, a taxpayer inadvertently omitted a large amount of gross income.

    (f) Same as (e), except that the omission was deliberate.

    (g) For 19X0, a taxpayer innocently overstated her deductions by a large amount.

14. During 19X2, T (an individual, calendar year taxpayer) had the following transactions, all of which were properly reported on a timely filed return:

| | | |
|---|---:|---:|
| Gross receipts | | $ 960,000 |
| Cost of goods sold | | (800,000) |
| Gross profit | | $ 160,000 |
| Capital gains and losses | | |
|    Capital gain | $ 72,000 | |
|    Capital loss | (24,000) | 48,000 |
| Total income | | $ 208,000 |

(a) Presuming the absence of fraud on T's part, how much of an omission from gross income would be required to make the six-year statute of limitations apply?

(b) Would it matter in your answer to (a) if cost of goods sold had been inadvertently overstated by $100,000?

15. On April 3, 19X2, T filed his 19X1 income tax return reflecting a tax of $40,000. On June 30, 19X3, he filed an amended 19X1 return showing an additional $12,000 tax, which was then paid. On May 20, 19X5, he filed a claim for refund of $18,000.

(a) Assuming T is correct concerning the claim for refund, how much tax can he recover?

(b) For what period is the interest payable on T's refund?

16. Ms. T had $40,000 withheld in 19X1. Because of heavy itemized deductions, she figured that she had no further tax to pay for the year. For this reason and because of personal problems and without securing an extension, she did not file her 19X1 return until July 1, 19X2. Actually, the return showed a refund of $2,400, which Ms. T ultimately received. On May 10, 19X5, Ms. T filed a $16,000 claim for refund of her 19X1 taxes.

(a) How much, if any, of the $16,000 may Ms. T recover?

(b) Would it have made any difference if Ms. T had requested and secured from the IRS an extension of time for filing her 19X1 tax return?

17. R's Federal income tax returns (i. e., Form 1040) for the past three years (19X1–19X3) were prepared by the following persons:

| Preparer | 19X1 | 19X2 | 19X3 |
|:---:|:---:|:---:|:---:|
| R | X | | |
| S | | X | |
| T | | | X |

S is R's next-door neighbor and owns and operates a pharmacy. T is a licensed CPA and is engaged in private practice. In the event R is audited and all three returns are examined, comment on who may represent R before the IRS at the agent level. At the Appeals Division.

18. Indicate whether the following statements are true or false (Note: SRTP = Statements on Responsibilities in Tax Practice):

(a) When a CPA has reasonable grounds for not answering an applicable question on a client's return, a brief explanation of the reason for the omission should not be provided, because it would flag the return for audit by the IRS.

(b) In preparing a taxpayer's return for 19X4, a CPA finds out that the client had 50% of his medical expense deduction claimed for 19X2 disallowed on audit by the IRS. The CPA should feel bound by the prior administrative proceeding in determining his client's medical expense deduction for 19X4.

(c) If the client tells you that she had contributions of $500 for unsubstantiated cash donations to her church, you should deduct an odd amount on her return (e. g., $499), because an even amount (i. e., $500) would indicate to the IRS that her deduction was based on an estimate.

(d) Basing an expense deduction on the client's estimates is not acceptable under the SRTP.

(e) If a CPA knows that his or her client has a material error in a prior year's return, he or she should not, without the client's consent, disclose the error to the IRS.

(f) If a CPA's client will not correct a material error in a prior year's return, the CPA should not prepare the current year's return for the client.

(g) If a CPA discovers during an IRS audit that his or her client has a material error in the return under examination, he or she should immediately withdraw from the engagement.

(h) If a CPA renders tax advice to the client in early 19X3, the client should be able to rely on such advice until April 15, 19X4. (The client prepared her own tax return.)

(i) The SRTP have the same force and effect as the AICPA's Code of Professional Ethics.

## Research Problems

*Research Problem 1.* For tax years 1971–1975, T filed fraudulent income tax returns. In 1977, however, he filed nonfraudulent amended returns and paid the additional basic taxes shown thereon. In 1983, the IRS issues notices of deficiency, asserting liability under § 6653(b) for additions to tax on account of fraud. T invoked the three-year statute of limitations as a defense to the assessment. Which side will prevail? Why?

*Research Problem 2.* E Corporation was formed in early 1978, did business for a short while, and is currently without assets. H was a director, minority shareholder, treasurer, and executive vice-president of E Corporation from its creation to the date of his resignation on September 12, 1978. H was responsible for E Corporation's day-to-day operations, although J, the majority shareholder and CEO, had the final say on the resolution of more important matters. At the start of his tenure with E Corporation, H himself determined on several occasions which of the bills were to be paid. In May of 1978, he caused $8,000 in back taxes to be paid to the IRS on behalf of J's predecessor partnership (with which H had no connection). J became extremely upset with H's action and ordered H not to pay any more money to the IRS. In fact, J relieved H of his duties for several weeks.

Upon being reinstated, H was instructed by J not to pay any more bills without J's prior approval. Although J generally told H which creditors he should pay and when, H did issue small checks without J's approval on a number of occasions. From May 12, 1978, to July 6, 1978, H was the only authorized signatory on the main checking account of E Corporation and wrote most of the company's checks. From July 6, 1978, until September 7, 1978, H and C (the comptroller and an employee working under H's supervision) were the only authorized signatories on this account. The bank required only one signature on checks drawn on this account.

E Corporation incurred employment tax liability for the second, third, and fourth quarters of 1978 in the amount of $30,388.53. These taxes included Federal income taxes withheld from employees, the employee portion of FICA taxes withheld from the employees, and the employer portion of FICA taxes. H was aware that the taxes were due and owing to the IRS, at least in some amount, as early as June of 1978.

At some point during the summer of 1978, H contacted a senior IRS official who was also a deacon at his church and asked what he should do about E Corporation's unpaid taxes. Allegedly, the official suggested that H write a letter to the IRS explaining the situation. H did not immediately follow this advice but continued fulfilling his duties at E Corporation throughout the summer. In this connection, he wrote at least 36 checks to creditors other than the IRS.

In his resignation letter to J, H expressed concern over the unpaid taxes (estimated to be in excess of $30,000). This letter was followed by a letter to the IRS, placing it on notice as to the situation. At the time these letters were written, E Corporation still had a substantial amount of money on deposit at the bank, as well as substantial assets in the form of inventories and accounts receivable. The IRS did not move to collect the taxes until over two years later. By that time, E Corporation was without assets.

The IRS issued assessments in the amount of the unpaid taxes under § 6672(a) against both H and J. Unfortunately, the IRS was unable to effect personal service on J but pursued the assessment against H. After paying a portion of the amount involved, H sued for a refund in the District Court. The IRS counterclaimed for the balance of the unpaid assessment. How should this controversy be resolved?

*Research Problem 3.* B became a CPA in 1964 and has practiced public accounting since 1965. In 1979, he was hired by the accounting firm of GW who had, among other clients, R Corporation and R (the sole shareholder of R Corporation). In 1979, B was assigned the accounts of R Corporation and R and was designated to be the preparer of their 1978 income tax returns. In the past, GW had adopted the practice of sending a data questionnaire to its individual income tax clients that was to be completed by the client and returned to the firm or used by the client as a guide in collecting the information necessary for the firm to prepare the returns. Such a questionnaire was not used by B when he prepared R's individual income tax return. Instead, the information necessary was supplied to B by R Corporation's bookkeeper. Such information was reconciled by B with R's prior return, processed, and eventually timely filed with the IRS. B also prepared and filed the Form 1120 for R Corporation based on a trial balance sheet submitted by the same bookkeeper. Unknown to B, R Corporation (due to high interest rates) had changed its borrowing policy. Instead of financing its operations through banking institutions, the credit source became R. Thus, an interest deduction of $15,000 was claimed on R Corporation's Form 1120 but was not reported as income on R's Form 1040. When B prepared the returns for the same clients as to tax year 1979, the same procedure was followed. Thus, as to the omitted interest income, history repeated itself. When the IRS caught the oversight, it assessed the $100 tax preparer penalty against B for both 1978 and 1979. How should this matter be resolved?

*Research Problem 4.* T's 1976 tax return listed his address as being in Allentown, Pennsylvania. Twelve days before the three-year statute of limitations was to expire, T orally notified the IRS of his new address in Niles, Michigan. That same day, the IRS mailed to T at the new address a Form 872 to extend the statute of limitations for 1976. T signed and mailed the Form 872, but the form was not received by the IRS before the expiration of the three-year period. On the last day of the limitation period, the IRS mailed a statutory notice of deficiency (i. e., the 90-day letter) to T at his old address. The U. S. Postal Service forwarded the notice to T at the new Niles address. Within 90 days of the mailing of the notice, T filed a timely petition with the U. S. Tax Court. In his petition, T made a motion to dismiss for lack of a timely notice of deficiency. How should this controversy be resolved?

*Research Problem 5.* Dr. P executed a single Form 872 that purported to extend the period for assessment for his 1974, 1975, and 1977 taxable years to June 30, 1981. Before accepting this form, and at a time at least 55 days prior to the expiration of the period for assessment, the IRS struck through the reference to the 1977 taxable year. The IRS did not seek the consent of Dr. P to this alteration, and when Dr. P received the modified Form 872, he called the IRS, vented his anger, and repudiated the change. The IRS issued a statutory notice of deficiency on March 27, 1981. Is the notice of deficiency valid? Why or why not?

*Research Problem 6.* Shortly before the statute of limitations was about to expire on a net operating loss carryback, T conferred with a nearby IRS office to obtain taxpayer assistance. The agent gave T several copies of Form 1045 (Application for Tentative Refund from Carryback of Net Operating Loss, Unused Investment Credit). One of these was properly completed by T and duly mailed to and received by the District Director two days prior to the expiration of the statute of limitations. Five days later, T received a form letter from the District Director's office informing him that he had used the wrong form and should, instead, file Form 1040X. The letter enclosed T's completed Form 1045. On the same day, T completed Form 1040X and sent it by registered mail to the District Director. One month thereafter, T received notice that his claim was barred by the statute of limitations. What are T's rights under the circumstances?

*Research Problem 7.* The heirs of an estate engaged an attorney to handle its probate and relied upon him to perform all necessary acts. In turn, the attorney arranged to have an assistant of his named administrator and depended upon him to timely file the death tax return. Such return was not timely filed, and no explanation was presented for the failure to do so. Is the estate liable for the addition to tax under § 6651(a)?

*Research Problem 8.* While working in an abandoned garage, T finds $2,438,110 in old currency which he turns over to the local authorities. After a lengthy series of legal actions (to which T is not a party), the money is identified as belonging to a convicted mobster and is turned over to the IRS in part payment of his delinquent taxes. The IRS rewards T with a cash payment of approximately 1.32% of the amount of currency he found. T feels he has been cheated, so he files suit in the U. S. Claims Court for the difference between 1.32% and 10%. Does T have a chance?

# APPENDIX A
# TAX RATES AND TABLES

# INDIVIDUALS—1986 TAX RATE SCHEDULES

## 1986 Tax Rate Schedules

**Caution:** Do not use these Tax Rate Schedules to figure your 1985 taxes. Use only to figure your 1986 estimated taxes.

### SCHEDULE X—Single Taxpayers

| If taxable income is: Over— | but not over— | The tax is: | of the amount over— |
|---|---|---|---|
| $0 | $2,480 | —0— | |
| 2,480 | 3,670 | -------- 11% | $2,480 |
| 3,670 | 4,750 | $130.90 + 12% | 3,670 |
| 4,750 | 7,010 | 260.50 + 14% | 4,750 |
| 7,010 | 9,170 | 576.90 + 15% | 7,010 |
| 9,170 | 11,650 | 900.90 + 16% | 9,170 |
| 11,650 | 13,920 | 1,297.70 + 18% | 11,650 |
| 13,920 | 16,190 | 1,706.30 + 20% | 13,920 |
| 16,190 | 19,640 | 2,160.30 + 23% | 16,190 |
| 19,640 | 25,360 | 2,953.80 + 26% | 19,640 |
| 25,360 | 31,080 | 4,441.00 + 30% | 25,360 |
| 31,080 | 36,800 | 6,157.00 + 34% | 31,080 |
| 36,800 | 44,780 | 8,101.80 + 38% | 36,800 |
| 44,780 | 59,670 | 11,134.20 + 42% | 44,780 |
| 59,670 | 88,270 | 17,388.00 + 48% | 59,670 |
| 88,270 | -------- | 31,116.00 + 50% | 88,270 |

### SCHEDULE Z—Heads of Household

| If taxable income is: Over— | but not over— | The tax is: | of the amount over— |
|---|---|---|---|
| $0 | $2,480 | —0— | |
| 2,480 | 4,750 | -------- 11% | $2,480 |
| 4,750 | 7,010 | $249.70 + 12% | 4,750 |
| 7,010 | 9,390 | 520.90 + 14% | 7,010 |
| 9,390 | 12,730 | 854.10 + 17% | 9,390 |
| 12,730 | 16,190 | 1,421.90 + 18% | 12,730 |
| 16,190 | 19,640 | 2,044.70 + 20% | 16,190 |
| 19,640 | 25,360 | 2,734.70 + 24% | 19,640 |
| 25,360 | 31,080 | 4,107.50 + 28% | 25,360 |
| 31,080 | 36,800 | 5,709.10 + 32% | 31,080 |
| 36,800 | 48,240 | 7,539.50 + 35% | 36,800 |
| 48,240 | 65,390 | 11,543.50 + 42% | 48,240 |
| 65,390 | 88,270 | 18,746.50 + 45% | 65,390 |
| 88,270 | 116,870 | 29,042.50 + 48% | 88,270 |
| 116,870 | -------- | 42,770.50 + 50% | 116,870 |

### SCHEDULE Y—Married Taxpayers and Qualifying Widows and Widowers

**Married Filing Joint Returns and Qualifying Widows and Widowers**

| If taxable income is: Over— | but not over— | The tax is: | of the amount over— |
|---|---|---|---|
| $0 | $3,670 | —0— | |
| 3,670 | 5,940 | -------- 11% | $3,670 |
| 5,940 | 8,200 | $249.70 + 12% | 5,940 |
| 8,200 | 12,840 | 520.90 + 14% | 8,200 |
| 12,840 | 17,270 | 1,170.50 + 16% | 12,840 |
| 17,270 | 21,800 | 1,879.30 + 18% | 17,270 |
| 21,800 | 26,550 | 2,694.70 + 22% | 21,800 |
| 26,550 | 32,270 | 3,739.70 + 25% | 26,550 |
| 32,270 | 37,980 | 5,169.70 + 28% | 32,270 |
| 37,980 | 49,420 | 6,768.50 + 33% | 37,980 |
| 49,420 | 64,750 | 10,543.70 + 38% | 49,420 |
| 64,750 | 92,370 | 16,369.10 + 42% | 64,750 |
| 92,370 | 118,050 | 27,969.50 + 45% | 92,370 |
| 118,050 | 175,250 | 39,525.50 + 49% | 118,050 |
| 175,250 | -------- | 67,553.50 + 50% | 175,250 |

**Married Filing Separate Returns**

| If taxable income is: Over— | but not over— | The tax is: | of the amount over— |
|---|---|---|---|
| $0 | $1,835 | —0— | |
| 1,835 | 2,970 | -------- 11% | $1,835 |
| 2,970 | 4,100 | $124.85 + 12% | 2,970 |
| 4,100 | 6,420 | 260.45 + 14% | 4,100 |
| 6,420 | 8,635 | 585.25 + 16% | 6,420 |
| 8,635 | 10,900 | 939.65 + 18% | 8,635 |
| 10,900 | 13,275 | 1,347.35 + 22% | 10,900 |
| 13,275 | 16,135 | 1,869.85 + 25% | 13,275 |
| 16,135 | 18,990 | 2,584.85 + 28% | 16,135 |
| 18,990 | 24,710 | 3,384.25 + 33% | 18,990 |
| 24,710 | 32,375 | 5,271.85 + 38% | 24,710 |
| 32,375 | 46,185 | 8,184.55 + 42% | 32,375 |
| 46,185 | 59,025 | 13,984.75 + 45% | 46,185 |
| 59,025 | 87,625 | 19,762.75 + 49% | 59,025 |
| 87,625 | -------- | 33,776.75 + 50% | 87,625 |

# ESTATES AND TRUSTS—TAX RATE SCHEDULES

### For taxable years beginning in 1984.—

| If taxable income is: | The tax is: |
|---|---|
| Not over $1,050 | 11% of taxable income. |
| Over $1,050 but not over $2,100 | $115.50, plus 12% of the excess over $1,050. |
| Over $2,100 but not over $4,250 | $241.50, plus 14% of the excess over $2,100. |
| Over $4,250 but not over $6,300 | $542.50, plus 16% of the excess over $4,250. |
| Over $6,300 but not over $8,400 | $870.50, plus 18% of the excess over $6,300. |
| Over $8,400 but not over $10,600 | $1,248.50, plus 22% of the excess over $8,400. |
| Over $10,600 but not over $13,250 | $1,732.50, plus 25% of the excess over $10,600. |
| Over $13,250 but not over $15,900 | $2,395, plus 28% of the excess over $13,250. |
| Over $15,900 but not over $21,200 | $3,137, plus 33% of the excess over $15,900. |
| Over $21,200 but not over $28,300 | $4,886, plus 38% of the excess over $21,200. |
| Over $28,300 but not over $41,100 | $7,584, plus 42% of the excess over $28,300. |
| Over $41,100 but not over $53,000 | $12,960, plus 45% of the excess over $41,100. |
| Over $53,000 but not over $79,500 | $18,315, plus 49% of the excess over $53,000. |
| Over $79,500 | $31,300, plus 50% of the excess over $79,500. |

### For taxable years beginning in 1985.—

| If taxable income is: | The tax is: |
|---|---|
| Not over $1,090 | 11% of taxable income. |
| Over $1,090 but not over $2,185 | $119.90, plus 12% of the excess over $1,090. |
| Over $2,185 but not over $4,425 | $251.30, plus 14% of the excess over $2,185. |
| Over $4,425 but not over $6,555 | $564.90, plus 16% of the excess over $4,425. |
| Over $6,555 but not over $8,740 | $905.70, plus 18% of the excess over $6,555. |
| Over $8,740 but not over $11,030 | $1,299.00, plus 22% of the excess over $8,740. |
| Over $11,030 but not over $13,790 | $1,802.80, plus 25% of the excess over $11,030. |
| Over $13,790 but not over $16,545 | $2,492.80, plus 28% of the excess over $13,790. |
| Over $16,545 but not over $22,065 | $3,264.20, plus 33% of the excess over $16,545. |
| Over $22,065 but not over $29,455 | $5,085.80, plus 38% of the excess over $22,065. |
| Over $29,455 but not over $42,775 | $7,894.00, plus 42% of the excess over $29,455. |
| Over $42,755 but not over $55,160 | $13,488.40, plus 45% of the excess over $42,755. |
| Over $55,160 but not over $82,740 | $19,061.65, plus 49% of the excess over $55,160. |
| Over $82,740 | $32,575.85, plus 50% of the excess over $82,740. |

### For taxable years beginning in 1986.—

| If taxable income is: | The tax is: |
|---|---|
| Not over $1,135 | 11% of taxable income. |
| Over $1,135 but not over $2,265 | $124.85 plus 12% of the excess over $1,135. |
| Over $2,265 but not over $4,585 | $260.45 plus 14% of the excess over $2,265. |
| Over $4,585 but not over $6,800 | $585.25 plus 16% of the excess over $4,585. |
| Over $6,800 but not over $9,065 | $939.65 plus 18% of the excess over $6,800. |
| Over $9,065 but not over $11,440 | $1,347.35 plus 22% of the excess over $9,065. |
| Over $11,440 but not over $14,300 | $1,869.85 plus 25% of the excess over $11,440. |
| Over $14,300 but not over $17,160 | $2,584.85 plus 28% of the excess over $14,300. |
| Over $17,160 but not over $22,875 | $3,385.65 plus 33% of the excess over $17,160. |
| Over $22,875 but not over $30,540 | $5,271.60 plus 38% of the excess over $22,875. |
| Over $30,540 but not over $44,350 | $8,184.30 plus 42% of the excess over $30,540 |
| Over $44,350 but not over $57,195 | $13,984.50 plus 45% of the excess over $44,350 |
| Over $57,195 but not over $85,790 | $19,764.75 plus 49% of the excess over $57,195 |
| Over $85,790 | $33,776.30, plus 50% of the excess over $85,790. |

# CORPORATIONS—TAX RATE SCHEDULES

## Corporate Regular Income Tax Rates

| Taxable Income | Tax Years Beginning in | | |
|---|---|---|---|
| | 1979, 1980 and 1981 | 1982 | 1983 and after |
| $ 1–$ 25,000 | 17% | 16% | 15% |
| 25,001– 50,000 | 20 | 19 | 18 |
| 50,001– 75,000 | 30 | 30 | 30 |
| 75,001– 100,000 | 40 | 40 | 40 |
| Over $100,000 | 46 | 46 | 46 |

*Note to fiscal year corporations.* Whenever there is a change in rates from one calendar year to the next, the proration rules of § 15 (formerly § 21) apply.
*Note regarding the effect of the Deficit Reduction Act of 1984 on large corporations:* A surtax of 5 percent is imposed on the taxable income in the $1,000,000 to $1,405,000 range for taxable years beginning after December 31, 1983.

# UNIFIED TRANSFER TAX RATE SCHEDULE

## For Gifts Made and For Deaths After 1976 and Before 1982

| If the amount with respect to which the tentative tax to be computed is: | The tentative tax is: |
| --- | --- |
| Not over $10,000 | 18 percent of such amount. |
| Over $10,000 but not over $20,000 | $1,800, plus 20 percent of the excess of such amount over $10,000. |
| Over $20,000 but not over $40,000 | $3,800, plus 22 percent of the excess of such amount over $20,000. |
| Over $40,000 but not over $60,000 | $8,200, plus 24 percent of the excess of such amount over $40,000. |
| Over $60,000 but not over $80,000 | $13,000, plus 26 percent of the excess of such amount over $60,000. |
| Over $80,000 but not over $100,000 | $18,200, plus 28 percent of the excess of such amount over $80,000. |
| Over $100,000 but not over $150,000 | $23,800, plus 30 percent of the excess of such amount over $100,000. |
| Over $150,000 but not over $250,000 | $38,800, plus 32 percent of the excess of such amount over $150,000. |
| Over $250,000 but not over $500,000 | $70,800, plus 34 percent of the excess of such amount over $250,000. |
| Over $500,000 but not over $750,000 | $155,800, plus 37 percent of the excess of such amount over $500,000. |
| Over $750,000 but not over $1,000,000 | $248,300, plus 39 percent of the excess of such amount over $750,000. |
| Over $1,000,000 but not over $1,250,000 | $345,800, plus 41 percent of the excess of such amount over $1,000,000. |
| Over $1,250,000 but not over $1,500,000 | $448,300, plus 43 percent of the excess of such amount over $1,250,000. |
| Over $1,500,000 but not over $2,000,000 | $555,800, plus 45 percent of the excess of such amount over $1,500,000. |
| Over $2,000,000 but not over $2,500,000 | $780,800, plus 49 percent of the excess of such amount over $2,000,000. |
| Over $2,500,000 but not over $3,000,000 | $1,025,800, plus 53 percent of the excess of such amount over $2,500,000. |
| Over $3,000,000 but not over $3,500,000 | $1,290,800, plus 57 percent of the excess of such amount over $3,000,000. |
| Over $3,500,000 but not over $4,000,000 | $1,575,800, plus 61 percent of the excess of such amount over $3,500,000. |
| Over $4,000,000 but not over $4,500,000 | $1,880,800, plus 65 percent of the excess of such amount over $4,000,000. |
| Over $4,500,000 but not over $5,000,000 | $2,205,800, plus 69 percent of the excess of such amount over $4,500,000. |
| Over $5,000,000 | $2,550,800, plus 70 percent of the excess of such amount over $5,000,000. |

# UNIFIED TRANSFER TAX RATE SCHEDULE

## For Gifts Made and For Deaths in 1982

**If the amount with respect to which the tentative tax to be computed is:**          **The tentative tax is:**

Not over $10,000 .............................. 18 percent of such amount.

Over $10,000 but not over $20,000............... $1,800, plus 20 percent of the excess of such amount over $10,000.

Over $20,000 but not over $40,000............... $3,800, plus 22 percent of the excess of such amount over $20,000.

Over $40,000 but not over $60,000............... $8,200, plus 24 percent of the excess of such amount over $40,000.

Over $60,000 but not over $80,000............... $13,000, plus 26 percent of the excess of such amount over $60,000.

Over $80,000 but not over $100,000 ............. $18,200, plus 28 percent of the excess of such amount over $80,000.

Over $100,000 but not over $150,000 ............ $23,800, plus 30 percent of the excess of such amount over $100,000.

Over $150,000 but not over $250,000 ............ $38,800, plus 32 percent of the excess of such amount over $150,000.

Over $250,000 but not over $500,000 ............ $70,800, plus 34 percent of the excess of such amount over $250,000.

Over $500,000 but not over $750,000 ............ $155,800, plus 37 percent of the excess of such amount over $500,000.

Over $750,000 but not over $1,000,000 .......... $248,300, plus 39 percent of the excess of such amount over $750,000.

Over $1,000,000 but not over $1,250,000 ........ $345,800, plus 41 percent of the excess of such amount over $1,000,000.

Over $1,250,000 but not over $1,500,000 ........ $448,300, plus 43 percent of the excess of such amount over $1,250,000.

Over $1,500,000 but not over $2,000,000 ........ $555,800, plus 45 percent of the excess of such amount over $1,500,000.

Over $2,000,000 but not over $2,500,000 ........ $780,800, plus 49 percent of the excess of such amount over $2,000,000.

Over $2,500,000 but not over $3,000,000 ........ $1,025,800, plus 53 percent of the excess of such amount over $2,500,000.

Over $3,000,000 but not over $3,500,000 ........ $1,290,800, plus 57 percent of the excess of such amount over $3,000,000.

Over $3,500,000 but not over $4,000,000 ........ $1,575,800, plus 61 percent of the excess of such amount over $3,500,000.

Over $4,000,000................................ $1,880,800, plus 65 percent of the excess of such amount over $4,000,000.

# UNIFIED TRANSFER TAX RATE SCHEDULE

## For Gifts Made and For Deaths in 1983

| If the amount with respect to which the tentative tax to be computed is: | The tentative tax is: |
| --- | --- |
| Not over $10,000 | 18 percent of such amount. |
| Over $10,000 but not over $20,000 | $1,800, plus 20 percent of the excess of such amount over $10,000. |
| Over $20,000 but not over $40,000 | $3,800, plus 22 percent of the excess of such amount over $20,000. |
| Over $40,000 but not over $60,000 | $8,200, plus 24 percent of the excess of such amount over $40,000. |
| Over $60,000 but not over $80,000 | $13,000, plus 26 percent of the excess of such amount over $60,000. |
| Over $80,000 but not over $100,000 | $18,200, plus 28 percent of the excess of such amount over $80,000. |
| Over $100,000 but not over $150,000 | $23,800, plus 30 percent of the excess of such amount over $100,000. |
| Over $150,000 but not over $250,000 | $38,800, plus 32 percent of the excess of such amount over $150,000. |
| Over $250,000 but not over $500,000 | $70,800, plus 34 percent of the excess of such amount over $250,000. |
| Over $500,000 but not over $750,000 | $155,800, plus 37 percent of the excess of such amount over $500,000. |
| Over $750,000 but not over $1,000,000 | $248,300, plus 39 percent of the excess of such amount over $750,000. |
| Over $1,000,000 but not over $1,250,000 | $345,800, plus 41 percent of the excess of such amount over $1,000,000. |
| Over $1,250,000 but not over $1,500,000 | $448,300, plus 43 percent of the excess of such amount over $1,250,000. |
| Over $1,500,000 but not over $2,000,000 | $555,800, plus 45 percent of the excess of such amount over $1,500,000. |
| Over $2,000,000 but not over $2,500,000 | $780,800, plus 49 percent of the excess of such amount over $2,000,000. |
| Over $2,500,000 but not over $3,000,000 | $1,025,800, plus 53 percent of the excess of such amount over $2,500,000. |
| Over $3,000,000 but not over $3,500,000 | $1,290,800, plus 57 percent of the excess of such amount over $3,000,000. |
| Over $3,500,000 | $1,575,800, plus 60 percent of the excess of such amount over $3,500,000. |

# UNIFIED TRANSFER TAX RATE SCHEDULE

## For Gifts Made and For Deaths in 1984 through 1987

| If the amount with respect to which the tentative tax to be computed is: | The tentative tax is: |
| --- | --- |
| Not over $10,000 | 18 percent of such amount. |
| Over $10,000 but not over $20,000 | $1,800, plus 20 percent of the excess of such amount over $10,000. |
| Over $20,000 but not over $40,000 | $3,800, plus 22 percent of the excess of such amount over $20,000. |
| Over $40,000 but not over $60,000 | $8,200, plus 24 percent of the excess of such amount over $40,000. |
| Over $60,000 but not over $80,000 | $13,000, plus 26 percent of the excess of such amount over $60,000. |
| Over $80,000 but not over $100,000 | $18,200, plus 28 percent of the excess of such amount over $80,000. |
| Over $100,000 but not over $150,000 | $23,800, plus 30 percent of the excess of such amount over $100,000. |
| Over $150,000 but not over $250,000 | $38,800, plus 32 percent of the excess of such amount over $150,000. |
| Over $250,000 but not over $500,000 | $70,800, plus 34 percent of the excess of such amount over $250,000. |
| Over $500,000 but not over $750,000 | $155,800, plus 37 percent of the excess of such amount over $500,000. |
| Over $750,000 but not over $1,000,000 | $248,300, plus 39 percent of the excess of such amount over $750,000. |
| Over $1,000,000 but not over $1,250,000 | $345,800, plus 41 percent of the excess of such amount over $1,000,000. |
| Over $1,250,000 but not over $1,500,000 | $448,300, plus 43 percent of the excess of such amount over $1,250,000. |
| Over $1,500,000 but not over $2,000,000 | $555,800, plus 45 percent of the excess of such amount over $1,500,000. |
| Over $2,000,000 but not over $2,500,000 | $780,800, plus 49 percent of the excess of such amount over $2,000,000. |
| Over $2,500,000 but not over $3,000,000 | $1,025,800, plus 53 percent of the excess of such amount over $2,500,000. |
| Over $3,000,000 | $1,290,800, plus 55 percent of the excess of such amount over $3,000,000. |

# UNIFIED TRANSFER TAX RATE SCHEDULE

## For Gifts Made and For Deaths After 1987

| If the amount with respect to which the tentative tax to be computed is: | The tentative tax is: |
|---|---|
| Not over $10,000 | 18 percent of such amount. |
| Over $10,000 but not over $20,000 | $1,800, plus 20 percent of the excess of such amount over $10,000. |
| Over $20,000 but not over $40,000 | $3,800, plus 22 percent of the excess of such amount over $20,000. |
| Over $40,000 but not over $60,000 | $8,200, plus 24 percent of the excess of such amount over $40,000. |
| Over $60,000 but not over $80,000 | $13,000, plus 26 percent of the excess of such amount over $60,000. |
| Over $80,000 but not over $100,000 | $18,200, plus 28 percent of the excess of such amount over $80,000. |
| Over $100,000 but not over $150,000 | $23,800, plus 30 percent of the excess of such amount over $100,000. |
| Over $150,000 but not over $250,000 | $38,800, plus 32 percent of the excess of such amount over $150,000. |
| Over $250,000 but not over $500,000 | $70,800, plus 34 percent of the excess of such amount over $250,000. |
| Over $500,000 but not over $750,000 | $155,800, plus 37 percent of the excess of such amount over $500,000. |
| Over $750,000 but not over $1,000,000 | $248,300, plus 39 percent of the excess of such amount over $750,000. |
| Over $1,000,000 but not over $1,250,000 | $345,800, plus 41 percent of the excess of such amount over $1,000,000. |
| Over $1,250,000 but not over $1,500,000 | $448,300, plus 43 percent of the excess of such amount over $1,250,000. |
| Over $1,500,000 but not over $2,000,000 | $555,800, plus 45 percent of the excess of such amount over $1,500,000. |
| Over $2,000,000 but not over $2,500,000 | $780,800, plus 49 percent of the excess of such amount over $2,000,000. |
| Over $2,500,000 | $1,025,800, plus 50 percent of the excess of such amount over $2,500,000. |

**Appendix A**

## TABLE FOR COMPUTATION OF GROSS ESTATE TAX—FOR DEATHS PRIOR TO JANUARY 1, 1977

| (A)<br>Taxable estate equal to or more than— | (B)<br>Taxable estate less than— | (C)<br>Tax on amount in column (A) | (D)<br>Rate of tax on excess over amount in column (A) |
|---|---|---|---|
| | | | Percent |
| 0 | $5,000 | 0 | 3 |
| $5,000 | 10,000 | $150 | 7 |
| 10,000 | 20,000 | 500 | 11 |
| 20,000 | 30,000 | 1,600 | 14 |
| 30,000 | 40,000 | 3,000 | 18 |
| 40,000 | 50,000 | 4,800 | 22 |
| 50,000 | 60,000 | 7,000 | 25 |
| 60,000 | 100,000 | 9,500 | 28 |
| 100,000 | 250,000 | 20,700 | 30 |
| 250,000 | 500,000 | 65,700 | 32 |
| 500,000 | 750,000 | 145,700 | 35 |
| 750,000 | 1,000,000 | 233,200 | 37 |
| 1,000,000 | 1,250,000 | 325,700 | 39 |
| 1,250,000 | 1,500,000 | 423,200 | 42 |
| 1,500,000 | 2,000,000 | 528,200 | 45 |
| 2,000,000 | 2,500,000 | 753,200 | 49 |
| 2,500,000 | 3,000,000 | 998,200 | 53 |
| 3,000,000 | 3,500,000 | 1,263,200 | 56 |
| 3,500,000 | 4,000,000 | 1,543,200 | 59 |
| 4,000,000 | 5,000,000 | 1,838,200 | 63 |
| 5,000,000 | 6,000,000 | 2,468,200 | 67 |
| 6,000,000 | 7,000,000 | 3,138,200 | 70 |
| 7,000,000 | 8,000,000 | 3,838,200 | 73 |
| 8,000,000 | 10,000,000 | 4,568,200 | 76 |
| 10,000,000 | | 6,088,200 | 77 |

# GIFT TAX RATES—FOR GIFTS PRIOR TO JANUARY 1, 1977

| (A)<br><br>Amount of taxable gifts equal to or more than— | (B)<br><br>Amount of taxable gifts less than— | (C)<br><br>Tax on amount in column (A) | (D)<br>Rate of tax on excess over amount in column (A) |
|---:|---:|---:|:---|
| | | | Percent |
| 0 | $5,000 | 0 | 2¼ |
| $5,000 | 10,000 | $112.50 | 5¼ |
| 10,000 | 20,000 | 375.00 | 8¼ |
| 20,000 | 30,000 | 1,200.00 | 10½ |
| 30,000 | 40,000 | 2,250.00 | 13½ |
| 40,000 | 50,000 | 3,600.00 | 16½ |
| 50,000 | 60,000 | 5,250.00 | 18¾ |
| 60,000 | 100,000 | 7,125.00 | 21 |
| 100,000 | 250,000 | 15,525.00 | 22½ |
| 250,000 | 500,000 | 49,275.00 | 24 |
| 500,000 | 750,000 | 109,275.00 | 26¼ |
| 750,000 | 1,000,000 | 174,900.00 | 27¾ |
| 1,000,000 | 1,250,000 | 244,275.00 | 29¼ |
| 1,250,000 | 1,500,000 | 317,400.00 | 31½ |
| 1,500,000 | 2,000,000 | 396,150.00 | 33¾ |
| 2,000,000 | 2,500,000 | 564,900.00 | 36¾ |
| 2,500,000 | 3,000,000 | 748,650.00 | 39¾ |
| 3,000,000 | 3,500,000 | 947,400.00 | 42 |
| 3,500,000 | 4,000,000 | 1,157,400.00 | 44¼ |
| 4,000,000 | 5,000,000 | 1,378,650.00 | 47¼ |
| 5,000,000 | 6,000,000 | 1,851,150.00 | 50¼ |
| 6,000,000 | 7,000,000 | 2,353,650.00 | 52½ |
| 7,000,000 | 8,000,000 | 2,878,650.00 | 54¾ |
| 8,000,000 | 10,000,000 | 3,426,150.00 | 57 |
| 10,000,000 | | 4,566,150.00 | 57¾ |

# TABLE FOR COMPUTATION OF MAXIMUM CREDIT FOR STATE DEATH TAXES

| (A)<br><br>Adjusted Taxable estate* equal to or more than— | (B)<br><br>Adjusted Taxable estate* less than— | (C)<br><br><br>Credit on amount in column (A) | (D)<br>Rates of credit on excess over amount in column (A) |
|---|---|---|---|
| | | | Percent |
| 0 | $40,000 | 0 | None |
| $40,000 | 90,000 | 0 | 0.8 |
| 90,000 | 140,000 | $400 | 1.6 |
| 140,000 | 240,000 | 1,200 | 2.4 |
| 240,000 | 440,000 | 3,600 | 3.2 |
| 440,000 | 640,000 | 10,000 | 4.0 |
| 640,000 | 840,000 | 18,000 | 4.8 |
| 840,000 | 1,040,000 | 27,600 | 5.6 |
| 1,040,000 | 1,540,000 | 38,800 | 6.4 |
| 1,540,000 | 2,040,000 | 70,800 | 7.2 |
| 2,040,000 | 2,540,000 | 106,800 | 8.0 |
| 2,540,000 | 3,040,000 | 146,800 | 8.8 |
| 3,040,000 | 3,540,000 | 190,800 | 9.6 |
| 3,540,000 | 4,040,000 | 238,800 | 10.4 |
| 4,040,000 | 5,040,000 | 290,800 | 11.2 |
| 5,040,000 | 6,040,000 | 402,800 | 12.0 |
| 6,040,000 | 7,040,000 | 522,800 | 12.8 |
| 7,040,000 | 8,040,000 | 650,800 | 13.6 |
| 8,040,000 | 9,040,000 | 786,800 | 14.4 |
| 9,040,000 | 10,040,000 | 930,800 | 15.2 |
| 10,040,000 | | 1,082,800 | 16.0 |

*The term "adjusted taxable estate" means the taxable estate reduced by $60,000.

# VALUATION TABLES
## (After 1970 and before December 1, 1983)

### Table A–6%

| Male | | | | Female | | | |
|---|---|---|---|---|---|---|---|
| 1 Age | 2 Annuity | 3 Life Estate | 4 Remainder | 1 Age | 2 Annuity | 3 Life Estate | 4 Remainder |
| 0 | 15.6175 | .93705 | .06295 | 0 | 15.8972 | .95383 | .04617 |
| 1 | 16.0362 | .96217 | .03783 | 1 | 16.2284 | .97370 | .02630 |
| 2 | 16.0283 | .96170 | .03830 | 2 | 16.2287 | .97372 | .02628 |
| 3 | 16.0089 | .96053 | .03947 | 3 | 16.2180 | .97308 | .02692 |
| 4 | 15.9841 | .95905 | .04095 | 4 | 16.2029 | .97217 | .02783 |
| 5 | 15.9553 | .95732 | .04268 | 5 | 16.1850 | .97110 | .02890 |
| 6 | 15.9233 | .95540 | .04460 | 6 | 16.1648 | .96989 | .03011 |
| 7 | 15.8885 | .95331 | .04669 | 7 | 16.1421 | .96853 | .03147 |
| 8 | 15.8508 | .95105 | .04895 | 8 | 16.1172 | .96703 | .03297 |
| 9 | 15.8101 | .94861 | .05139 | 9 | 16.0910 | .96541 | .03459 |
| 10 | 15.7663 | .94598 | .05402 | 10 | 16.0608 | .96365 | .03635 |
| 11 | 15.7194 | .94316 | .05684 | 11 | 16.0293 | .96176 | .03824 |
| 12 | 15.6698 | .94019 | .05981 | 12 | 15.9958 | .95975 | .04025 |
| 13 | 15.6180 | .93708 | .06292 | 13 | 15.9607 | .95764 | .04236 |
| 14 | 15.5651 | .93391 | .06609 | 14 | 15.9239 | .95543 | .04457 |
| 15 | 15.5115 | .93069 | .06931 | 15 | 15.8856 | .95314 | .04686 |
| 16 | 15.4576 | .92746 | .07254 | 16 | 15.8460 | .95076 | .04924 |
| 17 | 15.4031 | .92419 | .07581 | 17 | 15.8048 | .94829 | .05171 |
| 18 | 15.3481 | .92089 | .07911 | 18 | 15.7620 | .94572 | .05428 |
| 19 | 15.2918 | .91751 | .08249 | 19 | 15.7172 | .94303 | .05697 |
| 20 | 15.2339 | .91403 | .08597 | 20 | 15.6701 | .94021 | .05979 |
| 21 | 15.1744 | .91046 | .08954 | 21 | 15.6207 | .93724 | .06276 |
| 22 | 15.1130 | .90678 | .09328 | 22 | 15.5687 | .93412 | .06588 |
| 23 | 15.0487 | .90292 | .09702 | 23 | 15.5141 | .93085 | .06915 |
| 24 | 14.9807 | .89884 | .10116 | 24 | 15.4565 | .92739 | .07261 |
| 25 | 14.9075 | .89445 | .10555 | 25 | 15.3959 | .92375 | .07625 |
| 26 | 14.8287 | .88972 | .11028 | 26 | 15.3322 | .91993 | .08007 |
| 27 | 14.7442 | .88465 | .11535 | 27 | 15.2652 | .91591 | .08409 |
| 28 | 14.6542 | .87925 | .12075 | 28 | 15.1946 | .91168 | .08832 |
| 29 | 14.5588 | .87353 | .12647 | 29 | 15.1208 | .90725 | .09275 |
| 30 | 14.4584 | .86750 | .13250 | 30 | 15.0432 | .90259 | .09741 |
| 31 | 14.3528 | .86117 | .13883 | 31 | 14.9622 | .89773 | .10227 |
| 32 | 14.2418 | .85451 | .14549 | 32 | 14.8775 | .89265 | .10735 |
| 33 | 14.1254 | .84752 | .15248 | 33 | 14.7888 | .88733 | .11267 |
| 34 | 14.0034 | .84020 | .15980 | 34 | 14.6960 | .88176 | .11824 |
| 35 | 13.8758 | .83255 | .16745 | 35 | 14.5989 | .87593 | .12407 |
| 36 | 13.7425 | .82455 | .17545 | 36 | 14.4975 | .86985 | .13015 |
| 37 | 13.6036 | .81622 | .18378 | 37 | 14.3915 | .86349 | .13651 |
| 38 | 13.4591 | .80755 | .19245 | 38 | 14.2811 | .85687 | .14313 |
| 39 | 13.3090 | .79854 | .20146 | 39 | 14.1663 | .84998 | .15002 |
| 40 | 13.1538 | .78923 | .21077 | 40 | 14.0468 | .84281 | .15719 |
| 41 | 12.9934 | .77960 | .22040 | 41 | 13.9227 | .83536 | .16464 |
| 42 | 12.8279 | .76967 | .23033 | 42 | 13.7940 | .82764 | .17236 |
| 43 | 12.6574 | .75944 | .24056 | 43 | 13.6604 | .81962 | .18038 |
| 44 | 12.4819 | .74891 | .25109 | 44 | 13.5219 | .81131 | .18869 |
| 45 | 12.3013 | .73808 | .26192 | 45 | 13.3781 | .80269 | .19731 |
| 46 | 12.1158 | .72695 | .27305 | 46 | 13.2290 | .79374 | .20626 |

# VALUATION TABLES
## (After 1970 and Before December 1, 1983, *cont.*)

### Table A–6%

| Male | | | | Female | | | |
|------|------|------|------|------|------|------|------|
| **1**<br>Age | **2**<br>Annuity | **3**<br>Life Estate | **4**<br>Remainder | **1**<br>Age | **2**<br>Annuity | **3**<br>Life Estate | **4**<br>Remainder |
| 56 | 10.0777 | .60466 | .39534 | 56 | 11.4353 | .68612 | .31388 |
| 57 | 9.8552 | .59131 | .40869 | 57 | 11.2200 | .67320 | .32680 |
| 58 | 9.6297 | .57778 | .42222 | 58 | 10.9980 | .65988 | .34012 |
| 59 | 9.4028 | .56417 | .43583 | 59 | 10.7703 | .64622 | .35378 |
| 60 | 9.1753 | .55052 | .44948 | 60 | 10.5376 | .63226 | .36774 |
| 61 | 8.9478 | .53687 | .46313 | 61 | 10.3005 | .61803 | .38197 |
| 62 | 8.7202 | .52321 | .47679 | 62 | 10.0587 | .60352 | .39648 |
| 63 | 8.4924 | .50954 | .49046 | 63 | 9.8118 | .58871 | .41129 |
| 64 | 8.2642 | .49585 | .50415 | 64 | 9.5592 | .57355 | .42645 |
| 65 | 8.0353 | .48212 | .51788 | 65 | 9.3005 | .55803 | .44197 |
| 66 | 7.8060 | .46836 | .53164 | 66 | 9.0352 | .54211 | .45789 |
| 67 | 7.5763 | .45458 | .54542 | 67 | 8.7639 | .52583 | .47417 |
| 68 | 7.3462 | .44077 | .55923 | 68 | 8.4874 | .50924 | .49076 |
| 69 | 7.1149 | .42689 | .57311 | 69 | 8.2068 | .49241 | .50759 |
| 70 | 6.8823 | .41294 | .58706 | 70 | 7.9234 | .47540 | .52460 |
| 71 | 6.6481 | .39889 | .60111 | 71 | 7.6371 | .45823 | .54177 |
| 72 | 6.4123 | .38474 | .61526 | 72 | 7.3480 | .44088 | .55912 |
| 73 | 6.1752 | .37051 | .62949 | 73 | 7.0568 | .42341 | .57659 |
| 74 | 5.9373 | .35624 | .64376 | 74 | 6.7645 | .40587 | .59413 |
| 75 | 5.6990 | .34194 | .65806 | 75 | 6.4721 | .38831 | .61167 |
| 76 | 5.4602 | .32761 | .67239 | 76 | 6.1788 | .37073 | .62927 |
| 77 | 5.2211 | .31327 | .68673 | 77 | 5.8845 | .35307 | .64693 |
| 78 | 4.9825 | .29895 | .70105 | 78 | 5.5910 | .33546 | .66454 |
| 79 | 4.7469 | .28481 | .71519 | 79 | 5.3018 | .31811 | .68189 |
| 80 | 4.5164 | .27098 | .72902 | 80 | 5.0195 | .30117 | .69883 |
| 81 | 4.2955 | .25773 | .74227 | 81 | 4.7482 | .28489 | .71511 |
| 82 | 4.0879 | .24527 | .75473 | 82 | 4.4892 | .26935 | .73065 |
| 83 | 3.8924 | .23354 | .76646 | 83 | 4.2398 | .25439 | .74561 |
| 84 | 3.7029 | .22217 | .77783 | 84 | 3.9927 | .23956 | .76044 |
| 85 | 3.5117 | .21070 | .78930 | 85 | 3.7401 | .22441 | .77559 |
| 86 | 3.3259 | .19955 | .80045 | 86 | 3.5016 | .21010 | .78990 |
| 87 | 3.1450 | .18820 | .81130 | 87 | 3.2790 | .19674 | .80326 |
| 88 | 2.9703 | .17872 | .82178 | 88 | 3.0719 | .18431 | .81569 |
| 89 | 2.8052 | .16831 | .83169 | 89 | 2.8808 | .17285 | .82715 |
| 90 | 2.6536 | .15922 | .84078 | 90 | 2.7068 | .16241 | .83759 |
| 91 | 2.5162 | .15097 | .84903 | 91 | 2.5502 | .15301 | .84699 |
| 92 | 2.3917 | .14350 | .85650 | 92 | 2.4116 | .14470 | .85530 |
| 93 | 2.2801 | .13681 | .86319 | 93 | 2.2901 | .13741 | .86259 |
| 94 | 2.1802 | .13081 | .86919 | 94 | 2.1839 | .13103 | .86897 |
| 95 | 2.0891 | .12535 | .87465 | 95 | 2.0891 | .12535 | .87465 |
| 96 | 1.9997 | .11998 | .88002 | 96 | 1.9997 | .11998 | .88002 |
| 97 | 1.9145 | .11487 | .88513 | 97 | 1.9145 | .11487 | .88513 |
| 98 | 1.8331 | .10999 | .89001 | 98 | 1.8331 | .10999 | .89001 |
| 99 | 1.7554 | .10532 | .89468 | 99 | 1.7554 | .10532 | .89468 |
| 100 | 1.6812 | .10087 | .89913 | 100 | 1.6812 | .10087 | .89913 |
| 101 | 1.6101 | .09661 | .90339 | 101 | 1.6101 | .09661 | .90339 |
| 102 | 1.5416 | .09250 | .90750 | 102 | 1.5416 | .09250 | .90750 |
| 103 | 1.4744 | .08846 | .91154 | 103 | 1.4744 | .08846 | .91154 |
| 104 | 1.4065 | .08439 | .91561 | 104 | 1.4065 | .08439 | .91561 |
| 105 | 1.3334 | .08000 | .92000 | 105 | 1.3334 | .08000 | .92000 |
| 106 | 1.2452 | .07471 | .92529 | 106 | 1.2452 | .07471 | .92529 |
| 107 | 1.1196 | .06718 | .93282 | 107 | 1.1196 | .06718 | .93282 |
| 108 | .9043 | .05426 | .94574 | 108 | .9043 | .05426 | .94574 |
| 109 | .4717 | .02830 | .97170 | 109 | .4717 | .02830 | .97170 |

## VALUATION TABLES
### (After 1970 and Before December 1, 1983, *cont.*)

#### Table B—6%

| 1 Number of Years | 2 Annuity | 3 Term Certain | 4 Remainder | 1 Number of Years | 2 Annuity | 3 Term Certain | 4 Remainder |
|---|---|---|---|---|---|---|---|
| 1 | 0.9434 | .056604 | .943396 | 31 | 13.9291 | .835745 | .164255 |
| 2 | 1.8334 | .110004 | .889996 | 32 | 14.0840 | .845043 | .154957 |
| 3 | 2.6730 | .160381 | .839619 | 33 | 14.2302 | .853814 | .146186 |
| 4 | 3.4651 | .207906 | .792094 | 34 | 14.3681 | .862088 | .137912 |
| 5 | 4.2124 | .252742 | .747258 | 35 | 14.4982 | .869895 | .130105 |
| 6 | 4.9173 | .295039 | .704961 | 36 | 14.6210 | .877259 | .122741 |
| 7 | 5.5824 | .334943 | .665057 | 37 | 14.7368 | .884207 | .115793 |
| 8 | 6.2098 | .372588 | .627412 | 38 | 14.8460 | .890761 | .109239 |
| 9 | 6.8017 | .408102 | .591898 | 39 | 14.9491 | .896944 | .103056 |
| 10 | 7.3601 | .441605 | .558395 | 40 | 15.0463 | .902778 | .097222 |
| 11 | 7.8869 | .473212 | .526788 | 41 | 15.1380 | .908281 | .091719 |
| 12 | 8.3838 | .503031 | .496969 | 42 | 15.2245 | .913473 | .086527 |
| 13 | 8.8527 | .531161 | .468839 | 43 | 15.3062 | .918370 | .081630 |
| 14 | 9.2950 | .557699 | .442301 | 44 | 15.3832 | .922991 | .077009 |
| 15 | 9.7122 | .582735 | .417265 | 45 | 15.4558 | .927350 | .072650 |
| 16 | 10.1059 | .606354 | .393646 | 46 | 15.5244 | .931462 | .068538 |
| 17 | 10.4773 | .628636 | .371364 | 47 | 15.5890 | .935342 | .064653 |
| 18 | 10.8276 | .649656 | .350344 | 48 | 15.6500 | .939002 | .060998 |
| 19 | 11.1581 | .689487 | .330513 | 49 | 15.7076 | .942454 | .057546 |
| 20 | 11.4699 | .688195 | .311805 | 50 | 15.7619 | .945712 | .054288 |
| 21 | 11.7641 | .705845 | .294155 | 51 | 15.8131 | .948785 | .051215 |
| 22 | 12.0416 | .722495 | .277505 | 52 | 15.8614 | .951684 | .048316 |
| 23 | 12.3034 | .738203 | .261797 | 53 | 15.9070 | .954418 | .045582 |
| 24 | 12.5504 | .753021 | .246979 | 54 | 15.9500 | .956999 | .043001 |
| 25 | 12.7834 | .767001 | .232999 | 55 | 15.9905 | .959433 | .040567 |
| 26 | 13.0032 | .780190 | .219810 | 56 | 16.0288 | .961729 | .038271 |
| 27 | 13.2105 | .792632 | .207368 | 57 | 16.0649 | .963895 | .036105 |
| 28 | 13.4062 | .804370 | .195630 | 58 | 16.0990 | .965939 | .034061 |
| 29 | 13.5907 | .815443 | .184557 | 59 | 16.1311 | .967867 | .032133 |
| 30 | 13.7648 | .825890 | .174110 | 60 | 16.1614 | .969686 | .030314 |

# VALUATION TABLES (After November 30, 1983)

## Table A–10%
Single Life, Unisex, Showing the Present Worth of an
Annuity, of a Life Interest, and of a Remainder Interest
[Reg. § § 20.2031–7(f) and 25.2512–5(f)]

| Age (1) | Annuity (2) | Life Estate (3) | Remainder (4) | Age (1) | Annuity (2) | Life Estate (3) | Remainder (4) |
|---|---|---|---|---|---|---|---|
| 0 | 9.7188 | 0.97188 | 0.02812 | 55 | 8.0046 | .80046 | .19954 |
| 1 | 9.8988 | .98988 | .01012 | 56 | 7.9006 | .79006 | .20994 |
| 2 | 9.9017 | .99017 | .00983 | 57 | 7.7931 | .77931 | .22069 |
| 3 | 9.9008 | .99008 | .00992 | 58 | 7.6822 | .76822 | .23178 |
| 4 | 9.8981 | .98981 | .01019 | 59 | 7.5675 | .75675 | .24325 |
| 5 | 9.8938 | .98938 | .01062 | 60 | 7.4491 | .74491 | .25509 |
| 6 | 9.8884 | .98884 | .01116 | 61 | 7.3267 | .73267 | .26733 |
| 7 | 9.8822 | .98822 | .01178 | 62 | 7.2002 | .72002 | .27998 |
| 8 | 9.8748 | .98748 | .01252 | 63 | 7.0696 | .70696 | .29304 |
| 9 | 9.8663 | .98663 | .01337 | 64 | 6.9352 | .69352 | .30648 |
| 10 | 9.8565 | .98565 | .01435 | 65 | 6.7970 | .67970 | .32030 |
| 11 | 9.8453 | .98453 | .01547 | 66 | 6.6551 | .66551 | .33449 |
| 12 | 9.8329 | .98329 | .01671 | 67 | 6.5098 | .65098 | .34902 |
| 13 | 9.8198 | .98198 | .01802 | 68 | 6.3610 | .63610 | .36390 |
| 14 | 9.8066 | .98066 | .01934 | 69 | 6.2086 | .62086 | .37914 |
| 15 | 9.7937 | .97937 | .02063 | 70 | 6.0522 | .60522 | .39478 |
| 16 | 9.7815 | .97815 | .02185 | 71 | 5.8914 | .58914 | .41086 |
| 17 | 9.7700 | .97700 | .02300 | 72 | 5.7261 | .57261 | .42739 |
| 18 | 9.7590 | .97590 | .02410 | 73 | 5.5571 | .55571 | .44429 |
| 19 | 9.7480 | .97480 | .02520 | 74 | 5.3862 | .53862 | .46138 |
| 20 | 9.7365 | .97365 | .02635 | 75 | 5.2149 | .52149 | .47851 |
| 21 | 9.7245 | .97245 | .02755 | 76 | 5.0441 | .50441 | .49559 |
| 22 | 9.7120 | .97120 | .02880 | 77 | 4.8742 | .48742 | .51258 |
| 23 | 9.6986 | .96986 | .03014 | 78 | 4.7049 | .47049 | .52951 |
| 24 | 9.6841 | .96841 | .03159 | 79 | 4.5357 | .45357 | .54643 |
| 25 | 9.6678 | .96678 | .03322 | 80 | 4.3659 | .43659 | .56341 |
| 26 | 9.6495 | .96495 | .03505 | 81 | 4.1967 | .41967 | .58033 |
| 27 | 9.6290 | .96290 | .03710 | 82 | 4.0295 | .40295 | .59705 |
| 28 | 9.6062 | .96062 | .03938 | 83 | 3.8642 | .38642 | .61358 |
| 29 | 9.5813 | .95813 | .04187 | 84 | 3.6998 | .36998 | .63002 |
| 30 | 9.5543 | .95543 | .04457 | 85 | 3.5359 | .35359 | .64641 |
| 31 | 9.5254 | .95254 | .04746 | 86 | 3.3764 | .33764 | .66236 |
| 32 | 9.4942 | .94942 | .05058 | 87 | 3.2262 | .32262 | .67738 |
| 33 | 9.4608 | .94608 | .05392 | 88 | 3.0859 | .30859 | .69141 |
| 34 | 9.4250 | .94250 | .05750 | 89 | 2.9526 | .29526 | .70474 |
| 35 | 9.3868 | .93868 | .06132 | 90 | 2.8221 | .28221 | .71779 |
| 36 | 9.3460 | .93460 | .06540 | 91 | 2.6955 | .26955 | .73045 |
| 37 | 9.3026 | .93026 | .06974 | 92 | 2.5771 | .25771 | .74229 |
| 38 | 9.2567 | .92567 | .07433 | 93 | 2.4692 | .24692 | .75308 |
| 39 | 9.2083 | .92083 | .07917 | 94 | 2.3728 | .23728 | .76272 |
| 40 | 9.1571 | .91571 | .08429 | 95 | 2.2887 | .22887 | .77113 |
| 41 | 9.1030 | .91030 | .08970 | 96 | 2.2181 | .22181 | .77819 |
| 42 | 9.0457 | .90457 | .09543 | 97 | 2.1550 | .21550 | .78450 |
| 43 | 8.9855 | .89855 | .10145 | 98 | 2.1000 | .21000 | .79000 |
| 44 | 8.9221 | .89221 | .10779 | 99 | 2.0486 | .20486 | .79514 |
| 45 | 8.8558 | .88558 | .11442 | 100 | 1.9975 | .19975 | .80025 |
| 46 | 8.7863 | .87863 | .12137 | 101 | 1.9532 | .19532 | .80468 |
| 47 | 8.7137 | .87137 | .12863 | 102 | 1.9054 | .19054 | .80946 |
| 48 | 8.6374 | .86374 | .13626 | 103 | 1.8437 | .18437 | .81563 |
| 49 | 8.5578 | .85578 | .14422 | 104 | 1.7856 | .17856 | .82144 |
| 50 | 8.4743 | .84743 | .15257 | 105 | 1.6962 | .16962 | .83038 |
| 51 | 8.3874 | .83874 | .16126 | 106 | 1.5488 | .15488 | .84512 |
| 52 | 8.2969 | .82969 | .17031 | 107 | 1.3409 | .13409 | .86591 |
| 53 | 8.2028 | .82028 | .17972 | 108 | 1.0068 | .10068 | .89932 |
| 54 | 8.1054 | .81054 | .18946 | 109 | .4545 | .04545 | .95455 |

## VALUATION TABLES (After November 30, 1983, *cont.*)

### Table B–10%
Table Showing the Present Worth of an Annuity for
a Term Certain, of an Income Interest for a Term Certain and of
a Remainder Interest Postponed for a Term Certain
[Reg. § § 20.2031–7(f) and 25.2512–5(f)]

| (1) Number of Years | (2) Annuity | (3) Term Certain | (4) Remainder | (1) Number of Years | (2) Annuity | (3) Term Certain | (4) Remainder |
|---|---|---|---|---|---|---|---|
| 1 | .9091 | .090909 | .909091 | 31 | 9.4790 | .947901 | .052099 |
| 2 | 1.7355 | .173554 | .826446 | 32 | 9.5264 | .952638 | .047362 |
| 3 | 2.4869 | .248685 | .751315 | 33 | 9.5694 | .956943 | .043057 |
| 4 | 3.1699 | .316987 | .683013 | 34 | 9.6086 | .960857 | .039143 |
| 5 | 3.7908 | .379079 | .620921 | 35 | 9.6442 | .964416 | .035584 |
| 6 | 4.3553 | .435526 | .564474 | 36 | 9.6765 | .967651 | .032349 |
| 7 | 4.8684 | .486842 | .513158 | 37 | 9.7059 | .970592 | .029408 |
| 8 | 5.3349 | .533493 | .466507 | 38 | 9.7327 | .973265 | .026735 |
| 9 | 5.7590 | .575902 | .424098 | 39 | 9.7570 | .975696 | .024304 |
| 10 | 6.1446 | .614457 | .385543 | 40 | 9.7791 | .977905 | .022095 |
| 11 | 6.4951 | .649506 | .350494 | 41 | 9.7991 | .979914 | .020086 |
| 12 | 6.8137 | .681369 | .318631 | 42 | 9.8174 | .981740 | .018260 |
| 13 | 7.1034 | .710336 | .289664 | 43 | 9.8340 | .983400 | .016600 |
| 14 | 7.3667 | .736669 | .263331 | 44 | 9.8491 | .984909 | .015091 |
| 15 | 7.6061 | .760608 | .239392 | 45 | 9.8628 | .986281 | .013718 |
| 16 | 7.8237 | .782371 | .217629 | 46 | 9.8753 | .987528 | .012472 |
| 17 | 8.0216 | .802155 | .197845 | 47 | 9.8866 | .988662 | .011338 |
| 18 | 8.2014 | .820141 | .179859 | 48 | 9.8969 | .989693 | .010307 |
| 19 | 8.3649 | .836492 | .163508 | 49 | 9.9063 | .990630 | .009370 |
| 20 | 8.5136 | .851356 | .148644 | 50 | 9.9148 | .991481 | .008519 |
| 21 | 8.6487 | .864869 | .135131 | 51 | 9.9226 | .992256 | .007744 |
| 22 | 8.7715 | .877154 | .122846 | 52 | 9.9296 | .992960 | .007040 |
| 23 | 8.8832 | .888322 | .111678 | 53 | 9.9360 | .993600 | .006400 |
| 24 | 8.9847 | .898474 | .101526 | 54 | 9.9418 | .994182 | .005818 |
| 25 | 9.0770 | .907704 | .092296 | 55 | 9.9471 | .994711 | .005289 |
| 26 | 9.1609 | .916095 | .083905 | 56 | 9.9519 | .995191 | .004809 |
| 27 | 9.2372 | .923722 | .076278 | 57 | 9.9563 | .995629 | .004371 |
| 28 | 9.3066 | .930657 | .069343 | 58 | 9.9603 | .996026 | .003974 |
| 29 | 9.3696 | .936961 | .063039 | 59 | 9.9639 | .996387 | .003613 |
| 30 | 9.4269 | .942691 | .057309 | 60 | 9.9672 | .996716 | .003284 |

# APPENDIX B
# TAX FORMS

Form **709**

(Rev. June 1985)

Department of the Treasury
Internal Revenue Service

# United States Gift Tax Return

(Section 6019 of the Internal Revenue Code) (For gifts made after December 31, 1981, and before January 1, 1988)

**Calendar year 19 _____.**

▶ For "Privacy Act" Notice, see the Instructions for Form 1040.

OMB No. 1545-0020
Expires 4-30-88

| Donor's first name and middle initial | Donor's last name | Social security number |
|---|---|---|
| Address (number and street) | | Domicile |
| City, State, and ZIP code | | Citizenship |

| | Yes | No |
|---|---|---|
| If the donor died during the year, check here ▶ ☐ and enter date of death _____ , 19 _____ . | | |
| If you received an extension of time to file this Form 709, check here ▶ ☐ and attach the Form 4868, 2688, 2350 or extension letter. | | |
| If you (the donor) filed a previous Form 709 (or 709-A), has your address changed since the last Form 709 (or 709-A) was filed? . . . . | | |

**A**   Gifts by husband or wife to third parties.—Do you consent to have the gifts made by you and by your spouse to third parties during the calendar year considered as made one-half by each of you? (See instructions) . . . . . . . . . .

*(If the answer is "Yes," the following information must be furnished and your spouse is to sign the consent shown below. If the answer is "No," skip lines 1-5 and go to Schedule A.)*

| **1a** Name of consenting spouse | **1b** Social security number |
|---|---|

**2**   Were you married to one another during the entire calendar year? (see instructions) . . . . . . . . . . . . . .

**3**   If the answer to 2 is "No," check whether ☐ married ☐ divorced or ☐ widowed, and give date (see instructions) ▶

**4**   Will a gift tax return for this calendar year be filed by your spouse? . . . . . . . . . . . . . . . .

**5**   **Consent of Spouse**—I consent to have the gifts made by me and by my spouse to third parties during the calendar year considered as made one-half by each of us. We are both aware of the joint and several liability for tax created by the execution of this consent.

Consenting spouse's signature ▶                    Date ▶

| | | | |
|---|---|---|---|
| **1** | Enter the amount from Schedule A, line 13 . . . . . . . . . . . . . . | 1 | |
| **2** | Enter the amount from Schedule B, line 3 . . . . . . . . . . . . . . | 2 | |
| **3** | Total taxable gifts (add lines 1 and 2) . . . . . . . . . . . . . . | 3 | |
| **4** | Tax computed on amount on line 3 (see Table A in separate instructions) . . . . . . | 4 | |
| **5** | Tax computed on amount on line 2 (see Table A in separate instructions) . . . . . . | 5 | |
| **6** | Balance (subtract line 5 from line 4) . . . . . . . . . . . . . . . | 6 | |
| **7** | Enter the unified credit from Table B (see instructions) . . . . . . . . . . . | 7 | |
| **8** | Enter the unified credit against tax allowable for all prior periods (from Sch. B, line 1, col. (c)) | 8 | |
| **9** | Balance (subtract line 8 from line 7) . . . . . . . . . . . . . . . | 9 | |
| **10** | Enter 20% of the amount allowed as specific exemption after September 8, 1976, and before January 1, 1977 (see instructions) . . . . . . . . . . . . . . | 10 | |
| **11** | Balance (subtract line 10 from line 9) . . . . . . . . . . . . . . . | 11 | |
| **12** | Unified credit (enter the smaller of line 6 or line 11) . . . . . . . . . . . | 12 | |
| **13** | Credit for foreign gift taxes (see instructions) . . . . . . . . . . . . | 13 | |
| **14** | Total credits (add lines 12 and 13). . . . . . . . . . . . . . . . | 14 | |
| **15** | Balance (subtract line 14 from line 6) (do not enter less than zero) . . . . . . . . | 15 | |
| **16** | Gift taxes prepaid with extension of time to file . . . . . . . . . . . . | 16 | |
| **17** | If line 16 is less than line 15, enter BALANCE DUE (see instructions) . . . . . . . | 17 | |
| **18** | If line 16 is greater than line 15, enter AMOUNT TO BE REFUNDED . . . . . . . . | 18 | |

*Please attach the necessary supplemental documents; see instructions.*

Under penalties of perjury, I declare that I have examined this return, including any accompanying schedules and statements, and to the best of my knowledge and belief it is true, correct, and complete. Declaration of preparer (other than donor) is based on all information of which preparer has any knowledge.

Donor's signature ▶                    Date ▶

Preparer's signature
(other than donor) ▶                Date ▶

Preparer's address
(other than donor) ▶

*(Left margin: Tax Computation / Please attach check or money order here)*

**For Paperwork Reduction Act Notice, see page 1 of the separate instructions to this form.**        Form **709** (Rev. 6-85)

Form 709 (Rev. 6-85)                                                                                    Page **2**

**SCHEDULE A.—Computation of Taxable Gifts** Gifts less political organization, medical and educational exclusions—see instructions

| Item number | Donee's name and address and description of gift. If the gift was made by means of a trust, enter trust's identifying number below and attach a copy of the trust instrument. If the gift was securities, enter the CUSIP number(s), if available. | Donor's adjusted basis of gift | Date of gift | Value at date of gift |
|---|---|---|---|---|
| 1 | | | | |

| | | | |
|---|---|---|---|
| 1 | Total gifts of donor (see instructions) | 1 | |
| 2 | One-half of items _____ attributable to spouse (see instructions) | 2 | |
| 3 | Balance (subtract line 2 from line 1) | 3 | |
| 4 | Gifts of spouse to be included (from Schedule A, line 2 of spouse's return—see instructions) | 4 | |
| 5 | Total gifts (add lines 3 and 4) | 5 | |
| 6 | Total annual exclusions for gifts listed on Schedule A (including line 4) (see instructions) | 6 | |
| 7 | Total included amount of gifts, subtract line 6 from line 5 | 7 | |

**Deductions** (see instructions)

| | | | |
|---|---|---|---|
| 8 | Gifts of interests to spouse for which a marital deduction will be claimed, based on items _____ of Schedule A | 8 | |
| 9 | Exclusions attributable to gifts on line 8 | 9 | |
| 10 | Marital deduction—subtract line 9 from line 8 | 10 | |
| 11 | Charitable deduction, based on items ____ to ____ less exclusions | 11 | |
| 12 | Total deductions—add lines 10 and 11 | 12 | |
| 13 | Taxable gifts (subtract line 12 from line 7) | 13 | |

**Terminable Interest Marital Deduction.** (See instructions.)

☐ ◄ Check here if you elected, under the rules of section 2523(f), to include gifts of qualified terminable interest property on line 8, above. Enter the item numbers (from Schedule A, above) of the gifts for which you made this election ► _____

**SCHEDULE B.—** Did you (the donor) file gift tax returns for prior periods? (If "Yes," see instructions for completing Schedule B below.)   ☐ Yes   ☐ No

| (a) Calendar year or calendar quarter (see instructions) | (b) Internal Revenue office where prior return was filed | (c) Amount of unified credit against gift tax for periods after December 31, 1976 | (d) Amount of specific exemption for prior periods ending before January 1, 1977 | (e) Amount of taxable gifts |
|---|---|---|---|---|
| | | | | |

| | | | |
|---|---|---|---|
| 1 | Totals for prior periods (without adjustment for reduced specific exemption) | 1 | |
| 2 | Amount, if any, by which total specific exemption, line 1, column (d), is more than $30,000 | 2 | |
| 3 | Total amount of taxable gifts for prior periods (add amount, column (e), line 1, and amount, if any, on line 2) | 3 | |

*(If more space is needed, attach additional sheets of same size.)*

Department of the Treasury
Internal Revenue Service

# Instructions for Form 709

(Revised June 1985)

## United States Gift Tax Return

(For gifts made after December 31, 1981, and before January 1, 1988)

For Privacy Act Notice, see the Instructions for Form 1040

(Section references are to the Internal Revenue Code unless otherwise noted.)

If you are filing this form solely to elect gift-splitting for gifts of not more than $20,000 per donee, you may be able to use Form 709-A, United States Short Form Gift Tax Return, instead of this form. See the instructions for "Who Must File," below.

If you made gifts before January 1, 1982, do not use this Form 709 to report these gifts. Instead, use the November 1981 revision of Form 709.

Paperwork Reduction Act Notice.—We ask for this information to carry out the Internal Revenue laws of the United States. We need it to ensure that taxpayers are complying with these laws and to allow us to figure and collect the right amount of tax. You are required to give us this information.

## General Instructions

Purpose of Form.—Form 709 is used to report transfers subject to the Federal gift tax and to figure the gift tax, if any, due on those transfers.

All gift taxes are computed and filed on a calendar year basis regardless of your income tax accounting period.

Transfers Subject to the Gift Tax.—Generally, the Federal gift tax applies to any transfer by gift of real or personal property, whether tangible or intangible, that you made directly, in trust, or by any other means to a donee.

The gift tax applies not only to the gratuitous transfer of any kind of property, but also to sales or exchanges, not made in the ordinary course of business, where money or money's worth is exchanged but the value of the money received is less than the value of what is sold or exchanged. The gift tax is in addition to any other tax, such as Federal income tax, paid or due on the transfer.

The exercise or release of a power of appointment may be a gift by the individual possessing the power.

The gift tax may also apply to the forgiveness of a debt, to interest-free (or below market interest rate) loans, to the assignment of the benefits of an insurance policy, to certain property settlements in divorce cases, and to certain survivorship annuities.

Bonds that are exempt from Federal income taxes are not exempt from Federal gift taxes unless specifically exempted by a gift tax provision of the Code.

Publication 448, Federal Estate and Gift Taxes, contains further information on the gift tax.

Transfers Not Subject to the Gift Tax.—Three types of transfers are not subject to the gift tax. These are: transfers to political organizations and payments that qualify for the educational and medical exclusions. These transfers are not "gifts" as that term is used on Form 709 and its instructions. You need not file a Form 709 to report these transfers and should not list them on Schedule A of Form 709.

Political organizations.—The gift tax does not apply to a gift to a political organization (defined in section 527(e)(1)) for the use of the organization.

Educational exclusion.—The gift tax does not apply to an amount you paid on behalf of an individual to a qualifying domestic or foreign educational organization as tuition for the education or training of the individual. A qualifying educational organization is one that normally maintains a regular faculty and curriculum and normally has a regularly enrolled body of pupils or students in attendance at the place where its educational activities are regularly carried on. See section 170(b)(1)(A)(ii) and its regulations.

The payment must be made directly to the qualifying educational organization and it must be for tuition. No educational exclusion is allowed for amounts paid for books, supplies, dormitory fees, board or other similar expenses that do not constitute direct tuition costs. To the extent that the payment to the educational institution was for something other than tuition, it is a gift to the individual for whose benefit it was made, and may be offset by the annual exclusion if it is otherwise available.

Medical exclusion.—The gift tax does not apply to an amount you paid on behalf of an individual to a person or institution that provided medical care for the individual. The payment must be to the care provider. The medical care must meet the requirements of section 213(d) (section 213(e) prior to January 1, 1984) (definition of medical care for income tax deduction purposes). Medical care includes expenses incurred for the diagnosis, cure, mitigation, treatment or prevention of disease, or for the purpose of affecting any structure or function of the body, or for transportation primarily for and essential to medical care. Medical care also includes amounts paid for medical insurance on behalf of any individual.

The medical exclusion does not apply to amounts paid for medical care that are reimbursed by the donee's insurance. If payment for a medical expense is reimbursed by the donee's insurance company, your payment for that expense, to the extent of the reimbursed amount, is not eligible for the medical exclusion and you have made a gift to the donee on the date the reimbursement is received by the donee.

To the extent that the payment was for something other than medical care, it is a gift to the individual on whose behalf the payment was made, and may be offset by the annual exclusion if it is otherwise available.

The medical and educational exclusions are allowed without regard to the relationship between you and the donee. For examples illustrating these exclusions, see regulations section 25.2503-6.

Disclaimers.—For the rules governing when a qualified disclaimer is not subject to the gift tax, see Publication 448.

## Who Must File

Only individuals are required to file gift tax returns. If a trust, estate, partnership, or corporation makes a gift, the individual beneficiaries, partners, or stockholders are considered donors and may be liable for the gift tax.

If a donor dies before filing a return, the donor's executor must file the return.

A married couple may not file a joint gift tax return. However, see "Split Gifts" on page 2.

If a gift is of community property, it is considered made one-half by each spouse. For example, a gift of $100,000 of community property is considered a gift of $50,000 made by each spouse, and each spouse must file a gift tax return.

Citizens or Residents of the United States.—If you are a citizen or resident of the United States you must file a gift tax return (whether or not any gift tax is ultimately due) in the following situations:

Gifts to your spouse.—Except as described below, you do not have to file a gift tax return to report gifts to your spouse regardless of the amount of these gifts and regardless of whether the gifts are present or future interests.

However, you must file a gift tax return if you made any gift of a terminable interest that does not meet the "Life estate with power of appointment" exception described on page 3. You must also file a gift tax return to make a QTIP (Qualified Terminable Interest Property) election described on page 3.

Gifts to donees other than your spouse (including charitable donees).—You must file a gift tax return if you gave gifts to any such donee that are not fully excluded under the $10,000 annual exclusion (as described below). Thus, you must file a gift tax return to report any gift of a future interest (regardless of amount) or to report gifts to any donee that total more than $10,000 for the year.

Gift splitting.—You must file a gift tax return to split gifts (regardless of amount) with your spouse as described on page 2.

The term citizen of the United States includes a person who, at the time of making the gift:
- was domiciled in a possession of the United States;
- was a U.S. citizen; and
- became a U.S. citizen for a reason other than being a citizen of a U.S. possession or being born or residing in a possession.

Annual Exclusion.—The first $10,000 of gifts of present interests to each donee during the calendar year is subtracted in figuring the amount of taxable gifts.

All of the gifts made during the calendar year to a donee are fully excluded under the annual exclusion if they are all gifts of present interests and if they altogether total $10,000 or less.

No part of a gift of a future interest can ever be excluded under the annual exclusion.

A gift is considered a present interest if the donee has all immediate rights to the use, possession, and enjoyment of the property and income from the property. A gift is considered a future interest if the donee's rights to the use, possession, and enjoyment of the property and income from the property will not begin until some future date. Future interests include reversions, remainders, and other similar interests or estates.

In the case of transfers for the benefit of a minor and for the transitional rules for certain trusts with a power of appointment referenced to the annual exclusion, see Publication 448.

Nonresident Aliens.—Nonresident aliens are subject to gift taxes for gifts of tangible property situated in the United States. Under certain circumstances they are also subject to gift taxes for gifts of certain intangible property. (See section 2501(a).)

If you are a nonresident alien who made a gift subject to gift tax, you must file a gift tax return if (1) you gave any gifts of future interests or if (2) your gifts of present interests to any donee (including your spouse) total more than $10,000.

## When To File

Form 709 is an annual return.

Generally, you must file Form 709 on or after January 1 but not later than April 15 of the year following the calendar year when the gifts were made.

If the donor of the gifts died during the year in which the gifts were made, the executor must file the donor's Form 709 not later than the earlier of (1) the due date (with extensions) for filing the donor's estate tax return, or (2) April 15 of the year following the calendar year when the gifts were made. Under this rule, Form 709 may be due before April 15 if the donor died before July 15 of the year in which the gifts were made. If the donor died after July 14, the due date for Form 709 (without extensions) will always be April 15 of the following year. If no estate tax return is required to be filed, the due date for Form 709 (without extensions) is April 15. For more information, see regulations section 25.6075-1.

**Extension of Time To File.—** There are two methods of extending the time to file the gift tax return. *Neither method extends the time to pay the gift tax.* If you want an extension of time to pay the gift tax, you must request that separately. (See regulations section 25.6161-1.)

*(1) By letter.—*You can request an extension of time to file your gift tax return by writing to the district director or service center for your area. You must explain the reasons for the delay; or

*(2) By form.—*Any extension of time granted for filing your calendar year income tax return will also extend the time to file any gift tax return. Income tax extensions are made by using Forms 4868, 2688 or 2350, which have check boxes for Form 709.

**Any extension of time to file will not extend the April 15 deadline for making a QTIP election (explained on page 3).**

### Where To File

File Form 709 with the Internal Revenue Service center where you would file your Federal income tax return. See the Form 1040 instructions for a list of filing locations.

### Penalties

The law provides for penalties for both late filing of returns and late payment of tax unless you have reasonable cause. There are also penalties for valuation understatements that cause an underpayment of the gift tax, willful failure to file a return on time, and for willful attempt to evade or defeat payment of tax.

### Joint Tenancy

If you buy property with your own funds and have it titled with yourself and the donee as joint tenants with right of survivorship and if either you or the donee may give up those rights by severing your interest, you have made a gift to the donee in the amount of half the value of the property. If you create a joint bank account for yourself and the donee (or a similar kind of ownership by which you can get back the entire fund without the donee's consent), you have made a gift to the donee when the donee draws on the account for his or her own benefit. The amount of the gift is the amount that the donee took out without any obligation to repay you. If you buy a U.S. savings bond registered as payable to yourself or the donee, there is a gift to the donee when he or she cashes the bond without any obligation to account to you.

### Transfer of Certain Life Estates

If you received a qualifying terminable interest from your spouse for which a marital deduction was elected on your spouse's estate or gift tax return, you will be subject to the gift tax if you dispose of (by gift, sale or otherwise) all or part of your life income interest.

The entire value of the property involved, less the amount you received on the disposition, and less the amount (if any) of the life income interest you retained after the transfer, will be treated as a taxable gift. That portion of the property's value that is attributable to the remainder interest is a gift of a future interest for which no annual exclusion is allowed. To the extent you made a gift of the life income interest, you may claim an annual exclusion, treating the person to whom you transferred the interest as the donee for purposes of computing the $10,000 limitation.

## Specific Instructions

### Gifts by Husband or Wife to Third Parties—Split Gifts

A married couple may not file a joint gift tax return.

If you and your spouse agree, all gifts either of you make to third parties during the calendar year may be considered as made one-half by each of you if:

- you and your spouse were married to one another at the time of the gift;
- you did not remarry during the rest of the calendar year;
- neither of you was a nonresident alien at the time of the gift; and
- you did not give your spouse a general power of appointment over the property interest transferred.

If you transferred property partly to your spouse and partly to third parties, you can only split the gifts if the interest transferred to the third parties is ascertainable at the time of the gift.

If you meet these requirements and want your gifts to be considered made one-half by you and one-half by your spouse, check the "Yes" box on line A, page 1; complete lines 1 through 4; and have your spouse sign the consent on line 5. If you are not married or do not wish to split gifts, skip to Schedule A.

**Line 2.—**If you were married to one another for the entire calendar year, check the "Yes" box and skip to line 4. If you were married for only part of the year, check the "No" box and go to line 3.

**Line 3.—**Check the box that explains the change in your marital status during the year and give the date you were either married, divorced, or widowed.

### Consent of Spouse

To have your gifts considered as made one-half by each of you, your spouse must sign the consent. The consent may generally be signed at any time after the end of the calendar year. However, there are two exceptions. They are:

1. The consent may not be signed after April 15 following the end of the year. (But, if neither you nor your spouse has filed a gift tax return for the year on or before that date, the consent must be made on the first gift tax return for the year filed by either of you.)

2. The consent may not be signed after a notice of deficiency for the gift tax for the year has been sent to either you or your spouse.

The executor for a deceased spouse or the guardian for a legally incompetent spouse may sign the consent.

The consent is effective for the entire calendar year; therefore, all gifts made by both you and your spouse to third parties during the calendar year (while you were married) must be split.

If the consent is effective, the liability for the entire gift tax of each spouse is joint and several.

**When the consenting spouse must also file a gift tax return.—**If the spouses elect gift splitting (described under "Split Gifts," above), then both the donor spouse and the consenting spouse must each file separate gift tax returns unless all the requirements of either Exceptions 1 or 2 below are met:

*Exception 1.—*During the calendar year:

- Only one spouse made any gifts;
- The total value of these gifts to each third-party donee does not exceed $20,000, and
- All of these gifts constitute present interests.

*Exception 2.—*During the calendar year:

- Only one spouse (the donor spouse) made gifts of more than $10,000 but not more than $20,000 to any third-party donee;
- The only gifts made by the other spouse (the consenting spouse) were gifts of not more than $10,000 to third-party donees other than those to whom the donor spouse made gifts, and
- All of the gifts by both spouses constitute present interests.

If either of Exceptions 1 or 2 is met, only the donor spouse needs to file a return and the consenting spouse signifies consent on that return. This return may probably be made on **Form 709-A,** United States Short Form Gift Tax Return. This form is much easier to complete than Form 709, and you should consider filing it whenever your gifts to each third-party donee are not more than $20,000 for the year.

### Schedule A.—Computation of Taxable Gifts

Do not enter on Schedule A any gift or part of a gift that qualifies for the political organization, educational or medical exclusions. In the instructions below, "gifts" means gifts (or parts of gifts) that do not qualify for the political organization, educational or medical exclusions.

**Gifts to donees other than your spouse.—**You must always enter all gifts of *future interests* that you made during the calendar year regardless of their value.

*If you do not elect gift splitting.—*If the total gifts of *present interests* to any donee are more than $10,000 in the calendar year, then you must enter *all such gifts* that you made during the year to or on behalf of that donee, including those gifts that will be excluded under the annual exclusion. If the total is $10,000 or less you need not enter on Schedule A any gifts (except gifts of future interests) that you made to that donee.

*If you elect gift splitting.—*Enter on Schedule A the entire value of every gift you made during the calendar year while you were married, even if the gift's value will be less than $10,000 after it is split on line 2.

**Gifts to your spouse.—**If you were a citizen or resident during the entire calendar year, you do not need to enter any of the gifts to your spouse on Schedule A unless you gave a gift of a terminable interest to your spouse. If you gave your spouse any terminable interest that does not qualify as a life estate with power of appointment (defined below), you must report on Schedule A *only* gifts of terminable interests you made to your spouse during the year. You should not report any gifts you made to your spouse that are not terminable interests; however, you must report all terminable interests, whether or not they can be deducted.

*Charitable remainder trusts.—*If you make a gift to a charitable remainder trust and your spouse is the only noncharitable beneficiary (other than yourself), the interest you gave to your spouse is not considered a terminable interest and therefore should not be shown on Schedule A. For rules and definitions concerning these trusts, see section 2056(b)(8)(B).

*Nonresident aliens.—*If you were a nonresident alien at any time during the year, you must enter *all* gifts you made to your spouse during the year.

If you need more space than that provided, attach a separate sheet, using the same format as Schedule A.

Group the gifts in four categories: gifts made to your spouse; gifts made to third parties that are to be split with your spouse; charitable gifts (if you are not splitting gifts with your spouse); and other gifts. If a transfer results in gifts to two individuals (such as a life estate to one with remainder to the other), list the gift to each separately.

Number and describe all gifts (including charitable, public, and similar gifts) in the columns provided in Schedule A. Describe each gift in enough detail so that the property can be easily identified, as explained below.

For real estate provide:

- a legal description of each parcel;
- the street number, name, and area if the property is located in a city; and
- a short statement of any improvements made to the property.

For bonds, give:

- the number of bonds transferred;
- the principal amount of each bond;
- name of obligor;
- date of maturity;
- rate of interest;
- date or dates when interest is payable;
- series number if there is more than one issue;
- exchanges where listed; principal business office of corporation, if unlisted; and
- CUSIP number, if available. The CUSIP number is a nine digit number assigned by the American Banking Association to traded securities.

For stocks:

- give number of shares;
- state whether common or preferred;
- if preferred, give the issue, par value, quotation at which returned, and exact name of corporation;
- if unlisted, give location of principal business office, State in which incorporated, and date of incorporation;
- if listed, give principal exchange where sold; and
- give CUSIP number, if available. The CUSIP number is a nine digit number assigned by the American Banking Association to traded securities.

For interests in property based on the length of a person's life, give the date of birth of the person.

For life insurance policies, give the name of the insurer and the policy number.

**Donor's Adjusted Basis of Gifts.**—Show the basis you would use for income tax purposes if the gift were sold or exchanged. Generally, this means cost plus improvements, less applicable depreciation, amortization, and depletion.

For more information on adjusted basis, please see **Publication 551,** Basis of Assets.

**Date and Value of Gift.**—The value of a gift is the fair market value of the property on the date the gift is made. The fair market value is the price at which the property would change hands between a willing buyer and a willing seller, when neither is forced to buy or to sell, and when both have reasonable knowledge of all relevant facts. Fair market value may not be determined by a forced sale price, nor by the sale price of the item in a market other than that in which the item is most commonly sold to the public. The location of the item must be taken into account wherever appropriate.

Stock of close corporations or inactive stock must be valued on the basis of net worth, earnings, earning and dividend capacity, and other relevant factors.

**Supplemental Documents.**—To support the value of your gifts, you must provide information showing how it was determined.

For stock of close corporations or inactive stock, attach balance sheets, particularly the one nearest the date of the gift, and statements of net earnings or operating results and dividends paid for each of the five preceding years.

For each life insurance policy, attach **Form 712,** Life Insurance Statement.

**Note for single premium or paid-up policies:** *In certain situations, for example, where the surrender value of the policy exceeds its replacement cost, the true economic value of the policy will be greater than the amount shown on line 56 of Form 712. In these situations you should report the full economic value of the policy on Schedule A. See Rev. Rul. 78-137, 1978-1 C.B. 280 for details.*

If the gift was made by means of a trust, attach a certified or verified copy of the trust instrument.

Also attach appraisal lists, such as any appraisal used to determine the value of real estate.

If you do not attach this information, you must include in Schedule A full information to explain how the value was determined.

**Line 1.**—Add the value of all your gifts. Enter the total on line 1.

**Line 2.**—If you are not splitting gifts with your spouse, skip this line and enter the amount from line 1 on line 3. If you are splitting gifts with your spouse, show half of the gifts you made to third parties on line 2. On the dotted line indicate which numbered items from the top of Schedule A you treated this way.

**Line 4.**—If you are not splitting gifts, skip this line and go to line 5. If you gave all of the gifts, and your spouse is only filing to show his or her half of those gifts, you need not enter any gifts on line 4 of your return, or include your spouse's half anywhere else on your return. Your spouse should enter the amount from Schedule A, line 2 of your return on Schedule A, line 4 of his or her return. If both you and your spouse make gifts for which a return is required, the amount each of you shows on Schedule A, line 2 of his or her return must be shown on Schedule A, line 4 of the other's return.

**Line 6.**—Enter the total annual exclusions you are claiming for the gifts listed on Schedule A (including gifts listed on line 4). See "Annual Exclusion," on page 1. If you split a gift with your spouse, the annual exclusion you claim against that gift may not be more than your half of the gift.

## Deductions

**Line 8.**—Enter on line 8 all of the terminable interest gifts to your spouse which you listed on Schedule A and for which you are claiming a marital deduction. **Do not enter any gift that you did not include on Schedule A.** On the dotted line on line 8 indicate which numbered items from the top of Schedule A are gifts to your spouse for which you are claiming the marital deduction.

*Nonresident aliens.*—If you were a nonresident alien for the entire calendar year, enter "-0-" in line 8. If you were a citizen or resident of the U.S. for part of the calendar year you may claim a marital deduction for gifts you made to your spouse while you were a citizen or resident of the U.S. even if your spouse was a nonresident alien. You may deduct all gifts of nonterminable interests made during this time that you entered on Schedule A regardless of amount, and certain gifts of terminable interests as outlined below. **Do not enter on line 8 any gifts to your spouse that were made while you were a nonresident alien.**

*Citizens or residents of the U.S.*—Only terminable interest gifts to your spouse should have been listed on Schedule A. They are deducted according to the rules below.

**Terminable interests.**—Generally, you cannot take the marital deduction if the gift to your spouse is a terminable interest.

Some examples of terminable interests are:

- a life estate;
- an estate for a specified number of years; or
- any other property interest that after a period of time will terminate or fail.

If you transfer an interest to your spouse as sole joint tenant with yourself or as a tenant by the entirety, the interest is not considered a terminable interest just because the tenancy may be severed. A retiring Federal employee who receives a reduced annuity so that his or her spouse can get a survivor annuity after he or she dies, gives a terminable interest to the spouse when he or she retires. In that case, no marital deduction election would be allowed and no amount could be deducted for the annual exclusion because the gift of the survivor annuity is a future interest. Refer to **Publication 721,** Comprehensive Tax Guide to U.S. Civil Service Retirement Benefits, for additional information concerning the gift of a Federal annuity.

*Life estate with power of appointment.*—You may deduct, without an election, a gift of a terminable interest if all four requirements below are met:

1. your spouse is entitled for life to all of the income from the entire interest;
2. the income is paid yearly or more often;
3. your spouse has the unlimited power, while he or she is alive or by will, to appoint the entire interest in all circumstances; and
4. no part of the entire interest is subject to another person's power of appointment (except to appoint it to your spouse).

If only part of the property interest meets the above, see Publication 448 for the part that qualifies for the marital deduction.

**Election to deduct qualified terminable interest property (QTIP).**—You may *elect* to deduct a gift of a terminable interest if it meets requirements 1, 2, and 4 above, even though it does not meet requirement 3.

Make the election by checking the block above Schedule B and entering the appropriate item numbers from Schedule A. You must make this election before April 15 of the year following the year in which you made the gifts to your spouse. You may not make the election on a late filed Form 709. You may not make the election on a Form 709 filed after April 15 even if you have received an extension of time to file.

If you make this election, the terminable interest property involved will be included in your spouse's gross estate upon his or her death (section 2044). If your spouse disposes (by gift or otherwise) of all or part of the qualifying life income interest, he or she will be considered to have made a transfer of the entire property that is subject to the gift tax (see "Transfer of Certain Life Estates," above).

**Line 9.**—Enter the value of the annual exclusion that was claimed against the gifts you listed on line 8.

**Line 11.**—You may deduct from the total gifts made during the calendar year all gifts you gave to or for the use of:

- The United States, a State or political subdivision of a State or the District of Columbia, for public purposes only.
- Any corporation, trust, community chest, fund, or foundation organized and operated only for religious, charitable, scientific, literary, or educational purposes, or to prevent cruelty to children or animals, or to foster national or international amateur sports competition (if none of its activities involve providing athletic equipment (unless it is a qualified amateur sports organization)), as long as no part of the earnings benefits any one person, no substantial propaganda is produced, and no lobbying or campaigning for any candidate for public office is done.
- A fraternal society, order, or association operating under a lodge system, if the transferred property is to be used only for religious, charitable, scientific, literary, or educational purposes including the encouragement of art and the prevention of cruelty to children or animals.
- Any war veterans organization organized in the United States (or any of its possessions), or any of its auxiliary departments or local chapters or posts, as long as no part of any of the earnings benefits any one person.

On line 11, show your total charitable, public, or similar gifts (minus exclusions allowed). On the dotted line indicate which numbered items from the top of Schedule A are charitable gifts.

See Publication 448 for more information.

## Schedule B

If you did not file gift tax returns for previous periods, check the "No" box at the top of Schedule B and skip to the Tax Computation on page 1. If you filed gift tax returns for previous periods, check the "Yes" box and complete Schedule B by listing the years or quarters in chronological order as described below. If you need more space than that provided, attach a separate sheet, using the same format as Schedule B.

If you filed returns for gifts made before 1971 or after 1981, show the calendar years in column (a). If you filed returns for gifts made after 1970 and before 1982, show the calendar quarters.

In column (b), identify the Internal Revenue Service office where you filed the returns. If you have changed your name, be sure to list any other names under which the returns were filed. If there was any other variation in the names under

which you filed, such as the use of full given names, instead of initials, please explain.

In column (e), show the correct amount (the amount finally determined) of the taxable gifts for each earlier period.

## Tax Computation

**Line 7.**—If you are a citizen or resident of the United States, you must take any available unified credit against gift tax for gifts made after December 31, 1976. If you are not a citizen or resident of the United States, you may not claim a unified credit.

Using Table B below, figure the amount of unified credit according to when you made the gift. Report the total credit for the period for which you are filing this return on line 7.

**Line 10.**—Enter 20% of the amount allowed as a specific exemption for gifts made after

September 8, 1976, and before January 1, 1977. (These amounts will be among those listed in column (d) of Schedule B, for gifts made in the third and fourth quarters of 1976.)

**Line 13.**—Gift tax conventions are in effect with France, the United Kingdom, Australia and Japan. If you are claiming a credit for payment of foreign gift tax, figure the credit on an attached sheet and attach evidence that the foreign taxes were paid. See the applicable convention for details of computing the credit.

**Line 17.**—Make check or money order payable to "Internal Revenue Service" and write the donor's social security number on it.

**Signature.**—You as donor must sign the return. If you pay another person, firm, or corporation to prepare your return, that person must also sign the return as preparer, unless he or she is your regular full-time employee.

### Table A—Table for Computing Tax

| Column A | Column B | Column C | Column D |
|---|---|---|---|
| Taxable amount over— | Taxable amount not over— | Tax on amount in Column A | Rate of tax on excess over amount in Column A |
| -------- | $10,000 | -------- | 18% |
| $10,000 | 20,000 | $1,800 | 20% |
| 20,000 | 40,000 | 3,800 | 22% |
| 40,000 | 60,000 | 8,200 | 24% |
| 60,000 | 80,000 | 13,000 | 26% |
| 80,000 | 100,000 | 18,200 | 28% |
| 100,000 | 150,000 | 23,800 | 30% |
| 150,000 | 250,000 | 38,800 | 32% |
| 250,000 | 500,000 | 70,800 | 34% |
| 500,000 | 750,000 | 155,800 | 37% |
| 750,000 | 1,000,000 | 248,300 | 39% |
| 1,000,000 | 1,250,000 | 345,800 | 41% |
| 1,250,000 | 1,500,000 | 448,300 | 43% |
| 1,500,000 | 2,000,000 | 555,800 | 45% |
| 2,000,000 | 2,500,000 | 780,800 | 49% |
| 2,500,000 | See Table A(1), A(2) or A(3) for year in which the gift was made. | | |

### Table A(1)—Gifts Made in 1982

| Column A | Column B | Column C | Column D |
|---|---|---|---|
| Taxable amount over— | Taxable amount not over— | Tax on amount in Column A | Rate of tax on excess over amount in Column A |
| $2,500,000 | $3,000,000 | $1,025,800 | 53% |
| 3,000,000 | 3,500,000 | 1,290,800 | 57% |
| 3,500,000 | 4,000,000 | 1,575,800 | 61% |
| 4,000,000 | ---------- | 1,880,800 | 65% |

### Table A(2)—Gifts Made in 1983

| Column A | Column B | Column C | Column D |
|---|---|---|---|
| Taxable amount over— | Taxable amount not over— | Tax on amount in Column A | Rate of tax on excess over amount in Column A |
| $2,500,000 | $3,000,000 | $1,025,800 | 53% |
| 3,000,000 | 3,500,000 | 1,290,800 | 57% |
| 3,500,000 | ---------- | 1,575,800 | 60% |

### Table A(3)—Gifts Made in 1984, 1985, 1986 or 1987

| Column A | Column B | Column C | Column D |
|---|---|---|---|
| Taxable amount over— | Taxable amount not over— | Tax on amount in Column A | Rate of tax on excess over amount in Column A |
| $2,500,000 | $3,000,000 | $1,025,800 | 53% |
| 3,000,000 | ---------- | 1,290,800 | 55% |

### Table B

| Maximum Unified Credit Against Gift Tax | |
|---|---|
| For gifts made in— | The credit is— |
| 1981 and earlier | Use the November 1981 revision of Form 709 |
| 1982 | $62,800 |
| 1983 | 79,300 |
| 1984 | 96,300 |
| 1985 | 121,800 |
| 1986 | 155,800 |
| 1987 and later | 192,800 |

**Page 4**

# Form 1120-A

## U.S. Short-Form Corporation Income Tax Return
To see if you qualify to file Form 1120-A, see Instructions.

1234

Department of the Treasury
Internal Revenue Service

For calendar 1985 or tax year beginning _____, 1985, ending _____, 19__
▶ For Paperwork Reduction Act Notice, see page 1 of the instructions.

OMB No. 1545-0890

1985

| See Instructions for list of principal business: | | Use IRS label. Otherwise please type or machine print | Name | | D Employer identification number (EIN) | |
|---|---|---|---|---|---|---|
| A Activity | | | | | | |
| B Product or service | | | Number and street | | E Date incorporated | |
| C Code | | | City or town, state, and ZIP code | | F Total assets (see Specific Instructions) | |
| | | | | | Dollars | Cents |
| | | | | | $ | |

**G** Check method of accounting: **(1)** ☐ Cash **(2)** ☐ Accrual **(3)** ☐ Other (specify) ▶ _____

**H** Check box if there has been a change in address from the previous year . . . . . . . . . . . . . . ▶

| | | | | | |
|---|---|---|---|---|---|
| **Income** | **1 a** Gross receipts or sales _____ **b** Less returns and allowances _____ Balance ▶ | | | **1c** | |
| | **2** Cost of goods sold and/or operations (see instructions) . . . . . . . . | | | **2** | |
| | **3** Gross profit (line 1c less line 2) . . . . . . . . . . | | | **3** | |
| | **4** Domestic corporation dividends subject to the 85% deduction . . . . . | | | **4** | |
| | **5** Interest . . . . . . . . . . . . . . . . . . | | | **5** | |
| | **6** Gross rents . . . . . . . . . . . . . . . . . | | | **6** | |
| | **7** Gross royalties . . . . . . . . . . . . . . . . | | | **7** | |
| | **8** Capital gain net income (attach separate Schedule D (Form 1120)) . . . . | | | **8** | |
| | **9** Net gain or (loss) from Form 4797, line 17, Part II (attach Form 4797) . . . | | | **9** | |
| | **10** Other income (see instructions) . . . . . . . . . . . | | | **10** | |
| | **11** TOTAL income—Add lines 3 through 10 . . . . . . . . | | | **11** | |
| **Deductions** | **12** Compensation of officers (see instructions) . . . . . . . . . | | | **12** | |
| | **13 a** Salaries and wages _____ **b** Less jobs credit _____ Balance ▶ | | | **13c** | |
| | **14** Repairs . . . . . . . . . . . . . . . . . . | | | **14** | |
| | **15** Bad debts (If reserve method is used, answer Question K on page 2) . . . | | | **15** | |
| | **16** Rents . . . . . . . . . . . . . . . . . . . | | | **16** | |
| | **17** Taxes . . . . . . . . . . . . . . . . . . . | | | **17** | |
| | **18** Interest . . . . . . . . . . . . . . . . . . | | | **18** | |
| | **19** Contributions **(see instructions for 10% limitation)** . . . . . . | | | **19** | |
| | **20** Depreciation (attach Form 4562) . . . . . . . . . | **20** | | | |
| | **21** Less depreciation claimed elsewhere on return . . . . . . | **21a** | | **21b** | |
| | **22** Other deductions (attach schedule) . . . . . . . . . | | | **22** | |
| | **23** TOTAL deductions—Add lines 12 through 22 . . . . . . | | | **23** | |
| | **24** Taxable income before net operating loss deduction and special deductions (line 11 less line 23) . . . | | | **24** | |
| | **25 Less: a** Net operating loss deduction (see instructions) . . . . | **25a** | | | |
| | **b** Special deductions (see instructions) . . . . . . . | **25b** | | **25c** | |
| **Tax and Payments** | **26** Taxable income (line 24 less line 25c) . . . . . . . . . | | | **26** | |
| | **27** TOTAL TAX (from Part I, line 6 on page 2) . . . . . . . | | | **27** | |
| | **28 Payments:** | | | | |
| | **a** 1984 overpayment allowed as a credit . . . . | | | | |
| | **b** 1985 estimated tax payments . . . . . . | | | | |
| | **c** Less 1985 refund applied for on Form 4466 . . ( _____ ) | | | | |
| | **d** Tax deposited with Form 7004 . . . . . . | | | | |
| | **e** Credit from regulated investment companies (attach Form 2439) . . . | | | | |
| | **f** Credit for Federal tax on gasoline and special fuels (attach Form 4136) . . | | | **28** | |
| | **29** Enter any **PENALTY** for underpayment of estimated tax—Check ▶ ☐ if Form 2220 is attached . . . | | | **29** | |
| | **30** TAX DUE—If the total of lines 27 and 29 is larger than line 28, enter AMOUNT OWED . . . . . | | | **30** | |
| | **31** OVERPAYMENT—If line 28 is larger than the total of lines 27 and 29, enter AMOUNT OVERPAID . . . | | | **31** | |
| | **32** Enter amount of line 31 you want: **Credited to 1986 estimated tax** ▶ _____ Refunded ▶ | | | **32** | |

**Please Sign Here**

Under penalties of perjury, I declare that I have examined this return, including accompanying schedules and statements, and to the best of my knowledge and belief, it is true, correct, and complete. Declaration of preparer (other than taxpayer) is based on all information of which preparer has any knowledge.

▶ _____          _____          ▶ _____
Signature of officer                          Date                          Title

**Paid Preparer's Use Only**

| Preparer's signature ▶ | | Date | | Check if self-employed ▶ ☐ | Preparer's social security number |
|---|---|---|---|---|---|
| Firm's name (or yours, if self-employed) and address ▶ | | | | E.I. No. ▶ | |
| | | | | ZIP code ▶ | |

Form **1120-A** (1985)

Form 1120-A (1985)    **Part I**    **Tax Computation** (See Instructions) Page 2          Enter EIN ▶

| | |
|---|---|
| **1** Income tax (see instructions to figure the tax, enter lesser of this tax or alternative tax from Schedule D. Check if from Schedule D ▶ ☐ . . | 1 |
| **2** General business credit. Check if from ☐ Form 3800 ☐ Form 3468 ☐ Form 5884 ☐ Form 6478 ☐ Form 8007. | 2 |
| **3** Line 1 less line 2 . . . . . . . . . . . . . . . . . . . . . . . . | 3 |
| **4** Tax from recomputing prior-year investment credit (attach Form 4255) . . . . . | 4 |
| **5** Minimum tax on tax preference items (see instructions—attach Form 4626) . . . . | 5 |
| **6** Total tax—Add lines 3 through 5. Enter here and on line 27, page 1 . . . . . . | 6 |

**Additional Information** (See instruction F)

**I** Was a deduction taken for expenses connected with:

(1) An entertainment facility (boat, resort, ranch, etc.)? Yes ☐ No ☐

(2) Employees' families at conventions or meetings?   Yes ☐ No ☐

**J** Did any individual, partnership, estate or trust at the end of the tax year own, directly or indirectly, 50% or more of the corporation's voting stock? (For rules of attribution, see section 267(c).) If "Yes," complete (1) and (2) . . . . . . . . . . . . . . . Yes ☐ No ☐

(1) Attach a schedule showing name, address, and identifying number.

(2) Enter "highest amount owed;" include loans and accounts receivable/payable:

(a) Enter highest amount owed by the corporation to such owner during the year ▶ . . . .

(b) Enter highest amount owed to the corporation by such owner during the year ▶ . . . .

**K** If the reserve method is used for bad debts, complete (1) and (2) for the current year:

(1) Amount added to the reserve account:

(a) Current year's provision ▶

(b) Recoveries ▶ . . . . . . . .

(2) Amount charged against the reserve account ▶

**L** If an amount for cost of goods sold and/or operations is entered on line 2, page 1, complete (1) and (2):

(1) Purchases ▶ . . . . . . . .

(2) Other costs (attach schedule) ▶ . . .

**M** At any time during the tax year, did you have an interest in or a signature or other authority over a financial account in a foreign country (such as a bank account, securities account, or other financial account)? (See instruction F for filing requirements for Form TD F 90-22.1.) . . . . . Yes ☐ No ☐

If "Yes," write in the name of the foreign country

▶

**N** During this tax year was any part of your accounting/tax records maintained on a computerized system? . . . . . . . . . . Yes ☐ No ☐

**O** Enter amount of cash distributions and the book value of property (other than cash) distributions made in this tax year ▶

**Part II**    **Balance Sheets**

| | | (a) Beginning of tax year | (b) End of tax year |
|---|---|---|---|
| **Assets** | **1** Cash . . . . . . . . . . . . . . | | |
| | **2** Trade notes and accounts receivable . . . . . . . | | |
| | **a** Less allowance for bad debts . . . . . . . . . | ( ) | ( ) |
| | **3** Inventories . . . . . . . . . . . . . . | | |
| | **4** Federal and State government obligations . . . . . | | |
| | **5** Other current assets (attach schedule) · · · · · · · | | |
| | **6** Loans to stockholders . . . . . . . . . . | | |
| | **7** Mortgage and real estate loans . . . . . . . . | | |
| | **8** Depreciable, depletable, and intangible assets . . . | | |
| | **a** Less accumulated depreciation, depletion, and amortization . | ( ) | ( ) |
| | **9** Land (net of any amortization) . . . . . . . . | | |
| | **10** Other assets (attach schedule) . . . . . . . · | | |
| | **11** Total assets . . . . . . . . . . . . . . | | |
| **Liabilities and Stockholders' Equity** | **12** Accounts payable . . . . . . . . . . . . | | |
| | **13** Other current liabilities (attach schedule) . . . . . | | |
| | **14** Loans from stockholders . . . . . . . . . . | | |
| | **15** Mortgages, notes, bonds payable . . . . . . . . | | |
| | **16** Other liabilities (attach schedule) . . . . . . . . | | |
| | **17** Capital stock (Preferred and Common stock) . . . . | | |
| | **18** Paid-in or capital surplus . . . . . . . . . . | | |
| | **19** Retained earnings . . . . . . . . . . . | | |
| | **20** Less cost of treasury stock . . . . . . . . . | ( ) | ( ) |
| | **21** Total liabilities and stockholders' equity . . . . . . | | |

**Part III**    **Reconciliation of Income Per Books With Income Per Return** (See Instructions)

**1** Enter net income per books . . . . . . . .

**2** Federal income tax . . . . . . . . .

**3** Income subject to tax not recorded on books this year (itemize) ....................

**4** Expenses recorded on books this year not deducted in this return (itemize) . . . . . . . . .

**5** Income recorded on books this year not included in this return (itemize) ....................

**6** Deductions in this tax return not charged against book income this year (itemize) ....................

**7** Income (line 24, page 1). Enter the sum of lines 1, 2, 3, and 4 less the sum of lines 5 and 6 . . . .

# Form 1120

Department of the Treasury
Internal Revenue Service

## U.S. Corporation Income Tax Return

For calendar 1985 or tax year beginning _____ , 1985, ending _____ , 19 ____

▶ **For Paperwork Reduction Act Notice, see page 1 of the instructions.**

OMB No. 1545-0123

**1985**

Check if a—

**A** Consolidated return ☐

**B** Personal Holding Co. ☐

**C** Business Code No. (See the list in the Instructions)

Use IRS label. Otherwise please print or type.

| Name |
| Number and street |
| City or town, state, and ZIP code |

**D** Employer identification number

**E** Date incorporated

**F** Total assets (see Specific Instructions)

Dollars | Cents

**G** Check box if there has been a change in address from the previous year . . . . . . . . . . . . . . ▶ ☐  $

| | | Dollars | Cents |
|---|---|---|---|
| | **1 a** Gross receipts or sales _____ **b** Less returns and allowances _____ Balance ▶ | **1c** | |
| **Income** | **2** Cost of goods sold and/or operations (Schedule A) . . . . . . . . . . . | **2** | |
| | **3** Gross profit (line 1c less line 2) . . . . . . . . . . . . . . . | **3** | |
| | **4** Dividends (Schedule C) . . . . . . . . . . . . . . . | **4** | |
| | **5** Interest . . . . . . . . . . . . . . . . . . . | **5** | |
| | **6** Gross rents . . . . . . . . . . . . . . . . . . | **6** | |
| | **7** Gross royalties . . . . . . . . . . . . . . . . . | **7** | |
| | **8** Capital gain net income (attach separate Schedule D) . . . . . . . . | **8** | |
| | **9** Net gain or (loss) from Form 4797, line 17, Part II (attach Form 4797) . . . . . | **9** | |
| | **10** Other income (see instructions—attach schedule) . . . . . . . . . | **10** | |
| | **11** TOTAL income—Add lines 3 through 10 and enter here . . . . . . . ▶ | **11** | |
| **Deductions** | **12** Compensation of officers (Schedule E) . . . . . . . . . . . | **12** | |
| | **13 a** Salaries and wages _____ **b** Less jobs credit _____ Balance ▶ | **13c** | |
| | **14** Repairs . . . . . . . . . . . . . . . . . . . | **14** | |
| | **15** Bad debts (Schedule F if reserve method is used) . . . . . . . . . | **15** | |
| | **16** Rents . . . . . . . . . . . . . . . . . . . | **16** | |
| | **17** Taxes . . . . . . . . . . . . . . . . . . . | **17** | |
| | **18** Interest . . . . . . . . . . . . . . . . . . . | **18** | |
| | **19** Contributions (**see instructions for 10% limitation**) . . . . . . . | **19** | |
| | **20** Depreciation (attach Form 4562) . . . . . . . **20** | | |
| | **21** Less depreciation claimed in Schedule A and elsewhere on return . **21a** | **21b** | |
| | **22** Depletion . . . . . . . . . . . . . . . . . . | **22** | |
| | **23** Advertising . . . . . . . . . . . . . . . . . . | **23** | |
| | **24** Pension, profit-sharing, etc. plans . . . . . . . . . . . . | **24** | |
| | **25** Employee benefit programs . . . . . . . . . . . . . . | **25** | |
| | **26** Other deductions (attach schedule) . . . . . . . . . . . . | **26** | |
| | **27** TOTAL deductions—Add lines 12 through 26 and enter here . . . . . . ▶ | **27** | |
| | **28** Taxable income before net operating loss deduction and special deductions (line 11 less line 27) . | **28** | |
| | **29 Less: a** Net operating loss deduction (see instructions) . . . . . . **29a** | | |
| | **b** Special deductions (Schedule C) . . . . . . . **29b** | **29c** | |
| **Tax and Payments** | **30** Taxable income (line 28 less line 29c) . . . . . . . . . . . . | **30** | |
| | **31** TOTAL TAX (Schedule J) . . . . . . . . . . . . . . | **31** | |
| | **32 Payments:** | | |
| | **a** 1984 overpayment allowed as a credit . . . | | |
| | **b** 1985 estimated tax payments . . . . . | | |
| | **c** Less 1985 refund applied for on Form 4466 . . ( ) | | |
| | **d** Tax deposited with Form 7004 . . . . . | | |
| | **e** Credit from regulated investment companies (attach Form 2439) . . | | |
| | **f** Credit for Federal tax on gasoline and special fuels (attach Form 4136) | **32** | |
| | **33** Enter any **PENALTY** for underpayment of estimated tax—check ▶☐ if Form 2220 is attached . | **33** | |
| | **34 TAX DUE**—If the total of lines 31 and 33 is larger than line 32, enter AMOUNT OWED | **34** | |
| | **35 OVERPAYMENT**—If line 32 is larger than the total of lines 31 and 33, enter AMOUNT OVERPAID | **35** | |
| | **36** Enter amount of line 35 you want: **Credited to 1986 estimated tax** ▶ _____ Refunded ▶ | **36** | |

**Please Sign Here**

Under penalties of perjury, I declare that I have examined this return, including accompanying schedules and statements, and to the best of my knowledge and belief, it is true, correct, and complete. Declaration of preparer (other than taxpayer) is based on all information of which preparer has any knowledge.

▶ _____   _____   ▶ _____
Signature of officer      Date            Title

**Paid Preparer's Use Only**

| Preparer's signature ▶ | Date | Check if self-employed ▶ ☐ | Preparer's social security number |
| Firm's name (or yours, if self-employed) and address ▶ | | E.I. No. ▶ | |
| | | ZIP code ▶ | |

Form 1120 (1985)         Page **2**

### Schedule A   Cost of Goods Sold and/or Operations (See instructions for line 2, page 1)

| | | |
|---|---|---|
| 1 Inventory at beginning of year. | 1 | |
| 2 Purchases. | 2 | |
| 3 Cost of labor. | 3 | |
| 4 Other costs (attach schedule). | 4 | |
| 5 Total—Add lines 1 through 4. | 5 | |
| 6 Inventory at end of year. | 6 | |
| 7 Cost of goods sold and/or operations—Line 5 less line 6. Enter here and on line 2, page 1 | 7 | |

8 a Check all methods used for valuing closing inventory:
- (i) ☐ Cost
- (ii) ☐ Lower of cost or market as described in Regulations section 1.471–4 (see instructions)
- (iii) ☐ Writedown of "subnormal" goods as described in Regulations section 1.471–2(c) (see instructions)
- (iv) ☐ Other (Specify method used and attach explanation) ▶ _____

b Check if the LIFO inventory method was adopted this tax year for any goods (if checked, attach Form 970) . . . . . ☐

c If the LIFO inventory method was used for this tax year, enter percentage (or amounts) of closing inventory computed under LIFO . . . . . . . . . . **8c** | |

d If you are engaged in manufacturing, did you value your inventory using the full absorption method (Regulations section 1.471–11)? . . . . . . . . . . . . ☐ Yes ☐ No

e Was there any change in determining quantities, cost, or valuations between opening and closing inventory? . . . ☐ Yes ☐ No
If "Yes," attach explanation.

### Schedule C   Dividends and Special Deductions (See instructions for Schedule C)

| | (a) Dividends received | (b) % | (c) Special deductions: multiply (a) X (b) |
|---|---|---|---|
| 1 Domestic corporations subject to 85% deduction (other than debt-financed stock) | | 85 | |
| 2 Debt-financed stock of domestic corporations (section 246A) | | see instructions | |
| 3 Certain preferred stock of public utilities | | 59.13 | |
| 4 Foreign corporations subject to 85% deduction | | 85 | |
| 5 Wholly-owned foreign subsidiaries and FSCs subject to 100% deduction (sections 245(b) and (c)) | | 100 | |
| 6 Total—Add lines 1 through 5. See instructions for limitation | | | |
| 7 Affiliated groups subject to the 100% deduction (section 243(a)(3)) | | 100 | |
| 8 Other dividends from foreign corporations not included in lines 4 and 5 | | | |
| 9 Income from controlled foreign corporations under subpart F (attach Forms 5471) | | | |
| 10 Foreign dividend gross-up (section 78) | | | |
| 11 IC–DISC or former DISC dividends not included in line 1 and/or 2 (section 246(d)) | | | |
| 12 Other dividends | | | |
| 13 Deduction for dividends paid on certain preferred stock of public utilities (see instructions) | | | |
| 14 Total dividends—Add lines 1 through 12. Enter here and on line 4, page 1 ▶ | | | |
| 15 Total deductions—Add lines 6, 7 and 13. Enter here and on line 29b, page 1 ▶ | | | |

### Schedule E   Compensation of Officers (See instructions for line 12, page 1)
Complete Schedule E only if total receipts (line 1a, plus lines 4 through 10, of page 1, Form 1120) are $150,000 or more.

| (a) Name of officer | (b) Social security number | (c) Percent of time devoted to business | Percent of corporation stock owned (d) Common | (e) Preferred | (f) Amount of compensation |
|---|---|---|---|---|---|
| | | % | % | % | |
| | | % | % | % | |
| | | % | % | % | |
| | | % | % | % | |
| | | % | % | % | |
| | | % | % | % | |
| | | % | % | % | |

Total compensation of officers—Enter here and on line 12, page 1.

### Schedule F   Bad Debts—Reserve Method (See instructions for line 15, page 1)

| (a) Year | (b) Trade notes and accounts receivable outstanding at end of year | (c) Sales on account | Amount added to reserve (d) Current year's provision | (e) Recoveries | (f) Amount charged against reserve | (g) Reserve for bad debts at end of year |
|---|---|---|---|---|---|---|
| 1980 | | | | | | |
| 1981 | | | | | | |
| 1982 | | | | | | |
| 1983 | | | | | | |
| 1984 | | | | | | |
| 1985 | | | | | | |

Form 1120 (1985)        Page **3**

**Schedule J**   **Tax Computation**
(See instructions)

**1** Check if you are a member of a controlled group (see sections 1561 and 1563) . . . . . . . . ▶ ☐

**2** If line 1 is checked, see instructions and enter your portion of the $25,000 amount in each taxable income bracket:

     **a** $ _____ **b** $ _____ **c** $ _____ **d** $ _____

**3** Income tax (see instructions to figure the tax; enter this tax or alternative tax from Schedule D, whichever is less). Check if from Schedule D ▶ ☐ . . . . . . . . . . . . . . . . . . . **3**

| | | |
|---|---|---|
| **4 a** Foreign tax credit (attach Form 1118). . . . . . . . . . | **4a** | |
| **b** Possessions tax credit (attach Form 5735) . . . . . . . . | **b** | |
| **c** Orphan drug credit (attach Form 6765) . . . . . . . . | **c** | |
| **d** Credit for fuel produced from a nonconventional source (see instructions) . . . | **d** | |
| **e** Research credit (attach Form 6765) . . . . . . . . . | **e** | |
| **f** General business credit. Enter here and check which forms are attached ☐ Form 3800 ☐ Form 3468 ☐ Form 5884 ☐ Form 6478 ☐ Form 8007 . . . . . . . | **f** | |

**5** Total—Add lines 4a through 4f . . . . . . . . . . . . . **5**

**6** Line 3 less line 5 . . . . . . . . . . . . . . . . . **6**

**7** Personal holding company tax (attach Schedule PH (Form 1120)) . . . . . **7**

**8** Tax from recomputing prior-year investment credit (attach Form 4255) . . . . **8**

**9** Minimum tax on tax preference items (see instructions—attach Form 4626) . . . **9**

**10** Total tax—Add lines 6 through 9. Enter here and on line 31, page 1 . . . . . . . . . . **10**

**Additional Information** (See instruction F)    **Yes | No**

**H** Did the corporation claim a deduction for expenses connected with:

  **(1)** Entertainment facility (boat, resort, ranch, etc.)? . . . .

  **(2)** Living accommodations (except employees on business)? . .

  **(3)** Employees attending conventions or meetings outside the North American area? (See section 274(h).) . . . . .

  **(4)** Employees' families at conventions or meetings?
If "Yes," were any of these conventions or meetings outside the North American area? (See section 274(h).) . . . .

  **(5)** Employee or family vacations not reported on Form W-2? . .

**I (1)** Did the corporation at the end of the tax year own, directly or indirectly, 50% or more of the voting stock of a domestic corporation? (For rules of attribution, see section 267(c).) . .
If "Yes," attach a schedule showing: (a) name, address, and identifying number; (b) percentage owned; (c) taxable income or (loss) before NOL and special deductions (e.g., If a Form 1120: from Form 1120, line 28, page 1) of such corporation for the tax year ending with or within your tax year; (d) highest amount owed by the corporation to such corporation during the year; and (e) highest amount owed to the corporation by such corporation during the year.

  **(2)** Did any individual, partnership, corporation, estate or trust at the end of the tax year own, directly or indirectly, 50% or more of the corporation's voting stock? (For rules of attribution, see section 267(c).) If "Yes," complete (a) through (e) . . .

    **(a)** Attach a schedule showing name, address, and identifying number.

    **(b)** Enter percentage owned ▶ _____

    **(c)** Was the owner of such voting stock a person other than a U.S. person? (See instructions) (Note: If "Yes," the corporation may have to file Form 5472.) . . . . .
If "Yes," enter owner's country ▶ _____

    **(d)** Enter highest amount owed by the corporation to such owner during the year ▶ _____

    **(e)** Enter highest amount owed to the corporation by such owner during the year ▶ _____

**(Note:** *For purposes of I(1) and I(2), "highest amount owed" includes loans and accounts receivable/payable.*)

**Yes | No**

**J** Refer to the list in the instructions and state the principal:
Business activity ▶ _____
Product or service ▶ _____

**K** Was the corporation a U.S. shareholder of any controlled foreign corporation? (See sections 951 and 957.) . . . . . . .
If "Yes," attach Form 5471 for each such corporation.

**L** At any time during the tax year, did the corporation have an interest in or a signature or other authority over a financial account in a foreign country (such as a bank account, securities account, or other financial account)? · . . . . . . . . .
(See instruction F for exceptions and filing requirements for form TD F 90–22.1.)
If "Yes," write the name of the foreign country ▶ _____

**M** Was the corporation the grantor of, or transferor to, a foreign trust which existed during the current tax year, whether or not the corporation has any beneficial interest in it? . . . . .
If "Yes," the corporation may have to file Forms 3520, 3520-A or 926.

**N** During this tax year, did the corporation pay dividends (other than stock dividends and distributions in exchange for stock) in excess of the corporation's current and accumulated earnings and profits? (See sections 301 and 316.) . . . . . . . . . .
If "Yes," file Form 5452. If this is a consolidated return, answer here for parent corporation and on Form 851, Affiliations Schedule, for each subsidiary.

**O** During this tax year did the corporation maintain any part of its accounting/ tax records on a computerized system? . . . . .

**P** Check method of accounting:
  **(1)** ☐ Cash
  **(2)** ☐ Accrual
  **(3)** ☐ Other (specify) ▶ _____

Form 1120 (1985)　　　　　　　　　　　　　　　　　　　　　　　　　　　　Page **4**

## Schedule L　Balance Sheets

| Assets | Beginning of tax year | | End of tax year | |
|---|---|---|---|---|
| | (a) | (b) | (c) | (d) |
| 1 Cash . . . . . . . . . . | | | | |
| 2 Trade notes and accounts receivable . . . | | | | |
|   a Less allowance for bad debts . . . . . | | | | |
| 3 Inventories. . . . . . . . . . . | | | | |
| 4 Federal and State government obligations . . | | | | |
| 5 Other current assets (attach schedule). . . | | | | |
| 6 Loans to stockholders . . . . . . | | | | |
| 7 Mortgage and real estate loans . . . . . | | | | |
| 8 Other investments (attach schedule) . . . | | | | |
| 9 Buildings and other depreciable assets. . . | | | | |
|   a Less accumulated depreciation . . . . | | | | |
| 10 Depletable assets . . . . . . | | | | |
|   a Less accumulated depletion . . . . | | | | |
| 11 Land (net of any amortization) . . . . | | | | |
| 12 Intangible assets (amortizable only) . . . . | | | | |
|   a Less accumulated amortization . . . . | | | | |
| 13 Other assets (attach schedule) . . . . | | | | |
| 14 Total assets . . . . . . . . . | | | | |
| **Liabilities and Stockholders' Equity** | | | | |
| 15 Accounts payable . . . . . . . | | | | |
| 16 Mortgages, notes, bonds payable in less than 1 year | | | | |
| 17 Other current liabilities (attach schedule) . . | | | | |
| 18 Loans from stockholders . . . . . . | | | | |
| 19 Mortgages, notes, bonds payable in 1 year or more | | | | |
| 20 Other liabilities (attach schedule) . . . . | | | | |
| 21 Capital stock: a Preferred stock . . . . | | | | |
|   b Common stock . . . . | | | | |
| 22 Paid-in or capital surplus . . . . . . | | | | |
| 23 Retained earnings—Appropriated (attach schedule) | | | | |
| 24 Retained earnings—Unappropriated . . . | | | | |
| 25 Less cost of treasury stock . . . . . . | | ( ) | | ( ) |
| 26 Total liabilities and stockholders' equity . . | | | | |

## Schedule M–1　Reconciliation of Income Per Books With Income Per Return

Do not complete this schedule if the total assets on line 14, column (d), of Schedule L are less than $25,000.

| | | | |
|---|---|---|---|
| 1 Net income per books . . . . . . . | | 7 Income recorded on books this year not included in this return (itemize) | |
| 2 Federal income tax . . . . . . | | | |
| 3 Excess of capital losses over capital gains . . | |   a Tax-exempt interest $_____ | |
| 4 Income subject to tax not recorded on books this year (itemize) _____ | | | |
| _____ | | 8 Deductions in this tax return not charged against book income this year (itemize) | |
| 5 Expenses recorded on books this year not deducted in this return (itemize) | |   a Depreciation . . $_____ | |
|   a Depreciation . . $_____ | |   b Contributions carryover $_____ | |
|   b Contributions carryover $_____ | | _____ | |
| _____ | | 9   Total of lines 7 and 8 . . . . | |
| 6   Total of lines 1 through 5 . . . . . | | 10 Income (line 28, page 1)—line 6 less line 9 . | |

## Schedule M–2　Analysis of Unappropriated Retained Earnings Per Books (line 24, Schedule L)

Do not complete this schedule if the total assets on line 14, column (d), of Schedule L are less than $25,000.

| | | | |
|---|---|---|---|
| 1 Balance at beginning of year . . . . . | | 5 Distributions: a Cash . . . . | |
| 2 Net income per books . . . . . . . | |         b Stock . . . . . | |
| 3 Other increases (itemize) _____ | |         c Property . . . . | |
| _____ | | 6 Other decreases (itemize)_____ | |
| _____ | | _____ | |
| _____ | | _____ | |
| _____ | | 7   Total of lines 5 and 6 . . . . . | |
| 4   Total of lines 1, 2, and 3 . . . . . | | 8 Balance at end of year (line 4 less line 7) | |

| SCHEDULE PH (Form 1120) | Computation of U.S. Personal Holding Company Tax | OMB No. 1545-0123 |
|---|---|---|
| Department of the Treasury Internal Revenue Service | ▶ Attach to your tax return. | 1985 |

| Name | Employer identification number |
|---|---|
| | |

## Computation of Undistributed Personal Holding Company Income

**Additions**

| | | |
|---|---|---|
| 1 | Taxable income before net operating loss deduction and special deductions (Form 1120, line 28 as modified for section 465 losses, section 189 limitations, or section 280 limitations—see instructions for line 1) . . . . . . . . . . . . . . . . . . | 1 |
| 2 | Contributions deducted in figuring line 1 (Form 1120, line 19) . . . . . . . . . . | 2 |
| 3 | Excess expenses and depreciation under section 545(b)(6) (Schedule A, line 2) . . . . . . | 3 |
| 4 | Total—Add lines 1 through 3 . . . . . . . . . . . . . . . . . . . | 4 |

**Deductions**

| | | |
|---|---|---|
| 5 | Federal and foreign income, war profits, and excess profits taxes not deducted in figuring line 1 (attach schedule) . . . . . . . . . . . . . . . . . . . . | 5 |
| 6 | Contributions deductible under section 545(b)(2) (see line 6 instructions for limitation) . . | 6 |
| 7 | Net operating loss for the preceding tax year (deductible under section 545(b)(4)) . . . . . | 7 |
| 8a | Net capital gain (from separate Schedule D (Form 1120), line 10) | 8a |
| 8b | **Less:** Income tax on this net capital gain (see section 545(b)(5)—attach computation) . . | 8b |
| 8c | | 8c |
| 9 | Amounts used or irrevocably set aside to pay or retire qualified indebtedness (see instructions for line 9). . . . . . . . . . . . . . . . . . . . . . . | 9 |
| 10 | Deduction for dividends paid (other than dividends paid after the end of the tax year (Schedule B, line 5)). . . . . . . . . . . . . . . . . . . . . . . | 10 |
| 11 | Total—Add lines 5 through 10 . . . . . . . . . . . . . . . . . . | 11 |
| 12 | Subtract line 11 from line 4 . . . . . . . . . . . . . . . . . . . . | 12 |
| 13 | Dividends paid after the end of the tax year (other than deficiency dividends defined in section 547(d)) but not more than the smaller of line 12 or 20% of Schedule B, line 1 . . . . . . | 13 |
| 14 | Undistributed personal holding company income—Subtract line 13 from line 12. Foreign corporations—see instructions for line 14 . . . . . . . . . . . . . . . . | 14 |

**Tax**

| | | |
|---|---|---|
| 15 | Personal holding company tax (enter 50% of line 14 here and on: Schedule J (Form 1120), line 7; or the proper line of the appropriate tax return) . . . . . . . . . . | 15 |

**INFORMATION REQUIRED UNDER SECTION 6501(f).** If the information on income and stock ownership is not submitted with the corporation's return, the limitation period for assessment and collection of personal holding company tax is 6 years.

### Personal Holding Company Income

| | | | | |
|---|---|---|---|---|
| 1 | Dividends . . . . . . . . . . . . . . . . . . . . . . | | | 1 |
| 2 a | Interest . . . . . . . . . . . . . . . . . . . . . | 2a | | |
| b | **Less:** Amount excluded under section 543(b)(2)(C) (attach schedule) . | 2b | | 2c |
| 3 | Royalties (other than mineral, oil, gas or copyright royalties) . . . . . . . . . . . | | | 3 |
| 4 | Annuities . . . . . . . . . . . . . . . . . . . . . . . . | | | 4 |
| 5 a | Rents . . . . . . . . . . . . . . . . . . . . . . | 5a | | |
| b | **Less:** Adjustments described in section 543(b)(2)(A) (attach schedule) | 5b | | 5c |
| 6 a | Mineral, oil, and gas royalties . . . . . . . . . . . . . | 6a | | |
| b | **Less:** Adjustments described in section 543(b)(2)(B) (attach schedule) | 6b | | 6c |
| 7 | Copyright royalties . . . . . . . . . . . . . . . . . . . . . . | | | 7 |
| 8 | Produced film rents . . . . . . . . . . . . . . . . . . . . . | | | 8 |
| 9 | Compensation received for use of corporation property by shareholder . . . . . . . . | | | 9 |
| 10 | Amounts received under personal service contracts and from their sale . . . . . . . | | | 10 |
| 11 | Amounts received from estates and trusts . . . . . . . . . . . . . . . . | | | 11 |
| 12 | Total personal holding company income—Add lines 1 through 11 . . . . . . . . . . | | | 12 |

For Paperwork Reduction Act Notice, see page 1 of Form 1120 instructions.                    Schedule PH (Form 1120) 1985

**Stock Ownership.** Enter the names and addresses of the individuals who together owned, directly or indirectly at any time during the last half of the tax year, more than 50% in value of the outstanding stock of the corporation.

| (a) Name | (b) Address | Highest percentage of shares owned during last half of tax year | |
|---|---|---|---|
| | | (c) Preferred | (d) Common |
| | | % | % |
| | | % | % |
| | | % | % |
| | | % | % |
| | | % | % |

### Schedule A — Excess of Expenses and Depreciation Over Income From Property Not Allowable Under Section 545(b)(6) (See instruction for line 3)

| (a) Kind of property | (b) Date acquired | (c) Cost or other basis | (d) Depreciation | (e) Repairs, insurance, and other expenses (section 162) (attach schedule) | (f) Total of columns (d) and (e) | (g) Income from rent or other compensation | (h) Excess (col. (f) less col. (g)) |
|---|---|---|---|---|---|---|---|
| 1 | | | | | | | |
| | | | | | | | |
| | | | | | | | |
| | | | | | | | |
| | | | | | | | |

**2** Total excess of expenses and depreciation over rent or other compensation. Enter here and on line 3, page 1.
**Note:** *Attach a statement showing the names and addresses of persons from whom rent or other compensation was received for the use of, or the right to use, each property* . . . . . . . . . . . . . . . . . . . . . . . . . . . .

### Schedule B — Deduction for Dividends Paid (See instruction for line 10)

| | | | |
|---|---|---|---|
| **1** | Taxable dividends paid (do not include dividends considered as paid in the preceding tax year under section 563, or deficiency dividends as defined in section 547) . . . . . . . . . . . . . . | **1** | |
| **2** | Consent dividends (attach Forms 972 and 973) . . . . . . . . . . . . . . . . | **2** | |
| **3** | Taxable distributions—Add lines 1 and 2 . . . . . . . . . . . . . . . . . . | **3** | |
| **4** | Dividend carryover from first and second preceding tax years (attach computation) . . . . . . . | **4** | |
| **5** | Deduction for dividends paid—Add lines 3 and 4. Enter here and on line 10, page 1 . . . . . . . | **5** | |

## General Instructions

*(References are to the Internal Revenue Code, unless otherwise noted.)*

### Purpose of Form

This schedule is used to figure personal holding company tax.

### Who Must File

Every personal holding company must have this schedule attached to its income tax return.

### Definitions

**Personal Holding Company.**—A corporation is a personal holding company if:

● At least 60% of its adjusted ordinary gross income, defined in section 543(b)(2), for the tax year is personal holding company income as defined in section 543(a); **and**

● At any time during the last half of the tax year more than 50% in value of its outstanding stock is owned, directly or indirectly, by not more than 5 individuals.

For exceptions to the term "personal holding company," see section 542(c).

Certain personal holding companies may elect to be treated as a regulated investment company and be taxed at the highest corporate rate (46%) on their undistributed taxable income. For definitions, limitations, and procedures, see sections 851 and 852.

**Individual.**—An organization described in section 401(a), 501(c)(17), or 509(a), or a part of a trust permanently set aside or to be used exclusively for the purpose described in section 642(c) is also considered an individual, except as provided in section 701(o) of Public Law 95-600. See section 542(a)(2).

**Foreign Corporation.**—A foreign corporation is not a personal holding company if all of its outstanding stock during the last half of the tax year is owned by nonresident alien individuals, directly or indirectly. An exception is a foreign corporation that has income to which section 543(a)(7) applies.

**Foreign Corporations Must File a Return.**—If a foreign corporation that is a personal holding company does not file Schedule PH as required, the corporation will be charged a penalty. The penalty is 10% of the corporation's Federal income taxes (including the personal holding company tax) and is in addition to any other penalties charged the corporation. See section 6683.

**Note:** *For a foreign corporation all of whose outstanding stock during the last half of the tax year is owned directly or indirectly by nonresident alien individuals, taxable income for section 545(a) is only income received under a contract for personal services as described in section 543(a)(7). This income must be reduced by deductions for that income, and have special adjustments made to the income, as provided in section 545(b).*

## Specific Instructions

These instructions are numbered to correspond with the line numbers on page 1 of Schedule PH (Form 1120). Other line items on the form are self-explanatory.

### Additions

**Line 1—Taxable income before net operating loss deduction.**—Enter the amount shown on Form 1120, page 1, line 28. If you figured the income on line 28 using section 443(b), (placing the income on an annual basis), refigure it without that section. However, adjust it for sections 189, 280, and 465.

See section 189 for limitations on deductions for construction period interest and taxes on real property other than low income housing.

See section 280 for the limitation on deduction of certain expenditures incurred in the production of films, books, or similar property.

Section 465 contains special at risk rules that generally limit a personal holding company's losses. The at risk rules may apply to a personal holding company engaged in any activity as a trade or business or for the production of income. However, the rules do not apply to the holding of real property other than mineral property.

Section 465(d) losses are generally limited to the total for which the personal holding company is at risk for each separate activity at the end of the tax year. Generally, the corporation is at risk for an activity for amounts described in sections 465(b)(1) and (2). The amounts borrowed are not considered to be at risk if they are excluded under sections 465(b)(3) and (4).

If the corporation is involved in one, or more than one, activity, one or more of which incurs a loss for the year, report the losses for each activity separately. Attach **Form 6198**, Computation of Deductible Loss From an Activity Described in Section 465(c), showing the amount at risk and gross income and deductions for the activities with the losses.

If a loss from an activity is more than the amount the personal holding company is at risk for the activity at the end of the tax year, the amount of that loss that is included on line 28 of Form 1120 cannot be more than the amount at risk for the activity.

If the personal holding company disposes of an asset in, or its interest in (either total or partial), an activity to which the at risk rules apply, combine the gain or loss on the disposition with the profit or loss from the activity to determine the net profit or loss from the activity. If the personal holding company has a net loss, it may be limited because of the at risk rules.

Treat any loss from an activity not allowed for the corporation's 1984 tax year by section 465 as a deduction for the activity in 1985. Include this deduction on line 26 of Form 1120. See section 465(a).

If you are a foreign corporation (whether or not engaged in a trade or business within the United States) that qualifies as a personal holding company under section 542 but not as a foreign personal holding company under section 552, enter on line 1 the amount figured under section 861 and not under section 881(a).

**Line 2—Contributions.**—See instructions for Form 1120.

**Line 3—Expenses and depreciation.**— If the corporation earned rent or other compensation for the use of, or right to use, property that was less than the total allowable expenses and depreciation, complete Schedule A and enter the excess on line 3.

You must make this adjustment unless you establish, according to section 545(b)(6), that the rent or other compensation the corporation received was the highest obtainable. If none was received, you must show that none was obtainable. The property must be held in the course of a business carried on for profit. There must be a reasonable expectation that the property's operation would result in a profit, or that the property was necessary to conduct the business.

The burden of proof is on the corporation. For a corporation with excess deductions you must, instead of completing Schedule A, attach a statement reporting the deductions with the complete facts, circumstances, and arguments to support them. The statement must include the information required by Regulations section 1.545-2(h)(2).

Schedule PH (Form 1120) 1985

## Deductions

**Line 5—Federal and foreign income, war profits, and excess profits taxes.**—Attach a schedule showing the kind of tax, the tax year, and the amount. Under section 545(b)(1), the company can deduct Federal income taxes accrued during the tax year, but not the accumulated earnings tax under section 531 or the personal holding company tax under section 541.

The foreign tax credit is not allowed against personal holding company tax. A deduction is allowed, however, for income, war profits, and excess profits taxes accrued (or considered paid under sections 902(a) or 960(a)(1)) during the tax year to foreign countries and U.S. possessions. This is true if the corporation claims a credit for the taxes in figuring its income tax.

**Line 6—Contributions.**—Section 545(b)(2) provides a different limitation for charitable contributions for figuring the personal holding company tax than the 10% limitation used in determining the corporate income tax. The limitations on charitable deductions of individuals apply, but are applied to the taxable income to which the 10% limitation applied. However, figure taxable income without deducting the amount disallowed under section 545(b)(6), (excess expenses and depreciation).

The contribution carryover under section 170(d) is not allowed when figuring personal holding company tax.

**Line 7—Net operating loss.**—Section 545(b)(4) provides that instead of the net operating loss deduction provided in section 172, a deduction is allowed for the net operating loss (as defined in section 172(c)) for the preceding tax year figured without the deductions provided in Part VIII (except section 248) of Subchapter B.

**Line 9—Amounts used or irrevocably set aside.**—Subject to the limitations in section 545(c), section 545(c)(1) allows a deduction for amounts used, or irrevocably set aside, to the extent reasonable, to pay or retire qualified indebtedness as defined in section 545(c)(3). This deduction applies only to corporations described in section 545(c)(2).

Any corporation taking this deduction must provide detailed information and any necessary computation showing it is a corporation described in section 545(c)(2)(A). To the extent that it succeeds to the deduction by section 381(c)(15), it must submit detailed information showing that the distributor or transferor corporation was a corporation described in section 545(c)(2)(A).

A corporation succeeding to the deduction must adjust its qualified indebtedness to take this indebtedness into account.

The corporation must establish that the amount reported as a deduction is reasonable. Attach a statement giving a description of the indebtedness, date incurred or assumed, date due, and plan for payment or retirement of the obligations (indicating date and method of adoption). If the plan is covered by a mandatory sinking fund agreement or similar arrangement, include a copy of the indenture or agreement by which the fund was established and under which it is maintained.

The statement must also include:

• Amount of indebtedness on January 1, 1964; **and**

• Total amounts used or irrevocably set aside to pay or retire the indebtedness in earlier tax years beginning on and after January 1, 1964; **and**

• Amount actually used during the tax year to pay or retire the indebtedness; **and**

• Amount irrevocably set aside during the tax year to pay or retire the indebtedness but not actually used during the tax year for that purpose.

**Also,** the statement must indicate if the deduction claimed represents:

• An amount actually used during the tax year to pay or retire the indebtedness; **or**

• An amount irrevocably set aside during the tax year to pay or retire the indebtedness; **or**

• A combination of the two.

If the amount reported as a deduction on line 9 represents an

amount irrevocably set aside, and not used to pay or retire the indebtedness, attach a statement explaining the circumstances and method by which it was irrevocably set aside.

The corporation must also provide a schedule for amounts described in section 545(c)(5) that reduce the amounts used or irrevocably set aside to pay or retire qualified indebtedness.

Section 545(c)(4) allows corporations to elect to treat as nondeductible certain amounts used or irrevocably set aside to pay or retire qualified indebtedness that are otherwise deductible under section 545(c)(1). See Regulations section 1.545-3(e) for time and manner of making the election.

**Line 10—Deduction for dividends paid.**— Enter this deduction from Schedule B. The rules in section 562 apply in determining the deduction for dividends paid.

**Line 13—Dividends paid after the end of the tax year.**—Enter on line 13, and not in Schedule B, the dividends paid after the end of the tax year and before the 16th day of the third month following the end of the tax year, if the corporation elects to have the dividends considered as paid during that tax year.

Do not include on line 10 or line 13 deficiency dividends paid under section 547.

**Line 14—Undistributed personal holding company income of certain foreign corporations.**—If 10% or less in value of the outstanding stock of a foreign corporation is owned (see section 958(a)) during the last half of the tax year by U.S. persons, undistributed personal holding company income is determined by multiplying the undistributed personal holding company income (determined without this instruction) by the percentage in value of the corporation's outstanding stock. This percentage is figured by using the greatest percentage in value of its outstanding stock owned by the U.S. persons on any one day during the period.

Form **1120S**
Department of the Treasury
Internal Revenue Service

# U.S. Income Tax Return for an S Corporation

For calendar 1985 or tax year beginning _____, 1985, ending _____, 19 ____

▶ **For Paperwork Reduction Act Notice, see page 1 of the instructions.**

OMB No. 1545-0130

**1985**

| | | |
|---|---|---|
| **A** Date of election as an S corporation | Use IRS label. Other-wise, please print or type. | Name |
| **B** Business Code No. (see Specific Instructions) | | Number and street |
| | | City or town, state, and ZIP code |

**C** Employer identification number

**D** Date incorporated

**E** Total assets (see Specific Instructions)

**F.** Check box if there has been a change in address from the previous year  . . . . . . . . . . ▶ ☐  $

| | | | Dollars | Cents |
|---|---|---|---|---|
| **Income** | **1 a** Gross receipts or sales _____ **b** Less returns and allowances _____ Balance ▶ | **1c** | | |
| | **2** Cost of goods sold and/or operations (Schedule A, line 7). . . . . . . . . . | **2** | | |
| | **3** Gross profit (subtract line 2 from line 1c) . . . . . . . . . . . . | **3** | | |
| | **4** Taxable interest and nonqualifying dividends . . . . . . . . . . | **4** | | |
| | **5** Gross rents . . . . . . . . . . . . . . . . . . . . | **5** | | |
| | **6** Gross royalties . . . . . . . . . . . . . . . . . . . | **6** | | |
| | **7** Net gain or (loss) from Form 4797, line 17, Part II . . . . . . . . . | **7** | | |
| | **8** Other income (see instructions—attach schedule). . . . . . . . . . | **8** | | |
| | **9** TOTAL income (loss)—Combine lines 3 through 8 and enter here . . . . . . . . ▶ | **9** | | |
| **Deductions** | **10** Compensation of officers . . . . . . . . . . . . . . . . | **10** | | |
| | **11 a** Salaries and wages _____ **b** Less jobs credit _____ Balance ▶ | **11c** | | |
| | **12** Repairs . . . . . . . . . . . . . . . . . . . . . | **12** | | |
| | **13** Bad debts (see instructions) . . . . . . . . . . . . . . . | **13** | | |
| | **14** Rents . . . . . . . . . . . . . . . . . . . . . . | **14** | | |
| | **15** Taxes . . . . . . . . . . . . . . . . . . . . . . | **15** | | |
| | **16 a** Total deductible interest expense not claimed elsewhere on return (see instructions) . . . . . . . . . . **16a** | | | |
| | **b** Interest expense required to be passed through to shareholders on Schedule K-1, lines 9, 13a(2) and 13a(3) . . . **16b** | | | |
| | **c** Subtract line 16b from line 16a | **16c** | | |
| | **17 a** Depreciation from Form 4562 (attach Form 4562) . . . **17a** | | | |
| | **b** Depreciation claimed on Schedule A and elsewhere on return **17b** | | | |
| | **c** Subtract line 17b from line 17a . . . . . . . . . | **17c** | | |
| | **18** Depletion (**Do not deduct oil and gas depletion. See instructions**) . . . . . . | **18** | | |
| | **19** Advertising . . . . . . . . . . . . . . . . . . . | **19** | | |
| | **20** Pension, profit-sharing, etc. plans . . . . . . . . . . . . | **20** | | |
| | **21** Employee benefit programs . . . . . . . . . . . . . . | **21** | | |
| | **22** Other deductions (attach schedule) . . . . . . . . . . . . | **22** | | |
| | **23** TOTAL deductions—Add lines 10 through 22 and enter here . . . . . . . ▶ | **23** | | |
| | **24** Ordinary income (loss)—Subtract line 23 from line 9 . . . . . . . . . | **24** | | |
| **Tax and Payments** | **25** Tax: | | | |
| | **a** Excess net passive income tax (attach schedule) . . . . . **25a** | | | |
| | **b** Tax from Schedule D (Form 1120S), Part IV. . . . . **25b** | | | |
| | **c** Add lines 25a and 25b . . . . . . . . . . . . . . | **25c** | | |
| | **26** Payments: | | | |
| | **a** Tax deposited with Form 7004 . . . . . . . . **26a** | | | |
| | **b** Credit for Federal tax on gasoline and special fuels (attach Form 4136) . . **26b** | | | |
| | **c** Add lines 26a and 26b . . . . . . . . . . . . . | **26c** | | |
| | **27 TAX DUE** (subtract line 26c from line 25c). See instructions for Paying the Tax. . . ▶ | **27** | | |
| | **28 OVERPAYMENT** (subtract line 25c from line 26c) . . . . . . . . . . ▶ | **28** | | |

**Please Sign Here**

Under penalties of perjury, I declare that I have examined this return, including accompanying schedules and statements, and to the best of my knowledge and belief, it is true, correct, and complete. Declaration of preparer (other than taxpayer) is based on all information of which preparer has any knowledge.

▶ _____
Signature of officer        Date

▶ _____
Title

**Paid Preparer's Use Only**

| Preparer's signature ▶ | Date | Check if self-em-ployed ▶ ☐ | Preparer's social security number |
|---|---|---|---|
| Firm's name (or yours, if self-employed) and address ▶ | | E.I. No. ▶ | |
| | | ZIP code ▶ | |

Form **1120S** (1985)

**Schedule A** **Cost of Goods Sold and/or Operations** (See instructions for Schedule A)

| | | |
|---|---|---|
| 1 Inventory at beginning of year | **1** | |
| 2 Purchases | **2** | |
| 3 Cost of labor | **3** | |
| 4 Other costs (attach schedule) | **4** | |
| 5 Total—Add lines 1 through 4 | **5** | |
| 6 Inventory at end of year | **6** | |
| 7 Cost of goods sold and/or operations—Subtract line 6 from line 5. Enter here and on line 2, page 1 | **7** | |

8  a  Check all methods used for valuing closing inventory:

   (i)  ☐  Cost

   (ii)  ☐  Lower of cost or market as described in Regulations section 1.471–4 (see instructions)

   (iii)  ☐  Writedown of "subnormal" goods as described in Regulations section 1.471–2(c) (see instructions)

   (iv)  ☐  Other (Specify method used and attach explanation) ▶ ------------------------------------------------

   b  Check if the LIFO inventory method was adopted this tax year for any goods (if checked, attach Form 970) . . . . . . ☐

   c  If the LIFO inventory method was used for this tax year, enter percentage (or amounts) of closing inventory computed under LIFO . . . . . . . . . . . . . . . . . . . . . . . | **8c** |

   d  If you are engaged in manufacturing, did you value your inventory using the full absorption method (Regulations section 1.471–11)? . . . . . . . . . . . . . . . . . . . . . . . ☐ Yes  ☐ No

   e  Was there any change in determining quantities, cost, or valuations between opening and closing inventory? . . . ☐ Yes  ☐ No
   If "Yes," attach explanation.

## Additional Information Required

| | Yes | No |
|---|---|---|
| G Did you at the end of the tax year own, directly or indirectly, 50% or more of the voting stock of a domestic corporation? (For rules of attribution, see section 267(c)). . . . . . . . . . . . . . . . . | | |

If "Yes," attach a schedule showing:

**(1)** Name, address, and employer identification number;

**(2)** Percentage owned;

**(3)** Highest amount owed by you to such corporation during the year; and

**(4)** Highest amount owed to you by such corporation during the year.

**(Note:** *For purposes of G(3) and G(4), "highest amount owed" includes loans and accounts receivable/payable.)*

H  Refer to the listing of Business Activity Codes and state your principal:
Business activity ▶ ------------------------------; Product or service ▶ ------------------------------

I  Were you a member of a controlled group subject to the provisions of section 1561? . . . . . . . . . .

J  Did you claim a deduction for expenses connected with:

**(1)** Entertainment facilities (boat, resort, ranch, etc.)? . . . . . . . . . . . . . . . . . .

**(2)** Living accommodations (except for employees on business)? . . . . . . . . . . . . . .

**(3)** Employees attending conventions or meetings outside the North American area? (See section 274(h).) . . . . .

**(4)** Employees' families at conventions or meetings? . . . . . . . . . . . . . . . . .
If "Yes," were any of these conventions or meetings outside the North American area? (See section 274(h).) . . .

**(5)** Employee or family vacations not reported on Form W-2? . . . . . . . . . . . . . . . .

K  At any time during the tax year, did you have an interest in or a signature or other authority over a financial account in a foreign country (such as a bank account, securities account, or other financial account)? (See instructions for exceptions and filing requirements for form TD F 90-22.1.) . . . . . . . . . . . . . . . . . .
If "Yes," write the name of the foreign country ▶ ------------------------------

L  Were you the grantor of, or transferor to, a foreign trust which existed during the current tax year, whether or not you have any beneficial interest in it? If "Yes," you may have to file Forms 3520, 3520-A, or 926 . . . . . .

M  During this tax year did you maintain any part of your accounting/tax records on a computerized system? . . . . . .

N  Check method of accounting: **(1)** ☐ Cash  **(2)** ☐ Accrual  **(3)** ☐ Other (specify) ▶ ------------------------------

O  Check this box if the S corporation has filed or is required to file Form 8264, Application for Registration of a Tax Shelter . . . . . . . . . . . . . . . . . . . . . . . . . . . . ☐

**Schedule K**   Shareholders' Share of Income, Credits, Deductions, etc. (See Instructions.)

| (a) Distributive share items | | (b) Total amount |
|---|---|---|

**Income (Losses) and Deductions**

| | | | |
|---|---|---|---|
| 1 | Ordinary income (loss) (page 1, line 24) * . . . . . . . . . . . . . . . | 1 | |
| 2 | Dividends qualifying for the exclusion . . . . . . . . . . . . . . | 2 | |
| 3 | Net short-term capital gain (loss) (Schedule D (Form 1120S)) . . . . . . | 3 | |
| 4 | Net long-term capital gain (loss) (Schedule D (Form 1120S)) . . . . . . | 4 | |
| 5 | Net gain (loss) under section 1231 (other than due to casualty or theft). . . . . . | 5 | |
| 6 | Other income (loss) (attach schedule) . . . . . . . . . . . . . . | 6 | |
| 7 | Charitable contributions . . . . . . . . . . . . . . . . | 7 | |
| 8 | Expense deduction for recovery property (section 179 expense) * . . . . . . . . | 8 | |
| 9 | Other deductions (attach schedule) . . . . . . . . . . . . . . | 9 | |

**Credits**

| | | | |
|---|---|---|---|
| 10 | Jobs credit * . . . . . . . . . . . . . . . . . . . . | 10 | |
| 11 | Other credits (see instructions) * . . . . . . . . . . . . . . . . | 11 | |

**Tax Preference Items**

| | | | |
|---|---|---|---|
| 12 a | Accelerated depreciation on nonrecovery real property or 15-year or 18-year real property. . . . | 12a | |
| b | Accelerated depreciation on leased personal property or leased recovery property other than 15 (or 18)-year real property . . . . . . . . . . . . . . . . | 12b | |
| c | Depletion (other than oil and gas) . . . . . . . . . . . . . . . | 12c | |
| d (1) | Gross income from oil, gas, or geothermal properties . . . . . . . . . | 12d(1) | |
| (2) | Gross deductions allocable to oil, gas, or geothermal properties . . . . . . . | 12d(2) | |
| e (1) | Qualified Investment income included on page 1, Form 1120S . . . . . . . | 12e(1) | |
| (2) | Qualified Investment expenses included on page 1, Form 1120S . . . . . . | 12e(2) | |
| f | Other items (attach schedule) . . . . . . . . . . . . . . . . | 12f | |

**Investment Interest**

| | | | |
|---|---|---|---|
| 13 a (1) | Investment debts incurred before 12-17-69 . . . . . . . . . . . | 13a(1) | |
| (2) | Investment debts incurred before 9-11-75 but after 12-16-69 . . . . . . . | 13a(2) | |
| (3) | Investment debts incurred after 9-10-75 . . . . . . . . . . . . | 13a(3) | |
| b (1) | Investment income included on page 1, Form 1120S . . . . . . . . . | 13b(1) | |
| (2) | Investment expenses included on page 1, Form 1120S. . . . . . . . . | 13b(2) | |
| c (1) | Income from "net lease property" . . . . . . . . . . . . . | 13c(1) | |
| (2) | Expenses from "net lease property" . . . . . . . . . . . . . | 13c(2) | |
| d | Excess of net long-term capital gain over net short-term capital loss from investment property . . | 13d | |

**Foreign Taxes**

| | | | |
|---|---|---|---|
| 14 a | Type of income ........................................................ | | |
| b | Name of foreign country or U.S. possession ...................................... | | |
| c | Total gross income from sources outside the U.S. (attach schedule) . . . . . . . . . | 14c | |
| d | Total applicable deductions and losses (attach schedule) . . . . . . . . . . | 14d | |
| e | Total foreign taxes (check one): ▶ ☐ Paid ☐ Accrued . . . . . . | 14e | |
| f | Reduction in taxes available for credit (attach schedule) . . . . . . . . . | 14f | |
| g | Other (attach schedule) . . . . . . . . . . . . . . . . . | 14g | |

**Other Items**

| | | | |
|---|---|---|---|
| 15 | Total dividend distributions paid from accumulated earnings and profits contained in retained earnings (lines 23 and 24 of Schedule L) . . . . . . . . . . . . . . | 15 | |
| 16 | Total property distributions (including cash) other than dividend distributions reported on line 15 . . | 16 | |
| 17 | Other items and amounts not included in lines 1 through 16 that are required to be reported separately to shareholders (attach schedule). | | |

\* You are not required to complete lines 1, 8, 10, and 11. Completion of these lines is optional because the amounts which would appear in column (b) appear elsewhere on Form 1120S or on other IRS forms or schedules which are attached to Form 1120S.

| Schedule L   Balance Sheets | Beginning of tax year | | End of tax year | |
|---|---|---|---|---|
| **Assets** | (a) | (b) | (c) | (d) |
| 1 Cash. | | | | |
| 2 Trade notes and accounts receivable | | | | |
|    a   Less allowance for bad debts. | | | | |
| 3 Inventories. | | | | |
| 4 Federal and State government obligations. | | | | |
| 5 Other current assets (attach schedule). | | | | |
| 6 Loans to shareholders | | | | |
| 7 Mortgage and real estate loans | | | | |
| 8 Other investments (attach schedule) | | | | |
| 9 Buildings and other depreciable assets. | | | | |
|    a   Less accumulated depreciation. | | | | |
| 10 Depletable assets | | | | |
|    a   Less accumulated depletion. | | | | |
| 11 Land (net of any amortization) | | | | |
| 12 Intangible assets (amortizable only). | | | | |
|    a   Less accumulated amortization. | | | | |
| 13 Other assets (attach schedule) | | | | |
| 14 Total assets | | | | |
| **Liabilities and Shareholders' Equity** | | | | |
| 15 Accounts payable | | | | |
| 16 Mortgages, notes, bonds payable in less than 1 year | | | | |
| 17 Other current liabilities (attach schedule). | | | | |
| 18 Loans from shareholders | | | | |
| 19 Mortgages, notes, bonds payable in 1 year or more | | | | |
| 20 Other liabilities (attach schedule) | | | | |
| 21 Capital stock | | | | |
| 22 Paid-in or capital surplus | | | | |
| 23 Retained earnings—Appropriated (attach schedule) | | | | |
| 24 Retained earnings—Unappropriated (see instructions). | | | | |
| 25 Shareholders' undistributed taxable income previously taxed | | | | |
| 26 Accumulated adjustments account | | | | |
| 27 Other adjustments account | | (     ) | | (     ) |
| 28 Less cost of treasury stock | | | | |
| 29 Total liabilities and shareholders' equity | | | | |

**Schedule M**   Analysis of Shareholders' Undistributed Taxable Income Previously Taxed, Accumulated Adjustments Account, and Other Adjustments Account (If Schedule L, column (d), amounts for lines 25, 26, or 27 are not the same as corresponding amounts on line 9 of Schedule M, attach a schedule explaining any differences. See instructions.)

| | Shareholders' undistributed taxable income previously taxed | Accumulated adjustments account | Other adjustments account |
|---|---|---|---|
| 1 Balance at beginning of year | | | |
| 2 Ordinary income from page 1, line 24 | | | |
| 3 Other additions | | | |
| 4 Total of lines 1, 2, and 3 | | | |
| 5 Distributions other than dividend distributions | | | |
| 6 Loss from page 1, line 24 | | | |
| 7 Other reductions | | | |
| 8 Add lines 5, 6, and 7 | | | |
| 9 Balance at end of tax year—Subtract line 8 from line 4 | | | |

| SCHEDULE K-1 | Shareholder's Share of Income, Credits, | OMB No. 1545-0130 |
|---|---|---|
| **(Form 1120S)** | **Deductions, etc.** For calendar year 1985 or tax year | **1985** |
| Department of the Treasury Internal Revenue Service | beginning _____, 1985 and ending _____, 19____ | |

(Complete a separate Schedule K-1 for each shareholder—See instructions)

| Shareholder's identifying number ▶ | Corporation's identifying number ▶ |
|---|---|
| Shareholder's name, address, and ZIP code | Corporation's name, address, and ZIP code |

**A** Shareholder's percentage of stock ownership for tax year . . . . . . . . . . . . . . . . . ▶ _____ %

**B** Internal Revenue Service Center where corporation filed its return ▶

**C** Tax shelter registration number (see instructions) . . . . . . . . . ▶

| | (a) Distributive share items | (b) Amount | (c) 1040 filers enter the amount in column (b) on: |
|---|---|---|---|
| **Income (Losses) and Deductions** | **1** Ordinary income (loss) . . . . . . . . . . . | | Sch. E, Part II, col. (e) or (f) |
| | **2** Dividends qualifying for the exclusion . . . . . . . . | | Sch. B, Part II, line 4 |
| | **3** Net short-term capital gain (loss) . . . . . . . . | | Sch. D, line 4, col. (f) or (g) |
| | **4** Net long-term capital gain (loss) . . . . . . . | | Sch. D, line 12, col. (f) or (g) |
| | **5** Net gain (loss) under section 1231 (other than due to casualty or theft) . | | Form 4797, line 1 |
| | **6** Other income (loss) (attach schedule) . . . . . . . | | (Enter on applicable line of your return) |
| | **7** Charitable contributions . . . . . . . . | | See Form 1040 Instructions |
| | **8** Expense deduction for recovery property (section 179 expense) . . . | | See Shareholder's Instructions for Schedule K-1 (Form 1120S) |
| | **9** Other deductions (attach schedule) . . . . . . . . . | | (Enter on applicable line of your return) |
| **Credits** | **10** Jobs credit . . . . . . . . | | Form 5884 |
| | **11** Other credits (attach schedule) . . . . . . . . . | | (Enter on applicable line of your return) |
| **Tax Preference Items** | **12 a** Accelerated depreciation on nonrecovery real property or 15-year or 18-year real property . . . . . . . . | | Form 6251, line 4c |
| | **b** Accelerated depreciation on leased personal property or leased recovery property other than 15 (or 18)-year real property . . . . . | | Form 6251, line 4d |
| | **c** Depletion (other than oil and gas) . . . . . | | Form 6251, line 4i |
| | **d (1)** Gross income from oil, gas, or geothermal properties . . | | } See Form 6251 instructions |
| | **(2)** Gross deductions allocable to oil, gas, or geothermal properties . . | | |
| | **e (1)** Qualified investment income included on page 1, Form 1120S . . | | } See Shareholder's Instructions for Schedule K-1 (Form 1120S) |
| | **(2)** Qualified investment expenses included on page 1, Form 1120S . . | | |
| | **f** Other items (attach schedule) . . . . . . . | | |
| **Investment Interest** | **13 a** Interest expense on: | | |
| | **(1)** Investment debts incurred before 12/17/69 . . . . . | | Form 4952, line 1 |
| | **(2)** Investment debts incurred before 9/11/75 but after 12/16/69 . . | | Form 4952, line 15 |
| | **(3)** Investment debts incurred after 9/10/75 . . . . . . | | Form 4952, line 5 |
| | **b (1)** Investment income included on page 1, Form 1120S . . . | | } See Shareholder's Instructions for Schedule K-1 (Form 1120S) |
| | **(2)** Investment expenses included on page 1, Form 1120S . . . . | | |
| | **c (1)** Income from "net lease property" . . . . . . . | | |
| | **(2)** Expenses from "net lease property" . . . . . . . | | |
| | **d** Excess of net long-term capital gain over net short-term capital loss from investment property . . . . . . . | | Form 4952, line 20 |
| **Foreign Taxes** | **14 a** Type of income ▶_____ | | Form 1116, Check boxes |
| | **b** Name of foreign country or U.S. possession ▶_____ | | Form 1116, Part I |
| | **c** Total gross income from sources outside the U.S. (attach schedule) . . | | Form 1116, Part I |
| | **d** Total applicable deductions and losses (attach schedule) . . . . | | Form 1116, Part I |
| | **e** Total foreign taxes (check one): ▶ ☐ Paid ☐ Accrued . . . . | | Form 1116, Part II |
| | **f** Reduction in taxes available for credit (attach schedule). . . . . | | Form 1116, Part III |
| | **g** Other (attach schedule) . . . . . . . . . . . | | Form 1116 Instructions |

**For Paperwork Reduction Act Notice, see page 1 of Instructions for Form 1120S.**        **Schedule K-1 (Form 1120S) 1985**

Schedule K-1 (Form 1120S) (1985)

**Page 2**

| (a) Distributive share items | | | (b) Amount | (c) 1040 filers enter the amount in column (b) on: |
|---|---|---|---|---|

**Property Eligible for Investment Credit**

| | | | | | | | |
|---|---|---|---|---|---|---|---|
| **15** | Regular Percentage | Cost or other basis of new recovery property | **a** 3-year. . . . . | | | | Form 3468, line 1(a) |
| | | | **b** Other. . . . . | | | | Form 3468, line 1(b) |
| | | Cost or other basis of used recovery property | **c** 3-year. . . . . | | | | Form 3468, line 1(c) |
| | | | **d** Other. . . . . | | | | Form 3468, line 1(d) |
| | Section 48(q) Election to Reduce Credit (instead of adjusting basis) | Cost or other basis of new property | **e** 3-year. . . . . | | | | Form 3468, line 1(e) |
| | | | **f** Other. . . . . | | | | Form 3468, line 1(f) |
| | | Cost or other basis of used property | **g** 3-year. . . . . | | | | Form 3468, line 1(g) |
| | | | **h** Other. | | | | Form 3468, line 1(h) |
| | **i** Other property (see instructions for Schedule K-1 in the Instructions for Form 1120S) . | | | | | | See Shareholder's Instructions for Schedule K-1 (Form 1120S) |

**Property Subject to Recapture of Investment Credit**

| | | | A | B | C | |
|---|---|---|---|---|---|---|
| **16** | | Properties: | | | | |
| | **a** | Description of property (State whether recovery or nonrecovery property. If recovery property, state whether regular percentage method or section 48(q) election used.) . . . . . | | | | Form 4255, top |
| | **b** | Date placed in service . | | | | Form 4255, line 2 |
| | **c** | Cost or other basis . . | | | | Form 4255, line 3 |
| | **d** | Class of recovery property or original estimated useful life . . | | | | Form 4255, line 4 |
| | **e** | Date item ceased to be investment credit property . . . . . | | | | Form 4255, line 8 |

**Other Items**

| | | |
|---|---|---|
| **17** | Property distributions (including cash) other than dividend distributions reported to you on Form 1099-DIV . . . . . . . . . . | |
| **18** | Amount of loan repayments for "Loans from Shareholders" . . . . | See Shareholder's Instructions for Schedule K-1 (Form 1120S) |
| **19** | Other items and amounts not included in lines 1 through 18 that are required to be reported separately to each shareholder (attach schedule) . . . . . . . . . . . . . . . . . . . | |

**85**      Department of the Treasury
**Internal Revenue Service**

# Shareholder's Instructions
# for Schedule K-1 (Form 1120S)

Shareholder's Share of Income, Credits, Deductions, etc.

## (For Shareholder's Use Only)

*(Section references are to the Internal Revenue Code, unless otherwise noted.)*

## Purpose of Schedule K-1

The corporation uses Schedule K-1 (Form 1120S) to report to you your share of the corporation's income (reduced by any tax the corporation paid on the income), credits, deductions, etc. Please keep it for your records.

Although the corporation is subject to a capital gains tax and an excess net passive income tax, you, the shareholder, are liable for the income tax on your share of the corporation's income, whether or not distributed, and you must include your share on your tax return. **Your distributive share of S corporation income is not self-employment income and it is not subject to self-employment tax.** Please read **Limitation on Aggregate Losses and Deductions** under line 1 instructions to figure how much of your share of the corporation's loss is deductible.

You, as a shareholder, should use these instructions to help you report the items shown on Schedule K-1 on your tax return.

Where "(attach schedule)" appears next to lines 6, 9, 11, 12f, 14c, 14d, 14f, 14g, and 19, it means you should see the schedule that the corporation has attached (if applicable) for that line item.

The notation "(see instructions for Schedule K-1 in the Instructions for Form 1120S)" next to line 15i is directed to the corporation. You, as a shareholder, should ignore this notation.

Schedule K-1 does not show the amount of actual dividend distributions the corporation paid to you. The corporation must report such amounts totaling $10 or more during the calendar year to you on Form 1099-DIV. You report actual dividend distributions on Schedule B (Form 1040).

## General Instructions

**Basis in Corporate Stock.**—You are responsible for maintaining records to show the computation of your basis in stock of the corporation. Schedule K-1 provides you with information to help you make the computation at the end of each corporate tax year. Your basis in stock is adjusted as follows (this list is not all-inclusive):

**Increased for:**

(1) All income (including tax-exempt income) reported on Schedule K-1. Note: Taxable income must be reported on your tax return for it to increase your basis.

(2) The excess of the deduction for depletion over the basis of the property subject to depletion.

**Decreased for:**

(1) Property distributions made by the corporation (excluding dividend distributions reported on Form 1099-DIV and distributions in excess of basis) reported on Schedule K-1, line 17.

(2) All losses and deductions (including nondeductible expenses) reported on Schedule K-1.

**Inconsistent Treatment of Items Shown on this Schedule K-1 (and Any Attached Schedule or Similar Statements).**—You must treat corporate items on your return consistent with the way the corporation treated the items on its filed return. See sections 6242, 6243, and 6244 for more information.

If your treatment on your original or amended return is (or may be) inconsistent with the corporation's treatment, or if the corporation has not filed a return, you must file **Form 8082**, Notice of Inconsistent Treatment or Amended Return, with your original or amended return to identify and explain the inconsistency (or noting that a corporate return has not been filed).

If you are required to file Form 8082 but fail to do so, you may be subject to a penalty. Also, any deficiency that results from making the treatment of the inconsistent corporate item consistent with the corporate treatment may be assessed immediately.

**Errors.**—If you believe the corporation has made an error on your Schedule K-1, notify the corporation and ask for a corrected Schedule K-1. Do not change any items on your copy. Be sure that the corporation sends a copy of the corrected Schedule K-1 to the IRS. See above instructions on inconsistent treatment of items on Schedule K-1.

**Tax Shelters.**—If you receive a copy of **Form 8271**, Investor Reporting of Tax Shelter Registration Number, or if your S corporation is involved in a tax shelter, see the instructions for Form 8271 for the information you are required to furnish the Internal Revenue Service. Attach the completed forms to your income tax return. The tax shelter registration number can be found in item C at the top of your Schedule K-1.

**Windfall Profit Tax.**—If you are a producer of domestic crude oil, your corporation will inform you of your income tax deduction for windfall profit tax on **Form 6248**, Annual Information Return of Windfall Profit Tax, and not on this Schedule K-1. In addition,

generally, you must determine if you are entitled to a refund of overpaid windfall profit tax. See **Form 6249**, Computation of Overpaid Windfall Profit Tax. You will not be notified of any overpayment on this Schedule K-1.

**International Boycotts.**—Every S corporation that had operations in, or related to, a boycotting country, company, or national of a country, must file **Form 5713**, International Boycott Report. If the corporation did not cooperate with an international boycott and notifies you of that fact, you do not have to file Form 5713, unless you had other boycotting operations.

If the corporation cooperated with an international boycott, it must give you a copy of the Form 5713 that it filed. You also must file Form 5713 to report the activities of the corporation and any other boycott operations of your own. You may lose certain tax benefits if the corporation participated in, or cooperated with, an international boycott. Please see Form 5713 and the instructions for more information.

**Elections.**—Generally, the corporation decides how to figure taxable income from its operations. For example, it chooses the accounting method and depreciation methods it will use.

However, certain elections are made by you separately on your income tax return and not by the corporation. These elections are made under:

● Section 901 (foreign tax credit);

● Section 617 (deduction and recapture of certain mining exploration expenditures);

● Section 57(c) (net leases);

● Section 163(d)(6) (limitation on interest on investment indebtedness); and

● You may make an election under section 58(i) to deduct ratably over the period of time specified in section 58(i), certain qualified expenditures. For more information, see the instructions for line 19, item f.

**Additional Information.**—For more information on the treatment of S corporation income, credits, deductions, etc. see **Publication 589**, Tax Information on S Corporations, **Publication 535**, Business Expenses, **Publication 536**, Net Operating Losses and the At-Risk Limits, and **Publication 550**, Investment Income and Expenses.

## Specific Instructions

**Name, Address, and Identifying Number.**—Your name, address, and identifying number, the corporation's name, address, and identifying number, and items A and B should have been entered. If the corporation is involved in a tax shelter, item C will be completed.

**Lines 1–19**

If you are an individual shareholder, take the amounts shown in column (b) and enter them on the lines on your tax return as indicated in column (c). If you are an estate or trust, report the amounts shown in column (b) as instructed on **Form 1041**, U.S. Fiduciary Income Tax Return.

**Note:** *The line number references are to forms in use for tax years beginning in 1985. If you are a calendar year shareholder in a fiscal year 1985/1986 corporation, enter these amounts on the corresponding lines of the tax form in use for 1986.*

**Caution:** If you have losses, deductions, credits, etc., from a prior year that were not deductible or useable because of certain limitations, such as the at-risk rules, they may be taken into account in determining your income, loss, etc., for this year. However, do not combine the prior year amounts with any amounts shown on this Schedule K-1 to get a net figure to report on your return. Instead, report the amounts on your return on a year-by-year basis.

If you have amounts, other than line 1, to report on Schedule E (Form 1040), enter each item on a separate line of Part II of Schedule E, column (e) or (f), whichever applies. Enter any deduction items in column (e).

**Line 1. Ordinary Income (Loss).**—The amount shown reflects your share of ordinary income (loss) from all corporate business operations, including at-risk activities, without reference to your adjusted basis in stock and debt of the corporation, or the amount you are at-risk.

**Limitation on Aggregate Losses and Deductions.**—Generally, your deduction for your share of aggregate losses and deductions reported on Schedule K-1 is limited to your basis in stock and debt of the corporation. Your basis in stock is figured at year end. See Basis in Corporate Stock in the General Instructions. Your basis in loans made to the corporation is the balance the corporation now owes you less any reduction for losses in a prior year. See the instructions for line 18. Any loss not allowed for the tax year because of this limitation is available for indefinite carryover, limited to your basis in stock and debt in each subsequent tax year. See section 1366(d) for details.

If you have (1) a loss from any activity (except the holding of real property, other than mineral property) carried on as a trade or business or for the production of income by the corporation, and (2) amounts in the activity for which you are not at risk, you will have to complete **Form 6198**, Computation of Deductible Loss from an Activity Described in Section 465(c), to figure the allowable loss to report on your return.

Generally, your deductible loss from each activity for the tax year is limited to the amount you are at risk for the activity at the end of the corporation's tax year, or the amount of the loss, whichever is less. You are not at risk for the following:

**a.** Your basis in stock of the corporation or basis in loans you made to the corporation if the cash or other property used to purchase the stock or make the loans was from a source covered by nonrecourse indebtedness or protected against loss by a guarantee, stop-loss agreement, or other similar arrangement, or that is covered by indebtedness from a person who has an interest in the activity or from a related person to a person (other than the taxpayer) having such an interest, other than a creditor.

**b.** Any cash or property contributed to a corporate activity, or your interest in the corporate activity, that is covered by nonrecourse indebtedness or protected against loss by a guarantee, stop-loss agreement, or other similar arrangement, or that is covered by indebtedness from a person who has an interest in such activity or from a related person to a person (other than the taxpayer) having such an interest, other than a creditor.

Any loss from a section 465 activity not allowed for this tax year will be treated as a deduction allocable to the activity in the next tax year.

**Note:** *If the corporation sells or otherwise disposes of (1) an asset used in the activity to which the at risk rules apply or (2) any part of its interest in such an activity (or if you sell or dispose of your interest), you must combine the gain or loss on the sale or disposition with the profit or loss from the activity to determine the net profit or loss from the activity. If this is a net loss, it may be limited because of the at-risk rules.*

To help you complete Form 6198, if required, the corporation should tell you your share of the total pre-1976 loss(es) from a section 465(c)(1) activity (i.e., films or video tapes, leasing section 1245 property, farm, or oil and gas property) for which there existed a corresponding amount of nonrecourse liability at the end of the year in which the loss(es) occurred. In addition, you should get a separate statement of income, expenses, etc., for each activity from the corporation.

**Line 5. Net Gain (Loss) Under Section 1231 (Other Than Due to Casualty or Theft).**—The amount on this line is to be entered on line 1, column (g) or (h), whichever is applicable, of **Form 4797**, Gains and Losses From Sales or Exchanges of Assets Used in a Trade or Business and Involuntary Conversions. You do not have to complete the information called for on columns (b) through (f) of Form 4797. Write "From Schedule K-1 (Form 1120S)" across these columns.

**Line 6. Other Income (Loss).**—Amounts on this line are other items of income, gain, or loss not included on lines 1-5 such as:

**a.** Wagering gains and losses (section 165(d)).

**b.** Recoveries of bad debts, prior taxes, or delinquency amounts (section 111).

**c.** Gain or loss from section 1256 contracts where the corporation itself was a trader or dealer in section 1256 contracts. This income (loss) is treated as a gain or loss from the sale or exchange of a capital asset. See section 1256(f) and 1402(i).

**d.** Net gain (loss) from involuntary conversions due to casualty or theft. The corporation will give you a schedule that shows the amounts to be reported on Section B, line 16, columns (B)(i), (B)(ii), and (C) of **Form 4684**, Casualties and Thefts. If there was a gain (loss) from a casualty or theft to property not used in a trade or business or for income producing purposes, you will be notified by the corporation. You must complete Form 4684 for the type of casualty or theft based on the information the corporation provides.

The corporation should give you a description and the amount of your share of each of these items.

**Line 7. Charitable Contributions.**—The corporation will give you a schedule that shows which contributions it made were subject to the 50%, 30%, and 20% limitations. For further information, see the Form 1040 Instructions.

If property other than cash is contributed, and the fair market value of one item or group of similar items of property exceeds $5,000, the corporation is required to file **Form 8283**, Noncash Charitable Contributions, and give you a copy to attach to your tax return. Do not deduct the amount shown on Form 8283. It is the corporation's contribution. You should deduct the amount shown on line 7, Schedule K-1.

If the corporation provides you with information that the contribution was property other than cash and does not give you a Form 8283, see the Instructions for Form 8283 for filing requirements. A Form 8283 does not have to be filed unless the total claimed value of all contributed items of property exceeds $500.

**Line 8. Expense Deduction for Recovery Property (Section 179 Expense).**—See Schedule E (Form 1040) instructions for more information.

**Line 9. Other Deductions.**—Amounts on this line are other deductions not included on lines 7 or 8, such as:

**a.** Itemized deductions (Form 1040 filers enter on Schedule A (Form 1040)). If there was a gain (loss) from a casualty or theft to property not used in a trade or business or for income producing purposes, you will be notified by the corporation. You must complete Form 4684 for the type of casualty or theft based on the information the corporation provides.

**b.** Any penalty on early withdrawal of savings.

**c.** Soil and water conservation expenditures (section 175).

**d.** Expenditures for the removal of architectural and transportation barriers to the elderly and handicapped which the corporation has elected to treat as a current expense. The expenses are limited by section 190.

The corporation should give you a description and the amount of your share of each of these items.

**Line 11. Other Credits.**—Amounts on this line are credits other than investment credit and the jobs credit, such as:

**a.** Credit for backup withholding on dividends, interest income, and other types of income (see Form 1040 instructions on backup withholding under Total Federal Income Tax Withheld).

**b.** Credit for alcohol used as fuel. Enter this credit on **Form 6478**, Credit for Alcohol Used as Fuel.

**c.** Nonconventional source fuel credit. Enter this credit on a schedule you prepare yourself to determine the allowed credit to take on your tax return. See section 29 for rules on how to figure the credit.

**d.** Unused credits from cooperatives.

**e.** Credit for increasing research activities and the orphan drug credit (enter these credits on **Form 6765**, Credit for Increasing Research Activities).

The corporation will give you a description and the amount of your share of each of these items.

**Lines 12e(1) and (2). Qualified Investment Income and Qualified Investment Expenses.**—Use the amount on these lines to determine the amount to enter on line 2e(2) of **Form 6251**, Alternative Minimum Tax Computation.

**Caution:** Generally, the amount shown on each of these lines is not the total qualified investment income or total qualified investment expenses for this corporation. The corporation should attach a schedule which shows the amount of qualified investment income and the amount of qualified investment expenses included in the amount shown in column (b) for lines 2 through 9.

You will have to adjust lines 12e(1) and (2) for any other qualified investment income or qualified investment expenses included in lines 2 through 9 and dividends reported to you on Form 1099-DIV, to determine the total qualified investment income and total qualified investment expenses for this corporation.

To determine the amount to enter on line 2e(2) of Form 6251, add to the amount shown on lines 12e(1) and (2), the qualified investment income and qualified investment expenses from all other sources, including any qualified investment income and qualified investment expenses shown on lines 2 through 9 of this Schedule K-1, and enter the result (but not less than zero) on line 2e(2) of Form 6251.

**Note:** The amount on line 1 of Schedule K-1 has already been included in the amount shown on lines 12e(1) and (2).

**Line 13. Investment Interest.**—If the corporation paid or accrued interest on debts it incurred to buy or hold investment property, the amount of interest you can deduct may be limited. The corporation should have entered the interest on investment indebtedness; items of investment income and expenses; and gains and losses from the sale or exchange of investment property.

For more information see Publication 550 and **Form 4952**, Investment Interest Expense Deduction.

**Note:** Generally, if your total investment interest expense including investment interest expenses from all other sources (including carryovers, etc.) is less than $10,000 ($5,000 if married filing separately), you do not need to get Form 4952. Instead, you may enter the amounts of investment interest expense directly on Schedule A (Form 1040). The corporation will tell you if any of the amounts should be reported on Schedule E (Form 1040).

**Lines 13b(1) and (2). Investment Income and Investment Expenses.**—Use the amounts on these lines to determine the amount to enter on lines 2 or 10a of Form 4952.

**Caution:** Generally, the amount shown on each of these lines is not the total investment income or total investment expenses for this corporation. The corporation should attach a schedule which shows the amount of investment income and the amount of investment expenses included in the amount shown in column (b) for lines 2 through 9.

The amount on line 1 of Schedule K-1 has been included in the amount shown on lines 13b(1) and (2). To determine the amount to enter on Form 4952, add to the amount on lines 13b(1) and (2) the investment income and investment expenses from all other sources including any investment income and investment expenses shown on lines 2 through 9 of this Schedule K-1.

**Lines 13c(1) and (2). Income and Expenses from Net Lease Property.**—Use the amounts on these lines to determine the net amount to enter on lines 11 and 19 of Form 4952.

**Line 15. Property Eligible for Investment Credit.**—Your share of the corporation's investment in property that qualifies for the investment credit should be entered. You can claim a tax credit based on your pro rata share of this investment by filing **Form 3468**, Computation of Investment Credit. (For more information, see Form 3468 and the related instructions.)

In addition to the qualifying property reported on lines 15a through 15h, if applicable, the corporation will give you a separate schedule that shows your share of the corporation's investment in nonrecovery property, new commuter highway vehicle, used commuter highway vehicle, qualified rehabilitation expenditures and energy property that qualifies for the credit, and where to report these items.

**Line 16. Property Subject to Recapture of Investment Credit.**—When investment credit property is disposed of, ceases to qualify or there is a decrease in the percentage of business use before the "life-years category" or "recovery period" assigned, you will be notified. You may have to recapture (pay back) the investment credit taken in prior years. Use the information on line 16 to figure your recapture tax on **Form 4255**, Recapture of Investment Credit. See the Form 3468 on which you took the original credit for other information you need to complete Form 4255.

You may also need Form 4255 if you disposed of more than one-third of your interest in the corporation. See **Publication 572**, Investment Credit, for more information.

**Line 17.**—Reduce your basis in stock of the corporation by the distributions on line 17. If these distributions exceed your basis in stock, the excess is treated as gain from the sale or exchange of property.

**Line 18.**—If the line 18 payments are made on indebtedness with a reduced basis, the repayments result in income to you to the extent the repayments are more than the adjusted basis of the loan. See section 1367(b)(2) for information on reduction in basis of a loan and restoration in basis of a loan with a reduced basis. See Revenue Ruling 64-162, 1964-1 (Part 1) C.B. 304 and Revenue Ruling 68-537, 1968-2 C.B. 372 for other information.

**Line 19. Other.**—If applicable, the corporation will give you a description and the amount of your share for each of the following:

**a.** Tax-exempt income realized by the corporation. This income is not reported on your tax return but it does increase your basis in stock. Tax-exempt interest earned by the corporation will be stated separately to assist shareholders in figuring the taxable portion (if any) of their social security or railroad retirement benefits.

**b.** Nondeductible expenses realized by the corporation. These expenses are not deducted on your tax return but decrease your basis in stock.

**c.** Taxes paid on undistributed capital gains by a regulated investment company. (Form 1040 filers enter your share of these taxes on line 63 of Form 1040, and add the words "from Form 1120S". Also reduce your basis in stock of the S corporation by this tax.)

**d.** Gross income from oil and gas well property, share of production for the tax year, etc., needed to figure your depletion deduction for oil and gas wells. The corporation should also allocate to you a proportionate share of the adjusted basis of each corporate oil or gas property. The allocation of the basis of each property is made as specified in section 613A(c)(13). See Publication 535 for how to figure your depletion deduction. Also reduce your basis in stock by this deduction (section 1367(a)(2)(E)).

**e.** Recapture of expense deduction for recovery property (section 179). The corporation will tell you if the recapture of expense deduction for recovery property was caused by the disposition of property.

The recapture amount is limited to the deduction you took in a prior year. You will have to look at your prior year return(s) to determine the amount that you previously deducted. See Form 4797 for additional information.

**f.** Total qualified expenditures, and the applicable period paid or incurred during the tax year, to which an election under section 58(i) applies.

You may either deduct the total amount of these expenditures or you may make an election under section 58(i) to deduct them ratably over the period of time specified in section 58(i). If you choose to make the election under section 58(i), the expenditures will not be classified as tax preference items and thus will not be subject to the alternative minimum tax. Make the election on Form 4562.

If you choose not to make the election, deduct the section 58(i) expenditures in full on your return (subject to any other limitations, such as the at-risk or basis limitations). Individual shareholders should enter the deductible amount on Schedule E (Form 1040), Part II, column (e).

If intangible drilling costs or certain mining expenditures are passed through to you, see items g and h before making an election to deduct them under section 58(i).

g. Intangible drilling costs which may be deducted under section 263. See Publication 535 for more information. You may choose to deduct these costs under section 263 or under section 58(i), but not both.

h. Deduction and recapture of certain mining expenditures paid or incurred (section 617). You may choose to deduct section 617 expenditures under section 617 or 58(i), but not both.

i. Any information or statements you need to comply with requirements under section 6111 (registration of tax shelters) or 6661 (substantial understatement of tax liability).

j. Gross farming and fishing income. If you are an individual shareholder, enter this income on Schedule E (Form 1040), Part IV, line 37 Do not report this income elsewhere on Form 1040.

If you are a shareholder that is an estate or trust, report this income to your beneficiaries on line 10 of Schedule K-1 (Form 1041). Do not report it elsewhere on Form 1041.

k. Any other information you may need to file your individual tax return that is not shown elsewhere on Schedule K-1.

| Form **1065** | **U.S. Partnership Return of Income** | OMB No. 1545-0099 |
|---|---|---|
| Department of the Treasury Internal Revenue Service | ► For Paperwork Reduction Act Notice, see Form 1065 Instructions. <br> For calendar year 1985, or fiscal year beginning _____, 1985, and ending _____, 19___ | 19**85** |

| **A** Principal business activity | Use IRS label. Otherwise, please print or type. | Name | **D** Employer identification number |
|---|---|---|---|
| **B** Principal product or service | | Number and street | **E** Date business started |
| **C** Business code number | | City or town, state, and ZIP code | **F** Enter total assets at end of tax year $ |

**G** Check method of accounting: **(1)** ☐ Cash **(2)** ☐ Accrual **(3)** ☐ Other

**H** Check applicable boxes: **(1)** ☐ Final return **(2)** ☐ Change in address **(3)** ☐ Amended return

**I** Number of partners in this partnership ► _____

| | | Yes | No |
|---|---|---|---|
| **J** | Is this partnership a limited partnership (see page 3 of Instructions)? | | |
| **K** | Is this partnership a partner in another partnership? | | |
| **L** | Are any partners in this partnership also partnerships? | | |
| **M** | Does the partnership meet **all** the requirements shown on page 5 of the Instructions under **Question M**. | | |

| | | Yes | No |
|---|---|---|---|
| **N** | Was there a distribution of property or a transfer of a partnership interest during the tax year? If "Yes," see page 5 of the Instructions concerning an election to adjust the basis of the partnership's assets under section 754. | | |
| **O** | At any time during the tax year, did the partnership have an interest in or a signature or other authority over a bank account, securities account, or other financial account in a foreign country (see page 5 of Instructions)? If "Yes," write the name of the foreign country ► | | |
| **P** | Was the partnership the grantor of, or transferor to, a foreign trust which existed during the current tax year, whether or not the partnership or any partner has any beneficial interest in it? If "Yes," you may have to file Forms 3520, 3520-A, or 926 (see page 5 of Instructions). | | |
| **Q** | Check this box if the partnership has filed or is required to file **Form 8264**, Application for Registration of a Tax Shelter. ☐ | | |

**Income**

| | | |
|---|---|---|
| **1a** Gross receipts or sales $ _____ **1b** Minus returns and allowances $ _____ Balance ► | **1c** | |
| **2** Cost of goods sold and/or operations (Schedule A, line 7) | **2** | |
| **3** Gross profit (subtract line 2 from line 1c) | **3** | |
| **4** Ordinary income (loss) from other partnerships and fiduciaries | **4** | |
| **5** Taxable interest and nonqualifying dividends | **5** | |
| **6a** Gross rents $ _____ **6b** Minus rental expenses (attach schedule) $ _____ | | |
| **c** Balance net rental income (loss) ► | **6c** | |
| **7** Net income (loss) from royalties (attach schedule) | **7** | |
| **8** Net farm profit (loss) (attach Schedule F (Form 1040)) | **8** | |
| **9** Net gain (loss) (Form 4797, line 17) | **9** | |
| **10** Other income (loss) | **10** | |
| **11** **TOTAL** income (loss) (combine lines 3 through 10) | **11** | |

**Deductions**

| | | |
|---|---|---|
| **12a** Salaries and wages (other than to partners) $ _____ **12b** Minus jobs credit $ _____ Balance ► | **12c** | |
| **13** Guaranteed payments to partners (see page 7 of Instructions) | **13** | |
| **14** Rent | **14** | |
| **15a** Total deductible interest expense not claimed elsewhere on return (see page 7 of Instructions). **15a** | | |
| **b** Minus interest expense required to be passed through to partners on Schedule K–1(1065), lines 10, 15a (2), and 15a(3) **15b** | | |
| **c** Balance ► | **15c** | |
| **16** Taxes | **16** | |
| **17** Bad debts (see page 7 of Instructions) | **17** | |
| **18** Repairs | **18** | |
| **19a** Depreciation from Form 4562 (attach Form 4562) $ _____ **19b** Minus depreciation claimed on Schedule A and elsewhere on return $ _____ Balance ► | **19c** | |
| **20** Depletion (**Do not deduct oil and gas depletion.** See page 8 of Instructions.) | **20** | |
| **21a** Retirement plans, etc. (see page 8 of Instructions) | **21a** | |
| **b** Employee benefit programs (see page 8 of Instructions) | **21b** | |
| **22** Other deductions (attach schedule) | **22** | |
| **23** **TOTAL** deductions (add amounts in column for lines 12c through 22) | **23** | |
| **24** Ordinary income (loss) (subtract line 23 from line 11) | **24** | |

**Please Sign Here**

Under penalties of perjury, I declare that I have examined this return, including accompanying schedules and statements, and to the best of my knowledge and belief it is true, correct, and complete. Declaration of preparer (other than taxpayer) is based on all information of which preparer has any knowledge.

► Signature of general partner _____ ► Date _____

**Paid Preparer's Use Only**

| Preparer's signature ► | Date | Check if self-employed ► ☐ | Preparer's social security no. |
|---|---|---|---|
| Firm's name (or yours, if self-employed) and address ► | | E.I. No. ► | |
| | | ZIP code ► | |

Form 1065 (1985)                                                                    Page **2**

| **Schedule A** | **Cost of Goods Sold and/or Operations** (See Page 8 of Instructions.) | | |
|---|---|---|---|

| | | | |
|---|---|---|---|
| 1 | Inventory at beginning of year . . . . . . . . . . . . . . . . . . . . | **1** | |
| 2 | Purchases minus cost of items withdrawn for personal use . . . . . . . . . . . . . | **2** | |
| 3 | Cost of labor . . . . . . . . . . . . . . . . . . . . . . . | **3** | |
| 4 | Other costs (attach schedule) . . . . . . . . . . . . . . . . . | **4** | |
| 5 | Total (add lines 1 through 4). . . . . . . . . . . . . . . . . | **5** | |
| 6 | Inventory at end of year . . . . . . . . . . . . . . . . . . | **6** | |
| 7 | Cost of goods sold (subtract line 6 from line 5). Enter here and on page 1, line 2 . . . . . . . | **7** | |

**8a** Check all methods used for valuing closing inventory:

    **(i)** ☐ Cost

    **(ii)** ☐ Lower of cost or market as described in regulations section 1.471-4 (see page 8 of Instructions)

    **(iii)** ☐ Writedown of "subnormal" goods as described in regulations section 1.471-2(c) (see page 9 of Instructions)

    **(iv)** ☐ Other (specify method used and attach explanation) ▶ - - - - - - - - - - - - - - - - - - - - - - - - - - - - - - - - - - - - - - - - - - - - - -

  **b** Check if the LIFO inventory method was adopted this tax year for any goods (if checked, attach Form 970) . . . . ☐

  **c** If you are engaged in manufacturing, did you value your inventory using the full absorption method (regulations section 1.471-11)? ☐ Yes ☐ No

  **d** Was there any change in determining quantities, cost, or valuations between opening and closing inventory? . . . ☐ Yes ☐ No
    If "Yes," attach explanation.

| **Schedule B** | **Distributive Share Items** (See Pages 9-11, and 14 of Instructions.) | |
|---|---|---|
| | **(a) Distributive share items** | **(b) Total amount** |
| 1 | Net long-term capital gain (loss) . . . . . . . . . . . . . . . | **1** |
| 2 | Other net gain (loss) under section 1231 and specially allocated ordinary gain (loss) . . . . . . . | **2** |
| 3a | If the partnership had income from outside the United States, enter the name of the country or U.S. possession ▶ - - - - - - - - - - - - - - - - - - - - - - - - - - - - - - - - - | |
| b | Total gross income from sources outside the United States . . . . . . . . . . . . . . . | **3b** |

| **Schedule L** | **Balance Sheets** | | | | |
|---|---|---|---|---|---|
| | (See Pages 5 and 9 of Instructions and Question M on Page 1 Before Completing Schedules L and M.) | | | | |
| | | Beginning of tax year | | End of tax year | |
| | **Assets** | **(a)** | **(b)** | **(c)** | **(d)** |
| 1 | Cash . . . . . . . . . . | | | | |
| 2 | Trade notes and accounts receivable. . . . . . | | | | |
| a | Minus allowance for bad debts . . . . . . . . | | | | |
| 3 | Inventories . . . . . . . . . . . . . | | | | |
| 4 | Federal and state government obligations . . . . | | | | |
| 5 | Other current assets (attach schedule) . . . . . | | | | |
| 6 | Mortgage and real estate loans . . . . . . . . | | | | |
| 7 | Other investments (attach schedule) . . . . . | | | | |
| 8 | Buildings and other depreciable assets . . . . . | | | | |
| a | Minus accumulated depreciation . . . . . . . | | | | |
| 9 | Depletable assets . . . . . . . . . . . . | | | | |
| a | Minus accumulated depletion . . . . . . . . | | | | |
| 10 | Land (net of any amortization) . . . . . . . | | | | |
| 11 | Intangible assets (amortizable only) . . . . . . | | | | |
| a | Minus accumulated amortization . . . . . . . | | | | |
| 12 | Other assets (attach schedule) . . . . . . . . | | | | |
| 13 | **TOTAL** assets . . . . . . . . . . | | | | |
| | **Liabilities and Capital** | | | | |
| 14 | Accounts payable. . . . . . . . . . . . | | | | |
| 15 | Mortgages, notes, and bonds payable in less than 1 year | | | | |
| 16 | Other current liabilities (attach schedule) . . . . | | | | |
| 17 | All nonrecourse loans . . . . . . . . . . . | | | | |
| 18 | Mortgages, notes, and bonds payable in 1 year or more | | | | |
| 19 | Other liabilities (attach schedule) . . . . . . . | | | | |
| 20 | Partners' capital accounts . . . . . . . . . | | | | |
| 21 | **TOTAL** liabilities and capital . . . . . . . . . | | | | |

| **Schedule M** | **Reconciliation of Partners' Capital Accounts** (See Page 9 of Instructions.) | | | | | |
|---|---|---|---|---|---|---|
| | (Show reconciliation of each partner's capital account on Schedule K-1 (Form 1065), Question G.) | | | | | |
| **(a)** Capital account at beginning of year | **(b)** Capital contributed during year | **(c)** Ordinary income (loss) from page 1, line 24 | **(d)** Income not included in column (c), plus nontaxable income | **(e)** Losses not included in column (c), plus unallowable deductions | **(f)** Withdrawals and distributions | **(g)** Capital account at end of year |
| | | | | | | |

**SCHEDULE K**
**(Form 1065)**
Department of the Treasury
Internal Revenue Service

# Partners' Shares of Income, Credits, Deductions, etc.

▶ File this form if there are more than ten Schedules K-1 (Form 1065) to be filed with Form 1065.
▶ Attach to Form 1065. ▶ See Instructions for Schedule K (Form 1065) in the Instructions for Form 1065.

OMB No. 1545-0099

**1985**

Name of partnership

Employer identification number

| | | (a) Distributive share items | (b) Total amount |
|---|---|---|---|
| **Income (Loss)** | **1** | Ordinary income (loss) (page 1, line 24) . . . . . . . . . | *1 |
| | **2** | Guaranteed payments . . . . . . . . . . . . . . | 2 |
| | **3** | Dividends qualifying for exclusion . . . . . . . . . . | 3 |
| | **4** | Net short-term capital gain (loss) (Schedule D, line 4) . . . . . | *4 |
| | **5** | Net long-term capital gain (loss) (Schedule D, line 9) . . . . . | *5 |
| | **6** | Net gain (loss) under section 1231 (other than due to casualty or theft) . . . . . . | *6 |
| | **7** | Other (attach schedule) . . . . . . . . . . . . . | 7 |
| **Deduc-tions** | **8** | Charitable contributions (attach list) . . . . . . . . . | 8 |
| | **9** | Expense deduction for recovery property (section 179) from Form 4562 . . . . . | *9 |
| | **10** | Other (attach schedule) . . . . . . . . . . . . . | 10 |
| **Credits** | **11** | Credit for income tax withheld . . . . . . . . . . . | 11 |
| | **12** | Other (attach schedule) . . . . . . . . . . . . . | *12 |
| **Self-Employ-ment** | **13a** | Net earnings (loss) from self-employment . . . . . . . . | 13a |
| | **b** | Gross farming or fishing income . . . . . . . . . . . | 13b |
| | **c** | Gross non-farm income . . . . . . . . . . . . . | 13c |
| **Tax Preference Items** | **14a** | Accelerated depreciation on nonrecovery real property or 15-year or 18-year real property . . . . . . . . . . . . . . . . . . . . . . . | 14a |
| | **b** | Accelerated depreciation on leased personal property or leased recovery property other than 15-year or 18-year real property . . . . . . . . . . . . . . . . . . | 14b |
| | **c** | Depletion (other than oil and gas) . . . . . . . . . . | 14c |
| | **d (1)** | Gross income from oil, gas, and geothermal properties . . . . . | 14d(1) |
| | **(2)** | Deductions allocable to oil, gas, and geothermal properties . . . | 14d(2) |
| | **e (1)** | Qualified investment income included on page 1, Form 1065 . . . . | 14e(1) |
| | **(2)** | Qualified investment expenses included on page 1, Form 1065 . . . | 14e(2) |
| | **f** | Other (attach schedule) . . . . . . . . . . . . . | 14f |
| **Investment Interest** | **15a** | Interest expense on: | |
| | **(1)** | Investment debts incurred before 12/17/69 . . . . . . . . | 15a(1) |
| | **(2)** | Investment debts incurred before 9/11/75, but after 12/16/69 . . . . | 15a(2) |
| | **(3)** | Investment debts incurred after 9/10/75 . . . . . . . . . | 15a(3) |
| | **b (1)** | Investment income included on page 1, Form 1065 . . . . . . | 15b(1) |
| | **(2)** | Investment expenses included on page 1, Form 1065 . . . . . . | 15b(2) |
| | **c (1)** | Income from "net lease property" . . . . . . . . . . . | 15c(1) |
| | **(2)** | Expenses from "net lease property" . . . . . . . . . . | 15c(2) |
| **Foreign Taxes** | **16a** | Type of income | |
| | **b** | Foreign country or U.S. possession* | |
| | **c** | Total gross income from sources outside the U.S. (attach schedule) . . . . . | *16c |
| | **d** | Total applicable deductions and losses (attach schedule) . . . . . | 16d |
| | **e** | Total foreign taxes (check one): ▶ ☐ Paid ☐ Accrued . . . . | 16e |
| | **f** | Reduction in taxes available for credit (attach schedule) . . . . . . | 16f |
| | **g** | Other (attach schedule) . . . . . . . . . . . . . | 16g |
| **Other** | **17** | Other items and amounts not included in lines 1 through 16g that are required to be reported separately to partners. See instructions. **Caution:** *Attach a schedule that lists these items and amounts* . . . . . . . . . . . . . . . . . . . . | |

*You are not required to complete lines 1, 6, 9, 12 (see instructions), 16b, and 16c on Schedule K (Form 1065). Completion of these lines is optional because the amounts which would appear in column b appear elsewhere on Form 1065 or on other IRS forms or IRS schedules attached to Form 1065. Lines 4 and 5 must be completed only if any partner has a specially allocated capital gain (loss). (See instructions for line item.)

For Paperwork Reduction Act Notice, see Form 1065 Instructions.

Schedule K (Form 1065) 1985

**SCHEDULE K-1**
**(Form 1065)**

Department of the Treasury
Internal Revenue Service

**Partner's Share of Income, Credits, Deductions, etc.**

For calendar year 1985 or fiscal year
beginning _____, 1985, and ending _____, 19___.

OMB No. 1545-0099

**1985**

**Partner's identifying number ▶**

**Partnership's identifying number ▶**

Partner's name, address, and ZIP code

Partnership's name, address, and ZIP code

**A** Is partner a general partner (see page 3 of Instructions for
Form 1065)? . . . . . . . . . . . ☐ Yes ☐ No

**B** Partner's share of liabilities (see page 10 of Instructions for Form 1065):

Nonrecourse . . . . . . . . . . $ _____

Other . . . . . . . . . . . $ _____

**C** What type of entity is this partner? ▶ _____

**D** Enter partner's percentage of:

|  | (i) Before decrease or termination | (ii) End of year |
|---|---|---|
| Profit sharing . . . . . . . | _____% | _____% |
| Loss sharing . . . . . . . | _____% | _____% |
| Ownership of capital . . . . | _____% | _____% |

**E** IRS Center where partnership filed return ▶ _____

**F** Tax Shelter Registration Number ▶

**G** Reconciliation of partner's capital account:

| (a) Capital account at beginning of year | (b) Capital contributed during year | (c) Ordinary income (loss) from line 1 below | (d) Income not included in column (c), plus nontaxable income | (e) Losses not included in column (c), plus unallowable deductions | (f) Withdrawals and distributions | (g) Capital account at end of year |
|---|---|---|---|---|---|---|
|  |  |  |  |  |  |  |

| | | (a) Distributive share item | (b) Amount | (c) 1040 filers enter the amount in column (b) on: |
|---|---|---|---|---|
| **Income (Loss)** | 1 | Ordinary income (loss) . . . . . . . . . . | | Sch. E, Part II, col. (e) or (f) |
| | 2 | Guaranteed payments . . . . . . . . . | | Sch. E, Part II, column (f) |
| | 3 | Dividends qualifying for exclusion . . . . . . | | Sch. B, Part II, line 4 |
| | 4 | Net short-term capital gain (loss). . . . . . | | Sch. D, line 4, col. (f) or (g) |
| | 5 | Net long-term capital gain (loss) . . . . . . | | Sch. D, line 12, col. (f) or (g) |
| | 6 | Net gain (loss) under section 1231 (other than due to casualty or theft) | | Form 4797, line 1 |
| | 7 | Other (attach schedule) . . . . . . . . | | (Enter on applicable lines of your return) |
| **Deductions** | 8 | Charitable contributions . . . . . . . . | | See Form 1040 instructions |
| | 9 | Expense deduction for recovery property (section 179 ) . . . . . | | (See Partner's Instructions for Schedule K–1 (Form 1065)) |
| | 10 | Other (attach schedule) . . . . . . . . . | | (Enter on applicable lines of your return) |
| **Credits** | 11 | Credit for income tax withheld . . . . . . . | | See Form 1040 instructions, line 57 for Backup Withholding |
| | 12 | Other (attach schedule) . . . . . . . . . | | (Enter on applicable lines of your return) |
| **Self-employment** | 13 a | Net earnings (loss) from self-employment . . . . . . . . | | Sch. SE, Part I |
| | b | Gross farming or fishing income . . . . . . . . . | | (See Partner's Instructions for Schedule K–1 (Form 1065)) |
| | c | Gross nonfarm income . . . . . . . . . . . | | |
| **Tax Preference Items** | 14 a | Accelerated depreciation on nonrecovery real property or 15-year or 18-year real property. . . . . . . . . . | | Form 6251, line 4c |
| | b | Accelerated depreciation on leased personal property or leased recovery property other than 15-year or 18-year real property . . . . . . . . | | Form 6251, line 4d |
| | c | Depletion (other than oil and gas) . . . . . . . . | | Form 6251, line 4i |
| | d | (1) Gross income from oil, gas, and geothermal properties . . . . | | See Form 6251 instructions |
| | | (2) Deductions allocable to oil, gas, and geothermal properties . . . | | See Form 6251 instructions |
| | e | (1) Qualified investment income included in Schedule K-1, line 1 . . | | (See Partner's Instructions for Schedule K–1 (Form 1065)) |
| | | (2) Qualified investment expenses included in Schedule K-1, line 1 | | |
| | f | Other (attach schedule) . . . . . . . . . . . | | |

**For Paperwork Reduction Act Notice, see Form 1065 Instructions.**

**Schedule K–1 (Form 1065) 1985**

Schedule K-1 (Form 1065) (1985)      Page **2**

| (a) Distributive share item | | (b) Amount | (c) 1040 filers enter the amount in column (b) on: |
|---|---|---|---|
| **Investment Interest** 15a | Interest expense on: | | |
| | (1) Investment debts incurred before 12/17/69 . . . . . . . | | Form 4952, line 1 |
| | (2) Investment debts incurred before 9/11/75, but after 12/16/69 | | Form 4952, line 15 |
| | (3) Investment debts incurred after 9/10/75 . . . . . . . . | | Form 4952, line 5 |
| b | (1) Investment income included in Schedule K-1, line 1 . . . . . | | |
| | (2) Investment expenses included in Schedule K-1, line 1 . . . . | | See Partner's Instructions for Schedule K-1 (Form 1065) |
| c | (1) Income from "net lease property" . . . . . . . . . | | |
| | (2) Expenses from "net lease property" . . . . . . . . . | | |
| **Foreign Taxes** 16a | Type of income _____ | | Form 1116, Check boxes |
| b | Name of foreign country or U.S. possession _____ | | Form 1116, Part I |
| c | Total gross income from sources outside the U.S. (attach schedule) . | | Form 1116, Part I |
| d | Total applicable deductions and losses (attach schedule) . . . . | | Form 1116, Part I |
| e | Total foreign taxes (check one): ▶ ☐ Paid ☐ Accrued . . . . | | Form 1116, Part II |
| f | Reduction in taxes available for credit (attach schedule). . . . . | | Form 1116, Part III |
| g | Other (attach schedule) . . . . . . . . . . . . . . | | Form 1116 Instructions |
| **Other** 17 | Other items and amounts not included in lines 1 through 16g and 18 and 19 that are required to be reported separately to you. . . . . . | | (See Partner's Instructions for Schedule K-1 (Form 1065)) |

| **Property Eligible for Investment Credit** 18 | | | | (b) Amount | (c) |
|---|---|---|---|---|---|
| | Regular Percentage | Cost or other basis of new recovery property | **a** 3-Year . . . . | | Form 3468, line 1(a) |
| | | | **b** Other . . . . | | Form 3468, line 1(b) |
| | | Cost or other basis of used recovery property | **c** 3-Year . . . . | | Form 3468, line 1(c) |
| | | | **d** Other . . . . | | Form 3468, line 1(d) |
| | Section 48(q) Election to Reduce Credit (Instead of Adjusting Basis) | Cost or other basis of new recovery property | **e** 3-year . . . . | | Form 3468, line 1(e) |
| | | | **f** Other . . . . . | | Form 3468, line 1(f) |
| | | Cost or other basis of used recovery property | **g** 3-year . . . . | | Form 3468, line 1(g) |
| | | | **h** Other . . . . | | Form 3468, line 1(h) |
| | **i** | Other property (see instructions for Schedule K-1 in the Instructions for Form 1065) | | | See Partner's Instructions for Schedule K-1 (Form 1065) |

| **Property Subject to Recapture of Investment Credit** 19 | | A | B | C | |
|---|---|---|---|---|---|
| a | Properties: Description of property (State whether recovery or nonrecovery property. If recovery property, state whether regular percentage method or section 48(q) election used.) . . . . . | | | | Form 4255, top |
| b | Date placed in service . | | | | Form 4255, line 2 |
| c | Cost or other basis . . | | | | Form 4255, line 3 |
| d | Class of recovery property or original estimated useful life. . | | | | Form 4255, line 4 |
| e | Date item ceased to be investment credit property | | | | Form 4255, line 8 |

# 1985

**Department of the Treasury
Internal Revenue Service**

# Partner's Instructions for Schedule K-1 (Form 1065)

## (For Partner's Use Only)

*(Section references are to the Internal Revenue Code, unless otherwise noted.)*

## Purpose of Schedule K-1 (Form 1065)

The partnership uses Schedule K-1 (Form 1065) to report to you your share of the partnership's income, credits, deductions, etc. Please **keep it for your records. Do not file it with your tax return.** A copy has been filed with the IRS.

Although the partnership is not subject to income tax, you are liable for tax on your share of the partnership income, whether or not distributed, and you must include your share on your tax return. Your share of any partnership income, credit, deduction, etc., must also be reported on your return. Please read *Limitation on losses* under line 1 to figure how much of your share of any partnership loss is deductible.

Use these instructions to help you report the items shown on Schedule K-1 on your tax return.

Where "(attach schedule)" appears beside a line item (lines 7, 10, 12, 14f, 16c, 16d, 16f, and 16g), it means you should see the schedule that the partnership has attached to that line.

Where "(see instructions for Form 1065)" appears beside an item or line (Questions A, B and line 18i), it means the partnership should see the Instructions for Form 1065 before completing these lines. You may ignore this notation.

## General Information

**Inconsistent treatment of items shown on Schedule K-1 (and any attached schedules) or similar statement.**—You must treat partnership items on your return consistent with the way the partnership treated the items on its filed return. This rule does not apply if your partnership is within the "small partnership" exception and does not elect to have the section 6231(a)(I)(B)(ii) election apply. See section 6222 for the inconsistent treatment rules.

If your treatment on your original or amended return is (or may be) inconsistent with the partnership's treatment, or if the partnership was required to, but has not filed a return, you must file **Form 8082**, Notice of Inconsistent Treatment or Amended Return (Administrative Adjustment Request (AAR)), with your original or amended return to identify and explain the inconsistency (or to note that a partnership return has not been filed).

If you are required to file Form 8082 but do not do so, you may be subject to the negligence penalty under section 6653(a). This penalty is in addition to any tax that results from making your amount or treatment of the item consistent with that shown on the partnership's return. Any deficiency that results from making the amounts consistent may be assessed immediately.

**United States persons with interests in foreign partnerships.**—If you have an interest in a foreign partnership, you may be required to report changes in your partnership interest when: you acquire an interest in a foreign partnership; you dispose of any part of your interest in a foreign partnership; or your proportional interest in a foreign partnership changes substantially. See section 6046A and the related regulations for more information.

If you are a U.S. person in a foreign partnership that does not file a partnership return, any losses or credits from that partnership may be disallowed.

**Tax shelters.**—If you receive a copy of **Form 8271**, Investor Reporting of Tax Shelter Registration Number, or if your partnership is involved in a tax shelter, see the instructions for Form 8271 for the information you are required to furnish to the Internal Revenue Service. Attach the completed form(s) to your income tax return. The tax shelter registration number can be found on Question F of your Schedule K-1 (Form 1065).

**Tax treatment of partnership items.**—If a partnership return is filed by an entity for a tax year, but it is determined that the entity is not a partnership for that tax year, sections 6221 through 6233 apply to that entity and to persons holding an interest in that entity to the extent provided in the regulations. See section 6233 for more information.

**Section 1256 contracts and straddles.**—For information on how to report gains and losses from section 1256 contracts and straddles, see **Form 6781**, Gains and Losses From Section 1256 Contracts and Straddles.

**Windfall profit tax.**—Generally, if you are a producer of domestic crude oil, your partnership will inform you on **Form 6248**, Annual Information Return of Windfall Profit Tax-1985, of your income tax deduction for the windfall profit tax rather than on Schedule K-1 (Form 1065). You will have to determine if you are entitled to a refund of overpaid windfall profit tax. File

**Form 6249**, Computation of Overpaid Windfall Profit Tax, to obtain a refund.

**Note:** *If your partnership elects to be treated as authorized to act on behalf of the partners, the regulations under section 6232 and Revenue Procedure 84-4, 1984-1 C.B. 363, will apply.*

**Errors.**—If you believe the partnership has made an error on your Schedule K-1, notify the partnership and ask for a corrected Schedule K-1. Do not change any items on your copy. Be sure that the partnership sends a copy of the corrected Schedule K-1 to the Internal Revenue Service. However, see **Inconsistent treatment of items shown on Schedule K-1.**

**International boycotts.**—Every partnership that had operations in, or related to, a boycotting country, company, or a national of a country, must file **Form 5713**, International Boycott Report.

If the partnership tells you that it did not cooperate with an international boycott, you do not have to file Form 5713, unless you had other boycotting operations.

If the partnership cooperated with an international boycott, it must give you a copy of the form. You also must file Form 5713 to report the activities of the partnership and any other boycott operations of your own. You may lose certain tax benefits if the partnership participated in, or cooperated with, an international boycott. Please see Form 5713 and the instructions for more information.

**Definitions.**—

**General partner.**—A general partner is a member of the organization who is personally liable for the obligations of the partnership.

**Limited partner.**—A limited partner is one whose potential personal liability for partnership debts is limited to the amount of money or other property that the partner contributed or is required to contribute to the partnership.

**Limited partnership.**—A limited partnership is a partnership composed of at least one general partner and one or more limited partners.

**Nonrecourse loans.**—Nonrecourse loans are those liabilities of the partnership for which none of the partners have any personal liability.

**Elections.**—Generally, the partnership decides how to figure taxable income from its operations. For example, it chooses the accounting method and depreciation methods it will use.

However, certain elections are made by you separately on your income tax return and not by the partnership. These elections are made under:

● Section 57(c) (definition of net lease);

● Section 108(b)(5) or 108(d)(4) (income from discharge of indebtedness);

● Section 163(d)(6) (limitation on interest on investment indebtedness);

● Section 617 (deduction and recapture of certain mining exploration expenditures, paid or incurred); and

● Section 901 (foreign tax credit).

If you are an individual partner (including estates and trusts), you may make an election under section 58(i) to deduct ratably over the period of time specified in section 58(i), certain qualified expenditures. For more information, see the instructions for line 17, item g.

**Additional information.**—For more information on the treatment of partnership income, credits, deductions, etc., see: **Publication 541**, Tax Information on Partnerships; **Publication 535**, Business Expenses; **Publication 536**, Net Operating Losses and the At-Risk Limits; **Publication 550**, Investment Income and Expenses; and **Publication 556**, Examination of Returns, Appeal Rights, and Claims for Refund.

## Specific Instructions

**Name, address, and identifying number.**—Your name, address, and identifying number, as well as the partnership's name, address, and identifying number, should be entered.

**Question A. Is partner a general partner?**—Be sure the partnership has answered this question and that it is answered correctly.

**Question B. Partner's share of liabilities.**—Question B should show your share of the partnership's nonrecourse liabilities and other liabilities as of the end of the partnership's tax year. If you terminated your interest in the partnership during the tax year, Question B should show the share that existed immediately before the total disposition. (A partner's "other liability" is any partnership liability for which a partner is personally liable.)

Use the total of the two amounts for computing the adjusted basis of your partnership interest. Use the amount shown next to "Other" to compute your amount at risk. Do not include any amounts that are not at risk that may be included in "Other."

If your partnership is engaged in two or more different types of at-risk activities, or a combination of at-risk activities and any other activity, the partnership should give you a statement showing your share of nonrecourse liabilities and other liabilities for each activity.

See **Limitation on losses** under line 1 for more information.

**Lines 1-19**

If you are an individual partner, take the amounts shown in column (b) and enter them on the lines on your tax return as indicated in column (c). If you are not an individual partner, report the amounts in column (b) as instructed on your tax return.

The line numbers in column (c) are references to forms in use for calendar year 1985. If you file your tax return on a calendar year basis, but your partnership files a fiscal year 1985/1986 partnership return, enter these amounts on the corresponding lines of the tax forms in use for 1986.

If you have losses, deductions, credits, etc., from a prior year that were not deductible or useable because of certain limitations, such as the at-risk rules, they may be taken into account in determining

your net income, loss, etc., for this year. However, do not combine the prior-year amounts with any amounts shown on this Schedule K-1 to get a net figure to report on any supporting schedules, statements, or forms (such as **Schedule E (Form 1040),** Supplemental Income Schedule) attached to your return. Instead, report the amounts on the attached schedule, statement, or form on a year-by-year basis.

If you have amounts, other than line 1, to report on Schedule E (Form 1040), enter each item on a separate line of Part II of Schedule E, column (e) or (f), whichever applies. Enter any deduction items in column (e).

**Line 1. Ordinary income (loss).**—The amount shown should reflect your share of ordinary income (loss) from all partnership business operations, including at-risk activities, without reference to the adjusted basis of your partnership interest or your amount at risk.

*Limitation on losses.*—Generally, you may not claim your share of a partnership loss (including capital loss) that is greater than the adjusted basis of your partnership interest at the end of the partnership's tax year. See Publication 541 for a discussion on how to determine your correct adjusted basis for tax purposes.

However, if you have (1) a loss (including losses from the disposition of assets or any part of an interest), or other deductions such as the expense deduction for recovery property (section 179), from any activity (except the holding of real property, other than mineral property) carried on as a trade or business or for the production of income by the partnership, and (2) amounts in the activity for which you are not at risk (described below), use **Form 6198**, Computation of Deductible Loss From an Activity Described in Section 465(c), to figure the allowable loss or deduction to report on your return. (If you have a loss or other deductions but do not have any amounts not at risk, or you have a loss from a non at-risk activity, deduct the amount of the loss and other deductions or the adjusted basis of your partnership interest, whichever is less.)

Generally, you are not at risk for amounts such as the following:

● Nonrecourse loans used to finance the activity, to acquire property used in the activity, or to acquire your interest in the activity, that are not secured by your own property (other than that used in the activity).

● Cash, property, or borrowed amounts used in the activity (or contributed to the activity, or used to acquire your interest in the activity) that are protected against loss by a guarantee, stop-loss agreement, or other similar arrangement (excluding casualty insurance and insurance against tort liability).

● Amounts borrowed for use in the activity from a person who has an interest in the activity, other than as a creditor, or who is related, under section 168(e)(4), to a person (other than yourself) having such

an interest. An exception applies, however, to an interest as a shareholder in the case of amounts borrowed by a corporation from the shareholder.

To help you complete Form 6198, the partnership should give you your share of the total pre-1976 loss(es) from a section 465(c)(1) activity (i.e., films or video tapes, leasing section 1245 property, farm, or oil and gas property) for which there existed a corresponding amount of nonrecourse liability at the end of the year in which this loss(es) occurred. In addition, you should get a separate statement of income, expenses, etc., for each activity from the partnership.

Special transitional rules for movies, video tapes, and leasing activities can be found in section 204(c)(2) and (3) of the Tax Reform Act of 1976 and Publication 536.

**Lines 4 and 5. Net short-term and net long-term capital gain (loss).**—If any of the gain or loss is from investment property, the partnership should give you a statement breaking down the net short-term and long-term capital gain from investment property. You need this to compute the investment interest expense limitation. See **Form 4952,** Investment Interest Expense Deduction, for more information.

**Line 6. Net gain (loss) under section 1231 (other than due to casualty or theft).**—The amount on this line is to be entered on line 1, column (g) or (h), whichever is applicable, of **Form 4797,** Gains and Losses From Sales or Exchanges of Assets Used in a Trade or Business and Involuntary Conversions. You do not have to complete the information called for on columns (b) through (f). Write "From Schedule K-1 (Form 1065)" across these columns.

**Line 7. Other income (loss).**—Amounts on this line are other items of income, gain, or loss not included on lines 1-6, such as:

● Partnership gains from disposition of farm recapture property (see Form 4797) and other items to which section 1252 applies.

● Recoveries of bad debts, prior taxes, and delinquency amounts (section 111). Report on line 22, Form 1040.

● Gains and losses from wagers (section 165(d)).

● Any income, gain, or loss to the partnership under section 751(b). Report this amount on line 15, Form 4797.

● Specially allocated ordinary gain (loss). Report this amount on Form 4797, line 15.

● Net gain (loss) from involuntary conversions due to casualty or theft. The partnership will give you a schedule that shows the amounts to be entered on **Form 4684,** Casualties and Thefts, Section B, Part II, line 16, columns B(i), B(ii), and C.

The partnership should give you a description and the amount of your share for each of these items.

**Line 8. Charitable contributions.**—The partnership will give you a schedule that shows which contributions were subject to the 50%, 30%, and 20% limitations. For further information, see the Form 1040 Instructions.

If contributions of property other than cash are made and if the fair market value of one item or group of similar items of property exceeds $5,000, the partnership is required to file **Form 8283,** Noncash Charitable Contributions, and give you a copy to attach to your tax return. Do not deduct the amount shown on this form. It is the partnership's contribution. You should deduct the amount shown on line 8 of your Schedule K-1 (Form 1065).

If the partnership provides you with information that the contribution was property other than cash and does not give you a Form 8283, see the **Instructions for Form 8283** for filing requirements. A Form 8283 does not need to be filed unless the total claimed value of all contributed items of property exceeds $500.

**Line 9. Expense deduction for recovery property.**—See **Form 4562**, Depreciation and Amortization, for more information. If you are an individual partner, also see Schedule E (Form 1040), Part II, line 29, and the related instructions.

**Line 10. Other deductions.**—Amounts on this line are other deductions not included on lines 8-9, such as:

● Other itemized deductions (1040 filers enter on **Schedule A (Form 1040),** Itemized Deductions).

**Note:** *If there was a gain (loss) from a casualty or theft to property not used in a trade or business or for income-producing purposes, you will be notified by the partnership. You will have to complete your own Form 4684.*

● Any penalty on early withdrawal of savings.

● Soil and water conservation expenditures (section 175) and expenditures by farming partnerships for clearing land (section 182).

● Expenditures for the removal of architectural and transportation barriers to the elderly and handicapped incurred before January 1, 1986, which the partnership has elected to treat as a current expense (section 190).

● Payments for a partner to an IRA, Keogh, or a Simplified Employee Pension plan. See Form 1040 Instructions for line 26 of Form 1040 in order to figure your IRA deduction. Payments made to a Keogh or SEP plan will be entered on Form 1040, line 27. If the payments to a Keogh plan were to a defined benefit plan, the partnership should give you a statement showing the amount of the benefit accrued for the tax year.

The partnership should give you a description and the amount of your share for each of these items.

**Line 12. Other credits.**—Amounts on this line are other credits (other than investment credit which is reported on line 18) such as:

● Nonconventional source fuel credit.

● Unused credits from cooperatives.

● The credit for increasing research activities and orphan drug credit (enter these credits on **Form 6765**, Credit for Increasing Research Activities).

● Jobs Credit. Complete **Form 5884,** Jobs Credit, and attach it to your return. See the form for definitions, special rules, and limitations.

● Credit for alcohol used as fuel. Complete **Form 6478,** Credit for Alcohol Used as Fuel, and attach it to your return.

The partnership should give you a description and the amount of your share for each of these items.

**Lines 13a, 13b, and 13c:** If you and your spouse are both partners, each of you must complete and file your own **Schedule SE (Form 1040),** Computation of Social Security Self-Employment Tax, to report your partnership earnings (loss) from self-employment. Do not report the self-employment amounts for both of you on one Schedule SE (Form 1040).

**Line 13a. Net earnings (loss) from self-employment.**—Before entering this amount on Schedule SE (Form 1040), you must adjust it by any section 179 expense claimed, unreimbursed partnership expenses claimed, and depletion claimed on oil and gas properties.

If the amount on this line is a loss, enter only the deductible amount on Schedule SE (Form 1040). See *Limitation on losses* under the instructions for line 1.

If your partnership is an options dealer or a commodities dealer, see section 1402(i).

**Line 13b. Gross farming or fishing income.**—If you are an individual partner, enter the amount from this line on Schedule E (Form 1040), Part IV, line 37. You may also use this amount to figure self-employment income under the optional method on Schedule SE (Form 1040), Part II.

**Line 13c. Gross nonfarm income.**—If you are an individual partner, use this amount to figure self-employment income under the optional method on Schedule SE (Form 1040), Part II.

**Lines 14d(1) and (2), and 14e(1) and (2).**—Generally, the amounts shown on each of these lines are not the total gross income from, and total deductions allocable to, oil, gas, and geothermal properties and not the total qualified investment income or expenses for this partnership. The partnership should attach a schedule that shows the amount of gross income from, and deductions allocable to, oil, gas, and geothermal properties and the amount of qualified investment income and expenses included in the amount shown in column (b) for lines 2 through 10 and for line 17.

Do not use any part of the amount shown on line 1 of this Schedule K-1 to complete Form 6251. This amount has been included in the amounts shown on lines 14d and 14e.

**Lines 14d(1) and (2). Gross income from, and deductions allocable to, oil, gas, and geothermal properties.**—To determine the net amount to use in figuring the amount to be included on line 4k of **Form 6251,** Alternative Minimum Tax Computation, add to the amounts shown on lines 14d(1) and (2) the gross income from, and deductions allocable to, oil, gas, and geothermal properties from all other sources, including any such income and expenses shown on lines 2 through 10 and 17 of this Schedule K-1.

**Lines 14e(1) and (2). Qualified investment income and qualified investment expenses.**—To determine the net amount to enter on line 2e(2) of Form 6251, add to the amounts shown on lines 14e(1) and (2) the qualified investment income and expenses from all other sources, including any qualified investment income and expenses shown on lines 2 through 10 and 17 of this Schedule K-1. Enter the net result (but not less than zero) on line 2e(2) of Form 6251.

**Line 14f. Other.**—Enter the information on the schedule attached by the partnership for line 14f on the applicable lines of Form 6251.

**Line 15. Investment interest.**—If the partnership paid or accrued interest on debts it incurred to buy or hold investment property, the amount of interest you can deduct may be limited. The partnership should have entered the interest on investment debts and items of investment income and expenses.

For more information and the special provisions that apply to "out-of-pocket" expenses and rental income from property subject to a net lease, see section 163(d) and Publication 550. (Individuals, estates, and trusts, also see Form 4952.)

**Note:** *Generally, if your total investment interest expense including investment interest expense from all other sources (including carryovers, etc.) is less than $10,000 ($5,000 if married filing separately), you do not need to get Form 4952. Instead, you may enter the amounts of investment interest directly on Schedule A (Form 1040). The partnership will tell you if any of the amounts should be reported on Schedule E (Form 1040).*

**Lines 15b(1) and (2). Investment income and investment expenses.**—Use the amounts on these lines to determine the amount to enter on lines 2 or 10a of Form 4952.

**Caution:** *Generally, the amount shown on each of these lines is not the total investment income or expenses for this partnership. The partnership should attach a schedule which shows the amount of investment income and expenses included in the amount shown in column (b) for lines 2 through 10 and for line 17.*

*You will have to adjust lines 15b(1) and (2) for any other investment income or expenses included in lines 2 through 10 and 17 to determine the total investment income and total investment expenses for this partnership.*

*Do not use any part of the amount shown on line 1 of this Schedule K-1 to complete Form 4952. This amount has been included*

**Page 3**

*in the amount shown on lines 15b(1) and (2). To determine the amount to enter on Form 4952, add to the amount on lines 15b(1) and (2) the investment income and expenses from all other sources including any investment income and investment expenses shown on lines 2 through 10 and 17 of this Schedule K-1.*

Report the amounts on lines 15b(1) and (2) as follows:

● If (1) there is an entry on line 15a(1) or you had interest expense on investment debts incurred before 12/17/69; and (2) there is an entry on lines 15b(1) or (2) or you had investment income (loss) in 1985; combine the amount on lines 15b (1) and (2) with your other investment income and investment expenses from all sources and enter the result (but not less than zero) on line 2 of Form 4952. Complete lines 3 and 4 of Form 4952. Then enter the amount from line 4 of Form 4952 on line 10a of Form 4952.

● If there is not an entry on line 15a(1) and you do not have interest expense on investment debts incurred before 12/17/69, combine the amounts on lines 15b(1) and (2) with your other investment income and investment expenses from all sources and enter the result (but not less than zero) on line 10a of Form 4952.

**Lines 15c(1) and (2). Income and expenses from "net lease property."**—Use the amounts on these lines to determine the net amount to enter on lines 11 and 19 of Form 4952.

**Lines 16a-16g. Foreign taxes.**—Use the information on lines 16a through 16g, and on any attached schedules, to figure your foreign tax credit. For more information, see: **Form 1116,** Computation of Foreign Tax Credit—Individual, Fiduciary, or Nonresident Alien Individual, and the related instructions; **Form 1118,** Computation of Foreign Tax Credit—Corporations, and the related instructions; and **Publication 514**, Foreign Tax Credit for U.S. Citizens and Resident Aliens.

**Line 17. Other.**—Amounts included on the statement for this line are other amounts not included elsewhere such as:

a. Taxes paid on undistributed capital gains by a regulated investment company. (Form 1040 filers enter your share of these taxes on line 63, and add the words "From 1065.")

b. Number of gallons of the fuels used during the tax year and the appropriate tax rate for each type of use identified on **Form 4136,** Computation of Credit for Federal Tax on Gasoline and Special Fuels, and in the related instructions. Your share of the credit allowed for qualified diesel-powered highway vehicles as shown on Form 4136.

c. Your share of gross income from the property, share of production for the tax year, etc., needed to figure your depletion

deduction for oil and gas wells. The partnership should also allocate to you a share of the adjusted basis of each partnership oil or gas property. The allocation of the basis of each property is made as specified in section 613A(c)(7)(D). See Publication 535 for how to figure your depletion deduction.

d. If you are a corporation, any income allocable to you that is "timber preference income" under section 57(e).

e. Tax-exempt interest income earned by the partnership. If you are an individual partner, use this amount in determining the taxable part of any social security or railroad retirement benefits you may receive.

f. Recapture of expense deduction under section 179. If the recapture was caused by a disposition of the property, include the amount on Form 4797, line 14.

The amount to be recaptured will be limited to the amount you deducted in the prior year.

g. Total qualified expenditures (and the applicable period) paid or incurred during the tax year to which an election under section 58(i) applies and 58(i) type expenditures for corporate partners.

If you are an individual partner (including an estate or trust), you may either deduct the total amount of these expenditures or you may make an election under section 58(i) to deduct them ratably over the period of time specified in section 58(i). If you choose to make the election under section 58(i), these qualified expenditures will not be classified as tax preference items and thus will not be subject to the alternative minimum tax. See section 58(i) and make the election on **Form 4562,** Depreciation and Amortization.

If intangible drilling costs are passed through to you, see item h, which follows, before deducting them under section 58(i). If you are a limited partner, see section 58(i)(4).

h. Intangible drilling costs (IDCs) under section 263. See Publication 535 for more information. If you are an individual partner (including an estate or trust), you may choose to deduct IDCs under section 263 or under section 58(i), but not both.

i. Deduction and recapture of certain mining exploration expenditures paid or incurred. You may choose to deduct these expenditures under section 617 or under section 58(i), but not both.

If you are not eligible to make an election under section 58(i) or you choose not to make this election, deduct the section 58(i) expenditures in full on your return, subject to any other limitations, such as the at-risk limitations.

If you are an individual partner, enter the amount you are deducting on Schedule E (Form 1040), Part II, column (e).

j. Any items you need to determine the basis of your partnership interest for purposes of section 704(d) because Question G on Schedule K-1 is not completed; or any items (other than those shown in Question B) you need to figure your amount at risk.

k. Any information or statements you need to comply with section 6661 (regarding substantial understatement of tax liability) or section 6111 (regarding tax shelters).

l. Real property construction period interest and taxes for other than low-income housing or any real property acquired, constructed, or carried if the property is not and cannot reasonably be expected to be held in a trade or business, or in an activity conducted for profit. See section 189 for more information.

m. Any other information you may need to file your return that is not shown elsewhere on Schedule K-1.

The partnership should give you a description and the amount of your share for each of these items.

**Line 18. Property eligible for investment credit.**—Your share of the partnership's investment in property that qualifies for the investment credit should be entered. You can claim a tax credit based on your pro rata share of this investment by filing **Form 3468,** Computation of Investment Credit. In addition to the qualifying property reported on lines 18a through h, the partnership will give you a separate schedule that shows your share of the partnership's investment in nonrecovery property, new commuter highway vehicle property, used commuter highway vehicle property, qualified rehabilitation expenditures, and energy property that qualifies for the credit, and where to report these items.

**Line 19. Property subject to recapture of investment credit.**—When investment credit property is disposed of, ceases to qualify or there is a decrease in the percentage of business use before the "life-years category" or "recovery period" assigned, you will be notified. You may have to recapture (pay back) the investment credit taken in prior years. Use the information on line 19 to figure your recapture tax on **Form 4255,** Recapture of Investment Credit. See the Form 3468 on which you took the original credit for other information you need to complete Form 4255.

You may also need Form 4255 if you disposed of more than one-third of your interest in a partnership. See **Publication 572,** Investment Credit, for more information.

# U.S. Fiduciary Income Tax Return

Form **1041**
Department of the Treasury
Internal Revenue Service

**For the calendar year 1985 or fiscal year**

beginning............................................., 1985, and ending........................................., 19........

OMB No. 1545-0092

**1985**

**Check applicable boxes:**
- ☐ Decedent's estate
- ☐ Simple trust
- ☐ Complex trust
- ☐ Grantor type trust
- ☐ Ancillary return
- ☐ Bankruptcy estate
- ☐ Generation-skipping trust
- ☐ Family estate trust
- ☐ Pooled income fund
- ☐ Final return
- ☐ Amended return

Name of estate or trust (Grantor type trust, see instructions)

Name and title of fiduciary

Address of fiduciary (number and street)

City, state, and ZIP code

**For Paperwork Reduction Act Notice, see page 1 of the instructions.**

Employer identification number

Date entity created

Nonexempt charitable and split-interest trusts check applicable boxes (See instructions):
- ☐ Described in section 4947(a)(1)
- ☐ Not treated as a private foundation
- ☐ Described in section 4947(a)(2)

**Income**

| | | | |
|---|---|---|---|
| 1 | Dividends (enter full amount before exclusion) | 1 | |
| 2 | Interest income | 2 | |
| 3 | Partnership income or (loss) and income from another estate or trust | 3 | |
| 4 | Net rent or royalty income or (loss) (attach Schedule E (Form 1040)) | 4 | |
| 5 | Net business or farm income or (loss) (attach Schedules C and F (Form 1040)) | 5 | |
| 6 | Capital gain or (loss) (attach Schedule D (Form 1041)) | 6 | |
| 7 | Ordinary gain or (loss) (attach Form 4797) | 7 | |
| 8 | Other income (state nature of income) ........................................... | 8 | |
| 9 | **Total** income (add lines 1 through 8) ▶ | 9 | |

**Deductions**

| | | | |
|---|---|---|---|
| 10 | Interest | 10 | |
| 11 | Taxes | 11 | |
| 12 | Fiduciary fees | 12 | |
| 13 | Charitable deduction (from Schedule A, line 11) | 13 | |
| 14 | Attorney, accountant, and return preparer fees | 14 | |
| 15 | Other deductions (attach a separate sheet listing deductions) | 15 | |
| 16 | **Total** (add lines 10 through 15) ▶ | 16 | |
| 17 | Adjusted total income or (loss) (subtract line 16 from line 9) | 17 | |
| 18 | Income distribution deduction (from Schedule B, line 17) (see instructions) (attach Schedule K-1 (Form 1041)) | 18 | |
| 19 | Dividend exclusion (see instructions) | 19 | |
| 20 | Estate tax deduction (attach computation) | 20 | |
| 21 | Long-term capital gain deduction from Schedule D (Form 1041) (☐ Charity—see instructions) | 21 | |
| 22 | Exemption | 22 | |
| 23 | **Total** (add lines 18 through 22) ▶ | 23 | |
| 24 | Taxable income of fiduciary (subtract line 23 from line 17) ▶ | 24 | |

**Computation of Tax**

| | | | |
|---|---|---|---|
| 25 | **Tax: a** Tax rate schedule ....................................; **b** Other tax.....................; Total ▶ | 25c | |
| 26 | **Credits: a** Foreign tax................; **b** Nonconventional fuel ...............; **c** Research ...............; Total ▶ | 26d | |
| 27 | **Credits:** ☐ Form 3800  ☐ Form 3468 (see instructions)  ☐ Form 5884  ☐ Form 6478 | 27 | |
| 28 | **Total** (add lines 26d and 27) ▶ | 28 | |
| 29 | **Balance** (subtract line 28 from line 25c) | 29 | |
| 30 | Recapture of investment credit (attach Form 4255) | 30 | |
| 31 | Alternative minimum tax (attach Form 6251) | 31 | |
| 32 | **Total** (add lines 29 through 31) ▶ | 32 | |
| 33 | **Credits: a** Form 2439.................; **b** Form 4136.................; **c** Form 6249 ...................; Total ▶ | 33d | |
| 34 | **Federal income tax: a** Previously paid ▶.........................; **b** Withheld ▶...................; Total ▶ | 34c | |
| 35 | **Total** (add lines 33d and 34c) ▶ | 35 | |
| 36 | **Balance of tax due** (subtract line 35 from line 32) (see instructions) | 36 | |
| 37 | Overpayment (subtract line 32 from line 35) | 37 | |

**Please Sign Here**

Under penalties of perjury, I declare that I have examined this return, including accompanying schedules and statements, and to the best of my knowledge and belief, it is true, correct, and complete. Declaration of preparer (other than fiduciary) is based on all information of which preparer has any knowledge.

▶
Signature of fiduciary or officer representing fiduciary        Date

**Paid Preparer's Use Only**

| Preparer's signature ▶ | Date | Check if self-employed ▶ ☐ | Preparer's social security no. |
|---|---|---|---|
| Firm's name (or yours, if self-employed) and address ▶ | | E.I. No. ▶ | |
| | | ZIP code ▶ | |

Form **1041** (1985)

*Do not complete Schedules A and B for a simple trust or a pooled income fund.*

## SCHEDULE A.—Charitable Deduction

**(Write the name and address of each charitable organization to whom your contributions total $3,000 or more on an attached sheet.)**

| | | |
|---|---|---|
| 1 Amounts paid or permanently set aside for charitable purposes from current year's gross income . . . . | 1 | |
| 2 Tax-exempt interest allocable to charitable distribution (see instructions) . . . . . . . . . | 2 | |
| **(Complete lines 3 through 6 below only if gain on Schedule D (Form 1041), line 16, column (b), exceeds loss on Schedule D (Form 1041), line 15, column (b).)** | | |
| 3 Long-term capital gain included on line 1 (see instructions) . . . . . . . . . . . . | 3 | |
| 4 Enter gain from Schedule D (Form 1041), line 16, column (b), minus loss on Schedule D (Form 1041), line 15, column (b) | 4 | |
| 5 Enter gain from Schedule D (Form 1041), line 16, column (c), minus loss on Schedule D (Form 1041), line 15, column (c) | 5 | |
| 6 Enter 60% of the amount on line 3, 4, or 5, whichever is the smallest . . . . . . . . . | 6 | |
| 7 Add line 2 and line 6. | 7 | |
| 8 Balance (subtract line 7 from line 1) . . . . . . . . . . . . . . . . . | 8 | |
| 9 Enter the net short-term capital gain and 40% of the net long-term capital gain of the current tax year allocable to corpus, paid or permanently set aside for charitable purposes . . . . . . . . | 9 | |
| 10 Amounts paid or permanently set aside for charitable purposes from gross income of a prior year (see instructions) . . . . . . . . . . . . . . . . . . . . . . . | 10 | |
| 11 Total (add lines 8, 9, and 10). Enter here and on page 1, line 13 . . . . . . . . . . | 11 | |

## SCHEDULE B.—Income Distribution Deduction

| | | |
|---|---|---|
| 1 Adjusted total income (enter amount from page 1, line 17) (If net loss, enter zero) . . . . . . . | 1 | |
| 2 Adjusted tax-exempt interest, (see instructions) . . . . . . . . . . . . . . . | 2 | |
| 3 Net gain shown on Schedule D (Form 1041), line 17, column (a). If net loss, enter zero . . . . . | 3 | |
| 4 Enter amount from Schedule A, line 9 . . . . . . . . . . . . . . . . . | 4 | |
| 5 Enter 40% of the amount on Schedule A, line 3, 4, or 5 whichever is smallest . . . . . . . . | 5 | |
| 6 Short-term capital gain included on Schedule A, line 1 . . . . . . . . . . . . . | 6 | |
| 7 If the amount on page 1, line 6 is a capital loss enter here as a positive figure . . . . . . . | 7 | |
| 8 If the amount on page 1, line 6 is a capital gain enter here as a negative figure . . . . . . . | 8 | |
| 9 Distributable net income (combine lines 1 through 8) . . . . . . . . . . . . . | 9 | |
| 10 If a complex trust, amount of income for the tax year determined under the governing instrument (accounting income) . . . . . . . . . .  | 10 | |
| 11 Amount of income required to be distributed currently (see instructions) . . . . . . . . . | 11 | |
| 12 Other amounts paid, credited, or otherwise required to be distributed (see instructions) . . . . . | 12 | |
| 13 Total distributions (add lines 11 and 12) (If greater than line 10, see instructions) . . . . . . . | 13 | |
| 14 Enter the total of tax-exempt income included on line 13 . . . . . . . . . . . . | 14 | |
| 15 Tentative income distribution deduction (subtract line 14 from line 13) . . . . . . . . . | 15 | |
| 16 Tentative income distribution deduction (subtract line 2 from line 9) . . . . . . . . . | 16 | |
| 17 Income distribution deduction (enter the smaller of line 15 or line 16 here and on page 1, line 18) . . . | 17 | |

## Other Information

| | Yes | No |
|---|---|---|
| 1 If the fiduciary's name or address has changed enter the old information ▶ .................................................. | | |
| 2 Did the estate or trust receive tax-exempt income? (If "Yes," attach a computation of the allocation of expenses). . . . | | |
| 3 Did the estate or trust receive all or any part of the earnings (salary, wages, and other compensation) of any individual by reason of a contract assignment or similar arrangement? . . . . . . . . . . . . . . . . | | |
| 4 At any time during the tax year did the estate or trust have an interest in or a signature or other authority over a financial account in a foreign country (such as a bank account, securities account, or other financial account)? (See the instructions for question 4) | | |
| If "Yes," write the name of the foreign country ▶ .................................................. | | |
| 5 Was the estate or trust the grantor of, or transferor to, a foreign trust which existed during the current tax year, whether or not the estate or trust has any beneficial interest in it? (If "Yes," you may have to file Form 3520, 3520-A, or 926) . . | | |
| 6 Check this box, if this entity has filed or is required to file Form 8264, Application for Registration of a Tax Shelter . ▶ ☐ | | |
| 7 Check this box, if this entity is a complex trust making the section 663(b) election . . . . . . . . . . . ▶ ☐ | | |
| 8 Check this box, if a section 643(d)(3) election is made. (Attach Schedule D (Form 1041)) . . . . . . . . ▶ ☐ | | |
| 9 Check this box, if the decedent's estate has been open for more than two years. (See instructions) . . . . . . ▶ ☐ | | |

| SCHEDULE J (Form 1041)<br><br>Department of the Treasury<br>Internal Revenue Service | **Information Return**<br>**Trust Allocation of an Accumulation Distribution**<br>**(I.R.C. Section 665)**<br><br>▶ File with Form 1041. | OMB No. 1545-0092<br><br>19**84** |
|---|---|---|

| Name of trust | Employer identification number |
|---|---|

**Part I**   **Accumulation Distribution in 1984**

*For definitions and special rules, see the regulations under sections 665-668 of the Internal Revenue Code. See the Form 4970 instructions for certain income minors may exclude and special rules for multiple trusts.*

| | | |
|---|---|---|
| 1 Enter amount from Schedule B (Form 1041), line 12, for 1984 . . . . . . . . . . . . . . | **1** | |
| 2 Enter amount from Schedule B (Form 1041), line 9, for 1984 . . . . . . . . . | **2** | |
| 3 Enter amount from Schedule B (Form 1041), line 11, for 1984 . . . . . . . | **3** | |
| 4 Subtract line 3 from line 2. If line 3 is more than line 2, enter zero . . . . . . . . . | **4** | |
| 5 Subtract line 4 from line 1 . . . . . . . . . . . . . . . . . . . . . | **5** | |

**Part II**   **Ordinary Income Accumulation Distribution (Enter the applicable throwback years below.)**

| *If the distribution is thrown back to more than five years (starting with the earliest applicable tax year beginning after December 31, 1968), attach additional schedules. (If the trust was a simple trust see regulations section 1.665(e)-1A(b).)* | | Throwback year ending<br><br>19 .......... | Throwback year ending<br><br>19 .......... | Throwback year ending<br><br>19 .......... | Throwback year ending<br><br>19 .......... | Throwback year ending<br><br>19 .......... |
|---|---|---|---|---|---|---|
| 6 Distributable net income (see instructions) . . . . . . | **6** | | | | | |
| 7 Distributions (see instructions) | **7** | | | | | |
| 8 Subtract line 7 from line 6 . . | **8** | | | | | |
| 9 Enter amount from line 25 or line 31, Part III, as applicable . | **9** | | | | | |
| 10 Subtract line 9 from line 8 . . | **10** | | | | | |
| 11 Enter amount of prior accumulation distributions thrown back to any of these years . . . . . . . . . | **11** | | | | | |
| 12 Subtract line 11 from line 10 . | **12** | | | | | |
| 13 Allocate amount on line 5 that is an accumulation distribution to earliest applicable year first. Do not allocate an amount greater than line 12 for the same year . . . . . . . | **13** | | | | | |
| 14 Divide line 13 by line 10 and multiply result by line 9 . . . | **14** | | | | | |
| 15 Add lines 13 and 14 . . . . . | **15** | | | | | |
| 16 Tax-exempt interest included on line 13 (see instructions) . . | **16** | | | | | |
| 17 Subtract line 16 from line 15 . | **17** | | | | | |

For Paperwork Reduction Act Notice, see page 1 of the Instructions for Form 1041.      Schedule J (Form 1041) 1984

**Part III**   Taxes Imposed on Undistributed Net Income (Enter the applicable throwback years below.)

| If more than five throwback years are involved, attach additional schedules. If the trust received an accumulation distribution from another trust, see the regulations under sections 665-668 of the Internal Revenue Code. | | Throwback year ending 19........ | Throwback year ending 19........ | Throwback year ending 19........ | Throwback year ending 19........ | Throwback year ending 19........ |
|---|---|---|---|---|---|---|
| If trust elected alternative tax on capital gain, **OMIT** line 18 through line 25 **AND** complete line 26 through line 31. (The alternative tax on capital gain was repealed for tax years beginning after December 31, 1978.) | | | | | | |
| 18 Tax (see instructions) | 18 | | | | | |
| 19 Net short-term gain (see instructions) | 19 | | | | | |
| 20 Net long-term gain (see instructions) | 20 | | | | | |
| 21 Add line 19 and line 20 | 21 | | | | | |
| 22 Taxable income (see instructions) | 22 | | | | | |
| 23 Enter percent line 21 is of line 22, but not more than 100% | 23 | | | | | |
| 24 Multiply amount on line 18 by percent on line 23 | 24 | | | | | |
| 25 Subtract line 24 from line 18 and enter here and on line 9 | 25 | | | | | |
| If trust did not elect alternative tax on long-term capital gain, do **NOT** complete line 26 through line 31. | | | | | | |
| 26 Tax on income other than long-term capital gain (see instructions) | 26 | | | | | |
| 27 Net short-term gain (see instructions) | 27 | | | | | |
| 28 Taxable income less section 1202 deduction (see instructions) | 28 | | | | | |
| 29 Enter percent line 27 is of line 28, but not more than 100% | 29 | | | | | |
| 30 Multiply amount on line 26 by percent on line 29 | 30 | | | | | |
| 31 Subtract line 30 from line 26 and enter here and on line 9 | 31 | | | | | |

**Part IV**   Allocation to Beneficiary

Complete Part IV for each beneficiary. If the accumulation distribution is allocated to more than one beneficiary, attach an additional Schedule J with Part IV completed for each additional beneficiary. If more than five throwback years are involved, attach additional schedules.

| Beneficiary's name | | | Identifying number | | |
|---|---|---|---|---|---|
| Beneficiary's address (number and street including apartment number or rural route) | | | Enter amount from line 13 allocated to this beneficiary (a) | Enter amount from line 14 allocated to this beneficiary (b) | Enter amount from line 16 allocated to this beneficiary (c) |
| City, town or post office, State, and ZIP code | | | | | |
| 32 Throwback year 19 ..... | 32 | | | | |
| 33 Throwback year 19 ..... | 33 | | | | |
| 34 Throwback year 19 ..... | 34 | | | | |
| 35 Throwback year 19 ..... | 35 | | | | |
| 36 Throwback year 19 ..... | 36 | | | | |
| 37 Total (add amounts on line 32 through line 36) | 37 | | | | |

| SCHEDULE K-1<br>(Form 1041)<br><br>Department of the Treasury<br>Internal Revenue Service | **Beneficiary's Share of Income, Deductions, Credits, etc.—1985**<br>for the calendar year 1985, or fiscal year<br>beginning ................., 1985, ending ................, 19 .....<br>**Complete a separate Schedule K-1 for each beneficiary** | OMB No. 1545-0092<br><br>19**85** |

Name of estate or trust ▶

| Beneficiary's identifying number ▶ | Estate or trust's employer identification number ▶ |
|---|---|
| Beneficiary's name, address, and ZIP code | Fiduciary's name, address, and ZIP code |

**Your income from a fiscal year estate or trust must be included in your tax year during which the fiscal year of the estate or trust ends.**

| (a) Allocable share item | (b) Amount | (c) Form 1040 filers enter the amounts in column (b) on: |
|---|---|---|
| 1 Dividends (amount before exclusion) . . . . . . . . . . . . . . | | Schedule B, Part II, line 4 |
| 2 a Net short-term capital gain or (loss) . . . . . . . . . . . . | | Schedule D, line 4, column (f) or (g) |
| b Net long-term capital gain or (loss) . . . . . . . . . . . . . . | | Schedule D, line 12, column (f) or (g) |
| 3 Interest. . . . . . . . . . . . . . . . . . . . . . . . . . . . . . . | | |
| 4 Other taxable income (itemize): | | |
| a (1) ........................... | | |
| (2) ........................... | | |
| b Total (add lines 3, 4a(1) and (2)) . . . . . . . . . . . . . | | |
| c Depreciation (including cost recovery) and depletion . . . . | | |
| d Amortization deductions (itemize): | | |
| (1) ........................... | | |
| (2) ........................... | | |
| e Total (subtract lines 4c, 4d(1) and (2) from line 4b) . . . . | | Schedule E, Part II |
| 5 Estate tax deduction (attach computation) . . . . . . . . . . . | | Schedule A, line 22 |
| 6 Excess deductions on termination (attach computation) . . . . | | Schedule A, line 22 |
| 7 Tax preference items: | | |
| a Accelerated depreciation on: | | |
| (1) Real property . . . . . . . . . . . . . . . . . . . | | Form 6251, line 4c |
| (2) Personal property subject to a lease . . . . . . . . . . . | | Form 6251, line 4d |
| b Depletion . . . . . . . . . . . . . . . . . . . . . . . | | Form 6251, line 4i |
| c Other (itemize): | | |
| (1) ........................... | | Enter on applicable line of Form 6251 |
| (2) ........................... | | Enter on applicable line of Form 6251 |
| 8 Foreign taxes (list on a separate sheet) . . . . . . . . . . . . . | | Form 1116 or Schedule A (Form 1040), line 9 |
| 9 Property eligible for investment credit: | | |
| Cost or other basis of new recovery property    a 3-Year . . . . . . . . . . . . . . . | | Form 3468, line 1a |
| b Other . . . . . . . . . . . . | | Form 3468, line 1b |
| Cost of used recovery property    c 3-Year . . . . . . . . . . . . . . | | Form 3468, line 1c |
| d Other . . . . . . . . . . . . . | | Form 3468, line 1d |
| Section 48(q) Election to Reduce Credit (instead of adjusting basis)    e 3-Year . . . . . . . . . . . | | Form 3468, line 1e |
| f Other . . . . . . . . . . . . . | | Form 3468, line 1f |
| g 3-Year . . . . . . . . . . . . | | Form 3468, line 1g |
| h Other . . . . . . . . . . . . | | Form 3468, line 1h |
| Nonrecovery property (see instruction 9) (attach schedule) | | |
| 10 Other (itemize): | | |
| a ....................... | | ( Enter on applicable line ) |
| b ....................... | | ( of appropriate tax form ) |
| c ....................... | | |
| d ....................... | | |
| e ....................... | | |
| f | | |

For Paperwork Reduction Act Notice, see page 1 of the instructions for Form 1041.             Schedule K-1 (Form 1041) 1985

# Instructions for Beneficiary Filing Form 1040

## General Instructions

**Name, Address, and Identifying Number.**—Your name, address, and identifying number, the estate or trust name, address, and identifying number should have been entered on the Schedule K-1 you received.

**Tax Shelters.**—If you receive a copy of **Form 8271**, Investor Reporting of Tax Shelter Registration Number, and other tax shelter information from the estate or trust, or if the estate or trust is a tax shelter required to register under section 6111, see the Instructions for Form 8271 to determine your reporting requirements.

**Errors.**—If you believe the estate or trust has made an error on your Schedule K-1, notify the fiduciary of the estate or trust and ask for a corrected Schedule K-1. Do not change any items on your copy. Be sure that the estate or trust sends a copy of the corrected Schedule K-1 to the IRS.

## Specific Instructions

**Lines 1–10.**—Report the amount from line 1 (Schedule K-1) on your Schedule B (Form 1040), Part II, line 4. Report the amount from line 2a (Schedule K-1) on your Schedule D (Form 1040), line 4, column f or g. Report the amount from line 2b (Schedule K-1) on your Schedule D (Form 1040), line 12, column f or g. Report the amount from line 4e (Schedule K-1) on your Schedule E (Form 1040), Part II. Report on your appropriate tax form or schedule any other applicable items indicated on your Schedule K-1 according to the references printed or written on Schedule K-1.

If you have income from a fiscal year estate or trust, you must include it in income for the tax year during which the fiscal year of the estate or trust ends. For example, if the trust's fiscal year ends on June 30, 1985, you should report your income from the trust on your 1985 Form 1040. A fiscal year will be indicated at the top of your Schedule K-1 (Form 1041) by the dates shown on the fiscal year beginning and ending lines.

**Line 9. Property Eligible for Investment Credit.**—Your share of the estate's or trust's investment in property that qualifies for the investment credit should be entered. You can claim a tax credit based on your pro rata share of this investment by filing **Form 3468**, Computation of Investment Credit. (For more information, see Form 3468 and the related instructions.)

In addition to the qualifying property reported on lines 9a through 9h, if applicable, the estate or trust will give you a separate schedule that shows your share of the estate's or trust's investment in nonrecovery property, new commuter highway vehicle property, used commuter highway vehicle property, qualified rehabilitation expenditures and energy property that qualifies for the credit, and where to report it.

**Line 10a–f.**

*Tax-exempt income.*—If any tax-exempt income is entered on these lines by the estate or trust then you should report those amounts as a memo entry in the space to the left of Form 1040, line 21, if appropriate. This tax-exempt income figure is provided to assist retired individuals in figuring the taxable portion (if any) of their social security or railroad retirement benefits (see instructions to Form 1040, lines 21a and b).

*Gross farming and fishing income.*—The amount of gross farming and fishing income is included in "Other Income" on line 4. This income must also be separately stated on line 10 to assist beneficiaries in determining if they are subject to a penalty for underpayment of estimated tax.

● Individual Beneficiaries.—An individual beneficiary must report the income on Schedule E (Form 1040), Part IV, line 37.

● Beneficiaries that are Estates or Trusts.—Beneficiaries who are estates or trusts must pass through the amount of gross farming and fishing income included on line 10 of their Schedule K-1s to line 10 of their beneficiary's Schedule K-1s on a pro rata basis.

**Note:** *The fiduciary's instructions are contained in the Form 1041 instructions.*

# APPENDIX C
# GLOSSARY OF TAX TERMS

[NOTE: The words and phrases appearing below have been defined to reflect their conventional use in the field of taxation. Such definitions may, therefore, be incomplete for other purposes.]

## –A–

**A.**  See *acquiescence.*

**Accelerated cost recovery system.**  A method whereby the cost of a fixed asset is written off for tax purposes. Instituted by the Economic Recovery Tax Act of 1981, the system places assets into one of various recovery periods (i. e., class life of 3, 5, 10, 15, 18, and 19 years) and prescribes the applicable percentage of cost that can be deducted each year. In this regard, it largely resolves the controversy that used to arise with prior depreciation procedures in determining estimated useful life and in predicting salvage value. § 168.

**Accelerated depreciation.**  Various methods of depreciation that yield larger deductions in the earlier years of the life of an asset than the straight-line method. Examples include the double declining-balance and the sum of the years'-digits methods of depreciation. § 167(b)(2) and (3).

**Accounting method.**  The method under which income and expenses are determined for tax purposes. Major accounting methods are the cash basis and the accrual basis. Special methods are available for the reporting of gain on installment sales, recognition of income on construction projects (i. e., the completed-contract and percentage-of-completion methods), and the valuation of inventories (i. e., last-in first-out and first-in first-out). §§ 446–474. See *accrual basis, cash basis, completed-contract method, percentage-of-completion method,* etc.

**Accounting period.**  The period of time, usually a year, used by a taxpayer for the determination of tax liability. Unless a fiscal year is chosen, taxpayers must determine and pay their income tax liability by using the calendar year (i. e., January 1 through December 31) as the period of measurement. An example of a fiscal year is July 1 through June 30. A change in accounting periods (e. g., from a calendar year to a fiscal year) generally requires the consent of the IRS.

New taxpayers, such as a newly formed corporation or an estate created upon the death of an individual taxpayer, are free to select either a calendar or a fiscal year without the consent of the IRS. §§ 441–443.

**Accrual basis.**  A method of accounting that reflects expenses incurred and income earned for any one tax year. In contrast to the cash basis of accounting, expenses do not have to be paid to be deductible nor does income have to be received to be taxable. Unearned income (e. g., prepaid interest and rent) generally is taxed in the year of receipt regardless of the method of accounting used by the taxpayer. § 446(c)(2). See *accounting method, cash basis,* and *unearned income.*

**Accumulated adjustment account.**  An account which comprises an S corporation's post-1982 income, loss, and deductions for the tax year (including nontaxable income and nondeductible losses and expenses). After the year-end income and expense adjustments are made, the account is reduced by distributions made during the tax year.

**Accumulated earnings credit.**  A deduction allowed in arriving at accumulated taxable income for purposes of determining the accumulated earnings tax. See *accumulated earnings tax* and *accumulated taxable income.*

**Accumulated earnings tax.**  A special tax imposed on corporations that accumulate (rather than distribute) their earnings beyond the reasonable needs of the business. The accumulated earnings tax is imposed on accumulated taxable income (see below) in addition to the corporate income tax. §§ 531–537.

**Accumulated taxable income.**  The income upon which the accumulated earnings tax is imposed. Basically, it is the taxable income of the corporation as adjusted for certain items (e. g., the Federal income tax, excess charitable contributions, the 85% dividends received deduction) less the dividends paid deduction and the accumulated earnings credit. § 535.

**Accumulating trusts.** See *discretionary trusts.*

**Acq.** See *acquiescence.*

**Acquiescence.** In agreement with the result reached. The IRS follows a policy of either acquiescing (i. e., A, *Acq.*) or non-acquiescing (i. e., *NA, Non-Acq.*) in the results reached in the Regular decisions of the U. S. Tax Court.

**ACRS.** See *accelerated cost recovery system.*

**"Add-on" (or regular) minimum tax.** Prior to the Tax Equity and Fiscal Responsibility Act of 1982, the "add-on" (or regular) minimum tax covered both corporate and noncorporate taxpayers. As applied to individuals, the "add-on" minimum tax was 15 percent of the tax preference items (reduced by the greater of $10,000 or one-half of the income tax liability for the year). For taxable years beginning after 1982, the "add-on" minimum tax is repealed as to individuals. In its place, Congress chose to expand the scope of the alternative minimum tax. As to corporations, however, the "add-on" minimum tax is 15 percent of certain tax preference items in excess of the greater of $10,000 or the regular tax liability. An "add-on" minimum tax is to be distinguished from an alternative minimum tax in that the former is in addition to the regular income tax liability. In the case of an alternative minimum tax, moreover, the tax due is the higher of the regular income or the alternative minimum tax. See *alternative minimum tax.*

**Ad valorem tax.** A tax imposed on the value of property. The more common ad valorem tax is that imposed by states, counties, and cities on real estate. Ad valorem taxes can, however, be imposed on personalty. See *personalty.*

**Adjusted basis.** The cost or other basis of property reduced by depreciation allowed or allowable and increased by capital improvements. Other special adjustments are provided for in § 1016 and the Regulations thereunder. See *basis.*

**Adjusted gross estate.** The gross estate of a decedent reduced by § 2053 expenses (e.g., administration, funeral) and § 2054 losses (i.e., casualty). The determination of the adjusted gross estate is necessary in testing for

the 15-year extension of time for installment payout of estate taxes under § 6166. The concept of the adjusted gross estate also is utilized in meeting the more than 35 percent requirement of § 303 (redemption of stock to pay death taxes and administration expenses).

**Adjusted gross income.** A tax determination peculiar to taxpayers who are individuals. Generally, it represents the gross income of an individual less business expenses and any appropriate capital gain or loss adjustment.

**Adjusted ordinary gross income.** A determination peculiar to the personal holding company tax imposed by § 541. In testing to ascertain whether a corporation is a personal holding company, *personal holding company income divided by adjusted ordinary gross income* must equal 60% or more. Adjusted ordinary gross income is the corporation's gross income less capital gains, § 1231 gains, and certain expenses. Adjusted ordinary gross income is defined in § 543(b)(2) and the Regulations thereunder. See *personal holding company tax* and *personal holding company income.*

**Adjusted taxable estate.** The taxable estate reduced by $60,000. It is the adjusted taxable estate that is utilized in applying the table of § 2011 for determining the limit on the credit for state death taxes paid that will be allowed against the Federal estate tax.

**Administration.** The supervision and winding-up of an estate. The administration of an estate runs from the date of an individual's death until all assets have been distributed and liabilities paid. Such administration is conducted by an administrator or an executor. See *administrator* and *executor.*

**Administrator.** A person appointed by the court to administer (i. e., manage or take charge of) the assets and liabilities of a decedent (i. e., the deceased). Such person may be a male (i. e., administrator) or a female (i. e., administratrix). If the person performing these services is named by the decedent's will, he is designated as the executor, or she is designated as the executrix, of the estate.

**AFTR.** Published by Prentice-Hall, *American Federal Tax Reports* contain all of the Federal tax decisions issued by the U. S. District Courts, U. S. Court of Claims, U. S. Court of Appeals, and the U. S. Supreme Court.

**AFTR2d.** The second series of the *American Federal Tax Reports*. See *AFTR*.

**Alternate valuation date.** Property passing from a person by death may be valued for death tax purposes as of the date of death or the alternate valuation date. The alternate valuation date is six months from the date of death or the date the property is disposed of by the estate, whichever comes first. The use of the alternate valuation date requires an affirmative election on the part of the executor or administrator of the estate. The election of the alternate valuation date is not available unless it decreases the amount of the gross estate *and* reduces the estate tax liability.

**Alternative minimum tax.** For tax years beginning after 1982, individuals (including estates and trusts) will not be subject to an "add-on" minimum tax but, instead, will be covered by a new version of the alternative minimum tax. Simply stated, the alternative minimum tax is 20 percent of the alternative minimum taxable income (AMTI). AMTI is the taxpayer's adjusted gross income (1) increased by certain tax preference items; (2) decreased for certain alternative tax itemized deductions; and, (3) reduced by an exemption amount (e. g., $40,000 on a joint return). The taxpayer must pay the greater of the resulting alternative minimum tax (reduced by the foreign tax credit) or the regular income tax (reduced by all allowable tax credits). See *"add-on" minimum tax*.

**Alternative tax.** An option allowed to corporations in computing the tax on net capital gains. For tax years beginning after 1978, the rate is 28% of the net capital gains. For corporate taxpayers, failure to use the alternative tax means all of the long-term capital gain will be taxed in the appropriate income tax bracket.

**Amortization.** The write-off (or depreciation) for tax purposes of the cost or other basis of an intangible asset over its estimated useful life. Examples of amortizable intangibles include patents, copyrights, and leasehold interests. The intangible goodwill cannot be amortized for income tax purposes because it possesses no estimated useful life. As to tangible assets, see *depreciation*. As to natural resources, see *depletion*.

**Amount realized.** The amount received by a taxpayer upon the sale or exchange of property. The measure of the amount received is the sum of the cash and the fair market value of any property or services received. Determining the amount realized is the starting point for arriving at realized gain or loss. The amount realized is defined in § 1001(b) and the Regulations thereunder. See *realized gain or loss* and *recognized gain or loss*.

**Annual accounting period concept.** In determining a taxpayer's income tax liability, only those transactions taking place during a particular tax year are taken into consideration. For reporting and payment purposes, therefore, the tax life of taxpayers is divided into equal annual accounting periods. See *mitigation of the annual accounting period concept* and *accounting period*.

**Annual exclusion.** In computing the taxable gifts for any one year, each donor may exclude the first $10,000 of a gift to each donee. Usually, the annual exclusion is not available for gifts of future interests. § 2503(b). See *future interest*.

**Annuitant.** The party entitled to receive payments from an annuity contract. See *annuity*.

**Annuity.** A fixed sum of money payable to a person at specified times for a set period of time or for life. If the party making the payment (i. e., the obligor) is regularly engaged in this type of business (e. g., an insurance company), the arrangement is classified as a commercial annuity. A private annuity involves an obligor that is not regularly engaged in selling annuities (e. g., a charity or family member).

**Anticipatory assignment of income.** See *assignment of income*.

**Appellate court.** For Federal tax purposes, appellate courts include the Courts of Appeals and the Supreme Court. If the party losing in the trial (or lower) court is dissatisfied with the result, the dispute may be carried to the appropriate appellate court. See *trial court*.

**Arm's length.** The standard under which unrelated parties would carry out a particular transaction. Suppose, for example, X Corporation sells property to its sole shareholder for $10,000. In testing whether $10,000 is an "arm's length" price, one would ascertain for how much the corporation could have sold the property to a disinterested third party.

**Articles of incorporation.** The legal document specifying a corporation's name, period of existence, purpose and powers, authorized number of shares, classes of stock, and other conditions for operation. These articles are filed by the organizers of the corporation with the state of incorporation. If the articles are satisfactory and other conditions of the law are satisfied, the state will issue a charter recognizing the organization's status as a corporation.

**Assessment.** The process whereby the IRS imposes an additional tax liability. If, for example, the IRS audits a taxpayer's income tax return and finds gross income understated or deductions overstated, it will assess a deficiency in the amount of the tax that should have been paid in light of the adjustments made.

**Assignment of income.** A procedure whereby a taxpayer attempts to avoid the recognition of income by assigning the property that generates the income to another. Such a procedure will not avoid the recognition of income by the taxpayer making the assignment if it can be said that the income was earned at the point of the transfer. In this case, usually referred to as an anticipatory assignment of income, the income will be taxed to the person who earns it.

**Association.** An organization treated as a corporation for Federal tax purposes even though it may not qualify as such under applicable state law. What is designated as a trust or a partnership, for example, may be classified as an association if it clearly possesses corporate attributes. Corporate attributes include: centralized management, continuity of existence, free transferability of interests, and limited liability. § 7701(a)(3).

**Attribution.** Under certain circumstances, the tax law applies attribution rules to assign to one taxpayer the ownership interest of another taxpayer. If, for example, the stock of X Corporation is held 60% by M and 40% by S, M may be deemed to own 100% of X Corporation if M and S are mother and son. In such a case, the stock owned by S is attributed to M. Stated differently, M has a 60% "direct" and a 40% "indirect" interest in X Corporation. It can also be said that M is the "constructive" owner of S's interest.

**Audit.** Inspection and verification of a taxpayer's return or other transactions possessing tax consequences. See *correspondence audit, field audit,* and *office audit.*

## −B−

**Bail-out.** Various procedures whereby the owners of an entity can obtain its profits with favorable tax consequences. With corporations, for example, the bail-out of corporate profits at capital gain rates might well be the desired objective. The alternative of distributing the profits to the shareholders as dividends generally is less attractive since dividend income is taxed as ordinary income. See *preferred stock bail-out.*

**Bargain sale or purchase.** A sale of property for less than the fair market value of such property. The difference between the sale or purchase price and the fair market value of the property will have to be accounted for in terms of its tax consequences. If, for example, a corporation sells property worth $1,000 to one of its shareholders for $700, the $300 difference probably represents a constructive dividend to the shareholder. Suppose, instead, the shareholder sells the property (worth $1,000) to his or her corporation for $700. The $300 difference probably represents a contribution by the shareholder to the corporation's capital. Bargain sales and purchases among members of the same family may lead to gift tax consequences. See *constructive dividends.*

**Basis.** The amount assigned to an asset for income tax purposes. For assets acquired by purchase, basis would be cost [§ 1012]. Special rules govern the basis of property received by virtue of another's death [§ 1014] or by gift [§ 1015], the basis of stock received on a transfer of property to a controlled corporation [§ 358], the basis of the property transferred to the corporation [§ 362], and the basis of property received upon the liquidation of a corporation [§ § 334 and 338].

**Become of age.** See *legal age.*

**Beneficiary.** A party who will benefit from a transfer of property or other arrangement. Examples include the beneficiary of a trust, the beneficiary of a life insurance policy, and the beneficiary of an estate.

**Bequest.** A transfer by will of personalty. To bequeath is to leave such property by will. See *personalty.*

**Blockage rule.** A factor to be considered in valuing a large block of stock. Application of this rule generally justifies a discount in the fair market value since the disposition of a large amount of stock at any one time may well depress the value of such shares in the market place.

**Bona fide.** In good faith or real. In tax law, this term is often used in connection with a business purpose for carrying out a transaction. Thus, was there a bona fide business purpose for a shareholder's transfer of a liability to a controlled corporation? § 357(b)(1)(B). See *business purpose.*

**Book value.** The net amount of an asset after reduction by a related reserve. The book value of accounts receivable, for example, would be the amount of the receivables less the reserve for bad debts.

**Boot.** Cash or property of a type not included in the definition of a nontaxable exchange. The receipt of boot will cause an otherwise taxfree transfer to become taxable to the extent of the lesser of: the fair market value of such boot or the realized gain on the transfer. For example, see transfers to controlled corporations under § 351(b) and likekind exchanges under § 1031(b). See *realized gain or loss.*

**Brother-sister corporations.** More than one corporation owned by the same shareholders. If, for example, C and D each own one-half of the stock in X Corporation and Y Corporation, X and Y are brother-sister corporations.

**B.T.A.** The Board of Tax Appeals was a trial court which considered Federal tax matters. This Court is now designated as the U. S. Tax Court.

**Bulk sale.** A sale of substantially all the inventory of a trade or business to one person in one transaction. Under certain conditions, a corporation making a bulk sale pursuant to a complete liquidation will recognize neither gain or loss on such sale. § 337(b)(2).

**Burden of proof.** The requirement in a lawsuit to show the weight of evidence and, thereby, gain a favorable decision. Except in cases of tax fraud, the burden of proof in a tax case generally will be on the taxpayer.

**Business bad debts.** A tax deduction allowed for obligations obtained in connection with a trade or business which have become either partially or completely worthless. In contrast with nonbusiness bad debts, business bad debts are deductible as business expenses. § 166. See *nonbusiness bad debts.*

**Business purpose.** A justifiable business reason for carrying out a transaction. It has long been established that mere tax avoidance is not a business purpose. The presence of a business purpose is of crucial importance in the area of corporate readjustments.

**Buy and sell agreement.** An arrangement, particularly appropriate in the case of a closely-held corporation or a partnership, whereby the surviving owners (i. e., shareholders or partners) or the entity (i. e., corporation or partnership) agree to purchase the interest of a withdrawing owner (i. e., shareholder or partner). The buy and sell agreement provides for an orderly disposition of an interest in a business and may aid in setting the value of such interest for death tax purposes. See *cross-purchase buy and sell agreements* and *entity buy and sell agreements.*

# –C–

**Calendar year.** See *accounting period.*

**Capital asset.** Broadly speaking, all assets are capital except those specifically excluded. Major categories of *non-capital* assets include: property held for resale in the normal course of business (i. e., inventory), trade accounts and notes receivable, depreciable property and real estate used in a trade or business (i. e., "§ 1231 assets"). § 1221.

**Capital contribution.** Various means by which a shareholder makes additional funds available to the corporation (i. e., placed at the risk of the business) without the receipt of additional stock. Such contributions are added to the basis of the shareholder's existing stock investment and do not generate income to the corporation. § 118.

**Capital expenditure.** An expenditure which should be added to the basis of the property improved. For income tax purposes, this generally precludes a full deduction for the expenditure in the year paid or incurred. Any cost recovery in the form of a tax deduction would have to come in the form of depreciation. § 263.

**Capital gain.** The gain from the sale or exchange of a capital asset. See *capital asset.*

**Capital loss.** The loss from the sale or exchange of a capital asset. See *capital asset.*

**Cash basis.** A method of accounting that reflects deductions as paid and income as received in any one tax year. However, prepaid expenses that benefit more than one tax year (e. g., prepaid rent and prepaid interest) may have to be spread over the period benefited rather than deducted in the year paid. § 446(c)(1). See also, *constructive receipt of income.*

**Cash surrender value.** The amount of money an insurance policy would yield if cashed in with the insurance company that issued the policy.

**CCH.** Commerce Clearing House is the publisher of a tax service and of Federal tax decisions (i. e., USTC series).

**C corporation.** A regular corporation that is governed by Subchapter C of the Code. To be distinguished from S corporations that fall under Subchapter S of the Code.

**Centralized management.** A concentration of authority among certain persons who may make independent business decisions on behalf of the entity without the need for continuing approval by the owners of the entity. It is a characteristic of a corporation since its day-to-day business operations are handled by appointed officers and not by the shareholders. Reg. § 301.7701–2(c). See *association.*

**Cert. den.** By denying the Writ of Certiorari, the U. S. Supreme Court refuses to accept an appeal from a U. S. Court of Appeals. The denial of certiorari does not, however, mean that the U. S. Supreme Court agrees with the result reached by the lower court. See *certiorari.*

**Certiorari.** Appeal from a U. S. Court of Appeals to the U. S. Supreme Court is by Writ of Certiorari. The Supreme Court does not have to accept the appeal and usually does not (i. e., *cert. den.*) unless there is a conflict among the lower courts that needs to be resolved or a constitutional issue is involved. See *cert. den.*

**Cf.** Compare.

**Civil fraud.** See *fraud.*

**Claims Court.** A trial court (i. e., court of original jurisdiction) which decides litigation involving Federal tax matters. Previously known as the U. S. Court of Claims, appeal from the U. S. Claims Court is to the Court of Appeals for the Federal Circuit.

**Clifford trust.** A grantor trust whereby the grantor (i. e., creator) of the trust retains the right to possess again the property transferred in trust (i. e., a reversionary interest is retained) upon the occurrence of an event (e. g., the death of the beneficiary) or the expiration of a period of time. Unless the requirements of § 673 are satisfied, the income from the property placed in trust will continue to be taxed to the grantor. See *grantor trusts* and *reversionary interest.*

**Closely-held corporation.** A corporation, the stock ownership of which is not widely dispersed. Instead, a few shareholders are in control of corporate policy and are in a position to benefit personally from such policy.

**Collapsible corporation.** Generally, a corporation is collapsible only when it has not yet recognized two thirds of the income from the property it manufactured or constructed. If a corporation is collapsible, its liquidation may convert any long-term capital gain the shareholders might otherwise recognize into ordinary income. § 341.

**Collapsing.** To disregard a transaction or one of a series of steps leading to a result. See *telescoping, substance vs. form,* and *step transaction approach.*

**Common law state.** See *community property.*

**Community property.** The states with community property systems are: Louisiana, Texas, New Mexico, Arizona, California, Washington, Idaho, Nevada, and Wisconsin (as of January 1, 1986). The rest of the states are classified as common law jurisdictions. The difference between common law and community property systems centers around the property rights possessed by married persons. In a common law system, each spouse owns whatever he or she earns. Under a community property system, one-half of the earnings of each spouse is considered owned by the other spouse. Assume, for example, H and W are husband and wife and their only income is the $50,000 annual salary H receives. If they live in New York (a common law state), the $50,000 salary belongs to H. If, however, they live in Texas (a community property state), the $50,000 salary is divided equally, in terms of ownership, between H and W. See *separate property.*

**Completed-contract method.** A method of reporting gain or loss on certain long-term contracts. Under this method of accounting, gross income and expenses are recognized in the tax year in which the contract is completed. Reg. § 1.451–3. For another alternative, see *percentage-of-completion method of accounting.*

**Complex trusts.** Complex trusts are those that are not simple trusts. Such trusts may have charitable beneficiaries, accumulate income, and distribute corpus. § § 661–663. See *simple trusts.*

**Concur.** To agree with the result reached by another, but not necessarily with the reasoning or the logic used in reaching such a result. For example, Judge R agrees with Judges S and T (all being members of the same court) that the income is taxable but for a different reason. Judge R would issue a concurring opinion to the majority opinion issued by Judges S and T.

**Condemnation.** The taking of property by a public authority. The taking is by legal action and the owner of the property is compensated by the public authority. The power to condemn property is known as the right of eminent domain.

**Conduit concept.** An approach the tax law assumes in the tax treatment of certain entities and their owners. The approach permits specified tax characteristics to pass through the entity without losing their identity. Under the conduit concept, for example, long-term capital losses realized by a partnership are passed through as such to the individual partners. The same result does not materialize if the entity is a regular corporation. Varying forms of the conduit concept are applicable in the case of partnerships, trusts, estates, and S corporations.

**Consent dividends.** For purposes of avoiding or reducing the penalty tax on the unreasonable accumulation of earnings or the personal holding company tax, a corporation may declare a consent dividend. In a consent dividend no cash or property is distributed to the shareholders although the corporation obtains a dividends paid deduction. The consent dividend is taxed to the shareholders and increases the basis in their stock investment. § 565.

**Consolidated returns.** A procedure whereby certain affiliated corporations may file a single return, combine the tax transactions of each corporation, and arrive at a single income tax liability for the group. The election to file a consolidated return is usually binding on future years. See § § 1501–1505 and the Regulations thereunder.

**Consolidation.** The combination of two or more corporations into a newly created corporation. Thus, A Corporation and B Corporation combine to form C Corporation. A consolidation may qualify as a nontaxable reorganization if certain conditions are satisfied. § § 354 and 368(a)(1)(A).

**Constructive dividends.** A taxable benefit derived by a shareholder from his or her corporation although such benefit was not designated as a dividend. Examples include unreasonable compensation, excessive rent payments, bargain purchases of corporate property, and shareholder use of corporate property. Constructive dividends generally are a problem limited to closely-held corporations. See *closely-held corporations.*

**Constructive ownership.** See *attribution.*

**Constructive receipt of income.** If income is unqualifiedly available, it will be subject to the income tax although not physically in the taxpayer's possession. An example would be accrued interest on a savings account. Under the constructive receipt of income concept, such interest will be taxed to a depositor in the year it is available rather than the year actually withdrawn. The fact that the depositor uses the cash basis of accounting for tax purposes makes no difference. See Reg. § 1.451–2.

**Continuity of life or existence.** The death or other withdrawal of an owner of an entity will not terminate the existence of such entity. This is a characteristic of a corporation since the death or withdrawal of a shareholder will not affect its existence. Reg. § 301.7701–2(b). See *association.*

**Contributions to the capital of a corporation.** See *capital contribution.*

**Contributory qualified pension or profit-sharing plan.** A plan funded with both employer and employee contributions. Since the employee's contributions to the plan will be subject to the income tax, a later distribution of such contributions to the employee will be free of income tax. See *qualified pension or profit-sharing plan.*

**Corpus.** The main body or principal of a trust. Suppose, for example, G transfers an apartment building into a trust, income payable to W for life, remainder to S upon W's death. The corpus of the trust would be the apartment building.

**Correspondence audit.** An audit conducted by the IRS through the use of the mail. Typically, the IRS writes to the taxpayer requesting the verification of a particular deduction or exemption. The completion of a special form or the remittance of copies of records or other support is all that is requested of the taxpayer. See *field audit* and *office audit.*

**Court of Appeals.** Any of thirteen Federal courts which consider tax matters appealed from the U. S. Tax Court, a U. S. District Court, or the U. S. Claims Court. Appeal from a U. S. Court of Appeals is to the U . S. Supreme Court by Writ of Certiorari. See *appellate court.*

**Criminal fraud.** See *fraud.*

**Cross-purchase buy and sell agreement.** Under this type of arrangement the surviving owners of the business agree to buy out the withdrawing owner. Assume, for example, R and S are equal shareholders in T Corporation. Under a cross-purchase type of buy and sell agreement, R and S would contract to purchase the other's interest should he or she decide to withdraw from the business. See *buy and sell agreement* and *entity buy and sell agreement.*

**Current use valuation.** See *special use valuation.*

**Curtesy.** A husband's right under state law to all or part of his wife's property upon her prior death. See *dower.*

# –D–

**Death benefit.** A payment made by an employer to the beneficiary or beneficiaries of a deceased employee on account of the death of the employee. Under certain conditions, the first $5,000 of such payment will not be subject to the income tax. § 101(b)(1).

**Death tax.** A tax imposed on property transferred by the death of the owner. See *estate tax* and *inheritance tax.*

**Decedent.** A dead person.

**Deductions in respect of a decedent.** Deductions accrued to the point of death but not recognizable on the final income tax return of a decedent because of the method of accounting used. Such items are allowed as deductions on the estate tax return and on the income tax return of the estate (Form 1041) or the heir (Form 1040). An example of a deduction in respect of a decedent would be interest expense accrued up to the date of death by a cash basis debtor.

**Deemed transferor.** The person holding an interest in a trust the expiration of which will lead to the imposition of a generation-skipping tax. Assume, for example, GF creates a trust, income payable to S (GF's son) for life and, upon S's death, remainder to GS (GF's grandson). Upon S's death, he will be the "deemed transferor" and the trust will be included in his gross estate for purposes of determining the generation-skipping transfer tax. § 2612. See *generation-skipping trust.*

**Deferred compensation.** Compensation which will be taxed when received and not when earned. An example would be contributions by an employer to a qualified pension or profit-sharing plan on behalf of an employee. Such contributions will not be taxed to the employee until they are distributed (e. g., upon retirement). See *qualified pension or profit-sharing plan.*

**Deficiency.** Additional tax liability owed by a taxpayer and assessed by the IRS. See *assessment* and *statutory notice of deficiency.*

**Deficiency dividends.** Once the IRS has established a corporation's liability for the personal holding company tax in a prior year, the tax may be reduced or avoided by the issuance of a deficiency dividend under § 547. The deficiency dividend procedure is not available in cases where the deficiency was due to fraud with intent to evade tax or to a willful failure to file the appropriate tax return [§ 547(g)]. Nor does the deficiency dividend procedure avoid the usual penalties and interest applicable for failure to file a return or pay a tax.

**Deficit.** A negative balance in the earnings and profits account.

**Depletion.** The process by which the cost or other basis of a natural resource (e. g., an oil and gas interest) is recovered upon extraction and sale of the resource. The two ways to determine the depletion allowance are the cost and percentage (or statutory) methods. Under the cost method, each unit of production sold is assigned a portion of the cost or other basis of the interest. This is determined by dividing the cost or other basis by the total units expected to be recovered. Under the percentage (or statutory) method the tax law provides a special percentage factor for different types of minerals and other natural resources. This percentage is multiplied by the gross income from the interest to arrive at the depletion allowance. § § 613 and 613A.

**Depreciation.** The write-off for tax purposes of the cost or other basis of a tangible asset over its estimated useful life. As to intangible assets, see *amortization*. As to natural resources, see *depletion*. Also see *estimated useful life*.

**Descent and distribution.** See *intestate*.

**Determination letter.** Upon the request of a taxpayer, a District Director will pass upon the tax status of a completed transaction. Determination letters are most frequently used to clarify employee status, to determine whether a retirement or profit-sharing plan "qualifies" under the Code, and to determine the tax exempt status of certain non-profit organizations.

**Devise.** A transfer by will of real estate. For a transfer of personalty by will see *bequest*.

**Disclaimer.** The rejection, refusal, or renunciation of a claim, power, or property. Code § 2518 sets forth the conditions required to avoid gift tax consequences as the result of a disclaimer.

**Discretionary trusts.** Trusts where the trustee or another party has the right to accumulate (rather than pay out) the income for each year. Depending on the terms of the trust instrument, such income may be accumulated for future distributions to the income beneficiaries or added to corpus for the benefit of the remainderman. See *corpus, income beneficiary,* and *remainderman*.

**Disproportionate.** Not pro rata or ratable. Suppose, for example, S Corporation has two shareholders, C and D, each of whom owns 50% of its stock. If X Corporation distributes a cash dividend of $2,000 to C and only $1,000 to D, the distribution is disproportionate. The distribution would have been proportionate if C and D had received $1,500 each. See *substantially disproportionate* as to stock redemptions.

**Disregard of corporate entity.** To treat a corporation as if it did not exist for tax purposes. In such event, each shareholder would have to account for an allocable share of all corporate transactions possessing tax consequences. See *entity*.

**Dissent.** To disagree with the majority. If, for example, Judge B disagrees with the result reached by Judges C and D (all of whom are members of the same court), Judge B could issue a dissenting opinion.

**Distributable net income (DNI).** The measure that limits the amount of the distributions from estates and trusts that the beneficiaries thereof will have to include in income. Also, DNI limits the amount that estates and trusts can claim as a deduction for such distributions. § 643(a).

**Distributions in kind.** A transfer of property "as is." If, for example, a corporation distributes land to its shareholders, a distribution in kind has taken place. A sale of land followed by a distribution of the cash proceeds would not be a distribution in kind of the land. As to corporate liquidations, see § 336 for one type of distribution in kind.

**District Court.** A Federal District Court is a trial court for purposes of litigating Federal tax matters. It is the only trial court where a jury trial can be obtained. See *trial court*.

**Dividend exclusion.** The $100 exclusion allowed individuals for dividends received from certain qualifying domestic corporations. § 116. See *domestic corporation*.

**Dividends received deduction.** A deduction allowed a corporate shareholder for dividends received from a domestic corporation. The deduction usually is 85% of the dividends received but could be 100% if an affiliated group is involved. § § 243–246.

**Domestic corporation.** A corporation created or organized in the U. S. or under the law of the U. S. or any state or territory. § 7701(a)(4). Only dividends received from domestic corporations qualify for the dividend exclusion [§ 116] and the dividends received deduction [§ 243].

**Domicile.** A person's legal home.

**Donee.** The recipient of a gift.

**Donor.** The maker of a gift.

**Dower.** A wife's right to all or part of her deceased husband's property. It is a concept unique to common law states as opposed to community property jurisdictions.

## –E–

**Earned income.** Income from personal services to be distinguished from income generated by property. See § 911 and the Regulations thereunder.

**Earnings and profits.** A tax concept peculiar to corporate taxpayers which measures economic capacity to make a distribution to shareholders that is not a return of capital. Such a distribution will result in dividend income to the shareholders to the extent of the corporation's current and accumulated earnings and profits.

**Election to split gifts.** A special election for Federal gift tax purposes whereby husband and wife can treat a gift by one of them to a third party as being made one-half by each. If, for example, H (the husband) makes a gift of $20,000 to S, W (the wife) may elect to treat $10,000 of the gift as coming from her. The major advantage of the election is that it enables the parties to take advantage of the non-owner spouse's (W in this case) annual exclusion. § 2513. See *annual exclusion.*

**Eminent Domain.** See *condemnation.*

**En banc.** The case was considered by the whole court. For example, only one of the nineteen judges of the U. S. Tax Court will hear and decide a tax controversy. However, when the issues involved are unusually novel or of wide impact, the case will be heard and decided by the full Court sitting *en banc.*

**Encumbrance.** A liability, such as a mortgage. If the liability relates to a particular asset, the asset is encumbered.

**Entity.** An organization or being that possesses separate existence for tax purposes. Examples would be corporations, partnerships, estates and trusts. But see *disregard of corporate entity.*

**Entity buy and sell agreement.** A buy and sell agreement whereby the entity is to purchase the withdrawing owner's interest. When the entity is a corporation, the agreement generally involves a stock redemption on the part of the withdrawing shareholder. See *buy and sell agreement* and compare *cross-purchase buy and sell agreement.*

**Escrow.** Money or other property placed with a third party as security for an existing or proposed obligation. C, for example, agrees to purchase D's stock in X Corporation but needs time to raise the necessary funds. The stock is placed by D with E (i. e., the escrow agent) with instructions to deliver it to C when the purchase price is paid.

**Estate.** The assets and liabilities of a decedent.

**Estate tax.** A tax imposed on the right to transfer property by death. Thus, an estate tax is levied on the decedent's estate and not on the heir receiving the property. See *inheritance tax.*

**Estimated useful life.** The period over which an asset will be used by a particular taxpayer. Although such period cannot be longer than the estimated physical life of an asset, it could be shorter if the taxpayer does not intend to keep the asset until it wears out. Assets such as goodwill do not have an estimated useful life. The estimated useful life of an asset is essential to measuring the annual tax deduction for depreciation and amortization.

**Estoppel.** The process of being stopped from proving something (even if true) in court due to prior inconsistent action. It is usually invoked as a matter of fairness to prevent one party (either the taxpayer or the IRS) from taking advantage of a prior error.

**Excise tax.** A tax on the manufacture, sale, or use of goods or on the carrying on of an occupation or activity. Also a tax on the transfer of property. Thus, the Federal estate and gift taxes, are, theoretically, excise taxes.

**Executor.** A person designated by a will to administer (i. e., manage or take charge of) the assets and liabilities of a decedent. Such party may be a male (i. e., executor), female (i. e., executrix), or a trust company (i. e., executor). See *administrator.*

## −F−

**Fair market value.** The amount at which property would change hands between a willing buyer and a willing seller, neither being under any compulsion to buy or to sell and both having reasonable knowledge of the relevant facts. Reg. § 20.2031–1(b).

**Federal Register.** The first place that the rules and regulations of U. S. administrative agencies (e. g., the U. S. Treasury Department) are published.

**F.2d.** An abbreviation for the Second Series of the *Federal Reporter,* the official series where decisions of the U. S. Court of Claims and of the U. S. Court of Appeals are published.

**F. Supp.** The abbreviation for *Federal Supplement,* the official series where the reported decisions of the U. S. Federal District Courts are published.

**Fiduciary.** A person who manages money or property for another and who must exercise a standard of care in such management activity imposed by law or contract. A trustee, for example, possesses a fiduciary responsibility to the beneficiaries of the trust to follow the terms of the trust and the requirements of applicable state law. A breach of fiduciary responsibility would make the trustee liable to the beneficiaries for any damage caused by such breach.

**Field audit.** An audit by the IRS conducted on the business premises of the taxpayer or in the office of the tax practitioner representing the taxpayer. To be distinguished from a *correspondence audit* or an *office audit* (see these terms). Also see *audit*.

**First-in first-out (FIFO).** An accounting method for determining the cost of inventories. Under this method the inventory on hand is deemed to be the sum of the cost of the most recently acquired units.

**Fiscal year.** See *accounting period*.

**Flat tax.** In its pure form, a flat tax would eliminate all exclusions, deductions, and credits and impose a tax on gross income. Such a tax is receiving much attention as a reform proposal since our current tax system is perceived as being unduly complex and inequitable.

**Foreign corporation.** A foreign corporation is one which is not organized under the laws of one of the states or territories of the U. S. § 7701(a)(5). See *domestic corporation*.

**Foreign tax credit or deduction.** If a U. S. citizen or resident incurs or pays income taxes to a foreign country on income subject to U. S. tax, the taxpayer may be able to claim some of these taxes as a deduction or as a credit against the U. S. income tax. § § 27 and 901–905.

**Form 706.** The U. S. Estate Tax Return. In certain cases this form must be filed for a decedent who was a resident or citizen of the U. S.

**Form 709.** The U. S. Gift Tax Return.

**Form 709-A.** U. S. Short Form Gift Tax Return.

**Form 870.** The signing of Form 870 (Waiver of Restriction on Assessment and Collection of Deficiency in Tax and Acceptance of Overassessments) by a taxpayer permits the IRS to assess a proposed deficiency without the necessity of issuing a statutory notice of deficiency ("90–day letter"). This means the taxpayer must pay the deficiency and cannot file a petition to the U. S. Tax Court. § 6213(d).

**Form 872.** The signing of this form by a taxpayer extends the period of time in which the IRS can make an assessment or collection of a tax. In other words, Form 872 extends the applicable statute of limitations. § 6501(c)(4).

**Form 1041.** U. S. Fiduciary Income Tax Return. The form that is required to be filed by estates and trusts. See Appendix B for a specimen form.

**Form 1065.** U. S. Partnership Return of Income. See Appendix B for a specimen form.

**Form 1120.** U. S. Corporation Income Tax Return. See Appendix B for a specimen form.

**Form 1120-A.** U. S. Short-Form Corporation Income Tax Return.

**Form 1120S.** U. S. Small Business Corporation Income Tax Return. This form is required to be filed by S corporations. See Appendix B for a specimen form.

**Fraud.** Tax fraud falls into two categories: civil and criminal. Under civil fraud, the IRS may impose as a penalty an amount equal to 50% of the underpayment [§ 6653(b)]. Fines and/or imprisonment are prescribed for conviction of various types of criminal tax fraud [§ § 7201–7207]. Both civil and criminal fraud require a specific intent on the part of the taxpayer to evade the tax; mere negligence will not be enough. Criminal fraud requires the additional element of wilfulness (i. e., done deliberately and with evil purpose). In actual practice, it becomes difficult to distinguish between the degree of intent necessary to support criminal, as opposed to civil, fraud. In both situations, however, the IRS has the burden of proving fraud. See *burden of proof*.

**Free transferability of interest.** The capability of the owner of an entity to transfer his or her ownership interest to another without the consent of the other owners. It is a characteristic of a corporation since a shareholder usually can freely transfer the stock to others without the approval of the existing shareholders. Reg. § 301.7701–2(e). See *association*.

**Fringe benefits.** Compensation or other benefits received by an employee which are not in the form of cash. Some fringe benefits (e. g., accident and health plans, group-term life insurance) may be excluded from the employee's gross income and, therefore, not subject to the Federal income tax.

**Future interest.** An interest that will come into being at some future point in time. It is distinguished from a present interest which is already in existence. Assume, for example, that D transfers securities to a newly created trust. Under the terms of the trust instrument, income from the securities is to be paid each year to W for her life, with the securities passing to S upon her death. W has a present interest in the trust since she is currently entitled to receive the income from the securities. S has a future interest since he must wait for W's death to benefit from the trust. The annual exclusion of $10,000 is not allowed for a gift of a future interest. § 2503(b). See *annual exclusion*.

# –G–

**General partner.** A partner who is fully liable in an individual capacity for the debts of the partnership to third parties. In contrast to a limited partner, a general partner's liability is not limited to the investment in the partnership. See *limited partnership*.

**General power of appointment.** See *power of appointment*.

**Generation-skipping tax.** The transfer tax imposed upon a generation-skipping trust. See *generation-skipping trust*.

**Generation-skipping transfer.** A transfer which by-passes a generation younger than the transferor and, therefore, avoids the imposition of one transfer tax. For example, a grandmother gives property to her grandchildren. By by-passing the children, a transfer tax is avoided. If the property had been given to the children and they later pass it (by gift or death) to the grandchildren, no generation skipping takes place. A generation-skipping tax may be imposed if the generation-skipping approach utilizes the trust device. See *generation-skipping trust*.

**Generation-skipping trust.** A trust which skips a transfer tax on a generation of beneficiaries younger than the grantor of the trust. In the classic situation, D creates a trust with income payable to his children for life and remainder to the grandchildren

upon the death of the children. Until the Tax Reform Act of 1976 enacted Code §§ 2601–2603 and 2611–2614, there was no transfer tax imposed upon the death of D's children. Thus, one generation (i. e., D's children) was able to avoid both the gift and death tax when the trust property passed to the grandchildren. Under current law, barring certain exceptions, the trust must pay a transfer tax on the death of the children as if the trust corpus had been included in their gross estates. See *deemed transferor*.

**Gift.** A transfer of property for less than adequate consideration. Gifts usually occur in a personal setting (such as between members of the same family).

**Gift loans.** Bona fide loans that carry no interest (or a below market rate). If made in a nonbusiness setting, the imputed interest element is treated as a gift from the lender to the borrower. If made by a corporation to a shareholder, a constructive dividend could result. In either event, the lender may have interest income to recognize. § 7872.

**Gift splitting.** See *election to split gifts*.

**Gift tax.** A tax imposed on the transfer of property by gift. Such tax is imposed upon the donor of a gift and is based on the fair market value of the property on the date of the gift.

**Gifts within three years of death.** Some taxable gifts made after 1981 automatically are included in the gross estate of the donor if death occurs within three years of the gift. § 2035.

**Goodwill.** The reputation and built-up business of a company. For accounting purposes, goodwill has no basis unless purchased. In the purchase of a business, goodwill generally is the difference between the purchase price and the value of the assets acquired. The intangible asset goodwill cannot be amortized for tax purposes. Reg. § 1.167(a)–3. See *amortization*.

**Grantor.** A transferor of property. The creator of a trust is usually designated as the grantor of the trust.

**Grantor trusts.** Trusts whereby the grantor retains control over the income or corpus, or both, to such an extent that such grantor will be treated as the owner of the property and its income for income tax purposes. The result is to make the income from a grantor trust taxable to the grantor and not to the beneficiary who receives it. § § 671–677. See *grantor*.

**Gross estate.** The property owned or previously transferred by a decedent that will be subject to the Federal death tax. It can be distinguished from the probate estate which is property actually subject to administration by the administrator or executor of an estate. § § 2031–2046.

**Gross income.** Income subject to the Federal income tax. Gross income does not include income such as interest on municipal bonds. In the case of a manufacturing or merchandising business, gross income means gross profit (i. e., gross sales or gross receipts less cost of goods sold). § 61 and Reg. § 1.61–3(a).

**"Gross-up".** To add back to the value of the property or income received the amount of the tax that has been deducted. In the case of gifts made within three years of the gift, any gift tax paid on the transfer is added to the gross estate. § 2035.

**Group-term life insurance.** Life insurance coverage permitted by an employer for a group of employees. Such insurance is renewable on a year-to-year basis and does not accumulate in value (i. e., no cash surrender value is built up). The premiums paid by the employer on such insurance are not taxed to the employees on coverage of up to $50,000 per person. § 79 and Reg. § 1.79–1(b).

**Guardian.** See *guardianship*.

**Guardianship.** A legal arrangement whereby one person (i. e., a guardian) has the legal right and duty to care for another (i. e., the ward) and his or her property. A guardianship is established because of the ward's inability to legally act on his or her own behalf due to minority (i. e., not of age) or mental or physical incapacity.

## –H–

**Head of household.** An unmarried individual who maintains a household for another and satisfies certain conditions set forth in § 2(b). Such status enables the taxpayer to use a set of income tax rates [see § 1(b)] that are lower than those applicable to other unmarried individuals [§ 1(c)] but higher than those applicable to surviving spouses and married persons filing a joint return [§ 1(a)].

**Heir.** A person who inherits property from a decedent.

**Hobby.** An activity not engaged in for profit. § 183.

**Holding period.** The period of time property has been held for income tax purposes. The holding period is of crucial significance in determining whether or not gain or loss from the sale or exchange of a capital asset is long- or short-term. § 1223.

**H.R. 10 plans.** See *Keogh plans*.

**Hot assets.** This term is used to refer to unrealized receivables and substantially appreciated inventory under § 751. When hot assets are present, the sale of a partnership interest or the disproportionate distribution of such assets can cause ordinary income to be recognized.

**Household effects.** See *personal and household effects*.

## –I–

**Imputed interest.** In the case of certain long-term sales of property, the IRS has the authority to convert some of the gain from the sale into interest income if the contract does not provide for a minimum rate of interest to be paid by the purchaser. The application of this procedure has the effect of forcing the seller to recognize less long-term capital gain and more ordinary income (i. e., interest income). § 483 and the Regulations thereunder.

**Incident of ownership.** An element of ownership or degree of control over a life insurance policy. The retention by an insured of an incident of ownership in a life insurance policy will cause the policy proceeds to be included in his or her gross estate upon death. § 2042(2) and Reg. § 20.2042–1(c). See *gross estate* and *insured*.

**Includible gain.** Section 644 imposes a special tax on trusts which sell or exchange property at a gain within two years after the date of its transfer in trust by the transferor. The provision only applies if the fair market value of the property at the time of the initial transfer exceeds the adjusted basis of the property immediately after the transfer. The tax imposed by § 644 is the amount of additional tax the transferor would have to pay (including any minimum tax) if the gain had been included in his or her gross income for the tax year of the sale. However, the tax applies only to an amount known as *includible gain*. This term is defined as the lesser of:

—The gain recognized by the trust on the sale or exchange of any property, or

—The excess of the fair market value of such property at the time of the initial transfer in trust by the transferor over the adjusted basis of such property immediately after the transfer.

**Income averaging.** A special method whereby the income tax for any one year is determined by taking into account the taxable income of the past three years. The income averaging procedure provides relief from the annual accounting period concept where a taxpayer goes from a "rags to riches" income position and has a relatively large amount of income bunched in a particular year. See Schedule G of Form 1040 and §§ 1301–1305.

**Income beneficiary.** The party entitled to income from property. A typical example would be a trust where A is to receive the income for life with corpus or principal passing to B upon A's death. In this case, A would be the income beneficiary of the trust.

**Income in respect of a decedent.** Income earned by a decedent at the time of death but not reportable on the final income tax return because of the method of accounting utilized. Such income is included in the gross estate and will be taxed to the eventual recipient (i. e., either the estate or heirs). The recipient will, however, be allowed an income tax deduction for the estate tax attributable to the income. § 691.

**Incomplete transfer.** A transfer made by a decedent during lifetime which, because of certain control or enjoyment retained by the transferor, will not be considered complete for Federal estate tax purposes. Thus, some or all of the fair market value of the property transferred will be included in the transferor's gross estate. §§ 2036–2038. See *gross estate*.

**Incorporated pocketbook.** For individuals in high income tax brackets it was often advantageous to transfer income-producing property (e.g., stocks and bonds) to a specially created corporation. In this manner, the income from such property would be shifted to the corporation and taxed at a lower rate. The incorporated pocketbook approach led to the enactment of the penalty tax on personal holding companies.

**Individual retirement account.** Individuals with earned income are permitted to set aside up to 100% of such income per year (not to exceed $2,000) for a retirement account. The amount so set aside can be deducted by the taxpayer and will be subject to income tax only upon withdrawal. § 219. See *simplified employee pensions*.

**Inheritance tax.** A tax imposed on the right to receive property from a decedent. Thus, an inheritance tax, theoretically, is imposed on the heir. The Federal estate tax is imposed on the estate.

**In-kind.** See *distributions in kind*.

**Installment method.** A method of accounting enabling a taxpayer to spread the recognition of gain on the sale of property over the payout period. Under this procedure, the seller computes the gross profit percentage from the sale (i. e., the gain divided by the selling price) and applies it to each payment received to arrive at the gain to be recognized. § 453.

**Insured.** A person whose life is the subject of an insurance policy. Upon the death of the insured, the life insurance policy matures and the proceeds become payable to the designated beneficiary.

**Intangibles.** Property that is a "right" rather than a physical object. Examples would be patents, stocks and bonds, goodwill, trademarks, franchises, and copyrights. See *amortization*.

**Inter vivos transfer.** A transfer of property during the life of the owner. To be distinguished from testamentary transfers where the property passes at death.

**Interpolated terminal reserve.** The method used in valuing insurance policies for gift and estate tax purposes when the policies are not paid-up at the time of their transfer. For an illustration of the application of this method see Reg. § 20.2031–8(a)(3), Example (3).

**Intestate.** No will exists at the time of death. Under these circumstances, state law prescribes who will receive the decedent's property. The laws of intestate succession (also known as the laws of descent and distribution) generally favor the surviving spouse, children, and grandchildren and then move to parents and grandparents and to brothers and sisters.

**Intestate succession.** See *intestate*.

**Investment tax credit.** A special tax credit equal to 6 or 10 percent of the qualified investment in tangible personalty used in a trade or business.

**Investment tax credit recapture.** See *recapture of the investment tax credit*.

**Involuntary conversion.** The loss or destruction of property through theft, casualty, or condemnation. Any gain realized on an involuntary conversion can, at the taxpayer's election, be considered non-recognizable for Federal income tax purposes if the owner reinvests the proceeds within a prescribed period of time in property that is similar or related in service or use. § 1033.

**IRA.** See *individual retirement account*.

**Itemized deductions.** Certain personal expenditures allowed by the Code as deductions from adjusted gross income if they exceed the zero bracket amount. Examples include certain medical expenses, interest on home mortgages, state sales taxes, and charitable contributions. Itemized deductions are reported on Schedule A of Form 1040.

## –J–

**Jeopardy assessment.** If the collection of a tax appears in question, the IRS may assess and collect the tax immediately without the usual formalities. Also, the IRS has the power to terminate a taxpayer's taxable year before the usual date if it feels that the collection of the tax may be in peril because the taxpayer plans to leave the country. §§ 6851, 6861–6864.

**Joint and several liability.** Permits the IRS to collect a tax from one or all of several taxpayers. A husband and wife that file a joint income tax return usually are collectively or individually liable for the full amount of the tax liability. § 6013(d)(3).

**Joint tenancy.** The undivided ownership of property by two or more persons with the right of survivorship. Right of survivorship gives the surviving owner full ownership of the property. Suppose, for example, B and C are joint owners of a tract of land. Upon B's prior death, C becomes the sole owner of the property. As to the death tax consequences upon the death of a joint tenant, see § 2040. See *tenancy by the entirety* and *tenancy in common*.

**Joint venture.** A one-time grouping of two or more persons in a business undertaking. Unlike a partnership, a joint venture does not entail a continuing relationship among the parties. A joint venture is treated like a partnership for Federal income tax purposes. § 7701(a)(2).

## –K–

**Keogh plans.** A designation for retirement plans available to self-employed taxpayers. They are also referred to as H.R. 10 plans. Under such plans a taxpayer may deduct each year (starting in 1984) up to either 25% of net earnings from self-employment or $30,000, whichever is less.

**Kimbell-Diamond rule.** See *single transaction approach*.

## –L–

**Lapse.** The expiration of a right either by the death of the holder or upon the expiration of a period of time. Thus, a power of appointment lapses upon the death of the holder if such holder has not exercised the power during life or at death (i. e., through a will).

**Last-in first-out (LIFO).** An accounting method for valuing inventories for tax purposes. Under this method it is assumed that the inventory on hand is valued at the cost of the earliest acquired units. § 472 and the Regulations thereunder. See *first-in first-out (FIFO)*.

**Layperson.** Non-member of a specified profession. For example, a non-lawyer would be a layperson to a lawyer.

**Leaseback.** The transferor of property later leases it back. In a sale-leaseback situation, for example, R would sell property to S and subsequently lease such property from S. Thus, R becomes the lessee and S the lessor.

**Legacy.** A transfer of cash or other property by will.

**Legal age.** The age at which a person may enter into binding contracts or commit other legal acts. In most states a minor reaches legal age or majority (i. e., becomes of age) at age 18.

**Legal representative.** A person who oversees the legal affairs of another. Examples include the executor or administrator of an estate and a court appointed guardian of a minor or incompetent person.

**Legatee.** The recipient of property under a will and transferred by the death of the owner.

**Lessee.** One who rents property from another. In the case of real estate, the lessee is also known as the tenant.

**Lessor.** One who rents property to another. In the case of real estate, the lessor is also known as the landlord.

**Life estate.** A legal arrangement whereby the beneficiary (i. e., the life tenant) is entitled to the income from the property for his or her life. Upon the death of the life tenant, the property will go to the holder of the remainder interest. See *income beneficiary* and *remainder interest.*

**Life insurance.** A contract between the holder of a policy and an insurance company (i. e., the carrier) whereby the company agrees, in return for premium payments to pay a specified sum (i. e., the face value or maturity value of the policy) to the designated beneficiary upon the death of the insured. See *insured.*

**Lifetime exemption.** See *specific exemption.*

**Like-kind exchange.** An exchange of property held for productive use in a trade or business or for investment (except inventory and stocks and bonds) for property of the same type. Unless different property is received (i. e., "boot") the exchange will be nontaxable. § 1031. See *boot.*

**Limited liability.** The liability of an entity and its owners to third parties is limited to the investment in the entity. This is a characteristic of a corporation since shareholders generally are not responsible for the debts of the corporation and, at most, may lose the amount paid-in for the stock issued. Reg. § 301.7701–2(d). See *association.*

**Limited partner.** A partner whose liability to third party creditors of the partnership is limited to the amount invested by such partner in the partnership. See *limited partnership* and *general partner.*

**Limited partnership.** A partnership in which some of the partners are limited partners. At least one of the partners in a limited partnership must be a general partner. See *general partner* and *limited partner.*

**Lump-sum distribution.** Payment of the entire amount due at one time rather than in installments. Such distributions often occur from qualified pension or profit-sharing plans upon the retirement or death of a covered employee.

# –M–

**Majority.** See *legal age.*

**Malpractice.** Professional misconduct or an unreasonable lack of skill.

**Marital deduction.** A deduction allowed upon the transfer of property from one spouse to another. The deduction is allowed under the Federal gift tax for lifetime (i. e., inter vivos) transfers or under the Federal estate tax for death (i. e., testamentary) transfers. § § 2056 and 2523.

**Market value.** See *fair market value.*

**Merger.** The absorption of one corporation by another whereby the corporation being absorbed loses its identity. A Corporation is merged into B Corporation and the shareholders of A Corporation receive stock in B Corporation in exchange for their stock in A Corporation. After the merger, A Corporation ceases to exist as a separate legal entity. If a merger meets certain conditions, it will be nontaxable to the parties involved. § 368(a)(1)(A).

**Minimum tax.** See *"add-on" minimum tax* and *alternative minimum tax.*

**Minority.** See *legal age.*

**Mitigation.** To make less severe in terms of result. See *mitigation of the annual accounting period concept* and *mitigation of the statute of limitations.*

**Mitigation of the annual accounting period concept.** Various tax provisions that provide relief from the effect of the finality of the annual accounting period concept. For example, income averaging provisions provide relief for taxpayers with a large and unusual amount of income concentrated in a single tax year. See *annual accounting period concept.*

**Mitigation of the statute of limitations.** A series of tax provisions based on fairness that prevents either the IRS or a taxpayer from obtaining a double benefit from the application of the statute of limitations. It would be unfair, for example, to permit a taxpayer to depreciate an asset previously expensed, but which should have been capitalized, if the statute of limitations prevents the IRS from adjusting the tax liability for the year the asset was purchased. §§ 1311–1315. See *statute of limitations*.

**Monetary bequest.** A transfer by will of cash. It is often designated as a pecuniary bequest.

**Mortgagee.** The party who holds the mortgage; the creditor.

**Mortgagor.** The party who mortgages the property; the debtor.

**Most suitable use valuation.** For gift and estate tax purposes, property that is transferred normally is valued in accordance with its most suitable or highest and best use. Thus, if a farm is worth more as a potential shopping center, this value will control even though the transferee (i. e., the donee or heir) continues to use the property as a farm. For an exception to this rule concerning the valuation of certain kinds of real estate transferred by death see *special use valuation*.

**Multi-tiered partnerships.** See *tiered partnerships*.

# –N–

**NA.** See *nonacquiescence*.

**Necessary.** Appropriate and helpful in furthering the taxpayer's business or income producing activity. §§ 162(a) and 212. See *ordinary*.

**Negligence.** Failure to exercise the reasonable or ordinary degree of care of a prudent person in a situation that results in harm or damage to another. Code § 6653(a) imposes a 5 percent penalty on taxpayers who show negligence or intentional disregard of rules and Regulations with respect to the underpayment of certain taxes.

**Negligence penalty.** See *negligence*.

**Net operating loss.** In order to mitigate the effect of the annual accounting period concept, § 172 allows taxpayers to use an excess loss of one year as a deduction for certain past or future years. In this regard, a carryback period of three years and a carryforward period of fifteen years is allowed. See *mitigation of the annual accounting period concept*.

**Net worth method.** An approach used by the IRS to reconstruct the income of a taxpayer who fails to maintain adequate records.

Under this approach, the gross income for the year is the increase in net worth of the taxpayer (i. e., assets in excess of liabilities) with appropriate adjustment for nontaxable receipts and nondeductible expenditures. The net worth method often is used when tax fraud is suspected.

**Ninety-day letter.** See *statutory notice of deficiency*.

**Non-acq.** See *nonacquiescence*.

**Nonacquiescence.** Disagreement by the IRS on the result reached by the U. S. Tax Court in a Regular Decision. Sometimes abbreviated as *non-acq.* or *NA*. See *acquiescence*.

**Nonbusiness bad debts.** A bad debt loss not incurred in connection with a creditor's trade or business. Such loss is deductible as a short-term capital loss and will only be allowed in the year the debt becomes entirely worthless. In addition to family loans, many investor losses fall into the classification of nonbusiness bad debts. § 166(d). See *business bad debts*.

**Noncontributory qualified pension or profit-sharing plan.** A plan funded entirely by the employer with no contributions being made by the covered employees. See *qualified pension or profit-sharing plans*.

# –O–

**Obligee.** The party to whom someone else is obligated under a contract. Thus, if C loans money to D, C is the obligee and D is the obligor under the loan.

**Obligor.** See *obligee*.

**Office audit.** An audit by the IRS of a taxpayer's return which is conducted in the agent's office. It may be distinguished from a *correspondence audit* or a *field audit* (see these terms).

**On all fours.** A judicial decision which is exactly in point with another either as to result, facts, or both.

**One-month liquidation.** A special election available to certain shareholders of a corporation which determines how the distributions received in liquidation by the electing shareholders will be treated for Federal income tax purposes. In order to qualify for the election, the corporation must be completely liquidated within the time span of any one calendar month. §§ 333, 334(c).

**Ordinary.** Common and accepted in the general industry or type of activity in which the taxpayer is engaged. It comprises one of the tests for the deductibility of expenses incurred or paid in connection with a trade or business; for the production or collection of income; for the management, conservation, or maintenance of property held for the production of income; or in connection with the determination, collection, or refund of any tax. § § 162(a) and 212. See *necessary.*

**Ordinary and necessary.** See *ordinary* and *necessary.*

**Ordinary gross income.** A concept peculiar to personal holding companies and defined in § 543(b)(1). See *adjusted ordinary gross income.*

# –P–

**Partial liquidation.** A partial liquidation occurs when some of the corporation's assets are distributed to its shareholders (usually on a pro-rata basis) and the corporation continues doing business in a contracted form. § § 302(b)(4) and (e).

**Partner.** See *limited partner* and *general partner.*

**Partnership.** For income tax purposes, a partnership includes a syndicate, group, pool, joint venture, as well as ordinary partnerships. In an ordinary partnership two or more parties combine capital and/or services to carry on as co-owners a business for profit. § 7701(a)(2). See *limited partnership* and *tiered partnerships.*

**Passive investment income.** As defined in § 1362(d)(3)(D), "passive investment income" means gross receipts from royalties, certain rents, dividends, interest, annuities, and gains from the sale or exchange of stock and securities. With certain exceptions, if the passive investment income of a corporation exceeds 25 percent of its gross receipts for three consecutive years, S status is lost.

**Pecuniary bequest.** A bequest of money to an heir by a decedent. Also known as a monetary bequest. See *bequest.*

**Percentage depletion.** See *depletion.*

**Percentage-of-completion method of accounting.** A method of reporting gain or loss on certain long-term contracts. Under this method of accounting the gross contract price is included in income as the contract is completed. Reg. § 1.451–3. For another alternative see *completed-contract method of accounting.*

**Personal and household effects.** Usual reference is to the following items owned by a decedent at the time of death: clothing, furniture, sporting goods, jewelry, stamp and coin collections, silverware, china, crystal, cooking utensils, books, cars, televisions, radios, stereo equipment, etc.

**Personal holding company.** A corporation that satisfies the requirements of § 542. Qualification as a personal holding company means a penalty tax of 50% will be imposed on the corporation's undistributed personal holding company income for the year.

**Personal holding company income.** Income as defined by § 543. Such income includes interest, dividends, rents (in certain cases), royalties (in certain cases), income from the use of corporate property by certain shareholders, income from certain personal service contracts, and distributions from estates and trusts. Such income is relevant in determining whether a corporation is a personal holding company and is, therefore, subject to the penalty tax on personal holding companies. See *adjusted ordinary gross income* and *personal holding company.*

**Personal holding company tax.** See *personal holding company.*

**Personal property.** Generally, all property other than real estate. It is sometimes designated as personalty when real estate is termed realty. Personal property also can refer to property which is not used in a taxpayer's trade or business or held for the production or collection of income. When used in this sense, personal property could include both realty (e. g., a personal residence) and personalty (e. g., personal effects such as clothing and furniture).

**Personalty.** Personalty is all property not attached to real estate (i. e., realty) that is movable. Examples of personalty are machinery, automobiles, clothing, household furnishings, inventory, and personal effects. See *realty.*

**P–H.** Prentice-Hall is the publisher of a tax service and of Federal tax decisions (i. e., AFTR and AFTR2d series).

**Post–1953 securities.** Stock and securities (e. g., bonds) acquired by a corporation after December 31, 1953, and held by such corporation upon its complete liquidation. A shareholder's allocable share of these securities would be a determining factor in the amount of gain (and, in some cases, the nature of such gain) that must be recognized if the one-month liquidation treatment of § 333 has been elected. § § 333(e) and (f). See *one-month liquidation.*

**Power of appointment.** A legal right granted to someone by will or other document which gives the holder the power to dispose of property or the income from property. When the holder may appoint the property to his or her own benefit, the power usually is designated as a general power of appointment. If the holder cannot benefit himself or herself but may only appoint to certain other persons, the power is a special power of appointment. For example, assume G places $500,000 worth of securities in trust granting D the right to determine each year how the trustee is to divide the income between A and B. Under these circumstances, D has a special power of appointment. If D had the further right to appoint the income to himself, he probably possesses a general power of appointment. For the estate tax and gift tax effects of powers of appointment, see § § 2041 and 2514.

**Preferred stock bail-out.** A procedure whereby the issuance, sale, and later redemption of a preferred stock dividend was used by a shareholder to obtain long-term capital gains without any loss of voting control over the corporation. In effect, therefore, the shareholder was able to bail-out corporate profits without suffering the consequences of dividend income treatment. This procedure led to the enactment by Congress of § 306 which, if applicable, converts the prior long-term capital gain on the sale of the stock to ordinary income. Under these circumstances, the amount of ordinary income is limited to the shareholder's portion of the corporation's earnings and profits existing when the preferred stock was issued as a stock dividend.

**Present interest.** See *future interest.*

**Presumption.** An inference in favor of a particular fact. If, for example, the IRS issues a notice of deficiency against a taxpayer, a presumption of correctness attaches to the assessment. Thus, the taxpayer has the burden of proof of showing that he or she does not owe the tax listed in the deficiency notice.

**Previously taxed income.** Prior to the Subchapter S Revision Act of 1982, the undistributed taxable income (UTI) of a Subchapter S corporation was taxed to the shareholders as of the last day of its tax year. Because such income was taxed but not received, the UTI became previously taxed income (PTI) and usually could be withdrawn by the shareholders without tax consequences at some later point in time. The role served by the PTI concept has been taken over by the new accumulated adjustment account. See *accumulated adjustment account.*

**Principal.** Property as opposed to income. The term is often used to designate the corpus of a trust. If, for example, G places real estate in trust with income payable to A for life and the remainder to B upon A's death, the real estate is the principal or corpus of the trust.

**Pro se.** In tax litigation a pro se situation is one in which a taxpayer represents himself or herself before the court. The taxpayer handles his or her own case without the benefit of counsel.

**Probate.** The legal process whereby the estate of a decedent is administered. Generally, the probate process involves collecting a decedent's assets, liquidating liabilities, paying necessary taxes, and distributing property to heirs. These activities are carried on by the executor or administrator of the estate usually under the supervision of the state or local court of appropriate jurisdiction.

**Probate court.** The usual designation for the state or local court that supervises the administration (i. e., probate) of a decedent's estate.

**Probate estate.** The property of a decedent that is subject to administration by the executor or administrator of an estate. See *administration* and *probate.*

**Prop.Reg.** An abbreviation for Proposed Regulation. A Regulation may first be issued in proposed form to give interested parties the opportunity for comment. When, and if, a Proposed Regulation is finalized, it is designated as a Regulation (abbreviated "Reg.").

**Pro-rata.** Proportionately. Assume, for example, a corporation has ten shareholders each of whom owns 10% of the stock. A pro-rata dividend distribution of $1,000 would mean that each shareholder would receive $100.

**PTI.** See *previously taxed income.*

**Public policy limitation.** A concept developed by the courts precluding an income tax deduction for certain expenses related to activities which are deemed to be contrary to the public welfare. In this connection, Congress has incorporated into the Code specific disallowance provisions covering such items as illegal bribes, kickbacks, and fines and penalties [§ § 162(c) and (f)].

# –Q–

**Qualified dividends.** Those dividends that qualify for the $100 exclusion of § 116. Generally, these are taxable dividends paid by U. S. corporations.

**Qualified pension or profit-sharing plan.** An employer-sponsored plan that meets the requirements of § 401. If these requirements are met, none of the employer's contributions to the plan will be taxed to the employee until distributed to him or her [§ 402]. The employer will be allowed a deduction in the year the contributions are made [§ 404].

**QTIP.** See *qualified terminable interest property*.

**Qualified terminable interest property.** Generally, the marital deduction (for gift and estate tax purposes) is not available if the interest transferred will terminate upon the death of the transferee spouse and pass to someone else. Thus, if H (husband) places property in trust, life estate to W (wife), and remainder to their children upon W's death, this is a terminable interest that will not provide H (or his estate) with a marital deduction. If, however, the transfer in trust is treated as qualified terminable interest property (i.e., the QTIP election is made), the terminable interest restriction is waived and the marital deduction becomes available. As to gifts, the donor spouse is the one who has to make the QTIP election. As to property transferred by death, the executor of the estate of the deceased spouse has the right to make the election. § § 2056(b)(7) and 2523(f).

# –R–

**RAR.** A revenue agent's report which reflects any adjustments made by the agent as a result of an audit of the taxpayer. The RAR is mailed to the taxpayer along with the 30-day letter which outlines the appellate procedures available to the taxpayer.

**Realized gain or loss.** The difference between the amount realized upon the sale or other disposition of property and the adjusted basis of such property. § 1001. See *adjusted basis* and *basis*.

**Realty.** Real estate.

**Reasonable needs of the business.** The usual justification for avoiding the penalty tax on unreasonable accumulation of earnings. In determining the amount of taxable income subject to this tax (i. e., accumulated taxable income), § 535 allows a deduction for "such part of earnings and profits for the taxable year as are retained for the reasonable needs of the business." See, further, § 537.

**Rebuttable presumption.** A presumption that can be overturned upon the showing of sufficient proof. See *presumption*.

**Recapture.** To recover the tax benefit of a deduction or a credit previously taken. See *recapture of depreciation* and *recapture of the investment tax credit*.

**Recapture of depreciation.** Upon the disposition of depreciable property used in a trade or business, gain or loss is determined measured by the difference between the consideration received (i. e., the amount realized) and the adjusted basis of the property. Prior to the enactment of the recapture of depreciation provisions of the Code, any such gain recognized could be Section 1231 gain and usually qualified for long-term capital gain treatment. The recapture provisions of the Code (e. g., § § 1245 and 1250) may operate to convert some or all of the previous Section 1231 gain into ordinary income. The justification for recapture of depreciation is that it prevents a taxpayer from converting a dollar of deduction (in the form of depreciation) into forty cents of income (Section 1231 gain taxed as a long-term capital gain). The recapture of depreciation rules do not apply when the property is disposed of at a loss. See *Section 1231 gain*.

**Recapture of the investment tax credit.** When Section 38 property is disposed of or ceases to be used in the trade or business of the taxpayer, some of the investment tax credit claimed on such property may be recaptured as additional tax liability. The amount of the recapture is determined by reference to § 47(a). See *investment tax credit* and *Section 38 property*.

**Recapture potential.** Reference is to property which, if disposed of in a taxable transaction, would result in the recapture of depreciation (§ § 1245 or 1250) and/or of the investment tax credit (§ 47).

**Recognized gain or loss.** The portion of realized gain or loss that is subject to income taxation. See *realized gain or loss*.

**Reg.** An abbreviation for a U. S. Treasury Department Regulation.

**Regulations.** Treasury Department Regulations represent the position of the IRS as to how the Internal Revenue Code is to be interpreted. Their purpose is to provide taxpayers and IRS personnel with rules of general and specific application to the various provisions of the tax law. Regulations are published in the *Federal Register* and in all tax services.

**Remainder.** See *remainder interest*.

**Remainder interest.** The property that passes to a beneficiary after the expiration of an intervening income interest. If, for example, G places real estate in trust with income to A for life and remainder to B upon A's death, B has a remainder interest.

**Remainderman.** The holder of a remainder interest (usually as to property held in trust). In a will the remainderman is the party who will receive what is left of the decedent's property after all specific bequests have been satisfied. If, for example, D dies and her will leaves $10,000 in cash to A and the remainder of the estate to B, the remainderman is B.

**Remand.** To send back. An appellate court may remand a case to a lower court, usually for additional fact finding. In other words, the appellate court is not in a position to decide the appeal based on the facts determined by the lower court. Remanding is abbreviated "rem'g."

**Revenue neutral.** A change in the tax system that results in the same amount of revenue. Revenue neutral, however, does not mean that any one taxpayer will pay the same amount of tax as was previously the case. Thus, corporations could pay more taxes but the excess revenue will be offset by lesser taxes on individuals. One of the features of a flat tax (as currently proposed) would be that it would be revenue neutral. See *flat tax*.

**Revenue Procedure.** A matter of procedural importance to both taxpayers and the IRS concerning the administration of the tax laws is issued as a Revenue Procedure (abbreviated as "Rev.Proc."). A Revenue Procedure is first published in an Internal Revenue Bulletin (I.R.B.) and later transferred to the appropriate Cumulative Bulletin (C.B.). Both the Internal Revenue Bulletins and the Cumulative Bulletins are published by the U. S. Government.

**Revenue Ruling.** A Revenue Ruling (abbreviated "Rev.Rul.") is issued by the National Office of the IRS to express an official interpretation of the tax law as applied to specific transactions. Unlike a Regulation, it is more limited in application. A Revenue Ruling is first published in an Internal Revenue Bulletin (I.R.B.) and later transferred to the appropriate Cumulative Bulletin (C.B.). Both the Internal Revenue Bulletins and the Cumulative Bulletins are published by the U. S. Government.

**Reversed (Rev'd.).** An indication that a decision of one court has been reversed by a higher court in the same case.

**Reversing (Rev'g.).** An indication that the decision of a higher court is reversing the result reached by a lower court in the same case.

**Reversion.** See *reversionary interest*.

**Reversionary interest.** The property that reverts to the grantor after the expiration of an intervening income interest. Assume, for example, G places real estate in trust with income to A for eleven years and, upon the expiration of this term, the property returns to G. Under these circumstances, G has retained a reversionary interest in the property. A reversionary interest is the same as a remainder interest except that in the latter case the property passes to someone other than the original owner (e. g., the grantor of a trust) upon the expiration of the intervening interest. See *remainder interest*.

**Revocable transfer.** A transfer of property whereby the transferor retains the right to recover the property. The creation of a revocable trust is an example of a revocable transfer. § 2038. See *incomplete transfers*.

**Rev.Proc.** An abbreviation for an IRS Revenue Procedure. See *Revenue Procedure*.

**Rev.Rul.** An abbreviation for an IRS Revenue Ruling. See *Revenue Ruling*.

**Right of survivorship.** See *joint tenancy*.

# –S–

**Schedule PH.** A tax form required to be filed by corporations that are personal holding companies. The form must be filed in addition to Form 1120 (i. e., U. S. Corporation Income Tax Return).

**S corporation.** The designation for a Subchapter S corporation.

**Section 38 property.** Property which qualifies for the investment tax credit. Generally, this includes all tangible property (other than real estate) used in a trade or business. § 48.

**Section 306 stock.** Preferred stock issued as a nontaxable stock dividend which, if sold or redeemed, would result in ordinary income recognition. § 306(c). See *preferred stock bail-out*.

**Section 306 "taint".** The ordinary income that would result upon the sale or other taxable disposition of Section 306 stock. See *Section 306 stock*.

**Section 1231 assets.** Section 1231 assets are depreciable assets and real estate used in a trade or business and held for more than six months. Under certain circumstances, the classification also includes: timber, coal, domestic iron ore, livestock (held for draft, breeding, dairy, or sporting purposes), and unharvested crops. § 1231(b). See *Section 1231 gains and losses*.

**Section 1231 gains and losses.** If the combined gains and losses from the taxable dispositions of Section 1231 assets plus the net gain from business involuntary conversions (of both Section 1231 assets and long-term capital assets) is a gain, such gains and losses are treated as long-term capital gains and losses. In arriving at Section 1231 gains, however, the depreciation recapture provisions (e. g., § § 1245 and 1250) are first applied to produce ordinary income. If the net result of the combination is a loss, such gains and losses from Section 1231 assets are treated as ordinary gains and losses. § 1231(a). See *Section 1231 assets*.

**Section 1244 stock.** Stock issued under § 1244 by qualifying small business corporations. If § 1244 stock becomes worthless, the shareholders may claim an ordinary loss rather than the usual capital loss.

**Section 1245 property.** Property which is subject to the recapture of depreciation under § 1245. For a definition of § 1245 property see § 1245(a)(3). See *recapture of depreciation* and *Section 1245 recapture*.

**Section 1245 recapture.** Upon a taxable disposition of Section 1245 property, all depreciation claimed on such property after 1962 will be recaptured as ordinary income (but not to exceed recognized gain from the disposition).

**Section 1250 property.** Real estate which is subject to the recapture of depreciation under § 1250. For a definition of § 1250 property see § 1250(c). See *recapture of depreciation* and *Section 1250 recapture*.

**Section 1250 recapture.** Upon a taxable disposition of Section 1250 property, some of the depreciation or cost recovery claimed on the property may have to be recaptured as ordinary income.

**Separate property.** In a community property jurisdiction, separate property is that property which belongs entirely to one of the spouses. Generally, it is property acquired before marriage or acquired after marriage by gift or inheritance. See *community property*.

**Sham.** A transaction without substance that will be disregarded for tax purposes.

**Simple trusts.** Simple trusts are those that are not complex trusts. Such trusts may not have a charitable beneficiary, accumulate income, nor distribute corpus.

**Simplified employee pensions.** An employer may make contributions to an employee's individual retirement account (IRA) in amounts (beginning in 1984) not exceeding the lesser of 25% of compensation or $30,000 per individual. § 219(b)(2). See *individual retirement account*.

**Single-transaction approach.** An approach developed in the *Kimbell-Diamond* decision which led to the enactment of § 334(b)(2) and later § 338 of the Code. If one corporation purchases 80% or more of the stock in another corporation and, shortly thereafter, liquidates the acquired corporation, the court concluded that the purchase was of assets and not of stock. In other words, a single transaction (i. e., the purchase of assets) had occurred and not multiple transactions (i. e., the purchase of stock and the acquisition of assets through liquidation). Under this assumption, the basis of the subsidiary's assets to the parent corporation would be the cost of the stock and not the subsidiary's basis in such assets.

**Small business corporation.** A corporation which satisfies the definition of § 1361(b), § 1244(c)(2), or both. Satisfaction of § 1361(b) permits an S election, while satisfaction of § 1244 enables the shareholders of the corporation to claim an ordinary loss on the worthlessness of stock.

**Special power of appointment.** See *power of appointment.*

**Special use valuation.** An option which permits the executor of an estate to value, for death tax purposes, real estate used in a farming activity or in connection with a closely-held business at its current use value rather than at its most suitable or highest and best use value. Under this option, a farm would be valued at its value for farming purposes even though, for example, the property might have a higher value as a potential shopping center. In order for the executor of an estate to elect special use valuation, the conditions of § 2032A must be satisfied. See *most suitable use valuation.*

**Special valuation method.** See *special use valuation.*

**Specific bequest.** A bequest of ascertainable property or cash to an heir of a decedent. Thus, if D's will passes his personal residence to W and grants $10,000 in cash to S, both W and S receive specific bequests.

**Specific exemption.** For transfers made prior to 1977, each donor was allowed a specific exemption of $30,000. Available for the lifetime of a donor, the exemption could be used to offset any taxable gifts made. Section 2521 was repealed by the Tax Reform Act of 1976.

**Specific legatee.** The recipient of designated property under a will and transferred by the death of the owner.

**Spin-off.** A type of reorganization whereby, for example, A Corporation transfers some assets to B Corporation in exchange for enough B stock to represent control. A Corporation then distributes the B stock to its shareholders.

**Split-off.** A type of reorganization whereby, for example, A Corporation transfers some assets to B Corporation in exchange for enough B stock to represent control. A Corporation then distributes the B stock to its shareholders in exchange for some of their A stock.

**Split-up.** A type of reorganization whereby, for example, A Corporation transfers some assets to B Corporation and the remainder to Z Corporation in return for which it receives enough B and Z stock to represent control of each corporation. The B and Z stock is then distributed by A Corporation to its shareholders in return for all of their A stock. The result of the split-up is that A Corporation is liquidated and its shareholders now have control of B and Z Corporations.

**Statute of limitations.** Provisions of the law which specify the maximum period of time in which action may be taken on a past event. Code § § 6501–6504 contain the limitation periods applicable to the IRS for additional assessments while § § 6511–6515 relate to refund claims by taxpayers.

**Statutory depletion.** See *depletion.*

**Statutory notice of deficiency.** Commonly referred to as the 90-day letter, this notice is sent to a taxpayer upon request, upon the expiration of the 30-day letter, or upon exhaustion by the taxpayer of his or her administrative remedies before the IRS. The notice gives the taxpayer 90 days in which to file a petition with the U. S. Tax Court. If such a petition is not filed, the IRS will issue a demand for payment of the assessed deficiency. § § 6211–6216. See *thirty-day letter.*

**Step-down in basis.** A reduction in the income tax basis of property.

**Step-transaction approach.** Disregarding one or more transactions to arrive at the final result. Assume, for example, that the shareholders of A Corporation liquidate the corporation and thereby receive cash and operating assets. Immediately after the liquidation, the shareholders transfer the operating assets to newly formed B Corporation. Under these circumstances, the IRS may contend that the liquidation of A Corporation be disregarded (thereby depriving the shareholders of capital gain treatment). What may really have happened is a reorganization of A Corporation with a distribution of boot (ordinary income) to its shareholders. If this is so, there will be a carryover of basis in the assets transferred from A Corporation to B Corporation.

**Step-up in basis.** An increase in the income tax basis of property. The classic step-up in basis occurs when a decedent dies owning appreciated property. Since the estate or heir acquires a basis in the property equal to its fair market value on the date of death (or alternate valuation date if available and elected), any appreciation is not subject to the income tax. Thus, a step-up in basis is the result with no income tax consequences.

**Stock attribution.** See *attribution*.

**Straddle sale.** The sale of loss property prior to the adoption of a plan of liquidation. The objective of this approach is to avoid the disallowance of the loss that would result under § 337 (i. e., "12-month liquidation") if the property were sold after the adoption of the plan. See *twelve-month liquidation*.

**Subchapter C corporation.** A regular corporation subject to the rules contained in Subchapter C (§ § 301–385) of the Internal Revenue Code of 1954. To be distinguished from an S corporation which is governed by Subchapter S of the Code.

**Subchapter S.** Sections 1361–1379 of the Internal Revenue Code of 1954. See *Subchapter S corporation*.

**Subchapter S corporation.** An elective provision permitting certain small business corporations [§ 1361] and their shareholders to elect [§ 1362] to be treated for income tax purposes in accordance with the operating rules of § § 1363–1379. Of major significance is the fact that Subchapter S status usually avoids the corporate income tax, and corporate losses can be claimed by the shareholders.

**Substance vs. form.** To ascertain the true reality of what has occurred. Suppose, for example, a father sells stock to his daughter for $1,000. If the stock is really worth $50,000 at the time of the transfer, the substance of the transaction is probably a gift of $49,000.

**Substantially disproportionate.** A type of stock redemption that qualifies for exchange treatment under § 302(a). § 302(b)(2).

**Surviving spouse.** When a husband or wife predeceases the other, the survivor is known as a "surviving spouse." Under certain conditions, a surviving spouse may be entitled to use the income tax rates contained in § 1(a) [i. e., those applicable to married persons filing a joint return] for the two years after the year of death of his or her spouse. For the definition of a surviving spouse for this purpose see § 2(a).

**Survivorship.** See *joint tenancy*.

# –T–

**Taint.** See *Section 306 "taint"*.

**Tangible property.** All property which has form or substance and is not intangible. See *intangibles*.

**Tax benefit rule.** A rule which limits the recognition of income from the recovery of an expense or loss properly deducted in a prior tax year to the amount of the deduction that generated a tax benefit. Assume, for example, that last year T (an individual) had medical expenses of $2,000 and adjusted gross income of $30,000. Due to the 5 percent limitation, T was able to deduct only $500 of these expenses [i. e., $2,000 − (5% × $30,000)]. If, in this year, T is reimbursed by his insurance company for $600 of these expenses, the tax benefit rule limits the amount of income from the reimbursement to $500 (i. e., the amount previously deducted with a tax benefit).

**Tax Court.** The U. S. Tax Court is one of three trial courts of original jurisdiction which decides litigation involving Federal income, death, or gift taxes. It is the only trial court where the taxpayer must not first pay the deficiency assessed by the IRS. The Tax Court will not have jurisdiction over a case unless the statutory notice of deficiency (i. e., "90-day letter") has been issued by the IRS and the taxpayer files the petition for hearing within the time prescribed.

**Tax preference items.** Those items set forth in § 57 which may result in the imposition of the minimum tax. § § 55–58. See *"Add-on" minimum tax* and *alternative minimum tax*.

**Tax year.** See *accounting period*.

**Taxable estate.** Defined in § 2051, the taxable estate is the gross estate of a decedent reduced by the deductions allowed by § § 2053–2056 (e. g, administration expenses, marital and charitable deductions). The taxable estate is the amount that is subject to the unified transfer tax at death. See *gross estate*.

**Taxable gift.** Defined in § 2503, a taxable gift is the amount of the gift that is subject to the unified transfer tax. Thus, a taxable gift has been adjusted by the annual exclusion and other appropriate deductions (e. g., marital and charitable).

**Tax-free exchange.** Transfers of property specifically exempted from income tax consequences by the tax law. Examples are a transfer of property to a controlled corporation under § 351(a) and a like-kind exchange under § 1031(a).

**Tax-option corporation.** See *Subchapter S corporation.*

**T.C.** An abbreviation for the U. S. Tax Court. It is used to cite a Regular Decision of the U. S. Tax Court.

**T.C. Memo.** An abbreviation used to refer to a Memorandum Decision of the U. S. Tax Court.

**Telescoping.** To look through one or more transactions to arrive at the final result. It is also designated as the *step-transaction approach* or the *substance vs. form* concept (see these terms).

**Tenancy by the entirety.** Essentially, a joint tenancy between husband and wife. See *joint tenancy.*

**Tenancy in common.** A form of ownership whereby each tenant (i. e., owner) holds an undivided interest in property. Unlike a joint tenancy or a tenancy by the entirety, the interest of a tenant in common does not terminate upon his or her prior death (i. e., there is no right of survivorship). Assume, for example, B and C acquire real estate as equal tenants in common, each having furnished one-half of the purchase price. Upon B's prior death, his one-half interest in the property passes to his estate or heirs. For a comparison of results see *joint tenancy.*

**Terminable interest.** An interest in property which terminates upon the death of the holder or upon the occurrence of some other specified event. The transfer of a terminable interest by one spouse to the other spouse may not qualify for the marital deduction. § § 2056(b) and 2523(b). See *marital deduction.*

**Testamentary disposition.** The passing of property to another upon the death of the owner.

**Testamentary power of appointment.** A power of appointment that can only be exercised through the will (i. e., upon the death) of the holder. See *power of appointment.*

**Thin capitalization.** See *thin corporation.*

**Thin corporation.** When debt owed by a corporation to its shareholders becomes too large in relationship to its capital structure (i. e., stock and shareholder equity), the IRS may contend that the corporation is thinly capitalized. In effect, this means that some or all of the debt will be reclassified as equity. The immediate result is to disallow any interest deduction to the corporation on the reclassified debt. To the extent of the corporation's earnings and profits, interest payments and loan repayments are treated as dividends to the shareholders. § 385.

**Thirty-day letter.** A letter which accompanies a revenue agent's report (RAR) issued as a result of an IRS audit of a taxpayer (or the rejection of a taxpayer's claim for refund). The letter outlines the taxpayer's appeal procedure before the IRS. If the taxpayer does not request any such procedures within the 30-day period, the IRS will issue a statutory notice of deficiency (the "90-day letter").

**Tiered partnerships.** An ownership arrangement where one partnership (the parent or first-tier) is a partner in one or more partnerships (the subsidiary/subsidiaries or second-tier). Frequently, the first-tier is a holding partnership and the second-tier is an operating partnership(s).

**Transfer tax.** A tax imposed upon the transfer of property. See *unified transfer tax.*

**Transferee liability.** Under certain conditions, if the IRS is unable to collect taxes owed by a transferor of property, it may pursue its claim against the transferee of such property. The transferee's liability for taxes is limited to the extent of the value of the assets transferred. For example, the IRS can force a donee to pay the gift tax when such tax cannot be paid by the donor making the transfer. § §6901–6905.

**Treasury Regulations.** See *Regulations.*

**Trial court.** The court of original jurisdiction; the first court to consider litigation. In Federal tax controversies trial courts include: U. S. District Courts, the U. S. Tax Court, and the U. S. Claims Court. See *appellate court.*

**Twelve-month liquidation.** A provision of the Code that requires a corporation selling property within the 12-month period from the adoption of a plan of liquidation to its complete liquidation to recognize no gain or loss on such sales. Section 337(b) defines the "property" that qualifies for such treatment. Generally, inventory is not included within the definition unless a bulk sale occurs. See *bulk sale* and *straddle sale*.

## –U–

**Undistributed personal holding company income.** The penalty tax on personal holding companies is imposed on the corporation's undistributed personal holding company income for the year. The adjustments necessary to convert taxable income to undistributed personal holding company income are set forth in § 545.

**Undistributed taxable income.** The income of a Subchapter S corporation that had not been distributed to its shareholders but was, nevertheless, taxed to them as of the last day of the corporation's tax year. In view of the changes made by the Subchapter S Revision Act of 1982, the phrase "undistributed taxable income" or "UTI" no longer is used to describe the passthrough procedure applicable to S corporations.

**Unearned income.** Income that has been received but not yet earned. Normally, such income is taxed when received even in the case of accrual basis taxpayers.

**Unified transfer tax.** A set of tax rates applicable to transfers by gift and death made after 1976. § 2001(c).

**Unified transfer tax credit.** A credit allowed against any unified transfer tax. § § 2010 and 2505.

**Uniform Gift to Minors Act.** A means of transferring property (usually stocks and bonds) to a minor. The designated custodian of the property has the legal right to act on behalf of the minor without the necessity of a guardianship. Generally, the custodian possesses the right to change investments (e. g., sell one type of stock and buy another), apply the income from the custodial property to the minor's support, and even terminate the custodianship. In this regard, however, the custodian is acting in a fiduciary capacity on behalf of the minor. The custodian could not, for example, appropriate the property for his or her own use because it belongs to the minor. During the period of the custodianship, the income from the property is taxed to the minor. The custodianship terminates when the minor reaches legal age. See *guardianship* and *legal age*.

**Unrealized receivables.** Amounts earned by a cash basis taxpayer but not yet received. Because of the method of accounting used by the taxpayer, they have no income tax basis.

**Unreasonable compensation.** Under § 162(a)(1) a deduction is allowed for "reasonable" salaries or other compensation for personal services actually rendered. To the extent compensation is "excessive" (i. e., "unreasonable"), no deduction will be allowed. The problem of unreasonable compensation usually is limited to closely-held corporations where the motivation is to pay out profits in some form deductible to the corporation. Deductible compensation, therefore, becomes an attractive substitute for nondeductible dividends when the shareholders also are employed by the corporation.

**USSC.** An abbreviation for the U. S. Supreme Court.

**U. S. Tax Court.** See *Tax Court*.

**USTC.** Published by Commerce Clearing House, *U. S. Tax Cases* contain all of the Federal tax decisions issued by the U. S. District Courts, U. S. Claims Court, U. S. Courts of Appeals, and the U. S. Supreme Court.

## –V–

**Value.** See *fair market value*.

**Vested.** Absolute and complete. If, for example, a person holds a vested interest in property such interest cannot be taken away or otherwise defeated.

**Voting trust.** A trust which holds the voting rights to stock in a corporation. It is a useful device when a majority of the shareholders in a corporation cannot agree on corporate policy.

## –W–

**Wash sale.** A loss from the sale of stock or securities which is disallowed because the taxpayer has within 30 days before or after the sale acquired stock or securities substantially identical to those sold. § 1091.

# –Z–

**Zero bracket amount.** A deduction generally available to all individual taxpayers in arriving at taxable income. Unlike the standard deduction which it replaced, the zero bracket amount is not determined as a percentage of adjusted gross income but is a flat amount. This amount is $2,480 for single persons and head of household, $3,670 for married persons filing jointly, and $1,835 for married persons filing separate returns. The zero bracket amount does not have to be computed separately but is built into the tax rate tables and the tax rate schedules.

# APPENDIX D–1
# TABLE OF CODE SECTIONS CITED

**[See Title 26 U.S.C.A.]**

# APPENDIX D–2
# TABLE OF REGULATIONS CITED

# APPENDIX D-3
# TABLE OF REVENUE PROCEDURES AND REVENUE RULINGS CITED

## REVENUE PROCEDURES

## REVENUE RULINGS

# APPENDIX E
# TABLE OF CASES CITED

# SUBJECT INDEX

## A

AAA, *see* S corporations

Abandonment of Partnership Interest,
10-16, 10-17, 10-45

Accelerated Cost Recovery System (ACRS),
*see also* Depreciation
Background, 1-2
Corporations, 2-6, 2-10, 2-11
E & P computation, 4-3, 4-4
Estates, 13-13 to 13-15
Partnerships, 9-15
Trusts, 13-14, 13-15

Accounting Periods and Methods, 2-7

Accumulated Adjustments Account, *see* S
corporations

Accumulated Earnings Tax
Accounts payable in the operating cycle,
7-6, 7-7
Accumulated taxable income, 7-9 to 7-11
Appreciation of investments, 7-9
Compared with personal holding
company tax, 7-23, 7-24
Computation of tax, 7-9 to 7-11
Consent dividends, 7-10, 7-11, 7-19, 7-20
Constructive dividends, 7-1
Deduction for dividends paid, 7-9, 7-10,
7-20
Disguised dividends, 7-1
Dividend-paying record, 7-27
Element of intent, 7-2, 7-3, 7-24
Imposition of penalty tax, 7-3
Inventory situations—measuring
reasonable needs of the business,
7-5 to 7-7
Measuring the accumulation, 7-9
No justifiable needs, 7-8, 7-9
Noninventory situation—measuring
reasonable needs of the business,
7-7, 7-8
Purpose, 7-2
Reasonable needs of the business, 7-4 to
7-8, 7-25, 7-26
S corporation election, 7-27, 7-28
Tax planning, 7-25 to 7-28
Tax rates and credit, 7-3, 7-4
Vulnerability of closely and publicly
held corporations, 7-3
Working capital requirements, 7-5 to 7-8

Accumulation Distribution, *see* Throwback
Rule

Accumulation of Earnings
*See* Accumulated Earnings Tax

Acquiescence, *see* Citations—Tax Court

ACRS, *see* Accelerated Cost Recovery
System

Additions to the Tax Liability, *see* Interest;
Penalties

Adequate Consideration, 11-1, 11-7

Adequate Disclosure, 14-19, 14-20

Adjustment to Basis—Property Gifted or
Acquired by Death, *see* Basis

Administration Expenses, 4-28, 11-35,
11-36, 11-54 to 11-56, 12-19, 12-20,
13-13

Administrative Powers of the IRS, 14-24 to
14-26

Administrative Sources of the Tax Law,
1-27 to 1-30, 1-45, 1-46

Administrator, 11-18, 13-3

Adverse Party, 13-36

Aggregate Concept, *see* Conduit Concept

Allocation of Income to Beneficiaries,
13-23 to 13-30

Alternate Valuation Date
*See also* Estate Tax (Federal)
Applicable to all property of estate, 12-8
Background, 12-7
Earlier of two dates, 12-8
Elective provision, 12-8
Property generating income, 12-8
Tax planning, 12-22
Value change through lapse of time,
12-8

Alternative Rule for Determining Basis of
Partnership Interest, 9-13, 9-14

Annual Accounting Period Concept, 1-11
to 1-13

Annual Exclusion, 11-12, 11-13

Annuities
Defined, 11-24
Employment arrangements, 11-25, 11-26
Gross estate, 11-24
Survivorship annuities, 11-24, 11-25
Types, 11-24
Valuation for gift and estate tax
purposes, 12-5, 12-6

Appeal Process
*See also* Litigation Considerations
Protest, 14-9
Regional Appeals Division, 14-9 to 14-12
Scope of the Appeals Division, 14-9
Settlement at Regional Appeals Division
level (Form 870-AD), 14-11, 14-12,
14-40
Thirty-day letter, 14-9

Arm's Length Concept, 1-20, 4-42

Assessments of Tax
*See also* Statute of Limitations
Deficiency assessment, 14-24
Demand for payment, 14-25
Jeopardy assessments, 14-25
Special rules, 14-27

# F

Protective Claim for Refund, 14-42, 14-43
Public Utility Stock, 4-18

# Q

QTIP, *see* Qualified Terminable Interest
Property
Qualified Terminable Interest Property,
11-40, 11-41
Qualified Terminable Interest Trusts,
11-40, 11-41
Qualifying Heir, *see* Special Use Valuation
Method

# R

RAR, *see* Revenue Agent's Report
Rates, Corporate Tax, 2-18, 2-19
Recapture of the Investment Tax Credit
Distributions in kind in complete
liquidation, 5-6
Estates and trusts, 13-22
Gift property, 11-23, 11-24
Lifetime transfers of property, 11-23
Liquidation of corporation, 6-17
Liquidation of a subsidiary, 5-28
Partnership formation, 9-4, 9-5, 9-11,
9-12
Partnership property in nonliquidating
distribution, 9-42, 9-43
Property dividends, 4-13, 4-14
Sale of a partnership interest, 10-3, 10-4
Section 337 liquidations, 5-11
Section 351 transfers, 3-9, 3-10
S corporations, 8-28, 8-29, 8-35
Successor corporation, 6-39, 6-40
Testamentary dispositions, 11-23, 11-24
Twelve-month liquidations, 5-11
Reconciliation of Corporate Taxable and
Financial Net Income, 2-21, 2-22
Redemption of Preferred Stock, *see*
Preferred Stock Bailouts
Redemptions of Stock, *see* Stock
Redemptions
Refunds of Tax, 14-14, 14-15, 14-28, 14-29,
14-42, 14-43
Interest on, 14-14, 14-15
Protective claim, 14-42, 14-43
Regular Decisions, *see* Citations, Tax
Court
Regulations, *see* Treasury Department
Regulations
Related Corporations, 3-17 to 3-25, 3-30 to
3-32
Remainder Interest, 12-6, 12-18, 12-19,
13-2

Remainderman, 11-7, 13-2
Reorganizations
*See also* Carryover of Tax Attributes;
Distribution of Stock of a Controlled
Corporation, Section 355
requirements for nontaxability
Assumption of liabilities, in general,
6-33
Assumption of liabilities in type A
reorganization, 6-5
Basis of securities or property to
recipients, 6-3
Business purpose concept, 6-23 to 6-25
Change in identity, form, or place of
organization (type F), 6-22
Comparison with stock redemptions and
liquidations, 6-42 to 6-44
Comparison of type A and type C, 6-12,
6-13
Consideration in qualifying type A
reorganization, 6-4
Consideration "solely for voting stock"
in type B reorganization, 6-10 to
6-12
Consideration in type C reorganization,
6-14, 6-15
Continuity of business enterprise, 6-28
Continuity of interest concept, 6-25 to
6-27
Divisive reorganizations (type D), 6-15
to 6-20, 6-41, 6-42
Eighty percent control requirement
of a type B reorganization, 6-9, 6-10
Equity versus creditor interest of
transferors, 6-26, 6-27
Gain or loss recognition by acquired
corporation, 6-3
Gain or loss recognition by acquiring
corporation, 6-4
Gain recognition possibilities, 6-3
Letter Ruling, 6-1, 6-44
Liquidation-reincorporation, 6-30, 6-31
Merger and consolidation (type A), 6-4
to 6-8, 6-43
Nontaxability, 6-1
Party to a reorganization, 6-32
Plan of reorganization, 6-32
Possible alternatives, 6-40, 6-41
Recapitalization (type E), 6-20 to 6-22
Resolving shareholder disputes, 6-17,
6-41, 6-42
Reverse merger, 6-6 to 6-8
Section 355 requirements, 4-35 to 4-38,
6-19, 6-20
Spin-offs, split-offs, split-ups, 4-36, 6-2,
6-16 to 6-19, 6-41, 6-42
Statutory requirements of type A
reorganizations, 6-5
Step transaction approach, 6-28 to 6-30
Tax planning, 6-40 to 6-44

## W